Current Law STATUTES

1996

VOLUME FOUR

AUSTRALIA
The Law Book Company
Brisbane • Sydney • Melbourne • Perth

CANADA
Carswell
Ottawa • Toronto • Calgary • Montreal • Vancouver

Agents:
Steimatzky's Agency Ltd., Tel Aviv;
N. M. Tripathi (Private) Ltd., Bombay;
Eastern Law House (Private) Ltd., Calcutta;
M.P.P. House, Bangalore;
Universal Book Traders, Delhi;
Aditya Books, Delhi;
MacMillan Shuppan KK, Tokyo;
Pakistan Law House, Karachi

Current Law

STATUTES

1996

VOLUME FOUR

SWEET & MAXWELL EDITORIAL TEAM

SARAH ANDREWS
SHIRLEY ARCHER
RACHAEL ARMITAGE
MELANIE BHAGAT
HANNAH CASEY
CAROL LOCKE
CERI PICKERING
JANICE SAYER
MELISSA TEMPLE
SUZANNE WARREN

W. GREEN EDITORIAL TEAM

STEPHEN HARVEY
PETER NICHOLSON
JANIE BRASH

LONDON

SWEET & MAXWELL

EDINBURGH

W. GREEN

1997

Published by
SWEET & MAXWELL LIMITED
of 100 Avenue Road, London,
and W. GREEN LIMITED
of Alva Street, Edinburgh,
Typeset by MFK Information Services Limited, Hitchin, Herts.
and printed in Great Britain
by The Bath Press

ISBN This Volume only : 0 421 56600 0
As a set : 0 421 56610 8

CONTENTS

Chronological Table . . . . page v
Chronological Table—Volumes 1–4 vii
Alphabetical Index of Short Titles, Public General Acts . . xi
Alphabetical Index of Short Titles, Private Acts xiii

CHRONOLOGICAL TABLE

VOLUME FOUR

Public General Acts

c.61. Channel Tunnel Rail Link Act 1996
62. Theft (Amendment) Act 1996
Sir John Smith, C.B.E., Q.C., LL.D., Emeritus Professor of Law, University of Nottingham
63. Hong Kong Economic and Trade Office Act 1996

Private Acts

c.i. Edinburgh Assay Office Order Confirmation Act 1996
ii. Australia and New Zealand Banking Group Act 1996
iii. University College London Act 1996
iv. City of London (Approved Premises for Marriage) Act 1996
v. Henry Johnson, Sons & Co., Ltd Act 1996
vi. Belfast Charitable Society Act 1996
vii. Allied Irish Banks Act 1996
viii. City of Westminster Act 1996
ix. London Local Authorities Act 1996
x. City of Edinburgh Council Order Confirmation Act 1996
xi. Edinburgh Merchant Company Order Confirmation Act 1996
xii. Scottish Borders Council (Jim Clark Memorial Rally) Order Confirmation Act 1996
xiii. Western Isles Council (Berneray Causeway) Order Confirmation Act 1996

Commencement Orders

1. Commencement Diary 1996
2. Commencement Orders 1996 C.1–102 (C.31 was never issued.)

Numerical Table of Statutory Instruments

Listing of all Instruments released for 1996

Alphabetical Table of Statutes

Listing of all Public Acts passed, 1700–1996

Index 1996

CHRONOLOGICAL TABLE

VOLUMES 1–4

VOLUME 1

c.1. Humber Bridge (Debts) Act 1996
2. Hong Kong (Overseas Public Servants) Act 1996
3. Wild Mammals (Protection) Act 1996
4. Consolidated Fund Act 1996
5. Health Service Commissioners (Amendment) Act 1996
6. Chemical Weapons Act 1996
7. Prevention of Terrorism (Additional Powers) Act 1996
8. Finance Act 1996
9. Education (Student Loans) Act 1996
10. Audit (Miscellaneous Provisions) Act 1996
11. Northern Ireland (Entry to Negotiations, etc.) Act 1996
12. Ratings (Caravans and Boats) Act 1996
13. Non-Domestic Rating (Information) Act 1996
14. Reserve Forces Act 1996
15. National Health Service (Residual Liabilities) Act 1996
16. Police Act 1996
17. Industrial Tribunals Act 1996
18. Employment Rights Act 1996
19. Law Reform (Year and A Day Rule) Act 1996
20. Dogs (Fouling of Land) Act 1996
21. London Regional Transport Act 1996
22. Northern Ireland (Emergency Provisions) Act 1996

VOLUME 2

23. Arbitration Act 1996
24. Treasure Act 1996
25. Criminal Procedure and Investigations Act 1996
26. Offensive Weapons Act 1996
27. Family Law Act 1996
28. Commonwealth Development Corporation Act 1996
29. Sexual Offences (Conspiracy and Incitement) Act 1996
30. Community Care (Direct Payments) Act 1996
31. Defamation Act 1996
32. Trading Schemes Act 1996
33. Prisoners' Earnings Act 1996
34. Marriage Ceremony (Prescribed Words) Act 1996
35. Security Service Act 1996
36. Licensing (Amendment) (Scotland) Act 1996
37. Noise Act 1996

38. Energy Conservation Act 1996
39. Civil Aviation (Amendment) Act 1996
40. Party Wall, etc. Act 1996
41. Hong Kong (War Wives and Widows) Act 1996
42. Railway Heritage Act 1996
43. Education (Scotland) Act 1996
44. Deer (Amendment) (Scotland) Act 1996
45. Appropriation Act 1996
46. Armed Forces Act 1996
47. Trusts of Land and Appointment of Trustees Act 1996
48. Damages Act 1996
49. Asylum and Immigration Act 1996
50. Nursery Education and Grant-Maintained Schools Act 1996
51. Social Security (Overpayments) Act 1996
52. Housing Act 1996

VOLUME 3

53. Housing Grants, Construction and Regeneration Act 1996
54. Statutory Instruments (Production and Sale) Act 1996
55. Broadcasting Act 1996
56. Education Act 1996
57. School Inspections Act 1996
58. Deer (Scotland) Act 1996
59. Public Order (Amendment) Act 1996
60. Consolidated Fund (No. 2) Act 1996

VOLUME 4

61. Channel Tunnel Rail Link Act 1996
62. Theft (Amendment) Act 1996
63. Hong Kong Economic and Trade Office Act 1996

Private Acts

*c.*i. Edinburgh Assay Office Order Confirmation Act 1996
ii. Australia and New Zealand Banking Group Act 1996
iii. University College London Act 1996
iv. City of London (Approved Premises for Marriage) Act 1996
v. Henry Johnson, Sons & Co., Ltd Act 1996
vi. Belfast Charitable Society Act 1996
vii. Allied Irish Banks Act 1996
viii. City of Westminster Act 1996
ix. London Local Authorities Act 1996
x. City of Edinburgh Council Order Confirmation Act 1996
xi. Edinburgh Merchant Company Order Confirmation Act 1996
xii. Scottish Borders Council (Jim Clark Memorial Rally) Order Confirmation Act 1996
xiii. Western Isles Council (Berneray Causeway) Order Confirmation Act 1996

Commencement Orders

1. Commencement Diary 1996
2. Commencement Orders 1996 C.1–102 (C.31 was never issued.)

Numerical Table of Statutory Instruments

Listing of all Instruments released for 1996

Alphabetical Table of Statutes

Listing of all Public Acts passed, 1700–1996

Index 1996

ALPHABETICAL INDEX OF SHORT TITLES

PUBLIC GENERAL ACTS 1996

(References are to chapter numbers of 1996)

Appropriation Act 1996 45
Arbitration Act 1996 23
Armed Forces Act 1996 46
Asylum and Immigration Act 1996 49
Audit (Miscellaneous Provisions) Act 1996 10
Broadcasting Act 1996 55
Channel Tunnel Rail Link Act 1996 61
Chemical Weapons Act 1996 6
Civil Aviation (Amendment) Act 1996 39
Commonwealth Development Corporation Act 1996 28
Community Care (Direct Payments) Act 1996 30
Consolidated Fund Act 1996 4
Consolidated Fund (No. 2) Act 1996 60
Criminal Procedure and Investigations Act 1996 25
Damages Act 1996 48
Deer (Amendment) (Scotland) Act 1996 44
Deer (Scotland) Act 1996 58
Defamation Act 1996 31
Dogs (Fouling of Land) Act 1996 20
Education Act 1996 56
Education (Scotland) Act 1996 43
Education (Student Loans) Act 1996 9
Employment Rights Act 1996 18
Energy Conservation Act 1996 38
Family Law Act 1996 27
Finance Act 1996 8
Health Service Commissioners (Amendment) Act 1996 5
Hong Kong (Overseas Public Servants) Act 1996 2
Hong Kong (War Wives and Widows) Act 1996 41
Hong Kong Economic and Trade Office Act 1996 63
Housing Act 1996 52
Housing Grants, Construction and Regeneration Act 1996 53
Humber Bridge (Debts) Act 1996 1
Industrial Tribunals Act 1996 17
Law Reform (Year and A Day Rule) Act 1996 19
Licensing (Amendment) (Scotland) Act 1996 36
London Regional Transport Act 1996 21
Marriage Ceremony (Prescribed Words) Act 1996 34
National Health Service (Residual Liabilities) Act 1996 15

Noise Act 1996 37
Non-Domestic Rating (Information) Act 1996 13
Northern Ireland (Emergency Provisions) Act 1996 22
Northern Ireland (Entry to Negotiations, etc.) Act 1996 11
Nursery Education and Grant-Maintained Schools Act 1996 50
Offensive Weapons Act 1996 26
Party Wall, etc. Act 1996 40
Police Act 1996 16
Prevention of Terrorism (Additional Powers) Act 1996 7
Prisoners' Earnings Act 1996 33
Public Order (Amendment) Act 1996 59
Railway Heritage Act 1996 42
Ratings (Caravans and Boats) Act 1996 12
Reserve Forces Act 1996 14
School Inspections Act 1996 57
Security Service Act 1996 35
Sexual Offences (Conspiracy and Incitement) Act 1996 29
Social Security (Overpayments) Act 1996 51
Statutory Instruments (Production and Sale) Act 1996 54
Theft (Amendment) Act 1996 62
Trading Schemes Act 1996 32
Treasure Act 1996 24
Trusts of Land and Appointment of Trustees Act 1996 47
Wild Mammals (Protection) Act 1996 3

ALPHABETICAL INDEX OF SHORT TITLES

PRIVATE ACTS 1996

(References are to chapter numbers of 1996)

Allied Irish Banks Act 1996 .... *c.*vii
Australia and New Zealand Banking Group Act 1996........ ii
Belfast Charitable Society Act 1996........ vi
City of Edinburgh Council Order Confirmation Act 1996........ x
City of London (Approved Premises for Marriage) Act 1996........ iv
City of Westminster Act 1996........ viii
Edinburgh Assay Office Order Confirmation Act 1996........ i
Edinburgh Merchant Company Order Confirmation Act 1996........ xi
Henry Johnson, Sons & Co., Ltd Act 1996........ v
London Local Authorities Act 1996........ ix
Scottish Borders Council (Jim Clark Memorial Rally) Order Confirmation Act 1996........ xii
University College London Act 1996........ iii
Western Isles Council (Berneray Causeay) Order Confirmation Act 1996........ xiii

CHANNEL TUNNEL RAIL LINK ACT 1996

(1996 c. 61)

ARRANGEMENT OF SECTIONS

PART I

THE CHANNEL TUNNEL RAIL LINK

Works

SECT.
1. Construction and maintenance of scheduled works.
2. Further and supplementary provisions.
3. Highways.

Land

4. Acquisition within limits shown on deposited plans.
5. Acquisition outside limits shown on deposited plans.
6. Temporary possession and use.
7. Extinguishment of private rights of way.
8. Extinguishment of rights of statutory undertakers etc.

Planning and heritage

9. Planning: general.
10. Permitted development: time limits.
11. Fees for planning applications.
12. Heritage.
13. Heritage: rights of entry.

Operation

14. Operation and use of authorised works.
15. Bye-laws.

Application of railway legislation

16. Licensing.
17. Access agreements.
18. Closures.
19. Railway administration orders.
20. Other legislation.

Functions of the Rail Regulator

21. Duties as to exercise of regulatory functions.
22. Restriction of functions in relation to competition etc.

Competition

23. Restrictive trade practices.
24. Monopoly situations.
25. Anti-competitive practices.
26. Sections 23 to 25: supplementary provisions.

Trees

27. Power to deal with trees on neighbouring land.
28. Disapplication of controls.

Noise

29. Control of construction sites: appeals.
30. Proceedings in respect of statutory nuisance: defence.

Financial matters

31. Expenditure in connection with securing construction of works.
32. Reserved capacity on the rail link: expenditure.
33. Undertakings with respect to financial assistance etc.

Miscellaneous and general

34. Holder of functions of nominated undertaker.
35. Transfer of functions relating to works.
36. Compensation for injurious affection.
37. Duty to co-operate.
38. Disapplication and modification of miscellaneous controls.
39. Burial grounds.
40. Application of landlord and tenant law.
41. Variation of development agreement: disapplication of s.2 of Law of Property (Miscellaneous Provisions) Act 1989.
42. Related works: application of section 9 of the Transport and Works Act 1992.
43. Arbitration.

PART II

THE A2 AND M2 IMPROVEMENT WORKS

44. Authorised works.
45. Acquisition of land.
46. Blight: compensation for pre-enactment acquisition.

PART III

MISCELLANEOUS AND GENERAL

47. Time limit for powers of compulsory acquisition.
48. Power to acquire land by reference to combined effect of works.
49. Noise insulation regulations: procedure.
50. Overhead lines.
51. Replacement concrete batching facilities at St Pancras.
52. Protection of interests.
53. Correction of deposited plans.
54. Service of documents.
55. Financial provision.
56. Interpretation.
57. Short title.

SCHEDULES:

Schedule 1—Scheduled works.
Schedule 2—Works: further and supplementary provisions.
Schedule 3—Highways.
Schedule 4—Acquisition of land within limits shown on deposited plans.
Part I—Purposes for which certain land may be acquired or used.
Part II—Application of legislation relating to compulsory purchase.
Part III—Supplementary provisions.
Schedule 5—Temporary possession and use of land.
Schedule 6—Planning conditions.
Part I—Qualifying authorities.
Part II—Development in Greater London.
Part III—Development in Essex or Kent.
Part IV—Supplementary.
Schedule 7—Heritage.
Schedule 8—Heritage: rights of entry.
Schedule 9—Application of other railway legislation.
Part I—Railways Clauses Acts.
Part II—Other legislation.
Schedule 10—Disapplication and modification of miscellaneous controls.
Schedule 11—Burial grounds: removal of human remains and monuments.
Schedule 12—The A2 and M2 improvement works.
Part I—The authorised works.
Part II—Interference with highways and means of access.
Part III—Miscellaneous.
Schedule 13—A2 and M2 improvement works: purposes for which certain land may be acquired or used.
Schedule 14—Overhead lines: consent.

Schedule 15—Protective provisions.
Part I—Protection for highways and traffic.
Part II—Protection for electricity, gas, water and sewerage undertakers.
Part III—Protection of land drainage, flood defence, water resources and fisheries.
Part IV—Protection of telecommunications operators.
Part V—Protection of Port of Sheerness Limited.
Part VI—Protection of British Waterways Board.
Part VII—Protection of Port of London Authority.

An Act to provide for the construction, maintenance and operation of a railway between St Pancras, in London, and the Channel Tunnel portal at Castle Hill, Folkestone, in Kent, together with associated works, and of works which can be carried out in conjunction therewith; to make provision about related works; to provide for the improvement of the A2 at Cobham, in Kent, and of the M2 between junctions 1 and 4, together with associated works; to make provision with respect to compensation in relation to the acquisition of blighted land; and for connected purposes.

[18th December 1996]

PARLIAMENTARY DEBATES

Hansard, H.C. Vol. 267, col. 1054, Vol. 269, col. 116, Vol. 276, col. 608. H.L. Vol. 571, col. 1419, Vol. 572, cols. 791, 840. (1995–1996 session) H.C. Vol. 284, col. 235, Vol. 287, col. 174. H.L. Vol. 575, cols. 443, 1043, 1381. (1996–1997 session)

INTRODUCTION

This Act authorises the construction, operation and maintenance of the Channel Tunnel Rail Link, a high speed railway between St Pancras in London and the Channel Tunnel portal at Castle Hill, Folkestone, in Kent. Associated works are authorised, including the reinstatement of a disused line to provide access to the existing international station at Waterloo, London, connections to other existing lines, the outline of an intermediate station at Ebbsfleet in Kent, and the alteration and extension of St Pancras including advance works for Thameslink. The Act also secures powers for the Secretary of State to widen the A2 trunk road at Cobham and the M2 between Junctions 1 and 4 on the outskirts of the Medway towns.

PART I

THE CHANNEL TUNNEL RAIL LINK

Works

Construction and maintenance of scheduled works

1.—(1) The nominated undertaker may construct and maintain the works specified in Schedule 1 to this Act ("the scheduled works"), being—

(a) works for the construction of a railway between St Pancras in London and the Channel Tunnel portal at Castle Hill, Folkestone, Kent,

(b) works consequent on, or incidental to, the construction of the works mentioned in paragraph (a) above, and

(c) works which can conveniently be carried out at the same time as works included in paragraph (a) or (b) above.

(2) Subject to subsection (3) below, the scheduled works shall be constructed in the lines or situations shown on the deposited plans and in accordance with the levels shown on the deposited sections.

(3) In constructing or maintaining any of the scheduled works, the nominated undertaker may—

(a) deviate laterally from the lines or situations shown on the deposited plans to any extent within the limits of deviation for that work so shown, and

(b) deviate vertically from the level shown for that work on the deposited sections—

(i) to any extent not exceeding 3 metres upwards, and

(ii) to any extent downwards.

Further and supplementary provisions

2. Schedule 2 to this Act (which contains further and supplementary provisions about works) shall have effect.

Highways

3. Schedule 3 to this Act (which makes provision in relation to highways in connection with the works authorised by this Part of this Act) shall have effect.

Land

Acquisition within limits shown on deposited plans

4.—(1) The Secretary of State is authorised by this section to acquire compulsorily—

(a) so much of the land shown on the deposited plans within the limits of deviation for the scheduled works as may be required for or in connection with the works authorised by this Part of this Act, and

(b) so much of the land so shown within the limits of land to be acquired or used as may be so required.

(2) Without prejudice to the generality of subsection (1) above, the purposes for which land may be acquired under that subsection include, in the case of so much of any land specified in columns (1) and (2) of Part I of Schedule 4 to this Act as is within the limits of land to be acquired or used, the purpose specified in relation to that land in column (3) of that Part as one for which that land may be acquired or used.

(3) Part II of Schedule 4 to this Act (application of legislation relating to compulsory purchase) and Part III of that Schedule (supplementary provisions) shall have effect.

Acquisition outside limits shown on deposited plans

5.—(1) The Secretary of State may acquire compulsorily land outside the relevant limits which is required for or in connection with the works authorised by this Part of this Act.

(2) Without prejudice to the generality of subsection (1) above, the land which may be compulsorily acquired under that subsection shall include land which is or will be required—

(a) for use in mitigating the effect on the environment of any of the works authorised by this Part of this Act,

(b) for use in relocating apparatus which it is expedient to divert or replace in consequence of the carrying out of any of the works authorised by this Part of this Act, or

(c) for the purpose of being given in exchange for land forming part of a common, open space or fuel or field garden allotment which is acquired under section 4(1) above.

(3) The power of acquiring land compulsorily under subsection (1) above shall include power to acquire an easement or other right over land by the grant of a new right.

(4) The Acquisition of Land Act 1981 shall apply to the compulsory acquisition of land under subsection (1) above; and Schedule 3 to that Act shall apply to a compulsory acquisition by virtue of subsection (3) above.

(5) Part I of the Compulsory Purchase Act 1965, and the enactments relating to compensation for the compulsory purchase of land, shall apply to a compulsory acquisition by virtue of subsection (3) above with the modifications mentioned in paragraph 8(2)(a) and (b) of Schedule 4 to this Act.

(6) In this section—

"apparatus" includes a sewer, drain or tunnel and any structure for the lodging therein of apparatus or for gaining access to apparatus;

"common" includes any land subject to be enclosed under the Inclosure Acts 1845 to 1882, and any town or village green;

"fuel or field garden allotment" means any allotment set out as a fuel allotment, or a field garden allotment, under an Inclosure Act;

"open space" means any land laid out as a public garden, or used for the purposes of public recreation, or land which is a disused burial ground; and

"the relevant limits" means the limits of deviation for the scheduled works and the limits of land to be acquired or used.

Temporary possession and use

6. Schedule 5 to this Act (which contains provisions about temporary possession and use of land for the purposes of this Part of this Act) shall have effect.

Extinguishment of private rights of way

7.—(1) All private rights of way over land which is held by the Secretary of State as being required for or in connection with the works authorised by this Part of this Act shall be extinguished—

(a) in the case of land held by the Secretary of State immediately before the coming into force of this Act, on the coming into force of this Act, and

(b) in the case of land acquired by the Secretary of State after the coming into force of this Act, at the appropriate time.

(2) For the purposes of subsection (1)(b) above, the appropriate time is the time of acquisition, except where land—

(a) is acquired compulsorily, and

(b) is land in respect of which the power conferred by section 11(1) of the Compulsory Purchase Act 1965 (power of entry following notice to treat) is exercised,

in which case it is the time of entry under that provision.

(3) Any person who suffers loss by the extinguishment of any right of way under this section shall be entitled to be compensated by the nominated undertaker.

(4) Any dispute as to a person's entitlement to compensation under this section, or as to the amount of such compensation, shall be determined under and in accordance with Part I of the Land Compensation Act 1961.

(5) This section does not apply in relation to any right of way to which section 271 or 272 of the Town and Country Planning Act 1990 (extinguishment of rights of statutory undertakers etc.) applies.

Extinguishment of rights of statutory undertakers etc.

8.—(1) Sections 271 to 273 of the Town and Country Planning Act 1990 (extinguishment of rights of statutory undertakers etc.) shall apply in relation to land held by the Secretary of State as being land which is required for or in connection with the works authorised by this Part of this Act as they apply in relation to land acquired or appropriated as mentioned in section 271(1) of that Act.

(2) In the application of sections 271 to 273 of that Act by virtue of subsection (1) above, references to the acquiring or appropriating authority shall be construed as references to the nominated undertaker.

(3) In their application by virtue of subsection (1) above, sections 271 and 272 of that Act shall also have effect with the following modifications—

(a) in subsection (2), for the words from "with" to "appropriated" there shall be substituted "authorised by Part I of the Channel Tunnel Rail Link Act 1996", and

(b) in subsection (5), for the words from "local" to "or undertakers" there shall be substituted "a person other than a Minister, he".

(4) In the Town and Country Planning Act 1990, any reference to, or to any provision of, section 271, 272 or 273 shall include a reference to, or to that provision of, that section as applied by subsection (1) above.

(5) In their application by virtue of subsection (4) above, the following provisions of that Act shall have effect with the following modifications—

(a) in section 274(3), for "local authority or statutory undertakers" there shall be substituted "person", and

(b) in sections 274(5), 279(2) to (4) and 280(6), references to the acquiring or appropriating authority shall be construed as references to the nominated undertaker.

Planning and heritage

Planning: general

9.—(1) Subject to subsections (2) and (4) below, planning permission shall be deemed to be granted under Part III of the Town and Country Planning Act 1990 for the carrying out of development authorised by this Part of this Act.

(2) In the case of development consisting of the provision of parking at St Pancras in London, other than short term parking for coaches or taxis, subsection (1) above shall only apply to development which—

(a) is carried out on land within the limits of deviation for Works Nos. 1C, 1CC, 5C, 5D, 5D(1) or 5EE or the land in the London Borough of Camden numbered 37 and 61 on the deposited plans, and

(b) does not, when taken together with any other relevant development—

(i) so far as involving the provision of parking for cars, involve the provision of more than 750 parking spaces, and

(ii) so far as involving the provision of parking for coaches, involve the provision of more than 30 parking spaces.

(3) For the purposes of subsection (2)(b) above, relevant development is development consisting of the provision of parking, other than short term parking for coaches or taxis—

(a) which is carried out on such land as is mentioned in subsection (2)(a) above, and

(b) for which planning permission is deemed by subsection (1) above to be granted.

(4) In the case of development consisting of the provision of a combined international and domestic passenger station and parking at Ebbsfleet in Kent, subsection (1) above shall only apply to development which—

(a) is carried out on the land in the borough of Dartford, parish of Swanscombe and Greenhithe, numbered 25 to 33 on the deposited plans and the land in the borough of Gravesham, town of Gravesend, numbered 16, 17, 22 to 34, 45, 46, 109, 110 and 112 on those plans, and

(b) does not involve the provision of more than 9,000 parking spaces.

(5) Schedule 6 to this Act (which makes provision about planning conditions) shall have effect in relation to development for which planning permission is deemed by subsection (1) above to be granted, other than development to which subsection (2) or (4) above applies.

(6) The planning permission deemed by subsection (1) above to be granted shall, so far as relating to development to which subsection (2) or (4) above applies, be deemed to be granted subject to a condition specifying the matters mentioned in subsection (7) below as reserved matters for the subsequent approval of the relevant planning authority.

(7) The matters referred to above are—

(a) in the case of development to which subsection (2) above applies, the siting, design and external appearance of, and means of access to, the development, and

(b) in the case of development to which subsection (4) above applies, the siting, layout, design, external appearance and landscaping of the development.

(8) Development for which permission is deemed by this section to be granted shall be treated as not being development of a class for which planning permission is granted by the Town and Country Planning (General Permitted Development) Order 1995 (or any order replacing that order).

(9) Planning permission which is deemed by this section to be granted shall be treated as specific planning permission for the purposes of section 264(3)(a) of the Town and Country Planning Act 1990 (specific planning permission for the development of statutory undertakers' land relevant to whether the land is operational land).

(10) In subsections (2) and (4) above, references to development consisting of the provision of parking do not include development consisting of the provision of parking on working sites.

(11) In subsection (6) above, "relevant planning authority" means—

(a) in relation to Greater London, the local planning authority, and

(b) in relation to Essex or Kent, the district planning authority.

Permitted development: time limits

10.—(1) It shall be a condition of the planning permission deemed by section 9(1) above to be granted, so far as relating to—

(a) development consisting of the carrying out of a scheduled work, or

(b) development to which section 9(2) or (4) above applies,

that the development must be begun not later than the end of 10 years beginning with the day on which this Act is passed.

(2) The Secretary of State may, in relation to any development to which the condition imposed by subsection (1) above applies, by order extend the period by reference to which the condition operates.

(3) The power conferred by subsection (2) above shall be exercisable by statutory instrument which shall be subject to annulment in pursuance of a resolution of either House of Parliament.

(4) Nothing in section 91 of the Town and Country Planning Act 1990 (limit on duration of planning permission) shall apply to the planning permission deemed by section 9(1) above to be granted.

(5) Section 94 of that Act (completion notices) shall apply where development to which section 9(2) or (4) above applies has been begun within the period by reference to which the condition mentioned in subsection (1) above operates, but that period has elapsed without the development having been completed.

(6) In their application by virtue of subsection (5) above, sections 94(2) and (5) and 95(2) of that Act shall have effect with the insertion after "permission" of "deemed by section 9(1) of the Channel Tunnel Rail Link Act 1996 to be granted, so far as relating to the development,".

Fees for planning applications

11.—(1) The appropriate Ministers may by regulations make provision about fees for relevant planning applications.

(2) Regulations under subsection (1) above may, in particular—

(a) make provision for the payment to the authority to which a relevant planning application is made of a fee of a prescribed amount,

(b) make provision for the remission or refunding of a prescribed fee (in whole or part) in prescribed circumstances,

(c) make provision for a prescribed fee to be treated as paid in prescribed circumstances,

(d) make provision about the time for payment of a prescribed fee,

(e) make provision about the consequences of non-payment of a prescribed fee, including provision for the termination of the application concerned or any appeal against its refusal, and

(f) make provision for the resolution of disputes.

(3) Regulations under subsection (1) above may—

(a) make such supplementary, incidental or consequential provision as the appropriate Ministers think fit, and

(b) make different provision for different cases.

(4) The power to make regulations under subsection (1) above shall be exercisable by statutory instrument which shall be subject to annulment in pursuance of a resolution of either House of Parliament.

(5) Nothing in regulations under section 303 of the Town and Country Planning Act 1990 (fees for planning applications) shall apply to a relevant planning application.

(6) In this section—

"the appropriate Ministers" means the Secretary of State for the Environment and the Secretary of State for Transport acting jointly;

"prescribed" means prescribed in regulations under subsection (1) above; and

"relevant planning application" means a request for approval under the planning permission deemed by section 9(1) above to be granted.

Heritage

12. Schedule 7 to this Act (which makes provision for the disapplication or modification, in relation to authorised works, of controls relating to listed buildings, buildings in conservation areas and ancient monuments etc.) shall have effect.

Heritage: rights of entry

13. Schedule 8 to this Act (which makes provision about rights of entry for the Historic Buildings and Monuments Commission for England and the Royal Commission on the Historical Monuments of England) shall have effect.

Operation

Operation and use of authorised works

14.—(1) The nominated undertaker may, in relation to the works authorised by this Part of this Act—

(a) operate them for the purpose of providing infrastructure services, and

(b) use them for the purpose of providing services for the carriage of passengers or goods.

(2) In subsection (1) above, the reference to infrastructure services is to services which are network services or station services for the purposes of Part I of the Railways Act 1993.

Bye-laws

15. For the purposes of section 129 of the Railways Act 1993 (power of independent railway operator to make bye-laws), the nominated undertaker shall be treated as an independent railway operator.

Application of railway legislation

Licensing

16.—(1) Section 6(1) of the Railways Act 1993 (which prohibits any person from acting as the operator of a network, station or train being used on a network unless authorised by a licence under section 8 of that Act) shall not apply in relation to—

(a) any network comprised in the rail link,

(b) any rail link station, or

(c) any train being used, in circumstances in which subsection (2) below applies, on a network comprised in the rail link.

(2) This subsection applies if—

(a) the train is being used to provide a service involving travel through the Channel Tunnel, or

(b) the operator of the train is a rail link undertaker and the train is being used to provide a service for the carriage of goods which does not involve carriage outside the rail link.

(3) There shall not be included in a licence under section 8 of the Railways Act 1993 any condition relating to an activity in respect of which the licence holder is exempt from section 6(1) of that Act by virtue of subsection (1) above; and any condition which is included in such a licence shall be of no effect so far as relating to such an activity.

(4) For the purposes of subsection (1)(b) above, the following stations are rail link stations—

(a) St Pancras in London,

(b) any station constructed for the purposes of the rail link in exercise of the powers conferred by this Part of this Act, and

(c) any station constructed for the purposes of the rail link at Stratford, in the London Borough of Newham.

(5) Any expression used in this section and Part I of the Railways Act 1993 shall have the same meaning in this section as it has in that Part.

Access agreements

17.—(1) No directions under section 17(1) of the Railways Act 1993 (which enables the Rail Regulator to direct facility owners to enter into contracts for the use of their railway facilities) may be given to a rail link undertaker in relation to a rail link facility.

(2) Subject to subsection (3) below, section 18(1) of that Act (which restricts the freedom of a facility owner to enter into an access contract) shall not apply to the entry by a rail link undertaker into an access contract relating to a rail link facility.

(3) Where only part of a rail link facility is used for the purposes of or in connection with the provision of services on the rail link, subsection (2) above shall only apply if the access contract is restricted to that part of the facility.

(4) No directions under section 19(1) of that Act (which enables the Rail Regulator to direct installation owners to enter into contracts for the use of their installations) may be given to a rail link undertaker in relation to a network installation comprised in the rail link.

(5) In this section—

"access contract", "network installation" and "railway facility" have the same meanings as in Part I of the Railways Act 1993; and

"rail link facility" means a railway facility which is used wholly or partly for the purposes of or in connection with the provision of services for the carriage of passengers or goods on the rail link.

Closures

18. The following provisions of the Railways Act 1993—

section 38 (proposals to discontinue franchised etc. passenger services), and

section 48(3) (duties in relation to discontinuation of certain experimental passenger services),

shall not have effect in relation to services which involve travel on the rail link.

Railway administration orders

19.—(1) In section 59 of the 1993 Act (which defines a railway administration order as a court order under section 60, 61 or 62 of that Act in relation to a protected railway company) subsection (6) (paragraph (a) of which defines a "protected railway company" and paragraph (b) of which defines its "relevant activities") shall have effect, in relation to a rail link service operator—

(a) with the omission, in paragraph (a), of "both" and the words from "and the" to the end, and

(b) with the substitution for paragraph (b)(i) and (ii) of "its activities as the operator of a railway asset".

(2) For the purposes of the following provisions, namely—

(a) sections 60(1)(b), 61(1)(a)(ii) and (2)(b), and 62(2)(a)(ii), (3)(b), (5)(a)(ii), (6)(b) and (7)(b) of the 1993 Act, and

(b) sections 13(3)(b), 18(1)(b) and 27(1A) of the 1986 Act, as applied by Schedule 6 to the 1993 Act,

(which give the Director of Passenger Rail Franchising a role in relation to a protected railway company which is the holder of a passenger licence) a rail link service operator which is the holder of a passenger licence shall be treated as if it were not the holder of such a licence.

(3) Section 60 of the 1993 Act (railway administration orders made on special petitions), in its application to a rail link service operator, shall have effect with the following modifications—

(a) in subsection (1), for "either or both" there shall be substituted "any",

(b) in subsection (2), at the end there shall be inserted—

"(c) that an agreement between the Secretary of State and a relevant rail link undertaker has terminated.", and

(c) in subsection (7), at the end there shall be inserted—

" "rail link" has the same meaning as in the Channel Tunnel Rail Link Act 1996;

"relevant rail link undertaker" means a person who, under section 34 of that Act, is the nominated undertaker for any purpose of section 1(1) or 14(1)(a) of that Act, so far as relating to the rail link."

(4) Section 17 of the 1986 Act (duties of administrator), as applied by Schedule 6 to the 1993 Act, shall have effect, in relation to the administration of a rail link service operator, with the insertion after subsection (2) of—

"(2A) Subsection (2) shall only apply if the proposals have been approved by the Secretary of State and, where he approves them with modifications, shall apply as if the proposals prepared for the purposes of section 23 were the proposals as so modified."

(5) The following provisions of the 1986 Act, as applied by Schedule 6 to the 1993 Act, namely, sections 18(4), 21(2), 23(1) and (2) and 27(6) (which require documents to be sent to specified persons) shall not have effect to require any document relating to a rail link service operator to be sent to the Director of Passenger Rail Franchising.

(6) In Schedule 7 to the 1993 Act (transfer of relevant activities in connection with railway administration orders) paragraph 2 (making and modification of transfer schemes) shall have effect, where the company in relation

to which a railway administration order has been made is a rail link service operator, with the following modifications—

(a) in sub-paragraph (2), the words from "or" to the end shall be omitted,
(b) in sub-paragraph (3), the words "or the Franchising Director" shall be omitted,
(c) in sub-paragraph (6), the words "or the Franchising Director" shall be omitted, and
(d) in sub-paragraph (7), the words from "or, in a" to "Director" shall be omitted.

(7) An agreement by the Secretary of State shall be effective notwithstanding that, in the case of a rail link service operator, it fetters the Secretary of State in relation to a discretion under sections 60 to 65 of, and Schedules 6 and 7 to, the 1993 Act (the railway administration order provisions of the Act).

(8) The Secretary of State may by order repeal subsection (4) above.

(9) The power conferred by subsection (8) above shall be exercisable by statutory instrument which shall be subject to annulment in pursuance of a resolution of either House of Parliament.

(10) In this section—

"operator", in relation to a railway asset, means the person having the management of that railway asset for the time being;

"passenger licence" and "railway asset" have the same meanings as in Part I of the 1993 Act;

"rail link service operator" means a person who, under section 34 below, is the nominated undertaker for any purpose of section 14(1)(b) above, so far as relating to the rail link;

"the 1986 Act" means the Insolvency Act 1986; and

"the 1993 Act" means the Railways Act 1993.

Other legislation

20. Schedule 9 to this Act (which makes provision with respect to the incorporation of the Railways Clauses Acts and the application of miscellaneous other enactments relating to railways) shall have effect.

Functions of the Rail Regulator

Duties as to exercise of regulatory functions

21.—(1) The Rail Regulator shall have an overriding duty to exercise his regulatory functions in such a manner as not to impede the performance of any development agreement.

(2) In exercising his regulatory functions in relation to the use by a rail link undertaker of any existing network—

(a) for trains used in connection with the construction of the rail link, or
(b) for trains used to provide international services,

the Rail Regulator shall also be under a duty to have regard to the financial position of the rail link undertaker.

(3) The Rail Regulator may by notice require a person to whose financial position he is required by subsection (2) above to have regard to furnish to him, in such form and manner as may be specified in the notice, such information relating to that person's financial position as may be so specified, being information which the Rail Regulator considers necessary for the purpose of facilitating the performance of his duty under that subsection.

(4) If any person makes default in complying with a notice under subsection (3) above, the High Court may, on the application of the Rail Regulator, make such order as it thinks fit for requiring the default to be made good.

(5) An order under subsection (4) above may provide that all the costs or expenses of and incidental to the application under that subsection shall be

borne by the person in default or, in the case of a company or other association, by any of its officers who are responsible for its default.

(6) In this section—

"existing", in relation to a network, means not comprised in the rail link;

"international services" means services involving travel through the Channel Tunnel;

"network" has the same meaning as in Part I of the Railways Act 1993; and

references to the Rail Regulator's regulatory functions are to the functions assigned or transferred to him under or by virtue of Part I of the Railways Act 1993.

Restriction of functions in relation to competition etc.

22.—(1) The Rail Regulator shall not be entitled to exercise any functions under section 67(1) of the Railways Act 1993 (under which he may be required to exercise the Director General of Fair Trading's consumer protection functions under Part III of the Fair Trading Act 1973, so far as relating to courses of conduct detrimental to consumers of railway services) in relation to a course of conduct persisted in by a rail link undertaker in relation to the supply of railway services, so far as relating to the rail link.

(2) The functions of the Rail Regulator, so far as relating to monopoly situations which exist or may exist in relation to the supply of railway services, shall not be exercisable by him in relation to the supply by a rail link undertaker of railway services, so far as relating to the rail link.

(3) The functions of the Rail Regulator, so far as relating to courses of conduct which have or are intended to have or are likely to have the effect of restricting, distorting or preventing competition in connection with the supply of railway services, shall not, in the case of a course of conduct pursued by a rail link undertaker, be exercisable by the Regulator by reference to the effect of the course of conduct on the supply of railway services, so far as relating to the rail link.

(4) Section 67(4) of the Railways Act 1993 (duty of the Director General of Fair Trading to consult the Rail Regulator about the exercise of concurrent functions) shall not have effect to require the Director to consult the Regulator about the exercise of any function which the Regulator is prevented by subsection (2) or (3) above from exercising.

(5) In this section, "railway services" has the same meaning as in the Railways Act 1993.

Competition

Restrictive trade practices

23.—(1) The Restrictive Trade Practices Act 1976 ("the 1976 Act") shall not apply to any development agreement and shall be deemed never to have applied to any such agreement.

(2) Where two or more persons are specified under section 34 below as the nominated undertaker for the same purpose of the same provision, the Secretary of State may by order provide that the persons so specified and any body corporate which is a member of the same group as any of them shall be deemed to be members of one and the same group of interconnected bodies corporate for the purposes of the 1976 Act in relation to any scheduled works agreement.

(3) Section 24 of the 1976 Act (time limit for registering particulars of agreements subject to registration) shall apply in relation to an agreement which becomes subject to registration under that Act by virtue of the revocation of an order under subsection (2) above as it applies in relation to an agreement which becomes subject to registration under that Act by virtue of

the expiry or revocation of an order under section 29 of that Act (power to exempt agreements of importance to the national economy from registration).

(4) The Secretary of State may, in relation to a scheduled works agreement, make an order under section 29 of the 1976 Act after, as well as on or before, the conclusion of the agreement; and, on the coming into force of an order made by virtue of this subsection, that Act shall be deemed not to have applied to the agreement concerned.

(5) Before making an order under section 29 of the 1976 Act in relation to a scheduled works agreement, the Secretary of State shall consult the Director General of Fair Trading.

(6) Section 29(2) of the 1976 Act (conditions which the Secretary of State must be satisfied are met before approving an agreement) shall have effect, in relation to a scheduled works agreement, with the substitution for paragraph (b) of—

"(b) that its object or main object is the facilitation of the design, construction, financing, maintenance or operation of any of the scheduled works within the meaning of the Channel Tunnel Rail Link Act 1996;".

(7) Without prejudice to the powers of revocation conferred by subsection (5) of section 29 of the 1976 Act, the Secretary of State may at any time by order revoke an order made under that section in relation to a scheduled works agreement if—

(a) he is requested to do so by a party to the agreement, and
(b) he has given to each of the parties to the agreement at least 28 days' notice of his intention to make the order.

(8) Where the Secretary of State approves a scheduled works agreement for the purposes of section 29 of the 1976 Act, he may by order provide that, in relation to any agreement made in pursuance of the approved agreement which is of a class specified in the order, such of the parties to the approved agreement as may be so specified and any body corporate which is a member of the same group as any of them shall be deemed to be interconnected bodies corporate for the purposes of that Act.

Monopoly situations

24.—(1) Where two or more persons are specified under section 34 below as the nominated undertaker for the same purpose of the same provision, the Secretary of State may by order provide that the persons so specified and any body corporate which is a member of the same group as any of them shall be deemed to be members of one and the same group of interconnected bodies corporate for the purposes of the relevant monopoly provisions of the Fair Trading Act 1973 ("the 1973 Act").

(2) Where the Secretary of State approves a scheduled works agreement for the purposes of section 29 of the Restrictive Trade Practices Act 1976, he may by order provide that, in relation to any relevant goods or services, such of the parties to the agreement as may be specified in the order and any body corporate which is a member of the same group as any of them shall be deemed for the purposes of the relevant monopoly provisions of the 1973 Act to be members of one and the same group of interconnected bodies corporate.

(3) In subsection (2) above, the reference to any relevant goods or services is to any goods or services which are—

(a) supplied in connection with the design, construction, financing, maintenance or operation of any of the scheduled works, and
(b) of a description specified in the order.

(4) For the purposes of subsections (1) and (2) above, the relevant monopoly provisions of the 1973 Act are sections 6(1)(b) (monopoly situation in

relation to the supply of goods by or to members of one and the same group of interconnected companies) and 7(1)(b) (corresponding provision in relation to the supply of services).

Anti-competitive practices

25.—(1) Where two or more persons are specified under section 34 below as the nominated undertaker for the same purpose of the same provision, the Secretary of State may by order provide that the persons so specified and any body corporate which is a member of the same group as any of them shall be deemed to be persons who are to be treated as associated for the purposes of section 2 of the Competition Act 1980.

(2) Where the Secretary of State approves a scheduled works agreement for the purposes of section 29 of the Restrictive Trade Practices Act 1976, he may by order provide that, in relation to any relevant course of conduct, such of the parties to the agreement as may be specified in the order and any body corporate which is a member of the same group as any of them shall be deemed to be persons who are to be treated as associated for the purposes of section 2 of the Competition Act 1980.

(3) In subsection (2) above, the reference to any relevant course of conduct is to any course of conduct engaged in connection with the design, construction, financing, maintenance or operation of any of the scheduled works.

Sections 23 to 25: supplementary provisions

26.—(1) Before exercising the power conferred by section 23(2) or (8), 24(1) or (2) or 25(1) or (2) above, the Secretary of State shall consult the Director General of Fair Trading.

(2) An order under section 23(2) or (8), 24(1) or (2) or 25(1) or (2) above may impose, on any person to whom any provision made under that subsection relates, such requirements as the Secretary of State considers it expedient to impose in connection with that provision.

(3) Subsections (3) and (4) of section 93 of the Fair Trading Act 1973 (enforcement of directions) shall apply in relation to requirements imposed under subsection (2) above as they apply in relation to directions under section 90(7) of that Act.

(4) Orders under section 23(2) or (8), 24 or 25 above, and orders made by virtue of section 23(4) above, shall be made by statutory instrument which shall be subject to annulment in pursuance of a resolution of either House of Parliament.

(5) In sections 23 to 25 above, "group" means a body corporate and all other bodies corporate which are its subsidiaries within the meaning of the Companies Act 1985.

Trees

Power to deal with trees on neighbouring land

27.—(1) Where any tree overhangs land used for the purposes of the nominated undertaker's undertaking under this Part of this Act, the nominated undertaker may by notice to the occupier of the land on which the tree is growing require the tree to be removed, topped or lopped if it is necessary for that to be done—

(a) to enable the works authorised by this Part of this Act to be maintained, or

(b) for reasons of safety in connection with the operation of any railway comprised in those works.

(2) If, within the period of 28 days beginning with the giving by the nominated undertaker of a notice under subsection (1) above, the occupier of the

land on which the tree to which the notice relates is growing gives the nominated undertaker a counter-notice objecting to the removal, topping or lopping of the tree, the notice shall have effect only if confirmed by an order of the county court.

(3) If at any time a notice under subsection (1) above has not been complied with and either—

(a) a period of 28 days beginning with the giving of the notice has expired without a counter-notice having been given, or

(b) an order of the court confirming the notice has come into force,

the nominated undertaker may itself cause the tree to which the notice relates to be removed, topped or lopped as mentioned in subsection (1) above.

(4) Where the power conferred by subsection (3) above is exercisable in relation to any tree, the nominated undertaker may—

(a) enter the land on which the tree is growing for the purpose of exercising that power in relation to it, and

(b) take with it such vehicles and equipment as are necessary for that purpose.

(5) Where the nominated undertaker tops or lops a tree in exercise of the power conferred by subsection (3) above, it shall do so in a husband-like manner and in such a way as to cause the minimum of damage to the tree.

(6) Where—

(a) a notice under subsection (1) above is complied with either without a counter-notice having been given or after the notice has been confirmed, or

(b) the nominated undertaker exercises the power conferred by subsection (3) above,

the county court shall, on application made by a person who has suffered loss or damage in consequence of the removal, topping or lopping of the tree concerned or who has incurred expenses in complying with the notice, order the nominated undertaker to pay that person such compensation in respect of the loss, damage or expenses as it thinks fit.

Disapplication of controls

28.—(1) The following, namely—

(a) an order under section 198(1) of the Town and Country Planning Act 1990 (tree preservation orders), and

(b) section 211(1) of that Act (which prohibits the doing in a conservation area of any act which might be prohibited by a tree preservation order),

shall not apply to any tree works which are authorised for the purposes of this section.

(2) Tree works are authorised for the purposes of this section if—

(a) they are carried out in compliance with a notice under subsection (1) of section 27 above or in exercise of the power conferred by subsection (3) of that section,

(b) they are carried out in relation to a tree growing on land within the relevant limits and for the purposes of or in connection with the construction of the works authorised by this Part of this Act, or

(c) they are carried out in relation to a tree growing on land used for the purpose of the nominated undertaker's undertaking under this Part of this Act and in circumstances where it is necessary for them to be carried out—

(i) to enable the works authorised by this Part of this Act to be maintained, or

(ii) for reasons of safety in connection with the operation of any railway comprised in those works.

(3) In subsection (2)(b) above, the reference to land within the relevant limits is to land within the limits of deviation for the scheduled works or within the limits of land to be acquired or used.

(4) In this section, references to tree works are to works consisting of the removal, topping or lopping of a tree.

Noise

Control of construction sites: appeals

29.—(1) In the Control of Pollution Act 1974, sections 60 (control of noise on construction sites) and 61 (prior consent for work on construction sites) shall have effect, in relation to works carried out in exercise of the powers conferred by this Part of this Act, with the following modifications.

(2) In subsection (7) (appeal against failure to give consent or the giving of qualified consent), for "a magistrates' court" there shall be substituted "the Secretary of State".

(3) After that subsection there shall be inserted—

"(7A) If within seven days of the giving of notice of appeal under subsection (7) of this section the appellant and the local authority so agree, the appeal shall, instead of being determined by the Secretary of State, be referred to arbitration."

(4) The Secretary of State for the Environment and the Secretary of State for Transport acting jointly may by regulations made by statutory instrument make in relation to appeals which are referred to arbitration under subsection (7A) of section 60 or 61 of the Control of Pollution Act 1974 any such provision as may be made by regulations under section 70 of that Act in relation to appeals under Part III of that Act to the Secretary of State.

Proceedings in respect of statutory nuisance: defence

30.—(1) Where proceedings are brought under section 82(1) of the Environmental Protection Act 1990 (summary proceedings by person aggrieved by statutory nuisance) in relation to a nuisance falling within paragraph (g) of section 79(1) of that Act (noise emitted from premises so as to be prejudicial to health or a nuisance) no order shall be made, and no fine may be imposed, under section 82(2) of that Act if the defendant shows—

(a) that the nuisance relates to premises used by the nominated undertaker for the purposes of or in connection with the exercise of the powers conferred by this Part of this Act with respect to works, and

(b) that the nuisance is attributable to the carrying out of works which are being carried out in accordance with a notice served under section 60, or a consent given under section 61 or 65, of the Control of Pollution Act 1974.

(2) The following provisions of the Control of Pollution Act 1974, namely—

(a) section 61(9) (consent for work on construction site to include statement that it does not of itself constitute a defence to proceedings under section 82 of the Environmental Protection Act 1990), and

(b) section 65(8) (corresponding provision in relation to consent for registered noise level to be exceeded),

shall not apply where the consent relates to the use of premises by the nominated undertaker for the purposes of or in connection with the exercise of the powers conferred by this Part of this Act with respect to works.

Financial matters

Expenditure in connection with securing construction of works

31.—(1) The Secretary of State may make payments under any agreement entered into by him for the purpose of securing the construction of—

(a) any of the works authorised by this Part of this Act, or
(b) any related works.

(2) For the purposes of this section, the following are related works—
(a) a station at Stratford, in the London Borough of Newham, for use in connection with the rail link, and
(b) a railway providing access between the rail link and the West Coast Main Line by means of a connection to the North London Line.

Reserved capacity on the rail link: expenditure

32.—(1) The Secretary of State may make payments to the nominated undertaker, or its nominee, in pursuance of an agreement for the payment, for such period as may be specified in the agreement, of such sum as may be so specified for the reservation of rights of use in relation to the rail link.

(2) The Secretary of State may make, to any person charged with responsibility in relation to the selection of persons to exercise rights of use in relation to the rail link which are reserved to the Secretary of State under an agreement with the nominated undertaker ("reserved rights of use"), such payments in respect of the discharge of that responsibility as the Secretary of State thinks fit.

(3) The Secretary of State may give to any person exercising reserved rights of use such financial assistance in relation to the exercise of those rights as he thinks fit.

(4) Financial assistance under subsection (3) above shall be on such terms and subject to such conditions as the Secretary of State thinks fit.

Undertakings with respect to financial assistance etc.

33.—(1) Any undertaking of the Secretary of State which—
(a) is given with respect to applications for assistance of a kind to which subsection (2) below applies, and
(b) is contained in a development agreement,
shall be effective notwithstanding that it fetters his discretion.

(2) This subsection applies to—
(a) any kind of financial or other assistance in relation to an existing railway line which might allow it to be used to provide a line speed in excess of 200 kilometres per hour before 31st December 2030, and
(b) any kind of financial or other assistance which before that date would enable or assist a person to provide services or facilities for international rail passenger services.

Miscellaneous and general

Holder of functions of nominated undertaker

34.—(1) The Secretary of State may by order provide that a person specified in the order shall be the nominated undertaker for such purposes of such provisions of this Part of this Act as may be so specified.

(2) Where, in the case of any provision of this Part of this Act which refers to the nominated undertaker, there is any purpose of the provision for which there is no one who is the nominated undertaker under subsection (1) above, any reference in the provision to the nominated undertaker shall be construed, in relation to that purpose, as a reference to the Secretary of State.

(3) An agreement by the Secretary of State with respect to the exercise of his discretion under subsection (1) above shall be effective notwithstanding that it fetters his discretion.

(4) An order under subsection (1) above may contain such supplementary, incidental, consequential or transitional provision as the Secretary of State considers necessary or expedient in connection with the order.

(5) The Secretary of State may by order make such modifications of any provision of this Part of this Act referring to the Secretary of State, so far as applying for a purpose in relation to which subsection (2) above has effect, as appear to him to be necessary or expedient in consequence of his having functions by virtue of that subsection.

(6) The power to make an order under this section shall be exercisable by statutory instrument.

(7) A statutory instrument containing an order under subsection (5) above shall be subject to annulment in pursuance of a resolution of either House of Parliament.

Transfer of functions relating to works

35.—(1) If the Secretary of State acquires any land for the purposes of this Part of this Act from a railway operator and there are situated on the land works authorised by statute, he may by order provide for the transfer of any statutory power or duty relating to the works previously exercisable by the railway operator—

(a) to him, or

(b) to a person specified under section 34 above.

(2) The Secretary of State may by order provide for the further transfer—

(a) to him, or

(b) to a person specified under section 34 above,

of a power or duty transferred under subsection (1) above or this subsection.

(3) If a railway operator acquires from the Secretary of State any land on which there are situated works authorised by this Part of this Act, the Secretary of State may, with the consent of the railway operator, by order provide for the transfer to the railway operator of any duty under this Part of this Act relating to the works.

(4) An order under this section may contain such supplementary, incidental, consequential or transitional provision as the Secretary of State considers necessary or expedient in connection with the order.

(5) In subsections (1) and (3) above, references to a railway operator are to a person who has the management for the time being of any network, station or light maintenance depot.

(6) In this section, "light maintenance depot", "network" and "station" have the same meanings as in Part I of the Railways Act 1993.

Compensation for injurious affection

36. Section 10(1) of the Compulsory Purchase Act 1965 (compensation for injurious affection) shall have effect, in relation to land injuriously affected by the execution of works under this Part of this Act, with the substitution for "acquiring authority have" of "nominated undertaker has".

Duty to co-operate

37.—(1) Where the nominated undertaker considers that a matter affects—

(a) the construction, maintenance or operation of the rail link, and

(b) the construction, maintenance or operation of a railway asset which is not a rail link asset,

it may by notice in writing require the operator of the asset to enter into an agreement with it about how the matter is to be dealt with.

(2) Where the operator of a railway asset which is not a rail link asset considers that a matter affects—

(a) the construction, maintenance or operation of the asset, and

(b) the construction, maintenance or operation of the rail link,

it may by notice in writing require the nominated undertaker to enter into an agreement with it about how the matter is to be dealt with.

(3) The terms of an agreement under subsection (1) or (2) above shall be such as the nominated undertaker and the operator of the asset may agree or, in default of agreement, as may be determined by arbitration.

(4) For the purposes of subsections (1) and (2) above a railway asset is a rail link asset if—

(a) in the case of a railway asset consisting of any network, station or light maintenance depot, it is comprised in the rail link, and

(b) in the case of a railway asset consisting of any train being used on a network, the network is comprised in the rail link.

(5) In this section—

"light maintenance depot", "network", "railway asset" and "station" have the same meanings as in Part I of the Railways Act 1993; and

"operator", in relation to a railway asset, means the person having the management of the asset for the time being.

Disapplication and modification of miscellaneous controls

38. Schedule 10 to this Act (which makes provision for the disapplication and modification of miscellaneous statutory and other controls in relation to things done under this Part of this Act and otherwise for the purposes of this Part of this Act) shall have effect.

Burial grounds

39.—(1) Nothing in any enactment relating to burial grounds and no obligation or restriction imposed under ecclesiastical law or otherwise shall have effect to prohibit, restrict or impose any condition on the use of any land comprised in a burial ground for the purpose of constructing any of the works authorised by this Part of this Act.

(2) Subsection (1) above shall not apply in relation to land in which human remains are interred unless—

(a) the remains have been removed and reinterred or cremated in accordance with the provisions of Schedule 11 to this Act, and

(b) any monument to the deceased has been dealt with in accordance with those provisions,

and the other requirements of that Schedule, so far as relating to the nominated undertaker, have been complied with.

(3) Subsection (2) above shall not apply where the use of the land for the purpose mentioned in subsection (1) above does not involve disturbing the human remains which are interred in it.

(4) In this section (and Schedule 11 to this Act)—

"enactment" includes an enactment in any local or private Act of Parliament, and an order, rule, regulation, byelaw or scheme made under an Act of Parliament; and

"monument" includes a tombstone or other memorial;

and references to a monument to any person are to a monument commemorating that person, whether or not also commemorating any other person.

Application of landlord and tenant law

40.—(1) No enactment or rule of law regulating the rights and obligations of landlords and tenants shall apply in relation to the rights and obligations of the parties to a development agreement lease or a lease to which subsection (2) below applies—

(a) so as to exclude or in any respect modify any of the rights and obligations of those parties under the terms of the lease, whether with respect to the termination of the tenancy or any other matter,

(b) so as to confer or impose on either party any right or obligation arising out of or connected with anything done or omitted on or in relation to land which is the subject of the lease, in addition to any such right or obligation provided for by the terms of the lease, or

(c) so as to restrict the enforcement (whether by action for damages or otherwise) by either party to the lease of any obligation of the other party under the lease.

(2) This subsection applies to a lease if it is granted by the Secretary of State and—

(a) it is one on the grant of which a development agreement, or an agreement connected with such an agreement, is conditional, or

(b) it contains a statement to the effect that it is granted for purposes connected with the construction or operation of the rail link.

(3) In this section, "development agreement lease" means a lease granted by the Secretary of State in pursuance of a development agreement, or an agreement connected with such an agreement, and references to a development agreement lease include any provisions of a development agreement, or an agreement connected with such an agreement, providing for the grant of a lease of any land by the Secretary of State.

(4) For the purposes of this section, an agreement is connected with a development agreement if the development agreement is expressed to be conditional upon it being entered into.

(5) This section shall be deemed to have come into force on 4th July 1995.

Variation of development agreement: disapplication of s.2 of Law of Property (Miscellaneous Provisions) Act 1989

41.—(1) Section 2(1) to (6) of the Law of Property (Miscellaneous Provisions) Act 1989 (under which a contract for the sale etc. of land can only be made by incorporating all the terms agreed in one document) shall not apply in relation to the variation of a development agreement.

(2) This section shall be deemed to have come into force on 31st May 1996.

Related works: application of section 9 of the Transport and Works Act 1992

42.—(1) If an application under section 6 of the Transport and Works Act 1992 (application for an order under section 1 of that Act) is made by a relevant undertaker, section 9 of that Act (procedure where the Secretary of State considers an application relates to proposals of national significance) shall have effect in relation to the application with the insertion at the end of subsections (1) and (2) of "or relate to, or to matters ancillary to, the construction of works which are related works for the purposes of section 31 of the Channel Tunnel Rail Link Act 1996".

(2) In subsection (1) above, the reference to a relevant undertaker is to a person who, under section 34 above, is the nominated undertaker for any purpose of section 1(1) above, so far as relating to the rail link.

Arbitration

43.—(1) Where under this Part of this Act any difference is to be referred to arbitration, the difference shall be referred to, and settled by, a single arbitrator to be agreed between the parties or, in default of agreement, to be appointed on the application of either party, after notice in writing to the other, by the President of the Institution of Civil Engineers.

(2) The Secretary of State for the Environment and the Secretary of State for Transport acting jointly may by rules made by statutory instrument make provision about procedure in relation to arbitration under this Part of this Act.

PART II

THE A2 AND M2 IMPROVEMENT WORKS

Authorised works

44.—(1) The Secretary of State may construct the works specified in Part I of Schedule 12 to this Act ("the A2 and M2 improvement works").

(2) Part II of that Schedule shall have effect for conferring on the Secretary of State powers in relation to—

(a) the stopping up of highways and the extinguishment of rights of way over them,
(b) the stopping up of access to premises, and
(c) temporary interference with highways,

for the purposes of or in connection with the construction of any of the A2 and M2 improvement works.

(3) Part III of that Schedule shall have effect—

(a) for treating highways constructed by the Secretary of State in pursuance of that Schedule as highways of specified descriptions,
(b) for transferring such of those highways as do not become trunk roads to the Kent County Council,
(c) for treating operations and works in pursuance of that Schedule as authorised under specified provisions of the Highways Act 1980,
(d) for treating certain provisions of that Schedule as provisions of instruments made under specified provisions of that Act, and
(e) for enabling traffic on any highway constructed in pursuance of that Schedule to be subject to regulation under the Road Traffic Regulation Act 1984 as soon as it is open for public use.

(4) Subject to subsection (5) below, the A2 and M2 improvement works shall be constructed in the lines or situations shown on the deposited plans and in accordance with the levels shown on the deposited sections.

(5) In constructing any of the A2 and M2 improvement works, the Secretary of State may—

(a) deviate laterally from the lines or situations shown on the deposited plans to any extent within the limits of deviation for that work so shown, and
(b) deviate vertically from the level shown for that work on the deposited sections—
    (i) to any extent not exceeding 3 metres upwards, and
    (ii) to any extent downwards.

Acquisition of land

45.—(1) The Secretary of State is authorised by this section to acquire compulsorily—

(a) so much of the land shown on the deposited plans within the limits of deviation for the A2 and M2 improvement works as may be required for or in connection with the works authorised by this Part of this Act, and
(b) so much of the land so shown within the limits of land to be acquired or used as may be so required.

(2) Without prejudice to the generality of subsection (1) above, the purposes for which land may be acquired under that subsection include, in the case of any land specified in columns (1) and (2) in Schedule 13 to this Act, the purpose specified in relation to that land in column (3) in that Schedule as one for which that land may be acquired or used.

(3) Part I of the Compulsory Purchase Act 1965, so far as not inconsistent with this Part of this Act, shall apply to an acquisition of land under subsection (1) above as it applies to a compulsory purchase to which Schedule 1 of

the Acquisition of Land Act 1981 applies and as if this Part of this Act were a compulsory purchase order under that Act.

(4) In its application by virtue of subsection (3) above, the Compulsory Purchase Act 1965 shall have effect with the modifications set out in paragraph 3(2) to (4) of Schedule 4 to this Act.

(5) The Compulsory Purchase (Vesting Declarations) Act 1981 shall apply as if this Part of this Act were a compulsory purchase order.

(6) In its application by virtue of subsection (5) above, the Compulsory Purchase (Vesting Declarations) Act 1981 shall have effect with the modifications set out in paragraph 5(2) to (7) of Schedule 4 to this Act, except that, in paragraph 5(7) of that Schedule, for "section 4(1)" there shall be substituted "section 45(1)".

(7) The Lands Clauses Consolidation Act 1845 shall not apply to the acquisition of land under subsection (1) above.

Blight: compensation for pre-enactment acquisition

46.—(1) This section applies to land which is blighted land under paragraph 16 of Schedule 13 to the Town and Country Planning Act 1990 (route of proposed special road "blighted land" for the purposes of Chapter II of Part VI of that Act on the Secretary of State notifying the local planning authority of his intention and identifying the proposed route) by virtue of steps taken by the Secretary of State in relation to the A2 and M2 improvement works.

(2) Where by virtue of section 154(2) of the Town and Country Planning Act 1990 (effect of valid blight notice) the Secretary of State is deemed—

(a) to have served a notice to treat in respect of an interest in land to which this section applies, and

(b) to have done so on a date prior to the day on which this Act is passed,

this Act shall be deemed, for the purpose of applying section 6 of the Land Compensation Act 1961 (disregard of actual or prospective development in certain cases) to the assessment of compensation for the acquisition of the interest, to have been passed before the date on which the notice to treat is deemed to have been served.

(3) In this section, "blight notice" means a notice served under section 150, 161 or 162 of the Town and Country Planning Act 1990.

(4) This section shall be deemed to have come into force on 23rd November 1994.

PART III

MISCELLANEOUS AND GENERAL

Time limit for powers of compulsory acquisition

47.—(1) After the end of the period of 5 years beginning with the day on which this Act is passed—

(a) no notice to treat shall be served under Part I of the Compulsory Purchase Act 1965, as applied to the acquisition of land under section 4(1) or 45(1) above, and

(b) no declaration shall be executed under section 4 of the Compulsory Purchase (Vesting Declarations) Act 1981, as applied by section 45(5) above or paragraph 4 of Schedule 4 to this Act.

(2) The Secretary of State may by order extend the period under subsection (1) above in relation to any land.

(3) An order under subsection (2) above shall be subject to special Parliamentary procedure.

Power to acquire land by reference to combined effect of works

48.—(1) The Secretary of State may acquire by agreement land the enjoyment of which is, or will in his opinion be, seriously affected by the combined effect of—

(a) the carrying out of works for the construction of any of the rail link works or the use of any of those works, and

(b) the carrying out of works for the construction of any of the A2 and M2 improvement works or the use of any of those works,

if the interest of the vendor is a qualifying interest.

(2) Subsection (1) above shall not apply in relation to land which may be acquired, by reference to the A2 and M2 improvement works, under section 246(2) or (2A) of the Highways Act 1980.

(3) Subsection (1) above shall not apply in relation to an interest which is the subject of a claim for compensation under Part I of the Land Compensation Act 1973 (compensation for depreciation caused by use of public works).

(4) The power conferred by subsection (1) above—

(a) so far as exercisable by reference to the carrying out of works for the construction of any work, shall only be exercisable if the acquisition is begun before the work's opening date, and

(b) so far as exercisable by reference to the use of any work, shall only be exercisable if the acquisition is begun before the end of one year after the work's opening date.

(5) For the purposes of subsection (4) above—

(a) the acquisition of any land shall be treated as begun when the agreement for its acquisition is made, and

(b) a work's opening date is—

(i) in the case of a work consisting of a highway, the date on which it is first opened to public traffic, and

(ii) in the case of any other work, the date on which it is first used after completion.

(6) In this section—

"qualifying interest" has the meaning given in section 149(2) of the Town and Country Planning Act 1990, taking references to the relevant date as references to the date on which the purchase agreement is made; and

"rail link works" means the scheduled works, so far as relating to the rail link.

Noise insulation regulations: procedure

49. Section 20 of the Land Compensation Act 1973 (sound-proofing of buildings affected by public works) shall have effect, in relation to regulations under that section which relate only to noise caused or expected to be caused by the construction or use of works authorised by this Act, with the substitution for subsection (9) of—

"(9) An instrument containing regulations under this section shall be subject to annulment in pursuance of a resolution of either House of Parliament."

Overhead lines

50.—(1) Section 37(1) of the Electricity Act 1989 (which requires the consent of the Secretary of State to overhead lines) shall not apply in relation to any electric line which—

(a) for the purposes of or in connection with the exercise of any of the powers conferred by Part I of this Act with respect to works, or
(b) in pursuance of any provision of Schedule 15 to this Act,

is installed above land within the limits of deviation for the scheduled works or within the limits of land to be acquired or used.

(2) Schedule 14 to this Act (which makes alternative provision for consent in relation to lines to which subsection (1) above applies) shall have effect.

(3) On the revocation or expiry of consent under Schedule 14 to this Act, the line to which the consent relates shall cease to be a line to which subsection (1) above applies.

(4) On granting consent under Schedule 14 to this Act to electricity undertakers, the appropriate Ministers may direct that planning permission shall be deemed to be granted for the carrying out of development to which the consent relates, subject to such conditions (if any) as may be specified in the direction.

(5) In subsection (4) above—
(a) "electricity undertakers" means the holder of a licence under section 6 of the Electricity Act 1989, and
(b) the reference to the appropriate Ministers is to the Secretary of State for Trade and Industry and the Secretary of State for Transport acting jointly.

Replacement concrete batching facilities at St Pancras

51.—(1) Planning permission shall be deemed to be granted under Part III of the Town and Country Planning Act 1990 for the construction of concrete batching facilities on land at St Pancras in London within the relevant limits.

(2) The planning permission deemed by subsection (1) above to be granted shall be deemed to be granted subject to a condition specifying the siting, design, external appearance and landscaping of the development as reserved matters for the subsequent approval of the local planning authority.

(3) Section 10 above shall apply in relation to the planning permission deemed by subsection (1) above to be granted as it applies in relation to the planning permission deemed by subsection (1) of section 9 above to be granted, so far as relating to development to which subsection (2) or (4) of that section applies.

(4) The carrying out or maintenance of any work on land within the relevant limits is authorised by virtue of this section if it is done in accordance with the planning permission deemed by subsection (1) above to be granted, notwithstanding that it involves—
(a) interference with an interest or right to which subsection (5) below applies, or
(b) a breach of a restriction as to the user of land by virtue of a contract.

(5) The interests and rights to which this subsection applies are any easement, liberty, privilege, right or advantage annexed to land and adversely affecting other land, including any natural right of support.

(6) In respect of any interference or breach in pursuance of subsection (4) above, compensation shall be—
(a) payable under section 7 or 10 of the Compulsory Purchase Act 1965, and
(b) assessed in the same manner and subject to the same rules as in the case of other compensation under those sections in respect of injurious affection where—

(i) the compensation is to be estimated in connection with a purchase under that Act, or

(ii) the injury arises from the execution of works on land acquired under that Act.

(7) Nothing in subsection (4) above shall be construed as authorising any act or omission on the part of any person which is actionable at the suit of any person on any grounds other than such an interference or breach as is mentioned in that subsection.

(8) In this section, references to the relevant limits are to the limits of land for concrete batching facilities which are shown on the deposited plans.

Protection of interests

52.—(1) Schedule 15 to this Act shall have effect for protecting the interests of the bodies and persons specified in that Schedule (being bodies and persons who may be affected by other provisions of this Act).

(2) The provisions of Schedule 15 to this Act shall be treated for the purposes of Part I of this Act as provisions of that Part.

Correction of deposited plans

53.—(1) If the deposited plans or the book of reference to those plans are inaccurate in their description of any land, or in their statement or description of the ownership or occupation of any land, the Secretary of State, after giving not less than 10 days' notice to the owners and occupiers of the land in question, may apply to two justices having jurisdiction in the place where the land is situated for the correction of the plans or book of reference.

(2) If on such an application it appears to the justices that the misstatement or wrong description arose from mistake or inadvertence, the justices shall certify accordingly and shall in their certificate state in what respect a matter is misstated or wrongly described.

(3) The certificate shall be deposited in the office of the Clerk of the Parliaments and a copy of it in the Private Bill Office of the House of Commons and with the proper officer of each county council or London borough council in whose area the land to which the certificate relates is situated, and thereupon the deposited plans or book of reference shall be deemed to be corrected according to the certificate and it shall be lawful for the Secretary of State, in accordance with the certificate, to proceed under this Act as if the deposited plans or book of reference had always been in the corrected form.

(4) A copy certificate deposited under subsection (3) above shall be kept with the documents to which it relates.

(5) A justice of the peace may act under this section in relation to land which is partly in one area and partly in another if he may act as respects land in either area.

(6) In this section, "book of reference" means the book deposited in connection with the Channel Tunnel Rail Link Bill in the office of the Clerk of the Parliaments and the Private Bill Office of the House of Commons in November 1994 together with the books so deposited in November and December 1995.

Service of documents

54.—(1) Any document required or authorised to be served on any person under this Act may be served—

(a) by delivering it to him or by leaving it at his proper address or by sending it by post to him at that address, or

(b) if the person is a body corporate, by serving it in accordance with paragraph (a) above on the secretary of that body, or

(c) if the person is a partnership, by serving it in accordance with paragraph (a) above on a partner or a person having control or management of the partnership business.

(2) For the purposes of this section and section 7 of the Interpretation Act 1978 (which relates to the service of documents by post) in its application to this section, the proper address of any person on whom a document is to be served shall be his last known address, except that—

(a) in the case of service on a body corporate or its secretary, it shall be the address of the registered or principal office of the body;

(b) in the case of service on a partnership or a partner or a person having the control or management of a partnership business, it shall be the address of the principal office of the partnership;

and for the purposes of this subsection the principal office of a company registered outside the United Kingdom or of a partnership carrying on business outside the United Kingdom is its principal office within the United Kingdom.

(3) If a person to be served under this Act with any document by another has specified to that other an address within the United Kingdom other than his proper address (as determined under subsection (2) above) as the one at which he or someone on his behalf will accept documents of the same description as that document, that address shall also be treated as his proper address for the purposes of this section and for the purposes of section 7 of the Interpretation Act 1978 in its application to this section.

(4) Where a document is required or authorised to be served under this Act on a person in his capacity as the owner of an interest in, or occupier of, any land and his name or address cannot be ascertained after reasonable enquiry, the document may be served by addressing it to him by name or by the description of "owner" or "occupier", as the case may be, of the land and—

(a) leaving it with a person who is, or appears to be, resident or employed on the land, or

(b) leaving it conspicuously affixed to some building or object on or near the land.

(5) In this section "secretary", in relation to a local authority within the meaning of the Local Government Act 1972, means the proper officer within the meaning of that Act.

Financial provision

55. There shall be paid out of money provided by Parliament any expenditure of the Secretary of State under this Act.

Interpretation

56.—(1) In this Act, except where the context otherwise requires—

"A2 and M2 improvement works" has the meaning given by section 44(1) above;

"bridleway", "carriageway", "cycle track", "footpath", "footway", "highway", "highway authority" and "local highway authority" have the same meanings as in the Highways Act 1980;

"burial ground" means a churchyard, cemetery or other ground, whether consecrated or not, which has at any time been set apart for the purposes of interment;

"deposited plans" and "deposited sections" mean respectively the following plans and sections deposited in connection with the Channel Tunnel Rail Link Bill in the office of the Clerk of the Parliaments and the Private Bill Office of the House of Commons, namely—

(a) the plans and sections shown on Sheets Nos. 1 to 6 and 9 to 24 of the plans and sections deposited in November 1995 in connection with the Barking Extended Tunnel,

(b) the plans and sections deposited in November 1995 otherwise than in connection with the Barking Extended Tunnel,

(c) the plans and sections deposited in December 1995, and

(d) the plans and sections deposited in November 1994, so far as not superseded by the plans and sections mentioned in paragraphs (a) to (c) above;

"development agreement" means an agreement (including one entered into before the passing of this Act) to which the Secretary of State is a party and under which another party has responsibilities in relation to the design, construction, financing or maintenance of the rail link;

"limits of deviation" means the limits of deviation which are shown on the deposited plans;

"limits of land to be acquired or used" means the limits of land to be acquired or used which are shown on the deposited plans;

"owner" has the same meaning as in the Acquisition of Land Act 1981;

"rail link" means—

(a) the railway between St Pancras, in London, and the Channel Tunnel portal at Castle Hill, Folkestone, in Kent, authorised to be constructed by section 1(1) above, together with its associated works, facilities and installations, and

(b) the railway comprised in Works Nos. 11, 11A and 11B (which connects the railway mentioned in paragraph (a) above with the Chatham to Victoria Line), together with its associated works, facilities and installations;

"rail link undertaker" means a person who, under section 34 above, is the nominated undertaker for any purpose of section 1(1) or 14(1) above, so far as relating to the rail link;

"scheduled works" has the meaning given by section 1(1) above; and

"scheduled works agreement" means an agreement relating to the design, construction, financing, maintenance or operation of any of the scheduled works.

(2) References in this Act to the nominated undertaker shall be read in accordance with section 34 above.

(3) In this Act—

(a) a reference to a highway or any other place identified by letters and numbers is a reference to the highway or place shown as such on the deposited plans,

(b) a reference to a work identified by a number (or a number and a letter) is a reference to the scheduled work or, as the case may be, the A2 and M2 improvement work of that number (or number and letter),

(c) references to specified distances shall be construed as if the words "or thereabouts" were inserted after each such distance, distances between points on a road or railway being measured along the centre line of the road or railway.

Short title

57. This Act may be cited as the Channel Tunnel Rail Link Act 1996.

SCHEDULES

Section 1

SCHEDULE 1

Scheduled Works

Description of works

1. The works which the nominated undertaker is authorised by section 1 above to construct and maintain are the following—

In the London Boroughs of Camden and Islington—

St Pancras to Highbury Corner

Work No. 1—Railways between St Pancras and Highbury Corner and related works comprising the following railways, including a station terminus at St Pancras for international and domestic services and the provision of facilities in connection therewith—

International High Speed Railway

Work No. 1A—A railway (741 metres in length) commencing in the intended St Pancras Station, passing north-westwards over the new road (Work No. 5D), then northwards over the realigned Camley Street (Work No. 5A) and terminating at a point 33 metres south of the southern abutment of the existing bridge over the Regent's Canal, including bridges over Works Nos. 5A and 5D;

Work No. 1AA—A railway (2,189 metres in length) commencing by a junction with the railway (Work No. 1A) at its termination, passing northwards over the Regent's Canal and the railway (Work No. 2) in tunnel, then passing north-eastwards over the diverted York Way (Work No. 5Q), the railways (Works Nos. 2AA and 2BB) in tunnel and the East Coast Main Line to a tunnel portal 65 metres to the east of that railway, then passing in tunnel over the Piccadilly Line then beneath Caledonian Road, Westbourne Road and Liverpool Road and terminating at Highbury Corner beneath the junction of that road with Highbury Place, including bridges over the Regent's Canal, Work No. 5Q and the East Coast Main Line;

Work No. 1B—A railway (737 metres in length) commencing in the intended St Pancras Station, passing north-westwards over the new road (Work No. 5D), then northwards over the realigned Camley Street (Work No. 5A) and terminating at a point 30 metres south of the southern abutment of the existing bridge over the Regent's Canal, including bridges over Works Nos. 5A and 5D;

Work No. 1BB—A railway (2,182 metres in length) commencing by a junction with the railway (Work No. 1B) at its termination, passing northwards over the Regent's Canal and the railway (Work No. 2) in tunnel, then passing north-eastwards in tunnel beneath the railway (Work No. 1CC) for a distance of 150 metres, then over the diverted York Way (Work No. 5Q), the railways (Works Nos. 2AA and 2BB) in tunnel and the East Coast Main Line to a tunnel portal 65 metres to the east of that railway, then passing in tunnel over the Piccadilly Line then beneath Caledonian Road, Westbourne Road and Liverpool Road and terminating at Highbury Corner beneath the junction of that road with Highbury Place, including bridges over the Regent's Canal, Work No. 5Q and the East Coast Main Line;

Domestic Railway

Work No. 1C—A railway (533 metres in length) commencing in the intended St Pancras Station at a point 15 metres north-west of the existing junction of Clarence Passage with Pancras Road, passing north-westwards on the eastern side of the existing Midland Main Line, over the new road (Work No. 5D) and the realigned Camley Street (Work No. 5A), and terminating at a point 25 metres south of the southern abutment of the existing bridge over the Regent's Canal, including bridges over Works Nos. 5A and 5D;

Work No. 1CC—A railway (650 metres in length) commencing by a junction with the railway (Work No. 1C) at its termination, passing northwards over the Regent's Canal, then passing north-eastwards over the railways (Works Nos. 1BB and 1DD) in tunnel, then over the diverted York Way (Work No. 5Q) and terminating by a junction with the railway (Work No. 1AA) at a point 100 metres north-east of the existing York Way bridge, including bridges over the Regent's Canal and Work No. 5Q;

Work No. 1D—A railway (534 metres in length) commencing in the intended St Pancras Station at a point 15 metres north-west of the existing junction of Clarence Passage with Pancras Road, passing north-westwards on the eastern side of the existing Midland Main Line, over the new road (Work No. 5D) and the realigned Camley Street (Work No. 5A), and terminating at a point 30 metres south of the southern abutment of the existing bridge over the Regent's Canal, including bridges over Works Nos. 5A and 5D;

Work No. 1DD—A railway (680 metres in length) commencing by a junction with the railway (Work No. 1D) at its termination, passing northwards over the railway (Work No. 2) in tunnel and the Regent's Canal, then passing north-eastwards in tunnel beneath the railway (Work No. 1CC) for a distance of 150 metres, then over the diverted York Way (Work No. 5Q) and the railways (Works Nos. 2AA and 2BB) in tunnel, and terminating by a junction with the railway (Work No. 1BB) at a point 125 metres north-east of the existing York Way bridge, including bridges over the Regent's Canal and Work No. 5Q;

Work No. 1EE—A railway (767 metres in length) commencing by a junction with the railway (Work No. 1AA) at a point on the existing bridge over the Regent's Canal, passing northwards over the Midland City Line (Thameslink) in tunnel, then north-westwards and westwards, then on viaduct over the Midland City Line (Thameslink), the diverted Midland Main Line (Work No. 3B) and the railways (Works Nos. 1HH and 3C) and terminating by a junction with the North London Line at a point 15 metres east of the bridge carrying that railway over St Pancras Way, including the said viaduct;

Work No. 1FF—A railway (394 metres in length) commencing by a junction with the railway (Work No. 1EE) at a point 95 metres north of the northern abutment of the existing bridge over the Regent's Canal, passing northwards and north-eastwards under the railway (Work No. 1GG) and terminating by a junction with the realigned North London Incline Railway (Work No. 1JJ) at a point 30 metres west of the bridge carrying York Way over that railway;

Work No. 1GG—A railway (696 metres in length) commencing by a junction with the railway (Work No. 1EE) at a point 40 metres east of the bridge carrying the North London Line over St Pancras Way, passing eastwards on viaduct over the diverted Midland Main Line (Work No. 3B), the railways (Works Nos. 1HH and 3C) and the Midland City Line (Thameslink), then continuing on viaduct, passing south-eastwards over the new road (Work No. 5EE) and the railway (Work No. 1FF) and terminating by a junction with the railway (Work No. 1AA) at a point 40 metres west of the bridge carrying York Way over the North London Incline Railway, including the said viaduct;

Work No. 1HH—A railway (610 metres in length) commencing by a junction with the railway (Work No. 1EE) at a point 55 metres north of the northern abutment of the existing bridge over the Regent's Canal, passing northwards over the Midland City Line (Thameslink) in tunnel, then under the railways (Works Nos. 1EE, 1GG and 1JJ) and the existing bridge carrying the North London Line over the Midland Main Line and terminating by a junction with that railway at a point beneath the southern parapet of the bridge carrying Agar Grove over that railway;

Work No. 1JJ—A railway (955 metres in length), forming a realignment of the North London Incline Railway, commencing by a junction with the North London Line at a point 130 metres east of the bridge carrying that railway over St Pancras Way, passing eastwards then south-eastwards, then on viaduct over the diverted Midland Main Line (Work No. 3B), the railways (Works Nos. 1HH and 3C), the Midland City Line (Thameslink) and the new road (Work No. 5EE), then over the diverted York Way (Work No. 5Q), then passing northwards under the North London Line on viaduct and terminating by a junction with the Great Northern Suburban Line at the southern portal of the western bore of the Copenhagen Tunnel, including the said viaduct and a bridge over Work No. 5Q;

Work No. 1K—A railway (103 metres in length), forming a cross-over between the diverted Midland Main Line (Work No. 3B) and the railway (Work No. 1A), commencing by a junction with Work No. 3B at its commencement and terminating by a junction with Work No. 1A at its termination;

Thameslink, St Pancras and King's Cross

Work No. 2—A railway (876 metres in length), including a station tunnel on the Midland City Line (Thameslink) beneath St Pancras Station, commencing by a junction with that railway in tunnel at a point beneath Midland Road 145 metres north-east of the existing junction of that road with Euston Road, passing in tunnel north-westwards and northwards beneath the Regent's Canal and terminating by a junction with that railway in tunnel at a point beneath the existing Midland Main Line 55 metres north of the northern abutment of the bridge carrying that last-mentioned railway over that canal;

Work No. 2A—A railway (325 metres in length) commencing by a junction with the railway (Work No. 2) in tunnel at a point beneath the existing Midland Main Line 250 metres south of the southern abutment of the bridge carrying that railway over Camley Street, passing in tunnel northwards on the western side of Work No. 2 beneath the railways (Works Nos. 1A and 1B) and the realigned Camley Street (Work No. 5A) and terminating in tunnel at a point beneath the railway (Work No. 1D) 90 metres south of the southern abutment of the existing bridge over the Regent's Canal;

Work No. 2AA—A railway (883 metres in length) commencing by a junction with the railway (Work No. 2A) at its termination, passing in tunnel north-eastwards beneath the railways (Works Nos. 1C and 2), St Pancras Basin, the Regent's Canal and the diverted York Way (Work No. 5Q), then passing north-eastwards and northwards under the railways (Works Nos. 1AA, 1BB and 1DD) to a tunnel portal at a point 40 metres south of the southern side of the viaduct carrying the North London Line over the East Coast Main Line, then continuing under the North London Line on viaduct and terminating by a junction with the Great Northern Suburban Line at the southern portal of the western bore of the Copenhagen Tunnel on that railway;

Work No. 2B—A railway (255 metres in length) commencing by a junction with the railway (Work No. 2) in tunnel at the said point beneath the existing Midland Main Line 250 metres south of the southern abutment of the bridge carrying that railway over Camley Street, passing in tunnel northwards on the eastern side of Work No. 2 beneath the railways (Works Nos. 1A, 1B, 1C and 1D) and terminating in tunnel at a point beneath the realigned Camley Street (Work No. 5A) 150 metres south-east of the southern abutment of the existing bridge over the Regent's Canal;

Work No. 2BB—A railway (928 metres in length) commencing by a junction with the railway (Work No. 2B) at its termination, passing in tunnel north-eastwards beneath St Pancras Basin, the Regent's Canal and the diverted York Way (Work No. 5Q), then passing north-eastwards and northwards under the railways (Works Nos. 1AA, 1BB and 1DD) to a tunnel portal at a point 35 metres south of the southern side of the viaduct carrying the North London Line over the East Coast Main Line, then continuing under the North London Line on viaduct and terminating by a junction with the Great Northern Suburban Line at the said southern portal of the western bore of the Copenhagen Tunnel on that railway;

Work No. 2C—A railway (80 metres in length), forming a cross-over between the northbound and southbound rails of the Great Northern Suburban Line in tunnel within the western bore of the Copenhagen Tunnel, commencing and terminating by junctions with that railway at points respectively 50 metres and 130 metres north of the southern portal of that tunnel;

Work No. 2D—A railway (240 metres in length), forming cross-overs between the northbound and southbound rails of the City Widened Lines (Thameslink) partly within the Clerkenwell No. 3 Tunnel, commencing by a junction with that railway in tunnel beneath the junction of Frederick Street with the Kings Cross Road, passing northwestwards beneath Acton Street, Swinton Street, Wicklow Street and Britannia Street and terminating by a junction with that railway at a point 10 metres south-east of the bridge carrying Leeke Street over that railway;

Work No. 2E—A railway (349 metres in length), forming a cross-over between the Midland City Line (Thameslink) and the Midland Main Line at Kentish Town, commencing by a junction with that first named railway at a point 20 metres south-east of the south-eastern side of the bridge carrying Islip Street over that railway, passing south-eastwards and terminating by a junction with that last named railway at a point 85 metres north-west of the north-western portal of the Camden Road Tunnel;

Midland Main Line

Work No. 3—A railway (645 metres in length), forming a diversion of the Midland Main Line at St Pancras Station, commencing at its terminus in that station, passing northwestwards on the western side of the existing railway, including a western extension of the station over Midland Road and Pancras Road, then northwards over the new road (Work No. 5D) and the realigned Camley Street (Work No. 5A) and terminating at a point on the northern side of Work No. 5A 140 metres south of the existing bridge over the Regent's Canal, including bridges over Works Nos. 5A and 5D;

Work No. 3B—A railway (846 metres in length), forming a continuation of the diversion of the Midland Main Line at St Pancras Station, commencing by a junction with the railway (Work No. 3) at its termination, passing northwards over the Regent's Canal, under the railways (Works Nos. 1EE, 1GG and 1JJ) on viaduct and the existing bridge carrying the North London Line over the Midland Main Line and terminating by a junction with that railway beneath a point 30 metres north of the southern parapet of the bridge carrying Agar Grove over that railway, including a bridge over the Regent's Canal;

Work No. 3C—A railway (876 metres in length), forming a siding on the western side of the diverted Midland Main Line (Works Nos. 3 and 3B) north of St Pancras Station, commencing at a point 60 metres south of the bridge carrying that railway over the realigned Camley Street (Work No. 5A), passing northwards over Work No. 5A and the Regent's Canal, under the railways (Works Nos. 1EE, 1GG and 1JJ) on viaduct and the existing bridge carrying the North London Line over the Midland Main Line and terminating by a junction with that railway beneath a point 15 metres south of the said southern parapet of the bridge carrying Agar Grove over that railway, including bridges over Work No. 5A and the Regent's Canal;

Work No. 3D—A railway (71 metres in length), forming a cross-over between the northbound and southbound rails of the Midland Main Line, commencing by a junction with that railway at the northern portal of the Camden Road Tunnel on that railway, passing northwards and terminating by a junction with that railway at a point 70 metres north of its commencement;

Work No. 3E—A railway (829 metres in length), for construction purposes, commencing by a junction with the railway (Work No. 1HH) at a point 110 metres south-east of the southern side of the bridge carrying the North London Line over the Midland Main Line, passing south-eastwards, then eastwards and north-eastwards under the diverted York Way (Work No. 5Q), then passing northwards and terminating by a junction with the Great Northern Suburban Line at a point 65 metres south of the southern side of the viaduct carrying the North London Line over that railway;

London Underground: ticket halls and subways

Work No. 4—Ticket halls and subways, including alteration of existing ticket halls and subways, of the London Underground Railways comprising—

Work No. 4A—A passenger subway commencing on the eastern side of the intended St Pancras Station beneath a point 22 metres north of the existing junction of Clarence Passage with Pancras Road, passing south-eastwards to a ticket hall beneath the northern side of the forecourt of the Great Northern Hotel and terminating by a junction with the passenger subways (Works Nos. 4AA and 4F) beneath a point 26 metres north of the north-eastern corner of the Great Northern Hotel, including the said ticket hall;

Work No. 4AA—A passenger subway commencing by a junction with the passenger subway (Work No. 4A) at its termination and the passenger subway (Work No. 4F) at its commencement, passing eastwards to junctions with the passenger subway (Work No. 4MM) then continuing south-eastwards to a junction with the passenger subway (Work No. 4D), continuing eastwards and terminating by a junction with the existing passenger subway beneath a point 14 metres west of the junction of Caledonian Road with Pentonville Road;

Work No. 4B—A ticket hall in the German Gym off Pancras Road and a passenger subway commencing on the south-western side of that building at a point 40 metres west of the existing junction of Wellers Court with Cheney Road, passing south-eastwards, then south-westwards and terminating by a junction with the subway (Work No. 4A) beneath a point 23 metres east of the junction of Wellers Court with Pancras Road;

Work No. 4C—A passenger subway, forming a cross-passage between northbound and southbound station tunnels of the Victoria Line, commencing beneath a point 29 metres north-west of the junction of Caledonian Road with Pentonville Road; and terminating beneath a point 45 metres north-west of that road junction;

Work No. 4D—A passenger subway, including a lift shaft, commencing by a junction with the cross-passage (Work No. 4C) beneath a point 35 metres north-west of the junction of Caledonian Road with Pentonville Road, passing south-westwards to a junction with the passenger subway (Work No. 4A) at its termination and terminating by a junction with the cross-passage (Work No. 4E) beneath a point 55 metres west of that road junction;

Work No. 4E—A passenger subway, forming a cross-passage between northbound and southbound station tunnels of the Victoria Line, commencing and terminating beneath points 95 metres and 80 metres respectively south-east of the junction of Caledonia Street with York Way;

Work No. 4F—A passenger subway commencing by a junction with the passenger subway (Work No. 4A) at its termination and the passenger subway (Work No. 4AA) at its commencement beneath a point 26 metres north of the north-eastern corner of the Great Northern Hotel, passing south-westwards and terminating by a junction with the passenger subway (Work No. 4G) beneath a point in Pancras Road 40 metres south-west of the south-western corner of that building;

Work No. 4G—A passenger subway, including a lift shaft, commencing by a junction with the cross-passage (Work No. 4Q), passing eastwards to junctions with the cross-passage (Work No. 4R) and with the passenger subway (Work No. 4F) at its termination, and terminating by a junction with the existing cross-passage between northbound and southbound station tunnels of the Northern Line beneath a point 60 metres north-east of the existing junction of Pancras Road with Euston Road;

Work No. 4H—A passenger subway commencing in the ticket hall (part of Work No. 4A) beneath a point 48 metres north of the north-eastern corner of the Great Northern Hotel, passing south-eastwards and terminating by a junction with the existing passenger subway beneath a point 40 metres south-east of that corner of that building;

Work No. 4J—A passenger subway commencing in the existing ticket hall beneath the station concourse of King's Cross Station beneath a point 40 metres north of the junction of Pancras Road with Euston Road and terminating in St Pancras Station beneath a point 60 metres north-west of that road junction;

Work No. 4K—A ticket hall beneath the forecourt of St Pancras Station off Euston Road and a passenger subway commencing in that ticket hall beneath a point 100 metres west of the junction of Pancras Road with Euston Road, passing south-eastwards then north-eastwards and terminating by a junction with the Circle and Metropolitan Line Station concourse beneath a point 95 metres south-west of that road junction;

Work No. 4L—A passenger subway commencing in St Pancras Station at a point 75 metres west of the junction of Pancras Road with Euston Road, passing south-eastwards beneath Euston Road and terminating in the footway on the southern side of Euston Road at a point 75 metres south-west of that road junction, including a junction with the new ticket hall (part of Work No. 4K) and a permanent opening in Euston Road at that termination;

Work No. 4MM—A passenger subway, including a lift shaft, commencing by a junction with the existing Piccadilly Line Station concourse beneath a point 56 metres north-west of the junction of York Way with Euston Road, passing northwards to junctions with the passenger subway (Work No. 4AA) and the cross passage (Work No. 4N) then continuing south-eastwards and terminating by a junction with the passenger subway (Work No. 4AA) beneath a point 45 metres north-east of that road junction;

Work No. 4N—A passenger subway, forming a cross-passage between westbound and eastbound station tunnels of the Piccadilly Line, commencing beneath a point 35 metres west of the junction of Caledonia Street with York Way and terminating beneath a point 46 metres west of that road junction;

Work No. 4P—A passenger subway, including a lift shaft, commencing in the ticket hall (part of Work No. 4A) beneath a point 17 metres east of the north-eastern corner of the Great Northern Hotel, passing south-eastwards, then south-westwards and south-eastwards and terminating beneath that building at a point 11 metres north-west of the south-eastern corner of that hotel;

Work No. 4Q—A passenger subway, forming a cross-passage between southbound and northbound station tunnels of the Northern Line, commencing beneath a point 70 metres south of the existing junction of Cheney Road with Pancras Road and terminating beneath a point 82 metres south of that road junction;

Work No. 4R—A passenger subway, forming a cross-passage between southbound and northbound station tunnels of the Northern Line, commencing beneath a point 72 metres south of the existing junction of Cheney Road with Pancras Road and terminating beneath a point 84 metres south of that road junction;

Work No. 4S—A passenger subway, including a lift shaft, commencing in the existing passenger subway beneath a point 33 metres north of the junction of Belgrove Street with Euston Road and terminating at the Circle and Metropolitan Line Station concourse beneath a point 20 metres north of that road junction;

Associated Works

Work No. 5—Roadworks and sewer diversions associated with Works Nos. 1 to 4 comprising—

Roadworks

Work No. 5A—Realignment of Camley Street commencing at a point in that road 50 metres south of its junction with Granary Street, passing south-eastwards then eastwards under the railways (Works Nos. 1A to 1D and 3), then south-eastwards and terminating by a junction with Camley Street (Work No. 5C) at a point on the western side of that road 44 metres north-west of its existing junction with Goods Way;

Work No. 5B—A road commencing in Pancras Road at a point 20 metres south-east of the entrance from that road to St Pancras Old Church, passing south-eastwards then southwards to a junction with Brill Place and terminating in Midland Road at its existing junction with Euston Road, including access to a service area in St Pancras Station;

Work No. 5C—A road commencing by a junction with Camley Street (Work No. 5A) at a point 45 metres north-west of its existing junction with Goods Way, passing south-eastwards to a point 5 metres east of the existing junction of Wellers Court with Cheney Road, then south-westwards to a point 55 metres south of the existing junction of Wellers Court with Pancras Road, then passing south-eastwards along the line of that road and terminating in that road at its existing junction with Euston Road, including access to a service area in St Pancras Station and a parcels depot;

Work No. 5D—A road commencing by a junction with Work No. 5B at a point 175 metres south-east of its commencement, passing north-eastwards beneath the intended St Pancras Station (Works Nos. 1A to 1D and 3), across Work No. 5C at a point 7 metres south of its commencement and terminating by a junction with Goods Way at a point 155 metres from the junction of that road with York Way;

Work No. 5D(1)—A road, for construction purposes, commencing at a point 43 metres north-west of Battle Bridge Road at its termination west of Kings Cross Station, passing northwards, then north-westwards over Goods Way (Work No. 5D) at the termination of that work and over the Regent's Canal, then south-westwards and terminating by a junction with Wharf Road at a point 45 metres west of the existing bridge between Wharf Road and Goods Way, including bridges over Goods Way and the Regent's Canal;

Work No. 5D(2)—Widening of Wharf Road on its northern side between a point 50 metres west of the western side of the existing bridge over the Regent's Canal between Wharf Road and Goods Way and a point 15 metres east of the eastern side of that bridge;

Work No. 5EE—A road commencing by a junction with the diverted York Way (Work No. 5Q) at a point 70 metres south of the bridge carrying the North London Line over that road, passing westwards then south-westwards and southwards under the realigned North London Incline Railway (Work No. 1JJ) and the railway (Work No. 1GG) and terminating at a point 150 metres south-east of the existing bridge carrying the North London Line over the Midland Main Line;

Work No. 5F—A road commencing by a junction with Pancras Road (Work No. 5C) at a point 75 metres from its termination, passing north-eastwards, then northwards and north-westwards and terminating by a junction with Work No. 5C at the south-eastern corner of the German Gym in Cheney Road as existing, including access to a parcels depot;

Work No. 5F(1)—A road commencing by a junction with Work No. 5F at a point 65 metres from the commencement of that work, passing westwards and north-westwards along the frontage of the Great Northern Hotel, then continuing northwards and north-eastwards and terminating by a junction with Work No. 5F at a point 75 metres from the termination of that work;

Work No. 5G—Widening of Euston Road on its southern side between its junctions with Crestfield Street and Birkenhead Street;

Work No. 5H—Widening of Euston Road on its northern side between its junction with Euston Square and a point 45 metres north-east of that road junction;

Work No. 5Q—A road, forming a diversion of York Way, commencing at a point in that road 80 metres north of the junction of Copenhagen Street with York Way, passing northwards then north-westwards over the railway (Work No. 3E) and the railways (Works Nos. 2AA and 2BB) in tunnel, then northwards under the railways (Works Nos. 1AA, 1BB, 1CC, 1DD and 1JJ) to a junction with the new road (Work No. 5EE), then continuing northwards under the North London Line and terminating at a point in York Way 10 metres north-west of the junction of Vale Royal with York Way;

Work No. 5Q(1)—A road, forming a diversion of Randell's Road, commencing by a junction with the diverted York Way (Work No. 5Q) at a point 20 metres west of the existing junction of Randell's Road with York Way, passing eastwards and terminating at a point in Randell's Road 55 metres east of that existing road junction;

Sewer diversions

Work No. 5J—A sewer, forming a diversion of part of the Fleet Sewer, commencing by a junction with that sewer beneath a point in Pancras Road 35 metres south-east of the junction of Chenies Place with that street, passing along the line of Work No. 5B to its junction with Brill Place, then passing eastwards beneath the intended St Pancras Station, then southwards on the eastern side of that station and terminating beneath a point in Pancras Road 5 metres north of the existing junction of Wellers Court with that road, including a weir chamber at its junction with the Fleet Storm Relief Sewer;

Work No. 5K—A sewer, forming a diversion of the Midland Road sewer, commencing by a junction with that sewer beneath a point in Midland Road 140 metres north of its existing junction with Euston Road, passing north-westwards then northwards beneath land adjoining Midland Road and terminating by a junction with Work No. 5J beneath a point on the north-western side of Brill Place at its existing junction with Midland Road;

Work No. 5LL—A sewer, forming a diversion of part of the Camden Sewer, commencing by a junction with that sewer beneath a point 10 metres north of the bridge carrying the North London Line over the diverted York Way (Work No. 5Q), passing southwards, south-eastwards, then southwards and south-westwards and terminating by a junction with that sewer beneath a point 110 metres west of the Maiden Lane Bridge carrying York Way over the Regent's Canal;

Work No. 5N—A sewer, forming a diversion of the Camley Street Sewer, commencing by a junction with that sewer beneath a point in that street (Work No. 5A) 93 metres from the termination of that work, passing southwards along the line of that work and Work No. 5C to a point 15 metres south of Battle Bridge Road, then passing south-eastwards and terminating by a junction with the sewer (Work No. 5J) at a point on the northern side of Stanley Passage 35 metres north-east of its existing junction with Pancras Road;

Work No. 5P—A sewer, forming a diversion of the Goods Way Sewer, commencing by a junction with the sewer (Work No. 5N) at a point 105 metres south of the commencement of that work, passing eastwards on the line of the new road (Work No. 5D) and terminating by a junction with the Goods Way sewer beneath a point in Goods Way 180 metres west of its junction with York Way;

Work No. 5R—A sewer, forming a diversion of part of the St Pancras Sewer, commencing by a junction with that sewer beneath a point 38 metres north-west of the junction of Pancras Road with Euston Road, passing northwards, then westwards, north-westwards, then north-eastwards and terminating by a junction with the Fleet Sewer beneath a point 10 metres south-west of the south-eastern gable of the Great Northern Hotel;

In the London Boroughs of Islington, Hackney, Newham and Waltham Forest—

Highbury Corner to Stratford

Work No. 6—A railway (7,229 metres in length) commencing by a junction with the railways (Works Nos. 1AA and 1BB) at their termination, passing eastwards in tunnel beneath the North London Line, or land adjoining on the northern or southern side thereof, beneath Highbury Corner, Highbury Grove, Wallace Road, Mildmay Park, King Henry's Walk, Kingsland High Street, Dalston Lane, the Liverpool Street and Cambridge Railway, Mare Street, Barnabas Road, Kenworthy Road, the East Cross Route on the northern side of the North London Line, Eastway, the River Lea Navigation, Waterden Road and the River Lea, including ventilation shafts on lands off Corsica Street and Graham Road, then in retained cutting from chainage 6,147 metres for a distance of 1,067 metres, partly in tunnel beneath the railways (Works Nos. 6B and 6C) and the access roads (Works Nos. 6H and 6J), in land west of the High Meads Loop Railway, in the International Freight Terminal and the site of the former Chobham Farm Container Depot at Stratford, and terminating beneath a point on the western side of Angel Lane 60 metres north of the northern abutment of the bridge carrying that road over the Great Eastern Railway, including facilities for a railway crossover and junction at the International Freight Terminal and Depot at Stratford;

Work No. 6A—A railway (1,368 metres in length) commencing by a junction with the railway (Work No. 6) at the commencement of the retained cutting forming part of that work, passing eastwards between the eastbound and westbound lines of that railway to a point 210 metres west of the eastern face of the tunnel beneath the railway (Work No. 6C), then passing north-eastwards over the eastbound line of Work No. 6 and northwards in tunnel beneath the Old Yard Sidings (Work No. 6C) and the Lea Valley Line, then continuing north-westwards on the eastern side of that railway and terminating at a point under the bridge carrying Temple Mill Lane over that railway;

Work No. 6B—A railway (426 metres in length), for construction purposes, commencing by a junction with the North London Line at a point 10 metres north-west of the junction of that railway with the Channelsea Curve at Stratford Station, passing northwards, on the eastern side of the High Meads Curve, then north-eastwards over the railways (Works Nos. 6 and 6A) in tunnel and terminating by a junction with the High Meads Sidings at a point 30 metres north-east of the termination of the said tunnel over Works Nos. 6 and 6A;

Work No. 6C—A railway (836 metres in length) for construction purposes, commencing by a junction with the Lea Valley Line at a point 120 metres north-east of the junction of that railway with the Great Eastern Railway at Stratford Station, passing northwards and north-eastwards through the Old Yard Sidings and terminating by a junction with the Lea Valley Line at a point 130 metres south of the bridge carrying Temple Mill Lane over that railway;

Work No. 6D—A railway (1,032 metres in length) commencing in the existing Traction Maintenance Depot at a point 25 metres south-west of the south-western corner of the diesel repair shed in that depot, passing north-eastwards and northwards, then north-westwards on the western side of the Lea Valley Line to a junction with that railway 60 metres south of the bridge carrying Temple Mill Lane over that railway, passing under that bridge, then continuing on the eastern side of the Lea Valley Line and terminating by a junction with the railway (Work No. 6E) at a point 390 metres north of that bridge;

Work No. 6E—A railway (2,720 metres in length) commencing by a junction with the railway (Work No. 6A) at its termination, passing north-westwards and westwards through the former Temple Mills Marshalling Yard under Ruckholt Road and terminating at a point on the northern side of the Lea Valley Line 15 metres south-east of the eastern side of the bridge carrying Lea Bridge Road over that railway;

Work No. 6E(1)—A railway (410 metres in length), for construction purposes, commencing by a junction with the Lea Valley Line at a point 345 metres south-east of the bridge carrying Lea Bridge Road over that railway, passing eastwards and terminating by a junction with the railway (Work No. 6E) at chainage 1,922 metres;

Work No. 6F—A railway (509 metres in length) commencing by a junction with the railway (Work No. 6E) at a point 30 metres south-east of the bridge carrying Ruckholt Road over the Lea Valley Line, passing westwards under that bridge then south-westwards and terminating by a junction with that railway at a point 459 metres north-west of that bridge;

Work No. 6G—A cut, forming a diversion of the Channelsea River at its confluence with the River Lea, commencing in the Channelsea River at a point 26 metres south of the former sluice on that river at Bully Fen, passing south-westwards and terminating at the confluence of those rivers;

Work No. 6H—An access road commencing by a junction with the access road to the International Freight Terminal on the eastern side of the Container Terminal, passing south-westwards, over Works Nos. 6 and 6A in tunnel, and southwards through the

International Freight Terminal, then south-eastwards, eastwards and north-eastwards on the northern side of the North London Line, then continuing northwards, then eastwards and terminating by a junction with the access road to the Channelsea site, north of Stratford Station;

Work No. 6J—An access road commencing at a point in the existing Traction Maintenance Depot on the western side of the diesel repair shed in that depot, passing south-westwards, then westwards on the northern side of the retained cutting forming part of Work No. 6, then south-westwards over that railway and Work No. 6A in tunnel, then southwards and south-westwards and terminating by a junction with Work No. 6H in the International Freight Terminal;

In the London Boroughs of Newham, Redbridge, Barking and Dagenham and Havering—

Stratford to Barrington Road

Work No. 7—A railway (4,560 metres in length) commencing by a junction with the railway (Work No. 6) at its termination, passing eastwards in tunnel beneath Angel Lane, The Grove, Atherton Road, Woodgrange Road, Romford Road, Woodgrange Park Cemetery and Browning Road, including a ventilation shaft on land off Woodgrange Road and terminating beneath a point 60 metres east of the junction of Reesland Close with Barrington Road;

Barrington Road to Dagenham Dock

Work No. 22—A railway (6,700 metres in length) commencing by a junction with the railway (Work No. 7) at its termination, passing eastwards in tunnel beneath the North Circular Road and the River Roding, then south-eastwards beneath Barking Station, Station Parade, Ripple Road and Alfred's Way, then eastwards beneath Renwick Road and the Ripple Lane Freightliner Terminal to a portal at a point 462 metres south-east of the junction of Morrison Road with Julia Gardens, then continuing eastwards under the railway (Work No. 22A) and the new road (Work No. 22H(1)), across Chequers Lane (to be stopped up) and under Kent Avenue and terminating at a point 85 metres east of the bridge carrying Kent Avenue over the Tilbury Loop Railway, including ventilation shafts on lands off Barrington Road and Alfred's Way and a footbridge over the railway at Chequers Lane;

Work No. 22A—A railway (2,201 metres in length), forming a diversion of the Tilbury Loop Railway westbound line, commencing by a junction with that railway at a point 253 metres east of the junction of Stebbing Way with Wivenhoe Road, passing eastwards under Renwick Road, then south-eastwards and eastwards over the railway in tunnel (Work No. 22), under the new road (Work No. 22H(1)) and terminating by a junction with the Tilbury Loop Railway westbound line at a point 2 metres west of the western end of Dagenham Dock Station platforms;

Work No. 22B—A railway (2,252 metres in length), forming holding sidings, commencing by a junction with the railway (Work No. 22A) at a point 15 metres west of the bridge carrying Renwick Road over the Tilbury Loop Railway, passing south-eastwards and eastwards, under the new road (Work No. 22H(1)) and across Chequers Lane and terminating at a point 120 metres south-east of the eastern end of Dagenham Dock Station platforms, including a footbridge over the railway at Chequers Lane;

Work No. 22C—A railway (1,523 metres in length), for construction purposes, commencing by a junction with the Tilbury Loop Railway at a point 166 metres south-east of the bridge carrying Renwick Road over the railway, passing south-eastwards and eastwards, and terminating at a point 38 metres south-west of the point where the new road (Work No. 22H(1)) passes over the railway (Work No. 22B), including railway sidings;

Work No. 22D—A railway (280 metres in length) forming a connection between the Tilbury Loop Railway goods line and the railway (Work No. 22A), commencing by a junction with the said goods line at a point 468 metres south-east of the bridge carrying Renwick Road over that goods line, passing south-eastwards and terminating by a junction with Work No. 22A at a point 742 metres south-east of the said bridge;

Work No. 22E—A railway (1,095 metres in length) forming a connecting line between the railway (Work No. 22A) and the railway (Work No. 8E), commencing by a junction with Work No. 22A at a point 342 metres south of the junction of Morrison Road with Julia Gardens, passing eastwards under the new road (Work No. 22H(1)) and across Chequers Lane and terminating by a junction with Work No. 8E at a point 180 metres south-east of the eastern end of Dagenham Dock Station platforms, including a footbridge over the railway at Chequers Lane;

Work No. 22F—A railway (648 metres in length) forming a connecting line between the railway (Work No. 22A) and the railway (Work No. 22), commencing by a junction with Work No. 22A at a point 378 metres south-east of the junction of Morrison Road with Julia Gardens, passing eastwards under the new road (Work No. 22H(1)) and terminating by a junction with Work No. 22 at a point 150 metres west of the eastern end of Dagenham Dock Station platforms;

Work No. 22G—A railway (715 metres in length), for construction purposes, commencing by a junction with the railway (Work No. 22B) at a point 27 metres west of the point where the new road (Work No. 22H(1)) passes over Work No. 22B, passing eastwards then southwards, and terminating at a point 270 metres south-east of the eastern end of Dagenham Dock Station platforms, including railway sidings;

Work No. 22J—A jetty commencing on the northern bank of the River Thames at a point 190 metres north-west of The Gores outfall sluice, extending in a south-westerly direction into the said river for a distance of 230 metres and there terminating, including a jetty head with mooring dolphins and berthing facilities;

Dagenham Dock to Wennington

Work No. 8—A railway (5,200 metres in length) commencing by a junction with the railway (Work No. 22) at its termination, passing eastwards under Thames Avenue (Work No. 8R), over the Beam River, and under the intended A13 link road (under construction), then continuing south-eastwards on viaduct over the new road (Work No. 8S) and Rainham Creek, and terminating beneath the intended A13 (under construction) at a point 20 metres south-west of the Tilbury Loop Railway;

Work No. 8E—A railway (906 metres in length), forming a connection between the railway (Work No. 22E) and the westbound line of the railway (Work No. 8), commencing by a junction with Work No. 22E at its termination, passing south-eastwards under Kent Avenue (Work No. 8Q) and terminating by a junction with the railway (Work No. 8) at a point 30 metres west of the intended Thames Avenue bridge (Work No. 8R);

Work No. 8G—A railway (1,330 metres in length), forming a connection between the Tilbury Loop Railway and the eastbound line of the railway (Work No. 8), commencing by a junction with the Tilbury Loop Railway 10 metres east of the eastern end of Dagenham Dock Station, passing eastwards on the southern side of that line under Kent Avenue (Work No. 8Q) and Thames Avenue (Work No. 8R), over the Beam River and terminating by a junction with Work No. 8 at a point 215 metres east of the intended Thames Avenue bridge (Work No. 8R), including a bridge over the Beam River;

Work No. 8H—A railway (279 metres in length), connecting the goods line (Work No. 22B) with a private siding west of Kent Avenue, commencing by a junction with Work No. 22B at its termination, passing south-eastwards and southwards, under the intended A13 and terminating by a junction with the said siding at a point 55 metres south of the footpath crossing the siding east of Breach Lane;

Work No. 8J—A railway (1,452 metres in length), connecting the goods line (Work No. 22B) with private sidings east of Kent Avenue, commencing by a junction with Work No. 22B at its termination, passing eastwards under Kent Avenue (Work No. 8Q) and Thames Avenue (Work No. 8R), over the Beam River and terminating at a point 33 metres west of the bridge carrying the intended A13 link road (under construction) over the Tilbury Loop Railway and the railway (Work No. 8), including a bridge over the Beam River and railway sidings;

Work No. 8K—A railway (496 metres in length) commencing by a junction with a private siding on the eastern side of Kent Avenue at a point 10 metres south of the southern end of the viaduct carrying that road and railway across Dagenham Breach, passing northwards on the existing viaduct, under the intended A13, then eastwards and terminating by a junction with the railway (Work No. 8J) at a point 300 metres east of the intended Kent Avenue bridge (Work No. 8Q);

Work No. 8L—A railway (301 metres in length) commencing by a junction with the railway (Work No. 8J) at a point 245 metres west of the intended Thames Avenue bridge (Work No. 8R), passing eastward then southwards and terminating by a junction with a private siding at a point 30 metres north of Lake Road on the western side of Thames Avenue;

Work No. 22H(1)—A road commencing by a junction with Ripple Road at a point on its southern side 23 metres east of the junction of Pooles Lane with the road, passing southwards on the eastern side of Pooles Lane, then south-eastwards and southwards on the line of Choats Manor Way, over a private siding, the diverted Tilbury Loop Railway (Work No. 22A) and the railways (Works Nos. 22, 22B, 22E, 22F and 22G), and terminating at a point 100 metres south-west of the junction of Choats Road with Hindmans Way, including a bridge over the said railways;

Work No. 22H(2)—A road commencing at a point 25 metres west of Pooles Lane at the southern end of that road, passing eastwards and north-eastwards and terminating by a junction with the new road (Work No. 22H(1)) at a point 240 metres from its commencement;

Work No. 8P(3)—A road commencing by a junction with Choats Road at a point 240 metres west of its junction with Hindmans Way, passing eastwards along the line of Choats Road and Hindmans Way to a point 80 metres west of the junction of Hindmans Way with Chequers Lane, then turning southwards and terminating by a junction with Chequers Lane at a point 120 metres south of that last-mentioned road junction;

Work No. 8P(4)—A road commencing by a junction with the new road (Work No. 8P(3)) at a point 100 metres from its termination, passing north-eastwards and terminating by a junction with Chequers Lane at a point 60 metres north of its junction with Hindmans Way;

Work No. 8Q—Realignment of Kent Avenue, including a bridge over a private siding, the Tilbury Loop Railway and the railways (Works Nos. 8, 8E, 8G and 8J), commencing in that road at a point 205 metres south of its junction with New Road, Hornchurch, passing southwards over the said railways and terminating in Kent Avenue at a point 10 metres north of the northern end of the viaduct carrying that road over Dagenham Breach;

Work No. 8R—Realignment of Thames Avenue, including a bridge over the Tilbury Loop Railway, the railways (Works Nos. 8, 8G and 8J) and private sidings, commencing in that road at a point 25 metres south of its junction with New Road, Hornchurch, passing southwards over those railways and terminating in Thames Avenue at the junction of Lake Road with that road;

Work No. 8S—A road commencing by a junction with Bridge Road at the roundabout on that road 200 metres south of its junction with New Road, Hornchurch, passing westwards over Rainham Creek, then south-westwards under the Tilbury Loop Railway and the railway (Work No. 8), then passing southwards over Rainham Creek at a point 140 metres downstream from the bridge carrying the Tilbury Loop Railway over that river, then south-eastwards and terminating by a junction with Ferry Lane at the southernmost junction of Lamson Road with that road;

Work No. 8T—A road, forming an access to the Riverside Sewage Treatment works at Rainham off the new road (Work No. 8S), commencing in the said Treatment Works at Creekside Cottages, passing south-eastwards and eastwards and terminating by a junction with Work No. 8S at a point 70 metres south-west of the intended viaduct carrying the railway (Work No. 8) over that new road;

Work No. 8U(4)—A cut, forming a diversion of the Ship and Shovel Relief Channel, commencing by a junction with that watercourse at a point 148 metres from its confluence with The Gores, passing eastwards, then south-eastwards and terminating in The Gores at that confluence;

Work No. 8U(13)—A cut, forming a diversion of The Gores, commencing at the confluence of the Ship and Shovel Relief Channel (Work No. 8U(4)) with that stream, passing eastwards then northwards under the railways (Works Nos. 22, 22A, 22B, 22E, 22F and 22G), and terminating by a junction with The Gores at a point 70 metres east of the northern end of its existing culvert under the Tilbury Loop Railway;

Work No. 8U(6)—A cut, forming a diversion of Pooles Sewer, commencing by a junction with that watercourse 85 metres south of the southern side of the existing Manor Way level crossing on the Tilbury Loop Railway, passing eastwards and south-eastwards, then northwards under the railway (Work No. 8) and terminating by a junction with that watercourse at the southern end of its culvert under the Tilbury Loop Railway;

Work No. 8U(7)—A cut, forming a diversion of the Ferry Lane Sewer, commencing by a junction with that watercourse at the northern end of its culvert under the Tilbury Loop Railway west of Rainham Station, passing southwards under that railway and the railway (Work No. 8), then eastwards and southwards and terminating in that watercourse on the western side of Ferry Lane at a point 48 metres south of the existing Ferry Lane level crossing on the Tilbury Loop Railway;

Work No. 8U(8)—A cut, forming a diversion of the Rainham Cross Sewer, commencing at a point on the southern side of the Tilbury Loop Railway 375 metres east of the eastern end of Rainham Station, passing eastwards for a distance of 95 metres and there terminating by a junction with that watercourse;

Work No. 8U(9)—A cut, forming an improvement of the Rainham Main Sewer, commencing in that watercourse at a point 15 metres north of the northern end of its existing culvert under the Tilbury Loop Railway, passing under that railway and the railway (Work No. 8) and terminating in that watercourse at a point 52 metres south of the southern end of that existing culvert;

Work No. 8U(10)—A cut, forming a diversion of the Wennington Main Sewer, commencing by a junction with the cut (Work No. 8U(9)) at a point 10 metres north of its termination, passing south-eastwards on the southern side of the existing watercourse and terminating by a junction with that watercourse at a point 100 metres south of the southern end of a branch of that watercourse south of Manstead Gardens;

Work No. 8U(11)—A cut, forming an improvement of the Common Watercourse (Southall Sewers), commencing in that watercourse at a point 10 metres north-east of the northern end of its existing culvert under the Tilbury Loop Railway, passing south-westwards under that railway and the railway (Work No. 8) and terminating in that watercourse at a point 47 metres south-west of the southern end of that existing culvert;

Work No. 8U(12)—A cut, forming a diversion of Wennington Branch Sewer, commencing in that watercourse at a point 10 metres north-east of the northern end of its existing culvert under the Tilbury Loop Railway, passing under that railway and the railway (Work No. 8) and terminating in that watercourse at a point 40 metres south-west of the southern end of that existing culvert;

In the London Borough of Havering and in the borough of Thurrock, in the county of Essex—

Wennington to Purfleet

Work No. 23—A railway (3,835 metres in length) commencing by a junction with the railway (Work No. 8) at its termination, passing south-eastwards on the southern side of the realigned Tilbury Loop Railway (Work No. 23A) then on viaduct over that railway, then over the diverted Aveley Sewer (Work No. 23D) and under the new road (Work No. 23B(1)), then continuing over Mar Dyke and under the new road (Work No. 23C(2)), passing on the southern side of the Purfleet Bypass and terminating at a point 250 metres east of the junction of London Road, Purfleet with the Purfleet Bypass, including the said viaduct and a bridge over Mar Dyke;

Work No. 23A—A railway (1,185 metres in length), being a realignment of the Tilbury Loop Railway, commencing by a junction with that railway at a point 230 metres south-east of the Wennington Branch Sewer where that sewer passes in culvert under that railway, passing south-eastwards in tunnel under the railway (Work No. 23) and terminating by a junction with the Tilbury Loop Railway at a point 240 metres south-west of the point where Tank Hill Road is crossed on the level by the Tilbury Loop Railway;

In the borough of Thurrock, in the county of Essex—

Work No. 23B(1)—A road, forming a diversion of Tank Hill Road (A1090), commencing by a junction with Arterial Road, Purfleet (A13) at a point 165 metres north of its junction with Tank Hill Road, passing south-westwards then southwards over the diverted Aveley Sewer (Work No. 23D), the railway (Work No. 23), the Tilbury Loop Railway and Mar Dyke and terminating in that road at a point 15 metres north of the junction of Marlow Avenue with Tank Hill Road, including bridges over Works Nos. 23 and 23D, the Tilbury Loop Railway and Mar Dyke;

Work No. 23B(2)—A road, forming an access road into the Purfleet Industrial Estate, commencing by a junction with the new road (Work No. 23B(1)) at a point 130 metres west of the junction of Tank Hill Road with Arterial Road, Purfleet (A13), passing westwards then northwards and terminating at a point in the said estate 155 metres north-west of its commencement;

Work No. 23B(3)—A road, forming an access road, commencing by a junction with the new road (Work No. 23B(1)) at a point 110 metres south-west of the point where Tank Hill Road is crossed on the level by the Tilbury Loop Railway, passing eastwards and terminating at a point 105 metres south of that level crossing;

Work No. 23C—Diversion of Arterial Road, Purfleet, and Purfleet Bypass and diversion of Tank Lane and Botany Way, comprising—

Work 23C(1)—Diversion of the A13 (Arterial Road, Purfleet) commencing in that road at a point 360 metres west of its existing junction with Purfleet Bypass, passing eastwards by way of the northern junction roundabout forming part of Work No. 23C(2), and terminating in the A13 at a point 235 metres east of the said existing road junction;

Work No. 23C(2)—A road, including junction roundabouts at its commencement and termination, commencing by a junction with the diverted Arterial Road, Purfleet (Work No. 23C(1)) at a point 48 metres north-east of the existing junction of Arterial Road with Purfleet Bypass, passing south-westwards over the railway

(Work No. 23) and terminating by a junction with the diverted Tank Lane (Works Nos. 23C(4) and 23C(5)) at a point 150 metres west of the existing junction of Tank Lane with Botany Way, including a bridge over Work No. 23;

Work No. 23C(3)—Diversion of Purfleet Bypass at its junction with the A13 commencing by a junction with that road at the northern junction roundabout forming part of Work No. 23C(2), passing southwards and south-eastwards and terminating in Purfleet Bypass at a point 160 metres north-west of its junction with North Road;

Work No. 23C(4)—Diversion of Tank Lane commencing at a point 165 metres north of the bridge carrying Tank Lane over the Tilbury Loop Railway, passing southwards then eastwards along the northern side of Tank Lane, then south-eastwards along the line of that road and terminating at the southern junction roundabout forming part of Work No. 23C(2), at a point 150 metres west of the existing junction of Tank Lane with Botany Way;

Work No. 23C(5)—Diversion of Tank Lane and Botany Way, commencing at the southern junction roundabout forming part of Work No. 23C(2) at a point 150 metres north-west of its existing junction with Botany Way, passing eastwards then southwards on the line of Botany Way and terminating by a junction with that road at a point 115 metres south-west of its existing junction with Purfleet Bypass;

Work No. 23D—A cut, forming a diversion of the Aveley Sewer, commencing in that watercourse at a point 25 metres south-west of the southern end of its existing culvert under the Tilbury Loop Railway, passing in a north-easterly direction under the railways (Works Nos. 23 and 23A) and the new road (Work No. 23B(1)), then passing northwards and terminating at a point in a new balancing pond 95 metres north-west of the junction of Tank Hill Road with Arterial Road, Purfleet;

Purfleet to West Thurrock

Work No. 9—A railway (1,537 metres in length) commencing by a junction with the railway (Work No. 23) at its termination, passing south-eastwards on viaduct over the A1090 (London Road, Purfleet), the Tilbury Loop Railway and the northbound Dartford Tunnel Approach Road (Canterbury Way), under a span of the southbound approach to the Queen Elizabeth II Bridge, and over Oliver Close (North) (Work No. 9B) in the West Thurrock Industrial Estate to a point 90 metres west of the existing southernmost junction of Oliver Close with Oliver Road, then under Oliver Road (Work No. 9C) and terminating at a point 160 metres south-east of that existing road junction, including the said viaducts and a bridge over Work No. 9A(1);

Work No. 9B—Diversion of Oliver Close (North) commencing in that road at a point 25 metres south of the westernmost corner of that road, passing northwards for a distance of 60 metres from that commencement under the railway (Work No. 9), then turning eastwards and terminating by a junction with Oliver Close (North) at a point 160 metres west of its junction with Oliver Road;

Work No. 9C—Diversion of Oliver Road, including a bridge over the railway (Work No. 9), commencing in that road at the existing junction of that road with Oliver Close (North), passing southwards over Work No. 9 on the eastern side of the existing road, and terminating by a junction with Oliver Road at a point 130 metres south of its existing junction with Burnley Road;

Work No. 9D—Realignment of Burnley Road and Watson Close commencing by a junction with Oliver Road (Work No. 9C) at the existing road junction, passing eastwards along the line of, and then to the south of, Burnley Road, then turning northwards and terminating in Watson Close at a point 60 metres north of its existing junction with Burnley Road;

Work No. 9F(1)—A railway (835 metres in length) commencing by a junction with the railway (Work No. 9F(2)) at a point 275 metres from its commencement, passing westwards, south-westwards, southwards and south-eastwards and terminating at a point on the western side of Watson Close (Work No. 9D) at a point 45 metres north of the existing junction of that road with Burnley Road;

Work No. 9F(2)—A deviation railway (849 metres in length), commencing by a junction with the Tilbury Loop Railway at a point 325 metres east of the bridge carrying the southbound approach to the Queen Elizabeth II Bridge over that railway, passing eastwards on the southern side of that railway and terminating at the eastern end of the existing sidings;

In the borough of Thurrock, in the county of Essex, and in the borough of Dartford, parishes of Swanscombe and Greenhithe, Southfleet and Longfield and New Barn, in the borough of

Gravesham, town of Gravesend, and in the district of Sevenoaks, parish of Horton Kirby and South Darenth, in the county of Kent—

West Thurrock and Ebbsfleet to Singlewell

Work No. 10—A railway (9,161 metres in length) commencing by a junction with the railway (Work No. 9) at its termination, passing south-eastwards to a point 249 metres from that commencement, then passing in tunnel beneath Burnley Road and Watson Close (Work No. 9D), then beneath the River Thames and Bell Wharf, Swanscombe, with shafts at Burnley Road, West Thurrock Power Station, Bell Wharf and Swanscombe Marsh, continuing in tunnel south-eastwards to a point 120 metres north-west of the existing junction of Green Manor Way with Lower Road, then passing south-eastwards and southwards, under Galley Hill Road (Work No. 10K), then in tunnel for a distance of 58 metres beneath the North Kent Railway, continuing under the railway (Work No. 10C) and the new road (Work No. 10S(1)), then on viaduct over the River Ebbsfleet, then in tunnel for a distance of 310 metres beneath the course of the former Gravesend West Branch Railway and the A2 (Watling Street) at a point 50 metres west of the southern abutment of the bridge carrying the B262 (Hall Road) over that road, then passing in tunnel for distances of 35 metres and 25 metres respectively beneath the B262 and the slip road to that road and Station Road on the southern side of the A2, then continuing south-eastwards on the southern side of the A2, then in tunnel for a distance of 80 metres beneath the railway (Work No. 11A) and on viaduct over the A227 (Wrotham Road) and terminating at a point 180 metres east of that road 340 metres south of the southern side of the bridge carrying the A2 over that road, including the said viaducts over the River Ebbsfleet and Wrotham Road;

Work No. 10A—A railway (1,732 metres in length), partly for construction purposes, commencing at the seaward end of the existing Swanscombe Jetty, passing south-eastwards from that jetty and terminating by a junction with the railway (Work No. 10B) at a point 40 metres south-east of the intended bridge (Work No. 10K) carrying Galley Hill Road over that railway;

Work No. 10B—A railway (2,281 metres in length) commencing by a junction with the railway (Work No. 10) at a point 113 metres north-west of the intended bridge (Work No. 10K) carrying Galley Hill Road over that railway, passing south-eastwards on the eastern side of that railway under that road, and in tunnel for a distance of 71 metres beneath the North Kent Railway, then passing eastwards over a private road between the Northfleet Cement Works and Springhead Road, then in tunnel for a distance of 60 metres beneath the North Kent Railway at a point 30 metres south-east of the eastern abutment of the bridge carrying that railway over the mineral railway at the entrance to Church Path Pit, then south-eastwards on the northern side of the North Kent Railway, under Springhead Road (Work No. 10N) and terminating by a junction with that railway at a point 110 metres east of the intended bridge forming part of Work No. 10N, including a bridge over the said private road;

Work No. 10C—A railway (2,324 metres in length) commencing by a junction with the railway (Work No. 10) at a point 140 metres north-west of the intended bridge (Work No. 10K) carrying Galley Hill Road over that railway, passing south-eastwards on the western side of that railway under that road and in tunnel for a distance of 54 metres beneath the North Kent Railway, then eastwards, over the railways (Works Nos. 10, 10D and 10E) and over the said private road between the Northfleet Cement Works and Springhead Road, then south-eastwards on viaduct across the northern bay of the Blue Lake south of the North Kent Railway and under Springhead Road (Work No. 10N) and terminating by a junction with that railway at a point 95 metres east of the intended bridge forming part of Work No. 10N, including the said viaduct and bridges over Works Nos. 10, 10D and 10E and the said private road;

Work No. 10D—A railway (1,523 metres in length) commencing by a junction with the railway (Work No. 10B) at a point 45 metres north-west of the northern portal of the intended tunnel by which that railway passes beneath the North Kent Railway, passing south-eastwards on the western side of Work No. 10B beneath the North Kent Railway in that tunnel, then continuing southwards on the eastern side of the railway (Work No. 10), under the railway (Work No. 10C) and the new road (Work No. 10S(1)) and terminating by a junction with Work No. 10 at a point 10 metres south of the commencement of the intended viaduct carrying that railway over the River Ebbsfleet;

Work No. 10E—A railway (1,445 metres in length) commencing by a junction with the railway (Work No. 10C) 7 metres north-west of the southern portal of the intended tunnel by which that railway passes beneath the North Kent Railway, passing south-eastwards on the eastern side of Work No. 10C, then under that railway and continuing on the western side of the railway (Work No. 10), under the new road (Work No. 10S(1)) and terminating by a junction with Work No. 10 at a point 5 metres north of the commencement of the said intended viaduct carrying that railway over the River Ebbsfleet;

Work No. 10F—A railway (532 metres in length) commencing by a junction with the railway (Work No. 10B) at a point 140 metres west of the bridge carrying the North Kent Railway over the mineral railway at the entrance to the Church Path Pit, passing eastwards under that bridge and terminating in that pit at a point 378 metres east of that railway bridge;

Work No. 10F(1)—A railway (200 metres in length) commencing by a junction with the North Kent Railway at a point 230 metres north-west of the western end of the westbound platform of Northfleet Station passing eastwards and terminating by a junction with the sidings of the mineral railway on the southern side of the North Kent Railway at the western end of those sidings;

Work No. 10G—Improvement of Manor Way (West) commencing at the junction of that road with the A226 (London Road), passing north-eastwards and eastwards along the line of Manor Way (West) and terminating at a point 20 metres east of the junction of that road with Pilgrims Road;

Work No. 10H—A road commencing by a junction with Manor Way (West) (Work No. 10G) at the termination of that work, passing eastwards, then south-eastwards and terminating at the existing roundabout at the west end of the central access road in the Northfleet Industrial Estate;

Work No. 10J—A road, forming a diversion of Lower Road and Green Manor Way, commencing by a junction with Manor Way (West) (Work No. 10G) at its termination, passing northwards on the line of the footpath DS2 to a point 280 metres north of its existing junction with Lower Road, then turning eastwards and south-eastwards on the eastern side of the railway (Work No. 10) to a point on the northern side of Lower Road 330 metres east of its existing junction with Green Manor Way, then passing north-eastwards and eastwards on the line of Lower Road and terminating by a junction with Lower Road at a point 60 metres north of its junction with Stonebridge Road and Galley Hill Road;

Work No. 10J(1)—A road commencing by a junction with Green Manor Way at a point 310 metres north of its existing junction with Lower Road, passing southwards then south-westwards and terminating by a junction with the new road (Work No. 10J) at a point 85 metres from that commencement;

Work No. 10J(2)—A road commencing by a junction with Manor Way (East) at a point 110 metres north of its existing junction with Lower Road, passing southwards and terminating by a junction with the new road (Work No. 10J) at a point 105 metres from that commencement;

Work No. 10K—Realignment of Galley Hill Road, including a bridge over the railways (Works Nos. 10, 10A, 10B and 10C), commencing in that road at a point 270 metres east of its junction with London Road, Swanscombe, and terminating in Galley Hill Road at a point 310 metres west of its junction with Stonebridge Road;

Work No. 10N—Realignment of Springhead Road, including a bridge over the railways (Works Nos. 10B and 10C) and the North Kent Railway, commencing in that road at a point 40 metres north of the northern abutment of the existing bridge carrying that road over the North Kent Railway and terminating in that road at a point 110 metres south of the southern abutment of that existing bridge;

Work No. 10P—Diversion of Downs Road commencing in that road at a point 310 metres south-east of its junction with the Hog Lane subway under the A2 (Watling Street), passing south-eastwards and eastwards then southwards over the railways (Works Nos. 10, 11A and 11B) and terminating in Downs Road at a point 330 metres south of the existing junction with that road of the road to Northfleet Green, including bridges over Works Nos. 10, 11A and 11B;

Work No. 10Q—Diversion of the road from Downs Road to Northfleet Green commencing in that road at a point 20 metres east of the access from that road to Hazells, passing south-eastwards and terminating by a junction with Downs Road (Work No. 10P) at a point 210 metres north of the termination of that work;

Work No. 10R—A road, for construction purposes, including a bridge over the A2, commencing in the course of the former Gravesend West Branch Railway at a point 35 metres north-east of the northern side of that road, passing south-westwards over that road and terminating in the disused railway at a point 50 metres south-west of the southern side of that road;

Work No. 10R(1)—A cut, forming a diversion of the Swanscombe Main Drain south of the sewage disposal works on Swanscombe Marshes, commencing in that drain at a point

60 metres north of the junction of Pilgrims Road with Manor Way (West), passing northwards, then in culvert north-westwards under the new road (Work No. 10J), then northwards and terminating in that drain at the south-western corner of the said sewage works;

Work No. 10R(2)—A drainage pumping main commencing at a point 300 metres south-west of the western end of the platform of Northfleet Station, passing north-eastwards, under the railway (Work No. 10F(1)) and the North Kent Railway, then continuing north-eastwards and eastwards in Stonebridge Road and Grove Road between its junctions with Stonebridge Road and College Road, then eastwards in the Creek to a point 40 metres east of the junction of that road with College Road, then passing north-eastwards and terminating at a point at low water on the south bank of the River Thames 15 metres east of Robins Creek;

Work No. 10S(1)—A road commencing by a junction with the access road between the Northfleet Cement Works and Springhead Road at a point 75 metres south of the southern end of the bridge carrying that road over the River Ebbsfleet, passing southwards over that river, over the railways (Works Nos. 10, 10D and 10E), then south-westwards and terminating by a junction with the new road (Work No. 10S(2)) at a point 140 metres north of the junction with the existing Southfleet Road of the access road to the Northfleet West Grid Substation, including roundabouts at that commencement and termination and bridges over the river and Works Nos. 10, 10D and 10E;

Work No. 10S(2)—A road commencing at a point adjoining Southfleet Road 310 metres north of the existing junction with that road of the said road access to the Northfleet West Grid Substation, passing southwards to a point 120 metres south of that existing road junction then passing south-eastwards and terminating at a point 60 metres east of Southfleet Road, 220 metres north of the existing junction with the A2 of the road access from that road to the Northfleet West Grid Substation, including a roundabout at that termination;

Work No. 10T(1)—A road commencing by a junction with the new road (Work No. 10S(2)) at its termination, passing eastwards, then south-eastwards to a junction with Work No. 10T(4) at its termination, then eastwards over the railway (Work No. 10) in tunnel and terminating in the existing eastbound exit slip road of the A2 at Pepper Hill at a point 80 metres north-west of the junction of that slip road with Hall Road;

Work No. 10T(3)—A road commencing by a junction with the road (Work No. 10T(1)) at a point 85 metres north-west of the access to the Springhead Nursery from the existing access road on the northern side of the A2, passing south-eastwards on the southern side of Work No. 10T(1), over the railway (Work No. 10) in tunnel, and terminating in the eastbound carriageway of the A2 at a point 250 metres south-east of the bridge carrying Hall Road over the A2;

Work No. 10T(4)—A road, forming an exit slip road from the eastbound carriageway of the A2, commencing in that carriageway at a point 325 metres east of the footbridge over the A2 between Blue House and Swanscombe Park, passing eastwards over the new roads (Works Nos. 10T(6) and 10T(8)) and terminating by a junction with the road (Work No. 10T(1)) at a point 260 metres from its commencement;

Work No. 10T(6)—A road, forming an entry slip road to the westbound carriageway of the A2, commencing by a junction with the new road (Work No. 10S(2)) at its termination, passing southwards under the A2 then south-westwards, westwards and north-westwards to a point 300 metres west of the bridge carrying the A2 over the B259 (Park Corner Road) continuing westwards and terminating in the westbound carriageway of the A2 at a point 130 metres east of the said footbridge over the A2;

Work No. 10T(7)—A road commencing by a junction with the slip road (Work No. 10T(6)) at a point 325 metres north of the junction of Park Corner Road with the road leading to North End Farm, passing southwards and terminating by a junction with Park Corner Road at a point 150 metres from that commencement;

Work No. 10T(8)—A station access road, forming an exit slip road from the westbound carriageway of the A2, commencing by a junction with the new road (Work No. 10S(2)) at its termination, passing southwards under the A2 on the western side of the slip road (Work No. 10T(6)) to a point on the western side of the B259 (Park Corner Road) 160 metres south of the southern end of the bridge carrying the A2 over that road, then turning south-westwards, north-westwards, northwards and north-eastwards, passing over the road and the slip road (Work No. 10T(6)) on the southern side of the A2, continuing eastwards and terminating in the westbound carriageway of the A2 at a point 190 metres north-west of the bridge carrying Hall Road over the A2;

Longfield to Singlewell

Work No. 11—A railway (4,402 metres in length) commencing by a junction with the London and Chatham Railway at a point 130 metres east of the eastern abutment of the bridge carrying that railway over Pinden Road, passing eastwards, then north-eastwards on the course of the former Gravesend West Branch Railway, over the B260 (Main Road, Longfield), under Whitehill Road (Work No. 11C), the B255 (Hook Green Road) (Work No. 11D) and the B259 (Dale Road) (Work No. 11E), then eastwards under New Barn Road (Work No. 11F), and terminating at a point 60 metres east of the intended bridge forming part of that work, including a bridge over the B260;

Work No. 11A—A railway (1,366 metres in length) commencing by a junction with the railway (Work No. 11) at its termination, passing eastwards over the railway (Work No. 10) in tunnel, then south-eastwards on the northern side of that railway under Downs Road (Work No. 10P) and terminating by a junction with that railway at a point 290 metres south-east of the intended bridge forming part of that work;

Work No. 11B—A railway (1,354 metres in length) commencing by a junction with the railway (Work No. 11) at its termination, passing south-eastwards on the southern side of the railway (Work No. 10) under Downs Road (Work No. 10P) and terminating by a junction with the railway at a point 275 metres south-east of the intended bridge forming part of that work;

Work No. 11C—Realignment of Whitehill Road, including a bridge over the railway (Work No. 11), commencing in Whitehill Road at a point 375 metres south of the southern abutment of the existing bridge carrying that road over the disused railway and terminating in that road at its junction with Hook Green Road;

Work No. 11D—Realignment of the B255 (Hook Green Road), including a bridge over the railway (Work No. 11), commencing in that road at a point 50 metres south-east of its junction with Whitehill Road and terminating in the B255 at a point 190 metres east of the eastern abutment of the existing bridge over the disused railway;

Work No. 11E—Realignment of the B259 (Dale Road), including a bridge over the railway (Work No. 11), commencing in that road at a point 60 metres south of the southern abutment of the existing bridge over that disused railway and terminating in that road at a point 70 metres south of its junction with the B262 (Station Road);

Work No. 11F—Realignment of New Barn Road, including a bridge over the railway (Work No. 11), commencing in that road at a point 25 metres south of the centre of the roundabout at the junction of that road with the B262 (Station Road) and terminating in New Barn Road at a point 370 metres south-west of that commencement;

In the borough of Gravesham, parishes of Cobham and Shorne, and in the city of Rochester-upon-Medway, town of Rochester and parish of Cuxton, in the county of Kent—

Singlewell to Strood

Work No. 12—A railway (7,700 metres in length) commencing by a junction with the railway (Work No. 10) at its termination, passing eastwards on the southern side of the A2 (Watling Street), under Henhurst Road (Work No. 12D), Scotland Lane (Work No. 12E), Watling Street (B395) (Work No. 12F) and Halfpence Lane (C492) (Work No. 32C), then in tunnel for a distance of 75 metres beneath Work No. 32B and an adjoining area, under Brewers Road (Work No. 12H), over the access road (Work No. 12K) and under the access road (Work No. 12L), then passing south-eastwards on the western side of the M2, under a land bridge in Temple Wood, and terminating at a point 435 metres north-west of the southern end of the subway by which the footpath RS203 passes under the M2 as existing, including a bridge over Work No. 12K;

Work No. 12A—A railway (2,520 metres in length) on the northern side of the railway (Work No. 12) commencing by a junction with that railway at a point 50 metres east of its commencement, passing eastwards under Henhurst Road (Work No. 12D) and terminating by a junction with Work No. 12 at a point 515 metres east of the intended bridge carrying that road over that railway;

Work No. 12B—A railway (2,520 metres in length) on the southern side of the railway (Work No. 12) commencing by a junction with that railway at the said point 50 metres east of its commencement, passing eastwards under Henhurst Road (Work No. 12D) and terminating by a junction with Work No. 12 at the said point 515 metres east of the intended bridge carrying that road over that railway;

Work No. 12C—Diversion of Church Road commencing in that road at a point 170 metres north of the entrance from that road to St Margaret's Church, Ifield Court, passing north-eastwards then south-eastwards and terminating by a junction with Henhurst

Road (Work No. 12D) at a point 100 metres south of the southern abutment of the intended bridge carrying that road over the railways (Works Nos. 12, 12A and 12B);

Work No. 12D—Diversion of Henhurst Road, including a bridge over the railways (Works Nos. 12, 12A and 12B), commencing in that road at a point 40 metres south of its junction with the exit slip road from the westbound carriageway of the A2 and terminating in Henhurst Road at a point 60 metres north of the access from that road to Henhurst Cottage;

Work No. 12E—Diversion of Scotland Lane (Byway NS 195), including a bridge over the railway (Work No. 12), commencing in Scotland Lane at a point 210 metres south of its existing junction with Watling Street (B395), passing north-eastwards then eastwards to a junction with the existing access to The Mount, then passing northwards over the railway and terminating by a junction with the new road (Work No. 12F) at a point 15 metres from the commencement of that work;

Work No. 12F—A road, forming a diversion of Watling Street (B395), including a bridge over the railway (Work No. 12), commencing in that road at a point 130 metres south-east of the southern abutment of the bridge carrying that road over the A2, passing eastwards on the northern side of that road, then southwards over the railway and terminating by a junction with Halfpence Lane (C492) (Work No. 32C) at a point 80 metres north of its existing junction with Brewers Road;

Work No. 12H—Diversion of Brewers Road, including bridges over the railway (Work No. 12) and the A2, commencing in Brewers Road at its junction with Halfpence Lane (C492) passing eastwards, then north-eastwards over that railway and terminating in Brewers Road at a point 160 metres north-east of its junction with the slip roads to and from the eastbound carriageway of the A2;

Work No. 12J—An access road commencing by a junction with Brewers Road (Work No. 12H) at a point 55 metres south-west of the termination of that work, passing south-eastwards, then eastwards along the northern side of the A2 and terminating within the curtilage of Park Pale;

Work No. 12K—An access road to the Rochester and Cobham Park Golf Course, including a bridge over the A2, commencing by a junction with the access road (Work No. 12J) on the northern side of the A2 at a point 250 metres west of Park Pale, passing northwards and eastwards then southwards over that road and the A2 (including Works Nos. 31A, 31B, 34A and 35A), then westwards and southwards under the railway (Work No. 12), and terminating in the golf course south of the railway;

Work No. 12L—Diversion of an access road to Knights Place, including a bridge over the railway (Work No. 12), commencing in the existing access road from the A2 at a point 170 metres south of that road, passing southwards over the railway and terminating in the existing access road at a point 110 metres north of the access from that road to Knights Cottage;

In the city of Rochester-upon-Medway, town of Rochester and parish of Cuxton, in the borough of Tonbridge and Malling, parishes of Wouldham, Aylesford and Burham and in the borough of Maidstone, parishes of Boxley and Detling in the county of Kent—

Strood to Detling

Work No. 13—A railway (14,100 metres in length) commencing by a junction with the railway (Work No. 12) at its termination, passing south-eastwards, on the western side of the M2, over new roads (Works Nos. 36C, 36D and 36E) forming part of Junction 2 of the motorway, under the A228 (Rochester Road) (Work No. 36F), over the London and Chatham Railway, then on viaduct over the Strood and Maidstone Railway, the River Medway and Wouldham Road, then continuing south-eastwards on the western side of the M2 to a point at Nashenden Bottom, 120 metres north-west of the northern end of the go-kart racing track at Buckmore Park, south of Rochester Airport, then passing in tunnel (the North Downs Tunnel) for a distance of 3,190 metres beneath Blue Bell Hill and the North Downs, then passing south-eastwards under the Pilgrims Way (Work No. 13F), over Boarley Lane (Work No. 13G), then in tunnel for a distance of 330 metres beneath Boxley Road (Work No. 13H), continuing south-eastwards, under the A249 (Sittingbourne Road) (Work No. 13J), and Hockers Lane (Work No. 13K) and terminating at a point 270 metres east of the northern abutment of the bridge carrying Hockers Lane over the M20, including bridges over Works Nos. 36C, 36D and 36E, the London and Chatham Railway, the said viaduct, and a bridge over Work No. 13G;

Work No. 13A—Slip roads forming part of Junction 2 of the M2 pending widening of that motorway, being roads to be stopped up on the construction of the slip roads (Works Nos. 36A to 36D), comprising—

Work No. 13A(1)—A road, forming an exit slip road from the existing eastbound carriageway of the M2, commencing in that carriageway at a point 75 metres south-east of the southern end of the subway by which the footpath RS 203 passes under the motorway, passing south-eastwards and terminating by a junction with the A228 (Rochester Road) (Work No. 13A(4)) at a point 70 metres east of the eastern abutment of the existing bridge carrying that road over the M2;

Work No. 13A(2)—A road, forming an entry slip road to the existing westbound carriageway of the M2, commencing in that carriageway at a point 345 metres south-east of the southern end of the subway by which the footpath NS 183 passes under the M2, passing south-eastwards and terminating by a junction with Work No. 36C at a point 100 metres west of the southern end of the said subway for the footpath RS 203;

Work No. 13A(3)—A road forming an exit slip road from the existing westbound carriageway of the M2, commencing in that carriageway at a point 25 metres south-east of the southern abutment of the bridge carrying the M2 over the London and Chatham Railway, passing north-westwards under the railway (Work No. 13) and terminating by a junction with the western junction roundabout (part of Work No. 36E);

Work No. 13A(4)—A road, forming a diversion of the A228 (Rochester Road), commencing by a junction with the road (Work No. 36F) at a point 395 metres north-east of the commencement of that work, passing north-eastwards and eastwards and terminating by a junction with the A228 at a point 140 metres north-east of the junction with that road of the existing slip roads to the eastbound carriageway of the M2;

Work No. 13B—Diversion of Burham Road (D422) commencing by a junction with Wouldham Road at a point 30 metres south-west of the existing junction of those roads, passing south-eastwards and terminating by a junction with Burham Road 325 metres south of that road junction;

Work No. 13C—Diversion of bridleway MR11 (Stony Lane), including a bridge over the railway (Work No. 13), commencing in that bridleway at the northern end of the subway by which it passes under the M2, passing south-westwards under the M2, then north-westwards and south-westwards over the railway, then southwards and south-eastwards and terminating by a junction with Stony Lane at the north-eastern corner of Upper Nashenden Farm;

Work No. 13D—An access, for construction purposes, commencing by a junction with the existing westbound carriageway of the M2 at a point 160 metres north-west of the southern end of the existing subway by which Stony Lane passes under the motorway, passing north-westwards and westwards to the southern side of the railway (Work No. 13), passing south-eastwards on that side of the railway between chainages 4,000 and 4,190 metres, then passing eastwards, northwards and north-westwards and terminating by a junction with that carriageway of the motorway at a point 180 metres south-east of the bridge carrying Borstal Farm access over the M2;

Work No. 13E—Diversion of byway MR401, commencing by a junction with the byway at a point 160 metres south of its junction with Lower Warren Road, passing southwards over the railway (Work No. 13) in tunnel, then south-westwards and south-eastwards and terminating by a junction with byway MR401 at a point 225 metres south of that commencement;

Work No. 13F—Realignment of Pilgrims Way, including a bridge carrying that byway over the railway (Work No. 13), commencing in that byway at a point 85 metres east of the northern end of the subway by which the Pilgrims Way passes under the A229 (Chatham Road), passing eastwards then north-eastwards over the railway and terminating in that byway at a point 130 metres east of that commencement;

Work No. 13G—Diversion of Boarley Lane (D898) commencing in that road at a point 100 metres south of Boarley Cottage, passing southwards and south-eastwards under the railway (Work No. 13) and terminating in Boarley Lane at a point 50 metres north-east of the access to Boarley Oast;

Work No. 13H—Diversion of Boxley Road (C97) commencing in that road at its junction with Sandy Lane, passing north-westwards then north-eastwards over the railway (Work No. 13) in tunnel and terminating in that road at a point 50 metres north-east of the access to Street Farm, Boxley;

Work No. 13J—Realignment of the A249 (Sittingbourne Road), including a bridge over the railway (Work No. 13), commencing in that road at a point 80 metres north-east of the junction with that road of the side road to Detling and terminating in Sittingbourne

Road at a point 110 metres north of the northern abutment of the eastern bridge of the roundabout through which that road passes over the M20;

Work No. 13K—Realignment of Hockers Lane, including a bridge over the railway (Work No. 13), commencing in that road at a point 230 metres north of the northern abutment of the bridge carrying that road over the M20 and terminating in Hockers Lane at a point on that bridge 260 metres south of that commencement;

In the borough of Maidstone, parishes of Detling, Thurnham, Hollingbourne, Broomfield, Harrietsham, Lenham and Boughton Malherbe, in the county of Kent—

Detling to Lenham Heath

Work No. 14—A railway (13,904 metres in length) commencing by a junction with the railway (Work No. 13) at its termination, passing south-eastwards over Thurnham Lane (Work No. 14A), Water Lane (Work No. 14B) and Crismill Lane (Work No. 14C), then over the Maidstone and Ashford Railway at a point 85 metres east of the bridge carrying the M20 over that railway, continuing south-eastwards in tunnel for a distance of 240 metres beneath the B2163 (Eyhorne Street) (Work No. 14D), then passing over Snagbrook Stream, under Hospital Road (Work No. 14E), over the A20 (Ashford Road) (Work No. 14F) and under Fairbourne Lane (Work No. 14H), over Bell Farm access (Work No. 14J), then under Runham Lane (Work No. 14K), Sandway Road (Work No. 14L), Old Ham Lane (Work No. 14M), in tunnel for a distance of 170 metres beneath Headcorn Road (Work No. 14N), then continuing under Boughton Road (Work No. 14P), Lenham Heath Road (Work No. 14Q) and Bowley Lane (Work No. 14S), over the Great Stour River at a point 40 metres north of the bridge carrying the M20 over that river, under the access road west of Hook Street (Work No. 14U) and terminating at a point 85 metres south of the junction of Bull Hill with Lenham Heath Road, including bridges over Works Nos. 14A, 14B and 14C, the Maidstone and Ashford Railway, Snagbrook Stream, Works Nos. 14F and 14J and the Great Stour River;

Work No. 14A—Diversion of Thurnham Lane commencing in that road at a point 10 metres north of the access from that road to Gorewood Farm, passing south-westwards and southwards under the railway (Work No. 14) and terminating in Thurnham Lane at a point 10 metres north of the southern side of the bridge carrying the M20 over that road;

Work No. 14B—Diversion of Water Lane commencing in that road at a point 185 metres north of the northern side of the bridge carrying the M20 over that road, passing south-westwards and southwards under the railway (Work No. 14) and terminating in Water Lane at a point 5 metres north of the southern side of that bridge;

Work No. 14C—Diversion of bridleway KH134 (Crismill Lane) commencing in that bridleway at a point 30 metres south of the entrance to the Poer Meadow Shaw Pumping Station of the Mid-Kent Water Company, passing south-westwards, then south-eastwards and south-westwards under the railway (Work No. 14) and terminating in Crismill Lane at a point 5 metres north of the northern end of the subway by which that bridleway passes under the M20;

Work No. 14D—Realignment of the B2163 (Eyhorne Street) commencing at a point in that road 140 metres north-east of the northern abutment of the bridge carrying that road over the M20, passing south-westwards over the railway (Work No. 14) in tunnel and terminating at a point 75 metres south-west of that commencement;

Work No. 14E—Diversion of Hospital Road (D971), including a bridge over the railway (Work No. 14), commencing in that road at a point 180 metres north-east of the northern end of the subway by which that road passes under the M20, passing south-westwards, north-westwards, then south-westwards over the railway and south-eastwards and south-westwards and terminating in Hospital Road at a point 10 metres north-east of the southern end of that subway;

Work No. 14F—Diversion of the A20 (Ashford Road) commencing in that road at a point 20 metres east of the southern side of the bridge carrying the M20 over that road west of Holm Mill, passing eastwards under the railway (Work No. 14), then south-eastwards on the northern side of Work No. 14 and terminating in the A20 at a point 25 metres south-east of its junction with Holm Mill Lane;

Work No. 14G—Diversion of Greenway Court Road (D946) at its junction with the A20 (Ashford Road), commencing in Greenway Court Road at a point 110 metres north-east of its junction with Greenway Lane, passing south-westwards, then southwards on the eastern side of the existing road and terminating by a junction with the A20 (Work No. 14F) at a point 105 metres east of the intended bridge carrying the railway (Work No. 14) over that road;

Work No. 14H—Realignment of Fairbourne Lane, including a bridge over the railway (Work No. 14), commencing in that road at a point 50 metres south of its junction with the A20 (Ashford Road), passing southwards over the railway and terminating at a point 45 metres south of the northern end of the bridge carrying that road over the M20;

Work No. 14J—Diversion of the Bell Farm access from Sandway Road, Harrietsham, commencing by a junction with Sandway Road at a point 130 metres south-east of its junction with East Street, passing south-eastwards, then south-westwards and southwards under the railway (Work No. 14) and terminating in that access road at a point 35 metres south of the northern end of the subway by which it passes under the M20;

Work No. 14K—Realignment of Runham Lane, including a bridge over the railway (Work No. 14), commencing in that road at a point 60 metres south-west of its junction with Sandway Road, passing south-westwards over the railway and terminating in Runham Lane at a point 10 metres south-west of the north-eastern end of the bridge carrying that road over the M20;

Work No. 14L—Diversion of Sandway Road (C92), including a bridge over the railway (Work No. 14), commencing in that road at a point 180 metres south-east of its junction with Runham Lane, passing south-eastwards on the eastern side of Sandway Road, then southwards over the railway and terminating in that road at a point 190 metres north-west of its junction with Old Ham Lane;

Work No. 14M—Diversion of Old Ham Lane (D986), including a bridge over the railway (Work No. 14), commencing in that road at a point 360 metres north of its junction with Sandway Road and Lenham Heath Road, passing southwards over the railway and terminating in Old Ham Lane at that road junction;

Work No. 14N—Realignment of Headcorn Road commencing in that road at a point 220 metres north-east of its junction with Lenham Heath Road, passing south-westwards over the railway (Work No. 14) in tunnel and terminating in Headcorn Road at a point 130 metres north-east of that road junction;

Work No. 14P—Realignment of Boughton Road, including a bridge over the railway (Work No. 14) commencing in that road at a point 140 metres north of its junction with Lenham Heath Road, passing southwards over the railway and terminating in Boughton Road at a point 70 metres north of that road junction;

Work No. 14Q—Diversion of Lenham Heath Road (C92) at Sandway, including a bridge over the railway (Work No. 14), commencing in that road at a point 225 metres south-east of its junction with Boughton Road, passing south-eastwards then north-eastwards over the railway, then south-eastwards and eastwards and terminating in Lenham Heath Road at a point 590 metres north-west of its existing junction with Bowley Lane;

Work No. 14R—Diversion of Lenham Heath Road (C92) at Chapel Mill commencing in that road at a point 260 metres north-west of its existing junction with Bowley Lane, passing south-eastwards over the Great Stour River and terminating in Lenham Heath Road at a point 310 metres south-east of that existing road junction, including a bridge over the Great Stour River;

Work No. 14S—Diversion of Bowley Lane at its junction with Lenham Heath Road, including bridges over the railway (Work No. 14) and the M20, commencing by a junction with Lenham Heath Road (Work No. 14R) at a point 225 metres south-east of the commencement of that work, passing southwards and south-westwards, over the railway and the motorway, and terminating in Bowley Lane at a point 165 metres south of the southern end of the existing bridge carrying that road over the M20;

Work No. 14T—An access road, for construction purposes, commencing by a junction with the eastbound carriageway of the M20 at a point 75 metres north-west of the western side of the existing bridge carrying Bowley Lane over the motorway, passing south-eastwards and eastwards to a point on the southern side of the railway (Work No. 14) 220 metres south-east of the intended bridge carrying that road over the railway, then passing southwards and south-eastwards and terminating by a junction with that carriageway of the M20 at a point 210 metres north-west of the western side of the bridge carrying Hubbard's Farm access road over the motorway;

Work No. 14U—An access road on the line of Hubbard's Farm access road west of Hook Street, including a bridge over the railway (Work No. 14), commencing by a junction with Lenham Heath Road at a point 75 metres west of its junction with Bull Hill, passing southwards over the railway and terminating in the existing access road at the southern end of the bridge carrying it over the M20;

Work No. 14V—An access road on the southern side of the railway (Work No. 14) commencing in the curtilage of Old Cottage, passing south-eastwards to a junction with the new road (Work No. 14U) at a point 120 metres south of its commencement, then continuing south-eastwards and terminating in the curtilage of Yew Tree Cottage off Hook Street (to be stopped up);

In the borough of Maidstone, parish of Lenham, and in the borough of Ashford, town of Ashford and parishes of Charing, Hothfield and Westwell, in the county of Kent—

Lenham Heath to Ashford Barracks

Work No. 15—A railway (11,342 metres in length) commencing by a junction with the railway (Work No. 14) at its termination, passing south-eastwards under Egerton Road (Work No. 15C), Newlands Road (Work No. 15F) and Pluckley Road (Work No. 15G), passing eastwards in tunnel for a distance of 115 metres beneath Leacon Lane (Work No. 15J), and under the A20 (Maidstone Road) (Work No. 15K) then continuing south-eastwards over the M20 at a point 50 metres west of the bridge carrying the Maidstone and Ashford Railway over the motorway at Tutt Hill, passing under Westwell Lane (Work No. 15M) and over Station Road (Work No. 15N), under the A20 (Work No. 15P) and over Godinton Lane (Work No. 15Q) and terminating at a point in Rowcroft Barracks 530 metres north-west of the existing junction of Godinton Road with Chart Road, including bridges over the M20, Station Road and Godinton Lane;

Work No. 15A—A railway (2,576 metres in length) on the northern side of the railway (Work No. 15) commencing by a junction with that railway at a point 360 metres east of its commencement, passing eastwards under Egerton Road (Work No. 15C) and terminating by a junction with Work No. 15 at a point 125 metres north-west of the intended bridge carrying Newlands Road (Work No. 15F) over that railway;

Work No. 15B—A railway (2,576 metres in length) on the southern side of the railway (Work No. 15) commencing by a junction with that railway at the said point 360 metres east of its commencement, passing eastwards under Egerton Road (Work No. 15C) and terminating by a junction with Work No. 15 at the said point 125 metres north-west of the intended bridge carrying Newlands Road (Work No. 15F) over that railway;

Work No. 15C—Realignment of Egerton Road, including a bridge over the railways (Works Nos. 15,15A and 15B), commencing in that road at a point 5 metres south-west of the southern end of the bridge carrying it over the M20, passing north-eastwards over those railways and terminating in Egerton Road at a point 130 metres north-east of its junction with Vicarage Lane;

Work No. 15D—Realignment of Vicarage Lane commencing in that road at a point 65 metres north of its junction with Egerton Road and terminating at that road junction;

Work No. 15E—Diversion of Hurst Lane (D1198) at its junction with Newlands Road commencing in Hurst Lane at a point 260 metres north-west of that existing road junction, passing eastwards and terminating by a junction with Newlands Road (Work No. 15F) at a point 75 metres north of the said existing road junction;

Work No. 15F—Realignment of Newlands Road (D1199), including a bridge over the railway (Work No. 15), commencing in that road at a point 15 metres north of the northern abutment of the bridge carrying that road over the M20, passing northwards over the railway, then north-eastwards and terminating in Newlands Road at a point 135 metres north-east of its junction with Hurst Lane;

Work No. 15G—Realignment of Pluckley Road (C493), including a bridge over the railway (Work No. 15), commencing in that road at a point 25 metres south-west of the southern end of the bridge carrying it over the M20, passing north-eastwards and northwards over the motorway and the railway and terminating in Pluckley Road at a point 65 metres north of its existing junction with Leacon Lane;

Work No. 15H—Diversion of Leacon Lane between Pluckley Road and Leacon Alders commencing by a junction with Pluckley Road at its existing junction with Leacon Lane, passing eastwards then south-eastwards under the railway (Work No. 15) and terminating in Leacon Lane at a point 195 metres west of the bridge carrying that road over the stream at Leacon Alders, including access to Oakover Nursery and Raywood Cottages and to the emergency access to the M20;

Work No. 15J—Realignment of Leacon Lane east of Leacon Alders commencing in that road at a point 240 metres east of its junction with Hurstford Lane, passing north-eastwards over the railway (Work No. 15) in tunnel, and terminating in Leacon Lane at a point 200 metres south-west of its junction with the A20 (Maidstone Road);

Work No. 15K—Diversion of the A20 (Maidstone Road), including a bridge over the railway (Work No. 15), commencing in that road at a point 25 metres north of its junction with Leacon Lane, passing south-eastwards over the railway on the western side of the existing road and terminating in the A20 at the north-western end of the bridge carrying that road over the M20, including access to Leda Cottages at a point 35 metres north-west of that termination;

Work No. 15L—A road for access to premises on the eastern side of the existing A20 commencing by a junction with the A20 (Work No. 15K) at a point on its eastern side 205 metres south-east of its commencement, passing eastwards, then south-eastwards and terminating by a junction with the remaining part of the existing road at a point 285 metres south-east of the commencement of Work No. 15K;

Work No. 15M—Diversion of Westwell Lane (D1227) commencing in that road at the southern end of the bridge carrying it over the M20, passing southwards on the eastern side of the existing road, then south-westwards over the Maidstone and Ashford Railway and the railway (Work No. 15), then passing south-eastwards and southwards and terminating in that road at a point 180 metres south of the southern abutment of the existing bridge carrying that road over the Maidstone and Ashford Railway, including a bridge over that railway and Work No. 15;

Work No. 15N—Realignment of Station Road, Westwell, commencing in that road at a point 15 metres south-west of the bridge carrying the Maidstone and Ashford Railway over that road, passing south-westwards under the railway (Work No. 15) and terminating in Station Road at a point 220 metres south-west of that commencement;

Work No. 15P—Diversion of the A20 (Maidstone Road), including a bridge over the railway (Work No. 15), commencing in that road at a point 405 metres north-west of the entrance to Yonsea Farm, passing eastwards on the northern side of the existing road, over the railway, then south-eastwards and terminating in that road at a point at Potters Corner 25 metres south-east of the junction with that road of Godinton Lane;

Work No. 15Q—Diversion of Godinton Lane commencing in that road at a point 225 metres south-west of its junction with the A20, passing south-westwards on the western side of the existing road, under the railway (Work No. 15) and terminating in Godinton Lane at a point 10 metres north-east of the access to North Lodge;

In the borough of Ashford, town of Ashford and parish of Sevington, in the County of Kent—

Ashford Barracks to Sevington

Work No. 16—A railway (4,535 metres in length) commencing by a junction with the railway (Work No. 15) at its termination, passing south-eastwards to a point 130 metres north-west of the existing junction of Godinton Road with Chart Road, then in tunnel for a distance of 565 metres beneath Chart Road (Work No. 16F) and Godinton Road (Works Nos. 16G and 16H), the railway (Work No. 16A) and the Maidstone and Ashford Railway (Work No. 16C), then under Beaver Road (Work No. 16N), over the Great Stour and the East Stour Rivers, the Ashford and Canterbury Railway and the railways (Works Nos. 16C and 16D), then over the railways (Works Nos. 16A and 16E), under Boys Hall Road (Work No. 16Q), and terminating at a point 225 metres west of the western side of the existing bridge carrying Bad Munstereifel Road over the Ashford and Folkestone Railway at Sevington, including bridges over Works Nos. 16A, 16C, 16D and 16E, the Great Stour and the East Stour Rivers, the Ashford and Canterbury Railway, and the Aylesford Stream (Work No. 16S);

Work No. 16A—A railway (4,555 metres in length) commencing by a junction with the railway (Work No. 16) at a point 5 metres south-east of the commencement of that work, passing south-eastwards on the northern side of that railway, in tunnel for a distance of 405 metres beneath Chart Road (Work No. 16F), then passing southwards over the railway (Work No. 16) in tunnel, then south-eastwards and eastwards under Beaver Road (Work No. 16N), on existing bridges over the Great Stour and the East Stour Rivers, under Work No. 16, and Boys Hall Road (Work No. 16Q) and terminating by a junction with Work No. 16 at its termination, including bridges over Work No. 16K and the Aylesford Stream (Work No. 16S);

Work No. 16B—A railway (4,550 metres in length) commencing by a junction with the railway (Work No. 16) at a point 5 metres south-east of the commencement of that work, passing south-eastwards on the southern side of that railway, in tunnel for a distance of 475 metres beneath Chart Road (Work No. 16F) and Godinton Road (Works Nos. 16G and 16H), passing south-eastwards and eastwards under Beaver Road (Work No. 16N), on existing bridges over the Great Stour and East Stour Rivers, under Boys Hall Road (Work No. 16Q) and terminating by a junction with Work No. 16 at its termination, including bridges over Work No. 16K and the Aylesford Stream (Work No. 16S);

Work No. 16C—A railway (2,228 metres in length) commencing by a junction with the Maidstone and Ashford Railway at a point 200 metres north-west of the bridge carrying the Godinton Road over that railway, passing south-eastwards over the railway

(Work No. 16) in tunnel, under Beaver Road (Work No. 16N), on existing bridges over the Great Stour and East Stour Rivers and terminating by a junction with the Ashford and Canterbury Railway at a point 70 metres east of the intended bridge carrying Work No. 16 over that railway, including a bridge over Work No. 16K;

Work No. 16D—A railway (954 metres in length), forming sidings on the Ashford and Canterbury and Ashford and Folkestone Railways, commencing at a point 45 metres south-east of the eastern abutment of the bridge carrying that railway over the East Stour River, passing south-eastwards on the southern side of the railway (Work No. 16C) to a junction with the Ashford and Canterbury Railway, then passing eastwards under the railway (Work No. 16) then south-eastwards and terminating at a point 125 metres north-west of the junction of Bentley Road with Hunter Avenue and Aylesford Place, including railway sidings;

Work No. 16E—A railway (748 metres in length) commencing by a junction with the railway (Work No. 16A) at a point 140 metres north-west of the intended bridge carrying the railway (Work No. 16) over that railway, passing south-eastwards under Work No. 16, on the northern side of Work No. 16A and terminating at a point 92 metres south-east of the eastern side of the existing Aylesford Place level crossing (to be stopped up), including railway sidings;

Work No. 16F—Realignment of the A28 (Chart Road) commencing in that road at a point 45 metres east of the junction of Hilton Road with that road, passing eastwards over the railways (Works Nos. 16, 16A and 16B) in tunnel and terminating in that road at a point 3 metres west of the western side of the bridge carrying the Maidstone and Ashford Railway over that road;

Work No. 16G—Realignment of Godinton Road (B2074) and Carlton Road (E1467) commencing by a junction with Chart Road (Work No. 16F) at the existing junction of that road with Godinton Road, passing south-eastwards on the line of that road over the railway (Work No. 16B) in tunnel, then passing south-westwards on the line of Carlton Road and terminating in that road at a point 63 metres south-west of its junction with Godinton Road;

Work No. 16H—A road commencing by a junction with Godinton Road (Work No. 16G) at a point 80 metres south-east of its existing junction with Chart Road, passing north-eastwards over the railways (Works Nos. 16, 16A and 16B) in tunnel, then south-eastwards over the Maidstone and Ashford Railway (Work No. 16C) and terminating in Godinton Road at a point 45 metres north-west of its junction with James Street, including a bridge over the Maidstone and Ashford Railway (Work No. 16C);

Work No. 16J—Realignment of Bridge Road commencing in that road at a point 45 metres south-west of its existing junction with Godinton Road, passing north-eastwards, and terminating by a junction with Work No. 16G at that road junction;

Work No. 16K—An access road and cycle track commencing in Gasworks Lane at a point 30 metres south of its junction with the A292 (Elwick Road), passing south-westwards for a distance of 108 metres, on the western side of Gasworks Lane (to be stopped up), over the railway (Work No. 16), then continuing as a cycle track south-westwards, then eastwards and westwards, under the railways (Works Nos. 16A, 16B and 16C) and the Tonbridge and Ashford Railway, and terminating in Gasworks Lane at a point 10 metres south of the southern end of the existing bridge carrying that last mentioned railway over that road, including a bridge over Work No. 16;

Work No. 16L—A road commencing by a junction with Leacon Road at its junction with Norfolk Drive, passing eastwards and terminating by a junction with Gasworks Lane at a point 120 metres south of the southern end of the bridge carrying the Tonbridge and Ashford Railway over that road;

Work No. 16M—A cycle track commencing by a junction with the footpath AU 37 at a point 32 metres south of its junction with the A292 (Elwick Road), passing south-westwards over the railways (Works Nos. 16, 16A, 16B and 16C), the Maidstone and Ashford and the Tonbridge and Ashford Railways, then passing westwards, then eastwards and terminating by a junction with the footpath at a point 5 metres south-west of the southern end of the footbridge carrying that footpath over the Tonbridge and Ashford Railway;

Work No. 16N—Diversion of the A2070 (Beaver Road) commencing in that road at its junction with the A292 (Elwick Road and Station Road), passing southwards over the railways (Works Nos. 16, 16A, 16B and 16C) and terminating in the A2070 at its junction with the Romney Marsh Road, including a bridge over the said railways and a junction roundabout at that termination;

Work No. 16P—A cycle track commencing at the southern end of Alsops Road, passing eastwards, then westwards and eastwards, then southwards over the railways (Works

Nos. 16, 16A and 16B) and the Ashford and Folkestone Railway, then continuing westwards and eastwards and terminating by a junction with Crowbridge Road at a point 60 metres west of the junction of that road with Gladstone Road;

Work No. 16QQ—Diversion of Boys Hall Road and Canterbury Road (E1466), including a bridge over the Ashford and Folkestone Railway in place of the existing bridge over that railway and over the railways (Works Nos. 16, 16A and 16B) and the new road (Work No. 16RR), commencing in Boys Hall Road at a point 215 metres north-east of the existing junction of Crowbridge Road with that road, passing south-westwards over Works Nos. 16, 16A and 16B, the Ashford and Folkestone Railway and Work No. 16RR on the eastern side of the existing road and terminating in Canterbury Road at a point 150 metres south-west of that existing road junction;

Work No. 16RR—A road, forming in part a realignment of Crowbridge Road (D4488), commencing in that road at a point 230 metres north-west of its existing junction with Canterbury Road, passing south-eastwards under Work No. 16QQ then passing southwards, south-westwards and south-eastwards and terminating at a roundabout in the northern corner of Orbital Park, Ashford, at a point 520 metres north-west of the junction of Bad Munstereifel Road (Work No. 17A) with the access road to Orbital Park, Ashford;

Work No. 16RR(1)—A road commencing by a junction with the new road (Work No. 16QQ) at a point 40 metres north-east of the junction of Mead Road with Canterbury Road, passing south-eastwards and terminating by a junction with Work No. 16RR at a point 120 metres south-east of that road junction;

Work No. 16S—A cut, forming a diversion of the Aylesford Stream, commencing in that stream at a point 185 metres upstream from the northern side of the bridge carrying the Ashford and Folkestone Railway over that stream, passing westwards under the railways (Works Nos. 16, 16A and 16B) and terminating in that stream at a point 5 metres north of the southern side of the said bridge;

Work No. 16T—A railway (1,201 metres in length), forming sidings, commencing by a junction with the Ashford to Canterbury Railway at a point 4 metres south of the southern side of the bridge carrying Hythe Road over that railway, passing southwards, westwards then north-westwards and terminating in the Ashford Goods Yard at a point 200 metres east of the south-western side of the bridge carrying the Ashford to Folkestone Railway over the East Stour river;

Work No. 16U—A railway (100 metres in length), forming a cross-over, commencing by a junction with the railway (Work No. 16E) at a point 60 metres west of the junction of Bentley Road with Hunter Avenue and Aylesford Place, passing south-eastwards and terminating by a junction with the railway (Work No. 16A) at a point 85 metres south of that road junction;

In the borough of Ashford, parishes of Sevington, Mersham, Smeeth and Aldington, and in the district of Shepway, parishes of Sellindge, Stanford, Saltwood and Postling, in the county of Kent—

Work No. 17—A railway (12,300 metres in length) commencing by a junction with the railway (Work No. 16) at its termination, passing south-eastwards on the northern side of the Ashford and Folkestone Railway, under Bad Munstereifel Road (Work No. 17A) and Highfield Lane (Work No. 17C), over Blind Lane (Work No. 17D), then in tunnel beneath Church Road, Mersham for a distance of 160 metres, then passing eastwards, under Station Road, Smeeth (Work No. 17H), over Church Lane, Sellindge, (Work No. 17K), then on the southern side of the Sellindge Converter Station, under Harringe Lane (Work No. 17L), over the A20 (Ashford Road) at Sellindge (Work No. 17M) and the East Stour River west of Stone Street, Westenhanger, under the B2068 Link Road (Work No. 17P) and the A20 (Ashford Road) (Work No. 17Q) to a point alongside the western portal of the tunnel on the Ashford and Folkestone Railway beneath the access to Sandling Park, then in tunnel for a distance of 90 metres beneath that access and terminating at a point 427 metres east of the eastern portal of that tunnel at the access to Sandling Park, including bridges over Works Nos. 17D, 17K and 17M;

Work No. 17A—Realignment of Bad Munstereifel Road, including a bridge over the railway (Work No. 17) and the Ashford and Folkestone Railway in place of the existing bridge over that railway, commencing in that road at a point 330 metres north-east of the north-eastern abutment of the said existing bridge passing south-westwards over the two railways and terminating in that road at a point 420 metres south-west of the south-western abutment of that existing bridge;

Work No. 17B—Diversion of Highfield Lane and Church Road north of the bridge carrying Highfield Lane over the Ashford and Folkestone Railway, commencing in Church

Road at a point 260 metres south of its junction with Bad Munstereifel Road, passing southwards, then eastwards on the line of Church Road to its junction with Highfield Lane, then passing north-eastwards on the line of that road to a point 120 metres north-east of that road junction, then passing eastwards and terminating by a junction with Highfield Lane (Work No. 17C) at a point 120 metres south-west of the commencement of that work;

Work No. 17C—A new road, forming a diversion of Highfield Lane and Church Road, including a bridge over the railway (Work No. 17) and the Ashford and Folkestone Railway in place of the existing bridge carrying Highfield Lane over that railway, commencing by a junction with Highfield Lane at a point 260 metres north-east of its existing junction with Church Road, passing westwards, then south-westwards and southwards on the eastern side of the existing road, over the two railways, and terminating by a junction with Highfield Lane at a point 40 metres south of the access from that road to The Dean;

Work No. 17C(1)—A road for access to premises on the eastern side of Highfield Lane south of the Ashford and Folkestone Railway, commencing by a junction with the new road (Work No. 17C) at a point 100 metres north of the termination of that work, passing eastwards and terminating by a junction with the remaining part of Highfield Lane at a point 80 metres north of the access to The Dean;

Work No. 17D—Realignment of Blind Lane commencing in that road at a point 180 metres north-east of the existing bridge carrying the Ashford and Tonbridge Railway over that road, passing under that railway and the railway (Work No. 17) and terminating in Blind Lane at a point 90 metres south-west of the said existing bridge;

Work No. 17E—A tunnel over the Ashford and Folkestone Railway coterminous with the tunnel forming part of the railway (Work No. 17), beneath Church Road, Mersham (Work No. 17F);

Work No. 17F—A road, forming a diversion of Church Road, Mersham, commencing in that road at a point 240 metres south-west of its junction with Bower Road, passing south-westwards and southwards on the eastern side of the existing road, over the railway (Work No. 17) in tunnel and the Ashford and Folkestone Railway in tunnel (Work No. 17E), and terminating in Church Road at a point 190 metres north of its junction with Jemmett Lane;

Work No. 17G—A road for access to premises on the western side of Church Road, Mersham, north of the Ashford and Folkestone Railway, commencing in the remaining part of Church Road at a point opposite Bridge Cottage and terminating by a junction with Church Road (Work No. 17F) at a point 180 metres south-west of its commencement;

Work No. 17H—Diversion of the B2069 (Station Road, Smeeth), including a bridge over the railway (Work No. 17) and the Ashford and Folkestone Railway in place of the existing bridge carrying that road over that railway, commencing in Station Road at a point 260 metres south-west of the access to Park Wood Cottage, passing northwards on the western side of the existing road over the two railways, and terminating in Station Road at a point 130 metres north of the northern abutment of that existing bridge;

Work No. 17J(1)—A cut, forming a diversion of a tributary of the East Stour River west of Church Lane, Sellindge, commencing in that stream at a point 130 metres east of the northern end of the culvert by which it passes under the Ashford and Folkestone Railway, passing westwards, then southwards and terminating in that stream at a point 10 metres north of the northern end of that culvert;

Work No. 17J(2)—A cut, forming a diversion of the East Stour River, commencing in that river at a point 60 metres south-west of the southern end of the culvert by which that river passes under the Ashford and Folkestone Railway 290 metres east of Grove Bridge, passing eastwards then southwards and terminating in that river at a point 80 metres south of the southern end of the culvert by which that river passes under that railway 750 metres east of Grove Bridge;

Work No. 17J(3)—A cut, forming a diversion of the East Stour River at Westenhanger, commencing in that river at the northern end of the culvert by which that river passes under the Ashford and Folkestone Railway west of Stone Street, passing eastwards on the northern side of the railway (Work No. 17), and terminating in that river at a point 170 metres north-east of that commencement;

Work No. 17K—A diversion of Church Lane, Sellindge, commencing in that road at a point 20 metres north of the northern side of the existing bridge carrying the Ashford and Folkestone Railway over that road, passing south-eastwards under the railway (Work No. 17) and the Ashford and Folkestone Railway and terminating in Church Lane at a point 280 metres south of the southern side of that existing bridge;

Work No. 17L—A realignment of Harringe Lane, including a bridge over the railway (Work No. 17) and the Ashford and Folkestone Railway in place of the existing bridge carrying that road over that railway, commencing in that road at a point 50 metres north of the northern end of the bridge carrying that road over the M20, passing southwards over the motorway and over the two railways and terminating in Harringe Lane at a point 50 metres north of the bridge carrying that road over the East Stour River;

Work No. 17M—Realignment of the A20 (Ashford Road) at Sellindge commencing in that road at the southern side of the bridge carrying the M20 over that road, passing southwards on the line of the A20, under the railway (Work No. 17) and the Ashford and Folkestone Railway, and terminating in that road at a point 50 metres south of the southern side of the bridge carrying that last-mentioned railway over that road;

Work No. 17N—A road commencing by a junction with Stone Street at a point 80 metres west of the southern end of the bridge carrying the emergency services access road over the M20 at Stanford, passing south-eastwards then eastwards on the northern side of the railway (Work No. 17), then northwards, and terminating by a junction with the roundabout at Junction 11 of the M20 at a point 70 metres west of the junction with that roundabout of the westbound slip road of the B2068 Link Road;

Work No. 17P—Realignment of the B2068 Link Road, including a bridge over the railway (Work No. 17) and the Ashford and Folkestone Railway in place of the existing bridge carrying that road over that railway, commencing in that road at the existing junction of that road with the roundabout at Junction 11 of the M20, passing southwards over those two railways and terminating in that road at the existing roundabout at its junction with the A20 (Ashford Road);

Work No. 17Q—Diversion of the A20 (Ashford Road) at Sandling, including a bridge over the railway (Work No. 17) and the Ashford and Folkestone Railway in place of the existing bridge carrying that road over that railway, commencing in that road at the existing roundabout at its junction with the B2068 Link Road, passing north-eastwards over those two railways and terminating in that road at a point 220 metres north-east of the northern abutment of that existing bridge;

In the district of Shepway, parishes of Saltwood and Newington and town of Folkestone, in the county of Kent—

Saltwood to Folkestone

Work No. 18A—A railway (3,476 metres in length) commencing by a junction with the railway (Work No. 17) at its termination, passing eastwards under Sandling Road (Work No. 18H) on the northern side of the Ashford and Folkestone Railway and the northern side of the Dollands Moor Freight Yard, then under the roundabout (part of Work No. 18J) and terminating at a point on the western side of the M20 at Newington 215 metres south-west of the junction of Newington Road with the A20;

Work No. 18AA—A railway (1,700 metres in length) commencing by a junction with the railway (Work No. 18A) at its termination, passing eastwards over the M20 and the A20 and an access road within the Channel Tunnel Terminal and terminating by a junction with the Eurotunnel Railway at a point 1,430 metres east of the western end of the bridge carrying that railway over the A20, including bridges over the M20, the A20 and the said access road;

Work No. 18B—A railway (4,400 metres in length) commencing by a junction with the railway (Work No. 17) at its termination, passing eastwards on the northern side of the Ashford and Folkestone Railway, under Sandling Road (Work No. 18H), then over the Saltwood Tunnel on that railway, continuing on the southern side of that railway and the Dollands Moor Freight Yard, over the railway (Work No. 18E), under the B2065 (Hythe Road) (Work No. 18J), on existing bridges over the M20 and the A20 and terminating by a junction with the Eurotunnel Railway at a point 570 metres east of the eastern end of the bridge carrying that railway over the A20, including a bridge over Work No. 18E;

Work No. 18C—A railway (1,591 metres in length) commencing by a junction with the railway (Work No. 18B) at chainage 369 metres, passing eastwards on the southern side of the railway (Work No. 18A), then south-eastwards and terminating by a junction with the northern sidings of the Dollands Moor Freight Yard at a point 370 metres east of the eastern portal of the Saltwood Tunnel;

Work No. 18D—A railway (352 metres in length) commencing by a junction with the railway (Work No. 18A) at chainage 588 metres, passing eastwards and terminating by a junction with the railway (Work No. 18C) at chainage 571 metres;

Work No. 18E—A deviation railway (2,136 metres in length), forming a diversion of the Ashford and Folkestone Railway, commencing by a junction with that railway at the eastern portal of the Saltwood Tunnel, passing eastwards under the railway (Work No. 18B) and the B2065 (Hythe Road) (Work No. 18J) and terminating by a junction with the Ashford and Folkestone Railway at a point 470 metres west of the bridge carrying Cheriton High Street over that railway;

Work No. 18F—A railway (1,423 metres in length) commencing by a junction with the railway (Work No. 18E) at chainage 150 metres, passing eastwards under the B2065 (Hythe Road) (Work No. 18J), and terminating by a junction with the Eurotunnel Railway at a point 365 metres east of the existing bridge carrying that road over the Dollands Moor Freight Yard;

Work No. 18G—A railway (1,272 metres in length) commencing by a junction with the railway (Work No. 18E) at chainage 750 metres, passing eastwards under the B2065 (Hythe Road) (Work No. 18J) and terminating by a junction with the railway (Work No. 18B) at a point 90 metres east of the western end of the bridge carrying that railway over the M20;

Work No. 18H—Realignment of Sandling Road, including a bridge over the railways (Works Nos. 18A and 18B), commencing in that road at the bridge carrying that road over the Ashford and Folkestone Railway, passing north-westwards over those railways and terminating in Sandling Road at a point 140 metres south-east of the junction of that road with the A20 (Ashford Road), including a bridge over Works Nos. 18A and 18B;

Work No. 18J—Realignment of the B2065 (Hythe Road), including a roundabout at the junction of that road with the exit slip road from the Channel Tunnel Terminal (Work No. 18K) and bridges carrying that roundabout over the railway (Work No. 18A), commencing in the B2065 at a point 183 metres south of the centre of the roundabout at the Beechborough Cross Roads, passing southwards over Work No. 18A, then on viaduct over Dollands Moor Freight Yard and over the railways (Works Nos. 18B, 18E, 18F and 18G) and terminating in the B2065 at a point 215 metres north of its junction with the bridleway HE 260, including the said roundabout bridges and viaduct;

Work No. 18K—A road commencing by a junction with the north-eastern side of the roundabout (part of Work No. 18J), passing north-eastwards and eastwards and terminating by a junction with the exit slip road from the Channel Tunnel Terminal at a point 250 metres from the western end of the bridge carrying that road over the M20;

In the London Borough of Hammersmith and Fulham—

White City Sidings

Work No. 19—A railway (1,050 metres in length), forming a diversion of the northbound track of the West London Line between North Pole Junction and Kensington Olympia, commencing by a junction with that railway at a point 25 metres south-east of the bridge over that railway beneath Westway west of the junction of that road with West Cross Route, passing south-eastwards on the western side of that railway under the bridge carrying the Hammersmith and City Line of the London Underground over that railway and terminating by a junction with the West London Line at a point 170 metres north of the northern portal of the tunnel in which that railway passes beneath the junction of West Cross Route with Holland Park Avenue, Shepherds Bush Green and the Uxbridge Road;

Work No. 19A—A railway (715 metres in length), forming a siding of the West London Line, commencing by a junction with the railway (Work No. 19) at its commencement, passing south-eastwards on the eastern side of that railway, under the bridge carrying the Hammersmith and City Line of the London Underground over that railway and terminating at a point 258 metres south of the southern side of the said railway bridge;

In the borough of Gravesham, parishes of Shorne and Higham, in the county of Kent—

Hoo Sidings

Work No. 20A—A railway (1,111 metres in length), forming sidings of the Gravesend and Higham Railway at Hoo Junction, commencing by a junction with that railway on the eastern side of the Queens Farm Road level crossing on that railway, passing eastwards on the northern side of that railway, then north-eastwards on the southern side of the Grain Branch of that railway and terminating at a point 120 metres south of the south-western abutment of the bridge carrying that railway over the former Thames and Medway Canal;

Work No. 20B—A railway (827 metres in length), forming sidings of the Gravesend and Higham Railway at Hoo Junction, commencing by a junction with that railway on the eastern side of the Queens Farm Road level crossing on that railway, passing eastwards then south-eastwards on the southern side of that railway and terminating at the eastern end of the existing siding of that railway, including railway sidings;

In the districts of Dover and Thanet, parishes of Minster and Sandwich, in the county of Kent—

Richborough Sidings

Work No. 21—A railway (1,139 metres in length), forming sidings at the Richborough Power Station at Stonelees, commencing by a junction with the Margate and Dover Railway at a point 530 metres north-west of the north-western abutment of the bridge carrying that railway over the River Stour, passing south-eastwards and terminating at a point 470 metres west of the north-western end of the culvert carrying the A256 (Ramsgate Road) over Minster Stream, including railway sidings.

Interpretation

2. In paragraph 1 above—

references to the Tilbury Loop Railway are references to the Tilbury Line of the London Tilbury and Southend Railway;

references to the M2 and the M20 are references to the special roads so designated;

references to the A13 and the A20 are references to the trunk roads so designated and references to the intended A13 are to a new road to be constructed in substitution for part of the A13; and

"westbound" in any description of the direction of road or railway traffic signifies travel in the direction of London, whether or not London is the destination, and "eastbound" signifies travel in the opposite direction.

Section 2

SCHEDULE 2

Works: Further and Supplementary Provisions

Subsidiary works

1.—(1) The nominated undertaker may, for the purposes of or in connection with the scheduled works, do any of the following within the limits of deviation for those works or within the limits of land to be acquired or used—

(a) make, provide and maintain all such approaches, bridges, subways, interchanges, roundabouts, turning places, lifts, stairs, escalators, ramps, passages, means of access, shafts, stagings, buildings, apparatus, plant and machinery as may be necessary or convenient,

(b) make junctions and communications (including the provision of steps or ramps for the use of persons on foot) with any highway or access way intersected or interfered with by, or contiguous to, any of those works, and widen or alter any highway or access way for the purpose of connecting it with any of those works or another highway, or of crossing under or over the highway or access way,

(c) construct, provide and maintain all such embankments, aprons, abutments, retaining walls, wing walls, culverts and other works as may be necessary or convenient,

(d) alter or remove any structure erected upon any highway or adjoining land,

(e) alter the position of apparatus, including mains, sewers, drains and cables,

(f) alter the course of, or otherwise interfere with, non-navigable rivers, streams or watercourses, and

(g) carry out and maintain such other works, of whatever description, as may be necessary or expedient.

(2) Sub-paragraph (1) above shall not authorise the making of any cut for drainage purposes which is more than 3.35 metres wide at the bottom.

Highway accesses

2. Without prejudice to paragraph 1(1)(b) above, the nominated undertaker may, for the purposes of or in connection with the works authorised by this Part of this Act—

(a) form and lay out means of access, and

(b) improve existing means of access,

in the locations shown on the deposited plans.

Overhead line diversions

3.—(1) Without prejudice to paragraph 1(1)(e) above, the nominated undertaker may, for the purposes of, or in connection with, the works authorised by this Part of this Act, undertake the electric line diversions specified in the following table.

THE TABLE

(1) *Area*	(2) *Overhead line to be taken down*	(3) *New overhead line to be provided*
GREATER LONDON		
London Borough of Barking and Dagenham	Barking corridor 275kV overhead electric cable (ZBA) between points EC106, EC107 and EC108	New overhead electric cable to be provided on land within the relevant limits between points EC106, EC109 and EC108 or thereabouts.
London Borough of Barking and Dagenham and London Borough of Havering	Barking corridor 275kV overhead electric cable (ZBA) between points EC87, EC88, EC89, EC1, EC2, EC3, EC4, EC5, EC6, EC7, EC8, EC9, EC10, EC11 and EC12	New overhead electric cable to be provided on land within the relevant limits between points EC87, EC90, EC91, EC13, EC92, EC93, EC94, EC95, EC18, EC19, EC20, EC21, EC22 and EC12 or thereabouts.
London Borough of Havering	Havering overhead electric cable (ZBA) between points EC23, EC24 and EC25	New overhead electric cable to be provided on land within the relevant limits between points EC23, EC26 and EC25 or thereabouts.
COUNTY OF ESSEX		
Borough of Thurrock	Purfleet Road 400kV overhead electric cable (ZR) between points EC103, EC27, EC28, EC29 and EC30	New overhead electric cable to be provided on land within the relevant limits between points EC103, EC104, EC28, EC105 and EC30 or thereabouts.
	Aveley 275kV overhead electric cable (ZBA) between points EC96, EC97, EC98 and EC99	New overhead electric cable to be provided on land within the relevant limits between points EC96, EC100, EC101, EC102 and EC99 or thereabouts.
COUNTY OF KENT		
Borough of Dartford, Parish of Swanscombe and Greenhithe	Dartford 132kV overhead electric cable (south) (PK) between points EC48, EC49 and EC50	New overhead electric cable to be provided on land within the relevant limits between points EC48, EC51, EC52 and EC50 or thereabouts.
Borough of Dartford, Parish of Swanscombe and Greenhithe and Borough of Gravesham, Town of Gravesend	Dartford 132kV overhead electric cable (north) (PJ) between points EC40, EC41, EC42, EC43 and EC44	New overhead electric cable to be provided on land within the relevant limits between points EC40, EC45, EC42, EC46, EC47 and EC44 or thereabouts.
Borough of Dartford, Parish of Southfleet and Borough of Gravesham, Town of Gravesend	Dartford 400kV overhead electric cable (4TP) between points EC53, EC54, EC55 and EC56	New overhead electric cable to be provided on land within the relevant limits between points EC53, EC57, EC58 and EC56 or thereabouts.

(1) *Area*	(2) *Overhead line to be taken down*	(3) *New overhead line to be provided*
Borough of Gravesham, Town of Gravesend and Borough of Dartford, Parish of Swanscombe and Greenhithe	Gravesend 400kV overhead electric cable (ZR) between points EC33, EC34, EC35 and EC36	New overhead electric cable to be provided on land within the relevant limits between points EC33, EC37, EC38, EC39 and EC36 or thereabouts.
Borough of Gravesham, Town of Gravesend	Pepper Hill 400kV overhead electric cable (YN) between points EC59, EC60, EC61 and EC62	New overhead electric cable to be provided on land within the relevant limits between points EC59, EC63, EC64, EC65 and EC62 or thereabouts.
Borough of Gravesham, Parish of Shorne	Singlewell 400kV overhead electric cable (4YN) between points EC66, EC67 and EC68	New overhead electric cable to be provided on land within the relevant limits between points EC66, EC69 and EC68 or thereabouts.
Borough of Maidstone, Parish of Boxley	Pilgrims Way 400kV overhead electric cable (TP) between points EC70, EC71 and EC72	New overhead electric cable to be provided on land within the relevant limits between points EC70, EC73, EC74 and EC72 or thereabouts.
	Boxley 132kV overhead electric cable (PN) between points EC75, EC76, EC77 and EC78	New overhead electric cable to be provided on land within the relevant limits between points EC75, EC76, EC79 and EC78 or thereabouts.
Borough of Ashford, Parish of Aldington	Sellindge 400kV overhead electric cable (VO) between points EC80 and EC81	New overhead electric cable to be provided on land within the relevant limits between points EC80, EC82 and EC81 or thereabouts.
District of Shepway, Parish of Sellindge	Sellindge East 132kV overhead electric cable (PV) between points EC83, EC84 and EC85	New overhead electric cable to be provided on land within the relevant limits between points EC83, EC86 and EC85 or thereabouts.

(2) In sub-paragraph (1) above, references to land within the relevant limits are to land within the limits of deviation for the scheduled works or within the limits of land to be acquired or used.

Mitigation and protection works

4. The nominated undertaker may within the limits of deviation for the scheduled works or within the limits of land to be acquired or used—

(a) carry out and maintain landscaping and other works to mitigate any adverse effects of the construction, maintenance or operation of any of the works authorised by this Part of this Act, and

(b) carry out and maintain works for the benefit or protection of land affected by any of the works authorised by this Part of this Act.

Euston Road and York Way improvement works

5.—(1) The nominated undertaker may, within the limits of deviation for the scheduled works or within the limits of land to be acquired or used, carry out in Euston Road and York Way in the London Borough of Camden and their side roads, works for—

(a) the variation of the relative widths of carriageways and footways, or

(b) the division, or variation of the division, of carriageways (including the provision, or variation, of central reservations),

and works ancillary to any such works.

(2) The nominated undertaker may alter or remove any works executed by it under this paragraph.

(3) The exercise of the powers conferred by this paragraph shall be subject to the consent of the council of the London Borough of Camden, such consent not to be unreasonably withheld.

(4) Any dispute with the council of the London Borough of Camden under sub-paragraph (3) above shall, if the parties agree, be referred to arbitration, but shall otherwise be determined by the Secretary of State.

Underpinning of buildings

6.—(1) This paragraph applies where it is necessary or expedient in consequence of or in connection with the construction of any of the works authorised by this Part of this Act to underpin or strengthen a building within the relevant distance of the work.

(2) The nominated undertaker may underpin or strengthen the building on giving at least 28 days' notice to the owners and occupiers of the building of its intention to do so.

(3) If, within 21 days of the giving of a notice under sub-paragraph (2) above, the person to whom the notice has been given gives to the nominated undertaker notice disputing that this paragraph applies, the question of its application shall be referred to arbitration.

(4) If, under sub-paragraph (3) above, the arbitrator decides that this paragraph does apply, he shall, if one of the parties to the dispute so requires, prescribe how the underpinning or strengthening is to be carried out.

(5) Where the underpinning or strengthening of a building under this paragraph cannot be carried out reasonably conveniently without entering land adjacent to the building, the nominated undertaker may, on giving at least 14 days' notice to the owners and occupiers of the adjacent land, enter the land (but not any building on it) and carry out the work.

(6) In case of emergency, the power conferred by sub-paragraph (2) or (5) above shall be exercisable without notice.

(7) For the purpose of deciding how to exercise its powers under this paragraph, the nominated undertaker may at any reasonable time enter and survey—

(a) any building within the relevant distance of any of the works authorised by this Part of this Act, or

(b) any land adjacent to such a building (but not any building on any such land).

(8) Section 6 of the Acquisition of Land Act 1981 (service of documents) shall apply to the service of notices under this paragraph with, in subsection (4), the substitution for the words from "authority" to "document is to be served" of "nominated undertaker".

(9) In this paragraph—

"building" includes any structure and, in the case of a work under the surface of the ground, reference to a building within the relevant distance of that work includes a reference to any building within the relevant distance of any point on the surface below which the work is situated,

"notice" means notice in writing, and

"relevant distance", in relation to any work, means—

(i) where the work relates to an underground railway, 50 metres, and

(ii) where it does not, 35 metres.

7.—(1) This paragraph applies where it is necessary or expedient in consequence of or in connection with the construction of any of the works authorised by this Part of this Act further to underpin or strengthen a building which has been underpinned or strengthened under paragraph 6 above.

(2) The nominated undertaker may, at any time within the permitted period, further underpin or strengthen the building on giving at least 28 days' notice to the owners and occupiers of the building of its intention to do so.

(3) If, within 21 days of the giving of a notice under sub-paragraph (2) above, the person to whom the notice has been given gives to the nominated undertaker notice disputing that this paragraph applies, the question of its application shall be referred to arbitration.

(4) If, under sub-paragraph (3) above, the arbitrator decides that this paragraph does apply, he shall, if one of the parties to the dispute so requires, prescribe how the underpinning or strengthening is to be carried out.

(5) Where the underpinning or strengthening of a building under this paragraph cannot be carried out reasonably conveniently without entering land adjacent to the building, the nominated undertaker may, on giving at least 14 days' notice to the owners and occupiers of the adjacent land, enter the land (but not any building on it) and carry out the work.

(6) In case of emergency, the power conferred by sub-paragraph (2) or (5) above shall be exercisable without notice.

(7) For the purpose of deciding how to exercise its powers under this paragraph, the nominated undertaker may at any reasonable time enter and survey—

(a) any building which has been underpinned or strengthened under paragraph 6 above, or

(b) any land adjacent to such a building (but not any building on any such land).

(8) Section 6 of the Acquisition of Land Act 1981 (service of documents) shall apply to the service of notices under this paragraph with, in subsection (4), the substitution for the words from "authority" to "document is to be served" of "nominated undertaker".

(9) In sub-paragraph (2) above, the reference to the permitted period is to the period beginning with the completion of the underpinning or strengthening under paragraph 6 above and ending 5 years after the date on which the work which necessitated the underpinning or strengthening was brought into general use.

(10) In this paragraph, "notice" means notice in writing.

8.—(1) Where the nominated undertaker exercises any power under paragraph 6 or 7 above, it shall compensate the owners and occupiers of the building or land in relation to which the power is exercised for any loss which they may suffer by reason of the exercise of the power.

(2) Any dispute as to a person's entitlement to compensation under sub-paragraph (1) above, or as to the amount of the compensation, shall be determined under and in accordance with Part I of the Land Compensation Act 1961.

(3) Nothing in this paragraph shall affect liability to pay compensation under section 6 of the Railways Clauses Consolidation Act 1845, as incorporated with this Act, or section 10(2) of the Compulsory Purchase Act 1965, as applied to the acquisition of land under section 4(1) above, or under any other enactment, otherwise than for loss for which compensation is payable under sub-paragraph (1) above.

Discharge of water

9.—(1) The nominated undertaker may use any watercourse or any public sewer or drain for the drainage of water in connection with the construction or maintenance of the works authorised by this Part of this Act and for that purpose may lay down, take up and alter pipes and may, on any land within the limits of deviation for the scheduled works or within the limits of land to be acquired or used make connections with the watercourse, sewer or drain.

(2) The nominated undertaker shall not discharge any water into any public sewer or drain except with the consent of the person to whom it belongs; and such consent may be given subject to such terms and conditions as that person may reasonably impose but shall not be unreasonably withheld.

(3) The nominated undertaker shall not make any opening into any public sewer or drain except in accordance with plans approved by, and under the superintendence (if provided) of, the person to whom the sewer or drain belongs, but such approval shall not be unreasonably withheld.

(4) The nominated undertaker shall not, in the exercise of the powers conferred by this paragraph, damage or interfere with the beds or banks of any watercourse forming part of a main river.

(5) The nominated undertaker shall take such steps as are reasonably practicable to secure that any water discharged into a watercourse or public sewer or drain under the powers conferred by this paragraph is as free as may be practicable from gravel, soil or other solid substance or oil or matter in suspension.

(6) This paragraph does not authorise the doing of anything prohibited by section 85(1), (2) or (3) of the Water Resources Act 1991 (offences of polluting controlled waters).

(7) Any dispute as to the giving of consent under this paragraph shall, if the parties agree, be referred to arbitration, but shall otherwise be determined by the Secretary of State.

(8) In this paragraph—

(a) "public sewer or drain" means a sewer or drain which belongs to a sewerage undertaker, the Environment Agency, an internal drainage board, a local authority, an urban development corporation or a harbour authority within the meaning of the Harbours Act 1964,

(b) "watercourse" includes rivers, streams, ditches, drains, cuts, culverts, dykes, sluices, sewers and passages through which water flows, except a public sewer or drain, and

(c) other expressions used both in this paragraph and in the Water Resources Act 1991 have the same meanings as in that Act.

Entry for preparatory purposes

10.—(1) The nominated undertaker may, for the purposes of this Part of this Act—

(a) survey or investigate any land within the limits of deviation for the scheduled works or within the limits of land to be acquired or used or which may be affected by the works authorised by this Part of this Act,

(b) without prejudice to the generality of paragraph (a) above, make trial holes in such positions as it thinks fit on any such land to investigate the nature of the surface layer and subsoil and remove soil samples,

(c) without prejudice to the generality of paragraph (a) above, carry out archaeological investigations on any such land,

(d) take steps to protect or remove any flora or fauna on any such land which may be affected by the carrying out of the works authorised by this Part of this Act,

(e) place on, leave on and remove from any such land apparatus for use in connection with the exercise of any of the powers conferred by paragraphs (a) to (d) above, and

(f) enter on any such land for the purpose of exercising any of the powers conferred by paragraphs (a) to (e) above.

(2) No land may be entered, or equipment placed or left on or removed from land, under sub-paragraph (1) above unless at least 7 days' notice has been served on every owner and occupier of the land.

(3) The power conferred by paragraph (f) of sub-paragraph (1) above includes power to enter with such vehicles and equipment as are necessary for the purpose of exercising any of the other powers conferred by that sub-paragraph.

(4) Any person exercising the power conferred by sub-paragraph (1)(f) above on behalf of the nominated undertaker shall, if requested to do so, produce written evidence of his authority.

(5) This paragraph shall not authorise the making of trial holes in a carriageway or footway without the consent of the highway authority, but such consent shall not be unreasonably withheld.

(6) Any dispute as to the giving of consent under sub-paragraph (5) above shall, if the parties agree, be referred to arbitration, but shall otherwise be determined by the Secretary of State.

(7) The nominated undertaker shall compensate the owners and occupiers of land in respect of which the powers conferred by this paragraph are exercised for any loss which they may suffer by reason of the exercise of those powers.

(8) Any dispute as to a person's entitlement to compensation under sub-paragraph (7) above, or as to the amount of the compensation, shall be determined under and in accordance with Part I of the Land Compensation Act 1961.

Temporary interference with waterways

11.—(1) The powers conferred by this paragraph shall be exercisable for the purpose of, or in connection with, the exercise of the powers conferred by this Part of this Act in relation to Work No. 1A, 1AA, 1B, 1BB, 1C, 1CC, 1D, 1DD, 1EE, 1FF, 1HH, 1K, 2, 2A, 2AA, 2B, 2BB, 3, 3B, 3C, 5D(1), 6, 6G, 10, 10A, 10R(2), 13 or 22J.

(2) The nominated undertaker may—

(a) temporarily interfere with the relevant waterway, at any point within the limits of deviation for the scheduled works or within the limits of land to be acquired or used, by constructing or maintaining such temporary works, or by carrying out such dredging works, as it considers necessary or expedient,

(b) temporarily moor or anchor barges or other vessels or craft in the relevant waterway, or

(c) temporarily close the relevant waterway, or a part of it, to navigation.

(3) The power conferred by sub-paragraph (2)(c) above shall be exercised in a way which secures—

(a) that no more of the waterway is closed to navigation at any time than is necessary in the circumstances, and

(b) that, if complete closure of the waterway to navigation becomes necessary, all reasonable steps are taken to secure that the minimum obstruction, delay or interference is caused to vessels or craft which may be using or intending to use it.

(4) The nominated undertaker shall not be liable for any loss suffered, or costs or expenses incurred, by any person as a direct or indirect result of any closure of a waterway in accordance with this paragraph.

(5) In this paragraph, "relevant waterway" means—

(a) in relation to Works Nos. 1A, 1AA, 1B, 1BB, 1C, 1CC, 1D, 1DD, 1EE, 1FF, 1HH, 1K, 2, 2A, 2AA, 2B, 2BB, 3, 3B, 3C and 5D(1), the Regent's Canal,

(b) in relation to Works Nos. 6 and 6G, the River Lea,

(c) in relation to Works Nos. 10, 10A, 10R(2) and 22J, the River Thames, and

(d) in relation to Work No. 13, the River Medway.

Section 3

SCHEDULE 3

Highways

Stopping up: non-level crossings

1.—(1) Subject to the provisions of this paragraph, the nominated undertaker may, in connection with the construction of the works authorised by this Part of this Act, stop up each of the highways or parts of highways specified, by reference to the letters and numbers shown on the deposited plans, in columns (1) and (2) of the following table.

(2) No highway or part of a highway specified in columns (1) and (2) of Part I of the following table shall be stopped up under this paragraph unless all the land which abuts on it falls within one or more of the following categories, namely—

(a) land to which there is no right of access directly from the highway or part to be stopped up,

(b) land to which there is reasonably convenient access otherwise than directly from the highway or part to be stopped up,

(c) land the owners and occupiers of which have agreed to the stopping up of the highway or part, and

(d) land which is in the possession of the Secretary of State.

(3) No highway or part of a highway specified in columns (1) and (2) of Part II of the following table shall be stopped up under this paragraph if a new highway is specified in relation to it in column (3) of that Part of the table, by reference to the letters and numbers shown on the deposited plans or by reference to scheduled works, until—

(a) where the new highway is provided in exercise of the powers conferred by this Part of this Act, the later of the date of practical completion and the date on which it is first open for public use, and

(b) where it is not, the date on which it is first open for public use.

(4) Where a new highway specified in column (3) of Part II of the following table is provided in exercise of the powers conferred by this Part of this Act, the date of practical completion of the highway, or the date on which it is first open for public use, shall be taken for the purposes of sub-paragraph (3) above to be what it is taken to be for the purposes of paragraph 11(2) below.

The Table

Highways to be Stopped Up

Part I

Highways to be Stopped Up Without Provision of Substitute

(1) *Area*	(2) *Highway or part to be stopped up*
GREATER LONDON	
London Borough of Camden	Battlebridge Road between points E3 and E4
	Wellers Court between points F1 and F2
	Clarence Passage between points G1 and G2
	Stanley Passage between points H1 and H2

(1) *Area*	(2) *Highway or part to be stopped up*
London Borough of Barking and Dagenham	Footpath 47 between points M4 and M5
COUNTY OF ESSEX	
Borough of Thurrock	Oliver Close between points F4 and F5
COUNTY OF KENT	
Borough of Dartford, Parishes of Swanscombe and Greenhithe and Southfleet	Access road adjoining A2 between points D6, D7 and D8
Borough of Gravesham, Town of Gravesend	Footpath NU15 between points D3 and D4
Borough of Gravesham, Parish of Cobham	Old Watling Street (B395) between points K1 and K2
City of Rochester upon Medway, Parish of Cuxton	Footpath RS 205 between points D1 and D2 Footpath RR 27 between points D2 and D3
Borough of Maidstone, Parish of Hollingbourne	Musket Lane between points A4 and A3
Borough of Maidstone, Parish of Harrietsham	Footpath KH275 between points E5 and E3
Borough of Ashford, Parish of Charing	Footpath AW47 between points K1 and K2
Borough of Ashford, Town of Ashford	Gasworks Lane (D4543) between points E1 and E2
Borough of Ashford, Parish of Mersham	Footpath AE 386 between points C10 and C11
Borough of Ashford, Parish of Smeeth	Footpath AE 434 between points C3 and C2
District of Shepway, Parishes of Saltwood and Stanford	Footpath HE 346 between points A2 and A5 Stone Street between points B1 and B2
District of Shepway, Parish of Saltwood	Footpath HE 279 between points C9 and C10 Sandy Lane (D1752) between points C11 and C8

PART II

HIGHWAYS TO BE STOPPED UP ONLY ON PROVISION OF SUBSTITUTE

(1) *Area*	(2) *Highway or part to be stopped up*	(3) *New highway to be substituted for it*
GREATER LONDON		
London Borough of Camden	Midland Road between points B1 and B2	Work No. 5B
	Pancras Road between points C1, B2 and C2	Works Nos. 5B, 5C and 5D
	Taxi Road between points D1, D2 and D3	Works Nos. 5F and 5F(1)
	Cheney Road between points E1, E2 and E3	Work No. 5C

(1) *Area*	(2) *Highway or part to be stopped up*	(3) *New highway to be substituted for it*
	Goods Way between points K1 and K5	Work No. 5D
	Camley Street between points K4 and K6	Works Nos. 5A and 5C
	York Way between points L1 and L2	Work No. 5Q
London Borough of Islington	Randell's Road between points A1 and A2	Work No. 5Q(1)
London Borough of Barking and Dagenham	Pooles Lane between points M1 and M2	Work No. 22H(1) between its commencement and its junction with Work No. 22H(2), and Work No. 22H(2)
	Choats Manor Way between points M3 and M4	Work No. 22H(1) between its commencement and its junction with Work No. 8P(3)
	Choats Road between points L1 and L2	Work No. 8P(3)
	Hindmans Way between points L2 and L3	Work No. 8P(3)
	Chequers Lane between points L4 and L5	Works Nos. 8P(3) and 8P(4)
	Kent Avenue between points J1 and J2	Work No. 8Q
	Thames Avenue between points K1 and K2	Work No. 8R
London Borough of Havering	Creekside between points C1 and C2	Works Nos. 8S and 8T
	Lamson Road between points D1 and D3	Work No. 8S
COUNTY OF ESSEX		
Borough of Thurrock	Footpath FP145 between points L1 and L2	New footpath between points L1, L3, L4, L5, L6, L7 and L2
	Arterial Road, Purfleet between points M1 and M2	Work No. 23C(1)
	Purfleet Bypass between points M3 and M4	Work No. 23C(3)
	Tank Lane between points M5 and M6	Work No. 23C(5) and Work No. 23C(4) between point M5 and its termination
	Botany Way between points M8 and M9	Works Nos. 23C(2), 23C(3) and 23C(5)
	Footpath 167 between points N1 and N2	New footpath between points N1, N3 and N2
	Oliver Close (North) between points F1, F2 and F3	Work No. 9B

(1) *Area*	(2) *Highway or part to be stopped up*	(3) *New highway to be substituted for it*
	Oliver Road between points G1 and G2	Work No. 9C
	Burnley Road and Watson Close between points H1, H2 and H3	Work No. 9D
	A1090 (Tank Hill Road) between points J8 and J2	Work No. 23B(1) and new footpath between points J8 and J9
	Access road to Purfleet Industrial Park between points J5 and J6	Work No. 23B(1) between its commencement and its junction with Work No. 23B(2), and Work No. 23B(2)
COUNTY OF KENT		
Borough of Dartford, Parish of Swanscombe and Greenhithe	Green Manor Way between points B1 and B2	Works Nos. 10J and 10J(1)
	Footpath DS17 between points D1 and D2	New footpath between points D1, D3 and D2
Borough of Dartford, Parish of Swanscombe and Greenhithe and Borough of Gravesham, Town of Gravesend	Lower Road between points B3 and B4	Work No. 10J
Borough of Dartford, Parishes of Swanscombe and Greenhithe and Southfleet	Park Corner Road and Southfleet Road (B259) between points E1, E2 and E3	Works Nos. 10S(2) and 10(T)(6) to 10T(8)
	Access road between points F1 and F2	Works Nos. 10S(2), 10T(1), 10T(4), 10T(6) and 10T(8)
Borough of Dartford, Parish of Southfleet	Slip road from A2 to Park Corner Road between points C1 and C2	Work No. 10T(8)
	Footpath DR132 between points B1 and B2	New footpath between points B2 and B3
	New Barn Road between points A1 and A2	Work No. 11F
	Hook Green Road between points D1 and D2	Work No. 11D
Borough of Dartford, Parishes of Longfield and New Barn and Southfleet	Whitehill Road between points A1 and A2	Work No. 11C
Borough of Dartford, Parish of Longfield and New Barn and District of Sevenoaks, Parish of Horton Kirby and South Darenth	Footpath DR160 between points B1 and B2	New footpath between points B1, B3, B4 and B2
Borough of Gravesham, Town of Gravesend	Manor Way between points B5 and B6	Work No. 10J(2)

(1) *Area*	(2) *Highway or part to be stopped up*	(3) *New highway to be substituted for it*
	Footpath NU14 between points A1 and A2	New footpath between points A1, A3, A4 and A2
	Footpath NU7A between points B1 and B2	New footpath between points B1, B3 and B2
	Footpath NU14 between points C1 and C2	New footpath between points C1, C3 and C2
	Footpath NU16 between points D1 and D2	New footpath between points D1 and D5
	Bridleway NU24 between points F1 and F2	New bridleway between points F1, F5, F6 and F2
	Footpath NU23 between points F3 and F4	New footpath between points F4 and F2
	Downs Road between points G1 and G2	Work No. 10P
	Access road to Hazells between points H1 and H2	Work No. 10Q
	Bridleway NU27 between points J1 and J2	New bridleway between points J1, J3, J4 and J2
	Footpath NU29 between points L1 and L2	New footpath between points L1, K3, L3 and L2
	Footpath NU9 between points K1 and K2	New footpath between points K1 and K3
Borough of Gravesham, Town of Gravesend and Parish of Cobham	Footpaths NU18, NS193 and NG15 between points M1 and M4	New footpath between points M4 and M5
Borough of Gravesham, Parish of Cobham	Church Road between points A1 and A2	Work No. 12C and new footpath between points A3, A4, A5 and A2
	Footpaths NG16 and NS175 between points B1 and B3	Works Nos. 12C and 12D and new footpath between points B3 and B4
	Henhurst Road between points C1 and C2	Work No. 12D
	Footpath NS177 between points D1 and D2	Work No. 12D and new footpaths between points D1 and D3 and between points D4 and D2
	Access road between points E1, E4 and E2	New access roads between points E1, E3 and E2 and between points E3 and E4
	Scotland Lane (Byway NS195) between points F1 and F2	Works Nos. 12E and 12F
	Watling Street (B395) between points G1 and G2	Work No. 12F
	Access road between points F3 and F4	Works Nos. 12E and 12F

(1) *Area*	(2) *Highway or part to be stopped up*	(3) *New highway to be substituted for it*
	Halfpence Lane (C492) and slip road to A2 between points H1 and H3	Works Nos. 32B and 32C
	Slip road from A2 to Halfpence Lane between points H4 and H2	Work No. 32B
	Footpath NS179 between points L1 and L2	New footpaths between points L3 and L4 and between points L2 and L5
	Access road between points M1 and M2	Work No. 12L
Borough of Gravesham, Parish of Shorne	A2 eastbound slip road between points J3 and J4	Work No. 32A
Borough of Gravesham, Parishes of Cobham and Shorne	Brewers Road between points J1 and J2	Work No. 12H
	Access road between points K3 and K2	Work No. 12K
	Footpath NS180 between points K2 and K4	Work No. 12K
	Footpath NS161 between points K6, K2, K8 and K5	Work No. 12K and new footpath between points L5, K7 and K5
City of Rochester upon Medway, Town of Rochester and Parish of Cuxton	Footpath RS203 between points B2 and B3	New footpath between points B2, B5, B4 and B3
	A228 (Rochester Road) between points C1 and C3	Work No. 13A(4) and Work No. 36F between its commencement and its junction with Work No. 13A(4)
	M2 westbound entry slip road between points C6 and C7	Work No. 13A(2), Work No. 36C between its junction with Work No. 13A(2) and its termination, and Work No. 36E between its junction with Work No. 36C and its termination
	M2 westbound exit slip road between points C8 and C7	Work No. 13A(3) and Work No. 36E between its junction with Work No. 36C and its termination
	M2 eastbound exit slip road between points C9 and C4	Works Nos. 13A(1) and 13A(4) and Work No. 36F between its commencement and its junction with Work No. 13A(4)
City of Rochester upon Medway, Town of Rochester	Burham Road (D422) between points A1 and A2	Work No. 13B

(1) *Area*	(2) *Highway or part to be stopped up*	(3) *New highway to be substituted for it*
	Bridleway RR16 between points E4, E11 and E12	Work No. 13C between its junction with Work No. 38F and its termination, Work No. 38F between point E13 and its termination, and new bridleway between points E4 and E13 (having a junction at point E4 with bridleway RR16 as existing, so far as not stopped up under paragraph 3 of Schedule 12 below, or, if so stopped up, with Work No. 38C)
City of Rochester upon Medway, Town of Rochester and Borough of Tonbridge and Malling, Parish of Wouldham	Bridleway MR11 (Stony Lane) between points A1 and A2	Work No. 13C
	Bridleway MR12 between points E12 and A1	Work No. 13C
Borough of Tonbridge and Malling, Parish of Aylesford	Byway MR401 between points T1 and T2	Work No. 13E
Borough of Maidstone, Parish of Boxley	Boarley Lane (D898) between points A1 and A2	Work No. 13G
	Footpath KH25 between points B1 and B2	New footpath between points B1, B3 and B2
	Boxley Road (C97) between points C1 and C2	Work No. 13H
	Footpath KH15 between points D1 and D2	New footpath between points D1, D3 and D2
Borough of Maidstone, Parish of Thurnham	Footpath KH71 between points A1, A2 and A3	New footpath between points A1, A4, A5 and A6
	Thurnham Lane between points B1 and B2	Work No. 14A
	Bridleway KH123 between points C1, C2 and C3	New bridleway between points C1 and C4
	Water Lane between points D1 and D2	Work No. 14B
	Footpath KH130 between points E1, E4 and E2	New footpaths between points E1, E3 and E2 and between points E3 and E4
	Bridleway KH134 (Crismill Lane) between points F1 and F2	Work No. 14C
Borough of Maidstone, Parishes of Thurnham and Hollingbourne	Footpath KH141 between points G1 and G2	Work No. 14C and new footpath between points G3 and G2

(1) *Area*	(2) *Highway or part to be stopped up*	(3) *New highway to be substituted for it*
Borough of Maidstone, Parish of Hollingbourne	Footpath KH132A between points A1 and A2	New footpath between points A1 and A3
	Footpath KH198 between points C1, C2 and C3	New footpath between points C1, C4, C3 and C5
	Hospital Road (D971) between points D1 and D2	Work No. 14E
Borough of Maidstone, Parish of Broomfield	Footpath KH201 between points A1, A2 and A3	Works Nos. 14F and 14G and new footpath between points A1, A4 and A5
Borough of Maidstone, Parishes of Broomfield and Hollingbourne	Greenway Court Road (D946) between points E1 and E2	Works Nos. 14F and 14G
Borough of Maidstone, Parishes of Broomfield and Harrietsham	A20 (Ashford Road) between points B1 and B2	Work No. 14F
Borough of Maidstone, Parish of Harrietsham	Footpath KH343 between points A1 and A5	New footpaths between points A1, A2 and A4 and between points A2 and A3
	Bridleway between points C1 and C2	New bridleway between those points
	Footpath KH272 between points E1, E2, E3 and E4	New footpaths between points E1, E5 and E4 and between points E1 and E6
	Footpath KH272A between points F1, F2 and F3	New footpath between points F1, F4 and F5
	Access road between points G1 and G2	Work No. 14J
Borough of Maidstone, Parish of Lenham	Footpath KH416 between points A1 and A2	New footpath between points A1 and A3
	Sandway Road (C92) between points C1 and C2	Work No. 14L
	Footpath KH414B between points D1 and D2	Work No. 14L and new footpaths between points D3 and D1 and between points D4 and D5
	Old Ham Lane (D986) between points E1 and E2	Work No. 14M
	Footpath KH415 between points F3, F1 and F2	New footpath between points F4 and F5
Borough of Maidstone, Parishes of Boughton Malherbe and Lenham	Lenham Heath Road (C92) between points J1 and J2	Work No. 14Q
	Lenham Heath Road (C92) between points K1 and K2	Work No. 14R

(1) *Area*	(2) *Highway or part to be stopped up*	(3) *New highway to be substituted for it*
	Bowley Lane between points L1 and L2	Work No. 14S
Borough of Maidstone, Parish of Lenham	Access road to Water Street Cottage between points M1 and M2	Works Nos. 14U and 14V
	Hook Street between points P1 and P2	Works Nos. 14U and 14V
	Footpath KH408A between points Q1, Q2, Q3 and Q4	New footpath between points Q1 and Q4
	Footpath KH407A between points R1 and R2	New footpath between points R1, R3, R4 and R2
Borough of Ashford, Parish of Charing	Bridleway AW58 between points D1, D2 and C3 and footpath AW17 between points C1 and C3	New bridleway and footpath between points D1, C1 and D3
	Hurst Lane (D1198) between points E1 and E2	Works Nos. 15E and 15F
	Newlands Road (D1199) between points F1 and F2	Work No. 15F
	Footpath AW30 between points G1 and G2	New footpath between points G3 and G2
Borough of Ashford, Parishes of Charing and Little Chart	Leacon Lane (D1220) between points J1 and J2 and between points J3 and J4	Work No. 15H
Borough of Ashford, Parish of Charing	Footpath AW44 between points L1 and L2	New footpath between points L3, L4 and L2
	Footpath AW40 between points M1 and M2	New footpath between points M1, M3 and M2
Borough of Ashford, Parishes of Charing, Hothfield and Westwell	A20 (Maidstone Road) at West Leacon between points P1 and P2 and between points P3 and P4	Works Nos. 15K and 15L
Borough of Ashford, Parish of Westwell	Westwell Lane (D1227) between points B1 and B2	Work No. 15M
	Footpath AW123 between points A1 and A2	Work No. 15M and new footpath between points A1 and A3
	Footpath AW124 between points C1, C2 and C3	Works Nos. 15M and 15N and new footpath between points C4 and C5
	Footpath AW124 between points E1, E2 and E3	New footpath between points E1 and E3

(1) *Area*	(2) *Highway or part to be stopped up*	(3) *New highway to be substituted for it*
Borough of Ashford, Parishes of Hothfield and Westwell	A20 (Maidstone Road) at Yonsea between points F1 and F2	Work No. 15P
Borough of Ashford, Parish of Hothfield	Byway AW173 between points A1, A2 and A3	New byway between points A4 and A3
Borough of Ashford, Parish of Hothfield and Town of Ashford	Godinton Lane (C154) between points B1 and B2	Work No. 15Q
Borough of Ashford, Town of Ashford	Footpath AU67 between points A1 and A2	New footpath between points A1 and A3
	Godinton Road (B2074) between points C1 and C2	Works Nos. 16G and 16H
	Carlton Road (E1467) between points C4 and C5	Work No. 16G
	Footpath AU34 between points D1, D2 and D6	New footpath between points D1, D3, D4, D5 and D6
	Footpath AU37 between points F1 and F2	Work No. 16M
	Beaver Road (A2070) between points G1 and G2	Work No. 16N
	Footpath AU52 between points J1 and J2	New footpath between points J1, J3, J4, J5 and J2
	Boys Hall Road and Canterbury Road (E1466) between points P1 and P2	Work No. 16QQ
	Footpath AU51 between points Q1 and Q2	Work No. 16RR(1) and Work No. 16RR between its junction with Work No. 16RR(1) and point Q2
	Crowbridge Road (D4488) between points N1 and N2	Work No. 16RR(1) and Work No. 16RR between its commencement and its junction with Work No. 16RR(1)
Borough of Ashford, Parish of Sevington	Footpath AE341 between points A1 and A2	New footpath between points A1 and A5
	Footpath AE343 between points A2, A7 and A3	New footpath between points A5, A6 and A3
	Footpath AE342 between points A2 and A4	New footpath between points A5 and A8
	Highfield Lane between points B5, B4, B6 and B7 and between points B8 and B9	Works Nos. 17B, 17C and 17C(1)
Borough of Ashford, Parishes of Sevington and Mersham	Footpath AE344 between points C1 and C2 and footpath AE364 between points C2, C4 and C5	New footpath between points C6, C7, C8, C9, C3 and C5

(1) *Area*	(2) *Highway or part to be stopped up*	(3) *New highway to be substituted for it*
Borough of Ashford, Parish of Mersham	Church Road (C177) between points B1 and B2 and between points B3 and B4	Works Nos. 17F and 17G
	Footpath AE369 between points D1 and D2	New footpath between points D1 and D3
Borough of Ashford, Parishes of Mersham and Smeeth	Footpath AE373 between points E1 and E2	New footpath between points E1, E3 and E2
Borough of Ashford, Parish of Smeeth	Footpath AE428 between points A1, A2 and A3 and footpath AE430 between points A2 and A4	New footpath between points A3, A5, A1 and A4
	Station Road (B2069) between points B1 and B2	Work No. 17H
	Footpath AE435 between points C1 and C8	New footpath between points C1, C3, and C4
	Footpath AE437 between points C7 and C5	New footpath between points C7, C6, C4 and C5
Borough of Ashford, Parish of Aldington	Church Lane (B1424) between points E1 and E2	Work No. 17K
District of Shepway, Parish of Sellindge	Footpath HE309 between points A1, A3 and A4	New footpath between points A1, A2 and A4
	Bridleway HE271A between points C1, C2 and C3	New bridleway between points C1 and C4 and new footpath between points C1, C2 and C3
District of Shepway, Parish of Stanford	Footpath HE274 between points A1, A2 and A4	New footpath between points A1 and A4
District of Shepway, Parishes of Postling, Saltwood and Stanford	Footpath HE227 between points B3, C1, C2, C3 and C4	Work No. 17N and new footpaths between points B3, B4 and C5 and between points C6 and C4
District of Shepway, Parishes of Postling and Saltwood	A20 (Ashford Road) between points B1 and B2	Work No. 17Q and new footpath between points B3, B4 and B5
District of Shepway, Parish of Saltwood	Footpath HE294 between points A1 and A2	Work No. 18H and new footpath between points A1 and A3
	Footpath HE280 between points C1, C2 and C3	New footpath between points C4 and C5
	Footpath HE349 between points C3, C10, C6 and C7	New footpath between points C8, C9 and C7
	Bridleway HE350 between points C11 and C12	New bridleway between points C12 and C8

2.—(1) Subject to the provisions of this paragraph, the nominated undertaker may, in connection with the construction of the works authorised by this Part of this Act, stop up any bridleway or footpath, or part of a bridleway or footpath, which is—

(a) within the limits of deviation for the scheduled works or within the limits of land to be acquired or used, and

(b) not specified in columns (1) and (2) of the table in paragraph 1 above.

(2) The power conferred by sub-paragraph (1) above shall not be exercised unless the proposed stopping up has been confirmed by the appropriate Ministers upon application by the nominated undertaker.

(3) The appropriate Ministers shall grant an application under sub-paragraph (2) above if, but only if, they are satisfied—

(a) that an alternative bridleway or footpath has been provided,

(b) that an alternative bridleway or footpath will be provided before the proposed stopping up takes place, or

(c) that the provision of an alternative bridleway or footpath is not required.

(4) Where the appropriate Ministers grant an application under sub-paragraph (2) above, they shall notify the nominated undertaker of the basis on which the application is granted.

(5) Where the basis on which an application under sub-paragraph (2) above is granted is that an alternative bridleway or footpath will be provided, the proposed stopping up shall not take place until the alternative has been provided.

(6) Before making an application under sub-paragraph (2) above, the nominated undertaker shall publish in at least one local newspaper circulating in the relevant area a notice—

(a) specifying—

(i) the bridleway or footpath, or part, proposed to be stopped up,

(ii) what, if any, alternative bridleway or footpath is proposed, and

(iii) if no alternative is proposed, the reasons why,

(b) specifying a place in the relevant area where a map or plan illustrating the proposals may be inspected by any person free of charge at all reasonable hours during a period of 28 days from the date of publication of the notice ("the publication date"),

(c) stating that any person may within that period make representations about confirmation under sub-paragraph (2) above of the proposed stopping up, and

(d) specifying the manner in which such representations may be made.

(7) Not later than the publication date, the nominated undertaker shall—

(a) serve a copy of the notice, together with any map or plan to which it refers, on every local authority whose area includes any of the land on which the bridleway or footpath, or part, proposed to be stopped up is situated, and

(b) cause a copy of the notice to be displayed in a prominent position at the ends of the bridleway or footpath, or part, proposed to be stopped up.

(8) Before granting an application under sub-paragraph (2) above, the appropriate Ministers shall consider any representations made to them in accordance with the nominated undertaker's notice which have not been withdrawn.

(9) Unless they direct otherwise, the appropriate Ministers' functions in relation to an application under sub-paragraph (2) above shall, instead of being carried out by them, be carried out by a person appointed by them for the purpose.

(10) In sub-paragraph (6) above, references to the relevant area are to the area in which the bridleway or footpath, or part, proposed to be stopped up is situated.

(11) In sub-paragraph (7)(a) above, "local authority" means the council of a county, district, parish or London borough, a joint authority established by Part IV of the Local Government Act 1985, a housing action trust established under Part III of the Housing Act 1988 and the parish meeting of a rural parish not having a separate parish council.

(12) In this paragraph, references to the appropriate Ministers are to the Secretary of State for the Environment and the Secretary of State for Transport and, in relation to the carrying out of any functions, are to those Ministers acting jointly.

3.—(1) On a highway or part of a highway being stopped up under paragraph 1 or 2 above—

(a) all rights of way over or along it shall be extinguished, and

(b) the Secretary of State may appropriate and use, without making any payment, so much of the site of it as is bounded on both sides by land which he owns.

(2) The nominated undertaker shall compensate any person who suffers loss by the extinguishment under this paragraph of a private right of way.

(3) Any dispute as to a person's entitlement to compensation under sub-paragraph (2) above, or as to the amount of such compensation, shall be determined under and in accordance with Part I of the Land Compensation Act 1961.

(4) The Secretary of State shall not be entitled to any mines or minerals under land which he is entitled to appropriate and use under sub-paragraph (1)(b) above, with the exception of min-

erals necessarily extracted or used in the construction of the undertaking which the nominated undertaker is authorised to carry on by this Part of this Act.

(5) Part III of Schedule 2 to the Acquisition of Land Act 1981 (regulation of the working of mines or minerals underlying an authorised undertaking) shall apply in relation to the working of any mines or minerals underlying land which the Secretary of State is entitled to appropriate and use under sub-paragraph (1)(b) above with the following modifications—

(a) references to the undertaking shall be construed as references to the undertaking which the nominated undertaker is authorised to carry on by this Part of this Act,
(b) in paragraphs 3 to 5 and 7 to 9, references to the acquiring authority shall be construed as references to the nominated undertaker, and
(c) in paragraph 6, the first of the references to the acquiring authority shall be construed as a reference to the nominated undertaker.

Stopping up: level crossings

4.—(1) The nominated undertaker may, in connection with the construction of the works authorised by this Part of this Act, stop up each of the highways or parts of highways specified, by reference to the letters and numbers shown on the deposited plans, in columns (1), (2) and (3) of the following table.

(2) The nominated undertaker shall construct the footbridges referred to in column (3) of the following table, but the power conferred by sub-paragraph (1) above shall be independent of the duty imposed by this sub-paragraph.

(3) On a highway or part of a highway being stopped up under this paragraph—

(a) all rights of way over or along it shall be extinguished, and
(b) the place where the former highway crossed the railway shall cease to be a level crossing for the purposes of any enactment.

(4) The nominated undertaker shall compensate any person who suffers loss by the extinguishment under this paragraph of a private right of way.

(5) Any dispute as to a person's entitlement to compensation under sub-paragraph (4) above, or as to the amount of such compensation, shall be determined under and in accordance with Part I of the Land Compensation Act 1961.

THE TABLE

(1) *Area*	(2) *Name of highway at crossing*	(3) *Extent of closure and nature of work*
GREATER LONDON		
London Borough of Barking and Dagenham	Chequers Lane	Chequers Lane to be stopped up between points H1 and H2. Footbridge to be provided to carry a new footpath between points H3, H4, H5 and H6.
London Borough of Havering	Manor Way	Manor Way to be stopped up between points A1 and A2. Footbridge to be provided to carry a new footpath between points A1, A3, A4, A5, A6 and A2.
	Ferry Lane	Ferry Lane to be stopped up between points F1 and F2. Footbridge to be provided to carry a new footpath between points F3, F4, F5, F6, F7 and F2.
COUNTY OF ESSEX		
Borough of Thurrock	A1090 (Tank Hill Road)	A1090 (Tank Hill Road) to be stopped up between points J1 and J7.

(1) *Area*	(2) *Name of highway at crossing*	(3) *Extent of closure and nature of work*
COUNTY OF KENT		
Borough of Ashford, Town of Ashford	Aylesford Place	Aylesford Place to be stopped up between points H1 and H2.

Permanent obstruction

5.—(1) The powers conferred by paragraph 1 or 4 of Schedule 2 to this Act may be exercised in such a way as to obstruct the highway, but only with the consent of the highway authority, such consent not to be unreasonably withheld.

(2) Any dispute with a highway authority under sub-paragraph (1) above shall, if the parties agree, be referred to arbitration, but shall otherwise be determined by the Secretary of State.

(3) If a highway authority which receives an application for consent under sub-paragraph (1) above fails to notify the applicant of its decision on the application before the end of the period of 28 days beginning with the date on which the application was made, it shall be deemed to have granted it.

Temporary interference

6.—(1) For the purposes of the works authorised by this Part of this Act, the nominated undertaker may—

(a) temporarily stop up or alter or divert any highway or part of a highway,

(b) for any reasonable time—

(i) divert traffic from, and

(ii) prevent persons passing along,

any highway or part of a highway, and

(c) break up or interfere with any highway or part of a highway (including any sewer, drain or tunnel in it).

(2) The nominated undertaker shall provide reasonable access for pedestrians going to or from premises abutting on a highway affected by the exercise of the powers conferred by this paragraph if there would otherwise be no such access.

(3) It is hereby declared for the avoidance of doubt that there is no need to reinstate a highway or part of a highway in relation to which any of the powers conferred by sub-paragraph (1) above has been exercised where the exercise of the power comes to an end on the exercise, in relation to the highway or part, of the power conferred by paragraph 1(1) or 2(1) above.

Street works

7.—(1) The nominated undertaker may, for the purposes of the works authorised by this Part of this Act, enter upon any highway within the limits of deviation for the scheduled works or within the limits of land to be acquired or used and—

(a) place apparatus in it,

(b) maintain apparatus in it,

(c) change the position of apparatus in it,

(d) remove apparatus from it, and

(e) execute any works required for, or incidental to, any works authorised by paragraph (a), (b), (c) or (d) above.

(2) In this paragraph, "apparatus" has the same meaning as in Part III of the New Roads and Street Works Act 1991.

8.—(1) Works to which sub-paragraph (2) below applies shall be treated for the purposes of Part III of the New Roads and Street Works Act 1991 (street works) as major highway works if—

(a) they are of a description mentioned in any of paragraphs (a), (c) to (e), (g) and (h) of section 86(3) of that Act (which defines what highway authority works are major highway works), or

(b) they are works which, had they been executed under the powers of the highway authority, might have been carried out in exercise of the powers conferred by section 64 (dual carriageways and roundabouts) or 184 (vehicle crossings over footways and verges) of the Highways Act 1980.

(2) This sub-paragraph applies to any works executed under this Part of this Act in relation to a highway which consists of or includes a carriageway, other than those executed under power delegated to a highway authority by an agreement under paragraph 14(2) below.

(3) In Part III of the New Roads and Street Works Act 1991, references, in relation to major highway works, to the highway authority concerned shall, in relation to works which are major highway works by virtue of sub-paragraph (1) above, be construed as references to the nominated undertaker.

Construction

9.—(1) Where under this Part of this Act the nominated undertaker—

(a) constructs a new highway, or

(b) alters a highway, otherwise than by carrying out street works within the meaning of Part III of the New Roads and Street Works Act 1991,

the construction or alteration shall be completed to the reasonable satisfaction of the highway authority.

(2) Where work to which sub-paragraph (1) above applies has been completed to the reasonable satisfaction of a highway authority, it shall certify that fact in writing to the nominated undertaker.

(3) If the nominated undertaker requests a highway authority to issue a certificate under sub-paragraph (2) above and the highway authority does not before the end of the period of 28 days beginning with the date on which the request was made—

(a) issue a certificate under that sub-paragraph, or

(b) notify the nominated undertaker of its decision to refuse to issue such a certificate,

it shall be deemed to have issued such a certificate at the end of that period.

(4) Any dispute with a highway authority under this paragraph shall, if the parties agree, be referred to arbitration, but shall otherwise be determined by the Secretary of State.

10.—(1) Sub-paragraph (2) below applies where under this Part of this Act the nominated undertaker—

(a) realigns a highway which is constituted by or comprises a carriageway, or

(b) constructs a new highway which is constituted by or comprises a carriageway,

and the highway is one for which a local highway authority is the highway authority.

(2) The realignment, or construction, shall be carried out in accordance with plans, sections and specifications approved by the highway authority at the request of the nominated undertaker, such approval not to be unreasonably withheld.

(3) Any dispute with a highway authority under sub-paragraph (2) above shall, if the parties agree, be referred to arbitration, but shall otherwise be determined by the Secretary of State.

(4) If, on application by the nominated undertaker for the approval of plans, sections or specifications under sub-paragraph (2) above, the highway authority fails to notify the nominated undertaker of its decision on the application before the end of the period of 28 days beginning with the date on which the application was made, it shall be deemed to have approved the plans, sections or specifications as submitted.

Maintenance

11.—(1) Sub-paragraph (2) below applies where under this Part of this Act the nominated undertaker—

(a) constructs a new highway, or

(b) alters a highway, otherwise than by carrying out street works within the meaning of Part III of the New Roads and Street Works Act 1991.

(2) Unless otherwise agreed between the nominated undertaker and the highway authority, the new or altered highway shall be maintained by and at the expense of the nominated undertaker for a period of 12 months from the later of—

(a) the date of practical completion, and

(b) the date on which it is first open for public use;

and after the end of that period shall be maintained by and at the expense of the highway authority.

(3) Where in relation to a highway to which sub-paragraph (2) above applies the highway authority is satisfied that the highway is practically complete or is open for public use, it shall, at the request of the nominated undertaker, certify to it in writing the date of practical completion of the highway or, as the case may be, the date on which it was first open for public use.

(4) If the highway authority refuses a request to issue a certificate under sub-paragraph (3) above, or if the nominated undertaker disputes the date given in a certificate under that sub-

paragraph, the matter shall, if the parties agree, be referred to arbitration, but shall otherwise be determined by the Secretary of State.

(5) For the purposes of sub-paragraph (2) above, the date of practical completion of a highway, or the date on which it is first open for public use, shall be taken to be—

(a) where the date has been determined under sub-paragraph (4) above, the date so determined, and

(b) where it has not, the date certified under sub-paragraph (3) above.

(6) Sub-paragraph (2) above shall not have effect to impose any obligation in relation to—

(a) the structure of any bridge carrying a highway over, or

(b) the structure of any tunnel carrying a highway under,

any railway of the nominated undertaker.

(7) Nothing in this paragraph shall prejudice the operation of section 87 of the New Roads and Street Works Act 1991.

12. Notwithstanding anything in section 46 of the Railways Clauses Consolidation Act 1845, as incorporated with this Act, the nominated undertaker shall not be liable to maintain the surface of any highway under or over which the scheduled works shall be constructed, or the immediate approaches to any such highway.

Bridges carrying highways

13. Each of sections 116 and 117 of the Transport Act 1968 (duties as respects bridges carrying highways over railways) shall apply as if the nominated undertaker were one of the boards mentioned in that section.

Agreements with highway authorities etc.

14.—(1) Where under this Schedule the nominated undertaker is authorised to stop up or interfere with an existing highway or part of an existing highway, it may enter into agreements with the persons having the charge, management or control of the highway concerning the construction (or contribution towards the expense of the construction) of—

(a) any new highway to be provided in substitution,

(b) any alteration of the existing highway, and

(c) any other related matters.

(2) The nominated undertaker may, by agreement with any such persons, delegate to them the power of constructing any such new highway or any such alteration of an existing highway, including any bridge over any railway, and, where the nominated undertaker is responsible for maintaining the new or altered highway (or bridge), the power to maintain it.

Use of subsoil

15. The nominated undertaker may enter upon, take and use for the purposes of the works authorised by this Part of this Act so much of the subsoil of any highway within the limits of deviation for the scheduled works or within the limits of land to be acquired or used as shall be required for the purpose of the construction or maintenance of those works, without being required to acquire that subsoil or any interest therein.

Section 4

SCHEDULE 4

Acquisition of Land within Limits Shown on Deposited Plans

Part I

Purposes for which Certain Land may be Acquired or Used

(1) *Area*	(2) *Number of land shown on deposited plans*	(3) *Purpose for which land may be acquired or used*
GREATER LONDON		
London Borough of Camden	15, 16 and 159	The provision of car parking, a working site, and access for construction purposes.

(1) *Area*	(2) *Number of land shown on deposited plans*	(3) *Purpose for which land may be acquired or used*
	1 to 13, 149 to 151 and 153 to 158	Road improvement works and alterations to ventilation shafts.
	37	The provision of parking, a working site and access for construction purposes.
	61	The provision of parking and a working site.
	79	The provision of access for construction purposes.
	63, 64, 74 and 76 to 78	The provision of access for protective works.
	87	The provision of access for construction purposes and a working site.
	182 and 189 to 192	The provision of access for construction purposes.
	194, 196 and 197	The provision of access for construction purposes and permanent access for operational purposes.
	198 to 200	The provision of access for construction purposes and permanent access for operational purposes.
	203 and 204	The provision of access for construction purposes.
	227	The provision of access for construction purposes.
London Borough of Islington	1 and 2	Road improvement works.
	331, 333, 334, 336 and 337	The construction of a ventilation shaft, provision of permanent access thereto, and a working site.
	786 and 1048	The provision of electricity supply apparatus, access for construction purposes and permanent access for operational purposes.
	782 and 1050	The provision of access for construction purposes.
	787 and 788	The provision of access for construction purposes.
	792 and 794	The provision of protective works for public utilities' apparatus.
London Borough of Hackney	184 and 212	The construction of a ventilation shaft, provision of permanent access thereto, and a working site.
	773 to 777	The provision of access for construction purposes and river bank strengthening works.

(1) *Area*	(2) *Number of land shown on deposited plans*	(3) *Purpose for which land may be acquired or used*
	778 and 779	The provision of barge moorings and barge loading facilities.
	780	The provision of barge loading facilities, spoil handling plant and machinery, a temporary shaft to Work No. 6, a working site and access for construction purposes.
	781 and 782	The provision of access for construction purposes.
London Borough of Newham	1 and 2 (part)	The provision of a working site, access for construction purposes and river bank strengthening works.
	2 (part), 5 (part), 7 (part) and 8 (part)	Alteration of overhead electric cables for electricity supply for construction purposes.
	6	The provision of access for construction purposes.
	7 (part)	The provision of a working site.
	1, 4, 5 (part) and 8 (part)	The provision of a working site, drainage works and river bank strengthening works and diversion of a telephone cable.
	7 (part), 8 (part) and 11 (part)	The provision of permanent access for operational purposes and diversion of a telephone cable.
	8 (part) and 11 (part)	The provision of a working site and permanent access for operational purposes.
	8 (part)	The provision of a working site.
	8 (part), 12 (part), 14 and 15	The provision of a working site, access for construction purposes and permanent access for operational purposes.
	8 (part), 12 (part) and 13	The provision of a working site and access for construction purposes.
	519 to 521, 541 and 550	The construction of a ventilation shaft, provision of permanent access thereto, and a working site.
	1237 (part), 1244 and 1245	The construction of a ventilation shaft, provision of permanent access thereto, and a working site.
	1237 (part) and 1239	The provision of a working site.
	1253 and 1254 (part)	The provision of barge moorings and barge loading facilities.
	1254 (part)	The provision of spoil handling plant and machinery, a conveyor, a working site and access for construction purposes.

(1) *Area*	(2) *Number of land shown on deposited plans*	(3) *Purpose for which land may be acquired or used*
	1255 and 1260	The provision of spoil handling plant and machinery, a conveyor and access for construction purposes.
	1261	The provision of spoil handling plant and machinery and a conveyor.
	1262 and 1263 (part)	The provision of access for construction purposes.
	1263 (part) and 1264 (part)	The provision of a working site and access for construction purposes.
	1264 (part), 1265 and 1268	The provision of a temporary footbridge and raising of the existing footbridge.
	1269	The provision of a working site and access for construction purposes.
London Borough of Waltham Forest	1 and 3	The provision of a working site and a temporary tunnel segments manufacturing facility, a maintenance and servicing depot, access and drainage works.
	5 to 8 (part)	The provision of drainage works.
	8 (part) and 9	The provision of access for construction of drainage works.
	10	The provision of access for construction of drainage works.
	13 and 14	The provision of drainage works.
London Borough of Barking and Dagenham	161, 166 (part), 167 (part), 168 and 169	The provision of underground electric cables for electricity supply apparatus.
	195 and 199	The provision of a turning head.
	196 (part) and 197 (part)	Reinstatement of railway sidings.
	206 and 209	Alterations to a proposed service bridge and the provision of access for construction purposes.
	205	The provision of access for construction purposes.
	182	Road improvement works.
	195, 198 (part), 200 (part) to 202	The provision of access for construction purposes.
	198 (part)	The provision of a working site and diversion of high pressure gas pipelines and other public utilities' apparatus.
	208 (part)	The diversion of high pressure gas pipelines, a water pipe, overhead electric cables and other public utilities' apparatus.

(1) *Area*	(2) *Number of land shown on deposited plans*	(3) *Purpose for which land may be acquired or used*
	208 (part) and 210	The diversion of high pressure gas pipelines, a water pipe, overhead electric cables and other public utilities' apparatus.
	221 to 226 (part)	The diversion of gas pipelines, overhead electric cables and other public utilities' apparatus and provision of a working site.
	215 and 226 (part)	The provision of accesses for construction purposes.
	217 to 219	The provision of access for construction purposes.
	766 and 768	The construction of a ventilation shaft, provision of permanent access thereto and a working site.
	787, 788 and 790 to 793	The provision of protective works for public utilities' apparatus and access for construction purposes.
	789 and 795 (part)	The provision of a working site, access for construction purposes and permanent access for operational purposes.
	795 (part) and 798	The provision of electricity supply apparatus and permanent access for operational purposes.
	797	The provision of electricity supply apparatus and permanent access for operational purposes.
	800, 801 and 831	The provision of a working site, a conveyor, spoil handling plant and machinery, diversion of overhead electric cables and other public utilities' apparatus and access for construction purposes and permanent access for operational purposes.
	802	The diversion of public utilities' apparatus.
	803, 804, 808 and 809	The provision of a working site, a turning head and access for construction purposes, diversion of public utilities' apparatus and alteration of watercourses.
	805 to 807	The provision of access for construction purposes, diversion of overhead electric cables and other public utilities' apparatus and alteration of watercourses.
	814 and 815	Provision of a turning head, alteration of watercourses and access for construction purposes.

(1) *Area*	(2) *Number of land shown on deposited plans*	(3) *Purpose for which land may be acquired or used*
	829 and 830	The provision of a conveyor, spoil handling plant and machinery, and access for construction purposes.
	839	The use of a jetty and provision of moorings in the River Thames.
	841	The diversion of public utilities' apparatus.
	818, 819, 821, 822, 842 to 845 and 846 (part)	The diversion of overhead electric cables and other public utilities' apparatus.
	846 (part) and 847 to 849	The diversion of overhead electric cables, high pressure gas pipelines and other public utilities' apparatus.
London Borough of Havering	1 to 4	The provision of access for construction purposes.
	7, 8, 10 (part), 11 and 12	The provision of electricity supply apparatus, diversion of gas pipelines, overhead electric cables and other public utilities' apparatus and provision of a working site.
	10 (part) and 15, 16, 17 (part) and 18 (part)	The diversion of high pressure gas pipelines, overhead electric cables and other public utilities' apparatus.
	10 (part)	Connection of diverted high pressure gas pipelines to the existing network.
	10 (part)	The provision of a balancing pond, a working site, diversion of public utilities' apparatus and permanent access for operational purposes.
	19 to 22	The construction of a turning head and provision of a footbridge.
	17 (part) and 18 (part)	The diversion of public utilities' apparatus.
	18 (part)	The provision of permanent access for operational purposes.
	25 to 30 and 45	The provision of a working site and access for construction purposes.
	18 (part), 50 (part), 51, and 61	The provision of flood storage land at Rainham Creek.
	50 (part) and 59 to 66	The diversion of overhead electric cables.
	55 and 56	The provision of access for construction purposes.

(1) *Area*	(2) *Number of land shown on deposited plans*	(3) *Purpose for which land may be acquired or used*
	18 (part), 52, 53, 79 (part), 80 (part) and 81 to 83	The diversion of high pressure gas pipelines.
	57, 72 and 73	The construction of a turning head and provision of a new footbridge.
	79 (part) and 80 (part)	The provision of a working site, alteration of watercourses and diversion of overhead electric cables.
	79 (part)	The diversion of a high pressure gas pipeline and alteration of watercourses.
	79 (part), 80 (part) and 84 (part)	The diversion of a high pressure gas pipeline and provision of access for construction purposes.
	84 (part) and 86 (part)	The diversion of a high pressure gas pipeline, diversion of overhead electric cables, alteration of watercourses and landscaping.
	85	The provision of noise barriers.
	87 (part), and 88	The provision of access for construction purposes and permanent access for operational purposes.
	87 (part), 89 and 90 (part)	The provision of noise barriers and diversion of overhead electric cables.
	84 (part) and 86 (part)	The provision of landscaping, alteration of watercourses and permanent access for operational purposes.
	86 (part)	The alteration of watercourses.
	90 (part) to 92	The alteration of watercourses.
	93 and 94	The diversion of overhead electric cables, high pressure gas pipelines and other public utilities' apparatus.
	95 to 107	The diversion of overhead electric cables.
	108	The diversion of public utilities' apparatus.
	109	The diversion of overhead electric cables.
London Borough of Hammersmith and Fulham	1, 2 and 8 to 12	The provision of access for construction purposes and permanent access for operational purposes.
COUNTY OF ESSEX		
Borough of Thurrock	4 (part)	The alteration of watercourses.
	42 and 44	The diversion of water and gas pipes.

(1) *Area*	(2) *Number of land shown on deposited plans*	(3) *Purpose for which land may be acquired or used*
	39 and 45	The provision of a working site and permanent access for operational purposes.
	47 and 48 (part)	The provision of landscaping.
	46, 48 (part), 49 and 51	The provision of a working site, landscaping and access for construction purposes.
	48 (part) and 50	The provision of access for construction purposes.
	54 (part) and 55 (part)	The provision of access for construction purposes.
	52, 54 (part) and 55 (part to 67	The provision of access for construction purposes.
	81, 83, 84, 89, 93, 94, 96 and 98	The provision of a working site and access for construction purposes.
	91 and 92	The provision of a spoil disposal site.
	100	The construction of a ventilation shaft, provision of permanent access thereto and a working site.
	101 and 102	The provision of permanent access to a ventilation shaft and a working site.
	104	The diversion of overhead electric cables, provision of a working site and diversion of high pressure gas pipelines.
	107	The provision of a working site and permanent access for operational purposes.
	108 and 155	The provision of access for construction purposes and permanent access for operational purposes.
	109 to 114	The diversion of overhead electric cables.
	120 and 126	The provision of landscaping, diversion of overhead electric cables and provision of access for construction purposes.
	128 and 129	The diversion of overhead electric cables.
	130	The provision of landscaping, diversion of overhead electric cables and access for construction purposes.
	131, 137 and 138	The diversion of overhead electric cables.
	141 and 142	The provision of access to public utilities' apparatus.

(1) *Area*	(2) *Number of land shown on deposited plans*	(3) *Purpose for which land may be acquired or used*
COUNTY OF KENT		
Borough of Dartford, Parish of Swanscombe and Greenhithe	1 and 2	Use of working jetty and moorings in the River Thames.
	2 (part) and 3 (part)	The provision of working sites, spoil settlement lagoons, and spoil disposal.
	2 (part)	The provision of working sites, access for construction purposes and spoil disposal.
	2 (part)	The provision of a ventilation shaft and permanent access thereto, and a working site.
	2 (part) and 11 (part)	The provision of access for construction purposes.
	11, 13 and 14	The provision of access for construction purposes.
	15 (part)	The provision of access for construction purposes.
	15 (part), 18, 19, 20, 24 and 25 (part)	The provision of landscaping and access for construction purposes.
	25 (part), 26 to 32 and 33 (part)	The provision of an international and domestic passenger station with ancillary development and parking, diversion of overhead electric cables and provision of access for construction purposes.
	21, 22, 23 and 25 (part)	The provision of access for construction purposes.
	25 (part)	The diversion of overhead electric cables.
	36 and 39	The diversion of overhead electric cables and provision of a new access to Northfleet West Grid sub-station.
	25 (part), 41 and 42	The provision of access for construction purposes and diversion of overhead electric cables.
	33	The diversion of overhead electric cables.
Borough of Dartford, Parish of Southfleet	11	Alteration of overhead electric cables.
	12 and 13	The provision of access for construction purposes.
	16, 19 and 32 (part)	The diversion of underground electric cables.

(1) *Area*	(2) *Number of land shown on deposited plans*	(3) *Purpose for which land may be acquired or used*
	26	The provision of access for construction purposes.
	19 (part)	The provision of a working site, access for construction purposes and landscaping.
	19 (part)	The provision of a working site, and diversion of overhead electric cables.
	74	The provision of a working site, protective works and landscaping.
	49 (parts)	The provision of working sites.
	53	The provision of a working site and access for construction purposes.
	49 (part) and 54	The provision of access for construction purposes and permanent access to electrical apparatus.
	44	The provision of a balancing pond.
	11, 14 and 31, 32 (part), 33 and 34	The provision of a working site, access for construction purposes and diversion of overhead electric cables.
Borough of Dartford, Parish of Longfield and New Barn	2, 5 and 6	The provision of a balancing pond, landscaping, diversion of a high pressure gas pipeline and access for construction purposes.
	9 and 12	The diversion of a high pressure gas pipeline, provision of balancing ponds and access for construction purposes.
	10	The provision of a working site, protective works and landscaping.
Borough of Gravesham, Town of Gravesend	1	The provision of spoil settlement lagoons and spoil disposal.
	2, 3 and 4	The provision of access for construction purposes.
	10	The diversion of overhead electric cables.
	12 to 14	The provision of access for construction purposes.
	15, 16 (part) and 17 (part)	The diversion of overhead electric cables.
	16 (part) and 17 (part)	The diversion of overhead electric cables.
	16 (part), 17 (part), 22 to 30 (part), 31 (part), 32 (part), 33 (part), 34 (part), 45 (part) and 46 (part)	The provision of an international and domestic passenger station with ancillary development and parking and access for construction purposes.

(1) *Area*	(2) *Number of land shown on deposited plans*	(3) *Purpose for which land may be acquired or used*
	31 (part), 32 (part), 33 (part), 34 (part), 35 and 36	The diversion of overhead electric cables, landscaping and access for construction purposes.
	16 (part), 45 (part) and 46 (part)	The provision of access for construction purposes.
	30 (part)	The provision of protective works for a pumping station and access for construction purposes.
	44, 47, 48, 62 and 63	The provision of a working site, spoil disposal site and use of jetty and rail access.
	30 (part)	The provision of landscaping.
	42	The provision of access for construction purposes.
	70 (part)	The provision of a working site.
	68	The provision of access for construction purposes and permanent access for operational purposes.
	30 (part), 31 (part), 70 (part) and 71 (part)	The provision of access for construction purposes.
	37 and 74 to 79	The alteration of overhead electric cables, the provision of access for construction purposes, a working site and permanent access for operational purposes.
	72	The alteration of overhead electric cables.
	78, 80 and 81	The provision of access for work on overhead electric cables.
	88, 89 (part) and 90 to 93	The provision of a working site, a balancing pond, diversion of overhead electric cables and permanent access for operational purposes.
	99, 100 (part) and 101 (part)	The provision of a working site and landscaping.
	93, 100 (part), 101 (part) and 102	The provision of landscaping.
	97	The diversion of overhead electric cables and provision of landscaping.
	105, 107 and 108	The provision of a spoil disposal site and landscaping.
	109 to 112	The provision of pedestrian access, a footbridge, a working site and access for construction purposes.

(1) *Area*	(2) *Number of land shown on deposited plans*	(3) *Purpose for which land may be acquired or used*
District of Sevenoaks, Parish of Horton Kirby and South Darenth	3, 4 and 5	The provision of an electricity supply to an existing railway and permanent access for operational purposes.
	2	The diversion of a high pressure gas pipeline.
District of Sevenoaks, Parish of Swanley	1	The provision of electricity supply apparatus to existing railway.
Borough of Gravesham, Parish of Cobham	1 to 6 and 7 (part)	The provision of landscaping, a spoil disposal site and permanent access for operational purposes.
	7 (part)	The diversion of a high pressure gas pipeline.
	9 (part)	The provision of a spoil disposal site and diversion of overhead electric cables.
	9 (part), 10, 11 and 12	The provision of a balancing pond, landscaping, diversion of a high pressure gas pipeline, overhead electric cables, a connection to electricity supply apparatus and permanent access for operational purposes.
	9 (part)	The provision of electricity supply apparatus, connection to the electricity supply and permanent access for operational purposes.
	23, 25, and 26	The diversion of a water pipe.
	28	The provision of a working site and temporary road diversion.
	34 (part)	The diversion of a footpath.
	34 (part) and 40 (part)	Restoration of Repton Ponds.
	40 (part)	The provision of a working site.
	42 (part)	The provision of landscaping, diversion of a high pressure gas pipeline and permanent access for operational purposes.
	42 (part) and 47	The provision of a working site, access for construction purposes and permanent access for operational purposes.
	42 (part)	The provision of electricity supply apparatus.
	48	The diversion of pipelines, diversion of a footpath and landscaping.
Borough of Gravesham, Parish of Higham	9 and 10	The provision of access to a railhead to be used for construction purposes.

(1) *Area*	(2) *Number of land shown on deposited plans*	(3) *Purpose for which land may be acquired or used*
Borough of Gravesham, Parish of Shorne	1 and 2	Alteration of overhead electric cables.
	18	The provision of access to a railhead to be used for construction purposes.
City of Rochester Upon Medway, Parish of Cuxton	4	The diversion of pipelines, diversion of a footpath and landscaping.
	5 and 6	The provision of a working site, new woodland planting and landscaping.
	11 to 18, 21, 22, 27 and 29	The provision of a working site, permanent access for operational purposes to Medway Bridge (comprised in Work No. 13), access for construction purposes and landscaping.
City of Rochester Upon Medway, Town of Rochester	8, 9, 10 and 12	The provision of a spoil disposal site and access for construction purposes.
	27 to 30 (part), 33 (part) and 39 (part)	The provision of a working site and access to the River Medway for construction purposes.
	18 to 22, 30 (part), 33 (part) and 39 (part)	The provision of drainage works.
	36, 49, 52, 53 and 62	Access for construction purposes and permanent access for operational purposes.
	39 (part)	The provision of a working site, access for construction purposes and landscaping.
	40, 45, 46, 48, 51 and 63	The provision of a working site, landscaping, and protective works to water mains.
	64 and 67	The provision of landscaping.
	65, 68, 69 and 71	The provision of access for construction purposes.
Borough of Tonbridge and Malling, Parish of Wouldham	1 and 2	The provision of access for construction purposes.
	11 and 13	The provision of new woodland planting.
Borough of Tonbridge and Malling, Parish of Aylesford	1, 4, 29 and 41	The provision of a working site and access for construction purposes.
	190 (part)	The provision of a working site and landscaping.
	190 (part) and 193 to 195	The provision of a working site, access for construction purposes, landscaping, a balancing pond, diversion of overhead electric cables and permanent access for operational purposes.

(1) *Area*	(2) *Number of land shown on deposited plans*	(3) *Purpose for which land may be acquired or used*
	190 (part)	The provision of electricity supply apparatus and permanent access for operational purposes.
Borough of Maidstone, Parish of Boxley	38 (part)	The provision of electricity supply apparatus and permanent access for operational purposes.
	37, 38 (part), 39, 40, 41 and 42 (part)	The diversion of overhead electric cables and landscaping.
	38 (part), 42 (part) and 43	The provision of drainage works, landscaping and access for construction purposes.
	44 (part)	The provision of landscaping and diversion of overhead electric cables.
	44 (part)	The provision of a balancing pond and permanent access for operational purposes.
	44 (part) and 45 to 49	The provision of a working site, drainage works and landscaping.
	52 (part) and 53	The provision of landscaping and permanent access to a balancing pond and for operational purposes.
	52 (part) and 54 (part)	The provision of landscaping, footpath diversion and diversion of overhead electric cables.
	54 (part) and 58	The provision of drainage works.
	60	The provision of new woodland planting.
	73, 74, 80, 81, 82, and 86 (part)	The provision of a balancing pond, landscaping, diversion of a gas pipeline and permanent access for operational purposes.
	86 (part)	The provision of a working site and a footpath diversion.
	86 (part), 88 and 89 (part)	The provision of access for construction purposes.
	89 (part) and 90	The provision of new woodland planting.
Borough of Maidstone, Parish of Detling	1	The provision of a working site and access for construction purposes.
	4 and 7 (part)	The provision of access for construction purposes.
	5, 7 (part) and 8	The provision of a balancing pond, landscaping and permanent access for operational purposes.

(1) *Area*	(2) *Number of land shown on deposited plans*	(3) *Purpose for which land may be acquired or used*
	14 and 17	The provision of a balancing pond and permanent access for operational purposes.
Borough of Maidstone, Parish of Thurnham	1 and 3	The provision of new woodland planting.
	5	The provision of a working site and access for construction purposes.
	8	The provision of a balancing pond, diversion of a footpath, landscaping and permanent access for operational purposes.
	14	The provision of a site for nature conservation.
	18	The provision of a working site, landscaping and access for construction purposes.
Borough of Maidstone, Parish of Hollingbourne	1, 3, 4 (part) and 5	The provision of a working site, landscaping and access for construction purposes.
	4 (part), 6, 9 and 10 (part)	The provision of access for construction purposes and permanent access for operational purposes.
	7 (part) and 8	Alteration of a watercourse, provision of a balancing pond and permanent access for operational purposes.
	7 (part), 16, 17 and 18	The provision of drainage works.
	10 (part)	The provision of drainage works, a balancing pond and permanent access for operational purposes.
	11, 13 and 14	The provision of landscaping.
	19, 20, 24 and 26	The provision of permanent access for operational purposes.
	29, 32 and 33	The provision of balancing ponds and permanent access for operational purposes.
Borough of Maidstone, Parish of Leeds	1	The provision of access for construction purposes.
Borough of Maidstone, Parish of Harrietsham	8, 9 and 10	The provision of a balancing pond, drainage works and permanent access for operational purposes.
	13	The provision of drainage works, a balancing pond and a working site.
	2, 20, and 21.	The diversion of public utilities' apparatus.

(1) *Area*	(2) *Number of land shown on deposited plans*	(3) *Purpose for which land may be acquired or used*
	32, 34 and 35 to 38 (part)	The provision of balancing ponds, drainage works, a working site, access for construction purposes and footpath diversions, landscaping and permanent accesses for operational purposes.
	38 (part), 41 and 42	The provision of landscaping and access for construction purposes.
	43, 45 and 46	The provision of a waste disposal site, borrow pit, protective works, landscaping and access for maintenance and construction purposes.
Borough of Maidstone, Parish of Ulcombe	1	The provision of a balancing pond, drainage works and permanent access for operational purposes.
Borough of Maidstone, Parish of Lenham	6	The provision of a waste disposal site, borrow pit, protective works, landscaping and access for maintenance and construction purposes.
	10 and 11	The provision of drainage works and access for construction purposes.
	20 (part)	The provision of a spoil disposal site and a balancing pond.
	20 (part)	The provision of a spoil disposal site.
	33 and 34	The provision of a balancing pond.
	87 to 89 (part)	The provision of permanent access for operational purposes.
	89 (part), 90 and 91	The provision of permanent access for operational purposes.
Borough of Ashford, Parish of Charing	21 and 22	The provision of landscaping and new woodland planting.
	38 and 39	The provision of landscaping.
	51	The provision of replacement access to premises.
	66	The diversion of public utilities' apparatus.
	76 and 77	The provision of an accommodation access.
	68, 70, 71 and 72	The provision of drainage works.
Borough of Ashford, Parish of Hothfield	1 and 2	The provision of drainage works.
	6	The provision of access for construction purposes.
	7, 8 (part), 10 (part) and 12 (part)	The provision of access for construction purposes and permanent access for operational purposes.

(1) *Area*	(2) *Number of land shown on deposited plans*	(3) *Purpose for which land may be acquired or used*
	8 (part), 10 (part), 11, and 12 (part)	The provision of a working site, landscaping and permanent access for operational purposes.
	12 (part), 14 and 16	The provision of a working site, landscaping and permanent access for operational purposes.
Borough of Ashford, Parish of Westwell	1, 4, 5, and 20 (part)	The provision of a working site, spoil disposal site, landscaping and permanent access for operational purposes.
	16, 17, 18, 19, 20 (part) and 21 (part)	The provision of a working site and landscaping.
	21 (part), 24, 25, 26, 27, 40, 41 and 42	The provision of access for construction purposes, a working site and landscaping.
	44 and 45	The provision of landscaping.
	47 and 48	The provision of a spoil disposal site and landscaping.
	56, 57, 60 (part), 65 and 67	The provision of a borrow pit, spoil disposal site, access for construction purposes, an accommodation access and landscaping.
	49 and 60 (part)	The provision of access for construction purposes and permanent access for operational purposes.
Borough of Ashford, Town of Ashford	8	The provision of a working site and landscaping.
	6, 10, 12 (part) and 13	The provision of drainage works and diversion of a gas main.
	12 (part) and 14 (part)	The provision of accommodation access to premises, landscaping and a working site.
	14 (part) and 16	The provision of a working site.
	14 (part) and 15	The provision of a working site and access for construction purposes.
	34 to 37 and 48	The provision of a working site and access for construction purposes.
	59 to 73 and 76	The provision of a working site and access for construction purposes.
	78 (part)	The provision of a working site and access for construction purposes.
	46, 78 (part), 79 and 80	The provision of a working site and access for construction purposes.
	85, 86, 89, 94 and 95	The provision of a working site and access for construction purposes.

(1) *Area*	(2) *Number of land shown on deposited plans*	(3) *Purpose for which land may be acquired or used*
	84 and 88	The provision of access for construction purposes and permanent emergency access to the gas holder station and depot.
	92, 93, 98 (part), 99 and 100	The provision of access for construction purposes and permanent emergency access to the gas holder station and depot.
	110, 111, 117 and 122	The provision of a working site and access for construction purposes.
	125 (part) and 131	The provision of a working site and access for construction purposes.
	178, 181, 183, 194 and 195	The provision of flood storage lands and access for construction purposes.
	144, 145, 177, 179, 180, 184, 185 and 186	The provision of drainage works and access for construction purposes.
	238 to 241	The provision of a working site and access for construction purposes.
Borough of Ashford, Parish of Sevington	5	The provision of drainage works, a balancing pond and permanent access for operational purposes.
	7 and 8	The provision of a working site, access for construction purposes and permanent access for operational purposes.
	9 and 12 (part)	The provision of drainage works, a balancing pond and permanent access for operational purposes.
	12 (part), 16 and 19	The provision of a railhead, a working site, a balancing pond, access for construction purposes and permanent access for operational purposes.
	28	The provision of a working site.
	34	The provision of drainage works and access for construction purposes.
	33	The provision of a spoil disposal site.
	35	The provision of access for construction purposes, permanent access for operational purposes and dedication of road as a public highway connecting to Bad Munstereifel Road.

(1) *Area*	(2) *Number of land shown on deposited plans*	(3) *Purpose for which land may be acquired or used*
Borough of Ashford, Parish of Mersham	1	The provision of a spoil disposal site.
	4	The provision of drainage works, noise barriers and access for construction purposes.
	11, 14, 15, 17, 20 and 27	The provision of drainage works, a balancing pond, noise barriers, landscaping, access for construction purposes and permanent access for operational purposes.
	19, 21, 22, 25 and 26	The provision of landscaping, access for construction purposes and permanent access for operational purposes.
	37, 41, 42, 45 and 46	The provision of a working site, access for construction purposes, diversion of public utilities' apparatus, a balancing pond and permanent access for operational purposes.
	43	The provision of noise barriers and drainage works and access for construction purposes.
Borough of Ashford, Parish of Smeeth	6, 8, 13 and 16	The provision of drainage works, footpath diversions, landscaping and permanent access for construction purposes.
	24, 27	The provision of access for construction purposes.
	9, 10, 11 and 12	The provision of drainage works, a balancing pond, landscaping and permanent access for operational purposes.
	21 and 28	The provision of flood storage lands.
	30 (part) and 31	The provisions of a working site and access for construction purposes.
	30 (part)	The provision of electricity supply apparatus, landscaping and permanent access for operational purposes.
	32 to 34	The provision of access for construction purposes and alteration of overhead electric cables.
	35	The provision of noise barriers and access for construction purposes.
Borough of Ashford, Parish of Aldington	5 and 7 (part)	The provision of electricity supply apparatus, landscaping and permanent access for operational purposes.

(1) *Area*	(2) *Number of land shown on deposited plans*	(3) *Purpose for which land may be acquired or used*
	7 (part), 12, 13 (part) and 14	The provision of electricity supply apparatus and access for construction purposes.
	3, 6 and 10	The diversion of overhead electric cables.
	13 (part), 19 and 20	The provision of a working site, landscaping and access for construction purposes.
District of Shepway, Parish of Sellindge	3, 4 and 5	The provision of noise barriers and access for construction purposes.
	1, 2 and 6	The provision of a working site, diversion of overhead electric cables and access for construction purposes.
	8	Strengthening of railway embankment and diversion of overhead electric cables.
	9 and 11	The diversion of electric high voltage underground cables.
	12, 14 and 15	The diversion of electric high voltage underground cables and access for construction purposes.
	16, 26 and 32 (part)	The diversion of electric high voltage underground cables, the provision of noise barriers and access for construction purposes.
	32 (part), 33, 46 and 47	The alteration of overhead electric cables, provision of noise barriers and access for construction purposes.
	30	The alteration of overhead electric cables.
	44, 45 and 60	The provision of access for construction purposes.
District of Shepway, Parish of Stanford	1 (part)	The provision of noise barriers and access for construction purposes.
	1 (part) and 2	The provision of landscaping and access for construction purposes.
	8 and 9 (part)	The provision of drainage works, noise barriers, a working site and access for construction purposes.
	7, 9 (part), 17, 18 and 19	The provision of access for construction purposes.
District of Shepway, Parish of Saltwood	1 and 3	The provision of a working site, accommodation works and access for construction purposes.
	7	The provision of a balancing pond and permanent access for operational purposes.
	13 to 16	The provision of a working site and access for construction purposes.

(1) *Area*	(2) *Number of land shown on deposited plans*	(3) *Purpose for which land may be acquired or used*
	26	The provision of a footpath.
	30	The provision of drainage works.
	37, 38 and 39	The provision of a bridleway diversion, reconstruction of a bridleway bridge, provision of a working site, diversion of public utilities' apparatus and access for construction purposes.
District of Shepway, Parish of Postling	6 and 8	The provision of permanent access for operational purposes.
	11 and 14 to 18	The provision of a working site and access for construction purposes.
District of Shepway, Parish of Newington	3 and 4	The provision of a working site and access for construction purposes.
	6 and 9	The provision of access for construction purposes.
	17 and 27 (part)	The provision of a spoil disposal site and access for construction purposes.
	14, 15, 16, 19, 20, 21, 32 and 37	The provision of access for construction purposes.
	31 and 40	The provision of working sites and access for construction purposes.
	27 (part)	The provision of access for construction purposes.
	13, 25 and 29	The provision of access for construction purposes, and permanent access to a balancing pond and for operational purposes.
	60 and 61	The provision of access for construction purposes and permanent access for operational purposes.
	62	The provision of access for construction purposes.
District of Shepway, Parish of Hythe	1	The provision of access for construction purposes.
District of Shepway, Town of Folkestone	1	Alteration of railway track equipment.
	2 and 3	The provision of access for construction purposes, and permanent access to a balancing pond and for operational purposes.
	4 (part)	The provision of access for construction purposes and permanent access for operational purposes.

(1) *Area*	(2) *Number of land shown on deposited plans*	(3) *Purpose for which land may be acquired or used*
	4 (part)	The provision of lineside equipment and permanent access for operational purposes.
	6	The provision of a working site and access for construction purposes.
District of Thanet, Parish of Minster	2	The provision of access to a railhead to be used for construction purposes.
Borough of Dover, Parish of Sandwich	1	The provision of access to a railhead to be used for construction purposes.

PART II

APPLICATION OF LEGISLATION RELATING TO COMPULSORY PURCHASE

Lands Clauses Consolidation Act 1845

1. The Lands Clauses Consolidation Act 1845 shall not apply to the acquisition of land under section 4(1) above.

Compulsory Purchase Act 1965

2. Part I of the Compulsory Purchase Act 1965, so far as not inconsistent with this Part of this Act, shall apply to an acquisition of land under section 4(1) above as it applies to a compulsory purchase to which Schedule 1 to the Acquisition of Land Act 1981 applies and as if this Act were a compulsory purchase order under that Act.

3.—(1) In its application by virtue of paragraph 2 above, the Compulsory Purchase Act 1965 shall have effect with the following modifications.

(2) Section 4 (time limit for exercise of powers of compulsory purchase) shall be omitted.

(3) Section 11(1) (power to enter on and take possession of land the subject of a notice to treat after giving not less than fourteen days' notice) shall have effect—

(a) in a case where the notice to treat relates only to the acquisition of subsoil or undersurface of land or an easement or other right over land, with the substitution for "fourteen days" of "one month's", and

(b) in any other case, with the substitution for "fourteen days" of "three months' ".

(4) In Schedule 3 (alternative procedure for obtaining right of entry) paragraph 3(3) (requirement as to sureties in relation to bond for compensation) shall be omitted.

Compulsory Purchase (Vesting Declarations) Act 1981

4. The Compulsory Purchase (Vesting Declarations) Act 1981 shall apply as if this Act were a compulsory purchase order.

5.—(1) In its application by virtue of paragraph 4 above, the Compulsory Purchase (Vesting Declarations) Act 1981 shall have effect with the following modifications.

(2) In section 3 (preliminary notices) for subsection (1) there shall be substituted—

"(1) Before making a declaration under section 4 below with respect to any land which is subject to a compulsory purchase order the acquiring authority shall include the particulars specified in subsection (3) below in a notice which is—

(a) given to every person with a relevant interest in the land with respect to which the declaration is to be made (other than a mortgagee who is not in possession), and

(b) published in the London Gazette."

(3) In that section, in subsection (2), for "(1)(b)" there shall be substituted "(1)".

(4) In that section, subsections (5) and (6) shall be omitted and at the end there shall be inserted—

"(7) For the purposes of this section, a person has a relevant interest in land if—

(a) he is for the time being entitled to dispose of the fee simple of the land, whether in possession or reversion, or

(b) he holds, or is entitled to the rents and profits of, the land under a lease or agreement, the unexpired term of which exceeds one month."

(5) In section 5 (earliest date for execution of declaration)—

(a) in subsection (1), after "publication" there shall be inserted "in the London Gazette", and

(b) subsection (2) shall be omitted.

(6) In section 7 (constructive notice to treat) in subsection (1)(a), the words "(as modified by section 4 of the Acquisition of Land Act 1981)" shall be omitted.

(7) References to the Compulsory Purchase Act 1965 shall be construed as references to that Act as applied to the acquisition of land under section 4(1) above.

Part III

Supplementary Provisions

Acquisition of subsoil

6.—(1) In the case of land specified in the following table (non-pedestrian tunnels), the power conferred by section 4(1) above shall only be exercisable in relation to so much of the subsoil or under-surface of the land as lies more than 9 metres beneath the level of the surface of the land.

The Table

Area	*No. on deposited plans*
GREATER LONDON	
London Borough of Islington	307 to 318, 320 to 330, 332, 335, 338 to 739, 798, 799 and 803 to 1042
London Borough of Hackney	1 to 183, 185 to 211 and 213 to 772
London Borough of Newham	16 to 518, 522 to 540, 542 to 549, 551 to 1207, 1209 to 1223, 1235, 1236, 1238, 1240 to 1243 and 1246 to 1252
London Borough of Redbridge	8 to 14
London Borough of Barking and Dagenham	227 to 765, 767, 769 to 786, 794 and 796
COUNTY OF ESSEX	
Borough of Thurrock	99 and 103
COUNTY OF KENT	
Borough of Tonbridge and Malling, Parish of Aylesford	51 to 140 and 144 to 183
Borough of Tonbridge and Malling, Parish of Burham	1 to 9

(2) In the case of land specified in the following table (pedestrian tunnels and ground anchors), the power conferred by section 4(1) above shall only be exercisable in relation to so much of the subsoil or under-surface of the land as lies more than 2 metres beneath the level of the surface of the land.

The Table

Area	*No. on deposited plans*
GREATER LONDON	
London Borough of Camden	178
London Borough of Islington	740 to 771
COUNTY OF KENT	
Borough of Ashford, Parish of Mersham	39

(3) In the case of any other land, the power conferred by section 4(1) above shall be exercisable as well in relation to the subsoil or under-surface only as in relation to the land as a whole.

(4) Section 8(1) of the Compulsory Purchase Act 1965 (limitation on right to require a person to sell part only of any house, building, manufactory or park or garden belonging to a house) shall not apply where the power conferred by section 4(1) above is exercised in relation to the subsoil or under-surface of land only.

(5) For the purposes of sub-paragraphs (1) and (2) above, the level of the surface of the land shall be taken—

(a) in the case of any land on which a building is erected, to be the level of the surface of the ground adjoining the building, and

(b) in the case of a watercourse or other area of water, to be the level of the surface of the adjoining ground which is at all times above water level.

Acquisition of existing tunnels

7. In the case of land specified in the following table (existing railway tunnels), the power conferred by section 4(1) above shall only be exercisable in relation to so much of the land as is comprised in an existing railway tunnel.

THE TABLE

Area	*No. on deposited plans*
GREATER LONDON	
London Borough of Camden	117 to 120, 122 to 140 and 228 to 231
London Borough of Islington	20, 21 and 775 to 778
COUNTY OF KENT	
Borough of Gravesham, Town of Gravesend	49 to 61

Acquisition of new rights

8.—(1) The power conferred by section 4(1)(a) or (b) above shall include, in relation to any land to which the power relates, power to create and acquire such easements or other rights over land as may be required as mentioned in that provision instead of acquiring the land itself.

(2) Part I of the Compulsory Purchase Act 1965, as applied to the acquisition of land under section 4(1) above, and the enactments relating to compensation for the compulsory purchase of land, shall apply to a compulsory acquisition by virtue of sub-paragraph (1) above—

(a) with the modifications specified in paragraph 9 below, and

(b) with such other modifications as may be necessary.

9.—(1) The modifications referred to in paragraph 8(2)(a) above are as follows.

(2) For section 7 of the Compulsory Purchase Act 1965 there shall be substituted—

"**Measure of compensation in case of purchase of new right**

7. In assessing the compensation to be paid by the acquiring authority under this Act regard shall be had not only to the extent (if any) to which the value of the land over which the right is purchased is depreciated by the acquisition of the right but also to the damage (if any) to be sustained by the owner of the land by reason of its severance from other land of his, or injuriously affecting that other land by the exercise of the powers conferred by this or the special Act."

(3) In section 8 of that Act (provisions as to divided land) for subsection (1) there shall be substituted—

"(1) This subsection applies where—

(a) a notice to treat in respect of a right over land consisting of a house, building or manufactory or of a park or garden belonging to a house ("the relevant land") has been served on a person under section 5 of this Act,

(b) in consequence of the service of the notice, a question of disputed compensation in respect of the purchase of the right would, apart from this section, fall to be determined by the Lands Tribunal, and

(c) before the Lands Tribunal have determined that question, the person on whom the notice has been served satisfies them that the relevant conditions are met.

(1A) The relevant conditions are—

(a) that he has an interest which he is able and willing to sell in the whole of the relevant land;

(b) where the relevant land consists of a house, building or manufactory, that it cannot be made subject to the right without material detriment to it; and

(c) where the relevant land consists of a park or garden belonging to a house, that it cannot be made subject to the right without seriously affecting the amenity or convenience of the house.

(1B) Where subsection (1) above applies—

(a) the compulsory purchase order shall, in relation to the person on whom the notice to treat has been served—

(i) cease to authorise the purchase of the right to which the notice relates, and

(ii) be deemed to authorise the purchase of that person's interest in the whole of the relevant land including, where the land consists of a park or garden belonging to a house, the house,

and

(b) the notice to treat shall be deemed to have been served in respect of that interest on such date as the Lands Tribunal direct.

(1C) Any question as to the extent of the land in which the compulsory purchase order is deemed to authorise the purchase of an interest by virtue of subsection (1B)(a)(ii) of this section shall be determined by the Lands Tribunal.

(1D) Where the Lands Tribunal determine that the person on whom a notice to treat has been served has satisfied them as mentioned in subsection (1)(c) of this section, the acquiring authority may withdraw the notice at any time within the period of six weeks beginning with the date of the determination.

(1E) Subsection (1D) of this section is without prejudice to any other power of the acquiring authority to withdraw the notice to treat."

(4) The following provisions of that Act (which state the effect of a deed poll executed in various circumstances where there is no conveyance by persons with interests in the land) namely—

section 9(4) (failure of owners to convey),
paragraph 10(3) of Schedule 1 (owners under incapacity),
paragraph 2(3) of Schedule 2 (absent and untraced owners), and
paragraphs 2(3) and 7(2) of Schedule 4 (common land),

shall be so modified as to secure that, as against persons with interests in the land which are expressed to be overridden by the deed, the right which is to be purchased compulsorily is vested absolutely in the acquiring authority.

(5) Section 11 of that Act (powers of entry) shall be so modified as to secure that, as from the date on which the acquiring authority have served notice to treat in respect of any right, they have power, exercisable in the like circumstances and subject to the like conditions, to enter for the purpose of exercising that right (which shall be deemed for this purpose to have been created on the date of service of the notice); and sections 12 (penalty for unauthorised entry) and 13 (entry on sheriff's warrant in the event of obstruction) of that Act shall be modified correspondingly.

(6) Section 20 of that Act (compensation for short term tenants) shall apply with the modifications necessary to secure that persons with such interests in land as are mentioned in that section are compensated in a manner corresponding to that in which they would be compensated on a compulsory acquisition of the land but taking into account only the extent (if any) of such interference with such interests as is actually caused, or likely to be caused, by the exercise of the right in question.

(7) Section 22 of that Act (protection of acquiring authority's possession of land where interest accidentally omitted from purchase) shall be so modified as to enable the acquiring authority, in circumstances corresponding to those referred to in that section, to continue to be entitled to exercise the right acquired, subject to compliance with that section as respects compensation.

(8) References in that Act to land are, in appropriate contexts, to be read (according to the requirements of the particular context) as referring to, or as including references to—

(a) the right acquired or to be acquired, or

(b) the land over which the right is, or is to be, exercisable.

(9) In the Land Compensation Act 1973, for section 44 there shall substituted—

"**Compensation for injurious affection**

44.—(1) Where a right over land is purchased from any person for the purpose of works which are to be situated partly on that land and partly elsewhere, compensation for injurious affection of land retained by that person shall be assessed by reference to the whole of the works and not only the part situated on the land over which the right is exercisable.

(2) In this section "compensation for injurious affection" means compensation for injurious affection under section 7 or 20 of the Compulsory Purchase Act 1965 as applied by paragraph 8(2) of Schedule 4 to the Channel Tunnel Rail Link Act 1996."

(10) For section 58 of that Act there shall be substituted—

"Determination of material detriment where right over part of house etc. proposed for compulsory acquisition

58. In determining under section 8(1)(c) of the Compulsory Purchase Act 1965 as applied by paragraph 8(2) of Schedule 4 to the Channel Tunnel Rail Link Act 1996 whether—

(a) a right over part of a house, building or manufactory can be taken without material detriment to the house, building or manufactory, or

(b) a right over part of a park or garden belonging to a house can be taken without seriously affecting the amenity or convenience of the house,

the Lands Tribunal shall take into account not only the effect of the right on the whole of the house, building or manufactory or of the house and the park or garden but also the use to be made of the rights proposed to be acquired and, in a case where the right is proposed to be acquired for works or other purposes extending to other land, the effect of the whole of the works and the use to be made of the other land."

10.—(1) The Secretary of State may by order provide, in relation to land to which this paragraph applies, that section 4(1) above, so far as relating to acquisition by virtue of paragraph 8(1) above, shall be treated as also authorising acquisition by such person as may be specified in the order.

(2) This paragraph applies to land within the limits of deviation for the scheduled works or within the limits of land to be acquired or used which is or will be required for use in relocating any apparatus which it is expedient to divert or replace in consequence of the carrying out of any of the works authorised by this Part of this Act.

(3) The power to make an order under sub-paragraph (1) above includes power to make an order varying or revoking any order previously made under that provision.

Acquisition of part only of certain properties

11.—(1) Where—

(a) a notice to treat under Part I of the Compulsory Purchase Act 1965, as applied to the acquisition of land under section 4(1) above, is served in respect of land forming part only of a house, building or factory or part only of land consisting of a house with a park or garden, and

(b) a copy of this paragraph is served with the notice to treat,

the following provisions of this paragraph, with paragraph 12 below, shall apply instead of section 8(1) of the Compulsory Purchase Act 1965.

(2) The person on whom the notice to treat is served ("the owner") may within the period of 21 days beginning with the day on which the notice to treat is served on him, serve on the Secretary of State a counter-notice objecting to the sale of the part ("the land subject to the notice to treat") and stating that he is willing and able to sell the whole ("the land subject to the counter-notice").

(3) If no counter-notice is served under sub-paragraph (2) above, the owner shall be required to sell the land subject to the notice to treat.

(4) If a counter-notice is served under sub-paragraph (2) above and the Secretary of State agrees to take the land subject to the counter-notice, the notice to treat shall be deemed to be a notice to treat in addition for the remainder of the land subject to the counter-notice.

(5) If a counter-notice is served under sub-paragraph (2) above and the Secretary of State does not agree to take the land subject to the counter-notice, the question as to what land the owner is to be required to sell shall be referred to the Lands Tribunal.

(6) If, on a reference under sub-paragraph (5) above, the Lands Tribunal determine that the land subject to the notice to treat can be taken—

(a) without material detriment to the remainder of the land subject to the counter-notice, and

(b) where the land subject to the notice to treat consists of or includes garden only land, without seriously affecting the amenity and convenience of the relevant house,

the owner shall be required to sell the land subject to the notice to treat.

(7) If, on such a reference, the Lands Tribunal determine that only part of the land subject to the notice to treat can be taken as mentioned in sub-paragraph (6) above, the notice to treat shall, subject to sub-paragraph (8) below, be deemed to be a notice to treat for that part.

(8) Where the land subject to the notice to treat is not land which consists of or includes garden only land, sub-paragraph (7) above shall only have effect to deem the notice to treat to be a notice to treat for land which does consist of or include garden only land if the Lands Tribunal

determine that that land can be taken without seriously affecting the amenity and convenience of the relevant house.

(9) If, on such a reference, the Lands Tribunal determine—

(a) that none of the land subject to the notice to treat can be taken without material detriment to the remainder of the land subject to the counter-notice, but

(b) that the material detriment is confined to part of the remainder of that land,

then, except where sub-paragraph (10) below applies, the notice to treat shall be deemed to be a notice to treat in addition for the land to which the material detriment is confined.

(10) If, in a case where the land subject to the notice to treat consists of or includes garden only land, the Lands Tribunal determine on such a reference that none of the land subject to the notice to treat can be taken without seriously affecting the amenity or convenience of the relevant house, the notice to treat shall be deemed to be a notice to treat in addition for the remainder of the land subject to the counter-notice.

(11) If, on such a reference, the Lands Tribunal determine—

(a) that none of the land subject to the notice to treat can be taken without material detriment to the remainder of the land subject to the counter-notice, and

(b) that the material detriment is not confined to part of the remainder of that land,

the notice to treat shall be deemed to be a notice to treat in addition for the remainder of the land subject to the counter-notice.

(12) For the purposes of this paragraph, the land subject to the notice to treat consists of or includes garden only land if it consists of the whole or part of a park or garden belonging to a house or if it includes the whole or part of such a park or garden but does not include the house ("the relevant house") or any part of it.

12.—(1) Where under paragraph 11 above a notice to treat is deemed by virtue of a determination of the Lands Tribunal to be a notice to treat for less land or more land than that specified in the notice, the Secretary of State may, within the period of 6 weeks beginning with the day on which the determination is made, withdraw the notice.

(2) If the Secretary of State withdraws a notice to treat under sub-paragraph (1) above, he shall pay the person on whom the notice was served compensation for any loss or expense occasioned to that person by the giving and withdrawal of the notice, such compensation to be determined in case of dispute by the Lands Tribunal.

(3) Where under paragraph 11 above a person is required to sell part only of a house, building or factory or of land consisting of a house with a park or garden, the Secretary of State shall pay him compensation for any loss sustained by him due to the severance of that part in addition to the value of the interest acquired.

(4) A notice to treat shall have the effect which it is deemed to have under paragraph 11(4), (9), (10) or (11) above whether or not the additional land is, apart from that provision, land which the Secretary of State is authorised to acquire compulsorily under this Part of this Act.

Minerals

13.—(1) Parts II and III of Schedule 2 to the Acquisition of Land Act 1981 (exception of minerals from compulsory purchase and regulation of the working of mines or minerals underlying an authorised undertaking) shall have effect in relation to land to which section 4(1) above applies as if it were comprised in a compulsory purchase order providing for the incorporation with that order of those Parts of that Schedule.

(2) In their application by virtue of sub-paragraph (1) above, Parts II and III of Schedule 2 to the Acquisition of Land Act 1981 shall have effect with the following modifications—

(a) references to the acquiring authority, except the second reference in paragraph 6, shall be construed as references to the nominated undertaker, and

(b) references to the undertaking shall be construed as references to the undertaking which the nominated undertaker is authorised by this Part of this Act to carry on.

Power to require acquisition where time limit extended

14.—(1) If the Secretary of State makes an order under section 47(2) above the following provisions shall have effect as from the coming into operation of that order.

(2) If an owner or lessee of any of the land in relation to which the order is made gives notice in writing to the Secretary of State that he desires his interest in such of that land as is specified in the notice to be acquired by the Secretary of State, the Secretary of State shall, within the period of 3 months immediately following receipt of the notice—

(a) enter into an agreement with him for the acquisition of his interest in the whole or part of the land specified in the notice,

(b) exercise the relevant powers of compulsory acquisition in respect of his interest in the whole or part of the land specified in the notice, or

(c) serve on him notice in writing of the Secretary of State's intention not to proceed with the purchase of his interest in any of the land specified in the notice.

(3) Where—

(a) a person gives the Secretary of State notice under sub-paragraph (2) above, and

(b) the Secretary of State—

(i) fails to comply with the requirements of that sub-paragraph,

(ii) withdraws a notice to treat served in compliance with paragraph (b) of that sub-paragraph, or

(iii) serves on the owner notice in compliance with paragraph (c) of that sub-paragraph,

the relevant powers of compulsory acquisition shall cease to be exercisable in respect of that person's interest in any of the land specified in the notice under sub-paragraph (2) above.

(4) Where—

(a) a person gives the Secretary of State notice under sub-paragraph (2) above, and

(b) the Secretary of State acquires in pursuance of paragraph (a) or (b) of that sub-paragraph that person's interest in some, but not all, of the land specified in the notice,

the relevant powers of compulsory acquisition shall cease to be exercisable in respect of that person's interest in the remainder of that land.

(5) In this paragraph—

"lessee" means a person who holds an interest under a lease for a period of which not less than 21 years is unexpired at the date of the giving of any notice by that person under sub-paragraph (2) above,

"owner", in relation to any land, means a person, other than a mortgagee not in possession, who is for the time being entitled to dispose of the fee simple of the land, whether in possession or in reversion, and

references to the relevant powers of compulsory acquisition are to—

(a) the power to serve a notice to treat under Part I of the Compulsory Purchase Act 1965, as applied to the acquisition of land under section 4(1) above, and

(b) the power to execute a declaration under section 4 of the Compulsory Purchase (Vesting Declarations) Act 1981, as applied by paragraph 4 above.

15.—(1) Paragraph 14 above shall not apply to any subsoil or under-surface of land required only for the construction of a work at a level more than the relevant distance below the level of the surface of the land.

(2) In sub-paragraph (1) above, the reference to the relevant distance is—

(a) in the case of a work consisting of a pedestrian tunnel or ground anchor, 2 metres, and

(b) in the case of any other work, 9 metres.

(3) For the purposes of sub-paragraph (1) above, the level of the surface of the land shall be taken—

(a) in the case of any land on which a building is erected, to be the level of the surface of the ground adjoining the building, and

(b) in the case of a watercourse or other area of water, to be the level of the surface of the adjoining ground which is at all times above water level.

Compensation

16. Section 4 of the Acquisition of Land Act 1981 (assessment of compensation in relation to a compulsory purchase where unnecessary things done with a view to obtaining compensation) shall have effect in relation to a compulsory purchase under this Part of this Act as if it were a compulsory purchase for the purposes of that Act.

Section 6

SCHEDULE 5

TEMPORARY POSSESSION AND USE OF LAND

Occupation and use for construction of works

1.—(1) The nominated undertaker may, in connection with the construction of the scheduled work or works specified in column (1) of the following table (or any works which are necessary or expedient for the purposes of or in connection with that work or those works)—

(a) enter upon and take possession of the land specified in relation to that work or those works in columns (2) and (3) of that table for such purposes as are so specified in column (4) of that table, and

(b) for such purposes as are so specified—

(i) remove from the land any structure or vegetation, and

(ii) construct on the land temporary works (including the provision of means of access) and structures.

TABLE

(1) *Works*	(2) *Area*	(3) *Number of land shown on deposited plans*	(4) *Purpose for which temporary possession may be taken*
	GREATER LONDON		
1A, 1B, 1C, 1D, 1F and 5D(1)	London Borough of Camden	79	The provision of access for construction purposes.
1A, 1B, 1C, 1D and 1F		87	The provision of a working site and access for construction purposes.
1A, 1AA, 1B, 1BB, 1C, 1CC, 1D, 1DD, 1EE, 1K, 3, 3B, 3C and 5A		182 and 189 to 192	The provision of access for construction purposes.
1HH, 3B and 3C		203 and 204	The provision of access for construction purposes.
1JJ, 2AA and 2BB	London Borough of Islington	782 and 1050	The provision of access for construction purposes.
1AA, 1BB and 3E		787 and 788	The provision of access for construction purposes.
6	London Borough of Hackney	778 and 779	The provision of barge moorings and barge loading facilities.
6		780	The provision of barge loading facilities, spoil handling plant and machinery, a temporary shaft to Work No. 6, a working site and access for construction purposes.
6		781 and 782	The provision of access for construction purposes.
22	London Borough of Newham	1237 and 1239	The provision of a working site.
6, 6A, 6B, 6C, 6D, 6G, 6H, 6J and 7		1253 and 1254	The provision of barge moorings and barge loading facilities, spoil handling plant and machinery, a conveyor, a working site and access for construction purposes.

(1) *Works*	(2) *Area*	(3) *Number of land shown on deposited plans*	(4) *Purpose for which temporary possession may be taken*
6, 6A, 6B, 6C, 6D, 6G, 6H, 6J and 7		1255 to 1260	The provision of spoil handling plant and machinery, a conveyor and access for construction purposes.
6, 6A, 6B, 6C, 6D, 6G, 6H, 6J and 7		1261	The provision of spoil handling plant and machinery and a conveyor.
6, 6A, 6B, 6C, 6D, 6G, 6H, 6J and 7		1262 and 1263	The provision of access for construction purposes.
6, 6A, 6B, 6C, 6D, 6G, 6H, 6J and 7		1269	The provision of a working site and access for construction purposes.
6D and 6E	London Borough of Waltham Forest	6	The provision of access for construction purposes.
6D and 6E		10	The provision of access for construction of drainage works.
8Q	London Borough of Barking and Dagenham	205	The provision of access for construction purposes.
8H, 8P(3) and 8P(4)		195, 201 and 202	The provision of access for construction purposes.
8L and 8R		215 and 226	The provision of accesses for construction purposes.
8, 8G, 8J and 8R		217 to 219	The provision of access for construction purposes.
22, 22A, 22B, 22C, 22E, 22F, 22G, 22J and 8U(13)		829 and 830	The provision of a conveyor, spoil handling plant and machinery, and access for construction purposes.
22, 22A, 22B, 22C, 22E, 22F, 22G, 22J and 8U(13)		839	The use of a jetty and provision of moorings in the River Thames.
8, 8G, 8J and 8R	London Borough of Havering	1 to 4	The provision of access for construction purposes.

(1) *Works*	(2) *Area*	(3) *Number of land shown on deposited plans*	(4) *Purpose for which temporary possession may be taken*
8 and 8S		25 to 30 and 45	The provision of a working site and access for construction purposes.
8 and 8U(7)		55 and 56	The provision of access for construction purposes.
	COUNTY OF ESSEX		
9	Borough of Thurrock	52 and 56 to 67	The provision of access for construction purposes.
9, 9C, 9D, 9F(1) and 10		81, 83, 84, 89, 93, 94, 96 and 98	The provision of a working site and access for construction purposes.
	COUNTY OF KENT		
10, 10A, 10B, 10C and 10J	Borough of Dartford, Parish of Swanscombe and Greenhithe	13 and 14	The provision of access for construction purposes.
10B, 10D, 10F(1) and 10R(2)		21 to 23	The provision of access for construction purposes.
10, 10T(1), 10T(3), 10T(8), 10R, 10P, 10Q and 11 to 11F	Borough of Dartford, Parish of Southfleet	12 and 13	The provision of access for construction purposes.
10T(6), 10T(7) and 10T(8)		26	The provision of access for construction purposes.
11		53	The provision of a working site.
10J and 10J(2)	Borough of Gravesham, Town of Gravesend	2 to 4	The provision of access for construction purposes.
10, 10B, 10C, 10D, 10E and 10F(1)		12 to 14	The provision of access for construction purposes.
10R(2)		42	The provision of access for construction purposes.
10B, 10C and 10N		70	The provision of access for construction purposes.
12, 12F and 12H	Borough of Gravesham, Parish of Cobham	28	The provision of a working site and temporary road diversion.

(1) *Works*	(2) *Area*	(3) *Number of land shown on deposited plans*	(4) *Purpose for which temporary possession may be taken*
20A and 20B	Borough of Gravesham, Parish of Higham	9 and 10	The provision of access to a railhead to be used for construction purposes.
20A and 20B	Borough of Gravesham, Parish of Shorne	18	The provision of access to a railhead to be used for construction purposes.
13, 13B	City of Rochester Upon Medway, Town of Rochester	27 to 29	The provision of a working site and access to the River Medway for construction purposes.
13C and 13D		65, 68, 69 and 71	The provision of access for construction purposes.
13C and 13D	Borough of Tonbridge and Malling, Parish of Wouldham	1 and 2	The provision of access for construction purposes.
13	Borough of Tonbridge and Malling, Parish of Aylesford	1, 4, 29 and 41	The provision of a working site and access for construction purposes.
13	Borough of Maidstone, Parish of Boxley	88	The provision of access for construction purposes.
13 and 13J	Borough of Maidstone, Parish of Detling	1	The provision of a working site and access for construction purposes.
14 and 14A	Borough of Maidstone, Parish of Thurnham	5	The provision of a working site and access for construction purposes.
14	Borough of Maidstone, Parish of Leeds	1	The provision of access for construction purposes.
15	Borough of Ashford, Parish of Hothfield	6	The provision of access for construction purposes.
16, 16A, 16B and 16F		15	The provision of a working site and access for construction purposes.
16, 16A and 16B	Borough of Ashford, Town of Ashford	16	The provision of a working site.
16C and 16H		34 to 37 and 48	The provision of a working site and access for construction purposes.
16 and 16H		59 to 73 and 76	The provision of a working site and access for construction purposes.

(1) *Works*	(2) *Area*	(3) *Number of land shown on deposited plans*	(4) *Purpose for which temporary possession may be taken*
16 and 16K		78	The provision of a working site and access for construction purposes.
16A, 16B, 16C, 16K and 16L		46 and 78 to 80	The provision of a working site and access for construction purposes.
16, 16A, 16B, 16C, 16K and 16M		85, 86, 89, 94 and 95	The provision of a working site and access for construction purposes.
16, 16A, 16B, 16C and 16D		110, 111, 117 and 122	The provision of a working site and access for construction purposes.
16, 16A, 16B, 16C, 16D and 16E		125 and 131	The provision of a working site and access for construction purposes.
17, 17B and 17C	Borough of Ashford, Parish of Sevington	28	The provision of a working site.
17 and 17H	Borough of Ashford, Parish of Smeeth	24 and 27	The provision of access for construction purposes.
17, 17J(1) and 17K		31	The provision of a working site and access for construction purposes.
17 and 17J(2)	District of Shepway, Parish of Sellindge	44, 45 and 60	The provision of access for construction purposes.
17	District of Shepway, Parish of Stanford	7 and 17 to 19	The provision of access for construction purposes.
17 and 17Q	District of Shepway, Parish of Saltwood	13 to 16	The provision of a working site and access for construction purposes.
17, 17Q and 17P	District of Shepway, Parish of Postling	11 and 14 to 18	The provision of a working site and access for construction purposes.
18B, 18E, 18F and 18G	District of Shepway, Parish of Newington	3 and 4	The provision of a working site and access for construction purposes.
18J		6 and 9	The provision of access for construction purposes.

(1) *Works*	(2) *Area*	(3) *Number of land shown on deposited plans*	(4) *Purpose for which temporary possession may be taken*
18A, 18AA, 18B, 18F, 18G and 18K		14 to 16, 19 to 21, 32 and 37	The provision of a working site and access for construction purposes.
18A, 18AA, 18B and 18G		31 and 40	The provision of working sites and access for construction purposes.
18AA		62	The provision of access for construction purposes.
18E	District of Shepway, Parish of Hythe	1	The provision of access for construction purposes.
18AA	District of Shepway, Town of Folkestone	6	The provision of a working site and access for construction purposes.
13, 14, 15, 15A, 15B, 16, 16A, 16B, 16C, 16D, 16E, 17, 18A, 18AA, 18B, 18C, 18D, 18F, 18G and all railway works associated therewith	District of Thanet, Parish of Minster	2	The provision of access to a railhead to be used for construction purposes.
13, 14, 15, 15A, 15B, 16, 16A, 16B, 16C, 16D, 16E, 17, 18A, 18AA, 18B, 18C, 18D, 18F, 18G and all railway works associated therewith	District of Dover, Parish of Sandwich	1	The provision of access to a railhead to be used for construction purposes.

(2) Not less than 28 days before entering upon and taking possession of land under this paragraph, the nominated undertaker shall give notice to the owners and occupiers of the land of its intention to do so.

(3) The nominated undertaker may not remain in possession of any land under this paragraph after the end of the period of one year beginning with the date of completion of the work or

works specified in relation to the land in column (1) of the table in sub-paragraph (1) above unless the owners of the land agree.

(4) The nominated undertaker shall pay compensation to the owners and occupiers of land of which possession is taken under this paragraph for any loss which they may suffer by reason of the exercise in relation to the land of the powers conferred by this paragraph.

(5) Any dispute as to a person's entitlement to compensation under sub-paragraph (4) above, or as to the amount of compensation, shall be determined under and in accordance with Part I of the Land Compensation Act 1961.

(6) Nothing in this paragraph shall affect any liability to pay compensation under section 10(2) of the Compulsory Purchase Act 1965, as applied to the acquisition of land under section 4(1) above, or under any other enactment, otherwise than for loss for which compensation is payable under sub-paragraph (4) above.

(7) In this paragraph, "structure" includes any erection.

2.—(1) Before giving up possession of land of which possession has been taken under paragraph 1 above, the nominated undertaker shall, in accordance with a scheme agreed with the owners of the land and the relevant planning authority, put the land into such condition as the scheme may provide.

(2) If, in relation to any land of which possession has been taken under paragraph 1 above, no scheme has been agreed for the purposes of this paragraph within 6 months of the date of completion of the work or works specified in relation to the land in column (1) of the table in paragraph 1(1) above, the scheme shall be such as may be determined by the appropriate Ministers after consultation with the nominated undertaker, the owners of the land and the relevant planning authority.

(3) Unless the owners of the land and the nominated undertaker otherwise agree, a scheme determined under sub-paragraph (2) above shall provide for land to be restored to its former condition.

(4) Unless the nominated undertaker otherwise agrees, a scheme determined under sub-paragraph (2) above shall not provide for the nominated undertaker to replace any structure removed under paragraph 1 above other than a fence.

(5) Where the appropriate Ministers ask the relevant planning authority for assistance in connection with the carrying out by them of their function under sub-paragraph (2) above, they may require the nominated undertaker to reimburse to the planning authority any expenses which it reasonably incurs in meeting the request.

(6) The duty under sub-paragraph (1) above in relation to any land shall be owed separately to the owners of the land and to the relevant planning authority.

(7) Where a scheme for the purposes of this paragraph provides for any step to be taken by the nominated undertaker before a specified date and that step has not been taken before that date, the relevant planning authority may—

(a) enter the land concerned and take that step, and
(b) require the nominated undertaker to reimburse to it any expenses which it reasonably incurs in acting under paragraph (a) above.

(8) In this paragraph—

"appropriate Ministers" means the Secretary of State for the Environment and the Secretary of State for Transport acting jointly;

"relevant planning authority" means—

(a) in relation to Greater London, the local planning authority, and
(b) in relation to Essex or Kent, the district planning authority; and

"structure" includes any erection.

3.—(1) Where the power under paragraph 1 above to take possession of land is exercised in relation to any land to which section 4(1) above applies, the relevant powers of compulsory acquisition shall thereupon cease to be exercisable in relation to that land.

(2) Sub-paragraph (1) above shall not apply to compulsory acquisition by virtue of paragraph 8(1) of Schedule 4 to this Act.

(3) In sub-paragraph (1) above, the reference to the relevant powers of compulsory acquisition is to—

(a) the power to serve a notice to treat under Part I of the Compulsory Purchase Act 1965, as applied to the acquisition of land under section 4(1) above, and
(b) the power to execute a declaration under section 4 of the Compulsory Purchase (Vesting Declarations) Act 1981, as applied by paragraph 4 of Schedule 4 to this Act.

Occupation and use for maintenance of works

4.—(1) At any time during the maintenance period relating to any of the scheduled works, the nominated undertaker may—

(a) enter upon and take possession of any land which is—

(i) within 20 metres from that work, and

(ii) within the limits of deviation for the scheduled works or the limits of land to be acquired or used,

if such possession is reasonably required for the purpose of or in connection with maintaining the work or any ancillary works connected with it, and

(b) construct on the land such temporary works (including the provision of means of access) and structures as may be reasonably so required.

(2) Sub-paragraph (1) above shall not authorise the nominated undertaker to take possession of—

(a) a house,

(b) any other structure which is for the time being occupied, or

(c) a garden belonging to a house.

(3) Not less than 28 days before entering upon and taking possession of land under this paragraph, the nominated undertaker shall give notice to the owners and occupiers of the land of its intention to do so.

(4) The nominated undertaker may only remain in possession of land under this paragraph for so long as may be reasonably required to carry out the maintenance works for which possession of the land was taken.

(5) Before giving up possession of land of which possession has been taken under this paragraph, the nominated undertaker shall restore the land to the reasonable satisfaction of the owners of the land.

(6) The nominated undertaker shall pay compensation to the owners and occupiers of land of which possession is taken under this paragraph for any loss which they may suffer by reason of the exercise in relation to the land of the powers conferred by this paragraph.

(7) Any dispute as to a person's entitlement to compensation under sub-paragraph (6) above, or as to the amount of the compensation, shall be determined under and in accordance with Part I of the Land Compensation Act 1961.

(8) Nothing in this paragraph shall affect any liability to pay compensation under section 10(2) of the Compulsory Purchase Act 1965, as applied to the acquisition of land under section 4(1) above, or under any other enactment, otherwise than for loss for which compensation is payable under sub-paragraph (6) above.

(9) In this paragraph—

(a) "the maintenance period", in relation to any work, means the period beginning with the date on which the work is completed and ending 5 years after the date on which it is brought into general use,

(b) "structure" includes any erection, and

(c) any reference to land within a specified distance of a work includes, in the case of a work under the surface of the ground, a reference to land within the specified distance of any point on the surface below which the work is situated.

Suspension of private rights of way

5.—(1) All private rights of way over land of which the nominated undertaker takes possession under paragraph 1 or 4 above shall be suspended and unenforceable for as long as it remains in lawful possession of the land.

(2) Any person who suffers loss by the suspension of any right under this paragraph shall be entitled to compensation.

(3) Any dispute as to a person's entitlement to compensation under this paragraph, or as to the amount of such compensation, shall be determined under and in accordance with Part I of the Land Compensation Act 1961.

Section 9

SCHEDULE 6

Planning Conditions

Part I

Qualifying Authorities

Specification

1.—(1) As soon after the day on which this Act is passed as the Secretary of State considers reasonably practicable, he shall, by order made by statutory instrument, specify every relevant local authority which—

(a) had, on or before the day on which the Bill for this Act was reported from Select Committee in the House of Lords, given him undertakings with respect to the handling of planning matters arising under this Schedule which he considered satisfactory, and
(b) has not subsequently been released from its undertakings.

(2) Subject to the following provisions of this paragraph, an authority which is specified under sub-paragraph (1) above is a qualifying authority for the purposes of this Schedule.

(3) The Secretary of State may, if he considers it expedient to do so, by order made by statutory instrument provide that an authority shall cease to be a qualifying authority for the purposes of this Schedule.

(4) If, in relation to a relevant local authority which is not a qualifying authority for the purposes of this Schedule, the Secretary of State considers that the way in which the authority carries out its functions has been significantly affected by a change of circumstances occurring since the relevant day, he may by order made by statutory instrument provide that the authority shall be a qualifying authority for the purposes of this Schedule.

(5) Before making an order under sub-paragraph (3) or (4) above, the Secretary of State shall consult—
(a) the nominated undertaker, and
(b) unless the authority concerned has requested him to make the order, that authority.

(6) A statutory instrument containing an order under sub-paragraph (3) or (4) above shall be subject to annulment in pursuance of a resolution of either House of Parliament.

(7) In sub-paragraph (4) above, the reference to the relevant day is—
(a) in relation to an authority which has never been a qualifying authority for the purposes of this Schedule, to the day mentioned in sub-paragraph (1)(a) above, and
(b) in relation to an authority which has been a qualifying authority for the purposes of this Schedule, to the day on which it ceased, or last ceased, to be such an authority.

(8) For the purposes of this paragraph, a local authority is a relevant local authority if it has functions under Part II or III of this Schedule in relation to the giving of approval.

Transition

2.—(1) An order under paragraph 1 above may contain such transitional provision and savings as the Secretary of State thinks fit.

(2) Without prejudice to the generality of sub-paragraph (1) above, provision under that sub-paragraph may include provision with respect to the effect, in a case where the nominated undertaker has obtained, or requested, approval under this Schedule, of the authority which granted the approval, or to which the request has been made, ceasing to be, or becoming, a qualifying authority for the purposes of this Schedule.

(3) The Secretary of State may by agreement fetter the exercise of his discretion under sub-paragraph (1) above.

PART II

DEVELOPMENT IN GREATER LONDON

Introductory

3. This Part of this Schedule has effect in relation to development in Greater London.

Planning regimes

4.—(1) The requirement set out in paragraph 5 below shall be a condition of the deemed planning permission, so far as relating to relevant development in the area of a London borough council which is not a qualifying authority for the purposes of this Schedule.

(2) For the purposes of sub-paragraph (1) above, development is relevant development to the extent that it consists of or includes—
(a) the erection, construction, alteration or extension of any building, or
(b) the formation, laying out or alteration of any means of access to any highway used by vehicular traffic.

(3) The requirements set out in paragraphs 6 to 10 below shall be conditions of the deemed planning permission, so far as relating to development in the area of a London borough council which is a qualifying authority for the purposes of this Schedule.

(4) The requirements set out in paragraph 11 below shall be conditions of the deemed planning permission so far as relating to development in the area of any London borough council.

Conditions: non-qualifying authority

5.—(1) Development shall be carried out in accordance with plans and specifications for the time being approved by the local planning authority at the request of the nominated undertaker.

(2) The local planning authority may, on approving a plan or specification for the purposes of this paragraph, specify any respect in which it requires additional details of the development to be submitted for approval.

(3) Where the local planning authority exercises the power conferred by sub-paragraph (2) above, the plans and specifications in accordance with which the development is required under sub-paragraph (1) above to be carried out shall, as regards the specified respect, include a plan or specification showing the additional details.

(4) The only ground on which the local planning authority may refuse to approve plans or specifications for the purposes of this paragraph is—

(a) that the development to which they relate ought to, and could reasonably, be carried out elsewhere on land within the relevant limits, or

(b) that the design or external appearance of any building to which they relate ought to be modified to preserve the local environment or local amenity and is reasonably capable of being so modified.

(5) The ground mentioned in sub-paragraph (4)(a) above shall not apply in relation to development consisting of the provision of, or the carrying out of works to, a dam.

Conditions: qualifying authority

6.—(1) To the extent that development consists of any operation or work mentioned in the left-hand column of the table in sub-paragraph (4) below, it shall be carried out in accordance with plans and specifications for the time being approved by the local planning authority at the request of the nominated undertaker.

(2) The local planning authority may, on approving a plan or specification for the purposes of this paragraph, specify any respect in which it requires additional details of the development to be submitted for approval.

(3) Where the local planning authority exercises the power conferred by sub-paragraph (2) above, the plans and specifications in accordance with which the development is required under sub-paragraph (1) above to be carried out shall, as regards the specified respect, include a plan or specification showing the additional details.

(4) The only ground on which the local planning authority may refuse to approve for the purposes of this paragraph plans or specifications of any operation or work mentioned in the following table is a ground specified in relation to it in the right-hand column of that table.

THE TABLE

Operation or work	*Grounds*
1. *Construction works* (a) The erection, construction, alteration or extension of any building (except for anything within (b) or (c) below or item 2 or 6) or road vehicle park. (b) The construction, alteration or extension of any terracing, cuttings, embankments or other earth works. (c) The erection, construction, alteration or extension of any fences, walls or other barriers (including bunds) for visual or noise screening or dust suppression.	That the design or external appearance of the works ought to be modified— (a) to preserve the local environment or local amenity, (b) to prevent or reduce prejudicial effects on road safety or on the free flow of traffic in the local area, or (c) to preserve a site of archaeological or historic interest or nature conservation value, and is reasonably capable of being so modified. That the development ought to, and could reasonably, be carried out elsewhere within the limits of the land on which the works of which it forms part may be carried out under this Part of this Act.

Operation or work	Grounds
2. *Minor construction works* The erection, construction, alteration or extension of any transformers, telecommunications masts or pedestrian accesses to the railway line.	That the design or external appearance of the works ought to be modified to preserve the local environment or local amenity, and is reasonably capable of being so modified. That the development ought to, and could reasonably, be carried out on land elsewhere within the relevant limits.
3. *Fences and walls* The erection, construction, alteration or extension of any fences or walls (except for anything within item 1(c) above).	That the development ought to, and could reasonably, be carried out on land elsewhere within the relevant limits.
4. *Highway access* The formation, laying out or alteration of any means of access to a highway used, or proposed highway proposed to be used, by vehicular traffic.	That the development ought to be modified to prevent or reduce prejudicial effects on road safety or on the free flow of traffic in the local area, and is reasonably capable of being so modified.
5. *Gantries and overhead line supports* The erection or construction of any gantries or overhead line supports for so much of any railway comprised in Work No. 1 as lies between the northern end of the roof over St. Pancras station, as it is at the time of erection or construction, and the northern abutment of the existing bridge over the Regent's Canal.	That the design or external appearance of the work ought to be modified to preserve the local environment or local amenity, and is reasonably capable of being so modified.
6. *Artificial lighting* The erection, construction or installation of lighting equipment.	That the design of the equipment, with respect to the emission of light, ought to be modified to preserve the local environment or local amenity, and is reasonably capable of being so modified. That the development ought to, and could reasonably, be carried out elsewhere within the limits of land on which the works of which it forms part may be carried out under this Part of this Act.
7. *Waste and spoil disposal* The disposal of waste or spoil.	That— (a) the design or external appearance of disposal sites on land within the relevant limits, (b) the methods by which such sites are worked, or (c) the noise, dust, vibration or screening arrangements during the operation of such sites, ought to be modified and are reasonably capable of being modified.

Operation or work	*Grounds*
	That— (a) to preserve the local environment or local amenity, (b) to prevent or reduce prejudicial effects on road safety or on the free flow of traffic in the local area, or (c) to preserve a site of archaeological or historic interest or nature conservation value, the development ought to be carried out on land elsewhere within the relevant limits, and is reasonably capable of being so carried out.
8. *Borrow pits* The excavation of bulk materials from borrow pits.	That— (a) the design or external appearance of borrow pits on land within the relevant limits, (b) the methods by which such pits are worked, or (c) the noise, dust, vibration or screening arrangements during the operation of such pits, ought to be modified and are reasonably capable of being modified. That— (a) to preserve the local environment or local amenity, (b) to prevent or reduce prejudicial effects on road safety or on the free flow of traffic in the local area, or (c) to preserve a site of archaeological or historic interest or nature conservation value, the development ought to be carried out on land elsewhere within the relevant limits, and is reasonably capable of being so carried out.

Note:

1. In the case of items 1(b) and (c) and 6, the second of the grounds specified does not apply in relation to development which forms part of a scheduled work.
2. In the case of items 7 and 8, the second of the grounds specified does not apply in relation to development which—
   (a) is within the limits of deviation for the scheduled works, or
   (b) consists of the use of land specified in columns (1) and (2) of Part I of Schedule 4 for a purpose specified in relation to the land in column (3) of that Part.
3. Any reference in the left-hand column of the table to a description of works does not include works of that description of a temporary nature.

(5) Sub-paragraph (4) above shall apply in relation to the imposition of conditions on approval as it applies in relation to the refusal of approval.

7.—(1) Development shall be carried out in accordance with arrangements approved by the local planning authority at the request of the nominated undertaker with respect to the matters mentioned in the left-hand column of the table in sub-paragraph (2) below.

(2) The only ground on which the local planning authority may refuse to approve for the purposes of this paragraph arrangements with respect to a matter mentioned in the following table is—

(a) that the arrangements relate to development which, for the purposes of regulating the matter in question, ought to and can reasonably be considered in conjunction with other permitted development which is to be carried out in the authority's area, or

(b) the ground specified in relation to the matter in the right-hand column of the table.

THE TABLE

Matters	*Grounds*
1. *Road transport* Means and routes by which anything is to be transported on a highway by large goods vehicle to a working or storage site, a site where it will be re-used or a waste disposal site.	That the arrangements ought to be modified— (a) to preserve the local environment, local amenity or a site of archaeological or historic interest or nature conservation value, or (b) to prevent or reduce prejudical effects on road safety or on the free flow of traffic in the local area, and are reasonably capable of being so modified.
2. *Handling of re-useable spoil and top soil* Handling during removal, storage and re-use of any spoil or top soil removed during the course of carrying out the development.	That the arrangements ought to be modified to ensure that the spoil or top soil remain in good condition and are reasonably capable of being so modified.
3. *Storage sites* Sites on land within the relevant limits at which— (a) minerals, aggregates or other construction materials required for the development, or (b) spoil or top soil, are to be stored until used or re-used in carrying out the development or disposed of as waste.	That the arrangements ought to be modified— (a) to preserve the local environment, local amenity or a site of archaeological or historic interest or nature conservation value, or (b) to prevent or reduce prejudicial effects on road safety or on the free flow of traffic in the local area, and are reasonably capable of being so modified.
4. *Construction camps* Sites on land within the relevant limits which are to be used for the residential accommodation of persons engaged in carrying out the development.	As item 3.
5. *Screening* Provision where necessary on land within the relevant limits of any screening for working sites on such land required for the purposes of carrying out the development.	As item 3.

Matters	*Grounds*
6. *Hours of working* The hours and days of the week during which work on the development on land within the relevant limits is to be carried out.	That the arrangements ought to be modified to preserve the local environment or local amenity, and are reasonably capable of being so modified.
7. *Artificial lighting* The use of artificial lighting on land within the relevant limits for the purpose of carrying out the development.	As item 6.
8. *Suppression of noise, dust and vibration* The suppression of noise, dust and vibration caused by construction operations carried on on land within the relevant limits for the purpose of carrying out the development.	As item 6.
9. *Mud on highway* Measures to be taken on land within the relevant limits to prevent mud being carried onto any public highway as a result of carrying on the development.	That the arrangements ought to be modified— (a) to preserve the local environment or local amenity, or (b) to prevent or reduce prejudicial effects on road safety or on the free flow of traffic in the local area, and are reasonably capable of being so modified.
10. *Highway access* The formation, laying out or alteration of any means of access to any highway used, or proposed highway proposed to be used, on a temporary basis by vehicular traffic to serve a construction site or camp.	That the arrangements ought to be modified to prevent or reduce prejudicial effects on road safety or on the free flow of traffic in the local area, and are reasonably capable of being so modified.

(3) The local planning authority may only impose conditions on approval for the purposes of this paragraph with the agreement of the nominated undertaker.

(4) In this paragraph, "large goods vehicle" has the same meaning as in Part IV of the Road Traffic Act 1988.

8.—(1) To the extent that development consists of—

(a) the disposal of waste or spoil, or

(b) the excavation of bulk materials from borrow pits,

it shall not be begun unless the local planning authority has, at the request of the nominated undertaker, approved a scheme for the restoration of the land on which the development is to be carried out.

(2) The only ground on which the local planning authority may refuse to approve, or impose conditions on the approval of, a scheme for the purposes of this paragraph is that the scheme ought to be modified and is reasonably capable of being modified.

(3) The nominated undertaker shall carry out a scheme approved for the purposes of this paragraph once it has completed its use of the land to which the scheme relates for the purpose of carrying out development of a kind to which sub-paragraph (1) above applies.

(4) In sub-paragraph (1) above, the reference to restoration includes a reference to restoration in the longer term; and, accordingly, a scheme for the restoration of land may include provision about aftercare.

9.—(1) No work to which this paragraph applies shall be brought into use without the approval of the local planning authority.

(2) The works to which this paragraph applies are—

(a) any scheduled work,

(b) any station constructed in exercise of the powers conferred by this Part of this Act, and

(c) any depot constructed in exercise of those powers for use for or in connection with the maintenance of railway vehicles or track, whether or not constructed for use also for other purposes.

(3) The local planning authority shall, at the request of the nominated undertaker, grant approval for the purposes of sub-paragraph (1) above if—

(a) it considers that there are no reasonably practicable measures which need to be taken for the purpose of mitigating the effect of the work or its operation on the local environment or local amenity, or

(b) it has approved, at the request of the nominated undertaker, a scheme consisting of provision with respect to the taking of measures for that purpose.

(4) The local planning authority shall not refuse to approve, nor impose conditions on the approval of, a scheme submitted for the purposes of sub-paragraph (3)(b) above unless it is satisfied that it is expedient to do so on the ground that the scheme ought to be modified—

(a) to preserve the local environment or local amenity,

(b) to preserve a site of archaeological or historic interest, or

(c) in the interests of nature conservation,

and that the scheme is reasonably capable of being so modified.

(5) In this paragraph, "railway vehicle" and "track" have the same meanings as in Part I of the Railways Act 1993.

10.—Where the local planning authority approves a scheme for the purposes of paragraph 9(3)(b) above, the nominated undertaker shall be required—

(a) to carry out the scheme, and

(b) to comply with any condition subject to which the scheme is approved.

Conditions: general

11.—(1) Where development consists of or includes the carrying out on any site of operations ancillary to the construction of any of the scheduled works, those operations shall be discontinued as soon as reasonably practicable after the completion of the relevant scheduled work or works.

(2) The nominated undertaker shall, following discontinuation of the use of any site for carrying out operations ancillary to the construction of any of the scheduled works, restore the site in accordance with a scheme agreed with the local planning authority.

(3) If, in relation to a site used for carrying out operations ancillary to the construction of any of the scheduled works, no scheme has been agreed for the purposes of sub-paragraph (2) above within 6 months of the completion of the relevant scheduled work or works, the scheme shall be such as the appropriate Ministers may determine after consultation with the nominated undertaker and the local planning authority.

(4) Where, independently of any consultation under sub-paragraph (3) above, the appropriate Ministers ask the local planning authority for assistance in connection with the carrying out by them of their function under sub-paragraph (3) above, they may require the nominated undertaker to reimburse to the planning authority any expenses which it reasonably incurs in meeting the request.

(5) Sub-paragraph (2) above shall not apply to a site to the extent that it consists of land to which a scheme under paragraph 8 above applies.

(6) Sub-paragraph (2) above shall not apply where the site is one in relation to which the nominated undertaker is subject to an obligation under paragraph 2(1) of Schedule 5 above.

(7) In this paragraph, references to the relevant scheduled work or works, in relation to any site, are to the scheduled work or works to which the operations carried out on that site were ancillary.

PART III

DEVELOPMENT IN ESSEX OR KENT

Introductory

12. This Part of this Schedule has effect in relation to development in Essex or Kent.

Planning regimes: district councils

13.—(1) The requirement set out in paragraph 14 below shall be a condition of the deemed planning permission, so far as relating to relevant development in the area of a district council which is not a qualifying authority for the purposes of this Schedule.

(2) For the purposes of sub-paragraph (1) above, development is relevant development to the extent that it consists of or includes—

(a) the erection, construction, alteration or extension of any building, or

(b) the formation, laying out or alteration, otherwise than in connection with an excepted matter, of any means of access to any highway used by vehicular traffic.

(3) The requirements set out in paragraphs 15 and 16 below shall be conditions of the deemed planning permission, so far as relating to development, other than excepted development, in the area of a district council which is a qualifying authority for the purposes of this Schedule.

(4) For the purposes of sub-paragraph (3) above, excepted development is development consisting of—

(a) the formation, laying out or alteration, in connection with an excepted matter, of any means of access to any highway used by vehicular traffic,

(b) the disposal of waste or spoil, or

(c) the excavation of bulk materials from borrow pits.

(5) The requirements set out in paragraphs 17 and 18 below shall be conditions of the deemed planning permission, so far as relating to development in the area of a district council which is a qualifying authority for the purposes of this Schedule.

(6) The requirements set out in paragraph 19 below shall be conditions of the deemed planning permission, so far as relating to development in the area of any district council.

(7) For the purposes of this paragraph, the following are excepted matters—

(a) the transport of minerals,

(b) the transport of surplus spoil or top soil,

(c) the disposal of waste or spoil, and

(d) the excavation of bulk materials from borrow pits.

District conditions: non-qualifying authority

14.—(1) Development shall be carried out in accordance with plans and specifications for the time being approved by the district planning authority at the request of the nominated undertaker.

(2) The district planning authority may, on approving a plan or specification for the purposes of this paragraph, specify any respect in which it requires additional details of the development to be submitted for approval.

(3) Where the district planning authority exercises the power conferred by sub-paragraph (2) above, the plans and specifications in accordance with which the development is required under sub-paragraph (1) above to be carried out shall, as regards the specified respect, include a plan or specification showing the additional details.

(4) The only ground on which the district planning authority may refuse to approve plans or specifications for the purposes of this paragraph is—

(a) that the development to which they relate ought to, and could reasonably, be carried out elsewhere on land within the relevant limits, or

(b) that the design or external appearance of any building to which they relate ought to be modified to preserve the local environment or local amenity and is reasonably capable of being so modified.

District conditions: qualifying authority

15.—(1) To the extent that development consists of any operation or work mentioned in the left-hand column of the table in sub-paragraph (4) below, it shall be carried out in accordance with plans and specifications for the time being approved by the district planning authority at the request of the nominated undertaker.

(2) The district planning authority may, on approving a plan or specification for the purposes of this paragraph, specify any respect in which it requires additional details of the development to be submitted for approval.

(3) Where the district planning authority exercises the power conferred by sub-paragraph (2) above, the plans and specifications in accordance with which the development is required under sub-paragraph (1) above to be carried out shall, as regards the specified respect, include a plan or specification showing the additional details.

(4) The only ground on which the district planning authority may refuse to approve for the purposes of this paragraph plans or specifications of any operation or work mentioned in the following table is a ground specified in relation to it in the right-hand column of that table.

THE TABLE

Operation or work	*Grounds*
1. *Construction works* (a) The erection, construction, alteration or extension of any building (except for anything within (b) or (c) below or item 2 or 6) or road vehicle park. (b) The construction, alteration or extension of any terracing, cuttings, embankments or other earth works. (c) The erection, construction, alteration or extension of any fences, walls or other barriers (including bunds) for visual or noise screening or dust suppression.	That the design or external appearance of the works ought to be modified— (a) to preserve the local environment or local amenity, (b) to prevent or reduce prejudicial effects on road safety or on the free flow of traffic in the local area, or (c) to preserve a site of archaeological or historic interest or nature conservation value, and is reasonably capable of being so modified. That the development ought to, and could reasonably, be carried out elsewhere within the limits of the land on which the works of which it forms part may be carried out under this Part of this Act.
2. *Minor construction works* The erection, construction, alteration or extension of any transformers, telecommunications masts or pedestrian accesses to the railway line.	That the design or external appearance of the works ought to be modified to preserve the local environment or local amenity, and is reasonably capable of being so modified. That the development ought to, and could reasonably, be carried out on land elsewhere within the relevant limits.
3. *Fences and walls* The erection, construction, alteration or extension of any fences or walls (except for anything within item 1(c) above).	That the development ought to, and could reasonably, be carried out on land elsewhere within the relevant limits.
4. *Highway access* The formation, laying out or alteration of any means of access to a highway used, or proposed highway proposed to be used, by vehicular traffic.	That the development ought to be modified to prevent or reduce prejudicial effects on road safety or on the free flow of traffic in the local area, and is reasonably capable of being so modified.
5. *Gantries and overhead line supports* The erection or construction of any gantries or overhead line supports for so much of the railway comprised in Work No. 13 as lies between 1,000 and 2,400 metres from its western end.	That the design or external appearance of the work ought to be modified to preserve the local environment or local amenity, and is reasonably capable of being so modified.

Operation or work	*Grounds*
6. *Artificial lighting* The erection, construction or installation of lighting equipment.	That the design of the equipment, with respect to the emission of light, ought to be modified to preserve the local environment or local amenity, and is reasonably capable of being so modified. That the development ought to, and could reasonably be, carried out elsewhere within the limits of land on which the works of which it forms part may be carried out under this Part of this Act.

Note:

1. In the case of items 1(b) and (c) and 6, the second of the grounds specified does not apply in relation to development which forms part of a scheduled work.

2. Any reference in the left-hand column of the table to a description of works does not include works of that description of a temporary nature.

(5) Sub-paragraph (4) above shall apply in relation to the imposition of conditions on approval as it applies in relation to the refusal of approval.

16.—(1) Development shall be carried out in accordance with arrangements approved by the district planning authority at the request of the nominated undertaker with respect to the matters mentioned in the left-hand column of the table in sub-paragraph (2) below.

(2) The only ground on which the district planning authority may refuse to approve for the purposes of this paragraph arrangements with respect to a matter mentioned in the following table is—

(a) that the arrangements relate to development which, for the purposes of regulating the matter in question, ought to and can reasonably be considered in conjunction with other permitted development which is to be carried out in the authority's area, or

(b) the ground specified in relation to the matter in the right-hand column of the table.

THE TABLE

Matters	*Grounds*
1. *Handling of re-useable spoil and top soil* Handling during removal, storage and re-use of any spoil or top soil removed during the course of carrying out the development.	That the arrangements ought to be modified to ensure that the spoil or top soil remains in good condition and are reasonably capable of being so modified.
2. *Storage sites* Sites on land within the relevant limits at which— (a) minerals, aggregates or other construction materials required for the development, or (b) spoil or top soil, are to be stored until used or re-used in carrying out the development or disposed of as waste.	That the arrangements ought to be modified— (a) to preserve the local environment, local amenity or a site of archaeological or historic interest or nature conservation value, or (b) to prevent or reduce prejudicial effects on road safety or on the free flow of traffic in the local area, and are reasonably capable of being so modified.
3. *Construction camps* Sites on land within the relevant limits which are to be used for the residential accommodation of persons engaged in carrying out the development.	As item 2.

Matters	*Grounds*
4. *Screening* Provision where necessary on land within the relevant limits of any screening for working sites on such land required for the purpose of carrying out the development.	As item 2.
5. *Hours of working* The hours and days of the week during which work on the development on land within the relevant limits is to be carried out.	That the arrangements ought to be modified to preserve the local environment or local amenity, and are reasonably capable of being so modified.
6. *Artificial lighting* The use of artificial lighting on land within the relevant limits for the purpose of carrying out the development.	As item 5.
7. *Suppression of noise, dust and vibration* The suppression of noise, dust and vibration caused by construction operations carried on on land within the relevant limits for the purpose of carrying out the development.	As item 5.
8. *Mud on highway* Measures to be taken on land within the relevant limits to prevent mud being carried onto any public highway as a result of carrying on the development.	That the arrangements ought to be modified— (a) to preserve the local environment or local amenity, or (b) to prevent or reduce prejudicial effects on road safety or on the free flow of traffic in the local area, and are reasonably capable of being so modified.
9. *Highway access* The formation, laying out or alteration of any means of access to any highway used, or proposed highway proposed to be used, on a temporary basis by vehicular traffic to serve a construction site or camp.	That the arrangements ought to be modified to prevent or reduce prejudicial effects on road safety or on the free flow of traffic in the local area, and are reasonably capable of being so modified.

(3) The district planning authority may only impose conditions on approval for the purposes of this paragraph with the agreement of the nominated undertaker.

17.—(1) No work to which this paragraph applies shall be brought into use without the approval of the district planning authority.

(2) The works to which this paragraph applies are—

(a) any scheduled work,

(b) any station constructed in exercise of the powers conferred by this Part of this Act, and

(c) any depot constructed in exercise of those powers for use for or in connection with the maintenance of railway vehicles or track, whether or not constructed for use also for other purposes.

(3) The district planning authority shall, at the request of the nominated undertaker, grant approval for the purposes of sub-paragraph (1) above if—

(a) it considers that there are no reasonably practicable measures which need to be taken for the purpose of mitigating the effect of the work or its operation on the local environment or local amenity, or

(b) it has approved, at the request of the nominated undertaker, a scheme consisting of provision with respect to the taking of measures for that purpose.

(4) The district planning authority shall not refuse to approve, nor impose conditions on the approval of, a scheme submitted for the purposes of sub-paragraph (3)(b) above unless it is satisfied that it is expedient to do so on the ground that the scheme ought to be modified—

(a) to preserve the local environment or local amenity,
(b) to preserve a site of archaeological or historic interest, or
(c) in the interests of nature conservation,

and that the scheme is reasonably capable of being so modified.

(5) In this paragraph, "railway vehicle" and "track" have the same meanings as in Part I of the Railways Act 1993.

18. Where the district planning authority approves a scheme for the purposes of paragraph 17(3)(b) above, the nominated undertaker shall be required—

(a) to carry out the scheme, and
(b) to comply with any condition subject to which the scheme is approved.

District conditions: general

19.—(1) Where development consists of or includes the carrying out on any site of operations ancillary to the construction of any of the scheduled works, those operations shall be discontinued as soon as reasonably practicable after the completion of the relevant scheduled work or works.

(2) The nominated undertaker shall, following discontinuation of the use of any site for carrying out operations ancillary to the construction of any of the scheduled works, restore the site in accordance with a scheme agreed with the district planning authority.

(3) If, in relation to a site used for carrying out operations ancillary to the construction of any of the scheduled works, no scheme has been agreed for the purposes of sub-paragraph (2) above within 6 months of the completion of the relevant scheduled work or works, the scheme shall be such as the appropriate Ministers may determine after consultation with the nominated undertaker and the district planning authority.

(4) Where, independently of any consultation under sub-paragraph (3) above, the appropriate Ministers ask the district planning authority for assistance in connection with the carrying out by them of their function under sub-paragraph (3) above, they may require the nominated undertaker to reimburse to the planning authority any expenses which it reasonably incurs in meeting the request.

(5) Sub-paragraph (2) above shall not apply to a site to the extent that it consists of land to which a scheme under paragraph 24 below applies.

(6) Sub-paragraph (2) above shall not apply where the site is one in relation to which the nominated undertaker is subject to an obligation under paragraph 2(1) of Schedule 5 above.

(7) In this paragraph, references to the relevant scheduled work or works, in relation to any site, are to the scheduled work or works to which the operations carried out on that site were ancillary.

Planning regimes: county councils

20.—(1) The requirement set out in paragraph 21 below shall be a condition of the deemed planning permission, so far as relating to relevant development in the area of a county council which is not a qualifying authority for the purposes of this Schedule.

(2) For the purposes of sub-paragraph (1) above, relevant development is development consisting of the formation, laying out or alteration, in connection with an excepted matter, of any means of access to a highway used by vehicular traffic.

(3) The requirements set out in paragraphs 22, 23 and 24 below shall be conditions of the deemed planning permission, so far as relating to relevant development in the area of a county council which is a qualifying authority for the purposes of this Schedule.

(4) For the purposes of sub-paragraph (3) above, relevant development is development consisting of—

(a) the formation, laying out or alteration, in connection with an excepted matter, of any means of access to a highway used by vehicular traffic,
(b) the disposal of waste or spoil, or
(c) the excavation of bulk materials from borrow pits.

(5) The requirement set out in paragraph 25 below shall be a condition of the deemed planning permission, so far as relating to development in the area of a county council which is a qualifying authority for the purposes of this Schedule.

(6) For the purposes of this paragraph, the following are excepted matters—

(a) the transport of minerals,
(b) the transport of surplus spoil or top soil,
(c) the disposal of waste or spoil, and
(d) the excavation of bulk materials from borrow pits.

County conditions: non-qualifying authority

21.—(1) Development shall be carried out in accordance with plans and specifications for the time being approved by the county planning authority at the request of the nominated undertaker.

(2) The county planning authority may, on approving a plan or specification for the purposes of this paragraph, specify any respect in which it requires additional details of the development to be submitted for approval.

(3) Where the county planning authority exercises the power conferred by sub-paragraph (2) above, the plans and specifications in accordance with which the development is required under sub-paragraph (1) above to be carried out shall, as regards the specified respect, include a plan or specification showing the additional details.

(4) The only ground on which the county planning authority may refuse to approve plans or specifications for the purposes of this paragraph is that the development to which they relate ought to, and could reasonably, be carried out elsewhere on land within the relevant limits.

County conditions: qualifying authority

22.—(1) To the extent that development consists of any operation or work mentioned in the left-hand column of the table in sub-paragraph (4) below, it shall be carried out in accordance with plans and specifications for the time being approved by the county planning authority at the request of the nominated undertaker.

(2) The county planning authority may, on approving a plan or specification for the purposes of this paragraph, specify any respect in which it requires additional details of the development to be submitted for approval.

(3) Where the county planning authority exercises the power conferred by sub-paragraph (2) above, the plans and specifications in accordance with which the development is required under sub-paragraph (1) above to be carried out shall, as regards the specified respect, include a plan or specification showing the additional details.

(4) The only ground on which the county planning authority may refuse to approve for the purposes of this paragraph plans or specifications of any operation or work mentioned in the following table is a ground specified in relation to it in the right-hand column of that table.

THE TABLE

Operation or work	*Grounds*
1. *Highway access* The formation, laying out or alteration of any means of access to a highway used, or proposed highway proposed to be used, by vehicular traffic.	That the development ought to be modified to prevent or reduce prejudicial effects on road safety or on the free flow of traffic in the local area, and is reasonably capable of being so modified.
2. *Waste and spoil disposal* The disposal of waste or spoil.	That— (a) the design or external appearance of disposal sites on land within the relevant limits, (b) the methods by which such sites are worked, or (c) the noise, dust, vibration or screening arrangements during the operation of such sites, ought to be modified and are reasonably capable of being modified.
	That— (a) to preserve the local environment or local amenity, (b) to prevent or reduce prejudicial effects on road safety or on the free flow of traffic in the local area, or

Operation or work	*Grounds*
	(c) to preserve a site of archaeological or historic interest or nature conservation value, the development ought to be carried out on land elsewhere within the relevant limits, and is reasonably capable of being so carried out.
3. *Borrow pits* The excavation of bulk materials from borrow pits.	That— (a) the design or external appearance of borrow pits on land within the relevant limits, (b) the methods by which such pits are worked, or (c) the noise, dust, vibration or screening arrangements during the operation of such pits, ought to be modified and are reasonably capable of being modified. That— (a) to preserve the local environment or local amenity, (b) to prevent or reduce prejudicial effects on road safety or on the free flow of traffic in the local area, or (c) to preserve a site of archaeological or historic interest or nature conservation value, the development ought to be carried out on land elsewhere within the relevant limits, and is reasonably capable of being so carried out.

Note: In the case of items 2 and 3, the second of the grounds specified does not apply in relation to development which—

(a) is within the limits of deviation for the scheduled works, or

(b) consists of the use of land specified in columns (1) and (2) of Part I of Schedule 4 for a purpose specified in relation to the land in column (3) of that Part.

(5) Sub-paragraph (4) above shall apply in relation to the imposition of conditions on approval as it applies in relation to the refusal of approval.

23.—(1) Development shall be carried out in accordance with arrangements approved by the county planning authority at the request of the nominated undertaker with respect to the matters mentioned in the left-hand column of the table in sub-paragraph (2) below.

(2) The only ground on which the county planning authority may refuse to approve for the purposes of this paragraph arrangements with respect to a matter mentioned in the following table is—

(a) that the arrangements relate to development which, for the purposes of regulating the matter in question, ought to and can reasonably be considered in conjunction with other permitted development which is to be carried out in the authority's area, or

(b) the ground specified in relation to the matter in the right-hand column of the table.

THE TABLE

Matters	*Grounds*
1. *Handling of re-usable spoil and top soil* Handling during removal, storage, and re-use of any spoil or top soil removed during the course of carrying out the development.	That the arrangements ought to be modified to ensure that the spoil or top soil remains in good condition and are reasonably capable of being so modified.
2. *Storage sites* Sites on land within the relevant limits at which— (a) minerals, aggregates or other construction materials required for the development, or (b) spoil or top soil, are to be stored until used or re-used in carrying out the development or disposed of as waste.	That the arrangements ought to be modified— (a) to preserve the local environment, local amenity or a site of archaeological or historic interest or nature conservation value, or (b) to prevent or reduce prejudicial effects on road safety or on the free flow of traffic in the local area, and are reasonably capable of being so modified.
3. *Construction camps* Sites on land within the relevant limits which are to be used for the residential accommodation of persons engaged in carrying out the development.	As item 2.
4. *Screening* Provision where necessary on land within the relevant limits of any screening for working sites on such land required for the purpose of carrying out the development.	As item 2.
5. *Hours of working* The hours and days of the week during which work on the development on land within the relevant limits is to be carried out.	That the arrangements ought to be modified to preserve the local environment or local amenity, and are reasonably capable of being so modified.
6. *Artificial lighting* The use of artificial lighting on land within the relevant limits for the purpose of carrying out the development.	As item 5.
7. *Suppression of noise, dust and vibration* The suppression of noise, dust and vibration caused by construction operations carried on on land within the relevant limits for the purpose of carrying out the development.	As item 5.
8. *Mud on highway* Measures to be taken on land within the relevant limits to prevent mud being carried onto any public highway as a result of carrying on the development.	That the arrangements ought to be modified— (a) to preserve the local environment or local amenity, or (b) to prevent or reduce prejudicial effects on road safety or on the free flow of traffic in the local area, and are reasonably capable of being so modified.

Matters	*Grounds*
9. *Highway access* The formation, laying out or alteration of any means of access to any highway used, or proposed highway proposed to be used, on a temporary basis by vehicular traffic to serve a working site or camp.	That the arrangements ought to be modified to prevent or reduce prejudicial effects on road safety or on the free flow of traffic in the local area, and are reasonably capable of being so modified.

(3) The county planning authority may only impose conditions on approval for the purposes of this paragraph with the agreement of the nominated undertaker.

24.—(1) To the extent that development consists of—

(a) the disposal of waste or spoil, or

(b) the excavation of bulk materials from borrow pits,

it shall not be begun unless the county planning authority has, at the request of the nominated undertaker, approved a scheme for the restoration of the land on which the development is to be carried out.

(2) The only ground on which the county planning authority may refuse to approve, or impose conditions on the approval of, a scheme for the purposes of this paragraph is that the scheme ought to be modified and is reasonably capable of being modified.

(3) The nominated undertaker shall carry out a scheme approved for the purposes of this paragraph once it has completed its use of the land to which the scheme relates for the purpose of carrying out development of a kind to which sub-paragraph (1) above applies.

(4) In sub-paragraph (1) above, the reference to restoration includes a reference to restoration in the longer term; and, accordingly, a scheme for the restoration of land may include provision about aftercare.

25.—(1) Development shall be carried out in accordance with arrangements approved by the county planning authority at the request of the nominated undertaker with respect to the means and routes by which anything is to be transported on a highway by large goods vehicle to a working or storage site, a site where it will be re-used or a waste disposal site.

(2) The only ground on which the county planning authority may refuse to approve arrangements for the purposes of this paragraph is—

(a) that the arrangements relate to development which, for the purposes of regulating the matter in question, ought to and can reasonably be considered in conjunction with other permitted development which is to be carried out in the authority's area, or

(b) that the arrangements ought to be modified—

(i) to preserve the local environment, local amenity or a site of archaeological or historic interest or nature conservation value, or

(ii) to prevent or reduce prejudicial effects on road safety or on the free flow of traffic in the local area,

and are reasonably capable of being so modified.

(3) The county planning authority may only impose conditions on approval for the purposes of this paragraph with the agreement of the nominated undertaker.

(4) In this paragraph, "large goods vehicle" has the same meaning as in Part IV of the Road Traffic Act 1988.

PART IV

SUPPLEMENTARY

Programming of requests for planning approvals

26. A planning authority shall not be required to entertain a request for approval under Part II or III of this Schedule unless—

(a) the nominated undertaker has deposited with the authority a document setting out its proposed programme with respect to the making of requests under that Part to the authority, and

(b) the request is accompanied by a document explaining how the matters to which the request relates fit into the overall scheme of the works authorised by this Part of this Act.

Consultation

27.—(1) Where a planning authority considers that a request for approval under Part II or III of this Schedule relates to matters which may affect—

(a) nature conservation,

(b) the conservation of the natural beauty or amenity of the countryside, or

(c) a site of archaeological or historic interest,

it shall, within 5 days of receiving the request, invite the appropriate body or bodies to make representations.

(2) Where under sub-paragraph (1) above a planning authority has invited a body to make representations about a request for approval under Part II or III of this Schedule, it shall not make any decision about the request until—

(a) it has received representations from the body about the request,

(b) it has been informed by the body that it does not wish to make any representations about the request, or

(c) 21 days have elapsed since the date of the invitation.

(3) An invitation under sub-paragraph (1) above shall specify the time limit for making representations.

(4) For the purposes of this paragraph, the following are appropriate bodies in relation to the following matters—

Matter	*Body*
Nature conservation	The Nature Conservancy Council for England.
Conservation of the natural beauty or amenity of the countryside.	The Countryside Commission.
Sites of archaeological or historic interest.	The Historic Buildings and Monuments Commission for England.

28.—(1) Where a planning authority considers that a request for approval under Part II or III of this Schedule relates to matters which may affect—

(a) the conservation of the natural beauty or amenity of inland or coastal waters or land associated with such waters,

(b) the conservation of flora or fauna which are dependent on an aquatic environment, or

(c) the use of such waters or land for recreational purposes,

it shall, within 5 days of receiving the request, invite the Environment Agency to make representations.

(2) Where under sub-paragraph (1) above a planning authority has invited the Environment Agency to make representations about a request for approval under Part II or III of this Schedule, it shall not make any decision about the request until—

(a) it has received representations from the Agency about the request,

(b) it has been informed by the Agency that it does not wish to make any representations about the request, or

(c) 21 days have elapsed since the date of the invitation.

(3) An invitation under sub-paragraph (1) above shall specify the time limit for making representations.

29.—(1) Where a planning authority considers that a request for approval under Part II or III of this Schedule relates to matters which may affect the Lee Valley Regional Park, it shall, within 5 days of receiving the request, invite the Lee Valley Regional Park Authority to make representations.

(2) Where under sub-paragraph (1) above a planning authority has invited the Lee Valley Regional Park Authority to make representations about a request for approval under Part II or III of this Schedule, it shall not make any decision about the request until—

(a) it has received representations from the Authority about the request,
(b) it has been informed by the Authority that it does not wish to make any representations about the request, or
(c) 21 days have elapsed since the date of the invitation.

(3) An invitation under sub-paragraph (1) above shall specify the time limit for making representations.

Intervention by Secretary of State

30.—(1) The appropriate Ministers may by directions require a planning authority to refer any request for approval under Part II or III of this Schedule to them.

(2) In determining a request referred to them under this paragraph, the appropriate Ministers shall have the same powers as the authority making the reference.

(3) The determination by the appropriate Ministers of a request referred to them under this paragraph shall be final.

(4) Directions under this paragraph may—
(a) be given in relation to a specified request or requests of a specified description, and
(b) cancel or vary previous directions under this paragraph.

31.—(1) The appropriate Ministers may by directions restrict a planning authority's powers in relation to the grant of approval under Part II or III of this Schedule.

(2) Directions under this paragraph may—
(a) be given in relation to a specified approval or approvals of a specified description,
(b) be expressed to have effect without limit of time or during a specified period, and
(c) cancel or vary previous directions under this paragraph.

Appeals

32.—(1) Where the nominated undertaker is aggrieved by a decision of a planning authority on a request for approval under Part II or III of this Schedule (including a decision under sub-paragraph (2) of paragraph 5, 6, 14, 15, 21 or 22 above), it may appeal to the appropriate Ministers by giving notice of the appeal in the prescribed form to them and the authority whose decision is appealed against within 28 days of notification of the decision.

(2) On an appeal under this paragraph, the appropriate Ministers may allow or dismiss the appeal or vary the decision of the authority whose decision is appealed against, but may only make a determination involving the refusal of, or imposition of conditions on, approval on grounds open to that authority.

(3) Where, following receipt by a planning authority of a request by the nominated undertaker for relevant approval, the authority does not notify the undertaker within the appropriate period—
(a) of its decision on the request, or
(b) that the request has been referred to the appropriate Ministers in accordance with directions under paragraph 30 above,

this paragraph shall apply as if the authority had refused the request and notified the undertaker of its decision on the last day of the appropriate period.

(4) For the purposes of sub-paragraph (3) above, the appropriate period is the period of 8 weeks beginning with the date on which the request was received by the planning authority or such extended period as may at any time be agreed upon in writing between the authority and the nominated undertaker.

(5) The appropriate Ministers may by regulations make provision for the extension of the appropriate period for the purposes of sub-paragraph (3) above in connection with the payment of fees by means of cheque.

(6) The power to make regulations under sub-paragraph (5) above shall be exercisable by statutory instrument which shall be subject to annulment in pursuance of a resolution of either House of Parliament.

(7) In this paragraph, "prescribed" means prescribed by regulations made by the appropriate Ministers.

33. No appeal under section 78 of the Town and Country Planning Act 1990 (right to appeal against planning decisions and failure to take such decisions) may be made against a decision, or failure to notify a decision, in relation to which a right of appeal arises under paragraph 32 above.

34.—(1) Unless the appropriate Ministers direct otherwise, their functions in relation to the determination of an appeal under paragraph 32 above shall, instead of being carried out by them, be carried out by a person appointed by them for the purpose.

(2) The appropriate Ministers may by a further direction revoke a direction under sub-paragraph (1) above at any time before the determination of the appeal.

(3) A direction under sub-paragraph (1) or (2) above shall be served on the nominated undertaker and the planning authority whose decision is appealed against.

(4) At any time before the determination of an appeal by a person appointed for the purpose under this paragraph, the appropriate Ministers may revoke his appointment and appoint another person to determine the appeal instead.

(5) Where the function of determining an appeal under paragraph 32 above is transferred from one person to another, the person to whom the function is transferred shall consider the matter afresh, but the fact that the function is transferred shall not entitle any person to make fresh representations or to modify or withdraw any representations already made.

(6) If the appropriate Ministers determine an appeal which another person was previously appointed to determine, they may, in determining it, take into account any report made to them by that person.

35. The decision of the person appointed under paragraph 34 above, or, as the case may be, of the appropriate Ministers, on an appeal under paragraph 32 above shall be final.

36.—(1) An appeal under paragraph 32 above shall be dealt with on the basis of written representations, unless the person deciding the appeal directs otherwise.

(2) Subject to that, the appropriate Ministers may by regulations make such provision as they think fit about procedure in relation to appeals under paragraph 32 above.

(3) Regulations under sub-paragraph (2) above may, in particular—

(a) make provision for a time limit within which any person entitled to make representations must submit them in writing and any supporting documents,

(b) empower the person deciding an appeal to proceed to a decision taking into account only such written representations and supporting documents as were submitted within the time limit, and

(c) empower the person deciding an appeal, after giving written notice of his intention to do so to the nominated undertaker and the planning authority whose decision is appealed against, to proceed to a decision notwithstanding that no written representations were made within the time limit, if it appears to him that he has sufficient material before him to enable him to reach a decision on the merits of the case.

(4) Regulations under sub-paragraph (2) above may, in relation to such a time limit as is mentioned in sub-paragraph (3)(a) above—

(a) prescribe the time limit in the regulations, or

(b) enable the appropriate Ministers to give directions setting the time limit in a particular case or class of case.

37.—(1) Regulations under paragraph 32 or 36 above may make different provision for different cases.

(2) The power to make regulations under paragraph 32 or 36 above shall be exercisable by statutory instrument which shall be subject to annulment in pursuance of a resolution of either House of Parliament.

Interpretation

38.—(1) In this Schedule—

"building" includes any structure, other than—

(a) anything in the nature of plant or machinery,

(b) any gate, fence, wall or other means of enclosure, or

(c) any tunnel, earthwork or railway track bed,

but does not include anything temporary or, except where forming part of a station and intended for public use, anything underground;

"deemed planning permission" means the planning permission deemed by section 9 above to be granted;

"development" has the same meaning as in the Town and Country Planning Act 1990; and

"permitted development" means development to which the deemed planning permission relates.

(2) In this Schedule—

(a) references to the appropriate Ministers are to the Secretary of State for the Environment and the Secretary of State for Transport and, in relation to the carrying out of any function, are to those Ministers acting jointly, and

(b) references to land within the relevant limits are to land within the limits of deviation for the scheduled works or within the limits of land to be acquired or used.

(3) For the purposes of this Schedule, spoil or top soil is surplus if it is not used for the purposes of any of the works authorised by this Part of this Act.

Section 12

SCHEDULE 7

HERITAGE

Listed buildings and conservation areas

1.—(1) Subject to sub-paragraph (2) below, if a listed building was such a building immediately before 30th September 1994 and is specified in columns (1) and (2) of the following table—

(a) section 7 of the Planning (Listed Buildings and Conservation Areas) Act 1990 (restriction on works affecting listed buildings) shall not apply to works carried out in relation to the building in exercise of the powers conferred by this Part of this Act,

(b) to the extent that a notice issued in relation to the building under section 38(1) of that Act (enforcement) requires the taking of steps which would be rendered ineffective, or substantially ineffective, by works proposed to be carried out in exercise of the powers conferred by this Part of this Act, it shall not have effect or, as the case may be, shall cease to have effect,

(c) no steps may be taken in relation to the building under section 42(1) of that Act (execution of works specified in notice under section 38(1)) which would be rendered ineffective, or substantially ineffective, by such works as are mentioned in paragraph (b) above, and

(d) no works may be executed for the preservation of the building under section 54 of that Act (urgent works to preserve unoccupied listed buildings) which would be rendered ineffective, or substantially ineffective, by such works as are mentioned in paragraph (b) above.

(2) In the case of any building specified in columns (1) and (2) of the following table in relation to which any description of works is specified in column (3) of that table, sub-paragraph (1) above shall have effect as if the references to works carried out in exercise of the powers conferred by this Part of this Act were, so far as concerns works of demolition or alteration (as opposed to extension), to works so carried out which are of a description specified in relation to it in that column.

(3) Paragraphs (a) to (d) of sub-paragraph (1) above shall also apply in relation to a listed building which was not such a building immediately before 30th September 1994.

(4) If a building included in a conservation area and not a listed building—

(a) was not included in a conservation area immediately before 30th September 1994, or

(b) was included in such an area immediately before that date and is specified in columns (1) and (2) of the following table,

section 74 of the Planning (Listed Buildings and Conservation Areas) Act 1990 (control of demolition in conservation areas) shall not apply to the demolition of it in exercise of the powers conferred by this Part of this Act.

(5) Anything which, by virtue of section 1(5) of the Planning (Listed Buildings and Conservation Areas) Act 1990 (objects or structures fixed to, or within the curtilage of, a building), is treated as part of a building for the purposes of that Act shall be treated as part of the building for the purposes of this paragraph.

(6) In this paragraph, "building" and "listed building" have the same meanings as in the Planning (Listed Buildings and Conservation Areas) Act 1990.

THE TABLE

BUILDINGS AUTHORISED TO BE DEMOLISHED

(1) *Area*	(2) *Buildings authorised to be demolished*	(3) *Limit of authorised demolition or alteration*
GREATER LONDON		
London Borough of Camden	St Pancras Station and Chambers comprising trainshed, Chambers and ancillary buildings, including those in the forecourt. Grade I.	Demolition of structures at ground and upper levels to the north and on the west side of the trainshed and alterations and partial demolition elsewhere.

(1) *Area*	(2) *Buildings authorised to be demolished*	(3) *Limit of authorised demolition or alteration*
	Great Northern Hotel, Pancras Road. Grade II.	Partial demolitions and alterations in service yard and remedial alterations elsewhere.
	26 Pancras Road (German Gymnasium). Grade II.	Demolition of entrance, including stairs and passageway, and western hall and alterations and partial demolition elsewhere.
	Kings Cross Station. Grade I.	Demolition of porte cochere and part of west side offices and remedial alterations elsewhere.
	Front boundary wall to Euston Road Fire Brigade Station. Grade II.	
	Flats 1 to 20 Stanley Buildings, Stanley Passage (south side). Grade II.	Demolition of flats 1 to 10 and remedial alterations elsewhere.
	3 linked gas holders, Goods Way (west side). Grade II.	
	Water point north of St Pancras Station. Grade II.	
	Nos. 1 to 11 (odd) Euston Road.	
	Red Star Parcels office, Cheney Road.	
	Former Police buildings, Cheney Road.	
	Former Motorail Terminal, Cheney Road.	
	South Side Buildings, Wellers Court.	
	British Rail Staff Association Clubhouse, 2b Pancras Road.	
	Kings Cross taxi park cafe (temporary building), Pancras Road.	
	22, 24, 28, 30 and 32 Pancras Road.	
	Buildings at 40 Pancras Road.	
	1 to 4 Gas Works Cottages, Battle Bridge Road.	

(1) *Area*	(2) *Buildings authorised to be demolished*	(3) *Limit of authorised demolition or alteration*
	Single unlisted gas holder, associated gas governor and gas supply building and apparatus, Battle Bridge Road.	
	Units 1 to 6, 1 Battle Bridge Road.	
	The Battle Bridge Centre, 2 to 6 Battle Bridge Road.	
	Warehouse, 1 and 2 Goods Way.	
	1 Camley Street.	
	Fuel depot and electricity substation complex, Wharf Road.	
	Railway bridge (No. 8) over Regent's Canal.	
	Railway bridge (No. 6) over Camley Street.	
	Light industrial unit, Camley Street (south of railway bridge No. 6).	
	2 solid waste transfer stations, Camley Street.	
	2 unlisted gas holders, Camley Street (west side).	
	No. 1 Midland Road and railway bridge No. 1, at the junction of Pancras Road and Goods Way.	
	Arches 42 to 47 inclusive, 48 to 54 (even), 58 to 90(a) (even) (east side of Pancras Road) and disused coal drops above.	
	Boundary wall to Neville Close and arches 113–115 (west side of Pancras Road).	
	Walls along the west side of Midland Road, and along the south side of Brill Place, including incorporated structures at ground and upper levels.	

(1) *Area*	(2) *Buildings authorised to be demolished*	(3) *Limit of authorised demolition or alteration*
	Boundary walls and fences to east side of Pancras Road, south of Battle Bridge Road; north side of Clarence Passage; north and south sides of Stanley Passage; east and west side of Cheney Road; north and south sides of Battle Bridge Road; south side of Goods Way; north side of Goods Way, west of the concrete canal bridge; west side of Camley Street, south of the railway bridge; southern section of east side of Camley Street.	
	Any other walls, fences, parapets, bridge inverts, underground structures, plant, machinery and towpath works as required to be demolished to construct the works authorised by this Part of this Act within King's Cross/St Pancras, Regent's Canal, Camden Square and Bartholomew Estate Conservation Areas.	
London Borough of Islington	Caledonian Road and Barnsbury Station Ticket Office.	
COUNTY OF KENT		
Borough of Gravesham, Parish of Cobham	Parish boundary stone, Brewers Road. Grade II.	
Borough of Ashford, Parish of Charing	Brockton, Egerton Road, Charing Heath. Grade II.	
	Weatherboarded barn to the east of Brockton. Grade II.	
Borough of Ashford, Parish of Hothfield	Yonsea, Maidstone Road. Grade II.	
	Oasthouse to the south of Yonsea, Maidstone Road. Grade II.	
	Granary and cartshed to the north west of Yonsea, Maidstone Road. Grade II.	
	Yonsea Bungalow, Maidstone Road. Grade II.	

(1) *Area*	(2) *Buildings authorised to be demolished*	(3) *Limit of authorised demolition or alteration*
	Range of barns 50 metres to the north of Yonsea, Maidstone Road. Grade II.	
	Range of barns 50 metres to the west of Yonsea, Maidstone Road. Grade II.	
Borough of Ashford, Town of Ashford	2 Boys Hall Road. Grade II.	
	4 Boys Hall Road. Grade II.	
District of Shepway, Parish of Sellindge	Railway Cottages (Talbot House). Grade II.	

2.—(1) In the case of a listed building to which sub-paragraph (2) below applies—

(a) section 7 of the Planning (Listed Buildings and Conservation Areas) Act 1990 shall not apply to any works for the alteration or extension of the building which are carried out, in exercise of the powers conferred by this Part of this Act, for the purpose of maintaining or restoring its character as a building of special architectural or historical interest,

(b) to the extent that a notice issued in relation to the building under section 38(1) of that Act requires the taking of steps which would be rendered ineffective, or substantially ineffective, by works proposed to be carried out in exercise of the powers conferred by this Part of this Act, it shall not have effect or, as the case may be, shall cease to have effect,

(c) no steps may be taken in relation to the building under section 42(1) of that Act which would be rendered ineffective, or substantially ineffective, by such works as are mentioned in paragraph (b) above, and

(d) no works may be executed for the preservation of the building under section 54 of that Act which would be rendered ineffective, or substantially ineffective, by such works as are mentioned in paragraph (b) above.

(2) This sub-paragraph applies to a listed building if—

(a) it was not such a building immediately before 30th September 1994, or

(b) it was such a building immediately before that date and is specified in the following table.

(3) Anything which, by virtue of section 1(5) of the Planning (Listed Buildings and Conservation Areas) Act 1990, is treated as part of a building for the purposes of that Act shall be treated as part of the building for the purposes of this paragraph.

(4) In this paragraph, "building" and "listed building" have the same meanings as in the Planning (Listed Buildings and Conservation Areas) Act 1990.

THE TABLE

BUILDINGS AUTHORISED TO BE EXTENDED AND ALTERED

Area	*Building*
GREATER LONDON	
London Borough of Camden	Flats 21–30 Stanley Buildings, Clarence Passage (north side). Grade II.
	Lock Keepers Cottage, Camley Street. Grade II.
	The Granary, York Way. Grade II.
	Gas holder, Goods Way (east side). Grade II.

Area	Building
London Borough of Islington	302–304 Liverpool Road. Grade II.
	1–4 Highbury Place. Grade II.
	Church of St Jude, Mildmay Grove. Grade II.
	111 Mildmay Grove. Grade II.
London Borough of Hackney	Lodge to west entrance of the German Hospital, Ritson Road. Grade II.
	Main block and attached extension to the east of the German Hospital, Ritson Road. Grade II.
	Church of St Luke, Woodbine Terrace. Grade C.
	Mission Hall to the north of St Mary of Eton, Eastway. Grade II.
COUNTY OF ESSEX	
Borough of Thurrock	Barn to north of High House, London Road, Purfleet. Grade II.
COUNTY OF KENT	
Borough of Gravesham, Town of Gravesend	24/25 The Hill (Coach and Horses public house) Northfleet. Grade II.
Borough of Maidstone, Parish of Lenham	Oxley House, Boughton Road. Grade II.
	Old Cottage and Water Street Cottage, Lenham Heath Road. Grade II.
	Yew Tree Cottage, Hook Street, Lenham Heath. Grade II.
Borough of Ashford, Parish of Charing	Rose Cottage, Westwell Leacon. Grade II.
	The Old Parsonage Farmhouse, Maidstone Road. Grade II.
Borough of Ashford, Town of Ashford	Industrial building belonging to Knowles Removals and Storage, Station Road. Grade II.
	Willesborough and District Labour Club, Bentley Road. Grade II.
Borough of Ashford, Parish of Sevington	Orchard Cottage, Church Road. Grade II.
	Nos. 1 and 2 Maytree Cottages, Church Road. Grade II.
	Bridge Cottage, Highfield Lane, Sevington. Grade II.
Borough of Ashford, Parish of Mersham	Bridge House, Church Road. Grade II.
District of Shepway, Parish of Sellindge	Stream Cottage and Grove Bridge Cottage, Barrow Hill. Grade II.

3. Section 59 of the Planning (Listed Buildings and Conservation Areas) Act 1990 (acts causing or likely to result in damage to listed buildings) shall not apply to anything done in exercise of the powers conferred by this Part of this Act with respect to works.

Ancient monuments etc.

4.—(1) This paragraph has effect in relation to the Ancient Monuments and Archaeological Areas Act 1979.

(2) Section 2 (control of works affecting scheduled monuments) shall not apply to any works authorised by this Part of this Act.

(3) The powers of entry conferred by section 6(1) (entry to ascertain condition of scheduled monument), section 6A(1) (entry to enforce control of works affecting scheduled monuments) and section 26 (entry to record matters of archaeological or historical interest) shall not be exercisable in relation to land used for or in connection with the carrying out of any of the works authorised by this Part of this Act.

(4) The provisions of the Act with respect to the functions of a person as a guardian by virtue of the Act, and the provisions of any agreement under section 17 (agreement concerning ancient monuments and land in their vicinity), shall have effect subject to the powers conferred by this Part of this Act with respect to works.

(5) Section 19 (public access to monuments under public control) shall not apply in relation to a monument which is closed by the nominated undertaker for the purposes of, in connection with or in consequence of the carrying out of any of the works authorised by this Part of this Act.

(6) Regulations under section 19(3) or (4A) (which may include provision prohibiting or regulating any act or thing which would tend to injure or disfigure a monument or its amenities or disturb the public in their enjoyment of it) shall not apply to anything done in exercise of the powers conferred by this Part of this Act with respect to works.

(7) The power conferred by section 19(6) (power to refuse admission to monuments under public control) shall not be exercisable so as to prevent or restrict the exercise of the powers conferred by this Part of this Act with respect to works.

(8) In section 25 (treatment of ancient monuments)—

(a) subsection (2) (superintendence by the Historic Buildings and Monuments Commission for England) shall not authorise the superintendence of the carrying out of any of the works authorised by this Part of this Act, and

(b) subsection (3) (power of the Commission to charge for advice under subsection (1)) shall not apply in relation to advice given in connection with the carrying out of any of those works.

(9) Section 28 (offence of damaging certain ancient monuments) shall not apply to anything done in exercise of the powers conferred by this Part of this Act with respect to works.

(10) Section 35 (notice required of operations in areas of archaeological importance) shall not apply to operations carried out in exercise of the powers conferred by this Part of this Act with respect to works.

(11) Section 39(1) (power to investigate in advance of operations notice any site which may be acquired compulsorily) shall have effect as if operations carried out in exercise of the powers conferred by this Part of this Act with respect to works were exempt works for the purposes of that provision.

(12) Section 42(1) (prohibition on use of metal detectors in protected places without consent) shall not apply to the use of a metal detector for the purposes of or in connection with the exercise of the powers conferred by this Part of this Act with respect to works.

(13) Section 42(3) (prohibition on removal without consent of object discovered by use of a metal detector in a protected place) shall not apply to the removal of objects discovered by the use of a metal detector for the purposes of or in connection with the exercise of the powers conferred by this Part of this Act with respect to works.

5.—(1) The power of entry conferred by section 36(1) of the National Heritage Act 1983 (entry to obtain information about ancient monuments and historic buildings for the purposes of the records kept by the Historic Buildings and Monuments Commission for England) shall only be exercisable in relation to land used, or intended for use, for or in connection with the carrying out of any of the works authorised by this Part of this Act with the consent of the nominated undertaker, such consent not to be unreasonably withheld.

(2) Consent for the purposes of sub-paragraph (1) above may be granted subject to compliance with any reasonable requirements or conditions imposed for reasons of safety or for the purpose of preventing interference with or delay to the works.

(3) Section 36(6) of the National Heritage Act 1983 (which, in relation to land on which works are being carried out, regulates the exercise of the right to enter land to obtain information about ancient monuments and historic buildings for the purposes of the records kept by the Historic Buildings and Monuments Commission for England) shall not apply in relation to land on which works authorised by this Part of this Act are being carried out.

(4) Any dispute under this paragraph shall, if the parties agree, be referred to arbitration, but shall otherwise be determined by the appropriate Ministers acting jointly.

(5) In sub-paragraph (4) above, "appropriate Ministers" means—

(a) in relation to a dispute about entry for the purpose of obtaining information about an ancient monument, the Secretary of State for National Heritage and the Secretary of State for Transport, and

(b) in relation to a dispute about entry for the purpose of obtaining information about an historic building, the Secretary of State for the Environment and the Secretary of State for Transport.

(6) In sub-paragraph (5) above, "ancient monument" and "historic building" have the meanings given by section 33(8) of the National Heritage Act 1983.

Section 13

SCHEDULE 8

HERITAGE: RIGHTS OF ENTRY

Historic Buildings and Monuments Commission for England

1.—(1) Any person duly authorised in writing by the Commission may at any reasonable time enter any land on which (or in or under which) a scheduled monument is situated—

(a) for the purpose of observing or advising upon the exercise in relation to the land of any of the powers conferred by paragraph 10(1) of Schedule 2 to this Act, or

(b) for the purpose of inspecting, observing or advising upon the carrying out of any works on the land in exercise of any of the other powers conferred by this Part of this Act.

(2) Any person duly authorised in writing by the Commission may at any reasonable time enter any land in Greater London for the purpose of inspecting or observing the carrying out in relation to any building on the land of any decontrolled works.

(3) The right conferred by sub-paragraph (1) or (2) above shall not be exercisable at a time when the nominated undertaker reasonably considers that it is not safe to exercise it.

(4) A person exercising the right conferred by sub-paragraph (1) or (2) above shall comply with any directions given by the nominated undertaker for the purpose of securing compliance with relevant health and safety provisions.

(5) In this paragraph, "decontrolled works" means works to which section 7 or 74 of the Planning (Listed Buildings and Conservation Areas) Act 1990 would apply, but for paragraph 1(1)(a), (3) or (4) or 2(1)(a) of Schedule 7 to this Act.

Royal Commission on the Historical Monuments of England

2.—(1) The nominated undertaker shall not carry out any decontrolled works consisting of the demolition of a building unless—

(a) notice of the proposal to carry out the works has been given to the Royal Commission, and

(b) the appropriate period since the giving of the notice has elapsed.

(2) Subject to sub-paragraph (3) below, the appropriate period for the purposes of sub-paragraph (1)(b) above is 8 weeks or such longer period as may have been agreed between the nominated undertaker and the Royal Commission.

(3) In case of emergency, the appropriate period for the purposes of sub-paragraph (1)(b) above is such period as is reasonable in the circumstances.

(4) In determining whether the appropriate period for the purposes of sub-paragraph (1)(b) above has elapsed, there shall be disregarded any day on which entry to the building is refused under paragraph 3(2) below.

(5) In this paragraph, "decontrolled works" means works to which section 7 of the Planning (Listed Buildings and Conservation Areas) Act 1990 would apply, but for paragraph 1(1)(a) or (3) of Schedule 7 to this Act.

3.—(1) Following the giving of a notice under paragraph 2(1) above in relation to any building, any person duly authorised in writing by the Royal Commission may, at any reasonable time during the inspection period, enter the building for the purpose of recording it.

(2) The right conferred by sub-paragraph (1) above shall not be exercisable at a time when the nominated undertaker reasonably considers that it is not safe to exercise it.

(3) A person exercising the right conferred by sub-paragraph (1) above shall comply with any directions given by the nominated undertaker for the purpose of securing compliance with relevant health and safety provisions.

(4) For the purposes of sub-paragraph (1) above, the inspection period, in relation to a building which is the subject of a notice under paragraph 2(1) above, is the period beginning when the

notice under that provision is given and ending when the prohibition under that provision ceases to apply to the building.

Interpretation

4. In this Schedule—

"the Commission" means the Historic Buildings and Monuments Commission for England;

"the Royal Commission" means the Royal Commission on the Historical Monuments of England;

"scheduled monument" has the same meaning as in the Ancient Monuments and Archaeological Areas Act 1979.

Section 20

SCHEDULE 9

APPLICATION OF OTHER RAILWAY LEGISLATION

PART I

RAILWAYS CLAUSES ACTS

Railways Clauses Consolidation Act 1845 (c. 20)

1.—(1) The Railways Clauses Consolidation Act 1845, insofar as applicable for the purposes of this Act and not inconsistent with its provisions. is hereby incorporated with this Act.

(2) The following provisions are excepted from incorporation by virtue of sub-paragraph (1) above—

sections 1, 7 to 9, 11 to 15, 17, 19, 20, 22, 23, 42, 47, 48, 59 to 62, 74, 75, 77 to 85, 87, 88, 94, 95 and 112 to 124.

(3) In their application by virtue of sub-paragraph (1) above—

(a) section 2 shall have effect with the substitution for "so incorporated as aforesaid" of "incorporated",

(b) section 6 shall have effect with the omission of the words "and to take lands for that purpose", "taken or" and "for the value of the lands so taken or used, and",

(c) section 16, so far as relating to the erection and construction of new stations, shall only have effect, so far as concerns the railways comprised in the rail link or the accommodation works connected therewith, to authorise the erection and construction of stations at St Pancras in London and Ebbsfleet in Kent,

(d) sections 18 and 21 shall not apply in any case where the relations between the nominated undertaker and any other persons are regulated by sections 84 and 85 of the New Roads and Street Works Act 1991 or Part II of Schedule 15 to this Act,

(e) section 46 shall have effect with the omission of the proviso, and

(f) section 68 shall have effect with the omission of the words from "Such and" to "formation thereof" and from "together with all necessary gates" to "all necessary stiles".

Railways Clauses Act 1863 (c. 92)

2.—(1) Part I of the Railways Clauses Act 1863, insofar as applicable for the purposes of this Act and not inconsistent with its provisions, is hereby incorporated with this Act.

(2) The following provisions are excepted from incorporation by virtue of sub-paragraph (1) above—

sections 5 to 7 and 13 to 19.

PART II

OTHER LEGISLATION

Highway (Railway Crossings) Act 1839 (c. 45)

3. The Highway (Railway Crossings) Act 1839 shall not apply to a railway authorised by this Act.

Railway Regulation Act 1842 (c. 55)

4. Section 9 of the Railway Regulation Act 1842 shall not apply to a railway authorised by this Act.

Regulation of Railways Act 1871 (c. 78)

5. In section 2 of the Regulation of Railways Act 1871, in the definition of the term "railway", the reference to any special Act of Parliament shall be construed as including this Act.

Railway Companies (Accounts and Returns) Act 1911 (c. 34)

6. For the purposes of the Railway Companies (Accounts and Returns) Act 1911, a person shall not be a railway company by virtue of working a railway authorised by this Act.

British Transport Commission Act 1949 (c. xxix)

7.—(1) This paragraph has effect in relation to the British Transport Commission Act 1949.

(2) Section 55 (penalty for trespass on railways etc.) shall apply in relation to any railway, siding, tunnel, railway embankment, cutting or similar work comprised in the rail link as it applies in relation to any railway, siding, tunnel, railway embankment, cutting or similar work belonging to the British Railways Board.

(3) Section 56 (penalty for stone throwing etc. on railways) shall apply in relation to any railway or siding comprised in the rail link as it applies in relation to any railway or siding belonging to the British Railways Board.

Miscellaneous

8.—(1) In their application to—

(a) a rail link undertaker,

(b) the rail link, or

(c) any train of a rail link undertaker being used to provide services for the carriage of passengers or goods involving travel through the Channel Tunnel,

the enactments specified in column (1) of the following table (which create the offences broadly described in column (2) of the table) shall each have effect as if the maximum fine which may be imposed on summary conviction of any offence specified in the enactment were, instead of that specified in column (3) of the table, a fine not exceeding the level specified in column (4) of the table.

THE TABLE

(1) *Enactment*	(2) *Description of offence*	(3) *Maximum otherwise applicable (level on standard scale)*	(4) *Maximum fine (level on standard scale)*
Section 16 of the Railway Regulation Act 1840.	Obstruction of officers of railway company or trespass upon railway.	Level 1	Level 3
Section 17 of the Railway Regulation Act 1842.	Misconduct of persons employed on railways.	Level 1	Level 3
Section 22 of the Regulation of Railways Act 1868.	Provision and improper use of means of communication.	Level 1	Level 2
The Regulation of Railways Act 1889—			
section 5(1).	Failure to produce ticket, to pay fare or to give name and address.	Level 1	Level 2
section 5(3).	Travel with intent to avoid payment of fare.	Level 2	Level 3

(2) In such application—

(a) section 16 of the Railway Regulation Act 1840 shall have effect as if the court had, as an alternative to imposing a fine, the power to award imprisonment for a period not exceeding one month; and

(b) section 17 of the Railway Regulation Act 1842 shall have effect as if, instead of the power to award imprisonment for a period not exceeding two months, the court had power to award imprisonment for a period not exceeding three months; and

(c) section 5(2) of the Regulation of Railways Act 1889 (power to arrest passenger who fails to produce ticket and refuses to give his name and address) shall have effect as if after the word "refuses" there were inserted the words "or fails".

Section 38 SCHEDULE 10

DISAPPLICATION AND MODIFICATION OF MISCELLANEOUS CONTROLS

Ecclesiastical law

1.—(1) No obligation or restriction imposed under ecclesiastical law or otherwise in relation to consecrated land shall have effect to prohibit, restrict or impose any condition on the exercise of the powers conferred by this Part of this Act with respect to works.

(2) Sub-paragraph (1) above shall not apply in relation to the use of land comprised in a burial ground for the purpose of constructing any of the works authorised by this Part of this Act.

Overground wires

2. Nothing in the London Overground Wires &c. Act 1933, or in any byelaw made under that Act, shall extend or apply to any wire or part of a wire erected or placed, proposed to be erected or placed, or for the time being maintained, by the nominated undertaker in exercise of the powers conferred by this Part of this Act.

London Building Acts (Amendment) Act 1939

3.—(1) This paragraph has effect in relation to the London Building Acts (Amendment) Act 1939.

(2) The following provisions, namely—

(a) Part III (construction of buildings and structures generally),

(b) Part IV (construction of special and temporary buildings and structures), and

(c) Part V (means of escape in case of fire),

shall not apply to anything held by the Secretary of State or the nominated undertaker and used, or intended for use, by the nominated undertaker for the purposes of its undertaking under this Part of this Act.

(3) Sub-paragraph (2) above shall not apply in relation to a building which is a house or a hotel or which is used as offices or showrooms and does not form part of a railway station.

(4) No notice under section 45(1)(a) or (b) (notice before building at junction with adjoining land) shall be required before the building of any wall in exercise of the powers conferred by this Part of this Act.

(5) Sections 45(1)(c) and 46 (rights of adjoining owners) shall not have effect to confer rights in relation to—

(a) anything held by the Secretary of State or the nominated undertaker and used, or intended for use, by the nominated undertaker for the purposes of its undertaking under this Part of this Act, or

(b) land on which there is any such thing.

(6) Section 50 (underpinning of adjoining buildings) shall not apply in relation to a proposal to erect anything in exercise of the powers conferred by this Part of this Act.

Coast works

4. The following provisions of the Coast Protection Act 1949, namely—

(a) section 16(1) (consent of coast protection authority required for carrying out coast protection work),

(b) section 18(1) (prohibition of excavation or removal of materials from seashore), and

(c) section 34(1) (consent of Secretary of State required for works detrimental to navigation), shall not apply in relation to anything done within the limits of deviation for the scheduled works in exercise of the powers conferred by this Part of this Act in relation to those works, or any work in connection with them.

Highways etc.

5.—(1) The following enactments, namely—

(a) section 15(1) of the Greater London Council (General Powers) Act 1970, and

(b) section 169(1) of the Highways Act 1980,

(which control obstructions of the highway in connection with works related to buildings) shall not apply to anything erected, placed or retained in, upon or over a highway for the purposes of or in connection with the exercise of any of the powers conferred by this Part of this Act with respect to works.

(2) Section 141 of the Highways Act 1980 (restriction on planting trees or shrubs in or near carriageway) shall not apply to any tree or shrub planted for the purposes of or in connection with the exercise of any of the powers conferred by this Part of this Act with respect to works.

(3) Section 167 of the Highways Act 1980 (powers relating to retaining walls near streets) shall not apply to any length of a retaining wall erected on land held by the Secretary of State or the nominated undertaker and used, or intended for use, by the nominated undertaker for the purposes of its undertaking under this Part of this Act.

(4) Nothing in section 8(2) to (5) of the Greater London Council (General Powers) Act 1986 (powers of borough councils in relation to retaining walls supporting the carriageway or footway of certain highways) shall apply with respect to any retaining wall erected in exercise of the powers conferred by this Part of this Act.

Areas of special scientific interest

6. Sections 28(5) and 29(3) of the Wildlife and Countryside Act 1981 (which restrict, in relation to areas of special scientific interest, the carrying out of operations likely to damage the special flora, fauna or features) shall not apply to any operation carried out for the purposes of or in connection with the exercise of any of the powers conferred by this Part of this Act with respect to works.

Building regulations

7.—(1) Nothing in Part I of the Building Act 1984 with respect to building regulations, and nothing in any building regulations, shall apply in relation to a building held by the Secretary of State or the nominated undertaker and used, or intended for use, by the nominated undertaker for the purposes of its undertaking under this Part of this Act.

(2) Sub-paragraph (1) above shall not apply in relation to a building which is a house or a hotel or which is used as offices or showrooms and does not form part of a railway station.

(3) Any building to which sub-paragraph (2) above applies shall be disregarded for the purposes of section 4(1)(b) of the Building Act 1984 (exception for certain buildings belonging to statutory undertakers).

Deposits in the sea

8.—(1) Section 5 of the Food and Environment Protection Act 1985 (requirement of licences for deposit of substances and articles in the sea etc.) shall not apply to the deposit of substances and articles within the limits of deviation for Work No. 10, 10R(2), 13 or 22J in exercise of the powers conferred by this Part of this Act in relation to that work, or any work in connection with it.

(2) In the case of substances and articles which have been excavated or dredged, sub-paragraph (1) above shall only apply to deposit in the course of use as a construction material.

London lorries: general

9.—(1) This paragraph applies where an application for the issue of a permit under the London Lorry Ban Order is made under paragraph 10 below or is otherwise expressed to be made in connection with the carrying out of authorised works.

(2) The application shall be granted if the issue of a permit is reasonably required—

(a) for the purpose of enabling authorised works to be carried out in a timely and efficient manner, or

(b) for the purpose of enabling authorised works to be carried out in accordance with approved arrangements.

(3) If the application is granted, no condition may be imposed which is likely to obstruct the carrying out of authorised works—

(a) in a timely and efficient manner, or
(b) in accordance with approved arrangements.

(4) If the applicant is aggrieved by a decision under sub-paragraph (2) or (3) above, he may appeal to the Secretary of State by giving notice in writing of the appeal to him and the authority whose decision is appealed against within 28 days of notification of the decision.

(5) On an appeal under sub-paragraph (4) above, the Secretary of State may allow or dismiss the appeal or vary the decision of the authority whose decision is appealed against.

(6) If on an appeal under sub-paragraph (4) above against a decision under sub-paragraph (3) above the Secretary of State varies the decision, the variation shall have effect from and including the date on which the appeal was constituted or such later date as the Secretary of State may specify.

(7) The applicant may not challenge a decision under sub-paragraph (3) above otherwise than by an appeal under sub-paragraph (4) above.

(8) In this paragraph—

"approved arrangements" means arrangements approved for the purposes of any of the following provisions of Schedule 6 to this Act—
(a) paragraph 7, so far as relating to item 1 or 6 in the table in that paragraph,
(b) paragraph 16, so far as relating to item 5 in the table in that paragraph,
(c) paragraph 23, so far as relating to item 5 in the table in that paragraph, and
(d) paragraph 25;

"authorised works" means works authorised by this Part of this Act; and

"the London Lorry Ban Order" means the Greater London (Restriction of Goods Vehicles) Traffic Order 1985.

London lorries: emergency permits

10.—(1) This paragraph applies where a person proposes to undertake a journey before the end of the next complete eight working days, being a journey—
(a) proposed to be undertaken in connection with the carrying out of authorised works, and
(b) for which a permit under the London Lorry Ban Order will be required.

(2) The person may apply for a permit under the Order for the journey by giving the details mentioned in sub-paragraph (3) below to the authority concerned by telephone or by means of facsimile transmission.

(3) The details referred to above are—
(a) the identity of the applicant,
(b) a number on which he can be contacted by telephone or by means of facsimile transmission,
(c) the registration number of the vehicle to which the application relates,
(d) the authorised works in connection with which the journey is to be undertaken,
(e) whether any approved arrangements are relevant to the application, and, if so, what they are,
(f) the date when the journey is proposed to be undertaken,
(g) if it is proposed to stop anywhere in Greater London for the purpose of making a delivery or collection, the place or places at which, and the time or times when, it is proposed to stop for that purpose.

(4) In this paragraph—

"approved arrangements", "authorised works" and "the London Lorry Ban Order" have the same meanings as in paragraph 9 above; and

"working day" means any day which is not a Saturday or Sunday, Christmas Day, Good Friday or a bank holiday in England and Wales under the Banking and Financial Dealings Act 1971.

11.—(1) An authority responsible for dealing with applications for permits under the London Lorry Ban Order shall make arrangements enabling applications under paragraph 10 above to be made at any time.

(2) Once an application for a permit has been made under paragraph 10 above, then, for the purpose of any relevant journey, the application shall be treated as granted subject to such conditions as the Secretary of State may by order specify for the purposes of this provision.

(3) A journey is a relevant journey for the purposes of sub-paragraph (2) above if it is begun before the authority to which the application is made has communicated its decision on the application to the applicant by telephone or by means of facsimile transmission.

(4) If an application under paragraph 10 above has been granted, or is treated as granted, then, while the vehicle concerned is undertaking a journey covered by the application, paragraph 4 of the London Lorry Ban Order and of the Westminster Lorry Ban Order shall have effect in relation to it with the substitution for paragraph (a) of—

"(a) in relation to any goods vehicle being driven by any person in a restricted street during the prescribed hours in respect of which an application under paragraph 10 of Schedule 10 to the Channel Tunnel Rail Link Act 1996 has been granted, or is treated as granted, provided that any conditions subject to which the application is granted, or treated as granted, are complied with; or".

(5) The power to make an order under sub-paragraph (2) above includes—

(a) power to make different provision for different cases, and

(b) power to make an order varying or revoking any order previously made under that provision.

(6) In this paragraph—

"the London Lorry Ban Order" has the same meaning as in paragraph 9 above; and

"the Westminster Lorry Ban Order" means the City of Westminster (Restriction of Goods Vehicles) Traffic Order 1992.

Works under streets in Greater London

12. The following provisions of the Greater London Council (General Powers) Act 1986, namely—

(a) section 5(1) (consent of borough council required for demolition of works under a street),

(b) section 6(1) (consent of borough council required for works preventing access to premises under a street), and

(c) section 7(1) (consent of borough council required for infilling in premises under a street),

shall not apply to anything done in exercise of the powers conferred by this Part of this Act with respect to works.

Communication with public sewers in London

13. Section 106(8) of the Water Industry Act 1991 (which qualifies the general right to communicate with the public sewers of a sewerage undertaker) shall not apply where the proposed communication involves a drain or sewer serving the rail link.

Section 39

SCHEDULE 11

Burial Grounds: Removal of Human Remains and Monuments

Notice of removal

1.—(1) Before removing from the land in question any remains or any monument to the deceased, the nominated undertaker shall—

(a) publish in each of two successive weeks in a newspaper circulating in the area where the land is situated, and

(b) at the same time leave displayed in a conspicuous place on or near the land,

a notice complying with sub-paragraph (2) below.

(2) A notice under sub-paragraph (1) above shall—

(a) identify the land to which it relates,

(b) set out in general terms the effect of paragraphs 2 to 5 below,

(c) state where, and in what form, an application under paragraph 2(1) below may be made, and

(d) state how the nominated undertaker proposes to carry out its functions under this Schedule with respect to the disposal of the remains or monument.

(3) No notice shall be required under sub-paragraph (1) above before the removal of any remains or any monument to the deceased where the Secretary of State notifies the nominated undertaker that he is satisfied—

(a) that the remains were interred more than 100 years ago, and

(b) that no relative or personal representative of the deceased is likely to object to the remains or monument being removed in accordance with this Schedule.

(4) No notice shall be required under sub-paragraph (1) above before the removal of any remains or any monument to the deceased if—

(a) there is in force under section 25 of the Burial Act 1857 (bodies not to be removed from burial grounds without licence of the Secretary of State) a licence relating to the remains, and

(b) the holder of the licence is the nominated undertaker or a body corporate which is a member of the same group as the nominated undertaker.

(5) In sub-paragraph (4)(b) above, "group" means a body corporate and all other bodies corporate which are its subsidiaries within the meaning of the Companies Act 1985.

Removal of remains

2.—(1) In the case of remains in relation to which paragraph 1(1) above applies, the nominated undertaker shall issue a licence for the removal of the remains if—

(a) it receives an application in writing from a relative or personal representative of the deceased, and
(b) the application is received before the end of 56 days after the day on which notice relating to the remains is first published under paragraph (a) of that provision.

(2) In the case of remains in relation to which paragraph 1(3) above applies, the nominated undertaker shall issue a licence for the removal of the remains if—

(a) it receives an application in writing from a relative or personal representative of the deceased, and
(b) the application is received before the nominated undertaker has removed the remains under paragraph 3(1) below.

(3) For the purposes of sub-paragraphs (1) and (2) above, a person shall be taken to be a relative or personal representative of the deceased if the nominated undertaker is satisfied that he is or the county court has declared that he is.

(4) A licensee under this paragraph may remove the remains to which the licence relates and reinter them elsewhere or cremate them.

(5) The reasonable costs of removal and reinterment or cremation under this paragraph shall be paid by the nominated undertaker.

(6) An application for a declaration for the purposes of sub-paragraph (3) above shall be made to the county court for the district in which the remains are interred.

(7) In this paragraph, references to a relative of the deceased are to a person who—

(a) is a husband, wife, parent, grandparent, child or grandchild of the deceased, or
(b) is, or is a child of, a brother, sister, uncle or aunt of the deceased.

3.—(1) In the case of remains in relation to which paragraph 1(1) or (3) above applies, the nominated undertaker may remove the remains unless—

(a) it is required under paragraph 2(1) or (2) above to issue a licence for their removal, or
(b) not more than 28 days have passed since the issue under that provision of such a licence.

(2) In the case of remains in relation to which paragraph 1(4) above applies, the nominated undertaker may remove the remains and, if it does so, shall be treated for the purposes of this Act as acting under this paragraph and not under the licence under the Burial Act 1857.

(3) The nominated undertaker shall reinter any remains removed under this paragraph in a burial ground or cremate them in a crematorium.

Removal of monuments

4.—(1) Where a licence to remove any remains is issued under paragraph 2(1) or (2) above, the licensee may remove from the land any monument to the deceased and re-erect it elsewhere or otherwise dispose of it.

(2) The reasonable costs of removal and re-erection under sub-paragraph (1) above shall be paid by the nominated undertaker.

5.—(1) Where the nominated undertaker removes any remains under paragraph 3 above, it may also remove from the land any monument to the deceased.

(2) Where any remains are removed under a licence under paragraph 2(1) or (2) above, the nominated undertaker may remove from the land any monument to the deceased which is not removed by the licensee within 28 days of the issue of the licence.

(3) Where any remains are removed under a licence under section 25 of the Burial Act 1857, the nominated undertaker may remove from the land any monument to the deceased which is not removed by the licensee.

(4) The nominated undertaker may remove any monument removed under this paragraph to the place, if any, where the remains of the deceased are interred or to some other appropriate place.

(5) The nominated undertaker shall break and deface any monument removed under this paragraph which is not dealt with under sub-paragraph (4) above.

Records

6.—(1) Where any remains are removed under this Schedule, the nominated undertaker shall, within two months of the removal, provide the Registrar General with a certificate which—

(a) identifies the remains, so far as practicable,
(b) states the date on which, and the place from which, the remains were removed, and
(c) states the date and place of reinterment or cremation.

(2) Where any monument is removed under this Schedule, the nominated undertaker shall, within two months of the removal—

(a) deposit with the local authority in whose area the monument was situated prior to the removal a record which—

(i) identifies the monument,

(ii) gives any inscription on it,

(iii) states the date on which and the place from which it was removed, and

(iv) states the place, if any, to which it was moved or how it was disposed of,

and

(b) provide the Registrar General with a copy of the record deposited under paragraph (a) above.

(3) The nominated undertaker may require any person who removes remains or a monument under this Schedule to provide it with any information about the remains or monument removed which it needs to comply with sub-paragraph (1) or (2) above.

(4) In sub-paragraph (2)(a) above, "local authority" means a district or London borough council or the Common Council of the City of London.

Supplementary

7.—(1) Where the nominated undertaker removes remains in relation to the removal of which a licence has been granted under paragraph 2(1) or (2) above, it shall carry out in accordance with the reasonable requests of the licensee—

(a) its functions under paragraph 3 above with respect to disposal of the remains, and

(b) if it removes any monument to the deceased, its functions under paragraph 5 above with respect to disposal of the monument.

(2) The Secretary of State may give such directions as he thinks fit with respect to the carrying out of any function under this Schedule.

(3) No licence shall be required under section 25 of the Burial Act 1857 for the removal under this Schedule of any remains.

(4) Nothing in any enactment relating to burial grounds and no obligation or restriction imposed under ecclesiastical law or otherwise shall have effect to prohibit, restrict or impose any condition on the removal under this Schedule of any remains or monument.

Section 44

SCHEDULE 12

THE A2 AND M2 IMPROVEMENT WORKS

PART I

THE AUTHORISED WORKS

Description of works

1. The works which the Secretary of State is authorised by section 44 of this Act to construct are the following—

In the county of Kent—

In the borough of Gravesham, parishes of Cobham, Higham and Shorne—

Work No. 31—Improvement of the A2 between its junction with Halfpence Lane (C492) and its junction with the M2 at Junction 1, comprising—

Work No. 31A—Improvement and realignment of the eastbound carriageway of the A2 commencing at a point 115 metres east of the bridge carrying Brewers Road over that road, passing eastwards and terminating at a point 100 metres west of the bridge carrying the westbound slip road of the A2 over the M2 at Junction 1;

Work No. 31B—Improvement and realignment of the westbound carriageway of the A2 commencing at a point 340 metres west of the said bridge carrying Brewers Road over that road, passing eastwards and terminating at a point 220 metres west of the bridge carrying the said westbound slip road over that road;

Work No. 32—Improvement of the junction of Halfpence Lane (C492) and Brewers Road with the A2 at Cobham Junction, comprising—

Work No. 32A—A road, forming an entry slip road to the eastbound carriageway of the A2 (Work No. 31A), commencing by a junction with Brewers Road at a point 150 metres north-east of the north-eastern abutment of the bridge carrying that road over the A2, passing southwards and terminating by a junction with that carriageway at a point 410 metres east of that bridge;

Work No. 32B—A road, forming an exit slip road from the westbound carriageway of the A2 (Work No. 31B), commencing by a junction with the C492 at a point 150 metres south-west of the existing junction of Brewers Road with that road, passing northwards, then north-eastwards over the railway (Work No. 12) in tunnel, and terminating by a junction with that carriageway at a point 20 metres west of the said bridge over the A2, including a roundabout at the junction of the slip road with Brewers Road (Work No. 32C);

Work No. 32C—A road, forming an entry slip road to the westbound carriageway of the A2 from the C492 commencing at a point 30 metres south-east of that carriageway, passing southwards over the railway (Work No. 12), passing eastwards through the roundabout (part of Work No. 32B) along Brewers Road and terminating at a point 160 metres west of the said roundabout, including a bridge over Work No. 12;

In the borough of Gravesham, parishes of Cobham, Higham and Shorne, and in the city of Rochester-upon-Medway, town of Rochester and parish of Cuxton—

Work No. 33—Improvement of the M2 between Junction 1 and Junction 2, comprising—

Work No. 33A—Improvement and realignment of the M2 to form the eastbound carriageway of the motorway, commencing by a junction with Work No. 31A at its termination, passing south-eastwards under the A2 (Work No. 35A) at Junction 1 of the M2, over the existing subway by which footpath NS 183 passes under the M2, then over the road (Work No. 36E) and under Rochester Road (Work No. 36F) and the cycle track (Work No. 36G), over the London and Chatham Railway and terminating on the existing bridge carrying the M2 over that railway at a point 20 metres south-east of that railway, including a bridge over Work No. 36E;

Work No. 33B—A road, forming the westbound carriageway of the M2, commencing by a junction with Work No. 31B at its termination, passing south-eastwards under the A2 (Work No. 35A) at Junction 1 of the M2, over footpath NS 183, then over Work No. 36E and under Work No. 36F and Work No. 36G, over the London and Chatham railway and terminating at a point 180 metres south-east of that railway, including bridges over Work No. 36E and the said railway and extension of the subway for the footpath NS 183;

Work No. 34—Improvement of Junction 1 of the M2 comprising—

Work No. 34A—A road, forming the exit slip road from the eastbound carriageway of the A2, commencing by a junction with that carriageway (Work No. 31A) at a point 210 metres west of the existing bridge carrying the footpath between Park Pale and the Rochester and Cobham Park Golf Course, passing eastwards and terminating in the A2 at a point 20 metres east of the junction of Crutches Lane with that road;

Work No. 34B—A road, forming the entry slip road to the eastbound carriageway of the M2, commencing at a point on the northern side of Old Watling Street 270 metres east of its junction with Bowesden Lane and terminating in the M2 (Work No. 33A) at a point 30 metres north-west of the bridge carrying the A2 (Work No. 35A) over the M2;

Work No. 34C—A road, forming the exit slip road from the westbound carriageway of the M2, commencing in the intended eastbound entry slip road to the Wainscott Northern Bypass at a point 435 metres east of the bridge carrying the said footpath between Park Pale and the Rochester and Cobham Park Golf Course over the M2 and terminating in the M2 (Work No. 33B) at a point 190 metres from that commencement;

Work No. 35—Roads between the junction of the A2 and Halfpence Lane (C492) and Junction 1 of the M2, comprising—

Work No. 35A—Diversion of the A2 at Junction 1 commencing in the westbound carriageway of the A2 (Work No. 31B) at a point 660 metres east of the existing bridge carrying Brewers Road over the A2, passing eastwards on the southern side of the A2, then north-eastwards over the M2 (Works Nos. 33A and 33B) on the northern side of the existing bridge carrying the westbound slip road from the A2 over the M2, continuing eastwards and terminating in the westbound carriageway of the A2 at a point 20 metres east of the junction of Crutches Lane with that road, including bridges over Works Nos. 33A and 33B;

Work No. 35B—A road, forming a diversion of the access road to the Colewood Reservoirs of Southern Water Services Limited, commencing by a junction with the new road (Work No. 35A) at a point 230 metres west of the junction of the existing access road with the A2, passing southwards then eastwards and terminating by a junction with the existing access on the northern side of those reservoirs;

Work No. 36—Improvement of Junction 2 of the M2, comprising—

Work No. 36A—A road, forming the exit slip road from the eastbound carriageway of the M2 (Work No. 33A) at Junction 2, commencing by a junction with that carriageway at a point 550 metres north-west of the existing subway by which the footpath RS 203 passes under the M2, passing south-eastwards and terminating at the eastern junction roundabout (part of Work No. 36E);

Work No. 36B—A road, forming the entry slip road to the eastbound carriageway of the M2 (Work No. 33A) at Junction 2, commencing at the said eastern junction roundabout (part of Work No. 36E), passing southwards under Rochester Road (Work No. 36F) and the cycle track (Work No. 36G), over the London and Chatham Railway and terminating by a junction with Work No. 33A at its termination;

Work No. 36C—A road, forming the entry slip road on to the westbound carriageway of the M2 (Work No. 33B) at Junction 2, commencing by a junction with that carriageway at a point 590 metres north-west of the southern end of the said existing subway, passing south-eastwards under the railway (Work No. 13) and terminating at the western junction roundabout (part of Work No. 36E);

Work No. 36D—A road, forming the exit slip road from the westbound carriageway of the M2 (Work No. 33B) at Junction 2, commencing at the western junction roundabout (part of Work No. 36E), passing south-eastwards under the railway (Work No. 13), under Rochester Road (Work No. 36F) and the cycle track (Work No. 36G) and over the London and Chatham Railway and terminating by a junction with the westbound carriageway (Work No. 37B) at a point 160 metres south-east of that railway, including a bridge over the London and Chatham Railway;

Work No. 36E—A road, forming dual carriageways, commencing by junctions with Work No. 36A at its termination and Work No. 36B at its commencement at the eastern junction roundabout, the centre of which is at a point 180 metres south of the junction of Bootham Close with Rushdean Road, passing south-westwards under the M2 (Works Nos. 33A and 33B) and the railway (Work No. 13) to junctions with Work No. 36C at its termination and Work No. 36D at its commencement at the western junction roundabout, the centre of which is at a point 355 metres south-west of the junction of Bootham Close with Rushdean Road, then passing southwards and terminating by a junction with the A228 (Rochester Road) (Work No. 38F) at a roundabout, the centre of which is at a point 190 metres north-east of the northern end of the existing bridge carrying the A228 over the London and Chatham Railway, including those roundabouts;

Work No. 36F—A road, being a diversion of the A228, commencing in that road at the northern end of the said bridge carrying that road over the London and Chatham Railway, passing north-eastwards over the cycle track (Work No. 36H) to the roundabout (part of Work No. 36E), then north-eastwards over the railway (Work No. 13) and the M2 (Works Nos. 36B, 33A, 33B and 36D), over the cycle track (Work No. 36J) and terminating in the A228 at a point 30 metres south-west of the junction of Roman Way with that road, including bridges over Works Nos. 13, 33A, 33B, 36B, 36D 36H and 36J;

Work No. 36G—A cycle track on the southern side of the A228 (Work No. 36F) commencing by a junction with that work at a point 45 metres north-east of its commencement, passing north-eastwards on the eastern side of Work No. 36F to a junction with the cycle track (Work No. 36H), then over Work No. 13, the M2 and Work No. 36J and terminating by a junction with the A228 at a point 370 metres south-west of the termination of Work No. 36F;

Work No. 36H—A cycle track commencing by a junction with the A228 (Work No. 36F) at a point 60 metres north-east of its commencement, passing northwards then eastwards and south-eastwards under the A228 and terminating by a junction with Work No. 36G at a point 90 metres north-east of the commencement of that work;

Work No. 36J—A cycle track commencing by a junction with the A228 (Work No. 36F) at a point 370 metres south-west of its termination, passing westwards then southwards under the A228 and terminating by a junction with the cycle track (Work No. 36K) at a point 180 metres north-east of the termination of that work;

Work No. 36K—Realignment and improvement of the cycle track between the A228 and the bridge carrying the M2 over the River Medway, commencing by a junction with the cycle track (Work No. 36G) at a point 45 metres south-west of its termination, passing southwards to a junction with the cycle track (Work No. 36J), then south-westwards and south-eastwards and terminating by a junction with the existing cycle track at a point 5 metres south-east of the western abutment of the bridge carrying the M2 over the London and Chatham Railway;

In the city of Rochester-upon-Medway, town of Rochester and parish of Cuxton, and in the borough of Tonbridge and Malling, parishes of Wouldham and Aylesford—

Work No. 37—Improvement of the M2 between Junctions 2 and 3, comprising—

Work No. 37A—Improvement and realignment of the M2 to form the eastbound carriageway of the motorway, commencing by a junction with Work No. 33A at its termination, passing south-eastwards on the existing viaduct over the Strood and Maidstone Railway and the River Medway, then over Wouldham Road (Work No. 38B) and under Work No. 38F, then continuing south-eastwards to Junction 3 (Work No. 39), under the A229 (Work No. 40A) east of Buckmore Park, the new roundabout (Work No. 39E) and Robin Hood Lane (Work No. 41C) and over footpath MR 440 and terminating at a point 145 metres south-west of the junction of Woodbury Road with Walderslade Woods, including a bridge over Work No. 38B;

Work No. 37B—A road, forming the westbound carriageway of the M2, commencing by a junction with Work No. 33B at its termination, passing south-eastwards on viaduct over the Strood and Maidstone Railway and the River Medway, then over Work No. 38B and under Work No. 38F, then continuing south-eastwards to Junction 3 (Work No. 39), under Works Nos. 40A, 39E and 41C and over footpath MR 440 and terminating at a point 205 metres south of the junction of Woodbury Road with Walderslade Woods, including the said viaduct and a bridge over Work No. 38B and extension of the underpass for the said footpath;

Work No. 38—Roads between Junctions 2 and 3 of the M2, comprising—

Work No. 38A—A road, for construction purposes, commencing at a point 300 metres north-west of the western abutment of the bridge carrying the M2 over Wouldham Road (Work No. 38B), passing south-eastwards on the northern side of Work No. 37A and terminating by a junction with Work No. 38B at a point 30 metres north-west of the M2 eastbound carriageway;

Work No. 38B—Realignment of Wouldham Road commencing in that road at a point 20 metres north-east of the northern side of the existing bridge carrying the M2 over that road, passing south-westwards under Works Nos. 37A and 37B and terminating in Wouldham Road at a point 35 metres north-east of the junction of Burham Road with that road;

Work No. 38C—A road, forming a diversion of Nashenden Farm Lane and the access to Waterworks Cottages, commencing by a junction with Wouldham Road (Work No. 38B) at a point 110 metres south-west of its commencement, passing south-eastwards on the southern side of the M2 to a junction with Nashenden Farm Lane at a point 65 metres north-east of the access to Nashenden Farm Cottages, continuing southwards and terminating at a point 20 metres south-east of the entrance to Waterworks Cottages;

Work No. 38D—A road, for construction purposes, forming a diversion of the access to Nashenden Farm and Borstal Court Farm, commencing in Burham Road (Work No. 13B) at a point 100 metres south-east of the commencement of that work, passing eastwards, then south-eastwards on the southern side of Work No. 38C and terminating by a junction with the new road (Work No. 38C) at a point 225 metres from the commencement of that work;

Work No. 38E—A road, forming a diversion of the access track from the Roman Burial grounds to Stony Lane, commencing at a point 30 metres north of the existing bridge carrying that track over the M2, passing south-eastwards and terminating by a junction with Stony Lane (Work No. 38F) at a point 325 metres from its commencement;

Work No. 38F—A road, forming a diversion of bridleway MR11 (Stony Lane) commencing in Maidstone Road at its junction with Stony Lane, passing south-westwards and north-westwards, then south-westwards over the M2 (Works Nos. 37A and 37B) then southwards and terminating by a junction with the new access road (Work No. 13C) at a point 340 metres north-west of the western end of the subway by which Stony Lane passes under the M2, including a bridge over Works Nos. 37A and 37B;

Work No. 39—Improvements of the M2 at Junction 3, comprising—

Work No. 39A—Realignment of the exit slip road from the eastbound carriageway of the M2 (Work No. 37A), commencing by a junction with Work No. 37A at a point

185 metres south of the access from Rochester Road to the caravan site on the south side of Rochester Airport, passing south-eastwards under the A229 (Work No. 40A) and terminating at the north-eastern end of the roundabout (Work No. 39E);

Work No. 39B—Realignment of the entry slip road to the eastbound carriageway of the M2 (Work No. 37A), commencing at the north-eastern end of the roundabout (Work No. 39E), passing southwards under Robin Hood Lane (Work No. 41C), over footpath MR 440 and terminating by a junction with Work No. 37A at a point 145 metres south-west of the junction of Woodbury Road with Walderslade Woods;

Work No. 39C—A road, forming the entry slip road to the westbound carriageway of the M2 (Work No. 37B), commencing by a junction with Work No. 37B at a point 230 metres south of the access from Rochester Road to the said caravan site, passing south-eastwards under the A229 (Work No. 40A) and terminating at the south-western end of the roundabout (Work No. 39E);

Work No. 39D—A road, forming the exit slip road from the westbound carriageway of the M2 (Work No. 37B), commencing at the south-western end of the roundabout (Work No. 39E), passing south-eastwards under Robin Hood Lane (Work No. 41C), over footpath MR 440 and terminating by a junction with Work No. 37B at a point 205 metres west of the junction of Woodbury Road with Walderslade Woods;

Work No. 39E—Improvement of the Taddington Wood Loop Junction, forming a new roundabout over the M2 (Works Nos. 37A and 37B) including two bridges over those works;

Work No. 39F—A road commencing at the north-eastern end of the roundabout (Work No. 39E), passing eastwards and terminating by a junction with Walderslade Woods (Work No. 39G) at the Walderslade Woods Roundabout, the centre of which is 160 metres south of the junction of Hurst Hill with Taddington Wood Lane, including the said Walderslade Woods Roundabout;

Work No. 39G—Realignment of Walderslade Woods, forming dual carriageways, commencing at a point 140 metres south-east of the junction of that road with Taddington Wood Lane, passing south-eastwards to the roundabout (part of Work No. 39F) then continuing south-eastwards and terminating in Walderslade Woods at a point 310 metres from that commencement;

Work No. 39H—A road, forming dual carriageways, commencing at the south-western end of the roundabout (Work No. 39E), passing westwards and north-westwards and terminating by a junction with the A229 at the roundabout (Work No. 40N);

Work No. 39J—Realignment of Maidstone Road to form a junction with the new road (Work No. 39H) at Blue Bell Hill, commencing in that road at a point 40 metres north-west of its existing junction with Victoria Close, passing south-eastwards, then southwards to the junction with Work No. 39H, then continuing southwards and south-westwards and terminating in Maidstone Road at a point 120 metres north of its junction with Robin Hood Lane;

Work No. 40—Improvements of the A229 at Junction 3 of the M2, comprising—

Work No. 40A—Improvement and realignment of the A229 (Maidstone Road), forming dual carriageways, commencing at a point 345 metres north of the existing Bridgewood Roundabout at the junction of that road with Walderslade Woods and Rochester Road, passing southwards over the new roundabout at that road junction (Work No. 40F), the M2 (Works Nos. 37A, 37B, 39A and 39C), then under the roundabout (Work No. 40N) and terminating at a point 10 metres north of the bridge carrying Common Road over the A229, including bridges over Works Nos. 40F, 37A, 37B, 39A and 39C;

Work No. 40B—A road, forming the southbound exit slip road from the A229 (Work No. 40A), commencing by a junction with that road at a point 280 metres north of the existing Bridgewood Roundabout, passing southwards and terminating at the eastern end of the roundabout (Work No. 40F);

Work No. 40C—A road, forming the southbound entry slip road to the A229 (Work No. 40A), commencing at the eastern end of the roundabout (Work No. 40F), passing southwards and terminating by a junction with Work No. 40A at a point 145 metres south of the existing Bridgewood Roundabout;

Work No. 40D—A road, forming the northbound entry slip road to the A229 (Work No. 40A), commencing by a junction with that road at a point 280 metres north of the said existing Bridgewood Roundabout, passing southwards and terminating at the western end of the roundabout (Work No. 40F);

Work No. 40E—A road, forming the northbound exit slip road from the A229 (Work No. 40A), commencing at the western end of the roundabout (Work No. 40F), passing southwards and terminating by a junction with Work No. 40A at a point 145 metres south of the existing Bridgewood Roundabout;

Work No. 40F—A roundabout (the Bridgewood Roundabout) at the junction of Walderslade Woods, Rochester Road and the A229;

Work No. 40G—Realignment of Rochester Road commencing in that road at a point 160 metres north-west of its junction with the A229 at the existing Bridgewood Roundabout, passing south-eastwards and terminating at the western end of the roundabout (Work No. 40F);

Work No. 40H—Improvement and realignment of Walderslade Woods forming dual carriageways, commencing at the eastern end of the roundabout (Work No. 40F), passing eastwards and terminating in Walderslade Woods at a point 100 metres east of that commencement;

Work No. 40J—A road, forming the southbound exit slip road from the A229 (Work No. 40A), commencing by a junction with that road at a point 270 metres north of the intended Lord Lees Roundabout (Work No. 40N), passing southwards and terminating at the eastern end of that roundabout;

Work No. 40K—A road, forming the southbound entry slip road to the A229 (Work No. 40A), commencing at the eastern end of the intended Lord Lees Roundabout (Work No. 40N), passing southwards and terminating by a junction with Work No. 40A at a point 80 metres north-west of the bridge carrying Common Road over the A229;

Work No. 40L—A road, forming the northbound entry slip road to the A229 (Work No. 40A), commencing by a junction with that road at a point 300 metres north of the intended Lord Lees Roundabout (Work No. 40N), passing southwards and terminating at the western end of that roundabout;

Work No. 40M—A road, forming the northbound exit slip road from the A229 (Work No. 40A), commencing at the western end of the Roundabout (Work No. 40N), passing southwards and terminating by a junction with Work No. 40A at a point 70 metres north-east of the bridge carrying Common Road over the A229;

Work No. 40N—A roundabout (Lord Lees Roundabout) over the A229 (Work No. 40A) at Blue Bell Hill, including two bridges over Work No. 40A;

Work No. 40P—A road, forming an access road to the Buckmore Park Activity Centre and an access way for cycles and pedestrians at Shall Hook Wood, commencing in the existing access road at a point 250 metres north of the centre of the existing Lord Lees Roundabout, passing southwards and south-westwards on the western side of the slip road (Work No. 40L) and terminating at the western end of the roundabout (Work No. 40N);

Work No. 40Q—A road, forming an access road to the premises known as Nil Desperandum, commencing by a junction with the access road (Work No. 40P) at a point 40 metres west of the termination of that work, passing north-eastwards and terminating in the curtilage of those premises;

Work No. 40R—An access way to land on the northern side of the Common Road Sports Ground, commencing by a junction with the access way (Work No. 40S) at a point 90 metres north of the termination of that work, passing southwards on the western side of that work and Work No. 40M and terminating in the existing access way at a point 30 metres north of the said land;

Work No. 40S—A road, forming an access way for cycles and pedestrians, commencing by a junction with the access road (Work No. 40P) at a point 30 metres from the termination of that work, passing southwards and south-eastwards and terminating by a junction with the slip road (Work No. 40M) at a point 250 metres from the termination of that work;

Work No. 41—Associated works connected with improvements at Junction 3 of the M2, comprising—

Work No. 41A—A road, forming a southern extension of Hallsfield Road, commencing at a point 30 metres east of the western end of that road east of Maidstone Road, passing westwards, then southwards and terminating at a point 260 metres south of that commencement;

Work No. 41B—Realignment of Hallsfield Road commencing at a point 30 metres west of the junction of that road with Sadlers Close and terminating in Hallsfield Road at a point 95 metres north-west of that road junction;

Work No. 41C—Realignment of Robin Hood Lane commencing at a point 60 metres west of the existing junction of that road with the access road to the Medway Crematorium, passing eastwards over the M2 (Works Nos. 37A and 37B) and terminating at a point 180 metres east of that commencement, including a bridge over Works Nos. 37A, 37B, 39B and 39D;

Work No. 41D—Diversion of the said access road to the Medway Crematorium, commencing by a junction with Robin Hood Lane (Work No. 41C) at a point 15 metres west of its existing junction with that road and terminating in that access road at a point 80 metres south of that commencement;

In the borough of Tonbridge and Malling, parish of Aylesford, in the borough of Maidstone, parishes of Boxley and Bredhurst and in the borough of Gillingham, town of Gillingham—

Work No. 42—Improvement of the M2 between Junctions 3 and 4, comprising—

Work No. 42A—Improvement and realignment of the M2, to form the eastbound carriageway of that motorway, commencing by a junction with Work No. 37A at its termination, passing under the footpath KH 32 (Work No. 45), over Harp Farm Road (Work No. 43A), and under Lidsing Road and Forge Lane (Works Nos. 43C and 43E) and under Maidstone Road, then passing to Junction 4 (Work No. 44) and terminating at a point 190 metres east of the easternmost bridge at that Junction carrying the A278 (Hoath Way) over the M2, including a bridge over Harp Farm Road;

Work No. 42B—A road forming the westbound carriageway of the M2, being in part a new road and in part improvement and realignment of the existing westbound carriageway, commencing by a junction with Work No. 37B at its termination, passing over Work No. 43A, under Works Nos. 43C, 43E and 45 and under Maidstone Road, then passing to Junction 4 (Work No. 44) and terminating at a point 190 metres east of the said bridge over the M2, including a bridge over Harp Farm Road;

Work No. 43—Roads between Junctions 3 and 4, comprising—

Work No. 43A—Realignment of Harp Farm Road, commencing at a point 65 metres south of the centre of the roundabout at its junction with Walderslade Woods, passing southwards under the M2 (Works Nos. 42A and 42B) and terminating at a point 50 metres south-west of its existing junction with Yelsted Lane;

Work No. 43B—A road, forming a diversion of Yelsted Lane, commencing by a junction with Harp Farm Road (Work No. 43A) at a point 10 metres south of its existing junction with that road, passing eastwards on the southern side of the M2 (Work No. 42B) and terminating in Yelsted Lane at a point 345 metres east of that commencement;

Work No. 43C—Realignment of Lidsing Road commencing at a point 260 metres south of the southern end of the existing bridge carrying that road over the M2, passing northwards over the M2 (Works Nos. 42A and 42B) and terminating at a point 70 metres south of the junction of that road with Westfield Sole Road and Blind Lane, including a new bridge over Works Nos. 42A and 42B;

Work No. 43D—Realignment of an existing track between Blind Lane and Forge Lane on the northern side of the M2 (Work No. 42A), commencing at a point 370 metres north-east of the junction of that track with Blind Lane, passing north-eastwards on the northern side of the existing track then northwards and terminating by a junction with Forge Lane (Work No. 43E) at a point 260 metres south-east of its junction with Chapel Lane;

Work No. 43E—Realignment of Forge Lane commencing at its junction with Chapel Lane, passing south-eastwards over the M2 (Works Nos. 42A and 42B) and terminating at a point 40 metres south-east of the junction of Forge Lane with Blind Lane on the southern side of the motorway, including a bridge over the M2;

Work No. 44—Improvement of Junction 4 of the M2, comprising—

Work No. 44A—Realignment of the exit slip road from the eastbound carriageway of the M2 (Work No. 42A), commencing by a junction with Work No. 42A at a point 390 metres north-east of the existing bridge carrying Forge Lane over the M2, passing under Maidstone Road and terminating at the northern end of the roundabout over the M2 at Junction 4;

Work No. 44B—Realignment of the entry slip road to the westbound carriageway of the M2 (Work No. 42B) commencing by a junction with Work No. 42B at a point 155 metres north-east of the said bridge carrying Forge Lane over the M2, passing under Maidstone Road and terminating at the southern end of the roundabout over the M2 at Junction 4.

Work No. 45—Realignment of footpath KH 32, commencing at a point 12 metres south of the southern end of the footbridge carrying footpath KH 32A over Walderslade Wood, passing southwards over the M2 (Works Nos. 42A and 42B) on the eastern side of the existing bridge carrying that footpath over the M2 and terminating at a point 30 metres south of the southern end of that existing bridge, including a bridge over Works Nos. 42A and 42B;

Work No. 46—A cycle track commencing by a junction with the existing cycle track on the western side of the A229 (Maidstone Road) at a point 190 metres north of the centre of the Bridgewood Roundabout, passing westwards and terminating at a point on the eastern side of Rochester Road 200 metres west of the centre of that roundabout.

Interpretation of Part I

2. In paragraph 1 above—

references to the M2 are to the special road so designated;

references to the A2 are to the trunk road so designated;

references to the A228 and the A229 are to the principal roads so designated;

"Wainscott Northern Bypass" means the road scheme so named for a bypass between the A2 and the Medway Tunnel;

"westbound" in any description of the direction of traffic signifies travel in the direction of London, whether or not London is the destination, and "eastbound" signifies travel in the opposite direction.

PART II

INTERFERENCE WITH HIGHWAYS AND MEANS OF ACCESS

Stopping up of highways

3.—(1) Subject to the provisions of this paragraph, the Secretary of State may, in connection with the construction of the A2 and M2 improvement works, stop up—

(a) each of the highways or parts of highways specified, by reference to the letters and numbers shown on the deposited plans, in columns (1) and (2) of the following table, and

(b) any other bridleways or footpaths within the limits of deviation for the works authorised by this Part of this Act or within the limits of land to be acquired or used.

(2) No highway or part of a highway, other than one specified in columns (1) and (2) of Part II of the following table, shall be stopped up under this paragraph unless the Secretary of State is in possession of all lands abutting on it, except so far as the owners and occupiers of those lands may otherwise agree.

(3) No highway or part of a highway specified in columns (1) and (2) of Part II of the following table shall be stopped up under this paragraph until the Secretary of State is satisfied that the new highway specified in relation to it in column (3) of that Part of the table, by reference to the letters and numbers shown on the deposited plans or by reference to works authorised by this Part of this Act, has been completed and is open for public use.

(4) On a highway or part of a highway being stopped up under this paragraph, all rights of way over or along it shall be extinguished.

(5) The Secretary of State shall compensate any person who suffers loss by the extinguishment under this paragraph of a private right of way.

(6) Any dispute as to a person's entitlement to compensation under sub-paragraph (5) above, or as to the amount of such compensation, shall be determined under and in accordance with Part I of the Land Compensation Act 1961.

THE TABLE

HIGHWAYS TO BE STOPPED UP

PART I

HIGHWAYS TO BE STOPPED UP WITHOUT PROVISION OF SUBSTITUTE

(1) *Area*	(2) *Highway or part to be stopped up*
COUNTY OF KENT	
Borough of Gravesham, Parish of Shorne	Footpath NS312 for a distance of 45 metres north-eastwards from its junction with Watling Street (A2)

(1) *Area*	(2) *Highway or part to be stopped up*
Borough of Gravesham, Parish of Cobham	Old Watling Street (B395) between points K1 and K2
City of Rochester upon Medway, Parish of Cuxton	Footpath RS205 between points D1 and D2
	Footpath RR27 between points D2 and D3
Borough of Tonbridge and Malling, Parish of Aylesford	Access road to go-kart racing track between points S1 and S2
	Access road between points H1 and H2
	Victoria Close between points B3 and B4
	Footpath MR201 between points T1 and T3 and between points T3 and T4
	Footpath MR14 for a distance of 120 metres westwards from its junction with Maidstone Road (A229)

PART II

HIGHWAYS TO BE STOPPED UP ONLY ON PROVISION OF SUBSTITUTE

(1) *Area*	(2) *Highway or part to be stopped up*	(3) *New highway to be substituted for it*
COUNTY OF KENT		
Borough of Gravesham, Parish of Cobham	A2 westbound entry slip road between points H3 and H2	Work No. 32C
	A2 westbound exit slip road between points H4 and H2	Work No. 32B
	Halfpence Lane (C492) between points H1 and H2	Works Nos. 32B and 32C
	Footpath NS182 between points N9, P3 and N8	New footpath between points N7 and N8
	Access road between points N1 and N2 and points N3 and N4	Works Nos. 35A and 35B
Borough of Gravesham, Parish of Shorne	A2 eastbound entry slip road between points J3 and J4	Work No. 32A
Borough of Gravesham, Parishes of Cobham and Higham	A2 westbound slip road between points P1 and P2	Work No. 35A
City of Rochester upon Medway, Parish of Cuxton	Work No. 13A(2)	Work No. 36C between its commencement and its junction with Work No. 13A(2)
	Work No. 13A(3)	Work No. 36D

(1) *Area*	(2) *Highway or part to be stopped up*	(3) *New highway to be substituted for it*
City of Rochester upon Medway, Town of Rochester and Parish of Cuxton	Footpath RS203 between points B1 and B2	New footpath between points B1, B6, B5, B4 and B3
	Work No. 13A(4)	Work No. 36F between its junction with Work No. 13A(4) and its termination
	Work No. 13A(1)	Works Nos. 36A and 36E
City of Rochester upon Medway, Town of Rochester	A228 (Rochester Road) between points C1 and C2	Work No. 36F
	M2 eastbound exit slip road between points C9 and C4	Works Nos. 36A and 36E
	M2 westbound entry slip road between points C6 and C7	Works Nos. 36C and 36E
	M2 eastbound entry slip road between points C9 and C5	Works Nos. 36B and 36E
	M2 westbound exit slip road between points C8 and C7	Works Nos. 36D and 36E
	Footpath RS205A between points C9 and C10	Work No. 36K
	Nashenden Farm Lane between points E1 and E2	Work No. 38C
	Bridleway RR16 between points E3, E2 and E4	Work No. 38C
	Bridleway RR18 between points C1 and A3	Works Nos. 38F and 13C
City of Rochester upon Medway, Town of Rochester and Borough of Tonbridge and Malling, Parish of Wouldham	Work No. 13C between its commencement and its junction with Work No. 38F	Work No. 38F
Borough of Tonbridge and Malling, Parish of Wouldham	Bridleway MR11 between points A3, A2 and A1	Works Nos. 38F and 13C
Borough of Tonbridge and Malling, Parish of Aylesford	A229 (Maidstone Road) between points F1 and F2d	Works Nos. 40A, 40B, 40C, 40D, 40E, 40F and 41A
	Rochester Road between points F3 and F4	Work No. 40G
	A229 slip road between points B1 and B2	Work No. 40J
	A229 slip road between points C1 and C2	Work No. 40L
	A229 slip road between points D1 and D2	Work No. 40M

(1) *Area*	(2) *Highway or part to be stopped up*	(3) *New highway to be substituted for it*
	A229 slip road between points E1 and E2	Work No. 39H
	A229 slip road between points G1 and G2	Work No. 40K
	Walderslade Woods between points F5 and F6	Work No. 40H
	Walderslade Woods between points F7 and F8	Work No. 39G
	M2 eastbound exit slip road between points K1 and K2	Work No. 39A
	M2 eastbound entry slip road between points J1 and J2	Work No. 39B
	M2 westbound exit slip road between points M1 and M2	Work No. 39D
	M2 westbound entry slip road between points L1 and L2	Work No. 39C
	Maidstone Road between points N1 and N2	Work No. 39J
	Access way between points A1, A2 and A3	Work No. 40P
	Access way between points P3 and P4	Works Nos. 40R and 40S
	Access road between points P1, P3 and P2	Work No. 40Q
	Access road to Crematorium between points V3 and V4	Work No. 41D
	Footpath MR440 between points Q3 and Q4	New footpath between points Q3 and Q5
	Footpath MR438A between points R1 and R2	New footpath between those points
Borough of Maidstone, Parish of Boxley	Footpath KH32 between points Q1 and Q2	Work No. 45
	Yelsted Lane between points E3 and E4	Work No. 43B
	Lidsing Road between points F1 and F2	Work No. 43C
	Footpath KH9 between points G1, G3 and G4	New footpath between points G1, G2 and G4
	Footpath KH634 between points H1 and H2	Work No. 43D
Borough of Maidstone, Parishes of Boxley and Bredhurst	Forge Lane between points H3 and H4	Work No. 43E

(1) *Area*	(2) *Highway or part to be stopped up*	(3) *New highway to be substituted for it*
Borough of Gillingham, Town of Gillingham and Borough of Maidstone, Parish of Bredhurst	M2 westbound entry slip road between points A1 and A2	Work No. 44B
	M2 eastbound exit slip road between points A3 and A4	Work No. 44A

Note: In the event that Work No. 38F is not carried out after Work No. 13C, references in column (3) of the table to Work No. 13C shall be construed as references to so much of it as lies between its junction with Work No. 38F and its termination.

Stopping up of private access to premises

4.—(1) Subject to the provisions of this paragraph, the Secretary of State may, in connection with the construction of the A2 and M2 improvement works—

(a) stop up any private means of access to premises adjoining or adjacent to any land—

(i) comprised in the route of any highway which becomes, by virtue of paragraph 6 below, a special road, or

(ii) forming part of the site of any works authorised by this Part of this Act,

and

(b) provide a new means of access to any such premises.

(2) No means of access shall be stopped up under this paragraph unless the Secretary of State is satisfied—

(a) that no access to the premises is reasonably required, or

(b) that another reasonably convenient means of access to the premises is available or will be provided under this paragraph or otherwise.

(3) In determining for the purposes of sub-paragraph (2) above whether a means of access to any premises from a highway is or will be reasonably convenient, the Secretary of State shall have regard—

(a) to the need, if any, for a means of access from the highway to different places on those premises, and

(b) to any roads, paths or other ways on those or other premises which are or will be capable of providing such a means.

(4) The provision under this paragraph of a new means of access to any premises from a highway includes the provision of a road, path or other way on those or any other premises.

Temporary interference with highways

5.—(1) The Secretary of State may, for the purpose of constructing the A2 and M2 improvement works, temporarily stop up, open, break up or interfere with, or alter or divert, the whole or any part of any highway within the limits of deviation for the works authorised by this Part of this Act or the limits of land to be acquired or used, and may carry out and do all necessary works and things for, or in connection with, the stopping up, opening, breaking up, interference, alteration or diversion and for keeping the highway open for traffic.

(2) The Secretary of State shall provide reasonable access for all persons, with or without vehicles, going to or returning from premises abutting on any highway affected by the exercise of the powers conferred by this paragraph.

Part III

Miscellaneous

Status of new highways

6.—(1) On the date on which this Act is passed the highways comprised in Works Nos. 33B, 36A, 36B, 36C, 36D, 37B, 39A, 39B, 39C, 39D and 42B shall become trunk roads and special roads for the exclusive use of traffic of Classes I and II of the classes of traffic specified in Schedule 4 to the Highways Act 1980.

(2) The highways which become special roads by virtue of sub-paragraph (1) above shall be treated as provided by the Secretary of State under a scheme made by him under section 16 of the Highways Act 1980—

(a) prescribing the route of those highways as the route of the special roads authorised by the scheme,
(b) prescribing the classes of traffic mentioned in that sub-paragraph, and
(c) specifying the date on which this Act is passed as the date on which those special roads were to become trunk roads.

7. On the date on which this Act is passed—
(a) the highways comprised in Works Nos. 32A and 35A, and
(b) the highway comprised in Work No. 32B from the intersection of that work with Work No. 32C to its termination,

shall become trunk roads as if they had become so by virtue of an order under section 10(2) of the Highways Act 1980 specifying that date as the date on which they were to become trunk roads.

8.—(1) On the date certified by the Secretary of State as the date on which any highway constructed in pursuance of this Schedule, other than one to which paragraph 6 or 7 above applies, is open for public use, that highway shall be transferred to the Kent County Council and, following that transfer, shall be treated for the purposes of the Highways Act 1980 as if it had been so transferred by means of an order made under section 14(1)(b) or, as the case may be, 18(1)(d) of that Act.

(2) The Secretary of State may classify any highway proposed to be constructed in pursuance of this Schedule, other than one to which paragraph 6 or 7 above applies, in any manner in which, and for any purposes for which, he could classify that highway under section 12(3) of that Act.

(3) On the date of its transfer under sub-paragraph (1) above to the Kent County Council any highway classified under sub-paragraph (2) above shall become a highway classified in the manner and for the purposes in question as if so classified under section 12(3) of that Act.

Status of operations and works

9. The construction by the Secretary of State of a highway in pursuance of this Part of this Act shall be treated as the construction of a highway authorised by, and in pursuance of—
(a) a scheme under section 16 of the Highways Act 1980, in the case of the highways to which paragraph 6 above applies,
(b) section 24(1) of that Act, in the case of the highways to which paragraph 7 above applies, and
(c) an order under section 14 of that Act made in relation to the highways to which paragraph 7 above applies, in any other case.

10.—(1) The following operations and works, namely—
(a) the carrying out of any of the A2 and M2 improvement works which is not the construction of a highway,
(b) the stopping up of any highway in pursuance of Part II of this Schedule, and
(c) the stopping up of means of access to premises and the provision of new means of access in pursuance of Part II of this Schedule,

shall be treated as authorised by an order made by the Secretary of State under section 18 of the Highways Act 1980 in relation to the roads which become special roads by virtue of paragraph 6 above, and, in the case of operations and works falling within paragraph (c) above, as so authorised by virtue of section 125 of that Act.

(2) Subject to section 21 of that Act as it applies by virtue of sub-paragraph (1) above, the stopping up of any highway in pursuance of Part II of this Schedule shall not affect any rights—
(a) of statutory undertakers in respect of any apparatus of theirs which immediately before the date on which this Act is passed is under, in, on, over, along or across that highway; or
(b) of any sewerage undertakers in respect of any sewers or sewage disposal works of theirs which immediately before that date are under, in, on, over, along or across that highway.

Treatment of provisions of this Schedule for Highways Act purposes

11.—(1) Where, by virtue of any of the provisions of this Part of this Schedule, any operation or work is to be treated as authorised by an order under section 14 or 18 of the Highways Act 1980, any provision of Parts I and II of this Schedule relating to that operation or work shall be treated for the purposes of that Act as a provision of such an order.

(2) The provisions of paragraph 6 above relating to highways which are to be treated by virtue of that paragraph as provided under a scheme made under section 39 of the Highways Act 1980 shall be treated for the purposes of that Act as provisions of such a scheme.

Regulation of traffic on new roads

12.—(1) Subject to sub-paragraph (2) below, any power under the Road Traffic Regulation Act 1984 to make an order or to give a direction with respect to any road shall be exercisable in relation to any road forming or forming part of any of the A2 and M2 improvement works before that road is open for public use, in any case where it appears to the Secretary of State to be expedient that the order or (as the case may be) the direction should have effect immediately on the road's becoming open for public use.

(2) The procedure otherwise applicable under that Act in relation to the making of any such order or the giving of any such direction shall apply in any such case with such modifications as the Secretary of State may determine; and he shall publish notice of those modifications in such manner as appears to him to be appropriate for bringing them to the notice of persons likely to be affected by the provisions of any such order or (as the case may be) by any such direction.

Section 45

SCHEDULE 13

A2 and M2 Improvement Works: Purposes for which Certain Land May be Acquired or Used

(1) *Area*	(2) *Number of land shown on deposited plans*	(3) *Purpose for which land may be acquired or used*
COUNTY OF KENT		
Borough of Gravesham, Parish of Cobham	34	The provision of landscaping and planting.
	40	The provision of a balancing pond, landscaping and planting and pumping station.
	42 (part)	The provision of a balancing pond, landscaping and planting and permanent access for maintenance purposes.
	42 (part)	The provision of a working site.
City of Rochester Upon Medway, Parish of Cuxton	11 to 18, 21, 22, 27 and 29	The provision of a working site, landscaping, planting and access for construction purposes.
City of Rochester Upon Medway, Town of Rochester	14	The provision of a working site, landscaping and planting.
	65	The provision of a working site, landscaping and planting.
	94 to 98	The provision of landscaping and planting.
Borough of Tonbridge and Malling, Parish of Aylesford	4	The provision of landscaping and planting.
	10 to 13	The provision of landscaping and planting.
	23 to 28	The provision of landscaping and permanent access to adjacent houses fronting Maidstone Road.
	198 (part), 216, 217, 218, 243, 247, 248 and 249	The provision of a new footbridge, landscaping and planting.
	220 to 225	The provision of landscaping and planting.
	198 (part)	The provision of a working site, access for maintenance purposes, landscaping and planting.

(1) *Area*	(2) *Number of land shown on deposited plans*	(3) *Purpose for which land may be acquired or used*
	256	The provision of landscaping and planting.
Borough of Maidstone, Parish of Boxley	2	The provision of landscaping and planting.
	22	The provision of landscaping and planting.
	26, 29 and 30	The provision of landscaping and planting.
	32	The provision of landscaping and planting.
	34	The provision of landscaping and planting.
Borough of Maidstone, Parish of Bredhurst	12 and 15	The provision of landscaping and planting.
	16	The provision of landscaping and planting.
Borough of Gillingham, Town of Gillingham	1, 6, 7, 8 and 9	The provision of landscaping and planting.
	5	The provision of a working site.

Section 50

SCHEDULE 14

OVERHEAD LINES: CONSENT

Scope of Schedule

1. This Schedule applies to any electric line to which section 37(1) of the Electricity Act 1989 would apply, but for section 50(1) above.

Consent requirement

2.—(1) An electric line to which this Schedule applies shall not be installed or kept installed above ground except in accordance with a consent granted by the appropriate Ministers.

(2) Any person who without reasonable excuse contravenes the provisions of sub-paragraph (1) above shall be liable on summary conviction to a fine not exceeding level 3 on the standard scale.

(3) No proceedings shall be instituted in respect of an offence under this paragraph except by or on behalf of the Secretary of State.

Applications for consent

3.—(1) An application for consent under this Schedule shall be in writing and shall state—

(a) the length of the electric line to which it relates,

(b) the nominal voltage of that line, and

(c) whether the application to any extent relates to exercise of the power conferred by paragraph 3(1) of Schedule 2 to this Act.

(2) An application for consent under this Schedule shall be accompanied by a map showing—

(a) the land across which the electric line to which it relates is to be installed or kept installed, including details of the route of that line,

(b) the limits of deviation for the scheduled works and the limits of land to be acquired or used, so far as relevant to the application, and

(c) if the application to any extent relates to exercise of the power conferred by paragraph 3(1) of Schedule 2 to this Act, the extent to which it so relates.

4. An application for consent under this Schedule shall be supplemented, if the appropriate Ministers so direct in writing, by such additional information as may be specified in the direction.

Publicity

5.—(1) A person applying for consent under this Schedule shall publish notice of the application in two successive weeks in one or more local newspapers circulating in the area in which the land to which the application relates is situated (or in areas which together include that area).

(2) A notice under sub-paragraph (1) above shall—

(a) describe the route of the electric line to which the application relates,

(b) specify a place in the locality where a copy of the application may be inspected,

(c) state a time (not being less than 14 days from the date of publication) within which, and the manner in which, objections to the application may be made to the appropriate Ministers, and

(d) if it relates to an application by the nominated undertaker, explain the effect of paragraph 8(2)(b) below.

(3) Sub-paragraph (1) above shall not apply to an application for consent under this Schedule which relates only to exercise of the power conferred by paragraph 3(1) of Schedule 2 to this Act.

(4) If an application for consent under this Schedule relates partly to exercise of the power conferred by paragraph 3(1) of Schedule 2 to this Act, so much of the application as relates to exercise of that power shall be disregarded for the purposes of sub-paragraphs (1) and (2) above.

(5) If an application for consent under this Schedule is one in relation to which the applicant is subject to a duty under sub-paragraph (1) above, the appropriate Ministers shall not make any decision about the application until they are satisfied—

(a) that the applicant has performed his duty under that provision, and

(b) that the time allowed by the notice under that provision for making objections to the application has expired.

Consultation

6.—(1) Within 14 days of receiving an application for consent under this Schedule, the appropriate Ministers shall invite the relevant planning authority to make representations and shall not make any decision about the application until—

(a) they have received representations from the authority about it,

(b) they have been informed by the authority that it does not wish to make any representations about it, or

(c) 28 days have elapsed since the date of the invitation.

(2) An invitation under sub-paragraph (1) above shall specify the time limit for making representations.

(3) For the purposes of this paragraph, the relevant planning authority is—

(a) in the case of a line in Greater London, the local planning authority, and

(b) in the case of a line in Essex or Kent, the district planning authority.

7.—(1) If the appropriate Ministers consider that an application for consent under this Schedule relates to matters which may affect—

(a) nature conservation,

(b) the conservation of the natural beauty or amenity of the countryside, or

(c) a site of archaeological or historic interest,

they shall, within 14 days of receiving the application, also invite the appropriate body or bodies to make representations.

(2) Where under sub-paragraph (1) above the appropriate Ministers have invited a body to make representations about an application for consent under this Schedule, they shall not make any decision about the application until—

(a) they have received representations from the body about the request,

(b) they have been informed by the body that it does not wish to make any representations about the request, or

(c) 14 days have elapsed since the date of the invitation.

(3) An invitation under sub-paragraph (1) above shall specify the time limit for making representations.

(4) For the purposes of this paragraph, the following are appropriate bodies in the following matters—

Matter	Body
Nature conservation.	The Nature Conservancy Council for England.
Conservation of the natural beauty or amenity of the countryside.	The Countryside Commission.
Sites of archaeological or historic interest.	The Historic Buildings and Monuments Commission for England.

Grant of consent

8.—(1) This paragraph applies to an application for consent under this Schedule by the nominated undertaker.

(2) An application to which this paragraph applies may only be refused—

(a) to the extent that it relates to exercise of the power conferred by paragraph 3(1) of Schedule 2 to this Act, on the ground that the electric line ought to, and could reasonably, be installed elsewhere within the limits specified, in relation to the diversion concerned, in the third column of the table in paragraph 3(1) of Schedule 2 to this Act, and

(b) to the extent that it does not relate to exercise of that power, on the ground that the electric line ought to, and could reasonably, be installed elsewhere within the limits of deviation for the scheduled works or within the limits of land to be acquired or used.

9. A consent under this Schedule may include such conditions (including conditions as to the ownership and operation of the electric line to which it relates) as appear to the appropriate Ministers to be appropriate.

Variation and revocation of consent

10.—(1) A consent under this Schedule may be varied or revoked by the Secretary of State at any time after the end of such period as may be specified in the consent.

(2) The period which may be specified under sub-paragraph (1) above shall not be less than 10 years from the date of installation of the electric line to which the consent relates.

Duration of consent

11. Subject to paragraph 10 above, a consent under this Schedule shall continue in force for such period as may be specified in or determined by or under the consent.

Anticipatory applications

12.—(1) This paragraph applies where—

(a) an application to the appropriate Ministers has been made in anticipation of the coming into force of this Schedule,

(b) the application was made on or after 31st October 1996, and

(c) the person by, or on whose behalf, the application was made—

(i) is specified under section 34(1) above for purposes consisting of or including the construction of any works,

(ii) is a member of the same group as a person who is so specified, or

(iii) is the holder of a licence under section 6 of the Electricity Act 1989.

(2) In that case—

(a) the application,

(b) any notice of the application published by the applicant,

(c) any objections to the application made in response to any such notice,

(d) any invitation by the appropriate Ministers to make representations about the application, and

(e) any representations about the application, or statement about the wish to make representations about it, made in response to any such invitation,

shall have effect as if this Schedule had been in force at all material times.

(3) In sub-paragraph (1)(c)(ii) above, "group" means a body corporate and all other bodies corporate which are its subsidiaries within the meaning of the Companies Act 1985.

Interpretation

13. In this Schedule, references to the appropriate Ministers are to the Secretary of State for Trade and Industry and the Secretary of State for Transport acting jointly.

Section 52

SCHEDULE 15

PROTECTIVE PROVISIONS

PART I

PROTECTION FOR HIGHWAYS AND TRAFFIC

1.—(1) The following provisions of this Part of this Schedule shall, unless otherwise agreed in writing between the nominated undertaker and the highway authority concerned, have effect for the protection of the highway authorities referred to in this Part.

(2) In this Part of this Schedule—

"highway" means a highway for which the local highway authority is the highway authority;

"plans" includes sections and specifications; and

"property of the highway authority" means any apparatus of the highway authority affixed to or placed under any highway.

(3) Part III of the New Roads and Street Works Act 1991 shall not apply in relation to any matter which is regulated by this Part of this Schedule.

2. Wherever in this Part of this Schedule provision is made with respect to the approval or consent of the highway authority, that approval or consent shall be in writing and subject to such reasonable terms and conditions as the highway authority may require, but shall not be unreasonably withheld.

3.—(1) The nominated undertaker shall not exercise the powers conferred by paragraph 6(1) of Schedule 3 to this Act without the consent of the highway authority.

(2) In its application to this paragraph, paragraph 2 above shall have effect with the addition after "require" of "in the interest of public safety or convenience".

(3) If within 28 days after a request for consent has been submitted the highway authority has not given or refused such consent, it shall be deemed to have consented to the request as submitted.

(4) Where consent under this paragraph is given subject to a term or condition the performance of which is, or becomes, inconsistent with the performance by the nominated undertaker of any of the conditions to which the deemed planning permission is subject, the term or condition to which the consent under this paragraph is subject shall not have effect or, as the case may be, shall cease to have effect.

(5) In sub-paragraph (4) above, the reference to the deemed planning permission is to the planning permission deemed by section 9 above to be granted.

4. Before carrying out any work for the construction or maintenance of any part of the works authorised by Part I of this Act which will involve interference with a highway, or the traffic in any highway, or before temporarily stopping up any highway, the nominated undertaker shall consult the highway authority—

(a) as to the time when the work shall be commenced, and as to the extent of the surface of the highway which it may be reasonably necessary for the nominated undertaker to occupy, or the nature of the interference which may be caused to traffic in the carrying out of the work, or as to the time during which, and the extent to which, the highway shall be stopped up (as the case may be), and

(b) as to the conditions under which the work shall be carried out or the highway shall be stopped up (as the case may be),

so as to reduce so far as reasonably practicable inconvenience to the public and to ensure the safety of the public.

5. The nominated undertaker shall not, without the consent of the highway authority, construct any part of the works authorised by Part I of this Act under and within 8 metres of the surface of any highway which comprises a carriageway except in accordance with plans submitted to, and approved by, the highway authority and if within 28 days after such plans have been submitted the highway authority has not approved or disapproved them, it shall be deemed to have approved the plans as submitted.

6. In the construction of any part of the said works under a highway no part thereof shall, except with the consent of the highway authority, be so constructed as to interfere with the provision of proper means of drainage of the surface of the highway or be nearer than two metres to the surface of the highway.

7.—(1) The provisions of this paragraph have effect in relation to, and to the construction of, any new bridge, or any extension or alteration of an existing bridge, carrying any part of the works authorised by Part I of this Act over a highway or carrying a highway over any part of those works; and any such new bridge, or (as the case may be) any bridge so extended or altered, is in this paragraph referred to as "the bridge".

(2) Before commencing the construction of, or the carrying out of any work in connection with, the bridge which involves interference with a highway, the nominated undertaker shall submit to the highway authority for its approval plans, drawings and particulars (in this paragraph referred to as "plans") relating thereto, and the bridge shall not be constructed and the works shall not be carried out except in accordance with the plans submitted to, and approved by, the highway authority.

(3) If within 28 days after the plans have been submitted the highway authority has not approved or disapproved them, it shall be deemed to have approved the plans as submitted.

(4) If the bridge carries any part of the works authorised by Part I of this Act over any highway—

(a) it shall be constructed in such manner as to prevent so far as may be reasonably practicable the dripping of water from the bridge, and

(b) the highway authority may, at the cost of the nominated undertaker, provide and place such lamps and apparatus as may from time to time be reasonably necessary for efficiently lighting any highway under or in the vicinity of the bridge.

8. The nominated undertaker shall secure that so much of the works authorised by Part I of this Act as is constructed under any highway shall be so designed, constructed and maintained as to carry the appropriate loading recommended for highway bridges by the Secretary of State at the time of construction of the works, and the nominated undertaker shall indemnify the highway authority against, and make good to the highway authority, the expenses which the highway authority may reasonably incur in the maintenance or repair of any highway, or any tunnels, sewers, drains or apparatus therein, by reason of non-compliance with the provisions of this paragraph.

9. Any officer of the highway authority duly appointed for the purpose may at all reasonable times, on giving to the nominated undertaker such notice as may in the circumstances be reasonable, enter upon and inspect any part of the works authorised by Part I of this Act which—

(a) is in, over or under any highway, or

(b) which may affect any highway or any property of the highway authority,

during the carrying out of the work, and the nominated undertaker shall give to such officer all reasonable facilities for such inspection and, if he shall be of opinion that the construction of the work is attended with danger to any highway or to any property of the highway authority on or under any highway, the nominated undertaker shall adopt such measures and precautions as may be reasonably practicable for the purpose of preventing any damage or injury to the highway.

10.—(1) The nominated undertaker shall not alter, disturb or in any way interfere with any property of the highway authority on or under any highway, or the access thereto, without the consent of the highway authority, and any alteration, diversion, replacement or reconstruction of any such property which may be necessary shall be made by the highway authority or the nominated undertaker as the highway authority thinks fit, and the expense reasonably incurred by the highway authority in so doing shall be repaid to the highway authority by the nominated undertaker.

(2) If within 28 days after a request for consent has been submitted the highway authority has not given or refused such consent, it shall be deemed to have consented to the request as submitted.

11. The nominated undertaker shall not remove any soil or material from any highway except so much as must be excavated in the carrying out of the works authorised by Part I of this Act.

12.—(1) If the highway authority, after giving to the nominated undertaker not less than 28 days' notice (or, in case of emergency, such notice as is reasonably practicable) of its intention to do so, incurs any additional expense in the signposting of traffic diversions or the taking of other measures in relation thereto, or in the repair of any highway by reason of the diversion thereto of traffic from a road of a higher standard, in consequence of the construction of the works authorised by Part I of this Act, the nominated undertaker shall repay to the highway authority the amount of any such expense reasonably so incurred.

(2) An amount which apart from this sub-paragraph would be payable to the highway authority by virtue of this paragraph in respect of the repair of any highway shall, if the highway fell or would have fallen due for repair as part of the maintenance programme of the highway authority at any time within ten years of the repair being carried out by the nominated undertaker, so as to confer on the highway authority financial benefit (whether by securing the completion of overdue maintenance work for which the highway authority is liable or by deferment of the time for such work in the ordinary course), be reduced by the amount which represents that benefit.

13.—(1) The nominated undertaker shall not, except with the consent of the highway authority, deposit any soil or materials, or stand any plant, on or over any highway so as to obstruct or render less safe the use of the highway by any person, or, except with the like consent, deposit any soil or materials on any highway outside a hoarding, but if within 28 days after request therefor any such consent is neither given nor refused it shall be deemed to have been given.

(2) The expense reasonably incurred by the highway authority in removing any soil or materials deposited on any highway in contravention of this paragraph shall be repaid to the highway authority by the nominated undertaker.

14. The nominated undertaker shall, if reasonably so required by the highway authority, provide and maintain to the reasonable satisfaction of the highway authority, during such time as the nominated undertaker may occupy any part of a highway for the purpose of the construction of any part of the works authorised by Part I of this Act, temporary bridges and temporary ramps for vehicular or pedestrian traffic over any part of the works or in such other position as may be necessary to prevent undue interference with the flow of traffic in the highway.

15.—(1) Where any part of any highway has been broken up or disturbed by the nominated undertaker and not permanently stopped up or diverted the nominated undertaker shall make good the subsoil, foundations and surface of that part of the highway to the reasonable satisfaction of the highway authority, and shall maintain the same to the reasonable satisfaction of the highway authority for such time as may reasonably be required for the permanent reinstatement of the highway.

(2) The reinstatement of that part of the highway shall be carried out by the nominated undertaker to the reasonable satisfaction of the highway authority in accordance with such requirements as to specification of material and standards of workmanship as may be prescribed for equivalent reinstatement work by regulations made under section 71 of the New Roads and Street Works Act 1991.

16. If any damage to any highway or any property of the highway authority on or under any highway is caused by, or results from, the construction of any work authorised by Part I of this Act or any act or omission of the nominated undertaker, its contractors, agents or employees whilst engaged upon such work, the nominated undertaker may, in the case of damage to a highway, make good such damage to the reasonable satisfaction of the highway authority and, where the nominated undertaker does not make good, or in the case of damage to property of the highway authority, the nominated undertaker shall make compensation to the highway authority.

17. The fact that any act or thing may have been done in accordance with plans approved by the highway authority shall not (if it was not attributable to the act, neglect or default of the highway authority or of any person in its employ or its contractors or agents) exonerate the nominated undertaker from any liability, or affect any claim for damages, under this Part of this Schedule or otherwise.

18. Any dispute arising between the nominated undertaker and the highway authority under this Part of this Schedule shall, if the parties agree, be referred to arbitration, but shall otherwise be determined by the Secretary of State.

PART II

PROTECTION FOR ELECTRICITY, GAS, WATER AND SEWERAGE UNDERTAKERS

1.—(1) The following provisions of this Part of this Schedule shall, unless otherwise agreed in writing between the nominated undertaker and the undertakers concerned, have effect.

(2) In this Part of this Schedule—

"alternative apparatus" means alternative apparatus adequate to enable the undertakers to fulfil their functions as effectively as is achievable using the apparatus which the alternative apparatus is to replace;

"apparatus" means—

(a) in the case of electricity undertakers, electric lines or electrical plant (as defined in the Electricity Act 1989) belonging to, or maintained by, such undertakers;

(b) in the case of gas undertakers, mains, pipes or other apparatus belonging to, or maintained by, a public gas transporter for the purposes of gas supply;

(c) in the case of water undertakers, mains, pipes or other apparatus belonging to, or maintained by, such undertakers for the purposes of water supply; and

(d) in the case of sewerage undertakers, any sewer, drain or works vested in a sewerage undertaker under the Water Industry Act 1991 and includes a sludge main, disposal main (within the meaning of section 219 of that Act) or sewer outfall and any manholes, ventilating shafts, pumps or other accessories forming part of any such sewer, drain or works;

(not being, except in paragraph 17 below, apparatus in respect of which the relations between the nominated undertaker and the undertakers are regulated by the provisions of Part III of the New Roads and Street Works Act 1991) and includes any structure for the lodging therein of apparatus or for giving access to apparatus;

"construction" includes execution, placing, altering, replacing, relaying and removal and, in its application to works which include or comprise any operation, means the carrying out of that operation;

"functions" includes powers and duties;

"in" in a context referring to apparatus in land includes under, over, across, along or upon land;

"plans" includes sections and method statements;

"service obligations" means any service obligation imposed on the undertakers by or under the enactments authorising them to carry on their respective undertakings; and

"undertakers" means any of the following, namely, a licence holder within the meaning of Part I of the Electricity Act 1989, a public gas supplier within the meaning of Part I of the Gas Act 1986, a water undertaker within the meaning of the Water Industry Act 1991, a sewerage undertaker within Part I of that Act and any local authority which is a relevant authority for the purposes of section 97 of that Act; and, in relation to any apparatus, means the undertakers to whom it belongs or by whom it is maintained.

2.—(1) The following provisions of this paragraph have effect in any case where the Secretary of State or the nominated undertaker, in exercise of the powers of Part I of this Act, acquires any interest in or temporarily occupies any land in which apparatus is placed.

(2) Unless a certificate is issued by the appropriate Ministers under sub-paragraph (3) below the apparatus shall not be removed under this Part of this Schedule, and any right of the undertakers to maintain, repair, renew, adjust, alter or inspect the apparatus in that land shall not be extinguished—

(a) in the case of a right to adjust or alter apparatus, until 28 days after the nominated undertaker has given the undertakers in whom the right is vested a preliminary notice under paragraph 4 below in respect of land to which the right relates, or, if earlier, the date on which the nominated undertaker commences any work on that land, and

(b) in any other case, until any necessary alternative apparatus has been constructed and is in operation to the reasonable satisfaction of the undertakers.

(3) Where the appropriate Ministers certify in relation to any apparatus that—

(a) failure to remove the apparatus would cause undue delay to the construction of the scheduled works, and

(b) the removal of the apparatus before the provision of alternative apparatus in accordance with this paragraph would not substantially prejudice the ability of the undertakers to meet any relevant service obligations,

that apparatus may be removed (or required by the nominated undertaker to be removed) under this Part of this Schedule before any necessary alternative apparatus has been constructed or is in operation to the reasonable satisfaction of the undertakers.

(4) In this paragraph "appropriate Ministers" means the Secretary of State for Transport acting jointly with either the Secretary of State for the Environment or the Secretary of State for Trade and Industry.

3.—(1) Before exercising any right to adjust or alter apparatus pursuant to paragraph 2(2) above the undertakers concerned shall give the nominated undertaker not less than 28 days' written notice of the proposed alteration or adjustment, together with plans and specifications.

(2) Any altered or adjusted apparatus shall be constructed in such line or situation, at such depth and in accordance with such specification as the nominated undertaker may reasonably require for the purpose of securing that (so far as reasonably practicable at the time the requirement is imposed) the apparatus as altered or adjusted will accommodate any work authorised by Part I of this Act.

(3) Such apparatus shall be constructed in such manner, and in accordance with such programme, as is agreed between the undertakers and the nominated undertaker with a view to securing, among other things—

(a) the efficient implementation of the necessary work,

(b) the avoidance of delay or any other adverse effect on the programme for any works to be carried out by the nominated undertaker under Part I of this Act, and

(c) the continued fulfilment by the undertakers of their service obligations to a standard no less than that achieved prior to the making of the alteration or adjustment.

(4) If under sub-paragraph (2) above the nominated undertaker requires the altered or adjusted apparatus to be constructed in land other than that in which the undertakers have a right to construct it, paragraph 6(2) and (3) below shall apply to the provision of the requisite facilities and rights as if the apparatus were alternative apparatus.

(5) If any requirement made by the nominated undertaker under sub-paragraph (2) above involves cost in the construction of works under this paragraph exceeding that which would have been involved had the apparatus been altered or adjusted as proposed by the undertakers, and in the absence of the undertakers' proposals the nominated undertaker would have required the removal of the apparatus, the nominated undertaker shall repay to the undertakers the amount of the excess.

4. The nominated undertaker shall give the undertakers not less than 28 days' written preliminary notice of the nominated undertaker's intention to give notice under paragraph 6(1)(a) below in respect of apparatus in any land.

5.—(1) If the undertakers desire to alter or adjust any apparatus which has not been the subject of a notice under paragraph 6(1)(a) below after the extinguishment of their right to do so, they shall (except in the case of works of repair or renewal required in an emergency) submit to the nominated undertaker plans and specifications of the proposed work and such further particulars as the nominated undertaker may reasonably require.

(2) Any work in respect of which the undertakers are subject to an obligation under sub-paragraph (1) above shall not be constructed except in accordance with such plans as may be approved in writing by the nominated undertaker.

(3) Any approval of the nominated undertaker required under this paragraph—

(a) shall be deemed to have been given if it is neither given nor refused within 28 days of the submission of the plans for approval, and

(b) may be given subject to such requirements as the nominated undertaker may make for the purpose of securing that the work does not interfere with the construction or operation of any work authorised by Part I of this Act or for the protection of any such work.

(4) The requirements which the nominated undertaker may make under sub-paragraph (3) above include requirements as to the construction of protective works and the person by whom the works are to be constructed.

(5) Any work constructed under this paragraph shall be constructed with all reasonable despatch under the superintendence (if given) and to the reasonable satisfaction of the nominated undertaker.

6.—(1) This paragraph applies where—

(a) the nominated undertaker for the purpose of constructing any work authorised by Part I of this Act in, on or under any land, requires the removal of any apparatus placed in that land, and gives the undertakers not less than 28 days' written notice of that requirement, together with a plan of the proposed work, and of the proposed position of the alternative apparatus to be provided or constructed, or

(b) in consequence of the exercise of any of the powers of Part I of this Act, the undertakers reasonably require to remove any apparatus.

(2) Subject to sub-paragraph (3) below, the nominated undertaker or the Secretary of State shall afford the undertakers the requisite facilities and rights for the construction of any necessary alternative apparatus in other land which is available for the purpose and which is held or used, or intended for use, by the nominated undertaker for the purposes of its undertaking under this Act or held by the Secretary of State, or in which either of them has sufficient rights or interests and thereafter for the maintenance, repair, renewal and inspection of such apparatus.

(3) Sub-paragraph (4) below applies where facilities and rights required for the construction of apparatus under sub-paragraph (2) above are to be afforded elsewhere than in such other land and neither the nominated undertaker nor the Secretary of State is able to afford such facilities and rights.

(4) The undertakers shall, on receipt of a written notice from the nominated undertaker that this sub-paragraph applies, forthwith use their best endeavours to obtain the necessary facilities and rights; and neither the nominated undertaker nor the Secretary of State shall be under an obligation as to the provision of such facilities and rights in the other land.

(5) The obligation imposed by sub-paragraph (4) above shall not extend to the exercise by the undertakers of any power to acquire by way of compulsory purchase order any land or rights in land, other than any power which may be exercisable by them under paragraph 10 of Schedule 4 to this Act.

7.—(1) Any alternative apparatus to be constructed by the undertakers in pursuance of paragraph 6 above in land held or used, or intended for use, by the nominated undertaker for the purposes of its undertaking under this Act or held by the Secretary of State, or in which the undertakers have obtained the necessary facilities and rights, shall be constructed in such manner, and in such line or situation and in accordance with such programme, as is agreed between the undertakers and the nominated undertaker with a view to securing, among other things, the efficient implementation of the necessary work, the avoidance of unnecessary delay and the continued fulfilment by the undertakers of their service obligations to a standard no less than that achieved prior to the removal of the apparatus which the alternative apparatus replaces, or, in default of agreement, determined by arbitration under paragraph 18 below.

(2) If the undertakers fail to comply with an agreement made under sub-paragraph (1) above, or with the decision of an arbitrator under paragraph 18 below, they shall be liable to compensate the nominated undertaker in respect of any loss or damage (other than loss of, or arising from delayed receipt of, operating revenue due to delayed opening of the rail link) directly resulting from the failure.

8. The undertakers shall, after the manner of construction and the line and situation of any necessary alternative apparatus have been agreed or determined as aforesaid, and after the grant to or obtaining by the undertakers of any such facilities and rights as are referred to in paragraph 6 above, proceed with all reasonable despatch to construct and bring into operation the alternative apparatus and to remove any apparatus required by the nominated undertaker to be removed under the provisions of this Part of this Schedule and, in default, the nominated undertaker may remove that apparatus.

9.—(1) If the nominated undertaker gives notice in writing to the undertakers that it desires to carry out any part of so much of the work necessary in connection with the construction of the alternative apparatus, or the removal of the apparatus required to be removed, as is or will be situate in any lands held or used, or intended for use, by the nominated undertaker for the purposes of its undertaking under this Act or held by the Secretary of State, such work, instead of being carried out by the undertakers, shall be carried out by the nominated undertaker in accordance with plans and specifications and in a position agreed between the undertakers and the nominated undertaker, or, in default of agreement, determined by arbitration under paragraph 18 below, with all reasonable despatch under the superintendence (if given) and to the reasonable satisfaction of the undertakers.

(2) Nothing in this paragraph shall authorise the nominated undertaker to carry out any connection to or disconnection of any existing apparatus.

10.—(1) Where, in accordance with the provisions of this Part of this Schedule the nominated undertaker or the Secretary of State affords to the undertakers facilities and rights for the construction, maintenance, repair, renewal and inspection on land held or used, or intended for use, by the nominated undertaker for the purposes of its undertaking under this Act or held by the Secretary of State of alternative apparatus, those facilities and rights shall be granted upon such terms and conditions as may be agreed between the nominated undertaker or, as the case may be, the Secretary of State, and the undertakers or, in default of agreement, determined by arbitration under paragraph 18 below.

(2) In determining such terms and conditions as aforesaid in respect of alternative apparatus to be constructed across or along any works authorised by Part I of this Act the arbitrator shall—

(a) give effect to all reasonable requirements of the nominated undertaker for ensuring the safety and efficient operation of those works and for securing any subsequent alterations or adaptations of the alternative apparatus which may be required to prevent interference with any proposed works of the nominated undertaker or the use of the same, and

(b) so far as it may be reasonable and practicable to do so in the circumstances of the case, give effect to the terms and conditions (if any) applicable to the apparatus for which the alternative apparatus is to be substituted and have regard to the undertakers' ability to fulfil their service obligations.

(3) If the facilities and rights to be afforded by the nominated undertaker or the Secretary of State in respect of any alternative apparatus, and the terms and conditions subject to which those facilities and rights are to be granted are, in the opinion of the arbitrator, more or less favourable on the whole to the undertakers than the facilities, rights, terms and conditions applying to the apparatus to be removed, the arbitrator shall make such provision for the payment of compensation to or by the nominated undertaker or the Secretary of State to or by the undertakers in respect thereof as appears to him to be reasonable having regard to all the circumstances of the case.

11.—(1) Not less than 28 days before commencing to construct any work authorised by Part I of this Act which is near to, or will or may affect, any apparatus the removal of which has not been required by the nominated undertaker under paragraph 6 above, the nominated undertaker shall submit to the undertakers a plan and description of the work and of any protective measures which the nominated undertaker proposes to take in respect of that apparatus, together with a specification of such measures where appropriate.

(2) The work shall be constructed only in accordance with the plan and description submitted as aforesaid and in accordance with such reasonable requirements as may be made by the undertakers for the alteration or otherwise for the protection of the apparatus or for securing access thereto, and the undertakers shall be entitled by their officer to watch and inspect the construction of the work.

(3) If the undertakers within 14 days after the submission to them of any such plan and description shall, in consequence of the works proposed by the nominated undertaker, reasonably require the removal of any apparatus and give written notice to the nominated undertaker of that requirement, this Part of this Schedule shall have effect as if the removal of such apparatus had been required by the nominated undertaker under paragraph 6 above.

(4) Nothing in sub-paragraphs (1) to (3) above shall preclude the nominated undertaker from submitting at any time, or from time to time, but in no case less than 28 days before commencing the construction of the work, a new plan and description thereof in lieu of the plan and description previously submitted, and thereupon the provisions of those sub-paragraphs shall apply to and in respect of the new plan and description.

(5) The nominated undertaker shall not be required to comply with sub-paragraphs (1) to (3) above in a case of emergency but in such a case it shall give notice to the undertakers as soon as reasonably practicable and a plan and description of those works as soon as reasonably practicable thereafter, and shall comply with those sub-paragraphs so far as reasonably practicable in the circumstances.

12. If in consequence of the exercise of the powers of Part I of this Act the access to any apparatus is materially obstructed the nominated undertaker shall, so far as reasonably practicable, provide alternative means of access to such apparatus which is no less convenient than the access enjoyed by the undertakers prior to the obstruction.

13. Where, in consequence of Part I of this Act, any part of any highway in which any apparatus is situate ceases to be part of a highway, the undertakers may exercise the same rights of access to such apparatus as they enjoyed immediately before the passing of Part I of this Act, but nothing in this paragraph shall affect any right of the nominated undertaker or of the undertakers to require removal of that apparatus under this Part of this Schedule or the power of the nominated undertaker to construct works in accordance with paragraph 11 above.

14.—(1) Subject to the following provisions of this paragraph, the nominated undertaker shall repay to the undertakers the reasonable expenses incurred by the undertakers in, or in connection with—

(a) the removal and relaying or replacing, alteration or protection of any apparatus or the construction of any new apparatus under any provision of this Part of this Schedule,

(b) the cutting off of any apparatus from any other apparatus in consequence of the exercise by the nominated undertaker of any power under Part I of this Act, and

(c) any other work or thing rendered reasonably necessary in consequence of the exercise by the nominated undertaker of any such power.

(2) There shall be deducted from any sum payable under sub-paragraph (1) above the value of any apparatus removed under the provisions of this Part of this Schedule, that value being calculated after removal.

(3) If in pursuance of the provisions of this Part of this Schedule—

(a) alternative apparatus of better type, or greater capacity or of greater dimensions is placed in substitution for existing apparatus of worse type, of smaller capacity or of smaller dimensions, except where this has been solely due to using the nearest currently available type, or

(b) apparatus (whether existing apparatus or alternative apparatus) is placed at a depth greater than the depth at which the existing apparatus was situated,

and the placing of apparatus of that type or capacity or of those dimensions, or the placing of apparatus at that depth, as the case may be, is not agreed by the nominated undertaker or, in default of agreement, is not determined by arbitration to be necessary, then, if it involves cost in the construction of works under paragraph 6 above exceeding that which would have been involved if the apparatus placed had been of the existing type, capacity or dimensions, or at the existing depth, as the case may be, the amount which apart from this sub-paragraph would be payable to the undertakers by virtue of sub-paragraph (1) above shall be reduced by the amount of that excess.

(4) For the purposes of sub-paragraph (3) above—

(a) an extension of apparatus to a length greater than the length of existing apparatus shall not be treated as a placing of apparatus of greater dimensions than those of the existing apparatus except in a case where the apparatus as so extended serves a purpose (either additional to or instead of that served by the existing apparatus) which was not served by the existing apparatus, and

(b) where the provision of a joint in a cable is agreed, or is determined to be necessary, the consequential provision of a jointing chamber or of a manhole shall be treated as if it also had been agreed or had been so determined.

(5) An amount which apart from this sub-paragraph would be payable to the undertakers in respect of works by virtue of this paragraph shall, if the works include the placing of apparatus

provided in substitution for apparatus placed more than 7½ years earlier so as to confer on the undertakers any financial benefit by deferment of the time for renewal of the apparatus or of the system of which it forms part in the ordinary course, be reduced by the amount which represents that benefit.

(6) In any case where work is carried out by the nominated undertaker pursuant to paragraph 9 above and, if such work had been carried out by the undertakers, the repayment made to the undertakers under this paragraph would fall to be reduced pursuant to sub-paragraphs (3) to (5) above, the undertakers shall pay to the nominated undertaker such sum as represents the amount of that reduction.

15.—(1) Subject to sub-paragraphs (2) and (3) below, if by reason or in consequence of the construction of any of the works authorised by Part I of this Act, or any subsidence resulting from any of those works, any damage is caused to any apparatus (other than apparatus the repair of which is not reasonably necessary in view of its intended removal for the purposes of those works) or property of the undertakers, or there is any interruption in any service provided, or in the supply of any goods, by any of the undertakers, the nominated undertaker shall bear and pay the cost reasonably incurred by the undertakers in making good such damage or restoring the supply and shall—

(a) make reasonable compensation to the undertakers for loss sustained by them, and

(b) indemnify the undertakers against claims, demands, proceedings, costs, damages and expenses which may be made or taken against, or recovered from, or incurred by, the undertakers,

by reason or in consequence of any such damage or interruption.

(2) Nothing in sub-paragraph (1) above shall impose any liability on the nominated undertaker with respect to any damage or interruption to the extent that it is attributable to the act, neglect or default of the undertakers, their officers, servants, contractors or agents.

(3) The undertakers shall give the nominated undertaker reasonable notice of any such claim or demand and no settlement or compromise thereof shall be made without the consent of the nominated undertaker which, if it withholds such consent, shall have the sole conduct of any settlement or compromise or of any proceedings necessary to resist the claim or demand.

16. The nominated undertaker shall, so far as is reasonably practicable, so exercise its powers under paragraphs 6 and 7 of Schedule 2 to this Act as not to obstruct or render less convenient the access to any apparatus.

17. Notwithstanding the temporary stopping up or diversion of any highway under paragraph 6 of Schedule 3 to this Act, the undertakers may do all such works and things in any such highway as may be reasonably necessary to enable them to inspect, repair, maintain, renew, remove or use any apparatus which at the time of the stopping up or diversion was in that highway.

18.—(1) Any dispute arising between the nominated undertaker and the undertakers under this Part of this Schedule (other than a dispute under paragraph 5(1) to (4) above) shall be determined by an arbitrator who shall be appointed by agreement between the parties or, in default of such agreement, shall be the Secretary of State.

(2) In determining any such dispute the arbitrator may, if he thinks fit, require the nominated undertaker to construct any temporary or other works so as to avoid, so far as reasonably possible, interference with the use of any apparatus.

PART III

PROTECTION OF LAND DRAINAGE, FLOOD DEFENCE, WATER RESOURCES AND FISHERIES

1.—(1) The following provisions of this Part of this Schedule shall, unless otherwise agreed in writing between the nominated undertaker and the Agency, have effect.

(2) In this Part of this Schedule—

"the Agency" means the Environment Agency;

"construction" includes execution, placing, altering, replacing, relaying and removal;

"drainage work" means any watercourse and includes any land which is expected to provide flood storage capacity for any watercourse at intervals not less frequent than—

(a) in the case of land in a rural area, once in 50 years, and

(b) in the case of land in an urban area, once in 100 years,

or, if more frequent, the appropriate return period for the watercourse for which capacity is provided, and any bank, wall, embankment or other structure, or any appliance, constructed or used for land drainage, flood defence or tidal monitoring;

"fishery" means any waters containing fish and fish in, or migrating to or from such waters and the spawn, spawning grounds or food of such fish;

"plans" includes sections, drawings, specifications and method statements;

"specified work" means so much of any permanent or temporary work authorised by Part I of this Act (which includes, for the avoidance of doubt, any dredging and any geotechnical investigations that may be undertaken) as is likely to—

(a) affect any drainage work or the volumetric rate of flow of water in or flowing to or from any drainage work;

(b) affect the flow, purity or quality of water in any watercourse or other surface waters or ground water;

(c) cause obstruction to the free passage of fish or damage to any fishery; or

(d) affect the conservation, distribution or use of water resources; and

"watercourse" includes all rivers, streams, ditches, drains, cuts, culverts, dykes, sluices, sewers and passages through which water flows except a public sewer.

2.—(1) Before beginning to construct any specified work, the nominated undertaker shall submit to the Agency plans of the work and such further particulars available to it as the Agency may within 14 days of the submission of the plans reasonably require.

(2) Any such specified work shall not be constructed except in accordance with such plans as may be approved in writing by the Agency, or determined under paragraph 12 below.

(3) Any approval of the Agency required under this paragraph—

(a) shall not be unreasonably withheld;

(b) shall be deemed to have been given if it is neither given nor refused within 28 days of the submission of the plans for approval; and

(c) may be given subject to such reasonable requirements as the Agency may make for the protection of any drainage work or fishery or for the protection of water resources, or for the prevention of flooding or pollution.

3. The requirements which the Agency may make under paragraph 2 above include conditions requiring the nominated undertaker at its own expense to construct such protective works (including any new works as well as alterations to existing works) as are reasonably necessary—

(a) to safeguard any drainage work against damage, or

(b) to secure that its efficiency for flood defence purposes is not impaired,

during the construction of the specified work.

4.—(1) Any specified work, and all protective works required by the Agency under paragraph 2 above, shall be constructed to the reasonable satisfaction of the Agency and the Agency shall be entitled by its officer to watch and inspect the construction of such works.

(2) The nominated undertaker shall give to the Agency not less than 14 days' notice in writing of its intention to commence construction of any specified work and notice in writing of its completion not later than 7 days after the date on which it is brought into use.

(3) If any part of the works comprising a structure in, over or under a watercourse is constructed otherwise than in accordance with the requirements of this Part of this Schedule, the Agency may by notice in writing require the nominated undertaker at the nominated undertaker's own expense to comply with the requirements of this Part of this Schedule or (if the nominated undertaker so elects and the Agency in writing consents, such consent not to be unreasonably withheld) to remove, alter or pull down the work and, where removal is required, to restore the site to its former condition to such extent and within such limits as the Agency reasonably requires.

(4) Subject to sub-paragraph (5) below, if within a reasonable period, being not less than 28 days from the date when a notice under sub-paragraph (3) above is served upon the nominated undertaker, it has failed to begin taking steps to comply with the requirements of the notice and thereafter to make reasonably expeditious progress towards their implementation, the Agency may execute the works specified in the notice and any expenditure incurred by it in so doing shall be recoverable from the nominated undertaker.

(5) In the event of any dispute as to whether sub-paragraph (3) above is properly applicable to any work in respect of which notice has been served under that sub-paragraph, or as to the reasonableness of any requirement of such a notice, the Agency shall not except in an emergency exercise the powers conferred by sub-paragraph (4) above until the dispute has been finally determined.

5.—(1) Any work constructed under Part I of this Act for the purpose of providing a flood defence shall be maintained to the reasonable satisfaction of the Agency by the person who has control of the work.

(2) If any such work is not maintained to the reasonable satisfaction of the Agency, the Agency may by notice in writing require that person to repair and restore the work, or any part thereof, or (if the person having control of the work so elects and the Agency in writing consents, such consent not to be unreasonably withheld), to remove the work and restore the site (including any sea defences) to its former condition, to such extent and within such limits as the Agency reasonably requires.

(3) If, within a reasonable period being not less than 28 days beginning with the date on which a notice in respect of any work is served under sub-paragraph (2) above on the person who has control of that work, that person has failed to begin taking steps to comply with the reasonable requirements of the notice and has not thereafter made reasonably expeditious progress towards their implementation, the Agency may do what is necessary for such compliance and may recover any expenditure reasonably incurred by it in so doing from that person.

(4) In the event of any dispute as to the reasonableness of any requirement of a notice served under sub-paragraph (2) above, the Agency shall not except in a case of immediate foreseeable need exercise the powers of sub-paragraph (3) above until the dispute has been finally determined.

6.—(1) If by reason of the construction of any specified work or of the failure of any such work the efficiency of any drainage work for flood defence purposes is impaired, or that work is otherwise damaged, so as to require remedial action, such impairment or damage shall be made good by the nominated undertaker to the reasonable satisfaction of the Agency.

(2) If such impaired or damaged drainage work for flood defence purposes is not made good to the reasonable satisfaction of the Agency, the Agency may by notice in writing require the nominated undertaker to restore it to its former standard of efficiency or where necessary to construct some other work in substitution therefor.

(3) If, within a reasonable period being not less than 28 days beginning with the date on which a notice in respect of impaired or damaged drainage work for flood defence purposes is served under sub-paragraph (2) above on the nominated undertaker, the nominated undertaker has failed to begin taking steps to comply with the requirements of the notice and has not thereafter made reasonably expeditious progress towards its implementation, the Agency may do what is necessary for such compliance and may recover any expenditure reasonably incurred by it in so doing from the nominated undertaker.

(4) In the event of any dispute as to the reasonableness of any requirement of a notice served under sub-paragraph (2) above, the Agency shall not except in a case of immediate foreseeable need exercise the powers conferred by sub-paragraph (3) above until the dispute has been finally determined.

7.—(1) The nominated undertaker shall take all such measures as may be reasonably practicable to prevent any interruption of the free passage of fish in any fishery during the construction of any specified work.

(2) If by reason of—

(a) the construction of any specified work, or

(b) the failure of any such work,

damage to a fishery is caused, or the Agency has reason to expect that such damage may be caused, the Agency may serve notice on the nominated undertaker requiring it to take such steps as may be reasonably practicable to make good the damage or, as the case may be, to protect the fishery against such damage.

(3) If, within such time as may be reasonably practicable for that purpose after the receipt of written notice from the Agency of any damage or expected damage to a fishery, the nominated undertaker fails to take such steps as are described in sub-paragraph (2) above, the Agency may take those steps and may recover from the nominated undertaker the expense reasonably incurred by it in doing so.

(4) In any case where immediate action by the Agency is reasonably required in order to secure that the risk of damage to a fishery is avoided or reduced, the Agency may take such steps as are reasonable for the purpose, and may recover from the nominated undertaker the reasonable cost of so doing provided that notice specifying those steps is served on the nominated undertaker as soon as reasonably practicable after the Agency has taken, or commenced to take, the steps specified in the notice.

8.—(1) The nominated undertaker shall indemnify the Agency from all claims, demands, proceedings or damages, which may be made or taken against, or recovered from the Agency by reason of—

(a) any damage to any drainage work so as to impair its efficiency for flood defence purposes,

(b) any damage to a fishery,

(c) any raising or lowering of the water table in land adjoining the works authorised by this Act or any sewers, drains and watercourses, or

(d) any flooding or increased flooding of any such lands,

which is caused by, or results from, the construction of any specified work or any act or omission of the nominated undertaker, its contractors, agents or employees whilst engaged upon the work.

(2) The Agency shall give to the nominated undertaker reasonable notice of any such claim or demand and no settlement or compromise thereof shall be made without the consent of the

nominated undertaker which, if it withholds such consent, shall have the sole conduct of any settlement or compromise or of any proceedings necessary to resist the claim or demand.

9. Nothing in paragraph 8 above shall require the nominated undertaker to indemnify the Agency in respect of any claim, demand, proceedings or damages which the Agency could reasonably make, take against or recover from any other person.

10. The fact that any work or thing has been executed or done in accordance with a plan approved or deemed to be approved by the Agency, or to its satisfaction, or in accordance with any directions or award of an arbitrator, shall not relieve the nominated undertaker from any liability under the provisions of this Part of this Schedule.

11. For the purposes of section 5 of the Metropolis Management (Thames River Prevention of Floods) Amendment Act 1879 and Chapter II of Part II of the Water Resources Act 1991 (abstraction and impounding of water) and section 109 of that Act (as to structures in, over or under watercourses) as applying to the construction of any specified work, any consent or approval given or deemed to be given by the Agency under this Part of this Schedule with respect to such construction shall be deemed also to constitute an impounding licence under that Chapter or, as the case may be, a consent or approval under those sections, and the nominated undertaker shall not be obliged to serve any notice which would otherwise be required by section 30 of the said Act of 1991 (which relates to the construction of boreholes and similar works in respect of which a licence is not required).

12.—(1) Any dispute arising between the nominated undertaker and the Agency under this Part of this Schedule shall, if the parties agree, be determined by arbitration, but shall otherwise be determined by the appropriate Ministers acting jointly.

(2) In sub-paragraph (1) above, the reference to the appropriate Ministers—

(a) in the case of a dispute concerning fisheries, flood defence or land drainage, is to the Secretary of State for the Environment, the Secretary of State for Transport and the Minister of Agriculture, Fisheries and Food, and

(b) in the case of any other dispute, is to the Secretary of State for the Environment and the Secretary of State for Transport.

Part IV

Protection of Telecommunications Operators

1.—(1) The following provisions of this Part of this Schedule shall, unless otherwise agreed in writing between the nominated undertaker and telecommunications operator, have effect.

(2) In this Part of this Schedule—

"the authorised works" means the works authorised by Part I of this Act;

"construction" includes installation and "construct" shall be construed accordingly;

"telecommunications code" means the telecommunications code contained in Schedule 2 to the Telecommunications Act 1984;

"telecommunications operator" means the operator of a telecommunications code system; and

"operator", "telecommunication apparatus", "telecommunications code system" and "telecommunication system" have the same meanings as in Schedule 4 to the Telecommunications Act 1984.

2.—(1) Paragraph 21 of the telecommunications code shall not apply for the purposes of the authorised works to the extent that such works are regulated by Part XI of the Town and Country Planning Act 1990, sections 84 and 85 of the New Roads and Street Works Act 1991 (or regulations made under section 85 of that Act) or sub-paragraphs (3) to (8) of paragraph 4 below.

(2) Paragraph 23 of the telecommunications code shall apply for the purposes of the authorised works, save—

(a) insofar as such works are regulated by the New Roads and Street Works Act 1991 or any regulation made under that Act; or

(b) where the nominated undertaker exercises a right under subsection (4)(b) of section 272 of the Town and Country Planning Act 1990 or under an order made under that section to remove telecommunications apparatus.

3. The temporary stopping up or diversion of any highway under paragraph 6 of Schedule 3 to this Act shall not affect any right of a telecommunications operator under paragraph 9 of the telecommunications code in respect of any apparatus which at the time of the stopping up or diversion is in the highway.

4.—(1) Where a highway is stopped up under paragraph 1 or 2 of Schedule 3 to this Act, any telecommunications operator whose telecommunications apparatus is under, over, in, on, along or across that highway may exercise the same rights of access in order to inspect, maintain, adjust, repair or alter that apparatus as if this Act had not been passed, but nothing in this sub-paragraph shall affect any right of the nominated undertaker or the telecommunications operator to require removal of that apparatus under this Part of this Schedule or the power of the nominated undertaker to alter apparatus in accordance with paragraph 23 of the telecommunications code.

(2) The nominated undertaker shall give not less than 28 days' notice in writing of its intention to stop up any highway under paragraph 1 or 2 of Schedule 3 to this Act to any telecommunications operator whose apparatus is under, over, in, on, along or across the highway.

(3) Where a notice under sub-paragraph (2) above has been given, the telecommunications operator, if it reasonably considers that it is necessary for the safe and efficient operation and maintenance of the apparatus, may, and if reasonably requested so to do by the nominated undertaker in the notice, shall, as soon as reasonably practicable after the service of the notice—

(a) remove the apparatus and place it or other apparatus provided in substitution for it in such other position as the telecommunications operator may reasonably determine and have power to place it, or

(b) provide other apparatus in substitution for the existing apparatus and place it in such other position as aforesaid.

(4) Subject to the following provisions of this paragraph the nominated undertaker shall pay to any telecommunications operator an amount equal to the cost reasonably incurred by the telecommunications operator in or in connection with—

(a) the execution of relocation works required in consequence of the stopping up of the highway, and

(b) the doing of any other work or thing rendered necessary by the execution of relocation works.

(5) If in the course of the execution of relocation works under sub-paragraph (3) above—

(a) apparatus of better type, greater capacity or greater dimensions is placed in substitution for existing apparatus of worse type, smaller capacity or smaller dimensions, except where this has been solely due to using the nearest currently available type, capacity or dimension, or

(b) apparatus (whether existing apparatus or apparatus substituted for existing apparatus) is placed at a depth greater than the depth at which existing apparatus was,

and the placing of apparatus of that type or capacity or of those dimensions or the placing of apparatus at that depth, as the case may be, is not agreed by the nominated undertaker, or, in default of agreement, is not determined by arbitration to be necessary in consequence of the construction of the authorised works in order to ensure the continued efficient operation of the telecommunications system of the telecommunications operator then, if it involves cost in the execution of the relocation works exceeding that which would have been involved if the apparatus placed had been of the existing type, capacity or dimensions, or at the existing depth, as the case may be, the amount which apart from this paragraph would be payable to the telecommunications operator by virtue of sub-paragraph (4) above shall be reduced by the amount of that excess.

(6) For the purposes of sub-paragraph (5) above—

(a) an extension of apparatus to a length greater than the length of existing apparatus shall not be treated as a placing of apparatus of greater dimensions than those of the existing apparatus except in a case where the apparatus as so extended provides more than an equivalent service, and

(b) where the provision of a joint in a cable is agreed, or is determined to be necessary, the consequential provision of a jointing chamber or of a manhole (in either case of such type, capacity and dimensions as shall reasonably be appropriate) shall be treated as if it also had been agreed or had been so determined.

(7) The amount which apart from this sub-paragraph would be payable to a telecommunications operator in respect of works by virtue of sub-paragraph (4) above (and having regard, where relevant, to sub-paragraph (5) above) shall, if the works include the placing of apparatus provided in substitution for apparatus placed more than 7½ years earlier so as to confer on the telecommunications operator any financial benefit by deferment of the time for renewal of the apparatus in the ordinary course, be reduced by the amount which represents that benefit.

(8) Sub-paragraphs (4) to (7) above shall not apply where the authorised works constitute major transport works or major highway works for the purpose of Part III of the New Roads and Street Works Act 1991 (including that provision as applied by paragraph 8 of Schedule 3 to this Act), but instead—

(a) the allowable costs of any relocation works shall be determined in accordance with section 85 of that Act (sharing of costs of necessary measures) and any regulations for the time being having effect under that section, and

(b) the allowable costs shall be borne by the nominated undertaker and the telecommunications operator in such proportions as may be prescribed by any such regulations.

5.—(1) Subject to sub-paragraphs (2) to (4) below, if by reason or in consequence of the construction of the authorised works or any subsidence resulting from any of those works, any damage is caused to any telecommunications apparatus, other than apparatus the repair of which is not reasonably necessary in view of its intended removal for the purposes of those works, or property of the telecommunications operator, or there is any interruption in the supply of the service provided by the telecommunications operator, the nominated undertaker shall bear and pay the cost reasonably incurred by the operator in making good such damage or restoring the supply and shall—

(a) make reasonable compensation to the telecommunications operator for loss sustained by it, and

(b) indemnify the telecommunications operator against claims, demands, proceedings, costs, damages and expenses which may be made or taken against, or recovered from, or incurred by, the operator, by reason or in consequence of any such damage or interruption.

(2) Sub-paragraph (1) above shall not apply to any apparatus in respect of which the relations between the nominated undertaker and the telecommunications operator are regulated by the provisions of Part III of the New Roads and Street Works Act 1991 or to any damage, or any interruption, caused by electro-magnetic interference arising from the construction or use of the authorised works.

(3) Nothing in sub-paragraph (1) above shall impose any liability on the nominated undertaker with respect to any damage or interruption to the extent that it is attributable to the act, neglect or default of the telecommunications operator, its officers, servants. contractors or agents.

(4) The telecommunications operator shall give the nominated undertaker reasonable notice of any such claim or demand and no settlement or compromise thereof shall be made without the consent of the nominated undertaker which, if it withholds such consent, shall have the sole conduct of any settlement or compromise or of any proceedings necessary to resist the claim or demand.

6. Any dispute arising under this Part of this Schedule shall be determined by an arbitrator who shall be appointed by agreement between the parties or, in default of such agreement, shall be the Secretary of State.

Part V

Protection of Port of Sheerness Limited

1.—(1) The following provisions of this Part of this Schedule shall, unless otherwise agreed in writing between the nominated undertaker and the port authority, have effect for the protection of the port authority.

(2) In this Part of this Schedule—

"construction" includes execution, placing, altering, replacing, relaying and removal;

"plans" includes sections, drawings, specifications and method statements;

"the port authority" means the Port of Sheerness Limited;

"the river" means the River Medway;

"operations" includes temporary works, dredging works and temporary mooring of vessels authorised by paragraph 11 of Schedule 2 to this Act;

"tidal work" means so much of any work authorised by Part I of this Act as is on or over the surface of land below the level of mean high water springs forming part of the river.

2.—(1) Before beginning any operations for the construction of any tidal work, the nominated undertaker shall submit to the port authority plans of the work and such further particulars available to it as the port authority may within 14 days of the submission of the plans reasonably require.

(2) Such further particulars may include such relevant hydraulic and geological information as may be available to the nominated undertaker and is not in the possession of the port authority.

(3) A tidal work shall not be constructed except in accordance with such plans as may be approved by the port authority or determined under paragraph 14 below.

(4) Any approval of the port authority required under this paragraph shall not be unreasonably withheld and—

(a) shall be deemed to have been given if it is neither given nor refused (with an indication of the grounds for that refusal) within 28 days of the submission of the plans for approval; and

(b) may be given subject to such reasonable requirements as the port authority may make for the protection of traffic in, or the flow or regime of, the river.

3. The nominated undertaker shall carry out all operations for the construction of any tidal works with all reasonable despatch to the reasonable satisfaction of the port authority (and shall promptly remove all temporary works as soon as the same are no longer required) so that river traffic shall not suffer more interference than is reasonably practicable and the port authority shall be entitled by its officer at all reasonable times, on giving such notice as may be reasonable in the circumstances, to inspect such operations.

4.—(1) The nominated undertaker shall not, without the consent of the port authority, deposit in, or allow to fall or be washed into, the river any gravel, soil or other material.

(2) Any consent of the port authority under this paragraph shall not be unreasonably withheld and—

(a) shall be deemed to have been given if it is neither given nor refused within 28 days of the submission of the request therefor; and

(b) may be given subject to such reasonable requirements as the port authority may make for the protection of navigation in, or the flow or regime of, the river.

(3) In its application to the discharge of water into the river, paragraph 9(5) of Schedule 2 to this Act shall have effect subject to the terms of any conditions attached to a consent given under this paragraph.

(4) Nothing in this paragraph authorises the doing of anything prohibited by section 85(1), (2) or (3) of the Water Resources Act 1991 (offences of polluting controlled waters).

5. If any pile, stump or other obstruction to navigation becomes exposed in the course of constructing any tidal work (other than a pile, stump or other obstruction on the site of any permanent work), the nominated undertaker shall, as soon as reasonably practicable after the receipt of notice in writing from the port authority requiring such action, remove it from the river or, if it is not reasonably practicable to remove it, cut it off at such level below the bed of the river (not being more than two metres below bed level in the main navigation channel or one metre below bed level elsewhere in the river) as the port authority may reasonably direct and in the absence of such action within a reasonable period of time the port authority may carry out the removal and recover its reasonable expenses in so doing from the nominated undertaker.

6.—(1) If—

(a) by reason of the construction of any tidal work, it is necessary for the port authority to incur costs in altering, removing, resiting or reinstating relevant existing moorings, or laying down and removing relevant substituted moorings, or carrying out dredging operations for any such purpose not being costs which it would have incurred for any other reason; and

(b) the port authority gives to the nominated undertaker not less than 28 days' notice of its intention to incur such costs, and takes into account any representations which the nominated undertaker may make in response to the notice within 14 days of the receipt of the notice;

the nominated undertaker shall pay the costs reasonably so incurred by the port authority.

(2) For the purpose of this paragraph "relevant moorings" are moorings which are owned by the port authority, or moorings which are licensed by the port authority and in respect of which it is under an obligation to provide substitute moorings.

7. The nominated undertaker shall, at or near every tidal work, exhibit such lights, lay down such buoys and take such other steps for preventing danger to navigation as the port authority may from time to time reasonably require.

8.—(1) If any tidal work is abandoned or falls into decay, the port authority may by notice in writing to the nominated undertaker require it, either to repair and restore the work or any part of it, or (if the nominated undertaker no longer requires the work) to remove the work and restore the site to its former condition to such extent as the port authority reasonably requires.

(2) If—

(a) a work which consists of a tidal work and non-tidal work is abandoned or falls into decay; and

(b) the non-tidal work is in such a condition as to interfere with the right of navigation in the river,

the port authority may include the non-tidal work, or any part of it, in any notice under this paragraph.

(3) In sub-paragraph (2) above, references to a non-tidal work are to so much of any work authorised by Part I of this Act as is on or over land above the level of mean high water springs.

(4) If after such reasonable period as may be specified in a notice under this paragraph the work specified in the notice has not been carried out, the port authority may carry out that work and the nominated undertaker shall pay the amount of any expenditure reasonably incurred by the port authority in so carrying it out.

9.—(1) Without prejudice to the provisions of paragraph 7 above, the nominated undertaker shall provide, or afford reasonable facilities for the port authority to provide and maintain, at the viaduct over the river comprised in Work No. 13, such navigational lights or other apparatus for the benefit of navigation as the port authority may reasonably consider necessary by reason of construction of the viaduct or the carrying out of operations for its construction.

(2) The nominated undertaker shall pay to the port authority the costs reasonably incurred by it in connection with the provision and maintenance of that apparatus.

10. On the completion of the construction of the viaduct over the river comprised in Work No. 13 the nominated undertaker shall supply to the port authority a plan and sections and cross-sections on an appropriate scale showing the situation and level of the viaduct over the river.

11. The nominated undertaker shall not, except for the purpose of constructing a tidal work or any connected works, remove any gravel, soil or other materials from the bed, shores or banks of the river without the previous consent of the port authority signified in writing under the hand of its secretary (such consent not to be unreasonably withheld), but nothing in this paragraph shall prevent the use by the nominated undertaker of any gravel, soil or other material so removed for the purposes of the construction of other tidal works or any connected works.

12.—(1) The nominated undertaker shall indemnify the port authority from all claims, demands, proceedings or damages which may be made or given against or recovered from the port authority by reason of any damage to the river or its banks or any works or apparatus of the port authority in the river which is caused by or results from the construction of any tidal work or any act or omission of the nominated undertaker, its contractors, agents or employees whilst engaged upon the work, and from any costs reasonably incurred by the port authority in making good such damage.

(2) The port authority shall give to the nominated undertaker reasonable notice of any such claim or demand and no settlement or compromise thereof shall be made without the consent of the nominated undertaker which, if it notifies the port authority that it desires to do so, shall have the sole conduct of any settlement or compromise or of any proceedings necessary to resist the claim or demand.

(3) Nothing in sub-paragraph (1) above shall impose any liability on the nominated undertaker in respect of silting or scouring.

13. Nothing in paragraph 12 above shall impose any liability on the nominated undertaker with respect to any damage to the extent that it is attributable to the act, neglect or default of the port authority, its officers, servants, contractors or agents, but the fact that any work or thing has been executed or done in accordance with a plan approved or deemed to be approved by the port authority, or to its satisfaction, or in accordance with any directions or award of an arbitrator, shall not (in the absence of negligence on the part of the port authority, its officers, servants, contractors or agents) relieve the nominated undertaker from any liability under the provisions of this Part of this Schedule.

14. Any dispute arising between the nominated undertaker and the port authority under this Part of this Schedule shall, if the parties agree, be determined by arbitration, but shall otherwise be determined by the Secretary of State.

Part VI

Protection of British Waterways Board

1.—(1) The following provisions of this Part of this Schedule shall, unless otherwise agreed in writing between the nominated undertaker and the Board, have effect.

(2) In this Part of this Schedule—

"the Board" means the British Waterways Board;

"the canal" means the Regent's Canal (including the St Pancras Yacht Basin), the River Lee Navigation or the Waterworks River as the case may be, insofar as any of those waterways is owned or managed by the Board, and includes any works connected therewith for the maintenance of which the Board is responsible and any lands held or used by the Board for the purposes of the canal;

"construction" includes execution, placing, altering, replacing and relaying and includes removal;

"plans" includes sections, drawings, specifications and method statements;

"specified work" means so much of any permanent or temporary work authorised by Part I of this Act as is in, across, under, over or in the vicinity of the canal.

2. The Secretary of State shall not under the powers of section 4 above acquire compulsorily any land of the Board or any easement or other right over such land in the London Boroughs of Camden, Islington, Hackney or Newham other than such land, or easements or other rights thereover, as is reasonably necessary for, or in connection with, the construction, maintenance or operation of works authorised by Part I of this Act.

3.—(1) Before beginning to construct any specified work, the nominated undertaker shall submit to the Board plans of the work and such further particulars available to it as the Board may within 14 days of the submission of the plans reasonably require.

(2) Any specified work shall not be constructed except in accordance with such plans as may be approved in writing by the Board or determined under paragraph 11 below.

(3) Any approval of the Board required under this paragraph shall not be unreasonably withheld and—

(a) shall be deemed to have been given if it is neither given nor refused within 28 days of the submission of the plans for approval; and

(b) may be given subject to such reasonable requirements as the Board may make for the purpose of ensuring the safety or stability of the canal, including requirements as to the construction of protective works.

4.—(1) Any specified work, and any protective works required by the Board under paragraph 3(3)(b) above, shall be constructed with all reasonable despatch to the reasonable satisfaction of the Board, and in such manner as to cause as little damage to the canal as may be reasonably practicable and as little interference as may be reasonably practicable with the passage of vessels using the canal, and the Board shall be entitled by its officer at all reasonable times, on giving such notice as may be reasonable in the circumstances, to inspect the construction of such work or works.

(2) The nominated undertaker shall give to the Board not less than 28 days' notice in writing of its intention to commence construction of any specified work or any protective works and also, except in emergency (when the nominated undertaker shall give such notice as may be reasonably practicable), of its intention to carry out any works for the repair or maintenance of any specified work insofar as such works of repair or maintenance affect or interfere with the canal.

5. In constructing the bridge, or bridges, forming parts of Works Nos. 1AA, 1BB, 1CC, 1DD, 1EE, 3B and 3C over the canal, the nominated undertaker shall ensure that the soffit of any bridge at its lowest point is at a level of not less than 26.28 metres above Ordnance Datum Newlyn.

6.—(1) The nominated undertaker shall not deposit any polluting material on, in or over the canal and shall not without the consent of the Board—

(a) deposit any other materials on, in or over the canal; or

(b) notwithstanding anything in paragraph 9 of Schedule 2 to this Act (which authorises the discharge of water in connection with the construction or maintenance of works authorised under Part I of this Act), discharge any water directly or indirectly into the canal.

(2) Any consent of the Board required under this paragraph shall not be reasonably withheld and—

(a) shall be deemed to have been given if it is neither given nor refused within 28 days of the submission of the request therefor; and

(b) may be given subject to such reasonable requirements as the Board may make—

(i) in the case of a deposit, so as to ensure that the use of the canal is not obstructed or rendered less safe, and

(ii) in the case of a discharge, concerning the reimbursement by the nominated undertaker of expenses incurred by the Board in disposing of the water so discharged, being expenses which the Board would not have incurred but for the discharge.

7. In its application to the discharge of water into the canal, paragraph 9(5) of Schedule 2 to this Act shall have effect subject to the terms of any conditions attached to the consent under paragraph 6(2) above and, where such discharge includes a deposit to which consent has been given under paragraph 6(1) above, to any conditions attached to that consent.

8.—(1) If as a result of the construction of any specified work any part of the towing path beside the canal, or any public right of way giving access thereto, is temporarily closed to pedestrians or cyclists and there is no way which provides a reasonable alternative, the nominated undertaker shall, so far as reasonably practicable and to the extent that it is consistent with safety, provide a substitute path or paths for such time as the closure continues.

(2) This paragraph is without prejudice to the requirements of paragraph 6(2) of Schedule 3 to this Act and of paragraph 3(1) of Part I of this Schedule.

9.—(1) The nominated undertaker shall indemnify the Board from all claims, demands, proceedings or damages, which may be made or given against, or recovered from the Board by reason of any damage to the canal which is caused by, or results from, the construction of any specified work or protective work or any act or omission of the nominated undertaker, its contractors, agents or employees whilst engaged upon the work and from any costs reasonably incurred in making good such damage.

(2) The Board shall give to the nominated undertaker reasonable notice of any such claim or demand and no settlement or compromise thereof shall be made without the consent of the nominated undertaker which, if it notifies the Board that it desires to do so, shall have the sole conduct of any settlement or compromise or of any proceedings necessary to resist the claim or demand.

10. Nothing in paragraph 9 above shall impose any liability on the nominated undertaker with respect to any damage to the extent that it is attributable to the act, neglect or default of the Board, its officers, servants, contractors or agents but the fact that any work or thing has been executed or done in accordance with a plan approved or deemed to be approved by the Board, or to its satisfaction, or in accordance with any directions or award of an arbitrator, shall not (in the absence of negligence on the part of the Board, its officers, servants, contractors or agents) relieve the nominated undertaker from any liability under the provisions of this Part of this Schedule.

11.—(1) Any dispute arising between the nominated undertaker and the Board under this Part of this Schedule shall, if the parties agree, be determined by arbitration, but shall otherwise be determined by the appropriate Ministers acting jointly.

(2) In sub-paragraph (1) above, the reference to the appropriate Ministers—

(a) in the case of a dispute concerning land drainage or flood defence, is to the Secretary of State for the Environment, the Secretary of State for Transport and the Minister of Agriculture, Fisheries and Food, and

(b) in the case of any other dispute, is to the Secretary of State for the Environment and the Secretary of State for Transport.

Part VII

Protection of Port of London Authority

1.—(1) The provisions of this Part of this Schedule shall, unless otherwise agreed in writing between the nominated undertaker and the Port Authority, have effect for the protection of the Port Authority and the users of the river.

(2) In this Part of this Schedule—

"construction" includes execution, placing, altering, replacing, relaying and removal and, in its application to works which include or comprise any operation, means the carrying out of that operation;

"operations" includes temporary works, dredging and mooring of vessels authorised by paragraph 11 of Schedule 2 to this Act;

"plans" includes sections, drawings, specifications and method statements;

"the Port Authority" means the Port of London Authority;

"the river" means the waters within the limits of the port of London as described in Schedule 1 to the Port of London Act 1968;

"specified work" means so much of any permanent or temporary work authorised by Part I of this Act (which includes, for the avoidance of doubt, any removal of gravel or other material, any dredging or similar work and any geotechnical investigations that may be undertaken) as is on, in, under or over—

(a) the surface of land below the level of mean high water springs forming part of the river; or

(b) any land owned, occupied or used by the Port Authority for operational purposes.

2.—(1) Before beginning any operations for the construction of any specified work, the nominated undertaker shall submit to the Port Authority plans of the work and such further particulars available to it as the Port Authority may within 14 days of the submission of the plans reasonably require.

(2) A specified work shall not be constructed except in accordance with such plans as may be approved by the Port Authority or determined under paragraph 10 below.

(3) Any approval of the Port Authority required under this paragraph shall not be unreasonably withheld and—

(a) shall be deemed to be given if it is neither given nor refused (with an indication of the grounds for refusal) within 28 days of the submission of the plans; and

(b) may be given subject to such reasonable requirements as the Port Authority may make for the protection of—

(i) traffic in, or the flow or regime of, the river; or

(ii) the use of its operational land for the purposes of performing its statutory functions.

(4) The requirement for approval under this paragraph does not constitute any specified work a work subject to any of the controls in Part V of the Port of London Act 1968.

3. The nominated undertaker shall carry out all operations for the construction of any specified work with all reasonable despatch to the reasonable satisfaction of the Port Authority so that river traffic and the exercise of the Port Authority's statutory functions shall not suffer more interference than is reasonably practicable and the Port Authority shall be entitled by its officer at all reasonable times, on giving such notice as may be reasonable in the circumstances, to inspect such operations other than any operation relating to Work No. 10.

4.—(1) The nominated undertaker shall not, without the consent of the Port Authority, deposit in, or allow to fall or be washed into, the river any gravel, soil or other material.

(2) Any consent of the Port Authority under this paragraph shall not be unreasonably withheld and—

(a) shall be deemed to have been given if it is neither given nor refused within 28 days of the submission of the request therefor; and

(b) may be given subject to such reasonable requirements as the Port Authority may make for the protection of navigation in, or the flow or regime of, the river.

(3) In its application to the discharge of water into the river, paragraph 9(5) of Schedule 2 to this Act shall have effect subject to the terms of any conditions attached to a consent given under this paragraph.

(4) Nothing in this paragraph authorises the doing of anything prohibited by section 85(1), (2) or (3) of the Water Resources Act 1991 (offences of polluting controlled waters).

(5) The requirement for consent under this paragraph does not constitute any specified work or any operation a work or operation subject to any of the controls in Part V of the Port of London Act 1968.

5. If any pile, stump or other obstruction to navigation becomes exposed in the course of constructing any specified work (other than a pile, stump or other obstruction on the site of any permanent work), the nominated undertaker shall, as soon as reasonably practicable after the receipt of notice in writing from the Port Authority requiring such action, remove it from the river or, if it is not reasonably practicable to remove it, cut it off at such level below the bed of the river (not being more than two metres below the bed of the river) as the Port Authority may reasonably direct.

6. If—

(a) by reason of the construction of any specified work it is reasonably necessary for the Port Authority to incur costs in altering, removing, resiting or reinstating existing moorings owned by the Port Authority, or laying down and removing substituted moorings, or carrying out dredging operations for any such purpose, not being costs which it would have incurred for any other reason; and

(b) the Port Authority gives to the nominated undertaker not less than 28 days' notice of its intention to incur such costs, and take into account any representations which the nominated undertaker may make in response to the notice within 14 days of the receipt of the notice;

the nominated undertaker shall pay the costs reasonably so incurred by the Port Authority.

7. The nominated undertaker shall, at or near every specified work, and any other work of which the nominated undertaker is in possession in exercise of any of the powers of Part I of this Act, being in either case a work which is below the level of mean high water springs, exhibit such lights, lay down such buoys and take such other steps for preventing danger to navigation as the Port Authority may from time to time reasonably require.

8.—(1) If any specified work or any other work of which the nominated undertaker is in possession in exercise of any of the powers of Part I of this Act, being in either case a work which is below the level of mean high water springs is abandoned, the Port Authority may by notice in writing require the nominated undertaker to take such reasonable steps as may be specified in the notice to remove the work and (to such extent as the Port Authority reasonably requires) to restore the site to its former condition.

(2) If any specified work which is below the level of mean high water springs is in such condition that it is, or is likely to become, a danger to or to interfere with navigation in the river, the

Port Authority may by notice in writing require the nominated undertaker to take such reasonable steps as may be specified in the notice—

(a) to repair and restore the work or part of it, or

(b) if the nominated undertaker so elects, to remove the work and (to such extent as the Port Authority reasonably requires) to restore the site to its former condition.

(3) If—

(a) a specified work which consists of a tidal work and a non-tidal work is abandoned or falls into decay; and

(b) the non-tidal work is in such a condition as to interfere with the right of navigation in the river;

the Port Authority may include the non-tidal work, or any part of it, in any notice under this paragraph.

(4) In sub-paragraph (3) above "tidal work" means so much of any specified work as is below the level of mean high water springs and "non-tidal work" means so much of any such work as is above that level.

(5) If after such reasonable period as may be specified in a notice under this paragraph the nominated undertaker has failed to begin taking steps to comply with the requirements of the notice or after beginning has failed to make reasonably expeditious progress towards their implementation, the Port Authority may carry out the works specified in the notice and any expenditure reasonably incurred by it in so doing shall be recoverable from the nominated undertaker.

9. Paragraph 9(4) of Schedule 2 to this Act shall apply to any discharge of water under paragraph 9(1) of that Schedule in connection with the construction or maintenance of a specified work notwithstanding that the part of the river affected by the discharge is not a main river.

10. Any dispute arising between the nominated undertaker and the Port Authority under this Part of this Schedule shall, if the parties agree, be determined by arbitration but shall otherwise be determined by the Secretary of State.

INDEX

References are to sections and Schedules

ACQUISITION OF LAND,
by agreement, 48
see also COMPULSORY ACQUISITION
A2 AND M2 IMPROVEMENT WORKS,
acquisition of land, 45, Sched. 13
authorised works, 44, Sched. 12
blight: compensation for pre-enactment acquisition, 46

CHANNEL TUNNEL RAIL LINK,
arbitration, 43
burial grounds: removal of remains and monuments, 39, Sched. 11
bye-laws, 15
co-operation, duty as to, 37
competition,
anti-competitive practices, 25, 26
monopoly situations, 24, 26
Rail Regulator's functions, 22
restrictive trade practices, 23, 26
controls, disapplication of, 38, Sched. 10
development agreement, variation of, 41
financial matters,
expenditure for securing construction, 31
financial assistance: undertakings, 33
reserved capacity, 32
heritage,
disapplication of controls, 12, Sched. 7
rights of entry, 13, Sched. 8
injurious affection: compensation, 36
land,
compulsory acquisition of,
outside limits of deposited plans, 5
shown on deposited plans, 4, Sched. 4
private rights of way:
extinguishment, 7
statutory undertakers' rights:
extinguishment, 8
temporary possession and use, 6, Sched. 5
landlord and tenant law, application of, 40
noise,
control of construction sites: appeals, 29
statutory nuisance: defence, 30
nominated undertaker, 34
operation, 14
planning,
conditions, 9(5), Sched. 6
deemed permission, 9(1), 9(6)–(9)
fees for planning applications, 11
general, 9
permitted development: time limits, 10
Rail Regulator, functions of,
duty to exercise, 21
restriction of, in relation to competition, 22

CHANNEL TUNNEL RAIL LINK—*cont.*
railway legislation, application of, 20, Sched. 9
access agreements, 17
closures, 18
licensing, 16
railway administration orders, 19
Transport and Works Act 1992, application of, 42
trees,
disapplication of controls, 28
power to deal with neighbouring, 27
works,
construction and maintenance, 1
highways, 3, Sched. 3
scheduled works, 1(1), Sched. 1
supplementary provisions, 2, Sched. 2
transfer of functions relating to, 35
COMPULSORY ACQUISITION,
A2 and M2 improvement works, 45, Sched. 13
Channel Tunnel Rail Link, 4, 5, Sched. 4
time limit for powers, 47

DEPOSITED PLANS,
correction of, 53

FINANCIAL PROVISIONS, 55, *see also* CHANNEL TUNNEL RAIL LINK

INTERPRETATION, 56

NOISE INSULATION, 49

OVERHEAD LINES, 50, Sched. 14

PLANNING LAW,
concrete batching facilities at St. Pancras, 51
see also CHANNEL TUNNEL RAIL LINK
PROTECTIVE PROVISIONS, 52, Sched. 15

SERVICE OF DOCUMENTS, 54
SHORT TITLE, 57

THEFT (AMENDMENT) ACT 1996*

(1996 c. 62)

ARRANGEMENT OF SECTIONS

SECT.
1. Obtaining a money transfer by deception.
2. Dishonestly retaining a wrongful credit.
3. The new offences: jurisdiction.
4. Application to loans of offence of obtaining services by deception.
5. Short title and extent.

An Act to amend the Theft Act 1968 and the Theft Act 1978; and for connected purposes. [18th December 1996]

PARLIAMENTARY DEBATES

Hansard, H.L. Vol. 575, cols. 22, 1066; Vol. 576, cols. 796, 872, 940. H.C. Vol. 287, col. 586.

INTRODUCTION AND GENERAL NOTE

The purpose of this Act is to fill lacunae in the law of obtaining by deception under the Theft Act 1968 (c. 60) revealed by the decision of the House of Lords in *R. v. Preddy* [1996] 2 Cr. App. R. 524. Reversing the Court of Appeal, the House held that where D, dishonestly and by deception, procures a transaction whereby V's bank account is debited by £x and D's account is credited by £x, D is not guilty of obtaining property belonging to another, contrary to s.15 of the Theft Act 1968 (hereafter, "the 1968 Act"). The *effect* is exactly the same as if D *had* obtained £x belonging to V; but, in law, nothing which formerly belonged to V now belongs to D. A thing in action belonging to V has been diminished (or extinguished) and a different thing in action belonging to D has been enlarged (or created). The House held that the words "obtains property belonging to another" in s.15 of the 1968 Act must be interpreted literally. The decision caused consternation because of the many frauds, particularly "mortgage frauds," which had been prosecuted, it now appeared wrongly, under s.15. The Law Commission acted with great speed and, relying on an informal, but apparently very effective, consultation process instead of their normal procedure of publishing a consultation paper, proceeded directly to a Report, *Offences of Dishonesty: Money Transfers*, Law Com. No. 243, October 14, 1996. The Act closely follows the Draft Bill proposed by the Commission. They rejected the apparently obvious course of amending s.15 to cover *Preddy*. Finding that this could be done only by a great deal of undesirable "deeming," they preferred a direct approach. Consequently, the Act creates a new s.15A of the 1968 Act, "Obtaining a money transfer by deception," which provides, in effect, that "what Preddy did" is a specific offence.

The increased credit balance procured by Preddy was, before the decision of the House, stolen goods, and could be the subject of an offence of handling, contrary to s.22 of the 1968 Act. That is no longer so. The Act fills this lacuna by a new s.24A of the 1968 Act, creating an offence of "Dishonestly retaining a wrongful credit." This offence is wide enough to include some cases which were not offences even before the decision of the House in *Preddy*.

One reason for the heavy reliance by the prosecution on s.15 in mortgage fraud cases was the decision in *R. v. Halai* [1983] Crim. L.R. 624 that obtaining a mortgage advance was not the offence of obtaining services by deception contrary to s.1 of the Theft Act 1978. That decision was very heavily criticised and considered by some to have been made *per incuriam*. The Law Commission had already recommended its repeal in their Report, *Conspiracy to Defraud*, Law Com. No. 228 (1994) and they repeated their recommendation in Law Com. No. 243. It is effected by s.4 of the Act, "Application to loans of offence of obtaining services by deception." Before the present Act was passed, the Court of Appeal in *Graham* (October 25, 1996) had already overruled *Halai*, so that case is well and truly dead and buried.

COMMENCEMENT

The Act came into force on receiving the Royal Assent on December 18, 1996.

---

* Annotations by Sir John Smith, C.B.E., Q.C., LL.D., F.B.A., Emeritus Professor of Law, University of Nottingham.

Obtaining a money transfer by deception

1.—(1) After section 15 of the Theft Act 1968 insert—

"**Obtaining a money transfer by deception**

15A.—(1) A person is guilty of an offence if by any deception he dishonestly obtains a money transfer for himself or another.

(2) A money transfer occurs when—

(a) a debit is made to one account,

(b) a credit is made to another, and

(c) the credit results from the debit or the debit results from the credit.

(3) References to a credit and to a debit are to a credit of an amount of money and to a debit of an amount of money.

(4) It is immaterial (in particular)—

(a) whether the amount credited is the same as the amount debited;

(b) whether the money transfer is effected on presentment of a cheque or by another method;

(c) whether any delay occurs in the process by which the money transfer is effected;

(d) whether any intermediate credits or debits are made in the course of the money transfer;

(e) whether either of the accounts is overdrawn before or after the money transfer is effected.

(5) A person guilty of an offence under this section shall be liable on conviction on indictment to imprisonment for a term not exceeding ten years.

Section 15A: supplementary

15B.—(1) The following provisions have effect for the interpretation of section 15A of this Act.

(2) "Deception" has the same meaning as in section 15 of this Act.

(3) "Account" means an account kept with—

(a) a bank; or

(b) a person carrying on a business which falls within subsection (4) below.

(4) A business falls within this subsection if—

(a) in the course of the business money received by way of deposit is lent to others; or

(b) any other activity of the business is financed, wholly or to any material extent, out of the capital of or the interest on money received by way of deposit;

and "deposit" here has the same meaning as in section 35 of the Banking Act 1987 (fraudulent inducement to make a deposit).

(5) For the purposes of subsection (4) above—

(a) all the activities which a person carries on by way of business shall be regarded as a single business carried on by him; and

(b) "money" includes money expressed in a currency other than sterling or in the European currency unit (as defined in Council Regulation No. 3320/94/EC or any Community instrument replacing it)."

(2) Nothing in this section has effect in relation to anything done before the day on which this Act is passed.

GENERAL NOTE

Section 15A(1) and (2) describe what Preddy did and enact that it is an offence. Subsection (3) limits the offence to "money", meaning an obligation to pay money, notably the obligation of a banker to his customer. It excludes transfers of other things in action, such as bonds and securities. This limitation was criticised by Lord Donaldson of Lymington, whose Amendments designed to broaden the ambit of the offence were not accepted by the House of Lords: *Hansard*, H.L., Vol. 576, col. 796. Subsection (4) anticipates and excludes possible unmeritorious defences. The words, "in particular," make it clear that this is not an exclusive list. There are many matters which a court may properly hold to be immaterial, though not listed here.

Obtaining cheques. Preddy also settled that where D induces V to draw and deliver a cheque in favour of D, D is not guilty under s.15 of the 1968 Act of obtaining by deception the thing in action represented by the cheque. That thing in action was never "property belonging to" V. From the moment it came into existence, it belonged to D. When D presents the cheque and it is honoured, a debit is made to V's account and a corresponding credit to D's, so a money transfer as defined in s.15A(1) occurs. Arguably, in such a case, the *transfer* has not been obtained by deception but by D's presentation of the cheque (as where a key is obtained by deception and used to open a safe and steal: the money taken from the safe has been stolen, not obtained by deception). Subsection (4)(b) appears to assume that the transfer has been obtained by deception and, for practical purposes, probably puts the matter beyond all doubt. Even so, the new offence will not be committed until the cheque is honoured. D will, however, clearly be guilty of an attempt to commit that offence when he presents, or attempts to present the cheque for the credit of his account. Until he does so, he has probably done no act which is more than merely preparatory to the commission of the new offence. If he cashes the cheque he will not commit the new offence. The question may, therefore, still arise whether D has obtained the cheque form (as distinct from the thing in action), contrary to s.15. The problem is to find an intention permanently to deprive since D presumably knows that the form will be returned to V's bank. See the commentary on *R. v. Mitchell* [1993] Crim. L.R. 788.

For the meaning of "deception" in s.15 of the 1968 Act, see s.15(4) and Griew, *The Theft Acts* (7th ed.) (hereafter, "*Griew, Theft*") 8–10, Smith, *The Law of Theft* (7th ed.) (hereafter, "*Smith, Theft*"), Ch. 4. "Dishonestly" is not defined, but there can be no doubt that it will be construed in accordance with *R. v. Ghosh* [1982] Q.B. 1053.

Dishonestly retaining a wrongful credit

2.—(1) After section 24 of the Theft Act 1968 insert—

"**Dishonestly retaining a wrongful credit**

24A.—(1) A person is guilty of an offence if—

(a) a wrongful credit has been made to an account kept by him or in respect of which he has any right or interest;

(b) he knows or believes that the credit is wrongful; and

(c) he dishonestly fails to take such steps as are reasonable in the circumstances to secure that the credit is cancelled.

(2) References to a credit are to a credit of an amount of money.

(3) A credit to an account is wrongful if it is the credit side of a money transfer obtained contrary to section 15A of this Act.

(4) A credit to an account is also wrongful to the extent that it derives from—

(a) theft;

(b) an offence under section 15A of this Act;

(c) blackmail; or

(d) stolen goods.

(5) In determining whether a credit to an account is wrongful, it is immaterial (in particular) whether the account is overdrawn before or after the credit is made.

(6) A person guilty of an offence under this section shall be liable on conviction on indictment to imprisonment for a term not exceeding ten years.

(7) Subsection (8) below applies for purposes of provisions of this Act relating to stolen goods (including subsection (4) above).

(8) References to stolen goods include money which is dishonestly withdrawn from an account to which a wrongful credit has been made, but only to the extent that the money derives from the credit.

(9) In this section "account" and "money" shall be construed in accordance with section 15B of this Act."

(2) This section applies to wrongful credits made on or after the day on which this Act is passed.

General Note

Sections 22–24 of the 1968 Act are concerned with the offence of handling stolen goods and the offence created by s.24A is an offence of the same general character. Its effect is that D1, a person who has committed an offence under the new s.15A, commits a second offence under s.24A, if he does not take steps within a reasonable time to divest himself of his ill-gotten gains. The provision is not aimed at him but at D2, where D1 has, without D2's connivance, procured the crediting, not of his own, but of D2's account; or D3, where D1 has obtained "a wrongful credit" and transferred it, or part of it, to D3's account. The latter case would be covered by s.24A(4)(b). But the effect of s.24A(4)(a), (c) and (d) is that the section has a wider application, embracing cases not covered even before *Preddy*.

If D1 pays into his bank account money which he has stolen, or obtained by blackmail, or by selling stolen goods, and transfers the credit thereby created to D3's account, the credit in D3's account is a new item of property—a thing in action belonging to D3—which has never been "in the hands" of a thief or handler and so is not "stolen goods" within s.24(2) of the 1968 Act. D3, however, now commits an offence under s.24A(1) if he dishonestly fails to surrender "the wrongful credit" within a reasonable time. Any money which is withdrawn from a wrongful credit will be stolen goods and subject to the general law of handling: s.24A(8). There is no provision corresponding to s.24(3) of the 1968 Act (stolen goods cease to be "stolen" when they are restored to lawful custody or when the owner and any others claiming through him have ceased to have any right to restitution of the goods). Nor is there any exemption for the bona-fide purchaser such as is to be found in s.3 of the 1968 Act. If D sells his car in good faith to A who pays him with stolen money, D is not guilty of theft or any other offence if E has paid him in cash and, after learning the truth, he spends it. But if E has paid D by cheque, or if D has paid the cash into his own bank account, it appears that D will (subject to proof of dishonesty) commit an offence under s.24A when he spends the money because he has failed to take reasonable steps to disgorge. That would create not only an unsatisfactory anomaly but also a conflict with the civil law. A transferee of stolen currency for value and without notice gets a good title: *Miller v. Race* (1758) 1 Burr. 452. The money, whether in cash or in the bank, is surely his to dispose of as he chooses. It may be that a court will think it necessary to read into s.24A(1)(c) some such qualification as "except where no person has any right to restitution of the credit," on the ground that Parliament could not have intended to change, or create a conflict with, such a fundamental rule of the civil law. This would introduce a limitation to the same effect as that relating to stolen goods generally in s.24(4) of the 1968 Act.

The new offences: jurisdiction

3.—(1) In section 1(2) of the Criminal Justice Act 1993 (Group A offences for the purposes of the jurisdictional provisions) paragraph (a) (list of offences under the Theft Act 1968) shall be amended as follows.

(2) After the entry relating to section 15 insert—

"section 15A (obtaining a money transfer by deception);".

(3) After the entry relating to section 22 insert—

"section 24A (retaining credits from dishonest sources, etc.);".

General Note

The Criminal Justice Act 1993 (c. 36), ss.1–6, which have still not been brought into force, will extend the jurisdiction of the courts of England and Wales to prescribed offences which would not presently be triable here because they were wholly or partly committed abroad. See *Griew, Theft*, 17–02—17–12, *Smith, Theft*, 1–18—1–24. The offences created by this Act are added to the list of offences to which the sections will apply.

Application to loans of offence of obtaining services by deception

4.—(1) In section 1 of the Theft Act 1978 (obtaining services by deception) after subsection (2) (circumstances where there is an obtaining of services) insert—

"(3) Without prejudice to the generality of subsection (2) above, it is an obtaining of services where the other is induced to make a loan, or to cause or permit a loan to be made, on the understanding that any payment (whether by way of interest or otherwise) will be or has been made in respect of the loan."

(2) Nothing in this section has effect in relation to anything done before the day on which this Act is passed.

General Note

Following the overruling by *Graham* (above) of *Halai* (above) this provision is unnecessary but may be regarded as declaratory of the law under s.1 of the 1978 Act. It applies not merely to loans for the purpose of mortgages but to loans generally, provided that the loan ("the service") is to be "paid for" by the payment of interest or otherwise.

Short title and extent

5.—(1) This Act may be cited as the Theft (Amendment) Act 1996.

(2) Subject to subsection (3), this Act extends to England and Wales only.

(3) An Order in Council under paragraph 1(1)(b) of Schedule 1 to the Northern Ireland Act 1974 (legislation for Northern Ireland in the interim period) which contains a statement that it is made only for purposes corresponding to the purposes of this Act—

(a) shall not be subject to paragraph 1(4) and (5) of that Schedule (affirmative resolution of both Houses of Parliament); but

(b) shall be subject to annulment by resolution of either House.

INDEX

References are to sections

BLACKMAIL, 2
BUSINESS, 1

CREDITS, 1, 2

DEBITS, 1
DECEPTION, 1
DEPOSIT, 1
DISHONESTLY RETAINING A WRONGFUL CREDIT, 2

EXTENT, 5(2)–(3)

JURISDICTION, 3

LOANS, 4

MONEY TRANSFER, 1

OBTAINING A MONEY TRANSFER BY DECEPTION, 1
OBTAINING SERVICES BY DECEPTION, 4

SERVICES, 4
SHORT TITLE, 5(1)
STOLEN GOODS, 2

WRONGFUL CREDIT, 2

HONG KONG ECONOMIC AND TRADE OFFICE ACT 1996

(1996 c. 63)

An Act to make provision about privileges and immunities in relation to an economic and trade office established in the United Kingdom by the government of the Hong Kong Special Administrative Region.

[18th December 1996]

PARLIAMENTARY DEBATES

Hansard, H.C. Vol. 284, col. 795. H.C. Vol. 575, col. 570, Vol. 576, cols. 12, 907, 1276.

INTRODUCTION

This Act makes provision concerning privileges and immunities in relation to an Economic and Trade Office to be established in the U.K. from July 1, 1997 by the government of the Hong Kong Special Administrative region. The U.K.'s debt to Hong Kong has also required the passing earlier this year, of the Hong Kong (Overseas Public Servants) Act 1996 (c. 2) and the Hong Kong (War Wives and Widows) Act 1996 (c. 41). It remains to be seen whether any further legislation will be required before June 30, 1997.

Hong Kong Economic and Trade Office

1.—(1) This Act shall apply in relation to any office established in the United Kingdom by the government of the Hong Kong Special Administrative Region for the purposes of furthering the economic and trade interests of the Region.

(2) Where an office is located outside London, this Act shall apply in relation to it only if the Secretary of State so determines.

(3) The Schedule to this Act (which makes provision about privileges and immunities) shall have effect.

(4) If in any proceedings a question arises whether or not a privilege or immunity applies by virtue of the Schedule to this Act, a certificate issued by the Secretary of State stating any fact relating to that question shall be conclusive evidence of that fact.

Short title and extent

2.—(1) This Act may be cited as the Hong Kong Economic and Trade Office Act 1996.

(2) This Act extends to Northern Ireland.

(3) Her Majesty may by Order in Council direct that any of the provisions of this Act shall extend, with such modifications as appear to Her Majesty to be appropriate, to any of the Channel Islands or the Isle of Man.

Section 1(3)

SCHEDULE

PRIVILEGES AND IMMUNITIES

Premises and archives

1. The premises and archives of the Office shall have the same inviolability as is accorded to consular premises and archives in accordance with articles 31(1) to (4) and 33 of the Convention.

2. The premises of the Office and the residence of the head of the Office shall have the same exemptions as are accorded to consular premises and the residence of the career head of a consular post by virtue of article 32 of the Convention.

Legal proceedings

3.—(1) A person shall have immunity from suit and legal process in respect of things done or omitted to be done by him in the course of the performance of official duties as a member of the Office.

(2) Sub-paragraph (1) shall not apply in respect of civil proceedings relating to damage alleged to have been caused by a motor vehicle belonging to, or operated by or on behalf of, a member of the Office.

Exemptions and reliefs

4. The Treasury may by order confer in relation to the Office, to such extent as may be specified—

(a) exemption or relief (by way of refund or otherwise) from prohibitions, restrictions, duties and taxes on the importation of goods;

(b) relief of the kinds set out in paragraphs 6 and 7 of Schedule 1 to the International Organisations Act 1968 (importation and supply of hydrocarbon oil and other goods or services).

5. The Treasury may by order confer in relation to members of the Office and members of their families who form part of their households, to such extent as may be specified—

(a) exemption from income tax in respect of emoluments;

(b) the exemption set out in article 48 of the Convention (social security), construed in accordance with section 1(6) of the Consular Relations Act 1968;

(c) the exemption and privilege set out in paragraph 16 of Schedule 1 to the International Organisations Act 1968 (imports);

(d) exemption or relief (by way of refund or otherwise) from prohibitions, restrictions, duties and taxes on the importation or purchase of motor vehicles.

6.—(1) An order under paragraph 4 or 5 may provide for any exemption, relief or privilege to be subject to arrangements or conditions—

(a) specified in the order, or

(b) to be made or imposed by the Secretary of State or the Commissioners of Customs and Excise.

(2) An order under paragraph 4 or 5 may make different provision for different cases (including different provision for different persons).

(3) An order under paragraph 4 or 5 shall be made by statutory instrument and shall be subject to annulment in pursuance of a resolution of the House of Commons.

Waiver

7. A privilege or immunity which would apply by virtue of this Schedule shall not apply in any case in respect of which it is waived by the head of the Office.

Interpretation

8.—(1) In this Schedule—

"archives of the Office" includes all the papers, documents, correspondence, books, films, tapes, discs and registers of the Office (wherever found);

"the Convention" means the articles of the Vienna Convention on Consular Relations set out in Schedule 1 to the Consular Relations Act 1968;

"the head of the Office" means the person charged by the government of the Hong Kong Special Administrative Region with the duty of acting in that capacity;

"member of the Office" means, subject to sub-paragraph (3), a person employed by the government of the Hong Kong Special Administrative Region to carry on the business of the Office;

"the Office" means any office in relation to which this Act applies; and

"the premises of the Office" means the buildings or parts of buildings, together with any ancillary land, used exclusively for the official use of the Office.

(2) Where this Schedule refers to an article of the Convention, the article shall be construed for the purposes of the reference as if—

(a) references to the sending State were references to the Hong Kong Special Administrative Region; and

(b) references to the head of a consular post or diplomatic mission were references to the head of the office.

(3) If the Secretary of State notifies the government of the Hong Kong Special Administrative Region that a person—

(a) is not acceptable as a member of the Office, or

(b) is no longer considered to be a member of the Office,

that person shall not, while the notification is in force, be regarded as a member of the Office for the purposes of any provision of, or made by virtue of, this Schedule.

INDEX

References are to sections and the Schedule

EXTENT, 2(2)–(3)

HONG KONG SPECIAL ADMINISTRATIVE REGION, offices established in the U.K., 1

OFFICES OUTSIDE LONDON, 1(2)

PRIVILEGES AND IMMUNITIES, 1(3)–(4), Sched.

SHORT TITLE, 2(1)

EDINBURGH ASSAY OFFICE ORDER CONFIRMATION ACT 1996

(1996 c. i)

ARRANGEMENT OF SECTIONS

SECT.
1. Confirmation of Order in Schedule.
2. Short title.

SCHEDULE

EDINBURGH ASSAY OFFICE

1. Short title.
2. Interpretation.
3. Section 16 of Hallmarking Act 1973.
4. Additional activities of Incorporation.
5. Application of existing enactments.

An act to confirm a Provisional Order under the Private Legislation Procedure (Scotland) Act 1936, relating to Edinburgh Assay Office.

[29th February 1996]

PARLIAMENTARY PROGRESS

The Bill's progress through Parliament was as follows:

House of Commons: First Reading, January 24, 1996; Bill considered by Commons, January 30, 1996; Third Reading, January 31, 1996.

House of Lords: First Reading, January 31, 1996; Bill considered by Lords, February 5, 1996; Third Reading, February 8, 1996.

INTRODUCTION

This Act extends the activities of the Edinburgh Assay Office to the independent and objective testing, examination, investigation and evaluation of materials and articles of any kind, and of firms, corporations, systems, programmes and procedures, and to the purchase and sale of metals and other materials. The Act also amends retrospectively s.16 of the Hallmarking Act 1973 in its application to the Edinburgh Assay Office.

WHEREAS the Provisional Order set forth in the Schedule hereunto annexed has been made by the Secretary of State under the provisions of the Private Legislation Procedure (Scotland) Act 1936, and it is requisite that the said Order should be confirmed by Parliament.

Be it therefore enacted by the Queen's most Excellent Majesty, by and with the advice and consent of the Lords Spiritual and Temporal, and Commons, in this present Parliament assembled, and by the authority of the same, as follows:—

Confirmation of Order in Schedule

1. The Provisional Order contained in the Schedule hereunto annexed is hereby confirmed.

Short title

2. This Act may be cited as the Edinburgh Assay Office Order Confirmation Act 1996.

SCHEDULE

EDINBURGH ASSAY OFFICE

Provisional Order to amend section 16 of the Hallmarking Act 1973 in its application to the Edinburgh Assay Office; to extend the functions of the Office; and for other purposes incidental thereto.

WHEREAS—

(1) The Edinburgh Assay Office (hereinafter referred to as "the Incorporation"), of which the full name is The Incorporation of Goldsmiths of the City of Edinburgh, has been in existence for more than four hundred years:

(2) The Hallmarking Act 1973 (hereinafter referred to as "the Act of 1973") made fresh provision as to assay offices, and their powers and duties:

(3) Section 16 of the Act of 1973 gave the Secretary of State power to make orders (*inter alia*) for constituting and conferring powers on assay offices:

(4) In exercise of that power, the Secretary of State made the Edinburgh Assay Office Order 1979 (hereinafter referred to as "the Order of 1979"), altering the constitution of the Incorporation, conferring further powers upon it, repealing certain enactments affecting it, and making other provisions in relation to it:

(5) In further exercise of that power, the Secretary of State made the Edinburgh Assay Office (Amendment) Order 1993 (hereinafter referred to as "the Order of 1993"), amending the Order of 1979 and conferring a new power upon the Incorporation:

(6) The assaying of precious metals is believed to have been the earliest and, for a long time, the only form of consumer protection in the United Kingdom:

(7) It would be of public advantage if the Incorporation could extend its activities to the independent and objective testing, examination, investigation and evaluation of materials and articles of any kind, and of firms, corporations, systems, programmes and procedures, and to the purchase and sale of metals and other materials:

(8) For those reasons, and in order that it may respond to changed market conditions resulting from the Single European Market, the Incorporation wishes to have power to carry on, in addition to the business of an assay office, the other activities described in this Order, and to have, in relation to those activities, the ancillary powers so described:

(9) Doubts have arisen as to the extent to which the making of the Order of 1979 and the Order of 1993 was within the powers conferred upon the Secretary of State by section 16 of the Act of 1973, and it is desirable to set those doubts at rest, and to clarify the position for the future, by means of a retrospective amendment of that section in its application to the Incorporation:

(10) The purposes aforesaid cannot be effected without an Order confirmed by Parliament under the provisions of the Private Legislation Procedure (Scotland) Act 1936:

Now, therefore, in pursuance of the powers contained in the last-mentioned Act, the Secretary of State orders as follows:—

Short title

1. This Order may be cited as the Edinburgh Assay Office Order 1996.

Interpretation

2. In this order, unless the subject of context otherwise requires—

"the Act of 1973" means the Hallmarking Act 1973;

"the Incorporation" means the Edinburgh Assay Office, of which the full name is The Incorporation of Goldsmiths of the City of Edinburgh;

"materials" includes liquids, gases, dusts, wastes and tangible and intangible substances of any kind;

"the Order of 1979" means the Edinburgh Assay Office Order 1979; and

"the Order of 1993" means the Edinburgh Assay Office (Amendment) Order 1993.

Section 16 of Hallmarking Act 1973

3. In its application to the Incorporation, the Act of 1973 shall have effect, and be deemed always to have had effect, as if in section 16(1)(c)—

(a) "confer" were omitted;

(b) for "under" there were substituted "by"; and

(c) there were added at the end thereof—

"; or, on such an application, impose new duties or confer new powers on, or make alterations or additions to or omissions from the constitution of, the assay office.".

Additional activities of Incorporation

4.—(1) In addition to the functions which it has from time to time as an assay office, the Incorporation shall have power, in any part of the world—

(a) to undertake the provision of analytical services in relation to materials or articles of any kind, by means of chemical analysis or physical examination or testing or by any other method which is appropriate in the circumstances;

(b) to undertake investigation of the properties of materials or articles of any kind, their behaviour or likely behaviour under particular conditions, and their suitability for particular purposes;

(c) to undertake the examination of articles of any kind for the purpose of discovering whether and to what extent they comply with standards or other criteria which are published or have been made known to the Incorporation;

(d) to undertake the investigation of firms, corporate bodies or other persons, or of systems, documentation, programmes or procedures, for the purpose of discovering whether and to what extent they comply with standards or other criteria which are published or have been made known to the Incorporation;

(e) to undertake the valuation, on any basis and for any purpose, of materials or articles of any kind;

(f) to undertake the purchase or other acquisition, and the selling or other disposal, of metals or other materials;

(g) to undertake any other activities of a kind which the Incorporation may consider similar to, or suitable to be carried on with, the activities mentioned in paragraphs (a) to (f) above;

(h) to undertake or instigate, or join in undertaking or instigating, and to meet or contribute towards the cost of, research into, and the provision (including manufacture) and development of, plant, equipment, technology, methodology (including systems, procedures and computer and other programmes) and materials for use in, or in connection with, any of the foregoing activities; and

(i) to undertake, or join in undertaking, the marketing of, and the provision of maintenance, advisory, technical or other services in relation to, any plant, equipment, technology, methodology (including systems, procedures and computer and other programmes) and materials or articles of any kind used or capable of use in, or in connection with—

(i) any of the activities mentioned in paragraphs (a) to (g) above, or

(ii) any of the activities carried on in the course of the business of an assay office.

(2) The Incorporation may do anything which is calculated to facilitate or is incidental or conducive to the activities mentioned in subsection (1) above and (without prejudice to that generality) shall in particular have power—

(a) to issue certificates as to the results of any analysis, examination, test or investigation carried out under subsection (1) above;

(b) to provide advisory and supervisory services and to provide expert evidence for the purpose of legal or other proceedings;

(c) to make members of its staff available to advise on, or participate in, the formulation of standards or criteria of the kind referred to in paragraphs (c) and (d) of subsection (1) above;

(d) to register, maintain, protect and enforce in any part of the world intellectual property rights, including patents, trade marks and other marks, and to authorise the use of such intellectual property on such lawful terms and conditions as it sees fit;

(e) to promote or establish, or join in promoting or establishing, or to acquire interests in and take part in the management of, bodies corporate or unincorporate in any part of the world, having as their object, or as a main object, the carrying on of any or all of the activities mentioned in subsection (1) above;

(f) out of the income or other monies derived from such activities, to remunerate all or any of the members who for the time being constitute the Incorporation for work done or time spent in that capacity in connection with those activities (this power being without prejudice to the power given by article 8(9) of the Order of 1979, and extended by section 5(2) (Application of existing enactments) of this Order, to pay any member who may also be the Deacon or another of the wardens for services rendered in his capacity as such); and

(g) to receive grants and to accept gifts of money or other property to be used in meeting its expenses in connection with, or in furthering, any or all of such activities.

Application of existing enactments

5.—(1) In this section references to the Incorporation's other activities are references to the additional activities authorised by section 4 (Additional activities of Incorporation) of this Order or other the activities which the Incorporation is for the time being authorised to undertake in addition to its business of an assay office.

(2) Subject to the provisions of subsections (3) and (4) below, all the provisions of the Order of 1979 and the Order of 1993, and of any other enactments which relate to the Incorporation and to its business of an assay office, shall apply equally (so far as they are capable of doing so) to and in relation to its other activities, and to and in relation to the Incorporation in so far as its undertaking includes them (but, save as respects the reference in article 9(3) of the Order of 1979, specific references to articles brought to be assayed shall not extend to articles received by the Incorporation in the course of its other activities).

(3) The Incorporation shall keep accounts in respect of its other activities separate from the accounts kept in respect of its business of an assay office and (notwithstanding the provisions of paragraph (8) thereof) article 12 of the Order of 1979 shall apply in relation to the former accounts as it applies in relation to the latter, except that paragraph (5) of that Order shall not apply to the accounts kept in respect of the Incorporation's other activities; but references in this subsection to accounts do not include balance sheets and nothing in this subsection shall prevent the Incorporation from preparing a single balance sheet in respect of the whole of its undertaking.

(4) In so far as the business of the Incorporation consists of its other activities, the words in article 19 of the Order of 1979, "if so authorised by the British Hallmarking Council", shall not apply.

(5) Notwithstanding section 22(2) of the Act of 1973, an order under section 16(1)(c) of that Act in relation to the Incorporation shall, except so far as

it provides otherwise or the contrary otherwise appears, apply in relation to its other activities as well as to its business of an assay office; and such an order may consist of or include provisions which apply only to the Incorporation's other activities.

INDEX

References are to sections and the Schedule

CONFIRMATION OF PROVISIONAL ORDER, 1

HALLMARKING ACT 1973,
  amendments, Sched., para. 3

INCORPORATION,
  additional activities, Sched., para. 4

INCORPORATION—*cont.*
  application of 1973 Act, Sched., para. 3
  application of existing enactments, Sched., para. 5
  meaning of, Sched., para. 2
INTERPRETATION, Sched., para. 2

SHORT TITLE, 2, Sched., para. 2

AUSTRALIA AND NEW ZEALAND BANKING GROUP ACT 1996

(1996 c. ii)

ARRANGEMENT OF SECTIONS

PART I

PRELIMINARY

SECT.
1. Short title.
2. Interpretation.

PART II

REGISTRATION OF HOLDINGS AND GRINDLAYS

3. Registration in Victoria.
4. Removal from register in England and continuity of legal identity.

PART III

TRANSFER OF BUSINESS TO ANZ

5. Schemes for transfer to ANZ of property, liabilities, trusteeships and other appointments in United Kingdom.
6. Provisions as to trust and other property and liabilities in United Kingdom.
7. Supplementary provisions as to schemes and transfers in United Kingdom.
8. Evidence: books and documents.
9. Application of Bankers' Books Evidence Act 1879.
10. Evidence of transfer and vesting.
11. Savings in respect of transfers of property.

PART IV

MISCELLANEOUS

12. Application to Scotland and Northern Ireland.
13. Costs of Act.

An Act to provide for the registration of ANZ Holdings (UK) plc and ANZ Grindlays Bank plc as companies incorporated in the State of Victoria in the Commonwealth of Australia; for the cesser of application to those companies of the Companies Act 1985, consequent upon such registration; for the transfer to and vesting in Australia and New Zealand Banking Group Limited of the whole or parts of the undertakings in the United Kingdom of ANZ Grindlays Bank plc, National & Grindlays Bank Limited and ANZ Grindlays Executor & Trustee Company Limited; and for connected purposes. [17th June, 1996]

PARLIAMENTARY PROGRESS

The Bill's progress through Parliament was as follows:

House of Lords: First Reading, January 11, 1996, Second Reading, February 14, 1996, Bill committed, February 21, 1996, Bill committed to an unopposed committee, March 28, 1996, Third Reading, April 25, 1996.

House of Commons: First Reading, April 25, 1996, Second Reading, May 14, 1996, Bill committed, May 14, 1996, Bill committed to an unopposed committee, June 6, 1996, Third Reading, June 12, 1996.

INTRODUCTION AND GENERAL NOTE

This Act allows for ANZ Holdings (UK) plc and ANZ Grindlays Bank plc to be registered as incorporated companies in Victoria, Australia, and for their registration in England under the

Companies Act 1985 to cease, consequent upon such registration. The Act makes provision for the transfer to the Australia and New Zealand Banking Group Limited (ANZ) of all property, liabilities, trusteeships and other appointments in the UK of ANZ Grindlays Bank plc, National & Grindlays Bank Limited and ANZ Grindlays Executor & Trustee Company Limited.

Whereas Australia and New Zealand Banking Group Limited (hereinafter referred to as "ANZ") is a company deemed to be incorporated under the Companies Act 1961 of the State of Victoria in the Commonwealth of Australia (hereinafter referred to as "Victoria"):

And whereas ANZ carries on the business of banking and the provision of financial services in the Commonwealth of Australia, the United Kingdom and elsewhere:

And whereas ANZ Holdings (UK) plc (hereinafter referred to as "Holdings") and ANZ Grindlays Bank plc (hereinafter referred to as "Grindlays") are companies within the meaning of the Companies Act 1985 and are public companies limited by shares:

And whereas Holdings carries on the business of holding investments in the United Kingdom and Grindlays carries on the business of banking and the provision of financial services in the United Kingdom, Bahrain, Bangladesh, Greece, India, Jordan, Oman, Pakistan, Qatar, Sri Lanka, Switzerland, the United Arab Emirates and elsewhere:

And whereas National & Grindlays Bank Limited and ANZ Grindlays Executor & Trustee Company Limited each carries on trustee and executorship business in the United Kingdom:

And whereas Holdings is a wholly-owned subsidiary of ANZ:

And whereas ANZ holds 25%, and Holdings holds 75%, of the issued ordinary share capital of Grindlays and Holdings holds all of the deferred share capital and preference share capital of Grindlays:

And whereas each of National & Grindlays Bank Limited and ANZ Grindlays Executor & Trustee Company Limited is a wholly-owned subsidiary of Grindlays:

And whereas the registered office of each of Holdings, Grindlays, National & Grindlays Bank Limited and ANZ Grindlays Executor & Trustee Company Limited is in England:

And whereas, having regard to the fact that the area of operation of ANZ is largely in the Commonwealth of Australia, certain advantages would accrue to ANZ if Holdings and Grindlays were registered as companies incorporated under the laws of Victoria instead of under the laws of England and such registration would give ANZ, Holdings and Grindlays greater flexibility in the pursuit of their objectives:

And whereas no procedure exists whereby the registration of a company to which the Companies Act 1985 applies can be transferred from England to another country:

And whereas to proceed by way of winding-up and dissolution of Holdings and Grindlays and the transfer of assets to ANZ or a new company incorporated in Victoria would involve loss of the identity of Holdings and Grindlays, and the consequent disturbance of the financial structure and existing contracts of Holdings and Grindlays would interfere with the continuity of their respective operations and result in considerable attendant expense and inconvenience:

And whereas it is desirable that each of Holdings and Grindlays should be enabled to become registered as a company in Victoria and that thereupon the provisions of the Companies Act 1985 (with the exception of those provisions which apply to overseas companies) should cease to apply to them, but each should be the same company for all purposes as it was before registration as a company incorporated in Victoria:

And whereas it is expedient and desirable that the objects of this Act be given full faith and credit in every jurisdiction in which ANZ, Holdings and Grindlays carry on business:

And whereas for the more effective consolidation of the core businesses in the United Kingdom of ANZ, Grindlays, National & Grindlays Bank Limited and ANZ Grindlays Executor & Trustee Company Limited and the better conduct thereof it is expedient that provision be made for the transfer to and vesting in ANZ of the whole or parts of the undertakings in the United Kingdom of Grindlays, National & Grindlays Bank Limited and ANZ Grindlays Executor & Trustee Company Limited:

And whereas it is expedient that the said transfers and vesting should be effected without interference with the conduct and continuity of the businesses carried on by ANZ, Grindlays, National & Grindlays Bank Limited and ANZ Grindlays Executor & Trustee Company Limited:

And whereas it is expedient that the other provisions in this Act should be enacted:

And whereas the objects of this Act cannot be attained without the authority of Parliament:

May it therefore please Your Majesty that it may be enacted, and be it enacted, by the Queen's most Excellent Majesty, by and with the advice and consent of the Lords Spiritual and Temporal, and Commons, in this present Parliament assembled, and by the authority of the same, as follows:—

PART I

PRELIMINARY

Short title

1. This Act may be cited as the Australia and New Zealand Banking Group Act 1996.

Interpretation

2.—(1) In this Act, unless the subject or context otherwise requires—

"ANZ" means Australia and New Zealand Banking Group Limited;

"appointed day" in relation to a transfer scheme means such a day as may be specified under section 5(2) of this Act as the appointed day for the scheme;

"customer" includes any person having a bank account or other dealing, transaction, agreement or arrangement with a Transferor;

"the date of registration" means the date on which Holdings or Grindlays as the case may be respectively becomes registered as a company incorporated under the laws of Victoria;

"document" has the same meaning as in section 10 of the Civil Evidence Act 1968;

"enactment" means any enactment in this Act or in any general or local Act or in any order, rule or regulation made under any Act;

"existing" means existing, outstanding or in force immediately before the appointment day for a transfer scheme;

"first appointed day" in relation to a Transferor means such day as may be specified under section 5(2) of this Act as the earliest appointed day for a transfer scheme in relation to that Transferor;

"Grindlays" means ANZ Grindlays Bank plc;

"Holdings" means ANZ Holdings (UK) plc;

"liabilities" includes duties and obligations of every description;

"property" means property and assets of every description including property and assets held on trust or in a fiduciary capacity and rights, benefits and powers of every description;

"the registrar of companies" means the registrar or other officer performing under the Companies Act 1985 the duty of registration of companies in England;

"security" includes a mortgage or charge (whether legal or equitable), debenture, bill of exchange, promissory note, guarantee, lien, pledge (whether actual or constructive), hypothecation, assignment by way of security, indemnity, right of set-off, flawed asset arrangement, undertaking or other means of securing payment or discharge of a debt or liability;

"the Transferors" means Grindlays, National & Grindlays Bank Limited and ANZ Grindlays Executor & Trustee Company Limited and a reference to a "Transferor" is a reference to one of the Transferors;

"transfer scheme" means a scheme made under section 5 (Schemes for transfer to ANZ of property, liabilities, trusteeships and other appointments in United Kingdom) of this Act;

"trustee" includes a trustee or custodian trustee of any trust deed, settlement, covenant, agreement or will; executor of the will, or administrator of the estate, of a deceased person; judicial trustee appointed by order of any court; attorney for another person; or any other person acting in a fiduciary capacity;

"Victoria" means the State of Victoria in the Commonwealth of Australia; and

"will" includes a codicil and any other testamentary writing.

(2) Any reference in this Act to property or liabilities of a Transferor is a reference to property or liabilities wherever such property or liabilities are situated or arise and whether or not capable of being transferred or assigned by a Transferor and whether that Transferor is entitled or subject to the property or liabilities under the law of any part of the United Kingdom or under the law of any country or territory outside the United Kingdom.

PART II

REGISTRATION OF HOLDINGS AND GRINDLAYS

Registration in Victoria

3. Subject to the laws in force in Victoria and with such legislative governmental or other authority as is necessary in Victoria, Holdings and Grindlays may each become registered as a company incorporated under the laws of Victoria.

Removal from register in England and continuity of legal identity

4.—(1) (a) On or as soon as reasonably practicable after the date of registration of Holdings or Grindlays as the case may be, that company shall notify the registrar of companies thereof by telefax or telex and shall also transmit to him by registered or insured post a Queen's Printer's copy of this Act and a copy of the certificate of the registration of the company in Victoria.

(b) On receipt of any such copy the registrar of companies shall, with effect from the date of registration, remove the name of the company to which the certificate relates from the register in England.

(2) On and from the date of registration of Holdings or Grindlays as the case may be, the Companies Act 1985 (with the exception of those provisions which apply to oversea companies) shall not apply to that company, but that company shall (save for its registration as a company incorporated in Victoria) be the same company for all purposes as it was before the date of registration.

(3) The registrar of companies shall retain and register the copy of any certificate transmitted to him under subsection (1)(a) above.

PART III

TRANSFER OF BUSINESS TO ANZ

Schemes for transfer to ANZ of property, liabilities, trusteeships and other appointments in United Kingdom

5.—(1) Within five years from the passing of this Act ANZ may jointly with a Transferor make a scheme or schemes for—

(a) the transfer to ANZ of any of the property and liabilities to which, immediately before the appointed day for any such scheme, a Transferor is entitled or subject;

(b) the substitution of ANZ for a Transferor or of a director, officer, representative or employee of ANZ for a director, officer, representative or employee of a Transferor, in any position held by it or by such person as a trustee; and

(c) the substitution of ANZ for a Transferor, or of a director, officer, representative or employee of ANZ for a director, officer, representative or employee of a Transferor, as the holder of any office or appointment other than of trustee.

(2) A transfer scheme under subsection (1) above shall take effect on such day as may be specified in the scheme as the appointed day for the scheme; and in each case before the earliest day specified as an appointed day for a scheme in relation to any Transferor under this Act, ANZ shall publish in the London Gazette, the Edinburgh Gazette and the Belfast Gazette a notice stating that it is the earliest day so specified for a transfer scheme under this Act in relation to that Transferor.

(3) Not less than seven days before the appointed day for a transfer scheme a Transferor shall give written notice to every person having a bank account which is to be transferred by or in consequence of the scheme (or, in the case of a joint account, the first-named account holder) that the account is to become an account with ANZ and of the appointed day for the scheme:

Provided that a failure by the Transferor so to give such notice to any account holder shall not invalidate the scheme.

(4) On the appointed day for a transfer scheme any property and liabilities transferred by the scheme shall, by virtue of this Act and without further assurance, be transferred to and vested in ANZ to the intent that ANZ shall succeed to such property and liabilities as if for all purposes ANZ were the same person in law as the Transferor.

(5) Where the transfer of any propery or liability to which a transfer scheme relates is governed by the law of any country or territory outside the United Kingdom, the Transferor shall, if ANZ so requires, take all necessary steps to secure that the transfer of the property or liability to ANZ is fully effective under the law of that country or territory and pending such transfer any such property shall be held by the Transferor in trust for ANZ and ANZ shall be liable to the Transferor for any such liability.

Provisions as to trust and other property and liabilities in United Kingdom

6.—(1) Where a transfer scheme transfers to ANZ property or a liability to which immediately before the appointed day for the scheme a Transferor was then entitled or subject as a trustee or as the holder of any other office or appointment, whether alone or jointly with another person, it shall be held by ANZ, or ANZ shall be subject to it, on and from the appointed day, alone or, as the case may be, jointly with that other person, in that capacity upon the same trusts or terms and with and subject to the same powers and provisions as were applicable to the Transferor immediately before the appointed day.

(2) Where ANZ is substituted for a Transferor as a trustee or as the holder of any other office or appointment under paragraph (b) or (c) of section 5(1) above—

(a) any property to which the Transferor was then in that capacity entitled, whether alone or jointly with another person, shall, by virtue of this Act and without further assurance, be transferred to and held by ANZ alone or, as the case may be, jointly with that other person, upon the same trusts or terms and with and subject to the same powers, provisions and liabilities as were applicable to the Transferor immediately before the appointed day; and

(b) ANZ shall, by virtue of this Act and without further assurance, in the same capacity and upon the same terms, become subject to any liability to which the Transferor was then in that capacity subject, whether alone or jointly with another person.

(3) Where a director, officer, representative or employee of ANZ is substituted for a director, officer, representative or employee of a Transferor as a trustee or as the holder of any other office or appointment under paragraph (b) or (c) of section 5(1) above—

(a) any property to which that director, officer, representative or employee of the Transferor was then, as trustee or as the holder of that office or appointment, entitled, whether alone or jointly with another person, shall, by virtue of this Act and without further assurance, be transferred to and held by that director, officer, representative or employee of ANZ alone or, as the case may be, jointly with that other person upon the same trusts or terms and with and subject to the same powers, provisions and liabilities as were applicable to the director, officer, representative or employee of the Transferor immediately before the appointed day; and

(b) that director, officer, representative or employee of ANZ shall, by virtue of this Act and without further assurance, as trustee or as the holder of the office or appointment aforesaid, and upon the same terms, become subject to any liability to which the director, officer, representative or employee of the Transferor whom he is replacing was then, as trustee or as the holder of that office or appointment, subject, whether alone or jointly with another person.

(4) Any instrument or order of any court under or by virtue of which any property has been or is to become vested in a Transferor as a trustee or as the holder of any other office or appointment, and any provision therein, or any agreement or arrangement for the payment to, or retention by, a Transferor of remuneration for its services as a trustee or as the holder of any other office or appointment, shall, if that property is transferred by or in consequence of a transfer scheme, on and from the appointed day, be construed and have effect, so far as the context permits, as if for any reference therein to a Transferor, other than a reference (however worded and whether express or implied) to terms and conditions of, or to a scale of fees of, the Transferor, there were substituted a reference to ANZ.

Supplementary provisions as to schemes and transfers in United Kingdom

7.—(1) Without prejudice to the generality of the foregoing provisions of this Act but subject to any provision of this Act to the contrary effect, the following provisions shall have effect in relation to a transfer scheme and any property or liability transferred by or in consequence of a transfer scheme.

(2) A transfer scheme may—

(a) contain supplementary and incidental provisions for the purpose of giving full effect to the transfer by or in consequence of the scheme of property and liabilities and to the substitution of ANZ for a Transferor under paragraph (b) or (c) of section 5(1) above; and

(b) revoke or vary any provision of an earlier transfer scheme before the appointed day for that scheme.

(3) An agreement, transaction, or other thing (not contained in an enactment and not being a will) which has been made, effected or done by, to or in relation to, or with reference to, a Transferor and which—

(a) immediately before the appointed day for a transfer scheme is in force or effective; and

(b) relates to any property or liability to be transferred to ANZ by or in consequence of the scheme or to any position in respect of which ANZ is substituted for the Transferor under paragraph (b) or (c) of section 5(1) above,

shall on and after that day have effect as if made, effected or done by, to or in relation to, or with reference to, ANZ.

(4) Where any agreement, transaction or other thing has effect in accordance with subsection (3) above—

(a) any reference to the Transferor in any document incorporating or otherwise connected with the agreement, transaction or other thing shall on and after the appointed day for the transfer scheme be construed as a reference to ANZ; and

(b) any reference (however worded and whether express or implied) in the agreement, transaction or other thing to the directors, officers, representatives or employees (or to any director, officer, representative or employee) of the Transferor shall on and after the appointed day for the transfer scheme be construed as a reference to the directors, officers, representatives or employees of ANZ or, as the case may require, to such director, officer, representative or employee of ANZ, as ANZ may nominate for that purpose or, in default of nomination, to the director, officer, representative or employee of ANZ who corresponds as nearly as may be to the first-mentioned director, officer, representative or employee.

(5) Any agreement or transaction which relates to property or liabilities which are only partly transferred to ANZ by or in consequence or a transfer scheme shall be construed as if the agreement or transaction, to the extent to which it is enforceable by and against the Transferor, constituted two separate agreements or transactions, one of which is enforceable by and against ANZ as regards the part of the property or, as the case may be, liabilities so transferred to it and not as regards the other part, and the other of which is enforceable by and against the Transferor as regards the part of the property or, as the case may be, liabilities not so transferred to ANZ and not as regards the other part.

(6) Any account between a Transferor and a customer which is transferred by or in consequence of a transfer scheme shall be deemed for all purposes to be a single continuing account and, subject to the provisions of subsections (3) and (4) above and subsections (7) and (8) below, shall be subject to the same terms and conditions as those which applied before the transfer.

(7) Nothing in subsection (6) above shall preclude the exercise of any right of ANZ (in place of the Transferor) or of a customer to vary the terms and conditions subject to which the account of the customer is kept.

(8) Without prejudice to the generality of the foregoing, where by virtue of a transfer scheme and the operation of this Act ANZ becomes a party to an agreement, transaction or other thing in place of a Transferor, any reference in that agreement, transaction or other thing to a rate of interest prescribed by the Transferor shall be construed on and from the appointed day for the scheme as a reference to the equivalent rate of interest prescribed by ANZ.

(9) Any negotiable instrument, letter of credit or order for payment of money which is transferred by a transfer scheme and has been drawn on, or

given to, or accepted or endorsed by a Transferor, or is payable at a place of business of a Transferor, shall have the same effect as if it had been drawn on, or given to, or accepted or endorsed by, ANZ or were payable at a place of business of ANZ.

(10) The custody of any document or record, goods or other thing held by a Transferor as bailee in connection with any property or liabilities to be transferred by a transfer scheme shall pass to ANZ on the appointed day for the scheme, and the rights and obligations of a Transferor under any contract of bailment relating to any such document or record, goods or thing shall on that day become rights and obligations of ANZ.

(11) (a) Any security held immediately before the appointed day for a transfer scheme by a Transferor in connection with any property or liabilities to be transferred by or in consequence of the scheme, or by a nominee or agent of or trustee for a Transferor, shall, on and from that day, be held by, or as the case may require, by that nominee, agent or trustee for, ANZ and be available to ANZ (whether for its own benefit or, as the case may be, for the benefit of any other person);

(b) In relation to any security transferred to ANZ by or in consequence of a transfer scheme and to any liabilities thereby secured, ANZ shall be entitled to the same rights and priorities and be subject to the same obligations as those to which the Transferor would have been entitled or subject if it had continued to hold the security;

(c) Without prejudice to the generality of paragraph (b) above, in any case where any existing liability subsists between a Transferor and ANZ in respect of which the Transferor or ANZ, or a nominee or agent of or trustee for the Transferor or ANZ, holds security, that liability shall, for the purpose of enforcing or realising that security, be deemed to continue in effect notwithstanding a transfer to ANZ of the liability or the benefit of the liability by or in consequence of a transfer scheme.

(d) Any security referred to in the foregoing provisions of this subsection which extends to future advances, liabilities or indebtedness shall, on and from the appointed day for the transfer scheme, be available to ANZ (whether for its own benefit or, as the case may be, for the benefit of any other person) as security for the payment or discharge of future advances, liabilities and indebtedness to the same extent and in the same manner in all respects as it extends to future advances, liabilities or indebtedness immediately before that day.

(12) On and from the appointed day for a transfer scheme, ANZ and all other persons shall have the same rights, powers and remedies (and in particular the same rights and powers as to taking or resisting legal proceedings or making or resisting applications to any authority) for ascertaining, perfecting or enforcing the property or liability transferred by or in consequence of the scheme as if it had been property or a liability of ANZ for the period before the appointed day for the scheme during which it had been the property or liability of the Transferor; and any legal proceedings or applications to any authority pending immediately before the appointed day for the scheme by or against the Transferor may be continued by or against ANZ.

(13) Any judgment, order or award obtained by or against a Transferor relating to property or a liability transferred by or in consequence of a transfer scheme or to any position in respect of which ANZ is substituted for the Transferor under paragraph (b) or (c) of section 5(1) above and not fully satisfied before the appointed day for the scheme shall on and from that day, to the extent to which it was enforceable by or against the Transferor immediately before that day, be enforceable by or against ANZ and no longer by or against the Transferor.

(14) In respect of—

(a) any data transferred to ANZ by a transfer scheme, or

(b) any data relating to any property or a liability transferred to ANZ by or in consequence of a transfer scheme.

the Data Protection Registrar may, on and from the appointed day for that transfer scheme, serve on ANZ any notice under section 10 of the Data Protection Act 1984 which he could have served on a Transferor in respect of a breach of the data protection principles by the Transferor before that appointed day; but the transfer of property or liabilities to ANZ by or in consequence of a transfer scheme and any disclosure to ANZ of any information in contemplation or as a result thereof shall not amount to a breach of any duty of confidentiality to which the Transferor is or was subject immediately before the appointed day for the scheme or to a contravention by ANZ or the Transferor of the data protection principles.

Evidence: books and documents

8. All books and other documents which would, before the appointed day for a transfer scheme, have been evidence for or against the Transferor in respect of any matter to which the scheme relates shall be admissible in evidence in respect of the same matter for or against ANZ.

Application of Bankers' Books Evidence Act 1879

9.—(1) In this section "books" shall be construed in accordance with section 9(2) of the Bankers' Books Evidence Act 1879.

(2) On and from the appointed day for a transfer scheme the said Act of 1879 shall apply to those books of the Transferor which are transferred to ANZ by the scheme, and to entries made in those books before that day, as if such books were the books of ANZ.

(3) For the purposes of section 4 of the said Act of 1879, books so transferred to ANZ shall be deemed to have been the ordinary books of ANZ at the time of the making of any entry therein which purports to have been made before the appointed day for the scheme, and any such entry shall be deemed to have been made in the usual and ordinary course of business.

Evidence of transfer and vesting

10.—(1) In this section "convey" has the same meaning as in the Law of Property Act 1925.

(2) A certificate issued jointly by or on behalf of ANZ and a Transferor that by or in consequence of a transfer scheme any property or liabilities specified in the certificate have been transferred to ANZ shall be conclusive evidence for all purposes of that fact.

(3) A certificate issued under subsection (2) above, shall, in relation to any registered securities within the meaning of the Stock Transfer Act 1963 transferred to ANZ by or in consequence of a transfer scheme, operate for all the purposes of the said Act of 1963 as a duly executed stock transfer in respect of the transfer of such securities from the Transferor to ANZ.

(4) Without prejudice to subsection (2) above (but subject to that subsection)—

(a) any document made or executed on or after the relevant first appointed day whereby ANZ, whether alone or jointly with any other person, conveys or transfers, or purports to convey or transfer, to any person (whether for consideration or not), or applies to be registered as the holder or proprietor of, any property held by a Transferor immediately before that day, whether alone or jointly with any other person, shall be sufficient evidence that the interest of the Transferor in that property has been transferred to ANZ by or in consequence of a transfer scheme; and

(b) where there is any other transaction by ANZ on or after the relevant first appointed day in connection with, or in relation to, any property or liability which immediately before that day is property or a liability of a Transferor, it shall be deemed in favour of any other party to the transaction, or any person claiming through or under him, that ANZ has full power and authority for that transaction.

(5) Without prejudice to subsection (2) above (but subject to that subsection)—

(a) any document made or executed on or after the first appointed day whereby a Transferor, whether alone or jointly with any other person, conveys or transfers, or purports to convey or transfer, to any person (whether for consideration or not), or applies to be registered as the holder or proprietor of, any property held by it immediately before that day, whether alone or jointly with any other person, shall be sufficient evidence that its interest in that property has not been transferred to ANZ by or in consequence of a transfer scheme; and

(b) where there is any other transaction by a Transferor on or after the first appointed day in connection with, or in relation to, any property or liability which immediately before that day is property or a liability of the Transferor, it shall be deemed in favour of any other party to the transaction, or any person claiming through or under him, that the Transferor has full power and authority for that transaction.

(6) No person may rely upon the provisions of subsection (4) or (5) above if he has knowledge to the contrary and nothing in this section affects the liability of ANZ, or of a Transferor, to the other of them in respect of anything done, or purported to have been done, by one of them in connection with, or in relation to, any property or liabilities transferred by or in consequence of a transfer scheme.

Savings in respect of transfers of property

11. The transfer of any property or of a liability by or in consequence of a transfer scheme or the substitution of ANZ for a Transferor under paragraph (b) or (c) of section 5(1) above shall not—

(1) constitute a purchase or creation of an interest in land for the purposes of section 30(2) of the Landlord and Tenant Act 1954 or constitute a relevant disposal within the meaning of section 4 of the Landlord and Tenant Act 1987 for the purposes of that Act; or

(2) constitute an assignment, transfer, devolution, alienation, parting with possession or other disposition of property or of an interest in property for the purposes of any provision in any instrument, contract (whether in writing or not) or order of any court concerning that property or that interest; or

(3) give rise to any forfeiture; or

(4) invalidate or discharge any agreement, transaction, security or other thing; or

(5) require further registration in respect of any security transferred by or in consequence of the scheme; or

(6) cause the benefit of any agreement, licence or privilege enjoyed by a Transferor to be lost or surrendered or otherwise affected, or require the disposal by a Transferor of any interest, otherwise than as provided for in this Act; or

(7) relieve any person under an obligation to a Transferor of a corresponding obligation to ANZ; or

(8) constitute a breach of, or default under, or require any obligation to be performed sooner or later than would have otherwise been the case under, any agreement or arrangement to which ANZ or a Transferor is a party; or

(9) operate so as to merge any leasehold interest in the reversion expectant on it.

PART IV

MISCELLANEOUS

Application to Scotland and Northern Ireland

12.—(1) This Act other than Part II extends to Scotland and Northern Ireland.

(2) In the application of this Act to Scotland the following provisions shall have effect:—

(a) in the construction of this Act—

"assignment" includes an assignation;

"bailee" includes a custodian or a holder on deposit or pledge and "contract of bailment" includes any other contract regulating custody of things;

"convey" includes the execution of any deed or other instrument or document by which any property, or any estate, interest, security or other right in or over property, is constituted, completed disponed, assigned, transmitted or discharged;

"debenture" includes a floating charge or any instrument containing a floating charge;

"freehold land" includes heritable property;

"judgment" includes a decree;

"judicial trustee" includes a judicial factor;

"mortgage" includes a standard security, an assignation or disposition ex facie absolute and any agreement qualifying the same, a bond and disposition or assignation in security, a cash credit bond and disposition or assignation in security, an assignation in security and any real right or burden of whatever kind in the nature of a security whether or not constituted in respect of a heritable property; and

"will" includes a trust disposition and settlement and any deed taking effect on the death of any person whereby any part of his estate is disposed of, or under which a succession thereto arises;

(b) all standard securities and cash credit bonds and dispositions or assignations in security expressed to be in favour of a Transferor transferred to ANZ by or in consequence of a transfer scheme shall, on and from the appointed day for the scheme, have the same effect in favour of ANZ up to the maximum amounts stated therein respectively in all respects as if they had been originally granted in favour of ANZ for such maximum amounts;

(c) to enable ANZ to complete a title, if thought fit, to any property transferred to it by or in consequence of a transfer scheme, by notice of title or otherwise, or to deduce title, the transfer scheme shall be deemed to be, and may be used as, a general disposition, conveyance or, as the case may be, assignation of such property in favour of ANZ;

(d) for the reference in subsection (1) of section 2 (Interpretation) of this Act to section 10 of the Civil Evidence Act 1968 there shall be substituted reference to section 17 of the Law Reform (Miscellaneous Provisions) (Scotland) Act 1968.

(3) In the application of this Act to Northern Ireland—

(a) for the reference in subsection (1) of section 2 (Interpretation) of this Act to section 10 of the Civil Evidence Act 1968 there shall be substituted reference to section 6 of the Civil Evidence Act (Northern Ireland) 1971;

(b) for the reference in subsection (1) of section 10 (Evidence of transfer and vesting) of this Act to the Law of Property Act 1925 there shall be substituted reference to the Conveyancing Act 1881;

(c) the reference in subsection (3) of section 10 (Evidence of transfer and vesting) of this Act to the Stock Transfer Act 1963 shall include a reference to the Stock Transfer Act (Northern Ireland) 1963; and

(d) for paragraph (1) of section 11 (Savings in respect of transfers of property) of this Act, there shall be substituted the following:—

"(1) constitute a purchase or creation of an estate for the purposes of section 10(3) of the Business Tenancies Act (Northern Ireland) 1964; or".

Costs of Act

13. All costs, charges and expenses preliminary to, and of and incidental to, the preparing for, obtaining and passing of this Act, or otherwise in relation thereto, shall be paid by ANZ.

INDEX

References are to sections

ANZ Grindlays Bank plc,
continuation of legal identity, 4(2)
registration in Victoria, 3
removal from register in England, 4
ANZ Holdings (UK) plc,
continuation of legal identity, 4(2)
registration in Victoria, 3
removal from register on England, 4
Australia and New Zealand Banking Group Limited (ANZ),
schemes for transfer of property etc.,
books and documents, construction of, 8, 9
establishment of, 5
evidence,
books and documents, 8
of transfer and vesting, 10
Australia and New Zealand Banking Group Limited (ANZ)—*cont.*
schemes for transfer of property etc.—*cont.*
savings in respect of transfers, 11
supplementary provisions as to, 7
trust property and liabilities, 6

Costs of Act, 13

Extent, 12

Interpretation, 12

Short Title, 1

UNIVERSITY COLLEGE LONDON ACT 1996

(1996 c. iii)

ARRANGEMENT OF SECTIONS

SECT.
1. Short title.
2. Interpretation.
3. Appointed day.
4. Dissolution of existing bodies.
5. Transfer of property, etc.
6. Transfer of obligations, etc.
7. Savings for agreements, deeds, actions, etc.
8. Construction of bequests, etc., and powers of trustees.
9. Transfer of powers to appoint or nominate.
10. Name of medical school of College.
11. Restriction on use of names of existing bodies.

An Act to unite the Royal Free Hospital School of Medicine, the Institute of Neurology (Queen Square) and The Institute of Child Health with University College London; to transfer all rights, properties and liabilities from the said school and institutes to the said college; and for connected and other purposes. [4th July 1996]

PARLIAMENTARY PROGRESS

The Bill's progress through Parliament was as follows:

House of Commons: First Reading, January 23, 1996, Second Reading, January 30, 1996, Bill committed, March 18, 1996, Bill committed to an unopposed committee, April 25, 1996, Bill as amended by committee considered, May 15, 1996, Third Reading, May 25, 1996.

House of Lords: First Reading, May 8, 1996, Second Reading, June 3, 1996, Bill committed, June 3, 1996, Bill committed to an unopposed committee, June 12, 1996, Third Reading, June 20, 1996.

INTRODUCTION

This Act makes provision for the Royal Free Hospital School of Medicine, the Institute of Neurology (Queen Square) and the Institute of Child Health to be united with the University College London in order to enhance both academic strength and financial viability of the Medical schools by such a merger.

WHEREAS—

(1) University College London was founded in 1826, with the title "University of London", under a deed of settlement executed on 11th February 1826; the foundation stone of the then university building was laid on 30th April 1827, and courses of lectures began in October 1828:

(2) In 1836 a Royal Charter was granted, under which the proprietors of the institution then known as the University of London were reincorporated as University College London. On the same day a Royal Charter was granted to a separate body, to be known as the University of London (hereinafter referred to as "the University") with powers to examine and grant degrees to persons holding certificates of having pursued courses of instruction approved by the University at University College London or elsewhere:

(3) University College London was admitted as a school of the University in 1900, following the reconstitution of the University as a result of the University of London Act 1898 and was incorporated into the University in 1907 pursuant to the University College London (Transfer) Act 1905 with the title University of London, University College and was subsequently disincorporated from the University by a Royal Charter dated 9th December 1977 and reconstituted as University College London (hereinafter referred to as "the College") by the University College London Act 1979, the rights,

properties and liabilities of the University relating to the College being transferred to the College:

(4) University College Hospital grew out of the University Dispensary, which opened in September 1828 and medical classes started there on 1st October 1828; in May 1833 the foundation stone of the North London Hospital was laid on a site in Gower Street opposite the College and in 1837 the name was changed to University College Hospital (hereinafter referred to as "the Hospital"):

(5) In 1898 it was found that the University could no longer conveniently incorporate the Hospital nor that part of the Faculty of Medicine dealing with final medical studies and it was therefore decided that the teaching of final medical studies should be carried out by a new corporation and that the teaching of preliminary and intermediate medical studies should continue in the University of London, University College premises:

(6) The University College London (Transfer) Act 1905 accordingly provided for the formation of a separate body corporate by the name of North London or University College Hospital for the purposes of carrying on the Hospital and Medical School; from 1907 until 1948 the Hospital and Medical School were administered as one. Following the National Health Service Act 1946 the said Medical School by a new scheme of incorporation in 1948 became a body corporate having perpetual succession and a common seal and became administered separately from the Hospital as an independent school of the University:

(7) By the University College London Act 1979 the said Medical School was dissolved and ceased to exist as an entity separate from the College and all its property, rights, privileges, debts and liabilities were transferred to the College:

(8) By the University College London Act 1988, The Middlesex Hospital Medical School, the Institute of Laryngology and Otology, the Institute of Orthopaedics and the Institute of Urology were dissolved and all their property, rights, privileges, debts and liabilities were transferred to the College, that part of the College constituting its Medical School being known by the title "The University College and Middlesex School of Medicine of University College London":

(9) The Institute of Ophthalmology was incorporated on 22nd April 1950 as a company limited by guarantee with the principal objects of promoting the study of diseases of the eye and allied subjects. The said Institute's activities are now carried on principally in premises at 11–43 Bath Street, London EC1V 1LD and pursuant to an agreement dated 1st August 1995 now form part of the College:

(10) The London School of Medicine for Women was established in 1874 as an association incorporated under the Companies Acts 1862 and 1867 changing its name to The London (Royal Free Hospital) School of Medicine for Women in 1898 in recognition of its association with the Royal Free Hospital, founded in 1828, which provided clinical instruction for the students of the Medical School. It became a school of the University in 1900 under the name and style of the London (Royal Free Hospital) School of Medicine for Women (University of London):

(11) The London (Royal Free Hospital) School of Medicine for Women (University of London) was reconstituted as a body corporate by Royal Charter granted by His late Majesty King George the Sixth on 9th December 1938 which was subsequently revised on 21st May 1947, by the name and style of the Royal Free Hospital School of Medicine with the main object of acquiring and taking over the property and liabilities of the London (Royal Free Hospital) School of Medicine for Women, providing for the instruction of students to enable them to take degrees in the faculty of medicine of the University or to qualify as medical and dental practitioners and doing all such

other things as are incidental or conducive to advancing medical and surgical education, learning and research:

(12) The Institute of Neurology was incorporated on 11th June 1948 as the National Hospital (Queen Square) Institute of Neurology Limited, and on 24th July 1951 as the Institute of Neurology (Queen Square), under the Companies Acts 1929 and 1948 as a company limited by guarantee with the principal objects of promoting the study of diseases of the nervous system, carrying out research and investigation and providing education and practical training of duly qualified medical practitioners as specialists in the prevention, diagnosis and treatment of these diseases. The Institute became a federated institute of the British Postgraduate Medical Federation of the University on 1st August 1950, and its activities are now carried on principally in premises attached to the National Hospital for Neurology and Neurosurgery, Queen Square, London:

(13) The Institute of Child Health was recognised by resolution of the Senate of the University passed on 5th February 1945 as the research and teaching arm of the Hospital for Sick Children, Great Ormond Street and other related hospitals and was incorporated on 19th October 1949 as a company limited by guarantee and was admitted in July 1949 to the British Postgraduate Medical Federation of the University as an institution for postgraduate study in paediatrics. The Institute's activities are now carried on principally in premises attached to Great Ormond Street Hospital for Children NHS Trust.

(14) The Report of the Inquiry into London's Health Service, Medical Education and Research under the chairmanship of Sir Bernard Tomlinson dated October 1992 recommended the linking of London Medical Schools to multi-faculty colleges and it is consistent with the policy of the University that the academic strength and financial viability of the medical schools of the University should be enhanced by the merger of some of those schools with certain multi-faculty institutions of the University:

(15) The College, the School and the Institutes have agreed that it is expedient that provision should be made for the School and the Institutes to be united with the College in accordance with this Act:

(16) It is expedient that the other provisions contained in this Act should be enacted:

(17) The objects of this Act cannot be attained without the authority of Parliament:

May it therefore please Your Majesty that it may be enacted, and be it enacted, by the Queen's most Excellent Majesty, by and with the advice and consent of the Lords Spiritual and Temporal, and Commons, in this present Parliament assembled, and by the authority of the same, as follows:—

Short title

1. This Act may be cited as the University College London Act 1996.

Interpretation

2. In this Act, unless the subject or context otherwise requires—

"the appointed day", in reference to an existing body, means such day as may be agreed by the College and that body under section 3 below;

"the charter" means the charter incorporating the Royal Free Hospital School of Medicine, granted by His late Majesty King George the Sixth on 9th December 1938 and revised on 21st May 1947;

"the College" means University College London;

"existing body" means the Royal Free Hospital School of Medicine, the Institute of Neurology (Queen Square) or The Institute of Child Health.

Appointed day

3.—(1) The College and an existing body may agree a day to be the appointed day for the purposes of this Act in its application to that body.

(2) Not less than 28 days before any such day as may be agreed under subsection (1) above, the College shall—

(a) give notice to the Council of the University of London of the day so agreed; and

(b) publish in the London Gazette a notice stating the day so agreed.

Dissolution of existing bodies

4.—(1) On the appointed day—

(a) the Royal Free Hospital School of Medicine shall be dissolved and the charter shall be revoked; and

(b) the company incorporating respectively the Institute of Neurology (Queen Square) and The Institute of Child Health shall be dissolved.

(2) The College shall notify the registrar of the effect of paragraph (b) of subsection (1) above and of section 11 below within 14 days of the appointed day; and the registrar shall record the dissolution of the company in question.

(3) In subsection (2) above, "the registrar" has the meaning given in section 744 of the Companies Act 1985.

Transfer of property, etc.

5. All property, real and personal, of every description including things in action) and all rights and privileges of an existing body which immediately before the appointed day belonged to or were vested in or exercisable by that body shall on the appointed day, without any conveyance, transfer, assignment or other instrument, be transferred to and vested in, or be exercisable by, the College for all the estate and interest therein of that body.

Transfer of obligations, etc.

6. All debts and obligations of an existing body shall on the appointed day be transferred and attached to the College and shall thereafter be discharged and satisfied by the College.

Savings for agreements, deeds, actions, etc.

7. All agreements, appointments, awards, contracts, deeds and other instruments, and all actions and proceedings and causes of action, which immediately before the appointed day were existing or pending in favour of, or against, an existing body shall on and from the appointed day continue and may be carried into effect enforced and prosecuted by, or in favour of, or against, the College to the same extent and in like manner as if the College instead of the existing body had been party to, or interested in, the same respectively.

Construction of bequests, etc., and powers of trustees

8.—(1) Any scheme, will, deed or other instrument, whether made or executed before, on or after the appointed day, which contains any bequest, gift or trust or other benefit in favour of or connected with an existing body shall, on and after the appointed day, be read and have effect as if the College were named therein instead of that body:

Provided that the College shall administer that bequest, gift, trust or other benefit as nearly as may be for the purposes intended in the original scheme, will, deed or other instrument conferring such benefit and pursuant to the purposes of the existing body as those purposes were defined before that body's dissolution.

(2) Without prejudice to subsection (1) above, any persons who, immediately before the appointed day, had power, for all or any purposes relating to hospital services (including research) or to any other part of the health service associated with hospitals, to assist, support or otherwise benefit an existing body, shall, on and from that day, have power to assist, support or otherwise benefit the College as if it were a hospital or an institution within the health service associated with such a hospital for which those persons were appointed.

(3) In this section "the health service" and "hospital" have the same meaning as in the National Health Service Act 1977.

Transfer of powers to appoint or nominate

9. Any power or right of an existing body or of any officer or employee of an existing body to appoint or nominate a member of any education authority or of the governing body of any educational, charitable or other institution, shall on the appointed day be transferred to, and may be exercised by, the College or by the officer or employee of the College who in the opinion of the Council of the College most nearly performs the functions formerly performed by the former officer or employee in question.

Name of medical school of College

10.—(1) Subject to subsection (2) below, that part of the College constituting its medical school shall henceforth after the appointed day in reference to the Royal Free Hospital School of Medicine be known by the title the "Royal Free and University College Medical School of University College London":

Provided that the College shall, after the appointed day, administer the respective undertakings of The Institute of Child Health and the Institute of Neurology (Queen Square) within, and as part of, the medical school by those names and titles respectively.

(2) The Council of the College may, from time to time, by special procedure alter the name for the medical school referred to in subsection (1) above:

Provided that no such alteration shall be made for a period of 10 years from the appointed day of merger with the Royal Free Hospital School of Medicine.

(3) In subsection (2) above, "special procedure" shall comprise—

(a) the passing of a resolution by a majority of not less than two-thirds of those present and voting being an absolute majority of all the members of the Council at a meeting of the Council convened by 28 days' written notice specifying the substance of the resolution to be proposed at the meeting; and

(b) the passing of a second such resolution by a like majority at a meeting of the Council similarly convened and held not less than one month nor more than four months after the date of the first-mentioned meeting.

Restriction on use of names or existing bodies

11. No person other than the College shall, within a period of 25 years after the passing of this Act, without the consent of the College, and, in respect of the Royal Free Hospital School of Medicine, without consultation with the Royal Free Hampstead NHS Trust or its successor body, use the names "Royal Free Hospital School of Medicine", "Institute of Neurology", or "The Institute of Child Health".

INDEX

References are to sections

APPOINTED DAY, 3

BEQUESTS, 8

DISSOLUTION OF EXISTING BODIES, 4

INSTITUTE OF CHILD HEALTH,
  administration of undertakings, 10
  dissolution of, 4
  use of name, 11
INSTITUTE OF NEUROLOGY (QUEEN SQUARE),
  administration of undertakings, 10
  dissolution of, 4
  use of name, 11
INTERPRETATION, 2

NAME OF MEDICAL SCHOOL,
  from appointed day, 10(1)
NAME OF MEDICAL SCHOOL—*cont.*
  no alteration for 10 years, 10(2)
  special procedure for altering, 10(3)

ROYAL FREE AND UNIVERSITY COLLEGE MEDICAL SCHOOL OF UNIVERSITY COLLEGE LONDON, 10
ROYAL FREE HAMPSTEAD NHS TRUST, 11
ROYAL FREE HOSPITAL SCHOOL OF MEDICINE,
  dissolution of, 4
  use of name, 11

SAVINGS, 7
SHORT TITLE, 1

TRANSFER OF OBLIGATIONS, 6
TRANSFER OF POWERS TO APPOINT OR NOMINATE, 9
TRANSFER OF PROPERTY, 5
TRUSTEES' POWERS, 8

CITY OF LONDON (APPROVED PREMISES FOR MARRIAGE) ACT 1996

(1996 c. iv)

An Act to enable the approval of premises within the City of London (including the Temples) for the solemnization of civil marriages; and for connected purposes. [18th July 1996]

PARLIAMENTARY PROGRESS

The Bill's progress through Parliament was as follows:

House of Lords: First Reading, January 11, 1996, Second Reading, February 14, 1996, Bill committed, February 14, 1996, Bill committed to an unopposed Committee, June 5, 1996, Third Reading, June 13, 1996.

House of Commons: First Reading, June 13, 1996, Second Reading, June 25, 1996, Bill committed, June 25, 1996, Bill committed to an unopposed Committee, July 4, 1996, Third Reading, July 10, 1996.

INTRODUCTION

This Act empowers a London local authority to approve premises for the solemnization of marriages pursuant to s.26(1)(bb) of the Marriage Act 1949 (c. 76).

WHEREAS—

(1) The common council are responsible for providing the registration service for births, marriages and deaths within the City of London:

(2) It is expedient that the common council should be empowered to approve premises within the city for the solemnization of marriages pursuant to section 26(1)(bb) of the Marriage Act 1949:

(3) By ancient custom the Honourable Society of the Inner Temple and the Honourable Society of the Middle Temple exercise powers within the areas of the Inner Temple and the Middle Temple respectively ("the Temples") concerning (inter alia) the regulation and governance of the Temples:

(4) The Master of the Temple as holder from the Crown of the office of incumbent of the Temple Church exercises within the Temple those special privileges of the Crown which relate to his office:

(5) The objects of this Act cannot be attained without the authority of Parliament:

May it therefore please Your Majesty that it may be enacted, and be it enacted, by the Queen's most Excellent Majesty, by and with the advice and consent of the Lords Spiritual and Temporal, and Commons, in this present Parliament assembled, and by the authority of the same, as follows:—

Short title

1. This Act may be cited as the City of London (Approved Premises for Marriage) Act 1996.

Interpretation

2. In this Act, unless the context otherwise requires "the 1949 Act" means the Marriage Act 1949.

Approval of premises for marriage

3.—(1) The common council shall be a local authority for the purposes of section 46A of the 1949 Act and may accordingly, in accordance with regulations under that section, approve premises for the solemnization of marriage in pursuance of section 26(1)(bb) of that Act.

(2) In consequence of subsection (1) above, in section 46A(3) of the 1949 Act for "or London borough council" there shall be substituted "London borough council or the Common Council of the City of London".

Consultation with the Temples

4.—(1) As soon as practicable after receiving an application relating to any premises situated within the Inner Temple or the Middle Temple the common council shall notify the Sub-Treasurer of the Honourable Society of the Inner Temple (as respects premises in the Inner Temple) and the Under Treasurer of the Honourable Society of the Middle Temple (as respects premises in the Middle Temple).

(2) Before granting approval in relation to any such premises the common council shall consult the Sub-Treasurer or, as the case may be, the Under Treasurer.

(3) Where any matter that falls to be considered in determining an application for any such approval is one that is material to the exercise by the Sub-Treasurer or the Under Treasurer of his functions under any enactment and he objects, with reference to that matter, to the grant of approval, the common council shall refuse approval.

Saving for rights of the Temples and the Master of the Temple

5. Nothing in this Act shall prejudice or affect any right, power or privilege of the Honourable Society of the Inner Temple, the Honourable Society of the Middle Temple or the Master of the Temple.

INDEX

References are to sections

APPROVAL OF PREMISES, 3

INNER TEMPLE,
consultation with, 4
savings for, 5
INTERPRETATION, 2

MIDDLE TEMPLE,
consultation with, 4
savings for, 5

SHORT TITLE, 1

HENRY JOHNSON, SONS & CO., LIMITED ACT 1996

(1996 c. v)

An Act to make provision for the transfer to the Republic of France of the incorporation of Henry Johnson, Sons & Co., Limited; for the cesser of application to the company of provisions of the Companies Act 1985; and for the purposes incidental thereto. [18th July 1996]

Parliamentary Progress

The Bill's progress through Parliament was as follows:

House of Commons: First Reading, January 23, 1996, Second Reading, January 30, 1996, Bill committed, March 25, 1996, Bill committed to an unopposed Committee, April 24, 1996, Bill as amended by the Committee considered, Third Reading, May 14, 1996.

House of Lords: First Reading, May 14, 1996, Second Reading, June 12, 1996, Bill committed, June 12, 1996, Bill committed to an unopposed Committee, July 4, 1996, Third Reading, July 15, 1996.

Introduction

This Act allows for Henry Johnson, Sons & Co., Limited, an international transportation agent, to become registered under the laws of the Republic of France with its registered office in Paris. Section 4 sets out the procedures for removal from the register in England.

WHEREAS—

(1) Henry Johnson, Sons & Co., Limited (hereinafter in this Act referred to as "the Company") is a company within the meaning of the Companies Act 1985, and is a company limited by shares:

(2) The Company carries on the business of international transportation customs agents, transport commissioners, road haulage, services for the transportation of goods by public transport and the hiring of industrial vehicles with drivers for the road haulage of goods:

(3) The registered office of the Company is situated in England:

(4) Having regard to the fact that the area of operation of the Company is and has been for many years wholly in the Republic of France, certain advantages would accrue to the Company if it were incorporated under the laws of the Republic of France instead of under the laws of England:

(5) No procedure exists whereby the incorporation of a company to which the Companies Act 1985 applies can be transferred from England to another country:

(6) Under and subject to the law relating to corporations in the Republic of France the Company will be able, on the passing of this Act, to become a corporation incorporated and registered duly in that state:

(7) It is expedient that such provisions should be enacted as are in this Act contained:

(8) The objects of this Act cannot be attained without the authority of Parliament:

May it therefore please your Majesty that it may be enacted, and be it enacted, by the Queen's most Excellent Majesty, by and with the advice and consent of the Lords Spiritual and Temporal, and Commons, in this present Parliament assembled, and by the authority of the same, as follows:

Short title

1. This Act may be cited as the Henry Johnson, Sons & Co., Limited Act 1996.

Interpretation

2. In this Act—

"the date of registration" means the date on which the Company becomes a corporation incorporated and duly registered under the laws of the Republic of France;

"the registrar" means the registrar or other officer performing under the Companies Act 1985 the duty of registration of companies in England.

Registration in Republic of France

3. Subject to the laws in force in the Republic of France, and with such legislative, governmental, municipal or other authority, concession, licence or consent as may be necessary, the Company may become registered under the laws of the Republic of France with its registered office in Paris.

Removal from register in England

4.—(1) On the date of registration, the Company shall notify the registrar thereof by telex or cablegram and transmit to him as soon as is reasonably practicable by registered or insured post a Queen's Printer's copy of this Act and a copy of the certificate of registration of the Company issued by the registrar of the Commercial Court of Paris in the Republic of France, and on the receipt of that certificate the registrar shall, with effect from the date of registration, strike the name of the Company from the register of companies in England, and from that date the Companies Act 1985 (except in so far as the provisions of that Act apply to oversea companies) shall not apply to the Company, but the Company shall (save for its registration and incorporation in the Republic of France) for all purposes be the same company after the date of registration as it was before that date.

(2) The registrar shall retain and register the copy of the certificate of registration transmitted to him under this section.

INDEX

References are to sections

FRANCE,
registration in, 3

INTERPRETATION, 2

REGISTRATION OF COMPANY IN FRANCE, 3
REMOVAL FROM REGISTER IN ENGLAND, 4

SHORT TITLE, 1

BELFAST CHARITABLE SOCIETY ACT 1996

(1996 c. vi)

ARRANGEMENT OF SECTIONS

SECT.
1. Short title.
2. Definitions.
3. Continuance of Society.
4. Objects of Society.
5. Subsidiary powers of Society.
6. Regulations.
7. Board of Management.
8. Membership.
9. Validity of acts done at meetings.
10. Power to alter Act.
11. Repeals.

SCHEDULE—Repeals.

An Act to make provision as to the objects, powers, constitution and management of the Belfast Charitable Society; and for connected purposes. [18th July 1996]

PARLIAMENTARY PROGRESS

The Bill's progress through Parliament was as follows:

House of Lords: First Reading, January 11, 1996, Second Reading, February 14, 1996, Bill committed, February 22, 1996, Bill committed to an unopposed Committee, June 5, 1996, Third Reading, June 13, 1996, Commons' amendments considered by the House of Commons, July 19, 1996.

House of Commons: First Reading, June 13, 1996, Second Reading, June 25, 1996, Bill committed, June 25, 1996, Bill committed to an unopposed Committee, July 4, 1996, Bill as amended by the Committee considered, July 10, 1996, Third Reading, July 16, 1996.

INTRODUCTION

This Act modernises the objects, powers, constitution and management of the Belfast Charitable Society, in order for it to serve the present day and likely future needs of the community.

WHEREAS—

(1) By an Act of the Parliament of Ireland intituled "An Act for amending an Act made the last Session of Parliament, intitled, An Act for badging such Poor as shall be found unable to support themselves by Labour, and otherwise providing for them, and for restraining such as shall be found able to support themselves by Labour and Industry, from begging" the Belfast Charitable Society ("the Society") was incorporated in 1774 by the name of "the president and assistants of the Belfast charitable society" for the better carrying into execution under proper regulations the charitable and humane design of maintaining the poor of the town of Belfast with power to make laws, rules, orders and regulations for the government and management of the infirmary and poor house now known as Clifton House and to make byelaws and regulations and to exercise the same powers with respect to all idle and sturdy beggars within Belfast as certain corporations within counties and cities in Ireland were then enabled to do:

(2) Further provision was made with respect to the Society by subsequent Acts of the Parliament of Ireland, including limited powers to purchase and lease lands:

(3) The business of the Society is managed by a Board of Management established by regulations made under section 12 of the said Act of 1774:

(4) In order to ensure that the Society will be able to serve the present-day and likely future needs of the community it is necessary to modernise the objects and powers of the Society, together with its constitution and management:

(5) It is expedient that the other provisions of this Act should be enacted:

(6) The purposes of this Act cannot be effected without the authority of Parliament:

May it therefore please Your Majesty that it may be enacted, and be it enacted, by the Queen's most Excellent Majesty, by and with the advice and consent of the Lords Spiritual and Temporal, and Commons, in this present Parliament assembled, and by the authority of the same, as follows:—

Short title

1. This Act may be cited as the Belfast Charitable Society Act 1996.

Definitions

2. In this Act, unless the context otherwise requires—

"the 1774 Act" means the first Act mentioned in columns (1) and (2) of the Schedule to this Act;

"the 1800 Act" means the Act of the Parliament of Ireland intituled "An Act for paving, cleansing, and lighting, and improving the several Streets, Squares, Lanes and Passages within the Town of Belfast in the County of Antrim, and for removing and preventing all Encroachments, Obstructions and Annoyances therein, and also for establishing and maintaining a Nightly Watch throughout the said town and Precincts thereof, and for other Purposes";

"the Board" means the Board of Management of the Society;

"the existing enactments" means the Acts mentioned in columns (1) and (2) of the Schedule to this Act and the 1800 Act;

"the officers" means the persons who for the time being are respectively the President, the Chairman, the Honorary Treasurer and the Honorary Secretary of the Society;

"regulations" means regulations made under section 6 (Regulations) of this Act;

"the Society" means the President and Assistants of the Belfast Charitable Society.

Continuance of Society

3. The Society shall continue in being as a body corporate but the provisions of this Act as to the objects, powers, constitution and management of the Society shall have effect in place of the provisions for those purposes in the existing enactments.

Objects of Society

4. The objects of the Society are—

(a) to pursue all or any charitable activities which advance the interests or are for the benefit of persons appearing to the Society to be disadvantaged, primarily in Northern Ireland, including the care of the elderly, the relief of poverty, homelessness, distress, infirmity and sickness and providing for the educational and other needs of such persons; and

(b) to participate in and encourage all forms of co-operation among appropriate parties which are calculated to achieve any of the objects mentioned in paragraph (a) above.

Subsidiary powers of Society

5. Notwithstanding anything contained in the existing enactments, and without prejudice to the generality of section 4 (Objects of Society) of this Act, the Society shall in the furtherance of its objects have the following powers:—

(a) to dispose of any land, personal estate or property (including moneys secured on mortgage of or charged upon any land), or any rights or interests therein, vested in the Society or which shall hereafter be vested in or acquired by the Society, or any part thereof, and to do and execute all such acts, deeds, matters and things as may be necessary for effectuating and completing any such sale, mortgage, charge, letting, surrender, exchange, licence or other dealing;

(b) to purchase, take on lease in fee farm or in exchange or otherwise acquire any real and personal property and any rights and privileges;

(c) to construct, maintain, alter or demolish any buildings and improve or develop any property;

(d) without prejudice to paragraphs (a) to (c) above, to manage land or any other property and to effect any dealings in land or such property as the Society shall in its absolute discretion think fit;

(e) to form and promote, or join with any person in forming and promoting, any body corporate;

(f) to subscribe for or acquire shares, stock, debentures, debenture stock or any other security of a like nature of a body corporate;

(g) to dispose of any shares or other securities subscribed for or acquired under this section;

(h) without prejudice to paragraphs (a) to (g) above, to make such investments of whatever nature and wheresoever and whether involving liability or not as the Society shall in its absolute discretion think fit;

(i) to carry on businesses;

(j) to borrow or raise or secure the payment of money for any purpose and in any manner (including by way of mortgage) and secure the same or the repayment or performance of any debt, liability, contract, guarantee or other repayment incurred or to be entered into by the Society and so that no lender shall be concerned to see for what purpose any money is raised or as to the application thereof;

(k) to make appeals, advertise and conduct such other lawful activities as may be appropriate to raise funds for the Society or to make known its existence, purposes and work;

(l) to make loans, gifts or grants;

(m) to determine, demand and receive fees, subscriptions and deposits;

(n) to employ such persons as may be required for the purposes of the Society;

(o) to appoint any person being a bank, trust corporation or member of a recognised stock exchange or of a professional body to accept and hold in trust for the Society any property of the Society or in which it is interested and to execute and do all such deeds, acts and things as may be requisite in relation to any such trust and to provide for the remuneration of such trustee or trustees;

(p) to appoint any person or firm to act as investment advisers or investment managers and to permit any money, investments or other property belonging to or in the hands of the Society to be registered or held in the name of any nominee within the United Kingdom on behalf of the Society without being liable for any loss occasioned thereby in each case subject to such conditions and upon such terms (including the payment of remuneration) as may from time to time be agreed in writing between the Society and the person or firm concerned;

(q) to accept, receive and retain legacies, devises, gifts, grants, annuities, allowances and other benefits and consistently with the objects of the Society to undertake and perform any services or conditions attached to the acceptance, receipt or retention thereof;

(r) to promote or oppose any Bill, measure, order, scheme or application in Parliament or any other legislature or before any government department or court, authority or tribunal and to prosecute or defend any legal proceedings;

(s) to enter into and carry into effect any agreement or arrangement with any national or local authority or any institution, association or other body (whether incorporated or not) for co-operating with or assisting or being assisted by such authority, institution, association or other body in any manner and for any purpose which is consonant with any of the objects of the Society;

(t) to establish, maintain and administer unemployment, benevolent, superannuation, death benefit and provident funds for or in respect of employees and charitable funds;

(u) to combine, amalgamate or merge with any other body having charitable objects substantially similar to those of the Society;

(v) to do all such other things as shall be necessary for the attainment of any of the objects of the Society.

Regulations

6. Subject to the provisions of this Act, the Society may make regulations with respect to the membership, organisation and management of the Society and the government and administration of its affairs, undertaking, property and income.

Board of Management

7.—(1) The affairs of the Society shall continue to be managed by the Board.

(2) The regulations—

(a) may authorise the Board to delegate any of its functions to a committee of the Board; and

(b) may authorise such a committee to delegate any of its functions to a sub-committee.

Membership

8.—(1) The membership of the Society shall consist of the officers, the Board and such other members for the time being (including honorary members) as may be elected by the Board at its sole discretion in accordance with the regulations.

(2) Any person who, immediately before the passing of this Act, was a member of the Society by virtue of section 13 (1 guinea subscribers, members for 1 year) of the 1774 Act shall be deemed to have been duly elected under subsection (1) above on the passing of this Act.

Validity of acts done at meetings

9. No act done at a meeting of the Society, the Board or any committee or sub-committee of the Board shall be invalid by reason of any defect in the appointment or qualification of a person participating in the meeting.

Power to alter Act

10.—(1) The provisions of this Act may be altered from time to time in any manner whatever by order made by the Department of Health and Social Services upon the application of the Society.

(2) The power to make an order under this section shall be exercisable by statutory rule for the purposes of the Statutory Rules (Northern Ireland) Order 1979.

(3) An order under this section shall be subject to negative resolution within the meaning of section 41(6) of the Interpretation Act (Northern Ireland) 1954 as if it were a statutory instrument within the meaning of that Act; but during the interim period (as defined by subsection (4) of section 1 of the Northern Ireland Act 1974) an order made under this section shall be subject to annulment in pursuance of a resolution of either House of Parliament in like manner as a statutory instrument and section 5 of the Statutory Instruments Act 1946 shall apply accordingly.

Repeals

11. The enactments mentioned in the Schedule to this Act are hereby repealed to the extent mentioned in column (3) of that Schedule.

Sections 2 and 11

SCHEDULE

REPEALS

Chapter (1)	Title (2)	Extent of repeal (3)
13 & 14 Geo. 3 c.46 (1774) (Ir.).	An Act for amending an Act made the last Session of Parliament, intitled, An Act for badging such Poor as shall be found unable to support themselves by Labour, and otherwise providing for them, and for restraining such as shall be found able to support themselves by Labour and Industry, from begging.	In section 12, the words from "and the said president" to "discretion". Section 13. Section 14. Section 16. Section 18.
57 Geo. 3 c.lvii (1817).	An Act for giving further Powers to the President and Assistants of the Charitable Society of the Town of Belfast, in the County of Antrim, to supply the said Town with Water, and to improve their Estates.	Section 14. Section 68.
3 & 4 Vict. c.lxxxviii (1840).	An Act to amend the several Acts relating to the Belfast Charitable Society.	Sections 1 to 4.

INDEX

References are to sections and the Schedule

Board of Management, 7

Continuance of Society, 3

Definitions, 2

Membership, 8

Objects of Society, 4

Power to Alter Act, 10

Regulations, 6
Repeals, 11, Sched.

Short Title, 1
Subsidiary Powers of Society, 5

Validity of Acts Done at Meetings, 9

ALLIED IRISH BANKS ACT 1996

(1996 c. vii)

ARRANGEMENT OF SECTIONS

PART I

PRELIMINARY

SECT.
1. Short title.
2. Interpretation.

PART II

TRANSFER OF THE AIB GROUP BUSINESS

3. Appointed day for vesting of AIB Group business.
4. Vesting of AIB Group business in AIB NI.
5. Trust property.
6. Supplementary provisions.
7. Officers, etc., of transferor banks.
8. Evidence: books and documents.
9. Application of Bankers' Books Evidence Act 1879.
10. Evidence of vesting.
11. Interests in land.
12. Contracts of employment.

PART III

TRANSFER OF THE AIBF BUSINESS

13. Appointed day for vesting of AIBF business.
14. Vesting of AIBF business in AIB NI.
15. Application of supplementary provisions.

PART IV

MISCELLANEOUS

16. Saving for enactments concerning banking institutions.
17. Application to Scotland and Northern Ireland.
18. Costs of Act.

An Act to provide for the transfer to AIB Group Northern Ireland plc of part of the undertakings of Allied Irish Banks, p.l.c., AIB Capital Markets plc and AIB Finance Limited; and for related purposes. [24th July 1996]

PARLIAMENTARY PROGRESS

The Bill's progress through Parliament was as follows:

House of Commons: First Reading, January 23, 1996, Second Reading, January 30, 1996, Bill committed, May 13, 1996, Bill committed to an unopposed Committee, June 6, 1996, Bill as amended by the Committee considered, June 13, 1996, Third Reading, June 18, 1996.

House of Lords: First Reading, June 18, 1996, Second Reading, July 4, 1996, Bill committed, July 4, 1996, Bill committed to an unopposed Committee, July 10, 1996, Third Reading, July 18, 1996.

INTRODUCTION

By this Act, part of the undertakings of three banking companies carrying on business in the U.K.; the Allied Irish Banks, p.l.c., AIB Capital Markets plc and AIB Finance Limited, are transferred to AIB Group Northern Ireland plc, in order to better conduct those businesses in England, Scotland and Wales.

WHEREAS—

(1) Allied Irish Banks, p.l.c. (hereinafter called "AIB") is a public company incorporated in the Republic of Ireland under the Companies Acts 1963 to 1990 of that jurisdiction as a company limited by shares:

(2) AIB Capital Markets plc and AIB Finance Limited are also incorporated in the Republic of Ireland under the Companies Acts 1963 to 1990 of that jurisdiction as companies limited by shares and are wholly owned subsidiaries of AIB:

(3) All three companies carry on in the United Kingdom and elsewhere the businesses of banking, leasing, financial services and related activities and are European authorised institutions under the Second Banking Coordination (Second Council Directive) Regulations 1992; being companies incorporated outside the United Kingdom they have complied with the provisions of Part XXIII of the Companies Act 1985 and Part X of the Companies Act (Northern Ireland) 1960:

(4) AIB Group Northern Ireland plc (hereinafter called "AIB NI") is a public company incorporated in Northern Ireland under the Companies Acts (Northern Ireland) 1960 to 1982 as a company limited by shares and is a wholly owned subsidiary of AIB; it is an authorised institution under the Banking Act 1987 and carries on the business of banking in Northern Ireland:

(5) For the better conduct of the businesses of AIB, AIB Capital Markets plc and AIB Finance Limited in England, Scotland and Wales it is expedient to make provision for the fusion of those businesses by transferring them to and vesting them in AIB NI without interference with the conduct and continuity of those businesses:

(6) By virtue of the Allied Irish Banks Act 1993 there was transferred to AIB NI on 10th January 1994 the Northern Ireland banking business of AIB and it is now expedient, for the better conduct of the businesses of AIB NI and AIB Finance Limited in Northern Ireland, that the Northern Ireland undertaking of AIB Finance Limited should also be transferred to and vest in AIB NI:

(7) It is expedient that the other provisions in this Act should be enacted:

(8) The objects of this Act cannot be attained without the authority of Parliament:

May it therefore please Your Majesty that it may be enacted, and be it enacted, by the Queen's most Excellent Majesty, by and with the advice and consent of the Lords Spiritual and Temporal, and Commons, in this present Parliament assembled, and by the Authority of the same, as follows:—

PART I

PRELIMINARY

Short title

1. This Act may be cited as the Allied Irish Banks Act 1996.

Interpretation

2.—(1) In this Act, unless the subject or context otherwise requires—

"AIB" means Allied Irish Banks p.l.c.;

"the AIBF business" means the business of AIB Finance Limited carried on through its places of business in Northern Ireland, except the AIBF excluded items, including (without other limitation)—

(a) all banking accounts maintained with AIB Finance Limited at any office or branch of AIB Finance Limited in Northern Ireland and all rights and liabilities of AIB Finance Limited in respect of those accounts;

(b) the rights, obligations and duties of AIB Finance Limited as trustee of any debenture, debenture stock or loan stock;

(c) all real property (of whatever tenure and wheresoever situate) held by AIB Finance Limited for the purposes of or in connection with the AIBF business;

(d) all other property and liabilities of AIB Finance Limited wheresoever situate held for or otherwise relating to the AIBF business;

"the AIBF excluded items" means—

(a) documents required to be kept pursuant to the Companies Acts 1963 to 1990 of the Republic of Ireland;

(b) share capital and reserves of AIB Finance Limited;

(c) such other property, rights or liabilities of AIB Finance Limited as may on or before the appointed day be specified by the directors of AIB Finance Limited;

"the AIB Group business" means the business of the transferor banks carried on through their places of business in England, Scotland and Wales, except the excluded items, including (without other limitation)—

(a) all banking accounts maintained with a transferor bank at any office or branch of that bank in England, Scotland or Wales and all rights and liabilities of that bank in respect of those accounts;

(b) the rights, obligations and duties of a transferor bank as trustee of any debenture, debenture stock or loan stock;

(c) all real property (of whatever tenure and wheresoever situate) held by a transferor bank for the purposes of or in connection with the AIB Group business;

(d) all other property and liabilities of the transferor banks wheresoever situate held for or otherwise relating to the AIB Group business;

"AIB NI" means AIB Group Northern Ireland plc;

"the appointed day" means such day as may be appointed under section 3 (Appointed day for vesting of AIB Group business) or, as the case may be, under section 13 (Appointed day for vesting of AIBF business) of this Act;

"the excluded items" means—

(a) documents required to be kept pursuant to the Companies Acts 1963 to 1990 of the Republic of Ireland;

(b) shares in AIB Group Holdings (U.K.) Limited held or owned beneficially by AIB;

(c) shares in the following companies held or owned beneficially by AIB Capital Markets plc—

(i) LIFFE (Holdings) plc;

(ii) AIB (Local Authority Services) Limited; and

(iii) AIB Venture Capital Limited;

(d) share capital and reserves of the transferor banks;

(e) the business carried on by AIB under the style "AIB Group Treasury" out of its office at 12 Old Jewry, London EC2R 8DP including, in particular, managing funding and liquidity, the operations of Corporate Treasury and proprietary trading (including both on and off balance sheet instruments);

(f) the rights, obligations and duties of a transferor bank as an executor or trustee of any will or any settlement or trust arising under any will;

(g) such other property, rights or liabilities of any transferor bank as may on or before the appointed day be specified by the directors of that bank;

"existing" means existing, outstanding or in force immediately before the appointed day;

"liabilities" includes duties and obligations of every description whether present or future, actual or contingent;

"property" means property and assets of every description and rights of every description (whether present or future, actual or contingent), and includes property held on trust and securities, benefits and powers of every description;

"security" includes a mortgage or charge (whether legal or equitable), debenture, bill of exchange, promissory note, guarantee, lien, pledge (whether actual or constructive), hypothecation, assignment by way of security, indemnity, right of set-off, undertaking or other means of securing payment or discharge of a liability (whether present or future, actual or contingent); and

"the transferor banks" means AIB, AIB Capital Markets plc and AIB Finance Limited or any of them and a reference to "a transferor bank" is a reference to one of the transferor banks;

"will" includes a codicil and any other testamentary writing.

(2) Any reference in this Act to property or liabilities of a transferor bank is a reference to property or liabilities to which that bank is for the time being entitled or subject (whether beneficially or in any fiduciary capacity), wherever such property or liabilities are situated or arise and whether or not capable of being transferred or assigned by that bank, and whether that bank is entitled or subject to the property or liabilities under the law of any part of the United Kingdom or under the law of any country or territory outside the United Kingdom.

PART II

TRANSFER OF THE AIB GROUP BUSINESS

Appointed day for vesting of AIB Group business

3.—(1) The directors of AIB may appoint a day to be the appointed day for the purposes of this Part of this Act.

(2) Not less than 14 days before the day appointed under subsection (1) above AIB shall publish in the London Gazette, the Edinburgh Gazette and the Belfast Gazette a notice stating the day so appointed.

Vesting of AIB Group business in AIB NI

4.—(1) Subject as provided in subsection (2) below, on the appointed day the AIB Group business shall, by virtue of this Act and without further assurance, vest in AIB NI as if, as respects the AIB Group business, AIB NI were the same person in law as the transferor banks and to the intent that AIB NI shall succeed to the whole of the AIB Group business.

(2) Where the vesting of any part of the AIB Group business is governed wholly or partly by the law of any territory outside the United Kingdom, the transferor banks shall, if AIB NI so requires, take all necessary steps for the purpose of securing the vesting thereof in AIB NI and, pending such vesting, the transferor banks shall hold any such property in trust for AIB NI.

Trust property

5.—(1) Any property vested in AIB NI by virtue of this Act which immediately before the appointed day was held by a transferor bank, whether alone or jointly with any other person—

(a) as trustee or custodian trustee of any trust deed, settlement, covenant, agreement and whether originally so appointed or not, and whether appointed under hand or seal, or by order of any court or otherwise; or

(b) as judicial trustee appointed by order of any court; or

(c) in any other fiduciary capacity whatsoever;

shall, on and from the appointed day, be held by AIB NI alone or, as the case may be, jointly with such other person, in the same capacity, upon the trusts, and with and subject to the powers, provisions and liabilities, applicable thereto respectively.

(2) Any existing instrument or order of any court under or by virtue of which any such property became vested in a transferor bank in any such capacity, and any provision therein, and any existing contract or arrangement for the payment to, or retention by, a transferor bank of remuneration for its services in any such capacity, shall not fail by reason of anything in this Act, but shall be construed and have effect on and from the appointed day, so far as the context permits, as if for any reference therein to a transferor bank (not being a reference, however worded and whether express or implied, to terms and conditions of, or to a scale of fees of, that transferor bank) there were substituted a reference to AIB NI.

Supplementary provisions

6. Without prejudice to the generality of the foregoing provisions, but subject to any provision of this Act to the contrary effect, the following provisions of this section shall have effect on the appointed day to the extent that they relate to the property or liabilities comprising the AIB Group business—

(1) Every contract to which a transferor bank is a party (whether in writing or not) shall have effect on and from the appointed day as if—

(a) AIB NI had been a party thereto instead of that transferor bank;

(b) for any reference (however worded and whether express or implied) to that transferor bank there were substituted, as respects anything falling to be done on or after the appointed day, a reference to AIB NI; and

(c) any reference (however worded and whether express or implied) to the directors or to any director, officer or employee of that transferor bank were, as respects anything falling to be done on or after the appointed day, a reference to the directors of AIB NI or, as the case may require, to such director, officer or employee of AIB NI as AIB NI may appoint for that purpose or, in default of appointment, to the director, officer or employee of AIB NI who corresponds as nearly as may be to the first-mentioned director, officer or employee:

(2) Sub-paragraphs (b) and (c) of paragraph (1) above shall apply to—

(a) any statutory provision other than the provisions of this Act;

(b) any provision of any existing contract to which a transferor bank was not a party; and

(c) to any provision of any other existing document (not being a contract);

as they apply to a contract to which that paragraph applies, and every such provision shall be construed and have effect accordingly:

(3) Any account between a transferor bank and a customer shall, on the appointed day, become an account between AIB NI and the customer subject to the same conditions and incidents as theretofore; and such account shall be deemed for all purposes to be a single continuing account:

Provided that nothing herein shall affect any right of AIB NI or of the customer to vary the conditions or incidents subject to which any account is kept:

(4) Any existing instruction, order, direction, mandate, power of attorney, authority, undertaking or consent given to a transferor bank, either alone or jointly with another person (whether in writing or not and whether or not in relation to an account), shall have effect, on and from the appointed day, as if given to AIB NI:

(5) Any negotiable instrument or order for payment of money drawn on or given to, or accepted or endorsed by, a transferor bank or payable at

any place of business of a transferor bank whether so drawn, given, accepted, endorsed or payable before, on or after the appointed day, shall have the same effect on and from that day, as if it had been drawn on, or given to, or accepted or endorsed by, AIB NI, or were payable at the same place of business of AIB NI:

(6) The custody of any document or record, goods or other thing held by a transferor bank as bailee shall pass to AIB NI on the appointed day, and the rights and obligations of that transferor bank under any contract of bailment relating to any such document or record, goods or thing shall on that day become rights and obligations of AIB NI:

(7) (a) Any security held immediately before the appointed day by a transferor bank, or by a nominee or agent of or trustee for a transferor bank, as security for the payment or discharge of any liability shall, on and from that day, be held by, or, as the case may require, by that nominee, agent or trustee for, AIB NI, and be available to AIB NI (whether for its own benefit or, as the case may be, for the benefit of any other person) as security for the payment or discharge of that liability;

(b) In relation to any security vested in AIB NI in accordance with the provisions of this Act and any liabilities thereby secured, AIB NI shall be entitled to the rights and priorities and be subject to the obligations and incidents to which the transferor bank in question would have been entitled and subject if it had continued to hold the security;

(c) Any security referred to in the foregoing provisions of this paragraph which extends to future advances or liabilities shall, on and from the appointed day, be available to AIB NI (whether for its own benefit or, as the case may be, for the benefit of any other person) as security for the payment or discharge of future advances and future liabilities to the same extent and in the same manner in all respects as future advances by, or liabilities to, the transferor bank in question were secured thereby immediately before that day:

(8) Where by virtue of this Act any right or liability of a transferor bank becomes a right or liability of AIB NI, AIB NI and all other persons shall, on and from the appointed day, have the same rights, powers and remedies (and in particular the same rights and powers as to taking or resisting legal proceedings or making or resisting applications to any authority) for ascertaining, perfecting or enforcing that right or liability as if it had at all times been a right or liability of AIB NI; and any legal proceedings or application to any authority existing or pending immediately before the appointed day by or against the transferor banks may be continued by or against AIB NI:

(9) Any judgment or award obtained by or against a transferor bank and not fully satisfied before the appointed day shall on that day, to the extent to which it is enforceable by or against a transferor bank, become enforceable by or against AIB NI:

(10) The Data Protection Registrar may, on and from the appointed day, serve on AIB NI any notice under section 10 of the Data Protection Act 1984 which he could have served on a transferor bank in respect of a breach by that transferor bank of the data protection principles, but the transfer to, and vesting in AIB NI by this Act of the AIB Group business (and any disclosure to AIB NI of any information in contemplation or as a result thereof) shall not amount to a breach of any duty of confidentiality to which the existing banks are subject immediately before the appointed day or to a contravention by AIB NI or a transferor bank of the data protection principles.

Officers, etc., of transferor banks

7. No director, secretary or auditor of a transferor bank shall by virtue only of this Act become a director, secretary or, as the case may be, auditor of AIB NI.

Evidence: books and documents

8.—(1) All books and other documents which would before the appointed day have been evidence in respect of any matter for or against a transferor bank shall be admissible in evidence in respect of the same matter for or against AIB NI.

(2) In this section "documents" has the same meaning as in section 10 of the Civil Evidence Act 1968.

Application of Bankers' Books Evidence Act 1879

9.—(1) On and from the appointed day the Bankers' Books Evidence Act 1879 shall apply to the books of the transferor banks vested in AIB NI by virtue of this Act, and to entries made in those books before that day, as if such books had at all relevant times been the books of AIB NI.

(2) For the purposes of section 4 of the said Act of 1879, books which have become the books of AIB NI by virtue of this Act shall be deemed to have been the ordinary books of AIB NI at the time of the making of any entry therein which purports to have been made before the appointed day, and any such entry shall be deemed to have been made in the usual and ordinary course of business.

(3) In this section "books" shall be construed in accordance with section 9(2) of the said Act of 1879.

Evidence of vesting

10.—(1) The production of a Queen's Printer's copy of this Act shall, for all purposes, be conclusive evidence of the vesting of any property or liabilities of a transferor bank in AIB NI in accordance with the provisions of this Act.

(2) The following provisions of this section have effect without prejudice to the generality of subsection (1) above.

(3) A Queen's Printer's copy of this Act shall, in relation to any registered securities within the meaning of the Stock Transfer Act 1963 vested in AIB NI in accordance with the provisions of this Act, operate for all the purposes of the said Act of 1963 as a duly executed stock transfer in respect of the transfer of such securities from a transferor bank to AIB NI.

(4) Any document made or executed on or after the appointed day, whereby AIB NI or a transferor bank, whether alone or jointly with any other person, conveys or transfers, or purports to convey or transfer, to any person (whether for consideration or not), or applies to be registered as the holder or proprietor of, any property held by a transferor bank immediately before any such day, whether alone or jointly with any other person, shall be sufficient evidence that the interest of that transferor bank in that property—

(a) in the case of such a document referring to the property as property held by AIB NI, is vested in AIB NI under this Act; and

(b) in the case of such a document referring to the property as property held by a transferor bank, is not vested in AIB NI under this Act.

(5) Where there is any other transaction by AIB NI or a transferor bank on or after the appointed day in connection with, or in relation to, any property or liabilities which are property or liabilities of a transferor bank immediately before that day, it shall be deemed in favour of any other party to the transaction, or any person claiming through or under him, that AIB NI or, as the case may be, that transferor bank has full power and authority for that transaction as if—

(a) in the case of a transaction by AIB NI, the property or liabilities were vested in it under this Act; and
(b) in the case of a transaction by that transferor bank, the property or liabilities were not vested in AIB NI under this Act.

(6) A joint certificate given by or on behalf of a transferor bank and AIB NI, whether given before, on or after the appointed day, that any property or liabilities specified in the certificate is or is not at the date so specified vested in AIB NI under this Act, shall be conclusive evidence for all purposes of the fact so certified.

(7) Nothing in subsections (4) and (5) above affects the liability of a transferor bank or AIB NI to the other of them in respect of anything done, or purporting to have been done, by either of them in connection with, or in relation to, any property or liabilities.

(8) Nothing in this section applies to any vesting falling within subsection (2) of section 4 (Vesting of AIB Group business in AIB NI) of this Act.

(9) In this section "convey" has the same meaning as in the Law of Property Act 1925.

Interests in land

11. The vesting of an interest in land by or under this Act shall not—
(a) constitute a purchase or creation of an estate for the purposes of section 30(2) of the Landlord and Tenant Act 1954; or
(b) constitute an assignment, transfer, devolution, parting with possession, dealing with or other disposition of that interest for the purposes of any provision contained in any instrument concerning that interest; or
(c) give rise to any forfeiture; or
(d) invalidate or discharge any contract or security; or
(e) operate so as to merge any leasehold interest in the reversion which is expectant thereon.

Contracts of employment

12. Paragraph (1) of section 6 (Supplementary provisions) of this Act applies to a contract for the employment of any person by a transferor bank; and employment with that transferor bank and AIB NI under any such contract shall be deemed for all purposes to be a single continuing employment.

PART III

TRANSFER OF THE AIBF BUSINESS

Appointed day for vesting of AIBF business

13.—(1) The directors of AIB Finance Limited may appoint a day to be the appointed day for the purposes of this Part of this Act.

(2) Not less than 14 days before the day appointed under subsection (1) above AIB Finance Limited shall publish in the London Gazette, the Edinburgh Gazette and the Belfast Gazette a notice stating the day so appointed.

Vesting of AIBF business in AIB NI

14.—(1) Subject as provided in subsection (2) below, on the appointed day the AIBF business shall, by virtue of this Act and without further assurance, vest in AIB NI as if, as respects the AIBF business, AIB NI were the same person in law as AIB Finance Limited and to the intent that AIB NI shall succeed to the whole of the AIBF business.

(2) Where the vesting of any part of the AIBF business is governed wholly or partly by the law of any territory outside the United Kingdom, AIB

Finance Limited shall, if AIB NI so requires, take all necessary steps for the purpose of securing the vesting thereof in AIB NI and, pending such vesting, AIB Finance Limited shall hold any such property in trust for AIB NI.

Application of supplementary provisions

15. The provisions of sections 5 to 12 of this Act shall apply (subject to the provisions of section 17 (Application to Scotland and Northern Ireland) of this Act) in relation to the vesting of the AIBF business in AIB NI under section 14 (Vesting of AIBF business in AIB NI) of this Act as they apply in relation to the vesting of the AIB Group business in AIB NI under section 4 (Vesting of AIB Group business in AIB NI) of this Act and, accordingly, in those provisions as so applied—

(a) references to the transferor banks or any of them shall have effect as references to AIB Finance Limited;

(b) references to the AIB Group business shall have effect as references to the AIBF business; and

(c) references to the said section 4 shall have effect as references to the said section 14.

PART IV

MISCELLANEOUS

Saving for enactments concerning banking institutions

16. Except as otherwise expressly provided in this Act, nothing in this Act shall exempt any body corporate from any statutory provision relating to the carrying on of the business of banking.

Application to Scotland and Northern Ireland

17.—(1) This Act shall extend to Scotland and Northern Ireland.

(2) In the application of this Act to Scotland the following provisions shall have effect:—

(a) In the construction of this Act—

"assignment" includes an assignation;

"bailee" includes a custodian, and "contract of bailment" includes any other contract regulating custody of things;

"convey" includes the execution of any deed or other instrument or document by which any property, or any estate, interest, security or other right in or over property, is constituted, completed, disponed, assigned, transmitted or discharged;

"debenture" includes a floating charge or instrument containing a floating charge;

"forfeiture" includes an irritancy;

"judgment" includes a decree;

"judicial trustee" includes a judicial factor;

"mortgage" includes a standard security, an assignation or disposition ex facie absolute and any agreement qualifying the same, a bond and disposition or assignation in security, a cash credit bond and disposition or assignation in security, an assignation in security and any real right or burden of whatever kind in the nature of a security whether or not constituted in respect of a heritable security;

"will" includes a trust disposition and settlement and any deed taking effect on the death of any person whereby any part of his estate is disposed of, or under which a succession thereto arises;

(b) All standard securities and cash credit bonds and dispositions or assignations in security expressed to be in favour of a transferor bank vested in AIB NI by or under this Act shall, on and from the appointed day, have the same effect in favour of AIB NI up to such maximum amounts as may be stated therein respectively in all respects as if they had been originally granted in favour of AIB NI for such maximum amounts;

(c) To enable AIB NI to complete a title, if thought fit, to any property vested in it by virtue of this Act by notice of title or otherwise, or to deduce title, this Act shall be deemed to be, and may be used as, a general disposition, conveyance or, as the case may be, assignation of such property in favour of AIB NI;

(d) For the reference in subsection (2) of section 8 (Evidence: books and documents) of this Act to section 10 of the Civil Evidence Act 1968 there shall be substituted reference to section 17 of the Law Reform (Miscellaneous Provisions) (Scotland) Act 1968.

(3) In the application of this Act to Northern Ireland—

(a) for the reference in subsection (2) of section 8 (Evidence: books and documents) of this Act to section 10 of the Civil Evidence Act 1968 there shall be substituted reference to section 6 of the Civil Evidence Act (Northern Ireland) 1971;

(b) the references in subsection (3) of section 10 (Evidence of vesting) of this Act to the Stock Transfer Act 1963 shall include references to the Stock Transfer Act (Northern Ireland) 1963; and for the reference in subsection (9) of that section to the Law of Property Act 1925 there shall be substituted reference to the Conveyancing Act 1881.

Costs of Act

18. The costs, charges and expenses preliminary to, and of and incidental to, the preparing for, obtaining and passing of this Act, or otherwise in relation thereto, shall be paid by AIB and may in whole or in part be paid out of revenue.

INDEX

References are to sections

APPOINTED DAY FOR VESTING,
  AIB Finance Ltd business, 13
  AIB Group business, 3

BANKERS' BOOKS EVIDENCE ACT 1879,
  application of, 9

COSTS OF ACT, 18

EVIDENCE: BOOKS AND DOCUMENTS, 8
EXTENT, 17

INTERESTS IN LAND, 11
INTERPRETATION, 2

OFFICERS OF TRANSFEROR BANKS, 7

SAVINGS, 16
SCOTTISH PROVISIONS, 17
SHORT TITLE, 1
SUPPLEMENTARY PROVISIONS, 6, 15

TRUST PROPERTY, 5

VESTING OF AIB BUSINESS IN AIB NI,
  on appointed day, 4
  evidence of, 10
VESTING OF AIB FINANCE LIMITED BUSINESS IN AIB NI,
  on appointed day, 14

CITY OF WESTMINSTER ACT 1996

(1996 c. viii)

ARRANGEMENT OF SECTIONS

SECT.
1. Short title.
2. Interpretation.
3. Closure notice.
4. Closure order.
5. Appeals.
6. Enforcement.
7. Offences by bodies corporate.
8. Service of notices.

An Act to make further provision for the control of unlicensed sex establishments in the City of Westminster. [24th July 1996]

PARLIAMENTARY PROGRESS

The Bill's progress through Parliament was as follows:

House of Lords: First Reading, January 12, 1994, Second Reading, February 16, 1994, Bill committed to an unopposed Committee, May 23, 1994, Third Reading, June 14, 1994, Commons' amendments considered by the House of Lords, July 23, 1996.

House of Commons: First Reading, June 14, 1994, Second Reading, June 29, 1996, Bill committed, June 29, 1994, Bill committed to an unopposed Committee, July 7 to October 20, 1994, Motion to suspend the Bill, October 25, 1994, Bill as amended by the Committee considered, October 26, 1995, Motion to suspend the Bill, November 1, 1995, Motion to Revive the Bill, March 20, 1996, Bill as amended by the Committee considered, July 4, 1996, Third Reading, July 23, 1996.

INTRODUCTION

This Act allows Westminster City Council to serve a closure notice on premises in the city, where they are satisfied that such premises are being used as a sex establishment without a licence in breach of Schedule 3. Provisions are set out concerning service of such notices and the appeals procedure.

WHEREAS—

(1) The City of Westminster (hereinafter called "the city") is a London borough under the management and local government of the lord mayor and citizens of the city:

(2) The city has local, regional, national and international importance for shopping and tourism:

(3) The council of the city have certain powers under the Local Government (Miscellaneous Provisions) Act 1982 to control sex establishments but those powers are inadequate to control unlicensed sex establishments in the city:

(4) The purposes of this Act cannot be effected without the authority of Parliament:

(5) In relation to the promotion of the Bill for this Act the requirements of section 239 of the Local Government Act 1972 have been observed:

May it therefore please Your Majesty that it may be enacted, and be it enacted, by the Queen's most Excellent Majesty, by and with the advice and consent of the Lords Spiritual and Temporal, and Commons, in this present Parliament assembled, and by the authority of the same, as follows:—

Short title

1. This Act may be cited as the City of Westminster Act 1996.

Interpretation

2. In this Act—

"authorised officer" means an officer of the council authorised by the council in writing to act in relation to the relevant provision of this Act;
"the city" means the City of Westminster;
"the council" means the Westminster City Council;
"closure notice" means a notice served under subsection (2) of section 3 (Closure notice) of this Act;
"closure order" means an order made under section 4 (Closure order) of this Act;
"person having an interest in the premises" means the owner, leaseholder, licensee or occupier of the premises;
"premises" includes any premises, part of premises, vehicle, vessel or stall;
"Schedule 3" means Schedule 3 to the Local Government (Miscellaneous Provisions) Act 1982;
"sex establishment" has the same meaning as in Schedule 3.

Closure notice

3.—(1) Where the council are satisfied that premises in the city are being used as a sex establishment without a licence in breach of Schedule 3 they may serve a closure notice in respect of those premises.

(2) Where a closure notice is served—

(a) it shall be served on—

(i) at least one person having control of or an interest in the business carried on in the premises; and

(ii) the occupier of any other part of the building in which the premises are situated and to which, in the opinion of the council, access would be impeded if an order under section 4(5)(a) below were made in respect of the premises; and

(b) it may be served on any other person having an interest in the premises.

(3) A closure notice shall—

(a) specify the matter alleged to constitute a breach of Schedule 3;

(b) specify any steps which may be taken in order to remedy the breach described in paragraph (a) above including—

(i) the immediate closure of the premises to the public for the time being; or

(ii) the immediate discontinuance of the use of the premises as a sex establishment; and

(c) state the effect of section 4(1) below.

(4) The council may at any time withdraw a closure notice by serving further notice to that effect on all persons on whom the closure notice was served.

(5) For the purposes of subsection (2) above a person having an interest in the business carried on in the premises includes a person who—

(a) owns the business; or

(b) manages the business; or

(c) employs any person to manage the business; or

(d) is involved in the conduct of the business.

Closure order

4.—(1) Subject to subsection (2) below, the council may, not less than 14 days and no later than 6 months after the service of a closure notice, make a complaint to a justice of the peace acting for the petty sessions area in which the premises are situated for a closure order in respect of that closure notice.

(2) The council may not make a complaint under subsection (1) above if—

(a) (i) the premises have been closed to the public; or
(ii) they are satisfied that the use of the premises as a sex establishment has been discontinued; and
(b) they are satisfied that there is no reasonable likelihood that there will be a further breach of Schedule 3 in respect of those premises.

(3) Where a complaint has been made under subsection (1) above the justice of the peace may issue a summons directed to all persons upon whom the closure notice was served under section 3(2)(a)(i) above to answer to the complaint.

(4) Where a summons issued under subsection (3) above is served a notice stating the date, time and place at which the complaint will be heard shall be served on all persons upon whom the closure notice was served under section 3(2)(a)(ii) and (b) above.

(5) If, on hearing the complaint, the court is satisfied that—
(a) the closure notice was properly served;
(b) at the time the closure notice was served the premises were being used as a sex establishment in breach of Schedule 3; and
(c) (i) the breach of Schedule 3 has not been remedied; or
(ii) the breach of Schedule 3 has been remedied but considers that there is a reasonable likelihood that there will be a further breach of Schedule 3;

it may make an order under this section.

(6) The court may make such order under this section as it thinks fit and in particular may order that—
(a) the premises in respect of which the closure notice was served shall be closed immediately and remain closed until the council issues a certificate under subsection (11) below;
(b) the use of those premises as a sex establishment be discontinued immediately;
(c) the defendant pay into court such sum as the court determines and that the sum will not be released by the court to the defendant until the other requirements of the closure order are met:

Provided that no order may be made under paragraph (c) above unless the defendant has been convicted of an offence under Schedule 3 or this Act.

(7) A sum which has been ordered to be paid under subsection (6)(c) above shall be paid to the clerk of the court.

(8) Such conditions as the court thinks fit relating to the admission of specified individuals onto the premises may be applied by the court to an order made under subsection (6)(a) above.

(9) An order under subsection (6)(a) above shall not be made if closure of the premises would result in any person other than the occupier of the premises being impeded in his access to any other part of the building in which the premises are situated and of which he is the occupier.

(10) As soon as practicable after the making of a closure order the council shall give notice of the order by fixing a copy of it in a conspicuous position on the premises in respect of which it was made.

(11) An order made under subsection (6)(a) or (b) above shall cease to have effect and any sum paid by the defendant under subsection (6)(c) above shall be released by the court on the issue by the council of a certificate to the effect that they are satisfied that the alleged breach of Schedule 3 has been remedied and that the premises will not be used subsequently as a sex establishment in breach of Schedule 3.

(12) (a) Where a closure order has been made under subsection (6)(a) above, the defendant and any person having an interest in the premises may make a complaint to a justice of the peace acting for the petty sessions area in which the premises are situated for an order that the closure order be discharged.

(b) Where a complaint is made under paragraph (a) above, the justice may issue a summons directed to the council requiring them to appear before the magistrates' court to answer to the complaint.

(c) The court may not make an order under this subsection unless it is satisfied that the premises in respect of which the closure order was made would not be used as a sex establishment in breach of Schedule 3 if they were to be reopened.

Appeals

5.—(1) Any person—

(a) upon whom a closure notice has been served under subsection (2) of section 3 (Closure notice) of this Act and in respect of which closure notice a closure order has been made; or

(b) having an interest in the premises in respect of which a closure order has been made but on whom a closure notice was not served;

may at any time before the expiration of the period of 21 days beginning with the date on which the closure order was served appeal to the Crown Court.

(2) An appeal under subsection (1) above may be brought on one or both of the following grounds:—

(a) the person on whom the closure notice was served was not at the time at which it was served such a person as described in subsection (2) of the said section 3; or

(b) the premises in respect of which the closure order was made were not being used as a sex establishment in breach of Schedule 3 at the time at which the closure notice was served.

(3) On an appeal to the Crown Court under this section the court may make such order as it thinks fit and it shall be the duty of the council to give effect to such order.

Enforcement

6.—(1) Where a closure order has been made requiring premises to be closed, any authorised officer (on production, if so required, of a duly authenticated document of his authority) or police officer may at all reasonable times enter upon those premises and may do all things reasonably necessary for the purpose of securing that such requirement is met.

(2) Subsections (2), (3) and (4) of section 287 of the Public Health Act 1936 shall apply in respect of entry to premises for the purposes of subsection (1) above as they apply to entry to premises for the purposes of subsection (1) of that section.

(3) Any person who intentionally obstructs any person acting in the exercise of his powers under this section shall be guilty of an offence and shall be liable on summary conviction to a fine not exceeding level 5 on the standard scale.

(4) If any premises are opened or kept open in breach of a closure order then any person upon whom the closure notice was served under subsection (2)(a)(i) or (b) of section 3 (Closure notice) of this Act shall, unless he has reasonable excuse, be guilty of an offence and shall be liable on summary conviction to a fine not exceeding £20,000 or to imprisonment for a term not exceeding three months or to both.

Offences by bodies corporate

7.—(1) Where an offence under this Act committed by a body corporate is proved to have been committed with the consent or connivance of, or to be attributable to any neglect on the part of, any director, manager, secretary or other similar officer of the body corporate or any person who was purporting to act in any such capacity, he, as well as the body corporate, shall be guilty of that offence and shall be liable to be proceeded against and punished accordingly.

(2) Where the affairs of a body corporate are managed by its members subsection (1) above shall apply to the acts and defaults of a member in connection with his function of management as if he were a director of the body corporate.

Service of notices

8.—(1) Any notice, summons or other document required or authorised to be served or given under this Act may be served or given either—

(a) by delivering it to the person on whom it is to be served or to whom it is to be given; or

(b) by leaving it at the usual or last known place of abode or business of that person, or, in a case where an address for service has been given by that person, at that address; or

(c) by sending it in a prepaid registered letter, or by the recorded delivery service, addressed to that person at his usual or last known place of abode or business, or, in a case where an address for service has been given by that person, at that address; or

(d) in the case of a company or body incorporated in England or Wales, by delivering it to the secretary or clerk of the company or body at their registered or principal office, or sending it in a prepaid registered letter, or by the recorded delivery service, addressed to the secretary or clerk of the company or body at that office.

(2) Where the name of the person on whom the notice, summons or document is to be served cannot be ascertained after reasonable inquiry, or that person is a company or body incorporated outside England or Wales, the notice, summons or document shall be taken to be duly served if a copy of it is affixed conspicuously to some object on the premises and—

(a) it is addressed to that person either by name or by the description of "the owner" or "the manager", or as the case may be, "the occupier" of the premises (describing them) and is delivered or sent in the manner specified in subsection (1)(a), (b) or (c) above; or

(b) it is so addressed and is marked in such a manner that it is plainly identifiable as a communication of importance and—

(i) it is sent to the premises in a prepaid registered letter or by the recorded delivery service and is not returned to the authority sending it; or

(ii) it is delivered to some person on those premises.

(3) This section is without prejudice to section 233 of the Local Government Act 1972 (general provisions as to service of notices by local authorities).

INDEX

References are to sections

INTERPRETATION, 2

SEX ESTABLISHMENTS,
closure notices, 3
closure orders, 4
appeals against, 5
enforcement of, 6
offences by bodies corporate, 7
service of notices, 8

SHORT TITLE, 1

LONDON LOCAL AUTHORITIES ACT 1996

(1996 c. ix)

ARRANGEMENT OF SECTIONS

PART I

PRELIMINARY

SECT.
1. Citation and commencement.
2. Interpretation.

PART II

BUS LANES

3. Interpretation of Part II.
4. Penalty charge notices under Part II.
5. Exemption of fire brigade, ambulance and police vehicles under Part II.
6. Enforcement notices, etc., under Part II.
7. Financial provisions under Part II.
8. Fixing of penalty charges.
9. Penalty charge not payable in certain cases.

PART III

OCCASIONAL SALES

10. Meaning of "occasional sale".
11. Application of Part III.
12. Licensing of occasional sales.
13. Application for licence.
14. Grant of licence.
15. Part III appeals.
16. Display of names, etc.
17. Powers of entry.
18. Enforcement.
19. Restriction on right to prosecute.

PART IV

FIRE SAFETY AND ENTERTAINMENT LICENSING

20. Music and dancing, sports, boxing and wrestling licences.
21. Private places of entertainment.
22. Theatres.
23. Night cafés.

PART V

MISCELLANEOUS

24. Application of Environmental Protection Act 1990.
25. Amendment of London Local Authorities Act 1991.
26. Public charitable collections.
27. Application of London Local Authorities Act 1995 to Tower Hamlets.
28. Obstruction of authorised officer.
29. Defence of due diligence.
30. Liability of directors, etc.
31. Regulations.

SCHEDULES:
Schedule 1—Enforcement notices, etc., under Part II (Bus lanes) of this Act.
Schedule 2—Financial provisions relating to Part II (Bus lanes) of this Act.

An Act to confer further powers upon local authorities in London; and for related purposes. [17th October 1996]

PARLIAMENTARY DEBATES

The Bill's progress through Parliament was as follows:

House of Lords: First Reading, January 11, 1995, Second Reading, April 19, 1995, Bill Committed, April 19, 1995, Motion to suspend the Bill, October 26, 1995, Bill Committed to an Unopposed Committee, May 22, 1996, Third Reading, June 6, 1996.

House of Commons: First Reading, June 20, 1996, Second Reading, July 3, 1996, Bill Committed, July 3, 1996, Bill Committed to an Unopposed Committee, July 16–23, 1996, Bill as amended by the Committee considered, October 15, 1996, Third Reading, October 15, 1996.

INTRODUCTION

By this Act, it is intended to improve and develop local government services within London and thereby benefit persons residing therein. Therefore the powers of London borough councils and the Common Council of the City are extended and amended by this Act. Powers are granted for enforcement in relation to bus lanes (defined by s.3(1)) and for the control of occasional sales (defined by s.10). In addition, arrangements for the applications in relation to fire safety and entertainment and other licensing are amended, and other provisions are enacted.

WHEREAS—

(1) It is expedient that further and better provision should be made for the improvement and development of local government services in London and for the benefit of persons residing therein and that the powers of London borough councils and the Common Council of the City of London (hereinafter referred to as "London borough councils") should be extended and amended as provided in this Act:

(2) It is expedient that the London borough councils should have powers of enforcement in relation to bus lanes:

(3) It is expedient that the London borough councils should have power to control occasional sales:

(4) It is expedient that the arrangements for the applications in relation to fire safety and entertainment and other licensing be amended:

(5) It is expedient that the other provisions contained in this Act should be enacted:

(6) The purposes of this Act cannot be effected without the authority of Parliament:

(7) In relation to the promotion of the Bill for this Act the Westminster City Council have complied with the requirements of section 239 of the Local Government Act 1972 and the other London borough councils have complied with the requirements of section 87 of the Local Government Act 1985:

May it therefore please Your Majesty that it may be enacted, and be it enacted, by the Queen's most Excellent Majesty, by and with the advice and consent of the Lords Spiritual and Temporal, and Commons, in this present Parliament assembled, and by the authority of the same, as follows, that is to say:—

PART I

PRELIMINARY

Citation and commencement

1.—(1) This Act may be cited as the London Local Authorities Act 1996 and except where otherwise provided shall come into operation at the end of the period of two months beginning with the date on which it is passed.

(2) The London Local Authorities Act 1990, the London Local Authorities (No. 2) Act 1990, the London Local Authorities Act 1991, the London

Local Authorities Act 1994, the London Local Authorities Act 1995 and this Act may together be cited as the London Local Authorities Acts 1990 to 1996.

Interpretation

2. In this Act, except as otherwise expressly provided or unless the context otherwise requires—

"authorised officer" means an officer of a borough council authorised by the council in writing to act in relation to the relevant provision of this Act;

"borough council" means London borough council and includes the Common Council of the City of London; and "borough" and "council" shall be construed accordingly.

PART II

BUS LANES

Interpretation of Part II

3.—(1) In this Part of this Act—

"the Act of 1991" means the Road Traffic Act 1991;

"bus lane" has the meaning given in regulation 23 of the Traffic Signs Regulations 1994 and any regulation amending or revoking and re-enacting that regulation;

"bus lane offence" means an offence under section 8, 11 or 13 of the Road Traffic Regulation Act 1984 or section 36 of the Road Traffic Act 1988 which relates to the contravention of or failure to comply with an order or traffic sign in so far as it makes provision for or indicates a reservation of all or part of a carriageway of a road as a bus lane;

"Joint Committee" means the Joint Committee established under section 73 of the Act of 1991;

"prescribed device" means a device prescribed under section 20(9) of the Road Traffic Offenders Act 1988 or a device of a description specified in regulations made for the purposes of this section by the Secretary of State;

"road" has the same meaning as in section 142(1) of the Road Traffic Regulation Act 1984;

"vehicle" means a mechanically propelled vehicle intended or adapted for use on roads.

(2) For the purposes of this Part of and Schedule 1 to this Act, the owner of a vehicle shall be taken to be the person by whom the vehicle is kept.

(3) In determining, for the purposes of this Part of and Schedule 1 to this Act, who was the owner of a vehicle at any time, it shall be presumed that the owner was the person in whose name the vehicle was at that time registered under the Vehicle Excise and Registration Act 1994.

Penalty charge notices under Part II

4.—(1) Where a council, on the basis of information provided by the use of a prescribed device, has reason to believe that a penalty charge is payable under this Part of this Act with respect to a vehicle, they may serve a penalty charge notice on the person appearing to them to be the owner of the vehicle.

(2) For the purposes of this Part of this Act, a penalty charge is payable to a borough council with respect to a vehicle if the person in charge of the vehicle acts in contravention of or fails to comply with an order under section 6 or 9 or regulations under section 12 of the Road Traffic Regulation Act 1984 in so far as provision is made thereby for the reservation of all or part of a carriageway of a road as a bus lane.

(3) A penalty charge notice under this Part of this Act must state—

(a) the grounds on which the council believe that the penalty charge is payable with respect to the vehicle;

(b) the amount of the penalty charge which is payable;

(c) that the penalty charge must be paid before the end of the period of 28 days beginning with the date of the notice;

(d) that if the penalty charge is paid before the end of the period of 14 days beginning with the date of the notice, the amount of the penalty charge will be reduced by the specified proportion;

(e) that, if the penalty charge is not paid before the end of the 28 day period, an enforcement notice may be served by the council on the person appearing to them to be the owner of the vehicle;

(f) the address to which payment of the penalty charge must be sent; and

(g) the effect of paragraph 2 of Schedule 1 to this Act.

(4) In subsection (3)(d) above, "specified proportion" means such proportion, applicable in all cases, as may be determined for the purposes of this section by the borough councils acting through the Joint Committee.

Exemption of fire brigade, ambulance and police vehicles under Part II

5. No provision in this Part of this Act shall apply to any vehicle on an occasion when it is being used for fire brigade, ambulance or police purposes.

Enforcement notices, etc., under Part II

6.—(1) Schedule 1 to this Act shall have effect with respect to penalty charges under this Part of this Act, enforcement notices and other matters supplementary to the provisions of this Part of this Act; and the functions of traffic adjudicators under that Schedule shall be discharged by the persons who are appointed as parking adjudicators under section 73 of the Act of 1991.

(2) Regulations under section 73(11) of the Act of 1991 (provision as to procedure to be followed in relation to proceedings before parking adjudicators) may make provision with respect to proceedings before parking adjudicators when exercising the functions of traffic adjudicators; and any regulations under that subsection in force at the coming into operation of this Part of this Act shall, with any necessary modifications, apply in relation to such proceedings.

(3) The references to a parking adjudicator or parking adjudicators in section 73(13) to (15) and (17) and (18) of the Act of 1991 shall include references to a parking adjudicator or parking adjudicators exercising the functions of traffic adjudicators but section 73(15) of that Act shall not apply to a penalty charge under this Part of this Act which remains payable following an adjudication under paragraph 6 of Schedule 1 to this Act.

Financial provisions under Part II

7. Schedule 2 to this Act shall have effect with respect to financial provisions relating to the provisions of this Part of this Act.

Fixing of penalty charges

8. Section 74 of the Act of 1991 shall, with the omission of subsection (3), apply in relation to the levels of penalty charges under this Part of this Act as it applies in relation to the levels of (among other charges) penalty charges under Part II of that Act.

Penalty charge not payable in certain cases

9. No penalty charge shall be payable under this Part of this Act in respect of any conduct where—

(a) a notice is given to the driver under section 54(2) or (4) of the Road Traffic Offenders Act 1988 in respect of a bus lane offence constituted by that conduct; or
(b) notification of an intention to prosecute the driver in respect of such an offence is given by the Commissioner of Police of the Metropolis or of the City of London to the council of the borough in which the alleged offence took place before the expiry of the period of 14 days, beginning with the day on which the alleged offence takes place.

PART III

OCCASIONAL SALES

Meaning of "occasional sale"

10. In this Part of this Act "occasional sale" means a concourse of buyers and sellers of articles held otherwise than on a highway or in a building (except a car park) and comprising not less than five stalls, stands, vehicles (whether movable or not) or pitches from which articles are sold, but does not include—
(a) a market or fair the right to hold which was acquired by virtue of a grant (including a presumed grant) or acquired or established by statute;
(b) a sale by auction of farm livestock or deadstock;
(c) sales of a class which from time to time is by resolution of the borough council excluded from the operation of this Part of this Act;
(d) a market held in accordance with a planning permission granted under section 58(1)(b) of the Town and Country Planning Act 1990 (which provides for the granting of planning permission) or under a similar provision of a predecessor to that Act; or
(e) a market the holding of which commenced before 1st July 1948 and has continued without extinguishment.

Application of Part III

11.—(1) This Part of this Act applies to a borough as from such day as may be fixed in relation to that borough by resolution of the borough council, subject to and in accordance with the provisions of this section.

(2) The borough council shall cause to be published in a local newspaper circulating in the borough notice—
(a) of the passing of any such resolution and of a day fixed thereby; and
(b) of the general effect of the provisions of this Part of this Act;
and the day so fixed shall not be earlier than the expiration of three months from the publication of the said notice.

(3) Either a photostatic or other reproduction certified by the officer appointed for that purpose by the borough council to be a true reproduction of a page or part of a page of any such newspaper bearing the date of its publication and containing any such notice shall be evidence of the publication of the notice, and of the date of publication.

Licensing of occasional sales

12.—(1) Subject to the provisions of this Part of this Act it shall be unlawful for any person to hold an occasional sale within a borough unless that person is authorised to do so by a licence under this Part of this Act.

(2) No licence under this Part of this Act is required if the proceeds of the occasional sale are to be applied solely or principally for charitable, social, sporting, religious or political purposes.

(3) A person holds an occasional sale for the purposes of this Part of this Act if—

(a) he receives or is entitled to receive payment for any space or pitch hired or let on the site of the sale to persons wishing to trade at the sale; or

(b) as a person promoting the sale, or as the agent, licensee or assignee of a person promoting the sale, he receives or is entitled to receive payment from persons trading at the sale for goods sold or services rendered to persons attending the sale.

Application for licence

13.—(1) An application for a licence under this Part of this Act shall be made in writing to the borough council, not later than 42 days before the date on which the occasional sale is to be held:

Provided that nothing in this section shall prevent a borough council from granting a licence, notwithstanding that application has been made at a later date than aforesaid if they consider it reasonable in the circumstances so to do.

(2) An application made under this section shall be in writing and shall specify—

(a) the proposed date and time of commencement, expected duration and location of the intended occasional sale;

(b) the extent of the premises to be occupied or used for the purposes of the sale;

(c) the name and address (other than an address temporarily occupied for the purposes of the sale) of the person who proposes to hold the occasional sale, and the name and address of a person appointed to receive and answer complaints about the occasional sale;

(d) an estimate of the number of persons expected to attend the occasional sale;

(e) the arrangements proposed for accommodating vehicles of persons attending the occasional sale;

(f) the arrangements proposed for controlling road congestion, litter and noise.

(3) An applicant for the grant of a licence under this Part of this Act shall pay a reasonable fee determined by the borough council.

Grant of licence

14.—(1) The borough council may grant a licence under this Part of this Act, and in granting a licence may impose reasonable conditions relating to—

(a) the time of commencement of the occasional sale;

(b) the duration of the occasional sale;

(c) the arrangements to be made for accommodating the vehicles of persons attending the occasional sale;

(d) the arrangements to be made for controlling road congestion, litter and noise caused by the occasional sale;

(e) a requirement that the names and addresses of persons selling articles at the occasional sale are publicly displayed.

(2) If the borough council have not refused to grant a licence within 21 days of the receipt by them of an application duly made for a licence under subsection (1) of section 13 (Application for licence) of this Act, they shall be deemed to have granted a licence for an occasional sale in accordance with the details specified in the application.

(3) The borough council shall grant an application for a licence under this Part of this Act unless they consider that the application ought to be refused on one or more of the grounds specified in subsection (4) below.

(4) The borough council may refuse an application on any of the following grounds:—

(a) that inadequate arrangements have been proposed for accommodating the vehicles of persons attending the occasional sale;

(b) that inadequate arrangements have been proposed for controlling road congestion, litter or noise caused by the occasional sale; or

(c) that the applicant has been granted a licence by any borough council for an occasional sale within three years before the date of the application and failed to comply with conditions imposed in relation to that licence.

Part III appeals

15.—(1) If the borough council refuse to grant a licence under this Part of this Act they shall notify the applicant in writing—

(a) of their decision and of the ground or grounds for such refusal; and

(b) of his rights of appeal specified in this section.

(2) Any person aggrieved—

(a) by the refusal of a borough council to grant a licence; or

(b) by a condition imposed by a borough council under subsection (1) of section 14 (Grant of licence) of this Act;

may appeal to a magistrates' court acting for the area in which the proposed occasional sale is to be held.

(3) A person desiring to appeal against such refusal or condition shall give a written notice to the magistrates' court and to the borough council specifying the refusal or condition against which he wishes to appeal and the grounds upon which such appeal is made.

(4) On an appeal to the magistrates' court under this section, the court may make such order as it thinks fit and it shall be the duty of the borough council to give effect to the order.

Display of names, etc.

16.—(1) Any person who holds an occasional sale shall display his full name and business address and the full name and business address of the person appointed to receive and answer complaints about the occasional sale in a prominent position at the place where the sale is held.

(2) Any person who holds an occasional sale shall display on all notices, leaflets and posters given, distributed or exhibited by him or on his behalf in connection with the sale the full name and business address of—

(a) himself; and

(b) the person appointed to receive and answer complaints about the occasional sale.

Powers of entry

17. An authorised officer on producing if so required a duly authenticated document showing his authority, or any constable, may enter and inspect any premises if he has reasonable cause to believe that they are being, have been or are intended to be, used for or in connection with an occasional sale for the purpose of ascertaining whether there is or has been or is intended to be a contravention of this Part of this Act in, or in connection with, the premises.

Enforcement

18.—(1) Any person who contravenes section 12 (Licensing of occasional sales) of this Act shall be guilty of an offence and liable on summary conviction to a fine not exceeding level 4 on the standard scale.

(2) Any person who contravenes a condition imposed under section 14 (Grant of licence) of this Act shall be guilty of an offence and liable on summary conviction to a fine not exceeding level 3 on the standard scale.

(3) Any person who without reasonable excuse contravenes section 16 (Display of names, etc.) of this Act shall be guilty of an offence and liable on summary conviction to a fine not exceeding level 2 on the standard scale.

Restriction on right to prosecute

19. The written consent of the Director of Public Prosecutions is needed for the laying of an information of an offence created by this Part of this Act by any person other than an authorised officer or a constable.

PART IV

FIRE SAFETY AND ENTERTAINMENT LICENSING

Music and dancing, sports, boxing and wrestling licences

20. Schedule 12 to the London Government Act 1963 shall be amended as follows:—

(1) In paragraph 1(4), "occasional music licence" shall be substituted by the words "occasional licence".

(2) For paragraph 2 there shall be substituted the following paragraph:—

"2.—(1) An applicant for the grant, renewal or transfer of a licence under paragraph 1 or the variation of such a licence under paragraph 18 of this Schedule shall, not later than the day the application is made, send a copy of the application to the Commissioner of Police in whose area the premises are situated (in this Schedule referred to as "the Commissioner") and to the London Fire and Civil Defence Authority (in this Schedule referred to as "the fire authority") and, subject to sub-paragraph (2) below, no such application shall be considered by the Council unless the applicant complies with this sub-paragraph.

(2) Where an application for the grant, renewal, transfer or variation of a licence has been made and the applicant has failed to send a copy of the application in accordance with the requirement of sub-paragraph (1) above the Council may, in such cases as they think fit and after duly consulting with the party who was not supplied with a copy of the said application, waive such a requirement.

(3) In considering any such application the Council shall have regard to any observations submitted to them by the Commissioner and the fire authority within twenty-eight days of the making of the application and may have regard to any observation submitted by them thereafter.

(4) An applicant for any such grant, renewal, transfer or variation of a licence shall furnish such particulars and give such other notices, including the public advertisement of the application, as the Council may by regulation prescribe.

(5) Save where a shorter period is agreed by the Council, an applicant for the grant of an occasional licence shall make such application not less than twenty-eight days in advance of the occasion for which the occasional licence is sought and shall send a copy of the application to the Commissioner and to the fire authority.

(6) Regulations under sub-paragraph (4) above may prescribe the procedure for determining applications.".

(3) For paragraph 3B there shall be substituted the following paragraph:—

"3B.—(1) An applicant for the grant, renewal or transfer of a licence under paragraph 3A or the variation of such a licence under paragraph 18 of this Schedule shall, not later than the day the application is made, send a copy of the application to the Commissioner and to the fire authority and, subject to sub-paragraph (2) below, no such application shall be considered by the Council unless the applicant complies with this sub-paragraph.

(2) Where an application for the grant, renewal, transfer or variation of a licence has been made and the applicant has failed to send a copy of the application in accordance with the requirement of sub-paragraph (1) above the Council may, in such cases as they think fit and after duly consulting with the party who was not supplied with a copy of the said application, waive such a requirement.

(3) In considering any such application the Council shall have regard to any observations submitted to them by the Commissioner and the fire authority within twenty-eight days of the making of the application and may have regard to any observation submitted by them thereafter.

(4) An applicant for any such grant, renewal, transfer or variation of a licence shall furnish such particulars and give such other notices, including the public advertisement of the application, as the Council may by regulation prescribe.

(5) Regulations under sub-paragraph (4) above may prescribe the procedure for determining applications.".

(4) For paragraph 5 there shall be substituted the following paragraph:—

"5.—(1) An applicant for the grant, renewal, transfer or variation of a licence under paragraph 4 or the variation of such a licence under paragraph 18 of this Schedule shall not later than the day the application is made send a copy of the application to the Commissioner and to the fire authority and, subject to sub-paragraph (2) below, no such application shall be considered by the Council unless the applicant complies with this sub-paragraph.

(2) Where an application for the grant, renewal, transfer or variation of a licence has been made and the applicant has failed to send a copy of the application in accordance with the requirement of sub-paragraph (1) above the Council may, in such cases as they think fit and after duly consulting with the party who was not supplied with a copy of the said application, waive such a requirement.

(3) In considering any such application the Council shall have regard to any observations submitted to them by the Commissioner and the fire authority within twenty-eight days of the making of the application and may have regard to any observation submitted by them thereafter.

(4) An applicant for any such grant, renewal, transfer or variation of a licence shall furnish such particulars and give such other notices, including the public advertisement of the application, as the Council may by regulation prescribe.

(5) Regulations under sub-paragraph (4) above may prescribe the procedure for determining applications.".

Private places of entertainment

21. Section 3 of the Private Places of Entertainment (Licensing) Act 1967 shall apply to a borough as though—

(a) in subsection (1), after "inspection of the premises" there were inserted "including securing entry and inspection by an authorised officer of the fire authority"; and

(b) after subsection (4) the following subsections were inserted:—

"(5) The person making an application for any such grant, renewal, transfer or variation of a licence shall not later than the day the application is made send a copy of the application to the Commissioner of Police in whose area the premises are situated (in this section referred to as "the Commissioner") and to the London Fire and Civil Defence Authority (in this section referred to as the "fire authority") and, subject to subsection (6) below, no such application shall be considered by the licensing authority unless the applicant complies with this subsection.

(6) Where an application for the grant, renewal, transfer or variation of a licence has been made and the applicant has failed to send a copy of the application in accordance with the requirement of sub-paragraph (1) above the Council may, in such cases as they think fit and after duly consulting with the party who was not supplied with a copy of the said application, waive such a requirement.

(7) In considering any such application the licensing authority shall have regard to any observations submitted to them by the Commissioner and the fire authority within twenty-eight days of the making of the application and may have regard to any observation submitted by them thereafter.

(8) An applicant for any such grant, renewal, transfer or variation of a licence shall furnish such particulars and give such other notices, including the public advertisement of the application, as the licensing authority may by regulation prescribe.

(9) Regulations under subsection (8) above may prescribe the procedure for determining applications.".

Theatres

22. Schedule 1 to the Theatres Act 1968 shall apply in relation to applications for the grant, renewal, transfer or variation of licences in respect of premises within a borough as though the following paragraph were substituted for paragraph 2 of that Schedule:—

"2.—(1) An applicant for the grant, renewal, transfer or variation of a licence under this Act in respect of any premises shall not later than the day the application is made send a copy of the application to the Commissioner of Police in whose area the premises are situated (in this paragraph referred to as "the Commissioner") and to the London Fire and Civil Defence Authority (in this paragraph referred to as "the fire authority") and, subject to sub-paragraph (2) below, no such application shall be considered by the licensing authority unless the applicant complies with this sub-paragraph.

(2) Where an application for any such grant, renewal, transfer or variation of a licence has been made and the applicant has failed to send a copy of the application in accordance with the requirement of sub-paragraph (1) above the licensing authority may, in such cases as they think fit and after duly consulting with the party who was not supplied with a copy of the said application, waive such a requirement.

(3) In considering any such application the licensing authority shall have regard to any observations submitted to them by the Commissioner and the fire authority within twenty-eight days of the making of the application and may have regard to any observation submitted by them thereafter.

(4) An applicant for any such grant, renewal, transfer or variation of a licence shall furnish such particulars and give such other notices, including the public advertisement of the application, as the licensing authority may by regulation prescribe.

(5) Regulations under sub-paragraph (4) above may prescribe the procedure for determining applications.".

Night cafés

23. Section 17(1)(a) (Powers of entry) of the London Local Authorities Act 1990 shall be amended by the addition after "authorised officer" of the words "or officer of the fire authority, authorised by the fire authority in writing to act in relation to this Part of this Act".

Part V

Miscellaneous

Application of Environmental Protection Act 1990

24. The Environmental Protection Act 1990 shall have effect in a borough as though—

(1) in section 79 (which relates to statutory nuisances and inspections therefor)—

(a) in subsection (1), after paragraph (ga) there were inserted the following paragraph:—

"(gb) smoke, fumes or gases emitted from any vehicle, machinery or equipment on a street so as to be prejudicial to health or a nuisance other than from any vehicle, machinery or equipment being used for fire brigade purposes;";

(b) after subsection (6A) there were inserted the following subsection:—

"(6B) Subsection (1)(gb) above does not apply in relation to smoke, fumes or gases emitted from the exhaust system of a vehicle."; and

(c) in subsection (7), after the definition of "street" there were inserted—

" 'vehicle' means a mechanically propelled vehicle intended or adapted for use on roads, whether or not it is in a fit state for such use, and includes any trailer intended or adapted for use as an attachment to such a vehicle, any chassis or body, with or without wheels, appearing to have formed part of such a vehicle or trailer and anything attached to such a vehicle or trailer;";

(2) in section 80A(1), after "section 79(1)(ga)" there were inserted "or (gb)".

Amendment of London Local Authorities Act 1991

25.—(1) Section 23 (Audible intruder alarms) of the London Local Authorities Act 1991 shall be amended as follows:—

(a) by the substitution, in subsections (1)(a)(i), (1)(b)(i) and (2)(a) for "fitted with a device" of the words "fitted with a working device";

(b) by the insertion, after subsection (6), of the following subsection:—

"(6A) An authorised officer may de-activate an alarm where, under subsection (7) below, he has been authorised to enter premises to do so."; and

(c) by the insertion, in subsection (7)(a), after "operating" of the words "either continuously or intermittently,";

(d) by the insertion, after subsection (11) of the following subsections:—

"(11A) Where any premises are entered by virtue of subsection (7) above in a case where the occupier of those premises is convicted of an offence under subsection (6) above in respect of the premises any expenses reasonably incurred by the council in connection with the entry, turning off the alarm or complying with subsection (10) above may be recovered by the council from that occupier.

(11B) Nothing done by, or by a member of, a borough council or by an officer of or another person authorised by a borough council shall, if done in good faith for the purposes of this section, subject them or any of them personally to any action, liability, claim or demand whatsoever, other than any liability under section 19 or 20 of the Local Government Finance Act 1982.".

(2) The said section 23 shall apply additionally to the City of London, and references in that section to "borough" and "council" shall be construed as including references to the City of London and to the Common Council of the City of London.

Public charitable collections

26.—(1) Subsection (2) of section 21 (Interpretation of Part III) of the London Local Authorities Act 1990 shall be amended by the substitution of the following paragraph for paragraph (h):—

"(h) the doing of anything authorised by any permit or order under Part III of the Charities Act 1992;".

(2) This section shall come into operation on the day Part III of the Charities Act 1992 comes into operation.

Application of London Local Authorities Act 1995 to Tower Hamlets

27. The definition of "participating council" in section 2 (Interpretation) of the London Local Authorities Act 1995 shall be amended by the deletion of the words "other than Tower Hamlets".

Obstruction of authorised officer

28.—(1) Any person who—

(a) intentionally obstructs any authorised officer acting in the exercise of his powers under this Act; or

(b) without reasonable cause fails to give any authorised officer any assistance or information which the officer may reasonably require of him for the purposes of the exercise of the officer's functions under any provision of this Act;

shall be guilty of an offence and liable on summary conviction to a fine not exceeding level 3 on the standard scale.

(2) Subsection (1)(b) above applies in relation to a constable as it applies in relation to an authorised officer.

(3) A person shall be guilty of an offence if, in giving any information which is required of him by virtue of subsection (1)(b) above—

(a) he makes any statement which he knows is false in a material particular; or

(b) he recklessly makes a statement which is false in a material particular.

(4) A person guilty of an offence under subsection (3) above shall be liable on summary conviction to a fine not exceeding level 5 on the standard scale.

Defence of due diligence

29.—(1) In proceedings for an offence under this Act it shall be a defence for the person charged to prove that he took all reasonable precautions and exercised all due diligence to avoid the commission of the offence.

(2) If in any case the defence provided under subsection (1) above involves the allegation that the commission of the offence was due to the act or default

of another person, the person charged shall not, without leave of the court, be entitled to rely on that defence unless, no later than 7 clear days before the hearing, he has served on the prosecutor a notice in writing giving such information as was then in his possession identifying or assisting in the identification of that other person.

Liability of directors, etc.

30.—(1) Where an offence under this Act committed by a body corporate is proved to have been committed with the consent or connivance of, or to be attributable to any neglect on the part of, a director, manager, secretary or other similar officer of the body corporate or any person who was purporting to act in any such capacity, he, as well as the body corporate, shall be guilty of the offence.

(2) Where the affairs of the body corporate are managed by its members, subsection (1) above shall apply to the acts and defaults of a member in connection with his functions of management as if he were a director of the body corporate.

Regulations

31.—(1) Any power to make regulations conferred by this Act shall be exercised by statutory instrument.

(2) Any statutory instrument made under this Act shall be subject to annulment in pursuance of a resolution of either House of Parliament.

SCHEDULES

Sections 4 and 6

SCHEDULE 1

ENFORCEMENT NOTICES, ETC., UNDER PART II (BUS LANES) OF THIS ACT

Enforcement notices

1.—(1) Where—

(a) a penalty charge notice has been served with respect to a vehicle under section 4 (Penalty charge notices under Part II) of this Act or paragraph 4(1) below; and

(b) the period of 28 days for payment of the penalty charge has expired without that charge being paid; and

(c) representations have not been made in respect of that penalty charge notice under paragraph 2 below;

the council concerned may serve a notice (in this Schedule referred to as an "enforcement notice")—

(i) on the person who appears to them to have been the owner of the vehicle when the conduct giving rise to the service of the penalty charge is alleged to have taken place; or

(ii) where the penalty charge notice has been served under paragraph 4(1) below on the person on whom that notice was served.

(2) An enforcement notice must state—

(a) the amount of the penalty charge payable;

(b) the grounds on which the council believe that a penalty charge is payable with respect to the vehicle;

(c) that the penalty charge must be paid before the end of the period of 28 days beginning with the date on which the enforcement notice is served;

(d) that failure to pay the penalty charge may lead to an increased charge being payable;

(e) the amount of that increased charge;

(f) that the person on whom the notice is served may be entitled to make representations under paragraph 2 below; and

(g) the effect of paragraph 6 below.

(3) The Secretary of State may by regulations prescribe additional matters which must be dealt with in any enforcement notice.

Representations against penalty charge notice or enforcement notice

2.—(1) Where it appears to a person on whom a penalty charge notice has been served under section 4 (Penalty charge notices under Part II) of this Act, or paragraph 4(1) below, or a person on whom an enforcement notice has been served under paragraph 1 above (in this Schedule referred to as "the recipient") that one or other of the grounds mentioned in sub-paragraph (4) below is satisfied, he may make representations to that effect to the council who served the notice on him.

(2) Any representations under this paragraph must be made in such form as may be specified by the councils, acting through the Joint Committee.

(3) The council may disregard any such representations which are received by them after the end of the period of 28 days beginning with the date on which the penalty charge notice or enforcement notice in question was served.

(4) The grounds referred to in sub-paragraph (1) above are—

(a) where the penalty charge notice was served pursuant to the said section 4 or, where an enforcement notice was served, that the recipient—

(i) never was the owner of the vehicle in question;

(ii) had ceased to be its owner before the date on which the penalty charge was alleged to have become payable; or

(iii) became its owner after that date;

(b) that there was no breach of an order or regulations of the type described in subsection (2) of the said section 4;

(c) that at the time the alleged breach of such order or regulation took place the recipient was not in charge of the vehicle.

(5) Where the ground mentioned in sub-paragraph (4)(a)(ii) above is relied on in any representations made under this paragraph, those representations must include a statement of the name and address of the person to whom the vehicle was disposed of by the person making the representations (if that information is in his possession).

(6) Where the ground mentioned in sub-paragraph (4)(a)(iii) above is relied on in any representations made under this paragraph, those representations must include a statement of the name and address of the person from whom the vehicle was acquired by the person making the representations (if that information is in his possesssion).

(7) Where the ground mentioned in sub-paragraph (4)(c) above is relied on in any representations made under this paragraph, those representations must include a statement by the person making the representations of the name and address of the person whom he believed to be in charge of the vehicle at the time of the alleged breach of the order described in subsection (2) of the said section 4.

(8) A person who fails to comply with the requirements of sub-paragraph (7) above shall be guilty of an offence unless he shows to the satisfaction of the court that he did not know, and could not with reasonable diligence have ascertained, who was the driver of the vehicle.

(9) A person guilty of any offence under sub-paragraph (8) above shall be liable on summary conviction to a fine not exceeding level 3 on the standard scale.

(10) It shall be the duty of the council to whom representations are duly made under this paragraph—

(a) to consider them and any supporting evidence which the person making them provides; and

(b) to serve on that person notice of their decision as to whether they accept that the ground in question has been established.

Cancellation of penalty charge notice or enforcement notice

3.—(1) Where representations are made under paragraph 2 above and the council concerned accept that the ground in question has been established they shall—

(a) cancel the penalty charge notice or enforcement notice; and

(b) state in the notice served under sub-paragraph (10) of paragraph 2 above that the penalty charge notice or enforcement notice has been cancelled.

(2) The cancellation of a penalty charge notice or enforcement notice under this paragraph shall not be taken to prevent the council concerned serving a fresh penalty charge notice or enforcement notice on another person.

Reissue of penalty charge notice

4.—(1) Where representations are made under paragraph 2 above on the grounds mentioned in sub-paragraph (4)(c) of that paragraph and the council concerned accept that the ground in question has been established, they may, after cancelling the penalty charge notice or enforcement notice in accordance with paragraph 3(1)(a) above, serve a fresh penalty charge notice on any person mentioned in the statement made under paragraph 2(7) above or on any other person whom they have reasonable grounds to believe to have been in charge of the vehicle.

(2) Any penalty charge notice served under sub-paragraph (1) above must comply with the requirements of subsection (3) of section 4 (Penalty charge notices under Part II) of this Act.

Rejection of representations against enforcement notice

5. Where any representations are made under paragraph 2 above but the council concerned do not accept that a ground has been established, the notice served under sub-paragraph (10) of the said paragraph 2 (in this Schedule referred to as "the notice of rejection") must—

(a) state that a charge certificate may be served under paragraph 8 below unless before the end of the period of 28 days beginning with the date of service of the notice of rejection—
  (i) the penalty charge is paid; or
  (ii) the person on whom the notice is served appeals to a traffic adjudicator against the penalty charge; and

(b) describe in general terms the form and manner in which such an appeal must be made;

and may contain such other information as the council consider appropriate.

Adjudication by traffic adjudicator

6.—(1) Where a council serve a notice of rejection, the person who made the representations under paragraph 2 above in respect of which that notice was served may, before—

(a) the end of the period of 28 days beginning with the date of service of that notice; or

(b) such longer period as a traffic adjudicator may allow,

appeal to a traffic adjudicator against the council's decision.

(2) On an appeal under this paragraph, the traffic adjudicator shall consider the representations in question and any additional representations which are made by the appellant on any of the grounds mentioned in paragraph 2(4) above and may give the council concerned such directions as he considers appropriate.

(3) It shall be the duty of the council to whom a direction is given under sub-paragraph (2) above to comply with it forthwith.

Admissibility of certain evidence

7.—(1) Evidence of a fact relevant to proceedings under paragraph 6 above may be given by the production of—

(a) a record produced by a prescribed device; and

(b) (in the same or another document) a certificate as to the circumstances in which the record was produced signed by an authorised officer of the council of the borough in which the breach of the order or regulations described in subsection (2) of section 4 (Penalty charge notices under Part II) of this Act is alleged to have taken place.

(2) A record produced or measurement made by a prescribed device shall not be admissible as evidence of a fact relevant to proceedings under paragraph 6 above unless—

(a) the device is of a type approved by the Secretary of State; and

(b) any conditions subject to which the approval was given are satisfied.

(3) Any approval given by the Secretary of State for the purposes of this paragraph may be given subject to conditions as to the purposes for which, and the manner and other circumstances in which, any device of the type concerned is to be used.

(4) In proceedings under paragraph 6 above, evidence—

(a) of a measurement made by a device, or of the circumstances in which it was made; or

(b) that a device was of a type approved for the purposes of this paragraph, or that any conditions subject to which an approval was given were satisfied;

may be given by the production of a document which is signed as mentioned in sub-paragraph (1) above and which, as the case may be, gives particulars of the measurement or of the circumstances in which it was made, or states that the device was of such a type or that, to the best of the knowledge and belief of the person making the statement, all such conditions were satisfied.

(5) For the purposes of this paragraph a document purporting to be a record of the kind mentioned in sub-paragraph (1) above, or to be a certificate or other document signed as mentioned in that sub-paragraph or in sub-paragraph (4) above, shall be deemed to be such a record, or to be so signed, unless the contrary is proved.

(6) Nothing in sub-paragraph (1) or (4) above makes a document admissible as evidence in proceedings under paragraph 6 above unless a copy of it has not less than 7 days before the

hearing, been served on the appellant; and nothing in those paragraphs makes a document admissible as evidence of anything other than the matters shown on a record produced by a prescribed device if that person, not less than three days before the hearing or within such further time as the traffic adjudicator may in special circumstances allow, serves a notice on the council requiring attendance at the hearing or trial of the person who signed the document.

Charge certificates

8.—(1) Where a penalty charge notice or enforcement notice is served on any person and the penalty charge to which it relates is not paid before the end of the relevant period, the council serving the notice may serve on that person a statement (in this paragraph referred to as a "charge certificate") to the effect that the penalty charge in question is increased by 50 per cent.

(2) The relevant period, in relation to a penalty charge notice, is the period of 28 days beginning—

(a) where representations are made under paragraph 2 above and a notice of rejection is served by the borough council and no appeal against the notice of rejection is made, with the date on which the notice of rejection is served; or

(b) where there has been an unsuccessful appeal against a notice of rejection, with the date on which notice of the adjudicator's decision is served on the appellant.

(3) The relevant period, in relation to an enforcement notice is the period of 28 days beginning—

(a) where no representations are made under paragraph 2 above, with the date on which the enforcement notice is served;

(b) where such representations are made and a notice of rejection is served by the council concerned and no appeal against the notice of rejection is made with the date on which the notice of rejection is served; or

(c) where there has been an unsuccessful appeal against a notice of rejection, with the date on which notice of the adjudicator's decision is served on the appellant.

(4) Where an appeal against a notice of rejection is made but is withdrawn before the decision of the adjudicator is made the relevant period in relation to an enforcement notice is the period of 14 days beginning with the date on which the appeal is withdrawn.

Enforcement of charge certificate

9.—(1) Where a charge certificate has been served on any person and the increased penalty charge provided for in the certificate is not paid before the end of the period of 14 days beginning with the date on which the certificate is served, the council concerned may, if a county court so orders, recover the increased charge as if it were payable under a county court order.

(2) Any notice of any county court order made under this paragraph and being served on any person shall be accompanied by a copy of the penalty charge notice and, where appropriate, the enforcement notice to which the penalty charge relates.

(3) Section 78 of the Act of 1991 (which makes provision for the recovery of sums that are payable under or by virture of any provision of Part II of that Act and are recoverable as if they were payable under a county court order) shall have effect as though an increased penalty charge recoverable under sub-paragraph (1) above were a Part II debt for the purposes of that section.

Invalid notices

10.—(1) This paragraph applies where—

(a) a county court makes an order under paragraph 9 above;

(b) the person against whom it is made makes a statutory declaration complying with sub-paragraph (2) below; and

(c) that declaration is, before the end of the period of 21 days beginning with the date on which notice of the county court's order is served on him, served on the county court which made the order.

(2) The statutory declaration must state that the person making it—

(a) did not receive the enforcement notice in question;

(b) made representations to the council concerned under paragraph 2 above but did not receive a notice of rejection from that council; or

(c) appealed to a traffic adjudicator under paragraph 6 above against the rejection by that council of representations made by him under paragraph 2 above but had no response to the appeal.

(3) Sub-paragraph (4) below applies where it appears to a district judge, on the application of a person on whom a charge certificate has been served, that it would be unreasonable in the circumstances of his case to insist on him serving his statutory declaration within the period of 21 days allowed for by sub-paragraph (1) above.

(4) Where this sub-paragraph applies, the district judge may allow such longer period for service of the statutory declaration as he considers appropriate.

(5) Where a statutory declaration is served under sub-paragraph (1)(c) above—

(a) the order of the court shall be deemed to have been revoked;

(b) the charge certificate shall be deemed to have been cancelled;

(c) in the case of a statutory declaration under sub-paragraph (2)(a) above, the enforcement notice to which the charge certificate relates shall be deemed to have been cancelled; and

(d) the district judge shall serve written notice of the effect of service of the statutory declaration on the person making it and on the council concerned.

(6) Service of a declaration under sub-paragraph (2)(a) above shall not prevent the borough council serving a fresh enforcement notice but if, when it was served, the relevant order under paragraph 9 was accompanied by a copy of the enforcement notice to which the charge certificate relates, a fresh enforcement notice in the same terms shall be deemed to have been served on the person making the declaration on the same day as the declaration was served.

(7) Where a declaration has been served under sub-paragraph (2)(b) or (c) above, the borough council shall refer the case to the traffic adjudicator who may give such direction as he considers appropriate.

Offence of giving false information

11.—(1) A person who, in response to a penalty charge notice or enforcement notice served under this Schedule makes any representation under paragraph 2 or 6 above which is false in a material particular and does so recklessly or knowing it to be false in that particular is guilty of an offence.

(2) Any person guilty of such an offence shall be liable on summary conviction to a fine not exceeding level 5 on the standard scale.

Service by post

12. Any charge certificate, or notice under Part II (Bus lanes) of this Act or this Schedule—

(a) may be served by post; and

(b) where the person on whom it is to be served is a body corporate, is duly served if it is sent by post to the secretary or clerk of that body.

Section 7

SCHEDULE 2

Financial provisions relating to Part II (Bus lanes) of this Act

1. A borough council shall keep an account of their income and expenditure in respect of Part II (Bus lanes) of this Act.

2. At the end of each financial year any deficit in the account shall be made good out of the general rate fund, and (subject to paragraph 3 below) any surplus shall be applied for all or any of the purposes specified in paragraph 6 below and, in so far as it is not so applied, shall be appropriated to the carrying out of some specific project falling within those purposes and carried forward until applied to carrying it out.

3. If the borough council so determine, any amount not applied in any financial year, instead of being or remaining so appropriated, may be carried forward in the account kept under paragraph 1 above to the next financial year.

4. Each borough council shall, after each financial year, report to the Secretary of State on any action taken by them, pursuant to paragraph 2 or 3 above, in respect of any deficit or surplus in their account for the year.

5. The report under paragraph 4 above shall be made as soon after the end of the financial year to which it relates as possible.

6. The purposes referred to in paragraph 2 above are the following, that is to say:—

(a) the making good to the general rate fund of any amount charged to that fund under paragraph 2 above in the four years immediately preceding the financial year in question;

(b) meeting costs incurred, whether by the borough council or by some other person, in the provision or operation of, or of facilities for, public passenger transport services; and

(c) the purposes of a project connected with the carrying out by the appropriate highway authority (whether or not the borough council) of any operation which, within the meaning of the Highways Act 1980, constitutes the improvement of a highway in the borough council's area.

INDEX

References are to sections and Schedules

AMBULANCES,
  bus lanes regulations: exemption, 5
AUDIBLE INTRUDER ALARMS, 25

BUS LANES,
  exemptions to regulations, 5
  financial provisions, 7, Sched. 2
  interpretation, 3(1)
  penalty charge, 4, 6, Sched. 1
    cases where not payable, 9

CHARITIES,
  charitable collections, 26
CITATION, 1
COMMENCEMENT, 1

DEFENCE OF DUE DILIGENCE, 29
DIRECTORS' LIABILITY, 30

ENTRY POWERS,
  night cafés, 23
  occasional sales, 17
  private places of entertainment, 21

ENVIRONMENTAL PROTECTION,
  statutory nuisances, 24

FIRE SAFETY,
  bus lanes regulations: exemptions, 5
  entry rights, 21
  night cafés, 23
  occasional licences, 20
  private places of entertainment, 21
  theatres, 22

INTERPRETATION, 7

LICENSING,
  occasional licences: fire safety, 20

MUSIC AND DANCING,
  occasional licences, 20

NIGHT CAFÉS,
  entry powers, 23

OCCASIONAL SALES,
  application of Act, 11

CITY OF EDINBURGH COUNCIL ORDER CONFIRMATION ACT 1996

(1996 c. x)

An Act to confirm a Provisional Order under the Private Legislation Procedure (Scotland) Act 1936, relating to City of Edinburgh Council.

[18th December 1996]

PARLIAMENTARY PROGRESS

The Bill's progress through Parliament was as follows:

House of Commons: First Reading, October 30, 1996, Bill considered by Commons, November 5, 1996, Third Reading, November 6, 1996.

House of Lords: First Reading and Consideration by Lords, November 6, 1996, Report, November 14, 1996, Third Reading, November 28, 1996.

INTRODUCTION

By this Act, the Provisional Order which empowers the City of Edinburgh Council to create and maintain a general reserve fund is confirmed. This legislation is effective under the Private Legislation Procedure (Scotland) Act 1936.

Whereas the Provisional Order set forth in the Schedule hereunto annexed has been made by the Secretary of State under the provisions of the Private Legislation Procedure (Scotland) Act 1936, and it is requisite that the said Order should be confirmed by Parliament:

Be it therefore enacted by the Queen's most Excellent Majesty, by and with the advice and consent of the Lords Spiritual and Temporal, and Commons, in this present Parliament assembled, and by the authority of the same, as follows:—

Confirmation of Order in Schedule

1. The Provisional Order contained in the Schedule hereunto annexed is hereby confirmed.

Short title

2. This Act may be cited as the City of Edinburgh Order Confirmation Act 1996.

SCHEDULE

City of Edinburgh Council

Provisional Order to empower The City of Edinburgh Council to create and maintain a general reserve fund.

Whereas by virtue of section 2 of the Local Government (Scotland) Act 1973 the City of Edinburgh District Council (hereinafter referred to as "the former Council") were vested with all the functions of a district council for the area of the City of Edinburgh District as the said area was described in column 3 of Part III of Schedule 1 to the said Act of 1973:

And whereas in pursuance of the said Act of 1973 and the City of Edinburgh District Council Order 1991 (hereinafter referred to as "the Order of 1991") certain powers and functions were exercisable by and vested in the former Council:

And whereas in pursuance of section 36 of the Order of 1991 the former Council were empowered to continue to maintain, and did so continue to maintain, a general reserve fund until that section ceased to have effect on 1st January 1995:

And whereas by virtue of section 2 of the Local Government etc. (Scotland) Act 1994 The City of Edinburgh Council (hereinafter in this Order referred to as "the Council") are vested with all the functions of the former Council for the area of the City of Edinburgh as the said area is described in column 1 of Part I of Schedule 1 to the said Act of 1994:

And whereas it is expedient that provisions similar to section 36 of the Order of 1991 should be enacted and applied to the City of Edinburgh:

And whereas the purposes aforesaid cannot be effected without an Order confirmed by Parliament under the provisions of the Private Legislation Procedure (Scotland) Act 1936:

Now, therefore, in pursuance of the powers contained in the said Act of 1936 the Secretary of State orders as follows:—

Short title

1. This Order may be cited as the City of Edinburgh Council Order 1996.

General reserve fund

2.—(1) Subject to subsection (2) below, the Council may create and maintain a fund (to be called "the general reserve fund") and may apply it in defraying any expenditure which might be met out of the district rate.

(2) The Council may in any financial year pay into the general reserve fund such amounts as they think fit, so however that the general reserve fund shall not at any time exceed the sum produced by multiplying £20.00 by the relevant population of the Council's area as determined in accordance with subsection (4AA) of section 83 of the Local Government (Scotland) Act 1973 (power of local authorities to incur expenditure not otherwise authorised).

(3) The sum mentioned in subsection (2) above shall, from time to time, be increased or decreased (as the case may be) by an amount which bears the same proportion to that sum as shall be borne by any increase or decrease in the index of retail prices to the figure shown therein for the month in which this Order was enacted; and in this subsection "the index of retail prices" means the general index of retail prices (for all items) published in the monthly publication of the Office for National Statistics known as "Monthly Digest of Statistics", or any successor from time to time of that index.

INDEX

References are to sections and the Schedule

General Reserve Fund, Sched.

Order,
  confirmation of, 1
  terms of, Sched.

Short Title, 2

EDINBURGH MERCHANT COMPANY ORDER CONFIRMATION ACT 1996

(1996 c. xi)

ARRANGEMENT OF SECTIONS

SECT.
1. Confirmation of Order in Schedule.
2. Short title.

SCHEDULE

EDINBURGH MERCHANT COMPANY

PART I

PRELIMINARY

1. Short title.
2. Interpretation.
3. Confirmation of existing charters and repeal of Acts.

PART II

PROVISIONS AS TO MERCHANT COMPANY

A. Powers of Company

4. Powers of Company.

B. Election of members of Company

5. Qualifications for membership of Company.
6. Application for election.
7. Election of members.
8. Date of election of members.
9. Honorary members.

C. Election of office bearers

10. Election of Master, treasurer and assistants.
11. Master, treasurer and assistants may be re-elected.
12. Filling of vacancies among Master, treasurer and assistants.

D. Officials

13. Appointment of officials by Company.
14. Company may provide pensions, etc., for officials.

E. Fees, etc., payable by members

15. Entrance fees.
16. Election conditional on payment of entry money and other sums.
17. Powers of Company to vary entry money, etc.
18. Power to impose annual subscriptions, etc.

F. Funds and property of Company

19. Application of funds of Company.
20. Hall and offices of Company.
21. Power to contribute to widows' fund from general fund.

G. Meetings of Company

22. Stated general meetings of Company.
23. Special general meetings of Company.
24. Mode of calling Company meetings.
25. Chairman of meetings of Company.

26. Quorum of meetings of Company.
27. Voting at meetings of Company.
28. Company may make rules of procedure.

H. Miscellaneous

29. Company may make rules, etc.

PART III

MASTER'S COURT

30. Reconstitution of Master's court.
31. Meetings of Master's court.
32. Chairman of meetings of Master's court.
33. Quorum of meetings of Master's court.
34. Committees of Master's court.
35. Proceedings of Master's court not to be invalidated by vacancies, etc.
36. Duties of Master's court.
37. Accounts to be kept by Master's court and audited.
38. Company officials to act as officials of Master's court.

PART IV

DARLING FUND

39. Vesting, etc., of Darling fund in Master's court.
40. Payment of pensions out of Darling fund.

PART V

WIDOWS' FUND

A. Maintenance of widows' fund

41. Maintenance of widows' fund.
42. Closure of widows' fund to new contributors.

B. Contributors

43. Stated general meetings of contributors.
44. Special general meetings of contributors.
45. Mode of calling meetings of contributors.
46. Chairman of meetings of contributors.
47. Quorum of meetings of contributors.
48. Voting at meetings of contributors.
49. Appointment of officials by contributors.
50. Contributors may provide pensions, etc., for officials.
51. Contributors may make rules.

C. Powers of widows' fund

52. Powers of Trustees of widows' fund.
53. Constitution of trustees of widows' fund.
54. Elected trustees' eligibility for re-election.
55. Filling of vacancies among trustees.
56. Stated general meetings of trustees.
57. Special general meetings of trustees.
58. Mode of calling meetings of trustees.
59. Chairman of meetings of trustees.
60. Quorum of meetings of trustees.
61. Committees of trustees.
62. Proceedings of trustees not to be invalidated by vacancies, etc.
63. Widows' fund to be managed and administered by trustees.
64. Distribution of widows' fund.
65. Accounts of widows' fund to be kept by trustees and audited.

D. Payments, etc., by contributors

66. Payment of annual contributions.
67. Payment of half-yearly contributions and annuities by instalments.

68. Contributors may alter amount of half-yearly contributions.
69. Redemption of half-yearly contributions.
70. Half-yearly contributions not to be payable after death of married contributors.
71. Contributors may refund payments.
72. Contributor may discontinue payment of half-yearly contributions on death of wife.
73. Marriage tax payable on marriage after election.
74. Times of payment of marriage tax.
75. Alterations of marriage tax.
76. Particulars of marriage, etc., to be provided by contributors.
77. Penalty for failure to pay half-yearly contributions.
78. Interest on payments in arrear.
79. As to payment of half-yearly contributions, etc., of deceased contributors.

E. Payment of annuities

80. Payment of annuities to widows.
81. More than one annuity payable to widows.
82. Annuities to be alimentary.
83. Power to introduce new classes of beneficiaries.
84. Rate of annuity to continue until altered.

F. Alteration of amount of annuities

85. Periodical investigation of widows' fund.
86. Contributors may alter amount of annuity.
87. Conditions of increase of annuity.
88. Conditions of reduction of annuity.

G. Dissolution of widows' fund

89. Purchase of annuities.
90. Application of residue of widows' fund.
91. Widows' fund to be dissolved.

PART VI

ENDOWMENTS TRUST

A. Incorporation powers, etc., of endowments trust

92. Powers of endowments trust.
93. Endowments trust fund vested in endowments trust.
94. Constitution of endowments trust.
95. Election and period of office of members of endowments trust.
96. Filling of vacancies among elected members of endowments trust.
97. Meetings of endowments trust.
98. Chairman of endowments trust.
99. Quorum of meetings of endowments trust.
100. Committees of endowments trust.
101. Proceedings of endowments trust not to be invalidated by vacancies, etc.
102. Appointment of officials by endowments trust.
103. Endowments trust may provide pensions, etc., for officials.
104. Application of income of endowments trust fund.
105. Power of endowments trust to borrow.
106. Reserve fund of endowments trust.
107. Accounts to be kept by endowments trust and audited.

B. Payments, etc., to beneficiaries

108. Classes of beneficiaries.
109. Minimum amount and terms of pensions.
110. Endowments trust may provide houses, etc., for beneficiaries.
111. Election of beneficiaries.
112. Applications for pensions, etc.

C. Fraser Trust

113. Definitions for purposes of Head C.
114. Sir William Fraser Homes to be maintained.
115. Qualifications of persons to occupy Sir William Fraser Homes.
116. Election of occupants.
117. Rights of occupants of Sir William Fraser Homes.

118. Constitution of Fraser trustees.
119. Fraser trustees to be members of committees to administer Sir William Fraser Homes.
120. Application of funds retained by Fraser trustees.
121. Fraser trustees may transfer remaining assets to endowments trust.

D. Russell and Foster Endowment

122. Russell and Foster Endowment vested in endowments trust.
123. Income of Russell and Foster Endowment to be applied in payment of pensions.
124. Qualifications of Russell and Foster pensioners.
125. Amount, etc., of Russell and Foster pensions.
126. Designation of Russell and Foster beneficiaries.

E. Variation of trusts

127. Variation of trusts.

PART VII

JOINT COMMITTEE

128. Re-establishment of joint committee.
129. Election and period of office of members of joint committee.
130. Filling of vacancies in joint committee.
131. Meetings of joint committee.
132. Chairman of joint committee.
133. Quorum of meetings of joint committee.
134. Proceedings of joint committee not to be invalidated by vacancies, etc.
135. Powers of joint committee.

PART VIII

MISCELLANEOUS AND GENERAL

136. Execution of deeds.
137. Powers of investment.
138. Borrowing and lending inter se by Company, widows' fund, endowments trust and education board.
139. Donations, etc., may be received.
140. Notices.
141. Discharge of members, contributors, officials and others.
142. Saving for town and country planning.
143. Costs of Order.

An Act to confirm a Provisional Order under the Private Legislation Procedure (Scotland) Act 1936, relating to Edinburgh Merchant Company. [18th December 1996]

PARLIAMENTARY PROGRESS

The Bill's progress through Parliament was as follows:

House of Commons: First Reading, October 30, 1996, Bill considered by Commons, November 5, 1996, Third Reading, November 6, 1996.

House of Lords: First Reading and Consideration by Lords, November 6, 1996, Report, November 14, 1996, Third Reading, November 28, 1996.

INTRODUCTION

By this Act, the Provisional Order to continue the Company of Merchants of the City of Edinburgh is confirmed. The Order consolidates with amendments the Acts relating to the Company and, *inter alia*, makes provisions relating to the Master's court of the Company, the Alexander Darling Silk Mercer's fund and the Russell and Foster Endowment. This legislation is effective under the Private Legislation Procedure (Scotland) Act 1936.

Whereas the Provisional Order set forth in the Schedule hereunto annexed has been made by the Secretary of State under the provisions of the Private Legislation Procedure (Scotland) Act 1936, and it is requisite that the said Order should be confirmed by Parliament:

Be it therefore enacted by the Queen's most Excellent Majesty, by and with the advice and consent of the Lords Spiritual and Temporal, and Commons, in this present Parliament assembled, and by the authority of the same, as follows:

Confirmation of Order in Schedule

1. The Provisional Order contained in the Schedule hereunto annexed is hereby confirmed.

Short title

2. This Act may be cited as the Edinburgh Merchant Company Order Confirmation Act 1996.

SCHEDULE

Edinburgh Merchant Company

Provisional Order to continue in being the Company of Merchants of the City of Edinburgh and to consolidate with amendments the Acts relating to the Company and to the widows' fund and endowments trust of the Company; to reconstitute and confer powers on the Master's court of the Company and to vest in the Master's court the Alexander Darling Silk Mercer's fund and to make provision as to the management and administration thereof; to make provision for the dissolution of the widows' fund; to make provision as to the vesting in the said endowments trust of the Russell and Foster Endowment and to confer powers on the endowments trust; and for other purposes.

WHEREAS—

(1) The Company of Merchants of the City of Edinburgh (hereinafter referred to as "the Company") was incorporated by royal charter in 1681, ratified by an Act of the Parliament of Scotland in 1693 and further provision was made as to the regulation of the affairs of the Company by a royal charter granted in 1777:

(2) By the Edinburgh Merchant Company Act 1898 (hereinafter referred to as "the Act of 1898") the Company was reincorporated and the powers of the Company were amended and enlarged and further provision was made for the regulation, management and administration of its affairs and of the widows' fund established by the Company (hereinafter referred to as "the widows' fund") and of certain charitable endowments administered by the Company:

(3) By the Edinburgh Merchant Company Endowments Orders 1909 and 1952 further provision was made as to the charitable endowments administered by the Company:

(4) By the Edinburgh Merchant Company Widows' Fund (Amendment) Order 1947 the provisions of the Act of 1898 relative to the said widows' fund were amended:

(5) By the Edinburgh Merchant Company Order Confirmation Act 1960 (hereinafter referred to as "the Act of 1960") the Company was reincorporated as a body corporate under the same name and provisions of the Act of 1898; the said Orders of 1909, 1947 and 1952 were consolidated with certain amendments, modifications and additions; further provisions were made with respect to the constituting of the Master, treasurer and assistants of the Company as the Master's court of the Company and as to the functions of the said Master's court and with respect to the regulation, management and administration of the affairs of the Company and of the widows' fund and charitable endowments and provision was made whereby the benefits of the

widows' fund were extended to new classes of beneficiaries including the orphans of contributors to the widows' fund:

(6) The Alexander Darling Silk Mercer's Fund was vested by the Act of 1960 in the Master's court of the Company and powers contained in the Act of 1960 were conferred on the said Master's court:

(7) The Merchant Company Charities Board, as incorporated by the said Order of 1909, was reincorporated by the Act of 1960 as a corporate body under the name of "The Merchant Company Endowments Trust" (hereinafter referred to as "the endowments trust"):

(8) The property known as the Sir William Fraser Homes was by the Act of 1960 transferred to and vested in the endowments trust and is held and administered by the endowments trust as part of the endowments trust fund vested in the endowments trust:

(9) By his will and relative codicil the late Henry Walker Russell bequeathed property to be held and administered by the Merchant Company Charities Board as a separate fund to be known as "The Russell and Foster Endowment" for the purpose of paying annuities or pensions in accordance with the provisions of his said will:

(10) By the Act of 1960 "The Russell and Foster Endowment" was transferred to the endowments trust:

(11) It is expedient that the Company continue in being as a body corporate under the same name; that the provisions of the Act of 1960 be re-enacted with certain amendments, modifications and additions; that further provisions with respect to the categories of membership and the regulation, management and administration of the affairs of the Company should be enacted; that provision should be made to close the widows' fund and to dissolve the widows' fund:

(12) It is expedient to permit a variation of the terms of the Fraser Trust, the endowment trust and the Russell and Foster Endowment by means of a Petition to the Court of Session in Edinburgh:

(13) It is expedient that the other provisions of this Order shall be enacted:

(14) The purposes aforesaid cannot be effected without an Order confirmed by Parliament under the provisions of the Private Legislation Procedure (Scotland) Act 1936:

Now, therefore, in pursuance of the powers contained in the said Act of 1936, the Secretary of State orders as follows:—

PART I

PRELIMINARY

Short title

1. This Order may be cited as the Edinburgh Merchant Company Order 1996.

Interpretation

2. In this Order, except where the context otherwise requires—

"Act of 1960" means the Edinburgh Merchant Company Order Confirmation Act 1960;

"actuary" means the person holding the appointment of actuary of the Company for the time being;

"annual meeting" means the stated general meeting of the Company to be held annually on the second Thursday of November or such other date as the Company may prescribe pursuant to section 22 (Stated general meetings of Company) of this Order;

"annual meeting of the contributors" means the stated general meeting of the contributors to be held annually on the first Tuesday of October or such other date as the contributors may prescribe pursuant to section 43 (Stated general meetings of contributors) of this Order;
"assistant" means a person elected as an assistant pursuant to section 10 (Election of Master, treasurer and assistants) of this Order and for the time being holding the office of assistant and "senior assistant" means the assistant whose name stands highest in the list of assistants;
"commencement of this Order" means the date of the passing of the Act confirming this Order;
"Company" means the Company of Merchants of the City of Edinburgh;
"contributors" means the contributors to the widows' fund;
"Darling fund" means the fund constituted by the Darling trust disposition and settlement;
"Darling trust disposition and settlement" means the trust disposition and settlement of Alexander Darling LL.D. dated 31st August 1934, together with codicils dated 3rd June and 9th September 1936;
"Darling trustees" means the trustees for the time being of the Darling trust disposition and settlement;
"education board" means the Merchant Company Education Board constituted by the Edinburgh Merchant Company Educational Endowments Scheme 1960;
"endowments trust" means the Merchant Company Endowments Trust;
"endowments trust fund" means the fund vested in the endowments trust;
"existing" means existing immediately before the commencement of this Order;
"existing charters" means the royal charter of 1681 incorporating the Company and ratified by an Act of the Parliament of Scotland in 1693 and the royal charter of 1777;
"general fund" means the accumulated funds of the Company for the time being;
"joint committee" means the Merchant Company Joint Committee;
"Master's court" means the Master's court constituted by this Order;
"Master" means the Master of the Company for the time being;
"members" means the members of the Company for the time being and includes honorary members;
"old Master" means the person who last retired from the office of Master;
"registered auditor" means any person authorised by Part II of the Companies Act 1989 (which deals with the eligibility of persons for appointment as company auditors) to act as a company auditor;
"repealed Acts" means the Acts repealed by this Order;
"rules" means rules made by the Company or the contributors pursuant to the provisions of this Order;
"secretary" means the secretary of the Company for the time being;
"treasurer" means the treasurer of the Company for the time being;
"trustees" means the trustees of the widows' fund for the time being and "senior elected trustee" means the trustee whose name stands highest in the list of trustees elected in pursuance of section 53 (Constitution of trustees of widows' fund) of this Order;
"widow" includes widower;
"widows' fund" means the fund referred to in section 41 (Maintenance of widows' fund) of this Order.

Confirmation of existing charters and repeal of Acts

3.—(1) The existing charters, as amended by the provisions of this Order, are hereby ratified and confirmed.

(2) The following Acts are hereby repealed:—

(a) the Edinburgh Merchant Company Order Confirmation Act 1960; and

(b) the Edinburgh Merchant Company Order Confirmation Act 1976.

PART II

PROVISIONS AS TO MERCHANT COMPANY

A. Powers of Company

Powers of Company

4. The members shall continue in being under the name of "The Company of Merchants of the City of Edinburgh", as a body corporate with perpetual succession and a common seal; and with power to purchase, acquire, hold, sell, lease and dispose of lands and other property heritable, moveable, real and personal, and to sue and be sued, and with all other rights, powers and privileges of a body corporate.

B. Election of members of Company

Qualifications for membership of Company

5.—(1) Subject to the provisions of this Order, the persons eligible for election as members are the following:—

(a) merchants, bankers or traders who carry on or who have carried on business on their own account;

(b) persons who, as principals or agents, individually or in partnership with others, carry on or have carried on business on their own account in any department or description of commerce, trade, manufacture or handicraft, or as architects, engineers or surveyors;

(c) managing directors, managers and principal officers of banks (including managers of branch banks), insurance or other companies having their head office in the United Kingdom;

(d) such additional classes of persons as the Company may from time to time approve:

Provided that a person shall not be elected as a member of the Company (other than an honorary member) unless he is a guild brother of the City of Edinburgh and either—

(i) carries on or has carried on business on his own account or exercises or has exercised his office, within the City of Edinburgh or within 20 miles from Her Majesty's General Register House, Edinburgh or such other distance therefrom as the Company may from time to time determine; or

(ii) resides at the time of his election within the said city or within the said distance or such other distance as the Company may from time to time determine.

(2) Notice of a proposal to include any additional class of persons who shall be eligible for election as members of the Company shall be given at one of the stated general meetings of the Company and such class of persons shall not be eligible unless the proposal has been sanctioned by a resolution passed

by two-thirds of the members present and voting at the immediately following stated general meeting of the Company or at any adjournment thereof.

Application for election

6. Every person desiring to be elected as a member shall lodge with the secretary an application in such form and with such information as may from time to time be required by the Company.

Election of members

7. With respect to applications for election as members—

(1) Every application shall, in the first instance, be considered by the Master's court, who shall make a report as to the qualification and suitability of the applicant;

(2) The application along with such report shall thereafter be circulated to every member;

(3) Any member who wishes to object to an application must do so in writing to the secretary within 21 days of the date on which the said application is circulated;

(4) The application shall be remitted, within 42 days of the date on which the said application is circulated, to the Master's court;

(5) After considering any objections lodged as aforesaid, the Master's court may elect the applicant by a ballot in which at least 8 of their number vote for his election;

(6) If the application is refused by the Master's court, the applicant within 14 days of being notified of such refusal, may notify the secretary in writing that he wishes to appeal; and

(7) If the applicant does appeal as aforesaid, the application shall be submitted to a general meeting of the Company where the Company may elect the applicant by a ballot in which at least two-thirds of the members present and voting vote for his election.

Date of election of members

8. The date of election of a member shall be the date of his election by the Master's court or, in case of his election on appeal as provided for by the immediately preceding section of this Order, the date of his election by the Company.

Honorary members

9. The Company may elect as honorary members of the Company such persons, wheresoever resident or of whatsoever designation or calling, as may from their public eminence or public or private merits be deemed worthy to be elected.

C. Election of office bearers

Election of Master, treasurer and assistants

10.—(1) Subject to the provisions of this Order, the Company shall at every annual meeting elect the Master, the treasurer and 12 assistants.

(2) The Master and the treasurer shall be elected from amongst the members who at the time of election are, or who have been, assistants.

(3) The 12 assistants shall be elected from the members.

(4) The Master, the treasurer and the 12 assistants existing in office shall continue in their respective offices until the first annual meeting to be held

after the commencement of this Order and shall, subject to the provisions of this Order, be eligible for election pursuant to the provisions of this Order.

Master, treasurer and assistants may be re-elected

11.—(1) The Master and the treasurer or either of them may be re-elected by the Company at the annual meeting in any year.

(2) The assistants may be re-elected by the Company at any annual meeting:

Provided that four assistants shall not be eligible for re-election as assistants, such four assistants to be determined by the Company in accordance with the rules.

Filling of vacancies among Master, treasurer and assistants

12.—(1) In the event of any vacancy occurring at any time among the Master, treasurer and assistants, the Company shall fill such vacancy within four months of its occurrence either at a stated general meeting of the Company or at a special general meeting of the Company to be called for that purpose.

(2) In the case of a vacancy occurring among the assistants, the person elected to fill such vacancy shall be placed at the bottom of the list of assistants.

D. Officials

Appointment of officials by Company

13.—(1) The Company may appoint and employ all such officials (including a secretary) as the Company may deem necessary for the carrying on of its business:

Provided that—

(a) all existing officials of the Company shall, until the first annual meeting of the Company to be held after the commencement of this Order, hold their respective offices on their respective existing terms and conditions; and

(b) no person shall be qualified to be appointed as actuary unless he is either a Fellow of the Faculty of Actuaries in Scotland or a Fellow of the Institute of Actuaries.

(2) The secretary shall be elected annually at the annual meeting.

Company may provide pensions, etc., for officials

14. The Company may grant to its officials such pensions and life assurance cover as it may deem appropriate, and may join with any institution connected with the Company, for the purpose of contributing to a superannuation fund for such officials, or make payment to an insurance company for a like purpose.

E. Fees, etc., payable by members

Entrance fees

15. Subject to the provisions of this Order, every person shall on his election pay to the Company such sum of entry money and age tax, if any, as may for the time being be fixed by the Company.

Election conditional on payment of entry money and other sums

16. Subject to the provisions of this Order, the election of any person as a member shall be conditional on his paying to the Company the entry money and other sums due from him under this Order and the rules, and a person

who has been elected as a member shall not be deemed to be a member or be entitled to any rights or privileges in virtue of his election until such entry money and other sums due have been paid and if these are not so paid within 12 months of the date of his election, his election and all that has followed thereon shall be null and void.

Powers of Company to vary entry money, etc.

17. The Company may after investigation into the state of the general fund increase or reduce the amount of the entry money and age tax or either of them payable by persons on election as members, provided that such increase or reduction is sanctioned by a resolution passed by a majority of the members present and voting at a stated general meeting of the Company.

Power to impose annual subscriptions, etc.

18. The Company may impose an annual subscription or special levy on members, provided that such imposition and the amount thereof and any variations to them are sanctioned by a resolution passed by a majority of the members present and voting at a stated general meeting of the Company.

F. Funds and property of Company

Application of funds of Company

19. The general fund shall be held by the Company and managed, administered and applied by the Master's court in the following manner:—

(1) for payment of the expenses of management of the Company (including payments authorised under section 14 (Company may provide pensions, etc., for officials) of this Order);
(2) for payment of allowances or annuities to indigent members;
(3) for the good and utility of the Company;
(4) for any other purpose to which the general fund may be lawfully applied in terms of the existing charters and this Order and the customs and usages of the Company; and
(5) for payment of any sums of money to be transferred to the widows' fund pursuant to section 21 (Power to contribute to widows' fund from general fund) of this Order.

Hall and offices of Company

20. The title to the area of ground on which are erected the buildings including the hall and offices of the Company known as 20 and 22 Hanover Street, Edinburgh together with the officer's house at 18 Hanover Street, Edinburgh shall continue to be vested in and held by the Company, subject to the interests in the said property of the institutions connected with the Company, and the Company may at any time, by the Master's court, sell, burden or let or otherwise dispose of the said property or any part thereof in such manner and at such times as the Company may think fit and direct.

Power to contribute to widows' fund from general fund

21. The Company may, from time to time after an investigation into the state of the general fund and having regard to the state of the widows' fund, transfer from the general fund to the widows' fund such sums of money as the Company may fix to be applied for any of the following purposes:—

(1) in meeting any deficiency reported as a result of a periodical actuarial investigation into the state of the widows' fund;
(2) in providing for an increase of the annuities payable to the beneficiaries of the widows' fund; or

(3) generally in aiding or benefiting the widows' fund:
Provided that—

(a) any such transfer shall be sanctioned by a resolution passed by a majority of the members present and voting at a special general meeting of the Company called for that purpose; and

(b) there shall remain in the general fund after any such transfer such funds as shall, in the opinion of the actuary and of the Company, be sufficient to meet the claims against the Company then existing or that may arise, including the ordinary expenses of the Company.

G. Meetings of Company

Stated general meetings of Company

22.—(1) The Company shall hold stated general meetings each year on—

(a) the first Thursday of October; and

(b) the second Thursday of November;

or such other dates as the Company may prescribe.

(2) The Company may hold additional general meetings on such dates as the Company may prescribe.

Special general meetings of Company

23.—(1) The Master or in his absence the treasurer may convene a special general meeting of the Company at any time when he deems it necessary.

(2) If a requisition for a special general meeting of the Company signed by not less than 9 of the members is addressed to the Master he shall upon receiving such requisition convene a special general meeting which shall be held within two weeks of such requisition being received:

Provided that in the absence of the Master the treasurer shall act, or in his absence any of the assistants shall act, in his place for the purposes of this subsection.

Mode of calling Company meetings

24.—(1) All meetings of the Company shall be called by notice issued by the secretary and posted at least 7 days before the date of the meeting.

(2) The Company may adjourn any meeting as it sees fit.

Chairman of meetings of Company

25. The Master, or in his absence the treasurer, or in his absence the senior assistant present, shall preside as chairman at all meetings of the Company:

Provided that in the absence of the Master, the treasurer and all the assistants a chairman shall be chosen for the meeting from among the members present.

Quorum of meetings of Company

26. At all meetings of the Company not less than 30 of the members shall constitute a quorum.

Voting at meetings of Company

27.—(1) When a vote is required to be taken at any meeting of the Company such vote shall, unless otherwise provided in this Order or by any rules, be taken by a show of hands.

(2) In the event of any such vote being challenged by two or more members present the members present shall thereupon appoint tellers who shall ascertain the vote.

(3) The chairman of the meeting shall, in all cases of equality of votes, have a casting vote in addition to any other vote he may have.

Company may make rules of procedure

28. The Company may at any general meeting make rules for the purpose of regulating the procedure to be followed in the nomination and election of the Master, treasurer and assistants:

Provided that such rules are not inconsistent with the provisions of this Order and that the nomination of the persons to be proposed for election to the office of Master, treasurer or assistants shall (subject to the provisions of section 10 (Election of Master, treasurer and assistants) of this Order) take place annually at the stated general meeting of the Company to be held on the first Thursday of October or such other date as the Company may prescribe in every year.

H. Miscellaneous

Company may make rules, etc.

29. The Company may at any general meeting make such rules for the regulation of the affairs of the Company as it deems expedient and in particular the Company may make rules and prescribe terms and conditions on which any annual subscription or special levy imposed in pursuance of the provisions of this Order, shall be payable, and may impose penalties (including forfeiture of all interest and benefit in the Company and provision for possible reinstatement following such forfeiture) on members who allow the payment of such subscription or levy to fall into arrear for more than three years:

Provided that such rules, terms, conditions and penalties shall not be inconsistent with the provisions of this Order.

PART III

MASTER'S COURT

Reconstitution of Master's court

30. The Master, the treasurer and the assistants shall be and are hereby reconstituted as "The Master's Court of the Company of Merchants of the City of Edinburgh" for the purpose of exercising the powers conferred and carrying out the duties imposed on the Master's court by this Order, and performing the functions prescribed by this Order with respect to the Master's court, and under the said name may exercise the said powers and shall carry out the said duties and perform the said functions accordingly and the provisions of this Order relating to the Master's court shall apply to the Master's court as constituted by this section.

Meetings of Master's court

31.—(1) Meetings of the Master's court shall be held as the Master's court may direct or, in the absence of any direction, as the Master or, in his absence, the treasurer may direct and all such meetings shall be called by notice issued by the secretary and posted at least 7 days before the date of meeting.

(2) The Master's court may adjourn any meeting as it may see fit.

Chairman of meetings of Master's court

32.—(1) The Master, or in his absence the treasurer, or in his absence the senior assistant present, shall preside as chairman at all meetings of the Master's court.

(2) The chairman of every meeting shall, in all cases of equality of votes, have a casting vote in addition to any other vote he may have.

Quorum of meetings of Master's court

33. At all meetings of the Master's court not less than five members thereof shall constitute a quorum in all matters with the exception of the ballot for the admission of members in which case not less than 8 members of the Master's court shall form a quorum.

Committees of Master's court

34. The Master's court may appoint committees of their number and convenors of such committees and may confer on such committees all such powers and give them such instructions as may appear to the Master's court expedient and shall fix the quorum of each such committee.

Proceedings of Master's court not to be invalidated by vacancies, etc.

35. Proceedings of the Master's court or of any committee thereof shall not be invalidated or be illegal in consequence of there being any vacancy in the membership of the Master's court at the time of such proceedings, or in respect of any informality in the election of any member thereof.

Duties of Master's court

36.—(1) The Master's court shall manage and administer the general fund which shall be invested by and in the name of the Master's court and applied by them in the manner provided in this Order.

(2) The Master's court shall also bring before the Company such business as it considers proper, and dispose of or make reports and recommendations as to all business referred to it by the Company, and perform such acts and duties as the existing charters, this Order and the customs and usages of the Company may authorise or as the Company may prescribe.

Accounts to be kept by Master's court and audited

37.—(1) The Master's court shall keep accounts of the general fund showing the income and expenditure and assets and liabilities thereof, to be made up each year to 1st September.

(2) The said accounts shall be audited by a registered auditor on behalf of the Company and approved by the Company at a general meeting.

(3) A copy of the abstract of the accounts of the Company shall be sent each year to each member resident in Great Britain.

Company officials to act as officials of Master's court

38. The secretary and the other officials of the Company shall, after the commencement of this Order, also hold office in their several capacities as secretary and officials of the Master's court.

PART IV

DARLING FUND

Vesting, etc., of Darling fund in Master's court

39. The Darling fund shall continue to be vested in the Master's court, and shall be held, managed and administered by the Master's court as trustees, in accordance with the provisions of this Part of this Order.

Payment of pensions out of Darling fund

40.—(1) The full income of the Darling fund shall after meeting the expenses of management, be applied by the Master's court in the provision of pensions to be known as "Alexander Darling Silk Mercer's Fund Pensions", of not less than £15 per annum to women qualified as hereinafter provided in this section, who are in the opinion of the Master's court in need.

(2) The women qualified to receive such pensions shall be women of 55 years of age and over, of good character, preferably unmarried or widowed and being—

(a) (i) gentlewomen born in the City of Edinburgh; or

(ii) gentlewomen who for the greater part of their lives have been resident in the City of Edinburgh; or

(iii) gentlewomen who are the widows of men born in the City of Edinburgh; or

(iv) gentlewomen who are the widows of men who for the greater part of their lives were resident in the City of Edinburgh:

Provided that the Master's court shall be the sole judges of who are to be deemed gentlewomen for the purposes of this subsection; and

(b) women who have been employed at any time within the City of Edinburgh in the manufacture or sale of any textile garments for ladies and children or such articles of apparel including, without prejudice to the foregoing generalities, millinery, furs, laces and silks as are usually dealt in by a ladies' silk mercer:

Provided that women who have been wholly concerned in the manufacture or sale of garments for men's wear shall not be so qualified.

(3) In so far as is possible, the number of pensions available shall be apportioned one-half to gentlewomen qualified as mentioned in paragraph (a) of subsection (2) of this section and one-half to women qualified as mentioned in paragraph (b) of subsection (2) of this section.

(4) In the allocation of pensions under this section preference shall be given to women bearing the surname Darling or Millar or Scott or Small and to women born in the town of Lanark:

Provided that all those so named or so born are to be given equal preference and that the order of narrating the qualifications for preference is not in any way indicative of any preference inter se.

(5) The Master's court shall not pay a pension out of the Darling fund to any woman so qualified who is eligible for any national old age pension or allowance if such payment would cause the reduction of such national old age pension or allowance by an amount equal to or more than the amount of the pension payable out of the Darling fund and accordingly in any such case the amount of the pension payable out of the Darling fund shall from time to time be modified so that there shall be no such reduction of such national old age pension or allowance.

PART V

WIDOWS' FUND

A. Maintenance of widows' fund

Maintenance of widows' fund

41. The Company shall, subject to the provisions of this Order, continue and maintain the widows' fund.

Closure of widows' fund to new contributors

42. From the commencement of this Order no person shall be admitted as a contributor to the widows' fund.

B. Contributors

Stated general meetings of contributors

43.—(1) The contributors shall hold a stated general meeting each year on the first Thursday of October or such other date as the contributors may prescribe.

(2) The contributors shall also hold a general meeting immediately after any general meeting (other than a special general meeting) of the Company.

Special general meetings of contributors

44.—(1) The Master or in his absence the Treasurer may convene a special general meeting of the contributors at any time when he deems it necessary.

(2) If a requisition for a special general meeting of the contributors, signed by not less than 9 contributors is addressed to the Master he shall upon receiving such requisition convene a special general meeting which shall be held within two weeks of such requisition being received:

Provided that in the absence of the Master the treasurer shall act, or in his absence any of the assistants shall act, in his place for the purposes of this subsection.

Mode of calling meetings of contributors

45.—(1) All meetings of the contributors shall be called by notice issued by the secretary and posted at least 7 days before the date of meeting.

(2) The contributors may adjourn any meeting as they see fit.

Chairman of meetings of contributors

46. The Master, or in his absence the treasurer, or in his absence the old Master, or in his absence the senior elected trustee present, shall preside as chairman at all meetings of the contributors:

Provided that in the absence of the Master, the treasurer, the old Master and all the elected trustees a chairman shall be chosen from among the contributors present.

Quorum of meetings of contributors

47. At all meetings of the contributors 25 contributors entitled to vote shall constitute a quorum provided that the quorum shall be reduced to not less than one-tenth of the contributors entitled to vote in the event of there being fewer than 240 contributors.

Voting at meetings of contributors

48.—(1) When a vote is required to be taken at any meeting of the contributors, such vote shall, unless otherwise provided in this Order, be taken by a show of hands.

(2) In the event of any such vote being challenged by two or more contributors present, the contributors present at the meeting shall appoint tellers who shall ascertain the vote.

(3) A contributor whose contributions, or any part thereof, are at the date of the meeting in arrear shall not be entitled to vote.

(4) The chairman of the meeting shall, in all cases of equality of votes, have a casting vote in addition to any other vote he may have.

Appointment of officials by contributors

49. The contributors may appoint and employ all such officials as they may deem necessary for the carrying on of the business of the widows' fund:

Provided that—
(a) all existing officials appointed and employed by the contributors shall, until the first general meeting of the contributors to be held after the commencement of this Order, hold their respective offices on their respective existing terms and conditions; and
(b) the secretary shall also be secretary to the contributors.

Contributors may provide pensions, etc., for officials

50. The contributors may grant to their officials such pensions and life assurance cover as they may deem appropriate, and may join with the Company or any institution connected therewith, for the purpose of contributing to a superannuation fund for such officials, or make payment to an insurance company for a like purpose.

Contributors may make rules

51. The contributors may at any general meeting make such rules for the regulation of the affairs of the widows' fund as they deem expedient:

Provided that such rules shall not be inconsistent with the provisions of this Order.

C. Powers of widows' fund

Powers of trustees of widows' fund

52. The trustees of the widows' fund shall continue in being under the name of "The Trustees of the Widows' Fund of the Company of Merchants of the City of Edinburgh", as a body corporate with perpetual succession and a common seal; and with power to purchase, acquire, hold, sell, lease and dispose of lands and other property heritable, moveable, real and personal, and to sue and be sued, and with all other rights, powers and privileges of a body corporate.

Constitution of trustees of widows' fund

53.—(1) The trustees shall be 9 in number as follows:—
(a) the Master for the time being ex-officio;
(b) the treasurer for the time being ex-officio;
(c) the old Master for the time being ex-officio; and
(d) six persons to be elected annually by the contributors from amongst their number at the stated general meeting of the contributors held each year on the first Thursday of October or such other date as the contributors may prescribe.

(2) The existing trustees shall, subject to the provisions of this Order, continue in office until the expiry of their respective periods of office.

Elected trustees' eligibility for re-election

54.—(1) The trustee whose name at the time stands at the head of the list of the trustees elected by the contributors, shall not be eligible for re-election.

(2) The remaining five elected trustees shall be eligible for re-election.

Filling of vacancies among trustees

55. In the event of any vacancy occurring at any time among the elected trustees, the contributors shall fill such vacancy within four months of its occurrence either at a stated general meeting of the contributors or at a special general meeting of the contributors to be called for that purpose and the person elected to fill such vacancy shall be placed at the bottom of the list of elected trustees.

Stated general meetings of trustees

56.—(1) The trustees shall hold stated general meetings each year on—

(a) the fourth Thursday of April; and

(b) the fourth Thursday of October;

or such other dates as the trustees may prescribe.

(2) The trustees may hold additional general meetings on such dates as they may prescribe.

Special general meetings of trustees

57. The Master, or in his absence the treasurer, may convene a special general meeting of the trustees at any time when he deems it necessary.

Mode of calling meetings of trustees

58.—(1) All meetings of the trustees shall be called by notice issued by the secretary and posted at least 7 days before the date of meeting.

(2) The trustees may adjourn any meeting as they see fit.

Chairman of meetings of trustees

59.—(1) The Master or, in his absence the treasurer, or in his absence the old Master, or in his absence the senior elected trustee present, shall preside as chairman at all meetings of the trustees.

(2) The chairman of the meeting shall, in all cases of equality of votes, have a casting vote in addition to any other vote he may have.

Quorum of meetings of trustees

60. At all meetings of the trustees not less than three of them shall constitute a quorum in all matters.

Committees of trustees

61. The trustees may appoint committees of their number and convenors of such committees and may confer on such committees all such powers and give them such instructions as may appear to the trustees expedient and shall fix the quorum of each such committee.

Proceedings of trustees not to be invalidated by vacancies, etc.

62. Proceedings of the trustees or of any committee of the trustees shall not be invalidated in consequence of there being any vacancy in their membership at the time of such proceedings or in respect of any informality in the constitution or election of any of them.

Widows' fund to be managed and administered by trustees

63. The widows' fund shall be held, managed, administered and applied by the trustees in the following manner:—

(a) for payment of the expenses of management of the widows' fund (including payments authorised under section 50 (Contributors may provide pensions, etc., for officials) of this Order);

(b) for payment of annuities to the widows of contributors;

(c) for payment of annuities or benefits to such new class or classes of beneficiaries as may be created in pursuance of section 83 (Power to introduce new classes of beneficiaries) of this Order;

(d) for refund of payments in pursuance of section 71 (Contributors may refund payments) of this Order;

(e) for refund of payments made by female contributors who, at the commencement of this Order, were married to a contributor; and

(f) for the purchase of annuities for existing annuitants.

Distribution of widows' fund

64. The trustees may distribute the remainder of the widows' fund (after deducting outstanding expenses and liabilities of whatever kind) among the contributors for the time being pro rata to the level of their contributions, or in some such other equitable manner as shall be decided at his sole discretion by the actuary:

Provided that such distribution has been sanctioned by a resolution passed by at least two-thirds of the contributors present and voting at a general meeting or special general meeting of the contributors.

Accounts of widows' fund to be kept by trustees and audited

65.—(1) The trustees shall keep accounts of the widows' fund showing the income and expenditure and assets and liabilities thereof, to be made up each year to 1st September.

(2) The said accounts shall be audited by a registered auditor on behalf of the contributors and shall thereafter be examined by the trustees, and shall be laid before the contributors at the general meeting of the contributors held on the second Thursday of November or such other date as the contributors may prescribe.

(3) A copy of the abstract of the accounts of the widows' fund shall be sent each year to each contributor resident in Great Britain.

D. Payments, etc., by contributors

Payment of annual contributions

66.—(1) The annual contributions of all existing contributors shall continue to be payable in accordance with the existing provisions.

(2) Any contributor may elect to cease to make contributions in which case he, or any widow left by him, shall (without the need for any declarator) forfeit all right, interest and benefit in the widows' fund:

Provided that all the rights, interest and benefit of any widow shall be reinstated if she shall pay up the arrears due by her husband together with all interest thereon at the rate of five per cent over the Bank of Scotland plc's base rate from the time each payment fell due and any costs that may have been incurred in recovering the same.

Payment of half-yearly contributions and annuities by instalments

67. The contributors may permit the half-yearly contributions to the widows' fund, and the half-yearly payments of annuities to be paid in such instalments at such times and on such conditions as the actuary may recommend.

Contributors may alter amount of half-yearly contributions

68.—(1) The contributors, after an investigation by the actuary into the state of the widows' fund, may alter the amount of the half-yearly contributions payable to the widows' fund:

Provided that such alteration is sanctioned by a resolution passed by a majority of the contributors present and voting at a special general meeting of the contributors called for the purpose.

(2) Any alterations made by the contributors under this section may be wholly in respect of the half-yearly contributions or may be in the number of contributions or partly by all or any of such methods and in such proportions as the contributors may deem most expedient.

Redemption of half-yearly contributions

69. Every contributor may at any term of Whitsunday or Martinmas, having given one month's notice in writing to the secretary, redeem in whole or in part the half-yearly contributions payable by him, or such part thereof as may then remain unpaid, by making payment to the widows' fund of such sum as may be fixed by the actuary.

Half-yearly contributions not to be payable after death of married contributors

70. The half-yearly contributions of a contributor who is married and who dies before having paid all his contributions to the widows' fund, which would, but for the provisions of this section, fall due subsequent to the date of death of such contributor shall not be payable.

Contributors may refund payments

71. The contributors may resolve to refund in whole or in part to the representatives of deceased contributors any payments made by such contributors to the widows' fund.

Contributor may discontinue payment of half-yearly contributions on death of wife

72.—(1) A contributor who is married may, in the event of his wife predeceasing him, elect to continue to pay his half-yearly contributions, but in the event of his remarriage, he shall pay in respect of such marriage, any marriage tax prescribed by this Order with the half-yearly contribution which falls to be paid at the first term of Whitsunday or Martinmas following upon his remarriage.

(2) A contributor who is married may, in the event of his wife predeceasing him before he has paid all the half-yearly contributions due by him, suspend the payment of his half-yearly contributions to the widows' fund; but in the event of his remarriage if he wishes to benefit from the widows' fund, he shall—

(a) pay in respect of such marriage the following:—

(i) any marriage tax prescribed by this Order; and

(ii) all accumulated arrears of half-yearly contributions from the date of such suspension, with compound interest at such rate as may be fixed by the actuary; and

(b) thereafter resume payment of half-yearly contributions in the sum calculated by the actuary as being appropriate to his age at his next birthday until he has made two half-yearly payments for the number of years equal to the difference between his age at his next birthday following the resumption of payment and the age of 65 or such other date as may have been fixed by the contributors prior to the resumption of payment.

Marriage tax payable on marriage after election

73. Every contributor who marries or remarries, and whose age exceeds that of his wife by more than five years, shall pay to the widows' fund in respect of each such marriage, the marriage tax appropriate to his age at his next birthday following such marriage calculated by the actuary.

Times of payment of marriage tax

74. The marriage tax shall in the case of contributors who marry or remarry be payable at the first term of Whitsunday or Martinmas after their respective marriages.

Alterations of marriage tax

75. No alteration shall be made to the amount of the marriage tax payable to the widows' fund unless such alteration has been prepared by the actuary and approved by the contributors.

Particulars of marriage, etc., to be provided by contributors

76.—(1) Every contributor who marries shall, within three months after such marriage, provide the secretary with such evidence of marriage and birth as may be satisfactory to the trustees.

(2) If any contributor dies before having provided the secretary with such evidence of his marriage the widow of such contributor shall have no right or title to any benefit from the widows' fund:

Provided that the contributors may at any general meeting of the contributors grant to such widow such relief as they shall think fit.

Penalty for failure to pay half-yearly contributions

77. If any contributor allows any of the half-yearly contributions payable by him to fall into arrear for three years after the same first became due, he or any widow left by him shall (without the necessity for any declarator) forfeit all right, interest and benefit in the widows' fund:

Provided that the contributors may at any general meeting of the contributors reinstate any such contributor or his widow subject (in the case of a contributor) to his paying up the arrears due by him together with all interest thereon at the rate of five per cent over the Bank of Scotland plc's base rate from the time each payment falls due and any costs that may have been incurred in recovering the same or (in the case of a widow) to payment of the said arrears and other moneys due in accordance with the provisions of this Order.

Interest on payments in arrear

78. All payments to the widows' fund and all penalties imposed by this Order (if incurred) shall subject to the provisions of this Order bear interest at the rate of five per cent over the Bank of Scotland plc's base rate from time to time from the respective dates on which they are due until paid.

As to payment of half-yearly contributions, etc., of deceased contributors

79.—(1) If any contributor dies owing any money to the widows' fund, his widow shall not be entitled to receive an annuity until the sums owing together with interest have been paid:

Provided that the trustees may accept payment by deducting such sums and interest owing from the annuity by such instalments and at such times as they may think fit.

(2) The trustees (or the widow of such contributor who pays the sums owing) may take all competent legal action for recovering the same out of the estate of such contributor.

E. Payment of annuities

Payment of annuities to widows

80.—(1) There shall be paid out of the widows' fund to every existing widow who is entitled to an annuity, and to the widow of every contributor who, at the time of his death, may have an interest in the widows' fund and be entitled to the benefit thereof for his widow, such annuity as may from time to time be fixed by the contributors in pursuance of the provisions of this Order.

(2) The said annuities shall be paid at the terms of Whitsunday and Martinmas in equal portions.

(3) In the case of any annuity accruing to a widow after the commencement of this Order payment shall be made, at the first term of Whitsunday or Martinmas after her husband's death, of the proportion of the annuity corresponding to the time from the death of the husband to the first date of payment.

(4) The annuity of every widow entitled to an annuity shall continue to be paid during all her life, whether she remains a widow or marries again, and such proportion of the annuity as may be due at her death shall be paid to her legal representatives.

More than one annuity payable to widows

81. If the widow of any contributor marries another contributor and afterwards again becomes a widow she shall be entitled to an annuity in respect of each such marriage subject to the provisions of this Order.

Annuities to be alimentary

82. The annuities payable in accordance with the provisions of this Order shall be deemed to be alimentary and shall not be assignable by them or liable to be arrested or otherwise affected or attached by their creditors but shall be payable to each widow entitled to the same upon her own receipt, notwithstanding any assignation, arrestment or attachment, and such receipt shall sufficiently exonerate the trustees.

Power to introduce new classes of beneficiaries

83. The contributors may after a report by the actuary following an actuarial investigation, resolve to introduce a new class or classes of beneficiaries consisting of the minor orphan children of contributors or of certain classes of such children and may make such rules regarding such new classes of beneficiaries (including the amount of benefit which such beneficiaries may receive) as they deem necessary and such rules shall, unless and until altered by the contributors, have the same force and effect as if they had been enacted by this Order.

Rate of annuity to continue until altered

84. In the event of an alteration being made in the rate of the annuity payable under the provisions of this Order, the rate of annuity as so altered shall be and shall continue to be from and after the date of such alteration and until the rate of annuity is again altered (if any such further alteration be deemed necessary or expedient) the rate of payment of all the annuities payable out of the widows' fund.

F. Alteration of amount of annuities

Periodical investigation of widows' fund

85.—(1) The actuary shall make periodical investigations into the state of the widows' fund and its adequacy for payment of the annuities charged and that may become charged thereon and the circumstances connected therewith.

(2) The first investigation to be made under this Order shall be made at such date as shall be fixed by the contributors not being later than 1st September 1997 notwithstanding the date of the commencement of this Order and

such investigations shall thereafter be made at such intervals as shall be fixed by the contributors from time to time but not more than 7 years shall elapse between any two investigations.

Contributors may alter amount of annuity

86. The contributors may after any investigation into the state of the widows' fund resolve, subject to the provisions of this Order, that the amount of annuity which may be payable should for the time being—

(a) not be altered; or
(b) be increased; or
(c) be reduced;

and the contributors shall fix the amount of any such increase or reduction.

Conditions of increase of annuity

87. Subject to the provisions of this Order, an increase of the amount of annuity shall not be made unless—

(a) the actuary certifies that the value of the annuities at the increased rate payable to the widows then on the widows' fund, and which may become payable to the widows of the then existing contributors, together with an allowance for expenses and other liabilities, does not exceed the amount of the fund in hand (including any sums transferred or agreed to be transferred to the widows' fund from the general fund under the provisions of this Order) together with the value of the future contributions of the then existing contributors; and
(b) the increase is sanctioned by a resolution passed by a majority of the contributors present and voting at a special general meeting of the contributors called for that purpose.

Conditions of reduction of annuity

88. Subject to the provisions of this Order, a reduction of the amount of annuity shall not be made unless—

(a) the actuary reports that the amount of the fund in hand (including any sums transferred or agreed to be transferred to the widows' fund from the general fund under the provisions of this Order) together with the value of the future contributions of the then existing contributors is less than the value of the annuities payable to widows then on the widows' fund, and which may become payable to the widows of the then existing contributors, together with an allowance for expenses and other liabilities; and
(b) the actuary certifies that the amount of the reduction which is proposed to be made is necessary to place the widows' fund in a state of solvency; and
(c) the reduction is sanctioned by a resolution passed by a majority of the contributors present at a special general meeting of the contributors called for that purpose.

G. Dissolution of widows' fund

Purchase of annuities

89.—(1) At any time the trustees may, subject to a resolution passed by at least two-thirds of the contributors present and voting at a general meeting or special general meeting of the contributors, (but when there are less than 20 surviving annuitants the trustees shall)—

(a) purchase annuities for such surviving annuitants as the actuary shall in his sole discretion recommend; and
(b) out of the widows' fund, purchase from a life assurance company (being a member of the Association of British Insurers) and hold in

respect of spouses of existing contributors a deferred annuity so that the income may be paid to the surviving spouse on the death of the contributor.

(2) A deferred annuity purchased in respect of any contributor shall be in such sum as the actuary shall in his sole discretion recommend.

Application of residue of widows' fund

90.—(1) After they have fulfilled all their obligations under this Order or otherwise, the trustees may at any time in their absolute discretion invest the residue of the widows' fund or any part thereof (not being moneys forming part of any annuity or deferred annuity purchased by them) or pay the same or any part thereof to the endowments trust or such other charitable trust managed by the Company as the trustees in their absolute discretion shall determine.

(2) Upon the death of the last annuitant, and provided that at that date no person may yet come to be an annuitant, or upon it subsequently appearing that no person may yet come to be an annuitant, the trustees shall transfer the residue of the widows' fund to the endowments trust or such other charitable trust managed by the Company as shall be determined by the Company at a general meeting.

Widows' fund to be dissolved

91.—(1) Upon completion of the transfer of the residue of the fund in pursuance of section 90 (Application of residue of widows' fund) of this Order the widows' fund shall be dissolved:

Provided that such dissolution has been sanctioned by a resolution passed by a majority of the trustees.

(2) Notice of the passing of such resolution and of the date therein specified shall, as soon as may be after the passing thereof, be advertised in the Edinburgh Gazette.

PART VI

ENDOWMENTS TRUST

A. Incorporation powers, etc., of endowments trust

Powers of endowments trust

92. The former Merchant Company Endowments Trust incorporated by the Act of 1960, shall continue in being under the same name, as a body corporate with perpetual succession and a common seal; and with power to purchase, acquire, hold, sell, lease and dispose of lands and other property heritable, moveable, real and personal, to sue and be sued, and with all other rights, powers and privileges of a body corporate.

Endowments trust fund vested in endowments trust

93. The existing endowments trust fund shall, subject to the debts, liabilities, contracts and obligations affecting the same, continue to be vested in the endowments trust and shall be held, used and disposed of by the endowments trust for the purposes of and in accordance with the provisions of this Order.

Constitution of endowments trust

94.—(1) The endowments trust shall consist of 24 members as follows:—

(a) the Master, the treasurer and the 12 assistants of the Company for the time being ex-officio;

(b) five members of, and to be elected by, the council for the City of Edinburgh;

(c) two ministers of the Edinburgh Presbytery of the Church of Scotland to be elected by the said Presbytery; and

(d) three persons to be elected by the Company from among the members.

(2) The existing members of the endowments trust shall, subject to the provisions of this Order, continue in office until the second Thursday of November first occurring after the commencement of this Order.

Election and period of office of members of endowments trust

95.—(1) The election of the elected members of the endowments trust shall take place annually at any general meeting of the Company in October or November:

Provided that the election shall not take place after the date of the annual meeting from which date the elected members shall hold office until the following annual meeting.

(2) Any member of the endowments trust, upon the expiry of his term of office, shall be eligible for re-election if otherwise qualified under this Order.

Filling of vacancies among elected members of endowments trust

96. In the event of any vacancy occurring among the elected members of the endowments trust at any time the body which elected the person whose office has become vacant shall elect another person to fill such vacancy at a meeting of such electing body to be held within six weeks of such vacancy occurring and the person so elected shall, subject to the provisions of this Order, hold office during the unexpired portion of the period of office of the person in whose place he has been elected.

Meetings of endowments trust

97.—(1) Meetings of the endowments trust shall be held as the endowments trust may direct or, in the absence of any direction, as the Master, or in his absence, the treasurer, may direct and all such meetings shall be called by notice issued by the secretary and posted at least 7 days before the date of meeting.

(2) The endowments trust may adjourn any meeting as they see fit.

Chairman of endowments trust

98.—(1) The Master, or in his absence the treasurer, shall preside as chairman at all meetings of the endowments trust:

Provided that in the absence of the Master and the treasurer, a chairman shall be chosen from among the members of the endowments trust present.

(2) The chairman of the meeting shall, in all cases of equality of votes, have a casting vote in addition to any other he may have.

Quorum of meetings of endowments trust

99. At all meetings of the endowments trust not less than 10 members thereof shall constitute a quorum.

Committees of endowments trust

100. The endowments trust may, subject to the provisions of this Order, appoint committees and convenors of such committees and may confer on such committees such powers and give them all such instructions as may appear to the endowments trust expedient and shall fix the quorum of each such committee.

Proceedings of endowments trust not to be invalidated by vacancies, etc.

101. Proceedings of the endowments trust or any committee thereof shall not be invalidated in consequence of there being any vacancy in their membership at the time of such proceedings or in respect of any informality in the election of any of the elected members thereof.

Appointment of officials by endowments trust

102.—(1) The endowments trust may appoint and employ all such officials as they may deem necessary for carrying on of their business:

Provided that—

(a) all existing officials appointed and employed by the endowments trust shall continue to hold their respective offices on their respective terms and conditions; and

(b) the secretary shall also be secretary to the endowments trust.

(2) All the officials appointed and employed by the endowments trust shall hold their respective offices at the pleasure of the endowments trust.

Endowments trust may provide pensions, etc., for officials

103. The endowments trust may grant to their officials such pensions and life assurance cover as they may deem appropriate, and may join with the Company or any institution connected therewith, for the purpose of contributing to a superannuation fund for such officials, or make payment to an insurance company for a like purpose.

Application of income of endowments trust fund

104. Subject to the provisions of this Order, the free income of the endowments trust fund shall, after meeting the expenses of management (including payments authorised under section 103 (Endowments trust may provide pensions, etc., for officials) of this Order), be applied in the payment of annual pensions or gifts of money, and in providing (by way of gift, loan or on partial or full repayment) lodging, clothing, food, fuel, furnishings or other benefits to persons who are qualified as hereinafter mentioned in this Order to receive such benefits.

Power of endowments trust to borrow

105. The endowments trust may borrow or expend capital for the purposes of this Part of this Order (to which capital may properly be applied).

Reserve fund of endowments trust

106.—(1) The endowments trust may maintain a reserve fund by setting aside out of the revenue of the endowments trust fund such sums as they think fit.

(2) The reserve fund shall be applied by the endowments trust in such way and manner as they deem expedient for the benefit of the endowments trust fund and (inter alia) towards meeting—

(a) the excess of expenditure over revenue of the endowments trust fund occurring at the close of any financial year as ascertained by the registered auditor of the endowments trust for the time being;

(b) the losses which may be sustained by the endowments trust fund through the depreciation of securities or insolvency of debtors; and

(c) extraordinary expenditure on lands and buildings forming part of the endowments trust fund.

Accounts to be kept by endowments trust and audited

107.—(1) The endowments trust shall keep accounts of the endowments trust fund showing the income and expenditure and assets and liabilities thereof, to be made up to a date to be fixed by the endowments trust.

(2) The said accounts shall be audited by a registered auditor on behalf of the endowments trust.

(3) A copy of the abstract of the accounts of the endowments trust shall be sent each year to each member of the endowments trust resident in Great Britain.

B. Payments, etc., to beneficiaries

Classes of beneficiaries

108. The classes of persons qualified to be beneficiaries shall be—

(a) decent, peaceable and indigent men and women aged at least 55 on 1st July in the year of election (unless they are certified on medical grounds as being unable to earn their living) who are—

(i) members not exceeding 10 in number at any one time;

(ii) persons who have lived or worked in the City of Edinburgh;

(iii) persons who have lived or worked in Midlothian generally (excepting the City of Edinburgh):

Provided that in classes (ii) and (iii) preference shall be given to persons of the name of Gillespie or Gibb or Heriot and to those who have been connected with the building trade in the City of Edinburgh;

(b) persons qualified to occupy the Sir William Fraser Homes in accordance with the provisions of this Order.

Minimum amount and terms of pensions

109. Each pension from the endowments trust fund shall be not less than £10 per annum, and shall be payable in advance at such times as the endowments trust may decide to the beneficiary or to such other person as the endowments trust may from time to time determine to be applied for behoof of the beneficiary.

Endowments trust may provide houses, etc., for beneficiaries

110.—(1) The endowments trust may build, purchase, lease, alter and maintain and may fit up and furnish, wholly or partly houses, flats or other buildings, for the accommodation of beneficiaries, and may allow such beneficiaries in lieu of or in addition to the payment of their pension to occupy such houses, flats or other buildings during the pleasure of the endowments trust, or may enter into an arrangement with any other organisation having similar objects.

(2) The endowments trust may employ such persons as the endowments trust may consider necessary to assist and advise the beneficiaries.

(3) The endowments trust may defray all expenditure incurred by them, in the exercise of the powers conferred on them by this section, out of the endowments trust fund.

(4) The endowments trust may apply any money borrowed by them in the exercise of their powers, to the building or purchase of houses, flats or other buildings for the accommodation of beneficiaries or for any purpose connected therewith (to which capital may properly be applied).

Election of beneficiaries

111.—(1) The endowments trust shall, annually on a date or dates to be fixed by them, elect the number of beneficiaries for which in the opinion of the endowments trust the free income of the endowments trust fund will provide and shall determine the benefits which each beneficiary may receive during the ensuing year or such shorter period as the endowments trust may determine.

(2) Beneficiaries shall be designated Gillespie pensioners or Watherston donees or Gibb and Heriot pensioners as the endowments trust may decide when the beneficiary is elected.

Applications for pensions, etc.

112.—(1) The endowments trust shall, on request, issue to potential applicants for a pension or other benefit, a form of application with a schedule appended containing particulars of the information, certificates and documents required in support of their application.

(2) Every application shall be made on the form so supplied and shall be lodged with the endowments trust along with the required documents.

C. Fraser Trust

Definitions for purposes of Head C

113. For the purposes of this Head of this Part of this Order—

(a) "deed of directions" means the deed of directions executed by Sir William Fraser K.C.B., LL.D., pursuant to the Fraser trust disposition and dated 11th December 1896 and registered in the Books of Council and Session 22nd March 1898;

(b) "Fraser trust disposition" means the trust disposition and deed of settlement of the said Sir William Fraser dated 10th December 1896 and registered in the Books of Council and Session 22nd March 1898;

(c) "Fraser trustees" means the trustees for the time being of the Fraser trust disposition.

Sir William Fraser Homes to be maintained

114.—(1) The endowments trust shall maintain the property known as, and which shall continue to be known as, the Sir William Fraser Homes for occupation by the persons qualified in accordance with the provisions of this Head of this Part of this Order.

(2) The endowments trust may employ such staff as shall be deemed necessary for the proper maintenance of such homes and for the assistance of the occupants of such homes.

(3) The endowments trust may defray all expenditure incurred by them, in the exercise of the powers conferred on them by this section, out of the endowments trust fund.

(4) The endowments trust may apply any money borrowed by them towards the repair and rebuilding of such homes and in payment of any expenditure connected therewith, to which capital may properly be applied.

Qualifications of persons to occupy Sir William Fraser Homes

115. The classes of persons qualified to occupy the Sir William Fraser Homes shall be—

(a) poor persons resident in the City of Edinburgh or Midlothian who, in the opinion of the endowments trust and of the Fraser trustees, are of satisfactory character, preference being given to authors and artists otherwise qualified under this paragraph; and

(b) persons qualified to be beneficiaries of the endowments trust in accordance with the provisions of this Part of this Order.

Election of occupants

116.—(1) Vacancies arising in respect of occupants of the Sir William Fraser Homes appointed by the Fraser trustees shall be filled by the Fraser trustees provided that if they fail to fill such vacancy within six months of its arising the vacancy may be filled by the endowments trust. All other vacancies shall be filled by the endowments trust.

(2) The endowments trust shall before the election of any persons as occupants of the Sir William Fraser Homes consult with the Fraser trustees, and the Fraser trustees shall be entitled to receive due notice of and to attend and vote at any meeting of the endowments trust called for the purpose of electing such occupants.

Rights of occupants of Sir William Fraser Homes

117.—(1) The endowments trust may transfer the occupants of any house, whether elected before or after the commencement of this Order to any other house, in conformity with any scheme of division of the houses agreed between the Fraser trustees and the endowments trust:

Provided that an occupant elected by the Fraser trustees shall not be so transferred without the consent of the Fraser trustees.

(2) Occupants shall occupy the houses allocated to them during the pleasure of the endowments trust:

Provided the right of occupancy of any occupant elected by the Fraser trustees may not be terminated without the consent of the Fraser trustees.

(3) For the purposes of this section "house" means any house forming part of the Sir William Fraser Homes.

Constitution of Fraser trustees

118. For the purposes of this Head of this Part of this Order—

(a) the existing Fraser trustees shall continue to be Fraser trustees;

(b) the Lord Lyon King of Arms for the time being or his nominee shall be an ex officio Fraser trustee and the Sir William Fraser Professor of Ancient History and Palaeography for the time being in the University of Edinburgh or his nominee shall be an ex officio Fraser trustee;

(c) the Fraser trustees may from time to time appoint not more than one additional trustee to act with them, but so that there shall not at any one time be more than three Fraser trustees.

Fraser trustees to be members of committees to administer Sir William Fraser Homes

119. The Fraser trustees shall be members of any committee which may be appointed by the endowments trust to deal with the management and administration of the Sir William Fraser Homes. Such committee may, subject to the provisions of section 117 (Rights of occupants of Sir William Fraser Homes) of this Order, allocate the houses to be occupied by persons elected by the Fraser trustees and by the endowments trust respectively.

Application of funds retained by Fraser trustees

120. The Fraser trustees shall retain the existing assets held by them and shall apply the capital and income thereof in accordance with the deed of directions and the Fraser trust disposition including, without prejudice to the above generality, the decoration and internal improvement of the houses occupied by persons elected by the Fraser trustees.

Fraser trustees may transfer remaining assets to endowments trust

121. The Fraser trustees may at any time resolve to transfer, in whole or in part, to the endowments trust the remaining assets vested in them as the Fraser trustees.

D. Russell and Foster Endowment

Russell and Foster Endowment vested in endowments trust

122. All the lands, property, estate and securities forming the residue (together with the surplus income accumulated thereto) of the estate of the late Henry Walker Russell, held by and due to the trustees acting under his will dated 30th April 1948 and relative codicil registered in the Books of Council and Session 13th November 1954, shall, on the expiry of the last annuity payable in terms of the said will, continue to be vested in the endowments trust, and shall be held, managed and administered by the endowments trust in accordance with the provisions of this Order as a separate fund to be known as the "Russell and Foster Endowment".

Income of Russell and Foster Endowment to be applied in payment of pensions

123. Subject to the provisions of this Part of this Order the free income of the Russell and Foster Endowment shall, after meeting the expenses of management thereof, be applied by the endowments trust in the payment of annual pensions to persons qualified as hereinafter mentioned in this Order to receive such pensions.

Qualifications of Russell and Foster pensioners

124.—(1) The persons qualified to be beneficiaries of the Russell and Foster Endowment shall be respectable indigent Protestant men and women aged at least 55 at the date of their election, unless they are certified on medical grounds as being unable to earn their living, and who are resident in any part of Great Britain.

(2) The endowments trust shall be the sole judges of who are to be deemed respectable for the purposes of this section.

Amount, etc., of Russell and Foster pensions

125. Each pension to be paid by the endowments trust from the Russell and Foster Endowment shall be not less than £15 per annum, and shall be payable in advance at such times as the endowments trust may decide to the beneficiary or to such other person as the endowments trust may from time to time determine, to be applied for behoof of the beneficiary.

Designation of Russell and Foster beneficiaries

126. Beneficiaries under the Russell and Foster Endowment shall be designated Russell and Foster pensioners.

E. Variation of Trusts

Variation of trusts

127. In the event that the endowments trust or the Fraser trustees wish to vary or revoke all or any of the terms of the Russell and Foster Endowment or the Fraser trust disposition, as the case may be, or enlarge the powers of the trustees of managing or administering any of the property subject to the said trusts, the endowments trust or the Fraser trustees, as the case may be, may apply to the Court of Session by Petition for an Order of the Court for such variation, revocation or enlargement.

Part VII

Joint committee

Re-establishment of joint committee

128.—(1) The Merchant Company Joint Committee, as established by the Act of 1960, shall be and is hereby re-established under the same name.

(2) The joint committee shall consist of 9 members constituted and elected as follows:—

(a) the Master ex-officio;
(b) the treasurer ex-officio;
(c) one member to be elected by the Master's court from their number on behalf of the Company;
(d) one member to be elected by the trustees from their number on behalf of the contributors;
(e) three members to be elected by the education board from their number on behalf of the education board;
(f) two members to be elected by the endowments trust from their number on behalf of the endowments trust.

(3) The existing elected members of the joint committee shall continue in office until the date of the annual meeting first following the commencement of this Order.

Election and period of office of members of joint committee

129.—(1) The election of the elected members of the joint committee shall take place annually before the date of the annual meeting from which date the elected members shall hold office until the following annual meeting.

(2) Any member of the joint committee shall be eligible for re-election if otherwise qualified under this Order.

Filling of vacancies in joint committee

130. In the event of any vacancy occurring among the elected members of the joint committee at any time the body which elected the person whose office has become vacant shall fill such vacancy at the next stated meeting of such body or at a special meeting called for the purpose and the person so elected shall, subject to the provisions of this Order, hold office during the unexpired portion of the period of office of the person in whose place he has been elected.

Meetings of joint committee

131.—(1) Meetings of the joint committee shall be held as the joint committee may direct or, in the absence of any direction, as the Master, or in his absence, the treasurer, may direct and all such meetings shall be called by notice issued by the secretary and posted at least 7 days before the date of meeting.

(2) The joint committee may adjourn any of its meetings as it sees fit.

Chairman of joint committee

132.—(1) The Master or, in his absence the treasurer, shall preside as chairman of the joint committee:

Provided that in the absence of the Master and the treasurer, a chairman shall be chosen for the time from among the members of the joint committee present.

(2) The chairman of the meeting shall, in all cases of equality of votes, have a casting vote in addition to any other vote he may have.

Quorum of meetings of joint committee

133. At all meetings of the joint committee not less than three members thereof shall constitute a quorum.

Proceedings of joint committee not to be invalidated by vacancies, etc.

134. Proceedings of the joint committee shall not be invalidated in consequence of there being any vacancy in its membership at the time of such proceedings or in respect of any informality in the election of any of the elected members thereof.

Powers of joint committee

135.—(1) The joint committee may act for the purpose of transacting and disposing of any business common to the Company, the widows' fund, the education board and the endowments trust including, without prejudice to the foregoing generality—

(a) the expenses of management and the allocation of these expenses among the Company, the widows' fund, the education board and the endowments trust;

(b) the making of contracts;

(c) the apportionment of the accommodation required for the various departments in the office of the Company;

(d) the appointment, suspension and dismissal of employees (as opposed to office-holders);

(e) the fixing of the terms of appointment of any officials and any alterations thereof;

(f) the fixing of the rate of interest to be charged and paid from time to time on loans granted by any one of the Company, the widows' fund, the education board or the endowments trust respectively to any other of the Company, the widows' fund, the education board or the endowments trust respectively or granted from any of the funds under the management of either the education board or the endowments trust to any other of the said funds; and

(g) the consideration of reports upon all other matters which may be remitted to the joint committee.

(2) The joint committee may make such rules and orders for conducting its business as it may deem expedient:

Provided that such rules shall not be inconsistent with the provisions of this Order.

PART VIII

MISCELLANEOUS AND GENERAL

Execution of deeds

136. All deeds and other instruments requiring to be executed by the Company, the Master's court, the trustees, the endowments trust or the joint committee shall be validly executed if subscribed—

(a) in the case of the Company (either with or without the common seal of the Company being impressed) by any one of the Master, treasurer or assistants and by the secretary;

(b) in the case of the Master's court by any one of the Master, treasurer or assistants and by the secretary;
(c) in the case of the trustees (either with or without the common seal of the trustees being impressed) by any one of the trustees and by the secretary;
(d) in the case of the endowments trust (either with or without the common seal of the endowments trust being impressed) by any one of the members of the endowments trust and by the secretary; and
(e) in the case of the joint committee by any one of the members of the joint committee and by the secretary:

Provided that in the absence of the secretary any such deed or instrument may be signed by any other official appointed for the purpose by the body by which such deed or instrument is to be executed.

Powers of investment

137.—(1) The funds of the Company (which shall include the widows' fund, the funds administered by the Master's court, the endowments trust and the Darling trustees or any other funds subject to the control of the Company) may be invested in the purchase or upon the security of such shares, stock, securities or other investments or property of whatever nature including land, life assurance policies or annuities, and in any part of the world, whether involving liability or not, and whether producing income or not, as the Master's court, the trustees, the endowments trust, the Darling trustees or others as the case may be, shall in their sole discretion think fit in the same unrestricted manner as if they were beneficial owners thereof.

(2) Subject as hereinafter contained, the Master's court, the trustees, the endowments trust, the Darling trustees or others as the case may be, shall not be bound in any case to act personally but shall be at full liberty to employ an agent, servant, solicitor, accountant, factor, broker, investment manager, adviser or other to transact any business required to be done, and shall be entitled to be paid all charges and expenses so incurred, and shall not be responsible for the defaults of any such agent or others nor for any loss occasioned by their employment:

Provided always that nothing in the provisions of this section shall be construed as conferring on the Master's court, the trustees, the endowments trust, the Darling trustees or others as the case may be, the right to delegate any decision concerning the application or the distribution of the income or the capital of any trust funds pursuant to any charitable objects under their supervision.

(3) The Master's court, the trustees, the endowments trust, the Darling trustees or others as the case may be, shall have power to permit any moneys, bonds, certificates or other securities for money, or documents of title to property heritable or moveable, to be deposited with any bank, trust company or other like institution in the United Kingdom and permit any investments, securities or other heritable or moveable property which or any share or interest therein to be and remain invested in the name of nominees instead of in the name of the Company itself or of the trustees or the endowments trust or the Darling trustees as the case may be, upon such terms as to remuneration and in all other respects as the Master's court, the trustees, the endowments trust, the Darling trustees or others as the case may be, shall in their sole discretion think proper with power to delegate to such banks, trust companies or other institutions, or to such nominees such of the powers and discretions hereby or by law vested in the Company, the Master's court, the trustees, the endowments trust, the Darling trustees or others as the case may be, may consider expedient so to delegate:

Provided always that any such nominees shall report to the Master's court, the trustees, the endowments trust, the Darling trustees or others as the case may be, in writing fully and promptly in respect of such acts carried out by them on behalf of the Company or the Master's court, the trustees, the endowments trust, the Darling trustees or others as the case may be.

Borrowing and lending inter se by Company, widows' fund, endowments trust and education board

138. The Company (by the Master's court), the widows' fund (by the trustees), the Master's court and the endowments trust may lend to each other and to the education board and borrow from each other and the education board or any of the other funds or endowments connected with the Company, the widows' fund, the Master's court and the endowments trust (but excepting the Darling fund).

Donations, etc., may be received

139.—(1) The Company, the Master's court and the endowments trust may respectively receive donations or endowments for any of the purposes of this Order in so far as applicable to them respectively and may also receive donations or endowments for any special objects which shall not be inconsistent with or calculated to impede the due working of the provisions of this Order and may hold, exercise, administer and fulfil any trusts which may be confided to them.

(2) The endowments trust may enter into agreements with any persons who are the administrators of any charity or benevolent institution within the city of Edinburgh and for the transfer of the administration of such charity or benevolent institution to the endowments trust.

Notices

140. Any notice required to be given pursuant to the provisions of this Order may be sent by post.

Discharge of members, contributors, officials and others

141. The members, the contributors, the endowments trust and all officials appointed in pursuance of the repealed Acts and the heirs, executors and representatives of any of them who have predeceased or may predecease the confirming of this Order are hereby exonerated, acquitted and simpliciter discharged of their whole actings, transactions, intromissions and management in any way, and in whatever capacities, in consequence of or arising out of their membership or appointments to their respective offices or otherwise, and of all omissions which can or could be laid to their charge and of all claims and demands whatsoever which may be made against them.

Saving for town and country planning

142. This Order shall be deemed to be an enactment passed before and in force at the passing of the Town and Country Planning (Scotland) Act 1947 for the purposes of sections 11(4) and 112(1) of that Act or any subsequent re-enactment thereof.

Costs of Order

143. The costs, charges and expenses of and incident to the preparing, obtaining and confirming of this Order or otherwise in relation thereto shall be paid out of such funds as may be determined by the joint committee.

INDEX

References are to sections and the Schedule

CHARTERS, CONFIRMATION OF, Sched. para. 3(1)

INTERPRETATION, Sched. para. 1

MERCHANT COMPANY,
- borrowing powers, Sched. para. 138
- Darling fund, Sched. paras. 39–40
- discharge of members etc., Sched. para. 141
- donations, Sched. para. 139
- endowment trust,
  - payments to beneficiaries, Sched. paras. 108–112
  - powers of, Sched. paras. 92–107
- execution of deeds, Sched. para. 136
- fees payable, Sched. paras. 15–18
- Fraser Trust, Sched. paras. 113–121
- funds and property, Sched. paras. 19–21
- investment powers, Sched. para. 137
- joint committee, Sched. paras. 128–135
- master's court, Sched. paras. 30–38
- meetings, Sched. paras. 22–28
- members, election of, Sched. paras. 5–9
- notices, Sched. para. 140
- office bearers, election of, Sched. paras. 10–12

MERCHANT COMPANY—*cont.*
- officials, Sched. paras. 13–14
- powers of, Sched. para. 4
- rule-making, Sched. para. 29
- Russell and Foster Endowment. Sched. paras. 122–126
- variation of trusts, Sched. para. 127
- widows' fund,
  - annuities payable, Sched. paras. 80–88
  - contributors, Sched. paras. 43–51
  - dissolution of, Sched. paras. 89–91
  - maintenance of, Sched. paras. 41–42
  - payments of contributors. Sched. paras. 66–78
  - trustees' powers, Sched. paras. 52–65

ORDER,
- confirmation of, 1
- costs of, Sched. para. 143
- terms of, Sched.

REPEALS, Sched. para. 3(2)

SAVINGS, Sched. para. 142
SHORT TITLE, 1

SCOTTISH BORDERS COUNCIL (JIM CLARK MEMORIAL RALLY) ORDER CONFIRMATION ACT 1996

(1996 c. xii)

ARRANGEMENT OF SECTIONS

SECT.
1. Confirmation of Order in Schedule.
2. Short title.

SCHEDULE

SCOTTISH BORDERS COUNCIL (JIM CLARK MEMORIAL RALLY)

1. Short title.
2. Interpretation.
3. Authorised days.
4. Arrangements for rally.
5. Power to carry out works.
6. Power to close public roads.
7. Removal of vehicles.
8. Road traffic enactments not to apply to closed roads.
9. Road traffic regulations.
10. Compensation.
11. Application of New Roads and Street Works Act, 1991.
12. For protection of Post Office.
13. Discontinuance of rally and cesser of Order.

An Act to confirm a Provisional Order under the Private Legislation Procedure (Scotland) Act 1936, relating to Scottish Borders Council (Jim Clark Memorial Rally). [18th December 1996]

PARLIAMENTARY PROGRESS

The Bill's progress through Parliament was as follows:

House of Commons: First Reading, November 20, 1996, Bill considered by Commons, November 26, 1996, Third Reading, November 27, 1996.

House of Lords: First Reading and Consideration by Lords, November 27, 1996, Report, December 3, 1996, Third Reading, December 9, 1996.

INTRODUCTION

By this Act, the Provisional Order which authorises the Jim Clark Memorial Rally to take place on certain roads is confirmed. These roads are in the former district of Berwickshire in the Scottish Borders, and further powers are conferred on the Scottish Borders Council in relation thereto. This legislation is effective under the Private Legislation Procedure (Scotland) Act 1936.

Whereas the Provisional Order set forth in the Schedule hereunto annexed has been made by the Secretary of State under the provisions of the Private Legislation Procedure (Scotland) Act 1936, and it is requisite that the said Order should be confirmed by Parliament:

Be it therefore enacted by the Queen's most Excellent Majesty, by and with the advice and consent of the Lords Spiritual and Temporal, and Commons, in this present Parliament assembled, and by the authority of the same, as follows:

Confirmation of Order in Schedule

1. The Provisional Order contained in the Schedule hereunto annexed is hereby confirmed.

Short title

2. This Act may be cited as the Scottish Borders Council (Jim Clark Memorial Rally) Order Confirmation Act 1996.

SCHEDULE

Scottish Borders Council (Jim Clark Memorial Rally)

Provisional Order to authorise the Jim Clark Memorial Rally to take place on certain public roads in the former district of Berwickshire in the Scottish Borders; to confer powers on The Scottish Borders Council in relation thereto; and for other purposes.

WHEREAS—

(1) The Scottish Borders Council (hereinafter referred to as "the Council") are by virtue of sections 133 and 146 of the Local Government (Scotland) Act 1973 vested with the functions of roads authority for the area of the Scottish Borders:

(2) As roads authority and traffic authority the Council are responsible for administering the provisions of the Roads (Scotland) Act 1984 and the Road Traffic Regulation Act 1984:

(3) By virtue of Part VI of the Road Traffic Regulation Act 1984 public roads in the former district of Berwickshire (hereinafter referred to as "the district") are subject to speed limits for motor vehicles:

(4) For more than twenty years a motor car rally (hereinafter called "the rally") known as the Jim Clark Memorial Rally has taken place annually on private roads and tracks in the district in memory of the late Jim Clark, the Berwickshire farmer who became world motor-racing champion in 1963 and 1965 and was killed in a motor-racing accident at Hockenheim, Germany on 7th April 1968:

(5) It would generate more public interest in the rally and enhance its reputation and, by encouraging tourism in the district and benefiting the local economy, it would be of public and local advantage, if the rally were to take place on closed public roads in the district:

(6) For the purposes aforesaid it is expedient to authorise the Council to permit certain public roads in the district to be used for the rally on certain days of the year and for this purpose to empower the Council on certain days and at certain times to close to the public or restrict access to the whole or parts of those public roads in the district and to suspend the operation of certain enactments in respect of those roads:

(7) It is expedient that other provisions in this Order be enacted:

(8) The purposes aforesaid cannot be effected without an Order confirmed by Parliament under the provisions of the Private Legislation Procedure (Scotland) Act 1936:

Now therefore, in pursuance of the powers contained in the said Act of 1936, the Secretary of State orders as follows:

Short title

1. This Order may be cited as the Scottish Borders Council (Jim Clark Memorial Rally) Order 1996.

Interpretation

2. In this Order, except where the context otherwise requires—

"apparatus" means—

(a) in relation to a public gas supplier, mains, pipes and other apparatus belonging to or maintained by that supplier;

(b) in relation to a water and sewerage undertaker, water mains and communication and supply pipes as defined in section 109 of the Water (Scotland) Act 1980 and public sewers as defined in section 59 of the Sewerage (Scotland) Act 1968;

(c) in relation to a telecommunications operator, telecommunication apparatus as defined in paragraph 1(1) of Schedule 2 to the Telecommunications Act 1984, including such apparatus belonging to or used by British Telecommunications plc;

(d) in relation to Scottish Power plc, an electric line as defined in section 64 of the Electricity Act 1989;

"authorising agent" means the Royal Scottish Automobile Club;

"authorised days" has the meaning given by section 3 (Authorised days) of this Order;

"competition rules" shall mean the rules for the time being in force of the RAC Motor Sports Association Limited relative to motor rallies;

"Chief Constable" means the Chief Officer of Lothian and Borders Police;

"contravention" includes failure to comply;

"the Council" means The Scottish Borders Council;

"district" means the former local government area existing at 31st March 1996 known as the district of Berwickshire and shown delineated in red on the signed plan;

"motor vehicle" has the meaning given by sections 185 and 186 of the Road Traffic Act 1988;

"occupier" has the meaning given by section 151 of the Roads (Scotland) Act 1984;

"owner" has the meaning given by section 151 of the Roads (Scotland) Act 1984;

"premises" includes land and any interest in land or building thereon;

"promoter" means the person primarily responsible for the organisation and arrangement of the rally in the district;

"public road" means a road in the district which is a public road as defined in section 151 of the Roads (Scotland) Act 1984;

"Railtrack" means Railtrack PLC, a public limited company registered under the Companies Act 1985 to which there was transferred on 1st April 1994, under a scheme made on 30th March 1994, pursuant to section 85(1) of the Railways Act 1993 and by direction of the Secretary of State pursuant to section 85(4) of that Act, that part of the undertaking of the British Railways Board which consisted of the management of the railway network in Great Britain and related property, rights and liabilities;

"the rally" means the Jim Clark Memorial Rally, being a competition or trial of average speed consisting of one or more events;

"rally route", in respect of any year, means the route of the rally in so far as it—

(a) is on public roads, and

(b) has been approved by the Council in accordance with the provisions of section 4(3) of this Order;

"signed plan" means the plan marked "Scottish Borders Council (Jim Clark Memorial Rally) Order 1996: Berwickshire District: Boundary at 31st March 1996" of which five copies have been signed by Gavin Douglas QC, Senior Counsel to the Secretary of State for the purposes of the Private Legislation Procedure (Scotland) Act 1936, one of which copies has been deposited with the sheriff clerk of the Duns sheriff court district, one in the office of the Clerk of the Parliaments, House of Lords, one in the Private Bill Office of the House of Commons, one in the Scottish Office, London, and one in the Office of the Secretary of State, Edinburgh;

"statutory undertakers" means a public gas supplier, public water or sewerage undertaker, telecommunications operator or Scottish Power plc;

"telecommunications operator" means the operator of a telecommunications code system; and "operator" and "telecommunications code system" have the respective meanings given by paragraph 1 of Schedule 4 to the Telecommunications Act 1984; and

"traffic sign" has the meaning given by section 64 of the Road Traffic Regulation Act 1984.

Authorised days

3.—(1) In this Order the expression "authorised days" means in respect of any calendar year, any three consecutive days approved by the Council in consultation with the Chief Constable and the authorising agent on receipt of at least four months' written notice from the promoter.

(2) The promoter shall give not less than three months' notice of the authorised days to Railtrack and to any statutory undertakers having apparatus in, under or adjoining the rally route.

Arrangements for rally

4.—(1) Subject to the provisions of this Order the Council may authorise the organisation and arrangement of the rally in the district by the promoter on the authorised days.

(2) The rally shall follow the rally route, and a proposed route for that purpose will be notified to the Council in writing by the promoter at least four months prior to the authorised days and shall be subject to the approval of the Council in consultation with the Chief Constable and the authorising agent.

(3) The Council may approve the proposed route as the rally route if after such consultation they are satisfied that such provisions have been made with regard to public safety and alternative routes for vehicular and pedestrian traffic as they consider necessary, but if the Council are not so satisfied they may refuse to approve the proposed route as the rally route or approve it subject to such alterations as they think fit.

(4) Subject to such directives as may be given by—

(a) the Chief Constable;

(b) the Council; or

(c) the authorising agent;

the rally shall be run in accordance with the competition rules:

Provided that in case of conflict between any directives given under this subsection a directive given by the Chief Constable shall prevail over any conflicting directive given by the authorising agent or the Council and a directive given by the authorising agent shall prevail over any conflicting directive given by the Council.

Power to carry out works

5.—(1) The Council may carry out on public roads such works as they may consider to be necessary or convenient for the purposes of, or in connection with, the provisions of this Order.

(2) The cost of any works carried out by the Council under subsection (1) above may be recovered by the Council from the promoter.

(3) The Council shall not undertake any works under subsection (1) above which would render the road unsuitable for use at any time as a public road.

(4) The Council may give such assistance (other than such financial assistance as is not permitted by virtue of section 83 of the Local Government (Scotland) Act 1973) to the promoter as may be required to enable the promoter to carry out the purposes of this Order.

Power to close public roads

6.—(1) Subject to the provisions of subsections (2) to (6) below the Council may, for the purposes of this Order, on the authorised days close to the public or restrict access to the whole or part of any public road or roads comprised in the rally route and may exclude therefrom all or any persons, vehicles, goods and things (including persons seeking to go to or from any premises abutting any such road and whether or not in exercise or purported exercise of any public or private right of way over any part of the public roads) except with the consent of the Council in consultation with the promoter.

(2) The Council shall not on any of the authorised days close any part of the public roads comprised in the rally route—

(a) more than twice; or

(b) for a continuous period of more than five hours; or

(c) if that part has not been open to the public for at least two hours since the last closure.

(3) The Council shall ensure that, where any premises or any place of public religious worship is affected by the road closure or any restriction of access to a road under the powers contained in this section, the owner or occupier of such premises or any person attending such place (whether for the purpose of worship or education) shall have reasonable access to and egress from the said premises or place of public religious worship as the case may be in so far as it is safe to grant such access or egress, during the period of closure or restriction.

(4) Notice of the closing of public roads under this section and any revised traffic arrangements and alternative routes shall be indicated by traffic signs.

(5) The Council shall—

(a) not less than one month before the closing of a public road under this section cause to be published in a local newspaper circulating in the district notice thereof stating the public roads or parts of public roads to be closed and the periods during which such public roads shall be closed to vehicular and pedestrian traffic respectively;

(b) not later than the date on which such notice is published under paragraph (a) above serve a copy thereof on the Chief Constable, Railtrack and any statutory undertaker having apparatus in, under or adjoining the rally route;

(c) display copies of such notice in the public road or part of a public road to be closed in places where they can conveniently be read by the public for a period of not less than 14 days immediately preceding the closing.

(6) Either—

(a) a copy of any such newspaper containing any such notice, or

(b) a photostatic or other reproduction certified by the proper officer of the Council to be a true reproduction of a page, or part of a page, of any such newspaper bearing the date of its publication and containing any such notice,

shall be evidence of the publication of the notice and of the date of the publication.

(7) If any person without the consent of the Council knowingly and without reasonable excuse enters or remains upon any public road which is closed to him, or drives or causes or permits to be driven a vehicle upon any public road or part of a public road which is closed to that vehicle under this section, or fails to comply with any condition subject to which the Council have given their consent under this section, he shall be guilty of an offence and liable on summary conviction to a fine not exceeding level 4 on the standard scale.

(8) In proceedings for an offence under subsection (7) above, it shall be a defence for the person charged to prove that he took all reasonable pre-

cautions and exercised all due diligence to avoid the commission of the offence.

(9) Notwithstanding the closure of any public road or part of a public road by the Council under this section, in the case of emergency any emergency service of the Council, Railtrack, the police, the ambulance service, the fire service, the Borders Health Board or the statutory undertakers may require the promoter to stop the rally and may enter upon such public road or part of a public road with any necessary vehicles, plant and equipment for the purpose of exercising any of their functions in relation to the emergency.

(10) Nothing in this section shall prejudice or affect the operation of any of the relevant statutory provisions as defined in Part I of the Health and Safety at Work etc. Act 1974.

(11) The Council may recover from the promoter all or any of the costs incurred by them in exercising any of the powers contained in this section.

Removal of vehicles

7.—(1) Where a vehicle is on any public road or part of a public road which is closed in pursuance of section 6 (Power to close public roads) of this Order, otherwise than for the purposes of subsection (9) of that section, the Council may remove or arrange for the removal of the vehicle to a place other than the rally route.

(2) Any person removing a vehicle under subsection (1) above may do so by towing or driving the vehicle or in such other manner as he may reasonably think necessary and may take such measures in relation to the vehicle as he may reasonably think necessary to enable him to remove it as aforesaid.

(3) While the vehicle is in the custody of the Council in pursuance of this section it shall be the duty of the Council to take such steps as are reasonably necessary for the safe custody of the vehicle and for complying with a request for its return made by or on behalf of its owner.

(4) The owner of any vehicle removed by the Council in pursuance of this section shall be liable to pay the Council's costs incurred in carrying out such a removal.

(5) In this section "vehicle" means any vehicle whether or not it is in a fit state for use on public roads and includes any chassis or body with or without wheels appearing to have formed part of such a vehicle, and any load carried by, and anything attached to, such a vehicle.

Road traffic enactments not to apply to closed roads

8.—(1) Subject to subsections (2) and (3) below and to the provisions of section 9 (Road traffic regulations) of this Order, while the rally route is closed under section 6 (Power to close public roads) of this Order, no enactment relating to road traffic shall apply to any motor vehicle which is on the rally route with the consent of the Council or to any closed public road forming part of the rally route.

(2) The Motor Vehicles (Competitions and Trials) (Scotland) Regulations 1976 shall apply to the rally authorised by this Order so far as those regulations are not inconsistent with the provisions of this Order and the authorisation thereby of a rally on the rally route at speeds greater than the speed limit imposed under any enactment in respect of any public road which forms part of the rally route.

(3) Sections 4 to 11 of the Road Traffic Act 1988 are not disapplied by this section.

Road traffic regulations

9. In its application to the district, section 14 of the Road Traffic Regulation Act 1984 (which empowers a roads authority to make an order or give a notice temporarily prohibiting or restricting traffic on roads) shall have

effect on the authorised days in relation to any road other than a trunk road as if after the words "of serious damage to the road" where those words occur in subsection (1)(b) there were added the words "or in order to facilitate the operation of the Scottish Borders Council (Jim Clark Memorial Rally) Order 1996":

Provided that no order made or notice given under the said section 14, which could not have been made or given but for this Order, shall prevent any statutory undertaker obtaining access to any apparatus with any necessary plant and machinery.

Compensation

10.—(1) Without prejudice to any right to compensation enjoyed apart from this section, a person who sustains injury or damage by reason of the exercise of the powers of this Order shall be entitled to recover full compensation from the promoter to the extent that that person has not himself been in default.

(2) The promoter will maintain an insurance policy to provide such cover as will fulfil the obligations of the promoter under this section in an amount to be determined by, and to the satisfaction of, the RAC Motor Sports Association Limited.

Application of New Roads and Street Works Act 1991

11. The provisions contained in sections 142 to 144 of the New Roads and Street Works Act 1991 shall apply in relation to any works executed under section 5 (Power to carry out works) of this Order.

For protection of Post Office

12. For the protection of the Post Office the following provisions shall, unless otherwise agreed in writing between the Council, the promoter and the Post Office, apply and have effect:

(1) Not less than four months before the first of the days proposed by the promoter to be the authorised days in any year for the purposes of this Order, the promoter shall, in order to minimise disruption of rural postal collection and delivery services, consult the Post Office as to the proposed route of the rally, the proposed authorised days and the proposed periods during which roads are to be closed under the powers of this Order.

(2) The Council shall not approve the proposed rally route under section 4 (Arrangements for rally) of this Order unless they are satisfied that the promoter has consulted the Post Office in accordance with paragraph (1) above.

(3) After the authorised days have been determined in accordance with the provisions of this Order the promoter shall give not less than three months' notice to the Post Office of those days.

(4) After the route of the rally and the periods during which any public roads will be closed have been determined in accordance with the provisions of this Order the Council shall give not less than one month's notice to the Post Office of that route and those periods.

Discontinuance of rally and cesser of Order

13.—(1) Not later than 31st March in the year preceding any calendar year after the year 2001 in which the promoter intends to hold the rally, the promoter shall give written notice of such intention to the Secretary of State.

(2) If the Secretary of State is satisfied from a review of the effects of the rally that on grounds of public safety the rally should be discontinued or that it should be permitted to continue only upon certain terms or conditions, the Secretary of State may by order, within three months after the service of a

notice by the promoter under subsection (1) above, either prohibit the holding of the intended rally or permit it to continue subject to such terms or conditions as he thinks fit.

(3) If the Secretary of State prohibits the holding of the intended rally under subsection (2) above, the rally shall not take place in the year of the intended rally or in any later year and on 31st December following such prohibition this Order shall cease to have effect.

INDEX

References are to sections and the Schedule

AUTHORISED DAYS, Sched. para. 3

CLOSURE OF PUBLIC ROADS, Sched. para. 6
COMPENSATION, Sched. para. 10

INTERPRETATION, Sched. para. 2

ORDER,
  cesser of, Sched. para. 13(3)
  confirmation of, 1
  terms of, Sched.

POST OFFICE SERVICES, Sched. para. 12

RALLY,
  arrangements for, Sched. para. 4
  discontinuance of, Sched. para. 13(2)
  notice of, Sched. para. 13(1)
  prohibition of, Sched. para. 13(3)
REMOVAL OF VEHICLES, Sched. para. 7
ROAD TRAFFIC ENACTMENTS AND REGULATIONS, 9, Sched. para. 8

SHORT TITLE, 2

WORKS, 11, Sched. para. 5

WESTERN ISLES COUNCIL (BERNERAY CAUSEWAY) ORDER CONFIRMATION ACT 1996

(1996 c. xiii)

ARRANGEMENT OF SECTIONS

SECT.
1. Confirmation of Order in Schedule.
2. Short title.

SCHEDULE

WESTERN ISLES COUNCIL (BERNERAY CAUSEWAY)

PART I

PRELIMINARY

1. Short title.
2. Interpretation.

PART II

WORKS

3. Power to construct works.
4. Power to renew, etc., works.
5. Power to deviate.
6. Subsidiary works.
7. Works deemed to be within Western Isles Area.

PART III

MISCELLANEOUS

8. Tidal works not to be executed without approval of Secretary of State.
9. Lights on tidal works during construction.
10. Permanent lights on tidal works.
11. Survey of tidal works.
12. Provision against danger to navigation.
13. Abatement of works abandoned or decayed.
14. Saving for certain enactments, etc.
15. Saving for Coast Protection Act 1949.
16. For protection of Scottish Hydro-Electric plc.
17. Crown rights.

An Act to confirm a Provisional Order under the Private Legislation Procedure (Scotland) Act 1936, relating to Western Isles Council (Berneray Causeway). [18th December 1996]

PARLIAMENTARY PROGRESS

The Bill's progress through Parliament was as follows:

House of Commons: First Reading, November 20, 1996, Bill considered by Commons, November 26, 1996, Third Reading, November 27, 1996.

House of Lords: First Reading and Consideration by Lords, November 27, 1996, Report, December 3, 1996, Third Reading, December 9, 1996.

INTRODUCTION

This Act confirms the Provisional Order which authorises the Western Isles Council to construct a causeway for both pedestrians and vehicles between the islands of North Uist and Berneray in the Western Isles Area. This legislation is effective under the Private Legislation Procedure (Scotland) Act 1936.

Whereas the Provisional Order set forth in the Schedule hereunto annexed has been made by the Secretary of State under the provisions of the Private

Legislation Procedure (Scotland) Act 1936, and it is requisite that the said Order should be confirmed by Parliament:

Be it therefore enacted by the Queen's most Excellent Majesty, by and with the advice and consent of the Lords Spiritual and Temporal, and Commons, in this present Parliament assembled, and by the authority of the same, as follows:

Confirmation of Order in Schedule

1. The Provisional Order contained in the Schedule hereunto annexed is hereby confirmed.

Short title

2. This Act may be cited as the Western Isles Council (Berneray Causeway) Order Confirmation Act 1996.

SCHEDULE

Western Isles Council (Berneray Causeway)

Provisional Order to authorise the Western Isles Council to construct a causeway for pedestrian and vehicular traffic between the islands of North Uist and Berneray in the Western Isles Area.

WHEREAS—

(1) Under the Local Government etc. (Scotland) Act 1994 the Western Isles Council (hereinafter referred to as "the Council") are the local authority vested with the functions of an islands council in respect of the Western Isles Area which includes the islands of North Uist and Berneray:

(2) The inhabitants of the island of Berneray experience isolation and hardship due to the lack of convenient communication across the Sound of Berneray between that island and the island of North Uist and accordingly experience difficulty in transporting building materials, equipment, livestock and vehicles to and from the island of Berneray:

(3) It is the Council's policy to maintain remote communities and to procure that wherever possible they have reasonable access to the more populated and better provided-for localities within the islands:

(4) It is also the Council's policy to improve communications across the Sound of Harris to provide a link between the major population groupings of Lewis and Harris in the north of their area and the Uists in the south:

(5) The Council are the body statutorily responsible for the provision of roads in the Western Isles Area:

(6) The Council accordingly desire to construct between the islands of North Uist and Berneray a causeway across waters lying below the level of low water which will, in their opinion, help to maintain the present population of Berneray, relieve their hardship and also facilitate the introduction of a shorter and more frequent ferry service across the Sound of Harris:

(7) A plan and sections showing the lines, situations and levels of the works proposed to be authorised by this Order have been deposited with the sheriff clerk of the sheriff court district of Lochmaddy at Lochmaddy:

(8) The purposes of this Order cannot be effected without an Order confirmed by Parliament under the provisions of the Private Legislation Procedure (Scotland) Act 1936:

Now therefore, in pursuance of the powers contained in the said Act of 1936, the Secretary of State orders as follows:

PART I

PRELIMINARY

Short title

1. This Order may be cited as the Western Isles Council (Berneray Causeway) Order 1996.

Interpretation

2.—(1) In this Order, except where the context otherwise requires—

"the authorised works" means the works (or any of them) described in, and authorised by, section 3 below and includes such works as renewed, replaced or altered under section 4 below, and any works constructed or executed under section 6 below;

"the Council" means the Western Isles Council;

"the deposited plan" and "the deposited sections" mean respectively the plan and sections deposited on or before 20th November 1995 in Parliament, with the proper officer of the Council and with the sheriff clerk of the sheriff court district of Lochmaddy in connection with the application for this Order;

"the level of high water" means the level of mean high-water springs;

"the limits of deviation" means the limits of deviation shown on the deposited plan;

"tidal work" means so much of any of the authorised works as are on, under or over tidal waters or tidal lands below the level of high water.

(2) All directions, distances, lengths and widths stated in any description of works, powers or lands other than in section 5 below shall be construed as if the words "or thereby" were inserted after each such direction, distance, length and width.

(3) Map reference points specified in this Order shall be construed as references to Ordnance Survey National Grid reference points.

PART II

WORKS

Power to construct works

3. Subject to the provisions of this Order, the Council may, in the lines and situations and within the limits of deviation shown on the deposited plan and according to the levels shown on the deposited sections, construct, execute and maintain the work hereinafter described, with all necessary works and conveniences connected therewith in the parishes of North Uist and Harris in the Western Isles Area, that is to say—

A causeway providing an accessway for pedestrian and vehicular traffic between the islands of North Uist and Berneray commencing at a point at NF9074479389 on the island of North Uist and extending in a generally east-north-easterly direction for a distance of 569 metres and thence through a curve in a generally north-north-easterly direction for a distance of 299 metres and there terminating at a point at NF9140379924 on the island of Berneray having a width at the level of the metalled carriageway of 10 metres constructed on a mound of broken rock protected on each seaward face by rock armour.

Power to renew, etc., works

4. Subject to the provisions of this Order the Council may, within the limits of deviation, renew, replace, or otherwise alter temporarily or permanently the authorised works.

Power to deviate

5. Subject to the provisions of this Order, in the construction or execution of the authorised works the Council may deviate laterally from the lines or situations thereof shown on the deposited plan to the extent of the limits of deviation, and may deviate vertically from the levels shown in the deposited sections to any extent not exceeding 3 metres upwards and to any extent downward.

Subsidiary works

6. Subject to the provisions of this Order the Council, for the purposes of or in connection with the authorised works, may within the limits of deviation construct, execute and maintain all such subsidiary works and conveniences as may be necessary or expedient for or in connection with the authorised works.

Works deemed to be within Western Isles Area

7. So much of the authorised works constructed or executed pursuant to this Order as are not within the Western Isles Area shall be deemed for all purposes to be within that Area.

PART III

MISCELLANEOUS

Tidal works not to be executed without approval of Secretary of State

8.—(1) A tidal work shall not be constructed, executed, renewed, replaced or altered except in accordance with plans and sections approved by the Secretary of State and subject to any conditions and restrictions imposed by the Secretary of State before the work is begun.

(2) If a tidal work is constructed, executed, renewed, replaced or altered in contravention of this section—

(a) the Secretary of State may by notice in writing require the Council at their own expense to remove the tidal work or any part thereof and restore the site thereof to its former condition; and if, on the expiration of 30 days from the date when the notice is served upon the Council, they have failed to comply with the requirements of the notice, the Secretary of State may execute the works specified in the notice; or

(b) if it appears to the Secretary of State urgently necessary so to do, he may himself remove the tidal work or part of it and restore the site to its former condition;

and any expenditure incurred by the Secretary of State in so doing shall be recoverable from the Council.

Lights on tidal works during construction

9.—(1) The Council shall at or near a tidal work during the whole time of the construction, execution, renewal, replacement or alteration thereof exhibit every night from sunset to sunrise such lights, if any, and take such other steps for the prevention of danger to navigation as the Secretary of State shall from time to time direct.

(2) If the Council fail to comply in any respect with a direction given under this section they shall be guilty of an offence and liable on summary conviction to a fine not exceeding the statutory maximum and on conviction on indictment to a fine.

Permanent lights on tidal works

10.—(1) After the completion of a tidal work the Council shall exhibit every night from sunset to sunrise such lights, if any, and take such other steps for preventing danger to navigation as the Commissioners of Northern Lighthouses shall from time to time direct.

(2) If the Council fail to comply in any respect with a direction given under this section they shall be guilty of an offence and liable on summary conviction to a fine not exceeding the statutory maximum and on conviction on indictment to a fine.

Survey of tidal works

11. The Secretary of State may at any time if he deems it expedient order a survey and examination of a tidal work or of the site upon which it is proposed to construct and execute the work and any expenditure incurred by him in such survey and examination shall be recoverable from the Council.

Provision against danger to navigation

12.—(1) In the case of injury to or destruction or decay of a tidal work or any part thereof the Council shall forthwith notify the Commissioners of Northern Lighthouses and shall lay down such buoys, exhibit such lights and take such other steps for preventing danger to navigation as the Commissioners of Northern Lighthouses shall from time to time direct.

(2) If the Council fail to notify the Commissioners of Northern Lighthouses as required by this section or to comply in any respect with a direction given under this section they shall be guilty of an offence and liable on summary conviction to a fine not exceeding the statutory maximum and on conviction on indictment to a fine.

Abatement of works abandoned or decayed

13.—(1) Where a tidal work is abandoned or suffered to fall into decay the Secretary of State may by notice in writing require the Council at their own expense either to repair and restore the work or any part thereof, or to remove the work and restore the site thereof to its former condition, to such an extent and within such limits as the Secretary of State thinks proper.

(2) Where a work consisting partly of a tidal work and partly of works on or over land above the level of high water is abandoned or suffered to fall into decay and that part of the work on or over land above the level of high water is in such condition as to interfere or to cause reasonable apprehension that it may interfere with the right of navigation or other public rights over the foreshore, the Secretary of State may include that part of the work, or any portion thereof, in any notice under this section.

(3) If on the expiration of 30 days from the date when a notice under this section is served upon the Council, they have failed to comply with the requirements of the notice the Secretary of State may execute the works specified in the notice and any expenditure incurred by him in so doing shall be recoverable from the Council.

Saving for certain enactments, etc.

14.—(1) Nothing in this Order affects the operation of—

(a) the Control of Pollution Act 1974;

(b) any of the relevant statutory provisions as defined in section 53 of the Health and Safety at Work etc. Act 1974;

(c) Part II of the Food and Environment Protection Act 1985;

(d) the Environmental Protection Act 1990;

(e) the Environment Act 1995.

(2) Nothing in this Order affects prejudicially the jurisdiction or authority of the Commissioners of Northern Lighthouses.

Saving for Coast Protection Act 1949

15. Nothing in this Order shall exempt the Council from the provisions of Part I of the Coast Protection Act 1949.

For protection of Scottish Hydro-Electric plc

16. For the protection of Scottish Hydro-Electric plc the following provisions shall, save to the extent that the company may release the Council therefrom, apply and have effect:—

(1) In this section unless the subject or context otherwise requires—

"apparatus" means—

(a) any electrical plant or electric line as respectively defined in section 64 of the Electricity Act 1989; and

(b) any meter used for ascertaining the quantity of electricity supplied to any premises, not being a meter which is under the control of a consumer;

"the company" means Scottish Hydro-Electric plc;

"in" in a context referring to apparatus includes under, over, across, along or upon;

"plan" includes a section and description;

"position" includes depth.

(2)(a) Nothing in this Order shall relieve the Council from liability for damage caused by them to any apparatus in the exercise of the powers conferred on them by this Order and the Council shall indemnify the company against all claims, demands, costs, damages and expenses made or taken against or recovered from or incurred by the company by reason or in consequence of any damage done by the Council to any apparatus or of any interruption in the supply by the company of electricity which may without the written authority of the company be in any way occasioned either by reason of the exercise of any of the powers of this Order or by the acts or defaults (in, or in connection with, such exercise) of the Council.

(b) If in consequence of the exercise by the Council of the powers of this Order the access to any apparatus is materially obstructed, the Council shall provide an alternative means of access to such apparatus.

(3) If the Council in exercise of the powers of sections 3, 4 or 6 above require to cross over or under, remove, alter or otherwise interfere with any apparatus, or if the exercise of such powers is likely to affect any apparatus, the Council shall—

(a) give to the company not less than 28 days' prior notice in writing of such requirement or (as the case may be) of their intention to exercise such powers, together with a plan of the work proposed, and shall execute the work only in accordance with such plans and in accordance with such reasonable requirements as may within 21 days of the receipt of the plan be made by the company, and the company may under such requirements alter or otherwise protect the apparatus or provide alternative apparatus adequate to enable them to fulfil their statutory functions not less efficiently than before (hereinafter referred to as "alternative apparatus");

(b) afford to the company, where possible, any necessary facilities and rights for the construction, use, maintenance, repair, renewal and inspection of any alternative apparatus;

(c) pay to the company the expense reasonably incurred by them in and in connection with removing, re-laying, replacing, altering or protecting the apparatus or providing alternative apparatus less (in a case where alternative apparatus is provided) the value of any apparatus removed pursuant to this section.

(4) Alternative apparatus, if provided under this section shall be constructed in such manner and in such line or position as may be agreed between the Council and the company, and no apparatus shall be removed, altered or interfered with until any protective works required have been carried out or until alternative apparatus required has been provided and is operating to the reasonable satisfaction of the company.

(5)(a) Any difference arising between the Council and the company under this section shall be referred to and determined by an arbiter to be mutually agreed upon, or failing such agreement to be appointed on the application of either party (after notice in writing to the other) by the President of the Institution of Electrical Engineers.

(b) In settling any difference under this section the arbiter shall have regard to any duties or obligations which the company may be under in respect of any apparatus and may if he thinks fit require the Council to execute within the limits of deviation any temporary or other works so as to avoid so far as may be reasonably possible interference with any purpose for which the apparatus is used.

Crown rights

17.—(1) Nothing in this Order affects prejudicially any estate, right, power, privilege, authority or exemption of the Crown and in particular and without prejudice to the generality of the foregoing, nothing in this Order authorises the Council to take, use, enter upon or in any manner interfere with, any land or hereditaments (including any portion of the shore or bed of the sea or of any river, channel, creek, bay or estuary) or any rights of whatsoever description—

(a) belonging to Her Majesty in right of Her Crown and under the management of the Crown Estate Commissioners, without the consent in writing of those commissioners; or

(b) belonging to a government department or held in trust for Her Majesty for the purposes of a government department, without the consent in writing of that government department.

(2) A consent under subsection (1) above may be given unconditionally or subject to such conditions and upon such terms as shall be considered necessary or appropriate.

INDEX

References are to sections and the Schedule

INTERPRETATION, Sched., Pt. I

ORDER,
  confirmation of, 2
  terms of, Sched.

SHORT TITLE, 2

TIDAL WORKS, Sched., Pt. III

WORKS, Sched., Pt. II

CURRENT LAW STATUTES 1996

COMMENCEMENT DIARY

This table notes alphabetically by statute the commencement of statutes from January 1996 as initiated by Orders and by statutory provisions. This is up to date to **February 25, 1997** (Orders and Acts received). The full texts of the Orders can be found in the Commencement Orders section of Current Law Statutes.

Act Affected	Provision Brought Into Force	Commencement Date	Authority
Antarctic Act 1994 (c. 15)	s.7	November 1, 1996	S.I. 1996 No. 2666 (C.77)
Appropriation Act 1996 (c. 45)	All provisions	July 24, 1996	Royal Assent
Arbitration Act 1996 (c. 23)	ss.91 (part), 105, 107(1) (part), 107(2) (part), 108–110 Sched. 3, para. 36 (part), Sched. 4 (part)	December 17, 1996	S.I. 1996 No. 3146 (C.96)
Arbitration Act 1996 (c. 23)	All remaining provisions (except ss.85–87)	January 31, 1997	S.I. 1996 No. 3146 (C.96)
Armed Forces Act 1991 (c. 62)	All remaining provisions (ss.17, 18, 19, 20, 21, 22, 23, 24(3), 26(2) (part), Sched. 3 (part))	June 1, 1996	S.I. 1996 No. 1173 (C.19)
Armed Forces Act 1996 (c. 46)	ss.1, 34, 36	July 24, 1996	s.36(3)
Armed Forces Act 1996 (c. 46)	Repeal of s.1 of the Armed Forces Act 1991	September 1, 1996	s.36(4)
Armed Forces Act 1996 (c. 46)	ss.2, 6, 7, 11–14, 18, 19, 30–33, 35 (part), Scheds. 4, 6, paras. 1–3, 5, 6, 10–13, Sched. 7, Pt. III (part)	October 1, 1996	S.I. 1996 No. 2474 (C.65)
Asylum and Immigration Act 1996 (c. 49)	s.11, Sched. 1	July 24, 1996	Royal Assent
Asylum and Immigration Act 1996 (c. 49)	ss.3(3), (5), 9(1), (2) (for the purpose only of making orders), 9(3), 13	July 26, 1996	S.I. 1996 No. 2053 (C.46)
Asylum and Immigration Act 1996 (c. 49)	s.9 (except (3)(b)), 10 (part)	August 19, 1996	S.I. 1996 No. 2127 (C.50)

Act Affected	Provision Brought Into Force	Commencement Date	Authority
Asylum and Immigration Act 1996 (c. 49)	ss.2, 3 (except (3), (5)), 12 (for the purpose of Scheds. 2, 3, 4), Sched. 2, paras. 1, 2, 3, 5, Sched. 4 (part)	September 1, 1996	S.I. 1996 No. 2053 (C.46)
Asylum and Immigration Act 1996 (c. 49)	ss.4, 5, 6, 7, 12(1), (3) (for the purposes of Scheds. 2, 4), Sched. 2, paras. 1(2), (3), 2, 4, 5, 6, 7, 13, Sched. 4 (part)	October 1, 1996	S.I. 1996 No. 2053 (C.46)
Asylum and Immigration Act 1996 (c. 49)	ss.1 (for the purpose only of designating countries or territories), 10	October 7, 1996	S.I. 1996 No. 2127 (C.50)
Asylum and Immigration Act 1996 (c. 49)	s.1	October 21, 1996	S.I. 1996 No. 2127 (C.50)
Asylum and Immigration Act 1996 (c. 49)	Sched. 2, paras. 1(1), 3(1)	November 1, 1996	S.I. 1996 No. 2127 (C.50)
Asylum and Immigration Act 1996 (c. 49)	s.8	December 1, 1996 [for the purpose of making orders]	S.I. 1996 No. 2970 (C.90)
Asylum and Immigration Act 1996 (c. 49)	s.8	January 27, 1997	S.I. 1996 No. 2970 (C.90)
Audit (Miscellaneous Provisions) Act 1996 (c. 10)	All provisions except s.1	April 29, 1996	Royal Assent
Audit (Miscellaneous Provisions) Act 1996 (c. 10)	s.1	June 29, 1996	s.1(2)
Broadcasting Act 1996 (c. 55)	ss.73 (part), 74–78, 80, 83, 88, 90, 92, 131–136, 147(1), 148(1) (part), (2) (part), 149, 150, Sched. 2, paras. 7–9 (part), Scheds. 5–8, Sched. 10, paras. 15 (part), 19 (part), Sched. 11 (part)	July 24, 1996	s.149(1)

Act Affected	Provision Brought Into Force	Commencement Date	Authority
Broadcasting Act 1996 (c. 55)	ss.73 (part), 104, Sched. 2, Pt. IV, paras. 12, 13 of substituted Pt. IV of Sched. 2 to the Broadcasting Act 1990, Sched. 2, Pt. I (part), para. 11 (part)	August 10, 1996	S.I. 1996 No. 2120 (C.49)
Broadcasting Act 1996 (c. 55)	s.2 (for notification purposes only)	September 15, 1996	S.I. 1996 No. 2120 (C.49)
Broadcasting Act 1996 (c. 55)	1 to 40, 41 (part), 42 to 72, 73 (part), 79, 81, 84, 86, 91, 97 to 103, 105, 137, 138, 140, 141, 142, 147(2) (except (c)), 148 (part), Sched. 1, Sched. 2, para. 9, Sched. 9, Sched. 10, paras. 1 to 11, 14, 15, 16 (part), 19, 21(a), (c), 27 to 30, 31 (part), 32 (part), Sched. 11, Pt. I (part), Pt. II (part)	October 1, 1996	S.I. 1996 No. 2120 (C.49)
Broadcasting Act 1996 (c. 55)	ss.73 (part), 87, 89, 93, 94, 96, 139, 143 to 146, 148 (part), Sched. 2 (part), Sched. 10, paras. 13, 21(b), Sched. 11 (part)	November 1, 1996	S.I. 1996 No. 2120 (C.49)
Capital Allowances Act 1990 (c. 1)	s.33A (as inserted by s.94 Finance Act 1995, and amended by Sched. 35, para. 2 to the Finance Act 1996)	May 31, 1996 [Appointed day]	S.I. 1996 No. 1323 (C.23)
Carers (Recognition and Services) Act 1995 (c. 12)	All provisions	April 1, 1996	s.5(2)
Channel Tunnel Rail Link Act 1996 (c. 61)	All provisions	December 18, 1996	Royal Assent
Charities Act 1993 (c. 10)	All remaining provisions (ss.41–49, 69, Sched. 6, para. 21(3))	March 1, 1996	S.I. 1995 No. 2695 (C.54)
Chemical Weapons Act 1996 (c. 6)	s.39	April 3, 1996	s.39(1)

Act Affected	Provision Brought Into Force	Commencement Date	Authority
Chemical Weapons Act 1996 (c. 6)	All remaining provisions	September 16, 1996	S.I. 1996 No. 2054 (C.47)
Child Support Act 1995 (c. 34)	ss.9 (part), 11, 12 (rem.), 13, 14, 15	January 22, 1996	S.I. 1995 No. 3262 (C.76)
Child Support Act 1995 (c. 34)	ss.1(1) (part), (2) (part), 2 (part), 3 (part), 5 (part), 6(1) (part), (2) (part), 7 (part), 9 (part), 10, 26 (rem.), 30(5) (part), Sched. 1 (part), Sched. 2 (part), Sched. 3, paras. 1 (rem.), 20	October 14, 1996	S.I. 1996 No. 2630 (C.72)
Child Support Act 1995 (c. 34)	ss.1(1) (rem.), (2) (rem.), 2 (part), 3, 4, 5, 6(1), (2), 7, 8, 30(5) (part), Sched. 1 (rem.), Sched. 2 (rem.), Sched. 3, paras. 6, 7, 17	December 2, 1996	S.I. 1996 No. 2630 (C.72)
Children (Scotland) Act 1995 (c. 36)	s.4	September 1, 1996 [for the purpose of enabling regulations to be made]	S.I. 1996 No. 2203 (C.53) (S.179)
Children (Scotland) Act 1995 (c. 36)	s.91	October 1, 1996	S.I. 1996 No. 2203 (C.53) (S.179)

Act Affected	**Provision Brought Into Force**	**Commencement Date**	**Authority**
Children (Scotland) Act 1995 (c. 36)	Pt. 1, ss.54, 93, 98(1) (part), (2), 105(3) (part), (4) (part), (5) (part), Sched. 2, paras. 1, 7(a)(i), (b), (c), 8(a), 9(a), 11(b), (c), 12(b)(i), 13(a) (ii), (c)(ii), (d), 14, 17(b), 23, 26, 29(a) (iii), (v), (vi), Sched. 3, para. 7, Sched. 4, paras. 1–6, 7(1)–(5), (6)(a), 8, 9, 10(b), 11, 14, 15(1), (5), 17(a)(ii), 20(c), 28(d), (e), 18(3), 19, 20, 23(1), (4)(a) (part), (c), 24(1), (4), (5), (10), (11), 26(1), (2), (3), (4)(a), (c), (5)–(7), 27, 28(1), (5)(a), 29(1), (2), 30, 31, 33(1), (4), 34, 36, 37(1), (5), (6)(a)(i), (ii), 38, 39(1), (2)(a), (3)(a), (4), (5)(b), 41, 43, 46, 47, 48(1), (4), 50–52, 53(2), (4), (5), 54(1), (5), Sched. 5 (part)	November 1, 1996	S.I. 1996 No. 2203 (C.53) (S.179)
Children (Scotland) Act 1995 (c. 36)	ss.17, 19, 20, 31, 33, 38, 40, 42, 62, 70, 74, 75, 87, 94, 101	December 12, 1996 [for the purpose of enabling directions, rules or regulations to be made so as to come into force on or after April 1, 1997]	S.I. 1996 No. 3201 (C.102) (S.241)
Children (Scotland) Act 1995 (c. 36)	s.98, Sched. 2, paras. 3, 5, 19 (for the purpose of making insertions, substitutions and amendments to the Adoption (Scotland) Act 1978)	December 12, 1996 [for the purpose of enabling regulations to be made so as to come into force on or after April 1, 1997]	S.I. 1996 No. 3201 (C.102) (S.241)

Act Affected	**Provision Brought Into Force**	**Commencement Date**	**Authority**
Children (Scotland) Act 1995 (c. 36)	s.98, Sched. 2, para. 25	December 12, 1996 [for the purpose of enabling regulations to be made so as to come into force on or after April 1, 1998, or enabling Secretary of State to make a direction]	S.I. 1996 No. 3201 (C.102) (S.241)
Children (Scotland) Act 1995 (c. 36)	s.105(4), Sched. 4, para. 15 (amendment to the Social Work (Scotland) Act 1968)	December 12, 1996 [for the purpose of enabling regulations to be made, so as to come into force on or after April 1, 1997]	S.I. 1996 No. 3201 (C.102) (S.241)
Children (Scotland) Act 1995 (c. 36)	All remaining provisions (except s.98, Sched. 2, para. 25 insertion of s.51A into the Adoption (Scotland) Act 1978, Sched. 5 (part))	April 1, 1997	S.I. 1996 No. 3201 (C.102) (S.241)
Children (Scotland) Act 1995 (c. 36)	s.98, Sched. 2, para. 25 (insertion of s.51A into the Adoption (Scotland) Act 1978)	April 1, 1998	S.I. 1996 No. 3201 (C.102) (S.241)
Civil Aviation (Amendment) Act 1996 (c. 39)	All provisions	July 18, 1996	Royal Assent
Civil Evidence Act 1995 (c. 38)	All provisions except ss.10, 16(5)	January 31, 1997	S.I. 1996 No. 3217 (C.7)
Civil Evidence (Family Mediation) (Scotland) Act 1995 (c. 6)	All provisions	February 19, 1996	S.I. 1996 No. 125 (C.2) (S.9)
Commonwealth Development Corporation Act 1996 (c. 28)	All provisions	September 4, 1996	s.2(3)
Community Care (Direct Payments) Act 1996 (c. 30)	s.6	July 4, 1996	s.7(2)
Consolidated Fund Act 1996 (c. 4)	All provisions	March 21, 1996	Royal Assent
Consolidated Fund (No. 2) Act 1996 (c. 60)	All provisions	December 18, 1996	Royal Assent

Act Affected	Provision Brought Into Force	Commencement Date	Authority
Criminal Appeal Act 1995 (c. 35)	ss.1, 2, 4, 6, 7 (part), 26–28, 29 (part), 30, 31(1)(b), (2), 32–34, Sched. 2: paras. 1, 2, 4(1)–(3), 4(5), 5, 6, 12(1)–(4), 12(6), 15, 17, Sched. 3 (part)	January 1, 1996	S.I. 1995 No. 3061 (C.69)
Criminal Appeal Act 1995 (c. 93)	s.8, Sched. 1, paras. 1, 2	December 12, 1996 [for the purpose of making recommendations and appointments]	S.I. 1996 No. 3041 (C.93)
Criminal Appeal Act 1995 (c. 93)	s.8 (rem.), Sched. 1, paras. 1 (rem.), 2 (rem.), 31(1)(a), Sched. 1, paras. 3–11, Sched. 2, paras. 7–11	January 1, 1997	S.I. 1996 No. 3149 (C.97)
Criminal Justice and Public Order Act 1994 (c. 33)	s.22	March 8, 1996	S.I. 1996 No. 625 (C.12)
Criminal Justice and Public Order Act 1994 (c. 33)	s.149, Sched. 10, para. 70	July 1, 1996	S.I. 1996 No. 1608 (C.32)
Criminal Justice (Scotland) Act 1995 (c. 20)	ss.6(c), 14(4), 61(6) (for the purpose of enabling subordinate legislation to be made)	March 5, 1996	S.I. 1996 No. 517 (C.10) (S.51)
Criminal Justice (Scotland) Act 1995 (c. 20)	All remaining provisions except s.66	March 31, 1996	S.I. 1996 No. 517 (C.10) (S.51)
Criminal Law (Consolidation) (Scotland) Act 1995 (c. 39)	All provisions	April 1, 1996	s.53(2)
Criminal Procedure (Consequential Provisions) (Scotland) 1995 (c. 40)	All provisions	April 1, 1996	s.7(2)
Criminal Procedure and Investigations Act 1996 (c. 25)	All provisions	July 4, 1996	Royal Assent
Criminal Procedure and Investigations Act 1996 (c. 25)	ss.43, 48, 50, 53, 70, 71	October 1, 1996 [Appointed Day]	S.I. 1996 No. 2343 (C.60)

Act Affected	Provision Brought Into Force	Commencement Date	Authority
Criminal Procedure and Investigations Act 1996 (c. 25)	s.52	February 1, 1997 [Appointed Day]	S.I. 1997 No. 36 (C.3)
Criminal Procedure (Scotland) Act 1995 (c. 46)	All provisions	April 1, 1996	s.309(2)
Damages Act 1996 (c. 48)	All provisions	September 24, 1996	s.8(3)
Deer (Amendment) (Scotland) Act 1996 (c. 44)	All provisions	October 18, 1996	s.14(2)
Deer (Scotland) Act 1996 (c. 58)	All provisions	November 18, 1996	s.48(6)
Defamation Act 1996 (c. 31)	ss.18, 19, 20	July 4, 1996	s.19
Defamation Act 1996 (c. 31)	ss.1, 5, 6, 12, 13, 16, 17 (so far as relates to the above provisions), Sched. 2 (repeals, so far as relate to the above provisions)	September 4, 1996	s.19(2)
Deregulation and Contracting Out Act 1994 (c. 40)	All remaining provisions	January 1, 1996	S.I. 1995 No. 2835 (C.68)
Disability Discrimination Act 1995 (c. 50)	ss.50, 51, 52, Sched. 5	January 1, 1996	S.I. 1995 No. 3330 (C.78)
Disability Discrimination Act 1995 (c. 50)	ss.1, 2, 3, 16(3) (part), 28, 59, 62(1), (2), (7), 63(1), (2), (4), (5), (6), 67, 68, 69, 70(7), Sched. 1 (except para. 7), Sched. 2, Sched. 4, para. 4	May 17, 1996	S.I. 1996 No. 1336 (C.25)
Disability Discrimination Act 1995 (c. 50)	ss.5(6), (7), 6(8), (9), (10), 8(6), (7), 12(3), (6), 14(6), 16(5) (rem.), 17(3), 18(3), (4), 19(5)(c), 20(6), (7), (8), 24(5), 53, 54, 56, Sched. 4, Pt. I, para. 3	June 6, 1996	S.I. 1996 No. 1474 (C.27)
Disability Discrimination Act 1995 (c. 50)	ss.29(3), 30(1), (2), (3), (4), (5), (6), 31	July 31, 1996	S.I. 1996 No. 1474 (C.27)

Act Affected	**Provision Brought Into Force**	**Commencement Date**	**Authority**
Disability Discrimination Act 1995 (c. 50)	Guidance issued pursuant to s.3	July 31, 1996	S.I. 1996 No. 1996 (C.52)
Disability Discrimination Act 1995 (c. 50)	ss.4, 5(1), (2), (3), (4), (5), 6(1), (2), (3), (4), (5), (6), (7), (11), (12), 7, 8(1), (2), (3), (4), (5), (8), 9, 10, 11, 12(1), (2), (4), (5), 13, 14(1), (3), 16(1), (2), (4), 17(1), (2), (4), 18(1), (2), 19(1)(a), (c), (d), (2), (3), (4), (5)(a), (b), (6), 20(1), (3), (4), 22, 23, 24(1), (2), (3), (4), 25, 26, 55, 57, 58, 60, 61, 64, 65, 66, 68(2), (3), (4), (5), 70(4), 5 (part), Sched. 1, para. 7, Sched. 3, Sched. 4, Pt. I, paras. 1, 2, Sched. 6, Sched. 7	December 2, 1996	S.I. 1996 No. 1474 (C.27)
Disability Discrimination Act 1995 (c. 50)	Code of Practice issued pursuant to s.53	December 2, 1996	S.I. 1996 No. 1996 (C.52)
Disability Discrimination Act 1995 (c. 50)	s.16(3) (rem.)	December 2, 1996 [Appointed Day]	S.I. 1996 No. 3003 (C.92)
Dogs (Fouling of Land) Act 1996 (c. 20)	All provisions	August 17, 1996	s.8(2)
Education Act 1996 (c. 56)	s.317(6)	January 1, 1997	S.I. 1996 No. 2904 (C.86)
Education (Schools) Act 1992 (c. 38)	ss.2(3)(c), (d), 3(2), 6(3)(c), (d), 7(2)	May 15, 1996	S.I. 1996 No. 1325 (C.24)
Education (Scotland) Act 1996 (c. 43)	All provisions except ss.2–8, Sched. 5, paras. 6–9, Sched. 6 (repeal of s.129 Education (Scotland) Act 1980 (c.44))	September 18, 1996 [Appointed Day]	S.I. 1996 No. 2250 (C.63) (S.182)
Education (Student Loans) Act 1996 (c. 9)	All provisions	April 29, 1996	Royal Assent
Employment Rights Act 1989 (c. 38)	All remaining provisions	March 3, 1997	S.I. 1997 No. 134 (C.9)

Act Affected	**Provision Brought Into Force**	**Commencement Date**	**Authority**
Employment Rights Act 1996 (c. 18)	All provisions except ss.192, 219(3) (d), (4)(a)(iv)	August 22, 1996	s.243
Employment Rights Act 1996 (c. 18)	ss.46, 58–60, 102	October 6, 1996 [Appointed Day]	S.I. 1996 No. 2514 (C.68)
Energy Conservation Act 1996 (c. 38)	All provisions (Scotland only)	December 1, 1996	S.I. 1996 No. 2796 (C.81) (S.214)
Energy Conservation Act 1996 (c. 38)	All provisions (England and Wales)	January 14, 1997 [for the purpose of giving directions and guidance]	S.I. 1997 No. 47 (C.4)
Energy Conservation Act 1996 (c. 38)	All provisions (for all other purposes in England and Wales)	April 1, 1997	S.I. 1997 No. 47 (C.4)
Environment Act 1995 (c. 25)	ss.5(2), (5), 41 (part), 55(7)–(10), 80, 87–89, 90 (part), 91, 105 (part), 117, 118(1)–(3), (4) (part), (5) (part), (6), 119, 120(1) (part), (3) (part), Scheds. 11, paras. 2, 3, 5, Sched. 15, paras. 3, 5(1), Sched. 22, paras. 2, 13, 36, 37(2)(b), 43, 44, 67, 102, 103, 232(1), Sched. 24 (part)	February 1, 1996	S.I. 1996 No. 186 (C.3)
Environment Act 1995 (c. 25)	s.78 (part), s.115(1) (part), s.115(2) (part), s.115 (3), (4), (6) (part)	April 1, 1996	S.I. 1995 No. 2950 (C.65)

Act Affected	**Provision Brought Into Force**	**Commencement Date**	**Authority**
Environment Act 1995 (c. 25)	ss.2, 3(1), 5(1), (3), (4), 6, 8, 10, 11, 13–19, 25–29, 33–35, 37(3)–(8), 41 (rem.), 53, 54, 55(1)–(6), 81, 92, 104, 105 (part), 106–114, 115 (rem.), 120(1) (part), (2) (part), (3) (part), Sched. 15, paras. 1, 2, 4, 5(2), (3), 6–12, 14(2), (3), 6–12, 14(2), (3), 15, 16, 18, 19, 21–24, Sched. 22 paras. 1, 3, 5–12, 14, 17–27(a), 28, 29(1) (rem.), 29(2)–(20), 21(9)(ii), (23)–(25), (27)–(35), 30, 32–35, 37(3), (5)–(8), 40, 41, 45, 46(1)–(4), (6)–(11), 47–50, 51(4), 52, 54–66, 68(1), (2) (part), (3), (4), (6), (70)(1), (2), 72(2), 73(1), (2) (part) (3)–(6), 74 (part), 75, 76(2), (4)–(7), (8)(b), 77, 78, 80(3), 82 (rem.), 83–87, 90, 93, 94, 96–101, 103 (rem.), 104–132, 133(2), 134, 136, 140, 141, 144–146, 148–152, 154–160, 164–168, 171–181, 184, 185, 187(2), 188–191, 193–212, 213(a), (4)(5), 214–222, 223(1)(a)(b) (2), 224–231, 233, Sched. 23, paras. 1–6, 8–10, 12, 13, 14(1)–(4), (7), (8) (part), 16–24, Sched. 24 (part)	April 1, 1996	S.I. 1966 No. 186 (C.3)
Environment Act 1995 (c. 25)	s.120(1) (part), Sched. 22, paras. 142, 143, 169, 170, 183 (part)	November 21, 1996	S.I. 1996 No. 2909 (C.87)
Environment Act 1995 (c. 25)	ss.120(1) (rem.), (3) (part)	December 31, 1996	S.I. 1996 No. 2909 (C.87)

Act Affected	Provision Brought Into Force	Commencement Date	Authority
Environment Act 1995 (c. 25)	ss.96(1), (5), (6), 96(3), (4) (part), 120(3) (part), Scheds. 13, 14	January 1, 1997 [extends only to Scotland]	S.I. 1996 No. 2857 (C.84) (S.219)
Environment Act 1995 (c. 25)	ss.78 (part), 120(3) (part), Sched. 7, para. 7(2)	April 1, 1997	S.I. 1996 No. 2560 (C.71)
Environment Act 1995 (c. 25)	ss.105 (part), 120(2) (part) (3) (part)	January 1, 1999	S.I. 1995 No. 1988 (C.40)
Environmental Protection Act 1990 (c. 43)	s.162(2) (part)	December 16, 1996	S.I. 1996 No. 3056 (C.94)
Family Law Act 1996 (c. 27)	ss.65, 67	July 4, 1996	s.67(2)
Finance Act 1994 (c. 9)	s.105(3)(4)(b)	January 1, 1996	S.I. 1995 No. 3125 (C.72)
Finance Act 1994 (c. 9)	ss.244, 245	November 4, 1996	S.I. 1996 No. 2316 (C.59)
Finance Act 1995 (c. 4)	s.82	January 2, 1996	S.I. 1995 No. 2933 (C.63)
Finance Act 1996 (c. 8)	All provisions	April 29, 1996	Royal Assent
Finance Act 1996 (c. 8)	s.26, Sched. 3	June 1, 1996 [Appointed Day]	S.I. 1996 No. 1249 (C.21)
Finance Act 1996 (c. 8)	s.5 (part)	October 1, 1996 [Appointed Day]	S.I. 1996 No. 2314 (C.58)
Finance Act 1996 (c. 8)	s.8	November 1, 1996 [Appointed Day]	S.I. 1996 No. 2536 (C.70)
Finance Act 1996 (c. 8)	s.159(1), (3)	November 6, 1996 [Appointed Day]	S.I. 1996 No. 2646 (C.75)
Finance Act 1996 (c. 8)	s.6 (part), Sched. 1 (part)	November 15, 1996 [Appointed Day]	S.I. 1996 No. 2751 (C.80)
Finance Act 1996 (c. 8)	Sched. 35, para. 7(2)	January 31, 1997	S.I. 1997 No. 133 (C.8)
Further and Higher Education Act 1992 (c. 13)	ss.93(1) (so far as relates to Sched. 8, para. 10 remaining), 55(1), (2), (3), (7)(b) (remainder)	August 1, 1996	S.I. 1996 No. 1897 (C.41)
Gas Act 1995 (c. 45)	All remaining provisions	March 1, 1996	S.I. 1996 No. 218 (C.4)

Act Affected	**Provision Brought Into Force**	**Commencement Date**	**Authority**
Goods Vehicles (Licensing of Operators) Act 1995 (c. 23)	All provisions except s.50, Sched. 5	January 1, 1996	S.I. 1995 No. 2181 (C.44)
Health Authorities Act 1995 (c. 17)	s.1(1), 2(1), 4(1), 5(1) (rem.), Scheds. 1, 2, 3 (rem.)	April 1, 1996	s.1(2), 2(3), 4(2), 5(2)
Health Service Commissioners (Amendment) Act 1996 (c. 5)	All provisions	April 1, 1996 [ss.2(2), 4(2), 6(1) apply to actions beginning on or after April 1, 1996, and to actions before that date if reasonable to say that part of the same action occurs on or after that date]	S.I. 1996 No. 970 (C.15)
Home Energy Conservation Act 1995 (c. 10)	ss.3(1), 4(1), (2)	January 15, 1996	S.I. 1995 No. 3340 (C.79)
Home Energy Conservation Act 1995 (c. 10)	All remaining provisions (England only)	April 1, 1996	S.I. 1995 No. 3340 (C.79)
Home Energy Conservation Act 1995 (c. 10)	All provisions (Scotland only)	December 1, 1996	S.I. 1996 No. 2797 (C.82) (S.215)
Home Energy Conservation Act 1995 (c. 10)	ss.3(1), 4(1), (2)	January 10, 1997	S.I. 1996 No. 3181 (C.100)
Home Energy Conservation Act 1995 (c. 10)	All remaining provisions (Wales only)	April 1, 1997	S.I. 1996 No. 3181 (C.100)
Hong Kong Economic and Trade Office Act 1996 (c. 63)	All provisions	December 18, 1996	Royal Assent
Hong Kong (Overseas Public Servants) Act 1996 (c. 2)	All provisions	February 29, 1996	Royal Assent

Act Affected	Provision Brought Into Force	Commencement Date	Authority
Hong Kong (War Wives and Widows) Act 1996 (c. 41)	All provisions	July 18, 1996	Royal Assent
Housing Act 1996 (c. 52)	ss.2(7), (8), 5, 7 (part), 9(3), 17, 28(4), 36(1)–(6), 51 (part), 52, 53, 54, 55(1) (part), 55(2), (3), 56 to 64	August 1, 1996	S.I. 1996 No. 2048 (C.45)
Housing Act 1996 (c. 52)	ss.3(2), 7 (part), 24, 29 [so far as confer power to consult, make determinations, give consents and delegate functions]	August 1, 1996	S.I. 1996 No. 2048 (C.45)
Housing Act 1996 (c. 52)	ss.83(3) (part), 86(4) (part), (5) (part), 92 (part), 96 (part), 106 (part), 119 (part)	August 23, 1996	S.I. 1996 No. 2212 (C.55)
Housing Act 1996 (c. 52)	ss.219, 220, 222 (part), 227 (part)	September 24, 1996	S.I. 1996 No. 2402 (C.62)
Housing Act 1996 (c. 52)	ss.84, 88, 89, 90, 91, 92 (remainder), 93, 105, 107, 108, 109, 111 to 117, 227 (part)	October 1, 1996	S.I. 1996 No. 2212 (C.55)
Housing Act 1996 (c. 52)	ss.1, 2, 3, 4, 6, 7, 8, 9, 10–15, 22, 23, 30–34, 36(7), 37–50, 55(1) (part), 76, 77, 80(3), 129(3), (4), 135, 138(4)–(6), 139, 140, 141(2), (3), 142, 143, 160(4), (5), 165(1), (2), (5), 167(3)–(5), 169, 172, 174, 177 (3), 182, 183(2), 189(2)–(4), 199(5), 203(1), (2), (7), 210(2), 215, 217, 218, 222 (rem.), 227 (part)	October 1, 1996	S.I. 1996 No. 2402 (C.62)
Housing Act 1996 (c. 52)	ss.18(2), (7), 20(3), 21(3), 25, 27, 65, 66, 72, 75, 147, 161(2), (3), 162(4), 163(7), 185(2), (3), 194(6), 198(4)–(7), 207(4)–(6)	October 1, 1996 [so far as confers powers on the Corporation or the Secretary of State]	S.I. 1996 No. 2402 (C.62)

Act Affected	**Provision Brought Into Force**	**Commencement Date**	**Authority**
Housing Act 1996 (c. 52)	s.28(3)	October 1, 1996 [for enabling purposes]	S.I. 1996 No. 2402 (C.62)
Housing Act 1996 (c. 52)	s.167	October 23, 1996 [for consultation purposes]	S.I. 1996 No. 2658 (C.76)
Housing Act 1996 (c. 52)	ss.175, 176, 177 (rem.), 178–181, 183 (rem.), 184, 185 (rem.), 186–188, 189 (rem.), 190–193, 194 (rem.), 195–197, 198 (rem.), 199 (rem.), 200–202, 203 (rem.), 204–206, 207 (rem.), 208, 209, 210 (rem.), 211–214, 216, 227 (part)	January 20, 1997	S.I. 1996 No. 2959 (C.88)
Housing Act 1996 (c. 52)	ss.159, 160(1)–(3), 161 (rem.), 162 (rem.), 163 (rem.), 164, 165 (rem.), 166, 167 (rem.), 168, 170, 171, 173, 227 (part)	April 1, 1997	S.I. 1996 No. 2959 (C.88)
Housing Act 1997 (c. 52)	ss.124–128, 129(1), (2), (5), (6), 130–134, 136, 137, 138 (1)–(3), 141(1), 144–146, 147 (rem.)	February 12, 1997	S.I. 1997 No. 66 (C.5)
Housing Act 1996 (c. 52)	ss.96 (rem.), 97–104, 148–151, 227 (so far as relates to Sched. 19, Pt. IV)	February 28, 1997	S.I. 1997 No. 225 (C.12)
Housing Act 1996 (c. 52)	Part II; ss.65–80 (rem. except s.73)	March 3, 1997	S.I. 1997 No. 350 (C.16)
Housing and Planning Act 1986 (c. 63)	ss.53(1) (in so far as relates to Sched. 11, paras. 57, 58), 53(2) (in so far as relates to Sched. 12, Pt. IV repeals)	June 1, 1996	S.I. 1996 No. 1276 (C.22) (S.125)
Housing Grants, Construction and Regeneration Act 1996 (c. 53)	ss.146, 148–151	July 24, 1996	s.150(1)
Housing Grants, Construction and Regeneration Act 1996 (c. 53)	ss.74, 79, 86, 89, 94	September 11, 1996	S.I. 1996 No. 2352 (C.61)

Act Affected	Provision Brought Into Force	Commencement Date	Authority
Housing Grants, Construction and Regeneration Act 1996 (c. 53)	ss.2, 3, 7, 12, 17, 19, 25, 27, 30, 33, 44–47, 51, 52, 61, 63, 64, 67, 68, 76, 85, 87, 92, 101, 102, 104, 105, 106, 108, 114, 131–135, 139, 140	September 11, 1996 [so far as confers powers on Secretary of State or Lord Advocate]	S.I. 1996 No. 2352 (C.61)
Housing Grants, Construction and Regeneration Act 1996 (c. 53)	ss.126–130, 141, 142, 143–145, 147 (part), Sched. 3, Pt. III	September 24, 1996	s.150(2)
Housing Grants, Construction and Regeneration Act 1996 (c. 53)	s.125	October 1, 1996 [so far as relates to paras. 21(1) to (3) of Pt. III of Sched. 2]	S.I. 1996 No. 2352 (C.61)
Housing Grants, Construction and Regeneration Act 1996 (c. 53)	s.31 (part)	November 13, 1996 [so far as confers a power to make regulations]	S.I. 1996 No. 2842 (C.83)
Housing Grants, Construction and Regeneration Act 1996 (c. 53)	ss.1–59, 60–73, 75, 76–78, 80, 81–85, 87, 88, 90, 91, 92, 93, 95–103 (rem.), 147 (part)	December 17, 1996	S.I. 1996 No. 2842 (C.83)
Housing Grants, Construction and Regeneration Act 1996 (c. 53)	ss.118–125 (rem.), s.147 (part), Sched. 2	April 1, 1997	S.I. 1996 No. 2842 (C.83)
Humber Bridge (Debts) Act 1996 (c. 1)	All provisions	February 29, 1996	Royal Assent
Income and Corporation Taxes Act 1988 (c. 1)	s.51A	January 2, 1996 [Appointed Day]	S.I. 1995 No. 2932 (C.62)
Income and Corporation Taxes Act 1988 (c. 1)	s.737A	November 6, 1996 [Appointed Day]	S.I. 1996 No. 2645 (C.74)
Industrial Tribunals Act 1996 (c. 17)	All provisions	August 22, 1996	s.46
Industrial Tribunals Act 1996 (c. 17)	ss.12(3)–(6), 32(3)–(6) (for explanatory note see the Order)	December 18, 1996 [Appointed Day]	S.I. 1996 No. 3150 (C.98)
Insurance Companies (Reserves) Act 1995 (c. 29)	ss.1, 3	April 30, 1996	S.I. 1996 No. 945 (C.17)
Jobseekers Act 1995 (c. 18)	ss.28 (rem.), 29, 30, Sched. 3 (part)	April 1, 1996	S.I. 1995 No. 3228 (C.75)

Act Affected	Provision Brought Into Force	Commencement Date	Authority
Jobseekers Act 1995 (c. 18)	ss.27, 34(3), (7) (rem.)	April 6, 1996	S.I. 1995 No. 3228 (C.75)
Jobseekers Act 1995 (c. 18)	s.41(4) (so far as relates to paras. below), Sched. 2, paras. 38, 39, 40, 44, 45, 47, 52, 67, 68, 70, 73, 75, 76	April 22, 1996	S.I. 1996 No. 1126 (C.18)
Jobseekers Act 1995 (c. 18)	Sched. 2, paras. 10, 18, 21, 42, 46, 49, 50, 51, 53–64, 66, 71, 72, 74	June 11, 1996	S.I. 1996 No. 1509 (C.29)
Jobseekers Act 1995 (c. 18)	s.41(4) (so far as relates to following provisions), Sched. 2, paras. 2, 12, 14	September 2, 1996	S.I. 1996 No. 2208 (C.54)
Jobseekers Act 1995 (c. 18)	All remaining provisions	October 7, 1996	S.I. 1996 No. 2208 (C.54)
Landlord and Tenant (Covenants) Act 1995 (c. 30)	All provisions	January 1, 1996	S.I. 1995 No. 2963 (C.66)
Land Registers (Scotland) Act 1996 (c. 14)	All provisions	April 1, 1996	S.I. 1996 No. 94 (C.1) (S.4)
Land Registration (Scotland) Act 1979 (c. 33)	ss.2(1) (part), (2) (part), 3(3) (part)	April 1, 1997	S.I. 1996 No. 2490 (C.66) (S.195)
Law Reform (Miscellaneous Provisions) (Scotland) Act 1990 (c. 40)	ss.17 (rem.), 18 (rem.), 20, 21, 22 (part), 74 (part), Sched. 1, Pt. II, Sched. 8, paras. 19, 20, 22(1) (part), 22(2), 24, 25, 29(5) (part), 6(b) (part), Sched. 9 (repeals)	March 1, 1997	S.I. 1996 No. 2966 (C.89) (S.226) amending S.I. 1996 No. 2894 (C.85) (S.222)
Law Reform (Year and a Day Rule) Act 1996 (c. 19)	All provisions except for s.2	June 17, 1996	Royal Assent
Law Reform (Year and a Day Rule) Act 1996 (c. 19)	s.2	August 17, 1996	s.3(3)
Licensing (Amendment) (Scotland) Act 1996 (c. 36)	All provisions	October 21, 1996	S.I. 1996 No. 2670 (C.78) (S.209)

Act Affected	Provision Brought Into Force	Commencement Date	Authority
Local Government Act 1992 (c. 19)	Sched. 4, Pt. I (part) (relating to repeals in the Local Government, Planning and Land Act 1980 (c. 65))	August 8, 1996	S.I. 1996 No. 1888 (C.40)
Local Government and Housing Act 1989 (c. 42)	s.194(4) (part), Sched. 12, Pt. II (part)	July 22, 1996	S.I. 1996 No. 1857 (C.39)
Local Government etc. (Scotland) Act 1994 (c. 39)	ss.46, 180 (part), Sched. 13, paras. 176(2), (10), (12)(b), 16(a)–(c), Sched. 14 (repeals of certain provisions of the Local Government Finance Act 1992), Sched. 2, para. 8(5)(b) (part), para. 12(2)(b), (e), (f), Sched. 11, Pts. I, II, paras. 26, 27	February 19, 1996	S.I. 1996 No. 323 (C.6) (S.23)
Local Government etc. (Scotland) Act 1994 (c. 39)	ss.20, 33, 52, Sched. 6	April 1, 1996	S.I. 1995 No. 702 (C.18) (S.60)
Local Government etc. (Scotland) Act 1994 (c. 39)	ss.171 (rem.), 176	April 1, 1996	S.I. 1995 No. 2866 (C.60) (S.209)
Local Government Finance Act 1992 (c. 14)	Sched. 13, para. 39, Sched. 14 (part)	April 1, 1996	S.I. 1996 No. 918 (C.14) (S.102)
Local Government (Wales) Act 1994 (c. 19)	Sched. 17, para. 18(2)	January 1, 1996	S.I. 1995 No. 2816 (C.59)
Local Government (Wales) Act 1994 (c. 19)	s.66(6) (part), Sched. 16, para. 54(2)	January 1, 1996	S.I. 1995 No. 3178 (C.73)
Local Government (Wales) Act 1994 (c. 19)	s.66(8) (part), Sched. 1 (part)	January 1, 1996	S.I. 1995 No. 3198 (C.73)
Local Government (Wales) Act 1994 (c. 19)	ss.1(3) (part), (5), (6), (8), 8, 9, 10, 11, 12, 13, 16, 18(7), 20(1), (2), (3), 23(1), 49, 50, 66(6) (part), Sched. 2, paras. 1, 2, 3, 7, 10, 11, 12, Scheds. 4, 5, Sched. 16, para. 54(2)	April 1, 1996	S.I. 1995 No. 3198 (C.73)

Act Affected	Provision Brought Into Force	Commencement Date	Authority
Local Government (Wales) Act 1994 (c. 19)	ss.62, 66(7) (part), Sched. 17, paras. 15, 17	April 1, 1996	S.I. 1995 No. 3198 (C.73)
Local Government (Wales) Act 1994 (c. 19)	ss.17, 20(4) (part), 21, 22(1) (part), (2) (part), (3) (part), (4) (part), (5) (part), (6), 61, 66(5) (part), (6) (part), (7) (part), (8) (part), Sched. 6, paras. 1, 13–17, 19, 20, 22, 24(2)–(10) (9), 24(11)–(16), 24(17)(b)–27, Sched. 7, paras. 1–27(3), 28–43, Sched. 8, paras. 1–3(1), 3(3)–(11), Sched. 9, paras. 1–16, 17(1) (part), (2), (3), 17(5)–18, Sched. 10, paras. 1–10, 11(2)–13, Sched. 11, paras. 1, 2, 3(3)–(5), Sched. 15, paras. 2, 4, 5, 8(1)–(4), 9(1)–(4)(a), 10(2)–11(1), 12(a), 13–17, 21, 22, 24, 25, 27–51, 53, 54, 56, 62–66, Sched. 16, paras. 1–10, 13–25, 27–40(2)(a), 40(3)–54(1), 55, 56, 58–66, 68(1)–(5), 68(7) (part), 68(10)–(12), (17), (18), (20), 69, 71–81, 82(5) (part), 82(6)–83, 87, 89–92, 94, 95, 99–105, 107–109, Sched. 17, para. 16, Sched. 18 (part)	April 1, 1996	S.I. 1996 No. 396 (C.7)
London Regional Transport Act 1996 (c. 21)	All provisions	August 17, 1996	s.6(2)
Marriage Ceremony (Prescribed Words) Act 1996 (c. 34)	All provisions	February 1, 1997	S.I. 1996 No. 2506 (C.67)
Medical (Professional Performance) Act 1995 (c. 51)	ss.3, 4 (part), 5, 6, 7(1), (2) (part), Sched. paras. 1 (part), 4, 5, 6, 10(c), 22(b), 28(a), 29(a), 30(a)	May 1, 1996	S.I. 1996 No. 271 (C.5)

Act Affected	Provision Brought Into Force	Commencement Date	Authority
Medical (Professional Performance) Act 1995 (c. 51)	ss.4 (part), 7(2) (so far as relates to s.7(2)(b)), Sched., para. (so far as relates to para. 14), para. 14	September 1, 1996	S.I. 1996 No. 1631 (C.34)
Medical (Professional Performance) Act 1995 (c. 51)	ss.4 (part), 7(2) (so far as relates to s.7(2)(b)), Sched., para. 1 (so far as relates to para. 12), para. 12	September 1, 1996	S.I. 1996 No. 1631 (C.34)
Medical (Professional Performance) Act 1995 (c. 51)	ss.4 (part), 7(2) (so far as relates to s.7(2)(b)), Sched. para. 1 (so far as relates to other provisions of Sched. brought into force), para. 2, para. 12 (so far as not already in force), para. 13	January 1, 1997	S.I. 1996 No. 1631 (C.34)
Medicinal Products: Prescription by Nurses etc. Act 1992 (c. 28)	s.3	July 1, 1996	S.I. 1996 No. 1505 (C.28) (S.133)
Mental Health (Patients in the Community) Act 1995 (c. 52)	All provisions	April 1, 1996	s.7(2)
Merchant Shipping Act 1995 (c. 21)	All provisions	January 1, 1996	s.316(2)
Merchant Shipping Act 1995 (c. 21)	ss.171(1), 182(1)	May 30, 1996 [Appointed Day]	S.I. 1996 No. 1210 (C.20)
Motor Cycle Noise Act 1987 (c. 34)	All provisions	August 1, 1996	S.I. 1995 No. 2367 (C.47)
National Health Service (Amendment) Act 1995 (c. 31)	ss.7 (part), 8 (part), 9, 10, 11, 12, 14(2), Sched. (part)	January 1, 1996	S.I. 1995 No. 3214 (C.74) (S.240)
National Health Service (Amendment) Act 1995 (c. 31)	All remaining provisions	April 1, 1996	S.I. 1996 No. 552 (C.11)
National Health Service (Residual Liabilities) Act 1996 (c. 15)	All provisions	May 22, 1996	Royal Assent

Act Affected	Provision Brought Into Force	Commencement Date	Authority
Noise Act 1996 (c. 37)	ss.10(7), 13, 14(1), (2), (3), 10(8), (9), 11 (part), 12 (part), Sched. (part)	September 19, 1996	S.I. 1996 No. 2219 (C.56)
Non-Domestic Rating (Information) Act 1996 (c. 13)	All provisions	May 22, 1996	Royal Assent
Northern Ireland (Emergency Provisions) Act 1996 (c. 22)	All provisions	August 25, 1996	s.62(1)
Northern Ireland (Entry to Negotiations, etc.) Act 1996 (c. 11)	All provisions	April 29, 1996	Royal Assent
Nursery Education and Grant-Maintained Schools Act 1996 (c. 50)	All provisions except s.5 (so far as relates to following provisions), Sched. 1, paras. 6(1)(a), (2), (3) (so far as relates to inspections under para. 6(1)(a), (5)), paras. 8(2), 14 (so far as relate to inspections under para. 6(1)(A)), para. 16	September 1, 1996	S.I. 1996 No. 2022 (C.44)
Nursery Education and Grant-Maintained Schools Act 1996 (c. 50)	s.5 (so far as relates to Sched. 1, para. 6(1)(a))	December 10, 1996 [for the purpose of empowering the making of regulations]	S.I. 1996 No. 3192 (C.99)
Nursery Education and Grant-Maintained Schools Act 1996 (c. 50)	s.5 (so far as relates to Sched. 1, para. 6(5))	December 10, 1996	S.I. 1996 No. 3192 (C.99)
Nursery Education and Grant-Maintained Schools Act 1996 (c. 50)	s.5 (so far as relates to Sched. 1, paras. 6(2), (3), 8(2) (rem.), 16)	January 1, 1997	S.I. 1996 No. 3192 (C.99)
Nursery Education and Grant-Maintained Schools Act 1996 (c. 50)	s.5 (so far as relates to Sched. 1, para. 14 (rem.))	April 1, 1997	S.I. 1996 No. 3192 (C.99)
Offensive Weapons Act 1996 (c. 26)	All provisions except ss.4(1), (2), (3), 6(1), (2)	July 4, 1996	Royal Assent, ss.4(4), 6(3)

Act Affected	Provision Brought Into Force	Commencement Date	Authority
Offensive Weapons Act 1996 (c. 26)	s.4(1), (2), (3)	September 1, 1996	S.I. 1996 No. 2071 (C.48)
Offensive Weapons Act 1996 (c. 26)	s.6	January 1, 1997	S.I. 1996 No. 3063 (C.95)
Offshore Safety Act 1992 (c. 15)	ss.2(3)(b) (part), (c) (part), 3(3)(b) (part), 7(2) (part)	March 1, 1996	S.I. 1996 No. 487 (C.8)
Osteopaths Act 1993 (c. 21)	ss.1(1), (2) (part), (3) (part), (4) (part), 2(1), (2), (4), (5), (6), 34, 35(1), (2), (4), 36(1), (2), (4), (5), (6), 40, 41 (part), 42(1)–(6), (7) (part), Sched., Pt. I, paras. 1, 2, 4, 5, 6, 8, 11, 13, 14(2), (3) (part), 15, Pt. II	January 14, 1997 [Appointed Day]	S.I. 1997 No. 34 (C2)
Pensions Act 1995 (c. 26)	ss.39, 117 (part), 121 (part), 124 (part)	January 1, 1996	S.I. 1995 No. 3104 (C.71)
Pensions Act 1995 (c. 26)	ss.62–66, 120 (part), 121 (part), 124 (part), 174 (part), 175 (part)	January 1, 1996	S.I. 1995 No. 3104 (C.71)
Pensions Act 1995 (c. 26)	s.122 (part), Sched. 3, paras. 29, 32–37, 39(b), 42, 44(a)(i), 47	January 1, 1996	S.I. 1995 No. 3104 (C.71)
Pensions Act 1995 (c. 26)	ss.137(2)–(4), 137 (1)–(5), 138(5)	March 13, 1996 [for the purpose of authorising the making of orders]	S.I. 1996 No. 778 (C.13)
Pensions Act 1995 (c. 26)	ss.140(2), 142–144, 146	March 13, 1996 [for the purpose of authorising the making of regulations]	S.I. 1996 No. 778 (C.13)
Pensions Act 1995 (c. 26)	ss.1(1)–(4), (5) (part), (6), 2, Sched. 1, paras. 1–12, 14–17, 19, 20	April 1, 1996	S.I. 1996 No. 778 (C.13)

Act Affected	Provision Brought Into Force	Commencement Date	Authority
Pensions Act 1995 (c. 26)	ss.140(2), 142–144, 146	April 6, 1996	S.I. 1996 No. 778 (C.13)
Pensions Act 1995 (c. 26)	ss.119, 120 (rem.), 121 (rem.), 123(3), 124 (rem.), 148, 173 (part), 174 (rem.), 175 (rem.), 176, Sched. 6, para. 9, Sched. 7, Pt. III	April 6, 1996	S.I. 1996 No. 778 (C.13)
Pensions Act 1995 (c. 26)	ss.10(2), (3), 16–21, 27, 32, 33, 35, 37, 38, 40, 41, 47, 49, 50, 51, 56–61, 67, 68, 69, 73, 74(2), (3), (5)(b), 75, 76, 77, 87–89, 91–95, 136, 137, 139, 140(1), 141, 151 (part), 152–154, 155 (part), 173 (part), Sched. 5, para. 21 (part), Sched. 6, paras. 4, 5, 6(c), (e)	April 6, 1996 [for the purpose of authorising the making of regulations]	S.I. 1996 No. 778 (C.13)
Pensions Act 1995 (c. 26)	s.149	June 1, 1996 [for the purpose of authorising the making of regulations]	S.I. 1996 No. 778 (C.13)
Pensions Act 1995 (c. 26)	ss.10(1), 23, 151 (part), 81(1)(c), (2), (3)(f)(i), 82(1), 83(2), (3)(a), 84(1)(b), (2), (3), 86, 96(2), (5), 155 (part), 157(2), 158, 160, Sched. 5, para. 36	June 1, 1996 [for the purpose of authorising regulations]	S.I. 1996 No. 1412 (C.26)
Pensions Act 1995 (c. 26)	s.78(6)	June 1, 1996 [for the purpose of authorising regulations]	S.I. 1996 No. 1412 (C.26)
Pensions Act 1995 (c. 26)	s.1(5) (part), Sched. 1, para. 13	June 1, 1996	S.I. 1996 No. 1412 (C.26)
Pensions Act 1995 (c. 26)	s.167	July 15, 1996 [for the purpose of bringing into force provisions relating to the making of regulations in ss.10(8), (9), (10), 12A (8), (9), (10) of Family Law (Scotland) Act 1985]	S.I. 1996 No. 1843 (C.37) (S.151)

Act Affected	Provision Brought Into Force	Commencement Date	Authority
Pensions Act 1995 (c. 26)	s.116(1)	July 16, 1996	S.I. 1996 No. 1853 (C.38)
Pensions Act 1995 (c. 26)	s.78(1), (2), (3), (5), (7), (8) (part), 85(3)(a), Sched. 2, paras. 1–11, 13, 14(1), (2), (3), (4), 16, 17, 18(a), (b), 19, 20	August 1, 1996	S.I. 1996 No. 1412 (C.26)
Pensions Act 1995 (c. 26)	s.166 (subject to exceptions relating to MCA 1973)	August 1, 1996	S.I. 1996 No. 1675 (C.36)
Pensions Act 1995 (c. 26)	s.78(6)	August 1, 1996	S.I. 1996 No. 1412 (C.26)
Pensions Act 1995 (c. 26)	s.167	August 19, 1996	S.I. 1996 No. 1843 (C.37) (S.151)
Pensions Act 1995 (c. 26)	ss.21(3), 68, 117	October 6, 1996 [for the purpose of any transitional provisions contained in regulations made under ss.16–21]	S.I. 1996 No. 778 (C.13)
Pensions Act 1995 (c. 26)	ss.118, 122 (part), 125(2)–(4) (rem.), 151 (part)	October 16, 1996	S.I. 1996 No. 2637 (C.73)
Pensions Act 1995 (c. 26)	ss.3(2), 74(1), (5)(a), 165, Sched. 3, paras. 23, 44(a)(ii), Sched. 5, para. 80(f)	October 16, 1996 [for the purpose of making regulations]	S.I. 1996 No. 2637 (C.73)
Pensions Act 1995 (c. 26)	s.158	October 16, 1996 [for the purpose of making rules]	S.I. 1996 No. 2637 (C.73)
Pensions Act 1995 (c. 26)	s.136 (rem.), Part III (ss.135–151)	April 6, 1997	S.I. 1996 No. 778 (C.13)
Police Act 1996 (c. 16)	ss.44 (so far as relates to Sched. 5 of Police Act 1994), 52(2), (3), (4), 55, 61, 63(3), (8), (10), 93 (so far as relates to Pt. I of Sched. 9 to the Police Act 1994), Sched. 5 (part), Sched. 6, Sched. 9, Pt. I (part)	August 1, 1996	S.I. 1996 No. 1646 (C.35) (S.142)

Act Affected	Provision Brought Into Force	Commencement Date	Authority
Police Act 1996 (c. 16)	All provisions (except s.50(3), Pt. IV (including Scheds. 5, 6) other than s.88, Sched. 7, paras. 43, 45, 46, Sched. 8, para. 12, Sched. 9, Pt. II)	August 22, 1996	s.104
Police and Magistrates' Courts Act 1994 (c. 29)	s.51 (rem.)	January 1, 1996	S.I. 1994 No. 3075 (C.72) (S.163)
Police and Magistrates' Courts Act 1994 (c. 29)	ss.47(1)–(5), 49, 54, 63(9), 64 (all in rem.), 93 (part), Sched. 9, Pt. I	April 1, 1996	S.I. 1995 No. 492 (C.12) (S.34)
Prevention of Terrorism (Additional Powers) Act 1996 (c. 7)	All provisions	April 3, 1996	Royal Assent
Private International Law (Miscellaneous Provisions) Act 1995 (c. 42)	ss.5–8	January 8, 1996	s.16(2)
Private International Law (Miscellaneous Provisions) Act 1995 (c. 29)	Pt. III (ss.9–15)	May 1, 1996	S.I. 1996 No. 995 (C.16)
Private International Law (Miscellaneous Provisions) Act 1995 (c. 42)	ss.1, 2, 4	November 1, 1996	S.I. 1996 No. 2515 (C.69)
Proceeds of Crime (Scotland) Act 1995 (c. 43)	All provisions	April 1, 1996	s.50(2)
Public Order (Amendment) Act 1996 (c. 59)	All provisions	October 17, 1996	Royal Assent
Railway Heritage Act 1996 (c. 42)	All provisions	September 18, 1996	s.8(3)

Act Affected	Provision Brought Into Force	Commencement Date	Authority
Rating (Caravan and Boats) Act 1996 (c. 12)	All provisions	April 29, 1996	Royal Assent
Road Traffic (Driving Instruction by Disabled Persons) Act 1993 (c. 31)	All provisions	September 9, 1996	S.I. 1996 No. 1980 (C.43)
Road Traffic (New Drivers) Act 1995 (c. 13)	ss.5(1), (2), (8), (9), (10), 6 (part), 10(1), (5), Sched. 1, para. 11	March 1, 1997	S.I. 1997 No. 267 (C.13)
Road Traffic (New Drivers) Act 1995 (c. 13)	All remaining provisions	June 1, 1997	S.I. 1997 No. 267 (C.13)
School Inspections Act 1996 (c. 57)	All provisions	November 1, 1996	s.48(2)
Security Service Act 1996 (c. 35)	All provisions	October 14, 1996	S.I. 1996 No. 2454 (C.64)
Sex Discrimination Act 1975 (c. 65)	Codes of Practice relating to equal pay	March 26, 1997	S.I. 1997 No. 131 (C.6)
Sexual Offences (Conspiracy and Incitement) Act 1996 (c. 29)	All provisions	October 1, 1996	S.I. 1996 No. 2262 (C.57)
Shipping and Trading Interests (Protection) Act 1995 (c. 22)	All provisions	January 1, 1996	s.9(4)
Social Security (Overpayments) Act 1996 (c. 51)	All provisions	July 24, 1996	Royal Assent
Statute Law (Repeals) Act 1993 (c. 50)	s.1, Sched. 1	April 1, 1996	S.I. 1996 No. 509 (C.9)
Statutory Instruments (Production and Sale) Act 1996 (c. 54)	All provisions	July 24, 1996	Royal Assent
Theft (Amendment) Act 1996 (c. 62)	All provisions	December 18, 1996	Royal Assent
Trade Union Reform and Employment Rights Act 1993 (c. 19)	ss.7(2) (3), 51 (part), Sched. 10 (part)	April 1, 1996	S.I. 1993 No. 1908 (C.34)

Act Affected	**Provision Brought Into Force**	**Commencement Date**	**Authority**
Trading Schemes Act 1996 (c. 32)	All provisions	February 6, 1997	S.I. 1997 No. 29 (C.1)
Transport Act 1982 (c. 49)	s.18 (subject to qualifications)	August 1, 1996 [Appointed Day]	S.I. 1996 No. 1943 (C.42)
Transport and Works Act 1992 (c. 42)	ss.50, 52, 53, 54, 55, 56, 62, 65(1)(b) (part), 68(1) (part)	July 8, 1996	S.I. 1996 No. 1609 (C.33)
Trusts of Land and Appointment of Trustees Act 1996 (c. 47)	All provisions	January 1, 1997	S.I. 1996 No. 2974 (C.91)
Wild Mammals (Protection) Act 1996 (c. 3)	All provisions	April 29, 1996	s.7(2)

LAND REGISTRATION, SCOTLAND

REGISTERS AND RECORDS, SCOTLAND

THE LAND REGISTERS (SCOTLAND) ACT 1995 (COMMENCEMENT) ORDER 1996

(S.I. 1996 No. 94 (C. 1) (S. 4))

Made - - - - - 11th January 1996

INTRODUCTION

This Order brings into force on April 1, 1996, the Land Registers (Scotland) Act 1995 (c. 14).

The Secretary of State, in exercise of the powers conferred on him by section 2(2) of the Land Registers (Scotland) Act 1995 (c. 14) and of all other powers enabling him in that behalf, hereby makes the following Order:

Citation

1. This Order may be cited as the Land Registers (Scotland) Act 1995 (Commencement) Order 1996.

Appointed Day

2. The Land Registers (Scotland) Act 1995 shall come into force on 1st April 1996.

James Douglas-Hamilton
Minister of State,
Scottish Office

St Andrew's House, Edinburgh
11th January 1996

EVIDENCE

THE CIVIL EVIDENCE (FAMILY MEDIATION) (SCOTLAND) ACT 1995 (COMMENCEMENT AND TRANSITIONAL PROVISION) ORDER 1996

(S.I. 1996 No. 125 (C. 2) (S. 9))

Made - - - - - - *19th January 1996*

INTRODUCTION

This Order brings into force on February 19, 1996, the Civil Evidence (Family Mediation) (Scotland) Act 1995 (c. 6). The Act shall only apply to any evidence given or heard in any civil proceedings after that date.

The Lord Advocate, in exercise of the powers conferred on him by section 3(3) of the Civil Evidence (Family Mediation) (Scotland) Act 1995 (c. 6) and of all other powers enabling him in that behalf, hereby makes the following Order:

Citation

1. This Order may be cited as the Civil Evidence (Family Mediation) (Scotland) Act 1995 (Commencement and Transitional Provision) Order 1996.

Day appointed

2. Subject to article 3 below, 19th February 1996 is the day appointed for the coming into force of the Civil Evidence (Family Mediation) (Scotland) Act 1995.

Transitional provision

3.—(1) The said Act of 1995 shall not apply to any civil proceedings in which any evidence has been given or heard (in whole or in part) at any time prior to 19th February 1996.

(2) In paragraph (1) above, any such evidence includes evidence given by affidavit or on commission and evidence given in undefended family actions in terms of Part II of Chapter 49 of the Rules of the Court of Session 1994 (S.I. 1994/1443) or Part II of Chapter 33 of the Ordinary Cause Rules 1993 (S.I. 1993/1956).

Lord Advocate's Chambers
19th January 1996

Mackay of Drumadoon
Lord Advocate

ENVIRONMENTAL PROTECTION

THE ENVIRONMENT ACT 1995 (COMMENCEMENT NO. 5) ORDER 1996

(S.I. 1996 No. 186 (C. 3))

Made - - - - - - *31st January 1996*

INTRODUCTION

This Order, *inter alia*, brings into force provisions of the Environment Act 1995 (c. 25) concerning the Environment Agency and the Scottish Environment Protection Agency. Other provisions which are brought into force include those relating to air quality, mineral planning amendments, water undertakers' duties, national waste strategy and control of water pollution.

The Secretary of State, in exercise of his powers under section 125(3), (4) and (5) of the Environment Act 1995 (c. 25), hereby makes the following Order:

Citation

1. This Order may be cited as the Environment Act 1995 (Commencement No. 5) Order 1996.

Provisions coming into force on 1st February 1996

2. The following provisions of the Environment Act 1995 shall come into force on 1st February 1996—

section 5(2) and (5);
section 41 in so far as it confers power on the Secretary of State to make regulations and makes provision in relation to the exercise of that power;
section 55(7) to (10);
section 80;
sections 87 to 89;
section 90 in so far as it relates to paragraphs 2, 3 and 5 of Schedule 11;
section 91;
section 105 in so far as it relates to paragraphs 3 and 5(1) of Schedule 15;
section 117;
section 118(1) to (3);
section 118(4) and (5) in so far as they confer power to make an order or make provision in relation to the exercise of that power;
section 118(6);
section 119;
section 120(1) in so far as it relates to paragraphs 2, 13, 36, 37(2)(b), 43, 44, 67 in so far as it confers power to make regulations or makes provision in relation to the exercise of that power, 102, 103 in so far as it confers power to issue guidance or makes provision in relation to the exercise of that power, and 232(1) of Schedule 22; and
section 120(3) in so far as it relates to the repeals in Schedule 24 in relation to the Local Government etc. (Scotland) Act 1994 (c. 39), except the repeal in relation to section 165(6) of that Act.

Provisions coming into force on 1st April 1996

3. The following provisions of the Environment Act 1995 shall come into force on 1st April 1996—

section 2;
section 3(1);
section 5(1), (3) and (4);
section 6;

section 8;
sections 10 and 11;
sections 13 to 19;
sections 25 to 29;
sections 33 to 35;
section 37(3) to (8);
section 41 in so far as that section is not already in force;
sections 53 and 54;
section 55(1) to (6);
section 81;
section 92;
section 104;
section 105 in so far as it relates to paragraphs 1, 2, 4, 5(2) and (3), 6 to 12, 14(2) and (3), 15, 16, 18, 19 and 21 to 24 of Schedule 15;
sections 106 to 114;
section 115 in so far as that section is not already in force;
section 120(1) in so far as it relates to the following paragraphs of Schedule 22—

1, 3, 5 to 12, 14, 17 to 27(a), 28, 29(1) in so far as that sub-paragraph is not already in force, 29(2) to (20), (21)(a)(ii), (23) to (25) and (27) to (35), 30, 32 to 35, 37(3) and (5) to (8), 40, 41, 45, 46(1) to (4) and (6) to (11), 47 to 50, 51(4), 52, 54 to 66, 68(1), (2) in so far as it requires an application to be accompanied by the prescribed charge, (3), (4) and (6), 70(1) and (2), 72(2), 73(1), (2) in so far as it requires an application to be accompanied by the prescribed charge and (3) to (6), 74 in so far as it requires an application to be accompanied by the prescribed charge, 75, 76(2), (4) to (7) and (8)(b), 77, 78, 80(3), 82 in so far as that paragraph is not already in force, 83 to 87, 90, 93, 94, 96 to 101, 103 in so far as that paragraph is not already in force, 104 to 132, 133(2), 134, 136, 140, 141, 144 to 146, 148 to 152, 154 to 160, 164 to 168, 171 to 181, 184, 185, 187(2), 188 to 191, 193 to 212, 213(2)(a), (4) and (5), 214 to 222, 223(1)(a) and (b) and (2), 224 to 231 and 233;

section 120(2) in so far as it relates to paragraphs 1 to 6, 8 to 10, 12, 13, 14(1) to (4), (7) and (8) (in so far as that sub-paragraph relates to the definitions of "approval" and "the transfer date") and 16 to 24 of Schedule 23;
section 120(3) in so far as it relates to the following repeals in Schedule 24—

(i) the repeals in relation to the Public Health (Scotland) Act 1897 (60 & 61 Vict. c. 38);
(ii) the repeals in relation to the Alkali, &c, Works Regulation Act 1906 (6 Edw. 7. c. 14);
(iii) the repeals in relation to the Rivers (Prevention of Pollution) (Scotland) Act 1951 (14 & 15 Geo. 6. c. 66);
(iv) the repeal of section 151(5) of the Mines and Quarries Act 1954 (2 & 3 Eliz. 2. c. 70);
(v) the repeal of section 10(6)(a) of the Rivers (Prevention of Pollution) (Scotland) Act 1965 (c.13);
(vi) the repeal in relation to section 3(3)(b) of the Nuclear Installations Act 1965 (c. 57);
(vii) the repeals in relation to the Parliamentary Commissioner Act 1967 (c. 13);
(viii) the repeals in relation to the Sewerage (Scotland) Act 1968 (c. 47);
(ix) the repeal in relation to section 1(1)(g) of the Hovercraft Act 1968 (c. 59);

(x) the repeals in relation to the Agriculture Act 1970 (c. 40);
(xi) the repeal in relation to section 223(2) of the Local Government Act 1972 (c. 70);
(xii) the repeal of the Clyde River Purification Act 1972 (c. v);
(xiii) the repeals in relation to the Local Government (Scotland) Act 1973 (c. 65);
(xiv) the repeals in relation to section 28 of the Health and Safety at Work etc. Act 1974 (c. 37);
(xv) the repeals in relation to the Control of Pollution Act 1974 (c. 40) except that in relation to section 30(1) of that Act;
(xvi) the repeal of paragraph 1 of Schedule 2 to the Clean Air Enactments (Repeals and Modifications) Regulations 1974 (S.I. 1974/2170);
(xvii) the repeal in relation to Schedule 1 to the House of Commons Disqualification Act 1975 (c. 24);
(xviii) the repeal in relation to Schedule 1 to the Northern Ireland Assembly Disqualification Act 1975 (c. 25);
(xix) the repeals in relation to the Local Government (Scotland) Act 1975 (c. 30);
(xx) the repeals in relation to sections 5(2), 10 and 15 of the Salmon and Freshwater Fisheries Act 1975 (c. 51);
(xxi) the repeals in relation to the Water (Scotland) Act 1980 (c. 45);
(xxii) the repeal of paragraph 17(3) of Schedule 9 to the Roads (Scotland) Act 1984 (c. 54);
(xxiii) the repeal of regulations 2 and 4 of the Control of Industrial Air Pollution (Transfer of Powers of Enforcement) Regulations 1987 (S.I. 1987/180);
(xxiv) the repeal of sections 7(2) and (8) and 11(3) of the Control of Pollution (Amendment) Act 1989 (c. 14);
(xxv) the repeals in relation to the Water Act 1989 (c. 15);
(xxvi) the repeals in relation to the Environmental Protection Act 1990 (c. 43) except those in relation to sections 33(1), 36(11) and (12), 39(12) and (13), 54, 61, 75(3), 88, 143 of, and Schedule 8 to, that Act;
(xxvii) the repeals in relation to the Natural Heritage (Scotland) Act 1991 (c. 28);
(xxviii) the repeals in relation to the Water Industry Act 1991 (c. 56) except those in relation to section 4(6);
(xxix) in relation to the Water Resources Act 1991 (c. 57), the repeal of sections 1 to 14, 16 to 19, 58, 105(1), the repeal in relation to section 113(1), the repeal of sections 114, 117, 121 to 124, 131, 132, 144, 146, 150 to 153, 187, 196, 202(5), 206(2), 209(1), (2) and (4), 213 to 215, 218, the words "Subject to subsection (3) below," in section 219(2), section 219(3), the definitions of "the Authority" and "constituent council" in section 221(1) and Schedules 1, 3 and 4;
(xxx) the repeal in relation to section 72(1) of the Land Drainage Act 1991 (c. 59);
(xxxi) the repeals in relation to the Water Consolidation (Consequential Provisions) Act 1991 (c. 60);
(xxxii) the repeals in relation to the Clean Air Act 1993 (c. 11);
(xxxiii) the repeals in relation to the Radioactive Substances Act 1993 (c. 12);
(xxxiv) the repeals in relation to the Noise and Statutory Nuisance Act 1993 (c. 40);

(xxxv) the repeal of paragraph 17(4) of Schedule 9, and paragraph 3(1) and (2) of Schedule 11, to the Local Government (Wales) Act 1994 (c. 19);

(xxxvi) the repeal of the words "a river purification board" in section 165(6) of the Local Government etc. (Scotland) Act 1994 (c. 39).

Saving

4. Notwithstanding the coming into force on 1st April 1996 of the amendments made by paragraph 68(1) to (3) and (6) of Schedule 22 to the Environment Act 1995, section 36 of the Environmental Protection Act 1990 shall have effect in relation to England and Wales on and after that date in relation to any application for a licence under that section made, but not finally disposed of, before that date as if—

(a) those amendments had not been made;

(b) in subsection (4)(a) the words "the National Rivers Authority and" were omitted; and

(c) in subsection (4)(b) the words "the Authority or" were omitted.

Signed by authority of the Secretary of State,

James Clappison
Parliamentary Under Secretary of State,
Department of the Environment

31st January 1996

GAS

THE GAS ACT 1995 (APPOINTED DAY AND COMMENCEMENT) ORDER 1996

(S.I. 1996 No. 218 (C. 4))

Made - - - - - 5th February 1996

INTRODUCTION

This Order brings into force on March 1, 1996, s.12 of the Gas Act 1995 (c. 45). The Order also appoints that date for the purpose of s.18(2) of the 1995 Act.

The Secretary of State, in exercise of the powers conferred upon him by section 18(2) and (4) of the Gas Act 1995 (c. 45), hereby makes the following Order:

Citation

1. This Order may be cited as the Gas Act 1995 (Appointed Day and Commencement) Order 1996.

Appointment of appointed day

2. The day appointed for the purpose of section 18(2) of the Gas Act 1995 shall be 1st March 1996.

Commencement of section 12

3. Section 12 of the Gas Act 1995 shall come into force on 1st March 1996.

Tim Eggar,
Minister for Industry and Energy,
Department of Trade and Industry

5th February 1996

MEDICAL PROFESSION

THE MEDICAL (PROFESSIONAL PERFORMANCE) ACT 1995 (COMMENCEMENT NO. 1) ORDER 1996

(S.I. 1996 No. 271 (C. 5))

Made - - - - - 14th February 1996

INTRODUCTION

This Order brings into force on May 1, 1996 certain provisions of the Medical (Professional Performance) Act 1995 (c. 51). The provisions relate, *inter alia*, to the power of the General Medical Council through its appropriate Committees (i) to permit interim orders for suspension or conditional registration to be made for an initial period of six months rather than the original two months, and to make further interim orders for periods of up to three months at a time and (ii) to make an order for indefinite suspension in circumstances where the doctor's fitness to practise is judged by the General Medical Council's Health Committee to be seriously impaired by reason of his physical or mental condition and where the doctor concerned has already been suspended for at least two years.

At the Court at Buckingham Palace, the 14th day of February 1996

Present,

The Queen's Most Excellent Majesty in Council

Her Majesty, in exercise of the powers conferred upon Her by section 6 of the Medical (Professional Performance) Act 1995 (c. 51), and of all other powers enabling Her in that behalf, is pleased, by and with the advice of Her Privy Council, to order, and it is hereby ordered, as follows:

Citation and interpretation

1.—(1) This Order may be cited as the Medical (Professional Performance) Act 1995 (Commencement No. 1) Order 1996.

(2) In this Order—

(a) "the Act" means the Medical (Professional Performance) Act 1995; and

(b) "the 1983 Act" means the Medical Act 1983 (c. 54).

Appointed Day

2. 1st May 1996 is the day appointed for the coming into force of the provisions of the Act specified in column (1) of the Schedule to this Order (the subject matter of each provision being mentioned in column (2)).

N. H. Nicholls
Clerk of the Privy Council

Article 2

SCHEDULE

PROVISIONS OF THE ACT COMING INTO FORCE ON 1ST MAY 1996

(1) *Provision of the Act*	*(2)* *Subject matter*
Section 3	Preliminary Proceedings: interim orders
Section 4, so far as it relates to the provisions of the Schedule to the Act brought into force by this Order.	Supplementary and consequential amendments to the 1983 Act
Section 5	Expenses
Section 6	Commencement
Section 7(1)	Short title
Section 7(2), so far as it relates to the provisions of the Act brought into force by this Order.	Extent
In the Schedule, paragraph 1 (so far as it relates to the other provisions of the Schedule brought into force by this Order) and paragraphs 4, 5, 6, 10(c), 22(b), 28(a), 29(a) and 30(a)	Supplementary and consequential amendments to the 1983 Act, and to the National Health Service Act 1977 (c. 49), the National Health Service (Scotland) Act 1978 (c. 29), and the Health and Personal Social Services (Northern Ireland) Order 1972 (S.I. 1972/1265 (N.I. 14))

LOCAL GOVERNMENT, SCOTLAND
WATER SUPPLY, SCOTLAND

THE LOCAL GOVERNMENT ETC. (SCOTLAND) ACT 1994 (COMMENCEMENT NO. 7 AND SAVINGS) ORDER 1996

(S.I. 1996 No. 323 (C. 6) (S. 23))

Made - - - - - 9th February 1996

INTRODUCTION

This Order provides for the commencement on February 19, 1996, of certain provisions of the Local Government etc. (Scotland) Act 1994. Amendments and repeals to provisions of the Local Government Finance Act 1992 become effective, ensuring, *inter alia*, that new Scottish unitary councils will have responsibility for setting and collecting council tax in respect of financial years 1996/97 onwards. February 19, 1996 is also the commencement date for s.46, which relates to licensing boards.

The Order provides that the remaining provisions of the Act will become effective on April 1, 1996. These provisions relate principally to the transfer of functions.

The Secretary of State, in exercise of the powers conferred on him by section 184(2) and (3) of the Local Government etc. (Scotland) Act 1994 (c. 39) and of all other powers enabling him in that behalf, hereby makes the following Order:

Citation and interpretation

1.—(1) This Order may be cited as the Local Government etc. (Scotland) Act 1994 (Commencement No. 7 and Savings) Order 1996.

(2) In this Order, "the Act" means the Local Government etc. (Scotland) Act 1994.

Days appointed and savings

2.—(1) Subject to paragraph (2) below, 19th February 1996 is the day appointed for the coming into force of—

(a) section 46 of the Act (licensing boards);

(b) section 180 of the Act, so far as it relates to the provisions in Schedules 13 and 14 to the Act specified in sub-paragraphs (c) and (d) below;

(c) in Schedule 13 to the Act, paragraph 176(2), (10), (12)(b) and (16)(a) to (c); and

(d) in Schedule 14 to the Act, the repeals of the following provisions of the Local Government Finance Act 1992 (c. 14):—

(i) in section 93(1)(a) the words "regional, islands or district" and "as appropriate";

(ii) section 97(2);

(iii) section 112(2)(d);

(iv) in Schedule 2, in paragraph 8(5)(b), the words "or where the authority is a regional council, each amount set under section 93 of this Act", and, in paragraph 12(2), sub-sub-paragraph (b) and, in sub-sub-paragraphs (e) and (f), the word "levying"; and paragraph 19(7)(b); and

(v) in Schedule 11, Parts I and II and paragraphs 26 and 27.

(2) In the period until 1st April 1996, the provisions of the Local Government Finance Act 1992 which are amended or repealed by the provisions of the Act brought into force by paragraph (1)(b) to (d) above shall continue to apply (without amendment or repeal) in relation to any financial year which began prior to that date.

3. 31st March 1996 is the day appointed for the coming into force of—

(a) section 180 of the Act, so far as it relates to the provision in Schedule 13 to the Act specified in paragraph (b) below, and

(b) in Schedule 13 to the Act, paragraph 100(9)(b).

4.—(1) Subject to paragraph (2) below, 1st April 1996 is the day appointed for the coming into force of—

(a) the provisions of the Act specified in column 1 of Schedule 1 to this Order (which relate to the matters specified in column 2 of that Schedule);

(b) section 180 of the Act, so far as it relates to the provisions in Schedules 13 and 14 to the Act specified in sub-paragraphs (c) and (d) below;

(c) in Schedule 13 to the Act, paragraphs 1, 2, 4 (so far as not already in force), 5, 6, 8 to 26, 27 (so far as not already in force), 28 to 33, 35 to 37, 38(1) and (8), 39 to 56, 58, 59, 60 (so far as not already in force), 61, 63 to 66, 67 (so far as not already in force), 68 to 70, 71 (so far as not already in force), 72 (so far as already not in force), 73, 74, 75 (so far as not already in force), 76 to 84, 85(1), (2) and (3)(b)(ii) and (c), 86 to 91, 92 (other than sub-paragraphs (34), (35) and (48) and so far as not already in force), 93(1) and (3), 94, 95(3), (5) to (7) and (10), 96 to 99, 100(6) to (8) and (9)(a) to (i) (so far as not already in force), 101 to 115, 116(1) to (5), 117, 118, 119 (other than sub-paragraph (54)(a)(ii) and (h)(iii) and so far as not already in force), 120 to 128, 129 (so far as not already in force), 130 to 148, 150 to 155, 156 (so far as not already in force), 157 to 161, 163 to 166, 167 (other than sub-paragraphs (2), (4), (5), (7) and (9)), 168 to 175, 176 (so far as not already in force) and 178 to 184; and

(d) the repeals in Schedule 14 to the Act specified in Schedule 2 to this Order.

(2) The commencement, by virtue of paragraph (1)(d) above, of Schedule 14 to the Act so far as relating to the repeal of section 223 of the Local Government (Scotland) Act 1973 (c. 65) shall not affect the continuing operation of that section in relation to the councils constituted under section 2 of the Act for the areas of Orkney Islands, Shetland Islands and Western Isles.

George Kynoch
Parliamentary Under Secretary of State,
Scottish Office

St Andrew's House, Edinburgh
9th February 1996

Article 4(1)(a)

SCHEDULE 1

PROVISIONS OF THE ACT COMING INTO FORCE ON 1ST APRIL 1996

Column 1 *Provision of the Act*	*Column 2* *Subject matter*
Section 6	Date of elections.
Section 21	Application of section 211 of the Local Government (Scotland) Act 1973 (section 211 was amended by the Local Government and Housing Act 1989 (c. 42), s.159) to joint boards.
Section 22	Community councils.
Section 30	Rating authorities.
Section 31	Education.
Section 32	Co-operation between education authorities.
Section 35	Amalgamation schemes.
Section 41	Amendment of section 13 of the Transport Act 1968 (c. 73).
Section 45	Chief social work officer.
Section 48	Amendment of District Courts (Scotland) Act 1975 (c. 20).

Column 1 *Provision of the Act*	*Column 2* *Subject matter*
Section 51(1), (2), (4) and (5)	Registration of births, deaths and marriages.
Section 53	Records held by local authorities.
Section 54(1) to (4)	Use, acquisition and disposal of records.
Section 58 (so far as not already in force)	Further provision as to discharge of functions by authorities.
Section 65(1)	General duties of Secretary of State and of new authorities.
Section 68(2) and (3)	Functions of Customers Council.
Section 72	References to Monopolies and Mergers Commission.
Section 75	Maximum charges for services provided with help of new authority.
Section 78	Liability of occupiers etc. for charges.
Section 79(4)	Recovery of charges by diligence.
Section 80	Power to demand and recover charges not to affect duty to maintain domestic water supply etc.
Section 82	Arrears of charges: restrictions on voting.
Section 99	Compulsory acquisition of land.
Section 100	Disposal of land.
Section 102	Emptying of septic tanks.
Section 105	Restriction on references to Secretary of State of questions regarding water supply.
Section 106	Removal of restriction on supply of water to premises outwith water authority's limits of supply.
Section 107	Supply of water for use outwith Scotland.
Section 108	Further provisions as regards removal of restrictions on supply of water outwith limits of supply.
Section 109	Right of objection to proposed laying of mains.
Section 110	Vesting of certain supply pipes.
Section 111	Duty of water authority to keep map showing water mains etc.
Section 112	Simplification of provisions as respects opting for water supply by meter.
Section 117	Directions in the interests of national security.
Section 118(2) and (3)	Annual report.
Section 119	Records held by new authorities.
Section 120(2)	Notice of proposal to investigate new source of water supply.
Section 121	Power of new authorities to promote or oppose private legislation.
Section 127(1) (so far as not already in force)	The Principal Reporter.
Section 132	Duty of Administration to provide accommodation etc. for children's hearings.
Section 139	Report by local authority for purpose of investigation preliminary to children's hearing.
Section 140	Power of local authorities to provide assistance to voluntary organisations.
Section 142	Organisation of polling districts.
Section 144	Denominational schools: proposals under section 22D of Education (Scotland) Act 1980 (c. 44, s.22D was inserted by the Education (Scotland) Act 1981 (c. 58), s.6.

Column 1 *Provision of the Act*	*Column 2* *Subject matter*
Section 145	Provision of school transport and other facilities.
Section 162(2)	Abolition of Scottish Valuation Advisory Council.
Section 164(3), (4) and (5)	Calculation of limits on spending.
Section 174	Power of local authority to submit amending schemes to Secretary of State.
Section 183(2), (4) and (5)	Interpretation and amendment of statutory references.
Schedule 4	Amendments to the Town and Country Planning (Scotland) Act 1972 (c. 52).
Schedule 10	Recovery by diligence of charges payable to a collecting authority by virtue of section 79 of the Act.

Article 4(1)(d) SCHEDULE 2

REPEALS IN SCHEDULE 14 TO THE ACT COMING INTO FORCE ON 1ST APRIL 1996

Chapter	*Short title*	*Extent of repeal*
7 & 8 Geo. 6 c.26.	The Rural Water Supplies and Sewerage Act 1944.	The whole Act.
10 & 11 Geo. 6 c.41.	The Fire Services Act 1947.	In section 36, subsections (3) and (6).
10 & 11 Geo. 6 c.43.	The Local Government (Scotland) Act 1947.	In section 237(2)(b), the words from "and, if" to "determined".
11 & 12 Geo. 6 c.29.	The National Assistance Act 1948.	In section 33, subsection (2). In the Third Schedule, paragraphs 9 to 13.
12, 13 and 14 Geo. 6 c.74.	The Coast Protection Act 1949.	In section 20(5), the words "or the council of a district in Scotland".
12, 13 and 14 Geo. 6 c.97.	The National Parks and Access to the Countryside Act 1949.	In section 21(1), the words "general or district".
3 & 4 Eliz. 2 c.13.	The Rural Water Supplies and Sewerage Act 1955.	The whole Act.
4 & 5 Eliz. 2 c.60.	The Valuation and Rating (Scotland) Act 1956.	Section 1. Section 3. In section 43(1), the definition of "Advisory Council".
7 & 8 Eliz. 2 c.40.	The Deer (Scotland) Act 1959.	In section 25A, in subsection (2), the words "islands and district", and in subsections (4) and (5) the words "islands or district". In section 25D, in subsection (8), the words "islands or district".
1960 c.62.	The Caravan Sites and Control of Development Act 1960.	Section 24(8A).
1961 c.41.	The Flood Prevention (Scotland) Act 1961.	In section 4(2), the words "(whether a different authority from the local authority or not)". Section 12(2).
1965 c.49.	The Registration of Births, Deaths and Marriages (Scotland) Act 1965.	Section 15(4).

Chapter	*Short title*	*Extent of repeal*
1967 c.77.	The Police (Scotland) Act 1967.	Section 19(5). Section 21A.
1967 c.78.	The Water (Scotland) Act 1967.	The whole Act.
1967 c.86.	The Countryside (Scotland) Act 1967.	In section 49, subsection (5). In section 61, in each of subsections (5), (6) and (8), the word "local". In section 63, in each of subsections (2) and (4) to (9), the word "local" wherever it occurs, and in subsection (11), the word "local" where it first occurs and the words from "and any reference" to the end. In section 65(5), paragraph (c) and, in paragraph (f), the words "within the meaning of section 109(1) of the Water (Scotland) Act 1980"; and paragraph (g).
1968 c.16.	The New Towns (Scotland) Act 1968.	In section 34(1)(a), the words "water, sewerage or other".
1968 c.46.	The Health Services and Public Health Act 1968.	In section 71, subsection (3).
1968 c.47.	The Sewerage (Scotland) Act 1968.	Section 18. Section 40. Section 47. Section 52. In section 59(1), the definitions of "authorised officer", "local authority" and "trunk road".
1968 c.49.	The Social Work (Scotland) Act 1968.	Section 2. In section 5A(3), paragraph (b). Section 34(3). In section 36, subsections (1), (4) and (6). In section 76(2), the words "to which the case stands referred". In Schedule 3, in paragraph 3, sub-paragraph (i) and, in sub-paragraph (ii), the words "in any other case,".
1968 c.73.	The Transport Act 1968.	In section 9A(9)(b), the words "regional or islands". In section 56(4)(b), the words "regional or islands".
1970 c.6.	The Rural Water Supplies and Sewerage (Scotland) Act 1970.	The whole Act.
1971 c.49.	The Rural Water Supplies and Sewerage Act 1971.	The whole Act.
1972 c.52.	The Town and Country Planning (Scotland) Act 1972.	Section 4(5). Section 5(5) and (7). In section 8(1) the words from "and may provide for" to the end. In section 15(1), the words from "or of the provisions of Part IX" to "to be carried out, or", the words ", after holding a local inquiry or other hearing," and the words "carrying out the survey or are not". In section 22, the word "(1)" and subsection (2). Section 25(4). Section 28(3). Section 32(7). Section 49G.

Chapter	Short title	Extent of repeal
		Section 50(4). In section 52(4), the words "regional, general or district". In section 56F(1), the words from "and section 179" to "1973". In section 56K(10), the words "and section 179 of the Local Government (Scotland) Act 1973". Section 84A. In section 87A(1), the words "general and district". In section 102 in subsection (1) the words "to whom this subsection applies", and subsection (5). Section 169(8). Section 229A. In paragraphs (a) and (b) of section 231(2), the words "or as applied under section 181 of the Local Government (Scotland) Act 1973". Section 254(4). Section 265(9). In section 275(1), the definition of "district planning functions".
1973 c.65.	The Local Government (Scotland) Act 1973.	Section 1. Section 2. Section 3. Section 3A. Section 4. Section 5. Section 11. In section 24(5)(f), the words "regional, islands or district". Section 31(4). In section 47, in subsection (4), the words ", other than a water development board within the meaning of the Water (Scotland) Act 1980,", and subsection (5). In section 51, in subsection (1), the words "within the meaning of this Part of this Act" and subsection (3). In section 56(6), paragraphs (a) and (c). In section 56(9), paragraph (c). In section 63, in subsection (2), the words "or a district council" and, in subsection (5)(a), the words "or district council". In section 64(5), paragraphs (c) and (f). Section 69(4). Section 74(3). In section 83, in subsection (2), the words ", subject to subsection (3A) below,"; and subsections (2A), (2B) and (3A). In section 87, in subsection (1), the words "any other local authority in the area", in subsection (2), the words from "and where" to the end, and subsection (3). Section 90A. In section 106(1), paragraph (c) and the proviso. Section 109.

Chapter	*Short title*	*Extent of repeal*
		In section 111(1)(e), the words "or to a water development board within the meaning of the Water (Scotland) Act 1980.".
		Section 116(1) to (5), (7) and (8).
		In section 118, in subsection (1), the words "(a)" and paragraph (b) and, in subsection (5), the words "or any water development board within the meaning of the Water (Scotland) Act 1980".
		Section 127.
		Sections 131 and 132.
		In section 133, subsection (1).
		Section 134(1).
		Sections 137(1) and 138(1).
		Section 140.
		Sections 142 and 143.
		Section 146(7).
		Section 148(1).
		In section 153, in subsection (1), the words "regional or islands", in subsection (2), the words "regional or islands" and, wherever it occurs, "such" and, in subsection (3), the words "regional or islands" and, where it first occurs, "such".
		In section 154, in subsection (1), the words "Subject to subsection (3A) below" and "regional or islands", in subsection (2), the word "regional", in both places where it occurs, in subsection (3), the words "regional or islands" and "such" and subsections (3A) and (3B).
		Sections 154A and 154B.
		Sections 155(1) and 156(1).
		Section 159.
		Section 161.
		In section 163, subsection (1), in subsection (2), the words "as aforesaid" and subsection (3).
		In section 166, subsection (1) and, in subsection (2), paragraphs (a), (e) and (f).
		Section 168.
		Section 170A(5)(a).
		In section 170B(2), the words "or water development boards" where they first occur.
		Section 171(1) and (2).
		Section 173.
		Section 174.
		Section 176.
		Section 177.
		Section 179.
		Section 181.
		Section 182.
		Section 183.
		In section 202, in subsection (1), the words "Subject to subsection (1A) below"; and subsections (1A) and (13).
		In section 215, subsections (3) to (7).
		Sections 222 to 224.
		Section 226.
		Section 230.
		In section 235(1), the definitions of "area", "college council", "school council", "education committee" and "water authority".

Chapter	Short title	Extent of repeal
		In section 236(2), the words "Subject to section 74(3) of this Act and to section 20 of the Water (Scotland) Act 1980,"; and paragraph (e). Schedules 1 and 2. In Schedule 6, in paragraph 2, the letter "(a)". In Schedule 9, paragraph 53. Schedule 10. Schedules 13 and 14. In Schedule 17, in paragraph 1(1)(a), the words "or to a constituent board" and "or to a constituent water authority"; and paragraph 2. Schedule 20. Schedule 22. In Part II of Schedule 27, paragraphs 159, 180 and 182.
1974 c.40.	The Control of Pollution Act 1974.	Section 106(3).
1975 c.20.	The District Courts (Scotland) Act 1975.	Section 7(3). Section 18(3).
1975 c.24.	The House of Commons Disqualification Act 1975.	In Schedule 1, in Part IV, the entry relating to Her Majesty's Lord-Lieutenant or Lieutenant for an islands area in Scotland and, in the entry relating to Her Majesty's Lord-Lieutenant for the district of the city of Aberdeen, Dundee, Edinburgh, or Glasgow, the words "the district of".
1975 c.30.	The Local Government (Scotland) Act 1975.	In section 1, in subsection (3)(b), the words ", after consultation with the Advisory Council,", subsection (3)(c), and subsection (7). Section 4. Section 6(1A). In section 7(1A), the words "and, in the case of the non-domestic water rate, the net annual value and the apportioned net annual value of part residential subjects". Section 13. In section 16, the words ", water development boards". In section 23, subsections (1)(c) and (d) and (2)(c). In section 29A, in subsection (3)(a), the words from "or under" to "committees". In Schedule 3, paragraph 1(4); in paragraph 22, in sub-paragraph (2), the words from "(a)" to "or", where it occurs immediately following sub-paragraph (b); and in paragraph 28(1) the words "paragraph 1(4) above and" and ", a water development board". In Part II of Schedule 6, paragraphs 23 and 53.
1975 c.72.	The Children Act 1975.	In section 99(1), the word "or" immediately preceding paragraph (e).

Chapter	*Short title*	*Extent of repeal*
1976 c.66.	The Licensing (Scotland) Act 1976.	In section 1, subsection (3), in subsection (4), the words "district or islands" and, in subsection (5), the words "or electoral division". In section 3(2), the words "of the district or islands area". In section 5(8), the words "district or islands". In section 7, in subsection (1), the words "district and islands" and subsection (2).
1976 c.71.	The Supplementary Benefits Act 1976.	In Schedule 5, in paragraph 2(2), the words "and of", ", regions, islands areas" and "and", where it thirdly occurs, and, in paragraph 4(2), the words, ", a region, an islands area" and "or", where it secondly occurs.
1978 c.29.	The National Health Service (Scotland) Act 1978.	In section 16A(1), in paragraph (b), the words "of a regional or islands council's", in paragraph (c), the words "of a district or islands council's" and, in paragraph (d), the words "of a regional or islands council's".
1978 c.50.	The Inner Urban Areas Act 1978.	In section 1(2), the words "or region". In section 2(1), the words "or region", in both places where they occur. In section 7(1)(a), the words "or region".
1980 c.9.	The Reserve Forces Act 1980.	In section 131, in subsection (2), the words "the district of", subsections (3) and (4) and, in subsection (5), the words "the districts of".
1980 c.44.	The Education (Scotland) Act 1980.	In section 4, the words "regional or island authority". In section 6, in subsection (2), the letter "(a)" and paragraph (b) and subsection (3). Section 78. In section 86, in paragraph (a), the words from "or" to "authority", where thirdly occurring and in paragraph (e), the words "or by the director of education".
1980 c.45.	The Water (Scotland) Act 1980.	Sections 3 to 5. In section 10, in subsection (1), the words "or water development board"; in subsection (1A) the words "onto agricultural land or forestry land" and "or as the case may be water development board's"; and subsection (6). In section 11, in subsection (1), in paragraph (a), the words "or a water development board" and in paragraph (b) the words "or board"; in subsection (2), the words "or board"; in subsection (3), the words "or board" wherever they occur; in subsection (4), the words "or board" wherever they occur and "or "the transferee board" "; and in subsections (5) to (7), the words "or board" wherever they occur. In section 13, in subsection (1), the words "or water development board", in both places where they occur, "or board", in both places where they occur and "or area"; in subsection (2), the words "or water development board", "or board" wherever they

Chapter	Short title	Extent of repeal
		occur, "or area" and "or boards"; in subsection (3), the words "or water development board" and "or area, as the case may be"; and in subsection (6), the words "or water development board".
		Section 15.
		In section 16, in subsection (1), the words "or water development board"; and in each of subsections (2), (3) and (8), the words "or board" wherever they occur.
		In section 17, in subsection (1), the words "or water development board"; in subsection (2), the words "or water development board" and "or board"; in subsection (3), the words "or water development board" and, in both places where they occur, "or board"; and in subsection (4), the words "or water development board".
		In section 18, the words "or board" in both places where they occur.
		Section 20.
		In section 22, the words "or water development board".
		In section 23, in subsection (1), the words "or water development board"; in subsection (2), the words "or board"; and in subsection (3), the words "or water development board".
		In section 25(2), the words "or district", where they secondly occur.
		In section 27(1), the words "or district", where they secondly occur.
		In section 28, in subsection (1), the words "or a water development board"; and in subsection (2), the words "or water development board".
		In section 29, in subsection (2), the words "or water development board"; and in subsection (3), the words "or board".
		Section 30.
		In section 32, in subsection (1)(b), the words "subject to subsection (2),"; and subsection (2).
		In section 33, in subsection (1), the words "or water development board", "or their area, as the case may be" and "or board"; in subsection (3), the words "or water development board" in both places where they occur; and in each of subsections (4), (6)(b), (7), (8), (9) and (11), the words "or board" wherever they occur.
		Section 35(4).
		In section 38(1), the words "or water development board" and, in each of paragraphs (a), (c) and (d) "or board".
		Sections 40 and 41.
		Sections 42 to 46.
		In section 47(3), the word "and" where it first occurs.
		Sections 48 and 49.
		In section 54, subsection (2); and in subsection (3)(b), the words from "and in the case" to the end.

Chapter	*Short title*	*Extent of repeal*
		In section 58, in subsection (6), the words "or the district of a district council" and "or by that district council"; and subsection (8). Sections 60 and 61. Section 63(6). In section 68, in subsection (1), the words "or water development board" and "or board"; in the proviso to that subsection the words "or board"; and subsection (3). In section 70, in subsection (1), the words "or water development board"; in subsection (2), the words "or board"; in subsection (4), the words "or water development board"; and in the proviso to subsection (4), the words ", or as the case may be the Board,". In section 71, in subsection (1), the words "or water development board"; in subsection (5), the words "or board" and, where they secondly occur, "or boards"; and in subsection (6) the words "or boards". In section 72(2), the words "and water development board". In section 73, in subsection (1), the words "or water development board" and "or board"; and in each of subsections (2) and (3), the words "or board" wherever they occur. In section 76, in subsection (1), the words "or water development board" and "or board"; in subsection (2), the words "or water development board" and (wherever they occur, both in the subsection and in its proviso) "or board"; in subsection (3), the words "or water development board"; "or their area" and "or board"; and in the proviso to subsection (3), the words "or board"; and "or the area of that board". In section 76L(1), the definition of "local authority". Sections 80 to 92. In section 103, the words "or water development board" in both places where they occur. In section 107, in subsection (1)(b), the words "or a water development board" and "or board"; and in subsection (5), the words "or a water development board". In section 109, in subsection (1), the definitions of "the 1992 Act", "apportionment scheme", "apportionment note"; "Central Board", "constituent water authority", "contributing authority", "council water charge", "net annual value" and "part residential subjects"; and in subsection (3), the words "and water development board". In Schedule 1, in paragraph 3, the words "and the area of the water development board"; in paragraph 11, the words "where the river purification authority are not the same authority as the water authority"; in paragraph 12, the words "and the area of the board"; in paragraph 13, the words "not exceeding 10 pence"; in paragraph 14, the

Chapter	Short title	Extent of repeal
		words "or board"; in paragraph 17, the words "or board" and "or boards"; in paragraph 19, the words "or water development board" in both places where they occur and "or area"; in paragraph 20, the words "or water development board"; in paragraph 23, the words "or board" and "or boards"; in each of paragraphs 24, 26 and 27, the words "or water development board"; in paragraph 30, the words "or water development board" and "or board"; and in paragraph 31, the words "or board" in both places where they occur. In Schedule 2, in each of paragraphs 4 and 6, the words "or water development board" wherever they occur. In Schedule 3, in paragraph 1, the words "and water development board", "within their limits of supply or area" and from "and outside" to "removing mains" where they secondly occur; in paragraph 2(2), the words "or board" in both places where they occur; in paragraph 4(1), the words "within their limits of supply" and "within the said limits"; in paragraph 5, the words "within the limits of supply"; and paragraph 8. Schedules 7 and 8. In Schedule 10, Part II in so far as relating to the Local Government (Scotland) Act 1973.
1980 c.65.	The Local Government, Planning and Land Act 1980.	In section 8(1)(b), the words "(ii) a water authority; or". In section 20, in subsection (1), in the definition of "development body", sub-paragraph (i) of paragraph (b); and subsection (2A). In section 87(2), the word "(a)" and paragraph (b). In section 148(2), the words "exercising district planning functions". In Schedule 32, in paragraph 33, in sub-paragraph (4), the definition of "rates".
1981 c.23.	The Local Government (Miscellaneous Provisions) (Scotland) Act 1981.	Section 11. In Schedule 3, paragraphs 24, 28 and 38.
1982 c.16.	The Civil Aviation Act 1982.	In section 30, in subsection (1), the words ", other than a district council in Scotland," and the words from "and a" to "above" and, in subsection (2), the words ", other than a district council in Scotland," and, in section 88(10), the words ", other than a district council in Scotland.".
1982 c.43.	The Local Government and Planning (Scotland) Act 1982.	Sections 6 and 7. In section 14(2), the words "regional or islands council as". In section 27(4), the words from "Without" to "Act". Sections 33 and 34. In section 50, paragraph (c). Section 56. In Schedule 1, Part I. In Schedule 3, paragraph 16.

Chapter	*Short title*	*Extent of repeal*
1982 c.45.	The Civic Government (Scotland) Act 1982.	Section 87(6). Section 89(10). In section 122(2)(b), sub-paragraph (iii) and the word "and" immediately preceding it.
1983 c.2.	The Representation of the People Act 1983.	In section 18, in subsection (5), the words "any interested authority or", "(or in Scotland, the returning officer)", "or returning officer" in both places where they occur and, in the definition of "interested authority", sub-paragraph (iii) and, in subsection (6), the words "or returning officer". Section 25(3). In section 31(2), the words from "and for" to "polling district", where it secondly occurs. In section 204(1), in the definition of "electoral area", the words "division of".
1984 c.27.	The Road Traffic Regulation Act 1984.	In section 26(4), paragraph (b) and the word "and" immediately preceding it. In section 26(5), paragraph (b) and the word "or" immediately preceding it and the words "or, in Scotland, the district council,".
1984 c.54.	The Roads (Scotland) Act 1984.	In section 4(1), the words "or, in relation to cleansing, with a district council," and the words "or council". In section 95(2), the words "or by the district council". In Schedule 9, paragraphs 27(3)(a) and 64(5)(c).
1985 c.63.	The Water (Fluoridation) Act 1985.	Section 3. In section 4, in subsection (6), the words "or to terminate a preserved scheme"; and in subsection (7), the words "or terminate a preserved scheme".
1985 c.69.	The Housing Associations Act 1985.	In section 59, in subsections (1) and (2), the words "or regional council", wherever they appear.
1986 c.33.	The Disabled Persons (Services, Consultation and Representation) Act 1986.	In section 16, in the definition of "local authority", in paragraph (b), the words ", as read with section 2,".
1987 c.26.	The Housing (Scotland) Act 1987.	In section 61(11)(a), the words "council or", where first occurring. In section 212(4)(e), the words "or a water development board". Section 235. In Schedule 15, in paragraph 2(1), head (f). In Schedule 23, paragraph 23.
1989 c.9.	The Local Government Act 1988.	In section 1, in subsection (1), the words "and (k) a water development board in Scotland,"; and in subsection (3), the words "and (b) "water development board" has the same meaning as in section 109(1) of the Water (Scotland) Act 1980". In Schedule 2, the words "A water development board in Scotland and ", and (b) "water development board" has the same meaning as in section 109(1) of the Water (Scotland) Act 1980".

Chapter	Short title	Extent of repeal
1988 c.43.	The Housing (Scotland) Act 1988.	In section 55(1), the word "and" where it occurs immediately after the definition of "tenancy". In section 57(1), the word "neither" and the words from "nor" to "council", where thirdly occurring.
1988 c.47.	The School Boards (Scotland) Act 1988.	In section 22, in subsection (2), the definitions of "islands councillor" and "regional councillor". In Schedule 2, in paragraph 5, the words "Schedule 10 to" and "and Schedule 10 to".
1989 c.29.	The Electricity Act 1989.	In Schedule 5, in paragraph 8(a), the words "; and (iii) the water development board"; in paragraph 9, the words "and the water development board"; and in paragraph 14, the words ", or the area of any water development board.".
1989 c.42.	The Local Government and Housing Act 1989.	In section 2(6)(a), the words "or director of education" and the words from "or section" to "1980". In section 4(5), the words ", or Schedule 10 or 20 to,". In section 5(5), the words ", or Schedule 10 or 20 to,". In section 9(8)(b), the words ", or Schedule 10 or 20 to,". In section 14, subsections (2) and (3) and, in subsection (8), paragraphs (b), (c) and (d). In section 155(5), the letter "(d)". In Schedule 1, in paragraph 4, in sub-paragraph (1), in the definition of "ordinary committee", in paragraph (b), the words from "the authority's" to "or" and, in sub-paragraph (2), the definition of "social work committee" and the word "and" immediately preceding it. In Schedule 6, paragraphs 16 to 19. In Schedule 11, paragraph 43.
1990 c.43.	The Environmental Protection Act 1990.	In section 53, in subsection (4), the words "(other than an islands council)". In section 88(9), in paragraph (a), the words ", a regional council" and, in paragraph (b), the words ", regional council". In section 90(3), the words ", regional council". In section 92(1), the words ", regional council". In section 93(1), the words ", regional council". In section 95(1), the words ", regional council".
1991 c.22.	The New Roads and Street Works Act 1991.	In section 153, in subsection (1), the words "or district council" and "or council" and, in subsection (3), the words "or council".
1991 c.28.	The Natural Heritage (Scotland) Act 1991.	In section 22(1), in the definition of "compensation water", the words "or water development board". In section 24, in each of subsections (1)(a) and (9)(a), the words "or board".

Chapter	*Short title*	*Extent of repeal*
		In Schedule 7, in paragraph 5, in sub-paragraph (1), the words "or a water development board" and (in head (a)) "or board", in sub-paragraph (2), the words "or water development board" and in sub-paragraph (3), the words "or water development board" and "or board"; in paragraph 6, the words from ", including" to the end; and in paragraph 7, the words "or a water development board". In Schedule 8, in paragraph 1, in sub-paragraph (3), in the second column of the Table, in paragraph (a) of the entry relating to "All Orders", the words "or water development board (not being the applicant)".
1991 c.34.	The Planning and Compensation Act 1991.	In Schedule 13, paragraph 44.
1992 c.4.	The Social Security Contributions and Benefits Act 1992.	In section 127(1), the definition of "levying authority".
1992 c.5.	The Social Security Administration Act 1992.	In section 15A(3)(d), the words ", islands council". In section 191, the definition of "levying authority".
1992 c.14.	The Local Government Finance Act 1992.	In section 74(1), the words "regional, islands or district". In section 84, in subsection (1), the words "regional and islands" and, in subsection (2)(a), the words "regional or islands". In section 85, subsection (2), in subsections (3) and (5) the words "regional or islands" and, in subsection (4), the words "(a)" and "and" and paragraph (b). In section 86, in subsection (4) the words "region or islands" and, in subsections (10) and (11), the words "regional or islands". In section 87(9)(a), the words "regional or islands". In section 90(3)(a), the words "regional, islands or district". In section 94(9), the word "regional" and the words from "and may recover" to the end. Section 95. In section 99, in subsection (1), the definitions of "the 1968 Act", "council water charge", "levying authority", "public sewage treatment works", "public sewer" and "water authority" and in the definition of "housing body", paragraph (a); and in subsection (2), paragraphs (a)(ii) and (iii), (c) and (d). Section 107(1). In Schedule 9, paragraphs 9(c) and 25(d). In Schedule 11, paragraphs 24, 25, 31 to 34, 36, 37 and 38(a) to (c) and (e). In Schedule 13, paragraphs 37 and 93.
1993 c.43.	The Railways Act 1993.	In section 151(1), in the definition of "local authority", the words "regional council, islands council".

Chapter	Short title	Extent of repeal
		In Schedule 7, in paragraph 1, in sub-paragraph (1) the words "or a water development board" and "or board", in sub-paragraph (2) the words "or water development board" and in sub-paragraph (3), the words "or water development board" and "or board"; in paragraph 1 the words from ", meaning" to the end; and in paragraph [illegible] the words "or water development board".
		In Schedule 8, in paragraph 1, in sub-paragraph (1), in the second column of Table [illegible] in paragraph (a) of the entry [illegible] the words "or water development board [illegible] application)".
1991 c.34	The Planning and Compensation Act 1991	In Schedule 15, paragraph [illegible]
1992 c.4	The Social Security Contributions and Benefits Act 1992	In section [illegible](1), the definition of [illegible] authority".
1992 c.5	The Social Security Administration Act 1992	In section [illegible](3)(a), the words [illegible] authority". In section [illegible] the [illegible] authority".
1993 c.[illegible]	The [illegible] Act 1993	In section [illegible], the words [illegible]. [illegible] In section [illegible], the words "[illegible] and [illegible]" and [illegible] In subsection (1) the words "[illegible]" and [illegible]. In section [illegible], in paragraph (a) the words "[illegible] Scotland or [illegible]" and, in subsection (1)(b) and (c), the words "regional or islands" [illegible]. In section [illegible], the words "in Scotland or Islands" [illegible]. In section [illegible], the words "[illegible]". In section [illegible], the word "regional" and the words "and [illegible]" to the end. Section [illegible]. In section [illegible], in subsection (1), in the definitions of "the 1968 Act", "central water authority", "levying authority", "public sewage treatment works", "public sewer" and "water authority", and in the definition of "housing body", paragraph (a), and in subsection (2), paragraphs (a)(ii) and (iii), (c) and (d). Section [illegible](1). In Schedule [illegible], paragraphs [illegible] and [illegible]. In Schedule 11, paragraphs 2[illegible], 30, 3[illegible] and 38(a) to (c) and (f). In Schedule 1[illegible], paragraphs [illegible] and [illegible].
1993 c.45	The [illegible] Act 1993	In section 15(1), in the definition of "local authority", the words "regional", "council" or "district council".

LOCAL GOVERNMENT, ENGLAND AND WALES

WALES

THE LOCAL GOVERNMENT (WALES) ACT 1994 (COMMENCEMENT NO. 7) ORDER 1996

(S.I. 1996 No. 396 (C. 7))

Made - - - - - - *21st February 1996*

INTRODUCTION

This Order brings into force on April 1, 1996 various provisions of the Local Government (Wales) Act 1994 (c. 19). It is the final Commencement Order for this Act.

The Secretary of State for Wales, in exercise of the powers conferred upon him by section 66(3) of the Local Government (Wales) Act 1994 (c. 19), hereby makes the following Order:

Citation

1. This Order may be cited as the Local Government (Wales) Act 1994 (Commencement No. 7) Order 1996.

Interpretation

2. In this Order "the 1994 Act" means the Local Government (Wales) Act 1994.

Commencement of certain provisions of Part II of the 1994 Act

3. The provisions of Part II of, and Schedules 6, 7, 8, 9, 10 and 11 to, the 1994 Act which are specified in Schedule 1 to this Order shall come into force on 1st April 1996.

Commencement of certain provisions of Part VII of the 1994 Act

4. The provisions of Part VII of, and Schedules 15, 16, 17 and 18 to, the 1994 Act which are specified in Schedule 2 to this Order shall come into force on 1st April 1996.

Signed by authority of the Secretary of State for Wales

Gwilym Jones
Parliamentary Under Secretary of State,
Welsh Office

21st February 1996

Article 3 SCHEDULE 1

PROVISIONS OF PART II OF, AND SCHEDULES 6, 7, 8, 9, 10 AND 11 TO, THE 1994 ACT COMING INTO FORCE ON 1ST APRIL 1996

Provision of the 1994 Act	*Subject matter*
Section 17	General provision for transfer of functions.
Section 21	Local education authorities and minor authorities in Wales.
Section 22(6)	Transfer of specific functions; minor and consequential amendments to enactments.
Paragraphs 1 (paragraph 1 of Schedule 6 to the 1994 Act is amended by paragraph 38(1) of Schedule 10 to the Environment Act 1995 (c. 25)), 13 to 17, 19, 20, 22 (as a result of paragraph 30(6) of Schedule 10 to the Environment Act 1995 the paragraph (aa) inserted by paragraph 22 of Schedule 6 is re-numbered "(ab)"), 24(2) to (10)(a), 24(11) to (16) and 24(17)(b) to 27 of Schedule 6, and section 20(4) so far as it relates thereto	Minor and Consequential Amendments: Planning.
Paragraphs 1 to 27(3) and 28 to 43 of Schedule 7, and section 22(1) so far as it relates thereto	Highways, Road Traffic and Transport.
Paragraphs 1 to 3(1) and 3(3) to 11 of Schedule 8, and section 22(2) so far as it relates thereto	Housing.
Paragraphs 1 to 16, 17(1) (but only in respect of the insertion of paragraph (bb) into section 4(11) of the Environmental Protection Act 1990 (c. 43)), 17(2) (paragraph 17(2) of Schedule 9 to the 1994 Act is amended by paragraph 231 of Schedule 22 to the Environment Act 1995), 17(3) and 17(5) to 18 of Schedule 9, and section 22(3) so far as it relates thereto	Public Health.
Paragraphs 1 to 10 and 11(2) to 13 of Schedule 10, and section 22(4) so far as it relates thereto	Social Services.
Paragraphs 1, 2 and 3(3) to 5 of Schedule 11, and section 22(5) so far as it relates thereto	Water, Land Drainage and Coast Protection.

Article 4 SCHEDULE 2

PROVISIONS OF PART VII OF, AND SCHEDULES 15, 16, 17 AND 18 TO, THE 1994 ACT COMING INTO FORCE ON 1ST APRIL 1996

Provision of the 1994 Act	*Subject matter*
Section 61	Lieutenancies.
Paragraphs 2, 4, 5, 8(1) to (4), 9(1) to (4)(a), 10(2) to 11(1), 12(a), 13 to 17, 21, 22, 24, 25, 27 to 51, 53, 54, 56 and 62 to 66 of Schedule 15, and section 66(5) so far as it relates thereto	Minor and consequential amendments of the Local Government Act 1972.

Provision of the 1994 Act	*Subject matter*
Paragraphs 1 to 10, 13 to 25, 27 to 40(2)(a), 40(3) to 54(1), 55, 56, 58 to 66, 68(1) to (5), 68(7) (in respect of paragraph (b) of the new section 35(1A) of the Representation of the People Act 1983 (c. 2)), 68(10) to (12), 68(17), 68(18), 68(20), 69, 71 to 81, 82(5) (in respect of subsections (3) to (6) and (8) of the new section 4A of the Coroners Act 1988 (c. 13)), 82(6) to 83, 87, 89 to 92, 94, 95, 99 to 105 and 107 to 109 of Schedule 16, and section 66(6) so far as it relates thereto	Consequential amendments of miscellaneous enactments.
Paragraph 16 of Schedule 17, and section 66(7) so far as it relates thereto	Savings and Transitional Provisions: Planning.
In Schedule 18, the repeals to the Game Licences Act 1860 (c. 90), the Finance Act 1908 (c. 16), the Public Health Act 1936 (c. 49), the Education Act 1944 (c. 31), the Coast Protection Act 1949 (c. 74), the Disabled Persons (Employment) Act 1958 (c. 33), the Opencast Coal Act 1958 (c. 69), the Caravan Sites and Control of Development Act 1960 (c. 62), the Pipelines Act 1962 (c. 58), the Licensing Act 1964 (c. 26), the Harbours Act 1964 (c. 40), the Public Libraries and Museums Act 1964 (c. 75), the Gas Act 1965 (c. 36), the Agriculture Act 1967 (c. 22), the Slaughter of Poultry Act 1967 (c. 24), the Theatres Act 1968 (c. 54), the Mines and Quarries (Tips) Act 1969 (c. 10), the Post Office Act 1969 (c. 48), the Agriculture Act 1970 (c. 40), the Chronically Sick and Disabled Persons Act 1970 (c. 44), the Fire Precautions Act 1971 (c. 40), the Poisons Act 1972 (c. 66), sections 30, 60(5), 69(4), 76(2) and (3), 97(1), (2) and (3), 195(3), 213(1), 226(5), 227(1) and (2) and 245(6) to (9) of the Local Government Act 1972 (c. 70), paragraph 1(2)(c) and (d) of Schedule 11 to the Local Government Act 1972, paragraphs 4(a) and 11(1) of Schedule 26 to the Local Government Act 1972, the Employment Agencies Act 1973 (c. 35), the Breeding of Dogs Act 1973 (c. 60), the Slaughterhouses Act 1974 (c. 3), the Health and Safety at Work etc. Act 1974 (c. 37), the Consumer Credit Act 1974 (c. 39), the Control of Pollution Act 1974 (c. 40), the Reservoirs Act 1975 (c. 23), the Guard Dogs Act 1975 (c. 50), the Safety of Sports Grounds Act 1975 (c. 52), the Dangerous Wild Animals Act 1976 (c. 38), the Development of Rural Wales Act 1976 (c. 75), paragraph 4(5)(a) of Schedule 1 to the European Parliamentary Elections Act 1978 (c. 10), the Ancient Monuments and Archaeological Areas Act 1979 (c. 46), sections	Consequential repeals.

Provision of the 1994 Act	*Subject matter*
116(4)(a) and 165(9)(a) of, and paragraph 2(2)(a)(ii) of Schedule 32 to, the Local Government, Planning and Land Act 1980 (c. 65), the Zoo Licensing Act 1981 (c. 37), the Wildlife and Countryside Act 1981 (c. 69), the Civil Aviation Act 1982 (c. 16), sections 8(2), 18(2), 36(5), 39(6)(b) and 52(4)(a) of the Representation of the People Act 1983 (c. 2), the Level Crossings Act 1983 (c. 16), the Telecommunications Act 1984 (c. 12), the Road Traffic Regulation Act 1984 (c. 27), the Cinemas Act 1985 (c. 13), the Representation of the People Act 1985 (c. 50), the Transport Act 1985 (c. 67), the Airports Act 1986 (c. 31), the Gas Act 1986 (c. 44), the Building Societies Act 1986 (c. 53), the Fire Safety and Safety of Places of Sport Act 1987 (c. 27), the Road Traffic Act 1988 (c. 52), the Road Traffic Offenders Act 1988 (c. 53), the Electricity Act 1989 (c. 29), the Children Act 1989 (c. 41), paragraph 8(1) and (2)(a) of Schedule 1 to the Town and Country Planning Act 1990 (c. 8), the Planning (Listed Buildings and Conservation Areas) Act 1990 (c. 9), the Food Safety Act 1990 (c. 16), the Broadcasting Act 1990 (c. 42), sections 30(3)(a), 143(6)(b) and 149(11) of the Environmental Protection Act 1990 (c. 43), the Caldey Island Act 1990 (c. 44), the Road Traffic Act 1991 (c. 40), the Coal Mining Subsidence Act 1991 (c. 45), the Severn Bridges Act 1992 (c. 3), the Social Security Administration Act 1992 (c. 5), the Clean Air Act 1993 (c. 11), the Radioactive Substances Act 1993 (c. 12) and the Health Service Commissioners Act 1993 (c. 46); and section 66(8) so far as it relates thereto	
In Schedule 18, the repeals of sections 67(5)(f), 200 and 207 of the Local Government Act 1972, and section 66(8) so far as it relates thereto	Consequential repeals.

HEALTH AND SAFETY

THE OFFSHORE SAFETY ACT 1992 (COMMENCEMENT No. 2) ORDER 1996

(S.I. 1996 No. 487 (C. 8))

Made - - - - - *29th February 1996*

INTRODUCTION

This Order brings into force on March 1, 1996 various provisions of the Offshore Safety Act 1992 (c. 15) relating to the second repeal in the Gas Act 1986 (c. 44).

The Secretary of State, in exercise of the powers conferred on him by section 7(3) of the Offshore Safety Act 1992 (c. 15) and of all other powers enabling him in that behalf, hereby makes the following Order:—

1. This Order may be cited as the Offshore Safety Act 1992 (Commencement No. 2) Order 1996.

2. Sections 2(3)(b) and (c) and 3(3)(b) of the Offshore Safety Act 1992 and section 7(2) of that Act so far as relating to the second repeal in the Gas Act 1986 shall come into force on 1st March 1996.

Signed by order of the Secretary of State

Paul Beresford
Parliamentary Under Secretary of State,
Department of the Environment

29th February 1996

SHIPBUILDING INDUSTRY

THE STATUTE LAW (REPEALS) ACT 1993 (COMMENCEMENT) ORDER 1996

(S.I. 1996 No. 509 (C. 9))

Made - - - - - -	*1st March 1996*
Coming into force - - - -	*1st April 1996*

INTRODUCTION

This Order brings into force on April 1, 1996 the repeal of the Shipbuilding (Redundancy Payments) Act 1978 and of s.1 of the Shipbuilding Act 1985 by the Statute Law (Repeals) Act 1993. The 1978 Act provided, for a limited period, schemes to alleviate the hardship caused to redundant employees of British shipbuilders by the contraction of the international shipping market. However, the schemes have now expired and been replaced by non-statutory schemes.

The Lord Chancellor, in exercise of the powers conferred on him by section 4(3) of the Statute Law (Repeals) Act 1993 (c. 50), hereby makes the following Order:

Citation

1. This Order may be cited as the Statute Law (Repeals) Act 1993 (Commencement) Order 1996.

Appointed Day

2. The repeal by section 1 of, and Schedule 1 to, the Statute Law (Repeals) Act 1993 of—

(a) the Shipbuilding (Redundancy Payments) Act 1978 (c. 11); and
(b) section 1 of the Shipbuilding Act 1985 (c. 14),

shall come into force on 1st April 1996.

Dated 1st March 1996 *Mackay of Clashfern, C.*

CRIMINAL LAW, SCOTLAND

THE CRIMINAL JUSTICE (SCOTLAND) ACT 1995 (COMMENCEMENT NO. 2, TRANSITIONAL PROVISIONS AND SAVINGS) ORDER 1996

(S.I. 1996 No. 517 (C. 10) (S. 51))

Made - - - - - - 1st March 1996

INTRODUCTION

This Order provides for the commencement on March 5, 1996, of certain provisions of the Criminal Justice (Scotland) Act 1995, but only for the purpose of enabling subordinate legislation to be made under the provisions. All remaining provisions of the Act, except s.66, come into force on March 31, 1996.

The Secretary of State, in exercise of the powers conferred upon him by section 118(2) and (3) of the Criminal Justice (Scotland) Act 1995 (c. 20) and of all other powers enabling him in that behalf, hereby makes the following Order:

Citation and interpretation

1. This Order may be cited as the Criminal Justice (Scotland) Act 1995 (Commencement No. 2, Transitional Provisions and Savings) Order 1996.

2.—(1) In this Order—

"the Act" means the Criminal Justice (Scotland) Act 1995,

and, unless the context otherwise requires, any reference in this Order to a numbered section or Schedule is a reference to the section or Schedule bearing that number in the Act and, in article 5 of, and Schedule 2 to, this Order, includes a reference to any related repeal in Schedule 7 to the Act.

(2) For the purposes of this Order, criminal proceedings are commenced—

(a) in summary proceedings, on the date of the first calling of the case; and

(b) in solemn proceedings, on the date on whichever of the following first occurs:—

(i) the grant of a warrant to arrest and commit;

(ii) the intimation of a petition;

(iii) the service of an indictment.

Commencement of provisions

3.—(1) The provisions of the Act which are specified in column 1 of Schedule 1 to this Order shall come into force on 5th March 1996 but only for the purpose of enabling subordinate legislation to be made under the provisions specified in column 2 of that Schedule so as to come into force on or after 31st March 1996.

(2) Subject to the provisions of articles 4 to 6 of, and Schedule 2 to, this Order, all the provisions of the Act, except section 66, shall come into force on 31st March 1996 insofar as they are not then in force.

Transitional provisions and savings

4. The provisions of the Act specified in column 1 of Schedule 2 shall apply only in the cases, and in relation to the persons or matters, specified in column 2 of that Schedule.

5. Nothing in section 40, 54 or 113(3), Schedule 5 or paragraph 10 of Schedule 6 shall affect the powers of a court in relation to an offence committed before 31st March 1996.

6. Section 68 shall not apply in respect of the discharge of a debtor under section 54 of the Bankruptcy (Scotland) Act 1985 (c. 66) before 31st March 1996.

James Douglas-Hamilton
Minister of State,
Scottish Office

St Andrew's House, Edinburgh
1st March 1996

Article 3(1) SCHEDULE 1

Column 1 *Provision of the Act*	*Column 2* *Provision enabling subordinate legislation to be made*
Section 6(c)	Section 3(2) of the Jurors (Scotland) Act 1825 (c.22)
Section 14(4)	Section 337A(4) of the Criminal Procedure (Scotland) Act 1975 (c.21)
Section 61(6)	Section 56(7) of the Criminal Justice (Scotland) Act 1987 (c.41)

Article 4 SCHEDULE 2

Column 1 *Provision of the Act*	*Column 2* *Application*
Section 2	In relation to bail granted on or after 31st March 1996
Section 5	In relation to an application for bail made on or after 31st March 1996
Section 7(1)	In the case of a person excused from jury service on or after 31st March 1996
Section 7(2)	In the case of a person cited for jury service on or after 31st March 1996
Sections 11 and 13	In the case where the indictment is served on or after 31st March 1996
Section 15	In relation to criminal proceedings which are commenced on or after 31st March 1996
Sections 24 and 28	In the case where the trial commenced on or after 31st March 1996
Section 33	In relation to criminal proceedings which are commenced on or after 31st March 1996
Section 46	In the case of a new prosecution authorised under section 254(1)(c) or 452A(1)(c) of the Criminal Procedure (Scotland) Act 1975 (c.21; s.254 was substituted by the Criminal Justice (Scotland) Act 1980 (c.62), Sched. 2, para. 18; s.452A was inserted by the 1980 Act, Sched. 3, para. 11) on or after 31st March 1996
Section 58(2) to (4)	In the case of a person who is arrested or is detained under section 2(1) of the Criminal Justice (Scotland) Act 1980 (c.62) on or after 31st March 1996
Section 61	In relation to a conditional offer made under section 56 of the Criminal Justice (Scotland) Act 1987 (c.41) on or after 31st March 1996
Section 62	In relation to proceedings for an offence committed on or after 31st March 1996

Column 1 *Provision of the Act*	*Column 2* *Application*
Section 64, insofar as it inserts paragraph (da) in section 22(1) of the Legal Aid (Scotland) Act 1986 (c.47)	In relation to work done on or after 31st March 1996
In Schedule 6	
(a) paragraphs 14, 15 and 120	In relation to criminal proceedings which are commenced on or after 31st March 1996
(b) paragraphs 17(a) and 105(b)	In relation to bail granted on or after 31st March 1996
(c) paragraph 117(d)	In the case where a warrant under section 320 of the Criminal Procedure (Scotland) Act 1975 is served on or after 31st March 1996
(d) paragraph 179(2) and (3)	In the case of a person released on licence on or after 31st March 1996

NATIONAL HEALTH SERVICE, ENGLAND AND WALES
NATIONAL HEALTH SERVICE, SCOTLAND

THE NATIONAL HEALTH SERVICE (AMENDMENT) ACT 1995 (COMMENCEMENT No. 3) ORDER 1996

(S.I. 1996 No. 552 (C. 11))

Made - - - - - *4th March 1995*

INTRODUCTION

This Order brings into force on April 1, 1996, all remaining provisions of the National Health Service (Amendment) Act 1995 (c. 31) so far as they are not already in force. The provisions relate to powers of the National Health Service Tribunal (i) to direct the interim suspension of opticians, ophthalmic medical practitioners and pharmacists who are providing family health services under the National Health Service Act 1997 (c. 49), and under the National Health Service (Scotland) Act 1977 (c. 29), and (ii) when disqualifying them from inclusion in any list of such practitioners kept, to declare that they are not fit to be engaged in any capacity in the provision of those services.

The Secretary of State for Health, in exercise of the powers conferred on him by section 14(3) of the National Health Service (Amendment) Act 1995 (c. 31) and of all other powers enabling him in that behalf, hereby makes the following Order:—

Citation and interpretation

1. This Order may be cited as the National Health Service (Amendment) Act 1995 (Commencement No. 3) Order 1996.

Appointed day

2. 1st April 1996 is the day appointed for the coming into force of all the provisions of the National Health Service (Amendment) Act 1995 so far as they are not already in force.

Stephen Dorrell
4th March 1996 Secretary of State for Health

CHILDREN AND YOUNG PERSONS

THE CRIMINAL JUSTICE AND PUBLIC ORDER ACT 1994 (COMMENCEMENT NO. 9) ORDER 1996

(S.I. 1996 No. 625 (C. 12))

Made - - - - - *6th March 1996*

INTRODUCTION

This Order brings into force on March 8, 1996, the provisions of s.22 of the Criminal Justice and Public Order Act 1994 (c. 33) relating to the management of secure accommodation.

In exercise of the powers conferred upon him by section 172(2) of the Criminal Justice and Public Order Act 1994 (c. 33), the Secretary of State hereby makes the following Order:

1. This Order may be cited as the Criminal Justice and Public Order Act 1994 (Commencement No. 9) Order 1996.

2. Section 22 of the Criminal Justice and Public Order Act 1994 (management of secure accommodation) shall come into force on 8th March 1996.

Stephen Dorrell
One of Her Majesty's Principal Secretaries of State
6th March 1996 Department of Health

PENSIONS

THE PENSIONS ACT 1995 (COMMENCEMENT NO. 3) ORDER 1996

(S.I. 1996 No. 778 (C. 13))

Made - - - - - 12th March 1996

INTRODUCTION

Further provisions of the Pensions Act 1995 are brought into force by this Order on several commencement dates between March 13, 1996 and April 6, 1997. The provisions relate, *inter alia*, to the establishment of the Occupational Pensions Regulatory Authority, the regulation of occupational pension schemes, and the contracting-out by "hybrid schemes".

The Secretary of State for Social Security, in exercise of the power conferred on him by section 180(1) of the Pensions Act 1995 (c. 26) and of all other powers enabling him in that behalf, hereby makes the following Order:

Citation and interpretation

1.—(1) This Order may be cited as the Pensions Act 1995 (Commencement No. 3) Order 1996.

(2) In this Order, references to "the Act" are references to the Pensions Act 1995 and, except where the context otherwise requires, references to sections and Schedules are references to sections of, and Schedules to, the Act.

Appointed days

2.—(1) The day appointed for the coming into force of the provisions specified in Part I of the Schedule to this Order, for the purpose only of authorising the making of orders, is 13th March 1996.

(2) The day appointed for the coming into force of the provisions specified in Part II of the Schedule to this Order—

(a) for the purpose only of authorising the making of regulations, is 13th March 1996; and

(b) for all other purposes, is 6th April 1996.

(3) The day appointed for the coming into force of the provisions specified in Part III of the Schedule to this Order, is 1st April 1996.

(4) The day appointed for the coming into force of the provisions specified in Part IV of the Schedule to this Order, is 6th April 1996.

(5) The day appointed for the coming into force of—

(a) the provisions specified in Part V of the Schedule to this Order, for the purpose only of authorising the making of regulations, is 6th April 1996;

(b) sections 118 and 125, for the purpose only of authorising the making of regulations relating to those provisions of Part I of the Act specified in Part V of the Schedule to this Order, is 6th April 1996; and

(c) sections 21(3), 68 and 117, for the purpose only of any transitional provision contained in regulations made under sections 16 to 21 (member-nominated trustees and directors), is 6th October 1996.

(6) The day appointed for the coming into force of section 149 (hybrid occupational pension schemes), for the purpose only of authorising the making of regulations, is 1st June 1996.

(7) The day appointed for the coming into force of section 136 (new requirements for contracted-out schemes), insofar as not already in force, is

6th April 1997 and such day is designated as the principal appointed day for the purposes of Part III of the Act.

Signed by authority of the Secretary of State for Social Security.

Oliver Heald
Parliamentary Under Secretary of State,
Department of Social Security

12th March 1996

Article 2

SCHEDULE

PART I

PROVISIONS OF THE ACT COMING INTO FORCE ON 13TH MARCH 1996 FOR THE PURPOSE ONLY OF AUTHORISING THE MAKING OF ORDERS

Provisions of the Act	*Subject matter*
section 137(2) to (4)	reduced rates of Class 1 State scheme contributions in respect of members of salary related contracted-out schemes
section 137(1) and (5)	reduced rates of Class 1 State scheme contributions, and rebates, in respect of members of money purchase contracted-out schemes
section 138(5)	minimum contributions payable by the Secretary of State in respect of members of appropriate personal pension schemes

PART II

PROVISIONS OF THE ACT COMING INTO FORCE ON 13th MARCH 1996 FOR THE PURPOSE ONLY OF AUTHORISING THE MAKING OF REGULATIONS AND ON 6TH APRIL 1996 FOR ALL OTHER PURPOSES

Provisions of the Act	*Subject matter*
section 140(2)	reduction in State benefits for members of money purchase contracted-out schemes and appropriate schemes
sections 142 to 144	interim arrangements giving effect to protected rights
section 146	discharge of protected rights on winding up: insurance policies

PART III

PROVISIONS OF THE ACT COMING INTO FORCE ON 1ST APRIL 1996

Provisions of the Act	*Subject matter*
section 1(1) to (4) and (6)	establishment of Occupational Pensions Regulatory Authority

Provisions of the Act	*Subject matter*
section 2	reports by the Authority
Schedule 1, paragraphs 1 to 12, 14 to 17, 19 and 20 and section 1(5) insofar as it relates to those paragraphs	Occupational Pensions Regulatory Authority

PART IV

PROVISIONS OF THE ACT COMING INTO FORCE ON 6TH APRIL 1996

Provisions of the Act	*Subject matter*
section 119	calculations under regulations
section 120, insofar as not already in force	consultation about regulations
section 121, insofar as not already in force	Crown application
section 123(3)	meaning of "connected" and "associated" persons
section 124, insofar as not already in force	interpretation of Part I
section 148	Class 1 contributions where earner in more than one employment
section 174, insofar as not already in force	general provisions concerning regulations and orders
section 175, insofar as not already in force	Parliamentary control of regulations and orders
section 176	interpretation
Schedule 6, paragraph 9 and section 173 insofar as it relates to that paragraph	disclosure of information by the Secretary of State
in Schedule 7, Part III, the entry relating to section 48(2)(b) and (c) of the Pension Schemes Act 1993 (c.48) and section 177 insofar as it relates to that entry	repeals

PART V

PROVISIONS OF THE ACT COMING INTO FORCE ON 6TH APRIL 1996 FOR THE PURPOSE ONLY OF AUTHORISING THE MAKING OF REGULATIONS

Provisions of the Act	*Subject matter*
section 10(2) and (3)	civil penalties
sections 16 to 21	member-nominated trustees and directors
section 27	trustee not to be scheme auditor or actuary
section 32	decisions by majority of trustees
section 33	investment powers: duty of care
section 35	investment principles
section 37	payment of surplus to employer
section 38	power to defer winding-up
section 40	restriction on employer-related investments
section 41	provision of documents for members
section 47	professional advisers
section 49	receipts, payments and records
section 50	resolution of disputes

Provisions of the Act	Subject matter
section 51	annual increase in rate of pension
sections 56 to 61	minimum funding requirement
section 67	certification of detrimental amendments
section 68	power of trustees to modify schemes by resolution
section 69	grounds for applying to Authority for modification orders
section 73	preferential liabilities on winding up
section 74(2), (3) and (5)(b)	discharge of liabilities by insurance etc
section 75	deficiencies in the assets
section 76	excess assets on winding up
section 77	excess assets remaining after winding up: power to distribute
sections 87 to 89	money purchase schemes
sections 91 to 95	assignment, forfeiture, bankruptcy etc
section 136	new requirements for contracted-out schemes
section 137	State scheme contributions and rebates
section 139	money purchase and personal pension schemes: verification of ages
section 140(1)	reduction of State benefits for members of certified schemes
section 141	State scheme etc premiums and buyback into State scheme
sections 152 to 154	transfer values
section 155 but for the purpose only of authorising the making of regulations relating to section 113 of the Pension Schemes Act 1993	penalties for breach of regulations under the Pension Schemes Act 1993
Schedule 5, paragraph 21 (but only insofar as it relates to sections 11(5)(d), 34(2)(a), 50(4) and 163(6) of the Pension Schemes Act 1993), paragraph 22(a) (but only insofar as it relates to section 7(1) of that Act), and paragraphs 28(a), 33(b), 34(a), 35, 37, 39, 45(b), 46, 48(c), 49(a), 65, 70(c) and 84 and section 151 insofar as it relates to the above mentioned paragraphs	amendments relating to Part III of the Act
Schedule 6, paragraphs 4, 5 and 6(c) and (e) and section 173 insofar as it relates to those paragraphs	amendments relating to Part IV of the Act

LOCAL GOVERNMENT, SCOTLAND WATER SUPPLY, SCOTLAND

THE LOCAL GOVERNMENT FINANCE ACT 1992 (COMMENCEMENT NO. 10) ORDER 1996

(S.I. 1996 No. 918 (C. 14) (S. 102))

Made - - - - - *20th March 1996*

INTRODUCTION

This Order brings into force further provisions of the Local Government Finance Act 1992 on April 1, 1996. The provisions taking effect are Sched. 13, para. 39, the repeals in Sched. 14 of s.111(1)(a), (b), (c) of the Local Government (Scotland) Act 1973 relating to regulation-making powers with respect to rates, and s.9(6) of the Water (Scotland) Act 1980 relating to recovery of charges for non-domestic supply of water.

The Secretary of State, in exercise of the powers conferred upon him by section 119(2) of the Local Government Finance Act 1992 (c. 14) and of all other powers enabling him in that behalf, hereby makes the following Order:

Citation and interpretation

1.—(1) This Order may be cited as the Local Government Finance Act 1992 (Commencement No. 10) Order 1996.

(2) In this Order, "the Act" means the Local Government Finance Act 1992.

Commencement of provisions

2. The following provisions of the Act shall come into force on 1st April 1996—

(a) paragraph 39 of Schedule 13; and

(b) in Schedule 14, the repeals of—

(i) section 111(1)(a), (b) and (d) of the Local Government (Scotland) Act 1973 (c. 65); and

(ii) section 9(6) of the Water (Scotland) Act 1980 (c. 45).

George Kynoch
Parliamentary Under Secretary of State, Scottish Office

St Andrew's House, Edinburgh
20th March 1996

NATIONAL HEALTH SERVICE, ENGLAND AND WALES
NATIONAL HEALTH SERVICE, SCOTLAND

THE HEALTH SERVICE COMMISSIONERS (AMENDMENT) ACT 1996 (COMMENCEMENT) ORDER 1996

(S.I. 1996 No. 970 (C. 15))

Made - - - - - 27th March 1996

INTRODUCTION

The effect of this Order is to bring the whole of the Health Service Commissioners (Amendment) Act 1996 into force on April 1, 1996. This Order also brings certain actions which were begun before and continue after April 1, 1996, within the scope of the Health Service Commissioners Act 1993 by the 1996 Act.

In exercise of powers conferred by section 14 of the Health Service Commissioners (Amendment) Act 1996 (c. 5) and of all other powers enabling me in that behalf, I hereby make the following Order:

Citation and interpretation

1.—(1) This Order may be cited as the Health Service Commissioners (Amendment) Act 1996 (Commencement) Order 1996.

(2) In this Order, "the Act" means the Health Service Commissioners (Amendment) Act 1996.

Coming into force of the Act

2.—(1) The Act shall come into force on 1st April 1996.

(2) Sections 2(2), 4(2) and 6(1) of the Act shall apply in relation to—

(a) action beginning on or after 1st April 1996;

(b) action beginning before that date if it can reasonably be said that part of the same action occurs on or after that date.

Stephen Dorrell
One of Her Majesty's
Principal Secretaries of State

27th March 1996

PRIVATE INTERNATIONAL LAW

THE PRIVATE INTERNATIONAL LAW (MISCELLANEOUS PROVISIONS) ACT 1995 (COMMENCEMENT) ORDER 1996

(S.I. 1996 No. 995 (C. 16))

Made - - - - - *27th March 1996*

INTRODUCTION

This Order brings into force on May 1, 1996, ss.9–15 (Pt. III) of the Private International Law (Miscellaneous Provisions) Act 1995. These provisions establish new choice of law rules in respect of a tort or delict in relation to proceedings brought anywhere in the United Kingdom.

The Lord Chancellor and the Lord Advocate, in exercise of the power conferred on them by section 16(3) of the Private International Law (Miscellaneous Provisions) Act 1995 (c. 42), hereby make the following Order:

1. This Order may be cited as the Private International Law (Miscellaneous Provisions) Act 1995 (Commencement) Order 1996.

2. Part III of the Private International Law (Miscellaneous Provisions) Act 1995 shall come into force on 1st May 1996.

Mackay of Clashfern, C.
Dated 27th March 1996 *Mackay of Drumadoon*

INSURANCE

THE INSURANCE COMPANIES (RESERVES) ACT 1995 (COMMENCEMENT) ORDER 1996

(S.I. 1996 No. 945 (C. 17))

Made - - - - - 24th March 1996

INTRODUCTION

This Order brings into force on April 30, 1996, sections 1 and 3 of the Insurance Companies (Reserves) Act 1995 which relate to equalisation reserves.

The Secretary of State, in exercise of his powers under section 4(2) of the Insurance Companies (Reserves) Act 1995 (c. 29), hereby makes the following Order:

1. This Order may be cited as the Insurance Companies (Reserves) Act 1995 (Commencement) Order 1996.

2. Sections 1 and 3 of the Insurance Companies (Reserves) Act 1995 shall come into force on 30th April 1996.

Anthony Nelson
Minister of State,
24th March 1996 Department of Trade and Industry

SOCIAL SECURITY

THE JOBSEEKERS ACT 1995 (COMMENCEMENT NO. 2) ORDER 1996

(S.I. 1996 No. 1126 (C. 18))

Made - - - - - *18th April 1996*

INTRODUCTION

This Order brings into force on April 22, 1996, certain provisions in Schedule 2 of the Jobseekers Act 1995. References to this Act are inserted into the Social Security Administration Act 1992 (c. 5) and the Local Government Finance Act 1992 (c. 14).

The Secretary of State for Social Security, in exercise of the powers conferred upon him by section 41(2) and (3) of the Jobseekers Act 1995 (c. 18) and of all other powers enabling him in that behalf, hereby makes the following Order:

Citation

1. This Order may be cited as the Jobseekers Act 1995 (Commencement No. 2) Order 1996.

Appointed Day

2. 22nd April 1996 is the day appointed for the coming into force of—

(a) paragraphs 38, 39, 40, 44, 45, 47, 52, 67, 68, 69, 70, 73, 75 and 76 of Schedule 2 to the Jobseekers Act 1995 (which contain amendments to the Administration Act and the Local Government Finance Act 1992 (c. 14)); and

(b) section 41(4) of that Act in so far as it relates to those paragraphs.

Amendment of Commencement Order No. 1

3. In article 2(g) of the Jobseekers Act 1995 (Commencement No. 1) Order 1995 (S.I. 1995 No. 3228 (C. 75)), for the words "section 41(5)" there shall be substituted the words "section 41(4)".

Signed by authority of the Secretary of State for Social Security.

Roger Evans
Parliamentary Under-Secretary of State,
Department of Social Security

18th April 1996

DEFENCE

THE ARMED FORCES ACT 1991 (COMMENCEMENT NO. 2) ORDER 1996

(S.I. 1996 No. 1173 (C. 19))

Made - - - - - 24th April 1996

INTRODUCTION

This Order brings into force all remaining provisions of the Armed Forces Act 1991, on June 1, 1996. These provisions relate to the protection of children of service families, the repeal of obsolete provisions relating to the Channel Islands and the Isle of Man, and certain associated repeals.

The Secretary of State, in exercise of the powers conferred upon him by section 27(2) and (3) of the Armed Forces Act 1991 (c. 62), hereby makes the following Order:

1.—(1) This Order may be cited as the Armed Forces Act 1991 (Commencement No. 2) Order 1996.

2. Subject to article 3 of this Order, the following provisions of the Armed Forces Act 1991 shall come into force on 1st June 1996—
sections 17 to 23;
section 24(3);
section 26(2) and Schedule 3 insofar as they relate to the provisions specified in the Schedule to this Order.

3. The repeal of section 14 of the Armed Forces Act 1981 (c. 55; s.14 was amended by s.13 of the Armed Forces Act 1986 (c. 21)) (temporary removal to and detention in a place of safety abroad of children of service families in need of care and control) by virtue of article 2 of this Order shall not affect any order made under that section on or before 31st May 1996.

Michael Portillo
24th April 1996 Secretary of State for Defence

Article 2

SCHEDULE

REPEALS TAKING EFFECT ON 1ST JUNE 1996

Chapter	*Short title*	*Extent of repeal*
3 & 4 Eliz. 2 c. 18.	The Army Act 1955.	Section 216(4).
3 & 4 Eliz. 2 c. 19.	The Air Force Act 1955.	Section 214(4).
5 & 6 Eliz. 2 c. 53.	The Naval Discipline Act 1957.	Section 125(3).
1981 c. 55.	The Armed Forces Act 1981.	Section 14.
1986 c. 21.	The Armed Forces Act 1986.	Section 13.

MERCHANT SHIPPING

THE MERCHANT SHIPPING ACT 1995 (APPOINTED DAY NO. 1) ORDER 1996

(S.I. 1996 No. 1210 (C. 20))

Made - - - - - *30th April 1996*

INTRODUCTION

This Order provides that the appointed day for the purposes of ss.171(1) and 182(1) of the Merchant Shipping Act 1995 is May 30, 1996. These sections relate to transitory text and power to make transitional provisions. On this date the provisions set out in Sched. 4 as 'Chapter III' and 'Chapter IV' will no longer have effect.

The Secretary of State for Transport, in exercise of the powers conferred by sections 171(1) and 182(1) of the Merchant Shipping Act 1995 (c.21), hereby makes the following Order:

1. This Order may be cited as the Merchant Shipping Act 1995 (Appointed Day No. 1) Order 1996.

2. The day appointed for the purposes of sections 171(1) and 182(1) of the Merchant Shipping Act 1995 is 30th May 1996.

Signed by authority of the Secretary of State for Transport

Goschen
Parliamentary Under Secretary of State,
Department of Transport

30th April 1996

VALUE ADDED TAX

THE FINANCE ACT 1996, SECTION 26, (APPOINTED DAY) ORDER 1996

(S.I. 1996 No. 1249 (C. 21))

Made - - - - - *9th May 1996*

INTRODUCTION

This Order allows for the provisions of s.26 and Sched. 3 to the Finance Act 1996 to be brought into force on June 1, 1996, so far as they are not already in force on that date. These provisions relate to fiscal and other warehousing.

The Commissioners of Customs and Excise, in exercise of the power conferred on them by section 26(2) of the Finance Act 1996 (c. 8) and of all other powers enabling them in that behalf, hereby make the following Order:

1. This Order may be cited as the Finance Act 1996, section 26, (Appointed Day) Order 1996.

2. To the extent that they are not in force by virtue of section 26(3) of the Finance Act 1996, the day appointed as the day on which section 26 of and Schedule 3 to the Finance Act 1996 come into force is 1st June 1996.

Martin Brown
Commissioner of Customs and Excise

New King's Beam House
22 Upper Ground
London SE1 9PJ

9th May 1996

TOWN AND COUNTRY PLANNING, SCOTLAND

THE HOUSING AND PLANNING ACT 1986 (COMMENCEMENT NO. 19) (SCOTLAND) ORDER 1996

(S.I. 1996 No. 1276 (C. 22) (S. 125))

Made - - - - - 7th May 1996

INTRODUCTION

This Order brings into force on June 1, 1996, provisions of the Housing and Planning Act 1986. These provisions amend sections of the Town and Country Planning (Scotland) Act 1972 relating to listed buildings and local inquiries.

The Secretary of State, in exercise of the powers conferred on him by section 57(2) of the Housing and Planning Act 1986 (c. 63) and of all other powers enabling him in that behalf, hereby makes the following Order:

Citation

1. This Order may be cited as the Housing and Planning Act 1986 (Commencement No. 19) (Scotland) Order 1996.

Provisions coming into force on 1st June 1996

2. The following provisions of the Housing and Planning Act 1986 shall come into force on 1st June 1996:—

(a) section 53(1) (minor and consequential amendments) in so far as it relates to paragraphs 57 and 58 of Schedule 11; and

(b) section 53(2) (repeals) in so far as it relates to the repeals in Part IV of Schedule 12 specified in the Schedule to this Order.

Lindsay
Parliamentary Under Secretary of State,
Scottish Office

St Andrew's House, Edinburgh
7th May 1996

Article 2(b)

SCHEDULE

REPEALS IN PART IV OF SCHEDULE 12 COMING INTO FORCE ON 1ST JUNE 1996

Chapter	*Short title*	*Extent of repeal*
1968 c.14.	Public Expenditure and Receipts Act 1968.	In Schedule 3, in paragraph 6, the entry relating to section 355(8) of the Local Government (Scotland) Act 1947.
1972 c.52.	Town and Country Planning (Scotland) Act 1972.	In section 53(2), the word "only" and the words "(in this Act referred to as listed building consent)".
		In section 53(4) the words "under section 54 of this Act,".
1974 c.32.	Town and Country Amenities Act 1974.	Section 5.
1984 c.27.	Road Traffic Regulation Act 1984.	In section 129(1)(d) the words "(including" to "in the inquiry)".

INCOME TAX

THE CAPITAL ALLOWANCES ACT 1990, SECTION 33A, (APPOINTED DAY) ORDER 1996

(S.I. 1996 No. 1323 (C. 23))

Made - - - - - 16th May 1996

INTRODUCTION

This Order provides that the appointed day for the purpose of s.33A of the Capital Allowances Act 1990 (inserted by s.94 of the Finance Act 1995) is May 31, 1996. The section allows shipowners to make claims for the deferment of balancing charges on ship disposals which take place on or after April 21, 1996.

The Treasury, in exercise of the powers conferred on them by section 33F(3) of the Capital Allowances Act 1990 (c. 1; section 33F was inserted by section 97(1) of the Finance Act 1995 (c. 4) and amended by paragraph 6 of Schedule 35 to the Finance Act 1996 (c. 8)), hereby make the following Order:

1. This Order may be cited as the Capital Allowances Act 1990, section 33A, (Appointed Day) Order 1996.

2. The date appointed for the purposes of section 33A of the Capital Allowances Act 1990 (section 33A was inserted by section 94 of the Finance Act 1995 and amended by paragraph 2 of Schedule 35 to the Finance Act 1996) as the date before which no claim under that section may be made is 31st May 1996.

Derek Conway
Simon Burns
Two of the Lords Commissioners
of Her Majesty's Treasury

16th May 1996

EDUCATION, ENGLAND AND WALES

THE EDUCATION (SCHOOLS) ACT 1992 (COMMENCEMENT NO. 4) ORDER 1996

(S.I. 1996 No. 1538 (C. 24))

Made - - - - - *14th May 1996*

INTRODUCTION

This Order brings into force on May 15, 1996, sections 2(3)(c) and (d), 3(2), 6(3)(c) and (d), and 7(2) of the Education (Schools) Act 1992 relating to school inspections. All other provisions have been brought into force except paragraph 4(1) of Schedule 4, and in Schedule 5 the repeal of paragraph 5 of Schedule 1 to the Education Reform Act 1988.

In exercise of the power conferred on the Secretary of State by section 21(3) of the Education (Schools) Act 1992 (c. 38), the Secretary of State for Education and Employment as respects England, and the Secretary of State for Wales as respects Wales, hereby make the following Order:

1. This Order may be cited as the Education (Schools) Act 1992 (Commencement No. 4) Order 1996.

2. Sections 2(3)(c) and (d), 3(2), 6(3)(c) and (d), and 7(2) of the Education (Schools) Act 1992 shall come into force on 15th May 1996.

Robin Squire
Parliamentary Under Secretary of State,
30th April 1996 Department for Education and Employment

Rod Richards
Parliamentary Under Secretary of State,
14th May 1996 Welsh Office

DISABLED PERSONS

THE DISABILITY DISCRIMINATION ACT 1995 (COMMENCEMENT NO. 2) ORDER 1996

(S.I. 1996 No. 1336 (C. 25))

Made - - - - - *16th May 1996*

INTRODUCTION

This Order brings into force on May 17, 1996 various provisions of the Disability Discrimination Act 1995 relating to, *inter alia*, the definition of "disability" and "disabled person" (ss.1 and 2), and the provision of advice and assistance (s.28).

The Secretary of State for Social Security, in exercise of the powers conferred upon him by section 70(3) of the Disability Discrimination Act 1995 (c. 50), and of all other powers enabling him in that behalf, hereby makes the following Order:

Citation

1. This Order may be cited as the Disability Discrimination Act 1995 (Commencement No. 2) Order 1996.

Appointed day

2. The day appointed for the coming into force of the provisions of the Disability Discrimination Act 1995 specified in article 3 below is 17th May 1996.

Provisions commenced

3. The provisions referred to in article 2 above are—

(a) section 1 (Meaning of "disability" and "disabled person");
(b) section 2 (Past disabilities);
(c) section 3 (Guidance);
(d) section 16(3) in so far as it relates to the definitions of "sub-lease" and "sub-tenancy", and (5) in so far as it relates to paragraph 4 of Schedule 4 (Sub-leases etc);
(e) section 28 (Provision of advice and assistance);
(f) section 59 (Statutory authority and national security);
(g) section 62(1), (2) and (7) (Restriction of publicity: industrial tribunals);
(h) section 63(1), (2), (4), (5) and (6) (Restriction of publicity: Employment Appeal Tribunal);
(i) section 67 (Regulations and orders);
(j) section 68(1) (Interpretation);
(k) section 69 (Financial provisions);
(l) section 70(7) (House of Commons disqualification);
(m) Schedule 1 (with the exception of paragraph 7) (Provisions Supplementing Section 1);
(n) Schedule 2 (Past Disabilities);
(o) Schedule 4, paragraph 4 (Sub-leases etc.).

Signed by authority of the Secretary of State for Social Security.

MacKay of Ardbrecknish
Minister of State,
Department of Social Security

16th May 1996

PENSIONS

THE PENSIONS ACT 1995 (COMMENCEMENT NO. 4) ORDER 1996

(S.I. 1996 No. 1412 (C. 26))

Made - - - - - *31st May 1996*

INTRODUCTION

This Order brings into force further provisions of the Pensions Act 1995. Certain provisions for the purpose only of authorising the making of regulations shall come into effect on June 1, 1996, and those provisions relating to the establishment of the Pensions Compensation Board shall have effect on August 1, 1996.

The Secretary of State for Social Security, in exercise of the power conferred on him by section 180(1) of the Pensions Act 1995 (c. 26) and of all other powers enabling him in that behalf, hereby makes the following Order:

Citation and interpretation

1.—(1) This Order may be cited as the Pensions Act 1995 (Commencement No. 4) Order 1996.

(2) In this Order, references to "the Act" are references to the Pensions Act 1995 and, except where the context otherwise requires, references to sections and Schedules are references to sections of, and Schedules to, the Act.

Appointed days

2.—(1) The day appointed for the coming into force of the provisions specified in Part I of the Schedule to this Order, is 1st August 1996.

(2) The day appointed for the coming into force of the provisions specified in Part II of the Schedule to this Order, for the purpose only of authorising the making of regulations, is 1st June 1996.

(3) The day appointed for the coming into force of section 78(6) of the Act:

(a) for the purpose only of authorising the making of regulations, is 1st June 1996; and

(b) for all other purposes, is 1st August 1996.

(4) The day appointed for the coming into force of Schedule 1 paragraph 13 of the Act and section 1(5) in so far as it relates to that paragraph, is 1st June 1996.

Signed by authority of the Secretary of State for Social Security.

Roger Evans
Parliamentary Under-Secretary of State,
31st May 1996 Department of Social Security

Article 2

SCHEDULE

Part I

Provisions of the Act Coming into Force on 1st August 1996

Provisions of the Act	*Subject matter*
Section 78(1) to (3), (5) and (7)	establishment of the Pensions Compensation Board
section 85(3)(a)	investment of surplus funds held by the Pensions Compensation Board
Schedule 2 paragraphs 1 to 11, 13, 14(1) to (4), 16, 17, 18(a) and (b), 19 and 20 and section 78(8) in so far as it relates to those paragraphs	Pensions Compensation Board

Part II

Provisions of the Act Coming into Force on 1st June 1996 for the Purpose Only of Authorising the Making of Regulations

Provisions of the Act	*Subject matter*
section 10(1)	period for paying penalties
section 23	requirement for independent trustee
section 81(1)(c), (2) and (3)(f)(i)	cases where compensation provisions apply
section 82(1)	applications for payment
section 83(2) and (3)(a)	amount of compensation
section 84(1)(b), (2) and (3)	payments made in anticipation
section 86	modifications of compensation provisions
section 96(2) and (5)	review of decisions
section 155 in so far as not already in force for the purpose of making regulations	penalties for breach of regulations under the Pension Schemes Act 1993
section 157(2)	jurisdiction of the Pensions Ombudsman
section 158	payment of costs and expenses by the Pensions Ombudsman
section 160	interest on late payment of benefit
Schedule 5, paragraph 36 and section 151 in so far as it relates to that paragraph	investment and resources of schemes

DISABLED PERSONS

THE DISABILITY DISCRIMINATION ACT 1995 (COMMENCEMENT NO. 3 AND SAVING AND TRANSITIONAL PROVISIONS) ORDER 1996

(S.I. 1996 No. 1474 (C. 27))

Made - - - - - - 5th June 1996

INTRODUCTION

This Order brings into force provisions relating to the Disability Discrimination Act 1995. On June 6, 1996, those provisions authorising the making of regulations and relating to Codes of Practice come into force. On July 31, 1996, further provisions relating to the education and further education of disabled persons come into force. On December 2, 1996 various other sections of the Act are brought into force, including, *inter alia*, provisions relating to employment and provision of goods, facilities and services.

The Secretary of State for Social Security, in exercise of the power conferred upon him by sections 67(3) and 70(3) of the Disability Discrimination Act 1995 (c. 50), and of all other powers enabling him in that behalf, hereby makes the following Order:

Citation and interpretation

1.—(1) This Order may be cited as the Disability Discrimination Act 1995 (Commencement No. 3 and Saving and Transitional Provisions) Order 1996.

(2) In this Order, unless the context otherwise requires, references to sections and Schedules are references to sections of and Schedules to the Disability Discrimination Act 1995.

Appointed days

2.—(1) The day appointed for the coming into force of the provisions specified in Part I of the Schedule to this Order is 6th June 1996.

(2) The day appointed for the coming into force of the provisions specified in Part II of the Schedule to this Order is 31st July 1996.

(3) The day appointed for the coming into force of the provisions specified in Part III of the Schedule to this Order, subject to the saving and transitional provisions set out in article 3 below, is 2nd December 1996.

Saving and transitional provisions

3. Notwithstanding the repeal of sections 9 to 11, 12, 14 and 19 of the Disabled Persons Employment Act 1944 (c. 10) by the bringing into force by this Order of section 61 and Schedule 7:

(a) sections 9, 12 and 19 of the Disabled Persons (Employment) Act 1944 shall continue to have effect so as to allow prosecutions to be brought until 3rd December 1997 against persons alleged to have contravened section 9(2), section 9(5) or section 12(2) of that Act prior to 2nd December 1996:

(b) section 14 of the Disabled Persons (Employment) Act 1944 and regulation 9 of The Disabled Persons (General) Regulations 1945 (SR & O 1945/1558) shall continue to have effect so as to allow prosecutions to be brought until 3rd December 1997 against persons alleged to have contravened section 9(2), section 9(5) or section 12(2) of that Act prior to 2nd December 1996 and, where it is alleged that contravention of section 14(6) or section 14(7) of that Act hinders such prosecution, so as to allow prosecutions to be brought against persons alleged to have contravened those subsections.

Signed by authority of the Secretary of State for Social Security.

Alistair Burt
Minister of State,
Department of Social Security

5th June 1996

Article 2 SCHEDULE

PART I

PROVISIONS COMING INTO FORCE ON 6TH JUNE 1996

Provisions of the Disability Discrimination Act 1995	*Subject matter*
Section 5(6) and (7).	Meaning of "discrimination".
Section 6(8), (9) and (10).	Duty of employer to make adjustments.
Section 8(6) and (7).	Enforcement, remedies and procedure.
Section 12(3) and (6).	Discrimination against contract workers.
Section 14(6).	Meaning of "discrimination" in relation to trade organisations.
Section 16(5) to the extent not already in force.	Alterations to premises occupied under leases.
Section 17(3).	Occupational pension schemes.
Section 18(3) and (4).	Insurance services.
Section 19(5)(c).	Discrimination in relation to goods, facilities and services.
Section 20(6), (7) and (8).	Meaning of "discrimination".
Section 24(5).	Meaning of "discrimination".
Section 53.	Codes of practice prepared by the Secretary of State.
Section 54.	Further provision about codes issued under section 53.
Section 56.	Help for persons suffering discrimination.
Schedule 4, Part I, paragraph 3.	Premises occupied under leases—occupation by employer or trade organisation.

PART II

PROVISIONS COMING INTO FORCE ON 31ST JULY 1996

Provisions of the Disability Discrimination Act 1995	*Subject matter*
Section 29(3).	Education of disabled persons.
Section 30(1) to (6).	Further and higher education of disabled persons.
Section 31.	Further and higher education of disabled persons: Scotland.

PART III

PROVISIONS COMING INTO FORCE ON 2ND DECEMBER 1996

Provisions of the Disability Discrimination Act 1995	*Subject matter*
Section 4.	Discrimination against applicants and employees.
Section 5(1) to (5).	Meaning of "discrimination".
Section 6(1) to (7), (11) and (12).	Duty of employer to make adjustments.
Section 7.	Exemption for small businesses.
Section 8(1) to (5) and (8).	Enforcement, remedies and procedures.
Section 9.	Validity of certain agreements.
Section 10.	Charities and support for particular groups of persons.
Section 11.	Advertisements suggesting that employers will discriminate against disabled persons.
Section 12(1), (2), (4) and (5).	Discrimination against contract workers.
Section 13.	Discrimination by trade organisations.
Section 14(1) and (3).	Meaning of "discrimination" in relation to trade organisations.
Section 16(1), (2) and (4).	Alterations to premises occupied under leases.
Section 17(1), (2) and (4).	Occupational pension schemes.
Section 18(1) and (2).	Insurance services.
Section 19(1)(a), (c) and (d), (2), (3), (4), 5(a) and (b) and (6).	Discrimination in relation to goods, facilities and services.
Section 20(1), (3) and (4).	Meaning of "discrimination".
Section 22.	Discrimination in relation to premises.
Section 23.	Exemption for small dwellings.
Section 24(1) to (4).	Meaning of "discrimination".
Section 25.	Enforcement, remedies and procedure.
Section 26.	Validity and revision of certain agreements.
Section 55.	Victimisation.
Section 57.	Aiding unlawful acts.
Section 58.	Liability of employers and principals.
Section 60.	Appointment by Secretary of State of advisers.
Section 61.	Amendment of Disabled Persons (Employment) Act 1944.
Section 64.	Application to Crown etc.
Section 65.	Application to Parliament.
Section 66.	Government appointments outside Part II.
Section 68(2) to (5).	Interpretation.
Section 70(4).	Short title, commencement, extent etc.
Schedule 1, paragraph 7.	Persons deemed to be disabled.
Schedule 3.	Enforcement and Procedure.

Provisions of the Disability Discrimination Act 1995	*Subject matter*
Schedule 4, Part 1, paragraphs 1 and 2.	Premises occupied under leases.
Schedule 6.	Consequential Amendments.
Schedule 7 and section 70(5) insofar as is necessary to effect the repeal of sections 1, 6 to 14, 19 and 21 of The Disabled Persons (Employment) Act 1944 and section 2 of The Disabled Persons (Employment) Act 1958.	Repeals.

MEDICINES
NATIONAL HEALTH SERVICE, SCOTLAND

THE MEDICINAL PRODUCTS: PRESCRIPTION BY NURSES ETC. ACT 1992 (COMMENCEMENT NO. 2) ORDER 1996

(S.I. 1996 No. 1505 (C. 28) (S. 133))

Made - - - - - 5th June 1996

INTRODUCTION

This Order brings into force on July 1, 1996, s.3 of the Medicinal Products: Prescription by Nurses etc. Act 1992. All provisions of the Act are now in force.

The Secretary of State, in exercise of the powers conferred on him by section 6(2) of the Medicinal Products: Prescription by Nurses etc. Act 1992 (c. 28) and of all other powers enabling him in that behalf, hereby makes the following Order:

Citation

1. This Order may be cited as the Medicinal Products: Prescription by Nurses etc. Act 1992 (Commencement No. 2) Order 1996.

Appointed Day

2. 1st July 1996 is the day appointed for the coming into force of section 3 of the Medicinal Products: Prescription by Nurses etc. Act 1992.

James Douglas-Hamilton
Minister of State,
Scottish Office

St Andrew's House, Edinburgh
5th June 1996

SOCIAL SECURITY

THE JOBSEEKERS ACT 1995 (COMMENCEMENT NO. 3) ORDER 1996

(S.I. 1996 No. 1509 (C. 29))

Made - - - - - 10th June 1996

INTRODUCTION

This Order brings into force on June 11, 1996 certain provisions of Schedule 2 to the Jobseekers Act 1995. Consequential amendments are made to other legislation, including amendments to the Social Security Administration Act 1992.

The Secretary of State for Social Security, in exercise of the powers conferred upon him by section 41(2) and (3) of the Jobseekers Act 1995 (c. 18) and of all other powers enabling him in that behalf, hereby makes the following Order:

Citation

1. This Order may be cited as the Jobseekers Act 1995 (Commencement No. 3) Order 1996.

Appointed day

2. The day appointed for the coming into force of the provisions of Schedule 2 to the Jobseekers Act 1995 specified in the Schedule to this Order, and section 41(4) of that Act in so far as it relates to those provisions, is 11th June 1996.

Signed by authority of the Secretary of State for Social Security.

Roger Evans
Parliamentary Under-Secretary of State,
Department of Social Security

10th June 1996

Article 2

SCHEDULE

PROVISIONS COMING INTO FORCE ON 11TH JUNE 1996

Provisions of Schedule 2 to the Jobseekers Act 1995	*Subject matter*
Paragraph 10	Amendment of the Abolition of Domestic Rates Etc. (Scotland) Act 1987.
Paragraph 18	Amendment of the Local Government Finance Act 1988.
Paragraph 21	Amendment of the Criminal Justice Act 1991.
Paragraph 42	Amendment of the Social Security Administration Act 1992, section 20.
Paragraph 46	Amendment of the Social Security Administration Act 1992, section 68.
Paragraphs 49 to 51	Amendment of the Social Security Administration Act 1992, Part III.
Paragraphs 53 to 64	Amendment of the Social Security Administration Act 1992, Parts V to VIII.
Paragraph 66	Amendment of the Social Security Administration Act 1992, section 166.
Paragraphs 71, 72 and 74	Amendment of the Social Security Administration Act 1992, miscellaneous.

CRIMINAL LAW, ENGLAND AND WALES

THE CRIMINAL JUSTICE AND PUBLIC ORDER ACT 1994 (COMMENCEMENT NO. 9) ORDER 1996

(S.I. 1996 No. 1530 (C. 30))

Made - - - - - - *9th June 1996*

INTRODUCTION

This Order brings into force on July 1, 1996, s.149 of and para. 70 of Sched. 10 to the Criminal Justice and Public Order Act 1994. These provisions relate to incorporation of the Parole Board.

In exercise of the power conferred upon him by section 172(2) of the Criminal Justice and Public Order Act 1994 (c. 33), the Secretary of State hereby makes the following Order:

1. This Order may be cited as the Criminal Justice and Public Order Act 1994 (Commencement No. 9) Order 1996.

2. Section 149 of, and paragraph 70 of Schedule 10 to, the Criminal Justice and Public Order Act 1994 (incorporation of the Parole Board) shall come into force on 1st July 1996.

Home Office

Michael Howard
9th June 1996 One of Her Majesty's Principal Secretaries of State

[This Order was revoked by the Criminal Justice and Public Order Act 1994 (Commencement No. 10) Order 1996 (S.I. 1996 No. 1608 (C. 32))]

CRIMINAL LAW, ENGLAND AND WALES

THE CRIMINAL JUSTICE AND PUBLIC ORDER ACT 1994 (COMMENCEMENT NO. 10) ORDER 1996

(S.I. 1996 No. 1608 (C. 32))

Made - - - - - - *20th June 1996*

INTRODUCTION

This Order brings into force on July 1, 1996, s.149 of and para. 70 of Sched. 10 to the Criminal Justice and Public Order Act 1994. These provisions relate to incorporation of the Parole Board.

In exercise of the power conferred upon him by section 172(2) of the Criminal Justice and Public Order Act 1994 (c. 33), the Secretary of State hereby makes the following Order:

1. This Order may be cited as the Criminal Justice and Public Order Act 1994 (Commencement No. 10) Order 1996.

2. Section 149 of, and paragraph 70 of Schedule 10 to, the Criminal Justice and Public Order Act 1994 (incorporation of the Parole Board) shall come into force on 1st July 1996.

3. The Criminal Justice and Public Order Act 1994 (Commencement No. 9) Order 1996 (S.I. 1996 No. 1530 (C. 30)), made on 9th June 1996, is hereby revoked.

Home Office

Michael Howard

20th June 1996 One of Her Majesty's Principal Secretaries of State

TRANSPORT

THE TRANSPORT AND WORKS ACT 1992 (COMMENCEMENT NO. 6) ORDER 1996

(S.I. 1996 No. 1609 (C. 33))

Made - - - - - *17th June 1996*

INTRODUCTION

This Order brings into force on July 8, 1996, various provisions of the Transport and Works Act 1992, including, *inter alia*, provisions relating to the placement of signs and barriers at private crossings of railways and tramways.

The Secretary of State, in exercise of the powers conferred on him by section 70(1) and (2) of the Transport and Works Act 1992 (c. 42) and of all other powers enabling him in that behalf, hereby makes the following Order:—

Citation and interpretation

1.—(1) This Order may be cited as the Transport and Works Act 1992 (Commencement No. 6) Order 1996.

(2) In this Order "the Act" means the Transport and Works Act 1992.

Provisions coming into force

2. The provisions of the Act specified in the first column of the Schedule to this Order (which relate to the matters specified in the second column of that Schedule) shall come into force on 8th July 1996.

Savings

3. The repeal of section 124 of the Transport Act 1968 (c. 73) (except as it applies in Scotland) shall not affect the validity of an Order made under that section and in force immediately before 8th July 1996.

Signed by authority of the
Secretary of State for Transport

John Watts
Minister of State,
Department of Transport

17th June 1996

Article 2

SCHEDULE

PROVISIONS COMING INTO FORCE ON 8TH JULY 1996

Provisions of the Act	*Subject-matter of provisions*
Section 50.	Orders under section 124 of the Transport Act 1968 (c. 73).
Section 52.	Placing of signs and barriers.
Section 53.	Rights to enter land.
Section 54.	Default powers of Secretary of State.
Section 55.	Offence of failing to comply with sign.
Section 56.	Interpretation of sections 52 to 55.
Section 62.	Exclusion of hackney carriage legislation.
In Section 65(1)(b), the words "section 48,".	Section 48 of Tramways Act 1870 (c. 78).
Section 68(1) insofar as it relates to the entries in Schedule 4 referred to below.	Repeal of enactments.
In Part I of Schedule 4, in the entry relating to the Tramways Act 1870 the words "Section 48.", and in the entry relating to the Transport Act 1968 the words "Section 124 (except as it applies in Scotland).".	

MEDICAL PROFESSION

THE MEDICAL (PROFESSIONAL PERFORMANCE) ACT 1995 (COMMENCEMENT NO. 2) ORDER 1996

(S.I. 1996 No. 1631 (C. 34))

Made - - - - - - *26th June 1996*

INTRODUCTION

This Order brings into force on September 1, 1996 certain provisions of the Medical (Professional Performance) Act 1995, which makes amendments to the Medical Act 1983 by providing that rules made by the GMC must be approved by Privy Council before they can be brought into force. On January 1, 1996, further provisions provide for the establishment of two new Committees of the GMC.

At the Court at Buckingham Palace, the 26th day of June 1996

Present,

The Queen's Most Excellent Majesty in Council

Her Majesty, in exercise of the powers conferred upon Her by section 6 of the Medical (Professional Performance) Act 1995 (c. 51), and of all other powers enabling Her in that behalf, is pleased, by and with the advice of Her Privy Council, to order, and it is hereby ordered, as follows:—

Citation and interpretation

1.—(1) This Order may be cited as the Medical (Professional Performance) Act 1995 (Commencement No. 2) Order 1996.

(2) In this Order—

(a) "the Act" means the Medical (Professional Performance) Act 1995;

(b) "the 1983 Act" means the Medical Act 1983 (c. 54); and

(c) "the GMC" means the General Medical Council (*see* the 1983 Act, section 1).

Appointed Days

2.—(1) 1st September 1996 is the day appointed for the coming into force of the following provisions of the Act—

(a) section 7(2) (extent), so far as it relates to the provisions of the Act referred to in sub-paragraph (b);

(b) in the Schedule (supplementary and consequential amendments of the 1983 Act), paragraph 1 so far as it relates to paragraph 14, and paragraph 14; and section 4 so far as it relates to those paragraphs.

(2) 1st September 1996 is the day appointed for the coming into force of the following provisions of the Act, for the purpose of enabling the GMC in accordance with rules to determine the membership of its statutory committees (*see* the 1983 Act, section 1(3)) as from 1st January 1997—

(a) section 7(2) (extent), so far as it relates to the provisions of the Act referred to in sub-paragraph (b);

(b) in the Schedule (supplementary and consequential amendments of the 1983 Act), paragraph 1 so far as it relates to paragraph 12, and paragraph 12; and section 4 so far as it relates to those paragraphs.

(3) 1st January 1997 is the day appointed for the coming into force of the following provisions of the Act—

(a) section 7(2) (extent), so far as it relates to the provisions of the Act referred to in sub-paragraph (b);

(b) in the Schedule (supplementary and consequential amendments of the 1983 Act), paragraph 1 so far as it relates to the other provisions of the Schedule brought into force by this sub-paragraph, paragraph 2, paragraph 12 so far as not already in force, and paragraph 13; and section 4 so far as it relates to those paragraphs.

N. H. Nicholls
Clerk of the Privy Council

POLICE

THE POLICE AND MAGISTRATES' COURTS ACT 1994 (COMMENCEMENT NO. 10 AND SAVINGS) (SCOTLAND) ORDER 1996

(S.I. 1996 No. 1646 (C. 35) (S.142))

Made - - - - - - - -	*19th June 1996*
Laid before Parliament - - -	*11th July 1996*
Coming into force - - - - -	*1st August 1996*

INTRODUCTION

This Order brings into force on August 1, 1996, the remaining provisions of Pt. II of the Police and Magistrates' Courts Act 1994 together with related repeals. These provisions concern policing arrangements for Scotland.

The Secretary of State, in exercise of the powers conferred on him by section 94(1), (4) and (5) of the Police and Magistrates' Courts Act 1994 (c. 29) and of all other powers enabling him in that behalf, hereby makes the following Order:

Citation, commencement and interpretation

1.—(1) This Order may be cited as the Police and Magistrates' Courts Act 1994 (Commencement No. 10 and Savings) (Scotland) Order 1996 and shall come into force on 1st August 1996.

(2) In this Order—

"the 1967 Act" means the Police (Scotland) Act 1967 (c. 77);

"the 1967 Regulations" means the Police (Discipline) (Scotland) Regulations 1967 (S.I. 1967 No. 1021, amended by S.I. 1971 No. 843, 1975 No. 1544, 1976 No. 1073, 1982 No. 902, 1987 No. 2226 and 1995 No. 647);

"the 1969 Rules" means the Police (Appeals) (Scotland) Rules 1969 (S.I. 1969 No. 1632);

"the 1990 Regulations" means the Police (Discipline) (Senior Officers) (Scotland) Regulations 1990 (S.I. 1990 No. 1017, amended by S.I. 1995 No. 647);

"the 1994 Act" means the Police and Magistrates' Courts Act 1994;

"disciplinary offence" means a disciplinary offence set out in the Discipline Code in Schedule 1 to the 1967 Regulations;

"existing case" means any case where an act or omission was committed or made by a constable of a police force before 1st August 1996, which amounts or may amount to a disciplinary offence at the time when the act or omission was committed or made and, without prejudice to that generality, an existing case includes any such case irrespective of whether it is before, on or after that date that—

(a) a report, allegation or complaint is received in relation thereto;

(b) the constable is charged or found guilty of that disciplinary offence; or

(c) an appeal is made in relation to such a finding and any punishment imposed or only in relation to a punishment;

but, for the avoidance of doubt, it does not include any case where—

(i) the disciplinary offence consists of the conviction of the constable of a criminal offence as mentioned in paragraph 13 of Schedule 1 to the 1967 Regulations; and

(ii) such a conviction occurs on or after that date, even although the act or omission which constituted the criminal offence of which the constable was convicted was committed or made by the constable before that date;

"existing provisions" means—

(a) the provisions of section 44 of the Police Act 1964;

(b) the provisions of sections 7(3), 26, 30 and 42(1) of, and paragraph 2 of Schedule 2 and Schedule 3 to, the 1967 Act;

(c) the 1967 Regulations and the 1990 Regulations and any regulations made under section 26 of the 1967 Act on or after 1st August 1996 which amend either of those Regulations in relation to existing cases;

(d) the 1969 Rules and any rules made under paragraph 5 of Schedule 3 to the 1967 Act on or after 1st August 1996 which amend those Rules in relation to existing cases,

and any reference in this definition to a provision of the Police Act 1964 or the 1967 Act or to the 1969 Rules, the 1967 Regulations or the 1990 Regulations (but not to any rules or regulations amending those Rules or Regulations on or after 1st August 1996) is a reference to that provision or to those Rules or Regulations as in force immediately before 1st August 1996.

Provisions of the 1994 Act coming into force on 1st August 1996

2. The provisions of the 1994 Act which are specified in column 1 of the Schedule to this Order, and described by reference to the subject matter in column 2 of that Schedule, shall, insofar as not then in force, come into force on 1st August 1996 but, where a particular purpose is specified in relation to any provision in column 3 of that Schedule, that provision shall come into force on that day only for that purpose.

Savings

3. Notwithstanding any repeal or amendment effected by the provisions of the 1994 Act specified in the Schedule to this Order, the existing provisions shall continue to apply in relation to any existing case.

James Douglas-Hamilton
Minister of State,
Scottish Office

St Andrew's House, Edinburgh
19th June 1996

Article 2

SCHEDULE

PROVISIONS OF THE 1994 ACT WHICH COME INTO FORCE ON 1ST AUGUST 1996

Column 1 *Provision*	*Column 2* *Subject matter*	*Column 3* *Extent of commencement*
Section 44	Minor and consequential amendments	Only so far as it relates to the entries in Schedule 5 to the 1994 Act specified below.
Section 52(2)	Regulations for police forces	
Section 52(3)	Regulations for police forces	
Section 52(4)	Regulations for police forces	
Section 55	Appeals against dismissal etc.	
Section 61	Examination of handling of complaints against constables	
Section 63(3)	Other amendments of the 1967 Act	
Section 63(8)	Other amendments of the 1967 Act	
Section 63(10)	Other amendments of the 1967 Act	
Section 93	Repeals	Only so far as it relates to the entries in Part I of Schedule 9 to the 1994 Act specified below.
Schedule 5	Police: minor and consequential amendments	1. Only so far as extending to Scotland, paragraph 11. 2. In paragraph 39, the opening words and sub-paragraph (b). 3. In paragraph 40, sub-paragraphs (1) and (3).
Schedule 6	Schedule to be inserted in Police (Scotland) Act 1967: Appeals Tribunals	
Schedule 9, Part I	Repeals	1. The following entries in respect of the 1967 Act: In section 26, subsection (7). In section 42(1), the words "or to commit breaches of discipline". In Schedule 2, paragraph 2.

PENSIONS

THE PENSIONS ACT 1995 (COMMENCEMENT) (NO. 5) ORDER 1996

(S.I. 1996 No. 1675 (C. 36))

Made - - - - - *26th June 1996*

INTRODUCTION

This Order brings into force on August 1, 1996, s.166 of the Pensions Act 1995 subject to certain qualified exceptions. These exceptions allow for separate dates to be effective for inserted sections of the Matrimonial Causes Act 1973 which relate to the making of regulations, periodical payments, and proceedings commenced by petition.

The Lord Chancellor, in exercise of the powers conferred on him by sections 174(2) and (3) and 180(3) and (4) of the Pensions Act 1995 (c. 26), hereby makes the following Order:

1. This Order may be cited as the Pensions Act 1995 (Commencement) (No. 5) Order 1996.

2. In this Order—
(a) every reference to a section by number alone means the section so numbered in the Matrimonial Causes Act 1973 (c. 18);
(b) all words and phrases defined in section 25D(3) and (4) have the meanings assigned by that section.

3. Subject to the following articles of this Order, section 166 of the Pensions Act 1995 shall come into force on the following dates:—
(a) in relation to the amendment to the Matrimonial Causes Act 1973 consisting of the insertion of section 25D(2), (3) and (4), the day following the day on which this Order was made;
(b) for all other purposes, 1st August 1996.

4.—(1) Subject to paragraph (2), sections 25B and 25C shall have effect in relation to applications for an order under section 23—
(a) which are made on or after 1st August 1996, or
(b) which are made before that date and amended on or after that date pursuant to rule 3 of the Family Proceedings (Amendment) (No. 2) Rules 1996 (S.I. 1996/1674) so as to include provisions under section 25B or 25C.

(2) Where a petition for divorce, nullity of marriage or judicial separation was presented before 1st July 1996 the Matrimonial Causes Act 1973 shall have effect in relation to those proceedings, including any answer or cross petition filed in those proceedings, as if section 166 of the Pensions Act 1995 had not come into force.

5. No order under section 23 shall be made requiring the trustees or managers of a pension scheme to make periodical payments to the party without pension rights with effect from a date earlier than 6th April 1997.

Dated 26th June 1996 *Mackay of Clashfern*, C.

PENSIONS

THE PENSIONS ACT 1995 (COMMENCEMENT NO. 6) ORDER 1996

(S.I. 1996 No. 1843 (C. 37) (S.151))

Made - - - - - - - - *12th July 1996*

INTRODUCTION

This Order brings into force s.167 of the Pensions Act 1995 on August 19, 1996. No action for divorce, or action for declarator of nullity of marriage is affected if commenced before that date.

The Secretary of State, in exercise of the powers conferred on him by sections 174(2) and (3) and 180(1) of the Pensions Act 1995 (c. 26), hereby makes the following Order:

Citation and interpretation

1. This Order may be cited as the Pensions Act 1995 (Commencement No. 6) Order 1996.

2. In this Order—

"the Act" means the Pensions Act 1995.

Commencement

3. Subject to article 4 below, section 167 of the Act shall come into force on the following dates:

(a) 15th July 1996 but only for the purpose of bringing into force the provisions relating to the making of regulations in sections 10(8), (9) and (10) and 12A(8), (9) and (10) of Family Law (Scotland) Act 1985 (c. 37); and

(b) 19th August 1996, for all other purposes.

Savings

4. The coming into force of section 167 of the Act shall not affect any action for divorce commenced before 19th August 1996 or any action for declarator of nullity of marriage commenced before that date.

James Douglas-Hamilton
Minister of State,
Scottish Office

St Andrew's House, Edinburgh
12th July 1996

PENSIONS

THE PENSIONS ACT 1995 (COMMENCEMENT NO. 6) ORDER 1996

(S.I. 1996 No. 1853 (C. 38))

Made - - - - - 15th July 1996

INTRODUCTION

This Order brings s.116(1) of the Pensions Act 1995 (c. 26) into force on July 16, 1996. Section 116(1) makes provision as regards penalties for breach of regulations.

The Secretary of State for Social Security, in exercise of the power conferred on him by section 180(1) of the Pensions Act 1995 (c. 26) and of all other powers enabling him in that behalf, hereby makes the following Order:

Citation and interpretation

1. This Order may be cited as the Pensions Act 1995 (Commencement No. 6) Order 1996.

Appointed day

2. The day appointed for the coming into force of section 116(1) of the Pensions Act 1995, is the day following the day on which this Order is made.

Signed by authority of the Secretary of State for Social Security.

Oliver Heald
Parliamentary Under-Secretary of State,
15th July 1996 Department of Social Security

LOCAL GOVERNMENT, ENGLAND AND WALES

THE LOCAL GOVERNMENT AND HOUSING ACT 1989 (COMMENCEMENT NO. 18) ORDER 1996

(S.I. 1996 No. 1857 (C. 39))

Made - - - - - - 15th July 1996

INTRODUCTION

This Order brings into force provisions of the Local Government and Housing Act 1989 (c. 42) which repeal, *inter alia*, s.2 of the Education (Grants and Awards) Act 1984 (c. 11) (dealing with the limit on expenditure qualifying for education support grant, which ceased to apply with effect from April 1, 1990) and ss.1 and 3 of the Education (Amendment) Act 1986 (c. 1).

In exercise of the powers conferred on the Secretary of State by section 195(2) of the Local Government and Housing Act 1989 (c. 42) the Secretary of State for Education and Employment hereby makes the following Order—

1. This Order may be cited as the Local Government and Housing Act 1989 (Commencement No. 18) Order 1996.

2. Section 194(4) of the Local Government and Housing Act 1989, in so far as it relates to the following repeals in Part II of Schedule 12 to that Act, shall come into force on 22nd July 1996—

Chapter	*Short Title*	*Extent of Repeal*
1984 c.11	The Education (Grants and Awards) Act 1984	In section 1, in subsection (6) the words "or section 2 below" and in subsection (7) the words "in those sections". Section 2.
1986 c.1	The Education (Amendment) Act 1986	Sections 1 and 3

Robin Squire
Parliamentary Under-Secretary of State,
Department for Education and Employment

15th July 1996

LOCAL GOVERNMENT, ENGLAND AND WALES
LOCAL GOVERNMENT, SCOTLAND

THE LOCAL GOVERNMENT ACT 1992 (COMMENCEMENT NO. 5) ORDER 1996

(S.I. 1996 No. 1888 (C. 40))

Made - - - - - 18th July 1996

INTRODUCTION

This Order brings into force on August 8, 1996, the repeals contained in Part I of Schedule 4 to the Local Government Act 1992, which relate to the Local Government, Planning and Land Act 1980.

The Secretary of State, in exercise of the powers conferred on him by section 30(3) of the Local Government Act 1992 (c. 19; section 30(4)(c) was amended by paragraph 177 of Schedule 13 to the Local Government etc. (Scotland) Act 1994 (c. 39)), and all other powers enabling him in that behalf, hereby makes the following Order:

Citation

1. This Order may be cited as the Local Government Act 1992 (Commencement No. 5) Order 1996.

Provisions of the Local Government Act 1992 coming into force on 8th August 1996

2. The repeals in the Local Government, Planning and Land Act 1980 (c. 65) in Part I of Schedule 4 to the Local Government Act 1992 shall come into force on 8th August 1996.

Paul Beresford
Parliamentary Under-Secretary of State,
18th July 1996 Department of the Environment

EDUCATION, ENGLAND AND WALES

THE FURTHER AND HIGHER EDUCATION ACT 1992 (COMMENCEMENT NO. 3) ORDER 1996

(S.I. 1996 No. 1897 (C. 41))

Made - - - - - 9th July 1996

INTRODUCTION

This Order brings into force on August 1, 1996, s.93(1) of the Further and Higher Education Act 1992 so far as it relates to Sched. 8, para. 10 of that Act. An earlier Commencement Order (S.I. 1992 No. 2377 (C. 79)) purported to bring into effect para. 10, but Schedule 8 is only given effect by virtue of s.93(1).

Sections 55(1) to (3) and (7)(b) are already in force in relation to England, and are now brought into force in relation to Wales.

In exercise of the powers conferred by sections 89(4) and 94(3) of the Further and Higher Education Act 1992 (c. 13) the Secretary of State for Wales hereby makes the following Order:

1. This Order may be cited as the Further and Higher Education Act 1992 (Commencement No. 3) Order 1996.

2. Section 93(1) of the Further and Higher Education Act 1992 ("the Act"), so far as it relates to paragraph 10 of Schedule 8 to the Act and is not already in force, shall come into force on 1st August 1996.

3. Section 55(1) to (3) and (7)(b) of the Act shall (so far as not already in force) come into force on 1st August 1996.

Signed by authority of the Secretary of State for Wales

Jonathan Evans
Parliamentary Under Secretary of State,
Welsh Office

9th July 1996

ROAD TRAFFIC

THE TRANSPORT ACT 1982 (COMMENCEMENT NO. 7 AND TRANSITIONAL PROVISIONS) ORDER 1996

(S.I. 1996 No. 1943 (C. 42))

Made - - - - - 2nd July 1996

INTRODUCTION

This Order brings into force s.18 of the Transport Act 1982 (c. 49), on August 1, 1996. This section inserts new s.63A into the Road Traffic Act 1988 (c. 52) which provides for plated weights for goods vehicles to be altered without examination. In addition, transitional modifications are made to s.63A of the 1988 Act.

The Secretary of State for Transport, in exercise of the powers conferred by section 76 of the Transport Act 1982 (c. 49. Section 76 was amended by Schedule 14 to the Road Traffic Regulation Act 1984 (c. 27)), hereby makes the following Order:

1.—(1) This Order may be cited as the Transport Act 1982 (Commencement No. 7 and Transitional Provisions) Order 1996.

(2) For the purposes of this Order, the appointed day is 1st August 1996.

2. Subject to article 3 below, section 18 of the Transport Act 1982 (s.18 was amended by paragraphs 2 and 7 of Schedule 2 to the Road Traffic (Consequential Provisions) Act 1988 (c. 54)) shall come into force on the appointed day.

3. During the period beginning with the appointed day and ending immediately before the day on which section 8 of the Transport Act 1982 comes into force, section 63A(3)(a) of the Road Traffic Act 1988 (c. 52; section 63A is inserted by section 18 of the Transport Act 1982) shall have effect with the omission of the words "or by the prescribed testing authority".

Signed by authority of the Secretary of State for Transport

Steven Norris
Parliamentary Under Secretary of State,
Department of Transport

2nd July 1996

ROAD TRAFFIC

THE ROAD TRAFFIC (DRIVING INSTRUCTION BY DISABLED PERSONS) ACT 1993 (COMMENCEMENT) ORDER 1996

(S.I. 1996 No. 1980 (C. 43))

Made - - - - - *23rd July 1996*

INTRODUCTION

This Order brings into force all provisions of the Road Traffic (Driving Instruction by Disabled Persons) Act 1993 (c. 31) on September 9, 1996.

The Secretary of State for Transport, in exercise of the powers conferred by section 7(2) of the Road Traffic (Driving Instruction by Disabled Persons) Act 1993 (c. 31), hereby makes the following Order:

1. This Order may be cited as the Road Traffic (Driving Instruction by Disabled Persons) Act 1993 (Commencement) Order 1996.

2. The Road Traffic (Driving Instruction by Disabled Persons) Act 1993 shall come into force on 9th September 1996.

Signed by authority of the Secretary of State for Transport

Steven Norris
Parliamentary Under Secretary of State,
Department of Transport

23rd July 1996

EDUCATION, ENGLAND AND WALES

THE NURSERY EDUCATION AND GRANT-MAINTAINED SCHOOLS ACT 1996 (COMMENCEMENT NO. 1) ORDER 1996

(S.I. 1996 No. 2022 (C. 44))

Made - - - - - 31st July 1996

INTRODUCTION

By this Order, all the provisions of the Nursery Education and Grant-Maintained Schools Act 1996 (c. 50) (except those paragraphs of Sched. 1 and s.5 so far as they relate to inspection of nursery education funded under the Act), are brought into force on September 1, 1996.

In exercise of the powers conferred on the Secretary of State by section 11(3) of the Nursery Education and Grant-Maintained Schools Act 1996 (c. 50) the Secretary of State for Education and Employment hereby makes the following Order:

Citation and interpretation

1.—(1) This Order may be cited as the Nursery Education and Grant-Maintained Schools Act 1996 (Commencement No. 1) Order 1996.

(2) In this Order "the Act" means the Nursery Education and Grant-Maintained Schools Act 1996.

Commencement of provisions

2. Save as provided in article 3, the provisions of the Act shall come into force on 1st September 1996.

3. Article 2 shall not have effect for the purpose of bringing the following provisions of the Act into force:

(a) section 5, so far as it relates to the provisions of Schedule 1 not brought into force by this Order; and

(b) paragraph 6(1)(a), (2), (3) so far as it relates to inspections under paragraph 6(1)(a) and (5), paragraphs 8(2) and 14, so far as they relate to inspections under paragraph 6(1)(a), and paragraph 16 of Schedule 1.

Robin Squire
Parliamentary Under Secretary of State,
31st July 1996 Department for Education and Employment

HOUSING, ENGLAND AND WALES
HOUSING, SCOTLAND

THE HOUSING ACT 1996 (COMMENCEMENT NO. 1) ORDER 1996

(S.I. 1996 No. 2048 (C. 45))

Made - - - - - *30th July 1996*

INTRODUCTION

This Order brings into force on August 1, 1996 various provisions of the Housing Act 1996 (c. 52) including, *inter alia*, the criteria for registration of social landlords, and power to consult relating to consents for disposal of land by registered social landlords. Certain other provisions are brought into force in so far as they confer power to consult, to make determinations, to give consents and to delegate functions.

The Secretary of State, in exercise of the powers conferred upon him by section 232(3) and (4) of the Housing Act 1996 (c. 52), and of all other powers enabling him in that behalf, hereby makes the following Order:

Citation and interpretation

1.—(1) This Order may be cited as the Housing Act 1996 (Commencement No. 1) Order 1996.

(2) In this Order "the Act" means the Housing Act 1996.

Commencement

2.—(1) The following provisions of the Act shall come into force on 1st August 1996—

section 2(7) and (8),
section 5,
Section 7 in so far as it relates to paragraphs 3(1) and (2) and 16(1) and (2) of Schedule 1,
section 9(3),
section 17,
section 28(4),
section 36(1) to (6),
section 51 in so far as it relates to paragraphs 2 to 6, 10 and 11(1), (3) and (4) of Schedule 2, subject to the limitation in paragraph (2) of this article,
sections 52 to 54,
section 55(1) in so far as it relates to paragraphs 6 and 9 of Schedule 3,
section 55(2) and (3),
sections 56 to 64.

(2) Section 51 and the provisions of Schedule 2 specified in paragraph (1) of this article shall not come into force in relation to any complaint against any social landlord which is or at any time was registered with Housing for Wales.

3. So much of the following provisions of the Act as confer on the Secretary of State, the Housing Corporation or Housing for Wales a power to consult, to make determinations, to give consents and to delegate functions shall come into force on 1st August 1996—

section 3(2),
section 7 in so far as it relates to paragraphs 2(2)(f) and 27(4) of Schedule 1,
section 24,
section 29.

4. Section 55(1) of the Act in so far as it relates to paragraph 7 of Schedule 3 to the Act shall come into force on 1st August 1996 for the purposes of enabling a determination to be made under subsection (3) of section 87 of the

Housing Associations Act 1985 (c. 69; s.87 was substituted by s.183 of the Local Government and Housing Act 1989 (c. 42)) with respect to financial assistance under that section as amended by the Act.

John Selwyn Gummer

30th July 1996 One of Her Majesty's Principal Secretaries of State

IMMIGRATION

THE ASYLUM AND IMMIGRATION ACT 1996 (COMMENCEMENT NO. 1) ORDER 1996

(S.I. 1996 No. 2053 (C. 46))

Made - - - - - *25th July 1996*

INTRODUCTION

This Order brings into force various provisions of the Asylum and Immigration Act 1996. On July 26, 1996 the provisions specified in Part I of the Schedule to this Order are brought into force, including procedural rules contained in s.3(5). On September 1, 1996 provisions which relate, *inter alia*, to repeals and amendments are brought into force. On October 1, 1996, further provisions relating to, *inter alia*, increased penalties and powers of arrest are brought into force.

In exercise of the powers conferred upon him by section 13(3) of the Asylum and Immigration Act 1996 (c. 49), the Secretary of State hereby makes the following Order:

1.—(1) This Order may be cited as the Asylum and Immigration Act 1996 (Commencement No. 1) Order 1996.

(2) In this Order "the Act" means the Asylum and Immigration Act 1996.

2. The provisions of the Act which are specified in Part I of the Schedule to this Order shall come into force on 26th July 1996; the provisions specified in Part II of the Schedule shall come into force on 1st September 1996; and the provisions specified in Part III of the Schedule shall come into force on 1st October 1996.

Home Office
25th July 1996

Ann Widdecombe
Minister of State

Article 2

SCHEDULE

PART I

PROVISIONS OF THE ACT COMING INTO FORCE ON 26TH JULY 1996

Provision of Act	*Subject matter of provision*
Section 3(3)	Appointment of special adjudicators
Section 3(5)	Procedure rules
Section 9(1) and (2), for the purpose only of making orders, and section 9(3)	Orders
Section 13	Short title, interpretation, commencement and extent

PART II

PROVISIONS OF THE ACT COMING INTO FORCE ON 1ST SEPTEMBER 1996

Provision of Act	*Subject matter of provision*
Section 2	Removal etc. of asylum claimants to safe third countries
Section 3, except subsections (3) and (5)	Appeals against certificates under section 2
Section 12, for the purpose of the provisions of Schedules 2, 3 and 4 specified in this Part	Schedules
In Schedule 2, paragraphs 3 (2) and 8 to 12	Amendments of the Immigration Act 1971
In Schedule 3, paragraphs 1, 2, 3 and 5	Amendments of the Asylum and Immigration Appeals Act 1993
In Schedule 4, the entry relating to the Asylum and Immigration Appeals Act 1993	Repeals

PART III

PROVISIONS OF THE ACT COMING INTO FORCE ON 1ST OCTOBER 1996

Provision of Act	*Subject matter of provision*
Section 4	Obtaining leave by deception
Section 5	Assisting asylum claimants and persons seeking to obtain leave by deception
Section 6	Increased penalties
Section 7	Powers of arrest and search warrants
Section 12(1) and (3) for the purpose of the provisions of Schedules 2 and 4 specified in this Part	Schedules
In Schedule 2, paragraphs 1(2) and (3), 2, 4 to 7 and 13	Amendments of the Immigration Act 1971 and the Immigration Act 1988
In Schedule 4, the entry relating to the Immigration Act 1971	Repeals

CHEMICAL WEAPONS

THE CHEMICAL WEAPONS ACT 1996 (COMMENCEMENT) ORDER 1996

(S.I. 1996 No. 2054 (C. 47))

Made - - - - - 3rd August 1996

INTRODUCTION

This Order brings into force on September 16, 1996, all remaining provisions of the Chemical Weapons Act 1996. Section 39 was brought into force on the date of Royal Assent; April 3, 1996.

The Secretary of State, in exercise of the powers conferred on him by section 39(1) of the Chemical Weapons Act 1996 (c. 6), hereby makes the following Order:

Citation

1. This Order may be cited as the Chemical Weapons Act 1996 (Commencement) Order 1996.

Appointed day

2. The day appointed for the coming into force of the Chemical Weapons Act 1996, except for section 39, is 16th September 1996.

Anthony Nelson
Minister for Trade
3rd August 1996 Department of Trade and Industry

CRIMINAL LAW

THE OFFENSIVE WEAPONS ACT 1996 (COMMENCEMENT NO. 1) ORDER 1996

(S.I. 1996 No. 2071 (C. 48))

Made - - - - - *4th August 1996*

INTRODUCTION

This Order brings into force s.4(1), (2) and (3) of the Offensive Weapons Act 1996 on September 1, 1996. By these provisions it is an offence to have an article with a blade or point on school premises.

In exercise of the powers conferred upon him by section 4(4) of the Offensive Weapons Act 1996 (c. 26), the Secretary of State hereby makes the following Order:

1.—(1) This Order may be cited as the Offensive Weapons Act 1996 (Commencement No. 1) Order 1996.

(2) This Order extends to Northern Ireland.

2. Subsections (1) to (3) of section 4 of the Offensive Weapons Act 1996 shall come into force on 1st September 1996.

Home Office
4th August 1996

David Maclean
Minister of State

BROADCASTING

THE BROADCASTING ACT 1996 (COMMENCEMENT NO. 1 AND TRANSITIONAL PROVISIONS) ORDER 1996

(S.I. 1996 No. 2120 (C. 49))

Made - - - - - *9th August 1996*

INTRODUCTION

This Order brings into force various provisions of the Broadcasting Act 1996. The provisions which relate, *inter alia*, to determinations of the Independent Television Commission and the Radio Authority contained in the substituted Pt. IV of Sched. 2 to the Broadcasting Act 1990, become effective immediately. On October 1, 1996, various other provisions specified in Sched. 1 of this Order are brought into force. On November 1, 1996, those provisions specified in Sched. 2 to this Order are brought into force.

The Secretary of State, in exercise of the powers conferred upon her by section 149(2) and (3) of the Broadcasting Act 1996 (c. 55), and of all other powers enabling her in that behalf, hereby makes the following Order:

1.—(1) This Order may be cited as the Broadcasting Act 1996 (Commencement No. 1 and Transitional Provisions) Order 1996.

2. In this Order—
(a) "the 1990 Act" means the Broadcasting Act 1990 (c. 42); and
(b) "the 1996 Act" means the Broadcasting Act 1996.

3.—(1) Subject to paragraphs (2) and (3), the following provisions of the 1996 Act shall come into force on the day after this Order is made—
Section 73 so far as relating to the provisions on Schedule 2 brought into force by this Article;
Section 104;
Paragraphs 12 and 13 of the substituted Part IV of the Schedule to the 1990 Act;
Part I of Schedule 2 so far as relating to the interpretation of paragraphs 12 and 13 of the substituted Part IV of the Schedule 2 to the 1990 Act; and
Paragraph 11 of Schedule 2 so far as relating to paragraphs 12 and 13 of the substituted Part IV of Schedule 2 to the 1990 Act or to paragraphs 1, 2, 3, 9, 10, 11 and 14 of that substituted Part in their application to the interpretation of paragraphs 12 and 13.

(2) For the purposes of paragraph 12(5)(b) of the substituted Part IV of Schedule 2 to the 1990 Act, any determination made by the relevant authority before 1st November 1996 shall be taken to have been made on that date.

(3) The coming into force of the provisions referred to in paragraph (1) does not affect the continued operation until 1st November 1996 of the restrictions contained in Schedule 2 to the 1990 Act as it had effect immediately before the passing of the 1996 Act.

4.—(1) Subject to paragraphs (2) and (3) below, the provisions of the 1996 Act which are specified in Schedule 1 to this Order shall come into force on 1st October 1996.

(2) Section 2 shall come into force on 15th September 1996 for the purposes of the notification by the independent analogue broadcasters of their intention to provide their respective services for broadcasting in digital form, but not for any other purposes.

(3) Paragraph (1) above does not bring section 41 into force for the purposes of the notification by the independent national broadcasters of their intention to provide a service for broadcasting in digital form pursuant to section 41(2).

5.—(1) Subject to paragraph (2) below, the provisions of the 1996 Act which are specified in Schedule 2 to this Order shall come into force on 1st November 1996.

(2) Where the holder of any licence specified in paragraphs 9(4), 10(2), 11(1) and 11(3) of the substituted Part IV of Schedule 2 to the 1990 Act becomes connected with a national or local newspaper by virtue of the commencement of Part I of Schedule 2 to the 1996 Act, the "relevant day" shall for the purposes of paragraph 9(5) be 1st November 1996.

Inglewood
Parliamentary Under Secretary of State,
9th August 1996 Department of National Heritage

Article 4 SHEDULE 1

PROVISIONS OF THE 1996 ACT COMING INTO FORCE ON 1ST OCTOBER 1996 SUBJECT TO THE PROVISIONS OF ARTICLE 4 OF THE ORDER

Sections 1 to 72

Section 73, so far as relating to the provision of Schedule 2 mentioned below

Section 79

Sections 81 and 84

Section 86

Section 91

Sections 97 to 103

Section 105

Sections 137 and 138

Sections 140 to 142

In section 147, subsection (2) except paragraph (c)

Section 148, so far as relating the the provisions of Schedules 10 and 11 mentioned below.

Schedule 1

Paragraph 9 of Schedule 2

Schedule 9

In Schedule 10, paragraphs 1 to 11, pragraphs 14 and 15, paragraph 16 so far as relating to a multiplex service, paragraph 19, paragraphs 21(a) and (c), pragraphs 27 to 30, paragraph 31 so far as relating to anything done under Parts I or II of the 1996 Act, and paragraph 32 except so far as relating to anything done in pursuance of section 115(4) or (6), 116(5) or 117 of the 1996 Act.

In Part I of Schedule 11, the entries relating to the repeal of the 1990 Act except to the extent that the repeal concerns sections 104, 142 to 161 and 202 of, and Schedules 2, 13, 14 and 19 to, that Act.

In Part II of Schedule 11, the entry revoking the Cable (Excepted Programmes) Order 1991 (S.I. 1991 No. 1246).

Article 5 SHEDULE 2

PROVISIONS OF THE 1996 ACT COMING INTO FORCE ON 1ST NOVEMBER 1996, SUBJECT TO THE PROVISIONS OF ARTICLE 5 OF THE ORDER

Section 73, except so far as relating to the provisions of Schedule 2 excluded from the operation of Article 5 of this Order and this Schedule.

Section 87

Section 89

Sections 93 and 94

Section 96

Section 139

Sections 143 to 146

Section 148, so far as relating to the provisions of Schedules 10 and 11 mentioned below.

Schedule 2 (so far as not brought into force by Articles 3 and 4 of this Order) except paragraph 10 so far as relating to paragraphs 1(2)(b) and 2(7) of the substituted Part III of Schedule 2 to the 1990 Act and paragraph 11 so far as relating to paragraph 15 of the substituted Part IV of Schedule 2 to the 1990 Act.

In Schedule 10, paragraphs 13 and 21(b).

In Schedule 11, the entries in Part I relating to the repeal of section 104(5) and (6)(a) of, and Schedule 2 to, the 1990 Act and the entries in Part II relating to the revocation of the Broadcasting (Restrictions on the Holding of Licences) Order 1991 (S.I. 1991 No. 1176), the Broadcasting (Restrictions on the Holding of Licences) (Amendment) Order 1993 (S.I. 1993 No. 3199) and the Broadcasting (Restrictions of Holding Licences) (Amendment) Order 1995 (S.I. 1995 No. 1924).

IMMIGRATION

THE ASYLUM AND IMMIGRATION ACT 1996 (COMMENCEMENT NO. 2) ORDER 1996

(S.I. 1996 No. 2127 (C. 50))

Made - - - - - 11th August 1996

INTRODUCTION

This Order brings into force various provisions of the Asylum and Immigration Act 1996. On August 9, 1996, provisions relating to entitlement to housing accommodation and assistance (s.9), and prescribed conditions for eligibility for child benefit are brought into force (s.10). On October 7, 1996, provisions relating to entitlement to child benefit are brought into force (s.10), together with the Secretary of State's power to prescribe by order those countries in which generally there appears to be no serious risk of persecution (s.1).

Section 1 which relates to the extention of special asylum appeal procedures is brought into force on October 21, 1996, and Sched. 2, paras. 1(1) and 3(1) which amend the Immigration Act 1971 come into force on November 1, 1996.

In exercise of the powers conferred upon him by section 13(3) of the Asylum and Immigration Act 1996 (c. 49), the Secretary of State hereby makes the following Order:

1.—(1) This Order may be cited as the Asylum and Immigration Act 1996 (Commencement No. 2) Order 1996.

(2) In this Order "the Act" means the Asylum and Immigration Act 1996.

2. The provisions of the Asylum and Immigration Act 1996 specified in Part I of the Schedule to this Order shall come into force on 19th August 1996; the provisions specified in Part II of the Schedule shall come into force on 7th October 1996; the provision specified in Part III of the Schedule shall come into force on 21st October 1996; and the provisions specified in Part IV of the Schedule shall come into force on 1st November 1996.

Home Office
11th August 1996

Timothy Kirkhope
Parliamentary Under-Secretary of State

SCHEDULE

PART I

PROVISIONS OF THE ACT COMING INTO FORCE ON 19TH AUGUST 1996

Provision of Act	*Subject matter of provision*
Section 9, except subsection (3) (Subs. (3) was, and subss. (1) and (2) were partially, brought into force on July 26, 1996 by S.I. 1996 No. 2053.)	Entitlement to housing accommodation and assistance
Section 10, for the purpose only of prescribing conditions	Prescribed conditions

PART II

PROVISIONS OF THE ACT COMING INTO FORCE ON 7TH OCTOBER 1996

Provision of Act	*Subject matter of provision*
Section 1, for the purpose only of designating countries or territories	Designated countries
Section 10	Entitlement to child benefit

PART III

PROVISIONS OF THE ACT COMING INTO FORCE ON 21ST OCTOBER 1996

Provision of Act	*Subject matter of provision*
Section 1	Extension of special appeals procedures

PART IV

PROVISIONS OF THE ACT COMING INTO FORCE ON 1ST NOVEMBER 1996

Provision of Act	*Subject matter of provision*
In Schedue 2, paragraphs 1(1) and 3(1)	Amendments of the Immigration Act 1971

PENSIONS

THE PENSIONS ACT 1995 (COMMENCEMENT NO. 6 : S.I. 1996/1853 : C. 38) (AMENDMENT) ORDER 1996

(S.I. 1996 No. 2150 (C. 51))

Made - - - - - - *16th August 1996*

INTRODUCTION

By this Order, the Pensions Act 1995 (Commencement No. 6) Order 1996 (S.I. 1996 No. 1853 (c. 38)) is amended and renumbered as Commencement No. 7 Order.

The Secretary of State for Social Security, in exercise of the power conferred on him by section 180(1) of the Pensions Act 1995 (c. 26) and of all other powers enabling him in that behalf, hereby makes the following Order:

Citation

1.—(1) This Order may be cited as the Pensions Act 1995 (Commencement No. 6 : S.I. 1996/1853 : c. 38) (Amendment) Order 1996.

Amendment of S.I. 1996/1853

2. In article 1 of the Pensions Act 1995 (Commencement No. 6) Order 1996 made 15th July 1996 and registered as S.I. 1996/1853 (c. 38), for "No. 6" substitute "No. 7".

Signed by authority of the Secretary of State for Social Security.

Mackay of Ardbrecknish
Minister of State,
Department of Social Security

16th August 1996

PENSIONS

THE PENSIONS ACT 1995 (COMMENCEMENT NO. 6) (S.I. 1996/1853 (C.38)) (AMENDMENT) ORDER 1996

(S.I. 1996 No. 2150 (C.53))

Made ... 14th August 1996

INTRODUCTION

By this Order, the Pensions Act 1995 (Commencement No. 6) Order 1996 (S.I. 1996 No. 1853 (C.38)) is amended and renamed the Commencement No. 7 Order.

The Secretary of State for Social Security, in exercise of the power conferred on him by section 180(1) of the Pensions Act 1995 and of all other powers enabling him in that behalf, hereby makes the following Order:

Citation

1.—(1) This Order may be cited as the Pensions Act 1995 (Commencement No. 6) (S.I. 1996/1853 (C.38)) (Amendment) Order 1996.

Amendment of S.I. 1996/1853

2. In article 1 of the Pensions Act 1995 (Commencement No. 6) Order 1996, made 15th July 1996 and registered as S.I. 1996/1853 (c.38), for "No. 6" substitute "No. 7".

Signed by authority of the Secretary of State for Social Security.

Mackay of Ardbrecknish
Minister of State,
14th August 1996 Department of Social Security

DISABLED PERSONS

THE DISABILITY DISCRIMINATION (GUIDANCE AND CODE OF PRACTICE) (APPOINTED DAY) ORDER 1996

(S.I. 1996 No. 1996 (C. 52))

Made - - - - - - - 29th July 1996

INTRODUCTION

This Order appoints December 2, 1996 as the day on which the Code of Practice (issued pursuant to s.53 on July 25, 1996) of the Disability Discrimination Act 1995 shall come into force. This Code concerns the elimination of discrimination in the field of employment against disabled persons or persons who have had a disability.

WHEREAS—

(1) in pursuance of sections 3(4) and 54(1) of the Disability Discrimination Act 1995 (c. 50) the Secretary of State has consulted such persons in preparing a draft of the Guidance and such organisations in preparing a draft of the Code of Practice as she considered appropriate;

(2) in pursuance of sections 3(5) and 54(2) of the said Act the Secretary of State has published a draft of the Guidance and of the Code of Practice and has considered such representations that were made to her about the drafts and has modified her proposals in the light of those representations as she considered appropriate;

(3) in pursuance of sections 3(6) and 54(3) of the said Act the Secretary of State has laid the draft of the Guidance and the draft of the Code of Practice before both Houses of Parliament and neither House of Parliament has resolved not to approve the drafts within a period of 40-days beginning with the day on which they were laid;

(4) in pursuance of sections 3(8) and 54(5) of the said Act the Secretary of State has issued the said Guidance and Code of Practice in the form of the drafts laid before both Houses of Parliament on 6th June 1996;

Now, therefore, the Secretary of State for Education and Employment, in exercise of the powers conferred on her by sections 3(9) and 54(6) of the Disability Discrimination Act 1995, hereby makes the following Order:

Citation

1. This Order may be cited as the Disability Discrimination (Guidance and Code of Practice) (Appointed Day) Order 1996.

Appointed Day for Guidance

2. The day appointed as the day on which the Guidance (on the matters to be taken into account in determining questions relating to the definition of disability) (ISBN 0-11-270955-9) issued pursuant to section 3 of the Disability Discrimination Act 1995 on 25th July 1996 shall come into force is 31st July 1996.

Appointed Day for Code of Practice

3. The day appointed as the day on which the Code of Practice (for the elimination of discrimination in the field of employment against disabled persons or persons who have had a disability) (ISBN 0-11-270954-0) issued pursuant to section 53 of the Disability Discrimination Act 1995 on 25th July 1996 shall come into force is 2nd December 1996.

Henley
Minister of State,
29th July 1996 Department for Education and Employment

CHILDREN AND YOUNG PERSONS
FAMILY LAW
SOCIAL WORK, SCOTLAND

THE CHILDREN (SCOTLAND) ACT 1995 (COMMENCEMENT NO. 2 AND TRANSITIONAL PROVISIONS) ORDER 1996

(S.I. 1996 No. 2203 (C. 53) (S. 179))

Made - - - - - - - - *22nd August 1996*

INTRODUCTION

This Order brings into force various provisions of the Children (Scotland) Act 1995. On September 4, 1996, s.4 is brought into force, but only for the purpose of enabling regulations to be made under that section to come into force on November 1, 1996. Section 91 is brought into force on October 1, 1996 and the Schedule to this Order lists various provisions which are brought into force on November 1, 1996.

The Secretary of State, in exercise of the powers conferred upon him by section 105(1) and (2) of the Children (Scotland) Act 1995 (c. 36) and of all other powers enabling him in that behalf, hereby makes the following Order:

Citation

1. This Order may be cited as the Children (Scotland) Act 1995 (Commencement No. 2 and Transitional Provisions) Order 1996.

Interpretation

2. In this Order—

"the Act" means the Children (Scotland) Act 1995;

"the 1968 Act" means the Social Work (Scotland) Act 1968 (c. 49); and

"local authority" means a council constituted under section 2 of the Local Government etc. (Scotland) Act 1994 (c. 39).

Commencement of provisions

3.—(1) Section 4 of the Act shall come into force on 1st September 1996 but only for the purpose of enabling regulations to be made under that section so as to come into force on or after 1st November 1996.

(2) Section 91 of the Act shall come into force on 1st October 1996.

(3) Subject to the provisions of articles 4 to 7 of this Order, the provisions of the Act which are specified in column 1 of the Schedule to this Order and described by reference to the subject matter in column 2 of that Schedule shall, insofar as they are not then in force, come into force on 1st November 1996 but, where a particular purpose is specified in relation to any provision in column 3 of that Schedule, that provision shall come into force on that day only for that purpose.

Transitional provisions

4. Until the coming into force of section 70 of the Act, and without prejudice to the then operation of section 17(2)(b) of the Interpretation Act 1978 (c. 30), the reference in section 3(4) of the Act to a supervision requirement made under section 70 of the Act shall be construed as including a reference to a supervision requirement made under section 44 (s.44 was amended by the Children and Young Persons Act 1969 (c. 54), Sched. 5, para. 57, by the Children Act 1975 (c. 72), Sched. 3, para. 56, by the Law Reform (Miscellaneous Provisions) (Scotland) Act 1985 (c. 73), s.28, and by the Local

Government etc. (Scotland) Act 1994, Sched. 13, para. 76(15)) of the 1968 Act.

5. Until the coming into force of section 86 of the Act, and without prejudice to the then operation of section 17(2)(b) of the Interpretation Act 1978—

(a) in section 7(5) of the Act, the reference to an order under section 86 of the Act shall be construed as including a reference to a resolution under section 16 (s.16 was substituted by the Children Act 1975, s.74 and amended by the Adoption Act 1976 (c. 36), Sched. 3, para. 34; the Adoption (Scotland) Act 1978 (c. 28), Sched. 3, paras. 13 and 14; the Health and Social Services and Social Security Adjudications Act 1983 (c. 41), s.7(1); the Mental Health (Scotland) Act 1984 (c. 36), Sched. 3, para. 15; the Law Reform (Parent and Child) (Scotland) Act 1986 (c. 9), Sched. 1, para. 9 and the Age of Legal Capacity (Scotland) Act 1991 (c. 50), Sched. 1, para. 31; s.16(11)(e) was inserted by the Child Abduction and Custody Act 1985 (c. 60), s.25(6)) or 16A (s.16A was inserted by the Children Act 1975, s.75) of the 1968 Act; and

(b) in section 11(4)(d) of the Act, the reference to a case in which the parental responsibilities or parental rights have been transferred to a local authority by a parental responsibilities order shall be construed as including a reference to a case in which the relevant parental rights and powers in relation to the child (as defined in section 16(3) of the 1968 Act) have vested in a local authority or a voluntary organisation by a resolution under section 16 or 16A of the 1968 Act.

6. Until the coming into force of sections 52 and 69 of the Act, and without prejudice to the then operation of section 17(2)(b) of the Interpretation Act 1978—

(a) the reference in section 54(1) to a condition in section 52(2)(a) to (h), (j), (k) or (l) of the Act being satisfied with respect to a child shall be construed as including a reference to a condition in section 32(2)(a) to (f), (gg) and (i) of the 1968 Act (in s.32(2), paras. (b) and (c) were substituted by the Children Act 1975, Sched. 3, para. 54(a); para. (d) was amended by the Children Act 1975, Sched. 3, para. 54(b); para. (dd) was added by the Children Act 1975, Sched. 3, para. 54(c); para. (gg) was inserted by the Solvent Abuse (Scotland) Act 1983 (c. 33), s.1 and para. (i) was added by the Health and Social Services and Social Security Adjudications Act 1983, s.8(1)) being satisfied with respect to a child; and

(b) the reference in section 54(3)—

(i) to compulsory measures of supervision shall be construed as including a reference to compulsory measures of care within the meaning of section 32 of the 1968 Act;

(ii) to arranging a children's hearing to consider the case of the child under section 69 of the Act shall be construed as including a reference to arranging a children's hearing to consider the case of the child under sections 43 and 44 of the 1968 Act; and

(iii) to the application of section 69(1) of the Act shall be construed as including a reference to the application of sections 43 and 44 of the 1968 Act as if the condition specified by the court under section 54(1) of the Act as read with paragraph (a) above were a ground of referral established in accordance with section 42 (s.42 was amended by the Health and Social Services and Social Security Adjudications Act 1983, Sched. 2, para. 8 and the Law Reform (Miscellaneous Provisions) (Scotland) Act 1985, s.25; s.42(2A) was inserted by the Criminal Justice (Scotland) Act 1980 (c. 62), Sched. 7, para. 21) of the 1968 Act.

7.—(1) The following transitional provisions shall be made to each of the provisions of the Adoption (Scotland) Act 1978 ("the 1978 Act") (c. 28) until the repeal of that provision in Schedule 5 to the Act comes into force.

(2) In section 2(d) of the 1978 Act, the reference to "custody proceedings" shall be construed as including a reference to proceedings regarding a residence order under section 11(2)(c) of the Act.

(3) In section 32(4)(c) of the 1978 Act, the reference to an order awarding custody of a child should be construed as including a reference to a residence order under section 11(2)(c) of the Act.

James Douglas-Hamilton
Minister of State,
Scottish Office

St Andrew's House, Edinburgh
22nd August 1996

Article 3

SCHEDULE

PROVISIONS OF THE ACT WHICH COME INTO FORCE ON 1ST NOVEMBER 1996

Column 1 *Provisions of the Act*	*Column 2* *Subject matter*	*Column 3* *Purpose*
Part I	Parents, Children and Guardians	
Section 54	Reference to the Principal Reporter by court	
Section 93	Interpretation of Part II	
Section 98(1)	Amendments of the Adoption (Scotland) Act 1978	Only for the purpose of bringing into force the provisions of Schedule 2 to the Act specified in column 1
Section 98(2)	Interpretation of Part III	
Section 105(3)	Transitional provisions and savings	Only for the purpose of bringing into force the provisions of Schedule 3 to the Act specified in column 1
Section 105(4)	Amendments	Only for the purpose of bringing into force the provisions of Schedule 4 to the Act specified in column 1
Section 105(5)	Repeals	Only for the purpose of bringing into force the repeals in Schedule 5 to the Act which are referred to in column 1 below
In Schedule 2, paragraphs—	Amendments of the Adoption (Scotland) Act 1978	
1		
7(a)(i), (b) and (c)		
8(a)		
9(a)		
11(b) and (c)		

Column 1 *Provisions of the Act*	*Column 2* *Subject matter*	*Column 3* *Purpose*
12(b)(i)		
13(a)(ii), (c)(ii) and (d)		
14		
17(b)		
23		
26		
29(a)(iii), (v) and (vi)		
In Schedule 3, paragraph 7	Transitional provisions and savings	
In Schedule 4, paragraphs—	Amendment of enactments	
1 to 6		
7(1) to (5) and (6)(a)		
8 and 9		
10(b)		
11		
14		
15(1), (5), (17)(a)(ii), (20)(c) and (28)(d) and (e)		
18(3)		
19 and 20		
23(1)		
23(4)(a)		Only for the purpose of inserting paragraph (c) into section 7(2) of the Rehabilitation of Offenders Act 1974
23(4)(c)		
24(1), (4), (5), (10) and (11)		
26(1), (2), (3), (4)(a) and (c), and (5) to (7)		
27		
28(1) and (5)(a)		
29(1) and (2)		
30 and 31		
33(1) and (4)		
34		
36		
37(1), (5) and (6)(a)(i) and (ii)		
38		
39(1), (2)(a), (3)(a), (4) and (5)(b)		
41		

Column 1 *Provisions of the Act*	*Column 2* *Subject matter*	*Column 3* *Purpose*
43		
46 and 47		
48(1) and (4)		
50 to 52		
53(2), (4) and (5)		
54(1) and (5)		
In Schedule 5, the repeals specified in the Table below	Repeals	

TABLE

REPEALS

Chapter	*Short title*	*Extent of repeal*
8 & 9 Vict. c. 19.	Lands Clauses Consolidation (Scotland) Act 1845.	In section 7, the words "persons under legal disability by reason of nonage" in each place where they occur. In section 67, the words "persons under legal disability by reason of nonage". In section 69, the words "persons under legal disability by reason of nonage".
12 & 13 Vict. c. 51.	Judicial Factors Act 1849.	In section 1, the words from "the word "Guardian" " to "years;". Section 25(2). In section 27, the words "guardians and". In section 31, the word "guardian,". In section 32, the word "guardian,". In section 33, the words "guardians or". In section 34, in both places where it occurs, the word "guardian,". In section 36, the word "guardianships,". In section 37, the word "guardian,". In section 40, the word "guardians," in both places where it occurs.
27 & 28 Vict. c. 114.	Improvement of Land Act 1864.	In section 18, the words from "nor shall they" to the end. In section 21, the words from "or if the landowner" to "minors"; and the words "or circumstance" in both places where they occur.
43 & 44 Vict. c. 4.	Judicial Factors (Scotland) Act 1880.	In section 3, in the definition of "judicial factor", the words from "and" to "required".
7 Edw. 7 c. 51.	Sheriff Courts (Scotland) Act 1907.	Section 5(2C). Section 38C.
11 & 12 Geo. 5 c. 58.	Trusts (Scotland) Act 1921.	In section 2, in the definition of "trustee", the words from "guardian" to "years)".

Chapter	Short title	Extent of repeal
1 Edw. 8 & 1 Geo. 6 c. 37.	Children and Young Persons (Scotland) Act 1937.	In section 27, the first paragraph.
1 & 2 Geo. 6 c. 73.	Nursing Homes Registration (Scotland) Act 1938.	In section 4(1)(b)(iii), the words "custody or".
14 & 15 Geo. 6 c. 65.	Reserve and Auxiliary Forces (Protection of Civil Interests) Act 1951.	In section 8(1)(d), the words from "or any order" to the end.
6 & 7 Eliz. 2 c. 40.	Matrimonial Proceedings (Children) Act 1958.	Sections 8 to 10. Section 12.
1968 c. 49.	Social Work (Scotland) Act 1968.	In section 5B(5), the words from "and" at the end of the definition of child to the end of the subsection. In section 94(1), the definition of "guardian".
1972 c. 18.	Maintenance Orders (Reciprocal Enforcement) Act 1972.	Section 4(3).
1973 c. 29.	Guardianship Act 1973.	The whole Act.
1974 c. 53.	Rehabilitation of Offenders Act 1974.	In section 7(2) the words from "In the application" to the end.
1975 c. 72.	Children Act 1975.	Sections 47 to 49. Section 53.
1978 c. 28.	Adoption (Scotland) Act 1978.	In section 12, in subsection (3)(b), the words "or by"; and in subsection (4) the word "—(a)" and paragraph (b). In section 14(1), the words from "Subject" to "certain cases)". In section 15, in subsection (1), the words from "Subject" to "certain cases)"; and in subsection (3), the word "natural" wherever it occurs. In section 65(1), in the definition of "guardian", paragraph (b).
1984 c. 15.	Law Reform (Husband and Wife) (Scotland) Act 1984.	Section 3(2).
1984 c. 36.	Mental Health (Scotland) Act 1984.	Section 55(4).
1985 c. 37.	Family Law (Scotland) Act 1985.	In section 21, the words from "or an order" to "child".
1986 c. 9.	Law Reform (Parent and Child) (Scotland) Act 1986.	Sections 2 to 4. In section 8, the definitions of "child" and "parental rights". In Schedule 1, paragraph 3.
1986 c. 33.	Disabled Persons (Services, Consultation and Representation) Act 1986.	In section 16, in the definition of "guardian", paragraph (b).
1986 c. 55.	Family Law Act 1986.	In section 15(4), the words from "under section" to "1973". In section 17, in subsection (1), the words "Subject to subsection (2) below"; and subsection (2). In section 35(4)(c), the words "custody or".

Chapter	*Short title*	*Extent of repeal*
1988 c. 36.	Court of Session Act 1988.	Section 20.
1989 c. 41.	Children Act 1989.	In Schedule 13, paragraph 13.
1991 c. 48.	Child Support Act 1991.	In section 5(1), the words "(or, in Scotland, parental rights over)" in both places where they occur. In section 54, the definition of "parental rights".
1991 c. 50.	Age of Legal Capacity (Scotland) Act 1991.	In section 5(1), the words "or tutory". In section 9, the definition of "parental rights". In Schedule 1, paragraphs 3 to 5 and 7 to 15.
1993 c. 35.	Education Act 1993.	In Schedule 19, paragraph 36.

SOCIAL SECURITY

THE JOBSEEKERS ACT 1995 (COMMENCEMENT NO. 4) ORDER 1996

(S.I. 1996 No. 2208 (C. 54))

Made - - - - - - - - 27th August 1996

INTRODUCTION

This Order brings into force on September 2, 1996, paras. 2, 12, 14 of Sched. 2 to, and related part of s.41(4) of the Jobseekers Act 1995. All remaining provisions of the Act come into force on October 7, 1996.

The Secretary of State for Social Security, in exercise of the powers conferred upon him by section 41(2) and (3) of the Jobseekers Act 1995 (c. 18) and of all other powers enabling him in that behalf, hereby makes the following Order:

Citation

1. This Order may be cited as the Jobseekers Act 1995 (Commencement No. 4) Order 1996.

Appointed Day

2. The day appointed for the coming into force—

(a) of paragraphs 2, 12 and 14 of Schedule 2 to the Jobseekers Act 1995, and section 41(4) of that Act in so far as it relates to those paragraphs, is 2nd September 1996;

(b) of all other provisions of the Jobseekers Act 1995 in so far as not already in force, is 7th October 1996.

Signed by authority of the Secretary of State for Social Security.

Mackay of Ardbrecknish
Minister of State,
Department of Social Security

27th August 1996

HOUSING, ENGLAND AND WALES

THE HOUSING ACT 1996 (COMMENCEMENT NO. 2 AND SAVINGS) ORDER 1996

(S.I. 1996 No. 2212 (C. 55))

Made - - - - - - 22nd August 1996

INTRODUCTION

This Order brings into force on August 23, 1996, a number of provisions of the Housing Act 1996, which confer power to make orders, regulations or rules. On October 1, 1996, further provisions are brought into force, including, ss.105, 107 to 109, 111 to 117 which relate, *inter alia*, to collective enfranchisement.

The Secretary of State, in exercise of the powers conferred upon him by section 232(3) and (4) of the Housing Act 1996 (c. 52) and all other powers enabling him in that behalf, hereby makes the following Order—

Citation and interpretation

1.—(1) This Order may be cited as the Housing Act 1996 (Commencement No. 2 and Savings) Order 1996.

(2) In this Order:

"the Act" means the Housing Act 1996 and all reference to sections or Schedules (without more) are to sections of or Schedule to the Act; and

"the commencement date" means 1st October 1996.

Commencement

2.—(1) So much of the following provisions of the Act as confers on the Lord Chancellor or the Secretary of State the powers to make orders, regulations or rules shall come into force on 23rd August 1996—

section 83(3),
section 86(4) and (5)
section 92 in so far as it relates to paragraph 7 of Parv IV of Schedule 6,
section 96 in so far as it relates to the insertion by Schedule 7 of paragraphs 7(2)(a) and 9(2)(a) of Schedule 2A to the Housing Act 1988 (c. 50),
section 106 in so far as it relates to paragraph 1 of Schedule 9, and
section 119

(2) The following provisions of the Act shall come into force on the commencement date subject to the savings in the Schedule to this Order—

section 84,
section 88,
sections 89 to 91
section 92 (in so far as it will not already be in force),
section 93,
section 105,
sections 107 to 109,
sections 111 to 117, and
section 227 in so far as it relates to the repeals to the Landlord and Tenant Act 1987 (c. 31) in Part III of Schedule 19 and to the repeals in Part V of that Schedule (except the repeal to section 39(3) of the Leasehold Reform, Housing and Urban Development Act 1993 (c. 28)).

David Curry
Minister of State,
Department of the Environment

22nd August 1996

Article 2(2) SCHEDULE

SAVINGS

Compulsory acquisition of landlord's interest by qualifying tenants

1. Section 88 (period after which acquisition order may be made) shall not have effect in a case where, before the commencement date,—

(a) a notice under section 27 of the Landlord and Tenant Act 1987 (preliminary notice by tenants) has been served, or

(b) an application to court for an order dispensing with the requirement to service such a notice has been made.

The right of first refusal

2.—(1) Sections 89 to 93 and the repeals to the Landlord and Tenant Act 1987 in Part III of Schedule 19 (the right of first refusal) shall not have effect in a case where, before the commencement date,—

(a) a disposal has been made, or

(b) a notice under section 5 of the Landlord and Tenant Act 1987 (landlord's offer notice) has been served.

(2) In sub-paragraph (1), "disposal" has the same meaning as in Part I of the Landlord and Tenant Act 1987 as it will be amended by section 89.

Enfranchisement and lease extension: houses

3. The following section shall not have effect in a case where, before the commencement date,

(a) a notice has been given under section 8 or section 14 of the Leasehold Reform Act 1967 (c. 88) (notice of claim), or

(b) an application has been made under section 27 of that Act (enfranchisement where landlord cannot be found),—

section 105(1) and (2) (nil rateable values),
section 114 (amendment to section 1 of the Leasehold Reform Act 1967), and
section 115 (power for leasehold valuation tribunal to determine costs).

Collective enfranchisement and right to acquire new lease: flats

4. The following sections shall not have effect in a case where, before the commencement date,—

(a) a notice has been given under section 13 or 42 of the Leasehold Reform, Housing and Urban Development Act 1993 (notice of claim), or

(b) an application has been made to court under section 26 or 50 of that Act (applications where landlord cannot be found)—

section 105(3) (nil rateable values),
sections 107 to 109 (multiple freeholders, removal of professional valuation requirement and valuation principles),
sections 111 to 113 (trusts, residence condition and powers of trustees), and
section 227 is so far as it relates to the repeals in Part V of Schedule 19 (except the repeal of section 39(3) of the Leasehold Reform, Housing and Urban Development Act 1993).

ENVIRONMENTAL PROTECTION

NOISE ACT 1996 (COMMENCEMENT NO. 1) ORDER 1996

(S.I. 1996 No. 2219 (C. 56))

Made - - - - - - 28th August 1996

INTRODUCTION

This Order brings into force on September 19, 1996 various provisions of the Noise Act 1996, including s.10(7), which provides that the power of a local authority to abate a statutory nuisance includes power to seize and remove any equipment used in the emission of that noise.

The Secretary of State, in exercise of the powers conferred on him by section 14(2) of the Noise Act 1996 (c. 37) and of all other powers enabling him in that behalf, hereby makes the following Order:

Citation

1. This Order may be cited as the Noise Act 1996 (Commencement No. 1) Order 1996.

Provisions coming into force on 19th September 1996

2. The following provisions of the Noise Act 1996 shall come into force on 19th September 1996—

section 10(7), section 13 and section 14(1) to (3); and

section 10(8), section 10(9) and the Schedule, section 11 and section 12, in so far as those provisions relate to the power of a local authority under section 81(3) of the Environmental Protection Act 1990 (c. 43) to abate a statutory nuisance by virtue of section 79(1)(g) of that Act (noise emitted from premises).

Signed by authority of the Secretary of State.

Robert Jones
Minister of State,
Department of the Environment

28th August 1996

CRIMINAL LAW, ENGLAND AND WALES
CRIMINAL LAW, SCOTLAND
CRIMINAL LAW, NORTHERN IRELAND

THE SEXUAL OFFENCES (CONSPIRACY AND INCITEMENT) ACT 1996 (COMMENCEMENT) ORDER 1996

(S.I. 1996 No. 2262 (C. 57))

Made - - - - - - 2nd September 1996

INTRODUCTION

This Order brings all provisions of the Sexual Offences (Conspiracy and Incitement) Act 1996 into force on October 1, 1996.

In exercise of the power conferred upon him by section 7(2) of the Sexual Offences (Conspiracy and Incitement) Act 1996 (c. 29), the Secretary of State hereby makes the following Order:

1. This Order may be cited as the Sexual Offences (Conspiracy and Incitement) Act 1996 (Commencement) Order 1996.

2. The Sexual Offences (Conspiracy and Incitement) Act 1996 shall come into force on 1st October 1996.

Home Office
2nd September 1996

Ann Widdecombe
Minister of State

CUSTOMS AND EXCISE

THE FINANCE ACT 1996, SECTION 5(6), (APPOINTED DAY) ORDER 1996

(S.I. 1996 No. 2314 (C. 58))

Made - - - - - - - 9th September 1996

INTRODUCTION

This Order appoints October 1, 1996 as the day on which s.5 of the Finance Act 1996 is brought into effect in relation to the use of kerosene as fuel for certain engines. Among other matters, this section inserts new ss.13AA and 13AB into the Hydrocarbon Oil Duties Act 1979.

The Commissioners of Customs and Excise, in exercise of the powers conferred on them by section 5(6) of the Finance Act 1996 (c. 8), and of all other powers enabling them in that behalf, hereby make the following Order:

1. This Order may be cited as the Finance Act 1996, Section 5(6), (Appointed day) Order 1996.

2. The day appointed as the day on which section 5 of The Finance Act 1996 shall have effect in relation to cases where kerosene is—
(a) used as fuel, or
(b) taken into a fuel supply,
is 1st October 1996.

New King's Beam House
22 Upper Ground
London SE1 9PJ

D. J. Howard
9th September 1996 Commissioner of Customs and Excise

TAXES

THE FINANCE ACT 1994, SECTIONS 244 AND 245, (COMMENCEMENT) ORDER 1996

(S.I. 1996 No. 2316 (C. 59))

Made - - - - - - 9th September 1996

INTRODUCTION

This Order brings into force on November 4, 1996, ss.244 and 245 of the Finance Act 1994. These provisions relate to document production on transfer of land in Northern Ireland.

The Treasury, in exercise of the powers conferred on them by section 245(8) of the Finance Act 1994 (c. 9), hereby make the following Order:

1. This Order may be cited as the Finance Act 1994, sections 244 and 245, (Commencement) Order 1996.

2. Sections 244 and 245 of the Finance Act 1994 shall come into force on 4th November 1996.

Bowen Wells
Richard Ottaway
19th September 1996 Two of the Lords Commissioners of Her Majesty's Treasury

CRIMINAL LAW, ENGLAND AND WALES
CRIMINAL LAW, SCOTLAND
CRIMINAL LAW, NORTHERN IRELAND

THE CRIMINAL PROCEDURE AND INVESTIGATIONS ACT 1996 (APPOINTED DAY NO. 1) ORDER 1996

(S.I. 1996 No. 2343 (C. 60))

Made - - - - - - - 7th September 1996

INTRODUCTION

This Order appoints October 1, 1996 as the date on which ss.43, 48, 50, 53, 70, 71 of the Criminal Procedure and Investigations Act 1996 come into force. In particular, s.70 extends to England and Wales and Northern Ireland and has effect in its application to Northern Ireland subject to the modifications set out in para. 30 of Sched. 4.

The Secretary of State, in exercise of the powers conferred on him by sections 43(2), 48(5), 50(3), 53(3), 70(3), 71(6), 77(2) and (4) of the Criminal Procedure and Investigations Act 1996 (c. 25), hereby makes the following Order:

1. This Order may be cited as the Criminal Procedure and Investigations Act 1996 (Appointed Day No. 1) Order 1996.

2. 1st October 1996 is hereby appointed for the purposes of sections 48, 50, 53, 70 and 71 of the Criminal Procedure and Investigations Act 1996 ("the Act").

3.—(1) 1st October 1996 is hereby appointed for the purposes of section 43 of the Act (which relates to the application of Part IV of the Act).

(2) This article extends to England and Wales and Scotland only.

Home Office *Michael Howard*
7th September 1996 One of Her Majesty's Principal Secretaries of State

HOUSING, ENGLAND AND WALES CONSTRUCTION CONTRACTS ARCHITECTS

THE HOUSING GRANTS, CONSTRUCTION AND REGENERATION ACT 1996 (COMMENCEMENT NO. 1) ORDER 1996

(S.I. 1996 No. 2352 (C. 61))

Made - - - - - - 10th September 1996

INTRODUCTION

This Order brings into force various provisions of the Housing Grants, Construction and Regeneration Act 1996 on September 11, 1996. The provisions specified in art. 2(1) and (2) of this Order confer powers on the Secretary of State or the Lord Advocate to make orders, regulation and determinations, to give directions or guidance or to do other things.

This Order also brings into force on October 1, 1996, s.125 in so far as it relates to para. 21(1) to (3) in Pt. III of Sched. 2.

The Secretary of State, in exercise of the powers conferred on him by section 150(3) and (4) of the Housing Grants, Construction and Regeneration Act 1996 (c. 53) and all other powers enabling him in that behalf, hereby makes the following Order—

Citation and interpretation

1.—(1) This Order may be cited as the Housing Grants, Construction and Regeneration Act 1996 (Commencement No. 1) Order 1996.

(2) In this Order "the Act" means the Housing Grants, Construction and Regeneration Act 1996.

Commencement

2.—(1) The following provisions of the Act shall come into force on 11th September 1996—

section 74
section 79
section 86
section 89
section 94

(2) So much of the following provisions of the Act as confers on the Secretary of State or the Lord Advocate a power to consult, to make orders, regulations or determinations, to give directions, guidance, approvals or consents, to specify matters, or to impose conditions shall come into force on 11th September 1996—

sections 2 and 3
section 7
section 12
section 17
section 19
section 25
section 27
section 30
section 33
sections 44 to 47
sections 51 and 52
section 61
sections 63 and 64

sections 67 and 68
section 76
section 85
section 87
section 92
sections 101 and 102
sections 104 to 106
section 108
section 114
sections 131 to 135
section 139
section 140.

(3) Section 125 of the Act so far as it relates to paragraphs 21(1) to (3) of Part III of Schedule 2 shall come into force on 1st October 1996.

Signed by authority of the Secretary of State

Paul Beresford
Parliamentary Under Secretary of State,
Department of the Environment

10th September 1996

HOUSING, ENGLAND AND WALES

THE HOUSING ACT 1996 (COMMENCEMENT NO. 3 AND TRANSITIONAL PROVISIONS) ORDER 1996

(S.I. 1996 No. 2402 (C. 62))

Made - - - - - - - 16th September 1996

INTRODUCTION

This Order brings into force various provisions of the Housing Act 1996 (listed in art. 2), on September 24, 1996. On October 1, 1996 further provisions listed in art. 3 are brought into force. The majority of these provisions grant powers to the Secretary of State or Lord Chancellor to make regulations and orders, rules and directions and give guidance.

The Secretary of State, in exercise of the powers conferred on him by section 232(3) and (4) of the Housing Act 1996 (c. 52) and of all other powers enabling him in that behalf, hereby makes the following Order:

Citation and interpretation

1.—(1) This Order may be cited as the Housing Act 1996 (Commencement No. 3 and Transitional Provisions) Order 1996.

(2) In this Order—

"landlord" means a registered social landlord within the meaning of Part I of the 1996 Act;

"the 1985 Act" means the Housing Associations Act 1985 (c. 69);

"the 1988 Act" means the Housing Act 1988 (c. 50);

"the 1996 Act" means the Housing Act 1996.

Coming into force

2. The following provisions of the 1996 Act shall come into force on 24th September 1996—

section 219,

section 220,

section 222 in so far as it relates to paragraph 30 of Schedule 18, and

section 227 in so far as it relates to the entry in Part XIV of Schedule 19 for the Local Government (Wales) Act 1994 (c. 19).

3. Subject to the transitional provisions and savings in the Schedule to this Order, the following provisions of the 1996 Act shall come into force on 1st October 1996—

section 1,

section 2 to the extent that it is not already in force,

section 3 to the extent that it is not already in force,

section 4,

section 6,

section 7 to the extent that it is not already in force,

section 8,

section 9 to the extent that it is not already in force,

sections 10 to 15 inclusive,

sections 22 and 23,

sections 30 to 34 inclusive,

section 36(7),

sections 37 to 50 inclusive,

section 55(1) in so far as it relates to paragraphs 1(1) to (4), 2 to 5 inclusive, 7 (to the extent it is not already in force), 8, 10 and 11 of Schedule 3,

section 76,

section 77,
section 80(3),
section 129(3) and (4),
section 135,
section 138(4) to (6),
section 139,
section 140,
section 141(2) and (3),
section 142,
section 143,
section 160(4) and (5),
section 165(1), (2) and (5),
section 167(3) to (5),
section 169,
section 172,
section 174,
section 177(3),
section 182,
section 183(2),
section 189(2) to (4),
section 199(5),
section 203(1), (2) and (7),
section 210(2),
section 215,
section 217,
section 218,
section 222 in so far as it relates to paragraphs of Schedule 18 not already in force, and
section 227 in so far as it relates to—
(a) Part I of Schedule 19,
(b) Part IX of that Schedule except for the repeal in section 79(2)(a) of the 1988 Act, and
(c) Parts X to XIII of that Schedule.

4. So much of the following provisions of the 1996 Act as confer on the Corporation or the Secretary of State a power to consult, to make determinations, directions, orders or regulations or prepare schemes shall come into force on 1st October 1996—
section 18(2) and (7),
section 20(3),
section 21(3),
section 25,
section 27,
section 65,
section 66,
section 72,
section 75,
section 147,
section 161(2) and (3),
section 162(4),
section 163(7),
section 185(2) and (3),
section 194(6),
section 198(4) to (7), and
section 207(4) to (6).

5. Section 28(3) of the 1996 Act shall come into force on 1st October 1996 for the purpose of enabling a determination to be made under section 52(2) of the 1988 Act as amended by the 1996 Act.

Signed by authority of the Secretary of State

Paul Beresford
Parliamentary Under-Secretary of State,
Department of the Environment

16th September 1996

Article 3

SCHEDULE

TRANSITIONAL PROVISIONS AND SAVINGS

1.—(1) In accordance with article 3 of the Housing Act 1996 (Consequential Provisions) Order 1996 (S.I. 1996 No. 2325) and subject as follows, the provisions of Part I of the 1996 Act brought into force by this Order apply in relation to matters occurring before the commencement of the provisions as they apply in relation to matters arising on or after their commencement.

(2) Sub-paragraph (1) does not apply in relation to sections 39 to 50 of the 1996 Act.

2. The repeal of section 4(6) of the 1985 Act does not affect the priority of mortgages entered into before 1st October 1996.

3. The right of appeal under section 6 of the 1996 Act against a decision of the Corporation not to register a landlord or not to remove a landlord from the register does not apply to a decision made before 1st October 1996.

4. The repeal of section 24 of the 1985 Act does not affect the application of an order made under that section in relation to periods ending on or before 30th September 1996.

5. Paragraphs 16(3) to (5) and 19 of Schedule 1 to the 1996 Act apply in relation to accounts which relate to periods ending on or before 30th September 1996 and requirements under section 24 of the 1985 Act as they apply in relation to periods ending after that date and requirements under that paragraph 16.

6. Section 9(6) of the 1996 Act applies in relation to a body which was removed from the register under section 6(2) of the 1985 Act before 1st October 1996 as it applies in relation to a body removed from the register under section 4 of the 1996 Act.

7. The repeal of section 69(1)(e) and (g) of the 1985 Act does not affect applications made under section 69(2) of that Act before 1st October 1996.

8. The repeal of section 58 of the 1988 Act does not affect the application of section 79(2) of the 1985 Act, section 130 of the Housing Act 1985 or sections 11 to 15 of the 1996 Act in relation to a disposal made under section 58.

9. The amendment of section 79(2)(a) of the 1988 Act does not affect the power under section 79 of a housing action trust established under Part III of that Act to dispose of a house subject to a secure tenancy to a person approved under that section or section 94 of that Act.

10. The repeal of section 79(6) to (10) of the 1988 Act and of the words from "but" to the end in section 92(2) of that Act does not affect the application of these sections in relation to approvals given by the Corporation before 1st October 1996.

11. Sections 11 to 15 of the 1996 Act apply in relation to covenants and charges arising under Schedule 2 to the 1985 Act as they apply in relation to those arising under sections 11 to 15.

12.—(1) Part IV of the 1988 Act (change of landlords: secure tenants) and the provisions contained in Part IX of Schedule 19 shall continue to have effect in relation to applications under section 96 of that Act which have not been disposed of before 1st October 1996.

(2) That Part and those provisions shall also continue to have effect, as far as applicable, in relation to acquisitions made before that date, or by virtue of sub-paragraph (1).

(3) In its continued effect by virtue of this paragraph, section 105 of the Housing Act 1988 (consent for subsequent disposals) shall be construed as if in subsections (5) and (6) for the words "section 9 of the Housing Associations Act 1985" there were substituted "section 9 of the Housing Act 1996".

EDUCATION, SCOTLAND

THE EDUCATION (SCOTLAND) ACT 1996 (COMMENCEMENT) ORDER 1996

(S.I. 1996 No. 2250 (C. 63) (S. 182))

Made - - - - - - - 22nd August 1996

INTRODUCTION

This Order appoints September 18, 1996 as the day on which certain provisions of the Education (Scotland) Act 1996 are brought into force. All provisions in Pt. I are commenced other than those conferring substantive functions on the Scottish Qualifications Authority. Parts II and III are commenced entirely on this date, and also Pt. IV excluding minor consequential amendments and repeals of s.129 of the Education (Scotland) Act 1980.

The Secretary of State, in exercise of the powers conferred on him by section 37(2) of the Education (Scotland) Act 1996 (c. 43) and of all other powers enabling him in that behalf, hereby makes the following Order:

Citation and interpretation

1.—(1) This Order may be cited as the Education (Scotland) Act 1996 (Commencement) Order 1996.

(2) In this Order, "the Act" means the Education (Scotland) Act 1996.

Day appointed

2. 18th September 1996 is the day appointed for the coming into force of all the provisions of the Act other than those specified in article 3 below.

3. The provisions of the Act referred to in article 2 above are—

(a) sections 2 to 8;

(b) paragraphs 6 to 9 of Schedule 5; and

(c) Schedule 6 insofar as it provides for the repeal of section 129 of the Education (Scotland) Act 1980 (c. 44).

Raymond S. Robertson
Parliamentary Under Secretary of State,
Scottish Office

St Andrew's House, Edinburgh
22nd August 1996

SECURITY SERVICE

THE SECURITY SERVICE ACT 1996 (COMMENCEMENT) ORDER 1996

(S.I. 1996 No. 2454 (C. 64))

Made - - - - - - 23rd September 1996

INTRODUCTION

This Order brings into force all provisions of the Security Service Act 1996 on October 14, 1996.

In exercise of the powers conferred upon me by section 4(2) of the Security Service Act 1996 (c. 35), I hereby make the following Order:

1. This Order may be cited as the Security Service Act 1996 (Commencement) Order 1996.

2. The Security Service Act 1996 shall come into force on 14th October 1996.

Home Office *Michael Howard*
23rd September 1996 One of Her Majesty's Principal Secretaries of State

DEFENCE

THE ARMED FORCES ACT 1996 (COMMENCEMENT NO. 1) ORDER 1996

(S.I. 1996 No. 2474 (C. 65))

Made - - - - - - 25th September 1996

INTRODUCTION

This Order brings into force on October 1, 1996 various provisions of the Armed Forces Act 1996 including several repeals in Pt. III of Sched. 7.

The Secretary of State, in exercise of the powers conferred on him by section 36(2) and (5) of the Armed Forces Act 1996 (c. 46), hereby makes the following Order:

1. This Order may be cited as the Armed Forces Act 1996 (Commencement No. 1) Order 1996.

2. Subject to article 3 of this Order, the following provisions of the Armed Forces Act 1996 ("the Act") shall come into force on 1st October 1996—

section 2;
sections 6 and 7;
sections 11 to 14 and Schedule 4;
sections 18 and 19;
sections 30 to 33;
section 35 so far as is necessary to bring into force Schedules 6 and 7 to the extent specified below;
in Schedule 6, paragraphs 1 to 3, 5, 6, and 10 to 13;
Part III of Schedule 7 so far as it relates to the provisions specified in the Schedule to this Order.

3.—(1) Nothing in article 2 of this Order insofar as it relates to section 6 of the Act affects any service disciplinary proceedings, as defined in that section, which began on or before 30th September 1996.

(2) Sections 11 and 12 of the Act shall not have effect in relation to any conviction on or before 30th September 1996.

Nicholas Soames
Minister of State,
Ministry of Defence

25th September 1996

Article 2 SCHEDULE

REPEALS IN PART III OF SCHEDULE 7 TAKING EFFECT ON 1ST OCTOBER 1996

Chapter	*Short title*	*Extent of repeal*
1869 c.44.	Greenwich Hospital Act 1869.	Section 7.
1955 c.18.	Army Act 1955.	In section 122(1)(e), the words "for good conduct and industry". In Schedule 7, paragraph 8.
1955 c.19.	Air Force Act 1955.	In section 122(1)(e), the words "for good conduct and industry".
1957 c.53.	Naval Discipline Act 1957.	In section 82(1)(d), the words "for good conduct and industry". In section 111(2) the words "or the Women's Royal Naval Service". In section 132, in subsection (5), the words "the Women's Royal Naval Service,".
1974 c.53.	Rehabilitation of Offenders Act 1974.	In section 2, in subsection (1) the words "Subject to the following provisions of this section" and subsections (2) to (4). In section 6, in subsection (6) the words "Subject to subsection (7) below" and subsection (7).
1976 c.52.	Armed Forces Act 1976.	Section 17. In Schedule 9, paragraph 20(2).
S.I. 1978/1908 (N.I. 27).	Rehabilitation of Offenders (Northern Ireland) Order 1978.	In Article 4, in paragraph (1), the words "Subject to the following provisions of this Article," and paragraphs (2) to (4). In Article 7, in paragraph (6) the words "Subject to paragraph (7)" and paragraph (7).
1981 c.55.	Armed Forces Act 1981.	In section 20(2) the words "and the Women's Royal Naval Service". In Schedule 3, in paragraph 11(1) the words "and the Women's Royal Naval Service" and in paragraphs 11(2) and 12 to 14 the words "or the Women's Royal Naval Service". In Schedule 4, paragraphs 2(1) and 3(1).

LAND REGISTRATION, (SCOTLAND)

THE LAND REGISTRATION (SCOTLAND) ACT 1979 (COMMENCEMENT NO. 10) ORDER 1996

(S.I. 1996 No. 2490 (C. 66) (S.195))

Made - - - - - - - 25th September 1996

INTRODUCTION

This Order brings into force on April 1, 1997, ss.2(1), (2) and 3(3) of the Land Registration (Scotland) Act 1979 in the Counties of Ayr, Dumfries, the Stewartry of Kirkcudbright and Wigtown. These sections have already been brought into force by earlier commencement orders in the areas of Renfrew, Dumbarton, Lanark, Glasgow, Clackmannan, Stirling, West Lothian, Fife, Aberdeen and Kincardine.

The Secretary of State, in exercise of the powers conferred on him by section 30(2) of the Land Registration (Scotland) Act 1979 (c. 33) and all other powers enabling him in that behalf, hereby makes the following Order:

1. This Order may be cited as the Land Registration (Scotland) Act 1979 (Commencement No. 10) Order 1996.

2. Sections 2(1) and (2) and 3(3) of the Land Registration (Scotland) Act 1979 shall come into force on 1st April 1997 in the following areas, for the purpose of registration of writs:

(a) the County of Ayr;
(a) the County of Dumfries;
(a) the Country of the Stewartry of Kirkcudbright; and
(a) the County of Wigtown.

James Douglas-Hamilton
Minister of State,
Scottish Office

St Andrew's House, Edinburgh
25th September 1996

MARRIAGE

THE MARRIAGE CEREMONY (PRESCRIBED WORDS) ACT 1996 (COMMENCEMENT) ORDER 1996

(S.I. 1996 No. 2506 (C. 67))

Made - - - - - - - - *1st October 1996*

INTRODUCTION

This Order brings into force on February 1, 1997 all provisions of the Marriage Ceremony (Prescribed Words) Act 1996.

The Secretary of State, in exercise of the powers conferred on him by section 2(2) of the Marriage Ceremony (Prescribed Words) Act 1996 (c. 34), hereby makes the following Order:

1. This Order may be cited as the Marriage Ceremony (Prescribed Words) Act 1996 (Commencement) Order 1996.

2. The provisions of the Marriage Ceremony (Prescribed Words) Act 1996 shall come into force on 1st February 1997.

Home Office
1st October 1996

Blatch
Minister of State

TERMS AND CONDITIONS OF EMPLOYMENT

THE EMPLOYMENT RIGHTS ACT 1996 (RESIDUARY COMMENCEMENT NO. 1) ORDER 1996

(S.I. 1996 No. 2514 (C. 68))

Made - - - - - - - - *1st October 1996*

INTRODUCTION

By this Order, the appointed day for the purposes of Sched. 2, para. 15(1) to the Employment Rights Act 1996, is October 6, 1996, thereby bringing into force ss.46, 58–60 and 102 (relating to the employment rights of trustees of occupational pensions schemes).

The Secretary of State for Social Security, in exercise of the power conferred on him by paragraph 15(2)(b) of Schedule 2 to the Employment Rights Act 1996 (c. 18) and of all other powers enabling him in that behalf, hereby makes the following Order:

Citation

1. This Order may be cited as the Employment Rights Act 1996 (Residuary Commencement No. 1) Order 1996.

Appointed day

2. The day appointed as the relevant commencement date for the purposes of paragraph 15(1) of Schedule 2 to the Employment Rights Act 1996 (thereby bringing into force sections 46, 58 to 60 and 102 of that Act) is the 6th October 1996.

Signed by authority of the Secretary of State for Social Security.

Oliver Heald
Parliamentary Under-Secretary of State,
Department of Social Security

1st October 1996

PRIVATE INTERNATIONAL LAW

THE PRIVATE INTERNATIONAL LAW (MISCELLANEOUS PROVISIONS) ACT 1995 (COMMENCEMENT NO. 2) ORDER 1996

(S.I. 1996 No. 2515 (C. 69))

Made - - - - - - 26th September 1996

INTRODUCTION

This Order appoints November 1, 1996 as the date on which ss.1, 2 and 4 of the Private International Law (Miscellaneous Provisions) Act 1995 shall come into force. These are the final provisions to be brought into force, excepting s.3 which has been superseded by s.49 of the Arbitration Act 1996 and will be repealed when that section comes into effect.

The Lord Chancellor, in exercise of the power conferred on him by section 16(1) of the Private International Law (Miscellaneous Provisions) Act 1995 (c. 42), hereby makes the following Order:

1. This Order may be cited as the Private International Law (Miscellaneous Provisions) Act 1995 (Commencement No. 2) Order 1996.

2. Sections 1, 2 and 4 of the Private International Law (Miscellaneous Provisions) Act 1995 shall come into force on 1st November 1996.

Dated 26th September 1996 *Mackay of Clashfern, C.*

PRIVATE INTERNATIONAL LAW

THE PRIVATE INTERNATIONAL LAW (MISCELLANEOUS PROVISIONS) ACT 1995 (COMMENCEMENT NO. 2) ORDER 1996

(S.I. 1996 No. 2515 (C.[illegible]))

Made - - - - - - - - *20th September 1996*

Introduction

This Order appoints November 1, 1996 as the date on which s. 1 and s. 4 of the Private International Law (Miscellaneous Provisions) Act 1995 shall come into force. These are the only provisions of the Act not brought into force except s. 3 which has been superseded by s. 1 of the Arbitration Act 1996 and will be repealed when that Act comes into force.

The Lord Chancellor, in exercise of the power conferred on him by section 16(1) of the Private International Law (Miscellaneous Provisions) Act 1995 (c. 42), hereby makes the following Order:

1. This Order may be cited as the Private International Law (Miscellaneous Provisions) Act 1995 (Commencement No. 2) Order 1996.

2. Sections 1, 2 and 4 of the Private International Law (Miscellaneous Provisions) Act 1995 shall come into force on 1st November 1996.

20th September 1996 *Mackay of Clashfern, C.*

CUSTOMS AND EXCISE

THE FINANCE ACT 1996, SECTION 8, (APPOINTED DAY) ORDER 1996

(S.I. 1996 No. 2536 (C. 70))

Made - - - - - - - - 4th October 1996

INTRODUCTION

This Order appoints November 1, 1996 as the effective day for the purposes of s.8 of the Finance Act 1996. This section repeals s.18 and parts of s.19 of the Hydrocarbon Oil Duties Act 1979 which make provision for relief from excise duty on heavy hydrocarbon oil which is used as fuel for ships in home waters and oil used on certain fishing boats.

The Commissioners of Customs and Excise, in exercise of the powers conferred upon them by section 8(2) of the Finance Act 1996 (c. 8) and of all other powers enabling them in that behalf, hereby make the following Order:

1. This Order may be cited as the Finance Act 1996, section 8, (Appointed Day) Order 1996.

2. The day appointed as the day on which section 8 of the Finance Act 1996 comes into force is 1st November 1996.

New King's Beam House
22 Upper Ground
London
SE1 9PJ

D. J. Howard

4th October 1996 Commissioner of Customs and Excise

COUNTRYSIDE

THE ENVIRONMENT ACT 1995 (COMMENCEMENT NO. 6 AND REPEAL PROVISIONS) ORDER 1996

(S.I. 1996 No. 2560 (C. 71))

Made - - - - - - - *7th October 1996*

INTRODUCTION

This Order brings into force on April 1, 1997, various provisions of the Environment Act 1995. These provisions relate to the establishment of new National Park authorities under Pt. III of the Act. Each new National Park authority has, or will, with certain exceptions, become the sole local planning authority for the area of its Park.

The Secretary of State, in exercise of the powers conferred by section 125(3) and (4) of the Environment Act 1995 (c. 25), hereby makes the following Order:

Citation

1. This Order may be cited as the Environment Act (Commencement No. 6 and Repeal Provisions) Order 1996.

Provisions coming into force on 1st April 1997

2. The following provisions of the Environment Act 1995 shall come into force on 1st April 1997—

section 78 insofar as it relates to paragraphs 10(2)(b), 22(2), (4)(c), (6) and (7), 27, 32(14) and 33(6) to (8), 35 (insofar as that paragraph is not already in force), and 38(2) of Schedule 10;

section 120(3) insofar as it relates to the repeal of the enactments mentioned in Schedule 24 to the Environment Act 1995 (to the extent specified in the third column of that Schedule) and listed in column (1) of the Schedule to this Order, insofar as those repeals are not already in force, subject to the exceptions indicated in column (2); and paragraph 7(2) of Schedule 7.

Revocation

3. The following provisions of article 3 (provisions coming into force on 1st April 1996) of the Environment Act 1995 (Commencement No. 4 and Saving Provisions) Order 1995 (S.I. 1995 No. 2950 (C. 65)) are revoked with effect from 1st April 1997—

in paragraph (1), the words "—(1) Subject to paragraph (2),"; and paragraph (2).

Signed by authority of the Secretary of State for the Environment

David Curry
Minister of State
Department of the Environment

7th October 1996

Article 2

SCHEDULE

REPEALS

(1) **Enactment**	(2) **Exception from repeal**
National Parks and Access to the Countryside Act 1949 (c. 97)	
Caravan Sites and Control of Development Act 1960 (c. 62)	
Agriculture Act 1967 (c. 41)	
Countryside Act 1968 (c. 41)	
Local Government Act 1972 (c. 70) (the repeal relating to s.223(2) was brought into force on April 1, 1996 by the Environment Act 1995 (Commencement No. 5) Order 1996 (S.I. 1996 No. 186 (C. 3))	
Local Government Act 1974 (c. 7)	
Welsh Development Agency Act 1975 (c. 70)	
Race Relations Act 1976 (c. 74)	
Local Government, Planning and Land Act 1980 (c. 65)	The repeals relating to section 103(2)(c) and paragraph 9(2) and (3) of Schedule 2.
Highways Act 1980 (c. 66)	
Acquisition of Land Act 1981 (c. 67)	
Wildlife and Countryside Act 1981 (c. 69)	
Local Government (Miscellaneous Provisions) Act 1982 (c. 30)	
Derelict Land Act 1982 (c. 42)	
Litter Act 1983 (c. 35)	
Local Government Act 1985 (c. 51)	
Housing Act 1985 (c. 68)	
Norfolk and Suffolk Broads Act 1988 (c. 4)	
Local Government Act 1988 (c. 9)	
Local Government Finance Act 1988 (c. 41)	
Electricity Act 1989 (c. 29)	
Local Government and Housing Act 1989 (c. 42)	The repeal relating to the word "and" in section 21(1).
Town and Country Planning Act 1990 (c. 8) (the repeal relating to s.105 was brought into force on November 1, 1995 by the Environment Act 1995 (Commencement No. 3) Order 1995 (S.I. 1995 No. 2765 (C. 56))	
Planning (Listed Buildings and Conservation Areas) Act 1990 (c. 9)	
Planning (Hazardous Substances) Act 1990 (c. 10)	
Planning (Consequential Provisions) Act 1990 (c. 11)	
Environmental Protection Act 1990 (c. 43) (the repeals in Sched. 24, with the exception of those relating to ss.33(1), 36(11) and (12), 39(12) and (13), 54, 61, 75(3), 88 and 143 and Sched. 8, were brought into force on April 1, 1996 by the Environment Act 1995 (Commencement No. 5) Order 1996 (S.I. 1996 No. 186 (C. 3))	The repeals relating to sections 33(1), 54, 61, 75(3) and 143.
Planning and Compensation Act 1991 (c. 4)	
Water Industry Act 1991 (c. 56) (the repeals in Sched. 24, with the exception of those relating to s.4(6), were brought into force on April 1, 1996 by the Environment Act 1995 (Commencement No. 5) Order 1996)	

(1) **Enactment**	(2) **Exception from repeal**
Water Resources Act 1991 (c. 57) (the repeals relating to ss.68, 69(5), 126(6) and 124 were brought into force on September 21, 1995 by the Environment Act 1995 (Commencement No. 1) Order 1995 (S.I. 1995 No. 1983 (C. 40)). The repeals relating to ss.1 to 14, 16 to 19, 58, 105(1), 113(1), 114, 117, 121 to 124, 131, 132, 144, 146, 150 to 153, 187, 196, 202(5), 206(2), 209(1), (2) and (4), 213 to 215, 218, words in s.219(2), s.219(3), definitions in s.221(1) and Scheds. 1, 3 and 4 were brought into force on April 1, 1996 by the Environment Act 1995 (Commencement No. 5) Order 1996)	The repeal relating to section 190(1).
Land Drainage Act 1991 (c. 59) (the repeal relating to s.72(1) was brought into force on April 1, 1996 by the Environment Act 1995 (Commencement No. 5) Order 1996)	
Local Government Finance Act 1992 (c. 14)	The repeal relating to paragraph 95 of Schedule 13.
Local Government (Overseas Assistance) Act 1993 (c. 25)	
Local Government (Wales) Act 1994 (c. 19) (the repeals relating to para. 17(4) of Sched. 9 and para. 3(1) and (2) of Sched. 11 were brought into force on April 1, 1996 by the Environment Act 1995 (Commencement No. 5) Order 1996)	The repeals relating to paragraph 17(12) of Schedule 9 and paragraph 65(5) of Schedule 16.
Environment Act 1995 (c. 25)	The repeals relating to Schedule 22.

Environment	1. Water and drainage
Water Resources Act 1991 (c.57). The repeals relating to ss. 69(5), 120(1) and 174 were brought into force on September 21, 1995 by the Environment Act 1995 (Commencement No. 2) Order 1995 (S.I. 1995/1983) (C.40). The repeals relating to ss. [illegible] ... and ss. 213 to 215. The words in s. 190(1) ... [illegible] ... brought into force ... Environment Act 1995 (Commencement No. 1) Order 1995 ... Land Drainage Act 1991 (c.59) ... Environment Act 1995 (Commencement No. 5) Order 1996 ...	The repeals relating to section 190(1) ...
Local Government Act 1972 ...	The repeals relating to paragraph ... of Schedule ...
Environmental ...	
Local Government ... Act ... Food ... relating to ... and paragraph ... of Schedule ... Environmental Protection Act 1990 ... Environment Act 1995 (Commencement No. 5) Order 1996 ...	The repeal of ... paragraph 7(1) ... of Schedule ... paragraph 7(3) of Schedule 16.
Environment Act ...	In section ... relating ...

FAMILY LAW

CHILD SUPPORT

THE CHILD SUPPORT ACT 1995 (COMMENCEMENT NO. 3) ORDER 1996

(S.I 1996 No. 2630 (C. 72))

Made - - - - - - *14th October 1996*

INTRODUCTION

This Order brings into force most of the provisions of the Child Support Act 1995 which have not already been commenced. The provisions listed in Pt. I of the Schedule to this Order come into force on October 14, 1996, and those provisions in Pt. II come into force on December 2, 1996.

The Secretary of State for Social Security, in exercise of the power conferred upon him by section 30(4) of the Child Support Act 1995 (c. 34), hereby makes the following Order:

Citation and interpretation

1.—(1) This Order may be cited as the Child Support Act 1995 (Commencement No. 3) Order 1996.

(2) In this Order, unless the context otherwise requires, references to sections, Schedules and paragraphs of a Schedule are references to sections of, Schedules to, and paragraphs of a Schedule to the Child Support Act 1995.

Appointed days

2.—(1) The day appointed for the coming into force of the provisions specified in Part I of the Schedule to this Order is 14th October 1996.

(2) The day appointed for the coming into force of the provisions specified in Part II of the Schedule to this Order is 2nd December 1996.

Signed by authority of the Secretary of State for Social Security.

A. J. B. Mitchell
Parliamentary Under Secretary of State,
Department of Social Security

14th October 1996

Article 2

SCHEDULE

PART I

PROVISIONS COMING INTO FORCE ON 14TH OCTOBER 1996

Provisions of the Child Support Act 1995	*Subject matter*
Section 1(1), for the purposes only of making regulations under section 28A of the Child Support Act 1991 (c. 48) inserted by it	Application for a departure direction
Section 1(2) and Schedule 1, for the purposes only of making regulations under Schedule 4A to the Child Support Act 1991 inserted by Schedule 1	Application for a departure direction
Section 2, in respect of the insertion of section 28B(2) and (3) into the Child Support Act 1991, for the purposes only of making regulations under section 28B(2) of the Child Support Act 1991	Preliminary consideration of applications
Section 3, for the purposes only of making regulations under section 28C of the Child Support Act 1991 inserted by it	Imposition of a regular payments condition
Section 5, for the purposes only of making regulations under section 28E of the Child Support Act 1991 inserted by it	Matters to be taken into account
Section 6(1), for the purposes only of making regulations under section 28F of the Child Support Act 1991 inserted by it	Departure directions
Section 6(2) and Schedule 2, for the purposes only of making regulations under Schedule 4B to the Child Support Act 1991 inserted by Schedule 2	Departure directions
Section 7, for the purposes only of making regulations under section 28G of the Child Support Act 1991 inserted by it	Effect and duration of departure directions
Section 9, in respect of the insertion of section 28I(5) into the Child Support Act 1991	Transitional provisions
Section 10	Child maintenance bonus
Section 26, so far as not already in force	Regulations and orders
Schedule 3 in the respects specified below, and section 30(5) so far as it relates to them—	Minor and consequential amendments
paragraph 1, so far as not already in force	
paragraph 20	

PART II

PROVISIONS COMING INTO FORCE ON 2ND DECEMBER 1996

Provisions of the Child Support Act 1995	*Subject matter*
Section 1(1), so far as not already in force	Application for a departure direction
Section 1(2) and Schedule 1, inserting Schedule 4A into the Child Support Act 1991, so far as not already in force	Application for a departure direction
Section 2, in respect of the insertion of section 28B(1), (2) (so far as not already in force), (3) (so far as not already in force), (4) and (5) into the Child Support Act 1991	Preliminary consideration of applications
Section 3, so far as not already in force	Imposition of a regular payments condition
Section 4	Determination of applications
Section 5, so far as not already in force	Matters to be taken into account
Section 6(1), so far as not already in force	Departure directions
Section 6(2) and Schedule 2, inserting Schedule 4B into the Child Support Act 1991, so far as not already in force	Departure directions
Section 7, so far as not already in force	Effect and duration of departure directions
Section 8	Appeals in relation to applications for departure directions
Schedule 3 in the respects specified below and section 30(5) so far as it relates to them— paragraphs 6, 7 and 17	Minor and consequential amendments

PENSIONS

THE PENSIONS ACT 1995 (COMMENCEMENT NO. 8) ORDER 1996

(S.I. 1996 No. 2637 (C. 73))

Made - - - - - - 15th October 1996

INTRODUCTION

This Order brings into force on October 16, 1996 further provisions of the Pensions Act 1995 granting regulation and rule making powers.

The Secretary of State for Social Security, in exercise of the power conferred on him by section 180(1) of the Pensions Act 1995 (c. 26) and of all other powers enabling him in that behalf, hereby makes the following Order:

Citation and interpretation

1.—(1) This Order may be cited as the Pensions Act 1995 (Commencement No. 8) Order 1996.

(2) In this Order references to sections and Schedules are references to sections of, and Schedules to, the Pensions Act 1995.

Appointed days

2. The day appointed for the coming into force of sections 118 and 125(2) to (4) in so far as they are not already in force is 16th October 1996.

3. For the purposes of making regulations the day appointed for the coming into force of the following provisions is 16th October 1996—

(a) section 3(2),
(b) section 74(1) and (5)(a),
(c) section 165,
(d) Schedule 3, paragraphs 23 and 44(a)(ii) and section 122 in so far as it relates to those paragraphs, and
(e) Schedule 5, paragraph 80(f) and section 151 in so far as it relates to that paragraph.

4. For the purposes of making rules the day appointed for the coming into force of section 158 is 16th October 1996.

Signed by authority of the Secretary of State for Social Security.

Oliver Heald
Parliamentary Under-Secretary of State,
15th October 1996 Department of Social Security

INCOME TAX

THE INCOME AND CORPORATION TAXES ACT 1988, SECTION 737A, (APPOINTED DAY) ORDER 1996

(S.I. 1996 No. 2645 (C. 74))

Made - - - - - - 16th October 1996

INTRODUCTION

This Order appoints November 6, 1996 as the appointed day for the purposes of s.737A of the Income and Corporation Taxes Act 1988 in relation to agreements to sell overseas securities. Days have already been appointed in relation to agreements to sell U.K. equities and U.K. securities.

The Treasury, in exercise of the powers conferred on them by section 737B(9) of the Income and Corporation Taxes Act 1988 (c. 1, s.737B was inserted by s.122 of the Finance Act 1994 (c. 9)), hereby make the following Order:

1.—(1) This Order may be cited as the Income and Corporation Taxes Act 1988, section 737A, (Appointed Day) Order 1996.

2. The day appointed for the purposes of section 737A of the Income and Corporation Taxes Act 1988 (s.737A was inserted by s.122 of the Finance Act 1994 and amended by s.159(1) of, and Pt. V(21) of Sched. 41 to, the Finance Act 1996 (c. 8)) in relation to agreements to sell overseas securities entered into on or after that day is 6th November 1996.

Roger Knapman
Bowen Wells
Two of the Lords Commissioners
of Her Majesty's Treasury

16th October 1996

INCOME TAX

THE FINANCE ACT 1996, SECTION 159, (APPOINTED DAY) ORDER 1996

(S.I. 1996 No. 2646 (C. 75))

Made - - - - - - 16th October 1996

INTRODUCTION

The appointed day for the purposes of s.159(1) and (3) of the Finance Act 1996 is November 6, 1996. These provisions relate to sale and repurchase agreements, and the initial agreement to sell or transfer securities.

The Treasury, in exercise of the powers conferred on them by section 159(10) of the Finance Act 1996 (c. 8), hereby make the following Order:

1. This Order may be cited as the Finance Act 1996, section 159, (Appointed Day) Order 1996.

2. The day appointed for the purposes of section 159(1) and (3) of the Finance Act 1996 is 6th November 1996.

Roger Knapman
Bowen Wells
Two of the Lords Commissioners of Her Majesty's Treasury

16th October 1996

HOUSING, ENGLAND AND WALES

THE HOUSING ACT 1996 (COMMENCEMENT NO. 4) ORDER 1996

(S.I 1996 No. 2658 (C. 76))

Made - - - - - - 15th October 1996

INTRODUCTION

This Order brings into force s.167 of the Housing Act 1996 on October 23, 1996, for the purposes of requiring a local housing authority to consult on an allocation scheme prior to its adoption and enabling them to adopt the scheme.

The Secretary of State, in exercise of the powers conferred upon him by section 232(3) of the Housing Act 1996 (c. 52), and of all other powers enabling him in that behalf, hereby makes the following Order:

Citation

1. This Order may be cited as the Housing Act 1996 (Commencement No. 4) Order 1996.

Commencement

2. Section 167 of the Housing Act 1996 shall come into force on 23rd October 1996 for the purposes of requiring a local housing authority to consult on an allocation scheme prior to its adoption and enabling them to adopt the scheme.

Signed by authority of the Secretary of State.

David Curry
Minister of State,
Department of the Environment

15th October 1996

ANTARCTICA

THE ANTARCTIC ACT 1994 (COMMENCEMENT) ORDER 1996

(S.I. 1996 No. 2666 (C. 77))

Made - - - - - - - 3rd October 1996

INTRODUCTION

This Order brings into force on November 1, 1996, s.7 of the Antarctic Act 1994, which provides for protection of Antarctic fauna and flora.

The Secretary of State, in exercise of the powers conferred upon him by section 35 of the Antarctic Act 1994 (c. 15), and of all other powers enabling him in that behalf, hereby makes the following Order:

Citation

1. This Order may be cited as the Antarctic Act 1994 (Commencement) Order 1996.

Commencement of Section 7 of the Antarctic Act 1994

2. Section 7 of the Antarctic Act 1994 shall come into force on 1st November 1996.

Malcolm Rifkind
Secretary of State for
Foreign and Commonwealth Affairs

3rd October 1996

LICENSING (LIQUOR)

THE LICENSING (AMENDMENT) (SCOTLAND) ACT 1996 COMMENCEMENT ORDER 1996

(S.I. 1996 No. 2670 (C. 78) (S.209))

Made - - - - - - *14th October 1996*

INTRODUCTION

This Order brings into force on October 21, 1996, all provisions of the Licensing (Amendment) (Scotland) Act 1996.

The Secretary of State, in exercise of the powers conferred on him by section 3(2) of the Licensing (Amendment) (Scotland) Act 1996 (c. 36) and of all other powers enabling him in that behalf, hereby makes the following Order:

Citation

1. This Order may be cited as the Licensing (Amendment) (Scotland) Act 1996 Commencement Order 1996.

Appointed date

2. The date appointed as the date on which the Licensing (Amendment) (Scotland) Act 1996 shall come into force is 21st October 1996.

James Douglas-Hamilton
Minister of State,
Scottish Officer

St Andrew's House, Edinburgh
14th October 1996

CHILDREN AND YOUNG PERSONS

THE CHILDREN (SCOTLAND) ACT 1995 (COMMENCEMENT NO. 2 AND TRANSITIONAL PROVISIONS) (AMENDMENT) ORDER 1996

(S.I. 1996 No. 2708 (C. 79) (S. 210))

Made - - - - - - 18th October 1996

INTRODUCTION

This Order makes an amendment to the Children (Scotland) Act 1995 (Commencement No. 2 and Transitional Provisions) Order 1996. The entry relating to the Trusts (Scotland) Act 1921 is hereby omitted from the Table of repeals in the Schedule to that Order.

The Secretary of State in exercise of the powers conferred upon him by section 105(1) of the Children (Scotland) Act 1995 (c. 36) and of all other powers enabling him in that behalf, hereby makes the following Order:

Citation and interpretation

1.—(1) This Order may be cited as the Children (Scotland) Act 1995 (Commencement No. 2 and Transitional Provisions) (Amendment) Order 1996.

(2) In this Order "the second commencement order" means the Children (Scotland) Act 1995 (Commencement No. 2 and Transitional Provisions) Order 1996 (S.I. 1996 No. 2203).

Amendment of the second commencement order

2. In the Table of repeals in the Schedule to the second commencement order, the entry relating to the Trusts (Scotland) Act 1921 (c. 58) shall be omitted.

James Douglas Hamilton
Minister of State,
Scottish Office

St Andrew's House, Edinburgh
18th October 1996

CUSTOMS AND EXCISE

THE FINANCE ACT 1996, SECTION 6, (APPOINTED DAY) ORDER 1996

(S.I. 1996 No. 2751 (C. 80))

Made - - - - - - 28th October 1996

INTRODUCTION

This Order brings into force on November 15, 1996, s.6 of and Sched. 1 to the Finance Act 1996 in relation to the production of a mixture which is leaded or unleaded petrol, and the supply of a mixture of heavy oils. By s.6 new s.20AAA is inserted into the Hydrocarbon Oil Duties Act 1979.

The Commissioners of Customs and Excise, in exercise of the powers conferred on them by section 6(5) of the Finance Act 1996 (c. 8), and of all other powers enabling them in that behalf, hereby make the following Order:

1. This Order may be cited as the Finance Act 1996, Section 6, (Appointed Day) Order 1996.

2. The day appointed as the day on which section 6 of, and Schedule 1 to the Finance Act 1996 shall have effect in relation to—

(a) the production, on or after the date specified below, of a mixture which is leaded or unleaded petrol, and

(b) the supply, on or after that specified date, of a mixture of heavy oils,

is 15th November 1996.

New King's Beam House
22 Upper Ground
London
SE1 9PJ

D.J. Howard
Commissioner of Customs and Excise

28th October 1996

ENERGY CONSERVATION

THE ENERGY CONSERVATION ACT 1996 (COMMENCEMENT NO. 1) (SCOTLAND) ORDER 1996

(S.I. 1996 No. 2796 (C. 81) (S. 214))

Made - - - - - - 31st October 1996

INTRODUCTION

This Order brings into force, in Scotland, on December 1, 1996 all provisions of the Energy Conservation Act 1996. The Act amends the Home Energy Conservation Act 1995, which is brought into force in Scotland on the same day.

The Secretary of State, in exercise of the powers conferred upon him by section 2(2) of the Energy Conservation Act 1996 (c. 38) and of all other powers enabling him in that behalf, hereby makes the following Order:

Citation

1. This Order may be cited as the Energy Conservation Act 1996 (Commencement No. 1) (Scotland) Order 1996.

Commencement

2. The Energy Conservation Act 1996 shall come into force in Scotland on 1st December 1996.

Raymond S Robertson
Parliamentary Under Secretary of State,
Scottish Office

St Andrew's House, Edinburgh
31st October 1996

ENERGY CONSERVATION

THE HOME ENERGY CONSERVATION ACT 1995 (COMMENCEMENT NO. 3) (SCOTLAND) ORDER 1996

(S.I. 1996 No. 2797 (C. 82) (S.215))

Made - - - - - - *31st October 1996*

INTRODUCTION

This Order brings into force in Scotland, on December 1, 1996 all provisions of the Home Energy Conservation Act 1995. This Act is amended by the Energy Conservation Act 1996 which is brought into force in Scotland on the same day (by virtue of S.I. 1996 No. 2796 (C. 81) (S.214)).

The Secretary of State, in exercise of the powers conferred upon him by section 9(2) and (3) of the Home Energy Conservation Act 1995 (c. 10) and of all other powers enabling him in that behalf, hereby makes the following Order:

Citation

1. This Order may be cited as the Home Energy Conservation Act 1995 (Commencement No. 3) (Scotland) Order 1996.

Commencement

2. The Home Energy Conservation Act 1995 shall come into force in Scotland on 1st December 1996.

Raymond S Robertson
Parliamentary Under Secretary of State,
Scottish Office

St Andrew's House, Edinburgh
31st October 1996

ARCHITECTS
HOUSING, ENGLAND AND WALES

THE HOUSING GRANTS, CONSTRUCTION AND REGENERATION ACT 1996 (COMMENCEMENT NO. 2 AND REVOCATION, SAVINGS, SUPPLEMENTARY AND TRANSITIONAL PROVISIONS) ORDER 1996

(S.I. 1996 No. 2842 (C. 83))

Made - - - - - - 12th November 1996

INTRODUCTION

This Order brings into force various provisions of the Housing Grants, Construction and Regeneration Act 1996 (c.53), including those making provision on renovation grants, common parts grants, disabled facilities grants, HMO grants, restrictions on grant aid, participation in and variation of group repair schemes, home repair assistance and deferred action notices.

The Secretary of State, in exercise of the powers conferred by sections 102(5) and 150(3) and (4) of the Housing Grants, Construction and Regeneration Act 1996 (c. 53) hereby makes the following Order:

Citation and interpretation

1.—(1) This Order may be cited as the Housing Grants, Construction and Regeneration Act 1996 (Commencement No. 2 and Revocation, Savings, Supplementary and Transitional Provisions) Order 1996.

(2) In this Order—

"the 1996 Act" means the Housing Grants, Construction and Regeneration Act 1996;

"the 1989 Act" means the Local Government and Housing Act 1989 (c. 42. Pt. VIII is superseded, except as provided in s.102 of the Housing Grants, Construction and Regeneration Act 1996, by Chaps. I to III of Pt. I of that Act);

and expressions used in this Order and in Part VIII (grants towards cost of improvements and repairs, etc.) of the 1989 Act have the same meaning in this Order as they have in that Part.

Provision coming into force on 13th November 1996

2. So much of section 31 (determination of amount of grant in case of landlord's application) of the 1996 Act as confers on the Secretary of State a power to make regulations shall come into force on 13th November 1996.

Provisions coming into force on 17th December 1996

3. The following provisions of the 1996 Act (in so far as not already in force) (see S.I. 1996 No. 2352 (C. 61)) shall come into force on 17th December 1996—

sections 1 to 59 in Chapter 1 (the main grants),

sections 60 to 73 and 75 in Chapter II (group repair schemes) of Part I (grants, &c. for renewal of private sector housing),

sections 76 to 78 and 80 in chapter III (home repair assistance) of that Part,

sections 81 to 85, 87, 88, 90 and 91 in chapter IV (deferred action notices, &c.) of that Part,

sections 92, 93 and 95 to 103 in Chapter V (supplementary provisions) of that Part, and

subject to article 8, section 147 (repeals and revocations), in so far as it relates to Part I of Schedule 3.

Provisions coming into force on 1st April 1997

4. Part III (architects) (and Schedule 2) (in so far as not already in force) and section 147, in so far as it relates to Part II of Schedule 3, of the 1996 Act shall come into force on 1st April 1997.

Transitional and supplementary provision

5.—(1) This article applies to applications made after 2nd February 1996 under Part VIII of the 1989 Act for grant of a description mentioned in section 101 (grants for improvements and repairs) of that Act which have not been approved or refused before 17th December 1996.

(2) Where, in accordance with section 102(4) of the 1996 Act, an application to which this article applies is to be dealt with after 16th December 1996 as if sections 112 and 113 of the 1989 Act were omitted from that Part, that Part shall apply in relation to that application with the following further adaptations—

(a) in section 107 (certain dwellings and works excluded from grant aid)—

(i) for subsection (1) substitute—

"(1) In each of the cases in subsection (2) below, the local housing authority may not approve an application for a grant unless completion of the relevant works is necessary to comply with a notice under section 189 (repair notice requiring works to render premises fit for human habitation), section 190 (repair notice in respect of house in state of disrepair but not unfit) or section 352 (notice requiring works to render premises fit for number of occupants) of the Housing Act 1985." (c. 68);

(ii) for subsection (5) substitute—

"(5) A local housing authority may not approve an application for an HMO grant so far as it relates to works which related to means of escape from fire or other fire precautions unless completion of those works is necessary to comply with a notice under section 189, 190 or 352 of the Housing Act 1985.";

(b) in section 108 (restriction on grants for works already begun)—

(i) for subsection (2) substitute—

"(2) Subsection (1) above does not apply if completion of the relevant works is necessary to comply with a notice under section 189, 190 or 352 of the Housing Act."; and

(ii) in subsection (4), in paragraph (b), for the words "sections 112, 114 and 115 below" substitute the words "sections 114 and 115 below";

(c) after section 108 insert the following section—

"**Restriction on grants where more satisfactory course of action available**

108A.—(1) This subsection applies to applications for grant in respect of—

(a) works necessary to render a dwelling fit for human habitation;

(b) works to premises in a state of disrepair; or

(c) works to enable a house in multiple occupation to meet one or more of the requirements in section 352(1A) of the Housing Act 1985;

(whether or not any notice has been served under section 189, 190 or 352 of that Act in respect of the dwelling premises or house concerned).

(2) A local housing authority may not approve an application to which subsection (1) applies unless—

(a) they have determined that the dwelling, premises or house concerned is not fit for human habitation; and

(b) they are satisfied that completion of the relevant works is the most satisfactory course of action.

(3) Section 604 (fitness for human habitation) of the Housing Act 1985 applies for the purposes of this Part as it applies for the purposes of that Act.

(4) In deciding whether they are satisfied that the carrying out of the relevant works is the most satisfactory course of action in a case where the dwelling, premises or house concerned is unfit for human habitation, the local housing authority shall have regard to any guidance given under section 604A of the Housing Act 1985.
For that purpose the authority shall treat any guidance given in respect of the serving of a repair notice under section 189(1) of that Act as guidance given in respect of the completion of the relevant works." (Subsection (1A) of s.352 of the Housing Act 1985 was inserted by the Local Government and Housing Act 1989, Sched. 9, Pt. III, para. 49. Section 604A of the Housing Act 1985 was inserted by the Local Government and Housing Act 1989, Sched. 9, Pt. V, para. 84);

(d) in section 115 (discretionary approval of certain applications), in subsection (3)—
  (i) at the end of paragraph (f) omit the word "and";
  (ii) at the end of paragraph (g) insert—
    "(h) to ensure that the dwelling is fit for human habitation; and
    (i) to ensure that there is compliance with the requirements of any notice served under section 352 of the Housing Act 1985 with respect to the house.";

(e) in section 116 (approval and refusal of applications), in subsection (2), in paragraph (d) for the words "sections 109 to 115 above" substitute the words "sections 109 to 111, 114 and 115 above"; and

(f) in section 134 (cases in which grants may be re-calculated, withheld or repaid), in subsection (1), for paragraph (c) substitute—
  "(c) the authority ascertain that without their knowledge the eligible works were started before the application was approved and the application was not in respect of works whose completion was necessary to comply with a notice under section 198, 190 or 352 of the Housing Act 1985.".

Further supplementary provision

6.—(1) The local housing authority shall, not later than 11th March 1997, send a notice in writing to each person from whom they have received an application to which article 5 applies.

(2) A notice under paragraph (1) shall state—
(a) that the application is one to which section 102(4) of the 1996 Act applies;
(b) that the local housing authority are no longer required to approve the application; and
(c) that approval of the application is a matter for the discretion of the local housing authority.

(3) The local housing authority shall send with the notice under paragraph (1)—
(a) a copy of section 102 of the 1996 Act,
(b) a copy of this Order, and
(c) a summary of the general effect of that section and this Order.

Revocations

7. Subject to article 8(2), the subordinate legislation listed in the Schedule to this Order is hereby revoked.

Savings

8.—(1) Section 132 of the 1989 Act (contributions by the Secretary of State) shall continue to have effect for purposes connected with applications under section 461 (grant applications) of the Housing Act 1985 (c. 68. Pt. XV (grants for works of improvement, repair and conversion) was superseded, subject to saving and transitional provisions, by Pt. VIII of the Local Government and Housing Act 1989. See, in particular, the Local Government and Housing Act 1989 (Commencement No. 8 and Transitional Provisions) Order 1990 (S.I. 1990 No. 1274 (C. 36))) approved by a local housing authority before 1st July 1990.

(2) Subject to article 5, Part VIII of the 1989 Act and the subordinate legislation listed in the Schedule to this Order shall continue to have effect in relation to—

(a) any common parts grant, disabled facilities grant, HMO grant, renovation grant or minor works assistance approved under that Part before 17th December 1996;

(b) any group repair scheme approved under section 127 of the 1989 Act before that date; and

(c) any application made before that date for any such grant assistance as is mentioned in paragraph (a).

(3) For the purposes of paragraph (2)(b), the date of approval of a scheme not submitted for specific approval shall be taken to be the date on which the local housing authority that prepared the scheme decided that the scheme fulfilled the criteria for general approval (see Annex C to Department of the Environment Circular 7/93).

Signed by authority of the Secretary of State for the Environment.

David Curry
Minister of State,
Department of the Environment

12th November 1996

Article 7 SCHEDULE

REVOCATION OF SUBORDINATE LEGISLATION
PART I—STATUTORY INSTRUMENTS REVOKED

Title of instrument revoked	*Reference*
The Housing Renovation etc. Grants (Prescribed Forms and Particulars) (Welsh Forms and Particulars) (Amendment) Regulations 1996	S.I. 1996/1378
The Housing Renovation etc. Grants (Prescribed Forms and Particulars) (Amendment) Regulations 1996	S.I. 1996/1332
The Housing Renovation etc. Grants (Reduction of Grant) (Amendment) Regulations 1996	S.I. 1996/1331
The Housing Renovation etc. Grants (Prescribed Forms and Particulars) (Welsh Forms and Particulars) (Amendment) Regulations 1995	S.I. 1995/857
The Housing Renovation etc. Grants (Prescribed Forms and Particulars) (Amendment) Regulations 1995	S.I. 1995/839
The Housing Renovation etc. Grants (Reduction of Grant) (Amendment) Regulations 1995	S.I. 1995/838
The Housing Renovation etc. Grants (Prescribed Forms and Particulars) (Welsh Forms and Particulars) (Amendment) Regulations 1994	S.I. 1994/2765
The Housing Renovation etc. Grants (Prescribed Forms and Particulars) (Welsh Forms and Particulars) Regulations 1994	S.I. 1994/693
The Housing Renovation etc. Grants (Reduction of Grant) Regulations 1994	S.I. 1994/648
The Housing Renovation etc. Grants (Prescribed Forms and Particulars) Regulations 1994	S.I. 1994/565
The Housing Renovation etc. Grants (Grant Limit) (Amendment) Order 1993	S.I. 1993/2711
The Assistance for Minor Works to Dwellings (Amendment) Order 1993	S.I. 1993/554
The Housing Renovation etc. Grants (Grant Limit) Order 1993	S.I. 1993/553
The Assistance for Minor Works to Dwellings (Amendment) Regulations 1992	S.I. 1992/1845

Title of instrument revoked	*Reference*
The Assistance for Minor Works to Dwellings (Lead Pipes) Order 1992	S.I. 1992/1837
The Assistance for Minor Works to Dwellings Regulations 1990	S.I. 1990/388

PART II—OTHER REVOCATIONS

Title	*Reference*
The Housing Renovation, etc. Grants (Owner's Interest) Directions 1994	Department of the Environment Circular 8/94, Annex 1. Welsh Office Circular 25/94, Annex 1
Direction under section 110(2)(d) of the Local Government and Housing Act 1989 (grant determinations)	Department of the Environment Circular 7/93, Annex B. Welsh Office Circular 22/93, Annex B
General Approval to Group Repair Schemes 1993	Department of the Environment Circular 7/93, Annex C. Welsh Office Circular 22/93, Annex C
House Renovation Grants and Group Repair: Exchequer Contributions Determination 1990 (Amendment) Determination 1993	Department of the Environment Circular 7/93, Annex E
House Renovation Grants and Group Repair: Exchequer Contributions Conditions 1990 (Amendment) 1993	Department of the Environment Circular 7/93, Annex F. Welsh Office Circular 22/93, Annex E
Minor Works Assistance: Exchequer Contributions Determination (Wales) 1993	Welsh Office Circular 22/93, Annex F
Minor Works Assistance: Exchequer Contributions Determination 1990 (Amendment) Determination 1993	Department of the Environment Circular 7/93, Annex G
The Preliminary and Ancillary Fees and Charges Specification	Department of the Environment Circular 12/90, Annex B, Section 1. Welsh Office Circular 15/90, Annex B, Section 1
Direction under section 110(2)(d) of the Local Government and Housing Act 1989 (grant determinations)	Department of the Environment Circular 12/90, Annex B, Section 2. Welsh Office Circular 15/90, Annex B, Section 2
Specification under section 115(3)(f) of the Local Government and Housing Act 1989 (radon level)	Department of the Environment Circular 12/90, Annex B, Section 3. Welsh Office Circular 15/90, Annex B, Section 3
Consent under section 116(3)(a) of the Local Government and Housing Act 1989 (additional grant condition)	Department of the Environment Circular 12/90, Annex B, Section 4. Welsh Office Circular 15/90, Annex B, Section 4
House Renovation Grants and Group Repair: Exchequer Contributions Determination 1990	Department of the Environment Circular 12/90, Annex J

Title	*Reference*
House Renovation Grants and Group Repair: Exchequer Contributions (Wales) Determination 1990	Welsh Office Circular 15/90, Annex J
The House Renovation Grants and Group Repair: Exchequer Contributions Conditions 1990	Department of the Environment Circular 12/90, Annex J. Welsh Office Circular 15/90, Annex J
Determination as to payment of contributions towards expenditure on grants under Part XV of the Housing Act 1985	Department of the Environment Circular 12/90, Annex K. Welsh Office Circular 15/90, Annex K
Conditions relating to payment of contributions towards expenditure on grants under Part XV of the Housing Act 1985	Department of the Environment Circular 12/90, Annex K. Welsh Office Circular 15/90, Annex K
Minor Works Assistance: Exchequer Contributions Determination 1990	Department of the Environment Circular 4/90, Appendix B
Minor Works Assistance: Exchequer Contributions Conditions 1990	Department of the Environment Circular 4/90, Appendix B. Welsh Office Circular 13/90, Appendix B

TOWN AND COUNTRY PLANNING, SCOTLAND

THE ENVIRONMENT ACT 1995 (COMMENCEMENT NO. 7) (SCOTLAND) ORDER 1996

(S.I. 1996 No. 2857 (C. 84) (S.219))

Made - - - - - - - 8th November 1996

INTRODUCTION

This Order brings into force on January 1, 1997 in Scotland only, certain provisions of the Environment Act 1995, concerning, *inter alia*, mineral planning permissions and the repeal of s.251A of the Town and Country Planning (Scotland) Act.

The Secretary of State, in exercise of the powers conferred on him by section 125(3) of the Environment Act 1995 (c. 25) hereby makes the following Order:

Citation and extent

1.—(1) This Order may be cited as the Environment Act 1995 (Commencement No. 7) (Scotland) Order 1996.

(2) This Order extends to Scotland only.

Provisions coming into force on 1 January 1997

2. The following provisions of the Environment Act 1995 shall come into force on 1st January 1997:

section 96(1), (5) and (6) and Schedule 13 and 14 insofar as they apply in relation to Scotland;

96(3);

section 96(4) insofar as it relates to section 251A of the Town and Country Planning (Scotland) Act 1972 (c. 52, s.251A was substituted by s.51 and Sched. 8, para. 14, to the Planning and Compensation Act 1991 c. 34) ceasing to have effect;

section 120(3) insofar as it relates to the repeal in Schedule 24 of section 251A of the Town and Country Planning (Scotland) Act 1972.

George Kynoch
Parliamentary Under Secretary of State,
Scottish Office

Victoria Quay, Edinburgh
8th November 1996

LEGAL PROFESSION

THE LAW REFORM (MISCELLANEOUS PROVISIONS) (SCOTLAND) ACT 1990 (COMMENCEMENT NO. 13) ORDER 1996

(S.I. 1996 No. 2894 (C. 85) (S.222))

Made - - - - - - 6th November 1996

INTRODUCTION

This Order brings into force on December 5, 1996 certain provisions of the Law Reform (Miscellaneous Provisions) (Scotland) Act 1990. Where a provision has a special purpose listed in column 3 of the Schedule to this Order, it shall only come into force on that day and for that purpose.

The Secretary of State, in exercise of the powers conferred upon him by section 75(2) of the Law Reform (Miscellaneous Provisions) (Scotland) Act 1990 (c. 40) and of all other powers enabling him in that behalf, hereby makes the following Order:

Citation

1. This Order may be cited as the Law Reform (Miscellaneous Provisions) (Scotland) Act 1990 (Commencement No. 13) Order 1996.

Interpretation

2. In this Order—

"the Act" means the Law Reform (Miscellaneous Provisions) (Scotland) Act 1990; and

"the Board" means the Scottish Conveyancing and Executry Services Board.

Commencement

3. The provisions of the Act, which are specified in column 1 of the Schedule to this Order, and described by reference to the subject matter in column 2 of that Schedule, shall come into force on 5th December 1996 but, where a particular purpose is specified in relation to any provision in column 3 of that Schedule, that provision shall come into force on that day only for that purpose.

James Douglas-Hamilton
Minister of State,
Scottish Office

St Andrew's House, Edinburgh
6th November 1996

Article 3

SCHEDULE

THE PROVISIONS OF THE ACT WHICH COME INTO FORCE ON 5TH DECEMBER 1996

Column 1 *Provisions of the Act*	*Column 2* *Subject matter*	*Column 3* *Purpose*
Section 17, in so far as not already in force	Qualified conveyancers	
Section 18, in so far as not already in force	Executry practitioners	
Section 20	Professional misconduct, inadequate professional services, etc.	

Column 1 *Provisions of the Act*	Column 2 *Subject matter*	Column 3 *Purpose*
Section 21	Board's intervention powers	
Section 22, except subsection (1)(b) and (2)(c)	Disclosure of documents etc.	
In section 34—subsection (9)(d), (e) and (g)	Scottish legal services ombudsman	
In Schedule 1, Part II	Board's powers of investigation	
Section 74	Amendments and repeals	Only for the purpose of bringing into force the provisions of Schedules 8 and 9 to the Act specified or referred to in column 1 below
In Schedule 8, paragraphs—	Amendments of enactments	
19 and 20		
22(1)		For all purposes, except in relation to a recognised financial institution
22(2)		
24 and 25		
29(5) and (6)(b), insofar as not already in force		For all purposes, except in relation to a recognised financial institution
In Schedule 9—the repeals specified in the Table below	Repeals	

TABLE

REPEALS

Chapter	*Short title*	*Extent of Repeals*
1808 c. 149.	The Probate and Legacy Duties Act 1808.	In section 38, the words from "(which oath" to "administer").
1858 c. 56.	The Confirmation of Executors (Scotland) Act 1858.	Section 11.
1875 c. 41.	The Intestates Widows and Children (Scotland) Act 1875.	In section 6, the words from the beginning to "affirmations". In Schedule A, the words from "All which" to the end.
1876 c. 24.	The Small Testate Estates (Scotland) Act 1876.	Section 6. In Schedule A, the words from "All which" to the end.
1900 c. 55.	The Executors (Scotland) Act 1900.	Section 8.

EDUCATION, ENGLAND AND WALES

THE EDUCATION ACT 1996 (COMMENCEMENT NO. 1) ORDER 1996

(S.I. 1996 No. 2904 (C. 86))

Made - - - - - - 19th November 1996

INTRODUCTION

This Order brings into force on January 1, 1997, s.317(6) of the Education Act 1996. This section requires certain information relating to disabled pupils to be included in the annual reports of county, voluntary or grant-maintained schools. Only a small number of provisions of the Act remains to be brought into force.

In exercise of the powers conferred on the Secretary of State by section 583(3) of the Education Act 1996 (c. 56) the Secretary of State for Education and Employment hereby makes the following Order:

1. This Order may be cited as the Education Act 1996 (Commencement No. 1) Order 1996.

2. Section 317(6) of the Education Act 1996 shall come into force on 1st January 1997.

Henley
Minister of State,
Department for Education and Employment

19th November 1996

ENVIRONMENTAL PROTECTION

THE ENVIRONMENT ACT 1995 (COMMENCEMENT NO. 8 AND SAVING PROVISIONS) ORDER 1996

(S.I. 1996 No. 2909 (C. 87))

Made - - - - - - *20th November 1996*

INTRODUCTION

This Order brings into force on November 21, 1996, s.120(1) of, and paras. 142, 143, 169, 170 and 183 of Sched. 22 to, the Environment Act 1995 (c. 25) to the extent necessary to make regulations. These provisions relate to water pollution control registers of the Environment Agency and certain other procedures. The remainder of these provisions are brought into force on December 31, 1996 together with the s.120(3) related repeals.

The Secretary of State, in exercise of the powers conferred on him by section 125(3) and (4) of the Environment Act 1995 (c. 25), hereby makes the following Order:

Citation

1. This Order may be cited as the Environment Act 1995 (Commencement No. 8 and Saving Provisions) Order 1996.

Provisions coming into force on 21st November 1996

2. Section 120(1) of the Environment Act 1995 shall come into force on 21st November 1996 in so far as it relates to paragraphs 142, 143, 169, 170 and 183 of Schedule 22 in so far as the amendments made by those provisions confer any power to make regulations.

Provisions coming into force on 31st December 1996

3. Subject to article 4, the following provisions of the Environment Act 1995 shall come into force on 31st December 1996—

section 120(1) in so far as it relates to paragraphs 142, 143, 169, 170 and 183 of Schedule 22 in so far as those paragraphs are not already in force; and

section 120(3) in so far as it relates to the repeals made in Schedule 24 in relation to sections 91 and 190(1) of the Water Resources Act 1991 (c. 57).

Saving provisions

4.—(1) Nothing in this Order shall affect—

(a) the application of—

(i) paragraphs 1 to 5 of Schedule 10 to the Water Resources Act 1991 as originally enacted or as modified by the Control of Pollution (Discharges by the National Rivers Authority) Regulations 1989 (S.I. 1989 No. 1157; relevant amendments were made by para. 1(3) of Sched. 2 to the Water Consolidation (Consequential Provisions) Act 1991 (c. 60) and para. 233 of Sched. 22 to the Environment Act 1995 (c. 25)); and

(ii) regulations 2 to 6 of the Control of Pollution (Consents for Discharges etc.) (Secretary of State Functions) Regulations 1989 (S.I. 1989 No. 1151),

in relation to any application made under paragraph 1 of that Schedule (applications for discharge consents) before 31st December 1996 or any consent given under paragraph 5 of that Schedule (discharge consents granted without applications) before that date;

(b) the application of section 91 of the Water Resources Act 1991 as originally enacted (appeals in respect of consents under Chapter II of Part III of that Act), and regulations 2 and 7 of the Control of Pollution (Consents for Discharges etc.) (Secretary of State Functions) Regulations 1989, in relation to any appeal under that section made in relation to a decision taken before 31st December 1996;

(c) the power to amend or revoke any of the regulations mentioned in sub-paragraph (a) or (b) above.

(2) Paragraph (1)(a) above shall not apply in relation to an application made under paragraph 1 of Schedule 10 to the Water Resources Act 1991 before 31st December 1996 if—

(a) the application relates to discharges of a kind which the applicant, or a predecessor of his, was authorised to make by virtue of a consent to which paragraph 21 of Schedule 23 to the Environment Act 1995 (transitional provisions in relation to discharge consents) applied; and

(b) notice in accordance with sub-paragraph (2)(b)(ii) of that paragraph was not given by him or his predecessor.

Signed by authority of the Secretary of State for the Environment

Robert Jones
Minister of State,
Department of the Environment

20th November 1996

HOUSING, ENGLAND AND WALES

THE HOUSING ACT 1996 (COMMENCEMENT NO. 5 AND TRANSITIONAL PROVISIONS) ORDER 1996

(S.I. 1996 No. 2959 (C. 88))

Made - - - - - - - 25th November 1996

INTRODUCTION

This Order brings the provisions of Pts. VI and VII of the Housing Act 1996 (c. 52) fully into force on April 1, 1997 and January 20, 1997 respectively. These provisions concern the allocation of housing accommodation and homelessness. The Order is made subject to the transition provisions contained in the Schedule.

The Secretary of State, in exercise of the powers conferred upon him by section 232(3) and (4) of the Housing Act 1996 (c. 52), and of all other powers enabling him in that behalf, hereby makes the following Order:

Citation and interpretation

1.—(1) This Order may be cited as the Housing Act 1996 (Commencement No. 5 and Transitional Provisions) Order 1996.

(2) In this Order, "the Act" means the Housing Act 1996.

Commencement

2. Subject to the transitional provision in paragraph 1 of the Schedule to this Order, the following provisions of the Act shall come into force on 20th January 1997—

sections 175 and 176,
section 177 to the extent that it is not already in force,
sections 178 to 181,
section 183 to the extent that it is not already in force,
section 184,
section 185 to the extent that it is not already in force,
sections 186 to 188,
section 189 to the extent that it is not already in force,
sections 190 to 193,
section 194 to the extent that it is not already in force,
sections 195 to 197,
section 198 to the extent that it is not already in force,
section 199 to the extent that it is not already in force,
sections 200 to 202,
section 203 to the extent that it is not already in force,
sections 204 to 206,
section 207 to the extent that it is not already in force,
sections 208 and 209,
section 210 to the extent that it is not already in force,
sections 211 to 214,
section 216, and
section 227 in so far as it relates to Part VIII of Schedule 19.

3. Subject to the transitional provision in paragraph 2 of the Schedule to this Order, the following provisions of the Act shall come into force on 1st April 1997—

section 159,
sections 160 to 163 to the extent that they are not already in force,
section 164,

section 165 to the extent that it is not already in force,
section 166,
section 167 to the extent that it is not already in force,
section 168,
sections 170 and 171,
section 173, and
section 227 in so far as it relates to Part VII of Schedule 19.

Signed by authority of the Secretary of State

David Curry
Minister of State,
Department of the Environment

25th November 1996

Articles 2 and 3

SCHEDULE

TRANSITIONAL PROVISIONS

1. The repeals in Part VIII of Schedule 19 to the Act do not apply in relation to an applicant whose application for accommodation or assistance in obtaining accommodation was made before 20th January 1997.

2. The amendments made by paragraph 2 of Schedule 16 to the Act do not affect a tenancy granted before 1st April 1997.

LEGAL PROFESSION

THE LAW REFORM (MISCELLANEOUS PROVISIONS) (SCOTLAND) ACT 1990 (COMMENCEMENT NO. 13) (AMENDMENT) ORDER 1996

(S.I. 1996 No. 2966 (C. 89) (S.226))

Made - - - - - - 25th November 1996

INTRODUCTION

This Order amends the Law Reform (Miscellaneous Provisions) (Scotland) Act 1990 (Commencement No. 13) Order 1996 (S.I. 1996 No. 2894). The words "1st March 1997" now replace the words "5th December 1996", thereby amending the date that certain provisions of the Law Reform (Miscellaneous Provisions) (Scotland) Act 1990 are brought into force.

The Secretary of State, in exercise of the powers conferred upon him by section 75(2) of the Law Reform (Miscellaneous Provisions) (Scotland) Act 1990 (c. 40) and of all other powers enabling him in that behalf, hereby makes the following Order:

Citation and interpretation

1.—(1) This Order may be cited as the Law Reform (Miscellaneous Provisions) (Scotland) Act 1990 (Commencement No. 13) (Amendment) Order 1996.

(2) In this Order "the thirteenth commencement order" means the Law Reform (Miscellaneous Provisions) (Scotland) Act 1990 (Commencement No. 13) Order 1996 (S.I. 1996 No. 2984).

Amendment of thirteenth commencement order

2. In article 3 of and in the headnote to the Schedule to the thirteenth commencement order for the words "5th December 1996" there shall be substituted the words "1st March 1997".

James Douglas-Hamilton
Minister of State,
Scottish Office

St Andrew's House, Edinburgh
25th November 1996

IMMIGRATION

THE ASYLUM AND IMMIGRATION ACT 1996 (COMMENCEMENT NO. 3 AND TRANSITION PROVISIONS) ORDER 1996

(S.I. 1996 No. 2970 (C. 90))

Made - - - - - - 25th November 1996

INTRODUCTION

By this Order, s.8 of the Asylum and Immigration Act 1996 is brought into force on January 27, 1997. The section restricts the employment of persons subject to immigration control, with the Order providing that the section shall not apply to employment beginning before that date. The section is brought into force on December 1, 1996 only for the purpose of making Orders.

In exercise of the powers conferred on him by section 13(3) and (4) of the Asylum and Immigration Act 1996 (c. 49), the Secretary of State hereby makes the following Order:

1.—(1) This Order may be cited as the Asylum and Immigration Act 1996 (Commencement No. 3 and Transitional Provisions) Order 1996.

(2) In this Order "the Act" means the Asylum and Immigration Act 1996.

2.—(1) Subject to paragraphs (2) and (3) below, section 8 of the Act shall come into force on 27th January 1997.

(2) Section 8 of the Act shall not apply to employment which began before 27th January 1997.

(3) For the purpose only of making orders under subsections (1) and (2), section 8 of the Act shall come into force on 1st December 1996.

Home Office
25th November 1996

Ann Widdecombe
Minister of State

TRUSTS OF LAND

THE TRUSTS OF LAND AND APPOINTMENT OF TRUSTEES ACT 1996 (COMMENCEMENT) ORDER 1996

(S.I. 1996 No. 2944 (C. 91))

Made - - - - - -	*25th November 1996*
Coming into force - - - -	*1st January 1997*

INTRODUCTION

This Order brings into force on January 1, 1997, all provisions of the Trusts of Land and Appointment of Trustees Act 1996.

The Lord Chancellor, in exercise of the powers conferred on him by section 27(2) of the Trusts of Land and Appointment of Trustees Act 1996 (c. 47), hereby makes the following Order:

1. This Order may be cited as the Trusts of Land and Appointment of Trustees Act 1996 (Commencement) Order 1996.

2. The Trusts of Land and Appointment of Trustees Act 1996 shall come into force on 1st January 1997.

Dated 25th November 1996 *Mackay of Clashfern, C.*

DISABLED PERSONS

THE DISABILITY DISCRIMINATION ACT 1995 (COMMENCEMENT NO. 4) ORDER 1996

(S.I. 1996 No. 3003 (C. 92))

Made - - - - - 30th November 1996

INTRODUCTION

This Order brings into force on December 2, 1996, s.16(3) of the Disability Discrimination Act 1995 so far as it is not already in force.

The Secretary of State for Social Security, in exercise of the powers conferred upon him by section 70(3) of the Disability Discrimination Act 1995 (c. 50) and of all other powers enabling him in that behalf, hereby makes the following Order:

Citation

1. This Order may be cited as the Disability Discrimination Act 1995 (Commencement No. 4) Order 1996.

Appointed day

2. The day appointed for the coming into force of section 16(3) of the Disability Discrimination Act 1995 to the extent that it is not already in force is 2nd December 1996.

Signed by authority of the Secretary of State for Social Security.

Alistair Burt
Minister of State,
Department of Social Security

30th November 1996

CRIMINAL LAW, ENGLAND AND WALES
CRIMINAL LAW, NORTHERN IRELAND

THE CRIMINAL APPEAL ACT 1995 (COMMENCEMENT NO. 2) ORDER 1996

(S.I. 1996 No. 3041 (C. 93))

Made - - - - - - 4th December 1996

INTRODUCTION

This Order brings into force s.8 of and Sched. 1, paras. 1 and 2 to the Criminal Appeal Act 1995 on December 12, 1996. These provisions concern the making of recommendations for the appointment of members of the Criminal Cases Review Commission and also the making of such appointments.

In exercise of the powers conferred on him by section 32 of the Criminal Appeal Act 1995 (c. 35) the Secretary of State hereby makes the following Order:

1. This Order may be cited as the Criminal Appeal Act 1995 (Commencement No. 2) Order 1996.

2. For the purposes of making recommendations and appointments under section 8 of and paragraph 1 of Schedule 1 to the Criminal Appeal Act 1995, that section and paragraphs 1 and 2 of that Schedule shall come into force on 12th December 1996.

Home Office *Michael Howard*
4th December 1996 One of Her Majesty's Principal Secretaries of State

ENVIRONMENTAL PROTECTION

THE ENVIRONMENTAL PROTECTION ACT 1990 (COMMENCEMENT NO. 18) ORDER 1996

(S.I. 1996 No. 3056 (C. 94))

Made - - - - - - 28th November 1996

INTRODUCTION

This Order brings into force on December 16, 1996, s.162(2) of the Environmental Protection Act 1990 in so far as it relates to the repeal of the Alkali, etc. Works Regulation Act 1906, and the repeal of ss.(1)(d) and 5 of the Health and Safety at Work etc. Act 1974. Section 79(10) of the Environmental Protection Act 1990 makes reference to these repealed provisions, and is therefore also repealed on the same date. The repealed provisions concern the control of releases of noxious and offensive emissions into the air from certain premises.

The Secretary of State, in exercise of his powers under section 164(3) of the Environmental Protection Act 1990 (c. 43), hereby makes the following Order:

Citation

1. This Order may be cited as the Environmental Protection Act 1990 (Commencement No. 18) Order 1996.

Provisions coming into force on 16th December 1996

2. Section 162(2) of the Environmental Protection Act 1990 shall come into force on 16th December in so far as it relates to the following repeals in Part I of Schedule 16 to that Act and the repeals extend to England and Wales:

— the repeal of the whole of the Alkali, &c. Works Regulation Act 1906 (c. 14) so far as unrepealed;

— the repeal of section 1(1)(d) and the word "and" preceding it and section 5 of the Health and Safety at Work, etc. Act 1974 (c. 37);

— the repeal, in section 79(10) of the Environmental Protection Act 1990, of the words following "Part I".

Signed by authority of the Secretary of State.

Ferrers
Minister of State,
Department of the Environment

28th November 1996

CRIMINAL LAW

THE OFFENSIVE WEAPONS ACT 1996 (COMMENCEMENT NO. 2) ORDER 1996

(S.I. 1996 No. 3063 (C. 95))

Made - - - - - - 4th December 1996

INTRODUCTION

This Order brings into force s.6 of the Offensive Weapons Act 1996 on January 1, 1997, making it an offence to sell knives and certain weapons with blades or points to persons under 16. All provisions of the Act have now been brought into force.

In exercise of the powers conferred upon him by section 6(3) of the Offensive Weapons Act 1996 (c. 26), the Secretary of State hereby makes the following Order:

1.—(1) This Order may be cited as the Offensive Weapons Act 1996 (Commencement No. 2) Order 1996.

(2) This Order does not extend to Northern Ireland.

2. Section 6 of the Offensive Weapons Act 1996 shall come into force on 1st January 1997.

Home Office
4th December 1996

David Maclean
Minister of State

ARBITRATION

THE ARBITRATION ACT 1996 (COMMENCEMENT NO. 1) ORDER 1996

(S.I. 1996 No. 3146 (C. 96))

Made - - - - - - 16th December 1996

INTRODUCTION

This Order brings into force the provisions of the Arbitration Act 1996 (except for ss.85–87 which relate to domestic arbitration agreements). Enabling provisions which are necessary for the substantive provisions to be brought into force are commenced immediately. The substantive provisions come into force on January 31, 1997 subject to transitional provisions which are designed to ensure continuity of legal proceedings and to preserve the current law on "honourable engagement" clauses in relation to existing agreements.

The Secretary of State, in exercise of the powers conferred on him by section 109 of the Arbitration Act 1996 (c. 23), hereby makes the following Order:

1. This Order may be cited as the Arbitration Act 1996 (Commencement No. 1) Order 1996.

2. The provisions of the Arbitration Act 1996 ("the Act") listed in Schedule 1 to this Order shall come into force on the day after this Order is made.

3. The rest of the Act, except sections 85 to 87, shall come into force on 31st January 1997.

4. The transitional provisions in Schedule 2 to this Order shall have effect.

John M. Taylor,
Parliamentary Under-Secretary of State
for Corporate and Consumer Affairs,
Department of Trade and Industry

16th December 1996

CRIMINAL LAW, ENGLAND AND WALES
CRIMINAL LAW, NORTHERN IRELAND

THE CRIMINAL APPEAL ACT 1995 (COMMENCEMENT NO. 3) ORDER 1996

(S.I. 1996 No. 3149 (C. 97))

Made - - - - - - 16th December 1996

INTRODUCTION

This Order brings fully into force on January 1, 1997, certain provisions of the Criminal Appeal Act 1995. These provisions relate to the Criminal Cases Review Commission, which body is established under s.8 to consider claims of miscarriages of justice.

In exercise of the powers conferred on him by section 32 of the Criminal Appeal Act 1995 (c. 35) the Secretary of State hereby makes the following Order:

1. This Order may be cited as the Criminal Appeal Act 1995 (Commencement No. 3) Order 1996.

2. In this Order, "the 1995 Act" means the Criminal Appeal Act 1995.

3. Section 8 of and paragraphs 1 and 2 of Schedule 1 to the 1995 Act, for purposes for which they are not already in force (S.I. 1996 No. 3041 brought these provisions into force on December 12, 1996 for purposes of making recommendations for appointments to the Criminal Cases Review Commission, and making such appointments), and section 31(1)(a) of and paragraphs 3 to 11 of Schedule 1 and paragraphs 7 to 11 of Schedule 2 to the 1995 Act shall come into force on 1 January 1997.

Home Office *Michael Howard*
16th December 1996 One of Her Majesty's Principal Secretaries of State

INDUSTRIAL TRIBUNALS

THE INDUSTRIAL TRIBUNALS ACT 1996 (COMMENCEMENT) ORDER 1996

(S.I. 1996 No. 3150 (C. 98))

Made - - - - - 17th December 1996

INTRODUCTION

This Order appoints December 18, 1996 as the day on which ss.12(3) to (6) and 32(3) to (6) of the Industrial Tribunals Act 1996, have effect. These provisions relate to offences for breaching orders made by industrial tribunals and the Employment Appeal Tribunal restricting publicity in disability discrimination cases. They were contained in ss.62 and 63 of the Disability Discrimination Act 1995 and before they could be commenced, they were consolidated and repealed by the 1996 Act. Schedule 2, paras. 7(1), (2), (7) and (8) to the 1996 Act, state that in these circumstances the Act has effect with the omission of these provisions until the Secretary of State may appoint by order.

The Secretary of State, in exercise of the powers conferred on him by paragraphs 7(1), (2), (7) and (8) of Part II of Schedule 2 to the Industrial Tribunals Act 1996 (c. 17), hereby makes the following Order:

Citation

1. This Order may be cited as the Industrial Tribunals Act 1996 (Commencement) Order 1996.

Commencement

2. The day appointed as that from which the Industrial Tribunals Act 1996 has effect with the inclusion of sections 12(3) to (6) and 32(3) to (6) of the Act is the day after the day on which this Order is made.

John M Taylor,
Parliamentary Under-Secretary of State for
Corporate and Consumer Affairs,
17th December 1996 Department of Trade and Industry

EDUCATION, ENGLAND AND WALES

THE NURSERY EDUCATION AND GRANT-MAINTAINED SCHOOLS ACT 1996 (COMMENCEMENT NO. 2) ORDER 1996

(S.I. 1996 No. 3192 (C. 99))

Made - - - - - - 10th December 1996

INTRODUCTION

By this Order, the remaining provisions of the Nursery Education and Grant-Maintained Schools Act 1996 are brought into force. These remaining provisions relate to inspection of nursery education funded under the Act and come into force on January 1, 1997 except for certain regulation making powers which come into force on December 10, 1996 and Sched. 1, para. 14 (remaining) which comes into force on April 1, 1997.

In exercise of the powers conferred on the Secretary of State by section 11(3) of the Nursery Education and Grant-Maintained Schools Act 1996 (c. 50), the Secretary of State for Education and Employment makes the following Order:

Citation and interpretation

1.—(1) This Order may be cited as the Nursery Education and Grant-Maintained Schools Act 1996 (Commencement No. 2) Order 1996.

(2) In this Order "the Act" means the Nursery Education and Grant-Maintained Schools Act 1996.

Commencement of provisions

2. Section 5 of the Act shall come into force, so far as not in force, on the relevant dates relating to the provisions of Schedule 1 brought into force by this Order.

3. Paragraph 6(1)(a) of Schedule 1 to the Act shall come into force on 10th December 1996 for the purpose of empowering the making of regulations under that provision and on 1st January 1997 for all other purposes.

4. Paragraph 6(5) of Schedule 1 to the Act shall come into force on 10th December 1996.

5. The following paragraphs of Schedule 1 to the Act shall come into force on 1st January 1997:

6(2) and (3) insofar as it is not in force,
8(2) insofar as it is not in force,
16.

6. Paragraph 14 (insofar as it is not in force) shall come into force on 1st April 1997.

Signed by authority of the Secretary of State

Robin Squire
Parliamentary Under Secretary of State,
10th December 1996 Department for Education and Employment

ENERGY CONSERVATION
WALES

THE HOME ENERGY CONSERVATION ACT 1995 (COMMENCEMENT NO. 4) (WALES) ORDER 1996

(S.I. 1996 No. 3181 (C. 100))

Made - - - - - - *17th December 1996*

INTRODUCTION

This Order brings into force on April 1, 1997, all provisions of the Home Energy Conservation Act 1995 (c. 10) in Wales, except ss.3(1), 4(1) and (2) which come into force on January 10, 1997.

The Secretary of State for Wales, in exercise of the powers conferred upon him by section 9(2) and (3) of the Home Energy Conservation Act 1995 (c. 10) and of all other powers enabling him in that behalf, hereby makes the following Order—

Citation

1. This Order may be cited as the Home Energy Conservation Act 1995 (Commencement No. 4) (Wales) Order 1996.

Commencement

2.—(1) Subject to paragraph (2), the Home Energy Conservation Act 1995 shall come into force on 1st April 1997.

(2) Sections 3(1) and 4(1) and (2) of that Act shall come into force on 10th January 1997.

Application

3. This Order shall apply in relation only to energy conservation authorities whose areas are in Wales.

Signed by authority of the Secretary of State for Wales

Jonathan Evans
Parliamentary Under Secretary of State,
Welsh Office

17th December 1996

EVIDENCE

THE CIVIL EVIDENCE ACT 1995 (COMMENCEMENT NO. 1) ORDER 1996

(S.I. 1996 No. 3217 (C. 101))

Made - - - - - - - *19th December 1996*
Coming into force - - - - *31st January 1997*

INTRODUCTION

This Order brings into force on January 31, 1997, all provisions of the Civil Evidence Act 1995, except for ss.10 and 16(5).

The Lord Chancellor, in exercise of the powers conferred on him by section 16(2) of the Civil Evidence Act 1995 (c. 38), hereby makes the following Order—

1. This Order may be cited as the Civil Evidence Act 1995 (Commencement No. 1) Order 1996.

2. Except for sections 10 and 16(5), the Civil Evidence Act 1995 shall come into force on 31st January 1997.

Mackay of Clashfern, C.

Dated 19th December 1996

CHILDREN AND YOUNG PERSONS

THE CHILDREN (SCOTLAND) ACT 1995 (COMMENCEMENT NO. 3) ORDER 1996

(S.I. 1996 No. 3201 (C. 102) (S. 241))

Made - - - - - 11th December 1996

INTRODUCTION

This Order brings into force provisions of the Children (Scotland) Act 1995. Certain provisions are brought into force on December 12, 1996 for the purpose of enabling directions, rules or regulations to be made on or before to come into force on April 1, 1997. These provisions relate, *inter alia*, to the local authority duty to a child looked after by it, plans for services for children, and publication of information about such services. Certain insertions and amendments are made to the Adoption (Scotland) Act 1978 and amendments are also made to the Social Work (Scotland) Act 1968 on December 12, 1996 for the purpose of enabling regulations to be made so as to come into force on or after April 1, 1997.

All remaining provisions of the Act are brought into force on April 1, 1997 except the insertion of new s.51A in the Adoption (Scotland) Act 1978 which comes into force on April 1, 1998 and also a repeal of a provision in the Trusts (Scotland) Act 1921 made by Sched. 5.

The Secretary of State, in exercise of the powers conferred upon him by section 105(1) of the Children (Scotland) Act 1995 (c. 36) and of all other powers enabling him in that behalf, hereby makes the following Order:

Citation

1. This Order may be cited as the Children (Scotland) Act 1995 (Commencement No. 3) Order 1996.

Interpretation

2. In this Order "the Act" means the Children (Scotland) Act 1995.

Commencement

3.—(1) Sections 17, 19, 20, 31, 33, 38, 40, 42, 62, 70, 74, 75, 87, 94 and 101 of the Act shall come into force on 12th December 1996 but only for the purpose of enabling directions, rules or, as the case may be, regulations to be made under those sections so as to come into force on or after 1st April 1997.

(2) Section 98 of and paragraph 3 of Schedule 2 to the Act, insofar as not then in force, shall come into force on 12th December 1996 but only for the purpose of inserting after paragraph (a) of section 3(3) of the Adoption (Scotland) Act 1978 (c. 28) a new paragraph (aa) for the purpose only of enabling regulations to be made, so as to come into force on or after 1st April 1997.

(3) Section 98 of and paragraph 19 of Schedule 2 to the Act, insofar as not then in force, shall come into force on 12th December 1996 but only for the purpose of substituting new subsection (1) and (2) in section 27 of the Adoption (Scotland) Act 1978 for the purpose only of enabling regulations to be made, so as to come into force on or after 1st April 1997.

(4) Section 98 of and paragraph 5 of Schedule 2 of the Act shall come into force, insofar as not then in force, on 12th December 1996 but only for the purpose of amending section 9 of the Adoption (Scotland) Act 1978 and inserting a new subsection (3A) in that section of that Act for the purpose only of enabling regulations to be made thereunder so as to come into force on or after 1st April 1997.

(5) Section 98 of and paragraph 25 of Schedule 2 to the Act shall come into force on 12th December 1996 but only for the purpose of inserting new section 51A into the Adoption (Scotland) Act 1978 for the purpose only of enabling regulations to be made, so as to come into force on or after 1st April

1998 or, as the case may be, enabling the Secretary of State to make a direction.

(6) Section 105(4) of and paragraph 15 of Schedule 4 to the Act shall come into force on 12th December 1996 but only for the purpose of amending the Social Work (Scotland) Act 1968 (c. 49) for the purpose of enabling regulations to be made, so as to come into force on or after 1st April 1997.

(7) The provisions of the Act, insofar as not already in force, shall come into force on 1st April 1997 except—

(a) section 98 of and paragraph 25 of Schedule 2 to the Act insofar as they insert new section 51A into the Adoption (Scotland) Act 1978, which shall come into force on 1st April 1998; and

(b) the entry in Schedule 5 to the Act relating to the Trusts (Scotland) Act 1921 (c. 58).

St Andrew's House,
Edinburgh
11th December 1996

James Douglas-Hamilton
Minister of State,
Scottish Office

CURRENT LAW STATUTES

NUMERICAL TABLE OF STATUTORY INSTRUMENTS 1996

DOCUMENT DELIVERY

Copies of 1996 Statutory Instruments can be obtained from Legal Information Resources Ltd (part of Sweet & Maxwell). Please telephone for current rates and direct any orders to LIR on fax no. 01422 888001 or tel. no. 01422 888000.

This table details in numerical order a complete list of all Statutory Instruments released in 1996 (up to date to **February 25, 1997**). A numerical table of 1997 Statutory Instruments released as at **February 25, 1997** can be found on p. 65. For brief digests of Statutory Instruments see the Current Law Monthly Digest.

1................Insurance Companies (Pensions Business) (Transitional Provisions) (Amendment) Regulations 1996
2................Sea Fishing (Enforcement of Community Control Measures) (Amendment) Order 1996
5................Occupational Pension Schemes (Deficiency on Winding Up etc.) Amendment Regulations 1996
11................National Disability Council Regulations 1996
15................Weymouth Harbour Revision Order 1996
16................Road Vehicles (Construction and Use) (Amendment) Regulations 1996
21................Friendly Societies (Gilt-Edged Securities) (Periodic Accounting for Tax on Interest) Regulations 1996
22................Civil Aviation (Canadian Navigation Services) (Third Amendment) Regulations 1996
24................Town and Country Planning (Costs of Inquiries etc.) (Standard Daily Amount) Regulations 1996
25................Plant Health (Great Britain) (Amendment) Order 1996
26................Plant Health (Licence Fees) (England and Wales) Regulations 1996
27................Hill Livestock (Compensatory Allowances) (Amendment) Regulations 1996
28................Sheep and Goats (Records, Identification and Movement) Order 1996
29................Food Protection (Emergency Prohibitions) (Radioactivity in Sheep) (Wales) (Partial Revocation) Order 1996
30................Social Security (Persons from Abroad) Miscellaneous Amendments Regulations 1996
31................Food Protection (Emergency Prohibitions) (Radioactivity in Sheep) Partial Revocation Order 1996
32 (S. 1).....Prisons and Young Offenders Institutions (Scotland) Amendment Rules 1996
33................National Blood Authority (Transfer of Trust Property) Order 1996
34................National Blood Authority (Transfer of Trust Property) (No. 2) Order 1996
35................King's Mill Centre for Health Care Services National Health Trust (Transfer of Trust Property) Order 1996
41................A41 Trunk Road (Barnet) Red Route (No. 1) Experimental Traffic Order 1996

42................A41 Trunk Road (Barnet) Red Route (No. 2) Experimental Traffic Order 1996
43................Local Government Changes for England (Valuation and Community Charge Tribunals) Regulations 1996
48................Sheep Annual Premium and Suckler Cow Premium Quotas (Re-assessment of Eligibility) Regulations 1996
49................Sheep Annual Premium (Amendment) Regulations 1996
52................Judicial Pensions (Additional Voluntary Contributions) (Amendment) Regulations 1996
53................Kent County Council (Wainscott Northern Bypass) Motorway Scheme 1992 Confirmation Instrument 1996
54................Taxes (Interest Rate) (Amendment) Regulations 1996
56................Local Government Reorganisation (Wales) (Council Tax Reduction Scheme) Order 1996
57 (S. 2) .....Upper Spey and Associated Waters Protection (Renewal) Order 1993 Variation Order 1996
58 (S. 3) .....River Tay Catchment Area Protection (Renewal) Order 1993 Variation Order 1996
60................East of Abercynon–East of Dowlais Trunk Road (A4060) (Improvement of Mountain Hare to Dowlais Top) Order 1996
61................River Teign Mussel Fishery (Variation) (Oysters) Order 1996
62................Food Protection (Emergency Prohibitions) (Radioactivity in Sheep) (England) (Partial Revocation) Order 1996
63................A30 Trunk Road (Hounslow and Hillingdon) Red Route (Clearway) Traffic Order 1996
64................A41 Trunk Road (Barnet) Red Route (Prescribed Route) Experimental Traffic Order 1996
68................Civil Courts (Amendment) Order 1996
69................A30 Trunk Road (Great South West Road, Hounslow) Red Route (Prescribed Routes and Prohibitive Turns No. 1) Traffic Order 1996
70................A30 Trunk Road (Great South West Road, Hounslow) Red Route (Prescribed Routes and Prohibitive Turns No. 2) Traffic Order 1996
71................Leeds City Council (Leeds Inner Ring Road Stages 6 and 7 (A61) to M1 Motorway (Junction 46) Connecting Road) Scheme 1994 Confirmation Instrument 1996
72................Leeds City Council (M1 Motorway Junction 46 Slip Road Connecting Road) Scheme 1992 Confirmation Instrument 1996
73................Leeds City Council (Hunslet Viaduct) Scheme 1992 Confirmation Instrument 1996
74................City of Stoke-on-Trent (Lichfield Street Canal Bridge) Scheme, 1995 Confirmation Instrument 1996
75................Merchant Shipping (Distress Signals and Prevention of Collisions) Regulations 1996
76................Civil Aviation Act (Investigation of Accidents) Regulations 1996
88................Local Government Reorganisation (Wales) (Finance) Order 1996
90................London Ambulance Service National Health Service Trust (Establishment) Order 1996
91................Sussex Ambulance Service National Health Service Trust (Transfer of Trust Property) Order 1996
92................Hull and Holderness Community Health National Health Service Trust (Transfer of Trust Property) Order 1996
94 (C.1) (S. 4) Land Registers (Scotland) Act 1995 (Commencement) Order 1996
95 (S. 5) .....Non-domestic Rate (Scotland) Order 1996

97................Offshore Installations (Safety Zones) Order 1996
98................A1 Trunk Road (Haringey) Red Route Traffic Order 1993 Experimental Variation Order 1996
99................A1 Trunk Road (Islington) Red Route Traffic Order 1993 Experimental Variation No. 3 Order 1996
101................Industrial Training Levy (Construction Board) Order 1996
102................Industrial Training Levy (Engineering Construction Board) Order 1996
103 (S. 6).....Non-Domestic Rates (Levying) (Scotland) Regulations 1996
106................Tyne Riverside Enterprise Zones (North Tyneside) (Designation) (No. 1) Order 1996
107................Vehicle Excise Duty (Immobilisation, Removal and Disposal of Vehicles) Regulations 1996
111................Education (Grant Maintained Special Schools) (Amendment) Regulations 1996
115 (S. 7).....Housing Revenue Account General Fund Contribution Limits (Scotland) Order 1996
120 (S. 8).....Glasgow School of Art (Scotland) Order of Council 1996
124................North Staffordshire Combined Healthcare National Health Service Trust (Transfer of Trust Property) Order 1996
125 (C. 2) (S. 9) Civil Evidence (Family Mediation) (Scotland) Act 1995 (Commencement and Transitional Provision) Order 1996
127................Worthing and Southlands Hospitals National Health Service Trust (Transfer of Trust Property) Order 1996
131................Goods Vehicles (Authorisation of International Journeys) (Fees) Regulations 1996
137 (S. 10)...Valuation Appeal Panels and Committees (Scotland) Regulations 1996
138................Local Government Act 1988 (Defined Activities) (Exemption) (Royal Borough of Kingston-upon-Thames) Order 1996
139 (S. 11)...Scottish Environment Protection Agency (Transfer Date) Order 1996
140 (S. 12)...Act of Sederunt (Civil Evidence (Family Mediation)) 1996
141 (S. 13)...Coast Protection (Notices) (Scotland) Amendment Regulations 1996
142................Tameside (Ashton Northern By-pass Stage 1 Ashton-Under-Lyne) (Special Roads) Scheme 1994 Confirmation Instrument 1996
146................Health Authorities (Wales) Establishment Order 1996
147................Merchant Shipping (Delegation of Type Approval) Regulations 1996
148................Gateshead Hospitals National Health Service Trust (Transfer of Trust Property) Order 1996
149................Gateshead Healthcare National Health Service Trust (Transfer of Trust Property) Order 1996
154................Local Government Act 1988 (Competition) (Housing Management) (Rossendale) Regulations 1996
156................National Savings Stock Register (Amendment) Regulations 1996
158................County Council of Norfolk (Reconstruction of Acle Wey Bridge) Scheme 1995 Confirmation Instrument 1996
159................County Council of Norfolk (Reconstruction of Acle Wey Bridge—Temporary Bridge) Scheme 1995 Confirmation Instrument 1996
160................Sea Fish Industry Authority (Levy) Regulations 1995 Confirmation Order 1996
161................Mortgage Indemnities (Recognised Bodies) Order 1996

162................Housing (Right to Buy) (Priority of Charges) Order 1996
163................Road Vehicles (Construction and Use) (Amendment) (No. 2) Regulations 1996
164................Air Passenger Duty (Prescribed Rates of Interest) (Amendment) Order 1996
165................Value Added Tax Act 1994 (Interest on Tax) (Prescribed Rate) Order 1996
166................Insurance Premium Tax (Prescribed Rates of Interest) (Amendment) Order 1996
167................Public Services Vehicles (Carrying Capacity) (Amendment) Regulations 1996
175................Local Authorities (Alteration of Requisite Calculations) Regulations 1996
176................Local Government Changes for England (Council Tax) (Transitional Reduction) Regulations 1996
177 (S. 14)...National Health Service (General Dental Services) (Scotland) Regulations 1996
178................Contracting Out (Administration of the Teachers' Superannuation Scheme) Order 1996
179................Local Government (Wales) (Alternative Community Names) (Prescribed Steps) Regulations 1996
180................Charities (Exception from Registration) Regulations 1996
182................Social Security (Adjudication) and Child Support Amendment Regulations 1996
183................Local Government Reorganisation (Wales) (Charities) Order 1996
184................Housing (Change of Landlord) (Payment of Disposal Cost by Instalments) (Amendment) Regulations 1996
185................Local Government Pension Scheme (Appropriation Pension Fund) Regulations 1996
186 (C. 3).....Environment Act 1995 (Commencement No. 5) Order 1996
187................Land Registration Fees Order 1996
189................Companies Act 1985 (Miscellaneous Accounting Amendments) Regulations 1996
190................Copyright (Certification of Licensing Scheme for Educational Recording of Broadcasts) (Open University Educational Enterprises Limited) (Amendment) Order 1996
191................Copyright (Certification of Licensing Scheme for Educational Recording of Broadcasts and Cable Programmes) (Educational Recording Agency Limited) (Amendment) Order 1996
192................Equipment and Protective Systems Intended for Use in Potentially Explosive Atmospheres Regulations 1996
193................Social Security (Back to Work Bonus) Regulations 1996
194................Housing Benefit, Supply of Information and Council Tax Benefit (Amendment) Regulations 1996
195................Employer's Contributions Re-imbursement Regulations 1996
197................Newlyn Pier and Harbour (Revision of Constitution of Commissioners) Order 1996
201................A38 Trunk Road (A3064 St Budeaux Bypass Slip Roads) (Trunking) Order 1996
205................Education (Grant) (Henrietta Barnett School) (Amendment) Regulations 1996
206................Income Support (General) (Jobseeker's Allowance Consequential Amendments) Regulations 1996
207................Jobseeker's Allowance Regulations 1996
208................Local Government Act 1988 (Defined Activities) (Exemption) (London Borough of Hillingdon Council) Order 1996

210................Value Added Tax (Amendment) Regulations 1996
211................Motor Vehicles (Driving Licences) (Amendment) Regulations 1996
212................Motor Vehicles (Driving Licences) (Large Goods and Passenger Carrying Vehicles) (Amendment) Regulations 1996
215................A30 Trunk Road (Great South West Road) (Temporary Restriction of Traffic) Order 1996
216................A41 Trunk Road (Camden) Red Route Experimental Traffic Order 1996
217................A205 Trunk Road (Richmond and Wandsworth) Red Route Experimental Traffic Order 1995 (Amendment No. 1) Order 1996
218 (C. 4).....Gas Act 1995 (Appointed Day and Commencement) Order 1996
219................Gas Act 1995 (Transitional Provisions and Savings) (No. 1) Order 1996
221 (S. 15) ...Police (Promotion) (Scotland) Regulations 1996
223................Income Tax (Building Societies) (Dividends and Interest) (Amendment) Regulations 1996
230................Farm and Conservation Grant (Variation) Scheme 1996
232................Central Manchester Development Corporation (Planning Functions) Order 1996
233................Central Manchester Development Corporation (Transfer of Property, Rights and Liabilities) Order 1996
234................Environment Agency (Transfer Date) Order 1996
235................Education (Grants for Education Support and Training: Nursery Education) (England) Regulations 1996
236 (S. 16) ...Act of Sederunt (Fees of Solicitors in the Sheriff Court) (Amendment) 1996
237 (S. 17) ...Act of Sederunt (Rules of the Court of Session Amendment No. 1) (Fees of Solicitors) 1996
238 (S. 18) ...Act of Sederunt (Copyright, Designs and Patents) (Amendment) 1996
239................Community Drivers' Hours (Passenger and Goods Vehicles) (Temporary Exception) Regulations 1996
240................Drivers' Hours (Passenger and Goods Vehicles) (Exemption) Regulations 1996
243................Child Support Commissioners (Procedure) (Amendment) Regulations 1996
244................Carriage by Air (Sterling Equivalent) Order 1996
247................Sea Fishing (Enforcement of Community Quota Measures) Order 1996
248................Fishing Boats (European Economic Community) Designation (Variation) Order 1996
249................Hinckley College (Dissolution) Order 1996
251................National Health Service (Clinical Negligence Scheme) Regulations 1996
252................Gas Act 1995 (Consequential Modifications of Subordinate Legislation) Order 1996
253................Co-operation of Insolvency Courts (Designation of Relevant Countries) Order 1996
255................Bridgend and District National Health Service Trust (Dissolution) Order 1996
256................Glan Hafren National Health Service Trust (Dissolution) Order 1996
257................Bridgend and District National Health Service Trust (Establishment) Order 1996

258................Glan Hafren National Health Service Trust (Establishment) Order 1996
259................North Glamorgan National Health Service Trust (Establishment) Order 1996
262................Partnerships (Unrestricted Size) No. 11 Regulations 1996
263................Charter Trustees Regulations 1996
264................A316 Trunk Road (Richmond) (No. 2) Red Route Experimental Traffic Order 1996
265................Local Government Act 1988 (Defined Activities) (Specified Periods) (Wales) Regulations 1996
266................European Communities (Designation) Order 1996
267................European Communities (Definition of Treaties) (Statute of the European Schools) Order 1996
268................Bosnia and Herzegovina (High Representative) Order 1996
269................Child Abduction and Custody (Parties to Conventions) (Amendment) Order 1996
270................International Sea Bed Authority (Immunities and Privileges) Order 1996
271 (C. 5).....Medical (Professional Performance) Act 1995 (Commencement No. 1) Order 1996
272................International Tribunal for the Law of the Sea (Immunities and Privileges) Order 1996
273................Transfer of Functions (Registration and Statistics) Order 1996
274 (N.I. 1)..Education (Northern Ireland) Order 1996
275 (N.I. 2)..Gas (Northern Ireland) Order 1996
276................Crown Office (Forms and Proclamations Rules) (Amendment) Order 1996
277 (N.I. 3)..County Courts (Amendment) (Northern Ireland) Order 1996
278................Criminal Justice Act 1988 (Designated Countries and Territories) (Amendment) Order 1996
279................Extradition (Designated Commonwealth Countries) Order 1991 (Amendment) Order 1996
280................Merchant Shipping (Categorisation of Registries of Overseas Territories) (Gibraltar) Order 1996
281................Merchant Shipping (Gibraltar Colours) Order 1996
282................Merchant Shipping (Prevention of Pollution) (Law of the Sea Convention) Order 1996
283................Combined Probation Areas (Shropshire) Order 1996
284................Combined Probation Areas (Gwent and Mid Glamorgan) Order 1996
285................A1 Trunk Road (Barnet) (50 mph Speed Limit) Order 1996
293 (S. 19) ...Fossil Fuel Levy (Scotland) Regulations 1996
294................Mental Health (After-care under Supervision) Regulations 1996
295................Mental Health (Patients in the Community) (Transfers from Scotland) Regulations 1996
306 (S. 20) ...Educational Endowments (Fife Region) Transfer Scheme Order 1996
307 (S. 21) ...Educational Endowments (Highlands Region) Transfer Scheme Order 1996
308 (S. 22) ...Education Endowments (Borders Region) Transfer Scheme Order 1996
309................Local Government Reorganisation (Wales) (Council Tax Reduction Scheme) Regulations 1996
310................Council Tax (Demand Notices) (Wales) (Amendment) Regulations 1996
311................Non-Domestic Rating (Demand Notices) (Wales) (Amendment) Regulations 1996

312................Local Government Changes for England (Property Transfer and Transitional Payments) (Amendment) Regulations 1996
313................Transfer of Functions (Foreign Service Allowance) Order 1996
314................Mental Health Review Tribunal (Amendment) Rules 1996
315................Companies (Revision of Defective Accounts and Report) (Amendment) Regulations 1996
316................Wireless Telegraphy (Cordless Telephone Apparatus) (Exemption) Regulations 1996
319................Measuring Instruments (EEC Requirements) (Gas Volume Meters) (Amendment) Regulations 1996
323 (C. 6) (S. 23) Local Government etc. (Scotland) Act 1994 (Commencement No. 7 and Savings) Order 1996
324 (S. 24) ...West Glasgow Hospitals University National Health Service Trust (Establishment) (Amendment) Order 1996
325 (S. 25) ...Water Services Charges (Billing and Collection) (Scotland) Order 1996
326 (S. 26) ...Domestic Sewerage Charges (Reduction) (Scotland) Regulations 1996
330................Local Government Changes for England (Miscellaneous Provision) Regulations 1996
333................Local Government Changes for England (Council Tax) (Transitional Reduction) (Amendment) Regulations 1996
334................Education (Grants for Education Support and Training) (Wales) Regulations 1996
335................Local Government Reorganisation (Wales) (Calculation Tax Reduction Scheme) Regulations 1996
336................Potato Marketing Scheme (Commencement of Revocation Period) Order 1996
337................Agricultural Holdings (Fee) Regulations 1996
341................Health and Safety (Safety Signs and Signals) Regulations 1996
342................Local Authorities (Goods and Services) (Public Bodies) (Trunk Roads) Order 1996
344................Welsh Church Act Funds (Designation and Specification) Order 1996
345................Deregulation (Fair Trading Act 1973) (Amendment) (Merger Reference Time Limits) Order 1996
346................Deregulation (Restrictive Trade Practices Act 1976) (Amendment) (Variation of Exempt Agreements) Order 1996
347................Deregulation (Restrictive Trade Practices Act 1976) (Amendment) (Time Limits) Order 1996
348................Restrictive Trade Practices (Non-notifiable Agreements) (Turnover Threshold) Order 1996
349................Restrictive Trade Practices (Non-notifiable Agreements) (E.C. Block Exemptions) Order 1996
350................National Health Service Trusts (Originating Capital Debt) Order 1996
351................North Durham Acute Hospitals (Transfer of Trust Property) Order 1996
352................Community Health Care: North Durham National Health Service Trust (Transfer of Trust Property) Order 1996
353................Education (Grants for Nursery Education) (England) Regulations 1996
357................Trunk Road (A4) (Great West Road, Hounslow) (Restriction of Traffic) Order 1984 (Variation) Order 1996
360................Education (School Premises) Regulations 1996
362................Gas Act 1995 (Consequential Modifications of Local Acts and Orders) Order 1996

372................Redundancy Payments (Local Government) (Modification) (Amendment) Order 1996
374................Animals, Meat and Meat Products (Examination for Residues and Maximum Residue Limits) (Amendment) Regulations 1996
375................Human Fertilisation and Embryology (Statutory Storage Period for Embryos) Regulations 1996
377................Bath and North East Somerset District Council (Staff Transfer) Order 1996
378................East Riding of Yorkshire District Council (Staff Transfer) Order 1996
379................Wireless Telegraphy (Television Licence Fees) (Amendment) Regulations 1996
380................Coventry Healthcare National Health Service Trust (Transfer of Trust Property) Order 1996
381................Education (School Financial Statements) (Prescribed Particulars etc.) (Amendment and Revocation) Regulations 1996
382................Education (Individual Pupils' Achievements) (Information) (Wales) Regulations 1996
383................South Tyneside Health Care National Health Service Trust (Transfer of Trust Property) Order 1996
384................North Lincolnshire District Council (Staff Transfer) Order 1996
385................Restrictive Trade Practices (Gas Conveyance and Storage) Order 1996
386................North East Lincolnshire District Council (Staff Transfer) Order 1996
387................South Gloucestershire District Council (Staff Transfer) Order 1996
388................North Yorkshire (District of York) (Staff Transfer) Order 1996
389................National Health Service (Dental Charges) Amendment Regulations 1996
391................National Assistance (Sums for Personal Requirements) Regulations 1996
392 (S. 27) ...National Health Service Trusts (Originating Capital Debt) (Scotland) Order 1996
395................Education (Financial Delegation to Schools) (Mandatory Exceptions) (Revocation and Amendment) Regulations 1996
396 (C. 7).....Local Government (Wales) Act 1994 (Commencement No. 7) Order 1996
397................Humberside (Staff Transfer) Order 1996
398................Cleveland (Staff Transfer) Order 1996
399................Gas Act 1995 (Transitional Provisions and Savings) (No. 2) Order 1996
400................Avon (Staff Transfer) Order 1996
401................University College London Hospitals National Health Service Trust (Establishment) Order 1996
408................North Lincolnshire and East Riding of Yorkshire District Councils (Staff Transfer) Order 1996
409................Local Government Reorganisation (Wales) (Swansea Bay Port Health Authority) (Amendment) Order 1996
410................National Health Service (Travelling Expenses and Remission of Charges) Amendment Regulations 1996
412 (S. 28) ...Campbeltown (Ferry Terminal) Harbour Revision Order 1996
413 (S. 29) ...Lyon Court and Office Fees (Variation) Order 1996
414 (S. 30) ...Local Government Superannuation (Scotland) Amendment Regulations 1996

420................Railways Act 1993 (Consequential Modifications) (No. 5) Order 1996
422................Electricity and Pipe-line Works (Assessment of Environmental Effects) (Amendment) Regulations 1996
423................East Glamorgan National Health Service Trust (Transfer of Trust Property) Order 1996
424................Llandough Hospital and Community National Health Service Trust (Transfer of Trust Property) Order 1996
425................Social Security (Industrial Injuries and Diseases) (Miscellaneous Amendments) Regulations 1996
428................Noise Insulation (Railways and Other Guided Transport Systems) Regulations 1996
429 (S. 31)...National Health Service (Travelling Expenses and Remission of Charges) (Scotland) Amendment Regulations 1996
430 (S. 32)...Council Tax (Administrative and Enforcement) (Scotland) Amendment Regulations 1996
433................National Health Service (Appointment of Consultants) (Wales) Continuation and Transitional Provisions Order 1996
434................Civil Legal Aid (Assessment of Resources) (Amendment) Regulations 1996
435................Legal Advice and Assistance (Amendment) Regulations 1996
436................Legal Aid in Criminal and Care Proceedings (General) (Amendment) Regulations 1996
437................Veterinary Surgeons and Veterinary Practitioners (Registration) (Amendment) Regulations Order of Council 1996
438................Sex Discrimination and Equal Pay (Miscellaneous Amendments) Regulations 1996
439................Gas (Calculation of Thermal Energy) Regulations 1996
440................Cardiff Petty Sessional Division (Consequences of Local Government Changes) Order 1996
441................Vale of Glamorgan Petty Sessional Division (Consequences of Local Government Changes) Order 1996
442................Welshpool Petty Sessional Division (Consequences of Local Government Changes) Order 1996
443................A57 Trunk Road (Rotherham/Sheffield Boundary to Swallownest Roundabout) (Detrunking) Order 1996
444................British Nationality (Fees) Regulations 1996
445................Kent (Coroners' Districts) (Amendment) Order 1996
446................Local Government Changes for England (Miscellaneous Provision) Order 1996
448................Food Protection (Emergency Prohibitions) (Oil and Chemical Pollution of Fish and Plants) Order 1996
449................Gas Act 1986 (Exemptions) (No. 1) Order 1996
450................Gas Meters (Information of Connection and Disconnection) Regulations 1996
455................Local Government Changes for England (Staff) (Amendment) Regulations 1996
456................Local Government (Compensation for Redundancy) (Amendment) Regulations 1996
458................Assured and Protected Tenancies (Lettings to Students) (Amendment) Regulations 1996
462................Income-related Benefits Schemes (Miscellaneous Amendments) Regulations 1996
463................Petty Sessional Divisions (West Glamorgan) Order 1996
464 (S. 33)...New Town (Cumbernauld) (Transfer of Property, Rights and Liabilities) Order 1996

465 (S. 34)...New Town (East Kilbride) (Transfer of Property, Rights and Liabilities) Order 1996
466 (S. 35)...New Town (Glenrothes) (Transfer of Property, Rights and Liabilities) Order 1996
467 (S. 36)...Town and Country Planning (General Development Procedure) (Scotland) Amendment Order 1996
468................Lotteries (Gaming Board Fees) Order 1996
469................Local Authorities (Members' Allowances) (Amendment) Regulations 1996
470................Gas Act (Consequential Modifications of Subordinate Legislation) (No. 2) Order 1996
471................Gas Act 1986 (Exemptions) (No. 2) Order 1996
472 (S. 37)...National Health Service (Dental Charges) (Scotland) Amendment Regulations 1996
473 (S. 38)...National Health Service (Optical Charges and Payments) (Scotland) Amendment Regulations 1996
474 (S. 39)...Educational Endowments (Dumfries and Galloway Region) Transfer Scheme Order 1996
475 (S. 40)...Educational Endowments (Central Region) Transfer Scheme Order 1996
476................Gas (Application for Licences and Extensions and Restrictions of Licences) Regulations 1996
477 (S. 41)...Educational Endowments (Tayside Region) Transfer Scheme Order 1996
478 (S. 42)...Educational Endowments (Grampian Region) Transfer Scheme Order 1996
481................Child Support (Maintenance Assessments and Special Cases) and Social Security (Claims and Payments) Amendment Regulations 1996
482................Medicines (Homeopathic Medicinal Products for Human Use) Amendment Regulations 1996
484................Social Security (Incapacity for Work) (General) Amendment Regulations 1996
485................Guaranteed Minimum Pensions Increase Order 1996
486................Social Security (Contributions) Amendment Regulations 1996
487 (C. 8).....Offshore Safety Act 1992 (Commencement No. 2) Order 1996
488................Authorities for the Ashworth, Broadmoor and Rampton Hospitals (Establishment and Constitution) Order 1996
489................Ashworth, Broadmoor and Rampton Hospital Authorities (Functions and Membership) Regulations 1996
490................Special Hospitals Service Authority (Abolition) Order 1996
491................Gas (Street Works) (Compensation of Small Businesses) Regulations 1996
492 (S. 43)...Local Government (Transfer of Children's Hearings Cases) (Scotland) Order 1996
493 (S. 44)...Town and Country Planning (Costs of Inquiries etc.) (Standard Daily Amount) (Scotland) Regulations 1996
494................Cardiff (St. Mellons Community) Order 1996
495................Health Authorities (Wales) (Transfer of Trust Property) Order 1996
496 (S. 45)...Roads (Transitional Powers) (Scotland) Amendment Order 1996
497 (S. 46)...Food (Preparation and Distribution of Meat) (Scotland) Revocation Regulations 1996
498................Financial Services Act 1986 (Gas Industry Exemption) Order 1996

499................Safety of Sports Grounds (Accommodation of Spectators) Order 1996
500................Road Traffic Act 1991 (Amendment of Schedule 3) (England and Wales) Order 1996
501................Local Government Reorganisation (Wales) (Staff) Order 1996
502................Personal Injuries (Civilians) Amendment Scheme 1996
503................Salford Community Health Care National Health Service Trust (Transfer of Trust Property) Order 1996
504................Council Tax and Non-Domestic Rating (Demand Notices) (England) Amendment Regulations 1996
505................Financial Assistance for Environmental Purposes Order 1996
506................Environmental Protection (Controls on Substances that Deplete the Ozone Layer) Regulations 1996
507................Leicestershire (City of Leicester and District of Rutland) (Structural Change) Order 1996
508................Environmental Licences (Suspension and Revocation) Regulations 1996
509 (C. 9).....Statute Law (Repeals) Act 1993 (Commencement) Order 1996
510................Mental Health Review Tribunals (Regions) Order 1996
511................Authorities for London Post-Graduate Teaching Hospitals (Abolition) Order 1996
512................Authorities for London Post-Graduate Teaching Hospitals (Revocation) Regulations 1996
513 (S. 47)...Act of Adjournal (Criminal Procedure Rules) 1996
514 (S. 48)...Court of Session etc. Fees Amendment Order 1996
515 (S. 49)...Qualifications of Chief Social Work Officers (Scotland) Regulations 1996
516 (S. 50)...High Court of Justiciary Fees Amendment Order 1996
517 (C. 10) (S. 51) Criminal Justice (Scotland) Act 1995 (Commencement No. 2, Transitional Provisions and Savings) Order 1996
519 (S. 52)...Lands Tribunal for Scotland (Amendment) (Fees) Rules 1996
522................West Wales Ambulance National Health Service Trust (Transfer of Trust Property) Order 1996
523................West Wales Ambulance National Health Service Trust (Transfer of Trust Property) (No. 2) Order 1996
524................Gwent Community Health National Health Service Trust (Transfer of Trust Property) Order 1996
525................Local Government Reorganisation (Wales) (Consequential Amendments) Order 1996
526................Cardiff Community Healthcare National Health Service Trust (Transfer of Trust Property) Order 1996
527................Velindre Hospital National Health Service Trust (Transfer of Trust Property) Order 1996
528................Town and Country Planning (General Permitted Development) (Amendment) Order 1996
529................Rural Development Grants (Agriculture) (Wales) Regulations 1996
530................University Hospital of Wales Healthcare National Health Service Trust (Transfer of Trust Property) Order 1996
531................Rhondda Health Care National Health Service Trust (Transfer of Trust Property) Order 1996
532................Local Government Reorganisation (Wales) (Property etc.) Order 1996
533................Local Government Reorganisation (Wales) (Rent Officers) Order 1996
534................National Park Authorities (Wales) (Amendment) Order 1996

535................Development Board for Rural Wales (Area) Order 1996
536................Motor Vehicles (Driving Licences) (Amendment) (No. 2) Regulations 1996
537................Education (Grant-maintained and Grant-maintained Special Schools) (Finance) (Wales) Regulations 1996
538................Regional Flood Defence Committee (Welsh Region) Order 1996
539................Royal Liverpool Children's Hospital and Community Services National Health Service Trust (Change of Name) Order 1996
540................Mental Health (Hospital, Guardianship and Consent to Treatment) (Amendment) Regulations 1996
542................Value Added Tax (Annual Accounting) Regulations 1996
545................Norfolk and Suffolk Broads (Extension of Byelaws) Order 1996
546................Insurance (Fees) Regulations 1996
547................Local Government Changes for England (Housing Benefit and Council Tax Benefit) Amendment Regulations 1996
548 (S. 53) ...Local Government Changes for Scotland (Housing Benefit and Council Tax Benefit) Order 1996
549................Local Government Reorganisation (Wales) (Housing Benefit and Council Tax Benefit) Order 1996
550................Gas Safety (Installation and Use) (Amendment) Regulations 1996
551................Gas Safety (Management) Regulations 1996
552 (C. 11)...National Health Service (Amendment) Act 1995 (Commencement No. 3) Order 1996
557................London Residuary Body (Winding Up) Order 1996
561................Non-domestic Rating Contributions (England) (Amendment) Regulations 1996
563................Local Government Changes for England (Finance) (Amendment) Regulations 1996
568................Local Authorities (Capital Finance and Approved Investments) (Amendment) Regulations 1996
569................Financial Assistance for Industry (Increase of Limit) Order 1996
570................Royal West Sussex National Health Service Trust (Transfer of Trust Property) Order 1996
571................Chichester Priority Care Services National Health Service Trust (Transfer of Trust Property) Order 1996
572 (S. 54) ...Marriage Fees (Scotland) Regulations 1996
573................Injuries in War (Shore Employments) Compensation (Amendment) Scheme 1996
574 (S. 55) ...Registration of Births, Deaths, Marriages and Divorces (Fees) (Scotland) Amendment Regulations 1996
575................Public Record Office (Fees) Regulations 1996
576................Petty Sessions Areas (Divisions and Names) (Amendment) Regulations 1996
577................Youth Courts (Constitution) (Amendment) Rules 1996
578 (S. 56) ...Local Authorities (Property Transfer) (Scotland) Amendment Order 1996
579 (S. 57) ...Scottish Examination Board (Amendment) Regulations 1996
580 (S. 58) ...Rating, Valuation and Council Tax (Miscellaneous Provisions) (Scotland) Order 1996
581................Local Authorities (Capital Finance) (Rate of Discount for 1996/97) Regulations 1996
582................National Health Service (Optical Charges and Payments) Amendment Regulations 1996

583................National Health Service (Charges for Drugs and Appliances) Amendment Regulations
584................Education (Inner London Education Authority) (Property Transfer) (Modification) Order 1996
585................Local Government (Publication of Information about Unused and Underused Land) (England) (Revocation) Regulations 1996
586................Contracting Out (Management Functions in relation to certain Community Homes) Order 1996
587................Home Energy Efficiency Grants (Amendment) Regulations 1996
588................Civil Courts (Amendment) (No. 2) Order 1996
589................A1 Trunk Road (Islington) (Bus Lanes) Red Route Experimental 1996
590................Accounts and Audit Regulations 1996
591................A1 Trunk Road (Haringey) (Bus Lanes) Red Route Experimental 1996
592................Housing Associations (Permissible Additional Purposes) (England and Wales) Order 1996
593................Environment Act 1995 (Consequential Amendments) Regulations 1996
594................Companies (Forms) (Amendment) Regulations 1996
595................Companies (Welsh Language Forms and Documents) Regulations 1996
596................Misuse of Drugs (Licence Fees) (Amendment) Regulations 1996
597................Social Security (Contributions) (Rerating and National Insurance Fund Payments) Order 1996
598................Workmen's Compensation (Supplementation) (Amendment) Scheme 1996
599................Social Security Benefits Up-rating Order 1996
600................Energy Information (Washing Machines) Regulations 1996
601................Energy Information (Tumble Driers) Regulations 1996
602................National Assistance (Assessment of Resources) (Amendment) Regulations 1996
604................Public Airport Companies (Capital Finance) Order 1996
606................Income Support (General) Amendment Regulations 1996
608................Superannuation (Admission to Schedule 1 of the Superannuation Act 1972) Order 1996
609................Building Societies (General Charge and Fees) Regulations 1996
610................Charter Trustees (Amendment) Regulations 1996
611................Local Government Changes for England (Amendment) Regulations 1996
612................Industrial and Provident Societies (Credit Unions) (Amendment of Fees) Regulations 1996
613................Industrial and Provident Societies (Amendment of Fees) Regulations 1996
614................Friendly Societies (General Charge and Fees) Regulations 1996
615................Education (Areas to which Pupils and Students Belong) Regulations 1996
616 (S. 59)...Intermediate Diets (Scotland) Order 1996
617 (S. 60)...Criminal Justice (Scotland) Act 1987 Fixed Penalty Order 1996
618................Local Government Reorganisation (Wales) (Committees for Sea Fisheries Districts) (Amendment) Order 1996

619................Local Government Reorganisation (Wales) (Finance) (Miscellaneous Amendments and Transitional Provisions) Order 1996
620................Central Rating Lists (Amendment) Regulations 1996
621................Local Authorities (Companies) (Amendment) Order 1996
622................Medical Devices (Consultation Requirements) (Fees) Amendment Regulations 1996
623................National Health Service Contracts (Dispute Resolution) Regulations 1996
624................Health Authorities (England) Establishment Order 1996
625 (C. 12)...Criminal Justice and Public Order Act 1994 (Commencement No. 9) Order 1996
626 (S. 61) ...Jurors (Scotland) Act 1825 (Provision of Information) Order 1996
627 (S. 62) ...Criminal Legal Aid (Scotland) Amendment Regulations 1996
628 (S. 63) ...Sheriff Court Fees Amendment Order 1996
629 (S. 64) ...Educational Endowments (Strathclyde Region) Transfer Scheme Order 1996
630 (S. 65) ...Educational Endowments (Lothian Region) Transfer Scheme Order 1996
631 (S. 66) ...Council Tax (Amendment of Housing (Scotland) Act 1987) (Scotland) Regulations 1996
632 (S. 67) ...Housing (Forms) (Scotland) Amendment Regulations 1996
633................Local Government Reorganisation (Wales) (Capital Finance) Order 1996
634................Waste Management Regulations 1996
635................Child Support Departure Direction (Anticipatory Applications) Regulations 1996
636................Council Tax (Discount Disregards) Amendment Order 1996
637................Council Tax (Additional Provisions for Discount Disregards) Amendment Order 1996
638................Employment Protection (National Health Service) Order 1996
639................Railway Industry (Employees' Transport Vouchers) (Taxation) Order 1996
640................Community Health Councils Regulations 1996
641................Legal Advice and Assistance (Amendment) (No. 2) Regulations 1996
642................Civil Legal Aid (Assessment of Resources) (Amendment) (No. 2) Regulations 1996
643................Legal Aid in Contempt Proceedings (Remuneration) (Amendment) Regulation 1996
644................Legal Aid in Criminal and Care Proceedings (Costs) (Amendment) Regulations 1996
645................Legal Aid in Civil Proceedings (Remuneration) (Amendment) Regulations 1996
646................Legal Aid in Criminal and Care Proceedings (General) (Amendment) (No. 2) Regulations 1996
647................Legal Advice and Assistance (Duty Solicitor) (Remuneration) (Amendment) (No. 2) Regulations 1996
648................Legal Advice and Assistance at Police Stations (Remuneration) (Amendment) Regulations 1996
649................Civil Legal Aid (General) (Amendment) Regulations 1996
650................Legal Aid in Family Proceedings (Remuneration) (Amendment) Regulations 1996
651................Certification Officer (Amendment of Fees) Regulations 1996
653................National Health Service Trusts (Consultation on Establishment and Dissolution) Regulations 1996

654................National Health Service (Functions of Health Authorities in London) Regulations 1996
655................Local Government Reorganisation (Amendment of Coroners Act 1988) Regulations 1996
656................Avon (Coroners) Order 1996
657................Cleveland (Coroners) Order 1996
658................Humberside (Coroners) Order 1996
659................York and North Yorkshire (Coroners) Order 1996
660................Local Government Reorganisation (Compensation for Loss of Remuneration) (Amendment) Regulations 1996
661................Coroners' Districts (Wales) Order 1996
662................Coroners' Districts (Designation of Relevant Councils) (Wales) Order 1996
663................Social Security (Contributions) Amendment (No. 2) Regulations 1996
664................Railways Act 1993 (Extinguishment of Relevant Loans) (Railtrack plc) Order 1996
665................Nuclear Generating Stations (Security) Regulations 1996
666................Regional Health Authorities (Transfer of Trust Property) Order 1996
667................Environmental Protection (Applications, Appeals and Registers) (Amendment) Regulations 1996
668................Statutory Maternity Pay (Compensation of Employers) Amendment Regulations 1996
669................National Health Service (Functions of Health Authorities) (Complaints) Regulations 1996
670................Social Security Benefits Up-rating Regulations 1996
671................Social Security (Industrial Injuries) (Dependency) (Permitted Earnings Limits) Order 1996
672................Social Security (Claims and Payments Etc.) Amendment Regulations 1996
673................Exchange Gains and Losses (Insurance Companies) (Amendment) Regulations 1996
674................Local Government Changes for England (Magistrates' Courts) Regulations 1996
675................Magistrates' Courts (Wales) (Consequences of Local Government Changes) Order 1996
676................Commission Areas (Gwent, Mid Glamorgan and South Glamorgan) Order 1996
677................Housing Benefit (Permitted Totals) Order 1996
678................Council Tax Benefit (Permitted Totals) Order 1996
679................Sugar Beet (Research and Education) Order 1996
680 (S. 68)...Scottish Land Court (Fees) Order 1996
681 (S. 69)...Accounts Commission (Scotland) Regulations 1996
682 (S. 70)...Local Government (Transitional Financial Provisions) (Scotland) Order 1996
683................Medicines (Products for Human Use—Fees) Amendment Regulations 1996
686................National Health Service (Existing Liabilities Scheme) Regulations 1996
688................Civil Aviation (Canadian Navigation Services) Regulations 1996
689................Civil Aviation (Navigation Services Charges) (Amendment) Regulations 1996
690................Measuring Instruments (EEC Requirements) (Fees) (Amendment) Regulations 1996
691................Local Government Changes for England (Finance—Social Services Grants) Regulations 1996

692................Children (Homes and Secure Accommodation) (Miscellaneous Amendments) Regulations 1996
693................Isles of Scilly (Carers) Order 1996
694................Plastic Materials and Articles in Contact with Food (Amendment) Regulations 1996
695................Countryside Stewardship Regulations 1996
696................Common Agricultural Policy (Wine) Regulations 1996
697................Diseases of Animals (Approved Disinfectants) (Amendment) Order 1996
698................National Health Service (Pharmaceutical Services) Amendment Regulations 1996
699................Police (Amendment) Regulations 1996
700................Social Security (Contributions) Amendment (No. 3) Regulations 1996
701................National Health Service (Appointment of Consultants) Regulations 1996
702................National Health Service (General Medical Services) Amendment Regulations 1996
703................National Health Service (Service Committees and Tribunal) Amendment Regulations 1996
704................National Health Service (General Dental Services) Amendment Regulations 1996
705................National Health Service (General Ophthalmic Services) Amendment Regulations 1996
706................National Health Service (Fund-holding Practices) Regulations 1996
707................Health Authorities (Membership and Procedure) Regulations 1996
708................National Health Service (Functions of Health Authorities and Administration Arrangements) Regulations 1996
709................Health Authorities Act 1995 (Transitional Provisions) Order 1996
710................Local Government Changes for England (Education) (Miscellaneous Provisions) Regulations 1996
711................Local Government Pension Scheme (Environment Agency) Regulations 1996
712................Council Tax (Deductions from Income Support) Regulations 1993 Amendment Order 1996
713................Cambridge Water Company (Constitution and Regulation) Order 1996
714................Trade Marks (International Registration) Order 1996
715................Trade Marks (International Registration) (Fees) Rules 1996
716................United Nations (International Tribunal) (Former Yugoslavia) Order 1996
717................Health Service Commissioners for England (Authorities for the Ashworth, Broadmoor and Rampton Hospitals) Order 1996
718................Air Force Act 1955 (Bailiwick of Guernsey) Order 1996
719................Air Force Act 1955 (Isle of Man) Order 1996
720................Air Force Act 1955 (Jersey) Order 1996
721 (N.I. 4)..Appropriation (Northern Ireland) Order 1996
722................Army Act 1955 (Bailiwick of Guernsey) Order 1996
723................Army Act 1955 (Isle of Man) Order 1996
724................Army Act 1955 (Jersey) Order 1996
725 (N.I. 5)..Business Tenancies (Northern Ireland) Order 1996
726................Naval Discipline Act 1957 (Bailiwick of Guernsey) Order 1996
727................Naval Discipline Act 1957 (Isle of Man) Order 1996
728................Naval Discipline Act 1957 (Jersey) Order 1996

729................Trade Marks Act 1994 (Isle of Man) Order 1996
730................Double Taxation Relief (Taxes on Estates of Deceased Persons and Inheritances and on Gifts) (Netherlands) Order 1996
731 (S. 83) ...Lord-Lieutenants (Scotland) Order 1996
732................Naval, Military and Air Forces etc. (Disablement and Death) Service Pensions Amendment Order 1996
733................Local Authorities (Armorial Bearings) (Wales) Order 1996
734................Education (Grants for Education Support and Training) (England) Regulations 1996
735................Richmond Adult and Community College (Incorporation) Order 1996
736................Richmond Adult and Community College (Government) Regulations 1996
737................Wiltshire Health Care National Health Service Trust (Transfer of Trust Property) Order 1996
738 (S. 71) ...Environmentally Sensitive Areas (Breadalbane) Designation (Amendment) Order 1996
739 (S. 72) ...Local Government (Transitional and Consequential Provisions and Revocations) (Scotland) Order 1996
740 (S. 73) ...National Health Service (Charges for Drugs and Appliances) (Scotland) Amendment Regulations 1996
741 (S. 74) ...Housing (Valuation Bands for Improvement and Repairs Grants) (Scotland) Order 1996
742 (S. 75) ...Mental Health (Patients in the Community) (Transfer from England and Wales to Scotland) Regulations 1996
743 (S. 76) ...Mental Health (Prescribed Forms) (Scotland) Regulations 1996
744 (S. 77) ...Water and Sewerage Authorities (Rate of Return) (Scotland) Order 1996
745 (S. 78) ...Common Police Services (Scotland) Order 1996
746 (S. 79) ...Council Tax (Reduction of Liability) (Scotland) Regulations 1996
747 (S. 80) ...Local Authorities (Discretionary Expenditure) (Scotland) Regulations 1996
748 (S. 81) ...National Health Service (Fund-Holding Practices) (Scotland) Amendment Regulations 1996
749 (S. 82) ...Forth and Tay Road Bridge Order Confirmation Acts (Modification) Order 1996
750................Land Registry Trading Fund (Additional Assets) Order 1996
751................Plant Health (Forestry) (Great Britain) (Amendment) Order 1996
752................Gas (Extent of Domestic Supply Licences) Order 1996
753 (S. 84) ...European Parliamentary Elections (Returning Officers) (Scotland) Order 1996
754 (S. 85) ...Act of Sederunt (Rules of the Court of Session Amendment No. 2) (Fees of Short-hand Writers) 1996
755 (S. 86) ...Local Government Finance (Scotland) Order 1996
756 (S. 87) ...Revenue Support Grant (Scotland) Order 1996
757................Education (Grants) (Purcell School) Regulations 1996
767 (S. 88) ...Act of Sederunt (Fees of Shorthand Writers in the Sheriff Court) (Amendment) 1996
769................Medicines (Medicated Animal Feeding Stuffs) (Amendment) Regulations 1996
770................Local Government Act 1988 (Defined Activities) (Exemptions) (England and Wales) Order 1996
771................Adventure Activities (Licensing) (Designation) Order 1996
772................Adventure Activities Licensing Regulations 1996

773................Hydrographic Office Trading Fund Order 1996
774................Meteorological Office Trading Fund Order 1996
775................Occupational Pension Schemes (Discharge of Protected Rights on Winding Up) Regulations 1996
776................Personal and Occupational Pension Schemes (Miscellaneous Amendments) Regulations 1996
777................Social Security Contributions, Statutory Maternity Pay and Statutory Sick Pay (Miscellaneous Amendments) Regulations 1996
778 (C. 13)...Pensions Act 1995 (Commencement No. 3) Order 1996
779................Inter-American Development Bank (Eighth General Increase) Order 1996
780 (S. 89) ...Police Grant (Scotland) Order 1996
781................Lloyd's Underwriters (Tax) (Amendment) Regulations 1996
782................Lloyd's Underwriters (Tax) (1992/93 to 1996/97) (Amendment) Regulations 1996
783................Double Taxation Relief (Taxes on Income) (General) (Amendment) Regulations 1996
784 (S. 90) ...Local Government (Direct Labour Organisations) (Accounts) (Scotland) Regulations 1996
785................Children Act 1989 (Amendment) (Children's Services Planning) Order 1996
787................Humberside (Coroners) (Amendment) Order 1996
797................Weighing Equipment (Filling and Discontinuous Totalising Automatic Weighing Machines) (Amendment) Regulations 1996
800................Pensions Increase (Review) Order 1996
801................National Savings Bank (Amendment) Regulations 1996
802................A21 Trunk Road (Tonbridge Bypass to Pembury Bypass Dualling) Order 1996
804................Income Tax (Employments) (Amendment) Regulations 1996
805................Personal Pension Schemes (Deferred Annuity Purchase) (Acceptance of Contributions) Regulations 1996
807................A21 Trunk Road (Tonbridge Bypass to Pembury Bypass Dualling Slip Roads) Order 1996
808................A21 Trunk Road (Tonbridge Bypass to Pembury Bypass Dualling) (Detrunking) Order 1996
811 (S. 91) ...Advice and Assistance (Scotland) Amendment Regulations 1996
812 (S. 92) ...Civil Legal Aid (Scotland) Amendment Regulations 1996
813 (S. 93) ...Housing Support Grant (Scotland) Order 1996
814 (S. 94) ...Housing Support Grant (Scotland) Variation Order 1996
815................A41 Trunk Road (Barnet) Red Route (Clearway) (No. 1) Traffic Order 1996
816................Family Proceedings (Amendment) Rules 1996
817................A41 Trunk Road (Barnet) Red Route (Clearway) (No. 2) Traffic Order 1996
818................A41 Trunk Road (Barnet) Red Route (Clearway) (No. 3) Traffic Order 1996
819................A1 Trunk Road (Barnet) Red Route (Clearway) Traffic Order 1996
820................A406 Trunk Road (Barnet) Red Route (Clearway) Traffic Order 1996
821................A406 Trunk Road (Barnet) Red Route Experimental Traffic Order 1996
822................A501 Trunk Road (Marylebone Road, Westminster) (Temporary Prohibition of Traffic) Order 1996

823................Local Government Act 1988 (Defined Activities) (Specified Period) (Redbridge London Borough Council) Regulations 1996
824................Northumbrian and North East Water (Amendment of Local Enactments Etc.) Order 1996
825................Pipelines Safety Regulations 1996
826................Diseases of Animals (Waste Food) (Amendment) Order 1996
827................Animal By-products (Amendment) Order 1996
828................Solent Oyster Fishery (Variation) (Clams) Order 1996
830................Income Tax (Charge to Tax) (Payments out of Surplus Funds) (Relevant Rate) Order 1996
840 (S. 95)...National Health Service (Pharmaceutical Services) (Scotland) Amendment Regulations 1996
841 (S. 96)...National Health Service (General Dental Services) (Scotland) Amendment Regulations 1996
842 (S. 97)...National Health Service (General Medical Services) (Scotland) Amendment Regulations 1996
843 (S. 98)...National Health Service (General Ophthalmic Services) (Scotland) Amendment Regulations 1996
844................Tax-exempt Special Savings Account (Amendment) Regulations 1996
845................Trustee Investments (Division of Trust Fund) Order 1996
846................Personal Equity Plan (Amendment) Regulations 1996
847................Sussex Sea Fisheries District (Variation) Order 1996
848................Deregulation (Corn Returns Act 1882) Order 1996
850................Offshore Installations (Safety Zones) (No. 2) Order 1996
851................Central Manchester Development Corporation (Area and Constitution) Order 1996
853................A2 Trunk Road (West of Rochester) Detrunking Order 1996
854................M2 Motorway (West of Rochester Section) Scheme 1996
856................Food Protection (Emergency Prohibitions) (Oil and Chemical Pollution of Salmon and Migrating Trout) Order 1996
857................Local Government Act 1988 (Personnel Services) (Exemption) (England and Wales) Order 1996
858................Contracting Out (Functions in relation to the provision of Guardians Ad Litem and Reporting Officers Panels) Order 1996
867................Police Pensions (Amendment) Regulations 1996
871................Royal Free Hampstead National Health Service Trust (Amendment) Order 1996
872................Lincoln Hospitals National Health Service Trust (Change of Name) Order 1996
873................Hartlepool and East Durham National Health Service Trust (Establishment) Order 1996
874................Worcestershire Community Healthcare National Health Service Trust (Establishment) Order 1996
875................South Durham National Health Service Trust (Establishment) Order 1996
876................South West Durham Mental Health National Health Service Trust (Dissolution) Order 1996
877................Louth and District Healthcare National Health Service Trust (Dissolution) Order 1996
878 (S. 99)...Secretary of State's Trunk Road Functions (Contracting Out) (Scotland) Order 1996
879................Hartlepool and Peterlee Hospitals National Health Service Trust (Dissolution) Order 1996
880................South Durham Health Care National Health Service Trust (Dissolution) Order 1996

881................University College London National Health Service Trust (Dissolution) Order 1996
882................Birmingham Heartlands Hospital National Health Service Trust Dissolution Order 1996
883................Birmingham Heartlands and Solihull (Teaching) National Health Service Trust (Establishment) Order 1996
884................South Worcestershire Community National Health Service Trust Dissolution Order 1996
885................North East Worcestershire Community Health National Health Service Trust (Dissolution) Order 1996
886................Royal National Throat, Nose and Ear Hospital National Health Service Trust Dissolution Order 1996
887................Hartlepool Community Care National Health Service Trust (Dissolution) Order 1996
888................Protection of Water Against Agricultural Nitrate Pollution (England and Wales) Regulations 1996
889................Education (Grant-maintained and Grant-maintained Special Schools) (Finance) Regulations 1996
890................Marking of Plastic Explosives for Detection Regulations 1996
891................Prevention of Terrorism (Temporary Provisions) Act 1989 (Continuance) Order 1996
892................Prevention of Terrorism (Exclusion Orders) Regulations 1996
897................Returning Officers (Parliamentary Constituencies) (Wales) Order 1996
898................Returning Officers (Parliamentary Constituencies) (England) (Amendment) Order 1996
903................A41 Trunk Road (Gloucester Place, Westminster) (Temporary Prohibition of Traffic) Order 1996
904................Broadcasting (Prescribed Countries) Order 1996
905................Local Government Reorganisation (Wales) (Staff) (No. 2) Order 1996
906................Local Government Reorganisation (Wales) (Property Etc.) (Amendment) Order 1996
907................East Surrey and Sutton District Water (Amendment of Local Enactments Etc.) Order 1996
908................Farm Waste Grant (Nitrate Vulnerable Zones) (England and Wales) Scheme 1996
909................Income Support (General) Amendment (No. 2) Regulations 1996
910................Local Government Reorganisation (Wales) (Capital Finance and Miscellaneous Provisions) Order 1996
911................Non-Domestic Rating (Chargeable Amounts) (Amendment) Regulations 1996
912................Electricity Supply Industry and Water Undertakers (Rateable Values) Amendment Order 1996
913................Offshore Installations and Wells (Design and Construction, Etc.) Regulations 1996
916 (S. 100) .Waste Management Licensing (Scotland) Regulations 1996
917 (S. 101) .Local Government Act 1988 (Defined Activities) (Specified Periods) (Scotland) Regulations 1996
918 (C. 14) (S. 102) Local Government Act 1992 (Commencement No. 10) Order 1996
920................Environmentally Sensitive Areas (Somerset Levels and Moors) Designation (Amendment) Order 1996
921................Environmentally Sensitive Areas (The Broads) Designation (Amendment) Order 1996
922................Environmentally Sensitive Areas (West Penwith) Designation (Amendment) Order 1996

923................Environmentally Sensitive Areas (Pennine Dales) Designation (Amendment) Order 1996
924................Environmentally Sensitive Areas (South Downs) Designation (Amendment) Order 1996
925................A205 Trunk Road (Mortlake Road, Richmond upon Thames) (Vehicle Height Restriction) Order 1996
926................A16 Trunk Road (Fotherby Bypass) Order 1996
929................A41 Trunk Road (Park Road, Westminster) (Temporary Prohibition of Traffic) Order 1996
930................Combined Probation Areas (Suffolk) Order 1996
931................Combined Probation Areas (Nottinghamshire) Order 1996
932................Combined Probation Areas (Hampshire) Order 1996
933................Combined Probation Areas (Derbyshire) Order 1996
937................Elsecar Steam Railway Order 1996
938 (S. 103) .National Health Service (Service Committees and Tribunal) (Scotland) Amendment Regulations 1996
940................Social Security Benefits (Maintenance Payments and Consequential Amendments) Regulations 1996
941................Passenger and Goods Vehicles (Recording Equipment) Regulations 1996
942................Insurance Companies (Amendment) Regulations 1996
943................Insurance Companies (Accounts and Statements) Regulations 1996
944................Insurance Companies (Amendment No. 2) Regulations 1996
945 (C. 17)...Insurance Companies (Reserves) Act 1995 Commencement Order 1996
946................Insurance Companies (Reserves) Regulations 1996
951................Deregulation (Length of the School Day) Order 1996
956................Combined Probation Areas (West Glamorgan) Order 1996
957................Combined Probation Areas (West Sussex) Order 1996
958................Motor Vehicles (Type Approval and Approval Marks) (Fees) Regulations 1996
959................Rent Officers (Additional Functions) (Amendment) Order 1996
960................London Cab Order 1996
961................Beef (Emergency Control) Order 1996
962................Bovine Spongiform Encephalopathy (Amendment) Order 1996
963................Specified Bovine Material Order 1996
965................Housing Benefit (General) Amendment Regulations 1996
966................Central Manchester Development Corporation (Dissolution) Order 1996
967................Genetically Modified Organisms (Contained Use) (Amendment) Regulations 1996
968................National Health Service Litigation Authority (Amendment) Regulations 1996
969................Regional Health Authorities (Transfer of Trust Property) Amendment Order 1996
970 (C. 15)...Health Service Commissioners (Amendment) Act 1996 (Commencement) Order 1996
971................Health Authorities Act 1995 (Amendment of Transitional Provisions and Modification of References) Order 1996
972................Special Waste Regulations 1996
973 (S. 104) .Environment Act 1995 (Consequential and Transitional Provisions) (Scotland) Regulations 1996
974 (S. 105) .Local Government (Translation Amendments) (Scotland) Order 1996

975 (S. 106) .Rent Officers (Additional Functions) (Scotland) Amendment Order 1996
976................Chester-Holyhead Trunk Road (A5) (Llanfair Pwllgwyngyll to Bryngwran) Order 1996
977................Deregulation (Special Hours Certificates) Order 1996
978................Licensing (Special Hours Certificates) (Amendment) Rules 1996
979................Environmental Protection (Applications, Appeals and Registers) (Amendment No. 2) Regulations 1996
980................Income Tax (Employments) (Amendment No. 2) Regulations 1996
981................Income Tax (Sub-contractors in the Construction Industry) (Amendment) Regulations 1996
982................Walton Centre for Neurology and Neurosurgery National Health Service Trust (Establishment) Amendment Order 1996
983................South Manchester University Hospitals National Health Service Trust (Establishment) Amendment Order 1996
984................North Durham Acute Hospitals National Health Service Trust (Establishment) Amendment Order 1996
985................West Middlesex University Hospital National Health Service Trust (Establishment) Amendment Order 1996
986................Gloucestershire Royal National Health Service Trust (Establishment) Amendment Order 1996
987................Swindon and Marlborough National Health Service Trust (Establishment) Amendment Order 1996
988................Hull and Holderness Community Health National Health Service Trust (Establishment) Amendment Order 1996
989................Bishop Auckland Hospitals National Health Service Trust (Establishment) Amendment Order 1996
990................Hereford Hospitals National Health Service Trust (Establishment) Amendment Order 1996
991................Rochdale Healthcare National Health Service Trust (Establishment) Amendment Order 1996
992................Wellhouse National Health Service Trust (Establishment) Amendment Order 1996
993................Essex Rivers Healthcare National Health Service Trust (Establishment) Amendment Order 1996
994................Dartford and Gravesham National Health Service Trust (Establishment) Amendment Order 1996
995 (C. 16)...Private International Law (Miscellaneous Provisions) Act 1995 (Commencement) Order 1996
996................St James's and Seacroft University Hospitals National Health Service Trust (Establishment) Amendment Order 1996
997................Thameside Community Health Care National Health Service Trust (Establishment) Amendment Order 1996
998................South Buckinghamshire National Health Service Trust (Establishment) Amendment Order 1996
999................South Devon Health Care National Health Service Trust (Establishment) Amendment Order 1996
1000................Bexley Community Health National Health Service Trust (Establishment) Amendment Order 1996
1001................Norfolk and Norwich Health Care National Health Service Trust (Establishment) Amendment Order 1996
1002................East Yorkshire Community Healthcare National Health Service Trust (Establishment) Amendment Order 1996
1003................Education (School Teachers' Pay and Conditions) Order 1996

1004 (S. 107) .Registers of Scotland Executive Agency Trading Fund Order 1996
1005 (S. 108) .Sheriff Court Districts (Alteration of Boundaries) Order 1996
1006 (S. 109) .Sheriffdoms (Alteration of Boundaries) Order 1996
1007................Regional Flood Defence Committee (Welsh Region) (Amendment) Order 1996
1008................Local Government Reorganisation (Wales) (Consequential Amendments No. 2) Order 1996
1009 (S. 110) .Criminal Legal Aid (Scotland) (Prescribed Proceedings) Amendment Regulations 1996
1010 (S. 111) .Advice and Assistance (Financial Conditions) (Scotland) Regulations 1996
1011 (S. 112) .Advice and Assistance (Assistance by Way of Representation) (Scotland) Amendment Regulations 1996
1012 (S. 113) .Civil Legal Aid (Financial Conditions) (Scotland) Regulations 1996
1014................Lloyd's Underwriters (Gilt-edged Securities) (Periodic Accounting for Tax on Interest) (Amendment) Regulations 1996
1015................Gilt-edged Securities (Periodic Accounting for Tax on Interest) (Amendment) Regulations 1996
1021................Lands Tribunal (Fees) Rules 1996
1022................Lands Tribunal Rules 1996
1023................Employment Protection (Continuity of Employment of National Health Service Employees) (Modification) Order 1996
1024................Magistrates' Courts Committees (Bolton, Bury, Rochdale, Salford and Wigan) Amalgamation Order 1996
1027................A501 Trunk Road (Marylebone Road, Westminster) (Temporary Prohibition of Traffic) Order 1996
1029................Superannuation (Admission to Schedule 1 of the Superannuation Act 1972) (No. 2) Order 1996
1030................Environment Act 1995 (Isles of Scilly) Order 1996
1031................Capital Gains Tax (Gilt-edged Securities) Order 1996
1034................North Eastern Sea Fisheries District (Constitution of Committee and Expenses) (Variation) Order 1996
1035................Fishing Boats (Specified Countries) Designation Order 1996
1036................Third Country Fishing (Enforcement) Order 1996
1043................Beef (Emergency Control) (Amendment) Order 1996
1046................A23 Trunk Road (Purley Cross Junction Improvement) Trunking Order 1996
1047................Social Security (Contributions) Amendment (No. 4) Regulations 1996
1054................Social Security (Reduced Rates of Class 1 Contributions) (Salary Related Contracted-out Schemes) Order 1996
1055................Social Security (Reduced Rates of Class 1 Contributions and Rebates) (Money Purchase Contracted-out Schemes) Order 1996
1056................Social Security (Minimum Contributions to Appropriate Personal Pension Schemes) Order 1996
1063................Licensing (Fees) (Amendment) Order 1996
1064................Local Government Act 1988 (Defined Activities) (Exemption) (Stockport Borough Council) Order 1996
1065 (S. 114) .New Town (Glenrothes) Dissolution Order 1996
1066 (S. 115) .New Town (East Kilbride) Dissolution Order 1996
1076 (S. 116) .Statutory Nuisance (Appeals) (Scotland) Regulations 1996
1077................A41 Trunk Road (Gloucester Place/Ivor Place, Westminster) (Temporary Prohibition of Traffic) Order 1996

1078................A501 Trunk Road (Grays Inn Road, Camden) (Temporary Prohibition of Traffic) Order 1996
1080................Buying Agency Trading Fund (Amendment) Order 1996
1088................A406 Trunk Road (Ealing and Hounslow) Red Route Experimental Traffic Order 1996
1089................A406 Trunk Road (North Circular Road, Ealing) Red Route (Prescribed Routes and Turns No. 1) Experimental Traffic Order 1996
1090................A406 Trunk Road (North Circular Road, Hounslow) Red Route (Prescribed Route No. 1) Experimental Traffic Order 1996
1091................Beef (Emergency Control) (Amendment No. 2) Order 1996
1092................Chemicals (Hazard Information and Packaging for Supply) (Amendment) Regulations 1996
1093 (S. 117).North of Scotland Milk Marketing Board Dissolution Order 1996
1094 (S. 118).Aberdeen and District Milk Marketing Board Dissolution Order 1996
1097................Bath–Lincoln Trunk Road A46 (Upper Swainswick to A420 Cold Ashton Roundabout) Orders 1987 Revocation Order 1996
1100................A629 Trunk Road (Skipton to Kildwick Improvement and Slip Roads) Order 1996
1101................A629 Trunk Road (Ings Lane to Cononley Lane) (Detrunking) Order 1996
1104................Prohibition of Keeping of Live Fish (Crayfish) Order 1996
1105................Companies (Principal Business Activities) (Amendment) Regulations 1996
1106................Genetically Modified Organisms (Risk Assessment) (Records and Exemptions) Regulations 1996
1107 (S. 119).Prohibition of Keeping of Live Fish (Crayfish) (Scotland) Order 1996
1108................Smoke Control Areas (Exempted Fireplaces) Order 1996
1109................Gaming Clubs (Hours and Charges) (Amendment) Regulations 1996
1110................Road Traffic (Special Parking Area) (Royal Borough of Kingston upon Thames) (Amendment) Order 1996
1111................Animals and Animal Products (Import and Export) (Amendment) Regulations 1996
1112................Road Traffic (Special Parking Area) (London Borough of Newham) (Amendment) Order 1996
1113................A4 Trunk Road (Great West Road, Hounslow) (Prohibition of Use of Gap in Central Reserve) Order 1996
1124................Dual-Use and Related Goods (Export Control) (Amendment) Regulations 1996
1125................Fertilisers (Mammalian Meat and Bone Meal) Regulations 1996
1126 (C.18)....Jobseekers Act 1995 (Commencement No. 2) Order 1996
1132................Passenger Car Fuel Consumption (Amendment) Order 1996
1133................Social Security Revaluation of Earnings Factors Order 1996
1134................A406 Trunk Road (North Circular Road, Ealing) Red Route (Prescribed Turns No. 2) Experimental Traffic Order 1996
1135................A501 Trunk Road (Swinton Street, Camden) (Temporary Prohibition of Traffic) Order 1996
1136................A501 Trunk Road (Camden and Islington) Red Route Experimental Traffic Order 1996
1137................A501 Trunk Road (Camden, Islington and Westminster) Red Route Experimental Traffic Order 1996

1138................Hong Kong (Overseas Public Servants) (Retirement and Compensation) Order 1996
1139................Hong Kong (Overseas Public Servants) (Continuing Service: Compensation) Order 1996
1140................Prevention of Terrorism (Temporary Provisions) Act 1984 (Jersey) (Revocation) Order 1996
1141 (N.I. 6)..Juries (Northern Ireland) Order 1996
1142................Maximum Number of Judges Order 1996
1143................Merchant Shipping (Liability and Compensation for Oil Pollution Damage) (Transitional Provisions) Order 1996
1144 (S. 120).Gaming Clubs (Hours and Charges) (Scotland) Amendment Regulations 1996
1145................Smoke Control Areas (Authorised Fuels) (Amendment) Regulations 1996
1146................Education (Individual Pupils' Achievements) (Information) (Amendment) Regulations 1996
1148................Fresh Meat (Hygiene and Inspection) (Amendment) Regulations 1996
1151................Insurance Brokers Registration Council (Conduct of Investment Business) Rules Approval Order 1996
1157................A501 Trunk Road (Marylebone Road/Nottingham Place, Westminster) (Temporary Prohibition of Traffic) Order 1996
1163................A4 Trunk Road (Hillingdon) Red Route (Clearway) Traffic Order 1996
1165................Plant Health (Great Britain) (Amendment No. 2) Order 1996
1166................Beef (Emergency Control) (Amendment No. 3) Order 1996
1170................A4 Trunk Road (Hounslow) Red Route (Clearway) Traffic Order 1996
1171................Road Traffic (Permitted Parking Area and Special Parking Area) (County of Hampshire, City of Winchester) Order 1996
1172................Occupational Pension Schemes (Contracting-out) Regulations 1996
1173 (C. 19)...Armed Forces Act 1991 (Commencement) (No. 2) Order 1996
1174................Armed Forces (Protection of Children of Service Families) Regulations 1996
1176................London Cab (No. 2) Order 1996
1177 (L. 2).....Register of County Court Judgments (Amendment) Regulations 1996
1178................County Council of Northumberland (Duplicate North Seaton Bridge) Scheme 1995 Confirmation Instrument 1996
1179................European Investment Bank (Designated International Organisation) Order 1996
1180................Insurance Companies (Gilt-edged Securities) (Periodic Accounting for Tax on Interest) (Amendment) Regulations 1996
1181................Gilt-edged Securities (Periodic Accounting for Tax on Interest) (Amendment No. 2) Regulations 1996
1182................Lloyd's Underwriters (Gilt-edged Securities) (Periodic Accounting for Tax on Interest) (Amendment No. 2) Regulations 1996
1183................Aberystwyth Harbour Revision Order 1995
1184................Income Tax (Interest Relief) (Amendment) Regulations 1996
1185................Vocational Training (Tax Relief) (Amendment) Regulations 1996
1186................North Hull Housing Action Trust (Transfer of Property) Order 1996

1188................Deregulation (Friendly Societies Act 1992) Order 1996
1189................Deregulation (Credit Unions) Order 1996
1190................A303 Trunk Road (Sparkford to Ilchester Improvement and Slip Roads) (Detrunking) Order 1996
1191................A303 Trunk Road (Sparkford to Ilchester Improvement and Slip Roads) Order 1996
1192................Specified Bovine Material (No. 2) Order 1996
1193................Bovine Animals (Enforcement of Community Purchase Scheme) Regulations 1996
1194................Offshore Installations (Safety Zones) (No. 3) Order 1996
1196................Value Added Tax (Payments on Account) (Amendment) Order 1996
1197................Financial Services Act 1986 (Gas Industry Exemption) (Amendment) Order 1996
1198................Value Added Tax (Amendment No. 2) Regulations 1996
1199 (S. 121).Children's Hearings (Scotland) Amendment Rules 1996
1203................Public Telecommunication System Designation (Torch Communications Limited) Order 1996
1210 (C. 20)...Merchant Shipping Act 1995 (Appointed Day No. 1) Order 1996
1211 (S. 122).Deregulation (Salmon Fisheries (Scotland) Act 1868) Order 1996
1212................Food Protection (Emergency Prohibitions) (Oil and Chemical Pollution of Salmon and Migratory Trout) (Revocation) Order 1996
1213................Food Protection (Emergency Prohibitions) (Oil and Chemical Pollution of Fish and Plants) (Partial Revocation) Order 1996
1214................Local Government Reorganisation (Wales) (Staff) (No. 3) Order 1996
1215................Local Authorities (Members' Interests) (Amendment) Regulations 1996
1216................Occupational Pension Schemes (Member-nominated Trustees and Directors) Regulations 1996
1217................Housing Benefit and Council Tax Benefit (Subsidy) Order 1996
1218................General Medical Council Preliminary Proceedings Committee and Professional Conduct Committee (Procedure) (Amendment) Rules Order of Council 1996
1219................General Medical Council Health Committee (Procedure) (Amendment) Rules Order of Council 1996
1220................Elections (Northern Ireland) Order 1996
1222................A501 Trunk Road (Euston Road/Gower Street, Camden) (Temporary Prohibition of Traffic) Order 1996
1223................A501 Trunk Road (Marylebone Road/Glentworth Street, Westminster) (Temporary Prohibition of Traffic) Order 1996
1224................National Park Authorities (Wales) (Amendment No. 2) Order 1996
1225................Education (Coleg Normal Bangor Higher Education Corporation) (Dissolution) Order 1996
1226................Income Tax (Unapproved Manufactured Payments) Regulations 1996
1227................Income Tax (Manufactured Interest) (Amendment) Regulations 1996
1228................Income Tax (Stock Lending) (Amendment) Regulations 1996
1229................Income Tax (Manufactured Overseas Dividends) (Amendment) Regulations 1996

1230................A35 Trunk Road (Chideock Morecombelake Bypass) Order 1996
1240................Local Government Reorganisation (Compensation for Redundancy of Loss of Remuneration) (Education) Regulations 1996
1241 (S. 123).Local Government (Superannuation and Compensation for Premature Retirement) (Scotland) Amendment Regulations 1996
1242................Fishing Vessels (Decommissioning) Scheme 1996
1243................National Park Authorities (England) Order 1996
1244................Local Government Act 1988 (Defined Activities) (Exemption) (London Borough of Greenwich) Order 1996
1245................Social Security (Additional Pension) (Contributions Paid in Error) Regulations 1996
1249 (C. 21)...Finance Act 1996, section 26, (Appointed Day) Order 1996
1250................Value Added Tax (Amendment No. 3) Regulations 1996
1251................Hydrocarbon Oil (Designated Markers) Regulations 1996
1252................Income Support (Pilot Scheme) Regulations 1996
1255................Value Added Tax (Fiscal Warehousing) (Treatment of Transactions) Order 1996
1256................Value Added Tax (Cultural Services) Order 1996
1257................Civil Legal Aid (General) (Amendment) (No. 2) Regulations 1996
1258................Legal Aid in Criminal and Care Proceedings (General) (Amendment) (No. 3) Regulations 1996
1259................Motor Vehicles (Driving Licences) (Amendment) (No. 3) Regulations 1996
1260................Feeding Stuffs (Amendment) Regulations 1996
1261................Medicines (Animal Feeding Stuffs) (Enforcement) (Amendment) Regulations 1996
1266 (S. 124).Town and Country Planning (General Permitted Development) (Scotland) Amendment Order 1996
1267................Churnet Valley Light Railway Order 1996
1268................Charities (Trustees Investments Act 1961) Order 1996
1269................Housing (Change of Landlord) (Payment of Disposal Cost by Instalments) (Amendment No. 2) Regulations 1996
1270................Occupational Pension Schemes (Internal Dispute Resolution Procedures) Regulations 1996
1271................Personal and Occupational Pension Schemes (Pension Ombudsman) Amendment Regulations 1996
1276 (C. 22) (S. 125) Housing and Planning Act 1986 (Commencement No. 19) (Scotland) Order 1996
1279................Waste Management Licensing (Amendment) Regulations 1996
1288................Redundant Mineworkers (Payments Scheme) (Amendment and Consolidation) Order 1996
1290................European Communities (Definition of Treaties) (Partnership and Co-operation Agreement between the European Communities and their Member States and the Republic of Belarus) Order 1996
1291................European Communities (Definition of Treaties) (Partnership and Co-operation Agreement between the European Communities and their Member States and the Republic of Kazakhstan) Order 1996
1292................European Communities (Definition of Treaties) (Partnership and Co-operation Agreement between the European Communities and their Member States and Kyrgyz Republic) Order 1996

1293................European Communities (Definition of Treaties) (Partnership and Co-operation Agreement between the European Communities and their Member States and the Republic of Moldova) Order 1996
1294................Hong Kong (Overseas Public Servants) (Pension Supplements) Order 1996
1295................International Oil Pollution Compensation Fund 1992 (Immunities and Privileges) Order 1996
1296................United Nations (International Tribunal) (Rwanda) Order 1996
1297 (N.I. 7)..Commissioner for Complaints (Northern Ireland) Order 1996
1298 (N.I. 8)..Ombudsman (Northern Ireland) Order 1996
1299 (N.I. 9)..Proceeds of Crime (Northern Ireland) Order 1996
1300................Misuse of Drugs Act 1971 (Modification) Order 1996
1301................Air Navigation (Amendment) Order 1996
1306................Lotteries (Amendment) Regulations 1996
1307................Jobseeker's Allowance (Pilot Scheme) Regulations 1996
1308................Insolvent Partnerships (Amendment) Order 1996
1309................Fossil Fuel Levy (Amendment) Regulations 1996
1311................Personal Pension Schemes (Tables of Rates of Annuities) Regulations 1996
1312................Income Tax (Employments) (Amendment No. 3) Regulations 1996
1313................National Health Service (Appointment of Consultants) (Wales) Regulations 1996
1314................Housing Benefit and Council Tax Benefit (Subsidy) Amendment Regulations 1996
1316................Severn Bridges Regulations 1996
1319................Food Protection (Emergency Prohibitions) (Oil and Chemical Pollution of Fish and Plants) (Partial Revocation No. 2) Order 1996
1320 (N.I. 10) Road Traffic Offenders (Northern Ireland) Order 1996
1321................Taxes (Interest Rate) (Amendment No. 2) Regulations 1996
1322................Financial Services Act 1986 (Uncertificated Securities) (Extension of Scope of Act) Order 1996
1323 (C. 23)...Capital Allowances Act 1990, section 33A (Appointed Day) Order 1996
1325 (C. 24)...Education (Schools) Act 1992 (Commencement No. 4) Order 1996
1327................Electricity (Restrictive Trade Practices Act 1976) (Exemptions) Order 1996
1331................Housing Renovation etc. Grants (Reduction of Grant) (Amendment) Regulations 1996
1332................Housing Renovation etc. Grants (Prescribed Forms and Particulars) (Amendment) Regulations 1996
1333................Disability Discrimination (Sub-leases and Sub-tenancies) Regulations 1996
1334................Education (Grant-maintained and Grant-maintained Special Schools) (Finance) (Wales) (Amendment) Regulations 1996
1335................Statutory Maternity Pay (General) Amendment Regulations 1996
1336 (C. 25)...Disability Discrimination Act 1995 (Commencement No. 2) Order 1996
1338................Public Lending Right Scheme 1982 (Commencement of Variations) Order 1996
1339................Deregulation (Long Pull) Order 1996

1340................A501 Trunk Road (Marylebone Road/Park Crescent Mews West, Westminster) (Temporary Prohibition of Traffic) Order 1996
1341................Export of Goods (Control) (Amendment) Order 1996
1342................Fertilisers (Sampling and Analysis) Regulations 1996
1343................A501 Trunk Road (Camden and Islington) Red Route (Bus Lanes) Experimental Traffic Order 1996
1344................A501 Trunk Road (Camden) Red Route (Bus Lane) (No. 1) Experimental Traffic Order 1996
1345................Social Security and Child Support (Jobseeker's Allowance) (Consequential Amendments) Regulations 1996
1346................National Health Service (Travelling Expenses and Remission of Charges) Amendment (No. 2) Regulations 1996
1347................Exchange Gains and Losses (Alternative Method of Calculation of Gain or Loss) (Amendment) Regulations 1996
1348................Exchange Gains and Losses (Deferral of Gains and Losses) (Amendment) Regulations 1996
1349................Exchange Gains and Losses (Transitional Provisions) (Amendment) Regulations 1996
1350................Radioactive Material (Road Transport) (Great Britain) Regulations 1996
1351................Bovine Spongiform Encephalopathy Compensation (Amendment) Order 1996
1352................Brucellosis and Tuberculosis (England and Wales) Compensation (Amendment) Order 1996
1353................Recreational Craft Regulations 1996
1354................Gas Act (Exemptions) (No. 3) Order 1996
1355................Personal Equity Plan (Amendment No. 2) Regulations 1996
1356................Railways (Closure Provisions) (Exemptions) Order 1996
1358 (S. 126).Brucellosis and Tuberculosis Compensation (Scotland) Amendment Order 1996
1359................Deregulation (Gaming Machines and Betting Office Facilities) Order 1996
1360 (S. 127).Compensation for Redundancy or Premature Retirement (Scottish Environment Protection Agency and River Purification Boards Transitional Arrangements) (Scotland) Regulations 1996
1363................Income Support (General) (Standard Interest Rate Amendment) Regulations 1996
1366................Local Government Reorganisation (Wales) (Capital Finance) (Amendment) Order 1996
1370 (S. 128).Erskine Bridge Tolls Extension Order 1996
1371................Council Tax Limitation (England) (Maximum Amounts) Order 1996
1373................Notification of Existing Substances (Enforcement) (Amendment) Regulations 1996
1374................Prohibition of Keeping of Live Fish (Crayfish) Amendment Order 1996
1378................Housing Renovation etc. Grants (Prescribed Forms and Particulars) (Welsh Forms and Particulars) (Amendment) Regulations 1996
1382 (S. 129).Local Statutory Provisions (Exemption of St. Andrews Links Trust) (Scotland) Order 1996
1384................Public Telecommunication System Designation (SWEB Telecomms Ltd) Order 1996
1388................Rules of Procedure (Army) (Amendment) Rules 1996
1389................Rules of Procedure (Air Force) (Amendment) Rules 1996

1390................Civil Aviation (Air Travel Organiser's Licensing) (Amendment) Regulations 1996
1391................Local Government Act 1988 (Defined Activities) (Exemption) (Worthing Borough Council) Order 1996
1392................Aerodromes (Designation) (Facilities for Consultation) Order 1996
1393................Rules of the Air Regulations 1996
1401................A61 Trunk Road (B6131 Bar Lane, Mapplewell to Barnsley/ Wakefield Metropolitan Boundary) (Detrunking) Order 1996
1405................Pharmaceutical Qualifications (Recognition) Regulations 1996
1406................Pleasure Craft (Arrival and Report) Regulations 1996
1408................Northern Ireland Elections (Returning Officer's Charges) Order 1996
1410................National Disability Council (No. 2) Regulations 1996
1412 (C. 26)...Pensions Act 1995 (Commencement No. 4) Order 1996
1418................Family Credit (General) (Amendment) Regulations 1996
1419................Cromarty Firth Port Authority Harbour Revision Order 1996
1420................Armed Forces (Compensation Limits) Order 1996
1422................Amusement Machine Licence Duty (Small-prize Machines) Order 1996
1423................Amusement Machine Licence Duty (Special Licences) Regulations 1996
1427................Deposits in the Sea (Public Registers of Information) Regulations 1996
1428................Local Government Pension Scheme (Amendment) Regulations 1996
1429................A66 Trunk Road (Stainburn and Great Clifton Bypass) Order 1996
1430................A66 Trunk Road (Stainburn and Great Clifton Bypass) (Detrunking) Order 1996
1431 (S. 130) .Financial Assistance for Environmental Purposes (No. 2) Order 1996
1432................Nottingham Healthcare National Health Service Trust (Transfer of Trust Property) Order 1996
1433................Grantham and District Hospital National Health Service Trust (Transfer of Trust Property) Order 1996
1434................Welfare Food Regulations 1996
1435................Pension Schemes (Appropriate Schemes and Disclosure of Information) (Miscellaneous Amendments) Regulations 1996
1436................Social Security (Disability Living Allowance and Claims and Payments) Amendment Regulations 1996
1437................Dolgellau to South of Birkenhead Trunk Road (A494) (Drws y Nant Improvement) Order 1996
1443................Social Fund Maternity and Funeral Expenses (General) Amendment Regulations 1996
1444................Companies (Fees) (Amendment) Regulations 1996
1445................Consumer Credit (Exempt Agreements) (Amendment) Order 1996
1446................Cosmetic Products (Safety) (Amendments) Regulations 1996
1447................Defence Evaluation and Research Agency Trading Fund (Amendment) Order 1996
1448................National Enterprise Board (Dissolution) Order 1996
1449................Local Government Act 1988 (Defined Activities) (Exemption) (Bromley London Borough Council) Order 1996
1451................Oil and Fibre Plant Seeds (Amendment) Regulations 1996
1452................Vegetable Seeds (Amendment) Regulations 1996

1453................Fodder Plant Seeds (Amendment) Regulations 1996
1454................Home-grown Cereals Authority (Rate of Levy) Order 1996
1455................Disability Discrimination (Meaning of Disability) Regulations 1996
1458................Disability Discrimination (Employment) Regulations 1996
1459................A10 Trunk Road (Enfield and Haringey) Red Route (Bus Lanes) (No. 1) Traffic Order 1996
1460................Social Security (Claims and Payments) (Jobseeker's Allowance Consequential Amendments) Regulations 1996
1461................Protected Rights (Transfer Payment) Regulations 1996
1462................Contracting-out (Transfer and Transfer Payment) Regulations 1996
1463................A10 Trunk Road (Enfield) Red Route (Bus Lanes) (No. 2) Traffic Order 1996
1464................Wireless Telegraphy (Licence Charges) (Amendment) Regulations 1996
1469................Financial Markets and Insolvency Regulations 1996
1470................Inheritance Tax (Delivery of Accounts) Regulations 1996
1471................Deregulation (Resolutions of Private Companies) Order 1996
1472................Inheritance Tax (Delivery of Accounts) (Scotland) Regulations 1996
1473................Inheritance Tax (Delivery of Accounts) (Northern Ireland) Regulations 1996
1474 (C. 27)...Disability Discrimination Act 1995 (Commencement No. 3 and Saving and Transitional Provisions) Order 1996
1475 (S. 131).Inshore Fishing (Prohibition of Fishing Methods) (Scotland) Amendment Order 1996
1476................Overseas Service (Pensions Supplement) (Amendment) Regulations 1996
1477................Sweeteners in Food (Amendment) Regulations 1996
1478................Habitat (Former Set-aside Land) (Amendment) Regulations 1996
1479................Habitat (Salt-marsh) (Amendment) Regulations 1996
1480................Habitat (Water Fringe) (Amendment) Regulations 1996
1481................Countryside Stewardship (Amendment) (Extension to the Isles of Scilly) Regulations 1996
1482................Arable Area Payments (Amendment) Regulations 1996
1483................Highways (Road Humps) Regulations 1996
1484................Manchester Ship Canal (Bridgewater Canal) Act 1907 (Amendment) Order 1996
1485................Exchange Gains and Losses (Insurance Companies) (Amendment No. 2) Regulations 1996
1486................Seeds (Fees) (Amendment) Regulations 1996
1487................Pesticides (Maximum Residue Levels in Crops, Food and Feeding Stuffs) (Amendment) Regulations 1996
1488................Suckler Cow Premium (Amendment) Regulations 1996
1491................A19 Trunk Road (A19/A64 Fulford Interchange Improvement) Order 1996
1492................Offshore Installations (Safety Zones) (No. 4) Order 1996
1493................European Parliamentary (United Kingdom Representatives) Pensions (Amendment) Order 1996
1494................Civil Aviation Authority (Amendment) Regulations 1996
1495................Civil Aviation (Route Charges for Navigation Services) (Amendment) Regulations 1996
1496................Dental Qualifications (Recognition) Regulations 1996
1499................Food Labelling Regulations 1996
1500................Hill Livestock (Compensatory Allowances) Regulations 1996
1501................Bread and Flour (Amendment) Regulations 1996

1502................Food (Lot Marking) Regulations 1996
1503................National Health Service (Wheelchair Charges) Regulations 1996
1504 (S. 132) .National Health Service (General Medical Services, Pharmaceutical Services and Charges for Drugs and Appliances) (Scotland) Amendment Regulations 1996
1505 (C. 28) (S. 133) Medicinal Products: Prescription by Nurses etc. Act 1992 (Commencement No. 2) Order 1996
1507 (S. 134) .Ancient Monuments (Class Consents) (Scotland) Order 1996
1509 (C. 29)...Jobseekers Act 1995 (Commencement No. 3) Order 1996
1510................Housing Benefit, Council Tax Benefit and Supply of Information (Jobseeker's Allowance) (Consequential Amendments) Regulations 1996
1511................Social Security (Back to Work Bonus) (Amendment) Regulations 1996
1512 (S. 135) .Fossil Fuel Levy (Scotland) Amendment Regulations 1996
1513................Health and Safety (Consultation with Employees) Regulations 1996
1514................Medicines (Products Other Than Veterinary Drugs) (Prescription Only) Amendment Order 1996
1515................Jobseeker's Allowance (Transitional Provisions) (Amendment) Regulations 1996
1516................Jobseeker's Allowance (Amendment) Regulations 1996
1517................Jobseeker's Allowance and Income Support (General) (Amendment) Regulations 1996
1518................Social Security (Adjudication) Amendment Regulations 1996
1527................Landfill Tax Regulations 1996
1528................Landfill Tax (Qualifying Material) Order 1996
1529................Landfill Tax (Contaminated Land) Order 1996
1530 (C. 30)...Criminal Justice and Public Order Act 1994 (Commencement No. 9) Order 1996
1534 (S. 136) .Act of Sederunt (Requirements of Writing) 1996
1536................Occupational Pension Schemes (Minimum Funding Requirement and Actuarial Valuations Regulations 1996
1537................Personal and Occupational Pension Schemes (Protected Rights) Regulations 1996
1538................M11 Motorway (Junction 5, Loughton, Essex, North Facing Slip Roads) Scheme 1996
1547................Food Safety (Fishery Products and Live Bivalve Molluscs and Other Shellfish) (Miscellaneous Amendments) Regulations 1996
1551................Closure of Prisons (H.M. Young Offender Institution Finnamore Wood) Order 1996
1552................Medicines (Advertising) Amendment Regulations 1996
1553................Deregulation (Parking Equipment) Order 1996
1554................Legal Advice and Assistance at Police Stations (Remuneration) (Amendment No. 2) Regulations 1996
1555................Legal Aid in Family Proceedings (Remuneration) (Amendment No. 2) Regulations 1996
1557................Education (Recognised Awards) (Richmond College) Order 1996
1560................Disclosure of Interests in Shares (Amendment) Regulations 1996
1561................Insider Dealing (Securities and Regulated Markets) (Amendment) Order 1996
1564 (S. 137) .Protection of Water Against Agricultural Nitrate Pollution (Scotland) Regulations 1996

1567................Public Telecommunication System Designation (Atlantic Telecommunications Limited) Order 1996
1569................A406 Trunk Road (Hanger Lane, Ealing) (Temporary Prohibition of Traffic) Order 1996
1571................Stock Transfer (Addition and Substitution of Forms) Order 1996
1572................Northern Ireland (Emergency and Prevention of Terrorism Provisions) (Continuance) Order 1996
1576................Deregulation (Gun Barrel Proving) Order 1996
1577................Occupational Pension Schemes (Contracting-out) Amendment Regulations 1996
1578................Local Government Act 1988 (Defined Activities) (Exemption) (Waltham Forest London Borough Council) Order 1996
1579................Local Government Act 1988 (Defined Activities) (Exemption) (London Borough of Bexley) Order 1996
1582................Retirement Benefits Schemes (Restriction on Discretion to Approve) (Excepted Schemes) Regulations 1996
1583................Capital Gains Tax (Pension Funds Polling Schemes) Regulations 1996
1584................Stamp Duty and Stamp Duty Reserve Tax (Pension Funds Pooling Schemes) Regulations 1996
1585................Income Tax (Pension Funds Pooling Schemes) Regulations 1996
1586................Financial Services Act 1986 (Investment Advertisements) (Exemptions) Order 1996
1587................Financial Services Act 1986 (Exemption) Order 1996
1591................European Primary Medical Qualifications Regulations 1996
1592................Construction (Health, Safety and Welfare) Regulations 1996
1593................Arable Area Payments (Grazing of Bovine Animals on Set-Aside Land) (Temporary Provisions) Regulations 1996
1596................Education (School Performance Information) (England) (Amendment) Regulations 1996
1597................Misuse of Drugs (Amendment) Regulations 1996
1603................Education (Teachers) (Amendment) Regulations 1996
1605................Building Societies (Prescribed Contracts) (Amendment) Order 1996
1606................Building Societies (Supplementary Capital) (Amendment) Order 1996
1607................Aviation Security (Air Cargo Agents) (Amendment) Regulations 1996
1608 (C. 32)...Criminal Justice and Public Order Act 1994 (Commencement No. 10) Order 1996
1609 (C. 33)...Transport and Works Act 1992 (Commencement No. 6) Order 1996
1614................Yorkshire Regional Flood Defence Committee Order 1996
1615................Wessex Regional Flood Defence Committee Order 1996
1616................Severn-Trent Regional Flood Defence Committee Order 1996
1617................Northumbria Regional Flood Defence Committee Order 1996
1618................Anglian Regional Flood Defence Committee Order 1996
1619................Stansted Airport Aircraft Movement Limit (Amendment) Order 1996
1621................Insurance Companies (Taxation of Reinsurance Business) (Amendment) Regulations 1996
1622................A501 Trunk Road (Euston Road, Camden) (Temporary Prohibition of Traffic) Order 1996
1623................Project Work (Miscellaneous Provisions) Order 1996

1624................A12 Trunk Road (Redbridge) (No. 1) Red Route Traffic Order 1996
1625................A501 Trunk Road (Euston Road, Camden) Red Route (Prescribed Routes) Experimental Traffic Order 1996
1626................Registration of Births, Deaths and Marriages (Amendment) Regulations 1996
1627................Whitehaven Harbour Revision Order 1996
1628................Territorial Sea (Amendment) Order 1996
1629................United Nations Arms Embargoes (Former Yugoslavia) (Amendment) Order 1996
1630................General Medical Council (Constitutional) Amendment Order 1996
1631 (C. 34)...Medical (Professional Performance) Act 1995 (Commencement No. 2) Order 1996
1632 (N.I. 11) Deregulation and Contracting Out (Northern Ireland) Order 1996
1633 (N.I. 12) Food Safety (Amendment) (Northern Ireland) Order 1996
1634................Football Spectators (Corresponding Offences in Norway) Order 1996
1635................Football Spectators (Corresponding Offences in the Republic of Ireland) Order 1996
1636 (N.I. 13) Health and Personal Social Services (Residual Liabilities) (Northern Ireland) Order 1996
1637................Exempt Charities Order 1996
1638................Naval, Military and Air Forces etc. (Disablement and Death) Service Pensions Amendment (No. 2) Order 1996
1639................European Communities (Definition of Treaties) (The Energy Charter Treaty) Order 1996
1640................Education (Fees and Awards) (Amendment) Regulations 1996
1642 (S. 138) .Police (Conduct) (Scotland) Regulations 1996
1643 (S. 139) .Police (Efficiency) (Scotland) Regulations 1996
1644 (S. 140) .Police Appeals Tribunals (Scotland) Rules 1996
1645 (S. 141) .Police (Conduct) (Senior Officers) (Scotland) Regulations 1996
1646 (C. 35) (S. 142) Police and Magistrates' Courts Act 1994 (Commencement No. 10 and Savings) (Scotland) Order 1996
1647................Adventure Activities (Enforcing Authority and Licensing Amendment) Regulations 1996
1648................A556(M) Motorway (M6 to M56 Link) and Connecting Roads Scheme 1996
1649................A556(M) Motorway (M6 to M56 Link) Supplementary Connecting Roads Scheme 1996
1650................A556 Trunk Road (Church Farm–Turnpike Wood, Over Tabley) Order 1996
1651................A556 Trunk Road (Turnpike Wood, Over Tabley–A56 Bowdon Roundabout) (Detrunking) Order 1996
1654................Income Tax (Payments on Account) Regulations 1996
1655................Occupational Pension Schemes (Disclosure of Information) Regulations 1996
1656................Work in Compressed Air Regulations 1996
1657................Local Government Act 1988 (Defined Activities) (Exemption) (Gosport Borough Council) Order 1996
1658................Local Government Act 1988 (Defined Activities) (Exemption) (Horsham District Council and Wealdon District Council) Order 1996
1661................Value Added Tax (Anti-avoidance (Heating)) Order 1996
1662................Young Offender Institution (Amendment) Reules 1996
1663................Prison (Amendment) Rules 1996

1664................Education (Disability Statements for Further Education Institutions) Regulations 1996
1665................Education (School Performance Information) (Wales) (Amendment) Regulations 1996
1667................Charities (The Royal School for the Blind) Order 1996
1669................Financial Institutions (Prudential Supervision) Regulations 1996
1670................Contracting Out (Functions in Relation to the Welfare Food Scheme) Order 1996
1674 (L. 3).....Family Proceedings (Amendment No. 2) Rules 1996
1657 (C. 36)...Pensions Act 1995 (Commencement) (No. 5) Order 1996
1676................Divorce etc. (Pensions) Regulations 1996
1677................Public Telecommunication System Designation (National Transcommunications Limited) Order 1996
1678................Deregulation (Model Appeal Provisions) Order 1996
1679................Occupational Pension Schemes (Indexation) Regulations 1996
1680................Local Government (Discretionary Payments) Regulations 1996
1681 (S. 143) .Ayrshire and Arran Community Health Care National Health Service Trust (Establishment) Amendment Order 1996
1683................Deregulation (Improvement of Enforcement Procedures) (Food Safety Act 1990) Order 1996
1684................Runnymede and Spelthorne (Borough Boundaries) Order 1996
1685................Police (Promotion) Regulations 1996
1686................Cattle Passports Order 1996
1690................Local Government Reorganisation (Miscellaneous Provision) (Rush Common) Order 1996
1698................Northern Ireland (Emergency Provisions) Act 1991 (Codes of Practice) (No. 3) Order 1996
1699................Dairy Products (Hygiene) (Amendment) Regulations 1996
1700................Deregulation (Motor Vehicles Tests) Order 1996
1701................Kent and Canterbury Hospitals National Health Service Trust (Transfer of Trust Property) Order 1996
1702................St. Helier National Health Service Trust (Transfer of Trust Property) Order 1996
1703................Wandsworth National Health Service Trust (Transfer of Trust Property) Order 1996
1704................Heathlands Mental Health National Health Service Trust (Transfer of Trust Property) Order 1996
1706................Football Spectators (Seating) Order 1996
1707................North Downs Community National Health Service Trust (Transfer of Trust Property) Order 1996
1708................Royal Surrey County and St Luke's Hospitals National Health Service Trust (Transfer of Trust Property) Order 1996
1709................Mid Essex Hospital Services National Health Service Trust (Transfer of Trust Property) Order 1996
1710................Merton and Sutton Community National Health Service Trust (Transfer of Trust Property) Order 1996
1711................Mid Sussex National Health Service Trust (Transfer of Trust Property) Order 1996
1712................Food Protection (Emergency Prohibitions) (Oil and Chemical Pollution of Fish and Plants) (Partial Revocation No. 3) Order 1996
1713................Lewisham Hospital National Health Service Trust (Transfer of Trust Property) Order 1996

1714................Nottingham Community Health National Service Trust (Transfer of Trust Property) Order 1996
1715................Occupational Pension Schemes (Scheme Administration) Regulations 1996
1716................Criminal Justice Act 1988 (Confiscation Orders) Order 1996
1724................National Savings Bank (Amendment) (No. 2) Regulations 1996
1725................Eggs (Marketing Standards) (Amendment) Regulations 1996
1736................Dual-use and Related Goods (Export Control) (Amendment No. 2) Regulations 1996
1737................Education (School Inspection) (No. 2) (Amendment) Regulations 1996
1738................Deregulation (Industrial and Provident Societies) Order 1996
1739................North Hampshire Hospitals National Health Service Trust (Transfer of Trust Property) Order 1996
1740................Pathfinder National Health Service Trust (Transfer of Trust Property) Order 1996
1741................Protection of Wrecks (Designation No. 1) Order 1996
1742................Beef (Emergency Control) (Revocation) Order 1996
1743................Fresh Meat (Beef Controls) Regulations 1996
1744................Warwickshire College for Agriculture and Equine Studies (Dissolution) Order 1996
1745 (S. 144) .Sex Discrimination (Geoffrey Simpson Bequest Modification) Order 1996
1746................Contracting Out (Administration of Civil Service Pensions Schemes) Order 1996
1748................Northern Ireland Act 1974 (Interim Period Extension) Order 1996
1749................Merchant Shipping (Mandatory Ship Reporting) Regulations 1996
1750................Local Government Act 1988 (Defined Activities) (Exemption) (Lambeth London Borough Council) Order 1996
1751................Motor Vehicles (Tests) (Amendment) Regulations 1996
1754 (S. 145) .Student's Allowances (Scotland) Regulations 1996
1755................National Health Service Trusts (Membership and Procedure) Amendment Regulations 1996
1756 (S. 146) .Act of Sederunt (Rules of the Court of Session Amendment No. 3) (Miscellaneous) 1996
1757................Industrial Tribunals (Constitution and Rules of Procedure) (Amendment) Regulations 1996
1758................Industrial Tribunals (Constitution and Rules of Procedure) (Scotland) (Amendment) Regulations 1996
1759................Income-related Benefits Schemes (Miscellaneous Amendments) (No. 2) Regulations 1996
1760................Importation of Animals (Amendment) Order 1996
1761................Winchester School of Art Higher Education Corporation (Dissolution) Order 1996
1762................City of Bristol College (Incorporation) Order 1996
1763................Salford College of Technology Higher Education Corporation (Dissolution) Order 1996
1764................Monkwearmouth College, Sunderland and Wearside College, Sunderland (Dissolution) Order 1996
1765................City of Bristol College (Government) Regulations 1996
1766................Richmond Adult and Community College (Attribution of Surpluses and Deficits) Regulations 1996
1767................Social Security (Disability Living Allowance) Amendment Regulations 1996
1768................Cornwall and Isles of Scilly Learning Disabilities National Health Service Trust (Change of Name) Order 1996

1769................West Lambeth Community Care National Health Service Trust (Change of Name) Order 1996
1770................Radcliffe Infirmary National Health Service Trust (Transfer of Trust Property) Order 1996
1771................Horton General Hospital National Health Service Trust (Transfer of Trust Property) Order 1996
1772................Wireless Telegraphy (Television Licence Fees) (Amendment) (No. 2) Regulations 1996
1773................Oxford Radcliffe Hospital National Health Service Trust (Transfer of Trust Property) Order 1996
1774................Oxfordshire Mental Healthcare National Health Service Trust (Transfer of Trust Property) Order 1996
1775................Oxfordshire Community Health National Health Service Trust (Transfer of Trust Property) Order 1996
1776................Oxfordshire Learning Disability National Health Service Trust (Transfer of Trust Property) Order 1996
1777................Oxfordshire Ambulance National Health Service Trust (Transfer of Trust Property) Order 1996
1778 (L. 4).....Family Proceedings (Amendment No. 3) Rules 1996
1779................Income Tax (Interest on Quoted Eurobonds) Regulations 1996
1780................Income Tax (Paying and Collecting Agents) Regulations 1996
1781................Double Taxation Relief (Taxes on Income) (United States of America Dividends) (Amendment) Regulations 1996
1782................Double Taxation Relief (Taxes on Income) (Canadian Dividends and Interest) (Amendment) Regulations 1996
1783 (S. 147) .Grants for Pre-School Education (Scotland) Regulations 1996
1784 (S. 148) .Plant Health Fees (Scotland) Regulations 1996
1786................Private Crossings (Signs and Barriers) Regulations 1996
1790................War Pensions Committees (Amendment) Regulations 1996
1800................A47 Trunk Road (Hardwick Roundabout Flyover and Slip Roads) Order 1996
1801................A47 Trunk Road (Hardwick Roundabout to North Runcton) (Detrunking) Order 1996
1802................Birmingham–Great Yarmouth Trunk Road (King's Lynn Southern Bypass) Order 1971 Partial Revocation Order 1996
1803................Child Benefit, Child Support and Social Security (Miscellaneous Amendments) Regulations 1996
1807................St Mary's Music School (Aided Places) Amendment Regulations 1996
1808................Education (Assisted Places) (Scotland) Amendment Regulations 1996
1809................City of Salford (Pomona Bridge) Scheme 1995 Confirmation Instrument 1996
1811................Plant Breeders' Rights (Applications in Designated Countries) Order 1996
1812................Education (Student Loans) Regulations 1996
1813................Local Government Act 1988 (Defined Activities) (Exemption) (Kettering Borough Council) Order 1996
1814................Local Authorities (Goods and Services) (Public Bodies) (Trunk Roads) (No. 2) Order 1996
1815................Merchant Shipping (Navigational Warnings) Regulations 1996
1816................Education (School Teachers' Pay and Conditions) (No. 2) Order 1996
1817................Town and Country Planning (General Development Procedure) (Amendment) Order 1996

1826................Manufactured Overseas Dividends (French Indemnity Payments) Regulations 1996
1829................South Tynedale Railway (Light Railway) Order 1996
1830................A1 Motorway (North of Leeming to Scotch Corner Section and Connecting Roads) Scheme 1996
1831................A1 Trunk Road (Lengths of A1 Carriageway between Catterick and Barton) (Detrunking) Order 1996
1832................Education (Funding for Teacher Training) Designation Order 1996
1836................Disability Discrimination (Services and Premises) Regulations 1996
1841................A13 Trunk Road (Tower Hamlets) Red Route (No. 2) Experimental Traffic Order 1996
1842................Nottingham Healthcare National Health Service Trust (Transfer of Trust Property) (No. 2) Order 1996
1843 (C. 37) (S. 151) Pensions Act 1995 (Commencement No. 6) Order 1996
1844................Building Societies Act 1986 (Continuance of section 41) Order 1996
1845................A21 Trunk Road (Lamberhurst Bypass) Order 1996
1846................A21 Trunk Road (Lamberhurst Bypass Detrunking) Order 1996
1847................Occupational Pension Schemes (Transfer Values) Regulations 1996
1853 (C. 38)...Pensions Act 1995 (Commencement No. 6) Order 1996
1854................National Savings Bank (Investment Deposits) (Limits) (Amendment) Order 1996
1855................Anthrax (Amendment) Order 1996
1856................Jobseeker's Allowance (Pilot Scheme) (Amendment) Regulations 1996
1857 (C. 39)...Local Government and Housing Act 1989 (Commencement) (No. 18) Order 1996
1858................North Tees Health National Health Service Trust (Transfer of Trust Property) Order 1996
1860................Police and Criminal Evidence Act 1984 (Application to Customs and Excise) (Amendment) Order 1996
1862................Offshore Installations (Safety Zones) (No. 5) Order 1996
1863................Cheshire (Boroughs of Halton and Warrington) (Structural Change) Order 1996
1864................Deregulation (Wireless Telegraphy) Order 1996
1865................Devon (City of Plymouth and Borough of Torbay) (Structural Change) Order 1996
1866................Shropshire (District of The Wrekin) (Structural Change) Order 1996
1867................Hereford and Worcester (Structural, Boundary and Electoral Changes) Order 1996
1868................Lancashire (Boroughs of Blackburn and Blackpool) (Structural Change) Order 1996
1875................Essex (Boroughs of Colchester, Southend-on-Sea and Thurrock and District of Tendring) (Structural, Boundary and Electoral Changes) Order 1996
1876................Kent (Borough of Gillingham and City of Rochester upon Medway) (Structural Change) Order 1996
1877................Nottinghamshire (City of Nottingham) (Structural Change) Order 1996
1878................Cambridgeshire (City of Peterborough) (Structural, Boundary and Electoral Changes) Order 1996
1879................Berkshire (Structural Change) Order 1996

1880................Local Authorities (Contracting Out of Tax Billing, Collection and Enforcement Functions) Order 1996
1881................A1 Trunk Road (Islington) Red Route Traffic Order 1993 Variation Order 1996
1882................Local Government Changes for England (Direct Labour and Service Organisations) (Amendment) Regulations 1996
1883................Local Authorities (Contracting Out of Investment Functions) Order 1996
1887................Food Protection (Emergency Prohibitions) (Paralytic Shellfish Poisoning) Order 1996
1888 (C. 40)...Local Government Act 1992 (Commencement No. 5) Order 1995
1889................Income Support (General) (Standard Interest Rate Amendment) (No. 2) Regulations 1996
1891................A13 Trunk Road (Tower Hamlets) Red Route Traffic Order 1996
1892................A1400 Trunk Road (Redbridge) Red Route Traffic Order 1996
1893................A12 Trunk Road (Redbridge) Red Route Traffic Order 1996
1894................A13 Trunk Road (Havering) Red Route Traffic Order 1996
1895................A13 Trunk Road (Newham and Barking and Dagenham) Red Route Traffic Order 1996
1896................A13 Trunk Road (Barking and Dagenham) Red Route Traffic Order 1996
1897 (C. 41)...Further and Higher Education Act 1992 (Commencement No. 3) Order 1996
1898................Welsh Language Schemes (Public Bodies) Order 1996
1899................Local Government (Publication of Staffing Information) (Wales) Regulations 1996
1900 (S. 152) .Scottish Transport Group (Pension Schemes) Order 1996
1901 (S. 153) .Divorce etc. (Pensions) (Scotland) Regulations 1996
1905................Deregulation (Building) (Initial Notices and Final Certificates) Order 1996
1906................Building (Approved Inspectors etc.) (Amendment) Regulations 1996
1907 (S. 157) .Inshore Fishing (Monofilament Gill Nets) (Scotland) Order 1996
1908................Community Trade Mark Regulations 1996
1909................Insolvent Companies (Reports on Conduct of Directors) Rules 1996
1910 (S. 154) .Insolvent Companies (Reports on Conduct of Directors) (Scotland) Rules 1996
1911................Education (Grant-maintained and Grant-maintained Special Schools) (Finance) (Wales) (Amendment) (No. 2) Regulations 1996
1912................European Communities (Designation) (No.2) Order 1996
1913................Ministerial and other Salaries Order 1996
1914................Parliamentary Commissioner Order 1996
1915................Consular Fees Order 1996
1916................Outer Space Act 1986 (Gibraltar) Order 1996
1917 (N.I. 14) Appropriation (No. 2) (Northern Ireland) Order 1996
1918 (N.I. 15) Education (Student Loans) (Northern Ireland) Order 1996
1919 (N.I. 16) Employment Rights (Northern Ireland) Order 1996
1920 (N.I. 17) Explosives (Amendment) (Northern Ireland) Order 1996
1921 (N.I. 18) Industrial Tribunals (Northern Ireland) Order 1996
1922................Parliamentary Constituencies (England) (Miscellaneous Changes) Order 1996

1923 (N.I. 19) Personal Social Services (Direct Payments) (Northern Ireland) Order 1996
1924................Maximum Number of Stipendiary Magistrates Order 1996
1925................Recovery Abroad of Maintenance (Convention Countries) Order 1996
1926 (S. 155).European Parliamentary Constituencies (Scotland) Order 1996
1927................Social Security (Malta) Order 1996
1928................Social Security (Reciprocal Agreements) Order 1996
1929................Motor Vehicles (International Circulation) (Amendment) Order 1996
1930................Local Authorities (Armorial Bearings) (No. 2) (Wales) Order 1996
1931................European Communities (Definition of Treaties) (Euro-Mediterranean Agreement Establishing an Association between the European Communities and their Member States and the Republic of Tunisia) Order 1996
1932................Exempt Charities (No. 2) Order 1996
1933................Exempt Charities (No. 3) Order 1996
1934................Education (School Inspection) (Wales) (No. 2) (Amendment) Regulations 1996
1935................Education (Reorganisation in Inner London) (Compensation) (Amendment and Modification) Regulations 1996
1936................Education (School Information) (Wales) (Amendment) Regulations 1996
1937................A449 and A456 Trunk Roads (Kidderminster, Blakedown and Hagley Bypass and Slip Roads) Order 1996
1938 (S. 156).Community Service by Offenders (Hours of Work) (Scotland) Order 1996
1939................Sheep Annual Premium and Suckler Cow Premium Quotas (Amendment) Regulations 1996
1940................Plant Protection Products (Amendments) Regulations 1996
1941................Specified Bovine Material (No. 3) Order 1996
1942................Trade Mark (Fees) Rules 1996
1943 (C. 42)...Transport Act 1982 (Commencement No. 7 and Transitional Provisions) Order 1996
1944................Income-related Benefits Schemes and Social Fund (Miscellaneous Amendments) Regulations 1996
1945................Child Support (Miscellaneous Amendments) Regulations 1996
1946................Harbour Works (Assessment of Environmental Effects) (Amendment) Regulations 1996
1957................Food Protection (Emergency Prohibitions) (Oil and Chemical Pollution of Fish and Plants) (Partial Revocation No. 4) Order 1996
1960................County Council of Norfolk (Reconstruction of Stow Bridge) Scheme 1995 Confirmation Instrument 1996
1961................Department of Transport (Fees) (Amendment) Order 1996
1962 (S. 158).Environmentally Sensitive Areas (Machair of the Uists and Benbecula, Barra and Vatersay) Designation (Amendment) Order 1996
1963 (S. 159).Environmentally Sensitive Areas (Cairngorms Straths) Designation (Amendment) Order 1996
1964 (S. 160).Environmentally Sensitive Areas (Central Borders) Designation (Amendment) Order 1996
1965 (S. 161).Environmentally Sensitive Areas (Shetland Islands) Designation (Amendment) Order 1996

1966 (S. 162) .Environmentally Sensitive Areas (Argyll Islands) Designation (Amendment) Order 1996
1967 (S. 163) .Environmentally Sensitive Areas (Stewartry) Designation (Amendment) Order 1996
1968 (S. 164) .Environmentally Sensitive Areas (Western Southern Uplands) Designation (Amendment) Order 1996
1970 (S. 166) .Scottish Examination Board (Amendment No. 2) Regulations 1996
1971 (S. 167) .Colleges of Education (Local Government Re-organisation Consequential Provisions) (Scotland) Order 1996
1974................Driving Licences (Community Driving Licence) Regulations 1996
1975................Occupational Pension Schemes (Requirement to Obtain Audited Accounts and a Statement from the Auditor) Regulations 1996
1976................Occupational Pension Schemes (Pensions Compensation Board Limit on Borrowing) Regulations 1996
1977................Occupational Pension Schemes (Mixed Benefit Contracted-out Schemes) Regulations 1996
1978................Local Authorities (Charges for Overseas Assistance and Public Path Orders) Regulations 1996
1979................Pneumoconiosis etc. (Workers' Compensation) (Payment of Claims) Amendment Regulations 1996
1980 (C. 43)...Road Traffic (Driving Instruction by Disabled Persons) Act 1993 (Commencement) Order 1996
1981................Tyne Riverside Enterprise Zones (North Tyneside) (Designation) (No. 2) Order 1996
1982................Housing Accommodation and Homelessness (Persons Subject to Immigration Control) Order 1996
1983................Motor Cars (Driving Instruction) (Amendment) Regulations 1996
1994................Parochial Fees Order 1996
1995................Chessington Computer Centre Trading Fund (Revocation) Order 1996
1996 (C. 52)...Disability Discrimination (Guidance and Code of Practice) (Appointed Day) Order 1996
1997................Motor Vehicles (Driving Licences) (Amendment) (No. 4) Regulations 1996
2001................Mines (Substances Hazardous to Health) Regulations 1996
2005................Beef (Marketing Payment) Regulations 1996
2006................Income-related Benefits (Montserrat) Regulations 1996
2007................Bovine Spongiform Encephalopathy Order 1996
2008................Vehicle Excise Duty (Fee for Temporary Licences) Regulations 1996
2009................Local Government Changes for England (Sheriffs) Order 1996
2017................Road Traffic (Permitted Parking Area and Special Parking Area) (County of Hampshire, City of Winchester) (Amendment) Order 1996
2019................Special Waste (Amendment) Regulations 1996
2022 (C. 44)...Nursery Education and Grant Maintained Schools Act 1996 (Commencement No. 1) Order 1996
2032................Salford Royal Hospitals National Health Service Trust (Transfer of Trust Property) Order 1996
2033................Manchester Children's Hospitals National Health Service Trust (Transfer of Trust Property) Order 1996
2034................Grimsby Health National Health Service Trust (Change of Name) Order 1996

2035................Education (Assisted Places) (Incidental Expenses) (Amendment) Regulations 1996
2036................Education (Grants) (Music, Ballet and Choir Schools) (Amendment) Regulations 1996
2037................Harwich Parkeston Quay Harbour Revision Order 1996
2044................Control of Pollution (Silage, Slurry and Agricultural Fuel Oil) (Amendment) Regulations 1996
2045................Postal Privilege (Suspension) Order 1996
2046................Dartford Thurrock Crossing Tolls Order 1996
2047................Dartford Thurrock Crossing (Amendment) Regulations 1996
2048 (C. 45)...Housing Act 1996 (Commencement No. 1) Order 1996
2049................Education (Grant-maintained Schools) (Initial Governing Instruments) (Amendment) Regulations 1996
2050................Education (School Government) (Amendment) Regulations 1996
2051................National Health Service (General Dental Services) Amendment (No. 2) Regulations 1996
2052................Registration of Births, Deaths and Marriages (Accounting) Amendment Regulations 1996
2053 (C. 46)...Asylum and Immigration Act 1996 (Commencement No. 1) Order 1996
2054 (C. 47)...Chemical Weapons Act 1996 (Commencement) Order 1996
2060 (S. 168) .National Health Service (General Dental Services) (Scotland) Amendment (No. 2) Regulations 1996
2064................Road Vehicles (Construction and Use) (Amendment) (No. 3) Regulations 1996
2065................Immigration (Transit Visa) (Amendment) Order 1996
2068................Local Government Act 1988 (Defined Activities) (Exemptions) (Bedford Borough Council and Suffolk Coastal District Council) Order 1996
2069................National Health Service (Functions of Health Authorities in England) (General Dental Services Incentive Schemes) Regulations 1996
2070 (L. 5).....Asylum Appeals (Procedure) Rules 1996
2071 (C. 48)...Offensive Weapons Act 1996 (Commencement No. 1) Order 1996
2075................Health and Safety at Work etc. Act 1974 (Application to Environmentally Hazardous Substances) Regulations 1996
2082................Education (London Residuary Body) (Property Transfer) (Amendment) Order 1996
2083................Education (National Curriculum) (Exceptions) Regulations 1996
2084................Brunel College of Arts and Technology and South Bristol College (Dissolution) Order 1996
2085................Road Vehicles (Construction and Use) (Amendment) (No. 4) Regulations 1996
2086................Nursery Education Regulations 1996
2087................Education (Pupil Referral Units) (Application of Enactments) (Amendment) Regulations 1996
2088................Education (Mandatory Awards) (Amendment) Regulations 1996
2089................Carriage of Dangerous Goods by Rail Regulations 1996
2090................Packaging, Labelling and Carriage of Radioactive Material by Rail Regulations 1996
2091 (S. 169) .Fire Services (Appointments and Promotion) (Scotland) Amendment Regulations 1996
2092................Carriage of Dangerous Goods (Classification, Packaging and Labelling) and Use of Transportable Pressure Receptacles Regulations 1996

2093................Carriage of Explosives by Road Regulations 1996
2094................Carriage of Dangerous Goods by Road (Driver Training) Regulations 1996
2095................Carriage of Dangerous Goods by Road Regulations 1996
2096................Fire Services (Appointments and Promotion) (Amendment) Regulations 1996
2097................Fresh Meat (Beef Controls) (No. 2) Regulations 1996
2098................Value Added Tax (Amendment) (No. 4) Regulations 1996
2099................Insurance Premium Tax (Amendment) Regulations 1996
2100................Landfill Tax (Amendment) Regulations 1996
2101................AEA Technology plc (Capital Allowances) Order 1996
2102................Deregulation (Insurance Companies Act 1982) Order 1996
2103................Ilfracombe Harbour Revision Order 1996
2105................Environmentally Sensitive Areas (Upper Thames Tributaries) Designation (Amendment) Order 1996
2106................Environmentally Sensitive Areas (Blackdown Hills) Designation (Amendment) Order 1996
2107................Environmentally Sensitive Areas (Cotswold Hills) Designation (Amendment) Order 1996
2108................Environmentally Sensitive Areas (Essex Coast) Designation (Amendment) Order 1996
2109................Environmentally Sensitive Areas (Shropshire Hills) Designation (Amendment) Order 1996
2110................Environmentally Sensitive Areas (Dartmoor) Designation (Amendment) Order 1996
2113................Education (Assisted Places) (Amendment) Regulations 1996
2114................Education (National Curriculum) (Assessment Arrangements for the Core Subjects) (Key Stage 1) (England) Order 1996
2115................Education (National Curriculum) (Assessments for the Core Subjects) (Key Stage 2) (England) Order 1996
2116................Education (National Curriculum) (Key Stage 3 Assessment Arrangements) (England) Order 1996
2120 (C. 49)...Broadcasting Act 1996 (Commencement No. 1 and Transitional Provisions) Order 1996
2121................Local Authorities (Capital Finance) (Amendment No. 2) Regulations 1996
2125................General Medical Council (Constitution of Fitness to Practise Committees) Rules Order of Council 1996
2126................Closure of Prisons (H.M. Prison Oxford) Order 1996
2127 (C. 50)...Asylum and Immigration Act 1996 (Commencement No. 2) Order 1996
2128................Merchant Shipping (Prevention of Pollution) (Limits) Regulations 1996
2130................M62 (East) to M606 Link and Connecting Roads Scheme 1996
2131................Personal and Occupational Pension Schemes (Preservation of Benefit and Perpetuities) (Amendment) Regulations 1996
2132................Guarantee Payments (Exemption) (No. 30) Order 1996
2142................Chester-Bangor Trunk Road (A55) (Pont Dafydd to Waen Improvement, Detrunking) Order 1996
2145................Immigration (Restricted Right of Appeal Against Deportation) (Exemption) (Amendment) Order 1996
2146 (S. 170).Police Act 1996 (Scotland) Order 1996
2147 (S. 171).Act of Adjournal (Criminal Procedure Rules Amendment) (Miscellaneous) 1996
2148 (S. 172).Act of Sederunt (Civil Legal Aid Rules) (Amendment) 1996
2149 (S. 173).Act of Sederunt (Mental Health Rules) 1996

2150 (C. 51)...Pensions Act 1995 (Commencement No. 6: S.I. 1996 1853 (C.38)) (Amendment) Order 1996
2154................Merchant Shipping (Prevention of Oil Pollution) Regulations 1996
2156................Occupational Pension Schemes (Payments to Employers) Regulations 1996
2157................A4 Trunk Road (Hillingdon) (Prescribed Routes) Order 1996
2158................M66 Motorway (Bury Easterly Bypass Northern Section) (Junction 2 Southbound Off-Slip) (Detrunking) Order 1996
2159................M66 Motorway (Bury Easterly Bypass Northern Section) and Connecting Roads Scheme 1973 (Variation) Scheme 1996
2162................A501 Trunk Road (Marylebone Road/Upper Harley Street, Westminster) (Temporary Prohibition of Turns) Traffic Order 1996
2163................Agricultural Holdings (Units of Production) Order 1996
2164................A205 Trunk Road (Richmond and Wandsworth) Red Route Traffic Order 1996
2165................A41 Trunk Road (Camden and Westminster) Red Route (Bus Lane) Experimental Traffic Order 1996
2166................A41 Trunk Road (Westminster) Red Route Experimental Traffic Order 1966
2167 (S. 174) .Act of Sederunt (Family Proceedings in the Sheriff Court) 1996
2168 (S. 175) .Act of Sederunt (Rules of the Court of Session Amendment No. 4) (Miscellaneous) 1996
2177................Local Government Changes for England (Collection Fund Surpluses and Deficits) (Amendment) Regulations 1996
2180................Local Government Pension Scheme (Crown Prosecution Service) (Transfer of Pension Rights) Regulations 1996
2181 (L. 6).....County Courts (Amendment) Rules 1996
2182................Contracting Out of Functions (Court Staff) Order 1996
2184 (S. 176) .Act of Sederunt (Chancery Procedure Rules) 1996
2185................Advanced Television Services (Industrial Property Rights) Regulations 1996
2186................Goods Vehicles (Licensing of Operators) (Temporary Use in Great Britain) Regulations 1996
2192 (S. 177) .Sheriff Court Districts (Alteration of Boundaries) Amendment Order 1996
2194................Animal Test Certificates Regulations 1996
2195................Medicines (Exemptions from Licences) (Revocation) Order 1996
2196................Medicines (Products for Animal Use—Fees) (Amendment) Regulations 1996
2197................Medicines (Exemptions from Animal Test Certificates) (Revocation) Regulations 1996
2198................Assured and Protected Tenancies (Lettings to Students) (Amendment) (No. 2) Regulations 1996
2199................EC Competition Law (Articles 88 and 89) Enforcement Regulations 1996
2201................City of Manchester (Mancunian Way A57(M)) (Chester Road Roundabout) Motorway Scheme 1995 Confirmation Instrument 1996
2202 (S. 178) .Spring Traps Approval (Scotland) Order 1996
2203 (C. 53) (S. 179) Children (Scotland) Act 1995 (Commencement No. 2 and Transitional Provisions) Order 1996
2208 (C. 54)...Jobseekers Act 1995 (Commencement No. 4) Order 1996
2212 (C. 55)...Housing Act 1996 (Commencement No. 2 and Savings) Order 1996
2219 (C. 56)...Noise Act 1996 (Commencement No. 1) Order 1996

2228................Housing (Change of Landlord) (Payment of Disposal Cost by Instalments) (Amendment No. 3) Regulations 1996
2235................Deregulation (Slaughterhouses Act 1974 and Slaughter of Animals (Scotland) Act 1980) Order 1996
2247................Education (Transfer of Functions Relating to Grant-maintained Schools) Order 1996
2248 (S. 180) .Scottish Qualifications Authority (Establishment) (Scotland) Order 1996
2249 (S. 181) .Scottish Qualifications Authority (Transitional Provisions) (Scotland) Order 1996
2250 (S. 182) (C. 63) Education (Scotland) Act 1996 (Commencement) Order 1996
2251 (S. 183) .Building Standards (Scotland) Amendment Regulations 1996
2255................Cattle Passports (Fees) Order 1996
2256................Social Landlords (Permissible Additional Purposes or Objects) Order 1996
2259................Education (National Curriculum) (Exceptions) (Wales) (Revocation) Regulations 1996
2260................Bridgend and District National Health Service Trust (Transfer of Property) Order 1996
2261................North Glamorgan National Health Service Trust (Transfer of Property) Order 1996
2262 (C. 57)...Sexual Offences (Conspiracy and Incitement) Act 1996 (Commencement) Order 1996
2263................Special Trustees of the Middlesex Hospital (Transfer of Trust Property) Order 1996
2264................Heads of Sheep and Goats Order 1996
2265................Bovine Products (Despatch to Other Member States) Regulations 1996
2269................Teachers' Superannuation (Amendment) Regulations 1996
2278 (S. 184) .Local Government (Access to Information) (Scotland) Order 1996
2282................Teachers' Superannuation (Provision of Information and Administrative Expenses etc.) Regulations 1996
2283................Channel Tunnel (International Arrangements) (Amendment) Order 1996
2284................Road Traffic (Special Parking Area) (City of Westminster) (Amendment) Order 1996
2285................National Health Service (Transitional Functions of Health Authorities) (Administration Arrangements) Regulations 1996
2287................Cider and Perry (Amendment) Regulations 1996
2288................South and East Wales Ambulance National Health Service Trust (Establishment) (Amendment) Order 1996
2290................Contracting Out (Functions relating to Wireless Telegraphy) Order 1996
2291................Plant Health (Fees) (Forestry) (Great Britain) Regulations 1996
2303................Education (Grant-maintained Special Schools) (Amendment) (No. 2) Regulations 1996
2304................Offshore Installations (Safety Zone) (No. 6) Order 1996
2305................Rent Assessment Committee (England and Wales) (Leasehold Valuation Tribunal) (Amendment) Regulations 1996
2306................Social Security (Claims and Payments and Adjudication) Amendment Regulations 1996
2307................Legal Aid in Criminal and Care Proceedings (General) (Amendment) (No. 4) Regulations 1996
2308................Legal Advice and Assistance (Amendment) (No. 3) Regulations 1996

2309................Civil Legal Aid (Assessment of Resources) (Amendment) (No. 3) Regulations 1996
2310................Health Authorities Act 1995 (Transitional Provisions) Amendment Order 1996
2313................Hydrocarbon Oil (Payment of Rebates) Regulations 1996
2314 (C. 58)...Finance Act 1996, section 5(6), (Appointed Day) Order 1996
2316................Finance Act 1994, sections 244 and 245, (Commencement) Order 1996
2317 (S. 185).Teachers (Compensation for Premature Retirement and Redundancy) (Scotland) Regulations 1996
2320................National Health Service (General Ophthalmic Service) Amendment (No. 2) Regulations 1996
2325................Housing Act 1996 (Consequential Provisions) Order 1996
2326................Housing Benefit (Permitted Totals) (Amendment) Order 1996
2327................Child Benefit (General) Amendment Regulations 1996
2328................National Health Service (Optical Charges and Payments) Amendment (No. 2) Regulations 1996
2329................Road Vehicles (Construction and Use) (Amendment) (No. 5) Regulations 1996
2330................Motor Vehicles (Type Approval) (Great Britain) (Amendment) Regulations 1996
2331................Motor Vehicles (Type Approval for Goods Vehicles) (Amendment) Regulations 1996
2332................A3 Trunk Road (Kingston Upon Thames) Red Route Traffic Order 1996
2333................A3 Trunk Road (Merton) Red Route (Clearway) Traffic Order 1996
2334................A3 Trunk Road (Merton) Red Route Traffic Order 1996
2335................A205 Trunk Road (Hounslow) Red Route (Bus Lane) Experimental Traffic Order 1996
2336................A205 Trunk Road (Hounslow) Red Route Traffic Order 1996
2337................Education (National Curriculum) (Key Stage 3 Assessment Arrangements) (Wales) Order 1996
2338................A3 Trunk Road (Wandsworth) Red Route (Clearway) Traffic Order 1996
2339................A3 Trunk Road (Kingston Upon Thames) Red Route (Clearway) Traffic Order 1996
2343 (C. 60)...Criminal Procedure and Investigations Act 1996 (Appointed Day No. 1) Order 1996
2344................Social Security (Jobseeker's Allowance Consequential Amendments) (Deductions) Regulations 1996
2348................Stamp Duty (Production of Documents) (Northern Ireland) Regulations 1996
2349................Employment Protection (Recoupment of Jobseeker's Allowance and Income Support) Regulations 1996
2352 (C. 61)...Housing Grants, Construction and Regeneration Act 1996 (Commencement No. 1) Order 1996
2353 (S. 186).National Health Service (General Ophthalmic Services) (Scotland) Amendment (No. 2) Regulations 1996
2354 (S. 187).National Health Service (Optical Charges and Payments) (Scotland) Amendment (No. 2) Regulations 1996
2355................Food Protection (Emergency Prohibitions) (Oil and Chemical Pollution of Fish and Plants) (Partial Revocation No. 5) Order 1996
2359................Community Health Services, Southern Derbyshire National Health Service Trust (Transfer of Trust Property) Order 1996
2360................Solihull Health Authority (Transfer of Trust Property) Order 1996

2362................National Health Service (Travelling Expenses and Remission of Charges) Amendment (No. 3) Order 1996
2367................Social Security (Credits and Contributions) (Jobseeker's Allowance Consequential and Miscellaneous Amendments) Regulations 1996
2371................Tenant's Rights of First Refusal (Amendment) Regulations 1996
2374................European Communities (Recognition of Professional Qualifications) (Second General System) Regulations 1996
2378................Social Security and Child Support (Jobseeker's Allowance) (Transitional Provisions) (Amendment) Regulations 1996
2381................Income Tax (Employments) (Amendment No. 4) Regulations 1996
2382................Town and Country Planning (Costs of Inquiries etc.) (Examination in Public) Regulations 1996
2384................North Hampshire, Loddon Community National Health Service Trust (Transfer of Trust Property) Order 1996
2385................Teddington Memorial Hospital National Health Service Trust (Transfer of Trust Property) Order 1996
2387................A1400 Trunk Road (Southend Road, Redbridge) (Prohibition of Right Turn and U-Turns) Order 1996
2391 (S. 188) .National Health Service (Travelling Expenses and Remission of Charges) (Scotland) Amendment (No. 2) Regulations 1996
2393................Moorland (Livestock Extensification) (Amendment) Regulations 1996
2394................Rural Development Grants (Agriculture) (Amendment) Regulations 1996
2395................Deregulation (Still-Birth and Death Registration) Order 1996
2396................Taxation of Benefits under Pilot Schemes (Earnings Top-up) Order 1996
2402 (C. 62)...Housing Act 1996 (Commencement No. 3 and Transitional Provisions) Order 1996
2403................Cornwall (Coroner's Districts) (Amendment) Order 1996
2405................Community Charge and Council Tax (Administration and Enforcement) (Amendment) (Jobseeker's Allowance) Regulations 1996
2406................Parliamentary Pensions (Amendment) Regulations 1996
2407................Social Security (Contributions) Amendment (No. 5) Regulations 1996
2417................Local Government Act 1988 (Defined Activities) (Exemption) (London Borough of Brent) Order 1996
2418................Merchant Shipping (Survey and Certification) (Amendment) Regulations 1996
2419................Fishing Vessels (Safety Provisions) (Amendment) Rules 1996
2420................Medicines (Data Sheet) Amendment Regulations 1996
2421................Aerosol Dispensers (EEC Requirements) (Amendment) Regulations 1996
2424................National Health Service Pension Scheme (Provision of Information and Administrative Expenses etc.) Regulations 1996
2431................Income Support and Social Security (Claims and Payments) (Miscellaneous Amendments) Regulations 1996
2432................Council Tax Benefit and Housing Benefit (Miscellaneous Amendments) Regulations 1996
2433................Sea Fishing (Enforcement of Community Quota Measures) (Amendment) Order 1996
2435................Tyne Riverside Enterprise Zones (North Tyneside and South Tyneside) (Designation) Order 1996
2444 (S. 189) .Civil Legal Aid (Scotland) Regulations 1996

2445 (S. 190) .Act of Sederunt (Sheriff Court Ordinary Cause Rules Amendment) (Miscellaneous) 1996
2446 (S. 191) .Act of Sederunt (Proceeds of Crime Rules) 1996
2447 (S. 192) .Advice and Assistance (Scotland) (Consolidation and Amendment) Regulations 1996
2448 (S. 193) .A1 (Old Craighall Roundabout to East of Haddington) Special Road Regulations 1996
2450................Social Security (Adjudication) and Child Support Amendment (No. 2) Regulations 1996
2454 (C. 64)...Security Service Act 1996 (Commencement) Order 1996
2458................Bovine Spongiform Encephalopathy (Amendment) Order 1996
2462................Optimum Health Services National Health Service Trust (Transfer of Trust Property) Order 1996
2463................Plymouth Community Services National Health Service Trust (Transfer of Trust Property) Order 1996
2465 (S. 194) .Dairy Products (Hygiene) (Scotland) Amendment Regulations 1996
2466................Food Protection (Emergency Prohibitions) (Paralytic Shellfish Poisoning) Revocation Order 1996
2467................Northbrook Instrument of Management (Variation) Order 1996
2469................Local Government Act 1988 (Defined Activities) (Exemption) (The Common Council of the City of London) Order 1996
2473................Fertilisers (Mammalian Meat and Bone Meal) (Amendment) Regulations 1996
2474 (C. 65)...Armed Forces Act 1996 (Commencement No. 1) Order 1996
2475................Personal and Occupational Pension Schemes (Pensions Ombudsman) Regulations 1996
2477................Social Security (Contracting-out and Qualifying Earnings Factor) Regulations 1996
2479................Housing (Right to Buy) (Priority of Charges) Order 1996
2480................Yarmouth (Isle of Wight) Harbour Revision Order 1996
2483................HMSO Trading Fund (Revocation) Order 1996
2489................Local Authorities' Traffic Orders (Procedure) (England and Wales) Regulations 1996
2490 (C. 66) (S. 195) Land Registration (Scotland) Act 1979 (Commencement No. 10) Order 1996
2503................Chemical Weapons (Notification) Regulations 1996
2506 (C. 67)...Marriage Ceremony (Prescribed Words) Act 1996 (Commencement) Order 1996
2507 (S. 196) .Act of Sederunt (Sheriff Court Bankruptcy Rules) 1996
2511................United Kingdom Atomic Energy Authority (Extinguishment of Liabilities) Order 1996
2514 (C. 68)...Employment Rights Act 1996 (Residuary Commencement) (No. 1) Order 1996
2515 (C. 69)...Private International Law (Miscellaneous Provisions) Act 1995 (Commencement No. 2) Order 1996
2516 (L. 7).....County Courts (Interest on Judgment Debts) (Amendment) Order 1996
2517................Occupational Pension Schemes (Modification of Schemes) Regulations 1996
2518................Social Security (Non-dependant Deductions) Regulations 1996
2519................Social Security (Jobseeker's Allowance and Payments on Account) (Miscellaneous Amendments) Regulations 1996
2520................Local Government Act 1988 (Defined Activities) (Exemption) (Lewisham London Borough Council) Order 1996

2522................Fresh Meat (Beef Controls) (No. 2) (Amendment) Regulations 1996
2530................Child Benefit (General) Amendment (No. 2) Regulations 1996
2534................Local Authorities (Goods and Services) (Public Bodies) (The Julie Rose Stadium) Order 1996
2535................Gas Safety (Rights of Entry) Regulations 1996
2536 (C. 70)...Finance Act 1996, section 8 (Appointed Day) Order 1996
2537................Hydrocarbon Oil Duties (Marine Voyages Reliefs) Regulations 1996
2538................Social Security and Child Support (Jobseeker's Allowance) (Miscellaneous Amendments) Regulations 1996
2539................Local Authorities (Capital Finance) (Amendment No. 3) Regulations 1996
2540................Civil Aviation (Canadian Navigation Services) (Amendment) Regulations 1996
2541................Gas Safety (Installation and Use) (Amendment) (No. 2) Regulations 1996
2542................Local Government Act 1988 (Defined Activities) (Exemption) (Braintree and South Bedfordshire District Councils) Order 1996
2543................A406 Trunk Road (Enfield) Red Route Traffic Order 1996
2544................Social Fund Cold Weather Payments (General) Amendment Regulations 1996
2545................Income-related Benefits and Jobseeker's Allowance (Personal Allowances for Children and Young Persons) (Amendment) Regulations 1996
2546................National Park Authorities (England) (Amendment) Order 1996
2547................Local Government Changes (Rent Act Registration Areas) Order 1996
2548 (S. 197) .Prosecutor's Right of Appeal in Summary Proceedings (Scotland) Order 1996
2549 (S. 198) .Parental Responsibilities and Parental Rights Agreement (Scotland) Regulations 1996
2550 (S. 199) .Legal Aid in Contempt of Court Proceedings (Scotland) Amendment Regulations 1996
2551................Railtrack Group Plc (Target Investment Limit) Order 1996
2552................British Waterways Board (Sheffield and Tinsley Canal) (Reclassification) Order 1996
2553................Swindon and Marlborough National Health Service Trust (Transfer of Trust Property) Order 1996
2554................Income Tax (Employments) (Amendment No. 5) Regulations 1996
2555 (S. 200) .Criminal Legal Aid (Scotland) Regulations 1996
2556 (S. 201) .National Health Service (Optical Charges and Payments) (Scotland) Amendment (No. 3) Regulations 1996
2557................Foreign Satellite Service Proscription Order 1996
2558................Registration of Marriages (Amendment) Regulations 1996
2559................A3 Trunk Road (Woolmer Road Junction Improvement Slip Road) Order 1996
2560 (C. 71)...Environment Act (Commencement No. 6 and Repeal Provisions) Order 1996
2561................Beef (Marketing Payment) (Amendment) Regulations 1996
2563................Potatoes Originating in the Netherlands Regulations 1996
2564................Education (Recognised Awards) (Richmond College) (No. 2) Order 1996
2567................Jobseeker's Allowance (Transitional Provisions) Regulations 1996

2570................Social Security (Back to Work Bonus) (No. 2) Regulations 1996
2574................National Health Service (Optical Charges and Payments) Amendment (No. 3) Regulations 1996
2577................Education (School Performance Information) (England) Regulations 1996
2579................Civil Courts (Amendment No. 3) Order 1996
2585................Education (School Information) (England) Regulations 1996
2586 (S. 202) .Act of Sederunt (Sheriff Court Ordinary Cause Rules Amendments) (Miscellaneous) (Amendment) 1996
2587 (S. 203) .Act of Sederunt (Rules of the Court of Session Amendment No. 5) (Family Actions and Miscellaneous) 1996
2588................Central Nottinghamshire Healthcare National Health Service Trust (Establishment) Amendment Order 1996
2592................Criminal Justice Act 1988 (Application to Service Courts) (Evidence) Order 1996
2593................Antarctic Act 1994 (Gibraltar) Order 1996
2594................Education (Inspectors of Schools in England) Order 1996
2595................Child Abduction and Custody (Parties to Conventions) (Amendment) (No. 2) Order 1996
2596................European Convention on Extradition Order 1990 (Amendment) Order 1996
2597 (N.I. 20)Housing Benefit (Payment to Third Parties) (Northern Ireland) Order 1996
2598................Double Taxation Relief (Taxes on Income) (Mongolia) Order 1996
2599................Double Taxation Relief (Taxes on Income) (Venezuela) Order 1996
2600................European Convention on Cinematographic Co-Production (Amendment) Order 1996
2601................Parliamentary Commissioner (No. 2) Order 1996
2602................Essex Ambulance Service National Health Service Trust (Establishment) Amendment Order 1996
2614................Income Support (General) Amendment (No. 3) Regulations 1996
2615................Free Zone (Southampton) Designation (Variation of Area) Order 1996
2616................Income Tax (Interest Relief) (Housing Associations) (Amendment) Regulations 1996
2617................Airport Byelaws (Designation) Order 1996
2628................Specified Diseases (Notification) Order 1996
2629................Marketing Development (Limitation) Scheme 1996
2630 (C. 72)...Child Support Act 1995 (Commencement No. 3) Order 1996
2631................Income Tax (Employments) (Amendment No. 6) Regulations 1996
2632................Merchant Shipping (Fees) (Amendment) Regulations 1996
2635................Dangerous Substances and Preparations (Safety) (Consolidation) (Amendment) Regulations 1996
2636................Measuring Equipment (Measures of Length) (Amendment) Regulations 1996
2637 (C. 73)...Pensions Act 1995 (Commencement No. 8) Order 1996
2638................Personal and Occupational Pensions Schemes (Pensions Ombudsman) (Procedure) Amendments Rules 1996
2639................M4 Motorway (Maidenhead Windsor and Eton Flood Alleviation Scheme) (Temporary Diversion) Scheme 1996
2640 (S. 204) .River Stinchar Salmon Fishery District (Baits and Lures) Regulations 1996
2641 (S. 205) .River Forth Salmon Fishery District (Baits and Lures) Regulations 1996

2642................Manufactured Overseas Dividends (French Indemnity Payments) (Amendment) Regulations 1996
2643................Income Tax (Manufactured Overseas Dividends) (Amendment No. 2) Regulations 1996
2644................Taxes (Interest Rate) (Amendment No. 3) Regulations 1996
2645 (C. 74)...Income and Corporation Taxes Act 1988, section 737A (Appointed Day) Order 1996
2646 (C. 75)...Finance Act 1996 section 159 (Appointed Day) Order 1996
2647................Hull and Holderness Community Health National Health Service Trust (Transfer of Trust Property) (No. 2) Order 1996
2648................Safety of Sports Grounds (Designation) Order 1996
2649................Food Protection (Emergency Prohibitions) (Oil and Chemical Pollution of Fish and Plants) (Partial Revocation No. 6) Order 1996
2650................Road Traffic (Permitted Parking Areas and Special Parking Areas) (City of Oxford and Parish of North Hinksey) Order 1996
2651................Housing (Right to Buy) (Prescribed Persons) (Amendment) Order 1996
2652................Housing (Right to Buy) (Prescribed Forms) (Amendment) Order 1996
2653 (S. 206) .Sports Grounds and Sporting Events (Designation) (Scotland) Amendment Order 1996
2654................Double Taxation Relief (Manufactured Overseas Dividends) (Amendment) Regulations 1996
2655................Legal Aid in Criminal and Care Proceedings (Costs) (Amendment) (No. 2) Regulations 1996
2656................Legal Aid in Criminal and Care Proceedings (General) (Amendment) (No. 5) Regulations 1996
2657................Dairy Produce Quotas (Amendment) Regulations 1996
2658 (C. 76)...Housing Act 1996 (Commencement No. 4) Order 1996
2659................Social Security (Adjudication) Amendment (No. 2) Regulations 1996
2660................Duffield and Wirksworth Light Railway Order 1996
2661................A6 Trunk Road (Rothwell and Desborough Bypass and Detrunking) Order 1996
2663................Export of Goods (Control) (Amendment No. 2) Order 1996
2664 (S. 207) .Motorways Traffic (Scotland) Amendment Regulations 1996
2665 (S. 208) .Cycle Racing on Highways (Scotland) Amendment Regulations 1996
2666 (C. 77)...Antarctic Act 1994 (Commencement) Order 1996
2667................A41 London–Birmingham Trunk Road (East of Aylesbury to West of Tring) Detrunking Order 1991 (Amendment) Order 1996
2669................Chemical Weapons (Notification) (Amendment) Regulations 1996
2670 (C. 78) (S. 209) Licensing (Amendment) (Scotland) Act 1996 Commencement Order 1996
2671................Asylum (Designated Countries of Destination and Designated Safe Third Countries) Order 1996
2672................Northwick Park and St Mark's National Health Service Trust (Transfer of Trust Property) Order 1996
2677................Endangered Species (Import and Export) Act 1976 (Amendment) Order 1996
2678................Environmental Protection (Prescribed Processes and Substances etc.) (Amendment) (Petrol Vapour Recovery) Regulations 1996
2684................Endangered Species (Import and Export) Act 1976 (Amendment) Regulations 1996
2685................Seal Fisheries (North Pacific) Act 1912 (Amendment) Regulations 1996

2686................Import of Seal Skins Regulations 1996
2687................A41 Trunk Road (Camden and Westminster) Red Route (Bus Lanes) (No. 2) Experimental Traffic Order 1996
2688................A41 Trunk Road (Westminster) Red Route (No. 2) Experimental Traffic Order 1996
2689................A501 Trunk Road (Marylebone Road, Westminster) Red Route (Prescribed Routes and Prohibited Turns) (No. 1) Traffic Order 1996
2708 (C. 79 (S. 210) Children (Scotland) Act 1995 (Commencement No. 2 and Transitional Provisions) (Amendment) Order 1996
2709 (S. 211) .Act of Sederunt (Proceedings in the Sheriff Court under the Debtors (Scotland) Act 1987) (Amendment) 1996
2710................European Parliamentary Elections (Day of By-election) (Merseyside West Constituency) Order 1996
2711................Travel Concession Schemes (Amendment) Regulations 1996
2714................Greater Manchester (Light Rapid Transit System) (Eccles Extension) Order 1996
2715................Local Government Act 1988 (Defined Activities) (Exemption) (Reigate and Banstead Borough Council) Order 1996
2716................Electricity Act 1989 (Disclosure of Information) (Licence Holders) Order 1996
2721................Dual-Use and Related Goods (Export Control) Regulations 1996
2724................Leeds City Council (A64(M) Motorway Slip Road at Mabgate) Scheme 1995 Confirmation Instrument 1996
2726................A2 Trunk Road (Bexley) Red Route Traffic Order 1996
2727................A20 Trunk Road (Greenwich) Red Route Traffic Order 1996
2728................A20 Trunk Road (Bexley and Bromley) Red Route Traffic Order 1996
2731................Dorset Health Authority (Transfers of Trust Property) Order 1996
2732................Eastbourne and County Healthcare National Health Service Trust (Transfer of Trust Property) Order 1996
2733................United Leeds Teaching Hospitals National Health Service Trust (Transfer of Trust Property) Order 1996
2734................St. James's and Seacroft University Hospitals National Health Service Trust (Transfer of Trust Property) Order 1996
2744................Social Security (Invalid Care Allowance) Amendment Regulations 1996
2745................Social Security Benefit (Computation of Earnings) Regulations 1996
2746................Local Government Act 1988 (Defined Activities) (Exemption) (Merton London Borough Council) Order 1996
2751 (C. 80)...Finance Act 1996, section 6, (C.80) (Appointed Day) Order 1996
2752................Wine and Made-wine (Amendment) Regulations 1996
2753................Allocation of Housing Regulations 1996
2754................Homelessness Regulations 1996
2755 (S. 212) .Peterhead Harbours Revision Order 1996
2756................Stands for Carry-cots (Safety) (Revocation) Regulations 1996
2757................Trade Descriptions (Place of Production) (Marking) (Revocation) Order 1996
2758................Multiplex Licence (Broadcasting of Programmes in Gaelic) Order 1996
2759................Broadcasting (Percentage of Television Multiplex Revenue) Order 1996
2760................Independent Analogue Broadcasters (Reservation of Digital Capacity) Order 1996
2762................Dogs (Fouling of Land) Regulations 1996

2763................Dogs Fouling (Fixed Penalties) Order 1996
2765................International Carriage of Perishable Foodstuffs (Amendment) Regulations 1996
2766................Isle of Wight Community Healthcare National Health Service Trust Dissolution Order 1996
2767................St. Mary's Hospital National Health Service Trust Dissolution Order 1996
2768................Isle of Wight Healthcare National Health Service Trust (Establishment) Order 1996
2769 (S. 213) .Act of Sederunt (Rules of the Court of Session Amendment No. 6) 1996
2777................Teachers (Compensation for Redundancy and Premature Retirement) (Amendment) Regulations 1996
2791................Health and Safety (Fees) Regulations 1996
2792................A406 Trunk Road (Enfield) Red Route (Clearway) Traffic Order 1995 Variation Order 1996
2793................Disability Discrimination (Questions and Replies) Order 1996
2794................National Park Authorities (Levies) (England) Regulations 1996
2795................Gas Act 1986 (Exemptions) (No. 4) Order 1996
2796 (C. 81) (S. 214) Energy Conservation Act 1996 (Commencement No. 1) (Scotland) Order 1996
2797 (C. 82) (S. 215) Home Energy Conservation Act 1995 (Commencement No. 3) (Scotland) Order 1996
2798................Civil Aviation (Investigation of Air Accidents and Incidents) Regulations 1996
2799................A23 Trunk Road (Streatham High Road and Streatham Hill, Lambeth) (Prescribed Routes) Order 1996
2800................Vehicle Registration (Sale of Information) Regulations 1996
2803................Industrial Tribunals (Interest on Awards in Discrimination Cases) Regulations 1996
2809 (S. 216) .Local Government, Teachers' and National Health Service (Scotland) Pension Schemes (Provision of Information and Administrative Expenses etc.) Regulations 1996
2810 (L. 8).....County Court (Amendment No. 2) Rules 1996
2811 (L. 9).....County Court (Forms) (Amendment) Rules 1996
2817................Plastic Materials and Articles in Contact with Food (Amendment) (No. 2) Regulations 1996
2819................Residuary Body for Wales (Penlan Road Offices Carmarthen) Order 1996
2820................Joint Consultative Committee Order 1996
2821................Merchant Shipping and Fishing Vessels (Medical Stores) (Amendment) Regulations 1996
2824................Motor Vehicles (Driving Licences) Regulations 1996
2825................Local Government Changes for England (Property Transfer and Transitional Payments) (Amendment) No. 2) Regulations 1996
2826................Local Government Changes for England (Capital Finance) (Amendment) Regulations 1996
2827................Open-ended Investment Companies (Investment Companies with Variable Capital) Regulations 1996
2839................Approval of Codes of Management Practice (Residential Property) Order 1996
2840................A13 Trunk Road (A117 Junction Improvement, Trunk Road and Slip Roads) Order 1996
2841................A13 Trunk Road (Movers Lane Junction Improvement, Trunk Road and Slip Roads) Order 1996
2842 (C. 83)...Housing Grants, Construction and Regeneration Act 1996 (Commencement No. 2 and Revocation, Savings, Supplementary and Transitional Provisions) Order 1996

2843................Home-Grown Cereals Authority Levy (Variation) Scheme (Approval) Order 1996
2854................M23 Motorway (Balcombe Road Interchange) Connecting Roads Scheme 1996
2855 (S. 217) .Act of Sederunt (Fees of Messengers-at-Arms) 1996
2856 (S. 218) .Act of Sederunt (Lands Valuation Appeal Court) 1996
2857 (C. 84) (S. 219) Environment Act 1995 (Commencement No. 7) (Scotland) Order 1996
2858 (S. 220) .Act of Sederunt (Fees of the Sheriff Officers) 1996
2859................Offshore Installations (Safety Zones) (No. 7) Order 1996
2860................Royal Surrey County and St. Luke's Hospitals National Health Service Trust (Change of Name) Order 1996
2861................Leeds Community and Mental Health Services Teaching National Health Service Trust (Transfer of Trust Property) Order 1996
2862................Northumberland Health Authority (Transfer of Trust Property) Order 1996
2863 (S. 221) .Ayr Road Route (M77) (Speed Limit) Regulations 1996
2866................East Yorkshire Community Healthcare National Health Service Trust (Transfer of Trust Property) Order 1996
2867................Bodmin and Wenford Light Railway Order 1996
2874................Child Abduction and Custody (Parties to Conventions) (Amendment) (No. 3) Order 1996
2875................European Convention on Extradition (Dependent Territories) Order 1996
2876................Intelligence Services Act 1994 (Dependent Territories) (Amendment) Order 1996
2877................Criminal Justice Act 1988 (Designated Countries and Territories) (Amendment) (No. 2) Order 1996
2878................Criminal Justice (International Co-operation) Act 1990 (Enforcement of Overseas Forfeiture Orders) (Amendment) Order 1996
2879 (N.I. 21)Domestic Energy Efficiency Schemes (Northern Ireland) Order 1996
2880................Drug Trafficking Act 1994 (Designated Countries and Territories) Order 1996
2881................Maritime Security (Jersey) Order 1996
2882................Naval, Military and Air Forces etc. (Disablement and Death) Service Pensions Amendment (No. 3) Order 1996
2883................Group Repair (Qualifying Buildings) Regulations 1996
2884................Housing (Deferred Action and Charge for Enforcement Action) (Forms) Regulations 1996
2885................Housing (Fitness Enforcement Procedures) Order 1996
2886................Housing (Maximum Charge for Enforcement Action) Order 1996
2887................Home Repair Assistance Regulations 1996
2888................Disabled Facilities Grants and Home Repair Assistance (Maximum Amounts) Order 1996
2889................Housing Renewal Grants (Services and Charges) Order 1996
2890................Housing Renewal Grants Regulations 1996
2891................Housing Renewal Grants (Prescribed Form and Particulars) Regulations 1996
2892 (L. 10)...Rules of the Supreme Court (Amendment) 1996
2893................Judicial Pensions (Miscellaneous) (Amendment) Regulations 1996
2894 (C. 85) (S. 222) Law Reform (Miscellaneous Provisions) (Scotland) Act 1990 (Commencement No. 13) (Amendment) Order 1996
2900................Residuary Body for Wales (Levies) Regulations 1996

2902................Local Government Act 1988 (Defined Activities) (Exemption) (Harborough District Council) Order 1996
2903................Income Support (General) (Standard Interest Rate Amendment) (No. 3) Regulations 1996
2904 (C. 86)...Education Act 1996 (Commencement No. 1) Order 1996
2905................Conservation of Seals (England) Order 1996
2906................Horserace Totalisator Board (Extension of Powers) Order 1996
2907................Child Support Departure Direction and Consequential Amendments Regulations 1996
2908................Merchant Shipping (Ship Inspection and Survey Organisations) Regulations 1996
2909 (C. 87)...Environment Act 1955 (Commencement No. 8 and Saving Provisions) Order 1996
2910................A40 Trunk Road (Western Avenue, Hillingdon) (30 mph Speed Limit) Order 1996
2911................Utilities Contracts Regulations 1996
2912................Leicestershire Fire Services (Combination Scheme) Order 1996
2913................National Park Authorities (Levies) (Wales) (Amendment) Regulations 1996
2914................Denbighshire and Wrexham (Areas) Order 1996
2915................Bridgend and the Vale of Glamorgan (Areas) Order 1996
2916................Wiltshire Fire Services (Combination Scheme) Order 1996
2917................Staffordshire Fire Services (Combination Scheme) Order 1996
2918................Bedfordshire Fire Services (Combination Scheme) Order 1996
2919................Derbyshire Fire Services (Combination Scheme) Order 1996
2920................Dorset Fire Services (Combination Scheme) Order 1996
2921................Durham Fire Services (Combination Scheme) Order 1996
2922................East Sussex Fire Services (Combination Scheme) Order 1996
2923................Hampshire Fire Services (Combination Scheme) Order 1996
2924................Buckinghamshire Fire Services (Combination Scheme) Order 1996
2925................Cosmetic Products (Safety) Regulations 1996
2926................Occupational Pensions (Revaluation) Order 1996
2934 (S. 223) .Local Government Act 1988 (Defined Activities) (Exemption of Ground Maintenance in Trunk Road Work Agreements) (Scotland) Order 1996
2935 (S. 224) .Local Government, Planning and Land Act 1980 (Competition) (Scotland) Regulations 1996
2936 (S. 225) .Local Government, Planning and Land Act 1980 (Competition) (Scotland) Amendment Regulations 1996
2942................A41 Trunk Road (Watford Way/Hendon Way, Barnet) Temporary Prohibition of Traffic Order 1996
2945................Professions Supplementary to Medicine (Registration Rules) (Amendment) Order of Council 1996
2946................Petroleum (Production) (Seaward Areas) (Amendment) Regulations 1996
2948................Value Added Tax (Increase of Consideration for Fuel) Order 1996
2949................Value Added Tax (Pharmaceutical Chemists) Order 1996
2950................Value Added Tax (Increase of Registration Limits) Order 1996
2951................Retirement Benefits Schemes (Indexation of Earnings Cap) Order 1996
2952................Income Tax (Indexation) Order 1996

2953................Income Tax (Furnished Accommodation) (Basic Amount) Order 1996
2954................Income Tax (Cash Equivalents of Car Fuel Benefits) Order 1996
2955................Insurance Premium Tax (Taxable Insurance Contracts) Order 1996
2956................Inheritance Tax (Indexation) Order 1996
2957................Capital Gains Tax (Annual Exempt Amount) Order 1996
2958................Financial Services Act 1986 (Extension of Scope of Act) Order 1996
2959 (C. 88)...Housing Act 1996 (Commencement No. 5 and Transitional Provisions) Order 1996
2960................Value Added Tax (Amendment) (No. 5) Regulations 1996
2961................Local Government Act 1988 (Defined Activities) (Exemption) (North Hertfordshire District Council and Hertsmere Borough Council) Order 1996
2965................Local Government Act 1988 (Defined Activities) (Exemption) (Cleveland Police Authority) Order 1996
2966 (C. 89) (S. 226) Law Reform (Miscellaneous Provisions) (Scotland) Act 1990 (Commencement No. 13) (Amendment) Order 1996
2967................Copyright and Related Rights Regulations 1996
2968................Statistics of Trade (Customs and Excise) (Amendment) Regulations 1996
2969................Income Tax (Employments) (Notional Payments) (Amendment) Regulations 1996
2970 (C. 90)...Asylum and Immigration Act 1996 (Commencement No. 3 and Transitional Provisions) Order 1996
2971................Control of Pollution (Applications, Appeals and Registers) Regulations 1996
2972................Patents (Fees) Rules 1996
2973................Army Terms of Service (Amendment) Regulations 1996
2974 (C. 91)...Trusts of Land and Appointment of Trustees Act 1996 (Commencement) Order 1996
2975................Land Registration Rules 1996
2976................National Park Authorities (Levies) (England) (Amendment) Regulations 1996
2977................A66 Trunk Road (Long Newton Grade Separated Junction Slip Roads) Order 1996
2986................London Docklands Development Corporation (Alteration of Boundaries) (Surrey Docks) Order 1996
2987................Disability Discrimination Code of Practice (Goods, Services, Facilities and Premises) Order 1996
2988................Social Security (Claims and Payments) Amendment (No. 2) Regulations 1996
2989................Building Societies (Designated Capital Resources) (Amendment) Order 1996
2991................Insurance Companies (Reserves) (Tax) Regulations 1996
2992................Value Added Tax (Place of Supply of Services) (Amendment) Order 1996
2993................Deregulation (Bills of Exchange) Order 1996
2996................Financial Services Act 1986 (Restriction of Scope of Act and Meaning of Collective Investment Scheme) Order 1996
2997................A30 Trunk Road (Great South West Road, Hounslow) (Temporary Restriction of Traffic) Order 1996
2998................Dental Auxiliaries (Amendment) Regulations 1996
2999................Beef (Marketing Payment) (No. 2) Regulations 1996
3000................Bovine Products (Despatch to other Member States) (Amendment) Regulations 1996

3001................Surface Waters (Abstraction for Drinking Water) (Classification) Regulations 1996
3002................A406 London North Circular Trunk Road Popes Lane (B4491) to Western Avenue (A40) Improvement Orders 1988 Revocation Order 1996
3003 (C.92)....Disability Discrimination Act 1995 (Commencement No. 4) Order 1996
3008................Friendly Societies (Insurance Business) (Amendment) Regulations 1996
3009................Friendly Societies (Activities of a Subsidiary) Order 1996
3010................Merchant Shipping (Dangerous or Noxious Liquid Substances in Bulk) Regulations 1996
3011................Insurance (Lloyd's) Regulations 1996
3012................Mid-Essex Community and Mental Health National Health Service Trust (Establishment) Amendment Order 1996
3013................Motor Vehicles (Approval) Regulations 1996
3014................Motor Vehicles (Type Approval for Goods Vehicles) (Great Britain) (Amendment) (No. 2) Regulations 1996
3015................Motor Vehicles (Type Approval) (Great Britain) (Amendment) (No. 2) Regulations 1996
3016................Road Vehicles Lighting (Amendment) Regulations 1996
3017................Road Vehicles (Construction and Use) (Amendment) (No. 6) Regulations 1996
3018................Non-domestic Rating Contributions (Wales) (Amendment) Regulations 1996
3019................National Health Authorities Act 1995 (Transitional Provisions) (Wales) Amendment Order 1996
3020................Measuring Equipment (Measures of Length) (Amendment) (No. 2) Regulations 1996
3021................General Optical Council (Registration and Enrolment (Amendment) Rules) Order of Council 1996
3022................Health and Safety (Repeals and Revocations) Regulations 1996
3023 (S. 227).Town and Country Planning (General Permitted Development) (Scotland) Amendment (No. 2) Order 1996
3024 (S. 228).New Town (Cumbernauld) (Transfer of Property, Rights and Liabilities) (No. 2) Order 1996
3026................A41 Trunk Road (Leavesden Slip Road) Order 1996
3030................Chemicals Weapons (Licence Appeal Provisions) Order 1996
3031................Social Security (Contributions) Amendment (No. 6) Regulations 1996
3032................Civil Aviation (Joint Financing) (Second Amendment) Regulations 1996
3033................Road Vehicles (Construction and Use) (Amendment) (No. 7) Regulations 1996
3034................Medicines (Veterinary Drugs) (Pharmacy and Merchants' List) (Amendment) Order 1996
3035 (S. 229).Habitats (Scotland) Amendment Regulations 1996
3036 (S. 230).Heather Moorland (Livestock Extensification) (Scotland) Amendment Regulations 1996
3037 (S. 231).Set-Aside Access (Scotland) Amendment and Revocation Regulations 1996
3038................Road Traffic (Special Parking Area) (Royal Borough of Kingston upon Thames) Order 1996
3039................Personal Protective Equipment (EC Directive) (Amendment) Regulations 1996
3040................Bridlington Harbour Revision Order 1996
3041 (C. 93)...Criminal Appeal Act 1995 (Commencement No. 12) Order 1996

3042................Statutory Sick Pay (General) Amendment Regulations 1996
3043................Monmouth-Fishguard Trunk Road (A40) (Carmarthen Eastern Bypass) Order 1996
3046 (S. 232) .River Ythan Salmon Fishery District (Baits and Lures) Regulations 1996
3047 (S.233) ..Surface Waters (Abstraction for Drinking Water) (Classification) (Scotland) Regulations 1996
3049................Vocational Training (Public Financial Assistance and Disentitlement to Tax Relief) (Amendment) Regulations 1996
3050................A23 Trunk Road (Croydon) Red Route (Bus Lanes) Traffic Order 1996
3051................A23 Trunk Road (Croydon) Red Route (Clearway) Traffic Order 1996
3052................A316 Trunk Road (Richmond) (No. 1) Red Route Traffic Order 1996
3053................Motorways Traffic (England and Wales) (Amendment) Regulations 1996
3054................Medicines (Pharmacies) (Applications for Registration and Fees) Amendment Regulations 1996
3055................Litter (Fixed Penalty) Order 1996
3056 (C. 94)...Environmental Protection Act 1990 (Commencement No. 18) Order 1996
3058................Passenger Transport Executives (Capital Finance) (Amendment) Order 1996
3059................Road Traffic (Special Parking Area) (London Borough of Redbridge) (Amendment) Order 1996
3060................A23 Trunk Road (Croydon) Red Route (Prescribed Route) Traffic Order 1996
3061................Code of Practice on Environmental Procedures for Flood Defence Operating Authorities (Environment Agency) Order 1996
3062................Code of Practice on Environmental Procedures for Flood Defence Operating Authorities (Internal Drainage Boards and Local Authorities) Approval Order 1996
3063 (C. 95)...Offensive Weapons Act 1996 (Commencement No. 2) Order 1996
3064................Criminal Justice Act 1988 (Offensive Weapons) (Exemption) Order 1996
3065................Water Supply and Sewerage Service (Customer Service Standards) (Amendment) Regulations 1996
3066................Education (Grants for Education Support and Training) (England) (Amendment) Regulations 1996
3067................Broadcasting (Channel 3 Transmission and Shared Distribution Costs) Order 1996
3068................Youth Courts (Constitution) (Amendment No. 2) Rules 1996
3069................Grants to the Churches Conservation Trust Order 1996
3070 (S. 234) .Non-domestic Rating Contributions (Scotland) Regulations 1996
3071................Local Government Reorganisation (Wales) (Consequential Amendments No. 3) Order 1996
3072................Habitat (Species-rich Grassland) (Wales) (Amendment) Regulations 1996
3073................Habitat (Water Fringe) (Wales) (Amendment) Regulations 1996
3074................Habitat (Coastal Belt) (Wales) (Amendment) Regulations 1996
3075................Habitat (Broadleaved Woodland) (Wales) (Amendment) Regulations 1996

3076................Moorland (Livestock Extensification) (Wales) (Amendment No. 2) Regulations 1996
3077................Environmentally Sensitive Areas (Wales) Designation Orders (Amendment) Regulations 1996
3078 (S. 235).Grants for Pre-school Education (Social Security Information) (Scotland) Regulations 1996
3079 (S. 236).Grants for Pre-School Education (Prescribed Children) (Scotland) Order 1996
3080................Companies Act 1985 (Audit exemption) (Amendment) Regulations 1996
3081................Consumer Credit (Exempt Agreements) (Amendment) (No. 2) Order 1996
3082 (S. 237).Environmentally Sensitive Areas (Scotland) Orders Amendment Regulations 1996
3083 (S. 238).Organic Aid (Scotland) Amendment Regulations 1996
3084................Legal Officers (Annual Fees) Order 1996
3085................Ecclesiastical Judges and Legal Officers (Fees) Order 1996
3086................Payments to the Churches Conservation Trust Order 1996
3087................Community Bus (Amendment) Regulations 1996
3088................Minibus and Other Section 19 Permit Buses (Amendment) Regulations 1996
3089................Civil Aviation (Route Charges for Navigation Services) (Second Amendment) Regulations 1996
3090................Animals (Scientific Procedures) Act 1986 (Fees) (No. 1) Order 1996
3091................Animals (Scientific Procedures) Act 1986 (Fees) (No. 2) Order 1996
3092................Local Authorities (Goods and Services) (Public Bodies) (Sports Councils) Order 1996
3093................Channel 4 (Application of Excess Revenues) Order 1996
3094................Friendly Societies (General Charge Fees) (Amendment) Regulations 1996
3095................National Lottery etc. Act 1993 (Amendment of section 23) Order 1996
3096................Contracting Out of Functions (Court Staff) (Amendment) Order 1996
3097................Deregulation (Rag Flock and Other Filling Materials Act 1951) (Repeal) Order 1996
3098 (L. 11)...Attachment of Debts (Expenses) Order 1996
3099................Education (School Inspection) (No. 2) (Amendment) (No. 2) Regulations 1996
3100................Air Navigation (Dangerous Goods) (Amendment) Regulations 1996
3101................Nurses, Midwives and Health Visitors Act 1979 (Amendment) Regulations 1996
3102................European Nursing and Midwifery Qualifications Designation Order 1996
3103................Nurses, Midwives and Health Visitors (Admission to the Register and Training) Amendment Rules Approval Order 1996
3104................Environmentally Sensitive Areas (England) Designation Orders (Amendment) Regulations 1996
3105................Nitrate Sensitive Areas (Amendment) Regulations 1996
3106................Habitat (Water Fringe) (Amendment) (No. 2) Regulations 1996
3107................Habitat (Former Set-Aside Land) (Amendment) (No. 2) Regulations 1996
3108................Habitat (Salt March) (Amendment) (No. 2) Regulations 1996
3109................Organic Farming (Aid) (Amendment) Regulations 1996

3110................Moorland (Livestock Extensification) (Amendment) (No. 2) Regulations 1996
3111................Countryside Access (Amendment) Regulations 1996
3112................A13 Trunk Road (New Road, Havering) (Prohibition of U-Turns and Use of Gaps in Central Reserve) Order 1996
3113................Retirement Benefits Schemes (Tax Relief on Contributions) (Disapplication of Earnings Cap) (Amendment) Regulations 1996
3114................Retirement Benefits Schemes (Continuation of Rights of Members of Approved Schemes) (Amendment) Regulations 1996
3115................Occupational Pension Schemes (Transitional Provisions) (Amendment) Regulations 1996
3117................Nursery Education (Amendment) Regulations 1996
3118................Local Government (Changes for the Registration Service in Bedfordshire, Buckinghamshire, Derbyshire, Dorset, Durham, East Sussex, Hampshire, Leicestershire, Staffordshire and Wiltshire) Order 1996
3119................Housing Renewal Grants and Home Repair Assistance (Amendment) Regulations 1996
3120................Patents (Supplementary Protection Certificate Certificate for Plant Protection Products) Regulations 1996
3121................Industrial and Provident Societies (Forms and Precedure) Regulations 1996
3122................Allocation of Housing and Homelessness (Review Procedures and Amendment) Regulations 1996
3123................Countryside Stewardship (Amendment) (No. 2) Reuglations 1996
3124................Products of Animal Origin (Import and Export) Regulations 1996
3125................Fresh Meat (Import Conditions) Regulations 1996
3126................Occupational Pension Schemes (Winding Up) Regulations 1996
3127................Occupational Pension Schemes (Investment) Regulations 1996
3128................Occupational Pension Schemes (Deficiency on Winding Up etc.) Regulations 1996
3133................Road Vehicles (Construction and Use) (Amendment) (No. 8) Regulations 1996
3136................Berkshire College of Art and Design, Maidenhead (Dissolution) Order 1996
3137................Disability Working Allowance and Family Credit (General) Amendment Regulations 1996
3138................Control of Substances Hazardous to Health (Amendment) Regulations 1996
3139................Offshore Installations (Safety Zones) (No. 8) Order 1996
3140................Films (Exhibition Periods) Order 1996
3141 (L. 12)...High Court and County Courts Jurisdiction (Amendment) Order 1996
3142................Arable Area Payments Regulations 1996
3143................Council Tax (Discount Disregards) (Amendment) (No. 2) Order 1996
3144 (S. 239).Act of Sederunt (Commissary Court Books) (Amendment) 1996
3146 (C. 96)...Arbitration Act 1996 (Commencement No. 1) Order 1996
3147................Employment Protection (Continuity of Employment) Regulations 1996
3148................London Docklands Development Corporation (Alteration of Boundaries) (Limehouse and Wapping) Order 1996

3149 (C. 97)...Criminal Appeal Act 1995 (Commencement No. 3) Order 1996
3150 (C. 98)...Industrial Tribunals Act 1996 (Commencement) Order 1996
3151................Advanced Television Services Regulations 1997
3152................Registers of Births, Deaths and Marriages (Fees) Order 1996
3153................United Nations Arms Embargoes (Somalia, Liberia and Rwanda) (Isle of Man) Order 1996
3154................United Nations Arms Embargoes (Somalia, Liberia and Rwanda) (Channel Islands) Order 1996
3155................European Communites (Designation) (No. 3) Order 1996
3156................Child Abduction and Custody (Falkland Islands) Order 1996
3157................European Police Office (Legal Capacities) Order 1996
3158 (NI. 22).Licensing (Northern Ireland) Order 1996
3159 (NI. 23).Registration of Clubs (Northern Ireland) Order 1996
3160 (NI. 24).Criminal Justice (Northern Ireland) Order 1996
3161................Criminal Justice (Northern Ireland Consequential Amendments) Order 1996
3162 (NI. 25).Rates (Amendment) (Northern Ireland) Order 1996
3163 (NI. 26).Succession (Northern Ireland) Order 1996
3164................Double Taxation Relief (Taxes on Income) (China) Order 1996
3165................Double Taxation Relief (Taxes on Income) (Denmark) Order 1996
3166................Double Taxation Relief (Taxes on Income) (Finland) Order 1996
3167................Double Taxation Relief (Taxes on Income) (Latvia) Order 1996
3168................Double Taxation Relief (Taxes on Income) (Republic of Korea) Order 1996
3169................European Convention on Cinematographic Co-production (Amendment) (No. 2) Order 1996
3170................Judicial Committee (Fees) Order 1996
3171................Extraterritorial US Legislation (Sanctions against Cuba, Iran and Libya) (Protection of Trading Interests) Order 1996
3172................Education (Chief Inspector of Schools in Wales) Order 1996
3173................Hovercraft (General Amendment) Order 1996
3179................Local Government Act 1988 (Defined Activities) (Exemptions) (Wales) (Amendment) Order 1996
3180................Child Minding and Day Care (Registration and Inspection Fees) (Amendment) Regulations 1996
3181 (C. 100).Home Energy Conservation Act 1995 (Commencement No. 4) (Wales) Order 1996
3182................European Communities (Iron and Steel Employees Re-adaptation Benefits Scheme) (No. 2) (Amendment) Regulations 1996
3183................Bovine Spongiform Encephalopathy (No. 2) Order 1996
3184................Bovine Spongiform Encephalopathy Compensation Order 1996
3185................Specified Bovine Material (No. 3) (Amendment) Order 1996
3186................Selective Cull (Enforcement of Community Compensation Conditions) Regulations 1996
3187................Taxes (Interest Rate) (Amendment No. 4) Regulations 1996
3188................Merchant Shipping (High-speed Craft) Regulations 1996
3189 (L. 13)...County Court Fees (Amendment) 1996
3190 (L. 14)...Family Proceedings Fees (Amendment) Order 1996
3191 (L. 15)...Supreme Court Fees (Amendment) Order 1996
3192 (C. 99)...Nursery Education and Grant-Maintained Schools Act 1996 (Commencement No. 2) Order 1996

3193................Medicines (Products Other Than Veterinary Drugs) (Prescription Only) Amendment (No. 2) Order 1996
3194................Town and Country Planning (Atomic Energy Establishments Special Development) (Revocation) Order 1996
3195................Social Security (Child Maintenance Bonus) Regulations 1996
3196................Child Support (Miscellaneous Amendments) (No. 2) Regulations 1996
3197................Advanced Television Services (Amendment) Regulations 1996
3198................Motor Vehicles (Driving Licences) (Amendment) Regulations 1996
3199 (S. 240) .Road Works (Permission under Section 109) (Scotland) Regulations 1996
3200................Fireworks (Safety) Regulations 1996
3201 (C. 102) (S. 241) Children (Scotland Act 1995 (Commencement No. 3) Order 1996
3202 (S. 242) .Act of Sederunt (Civil Legal Aid Rules) (Amendment No. 2) 1996
3203................Gas Act 1995 (Repeal of Superseded Provisions of the Gas Act 1986) Order 1996
3204................Homelessness (Suitability of Accommodation) Order 1996
3205................Local Authorities (Contracting Out of Allocation of Housing and Homelessness Functions) Order 1996
3206................Driving Licences (Designation of Relevant External Law) Order 1996
3207................Social Security (Incapacity for Work and Miscellaneous Amendments) Regulations 1996
3208................Amusements with Prizes (Variation of Monetary Limits) Order 1996
3209................Combined Probation Areas (North Yorkshire) Order 1996
3210................Education Act 1996 (Amendment) Order 1996
3211................Unfair Arbitration Agreements (Specified Amount) Order 1996
3212................Severn Bridges Tolls Order 1996
3213................Naval Medical Compassionate Fund (Amendment) Order 1996
3214................Non-domestic Rating (Chargeable Amounts for Small Hereditaments) Regulations 1996
3215 (L. 16)...High Court and County Courts (Allocation of Arbitration Proceedings) Order 1996
3216................Employment Appeal Tribunal (Amendment) Rules 1996
3217 (C. 101).Civil Evidence Act 1995 (Commencement No. 1) Order 1996
3218 (L. 17)...County Court (Amendment No. 3) Rules 1996
3219 (L. 18)...Rules of the Supreme Court (Amendment No. 3) Rules 1996
3220................Charities (The Proby Trust Fund) Order 1996
3221 (S. 243) .Electricity (Scottish Nuclear Limited) (Target Investment Limited) Order 1996
3225................Immigration (Restrictions on Employment) Order 1996
3227................Motor Vehicle Tyres (Safety) (Amendment) Regulations 1996
3231................Civil Aviation Authority (Hovercraft) (Revocation) Regulations 1996
3232 (S. 244) .Police (Scotland) Amendment Regulations 1996
3233................Retirement Benefits Schemes (Continuation of Rights of Members of Approved Schemes) (Amendment No. 2) Regulations 1996
3234................Occupational Pension Schemes (Transitional Provisions) (Amendment No. 2) Regulations 1996

3235................Sole (Specified Sea Areas) (Prohibition of Fishing) Order 1996
3236................Haddock, Saithe, etc (Specified Sea Areas) (Prohibition of Fishing) Order 1996
3237................Public Lending Right Scheme 1982 (Commencement of Variations) (No. 2) Order 1996
3241................Beef Special Premium Regulations 1996
3242................Plant Health (Great Britain) (Amendment) (No. 3) Order 1996
3243................Merchant Shipping (Fees) Regulations 1996
3245................Non-Domestic Rating Contributions (England) (Amendment) (No. 2) Regulations 1996
3253................A23 Trunk Road (Croydon) Red Route (Prescribed Route No. 2) Traffic Order 1996
3254................A205 Trunk Road (Wandsworth and Richmond) Red Route Experimental Traffic Order 1996
3255 (S. 245).Secure Accommodation (Scotland) Regulations 1996
3256 (S. 246).Residential Establishments—Child Care (Scotland) Regulations 1996
3257 (S. 247).Adoption Allowance (Scotland) Regulations 1996
3258 (S. 248).Emergency Child Protection Measures (Scotland) Regulations 1996
3259 (S. 249).Refugees for Children (Scotland) Regulations 1996
3260 (S. 250).Children's Hearing (Transmission of Information etc) (Scotland) Regulations 1996
3261 (S. 251).Children's Hearings (Scotland) Rules 1996
3262 (S. 252).Arrangements to Look After Children (Scotland) Regulations 1996
3263 (S. 253).Fostering of Children (Scotland) Regulations 1996
3265................Markets, Sales and Lairs (Amendment) Order 1996
3266 (S. 254).Adoption Agencies (Scotland) Regulations 1996
3267 (S. 255).Children (Reciprocal Enforcement of Prescribed Orders etc (England and Wales and Northern Ireland) (Scotland) Regulations 1996
3268................Specified Bovine Material (No. 3) (Amendment) (No. 2) Order 1996
3269................Medicines (Phenacetin Prohibition) (Revocation) Order 1996
3272................Firearms (Amendment) Act 1988 (Firearms Consultative Committee) Order 1996
3273 (S. 256).Amusements with Prizes (Variation of Monetary Limits) (Scotland) Order 1996
3274................Housing Accommodation and Homelessness (Persons subject to Immigration and Control) Order (Northern Ireland) 1996
3275................Gas (Extent of Domestic Supply Licences) (Amendment) Order 1996
3278................Animals (Scientific Procedures) Act 1986 (Appropriate Methods of Humane Killing) Order 1996

ALPHABETICAL TABLE OF STATUTES

This is an alphabetical table of statutes from 1700–1996. It comprises a listing of Acts printed in the edition of the Record Commissioners known as Statutes of the Realm so far as it extends (1713), the Acts printed in Ruffhead's Edition so far as it extends (1785) and thereafter all Acts printed by the King's or Queen's Printer as Public Acts or (since 1797) Public General Acts. It should be noted that from 1797 Public Acts were divided into two series, Public General and Public Local and Personal Acts, prior to that date Acts which might now be classified as local were included in the definition Public Acts. Such Acts are therefore included in this list. For 1997 statutes see the most recent table in the Contents section of the Service File.

Abandonment of Animals Act 1960 (c.43)
Abandonment of Railways Act 1850 (c.83)
Abandonment of Railways Act 1869 (c.114)
Aberbrothock Beer Duties Act 1737 (c.4)
Aberbrothock Beer Duties Act 1763 (c.28)
Aberbrothock Beer Duties Act 1787 (c.46)
Aberdare Canal Act 1793 (c.95)
Aberdeen Beer Duties Act 1730 (c.13)
Aberdeen Commissary Court Records Act 1721 (c.28)
Aberdeen Harbour Act 1772 (c.29)
Aberdeen Harbour Act 1795 (c.41)
Aberdeen Harbour Act 1796 (c.68)
Aberdeen: Harbour Improvement Act 1797 (c.101)
Aberdeen Improvements Act 1795 (c.76)
Aberdeen Records Act 1722 (c.25)
Aberdeen Roads Act 1795 (c.161)
Abergavenny: Improvement Act 1794 (c.106)
Abergele and Rhydlan: Drainage Act 1794 (c.110)
Aberystwyth Harbour Act 1780 (c.26)
Abingdon: Improvement Act 1794 (c.89)
Abingdon to Swinford Roads Act 1768 (c.61)
Abingdon to Trowbridge Canal Act 1795 (c.52)
Abnormal Importations (Customs Duties) Act 1931 (c.1)
Abolition of Domestic Rates Etc. (Scotland) Act 1987 (c.47)
Abolition of Offices in Courts of Law Act 1845 (c.78)
Abolition of Slave Trade Act 1807 (c.36)
Abolition of Slavery Act 1836 (c.5)
Abolition of Slavery Act 1836 (c.16)
Abolition of Slavery Act 1836 (c.82)
Abolition of Slavery Act 1837 (c.3)
Abolition of Slavery Act 1838 (c.19)
Abolition of Slavery Act 1841 (c.18)
Abortion Act 1967 (c.87)
Absconding Debtors Act 1870 (c.76)
Access to Health Records Act 1990 (c.23)
Access to Medical Reports Act 1988 (c.28)
Access to Mountains Act 1939 (c.30)
Access to Neighbouring Land Act 1992 (c.23)
Access to Personal Files Act 1987 (c.37)
Accession Declaration Act 1910 (c.29)
Accessories and Abettors Act 1861 (c.94)
Accommodation Agencies Act 1953 (c.23)
Account of Civil List Revenues Act 1815 (c.15)
Accountant General in Chancery Act 1804 (c.82)
Accountant General of Court of Chancery Act 1813 (c.14)
Accounting for Certain Debentures Act 1706 (c.33)
Accounts, etc., of Barrack Master General Act 1807 (c.13)
Accounts of Barrack Office Act 1808 (c.89)
Accounts of Colonial Revenues Act 1814 (c.184)
Accounts of Expenditure in France Act 1814 (c.98)
Accounts of Expenditure in West Indies Act 1808 (c.91)
Accounts of Paymaster General Act 1808 (c.49)
Accumulations Act 1800 (c.98)
Accumulations Act 1892 (c.58)
Achurch Parish Church 1778 (c.9)
Acknowledgement of Deeds by Married Women Act 1854 (c.75)
Acknowledgement of Deeds by Married Women (Ireland) Act 1878 (c.23)
Acquisition of Land Act 1981 (c.67)
Acquisition of Land (Assessment of Compensation) Act 1919 (c.57)
Acquisition of Land (Assessment of Compensation) (Scotland) Act 1931 (c.11)
Acquisition of Land (Authorisation Procedure) Act 1946 (c.49)
Acquisition of Land (Authorisation Procedure) (Scotland) Act 1947 (c.42)
Act of Marriage 1929 (c.36)
Act of Settlement 1700 (c.2)
Act of Uniformity 1662 (c.4)
Act of Uniformity Amendment Act 1872 (c.35)
Actions Against Certain Spiritual Persons Act 1803 (c.34)
Actions Against Spiritual Persons Act 1813 (c.6)
Actions, etc., for Buying Oak Bark, etc. Act 1806 (c.152)
Actions for Gaming Act 1844 (c.3)
Actions for Gaming Act 1844 (c.58)
Activity Centres (Young Persons' Safety) Act 1995 (c.15)

Acts of Common Council, London Act 1745 (c.8)
Acts of Parliament (Commencement) Act 1793 (c.13)
Acts of Parliament (Expiration) 1808 (c.106)
Acts of Parliament (Mistaken References) Act 1837 (c.60)
Acts of Parliament Numbering and Citation Act 1962 (c.34)
Adam Buildings Act 1772 (c.75)
Aden, Perim and Kuria Muria Islands Act 1967 (c.71)
Addenbrooke's Hospital, Cambridge Act 1767 (c.99)
Adderbury and Oxford Road Act 1797 (c.170)
Addingham to Black Lane End Road Act 1781 (c.99)
Additional Income Tax Act 1884 (c.1)
Additional Taxes Act 1795 (c.14)
Admeasurement of Coals Act 1780 (c.34)
Administration Act 1868 (c.90)
Administration of Estates Act 1798 (c.87)
Administration of Estates Act 1869 (c.46)
Administration of Estates Act 1925 (c.23)
Administration of Estates Act 1971 (c.25)
Administration of Estates (Probate) Act 1800 (c.72)
Administration of Estates (Small Payments) Act 1965 (c.32)
Administration of Intestates' Estates Act 1856 (c.94)
Administration of Justice Act 1705 (c.3)
Administration of Justice Act 1813 (c.24)
Administration of Justice Act 1920 (c.81)
Administration of Justice Act 1925 (c.28)
Administration of Justice Act 1928 (c.26)
Administration of Justice Act 1932 (c.55)
Administration of Justice Act 1956 (c.46)
Administration of Justice Act 1960 (c.65)
Administration of Justice Act 1964 (c.42)
Administration of Justice Act 1965 (c.2)
Administration of Justice Act 1968 (c.5)
Administration of Justice Act 1969 (c.58)
Administration of Justice Act 1970 (c.31)
Administration of Justice Act 1973 (c.15)
Administration of Justice Act 1977 (c.38)
Administration of Justice Act 1982 (c.53)
Administration of Justice Act 1985 (c.61)
Administration of Justice (Appeals) Act 1934 (c.40)
Administration of Justice (Emergency Provisions) Act 1939 (c.78)
Administration of Justice (Emergency Provisions) Act 1939 (c.105)
Administration of Justice (Emergency Provisions) (Scotland) Act 1939 (c.79)
Administration of Justice (Emergency Provisions) (Scotland) Act 1979 (c.19)
Administration of Justice in Certain Boroughs Act 1836 (c.105)
Administration of Justice (Judges and Pensions) Act 1960 (c.3)
Administration of Justice (Miscellaneous Provisions) Act 1933 (c.36)
Administration of Justice (Miscellaneous Provisions) Act 1938 (c.63)
Administration of Justice, New South Wales, etc. Act 1838 (c.50)
Administration of Justice (Pensions) Act 1950 (c.11)
Administration of Justice (Scotland) Act 1809 (c.119)
Administration of Justice (Scotland) Act 1933 (c.41)
Administration of Justice (Scotland) Act 1948 (c.10)
Administration of Justice (Scotland) Act 1972 (c.59)
Administration of Justice, West Indies Act 1836 (c.17)
Admiralty and Prize Courts Act 1810 (c.118)
Admiralty and War Office Regulation Act 1878 (c.53)
Admiralty Court Act 1840 (c.65)
Admiralty Court Act 1861 (c.10)
Admiralty, etc. Acts Repeal Act 1865 (c.112)
Admiralty, etc., Courts, (Scotland) Act 1786 (c.47)
Admiralty Jurisdiction (Indian) Act 1860 (c.88)
Admiralty Lands Act 1843 (c.58)
Admiralty Lands and Works Act 1864 (c.57)
Admiralty Offences Act 1826 (c.38)
Admiralty Offences Act 1844 (c.2)
Admiralty Offences (Colonial) Act 1849 (c.96)
Admiralty Offences (Colonial) Act 1860 (c.122)
Admiralty Pensions Act 1921 (c.39)
Admiralty Powers etc. Act 1865 (c.124)
Admiralty Suits Act 1868 (c.78)
Admission of Vassals (Scotland) Act 1751 (c.20)
Adoption Act 1950 (c.26)
Adoption Act 1958 (c.5)
Adoption Act 1960 (c.59)
Adoption Act 1964 (c.57)
Adoption Act 1968 (c.53)
Adoption Act 1976 (c.36)
Adoption of Children Act 1926 (c.29)
Adoption of Children Act 1949 (c.98)
Adoption of Children (Regulation) Act 1939 (c.27)
Adoption of Children (Scotland) Act 1930 (c.37)
Adoption of Children (Workmen's Compensation) Act 1934 (c.34)
Adoption (Scotland) Act 1978 (c.28)
Adulteration of Coffee Act 1718 (c.11)
Adulteration of Food and Drugs Act 1872 (c.74)
Adulteration of Hops Act 1733 (c.19)
Adulteration of Seeds Act 1869 (c.112)
Adulteration of Seeds Act 1878 (c.17)
Adulteration of Tea Act 1730 (c.14)
Adulteration of Tea Act 1776 (c.29)
Adulteration of Tea and Coffee Act 1724 (c.30)

Advance by Bank of England Act 1781 (c.60)
Advance by Bank of England Act 1816 (c.7)
Advance by Bank of England Act 1816 (c.14)
Advance from Bank of England Act 1808 (c.3)
Advance of Money to Foreign States Act 1729 (c.5)
Advance of Unclaimed Dividends, etc. Act 1808 (c.4)
Advance of Unclaimed Dividends, etc. Act 1816 (c.97)
Advance Petroleum Revenue Tax Act 1986 (c.68)
Advance to Boyed, Benfield and Co. Act 1805 (c.78)
Advances by Bank of Ireland Act 1811 (c.35)
Advances for Public Works Act 1837 (c.51)
Advances for Public Works Act 1838 (c.88)
Advances for Public Works Act 1840 (c.10)
Advances for Public Works Act 1842 (c.9)
Advances for Public Works Act 1861 (c.80)
Advances for Public Works Act 1862 (c.30)
Advances for Railways (Ireland) Act 1847 (c.73)
Advances to County of Mayo Acts 1854 (c.110)
Advertisements (Hire Purchase) Act 1957 (c.41)
Advertisements (Hire-Purchase) Act 1967 (c.42)
Advertisements Regulation Act 1907 (c.27)
Advertisements Regulation Act 1925 (c.52)
Advertising Stations (Rating) Act 1889 (c.27)
Advowsons Act 1707 (c.18)
Aerial Navigation Act 1911 (c.4)
Aerial Navigation Act 1913 (c.22)
Affidavits in County of Durham Act 1763 (c.21)
Affidavits in County of Lancaster Act 1743 (c.7)
Affiliation Orders Act 1914 (c.6)
Affiliation Orders Act 1952 (c.41)
Affiliation Orders (Increase of Maximum Payment) Act 1918 (c.49)
Affiliation Proceedings Act 1957 (c.55)
Affiliation Proceedings (Amendment) Act 1972 (c.49)
Affirmation by Quakers Act 1701 (c.4)
Affirmations Act 1861 (c.66)
Affirmations by Quakers etc. Act 1859 (c.10)
Affirmations (Scotland) Act 1855 (c.25)
Affirmations (Scotland) Act 1865 (c.9)
African Company Act 1711 (c.34)
African Company Act 1750 (c.49)
African Company Act 1751 (c.40)
African Company Act 1783 (c.65)
African Slave Trade Act 1862 (c.40)
African Slave Trade Act 1862 (c.90)
African Slave Trade Treaty Act 1863 (c.34)
Age of Legal Capacity (Scotland) Act 1991 (c.50)
Age of Majority (Scotland) Act 1969 (c.39)
Age of Marriage Act 1929 (c.36)
Agent General for Volunteers, etc. Act 1812 (c.152)
Agent General for Volunteers, etc. Act 1815 (c.170)
Aggravated Vehicle-Taking Act 1992 (c.11)
Agricultural and Technical Instruction (Ireland) - Northern Irish Act 1899 (c.50)
Agricultural and Forestry Associations Act 1962 (c.29)
Agricultural and Forestry (Financial Provisions) Act 1991 (c.33)
Agricultural Children Act 1873 (c.67)
Agricultural Credits Act 1923 (c.34)
Agricultural Credits Act 1928 (c.43)
Agricultural Credits Act 1931 (c.35)
Agricultural Credits (Scotland) Act 1929 (c.13)
Agricultural Development Act 1939 (c.48)
Agricultural Development (Ploughing up of Land) Act 1946 (c.32)
Agricultural Gangs Act 1867 (c.130)
Agricultural Holdings Act 1900 (c.50)
Agricultural Holdings Act 1906 (c.56)
Agricultural Holdings Act 1908 (c.28)
Agricultural Holdings Act 1913 (c.21)
Agricultural Holdings Act 1914 (c.7)
Agricultural Holdings Act 1923 (c.9)
Agricultural Holdings Act 1948 (c.63)
Agricultural Holdings Act 1984 (c.41)
Agricultural Holdings Act 1986 (c.5)
Agricultural Holdings (Amendment) Act 1990 (c.15)
Agricultural Holdings (Amendment) (Scotland) Act 1983 (c.46)
Agricultural Holdings (England) Act 1875 (c.92)
Agricultural Holdings (England) Act (1875) Amendment Act 1876 (c.74)
Agricultural Holdings (England) Act 1883 (c.61)
Agricultural Holdings (Notices to Quit) Act 1977 (c.12)
Agricultural Holdings (Scotland) Act 1883 (c.62)
Agricultural Holdings (Scotland) Act 1889 (c.20)
Agricultural Holdings (Scotland) Act 1908 (c.64)
Agricultural Holdings (Scotland) Act 1923 (c.10)
Agricultural Holdings (Scotland) Act 1949 (c.75)
Agricultural Holdings (Scotland) Act 1991 (c.55)
Agricultural Holdings (Scotland) Amendment Act 1910 (c.30)
Agricultural Improvement Grants Act 1959 (c.31)
Agricultural Land (Removal of Surface Soil) Act 1953 (c.10)
Agricultural Land Sales (Restriction of Notice to Quit) Act 1919 (c.63)
Agricultural Land (Utilisation) Act 1931 (c.41)
Agricultural Marketing Act 1931 (c.42)
Agricultural Marketing Act 1933 (c.31)

Agricultural Marketing Act 1949 (c.38)
Agricultural Marketing Act 1958 (c.47)
Agricultural Marketing Act 1983 (c.3)
Agricultural Marketing (No. 2) Act 1933 (c.1)
Agricultural (Miscellaneous Provisions) Act 1949 (c.37)
Agricultural (Miscellaneous Provisions) Act 1950 (c.17)
Agricultural Mortgage Corporation Act 1956 (c.38)
Agricultural Mortgage Corporation Act 1958 (c.2)
Agricultural Produce (Grading and Marking) Act 1928 (c.19)
Agricultural Produce (Grading and Marking) Amendment Act 1931 (c.40)
Agricultural Rates Act 1896 (c.16)
Agricultural Rates Act, 1896, etc., Continuance Act 1901 (c.13)
Agricultural Rates Act, 1896, etc., Continuance Act 1905 (c.8)
Agricultural Rates Act 1923 (c.39)
Agricultural Rates Act 1929 (c.26)
Agricultural Rates (Additional Grant) Continuance Act 1925 (c.10)
Agricultural Rates, Congested Districts, and Burgh Land Tax Relief (Scotland) 1896 (c.37)
Agricultural Research Act 1955 (c.28)
Agricultural Research etc. (Pensions) Act 1961 (c.9)
Agricultural Returns Act 1925 (c.39)
Agricultural Statistics Act 1979 (c.13)
Agricultural Tenancies Act 1995 (c.8)
Agricultural Training Board Act 1982 (c.9)
Agricultural Training Board Act 1985 (c.36)
Agricultural Training Board Act 1987 (c.29)
Agricultural Wages Act 1948 (c.47)
Agricultural Wages (Regulation) Act 1924 (c.37)
Agricultural Wages (Regulation) Act 1947 (c.15)
Agricultural Wages (Regulation) Amendment Act 1939 (c.17)
Agricultural Wages (Regulation) (Scotland) Act 1937 (c.53)
Agricultural Wages (Regulation) (Scotland) Act 1939 (c.27)
Agricultural Wages (Scotland) Act 1949 (c.30)
Agriculture Act 1920 (c.76)
Agriculture Act 1937 (c.70)
Agriculture Act 1947 (c.48)
Agriculture Act 1957 (c.57)
Agriculture Act 1958 (c.71)
Agriculture Act 1967 (c.22)
Agriculture Act 1970 (c.40)
Agriculture Act 1986 (c.49)
Agriculture Act 1993 (c.37)
Agriculture (Amendment) Act 1921 (c.17)
Agriculture (Amendment) Act 1923 (c.25)
Agriculture (Amendment) Act 1984 (c.20)
Agriculture and Horticulture Act 1964 (c.28)
Agriculture and Technical Instruction (Ireland) Act 1902 (c.3)
Agriculture and Technical Instruction (Ireland) (No. 2) Act 1902 (c.33)
Agriculture (Artificial Insemination) Act 1946 (c.29)
Agriculture (Calf Subsidies) Act 1952 (c.62)
Agriculture (Emergency Payments) Act 1947 (c.32)
Agriculture (Fertilisers) Act 1952 (c.15)
Agriculture (Improvement of Roads) Act 1955 (c.20)
Agriculture (Miscellaneous Provisions) Act 1940 (c.14)
Agriculture (Miscellaneous Provisions) Act 1941 (c.50)
Agriculture (Miscellaneous Provisions) Act 1943 (c.16)
Agriculture (Miscellaneous Provisions) Act 1944 (c.28)
Agriculture (Miscellaneous Provisions) Act 1949 (c.37)
Agriculture (Miscellaneous Provisions) Act 1950 (c.17)
Agriculture (Miscellaneous Provisions) Act 1954 (c.39)
Agriculture (Miscellaneous Provisions) Act 1963 (c.11)
Agriculture (Miscellaneous Provisions) Act 1968 (c.34)
Agriculture (Miscellaneous Provisions) Act 1972 (c.62)
Agriculture (Miscellaneous Provisions) Act 1976 (c.55)
Agriculture (Miscellaneous War Provisions) Act 1940 (c.14)
Agriculture (Miscellaneous War Provisions) (No.2) Act 1940 (c.50)
Agriculture Mortgage Corporation Act 1956 (c.38)
Agriculture (Ploughing Grants) Act 1952 (c.35)
Agriculture (Poisonous Substances) Act 1952 (c.60)
Agriculture (Safety, Health and Welfare Provisions) Act 1956 (c.49)
Agriculture (Scotland) Act 1948 (c.45)
Agriculture (Small Farmers) Act 1959 (c.12)
Agriculture (Spring Traps) (Scotland) Act 1969 (c.26)
Agriculture and Horticulture Act 1964 (c.28)
Aid to Government of France Act 1794 (c.9)
Aid to Russia, etc. Act 1813 (c.13)
AIDS Control Act 1987 (c.33)
Air Corporations Act 1949 (c.91)
Air Corporations Act 1960 (c.13)
Air Corporations Act 1962 (c.5)
Air Corporations Act 1966 (c.11)
Air Corporations Act 1967 (c.33)
Air Corporations Act 1968 (c.30)
Air Corporations Act 1969 (c.43)
Air Corporations Act 1971 (c.5)
Air Force Act 1955 (c.19)

Air Force (Constitution) Act 1917 (c.51)
Air Force Reserve Act 1950 (c.33)
Air Force Reserve (Pilots and Observers) Act 1934 (c.5)
Air Guns and Shot Guns, etc. Act 1962 (c.49)
Air Ministry (Heston and Kenley Aerodromes Extension) Act 1939 (c.59)
Air Ministry (Kenley Common Acquisition) Act 1922 (c.40)
Air Navigation Act 1919 (c.3)
Air Navigation Act 1920 (c.80)
Air Navigation Act 1936 (c.44)
Air Navigation Act 1947 (c.18)
Air Navigation (Financial Provisions) Act 1938 (c.33)
Air Raid Precaution (Postponement of Financial Investigations) Act 1941 (c.10)
Air Raid Precautions Act 1937 (c.6)
Air Transport (Subsidy Agreements) Act 1930 (c.30)
Air Travel Reserve Fund Act 1975 (c.36)
Aircraft and Shipbuilding Industries Act 1977 (c.3)
Aire and Calder, Navigation Act 1774 (c.96)
Airports Act 1986 (c.31)
Airport Authority Act 1965 (c.16)
Airports Authority Act 1972 (c.8)
Airports Authority Act 1975 (c.78)
Airways Corporations Act 1949 (c.57)
Alcoholic Liquor Duties Act 1979 (c.4)
Alderney Harbour (Transfer) Act 1874 (c.92)
Alderney (Transfer of Property etc.) Act 1923 (c.15)
Alford to Cowbridge Road Act 1784 (c.62)
Aldwork Bridge, Ure Act 1772 (c.87)
Alehouses Act 1753 (c.31)
Alehouses Act 1756 (c.12)
Alexander Wilson (Provost of Edinburgh) Act 1736 (c.34)
Alice Holt Forest Act 1812 (c.72)
Aliens Act 1746 (c.44)
Aliens Act 1793 (c.4)
Aliens Act 1794 (c.82)
Aliens Act 1795 (c.24)
Aliens Act 1796 (c.109)
Aliens Act 1797 (c.92)
Aliens Act 1798 (c.50)
Aliens Act 1798 (c.77)
Aliens Act 1800 (c.24)
Aliens Act 1802 (c.92)
Aliens Act 1803 (c.155)
Aliens Act 1814 (c.155)
Aliens Act 1815 (c.54)
Aliens Act 1816 (c.86)
Aliens Act 1844 (c.66)
Aliens Act 1847 (c.83)
Aliens Act 1848 (c.20)
Aliens Act 1905 (c.13)
Aliens' Employment Act 1955 (c.18)
Aliens Restriction Act 1914 (c.12)
Aliens Restriction (Amendment) Act 1919 (c.92)
Alkali Act 1863 (c.124)
Alkali Act 1874 (c.43)
Alkali Act Perpetuation Act 1868 (c.36)
Alkali, etc., Works Regulation Act 1881 (c.37)
Alkali, etc., Works Regulation Act 1892 (c.30)
Alkali, etc., Works Regulation Act 1906 (c.14)
Alkali, etc., Works Regulation (Scotland) Act 1951 (c.21)
All Saints' Church, Newcastle Act 1786 (c.117)
All Saints' Church, Southampton Act 1791 (c.71)
All Saints' Church, Southampton Act 1793 (c.101)
Allied Forces Act 1939 (c.51)
Allied Powers (Maritime Courts) Act 1941 (c.21)
Allied Powers (War Service) Act 1942 (c.29)
Alloa Beer Duties Act 1754 (c.35)
Alloa Harbour Act 1786 (c.13)
Allotments Act 1887 (c.48)
Allotments Act 1890 (c.65)
Allotments Act 1922 (c.51)
Allotments Act 1925 (c.61)
Allotments Act 1950 (c.31)
Allotments and Cottage Gardens Compensation for Crops Act 1887 (c.26)
Allotments Extension Act 1882 (c.80)
Allotments Rating Exemption Act 1891 (c.33)
Allotments (Scotland) Act 1892 (c.54)
Allotments (Scotland) Act 1922 (c.52)
Allotments (Scotland) Act 1926 (c.5)
Allotments (Scotland) Act 1950 (c.38)
Allowance for Mint Prosecutions Act 1772 (c.52)
Allowance of Duty to Meux & Co. Act 1815 (c.189)
Allowance to Brewers Act 1785 (c.73)
Allowance to Distillers (Scotland) Act 1790 (c.39)
Allowances to Foreign Officers Act 1815 (c.126)
Allowing Time for First Meetings Act 1757 (c.13)
Alteration of Terms in Scotland Act 1708 (c.15)
Altrincham and Warrington Roads Act 1796 (c.145)
Alvingham, Lincoln, Navigation Act 1763 (c.39)
Amendment of c.10 of this Session Act 1800 (c.19)
Amendment of cc.26, 28 of this Session Act 1808 (c.71)
Amendment of c.29 of this Session Act 1793 (c.51)
American and European Payments (Financial Provisions) Act 1949 (c.17)
American Colonies Act 1766 (c.12)
American Loan Act 1915 (c.81)
American Loyalists Act 1783 (c.80)
American Loyalists Act 1785 (c.76)
American Loyalists Act 1786 (c.68)
American Loyalists Act 1787 (c.39)

American Loyalists Act 1788 (c.44)
American Loyalists Act 1789 (c.62)
American Loyalists Act 1790 (c.34)
American Prizes Act 1813 (c.63)
American Rebellion Act 1774 (c.39)
American Rebellion Act 1774 (c.45)
American Rebellion Act 1778 (c.13)
American Treaty Commissioners Act 1803 (c.135)
Amlwch Harbour Act 1793 (c.125)
Anatomy Act 1832 (c.75)
Anatomy Act 1871 (c.16)
Anatomy Act 1984 (c.14)
Anchors and Chain Cables Act 1899 (c.23)
Ancient Monument Act 1931 (c.16)
Ancient Monuments and Archaeological Areas Act 1979 (c.46)
Ancient Monuments Consolidation and Amendment Act 1913 (c.32)
Ancient Monuments Protection Act 1882 (c.73)
Ancient Monuments Protection Act 1900 (c.34)
Ancient Monuments Protection Act 1910 (c.3)
Ancient Monuments Protection (Ireland) Act 1892 (c.46)
Andover Canal Act 1789 (c.72)
Anglesey: Drainage, etc. Act 1788 (c.71)
Anglesey: Drainage Act 1790 (c.59)
Anglesey Roads Act 1765 (c.56)
Anglo-French Convention Act 1904 (c.33)
Anglo-French Treaty (Defence of France) Act 1919 (c.34)
Anglo-German Agreement Act 1890 (c.32)
Anglo-Italian Treaty (East African Territories) Act 1925 (c.9)
Anglo-Persian Oil Company (Acquisition of Capital) Act 1914 (c.37)
Anglo-Persian Oil Company (Acquisition of Capital) (Amendment) Act 1919 (c.86)
Anglo-Persian Oil Company (Payment of Calls) Act 1922 (c.26)
Anglo-Portuguese Commercial Treaty Act 1914 (c.1)
Anglo-Portuguese Commercial Treaty Act 1916 (c.39)
Anglo-Turkish (Armaments Credit) Agreement 1938 (c.60)
Anglo-Venezuelan Treaty (Island of Patos) Act 1942 (c.17)
Anguilla Act 1971 (c.63)
Anguilla Act 1980 (c.67)
Animal Boarding Establishments Act 1963 (c.43)
Animal Health Act 1981 (c.22)
Animal Health and Welfare Act 1984 (c.40)
Animals Act 1948 (c.35)
Animals Act 1971 (c.22)
Animals (Anaesthetics) Act 1919 (c.54)
Animals (Cruel Poisons) Act 1962 (c.26)
Animals (Restriction of Importation) Act 1964 (c.61)
Animals (Scientific Procedures) Act 1986 (c.14)
Animals (Scotland) Act 1987 (c.9.)
Annoyance Jurors, Westminster Acts 1861 (c.78)
Annual Revision of Rateable Property (Ireland) Amendment Act 1860 (c.4)
Annual Turnpike Acts Continuance Act 1850 (c.79)
Annual Turnpike Acts Continuance Act 1851 (c.37)
Annual Turnpike Acts Continuance Act 1853 (c.135)
Annual Turnpike Acts Continuance Act 1854 (c.58)
Annual Turnpike Acts Continuance Act 1859 (c.51)
Annual Turnpike Acts Continuance Act 1860 (c.73)
Annual Turnpike Acts Continuance Act 1861 (c.64)
Annual Turnpike Acts Continuance Act 1862 (c.72)
Annual Turnpike Acts Continuance Act 1863 (c.94)
Annual Turnpike Acts Continuance Act 1864 (c.75)
Annual Turnpike Acts Continuance Act 1865 (c.107)
Annual Turnpike Acts Continuance Act 1866 (c.105)
Annual Turnpike Acts Continuance Act 1867 (c.121)
Annual Turnpike Acts Continuance Act 1867 (c.129)
Annual Turnpike Acts Continuance Act 1868 (c.99)
Annual Turnpike Acts Continuance Act 1869 (c.90)
Annual Turnpike Acts Continuance Act 1870 (c.73)
Annual Turnpike Acts Continuance Act 1871 (c.115)
Annual Turnpike Acts Continuance Act 1872 (c.85)
Annual Turnpike Acts Continuance Act 1873 (c.90)
Annual Turnpike Acts Continuance Act 1874 (c.95)
Annual Turnpike Acts Continuance Act 1876 (c.39)
Annual Turnpike Acts Continuance Act 1877 (c.64)
Annual Turnpike Acts Continuance Act 1878 (c.62)
Annual Turnpike Acts Continuance Act 1879 (c.46)
Annual Turnpike Acts Continuance Act 1880 (c.12)
Annual Turnpike Acts Continuance Act 1881 (c.31)
Annual Turnpike Acts Continuance Act 1882 (c.52)
Annual Turnpike Acts Continuance Act 1883 (c.21)

Annual Turnpike Acts Continuance Act 1884 (c.52)
Annual Turnpike Acts Continuance Act 1885 (c.37)
Annuities Act 1704 (c.2)
Annuities Act 1799 (c.29)
Annuities Act 1799 (c.30)
Annuities, etc. Act 1702 (c.14)
Annuities, etc. Act 1704 (c.14)
Annuities (Ireland) Act 1807 (c.21)
Annuities (Prince of Wales, etc.) Act 1863 (c.1)
Annuities to Branches of Royal Family Act 1807 (c.39)
Annuities to Duke and Princess Mary of Cambridge Act 1850 (c.77)
Annuities to Duke, etc., of York 1792 (c.13)
Annuities to Duke of Sussex etc. Act 1802 (c.48)
Annuities to Lady Abercromby, etc. Act 1801 (c.59)
Annuities to Princesses Act 1812 (c.57)
Annuities to Retired Judges (Scotland) Act 1814 (c.94)
Annuities to Royal Family Act 1806 (c.145)
Annuity, Duchess of Mecklenburgh Strelitz Act 1843 (c.25)
Annuity, Duke of Albany Act 1882 (c.5)
Annuity, Duke of Edinburgh Act 1866 (c.8)
Annuity, Duke of Marlborough; Pension Act 1706 (c.6)
Annuity, etc., to Duke of Wellington Act 1814 (c.161)
Annuity (Heirs of Sir T. Clarges) Act 1799 (c.84)
Annuity, Lady Mayo Act 1872 (c.56)
Annuity (Lady of Havelock) Act 1858 (c.2)
Annuity (Lord Amherst) Act 1803 (c.159)
Annuity (Lord and Lady Raglan) Act 1855 (c.64)
Annuity, Lord Exmouth Act 1814 (c.164)
Annuity, Lord Gough Act 1846 (c.32)
Annuity Lord Hardinge Act 1846 (c.31)
Annuity (Lord Napier) Act 1868 (c.91)
Annuity (Lord Rodney) Act 1793 (c.77)
Annuity (Penn's Descendants) Act 1790 (c.46)
Annuity, Princess Beatrice Act 1885 (c.24)
Annuity, Princess Helena Act 1866 (c.7)
Annuity, Princess Mary of Cambridge Act 1866 (c.48)
Annuity, Princess Royal Act 1857 (c.2)
Annuity (Sir H. Brand) Act 1884 (c.1)
Annuity Tax in Edinburgh and Montrose Act 1860 (c.50)
Annuity Tax in Edinburgh and Montrose, etc. Act 1870 (c.87)
Annuity to Admiral Duckworth Act 1806 (c.40)
Annuity to Admiral Saumanez Act 1803 (c.37)
Annuity to Brook Watson, Esq. Act 1786 (c.93)
Annuity to Brook Watson, Esq. Act 1788 (c.43)
Annuity to Dr. Willis Act 1790 (c.44)
Annuity to Duchess of Brunswick Wolfenbuttel Act 1808 (c.59)
Annuity to Duke and Duchess of Edinburgh Act 1873 (c.80)
Annuity to Duke of Atholl, etc. Act 1805 (c.123)
Annuity to Duke of Brunswick Act 1810 (c.37)
Annuity to Duke of Clarence Act 1791 (c.34)
Annuity to Duke of Connaught Act 1871 (c.64)
Annuity to Duke of Gloucester Act 1785 (c.53)
Annuity to Duke of St. Albans Act 1788 (c.41)
Annuity to Duke of Wellington, etc. Act 1810 (c.8)
Annuity to Duke of Wellington, etc. Act 1812 (c.37)
Annuity to Family of Lord Kilwarden Act 1804 (c.76)
Annuity to Family of Sir G. Carlton Act 1788 (c.42)
Annuity to Lady Elgin Act 1864 (c.31)
Annuity to Lady Maria Carlton Act 1786 (c.88)
Annuity to Lady Nelson Act 1806 (c.4)
Annuity to Lord Beresford, etc. Act 1814 (c.162)
Annuity to Lord Camperdown Act 1797 (c.22)
Annuity to Lord Collingwood, etc. Act 1806 (c.13)
Annuity to Lord Combermere, etc. Act 1814 (c.163)
Annuity to Lord Hill Act 1814 (c.165)
Annuity to Lord Hutchinson, etc. Act 1802 (c.113)
Annuity to Lord Keane, etc. Act 1841 (c.1)
Annuity to Lord Lynedoch Act 1814 (c.166)
Annuity to Lord Nelson, etc. Act 1798 (c.1)
Annuity to Lord Rodney Act 1783 (c.86)
Annuity to Lord Rodney Act 1806 (c.147)
Annuity to Lord St. Vincent Act 1797 (c.21)
Annuity to Lord St. Vincent Act 1806 (c.50)
Annuity to Lord Walsingham Act 1815 (c.18)
Annuity to Major-Gen. Sir J. Stuart Act 1807 (c.4)
Annuity to Prince Leopold Act 1874 (c.65)
Annuity to Prince of Wales, etc. Act 1803 (c.26)
Annuity to Princess Alice Act 1861 (c.15)
Annuity to Princess Louise Act 1871 (c.1)
Annuity to Princess of Wales Act 1814 (c.160)
Annuity to Right Hon. Charles Shaw Lefevre Act 1857 (c.9)
Annuity to Sir G.A. Elliott Act 1783 (c.85)
Annuity to Sir J. Marriott Act (c.58)
Annuity to Sir J. Skynner Act 1787 (c.12)
Annuity to Sir R. Strachan Act 1806 (c.5)
Annuity to Sir Sidney Smith Act 1801 (c.5)
Annuity to Sir W.F. Williams Act 1856 (c.30)
Annuity to Viscount Lake, etc. Act 1808 (c.13)
Anstruther Easter Beer Duties Act 1748 (c.10)
Anstruther Easter Beer Duties Act 1775 (c.48)

Anstruther Union Harbour Act 1860 (c.39)
Antarctic Act 1994 (c.15)
Antarctic Minerals Act 1989 (c.21)
Antarctic Treaty Act 1967 (c.65)
Anthrax Prevention Act 1919 (c.23)
Antigua and Barbuda Act 1859 (c.13)
Anwick: Inclosure Act 1791 (c.93)
"Anzac" (Restriction on Trade Use of Word) Act 1916 (c.51)
Apothecaries Act 1702 (c.5)
Apothecaries Act 1815 (c.194)
Apothecaries Act Amendment Act 1874 (c.34)
Appeal (Forma Pauperis) Act 1893 (c.22)
Appeal in Revenue Cases (Ireland) Act 1812 (c.78)
Appeals on Civil Bills, Dublin Act 1848 (c.34)
Appellate Jurisdiction Act 1876 (c.59)
Appellate Jurisdiction Act 1887 (c.70)
Appellate Jurisdiction Act 1908 (c.51)
Appellate Jurisdiction Act 1913 (c.21)
Appellate Jurisdiction Act 1929 (c.8)
Appellate Jurisdiction Act 1947 (c.11)
Application of Bounties on Linen, etc. Act 1812 (c.96)
Application of Highway Rates to Turnpikes Act 1841 (c.59)
Appointment Act 1834 (c.22)
Appointment of a Judge at Bombay Act 1864 (c.16)
Appointment of Judges in Vacation Act 1799 (c.113)
Appointment of Revising Barristers Act 1872 (c.84)
Appointment of Superintending Magistrates, etc. Act 1814 (c.131)
Appointment of Vice-Chancellor Act 1851 (c.4)
Appointments in Cathedral Churches Act 1839 (c.14)
Apportionment Act 1820 (c.108)
Apportionment Act 1834 (c.22)
Apportionment Act 1870 (c.35)
Appraisers Licences Act 1806 (c.43)
Apprehension of Certain Offenders Act 1853 (c.118)
Apprehension of Endorsed Warrants Act 1750 (c.55)
Apprehension of Housebreakers Act 1706 (c.31)
Apprehension of Offenders Act 1804 (c.92)
Apprehension of Offenders Act 1814 (c.186)
Apprehension of Offenders Act 1843 (c.34)
Apprentices Act 1814 (c.96)
Apprentices (Settlement) Act 1757 (c.11)
Apprenticeship Indentures Act 1801 (c.22)
Appropriation Act 1775 (c.12)
Appropriation Act 1775 (c.42)
Appropriation Act 1776 (c.47)
Appropriation Act 1776 (c.49)
Appropriation Act 1778 (c.54)
Appropriation Act 1779 (c.71)
Appropriation Act 1780 (c.62)
Appropriation Act 1781 (c.57)
Appropriation Act 1782 (c.67)
Appropriation Act 1783 (c.78)
Appropriation Act 1784 (c.44)
Appropriation Act 1786 (c.61)
Appropriation Act 1787 (c.33)
Appropriation Act 1788 (c.26)
Appropriation Act 1789 (c.61)
Appropriation Act 1790 (c.32)
Appropriation Act 1791 (c.41)
Appropriation Act 1792 (c.35)
Appropriation Act 1793 (c.72)
Appropriation Act 1794 (c.49)
Appropriation Act 1795 (c.120)
Appropriation Act 1796 (c.126)
Appropriation Act 1797 (c.144)
Appropriation Act 1798 (c.90)
Appropriation Act 1799 (c.114)
Appropriation Act 1800 (c.14)
Appropriation Act 1802 (c.120)
Appropriation Act 1803 (c.162)
Appropriation Act 1804 (c.110)
Appropriation Act 1805 (c.129)
Appropriation Act 1806 (c.149)
Appropriation Act 1807 (c.76)
Appropriation Act 1808 (c.148)
Appropriation Act 1809 (c.128)
Appropriation Act 1810 (c.115)
Appropriation Act 1811 (c.117)
Appropriation Act 1812 (c.154)
Appropriation Act 1813 (c.136)
Appropriation Act 1814 (c.167)
Appropriation Act 1815 (c.187)
Appropriation Act 1835 (c.80)
Appropriation Act 1836 (c.98)
Appropriation Act 1837 (c.79)
Appropriation Act 1838 (c.111)
Appropriation Act 1839 (c.89)
Appropriation Act 1840 (c.112)
Appropriation Act 1841 (c.11)
Appropriation Act 1841 (c.53)
Appropriation Act 1842 (c.121)
Appropriation Act 1843 (c.99)
Appropriation Act 1844 (c.104)
Appropriation Act 1845 (c.130)
Appropriation Act 1846 (c.116)
Appropriation Act 1848 (c.126)
Appropriation Act 1849 (c.98)
Appropriation Act 1850 (c.107)
Appropriation Act 1851 (c.101)
Appropriation Act 1852 (c.82)
Appropriation Act 1853 (c.110)
Appropriation Act 1854 (c.121)
Appropriation Act 1855 (c.129)
Appropriation Act 1856 (c.105)
Appropriation Act 1857 (c.20)
Appropriation Act 1857 (c.69)
Appropriation Act 1858 (c.107)
Appropriation Act 1859 (c.23)
Appropriation Act 1859 (c.55)
Appropriation Act 1860 (c.131)
Appropriation Act 1861 (c.103)
Appropriation Act 1862 (c.71)

Appropriation Act 1863 (c.99)
Appropriation Act 1865 (c.123)
Appropriation Act 1866 (c.91)
Appropriation Act 1867 (c.120)
Appropriation Act 1868 (c.85)
Appropriation Act 1869 (c.93)
Appropriation Act 1870 (c.96)
Appropriation Act 1871 (c.89)
Appropriation Act 1872 (c.87)
Appropriation Act 1873 (c.79)
Appropriation Act 1874 (c.56)
Appropriation Act 1875 (c.78)
Appropriation Act 1876 (c.60)
Appropriation Act 1877 (c.61)
Appropriation Act 1878 (c.65)
Appropriation Act 1879 (c.51)
Appropriation Act 1880 (c.13)
Appropriation Act 1881 (c.56)
Appropriation Act 1882 (c.71)
Appropriation Act 1883 (c.50)
Appropriation Act 1884 (c.73)
Appropriation Act 1885 (c.64)
Appropriation Act 1886 (c.26)
Appropriation Act 1887 (c.50)
Appropriation Act 1888 (c.61)
Appropriation Act 1889 (c.70)
Appropriation Act 1890 (c.72)
Appropriation Act 1891 (c.55)
Appropriation Act 1892 (c.33)
Appropriation Act 1893 (c.60)
Appropriation Act 1894 (c.59)
Appropriation Act 1895 (c.6)
Appropriation Act 1895 (c.31)
Appropriation Act 1896 (c.46)
Appropriation Act 1897 (c.67)
Appropriation Act 1898 (c.61)
Appropriation Act 1899 (c.1)
Appropriation Act 1899 (c.49)
Appropriation Act 1900 (c.2)
Appropriation Act 1900 (c.57)
Appropriation Act 1901 (c.21)
Appropriation Act 1902 (c.27)
Appropriation Act 1903 (c.32)
Appropriation Act 1904 (c.17)
Appropriation Act 1905 (c.17)
Appropriation Act 1906 (c.26)
Appropriation Act 1907 (c.20)
Appropriation Act 1908 (c.30)
Appropriation Act 1909 (c.5)
Appropriation Act 1910 (c.14)
Appropriation Act 1911 (c.15)
Appropriation Act 1912 (c.7)
Appropriation Act 1913 (c.27)
Appropriation Act 1913 (c.35)
Appropriation Act 1914 (c.24)
Appropriation Act 1915 (c.77)
Appropriation Act 1916 (c.71)
Appropriation Act 1917 (c.52)
Appropriation Act 1918 (c.56)
Appropriation Act 1919 (c.88)
Appropriation Act 1921 (c.46)
Appropriation Act 1922 (c.3)
Appropriation Act 1922 (c.32)
Appropriation Act 1923 (c.35)
Appropriation Act 1924 (c.31)
Appropriation Act 1925 (c.57)
Appropriation Act 1926 (c.23)
Appropriation Act 1927 (c.11)
Appropriation Act 1928 (c.18)
Appropriation Act 1929 (c.22)
Appropriation Act 1930 (c.27)
Appropriation Act 1931 (c.29)
Appropriation Act 1931 (c.50)
Appropriation Act 1933 (c.34)
Appropriation Act 1934 (c.44)
Appropriation Act 1935 (c.28)
Appropriation Act 1936 (c.37)
Appropriation Act 1937 (c.55)
Appropriation Act 1938 (c.47)
Appropriation Act 1939 (c.46)
Appropriation Act 1939 (c.52)
Appropriation Act 1941 (c.38)
Appropriation Act 1942 (c.27)
Appropriation Act 1943 (c.31)
Appropriation Act 1944 (c.25)
Appropriation Act 1944 (c.30)
Appropriation Act 1946 (c.65)
Appropriation Act 1947 (c.52)
Appropriation Act 1948 (c.50)
Appropriation Act 1949 (c.48)
Appropriation Act 1950 (c.16)
Appropriation Act 1951 (c.44)
Appropriation Act 1952 (c.38)
Appropriation Act 1953 (c.35)
Appropriation Act 1954 (c.45)
Appropriation Act 1955 (c.16)
Appropriation Act 1956 (c.55)
Appropriation Act 1957 (c.63)
Appropriation Act 1959 (c.59)
Appropriation Act 1960 (c.45)
Appropriation Act 1961 (c.59)
Appropriation Act 1962 (c.45)
Appropriation Act 1963 (c.26)
Appropriation Act 1964 (c.62)
Appropriation Act 1965 (c.23)
Appropriation Act 1966 (c.3)
Appropriation Act 1967 (c.59)
Appropriation Act 1968 (c.43)
Appropriation Act 1969 (c.31)
Appropriation Act 1970 (c.25)
Appropriation Act 1971 (c.67)
Appropriation Act 1972 (c.56)
Appropriation Act 1973 (c.40)
Appropriation Act 1974 (c.2)
Appropriation Act 1975 (c.44)
Appropriation Act 1976 (c.43)
Appropriation Act 1977 (c.35)
Appropriation Act 1978 (c.57)
Appropriation Act 1979 (c.24)
Appropriation Act 1980 (c.54)
Appropriation Act 1981 (c.51)
Appropriation Act 1982 (c.40)
Appropriation Act 1983 (c.27)
Appropriation Act 1983 (c.48)
Appropriation Act 1984 (c.44)
Appropriation Act 1985 (c.55)

Appropriation Act 1986 (c.42)
Appropriation Act 1987 (c.17)
Appropriation Act 1988 (c.38)
Appropriation Act 1989 (c.25)
Appropriation Act 1990 (c.28)
Appropriation Act 1991 (c.32)
Appropriation Act 1992 (c.22)
Appropriation Act 1993 (c.33)
Appropriation Act 1994 (c.24)
Appropriation Act 1995 (c.19)
Appropriation Act 1996 (c.45)
Appropriation Acts Amendment Act 1842 (c.1)
Appropriation, etc. Act 1785 (c.60)
Appropriation, etc. Act 1801 (c.84)
Appropriation (No. 2) Act 1902 (c.30)
Appropriation (No. 2) Act 1910 (c.38)
Appropriation (No. 2) Act 1915 (c.86)
Appropriation (No. 2) Act 1921 (c.63)
Appropriation (No. 2) Act 1925 (c.78)
Appropriation (No. 2) Act 1926 (c.33)
Appropriation (No. 2) Act 1927 (c.25)
Appropriation (No. 2) Act 1931 (c.50)
Appropriation (No. 2) Act 1939 (c.63)
Appropriation (No. 2) Act 1941 (c.43)
Appropriation (No. 2) Act 1942 (c.33)
Appropriation (No. 2) Act 1943 (c.41)
Appropriation (No. 2) Act 1944 (c.37)
Appropriation (No. 2) Act 1955 (c.3)
Appropriation (No. 2) Act 1966 (c.26)
Appropriation (No. 2) Act 1970 (c.48)
Appropriation (No. 2) Act 1974 (c.31)
Appropriation (No. 2) Act 1979 (c.51)
Appropriation (No. 2) Act 1983 (c.48)
Appropriation (No. 2) Act 1987 (c.50)
Appropriation (No. 2) Act 1992 (c.47)
Appropriation (No. 3) Act 1942 (c.34)
Appropriation of Certain Duties Act 1799 (c.11)
Appropriation of Revenue Act 1700 (c.12)
Appropriation (Session 2) Act 1880 (c.40)
Appropriation (Session 2) Act 1886 (c.1)
Arbitration Act 1889 (c.49)
Arbitration Act 1934 (c.14)
Arbitration Act 1950 (c.27)
Arbitration Act 1975 (c.3)
Arbitration Act 1979 (c.42)
Arbitration Act 1996 (c.23)
Arbitration Clauses (Protocol) Act 1924 (c.39)
Arbitration (Foreign Awards) Act 1930 (c.15)
Arbitration (International Investment Disputes) Act 1966 (c.41)
Arbitration (Masters and Workmen) Act 1872 (c.46)
Arbitration (Scotland) Act 1894 (c.13)
Arbitrations Act 1844 (c.93)
Archbishops' etc., House of Residence Act 1839 (c.18)
Archbishops' Palace, Dublin Act 1804 (c.63)
Archdeaconries and Rural Deaneries Act 1874 (c.63)
Archdeaconry of Cornwall Act 1897 (c.9)
Archdeaconry of London (Additional Endowment) Act 1897 (c.45)
Archdeaconry of Rochester Act 1861 (c.131)
Architects Registration Act 1938 (c.54)
Architects (Registration) Act 1931 (c.33)
Architects (Registration) Act 1934 (c.38)
Argentine Treaty Act 1842 (c.40)
Argyll Roads and Bridges Act 1775 (c.63)
Argyllshire Valuation Act 1748 (c.29)
Architects Registration (Amendment) Act 1969 (c.42)
Argyllshire Valuation Act 1748 (c.29)
Arklow Harbour Act 1882 (c.13)
Armed Forces Act 1966 (c.45)
Armed Forces Act 1971 (c.33)
Armed Forces Act 1976 (c.52)
Armed Forces Act 1981 (c.55)
Armed Forces Act 1986 (c.21)
Armed Forces Act 1991 (c.62)
Armed Forces Act 1996 (c.46)
Armed Forces (Conditions of Service) Act 1939 (c.68)
Armed Forces (Housing Loans) Act 1949 (c.77)
Armed Forces (Housing Loans) Act 1953 (c.3)
Armed Forces (Housing Loans) Act 1958 (c.1)
Armed Forces (Housing Loans) Act 1965 (c.9)
Armorial Bearings Act 1798 (c.53)
Armorial Bearings Act 1799 (c.8)
Arms and Gunpowder (Ireland) Act 1807 (c.8)
Arms and Gunpowder (Ireland) Act 1836 (c.39)
Arms and Gunpowder (Ireland) Act 1838 (c.71)
Arms Control and Disarmament (Inspections) Act 1991 (c.41)
Arms Control and Disarmament (Privileges and Immunities) Act 1988 (c.2)
Arms, etc. (Ireland) Act 1843 (c.74)
Arms (Ireland) Act 1810 (c.109)
Arms (Ireland) Act 1813 (c.78)
Army Act 1774 (c.54)
Army Act 1811 (c.106)
Army Act 1812 (c.27)
Army Act 1812 (c.120)
Army Act 1881 (c.58)
Army Act 1955 (c.18)
Army Act 1992 (c.39)
Army (Amendment) Act 1915 (c.26)
Army (Amendment) No. 2 Act 1915 (c.58)
Army and Air Force Act 1961 (c.52)
Army and Air Force (Annual) Act 1921 (c.9)
Army and Air Force (Annual) Act 1922 (c.6)
Army and Air Force (Annual) Act 1923 (c.3)
Army and Air Force (Annual) Act 1924 (c.5)
Army and Air Force (Annual) Act 1925 (c.25)
Army and Air Force (Annual) Act 1926 (c.6)
Army and Air Force (Annual) Act 1927 (c.7)
Army and Air Force (Annual) Act 1928 (c.7)
Army and Air Force (Annual) Act 1929 (c.20)
Army and Air Force (Annual) Act 1930 (c.22)
Army and Air Force (Annual) Act 1931 (c.14)

Army and Air Force (Annual) Act 1932 (c.22)
Army and Air Force (Annual) Act 1933 (c.11)
Army and Air Force (Annual) Act 1934 (c.11)
Army and Air Force (Annual) Act 1935 (c.17)
Army and Air Force (Annual) Act 1936 (c.14)
Army and Air Force (Annual) Act 1937 (c.26)
Army and Air Force (Annual) Act 1938 (c.20)
Army and Air Force (Annual) Act 1939 (c.17)
Army and Air Force (Annual) Act 1940 (c.18)
Army and Air Force (Annual) Act 1941 (c.17)
Army and Air Force (Annual) Act 1942 (c.15)
Army and Air Force (Annual) Act 1943 (c.15)
Army and Air Force (Annual) Act 1944 (c.18)
Army and Air Force (Annual) Act 1945 (c.22)
Army and Air Force (Annual) Act 1946 (c.47)
Army and Air Force (Annual) Act 1947 (c.25)
Army and Air Force (Annual) Act 1948 (c.28)
Army and Air Force (Annual) Act 1949 (c.28)
Army and Air Force (Annual) Act 1950 (c.3)
Army and Air Force (Annual) Act 1951 (c.24)
Army and Air Force (Annual) Act 1952 (c.24)
Army and Air Force (Annual) Act 1953 (c.31)
Army and Air Force (Annual) Act 1954 (c.35)
Army and Air Force (Women's Service) Act 1948 (c.21)
Army and Navy Act 1797 (c.6)
Army and Navy Act 1798 (c.4)
Army and Navy Act 1800 (c.16)
Army and Navy Act 1800 (c.29)
Army and Navy Act 1800 (c.100)
Army and Navy Act 1807 (c.15)
Army and Navy Audit Act 1889 (c.31)
Army (Annual) Act 1882 (c.7)
Army (Annual) Act 1883 (c.6)
Army (Annual) Act 1884 (c.8)
Army (Annual) Act 1885 (c.8)
Army (Annual) Act 1886 (c.8)
Army (Annual) Act 1887 (c.2)
Army (Annual) Act 1888 (c.4)
Army (Annual) Act 1889 (c.3)
Army (Annual) Act 1890 (c.4)
Army (Annual) Act 1891 (c.5)
Army (Annual) Act 1892 (c.2)
Army (Annual) Act 1893 (c.4)
Army (Annual) Act 1894 (c.3)
Army (Annual) Act 1895 (c.7)
Army (Annual) Act 1896 (c.2)
Army (Annual) Act 1897 (c.3)
Army (Annual) Act 1898 (c.1)
Army (Annual) Act 1899 (c.3)
Army (Annual) Act 1900 (c.5)
Army (Annual) Act 1901 (c.2)
Army (Annual) Act 1902 (c.2)
Army (Annual) Act 1903 (c.4)
Army (Annual) Act 1904 (c.5)
Army (Annual) Act 1905 (c.2)
Army (Annual) Act 1906 (c.2)
Army (Annual) Act 1907 (c.2)
Army (Annual) Act 1908 (c.2)
Army (Annual) Act 1909 (c.3)
Army (Annual) Act 1910 (c.6)
Army (Annual) Act 1911 (c.3)
Army (Annual) Act 1912 (c.5)
Army (Annual) Act 1913 (c.2)
Army (Annual) Act 1914 (c.2)
Army (Annual) Act 1915 (c.25)
Army (Annual) Act 1916 (c.5)
Army (Annual) Act (1916) Amendment 1917 (c.10)
Army (Annual) Act 1917 (c.9)
Army (Annual) Act 1918 (c.6)
Army (Annual) Act 1919 (c.11)
Army Chaplains Act 1868 (c.83)
Army (Conditions of Enlistment) Act 1957 (c.50)
Army (Courts of Inquiry) Act 1916 (c.33)
Army Discipline and Regulation Act 1879 (c.33)
Army Discipline and Regulation (Annual) Act 1880 (c.9)
Army Discipline and Regulation (Annual) Act 1881 (c.9)
Army Enlistment Act 1849 (c.73)
Army Enlistment Act 1855 (c.4)
Army Enlistment Act 1858 (c.55)
Army Enlistment Act 1867 (c.34)
Army in Ireland Act 1768 (c.13)
Army Pensions Act 1830 (c.41)
Army Pensions Act 1914 (c.83)
Army Prize Money Act 1814 (c.86)
Army Prize Money Act 1848 (c.103)
Army Prize (Shares of Deceased) Act 1864 (c.36)
Army Reserve Act 1950 (c.32)
Army Reserve Act 1962 (c.10)
Army Reserve Act 1969 (c.23)
Army Schools Act 1891 (c.16)
Army (Supply of Food, Forage and Stores) Act 1914 (c.26)
Army (Suspension of Sentences) Act 1915 (c.23)
Army (Suspension of Sentences) Amendment Act 1916 (c.103)
Army (Transfer) Act 1915 (c.43)
Arrangements Between Debtors and Creditors Act 1844 (c.70)
Arranmore Polling District Act 1878 (c.75)
Arrears of Crown, etc., Rents (Ireland) Act 1816 (c.71)
Arrears of Crown Rents (Ireland) Act 1811 (c.91)
Arrears of Rent (Ireland) Act 1882 (c.47)
Arrest for Debtors Act 1851 (c.52)
Arrest in Personal Actions (Ireland) Act 1841 (c.17)
Arsenic Act 1851 (c.13)
Art Act 1866 (c.16)
Art Unions Act 1846 (c.48)
Art Unions Indemnity Act 1844 (c.109)
Art Unions Indemnity Act 1845 (c.57)
Arthur Jenkins Indemnity Act 1941 (c.1)
Articles of Commerce (Returns, &c.) Act 1914 (c.65)
Artificers Act 1718 (c.27)
Artificers etc. Act 1749 (c.13)
Artificial Cream Act 1929 (c.32)

Artillery and Rifle Ranges Act 1885 (c.36)
Artillery Corps, etc. Act 1795 (c.83)
Artizans and Labourers Dwellings Act 1868 (c.130)
Artizans and Labourers Dwellings Act (1868) Amendment 1879 (c.64)
Artizans' and Labourers' Dwellings Improvement Act 1875 (c.36)
Artizans and Labourers Dwellings Improvement Act 1879 (c.63)
Artizans and Labourers Dwellings Improvement (Scotland) Act 1875 (c.49)
Artizans and Labourers Dwellings Improvement (Scotland) Act 1880 (c.2)
Artizans' Dwellings Act (1868) Amendment Act (1879) Amendment 1880 (c.8)
Artizans Dwellings Act 1882 (c.54)
Arun, Sussex: Navigation Act 1785 (c.100)
Arundel: Improvement Act 1785 (c.90)
Ascertaining of Strength of Spirits Act 1791 (c.44)
Ashburton Roads Act 1776 (c.79)
Assaulting a Privy Counsellor Act 1710 (c.21)
Assaults (Ireland) Act 1814 (c.181)
Assaults (Ireland) Act 1815 (c.88)
Assaults (Ireland) Act 1839 (c.77)
Assaults (Ireland) Act 1844 (c.23)
Assaults (Ireland) Act 1849 (c.38)
Assaults with Intent to Rob Act 1733 (c.21)
Assay of Imported Watch-Cases (Existing Stocks Exemption) Act 1907 (c.8)
Assay of Plate Act 1702 (c.3)
Assessed Rates Act 1879 (c.10)
Assessed Taxes Act 1791 (c.5)
Assessed Taxes Act 1805 (c.13)
Assessed Taxes Act 1805 (c.105)
Assessed Taxes Act 1806 (c.78)
Assessed Taxes Act 1810 (c.104)
Assessed Taxes Act 1811 (c.72)
Assessed Taxes Act 1812 (c.93)
Assessed Taxes Act 1812 (c.147)
Assessed Taxes Act 1816 (c.66)
Assessed Taxes Act 1837 (c.61)
Assessed Taxes Act 1840 (c.38)
Assessed Taxes Act 1841 (c.26)
Assessed Taxes Act 1845 (c.36)
Assessed Taxes Act 1851 (c.33)
Assessed Taxes Act 1854 (c.1)
Assessed Taxes Composition Act 1850 (c.96)
Assessed Taxes and Income Tax Act 1846 (c.56)
Assessed Taxes, etc. Act 1839 (c.35)
Assessed Taxes, etc. (Ireland) Act 1807 (c.11)
Assessed Taxes, etc. (Ireland) Act 1816 (c.57)
Assessed Taxes (Ireland) Act 1807 (c.21)
Assessed Taxes (Ireland) Act 1808 (c.42)
Assessed Taxes (Ireland) Act 1815 (c.61)
Assessed Taxes (Ireland) Act 1815 (c.67)
Assessed Taxes (Ireland) Act 1815 (c.140)
Assessed Taxes, Property Tax and Duty on Pensions and Offices of Profit Act 1844 (c.46)
Assessionable Manors Award Act 1848 (c.83)
Assessment of Taxes Act 1808 (c.141)
Assessments in Edinburgh Act 1861 (c.27)
Assessor of Public Undertakings (Scotland) Act 1934 (c.22)
Assise and Making of Bread, London Act 1797 (c.98)
Assise of Bread Act 1798 (c.62)
Assise of Fuel Act 1710 (c.20)
Assise of Fuel Act 1711 (c.5)
Assistant Postmaster-General Act 1909 (c.14)
Assizes Act 1839 (c.72)
Assizes and Quarter Sessions Act 1908 (c.41)
Assizes for Cornwall Act 1715 (c.45)
Assizes (Ireland) Act 1825 (c.51)
Assizes (Ireland) Act 1835 (c.26)
Assizes (Ireland) Act 1850 (c.85)
Assizes (Ireland) Act 1850 (c.88)
Assizes Relief Act 1889 (c.12)
Association of County Councils (Scotland) Act 1946 (c.77)
Assurance Companies Act 1909 (c.49)
Assurance Companies Act 1946 (c.28)
Assurance Companies (Winding Up) Act 1933 (c.9)
Assurance Companies (Winding Up) Act 1935 (c.45)
Assurance on French Ships Act 1747 (c.4)
Asthall to Buckland Road Act 1777 (c.105)
Asylum and Immigration Act 1996 (c.49)
Asylum and Immigration Appeals Act 1993 (c.23)
Asylums and Certified Institutions (Officers Pensions) Act 1918 (c.33)
Asylums' Officers Superannuation Act 1909 (c.48)
Atomic Energy Act 1946 (c.80)
Atomic Energy Act 1989 (c.7)
Atomic Energy Authority Act 1954 (c.32)
Atomic Energy Authority Act 1959 (c.5)
Atomic Energy Authority Act 1971 (c.11)
Atomic Energy Authority Act 1986 (c.3)
Atomic Energy Authority Act 1995 (c.37)
Atomic Energy Authority (Special Constables) Act 1976 (c.23)
Atomic Energy Authority (Weapons Group) Act 1973 (c.4)
Atomic Energy (Miscellaneous Provisions) Act 1981 (c.48)
Atomic Weapons Establishment Act 1991 (c.46)
Attachment of Earnings Act 1971 (c.32)
Attachment of Goods (Ireland) Act 1850 (c.73)
Attainder of Bishop of Rochester Act 1722 (c.17)

Attainder of David Ogilvy: Disabilities Removed on Pardon Act 1783 (c.34)
Attainder of Duke of Ormonde Act 1714 (c.17)
Attainder of Earl of Kellie and Others Act 1745 (c.26)
Attainder of Earl of Mar and Others Act 1715 (c.32)
Attainder of Earl of Marischal and Others Act 1715 (c.42)
Attainder of George Kelley Act 1722 (c.16)
Attainder of John Plunket Act 1722 (c.15)
Attainder of Thomas Forster and Others Act 1715 (c.53)
Attainder of Viscount Bolingbroke Act 1714 (c.16)
Attempted Rape Act 1948 (c.19)
Attendance of Witnesses Act 1854 (c.34)
Attorneys Act 1809 (c.28)
Attorneys and Solicitors Act 1728 (c.23)
Attorneys and Solicitors Act 1732 (c.27)
Attorneys and Solicitors Act (1860) Amendment 1872 (c.81)
Attorneys and Solicitors Act 1870 (c.28)
Attorneys and Solicitors Act 1874 (c.68)
Attorneys and Solicitors (Ireland) Act 1866 (c.84)
Auction Duties Act 1815 (c.142)
Auction Duties, etc. Act 1779 (c.56)
Auction Duties (Ireland) Act 1807 (c.17)
Auction Duties (Ireland) Act 1814 (c.82)
Auction Duty Act 1792 (c.41)
Auction Duty Act 1807 (c.65)
Auction Duty Act 1812 (c.53)
Auction Duty, etc. Act 1790 (c.26)
Auctioneers Act 1845 (c.15)
Auctioneers' Licences Act 1776 (c.50)
Auctions (Bidding Agreements) Act 1927 (c.12)
Auctions (Bidding Agreements) Act 1969 (c.56)
Auctions Duties (Ireland) Act 1809 (c.100)
Audit (Local Authorities) Act 1927 (c.31)
Audit (Local Authorities etc.) Act 1922 (c.14)
Audit (Miscellaneous Provisions) Act 1996 (c.10)
Audit of Accounts Act 1813 (c.100)
Audit of Accounts, etc. Act 1813 (c.150)
Audit of Military Accounts (Ireland) Act 1812 (c.51)
Audit of Public Accounts Act 1780 (c.40)
Audit of Public Accounts Act 1780 (c.45)
Audit of Public Accounts Act 1780 (c.54)
Audit of Public Accounts Act 1782 (c.50)
Audit of Public Accounts Act 1784 (c.13)
Audit of Public Accounts Act 1785 (c.52)
Audit of Public Accounts Act 1785 (c.68)
Audit of Public Accounts Act 1786 (c.67)
Audit of Public Accounts Act 1794 (c.59)
Audit of Public Accounts Act 1805 (c.55)
Audit of Public Accounts Act 1806 (c.141)
Audit of Public Accounts (Ireland) Act 1812 (c.52)
Auditing of Public Accounts Act 1805 (c.91)
Auditing of Public Accounts Act 1809 (c.95)
Auditing of the Public Accounts Act 1783 (c.68)
Auditor of the Exchequer Act (1806) (c.1)
Auditors of Land Revenue Act 1799 (c.83)
Augmentation of Benefices Act 1854 (c.84)
Augmentation of 60th Regiment Act 1797 (c.13)
Augmentation of 60th Regiment Act 1799 (c.104)
Augmentation of 60th Regiment Act 1813 (c.12)
Australia Act 1986 (c.2)
Australian Colonies Act 1801 (c.44)
Australian Colonies Duties Act 1873 (c.22)
Australian Colonies Duties Act 1895 (c.3)
Australian Colonies, Waste Lands Act 1842 (c.36)
Australian Constitution (Public Record Copy) Act 1990 (c.17)
Australian Constitutions Act 1842 (c.76)
Australian Constitutions Act 1844 (c.74)
Australian Constitutions Act 1850 (c.59)
Australian Constitutions Act 1862 (c.11)
Australian Passengers Act 1861 (c.52)
Australian States Constitution Act 1907 (c.7)
Australian Waste Lands Act 1855 (c.56)
Austrian Loan Guarantee Act 1931 (c.5)
Austrian State Treaty Act 1955 (c.1)
Auxiliary Air Force and Air Force Reserve Act 1924 (c.15)
Auxiliary and Reserve Forces Act 1949 (c.96)
Auxiliary Forces Act 1953 (c.50)
Average Price of Brown Sugar Act 1809 (c.43)
Aviation and Maritime Security Act 1990 (c.31)
Aviation Security Act 1982 (c.36)
Axminster Roads Act 1754 (c.32)
Aylesbury Gaol and Shire Hall: Rate in Buckinghamshire Act 1736 (c.10)
Aylesbury to West Wycombe Road Act 1795 (c.149)
Ayre and Lamark Roads Act 1771 (c.90)
Ayr Bridge Act 1785 (c.37)
Ayr (County) Roads Act 1797 (c.162)
Ayr Harbour Act 1772 (c.22)
Ayr Harbour Act 1794 (c.99)
Ayr Roads Act 1757 (c.57)
Ayr Roads Act 1767 (c.106)
Ayr Roads Act 1774 (c.109)
Ayr Roads Act 1789 (c.79)
Ayr Roads Act 1791 (c.95)
Ayr Roads Act 1791 (c.107)
Ayr Roads Act 1792 (c.121)

Backing of Warrants (Republic of Ireland) Act 1965 (c.45)
Bacon Industry Act 1938 (c.71)
Bacon Industry (Amendment) Act 1939 (c.10)
Badgers Act 1973 (c.57)
Badgers Act 1991 (c.36)
Badgers (Further Protection) Act 1991 (c.35)
Badgers (Protection) Act 1992 (c.51)

Bagshot to Hertford Bridge Hill Road Act 1777 (c.84)
Bagshot to Winchester Road Act 1773 (c.88)
Bahama Islands (Constitution) Act 1963 (c.56)
Bahama Islands Trade Act 1812 (c.99)
Bahamas Independence Act 1973 (c.27)
Bail Act 1898 (c.7)
Bail Act 1976 (c.63)
Bail (Amendment) Act 1993 (c.26)
Bail Bonds Act 1808 (c.58)
Bail etc. (Scotland) Act 1980 (c.4)
Bail in Cases of Forgery, etc. (Scotland) Act 1835 (c.73)
Bail in Criminal Cases (Scotland) Act 1724 (c.26)
Bail in Criminal Cases (Scotland) Act 1799 (c.49)
Bail in Error Act 1845 (c.68)
Bail in Error Act 1853 (c.32)
Bail (Scotland) Act 1888 (c.36)
Bails Act 1869 (c.38)
Bakehouse Regulation Act 1863 (c.40)
Baking Industry (Hours of Work) Act 1938 (c.41)
Baking Industry (Hours of Work) Act 1954 (c.57)
Baking Trade Act 1810 (c.73)
Baking Trade, Dublin Act 1802 (c.8)
Balby to Worksop Road Act 1765 (c.67)
Balby to Worksop Road Act 1787 (c.84)
Bale and Dolgelly Roads Act 1796 (c.147)
Ballot Act 1872 (c.33)
Banbury Church Act 1790 (c.72)
Banbury Road Act 1780 (c.67)
Banbury to Lutterworth Road Act 1785 (c.128)
Bancroft's Patent Act 1785 (c.38)
Bangladesh Act 1973 (c.49)
Bank Act 1892 (c.48)
Bank Charter Act 1844 (c.32)
Bank Holiday (Ireland) Act 1903 (c.1)
Bank Holidays Act 1871 (c.17)
Bank Notes (Scotland) Act 1765 (c.49)
Bank Notes Act 1833 (c.83)
Bank Notes Act 1841 (c.50)
Bank Notes Act 1852 (c.2)
Bank Notes Act 1853 (c.2)
Bank Notes Forgery Act 1801 (c.57)
Bank Notes (Forgery) Act 1805 (c.89)
Bank Notes Forgery (Scotland) Act 1820 (c.92)
Bank Notes (Ireland) Act 1864 (c.78)
Bank Notes (Scotland) Act 1765 (c.49)
Bank Notes (Scotland) Act 1845 (c.38)
Bank of Ayr Act 1774 (c.21)
Bank of Bombay Failure Commissioners Act 1868 (c.63)
Bank of England Act 1694 (c.20)
Bank of England Act 1696 (c.20)
Bank of England Act 1707 (c.59)
Bank of England Act 1708 (c.30)
Bank of England Act 1709 (c.1)
Bank of England Act 1710 (c.7)
Bank of England Act 1716 (c.8)
Bank of England Act 1727 (c.8)
Bank of England Act 1728 (c.3)
Bank of England Act 1741 (c.13)
Bank of England Act 1745 (c.6)
Bank of England Act 1750 (c.4)
Bank of England Act 1784 (c.32)
Bank of England Act 1785 (c.83)
Bank of England Act 1791 (c.33)
Bank of England Act 1800 (c.28)
Bank of England Act 1833 (c.98)
Bank of England Act 1854 (c.1)
Bank of England Act 1861 (c.3)
Bank of England Act 1946 (c.27)
Bank of England (Advance) Act 1816 (c.96)
Bank of England Buildings Act 1764 (c.49)
Bank of England: Buildings Act 1766 (c.76)
Bank of England (Election of Directors) Act 1872 (c.34)
Bank of England Notes Act 1773 (c.79)
Bank of England Notes Act 1797 (c.28)
Bank of England Site Act 1793 (c.15)
Bank of England Stock Act 1796 (c.90)
Bank of Ireland Act 1808 (c.103)
Bank of Ireland Act 1860 (c.31)
Bank of Ireland Act 1865 (c.16)
Bank of Ireland Advances Act 1837 (c.59)
Bank of Ireland Advances Act 1838 (c.81)
Bank of Ireland Advances Act 1839 (c.91)
Bank of Ireland Charter Act 1872 (c.5)
Bank of Ireland, Transfer of Stocks Act 1862 (c.21)
Bank of Scotland Act 1774 (c.32)
Bank of Scotland Act 1784 (c.12)
Bank of Scotland Act 1792 (c.25)
Bank of Scotland Act 1794 (c.19)
Bank Post Bills Composition (Ireland) Act
Bank (Scotland) Act 1797 (c.40)
Bank (Scotland) Act 1797 (c.137)
Bankers' Books Evidence Act 1876 (c.48)
Bankers' Books Evidence Act 1879 (c.11)
Bankers' Composition Act 1856 (c.20)
Bankers' Composition (Scotland) Act 1853 (c.63)
Bankers' (Scotland) Act 1854 (c.73)
Bankers' Debt Act 1703 (c.9)
Bankers (Ireland) Act 1845 (c.37)
Bankers (Northern Ireland) Act 1928 (c.15)
Banking Act 1979 (c.37)
Banking Act 1987 (c.22)
Banking and Financial Dealings Act 1971 (c.80)
Banking Companies' (Shares) Act 1867 (c.29)
Banking Copartnerships Act 1864 (c.32)
Bankrupt and Insolvent Act 1857 (c.60)
Bankruptcy Act 1621 (c.18)
Bankruptcy Act 1716 (c.12)
Bankruptcy Act 1836 (c.27)
Bankruptcy Act 1839 (c.29)
Bankruptcy Act 1839 (c.86)
Bankruptcy Act 1842 (c.122)

Bankruptcy Act 1845 (c.48)
Bankruptcy Act 1852 (c.77)
Bankruptcy Act 1854 (c.119)
Bankruptcy Act 1861 (c.134)
Bankruptcy Act 1862 (c.99)
Bankruptcy Act 1869 (c.71)
Bankruptcy Act 1883 (c.52)
Bankruptcy Act 1890 (c.71)
Bankruptcy Act 1914 (c.59)
Bankruptcy (Agricultural Labourers' Wages) Act 1886 (c.28)
Bankruptcy Amendment Act 1868 (c.104)
Bankruptcy (Amendment) Act 1926 (c.7)
Bankruptcy and Cessio (Scotland) Act 1881 (c.22)
Bankruptcy and Deeds of Arrangement Act 1913 (c.34)
Bankruptcy and Real Securities (Scotland) Act 1857 (c.19)
Bankruptcy Appeals (County Courts) Act 1884 (c.9)
Bankruptcy Court Act 1853 (c.81)
Bankruptcy (Discharge and Closure) Act 1887 (c.66)
Bankruptcy Disqualification Act 1871 (c.50)
Bankruptcy, etc. Act 1847 (c.102)
Bankruptcy, etc. (Ireland) Act 1859 (c.62)
Bankruptcy Frauds and Disabilities (Scotland) Act 1884 (c.16)
Bankruptcy (Ireland) Act 1836 (c.14)
Bankruptcy (Ireland) Act 1837 (c.48)
Bankruptcy (Ireland) Act 1849 (c.107)
Bankruptcy (Ireland) Amendment Act 1872 (c.58)
Bankruptcy Law Consolidation Act 1849 (c.106)
Bankruptcy (Office Accommodation) Act 1885 (c.47)
Bankruptcy (Office Accommodation) Act 1886 (c.12)
Bankruptcy Repeal and Insolvent Court Act 1869 (c.83)
Bankruptcy (Scotland) Act 1839 (c.41)
Bankruptcy (Scotland) Act 1853 (c.53)
Bankruptcy (Scotland) Act 1856 (c.79)
Bankruptcy (Scotland) Act 1875 (c.26)
Bankruptcy (Scotland) Act 1913 (c.20)
Bankruptcy (Scotland) Act 1985 (c.66)
Bankruptcy (Scotland) Act 1993 (c.6)
Bankruptcy (Scotland) Amendment Act 1860 (c.33)
Bankrupts Act 1705 (c.4)
Bankrupts Act 1706 (c.22)
Bankrupts Act 1711 (c.25)
Bankrupts Act 1718 (c.24)
Bankrupts Act 1720 (c.19)
Bankrupts Act 1720 (c.31)
Bankrupts Act 1731 (c.30)
Bankrupts Act 1742 (c.27)
Bankrupts Act 1745 (c.32)
Bankrupts Act 1763 (c.33)
Bankrupts Act 1772 (c.47)
Bankrupts Act 1794 (c.57)
Bankrupts Act 1797 (c.124)
Bankrupts Act 1806 (c.135)
Bankrupts (England) and (Ireland) Act 1809 (c.121)
Bankrupts, etc. Act 1763 (c.36)
Bankrupts Release Act 1848 (c.86)
Banks (Scotland) Act 1797 (c.62)
Baptismal Fees Abolition Act 1872 (c.36)
Barbados Independence Act 1966 (c.37)
Barbed Wire Act 1893 (c.32)
Barking Act 1786 (c.115)
Barmouth Harbour Act 1797 (c.50)
Barnsley Canal Act 1793 (c.110)
Barnsley Canal Act 1793 (c.115)
Barnstaple Roads Act 1763 (c.35)
Barnstaple Roads Act 1783 (c.31)
Barrack Lane, Windsor Act 1867 (c.109)
Barracks Act 1890 (c.25)
Barristers Admission (Ireland) Act 1885 (c.20)
Barristers Admission, Stamp Duty Act 1874 (c.19)
Barristers (Qualifications for Office) Act 1961 (c.44)
Barthomley Church, Chester Act 1789 (c.11)
Basingstoke Canal Act 1778 (c.75)
Basingstoke Canal Act 1793 (c.16)
Basingstoke Roads Act 1797 (c.169)
Basingstoke to Winchester Road Act 1795 (c.162)
Basses Lights Act 1869 (c.77)
Basses Lights Act 1872 (c.55)
Bastard Children Act 1732 (c.31)
Bastard Children Act 1839 (c.85)
Bastards Act 1810 (c.51)
Bastards (Scotland) Act 1836 (c.22)
Bastardy Act 1809 (c.68)
Bastardy Act 1845 (c.10)
Bastardy Act 1923 (c.23)
Bastardy (Ireland) Act 1863 (c.21)
Bastardy Laws Act Amendment 1872 (c.65)
Bastardy Laws Amendment Act 1873 (c.9)
Bastardy Orders Act 1880 (c.32)
Bastardy (Witness Process) Act 1929 (c.38)
Bath City Prison Act 1871 (c.46)
Bath Highway, Streets, etc. Act 1707 (c.42)
Bath Highway, Streets, etc. Act 1720 (c.19)
Bath Hospital Act 1738 (c.31)
Bath Hospital Act 1779 (c.23)
Bath: Improvement Act 1766 (c.70)
Bath: Improvement Act 1789 (c.73)
Bath Roads Act 1757 (c.67)
Bath Roads Act 1758 (c.51)
Bath Roads Act 1760 (c.31)
Bath Roads Act 1793 (c.144)
Bath Roads, Streets, etc. Act 1738 (c.20)
Bath (Streets, Buildings, Watch etc.) 1757 (c.65)
Baths and Washhouses Act 1846 (c.74)
Baths and Washhouses Act 1847 (c.61)
Baths and Washhouses Act 1878 (c.14)
Baths and Washhouses Act 1882 (c.30)
Baths and Washhouses Act 1896 (c.59)

Baths and Washhouses Act 1899 (c.29)
Baths and Washhouses (Ireland) Act 1846 (c.87)
Bathwick Roads and Bridges, etc. Act 1769 (c.95)
Battersea Bridge Act 1766 (c.66)
Battersea Bridge and Embankment, etc. Act 1846 (c.39)
Battersea Parish Church Act 1774 (c.95)
Battersea Park Act 1846 (c.38)
Battersea Park Act 1851 (c.77)
Battersea Park Act 1853 (c.47)
Battle-axe Guards (Ireland) Act 1813 (c.54)
Bawtry to Markham Road Act 1793 (c.136)
Bawtry by Selby Road Act 1793 (c.166)
Beaconsfield and Redhill Road Act 1750 (c.32)
Beaconsfield and Stokenchurch Road Act 1759 (c.37)
Beaconsfield to Stokenchurch Road Act 1775 (c.70)
Beaconsfield to Stokenchurch Road Act 1794 (c.142)
Beccles: Improvement Act 1796 (c.51)
Bedford and Buckingham Highways Act 1708 (c.25)
Bedford and Buckingham Highways Act 1709 (c.25)
Bedford and Buckingham Roads Act 1727 (c.10)
Bedford and Buckingham Roads Act 1754 (c.21)
Bedford and Buckingham Roads Act 1754 (c.34)
Bedford and Buckingham Roads Act 1780 (c.68)
Bedford and Buckingham Roads Act 1790 (c.114)
Bedford and Hertford Roads Act 1742 (c.42)
Bedford and Hertford Roads Act 1775 (c.72)
Bedford and Hertford Roads Act 1786 (c.130)
Bedford and Hertford Roads Act 1795 (c.163)
Bedford and Hunts. Roads Act 1770 (c.83)
Bedford and Hunts. Roads Act 1791 (c.96)
Bedford and Northants Roads Act 1754 (c.33)
Bedford and Woburn Road Act 1796 (c.151)
Bedford Level Act 1754 (c.19)
Bedford Level Act 1756 (c.9)
Bedford Level Act 1772 (c.9)
Bedford Level Act 1780 (c.25)
Bedford Level Act 1783 (c.25)
Bedford Level Act 1789 (c.22)
Bedford Level Act 1796 (c.73)
Bedford Level and Swaffham Drainage Act 1767 (c.53)
Bedford Level: Drainage Act 1757 (c.18)
Bedford Level: Drainage Act 1771 (c.78)
Bedford Level: Drainage Act 1772 (c.40)
Bedford Level: Drainage Act 1772 (c.45)
Bedford Level: Drainage Act 1772 (c.49)
Bedford Level: Drainage Act 1775 (c.12)
Bedford Level: Drainage Act 1777 (c.65)
Bedford Level: Drainage Act 1779 (c.24)
Bedford Level: Drainage Act 1796 (c.33)
Bedford Roads Act 1731 (c.26)
Bedford Roads Act 1772 (c.89)
Bedford Roads Act 1772 (c.107)
Bedford Roads Act 1777 (c.94)
Bedford Roads Act 1793 (c.178)
Bedford: Poor Relief Act 1794 (c.98)
Bedford to Kimbolton Road Act 1795 (c.148)
Bedfordshire and Buckinghamshire Roads Act 1706 (c.4)
Bedfordshire and Buckinghamshire Roads Act 1739 (c.9)
Bedfordshire and Hertfordshire Roads Act 1763 (c.27)
Bedfordshire Highways Act 1706 (c.13)
Bedfordshire Roads Act 1724 (c.20)
Bedfordshire Roads Act 1736 (c.24)
Bedfordshire Roads Act 1753 (c.41)
Bee Pest Prevention (Ireland) Act 1908 (c.34)
Beef and Veal Customs Duties Act 1937 (c.8)
Beer Act 1761 (c.14)
Beer Act 1816 (c.58)
Beer and Malt (Ireland) Act 1809 (c.57)
Beer Dealers Retail Licences Act 1880 (c.6)
Beer Dealers, Retail Licences (Amendment) Act 1882 (c.34)
Beer, Devon, Harbour Act 1792 (c.92)
Beer Duties, Borrowstoness Act 1743 (c.21)
Beer Duties, Borrowstoness Act 1767 (c.90)
Beer Duties: Borrowstoness Act 1794 (c.91)
Beer, etc., Licences (Great Britain) Act 1816 (c.113)
Beer Licences Regulation (Ireland) Act 1877 (c.4)
Beer Retailers etc., Retail Licences (Ireland) Act 1900 (c.30)
Beerhouse Act 1840 (c.61)
Beerhouse Act 1870 (c.111)
Beerhouses (Ireland) Act 1864 (c.35)
Beerhouses (Ireland) Act (1864) Amendment 1871 (c.111)
Bees Act 1980 (c.12)
Behring Sea Award Act 1894 (c.2)
Belfast Borough Extension Act 1853 (c.114)
Belfast Commission Act 1886 (c.4)
Belfast Constabulary Act 1866 (c.46)
Belfast Custom House Act 1852 (c.30)
Belize Act 1981 (c.52)
Benefice (Ireland) Act 1865 (c.82)
Benefices Act 1807 (c.75)
Benefices Act 1808 (c.5)
Benefices Act 1898 (c.48)
Benefices (England) Act 1803 (c.84)
Benefices (England) Act 1803 (c.109)
Benefices (Ireland) Act 1808 (c.66)
Benefices (Ireland) Act 1860 (c.72)
Benefices (Scotland) Act 1843 (c.61)
Benefit Building Societies Act 1836 (c.32)
Benthall Bridge, Severn Act 1776 (c.17)
Berkshire Act 1751 (c.21)
Berkshire and Oxford Roads Act 1765 (c.55)
Berkshire and Southampton Roads Act 1772 (c.78)

Berkshire and Southampton Roads Act 1794 (c.141)
Berkshire and Wiltshire Roads Act 1770 (c.100)
Berkshire and Wiltshire Roads Act 1771 (c.97)
Berkshire and Wiltshire Roads Act 1781 (c.91)
Berkshire and Wiltshire Roads Act 1781 (c.101)
Berkshire and Wiltshire Roads Act 1793 (c.138)
Berkshire Highways Act 1713 (c.28)
Berkshire, Oxford, Buckinghamshire and Hertford Roads Act 1787 (c.81)
Berkshire Roads Act 1732 (c.16)
Berkshire Roads Act 1738 (c.11)
Berkshire Roads Act 1746 (c.6)
Berkshire Roads Act 1751 (c.21)
Berkshire Roads Act 1756 (c.77)
Berkshire Roads Act 1756 (c.81)
Berkshire Roads Act 1771 (c.70)
Berkshire Roads Act 1772 (c.104)
Berkshire Roads Act 1778 (c.99)
Berkshire Roads Act 1783 (c.100)
Berkshire Roads Act 1790 (c.106)
Berkshire Roads Act 1791 (c.105)
Berkshire Roads Act 1794 (c.132)
Bermuda Constitution Act 1967 (c.63)
Bermondsey, etc.: Streets Act 1785 (c.23)
Bermondsey (Poor Relief) Act 1757 (c.45)
Bermondsey: Poor Relief Act 1791 (c.19)
Bermuda Trade Act 1813 (c.50)
Berwick and Durham Roads Act 1793 (c.185)
Berwick-on-Tweed Act 1836 (c.103)
Berwick Roads Act 1753 (c.82)
Berwick Roads Act 1766 (c.73)
Berwick Roads Act 1772 (c.97)
Berwick Roads Act 1779 (c.79)
Berwick Roads Act 1781 (c.91)
Berwick Roads Act 1787 (c.89)
Berwick Roads Act 1792 (c.149)
Berwickshire County Town Act 1903 (c.5)
Berwickshire Courts Act 1853 (c.27)
Bethnal Green and Shoreditch: Improvement Act 1793 (c.88)
Bethnal Green: Completion of Church and Poor Relief Act 1745 (c.15)
Bethnal Green: Parish Act 1742 (c.28)
Bethnal Green: Poor Relief Act 1763 (c.40)
Bethnal Green: Poor Relief Act 1772 (c.53)
Bethnal Green Road Act 1756 (c.43)
Bethnal Green Road Act 1767 (c.105)
Betting Act 1853 (c.119)
Betting Act 1874 (c.15)
Betting and Gaming Act 1960 (c.60)
Betting and Gaming Duties Act 1972 (c.25)
Betting and Gaming Duties Act 1981 (c.63)
Betting and Loans (Infants) Act 1892 (c.4)
Betting and Lotteries Act 1934 (c.58)
Betting Duties Act 1963 (c.3)
Betting, Gaming and Lotteries Act 1963 (c.2)
Betting, Gaming and Lotteries Act 1964 (c.78)
Betting, Gaming and Lotteries (Amendment) Act 1969 (c.17)
Betting, Gaming and Lotteries (Amendment) Act 1971 (c.26)
Betting, Gaming and Lotteries (Amendment) Act 1980 (c.18)
Betting, Gaming and Lotteries (Amendment) Act 1984 (c.25)
Betting, Gaming and Lotteries (Amendment) Act 1985 (c.18)
Betting (Juvenile Messengers) (Scotland) Act 1928 (c.27)
Betting Levy Act 1961 (c.17)
Beverley and Kexby Bridge Road Act 1764 (c.76)
Beverley Improvement Act 1726 (c.4)
Beverley Improvement Act 1744 (c.13)
Beverley to Kexby Bridge Road Act 1785 (c.110)
Bewdley Bridge Act 1795 (c.78)
Bewdley Roads Act 1753 (c.39)
Bewdley Roads Act 1774 (c.112)
Bicester and Aylesbury Road Act 1770 (c.72)
Bicester Roads Act 1793 (c.180)
Bicester to Aylesbury Road Act 1791 (c.101)
Bicester to Aynho Road Act 1791 (c.103)
Bideford Roads Act 1764 (c.87)
Bideford Roads Act 1785 (c.119)
Bigamy Act 1795 (c.67)
Billiards (Abolition of Restrictions) Act 1987 (c.19)
Bill Chamber Procedure Act 1857 (c.18)
Bill of Exchange Act 1702 (c.8)
Bill of Exchange Act 1704 (c.8)
Bill of Exchange Act 1776 (c.30)
Bill of Exchange Act 1800 (c.42)
Bill of Exchange Act 1808 (c.88)
Bill of Exchange (Scotland) Act 1772 (c.72)
Bill of Sale Act 1891 (c.35)
Billeting of Civilians Act 1917 (c.20)
Bills and Notes Metropolis Act 1852 (c.1)
Bills and Notes Metropolis Act 1863 (c.2)
Bills Confirming Provisional Orders Act 1870 (c.1)
Bills of Exchange Act 1836 (c.58)
Bills of Exchange Act 1871 (c.74)
Bills of Exchange Act 1878 (c.13)
Bills of Exchange Act 1882 (c.61)
Bills of Exchange Act 1914 (c.82)
Bills of Exchange Act (1882) Amendment Act 1932 (c.44)
Bills of Exchange (Crossed Cheques) Act 1906 (c.17)
Bills of Exchange, etc. Act 1783 (c.7)
Bills of Exchange (Ireland) Act 1828 (c.24)
Bills of Exchange (Ireland) Act 1862 (c.23)
Bills of Exchange (Ireland) Act 1864 (c.7)
Bills of Exchange (Scotland) Act 1772 (c.72)
Bills of Exchange (Time of Noting) Act 1917 (c.48)
Bills of Lading Act 1855 (c.111)
Bills of Sale Act 1854 (c.36)
Bills of Sale (Ireland) Act 1854 (c.55)

Bills of Sale Act 1866 (c.96)
Bills of Sale Act 1878 (c.31)
Bills of Sale Act (1878) Amendment Act 1882 (c.43)
Bills of Sale Act 1890 (c.53)
Bills of Sale (Ireland) Act 1879 (c.50)
Bills of Sale (Ireland) Act (1879) Amendment Act 1883 (c.7)
Bingo Act 1992 (c.10)
Biological Standards Act 1975 (c.4)
Biological Weapons Act 1974 (c.6)
Birkenhead Enfranchisement Act 1861 (c.112)
Birmingham and Chesterfield Roads Act 1786 (c.149)
Birmingham and Stratford Roads Act 1825 (c.6)
Birmingham and Wednesbury Roads Act 1726 (c.14)
Birmingham Canal Act 1769 (c.53)
Birmingham Canal, Navigation Act 1768 (c.38)
Birmingham Canal, Navigation Act 1771 (c.67)
Birmingham Canal, Navigation Act 1783 (c.92)
Birmingham Canal, Navigation Act 1784 (c.4)
Birmingham Canal: Navigation Act 1785 (c.99)
Birmingham Canal: Navigation Act 1792 (c.81)
Birmingham Canal: Navigation Act 1794 (c.25)
Birmingham Canal: Navigation Act 1794 (c.87)
Birmingham Chapels Act 1772 (c.64)
Birmingham: Improvement Act 1769 (c.83)
Birmingham: Improvement Act 1772 (c.36)
Birmingham Police Act 1839 (c.88)
Birmingham: Poor Relief Act 1783 (c.54)
Birmingham to Edghill Road Act 1757 (c.58)
Birmingham to Stratford Roads Act 1725 (c.6)
Birmingham to Stratford Road Act 1771 (c.74)
Birmingham and Wednesbury Roads Act 1726 (c.14)
Birmingham Canal, Navigation Act 1784 (c.4)
Birstall to Huddersfield Roads Act 1786 (c.140)
Births and Deaths Registration Act 1836 (c.86)
Births and Deaths Registration Act 1837 (c.22)
Births and Deaths Registration Act 1858 (c.25)
Births and Deaths Registration Act 1874 (c.88)
Births and Deaths Registration Act 1901 (c.26)
Births and Deaths Registration Act 1926 (c.48)
Births and Deaths Registration Act 1947 (c.12)
Births and Deaths Registration Act 1953 (c.20)
Births and Deaths Registration (Ireland) Act 1880 (c.13)
Bishop of Calcutta Act 1874 (c.13)
Bishop of Quebec Act 1852 (c.53)
Bishopric of Bristol Act 1884 (c.66)
Bishopric of Bristol Amendment Act 1894 (c.21)
Bishopric of Bristol Amendment Act 1896 (c.29)
Bishopric of Christ Church, New Zealand Act 1852 (c.88)
Bishopric of St. Albans Act 1875 (c.34)
Bishopric of Southwark and Birmingham Act 1904 (c.30)
Bishopric of Truro Act 1876 (c.54)
Bishoprics Act 1878 (c.68)
Bishoprics, etc., in West Indies Act 1842 (c.4)
Bishoprics of Bradford and Coventry Act 1918 (c.57)
Bishoprics of Sheffield, Chelmsford and for the County of Suffolk Act 1913 (c.36)
Bishoprics of Southwark and Birmingham Act 1904 (c.30)
Bishops in Foreign Countries Act 1841 (c.6)
Bishops of London and Durham Act 1856 (c.115)
Bishops Trusts Substitution Act 1858 (c.71)
Bishops Resignation Act 1869 (c.111)
Bishops Resignation Act 1875 (c.19)
Bishops Resignation Act Continuance 1872 (c.40)
Bishopsgate: Poor Relief Act 1795 (c.61)
Black Game in Somerset and Devon Act 1810 (c.67)
Blackburn and Addingham Road Act 1796 (c.137)
Blackburn Roads Act 1776 (c.75)
Blackburn Roads Act 1796 (c.144)
Blackburn to Burscough Bridge Road Act 1793 (c.134)
Blackfriars Bridge Act 1756 (c.86)
Blackfriars Bridge Act 1756 (c.86)
Blackfriars Bridge (Sunday Tolls) Act 1786 (c.37)
Blackfriars Sewer Act 1795 (c.131)
Blackheath, etc., Small Debts Act 1770 (c.29)
Blackwater Bridge Act 1867 (c.57)
Blackwater Bridge Act 1873 (c.46)
Blackwater Bridge Debt Act 1873 (c.47)
Blandford Forum (Rebuilding after the Fire) Act 1731 (c.16)
Bleaching and Dyeing Works Act 1860 (c.78)
Bleaching and Dyeing Works Act Amendment Act 1863 (c.38)
Bleaching and Dyeing Works Act Ext. 1864 (c.98)
Bleaching Powder Act 1815 (c.38)
Bleaching Works Act 1862 (c.8)
Blind Persons Act 1938 (c.11)
Blind Voters Act 1933 (c.27)
Bloomsbury Churches Act 1730 (c.19)

Bloomsbury: Poor Relief Act 1774 (c.62)
Bloomsbury: Poor Relief Act 1774 (c.108)
Blything, Suffolk: Poor Relief, etc. Act 1764 (c.56)
Blything, Suffolk (Poor Relief, Guardians, etc.) Act 1793 (c.126)
Board of Agriculture Act 1889 (c.30)
Board of Agriculture and Fisheries Act 1903 (c.31)
Board of Agriculture and Fisheries Act 1909 (c.15)
Board of Education Act 1899 (c.33)
Board of Education (Scotland) Act 1877 (c.38)
Board of Trade Act 1909 (c.23)
Board of Trade Arbitrations etc. Act 1874 (c.40)
Boards of Guardians (Default) Act 1926 (c.20)
Boards of Management of Poor Law District Schools (Ireland) Act 1892 (c.41)
Bodies Corporate (Joint Tenancy) Act 1899 (c.20)
Bodmin Canal Act 1797 (c.29)
Bodmin Gaol Act 1778 (c.17)
Bodmin Roads Act 1769 (c.69)
Bodmin Roads Act 1786 (c.129)
Bogs (Ireland) Act 1811 (c.122)
Bogs (Ireland) Act 1812 (c.74)
Boiler Explosions Act 1882 (c.22)
Boiler Explosions Act 1890 (c.35)
Bolton and Nightingale's Road Act 1763 (c.31)
Bolton and Nightingale's Road Act 1763 (c.40)
Bolton and St. Helens Road Act 1796 (c.149)
Bolton, Blackburn and Twisey Roads Act 1797 (c.173)
Bolton Grammar School Act 1788 (c.81)
Bolton Police Act 1839 (c.95)
Bombay Civil Fund Act 1882 (c.45)
Bonded Corn Act 1842 (c.92)
Bonded Corn Act 1845 (c.103)
Bonded Warehouses Act 1805 (c.87)
Bonded Warehouses Act 1848 (c.122)
Bonding of Coffee, etc. Act 1807 (c.48)
Bonding of Spirits Act 1806 (c.27)
Bonding of Spirits (Ireland) Act 1804 (c.104)
Bonding of Sugar Act 1804 (c.36)
Bonding of Wine Act 1803 (c.103)
Bonding of Wines Act 1803 (c.14)
Bonding Warehouses Act 1806 (c.137)
Bonding Warehouses (Ireland) Act 1808 (c.32)
Bonded Warehouses (Ireland) Act 1810 (c.38)
Bonds of East India Company Act 1803 (c.3)
Booth's Charity, Salford Act 1776 (c.55)
Booth's Patent Act 1792 (c.73)
Borders Rivers (Prevention of Pollution) Act 1951 (c.7)
Borough and Local Courts of Record Act 1872 (c.86)
Borough and Watch Rates Act 1845 (c.110)
Borough Charters Confirmation Act 1842 (c.111)
Borough Clerks of the Peace (Ireland) Act 1868 (c.98)
Borough Constables Act 1883 (c.44)
Borough Coroners (Ireland) Act 1860 (c.74)
Borough Councillors (Alteration of Number) Act 1925 (c.11)
Borough Courts (England) Act 1839 (c.27)
Borough Electors Act 1868 (c.41)
Borough Fund in Certain Boroughs Act 1836 (c.104)
Borough Funds Act 1872 (c.91)
Borough Funds Act 1903 (c.14)
Borough Funds (Ireland) Act 1888 (c.53)
Borough Justices Act 1850 (c.91)
Borough of Hanley Act 1857 (c.10)
Borough Police Act 1848 (c.14)
Borough Quarter Sessions Act 1877 (c.17)
Borough Rates (England) Act 1854 (c.71)
Borough Recorders' Deputies Act 1869 (c.23)
Borough Watch Rates Act 1839 (c.28)
Boroughbridge and Darlington Road Act 1744 (c.8)
Boroughs, Relief from County Expenditure Act 1849 (c.82)
Borrowing (Control and Guarantees) Act 1946 (c.58)
Borrowstoness Canal Act 1783 (c.5)
Bosmere and Claydon, Suffolk (Poor Relief) Act 1764 (c.57)
Boston: Improvement Act 1792 (c.80)
Boston Pilotage Act 1776 (c.23)
Boston Pilotage Act 1792 (c.79)
Boston: Streets Act 1776 (c.25)
Boston Water Supply Act 1711 (c.44)
Botswana Independence Act 1966 (c.23)
Boundaries of Burghs Extension (Scotland) Act 1857 (c.70)
Boundaries of Burghs Extension (Scotland) Act 1861 (c.36)
Boundary Act 1868 (c.46)
Boundary Commissions Act 1992 (c.55)
Boundary Survey (Ireland) Act 1854 (c.17)
Boundary Survey (Ireland) Act 1857 (c.45)
Boundary Survey (Ireland) Act 1859 (c.8)
Bounties Act 1779 (c.27)
Bounties Act 1780 (c.40)
Bounties Act 1783 (c.21)
Bounties Act 1795 (c.21)
Bounties Act 1796 (c.56)
Bounties Act 1801 (c.13)
Bounties Act 1801 (c.34)
Bounties Act 1801 (c.92)
Bounties Act 1802 (c.59)
Bounties and Drawbacks Act 1805 (c.24)
Bounties and Drawbacks Act 1808 (cc.16, 17)
Bounties, etc., on Sugar Act 1809 (cc.10, 11)
Bounties, etc., on Sugar Act 1812 (c.15)
Bounties, etc., on Sugar Act 1813 (c.24)

Bounties for Destroying Spanish Ships Act 1785 (c.29)
Bounties for Destroying Spanish Ships Act 1786 (c.35)
Bounties (Great Britain) Act 1807 (c.29)
Bounties on Exportation Act 1744 (c.25)
Bounties on Importation Act 1800 (c.10)
Bounties on Importation Act 1800 (c.29)
Bounties on Pilchards Act 1812 (c.42)
Bounties on Sugar Act 1807 (c.22)
Bounties on Sugar Act 1808 (c.12)
Bounty for Taking L'Amazone Act 1784 (c.28)
Bounty of Exportation Act 1766 (c.45)
Bounty of Raw Sugar Act 1810 (c.9)
Bounty on British Calicoes Act 1807 (c.64)
Bounty on British Sail Cloth Exported Act 1797 (c.30)
Bounty on Certain Linens Exported Act 1799 (c.28)
Bounty on Cordage Exported Act 1786 (c.85)
Bounty on Corn Act 1780 (c.31)
Bounty on Corn, etc. Act 1750 (c.56)
Bounty on Exportation Act 1797 (c.76)
Bounty on Exportation Act 1806 (c.99)
Bounty on Exportation Act 1810 (c.40)
Bounty on Hemp Act 1779 (c.37)
Bounty on Importation Act 1800 (c.35)
Bounty on Pilchards Act 1797 (c.94)
Bounty on Pilchards Act 1799 (c.65)
Bounty on Pilchards Act 1808 (c.68)
Bounty on Rye Act 1800 (c.53)
Bounty on Silk Manufactures Act 1806 (c.110)
Bounty on Sugar Act 1816 (c.19)
Bounty on Sugar, etc. Act 1806 (c.109)
Bounty to Garrison of Gibraltar Act 1783 (c.16)
Bounty upon Importation Act 1763 (c.26)
Board of Trade (Parliamentary Secretary) Act 1867 (c.72)
Bourn, Lincs.: Navigation Act 1780 (c.22)
Bradford and Wakefield Road Act 1753 (c.83)
Bradford-on-Avon (Additional Overseer) Act 1783 (c.20)
Bradford to Idle Canal Act 1771 (c.89)
Bradford, Yorks: Water Supply Act 1790 (c.63)
Branding of Herrings (Northumberland) Act 1891 (c.28)
Brandon and Sams Cut Drain: Drainage Act 1757 (c.35)
Brandon and Waveney: Navigation Act 1750 (c.12)
Brazilian Slave Trade Repeal Act 1869 (c.2)
Bread Act 1762 (c.6)
Bread Act 1762 (c.11)
Bread Act 1772 (c.62)
Bread Act 1793 (c.37)
Bread Act 1836 (c.37)
Bread Acts Amendment Act 1922 (c.28)
Bread (Ireland) Act 1838 (c.28)
Brecknock and Abergavenny Canal Act 1793 (c.96)
Brecknock Forest Act 1815 (c.190)
Brecknock Water Supply Act 1776 (c.56)
Brecon Roads Act 1767 (c.60)
Brecon Roads Act 1772 (c.105)
Brecon Roads Act 1787 (c.75)
Brecon Roads Act 1793 (c.154)
Breeding of Dogs Act 1973 (c.60)
Breeding of Dogs Act 1991 (c.64)
Brent Bridge to Plymouth Road Act 1777 (c.81)
Brentford Road Act 1791 (c.124)
Bretton Woods Agreements Act 1945 (c.19)
Brewers' Licensing Act 1850 (c.67)
Brewn Roads Act 1772 (c.105)
Bribery at Elections Act 1842 (c.102)
Brick Duties Repeal Act 1850 (c.9)
Brick Making Act 1725 (c.35)
Brickmaking Act 1728 (c.15)
Brickmaking Act 1730 (c.22)
Bricks and Tiles Act 1770 (c.49)
Bricks and Tiles Act 1776 (c.42)
Bridewell Hospital Act 1780 (c.27)
Bridgeford Lane, Notts. to Kettering Road 1754 (c.39)
Bridges Act 1670 (c.12)
Bridges Act 1702 (c.12)
Bridges Act 1740 (c.33)
Bridges Act 1803 (c.59)
Bridges Act 1812 (c.110)
Bridges Act 1814 (c.90)
Bridges Act 1815 (c.143)
Bridges Act 1850 (c.64)
Bridges Act 1929 (c.33)
Bridges (Ireland) Act 1843 (c.42)
Bridges (Ireland) Act 1850 (c.4)
Bridges (Ireland) Act 1851 (c.21)
Bridges (Ireland) Act 1867 (c.50)
Bridges (Ireland) Act 1875 (c.46)
Bridges (Ireland) Act 1813 (c.77)
Bridges (Scotland) Act 1813 (c.117)
Bridgewell Hospital Act 1783 (c.27)
Bridgnorth Bridge Act 1797 (c.58)
Bridgnorth Church Act 1792 (c.30)
Bridgwater and Beverly Disfranchisement Act 1870 (c.21)
Bridgwater Canal Act 1795 (c.44)
Bridgwater Markets Act 1779 (c.36)
Bridgwater: Navigation Act 1794 (c.105)
Bridgwater Roads Act 1730 (c.34)
Bridgwater Roads Act 1779 (c.100)
Bridlington Pier Act 1715 (c.49)
Bridlington Pier Act 1718 (c.10)
Bridlington Pier Act 1789 (c.23)
Bridlington Piers Act 1720 (c.16)
Bridlington Piers Act 1753 (c.10)
Bridlington Roads Act 1767 (c.89)
Bridport, Dorset, Harbour Act 1721 (c.11)
Bridport: Improvement Act 1785 (c.91)
Brighton: Streets Act 1772 (c.34)
Brine Pumping (Compensation for Subsidence) Act 1891 (c.40)
Bringing of Coals, etc., to London, etc. Act 1805 (c.128)

Bringing of Coals, etc., to London Act 1807 (c.34)
Bringing of Coals, etc., to London, etc. Act 1808 (c.95)
Bringing of Coals, etc., to London, etc. Act 1810 (c.110)
Bringing of Coals, etc., to London Act 1811 (c.29)
Bringing of Coals, etc., to London, etc. Act 1817 (c.114)
Bringing of Coals to London, etc. Act 1806 (c.104)
Bringing of Coals to London, etc. Act 1813 (c.135)
Bringing of Coals to London, etc. 1815 (c.175)
Bringing of Coals to London, etc. Act 1816 (c.124)
Bristol and Exeter Railway Act 1836 (c.36)
Bristol Bridge Act 1759 (c.52)
Bristol Bridge Act 1786 (c.111)
Bristol: Building Act 1788 (c.66)
Bristol Charities Act 1858 (c.30)
Bristol Charities Act 1858 (c.31)
Bristol Churches Act 1750 (c.37)
Bristol Dock Act 1776 (c.33)
Bristol Gaol Act 1792 (c.82)
Bristol Guildhall, etc. Act 1788 (c.67)
Bristol Hospitals Act 1744 (c.38)
Bristol: Improvement Act 1788 (c.65)
Bristol Museum Act 1766 (c.18)
Bristol (Nightly Watch) Act 1755 (c.32)
Bristol, Paving, etc. Act 1748 (c.20)
Bristol, Poor Relief Act 1713 (c.32)
Bristol (Poor Relief) Act 1757 (c.56)
Bristol Roads Act 1726 (c.12)
Bristol Roads Act 1730 (c.22)
Bristol Roads Act 1748 (c.28)
Bristol Roads Act 1779 (c.117)
Bristol Roads Act 1797 (c.178)
Bristol Streets Act 1766 (c.34)
Bristol Theatre Act 1778 (c.8)
Bristol Watch Act 1756 (c.47)
British Aerospace Act 1980 (c.26)
British Airways Board Act 1977 (c.13)
British Calicoes Act 1811 (c.33)
British Caribbean Federation Act 1956 (c.63)
British Coal and British Rail (Transfer Proposals) Act 1993 (c.2)
British Columbia Act 1866 (c.67)
British Columbia Boundaries Act 1863 (c.83)
British Columbia Government Act 1858 (c.99)
British Columbia Government Act 1870 (c.66)
British Columbia (Loan) Act 1892 (c.52)
British Council and Commonwealth Institute Superannuation Act 1986 (c.51)
British Empire Exhibition (Amendment) Act 1922 (c.25)
British Empire Exhibition (Guarantee) Act 1920 (c.74)
British Empire Exhibition (Guarantee) Act 1925 (c.26)
British Ferries Society Act 1799 (c.100)
British Film Institute Act 1949 (c.35)
British Fisheries Act 1795 (c.56)
British Fisheries Act 1798 (c.58)
British Fisheries Act 1800 (c.85)
British Fisheries Act 1804 (c.86)
British Fisheries Act 1806 (c.34)
British Fisheries Act 1806 (c.156)
British Fisheries Act 1807 (c.51)
British Fisheries Act 1808 (c.86)
British Fisheries Act 1810 (c.54)
British Fisheries, etc. Act 1802 (c.79)
British Fisheries Society Act 1786 (c.106)
British Fishing Boats Act 1983 (c.8)
British Forces in India Act 1862 (c.27)
British Guiana Act 1928 (c.5)
British Honduras (Court of Appeal) Act 1881 (c.36)
British Hydrocarbon Oils Production Act 1934 (c.4)
British Industries Fair (Guarantees and Grants) Act 1954 (c.26)
British Kaffrania Act 1865 (c.5)
British Law Ascertainment Act 1859 (c.63)
British Leyland Act 1975 (c.43)
British Library Act 1972 (c.54)
British Mercantile Marine Uniform Act 1919 (c.62)
British Museum Act 1700 (c.7)
British Museum Act 1706 (c.30)
British Museum Act 1753 (c.22)
British Museum Act 1766 (c.18)
British Museum Act 1805 (c.127)
British Museum Act 1807 (c.36)
British Museum Act 1816 (c.99)
British Museum Act 1839 (c.10)
British Museum Act 1878 (c.55)
British Museum Act 1902 (c.12)
British Museum Act 1924 (c.23)
British Museum Act 1930 (c.46)
British Museum Act 1931 (c.34)
British Museum Act 1932 (c.34)
British Museum Act 1938 (c.62)
British Museum Act 1946 (c.56)
British Museum Act 1955 (c.23)
British Museum Act 1962 (c.18)
British Museum Act 1963 (c.24)
British Museum (Purchase of Land) Act 1894 (c.34)
British Nationality Act 1730 (c.21)
British Nationality Act 1772 (c.21)
British Nationality Act 1948 (c.56)
British Nationality Act 1958 (c.10)
British Nationality Act 1964 (c.22)
British Nationality Act 1965 (c.34)
British Nationality Act 1981 (c.61)
British Nationality and Status of Aliens Act 1918 (c.38)
British Nationality and Status of Aliens Act 1922 (c.44)
British Nationality and Status of Aliens Act 1933 (c.49)
British Nationality and Status of Aliens Act 1943 (c.14)

British Nationality (Falkland Islands) Act 1983 (c.6)
British Nationality (Hong Kong) Act 1990 (c.34)
British Nationality (No. 2) Act 1964 (c.54)
British North America Act 1840 (c.35)
British North America Act 1867 (c.3)
British North America Act 1870 (c.28)
British North America Act 1871 (c.28)
British North America Act 1886 (c.35)
British North America Act 1907 (c.11)
British North America Act 1915 (c.45)
British North America Act 1916 (c.19)
British North America Act 1930 (c.26)
British North America Act 1939 (c.36)
British North America Act 1940 (c.36)
British North America Act 1943 (c.30)
British North America Act 1946 (c.63)
British North America Act 1949 (c.22)
British North America Act 1951 (c.32)
British North America Act 1960 (c.2)
British North America Act 1964 (c.73)
British North America (No. 2) Act 1949 (c.81)
British North America (Quebec) Act 1774 (c.83)
British Overseas Airways Act 1939 (c.61)
British Railways Board (Finance) Act 1991 (c.63)
British Sailcloth, etc. Act 1793 (c.49)
British Settlements Act 1887 (c.54)
British Settlements Act 1945 (c.7)
British Settlements in Africa, etc. Act 1764 (c.44)
British Shipbuilders Act 1983 (c.15)
British Shipbuilders (Borrowing Powers) Act 1983 (c.58)
British Shipbuilders (Borrowing Powers) Act 1986 (c.19)
British Shipbuilders (Borrowing Powers) Act 1987 (c.52)
British Shipping (Assistance) Act 1935 (c.7)
British Shipping (Continuance of Subsidy) Act 1936 (c.12)
British Shipping (Continuance of Subsidy) Act 1937 (c.21)
British Ships Act 1772 (c.26)
British Ships Captured by the Enemy Act 1808 (c.70)
British Ships (Transfer Restriction) Act 1915 (c.21)
British Ships (Transfer Restriction) Act 1916 (c.42)
British Standard Time Act 1968 (c.45)
British Steel Act 1988 (c.35)
Btitish Subjects Act 1751 (c.39)
British Subjects in China Act 1843 (c.80)
British Sugar Industry (Assistance) Act 1931 (c.35)
British Sugar (Subsidy) Act 1925 (c.12)
British Sugar (Subsidy) Act 1934 (c.39)
British Sugar (Subsidy) Act 1935 (c.37)
British Technology Group Act 1991 (c.66)
British Telecommunications Act 1981 (c.38)
British White Herring Fishery Act 1811 (c.101)
British White Herring Fishery Act 1812 (c.153)
British White Herring Fishery Act 1814 (c.102)
Brixton: Small Debts Act 1757 (c.23)
Broadcasting Act 1980 (c.64)
Broadcasting Act 1981 (c.68)
Broadcasting Act 1987 (c.10)
Broadcasting Act 1990 (c.42)
Broadcasting Act 1996 (c.55)
Broadstairs Pier Act 1792 (c.86)
Brokers, Bristol Act 1730 (c.31)
Bromsgrove and Birmingham Roads Act 1776 (c.15)
Bromsgrove to Birmingham Road Act 1790 (c.101)
Brown Linen Manufacture (Ireland) Act 1815 (c.25)
Brunei and Maldives Act 1985 (c.3)
Brunei Appeals Act 1989 (c.36)
Bruntisland Beer Duties Act 1746 (c.26)
Bruntisland Beer Duties Act 1776 (c.20)
Bruntisland Beer Duties Act 1794 (c.8)
Bruton Roads Act 1756 (c.50)
Bubble Schemes, Colonies Act 1740 (c.37)
Bubwith Bridge Act 1793 (c.106)
Buckingham and Hanwell Road Act 1792 (c.134)
Buckingham and Middlesex Roads Act 1779 (c.83)
Buckingham and Oxford Roads Act 1770 (c.58)
Buckingham and Oxford Roads Act 1785 (c.127)
Buckingham to Banbury Road Act 1791 (c.133)
Buckingham to Hanwell Road Act 1769 (c.52)
Buckingham to Warmington Road Act 1743 (c.43)
Buckinghamshire and Oxford Roads Act 1769 (c.88)
Buckinghamshire and Oxford Roads Act 1791 (c.136)
Buckinghamshire Assizes Act 1747 (c.12)
Buckinghamshire Assizes Act 1849 (c.6)
Buckinghamshire Highways Act 1722 (c.13)
Buckinghamshire Roads Act 1720 (c.24)
Buckinghamshire Roads Act 1735 (c.11)
Buckinghamshire Roads Act 1735 (c.21)
Buckinghamshire Roads Act 1741 (c.5)
Buckinghamshire Roads Act 1741 (c.6)
Buckinghamshire Roads Act 1759 (c.43)
Buckinghamshire Roads Act 1767 (c.61)
Buckinghamshire Roads Act 1777 (c.82)
Bude Canal Act 1774 (c.53)
Building Act 1984 (c.55)
Building Control Act 1966 (c.27)
Building Materials and Housing Act 1945 (c.20)
Building of Churches, etc. (Ireland) Act 1809
Building of Churches, London and Westminster Act 1714 (c.23)

Building Restrictions (War-Time Contraventions) Act 1946 (c.35)
Building (Scotland) Act 1959 (c.24)
Building (Scotland) Act 1970 (c.38)
Building Sites for Religious and Other Purposes Act 1868 (c.44)
Building Societies Act 1874 (c.42)
Building Societies Act 1875 (c.9)
Building Societies Act 1877 (c.63)
Building Societies Act 1884 (c.41)
Building Societies Act 1894 (c.47)
Building Societies Act 1939 (c.55)
Building Societies Act 1960 (c.64)
Building Societies Act 1962 (c.37)
Building Societies Act 1986 (c.53)
Building Societies (Joint Account Holders) Act 1995 (c.5)
Bunhill Fields Burial Ground Act 1867 (c.38)
Burford Charities Act 1861 (c.22)
Burford to Preston Road Act 1780 (c.76)
Burgesses Qualification (Scotland) Act 1876 (c.12)
Burgesses (Scotland) Act 1860 (c.47)
Burgh Council Elections (Scotland) Act 1853 (c.26)
Burgh Customs (Scotland) Act 1870 (c.42)
Burgh Gas Supply (Scotland) Amendment Act 1918 (c.45)
Burgh Harbours (Scotland) Act 1853 (c.93)
Burgh Police (Amendment) (Scotland) Act 1964 (c.33)
Burgh Police, etc. (Scotland) Act 1847 (c.39)
Burgh Police (Scotland) Act 1892 (c.55)
Burgh Police (Scotland) Act 1892, Amendment 1894 (c.18)
Burgh Police (Scotland) Act 1893 (c.25)
Burgh Police (Scotland) Act 1903 (c.33)
Burgh Police (Scotland) Amendment Act 1911 (c.51)
Burgh Registers (Scotland) Act 1926 (c.50)
Burgh, Scotland (Petty Customs) Act 1879 (c.13)
Burgh Sewerage, Drainage and Water Supply (Scotland) Act 1901 (c.24)
Burgh Trading Act 1846 (c.17)
Burgh Voters' Registration (Scotland) Act 1856 (c.58)
Burgh Wards (Scotland) Act 1876 (c.25)
Burghs Gas Supply (Scotland) Act 1876 (c.49)
Burghs Gas Supply (Scotland) Act 1893 (c.52)
Burghs of Barony (Scotland) Act 1795 (c.122)
Burghs (Scotland) Act 1852 (c.33)
Burglaries, etc. Act 1706 (c.9)
Burglary Act 1837 (c.86)
Burglary Act 1896 (c.57)
Burial Act 1852 (c.85)
Burial Act 1853 (c.134)
Burial Act 1854 (c.87)
Burial Act 1855 (c.128)
Burial Act 1857 (c.81)
Burial Act 1859 (c.1)
Burial Act 1860 (c.64)
Burial Act 1862 (c.100)
Burial Act 1871 (c.33)
Burial Act 1900 (c.15)
Burial Act 1906 (c.44)
Burial and Registration Acts (Doubts Removal) Act 1881 (c.2)
Burial Boards (Contested Elections) Act 1885 (c.21)
Burial Grounds (Ireland) Act 1856 (c.98)
Burial Grounds (Ireland) Act 1860 (c.76)
Burial Grounds (Scotland) Act 1855 (c.68)
Burial Grounds (Scotland) Act, 1855, Amendment Act 1881 (c.27)
Burial Grounds (Scotland) Act 1857 (c.42)
Burial Grounds (Scotland) Amendment Act 1886 (c.21)
Burial in Burghs (Scotland) Act 1866 (c.46)
Burial (Ireland) Act 1868 (c.103)
Burial Laws Amendment Act 1880 (c.41)
Burial of Drowned Persons Act 1808 (c.75)
Burial of Drowned Persons Act 1886 (c.20)
Burma Independence Act 1947 (c.3)
Burma Legislature Act 1946 (c.57)
Burning of Buildings, etc. Act 1837 (c.89)
Burning of Farm Buildings Act 1844 (c.62)
Burning of Houses (Dublin) Act 1841 (c.10)
Burning of Land (Ireland) Act 1814 (c.115)
Burnley Roads Act 1795 (c.146)
Burnt Fen (Northampton): Drainage Act 1797 (c.89)
Bursledon Bridge, Southampton Act 1797 (c.131)
Burton-upon-Trent and Derby Road Act 1753 (c.59)
Burton-upon-Trent and Derby Road Act 1764 (c.51)
Burton-upon-Trent: Improvement Act 1779 (c.39)
Burtry Ford to Burnstone Road 1794 (c.125)
Bury and Bolton Roads Act 1797 (c.174)
Bury and Stratton Road Act 1755 (c.35)
Bury St. Edmunds (Poor Relief) Act 1749 (c.21)
Bury to Church Kirk Canal Act 1794 (c.77)
Burying in Woollen Act 1814 (c.108)
Bus Fuel Grants Act 1966 (c.46)
Bushey Heath to Aylesbury Road Act 1783 (c.93)
Business Names Act 1985 (c.7)
Butter and Cheese Trade Act 1844 (c.48)
Butter and Margarine Act 1907 (c.21)
Butter Trade (Ireland) Act 1812 (c.134)
Butter Trade (Ireland) Act 1813 (c.46)
Buxton and Manchester Road Act 1753 (c.53)
Buxton to Manchester Road Act 1729 (c.4)
Buxton to Manchester Road Act 1748 (c.12)
Byron's Shorthand Act 1741 (c.23)

Cable and Broadcasting Act 1984 (c.46)
Cable and Wireless Act 1946 (c.82)

Caddington Church Act 1740 (c.26)
Caithness Roads Act 1793 (c.120)
Calder and Hebb: Navigation Act 1769 (c.71)
Calder Canal Act 1774 (c.13)
Calder Navigation Act 1757 (c.72)
Caldey Island Act 1990 (c.44)
Caldon Canal Act 1797 (c.36)
Caledonian and Crinan Canals Amendment Act 1860 (c.46)
Caledonian Canal Act 1803 (c.102)
Caledonian Canal Act 1804 (c.62)
Caledonian Canal Act 1840 (c.41)
Caledonian Canal Act 1848 (c.54)
Caledonian Canal Act 1857 (c.27)
Calendar Act 1750 (c.30)
Calendar (New Style) Act 1750 (c.23)
Callington Roads Act 1764 (c.48)
Camberwell and Peckham: Streets Act 1776 (c.26)
Camberwell, Bristol and Nottingham Elections (Validation) Act 1946 (c.43)
Camberwell: Streets Act 1787 (c.52)
Cambrics Act 1744 (c.36)
Cambrics Act 1747 (c.26)
Cambridge and Arrington Roads Act 1797 (c.179)
Cambridge and Ely Roads Act 1763 (c.36)
Cambridge and Newmarket Road Act 1763 (c.30)
Cambridge and Norfolk Roads Act 1770 (c.97)
Cambridge Commissioners Act 1873 (c.73)
Cambridge: Improvement Act 1788 (c.64)
Cambridge: Improvement Act 1794 (c.104)
Cambridge Roads Act 1723 (c.12)
Cambridge Roads Act 1724 (c.14)
Cambridge Roads Act 1730 (c.37)
Cambridge Roads Act 1755 (c.36)
Cambridge Roads Act 1765 (c.74)
Cambridge Roads Act 1765 (c.76)
Cambridge Roads Act 1765 (c.79)
Cambridge Roads Act 1766 (c.84)
Cambridge Roads Act 1773 (c.110)
Cambridge Roads Act 1790 (c.94)
Cambridge Roads Act 1792 (c.129)
Cambridge to Royston Road Act 1793 (c.130)
Cambridge University Act 1856 (c.88)
Cambridge University Act 1858 (c.11)
Cambridge University, etc. Act 1859 (c.34)
Cambridgeshire Roads Act 1730 (c.24)
Cambridgeshire Roads Act 1741 (c.16)
Camps Act 1939 (c.22)
Camps Act 1945 (c.26)
Canada Act 1775 (c.40)
Canada Act 1982 (c.11)
Canada Civil List Act 1847 (c.71)
Canada Company's Amendment Act 1856 (c.23)
Canada Copyright Act 1875 (c.53)
Canada Defences Loan Act 1870 (c.82)
Canada Loan Guarantee Act 1842 (c.118)
Canada (Ontario Boundary) Act 1889 (c.28)
Canada (Public Works) Loan Act 1873 (c.45)
Canada Railway Loan Act 1867 (c.16)
Canada (Rupert's Land) Loan Act 1869 (c.101)
Canada Union Act 1848 (c.56)
Canadian Speaker (Appointment of Deputy) Act 1895 (c.3)
Canadian Stock Stamp Act 1874 (c.26)
Canal Boats Act 1877 (c.60)
Canal Boats Act 1884 (c.75)
Canal, Carmarthen Act 1766 (c.55)
Canal Carriers Act 1845 (c.42)
Canal (Carriers) Act 1847 (c.94)
Canal Tolls Act 1845 (c.28)
Canals (Continuance of Charging Powers) Act 1922 (c.27)
Canals (Continuance of Charging Powers) Act 1924 (c.2)
Canals, etc. (Scotland) Act 1806 (c.155)
Canals (Ireland) Act 1816 (c.55)
Canals (Offences) Act 1840 (c.50)
Canals Protection (London) Act 1898 (c.16)
Canals: Trent and Mersey Act 1797 (c.81)
Cancer Act 1939 (c.13)
Canterbury Association (New Zealand) Act 1850 (c.70)
Canterbury Association (New Zealand) Act 1851 (c.84)
Canterbury: Church of St. Andrew Act 1763 (c.49)
Canterbury: Poor Relief Act 1727 (c.20)
Canterbury: Streets Act 1787 (c.14)
Canterbury to Whitstable Road Act 1783 (c.97)
Canvey Island, Sea Defences Act 1792 (c.23)
Cape of Good Hope (Advance) Act 1885 (c.7)
Cape of Good Hope Trade Act 1796 (c.21)
Cape of Good Hope Trade Act 1806 (c.30)
Cape of Good Hope Trade Act 1807 (c.11)
Cape of Good Hope Trade Act 1808 (c.105)
Cape of Good Hope Trade Act 1809 (c.17)
Cape of Good Hope Trade Act 1816 (c.8)
Cape Race Lighthouse Act 1886 (c.13)
Cape Rock Lighthouse (Scotland) Act 1806 (c.132)
Capital Allowances Act 1968 (c.3)
Capital Allowances Act 1990 (c.1)
Capital Expenditure (Money) Act 1904 (c.21)
Capital Gains Tax Act 1979 (c.14)
Capital Punishment, etc. Act 1823 (c.46)
Capital Punishment Abolition Act 1835 (c.81)
Capital Punishment Abolition Act 1836 (c.4)
Capital Punishment Amendment Act 1868 (c.24)
Capital Punishment (Ireland) Act 1842 (c.28)
Capital Transfer Tax Act 1984 (c.51)
Captive Birds Shooting (Prohibition) Act 1921 (c.13)
Captures Act 1776 (c.40)
Car Tax (Abolition) Act 1992 (c.58)
Car Tax Act 1983 (c.53)
Caravan Sites Act 1968 (c.52)
Caravan Sites and Control of Development Act 1960 (c.62)

Caravans (Standard Community Charge and Rating) Act 1991 (c.2)
Cardiff Bay Barrage Act 1993 (c.42)
Cardiff: Improvement Act 1774 (c.9)
Cardigan Roads Act 1770 (c.55)
Cardigan Roads Act 1791 (c.97)
Care and Treatment of Lunatics Act 1853 (c.96)
Care, etc., of Lunatics Act 1841 (c.4)
Care of King During His Illness, etc. Act 1811 (c.1)
Care of King's Estate During His Illness Act 1812 (c.14)
Carers (Recognition and Services) Act 1995 (c.12)
Carlford, Suffolk: Poor Relief Act 1756 (c.79)
Carlford, Suffolk (Poor Relief) Act 1764 (c.58)
Carlisle and Eamont Bridge Road Act 1753 (c.40)
Carlisle and Newcastle Road Act 1750 (c.25)
Carlton Bridge, Yorks. Act 1774 (c.63)
Carmarthen and Pembroke Roads Act 1763 (c.34)
Carmarthen: Improvement Act 1792 (c.104)
Carmarthen Roads Act 1765 (c.76)
Carmarthen Roads Act 1779 (c.102)
Carmarthen Roads Act 1779 (c.103)
Carmarthen Roads Act 1783 (c.33)
Carmarthen Roads Act 1786 (c.150)
Carmarthen Roads Act 1788 (c.109)
Carmarthen Roads Act 1792 (c.156)
Carnarvon Harbour Act 1793 (c.123)
Carnarvon Roads Act 1769 (c.77)
Carnarvon Roads Act 1795 (c.143)
Carriage and Deposit of Dangerous Goods Act 1866 (c.69)
Carriage by Air Act 1931 (c.36)
Carriage by Air Act 1961 (c.27)
Carriage by Air and Road Act 1979 (c.28)
Carriage by Air (Supplementary Provisions) Act 1962 (c.43)
Carriage by Railway Act 1972 (c.33)
Carriage Duties Act 1795 (c.109)
Carriage of Corn, etc. Act 1702 (c.20)
Carriage of Goods by Road Act 1965 (c.37)
Carriage of Goods by Sea Act 1924 (c.22)
Carriage of Goods by Sea Act 1971 (c.19)
Carriage of Goods by Sea Act 1992 (c.50)
Carriage of Gunpowder (Great Britain) Act 1814 (c.152)
Carriage of Passengers by Road Act 1974 (c.35)
Carriers Act 1830 (c.68)
Carriers Act Amendment Act 1865 (c.94)
Carrying of Knives etc. (Scotland) Act 1993 (c.13)
Carts on Highways Act 1744 (c.33)
Casting Away of Vessels, etc. Act 1803 (c.113)
Castle Stewart and Nairn Road Assessment Act 1860 (c.37)
Casual Poor Act 1882 (c.36)
Catering Wages Act 1943 (c.24)
Cathedral Acts Amendment 1873 (c.39)
Cathedral Churches, etc. Act 1853 (c.35)
Cathedral Statutes Act 1707 (c.75)
Cathedrals Act 1864 (c.70)
Catterick Bridge to Durham Road Act 1788 (c.90)
Cattle Assurance Act 1866 (c.34)
Cattle Disease Act 1866 (c.15)
Cattle Disease (Ireland) Act 1866 (c.4)
Cattle Disease (Ireland) Act 1876 (c.51)
Cattle Disease (Ireland) Acts Amendment 1874 (c.6)
Cattle Disease (Ireland) Amendment Act 1872 (c.16)
Cattle Diseases (Ireland) Amendment Act 1870 (c.36)
Cattle Disease Prevention Amendment Act 1866 (c.110)
Cattle Diseases Prevention Act 1866 (c.2)
Cattle Distemper, Vagrancy, Marshalsea Prison Act 1753 (c.34)
Cattle Industry Act 1936 (c.46)
Cattle Industry (Emergency Provisions) Act 1934 (c.54)
Cattle Industry (Emergency Provisions) Act 1935 (c.12)
Cattle Industry (Emergency Provisions) (No. 2) Act 1935 (c.39)
Cattle sheds in Burghs (Scotland) Act 1866 (c.17)
Cattle Stealing Act 1740 (c.6)
Cattle Stealing Act 1741 (c.34)
Cattle Theft (Scotland) Act 1747 (c.34)
Catwater Harbour and Sutton Pool, Plymouth Act 1709 (c.4 (b))
Causey, Yarmouth to Caistor Act 1723 (c.8)
Cawdle Fen. etc. Drainage Act 1737 (c.34)
Cayman Islands Act 1863 (c.31)
Cayman Islands and Turks and Caicos Islands Act 1958 (c.13)
Celluloid and Cinematograph Film Act 1922 (c.35)
Cemeteries Clauses Act 1847 (c.65)
Census Act 1800 (c.15)
Census Act 1841 (c.7)
Census Act 1841 (c.9)
Census Act 1860 (cc.61, 62)
Census Act 1880 (c.37)
Census Act 1920 (c.41)
Census (Confidentiality) Act 1991 (c.6)
Census (England) Act 1870 (c.107)
Census (England and Wales) Act 1890 (c.61)
Census (Great Britain) Act 1811 (c.6)
Census (Great Britain) Act 1840 (c.99)
Census, Great Britain Act 1850 (c.53)
Census (Great Britain) Act 1900 (c.4)
Census (Great Britain) Act 1910 (c.27)
Census (Ireland) Act 1812 (c.133)
Census (Ireland) Act 1815 (c.120)
Census (Ireland) Act 1840 (c.100)
Census (Ireland) Act 1850 (c.44)
Census (Ireland) Act 1870 (c.80)
Census (Ireland) Act 1880 (c.28)

Census (Ireland) Act 1890 (c.46)
Census (Ireland) Act 1900 (c.6)
Census (Ireland) Act 1910 (c.11)
Census of Production Act 1906 (c.49)
Census of Production Act 1917 (c.2)
Census of Production Act 1939 (c.15)
Census (Scotland) Act 1860 (c.98)
Census (Scotland) Act 1870 (c.108)
Census (Scotland) Act 1880 (c.38)
Census (Scotland) Act 1890 (c.38)
Central Criminal Court Act 1837 (c.77)
Central Criminal Court Act 1846 (c.24)
Central Criminal Court Act 1856 (c.16)
Central Criminal Court (Prisons) Act 1881 (c.64)
Central Criminal Lunatic Asylum (Ireland) Act 1845 (c.107)
Cereals Marketing Act 1965 (c.14)
Certain Export Duties Repeal Act 1845 (c.7)
Certain Mutinous Crews Act 1797 (c.71)
Certain Parliamentary Grants Act 1801 (c.73)
Certificates for Killing Hares Act 1791 (c.21)
Certificates of Attorneys, etc. Act 1804 (c.59)
Cessio (Scotland) Act 1836 (c.56)
Cestui que Vie Act 1707 (c.72)
Ceylon Independence Act 1947 (c.7)
Chaff-Cutting Machines (Accidents) Act 1897 (c.60)
Chain Cable and Anchor Act 1864 (c.27)
Chain Cable and Anchor Act 1871 (c.101)
Chain Cable and Anchor Act 1872 (c.30)
Chain Cables and Anchors Act 1874 (c.51)
Chairman of District Councils Act 1896 (c.22)
Chairman of Quarter Sessions (Ireland) Act 1858 (c.88)
Chairman of Quarter Sessions (Ireland) Jurisdiction Act 1876 (c.71)
Chairman of Traffic Commissioners etc. (Tenure of Office) Act 1937 (c.52)
Chancel Repairs Act 1931 (c.20)
Chancery Amendment Act 1858 (c.27)
Chancery and Common Law Offices (Ireland) Act 1867 (c.129)
Chancery Appeal Court (Ireland) Act 1856 (c.92)
Chancery Court Act 1838 (c.54)
Chancery (Ireland) Act 1834 (c.78)
Chancery (Ireland) Act 1835 (c.16)
Chancery (Ireland) Act 1851 (c.15)
Chancery (Ireland) Act 1867 (c.44)
Chancery of Lancaster Act 1890 (c.23)
Chancery Receivers (Ireland) Act 1856 (c.77)
Chancery Regulation Act 1862 (c.42)
Chancery Regulation (Ireland) Act 1862 (c.46)
Chancery Rules and Orders Act 1860 (c.128)
Chancery Taxing Master (Ireland) Act 1845 (c.115)
Channel Tunnel Act 1987 (c.53)
Channel Tunnel (Initial Finance) Act 1973 (c.66)
Channel Tunnel Rail Link Act 1996 (c.61)
Chapel of Ease, Yarmouth Act 1713 (c.16(d))
Chapels of Ease Act 1836 (c.31)
Chapels of Ease, etc. (Ireland) Act 1849 (c.99)
Chaplains in Gaols, etc. (England) Act 1815 (c.48)
Chaplains in the Navy (1820) (c.106)
Charge of Certain Annuities Act 1813 (c.156)
Charge of Loan Act 1807 (c.55)
Charge of Loan Act 1811 (c.61)
Charges of Loan, etc., of Present Session Act 1810 (c.71)
Charge of Loans Act 1809 (c.92)
Charging Orders Act 1979 (c.53)
Charitable Corporation Act 1732 (c.2)
Charitable Corporation (Arrangements with Creditors) Act 1732 (c.36)
Charitable Corporation (Claims and Disputes) Act 1731 (c.31)
Charitable Corporation Frauds Act 1731 (c.3)
Charitable Corporation Lottery Act 1733 (c.11)
Charitable Corporation Lottery Act 1734 (c.14)
Charitable Donations and Bequest (Ireland) Act 1867 (c.54)
Charitable Donations and Bequests (Ireland) Act 1844 (c.97)
Charitable Donations and Bequests (Ireland) Act 1871 (c.102)
Charitable Donations Registration Act 1812 (c.102)
Charitable Funds Investment Act 1870 (c.34)
Charitable Loan Societies (Ireland) Act 1844 (c.38)
Charitable Loan Societies (Ireland) Act 1900 (c.25)
Charitable Loan Societies (Ireland) Act 1906 (c.23)
Charitable Pawn Offices (Ireland) Act 1842 (c.75)
Charitable Trust (Recovery) Act 1891 (c.17)
Charitable Trustees Incorporation Act 1872 (c.24)
Charitable Trusts Act 1853 (c.137)
Charitable Trusts Act 1860 (c.136)
Charitable Trusts Act 1862 (c.112)
Charitable Trusts Act 1869 (c.110)
Charitable Trusts Act 1887 (c.49)
Charitable Trusts Act 1914 (c.56)
Charitable Trusts Act 1925 (c.27)
Charitable Trusts Amendment Act 1855 (c.124)
Charitable Trusts Deeds Enrolment Act 1866 (c.57)
Charitable Trusts (Places of Religious Worship) Amendment Act 1894 (c.35)
Charitable Trusts (Validation) Act 1954 (c.58)
Charitable Uses Act 1735 (c.36)
Charitable Uses Act 1861 (c.9)
Charitable Uses Act 1862 (c.17)
Charities Act 1960 (c.58)
Charities Act 1985 (c.20)
Charities Act 1992 (c.41)

Charities Act 1993 (c.10)
Charities (Amendment) Act 1995 (c.48)
Charities (Enrolment of Deeds) Act 1864 (c.13)
Charities (Fuel Allotments) Act 1939 (c.26)
Charities Inquiries Commission Expenses Act 1837 (c.4)
Charities Inquiries (England) Act 1835 (c.71)
Charities of John Pierrepont Act 1708 (c.10)
Charities of Thomas Guy Act 1724 (c.12)
Charities Procedure Act 1812 (c.101)
Charities (Service of Notice) Act 1851 (c.56)
Charity Inquiries Expenses Act 1892 (c.15)
Charity Lands Act 1863 (c.106)
Charles Beattie Indemnity Act 1956 (c.27)
Charles Radcliffe's Estates Act 1788 (c.63)
Charlwood and Horley Act 1974 (c.11)
Charter Trustees Act 1985 (c.45)
Chartered and Other Bodies (Resumption of Elections) Act 1945 (c.6)
Chartered and Other Bodies (Temporary Provisions) Act 1939 (c.119)
Chartered and Other Bodies (Temporary Provisions) Act 1941 (c.19)
Chartered Associations (Protection of Names and Uniforms) Act 1926 (c.26)
Chartered Companies Act 1837 (c.73)
Chartered Companies Act 1884 (c.56)
Charterhouse Governors (Quorum) Act 1721 (c.29)
Charterhouse Square: Rates Act 1742 (c.6)
Chatham and Sheerness Stipendiary Magistrate Act 1867 (c.63)
Chatham and Sheerness Stipendiary Magistrate Act 1929 (c.30)
Chatham Dockyard Act 1861 (c.41)
Chatham Fortifications Act 1780 (c.49)
Chatham: Improvement Act 1776 (c.58)
Chatham Lands Purchase Act 1857 (c.30)
Chatham Roads Act 1797 (c.155)
Chatham: Streets Act 1772 (c.18)
Cheap Trains Act 1883 (c.34)
Cheap Trains and Canal Carriers Act 1858 (c.75)
Checkweighing in Various Industries Act 1919 (c.51)
Chelmsford and Blackwater Canal Act 1793 (c.93)
Chelmsford Gaol Act 1770 (c.28)
Chelmsford: Improvement Act 1789 (c.44)
Chelmsford Roads Act 1794 (c.137)
Chelsea and Greenwich Out-Pensioners Act 1847 (c.54)
Chelsea and Greenwich Out-Pensioners, etc. Act 1848 (c.84)
Chelsea and Kilmainham Hospitals Act 1826 (c.16)
Chelsea Bridge Act 1858 (c.66)
Chelsea Hospital Act 1755 (c.1)
Chelsea Hospital Act 1812 (c.109)
Chelsea Hospital Act 1815 (c.125)
Chelsea Hospital Act 1843 (c.31)
Chelsea Hospital Act 1858 (c.18)
Chelsea Hospital Act 1876 (c.14)
Chelsea Hospital Out-Pensioners Act 1842 (c.70)
Chelsea Hospital Out-Pensioners Act 1843 (c.95)
Chelsea Hospital Purchase Act 1855 (c.21)
Chelsea and Greenwich Hospitals Act 1815 (c.133)
Chelsea Pensions (Abolition of Poundage) Act 1847 (c.4)
Cheltenham Roads Act 1785 (c.125)
Cheltenham: Streets Act 1786 (c.116)
Chemical Weapons Act 1996 (c.6)
Chequers Estate Act 1917 (c.55)
Chequers Estate Act 1958 (c.60)
Cheques Act 1957 (c.36)
Cheques Act 1992 (c.32)
Cheshire Roads Act 1730 (c.3)
Cheshire Roads Act 1753 (c.62)
Cheshire Roads Act 1774 (c.100)
Cheshire Roads Act 1781 (c.82)
Cheshire Roads Act 1786 (c.139)
Chest of Greenwich Act 1806 (c.101)
Chester and Derby Roads Act 1770 (c.97)
Chester and Derby Roads Act 1789 (c.93)
Chester and Derby Roads Act 1790 (c.88)
Chester and Lancaster Roads Act 1770 (c.89)
Chester and Stafford Roads Act 1783 (c.101)
Chester and Stafford Roads Act 1788 (c.104)
Chester and Whitchurch Roads Act 1778 (c.86)
Chester Courts Act 1867 (c.36)
Chester Highways Act 1705 (c.26)
Chester: Improvement Act 1788 (c.82)
Chester, Lancaster and Yorks. Roads Act 1765 (c.100)
Chester Lighthouse Act 1776 (c.61)
Chester–Nantwich Canal Act 1772 (c.75)
Chester (Poor Relief, etc.) Act 1762 (c.45)
Chester Roads Act 1753 (c.84)
Chester Roads Act 1765 (c.98)
Chester Roads Act 1769 (c.65)
Chester Roads Act 1777 (c.76)
Chester Roads Act 1779 (c.113)
Chester Roads Act 1787 (c.93)
Chester Roads Act 1788 (c.111)
Chester Roads Act 1789 (c.99)
Chester Roads Act 1791 (c.125)
Chester Theatre Act 1776 (c.14)
Chester to Birmingham Road Act 1759 (c.51)
Chesterfield to Stockwith (Trent) Canal Act 1771 (c.75)
Chesterfield to Worksop Road Act 1786 (c.152)
Chevening Estate Act 1959 (c.49)
Chevening Estate Act 1987 (c.20)
Chichester Paving and Improvement Act 1791 (c.63)
Chichester: Poor Relief, etc. Act 1753 (c.100)
Chief Justice's Salary Act 1851 (c.41)
Chief Superintendent in China Act 1859 (c.9)
Child Abduction Act 1984 (c.37)

Child Abduction and Custody Act 1985 (c.60)
Child Benefit Act 1975 (c.61)
Child Care Act 1980 (c.5)
Child Stealing Act 1814 (c.101)
Child Support Act 1991 (c.48)
Child Support Act 1995 (c.34)
Children Act 1908 (c.67)
Children Act 1921 (c.4)
Children Act 1948 (c.43)
Children Act 1958 (c.65)
Children Act 1972 (c.44)
Children Act 1975 (c.72)
Children Act 1989 (c.41)
Children Act (1908) Amendment Act 1910 (c.25)
Children and Young Persons Act 1931 (c.46)
Children and Young Persons Act 1932 (c.46)
Children and Young Persons Act 1933 (c.12)
Children and Young Persons Act 1938 (c.40)
Children and Young Persons Act 1956 (c.24)
Children and Young Persons Act 1963 (c.37)
Children and Young Persons Act 1969 (c.54)
Children and Young Persons Act 1952 (c.50)
Children and Young Persons (Amendment) Act 1986 (c.28)
Children and Young Persons (Harmful Publications) Act 1955 (c.28)
Children and Young Persons (Protection from Tobacco) Act 1991 (c.23)
Children and Young Persons (Scotland) Act 1931 (c.47)
Children and Young Persons (Scotland) Act 1937 (c.37)
Children (Employment Abroad) Act 1913 (c.7)
Children (Scotland) Act 1995 (c.36)
Children's Dangerous Performances Act 1879 (c.34)
Children's (Employment Abroad) Act 1930 (c.21)
Children's Homes Act 1982 (c.20)
Chimney Sweepers Act 1788 (c.48)
Chimney Sweepers Act 1875 (c.70)
Chimney Sweepers Act 1894 (c.51)
Chimney Sweepers Acts (Repeal) Act 1938 (c.58)
Chimney Sweepers and Chimneys Regulation Act 1840 (c.85)
Chimney Sweepers Regulations Act 1864 (c.37)
China (Currency Stabilisation) Act 1939 (c.14)
China Indemnity (Application) Act 1925 (c.41)
China Indemnity (Application) Act 1931 (c.7)
Chinese Passengers Act 1855 (c.104)
Chippenham Roads Act 1726 (c.13)
Chiropractors Act 1994 (c.17)
Cholera, etc. Protection (Ireland) Act 1884 (c.69)
Cholera Hospitals (Ireland) Act 1883 (c.48)
Cholera Hospitals (Ireland) Act 1884 (c.59)
Cholera Hospitals (Ireland) Act 1885 (c.39)
Cholera Hospitals (Ireland) Act 1893 (c.13)
Chorley and Rufford Chapels, Lancaster Act 1793 (c.24)
Christ Church, Oxford Act 1867 (c.76)
Christ Church, Surrey Act 1737 (c.21)
Christ College of Brecknock Act 1853 (c.82)
Christchurch, Middlesex Act 1772 (c.38)
Christchurch, Middlesex: Improvement Act 1788 (c.60)
Christchurch, Middlesex: Light and Watch Act 1737 (c.35)
Christchurch, Stepney: Poor Relief Act 1753 (c.98)
Christchurch, Stepney: Poor Relief Act 1778 (c.74)
Christchurch, Surrey: Improvement Act 1791 (c.61)
Christchurch, Surrey, Streets Act 1793 (c.90)
Christmas Islands Act 1958 (c.25)
Chronically Sick and Disabled Persons Act 1970 (c.44)
Chronically Sick and Disabled Persons (Amendment) Act 1976 (c.49)
Chronically Sick and Disabled Persons (Northern Ireland) Act 1978 (c.53)
Chronically Sick and Disabled Persons (Scotland) Act 1972 (c.51)
Church at Coventry Act 1733 (c.27)
Church at Gravesend Act 1730 (c.20)
Church at Limerick Act 1844 (c.89)
Church at Woolwich Act 1731 (c.4)
Church, Buckingham Act 1776 (c.32)
Church Building Act 1818 (c.45)
Church Building Act 1819 (c.134)
Church Building Act 1822 (c.72)
Church Building Act 1824 (c.103)
Church Building Act 1827 (c.72)
Church Building Act 1831 (c.38)
Church Building Act 1832 (c.61)
Church Building Act 1837 (c.75)
Church Building Act 1838 (c.107)
Church Building Act 1839 (c.49)
Church Building Act 1840 (c.60)
Church Building Act 1845 (c.70)
Church Building Act 1848 (c.37)
Church Building Act 1851 (c.97)
Church Building Act 1854 (c.32)
Church Building Acts Amendment Act 1871 (c.82)
Church Building (Banns and Marriages) Act 1844 (c.56)
Church Building (Burial Service in Chapels) Act 1846 (c.68)
Church Building Commission Act 1848 (c.71)
Church Building Commission Act 1854 (c.14)
Church Building Commissioners (Transfer of Powers) Act 1856 (c.55)
Church Building etc. (Ireland) Act 1808 (c.65)
Church Building (Ireland) Act 1814 (c.117)
Church Discipline Act 1840 (c.86)
Church in Sheffield Act 1739 (c.12)
Church in Strand on Maypole Site: Stepney Advowsons Act 1712 (c.17)
Church, Macclesfield Act 1779 (c.7)

Church of Abthorpe and Foxcoate, Northants Act 1736 (c.21)
Church of Allhallows, City Act 1765 (c.65)
Church of Allhallows, City Act 1766 (c.75)
Church of All Saints, Worcester Act 1737 (c.5)
Church of England 1706 (c.8)
Church of England Act 1966 (c.2)
Church of England Assembly (Powers) Act 1919 (c.76)
Church of Ireland Act 1858 (c.59)
Church of Ireland Act 1863 (c.123)
Church of Ireland Acts Repeal Act 1851 (c.71)
Church of Ireland Act 1851 (c.72)
Church of Scotland Act 1921 (c.29)
Church of Scotland, etc. Act 1748 (c.21)
Church of Scotland Courts Act 1863 (c.47)
Church of Scotland (Property and Endowments) Act 1925 (c.33)
Church of Scotland (Property and Endowments) Amendment Act 1933 (c.44)
Church of St. George, Southwark Act 1732 (c.8)
Church of St. John, Wapping Act 1756 (c.89)
Church of St. Leonard, Shoreditch Act 1734 (c.27)
Church of St. Olave, Southwark Act 1736 (c.18)
Church of Scotland, etc. Act 1743 (c.11)
Church of Scotland (Property and Endowments) Act 1925 (c.33)
Church of Scotland (Property and Endowments) Act 1957 (c.30)
Church of Scotland (Property and Endowments) Amendment Act 1933 (c.44)
Church Patronage Act 1737 (c.17)
Church Patronage Act 1846 (c.88)
Church Patronage Act 1870 (c.39)
Church Patronage (Scotland) Act 1711 (c.21)
Church Patronage (Scotland) Act 1718 (c.29)
Church Patronage (Scotland) Act 1874 (c.82)
Church Seats Act 1872 (c.49)
Church Services (Wales) Act 1863 (c.82)
Church Temporalities Act 1854 (c.11)
Church Temporalities Act 1860 (c.150)
Church Temporalities (Ireland) Act 1836 (c.99)
Church Temporalities (Ireland) Act 1840 (c.101)
Church Temporalities (Ireland) Act 1867 (c.137)
Churches in London and Westminster Act 1711 (c.20 (c))
Churches (Scotland) Act 1905 (c.12)
Cider and Perry Act 1763 (c.7)
Cinemas Act 1985 (c.13)
Cinematograph Act 1909 (c.30)
Cinematograph Act 1952 (c.68)
Cinematograph (Amendment) Act 1982 (c.33)
Cinematograph Films Act 1927 (c.29)
Cinematograph Films Act 1937 (c.17)
Cinematograph Films Act 1948 (c.23)
Cinematograph Films Act 1957 (c.21)
Cinematograph Films Act 1960 (c.14)
Cinematograph Films Act 1975 (c.73)
Cinematograph Films (Animals) Act 1937 (c.59)
Cinematograph Film Production (Special Loans) Act 1949 (c.20)
Cinematograph Film Production (Special Loans) Act 1950 (c.18)
Cinematograph Film Production (Special Loans) Act 1952 (c.20)
Cinematograph Film Production (Special Loans) Act 1954 (c.15)
Cinque Ports Act 1811 (c.36)
Cinque Ports Act 1855 (c.48)
Cinque Ports Act 1857 (c.1)
Cinque Ports Act 1869 (c.53)
Cinque Ports Pilots Act 1813 (c.140)
Circulation of Notes, etc., Issued in France Act 1793 (c.1)
Circuit Clerks (Scotland) Act 1898 (c.40)
Circuit Courts and Criminal Procedure (Scotland) Act 1925 (c.81)
Circuit Courts (Scotland) Act 1828 (c.29)
Circuit Courts (Scotland) Act 1709 (c.16)
Circuits Courts Act 1711 (c.40)
Cirencester Roads Act 1726 (c.11)
Cirencester to Birdlip Hill Road Act 1795 (c.141)
Cirencester to Cricklade Road Act 1779 (c.116)
Citation Amendment (Scotland) Act 1871 (c.42)
Citation Amendment (Scotland) Act 1882 (c.77)
Citations (Scotland) Act 1846 (c.67)
City of London Burial Act 1857 (c.35)
City of London Elections Act 1724 (c.18)
City of London (Garbling of Spices and Admission of Brokers) Act 1707 (c.68)
City of London: Improvement Act 1759 (c.38)
City of London: Improvement Act 1765 (c.91)
City of London: Improvement Act 1785 (c.97)
City of London Militia Act 1662 (c.3)
City of London Militia Act 1813 (c.17)
City of London Militia Act 1813 (c.38)
City of London Parochial Charities Act 1883 (c.36)
City of London Sewerage Act 1771 (c.29)
City Streets Act 1783 (c.46)
Civic Amenities Act 1967 (c.69)
Civic Government (Scotland) Act 1982 (c.45)
Civic Restaurants Act 1947 (c.22)
Civil Aviation Act 1946 (c.70)
Civil Aviation Act 1949 (c.67)
Civil Aviation Act 1968 (c.61)
Civil Aviation Act 1971 (c.75)
Civil Aviation Act 1978 (c.8)
Civil Aviation Act 1980 (c.60)
Civil Aviation Act 1982 (c.16)
Civil Aviation (Air Navigation Charges) Act 1989 (c.9)
Civil Aviation (Amendment) Act 1982 (c.1)
Civil Aviation (Amendment) Act 1996 (c.39)

Civil Aviation Authority (Borrowing Powers) Act 1990 (c.2)
Civil Aviation (Declaratory Provisions) Act 1971 (c.6)
Civil Aviation (Eurocontrol) Act 1962 (c.8)
Civil Aviation (Eurocontrol) Act 1983 (c.11)
Civil Aviation (Licensing) Act 1960 (c.38)
Civil Bill Court (Ireland) Act 1865 (c.1)
Civil Bill Courts (Ireland) Act 1836 (c.75)
Civil Bill Courts (Ireland) Act 1851 (c.57)
Civil Bill Courts (Ireland) Act 1874 (c.66)
Civil Bill Courts Procedure Amendment (Ireland) Act 1864 (c.99)
Civil Bill Courts Procedure Amendment (Ireland) Act 1871 (c.99)
Civil Bill Decrees (Ireland) Act 1842 (c.33)
Civil Contingencies Fund Act 1919 (c.6)
Civil Contingencies Fund Act 1952 (c.2)
Civil Defence Act 1939 (c.31)
Civil Defence Act 1948 (c.6)
Civil Defence Act 1949 (c.5)
Civil Defence (Armed Forces) Act 1954 (c.66)
Civil Defence (Electricity Undertakings) Act 1954 (c.19)
Civil Defence (Suspension of Powers) Act 1945 (c.12)
Civil Evidence Act 1968 (c.64)
Civil Evidence Act 1972 (c.30)
Civil Evidence Act 1995 (c.38)
Civil Evidence (Family Mediation) (Scotland) Act 1995 (c.6)
Civil Evidence (Scotland) Act 1988 (c.32)
Civil Imprisonment (Scotland) Act 1882 (c.42)
Civil Jurisdiction and Judgments Act 1982 (c.27)
Civil Jurisdiction and Judgments Act 1991 (c.12)
Civil Liability (Contribution) Act 1978 (c.47)
Civil List Act 1714 (c.1)
Civil List Act 1727 (c.1)
Civil List Act 1760 (c.1)
Civil List Act 1776 (c.21)
Civil List Act 1785 (c.61)
Civil List Act 1804 (c.80)
Civil List Act 1837 (c.2)
Civil List Act 1901 (c.4)
Civil List Act 1910 (c.28)
Civil List Act 1936 (c.15)
Civil List Act 1937 (c.32)
Civil List Act 1952 (c.37)
Civil List Act 1972 (c.7)
Civil List Act 1975 (c.82)
Civil List and Secret Service Money Act 1782 (c.82)
Civil List Audit Act 1816 (c.46)
Civil List, During King's Illness Act 1812 (c.6)
Civil List (Ireland) Act 1805 (c.76)
Civil Procedure Acts Repeal 1879 (c.59)
Civil Protection in Peacetime Act 1986 (c.22)
Civil Rights of Convicts Act 1828 (c.32)
Civil Service, India Act 1837 (c.70)
Civil Service (Management Functions) Act 1992 (c.61)
Civil Service Superannuation Act 1857 (c.37)
Clackmannan and Perth Roads Act 1794 (c.139)
Clackmannan and Perth Roads Act 1797 (c.166)
Clan Gregour (Scotland) Act 1775 (c.29)
Clandestine Marriages Act 1753 (c.33)
Clandestine Running of Goods, etc. Act 1810 (c.10)
Clapham Church Act 1774 (c.12)
Clapham: Streets Act 1785 (c.88)
Claremont Estate Purchase (Grant of Life Interest) Act 1816 (c.115)
Clean Air Act 1956 (c.52)
Clean Air Act 1968 (c.62)
Clean Air Act 1993 (c.11)
Clean Rivers (Estuaries and Tidal Waters) Act 1960 (c.54)
Cleansing of Persons Act 1897 (c.31)
Clearance of Vessels, London Act 1811 (c.24)
Clergy Discipline Act 1892 (c.32)
Clergy Endowments (Canada) Act 1791 (c.31)
Clergy Ordination Act 1804 (c.43)
Clergy Reserves in Canada Act 1840 (c.78)
Clergy Residences Repair Act 1776 (c.53)
Clergy Residences Repair Act 1781 (c.66)
Clergymen Ordained Abroad Act 1863 (c.121)
Clerical Disabilities Act 1870 (c.91)
Clerical Subscription Act 1865 (c.122)
Clerkenwell Church Act 1788 (c.10)
Clerkenwell: Poor Relief Act 1775 (c.23)
Clerkenwell: Poor Relief Act 1783 (c.44)
Clerkenwell: Streets Act 1774 (c.24)
Clerkenwell: Streets Act 1777 (c.63)
Clerkenwell: Watching, etc. Act 1771 (c.33)
Clerk of Assize (Ireland) Act 1821 (c.54)
Clerk of the Crown (Ireland) Act 1832 (c.48)
Clerk of the Council Act 1859 (c.1)
Clerk of the Crown in Chancery Act 1844 (c.77)
Clerk of the Hanaper Act 1749 (c.25)
Clerks of Assize, etc. Act 1869 (c.89)
Clerks of Session (Scotland) Regulation Act 1889 (c.54)
Clerks of Session (Scotland) Regulation Act 1913 (c.23)
Clerks of the Peace (Removal) Act 1864 (c.65)
Cloth Manufacture Act 1733 (c.25)
Cloth Manufacture Act 1737 (c.28)
Cloth Manufacture Act 1740 (c.35)
Cloth Manufacturer Act 1724 (c.24)
Cloth Manufacture, Yorkshire Act 1765 (c.51)
Cloth Manufacture, Yorkshire Act 1766 (c.23)
Clothing of the Army, etc. Act 1810 (c.107)
Clubs (Temporary Provisions) Act 1915 (c.84)
Clyde Bridge Act 1758 (c.62)
Clyde Marine Society Act 1786 (c.109)
Clyde, Navigation Act 1774 (c.103)

Coaches, Bond Street Act 1792 (c.62)
Coadjutors to Bishops in Ireland Act 1812 (c.62)
Coal Act 1938 (c.52)
Coal Act 1943 (c.38)
Coal (Concurrent Leases) Act 1942 (c.19)
Coal Consumers' Councils (Northern Irish Interests) Act 1962 (c.22)
Coal Duty, Dublin Act 1811 (c.11)
Coal Duty, London Act 1845 (c.101)
Coal Industry Act 1949 (c.53)
Coal Industry Act 1951 (c.41)
Coal Industry Act 1956 (c.61)
Coal Industry Act 1960 (c.17)
Coal Industry Act 1961 (c.5)
Coal Industry Act 1962 (c.6)
Coal Industry Act 1965 (c.82)
Coal Industry Act 1967 (c.91)
Coal Industry Act 1971 (c.16)
Coal Industry Act 1973 (c.8)
Coal Industry Act 1975 (c.56)
Coal Industry Act 1977 (c.39)
Coal Industry Act 1980 (c.50)
Coal Industry Act 1982 (c.15)
Coal Industry Act 1983 (c.60)
Coal Industry Act 1985 (c.27)
Coal Industry Act 1987 (c.3)
Coal Industry Act 1990 (c.3)
Coal Industry Act 1992 (c.17)
Coal Industry Act 1994 (c.21)
Coal Industry Commission Act 1919 (c.1)
Coal Industry Nationalisation Act 1946 (c.59)
Coal Industry (No. 2) Act 1949 (c.79)
Coal Loading: Newcastle and Sunderland Act 1766 (c.22)
Coal Loading: Newcastle and Sunderland Act 1772 (c.22)
Coal Measurement, London Act 1776 (c.13)
Coal Metage, etc., London Act 1766 (c.23)
Coal Mines Act 1855 (c.107)
Coal Mines Act 1862 (c.79)
Coal Mines Act 1886 (c.40)
Coal Mines Act 1911 (c.50)
Coal Mines Act 1914 (c.22)
Coal Mines Act 1919 (c.48)
Coal Mines Act 1926 (c.17)
Coal Mines Act 1930 (c.34)
Coal Mines Act 1931 (c.27)
Coal Mines Act 1932 (c.29)
Coal Mines (Check Weigher) Act 1894 (c.52)
Coal Mines Control Agreement (Confirmation) Act 1918 (c.56)
Coal Mines (Decontrol) Act 1921 (c.6)
Coal Mines (Employment of Boys) Act 1937 (c.62)
Coal Mines Inspection Act 1850 (c.100)
Coal Mines (Minimum Wage) Act 1912 (c.2)
Coal Mines Regulation Act 1872 (c.76)
Coal Mines Regulation Act 1887 (c.58)
Coal Mines Regulation Act (1887) Amendment 1903 (c.7)
Coal Mines Regulation Act 1896 (c.43)
Coal Mines Regulation Act 1908 (c.57)
Coal Mines Regulation (Amendment) Act 1917 (c.8)
Coal Mines (Weighing of Minerals) Act 1905 (c.9)
Coal Mining (Subsidence) Act 1950 (c.23)
Coal Mining (Subsidence) Act 1957 (c.59)
Coal Mining Subsidence Act 1991 (c.45)
Coal (Registration of Ownership) Act 1937 (c.56)
Coal Trade Act 1710 (c.30)
Coal Trade Act 1730 (c.26)
Coal Trade Act 1730 (c.30)
Coal Trade Act 1788 (c.53)
Coal Trade Act 1836 (c.109)
Coal Trade, London Act 1745 (c.35)
Coal Trade, London Act 1758 (c.27)
Coal Trade, London Act 1786 (c.83)
Coal Trade, London Act 1796 (c.61)
Coal Trade: Westminster Act 1766 (c.35)
Coal Trade, Westminster Act 1786 (c.108)
Coal Vendors Act 1843 (c.2)
Coalport Bridge over Severn (Tolls, etc.) Act 1776 (c.12)
Coals Act 1743 (c.35)
Coals, Newcastle Act 1782 (c.32)
Coalwhippers, London Act 1851 (c.78)
Coalwhippers, Port of London Act 1846 (c.36)
Coast Protection Act 1939 (c.39)
Coast Protection Act 1949 (c.74)
Coast Trade Act 1792 (c.50)
Coastal Flooding (Emergency Provisions) Act 1953 (c.18)
Coastguard Act 1925 (c.88)
Coastguard Service Act 1856 (c.83)
Coasting Trade Act 1805 (c.81)
Coasting Trade Act 1854 (c.5)
Coatbridge and Springburn Elections (Validation) Act 1945 (c.3)
Cobham, Leatherhead and Godalming Bridges Act 1782 (c.17)
Cockburnspath Bridge, Berwick Act 1789 (c.42)
Cockermouth and Workington Road Act 1779 (c.105)
Cockerton Bridge to Staindrop Road Act 1793 (c.146)
Cockfighting Act 1952 (c.59)
Cocos Islands Act 1955 (c.5)
Codbreck Brook, Navigation Act 1767 (c.95)
Coffee and Cocoa-Nuts Act 1783 (c.79)
Coffee, etc. Act 1812 (c.149)
Coffee, etc. Act 1814 (c.47)
Coin Act 1732 (c.26)
Coin Act 1774 (c.70)
Coin Act 1816 (c.68)
Coin Act 1849 (c.41)
Coinage Act 1708 (c.24)
Coinage Act 1859 (c.30)
Coinage Act 1870 (c.10)
Coinage Act 1889 (c.58)
Coinage Act 1891 (c.72)
Coinage Act 1893 (c.1)
Coinage Act 1946 (c.74)

Coinage Act 1971 (c.24)
Coinage (Colonial Offences) Act 1853 (c.48)
Coinage Duties Act 1730 (c.12)
Coinage Duties Act 1738 (c.5)
Coinage Duties Act 1745 (c.14)
Coinage Duties Act 1760 (c.16)
Coinage Duties Act 1769 (c.25)
Coinage Duties, etc. Act 1754 (c.11)
Coinage in American Plantations Act 1707 (c.57)
Coinage Offences Act 1861 (c.99)
Coinage Offences Act 1936 (c.16)
Colewort Barracks, Portsmouth Act 1860 (c.49)
Collecting Societies and Industrial Assurance Companies Act 1896 (c.26)
Collection of Charity Money Act 1705 (c.25)
Collection of Malt Duties, etc. Act 1805 (c.53)
Collection of Revenue, etc. (Ireland) Act 1803 (c.98)
Collection of Revenue (Ireland) Act 1803 (c.43)
Collection of Revenue (Ireland) Act 1803 (c.97)
Collection of Revenue (Ireland) Act 1804 (c.105)
Collection of Revenues (Ireland) Act 1802 (c.36)
College Charter Act 1871 (c.63)
College of Physicians (Ireland) Act 1862 (c.15)
Collegiate Church of Manchester Act 1728 (c.29)
Collieries and Mines Act 1800 (c.77)
Collieries (Ireland) Act 1807 (c.45)
Colliers Act 1775 (c.28)
Colliers (Scotland) Act 1799 (c.56)
Collingham to York Road Act 1792 (c.142)
Colneis and Carlford Hundreds, Suffolk: Poor Relief Act 1790 (c.22)
Colne Oyster Fishery Act 1757 (c.71)
Colne River, Essex: Navigation Act 1718 (c.31)
Colonial Acts Confirmation Act 1863 (c.84)
Colonial Acts Confirmation Act 1894 (c.72)
Colonial Acts Confirmation Act 1901 (c.29)
Colonial Affidavits Act 1859 (c.12)
Colonial and Other Territories (Divorce Jurisdiction) Act 1950 (c.20)
Colonial Attorneys Relief Act 1857 (c.39)
Colonial Attorneys Relief Act 1874 (c.41)
Colonial Attorneys Relief Amendment Act 1884 (c.24)
Colonial Bishops Act 1852 (c.52)
Colonial Bishops Act 1853 (c.49)
Colonial Boundaries Act 1895 (c.34)
Colonial Branch Mint Act 1866 (c.65)
Colonial Clergy Act 1874 (c.77)
Colonial Copyright Act 1847 (c.95)
Colonial Courts of Admiralty Act 1890 (c.27)
Colonial Development Act 1929 (c.5)
Colonial Development and Welfare Act 1939 (c.40)
Colonial Development and Welfare Act 1944 (c.20)
Colonial Development and Welfare Act 1949 (c.49)
Colonial Development and Welfare Act 1950 (c.4)
Colonial Development and Welfare Act 1955 (c.6)
Colonial Development and Welfare Act 1959 (c.71)
Colonial Docks Loans Act 1865 (c.106)
Colonial Duties Act 1842 (c.49)
Colonial Fortifications Act 1877 (c.23)
Colonial Governors (Pensions) Act 1865 (c.113)
Colonial Governors (Pensions) Act 1872 (c.29)
Colonial Inland Post Office Act 1849 (c.66)
Colonial Laws Validity Act 1865 (c.63)
Colonial Leave of Absence Act 1782 (c.75)
Colonial Letters Patent Act 1863 (c.76)
Colonial Loans Act 1899 (c.36)
Colonial Loans Act 1949 (c.50)
Colonial Loans Act 1952 (c.1)
Colonial Loans Act 1962 (c.41)
Colonial Marriages Act 1865 (c.64)
Colonial Marriages (Deceased Wife's Sister) Act 1906 (c.30)
Colonial Naval Defence Act 1865 (c.14)
Colonial Naval Defence Act 1909 (c.19)
Colonial Naval Defence Act 1931 (c.9)
Colonial Naval Defence Act 1949 (c.18)
Colonial Officers (Leave of Absence) Act 1894 (c.17)
Colonial Offices Act 1830 (c.4)
Colonial Prisoners Removal Act 1869 (c.10)
Colonial Prisoners Removal Act 1884 (c.31)
Colonial Probates Act 1892 (c.6)
Colonial Probates (Protected States and Mandated Territories) Act 1927 (c.43)
Colonial Shipping Act 1868 (c.129)
Colonial Solicitors Act 1900 (c.14)
Colonial Stock Act 1877 (c.59)
Colonial Stock Act 1892 (c.35)
Colonial Stock Act 1900 (c.62)
Colonial Stock Act 1934 (c.47)
Colonial Stock Act 1948 (c.1)
Colonial Trade Act 1730 (c.28)
Colonial Trade Act 1734 (c.19)
Colonial Trade Act 1738 (c.30)
Colonial Trade Act 1760 (c.9)
Colonial Trade Act 1763 (c.27)
Colonial Trade Act 1768 (c.22)
Colonial Trade Act 1769 (c.27)
Colonial Trade Act 1812 (c.98)
Colonial War Risks Insurance (Guarantees) Act 1941 (c.35)
(Colonies) Evidence Act 1843 (c.22)
Colony of New York Act 1770 (c.35)
Colouring of Porter Act 1811 (c.87)
Combination of Workmen Act 1796 (c.111)
Combinations of Workmen Act 1801 (c.38)
Combination of Workmen Act 1859 (c.34)

Commerce with Certain Countries Act 1721 (c.8)
Commerce with Spain Act 1739 (c.27)
Commerce with Sweden Act 1716 (c.1)
Commerce with United States Act 1816 (c.15)
Commerce with United States Act 1816 (c.51)
Commercial Treaty with Portugal Act 1811 (c.47)
Commissariat Accounts Act 1821 (c.121)
Commissary Court of Edinburgh Act 1815 (c.97)
Commissary Court of Edinburgh, etc. Act 1836 (c.41)
Commissioners Clauses Act 1847 (c.16)
Commissioners for Oaths Act 1853 (c.78)
Commissioners for Oaths Act 1855 (c.42)
Commissioners for Oaths Act 1889 (c.10)
Commissioners for Oaths Act 1891 (c.50)
Commissioners for Oaths Amendment Act 1890 (c.7)
Commissioners for Oaths, Bail in Error, etc. Act 1859
Commissioners for Oaths, Bail in Error, etc. Act 1859 (c.16)
Commissioners for Oaths (Ireland) Act 1872 (c.75)
Commissioners for Oaths (Prize Proceedings) Act 1907 (c.25)
Commissioners of Customs Act 1845 (c.85)
Commissioners of Sewers (City of London) Act 1708 (c.32)
Commissioners of Supply Meetings (Scotland) Act 1865 (c.38)
Commissioners of Supply (Scotland) Act 1856 (c.93)
Commissioners of Supply (Scotland) Act 1857 (c.11)
Commissioners of the Treasury Act 1807 (c.20)
Commissioners of Woods (Audit) Act 1844 (c.89)
Commissioners of Woods (Thames Piers) Act 1879 (c.73)
Commissioners of Works Act 1852 (c.28)
Commissioners of Works Act 1894 (c.23)
Commissions of Sewers Act 1708 (c.33)
Commissions of the Peace Continuance Act 1837 (c.1)
Commissions to Foreign Protestants Act 1756 (c.5)
Commissions and Salaries of Judges Act 1760 (c.23)
Commission of Assize in County Palatine of Lancaster Act 1855 (c.45)
Common Informers Act 1951 (c.39)
Common Land (Rectification of Registers) Act 1989 (c.18)
Common Law Chambers Act 1867 (c.68)
Common Law Courts Act 1852 (c.73)
Common Law Courts (Fees) Act 1865 (c.45)
Common Law Courts (Fees and Salaries) Act 1866 (c.101)
Common Law Courts (Ireland) Act 1851 (c.17)
Common Law Offices (Ireland) Act 1844 (c.107)
Common Law Procedure Act 1838 (c.45)
Common Law Procedure Act 1852 (c.76)
Common Law Procedure Act 1854 (c.125)
Common Law Procedure Act 1860 (c.126)
Common Law Procedure Act 1864 (c.28)
Common Law Procedure Amendment (Ireland) Act 1853 (c.113)
Common Law Procedure Amendment (Ireland) Act 1856 (c.102)
Common Law Procedure Amendment (Ireland) Act 1870 (c.109)
Common Law Procedure (Ireland) Act 1855 (c.7)
Common Law Procedure (Ireland) Act 1860 (c.82)
Common Lodging House Act 1853 (c.41)
Common Lodging Houses Act 1851 (c.28)
Common Lodging Houses (Ireland) Act 1860 (c.26)
Common Pleas of Lancaster Act 1794 (c.46)
Common Pleas of Lancaster Act 1800 (c.105)
Common Pleas at Lancaster Amendment Act 1869 (c.37)
Common Recoveries, etc. Act 1740 (c.20)
Commonable Rights Compensation Act 1882 (c.15)
Commons Act 1876 (c.56)
Commons Act 1879 (c.37)
Commons Act 1899 (c.30)
Commons Act 1908 (c.44)
Commons (Expenses) Act 1878 (c.56)
Commons Registration Act 1965 (c.64)
Commonwealth Development Act 1963 (c.40)
Commonwealth Development Corporation Act 1978 (c.2)
Commonwealth Development Corporation Act 1982 (c.54)
Commonwealth Development Corporation Act 1986 (c.25)
Commonwealth Development Corporation Act 1995 (c.9)
Commonwealth Development Corporation Act 1996 (c.28)
Commonwealth Immigrants Act 1962 (c.21)
Commonwealth Immigration Act 1968 (c.9)
Commonwealth (India (Consequential) Provisions) Act 1949 (c.92)
Commonwealth Institute Act 1958 (c.16)
Commonwealth of Australia Constitution Act 1900 (c.12)
Commonwealth Scholarships Act 1959 (c.6)
Commonwealth Scholarships (Amendment) Act 1963 (c.6)
Commonwealth Secretariat Act 1966 (c.10)
Commonwealth Settlement Act 1957 (c.8)
Commonwealth Settlement Act 1962 (c.17)
Commonwealth Settlement Act 1967 (c.31)
Commonwealth Teachers Act 1960 (c.40)

Commonwealth Telecommunications Act 1968 (c.24)
Commonwealth Telegraphs Act 1949 (c.39)
Communications from Marylebone to Charing Cross Act 1813 (c.121)
Community Care (Direct Payments) Act 1996 (c.30)
Community Care (Residential Accommodation) Act 1992 (c.49)
Community Charges (General Reduction) Act 1991 (c.9)
Community Charges (Substitute Setting) Act 1991 (c.8)
Community Health Councils (Access to Information) Act 1988 (c.24)
Community Land Act 1975 (c.77)
Community Service by Offenders (Scotland) Act 1978 (c.49)
Companies Act 1862 (c.89)
Companies Act 1867 (c.131)
Companies Act 1877 (c.26)
Companies Act 1879 (c.76)
Companies Act 1880 (c.19)
Companies Act 1883 (c.28)
Companies Act 1886 (c.23)
Companies Act 1898 (c.26)
Companies Act 1900 (c.48)
Companies Act 1907 (c.50)
Companies Act 1908 (c.12)
Companies Act 1913 (c.25)
Companies Act 1928 (c.45)
Companies Act 1929 (c.23)
Companies Act 1947 (c.47)
Companies Act 1948 (c.38)
Companies Act 1967 (c.81)
Companies Act 1976 (c.69)
Companies Act 1980 (c.22)
Companies Act 1981 (c.62)
Companies Act 1985 (c.6)
Companies Act 1989 (c.40)
Companies (Beneficial Interests) Act 1983 (c.50)
Companies Clauses Act 1863 (c.118)
Companies Clauses Act 1869 (c.48)
Companies Clauses Consolidation Act 1845 (c.16)
Companies Clauses Consolidation Act 1888 (c.48)
Companies Clauses Consolidation Act 1889 (c.37)
Companies Clauses Consolidation (Scotland) Act 1845 (c.17)
Companies (Colonial Registers) Act 1883 (c.30)
Companies (Consolidation) Act 1908 (c.69)
Companies Consolidation (Consequential Provisions) Act 1985 (c.9)
Companies (Converted Societies) Act 1910 (c.23)
Companies (Defence) Act 1939 (c.75)
Companies (Floating Charges and Receivers) (Scotland) Act 1972 (c.67)
Companies (Floating Charges) (Scotland) Act 1961 (c.46)
Companies (Foreign Interests) Act 1917 (c.18)
Companies (Memorandum of Association) Act 1890 (c.62)
Companies (Particulars as to Directors) Act 1917 (c.28)
Companies (Winding-up) Act 1890 (c.63)
Companies (Winding-up) Act 1893 (c.58)
Company Directors (Disqualification) Act 1986 (c.46)
Company Seals Act 1864 (c.19)
Company Securities (Insider Dealing) Act 1985 (c.8)
Compassionate List of the Navy, etc. Act 1809 (c.45)
Compensation (Defence) Act 1939 (c.75)
Compensation for Injuries to Mills etc. Act 1801 (c.24)
Compensation for Works at Portsmouth Act 1815 (c.123)
Compensation of Displaced Officers (War Service) Act 1945 (c.10)
Compensation to American Loyalists, etc. Act 1788 (c.40)
Compensation to Patentee Officers (Ireland) Act 1808 (c.108)
Competency of Witnesses Act 1787 (c.29)
Competition Act 1980 (c.21)
Competition and Service (Utilities) Act 1992 (c.43)
Completing St. Paul's, etc. Act 1702 (c.12)
Completion of Somerset House Act 1780 (c.40)
Composition for a Certain Crown Debt Act 1770 (c.12)
Composition for a Crown Debt Act 1774 (c.35)
Composition for a Crown Debt Act 1775 (c.19)
Composition for a Crown Debt Act 1776 (c.31)
Composition for a Crown Debt Act 1776 (c.49)
Composition for a Crown Debt Act 1779 (c.77)
Composition for a Crown Debt Act 1784 (c.14)
Composition for a Crown Debt Act 1801 (c.60)
Compound Householders Act 1851 (c.14)
Comptroller of the Exchequer, etc. Act 1865 (c.93)
Compulsory Church Date Abolition 1868 (c.109)
Compulsory Purchase Act 1965 (c.56)
Compulsory Purchase (Vesting Declarations) Act 1981 (c.66)
Computer Misuse Act 1990 (c.18)
Concealment of Birth (Scotland) Act 1809 (c.14)
Concessionary Travel for Handicapped Persons (Scotland) Act 1980 (c.29)
Conciliation Act 1896 (c.30)

Concorde Aircraft Act 1973 (c.7)
Confirmation and Probate Amendment Act 1859 (c.30)
Confirmation of Certain Marriages Act 1781 (c.53)
Confirmation of Certain Marriages Act 1858 (c.46)
Confirmation of Certain Marriages Act 1889 (c.38)
Confirmation of Certain Proceedings Act 1842 (c.43)
Confirmation of Executors (Scotland) Act 1823 (c.98)
Confirmation of Executors (Scotland) Act 1858 (c.56)
Confirmation of Executors (War Service) (Scotland) Act 1917 (c.27)
Confirmation of Executors (War Service) (Scotland) Act 1939 (c.41)
Confirmation of Executors (War Service) (Scotland) Act 1940 (c.41)
Confirmation of Marriages Act 1853 (c.122)
Confirmation of Marriages Act 1854 (c.88)
Confirmation of Marriages Act 1855 (c.66)
Confirmation of Marriages Act 1856 (c.70)
Confirmation of Marriages Act 1857 (c.29)
Confirmation of Marriages Act 1859 (c.24)
Confirmation of Marriages Act 1859 (c.64)
Confirmation of Marriages Act 1860 (c.1)
Confirmation of Marriages Act 1861 (c.16)
Confirmation of Marriages, Blakedown Chapel Act 1868 (c.113)
Confirmation of Marriages (Cove Chapel) Act 1873 (c.1)
Confirmation of Marriages on Her Majesty's Ships Act 1879 (c.29)
Confirmation of Provision Order (Land Drainage) Act 1867 (c.22)
Confirmation of Provisional Orders, Turnpike Trusts Act 1867 (c.66)
Confirmation of Sales etc., by Trustees Act 1862 (c.108)
Confirmation to Small Estates (Scotland) Act 1979 (c.22)
Congenital Disabilities (Civil Liability) Act 1976 (c.28)
Congested Districts Board (Ireland) Act 1893 (c.35)
Congested Districts Board (Ireland) Act 1894 (c.50)
Congested Districts Board (Ireland) Act 1899 (c.18)
Congested Districts Board (Ireland) Act 1901 (c.34)
Congested Districts (Scotland) Act 1897 (c.53)
Conjugal Rights (Scotland) Amendment Act 1861 (c.86)
Conjugal Rights (Scotland) Amendment Act 1874 (c.31)
Consecration of Bishops Abroad Act 1786 (c.84)
Consecration of Churchyards Act 1867 (c.133)
Consecration of Churchyards Act 1868 (c.47)
Conservation of Seals Act 1970 (c.30)
Conservation of Wild Creatures and Wild Plants Act 1975 (c.48)
Consolidated Annuities (Ireland) Act 1853 (c.75)
Consolidated Fund Act 1806 (c.44)
Consolidated Fund Act 1816 (c.98)
Consolidated Fund Act 1947 (c.17)
Consolidated Fund Act 1950 (c.1)
Consolidated Fund Act 1951 (c.12)
Consolidated Fund Act 1952 (c.16)
Consolidated Fund Act 1953 (c.6)
Consolidated Fund Act 1954 (c.22)
Consolidated Fund Act 1955 (c.3)
Consolidated Fund Act 1956 (c.32)
Consolidated Fund Act 1957 (c.7)
Consolidated Fund Act 1958 (c.7)
Consolidated Fund Act 1960 (c.10)
Consolidated Fund Act 1963 (c.1)
Consolidated Fund Act 1965 (c.1)
Consolidated Fund Act 1966 (c.1)
Consolidated Fund Act 1968 (c.1)
Consolidated Fund Act 1969 (c.3)
Consolidated Fund Act 1970 (c.1)
Consolidated Fund Act 1971 (c.1)
Consolidated Fund Act 1972 (c.13)
Consolidated Fund Act 1973 (c.1)
Consolidated Fund Act 1974 (c.1)
Consolidated Fund Act 1975 (c.1)
Consolidated Fund Act 1976 (c.2)
Consolidated Fund Act 1977 (c.1)
Consolidated Fund Act 1978 (c.7)
Consolidated Fund Act 1979 (c.20)
Consolidated Fund Act 1980 (c.14)
Consolidated Fund Act 1981 (c.4)
Consolidated Fund Act 1982 (c.8)
Consolidated Fund Act 1983 (c.1)
Consolidated Fund Act 1984 (c.1)
Consolidated Fund Act 1985 (c.1)
Consolidated Fund Act 1986 (c.4)
Consolidated Fund Act 1987 (c.8)
Consolidated Fund Act 1988 (c.6)
Consolidated Fund Act 1989 (c.2)
Consolidated Fund Act 1990 (c.4)
Consolidated Fund Act 1991 (c.7)
Consolidated Fund Act 1992 (c.1)
Consolidated Fund Act 1993 (c.4)
Consolidated Fund Act 1994 (c.4)
Consolidated Fund Act 1995 (c.2)
Consolidated Fund Act 1996 (c.4)
Consolidated Fund (Civil List Provisions) Act 1951 (c.50)
Consolidated Fund (No. 1) Act 1879 (c.2)
Consolidated Fund (No. 1) Act 1880 (c.5)
Consolidated Fund (No. 1) Act 1881 (c.1)
Consolidated Fund (No. 1) Act 1882 (c.1)
Consolidated Fund (No. 1) Act 1883 (c.2)
Consolidated Fund (No. 1) Act 1884 (c.2)
Consolidated Fund (No. 1) Act 1884 (c.4)
Consolidated Fund (No. 1) Act 1886 (c.4)
Consolidated Fund (No. 1) Act 1887 (c.1)
Consolidated Fund (No. 1) Act 1888 (c.1)

Consolidated Fund (No. 1) Act 1889 (c.1)
Consolidated Fund (No. 1) Act 1890 (c.1)
Consolidated Fund (No. 1) Act 1891 (c.6)
Consolidated Fund (No. 1) Act 1892 (c.3)
Consolidated Fund (No. 1) Act 1893 (c.3)
Consolidated Fund (No. 1) Act 1894 (c.1)
Consolidated Fund (No. 1) Act 1895 (c.4)
Consolidated Fund (No. 1) Act 1896 (c.3)
Consolidated Fund (No. 1) Act 1897 (c.4)
Consolidated Fund (No. 1) Act 1898 (c.3)
Consolidated Fund (No. 1) Act 1899 (c.2)
Consolidated Fund (No. 1) Act 1900 (c.1)
Consolidated Fund (No. 1) Act 1901 (c.1)
Consolidated Fund (No. 1) Act 1902 (c.1)
Consolidated Fund (No. 1) Act 1903 (c.3)
Consolidated Fund (No. 1) Act 1904 (c.1)
Consolidated Fund (No. 1) Act 1905 (c.1)
Consolidated Fund (No. 1) Act 1906 (c.1)
Consolidated Fund (No. 1) Act 1907 (c.1)
Consolidated Fund (No. 1) Act 1908 (c.1)
Consolidated Fund (No. 1) Act 1909 (c.1)
Consolidated Fund (No. 1) Act 1910 (c.4)
Consolidated Fund (No. 1) Act 1911 (c.1)
Consolidated Fund (No. 1) Act 1912 (c.1)
Consolidated Fund (No. 1) Act 1913 (c.1)
Consolidated Fund (No. 1) Act 1914 (c.1)
Consolidated Fund (No. 1) Act 1916 (c.1)
Consolidated Fund (No. 1) Act 1917 (c.1)
Consolidated Fund (No. 1) Act 1918 (c.1)
Consolidated Fund (No. 1) Act 1919 (c.5)
Consolidated Fund (No. 1) Act 1921 (c.2)
Consolidated Fund (No. 1) Act 1922 (c.1)
Consolidated Fund (No. 1) Act 1923 (c.1)
Consolidated Fund (No. 1) Act 1924 (c.2)
Consolidated Fund (No. 1) Act 1925 (c.8)
Consolidated Fund (No. 1) Act 1926 (c.1)
Consolidated Fund (No. 1) Act 1927 (c.2)
Consolidated Fund (No. 1) Act 1928 (c.1)
Consolidated Fund (No. 1) Act 1928 (c.2)
Consolidated Fund (No. 1) Act 1929 (c.10)
Consolidated Fund (No. 1) Act 1932 (c.1)
Consolidated Fund (No. 1) Act 1932 (c.14)
Consolidated Fund (No. 1) Act 1934 (c.3)
Consolidated Fund (No. 1) Act 1935 (c.4)
Consolidated Fund (No. 1) Act 1936 (c.8)
Consolidated Fund (No. 1) Act 1937 (c.7)
Consolidated Fund (No. 1) Act 1938 (c.9)
Consolidated Fund (No. 1) Act 1939 (c.12)
Consolidated Fund (No. 1) Act 1940 (c.11)
Consolidated Fund (No. 1) Act 1941 (c.6)
Consolidated Fund (No. 1) Act 1943 (c.4)
Consolidated Fund (No. 1) Act 1944 (c.1)
Consolidated Fund (No. 1) Act 1944 (c.4)
Consolidated Fund (No. 1) Act 1945 (c.4)
Consolidated Fund (No. 1) Act 1946 (c.33)
Consolidated Fund (No. 1) Act 1948 (c.18)
Consolidated Fund (No. 1) Act 1949 (c.24)
Consolidated Fund (No. 1) (Session 2) Act 1880 (c.3)
Consolidated Fund (No. 1) (Session 2) Act 1914 (c.6)
Consolidated Fund (No. 1) (Session 2) Act 1931 (c.1)
Consolidated Fund (No. 1) (Session 2) Act 1941 (c.2)
Consolidated Fund (No. 2) Act 1879 (c.7)
Consolidated Fund (No. 2) Act 1881 (c.8)
Consolidated Fund (No. 2) Act 1882 (c.4)
Consolidated Fund (No. 2) Act 1883 (c.5)
Consolidated Fund (No. 2) Act 1884 (c.15)
Consolidated Fund (No. 2) Act 1885 (c.6)
Consolidated Fund (No. 2) Act 1886 (c.7)
Consolidated Fund (No. 2) Act 1887 (c.14)
Consolidated Fund (No. 2) Act 1888 (c.16)
Consolidated Fund (No. 2) Act 1889 (c.2)
Consolidated Fund (No. 2) Act 1890 (c.28)
Consolidated Fund (No. 2) Act 1891 (c.27)
Consolidated Fund (No. 2) Act 1892 (c.20)
Consolidated Fund (No. 2) Act 1893 (c.16)
Consolidated Fund (No. 2) Act 1894 (c.7)
Consolidated Fund (No. 2) Act 1895 (c.15)
Consolidated Fund (No. 2) Act 1896 (c.7)
Consolidated Fund (No. 2) Act 1898 (c.32)
Consolidated Fund (No. 2) Act 1900 (c.3)
Consolidated Fund (No. 2) Act 1901 (c.6)
Consolidated Fund (No. 2) Act 1905 (c.6)
Consolidated Fund (No. 2) Act 1909 (c.2)
Consolidated Fund (No. 2) Act 1910 (c.9(a))
Consolidated Fund (No. 2) Act 1911 (c.5)
Consolidated Fund (No. 2) Act 1913 (c.5)
Consolidated Fund (No. 2) Act 1915 (c.33)
Consolidated Fund (No. 2) Act 1916 (c.3)
Consolidated Fund (No. 2) Act 1917 (c.7)
Consolidated Fund (No. 2) Act 1918 (c.11)
Consolidated Fund (No. 2) Act 1919 (c.49)
Consolidated Fund (No. 2) Act 1921 (c.3)
Consolidated Fund (No. 2) Act 1922 (c.3)
Consolidated Fund (No. 2) Act 1924 (c.4)
Consolidated Fund (No. 2) Act 1929 (c.10)
Consolidated Fund (No. 2) Act 1930 (c.14)
Consolidated Fund (No. 2) Act 1931 (c.10)
Consolidated Fund (No. 2) Act 1933 (c.3)
Consolidated Fund (No. 2) Act 1935 (c.10)
Consolidated Fund (No. 2) Act 1936 (c.11)
Consolidated Fund (No. 2) Act 1937 (c.20)
Consolidated Fund (No. 2) Act 1939 (c.39)
Consolidated Fund (No. 2) Act 1941 (c.9)
Consolidated Fund (No. 2) Act 1942 (c.12)
Consolidated Fund (No. 2) Act 1943 (c.11)
Consolidated Fund (No. 2) Act 1944 (c.17)
Consolidated Fund (No. 2) Act 1945 (c.4)
Consolidated Fund (No. 2) Act 1957 (c.10)
Consolidated Fund (No. 2) Act 1958 (c.18)
Consolidated Fund (No. 2) Act 1961 (c.12)
Consolidated Fund (No. 2) Act 1962 (c.11)
Consolidated Fund (No. 2) Act 1963 (c.8)
Consolidated Fund (No. 2) Act 1964 (c.17)
Consolidated Fund (No. 2) Act 1965 (c.8)
Consolidated Fund (No. 2) Act 1967 (c.6)
Consolidated Fund (No. 2) Act 1968 (c.15)
Consolidated Fund (No. 2) Act 1969 (c.9)
Consolidated Fund (No. 2) Act 1970 (c.12)
Consolidated Fund (No. 2) Act 1971 (c.14)
Consolidated Fund (No. 2) Act 1972 (c.23)
Consolidated Fund (No. 2) Act 1973 (c.10)
Consolidated Fund (No. 2) Act 1974 (c.12)

Consolidated Fund (No. 2) Act 1975 (c.12)
Consolidated Fund (No. 2) Act 1976 (c.84)
Consolidated Fund (No. 2) Act 1977 (c.52)
Consolidated Fund (No. 2) Act 1978 (c.59)
Consolidated Fund (No. 2) Act 1979 (c.56)
Consolidated Fund (No. 2) Act 1980 (c.68)
Consolidated Fund (No. 2) Act 1981 (c.70)
Consolidated Fund (No. 2) Act 1983 (c.5)
Consolidated Fund (No. 2) Act 1984 (c.61)
Consolidated Fund (No. 2) Act 1985 (c.11)
Consolidated Fund (No. 2) Act 1986 (c.67)
Consolidated Fund (No. 2) Act 1987 (c.54)
Consolidated Fund (No. 2) Act 1988 (c.55)
Consolidated Fund (No. 2) Act 1989 (c.46)
Consolidated Fund (No. 2) Act 1990 (c.46)
Consolidated Fund (No. 2) Act 1991 (c.10)
Consolidated Fund (No. 2) Act 1992 (c.21)
Consolidated Fund (No. 2) Act 1993 (c.7)
Consolidated Fund (No. 2) Act 1994 (c.41)
Consolidated Fund (No. 2) Act 1995 (c.54)
Consolidated Fund (No. 2) Act 1996 (c.60)
Consolidated Fund (No. 2) (Session 2) Act 1880 (c.30)
Consolidated Fund (No. 3) Act 1879 (c.14)
Consolidated Fund (No. 3) Act 1881 (c.15)
Consolidated Fund (No. 3) Act 1882 (c.8)
Consolidated Fund (No. 3) Act 1883 (c.13)
Consolidated Fund (No. 3) Act 1885 (c.14)
Consolidated Fund (No. 3) Act 1888 (c.26)
Consolidated Fund (No. 3) Act 1889 (c.15)
Consolidated Fund (No. 3) Act 1893 (c.28)
Consolidated Fund (No. 3) Act 1894 (c.29)
Consolidated Fund (No. 3) Act 1915 (c.53)
Consolidated Fund (No. 3) Act 1916 (c.16)
Consolidated Fund (No. 3) Act 1917 (c.17)
Consolidated Fund (No. 3) Act 1918 (c.37)
Consolidated Fund (No. 3) Act 1930 (c.18)
Consolidated Fund (No. 3) Act 1939 (c.52)
Consolidated Fund (No. 3) Act 1941 (c.26)
Consolidated Fund (No. 3) Act 1942 (c.22)
Consolidated Fund (No. 3) Act 1943 (c.20)
Consolidated Fund (No. 3) Act 1944 (c.20)
Consolidated Fund (No. 3) Act 1945 (c.13)
Consolidated Fund (No. 3) Act 1951 (c.1)
Consolidated Fund (No. 3) Act 1953 (c.2)
Consolidated Fund (No. 3) Act 1971 (c.79)
Consolidated Fund (No. 3) Act 1972 (c.78)
Consolidated Fund (No. 3) Act 1974 (c.15)
Consolidated Fund (No. 3) Act 1975 (c.79)
Consolidated Fund (No. 3) Act 1983 (c.57)
Consolidated Fund (No. 3) Act 1985 (c.74)
Consolidated Fund (No. 3) Act 1987 (c.55)
Consolidated Fund (No. 3) Act 1991 (c.68)
Consolidated Fund (No. 3) Act 1992 (c.59)
Consolidated Fund (No. 3) Act 1993 (c.52)
Consolidated Fund (No. 4) Act 1879 (c.20)
Consolidated Fund (No. 4) Act 1881 (c.50)
Consolidated Fund (No. 4) Act 1882 (c.28)
Consolidated Fund (No. 4) Act 1883 (c.23)
Consolidated Fund (No. 4) Act 1893 (c.46)
Consolidated Fund (No. 4) Act 1915 (c.80)
Consolidated Fund (No. 4) Act 1916 (c.30)
Consolidated Fund (No. 4) Act 1917 (c.33)
Consolidated Fund (No. 4) Act 1974 (c.57)
Consolidated Fund (No. 5) Act 1916 (c.48)
Consolidated Fund (No. 5) Act 1917 (c.49)
Consolidated Fund (Permanent Charges Redemption) Act 1873 (c.57)
Consolidated Fund (Permanent Charges Redemption) Act 1883 (c.1)
Consolidation of Enactments (Procedure) Act 1949 (c.33)
Conspiracy and Protection of Property Act 1875 (c.86)
Constables Expenses Act 1801 (c.78)
Constables Near Public Works (Scotland) Act 1845 (c.3)
Constables Protection Act 1750 (c.44)
Constables (Scotland) Act 1875 (c.47)
Constabulary and Police (Ireland) Act 1883 (c.14)
Constabulary and Police (Ireland) Act 1914 (c.54)
Constabulary and Police (Ireland) Act 1916 (c.59)
Constabulary and Police (Ireland) Act 1918 (c.53)
Constabulary and Police (Ireland) Act 1919 (c.68)
Constabulary (Ireland) Act 1836 (c.13)
Constabulary (Ireland) Act 1846 (c.97)
Constabulary (Ireland) Act 1848 (c.72)
Constabulary (Ireland) Act 1851 (c.85)
Constabulary (Ireland) Act 1857 (c.17)
Constabulary (Ireland) Act 1859 (c.22)
Constabulary (Ireland) Act 1866 (c.103)
Constabulary (Ireland) Act 1875 (c.44)
Constabulary (Ireland) Act 1877 (c.20)
Constabulary (Ireland) Act 1897 (c.64)
Constabulary (Ireland) Act 1908 (c.60)
Constabulary (Ireland) Act 1922 (c.55)
Constabulary (Ireland) Amendment Act 1865 (c.70)
Constabulary (Ireland) Amendment) Act 1870 (c.83)
Constabulary (Ireland) Amendment Act 1882 (c.63)
Constabulary (Ireland) (Consular Advances) Act 1825 (c.87)
Constabulary (Ireland) (No. 2) Act 1836 (c.36)
Constabulary (Ireland) Redistribution Act 1885 (c.12)
Consular Conventions Act 1949 (c.29)
Consular Fees Act 1980 (c.23)
Consular Marriage Act 1868 (c.61)
Consular Marriages Act 1849 (c.68)
Consular Relations Act 1968 (c.18)
Consular Salaries and Fees Act 1891 (c.36)
Consuls in Ottoman Dominions Act 1836 (c.78)
Consumer Arbitration Agreements Act 1988 (c.21)
Consumer Credit Act 1974 (c.39)
Consumer Protection Act 1961 (c.40)
Consumer Protection Act 1971 (c.15)

Consumer Protection Act 1987 (c.43)
Consumer Safety Act 1978 (c.38)
Consumer Safety (Amendment) Act 1986 (c.29)
Consumption of Malt Liquors (Ireland) Act 1810 (c.46)
Contagious Diseases Act 1866 (c.35)
Contagious Diseases Act 1869 (c.96)
Contagious Diseases Acts Repeal 1886 (c.10)
Contagious Diseases (Animals) Act 1853 (c.62)
Contagious Diseases, Animals Act 1856 (c.101)
Contagious Diseases (Animals) Act 1867 (c.125)
Contagious Diseases (Animals) Act 1869 (c.70)
Contagious Diseases (Animals) Act 1878 (c.74)
Contagious Diseases (Animals) Act 1884 (c.13)
Contagious Diseases (Animals) Act 1886 (c.32)
Contagious Diseases (Animals) Act 1892 (c.47)
Contagious Diseases (Animals) Act 1893 (c.43)
Contagious Diseases (Animals) (Pleuro pneumonia) Act 1890 (c.14)
Contagious Diseases (Animals) (Scotland) Act 1875 (c.75)
Contagious Diseases (Animals) Transfer of Parts of Districts Act 1884 (c.47)
Contagious Diseases (Ireland) Amendment Act 1868 (c.80)
Contagious Diseases of Sheep Act 1858 (c.62)
Contagious Diseases Prevention Act 1864 (c.85)
Contagious Disorders (Sheep), etc. Act 1848 (c.107)
Contempt of Court Act 1981 (c.49)
Continental Shelf Act 1964 (c.29)
Continental Shelf Act 1989 (c.35)
Contingencies Fund Act 1970 (c.56)
Contingencies Fund Act 1974 (c.18)
Contingent Remainders Act 1877 (c.33)
Continuance etc. of Acts Act 1735 (c.18)
Continuance etc., of Acts Act 1757 (c.42)
Continuance etc. of Acts Act 1763 (c.25)
Continuance of Acts Act 1702 (c.13)
Continuance of Acts Act 1706 (c.34)
Continuance of Acts Act 1711 (c.24(e))
Continuance of Acts Act 1718 (c.25)
Continuance of Acts Act 1726 (c.27)
Continuance of Acts Act 1734 (c.18)
Continuance of Acts Act 1737 (c.18)
Continuance of Acts Act 1740 (c.34)
Continuance of Acts Act 1746 (c.47)
Continuance of Acts Act 1750 (c.57)
Continuance of Acts Act 1756 (c.28)
Continuance of Acts Act 1759 (c.16)
Continuance of Acts Act 1797 (c.9)
Continuance of Acts Act 1780 (cc.4, 5)
Continuance of Acts Act 1799 (c.9)
Continuance of Acts Act 1799 (c.12)
Continuance of Acts Act 1799 (c.38)
Continuance of Acts Act 1801 (c.45)
Continuance of Acts, etc. Act 1722 (c.8)
Continuance of Acts, etc. Act 1723 (c.17)
Continuance of Acts, etc. Act 1724 (c.29)
Continuance of Acts, etc. Act 1739 (c.28)
Continuance of Acts, etc. Act 1749 (c.26)
Continuance of Acts, etc. Act 1753 (c.32)
Continuance of Acts, etc. Act 1754 (c.18)
Continuance of Acts, etc. Act 1757 (c.1)
Continuance of Acts. etc. Act 1757 (c.35)
Continuance of Certain Duties, etc. Act 1708 (c.31)
Continuance of Certain Laws Act 1772 (c.56)
Continuance of Certain Laws, etc. Act 1771 (c.51)
Continuance of Criminal Law Act 1722 Act 1725 (c.30)
Continuance of Laws Act 1734 (c.21)
Continuance of Laws Act 1763 (c.11)
Continuance of Laws Act 1763 (c.12)
Continuance of Laws Act 1766 (c.44)
Continuance of Laws Act 1768 (c.1)
Continuance of Laws Act 1774 (c.67)
Continuance of Laws Act 1774 (c.80)
Continuance of Laws Act 1774 (c.86)
Continuance of Laws Act 1776 (c.44)
Continuance of Laws Act 1776 (c.54)
Continuance of Laws Act 1778 (c.45)
Continuance of Laws Act 1779 (c.22)
Continuance of Laws Act 1780 (c.19)
Continuance of Laws Act 1782 (c.13)
Continuance of Laws Act 1783 (c.6)
Continuance of Laws Act 1786 (c.53)
Continuance of Laws Act 1786 (c.80)
Continuance of Laws Act 1787 (c.36)
Continuance of Laws Act 1788 (cc.23, 24)
Continuance of Laws Act 1789 (c.55)
Continuance of Laws Act 1790 (c.18)
Continuance of Laws Act 1791 (c.43)
Continuance of Laws Act 1792 (c.36)
Continuance of Laws Act 1793 (c.40)
Continuance of Laws Act 1794 (c.36)
Continuance of Laws Act 1795 (c.38)
Continuance of Laws Act 1796 (c.40)
Continuance of Laws Act 1796 (c.108)
Continuance of Laws Act 1797 (c.35)
Continuance of Laws Act 1797 (c.99)
Continuance of Laws Act 1800 (c.5)
Continuance of Laws Act 1800 (c.20)
Continuance of Laws Act 1803 (c.4)
Continuance of Laws Act 1803 (c.29)
Continuance of Laws Act 1805 (c.80)
Continuance of Laws Act 1806 (c.29)
Continuance of Laws, etc. Act 1714 (c.26)
Continuance of Laws, etc. Act 1742 (c.26)
Continuance of Laws, etc. Act 1748 (c.46)
Contract (India Office) Act 1903 (c.11)
Contracts (Applicable Law) Act 1990 (c.36)

Contracts of Employment Act 1963 (c.49)
Contracts of Employment Act 1972 (c.53)
Controlled Drugs (Penalties) Act 1985 (c.39)
Control of Employment Act 1939 (c.104)
Control of Food Premises (Scotland) Act 1977 (c.28)
Control of Liquid Fuel Act 1967 (c.57)
Control of Office and Industrial Development Act 1965 (c.33)
Control of Office Development Act 1977 (c.40)
Control of Pollution Act 1974 (c.40)
Control of Pollution (Amendment) Act 1989 (c.14)
Control of Smoke Pollution Act 1989 (c.17)
Controverted Elections Act 1788 (c.52)
Controverted Elections Act 1796 (c.59)
Controverted Elections Act 1801 (c.101)
Controverted Elections Act 1802 (c.84)
Controverted Elections Act 1802 (c.106)
Controverted Elections Act 1807 (c.1)
Controverted Elections Act 1813 (c.71)
Controverted Elections Act 1841 (c.58)
Controverted Elections Act 1842 (c.73)
Controverted Elections Act 1843 (c.47)
Controverted Elections Act 1844 (c.103)
Controverted Elections, etc. Act 1792 (c.1)
Controverted Elections (Ireland) Act 1807 (c.14)
County Rates Act 1738 (c.29)
Convention (Ireland) Act Repeal 1879 (c.28)
Convention of Royal Burghs (Scotland) Act 1879 (c.27)
Convention of Royal Burghs (Scotland) Act 1879, Amendment Act 1895 (c.6)
Convention with United States Act 1855 (c.77)
Conversion of India Stock Act 1887 (c.11)
Conveyance by Release Without Lease Act 1841 (c.21)
Conveyance of Mails Act 1893 (c.38)
Conveyance of Prisoners (Ireland) Act 1815 (c.158)
Conveyance of Prisoners (Ireland) Act 1837 (c.6)
Conveyance of Real Property Act 1845 (c.119)
Conveyancers (Ireland) Act 1864 (c.8)
Conveyancing Act 1881 (c.41)
Conveyancing Act 1882 (c.39)
Conveyancing Act 1911 (c.37)
Conveyancing Amendment (Scotland) Act 1938 (c.24)
Conveyancing and Feudal Reform (Scotland) Act 1970 (c.35)
Conveyancing and Law of Property Act 1892 (c.13)
Conveyancing (Scotland) Act 1874 (c.94)
Conveyancing (Scotland) Act, 1874, Amendment 1879 (c.40)
Conveyancing (Scotland) Act 1924 (c.27)
Conveyancing (Scotland) Acts (1874 and 1879) Amendment 1887 (c.69)
Convict Prisons Act 1850 (c.39)
Convict Prisons Act 1853 (c.121)
Convict Prisons Abroad Act 1859 (c.25)
Convict Prisons Act 1854 (c.76)
Convict Prisons Returns Act 1876 (c.42)
Convicted Prisoners Removal, etc. Act 1853
Conway's Patent Kiln Act 1795 (c.68)
Conwy Tunnel (Supplementary Powers) Act 1983 (c.7)
Co-operative Development Agency 1978 (c.21)
Co-operative Development Agency and Industrial Development Act 1984 (c.57)
Copyhold Act 1843 (c.23)
Copyhold Act 1852 (c.51)
Copyhold Act 1887 (c.73)
Copyhold Act 1894 (c.46)
Copyhold Commission Act 1846 (c.53)
Copyhold Commission Act 1847 (c.101)
Copyhold Commission Act 1858 (c.53)
Copyhold Commission Cont. Act 1860 (c.81)
Copyhold, etc., Commission Act 1853 (c.124)
Copyhold, etc., Commission Act 1855 (c.52)
Copyhold, etc., Commission Act 1857 (c.8)
Copyhold, etc., Commission Cont. Act 1862 (c.73)
Copyhold Lands Act 1844 (c.55)
Copyholds Act 1722 (c.29)
Copyholds Act 1853 (c.57)
Copyholds Act 1858 (c.94)
Copyright Act 1709 (c.21(i))
Copyright Act 1775 (c.53)
Copyright Act 1798 (c.71)
Copyright Act 1801 (c.107)
Copyright Act 1814 (c.156)
Copyright Act 1836 (c.110)
Copyright Act 1842 (c.45)
Copyright Act 1911 (c.46)
Copyright Act 1956 (c.74)
Copyright Act 1956 (Amendment) Act 1982 (c.35)
Copyright (Amendment) Act 1983 (c.42)
Copyright (British Museum) Act 1915 (c.38)
Copyright (Computer Software) Amendment Act 1985 (c.41)
Copyright, Designs and Patents Act 1988 (c.48)
Copyright (Musical Compositions) Act 1882 (c.40)
Copyright (Musical Compositions) Act 1888 (c.17)
Copyright of Designs Act 1839 (c.13)
Copyright of Designs Act 1839 (c.17)
Copyright of Designs Act 1842 (c.100)
Copyright of Designs Act 1843 (c.65)
Copyright of Designs Act 1850 (c.104)
Copyright of Designs Act 1858 (c.70)
Copyright of Designs Act 1861 (c.73)
Copyright of Designs Act 1875 (c.93)
Cordage for Shipping Act 1785 (c.56)
Cork Infirmary Act 1861 (c.29)
Corn Act 1731 (c.12)
Corn Act 1766 (c.17)

Corn Act 1770 (c.39)
Corn Act 1774 (c.64)
Corn Act 1780 (c.50)
Corn Accounts and Returns Act 1864 (c.87)
Corn Duties Act 1847 (c.1)
Corn, etc. Act 1801 (c.13)
Corn Exportation Act 1737 (c.22)
Corn Production Act 1917 (c.46)
Corn Production Acts (Repeal) Act 1921 (c.48)
Corn Production (Amendment) Act 1918 (c.36)
Corn Rents Act 1963 (c.14)
Corn Returns Act 1882 (c.37)
Corn Sales Act 1921 (c.35)
Corneal Grafting Act 1952 (c.28)
Corneal Tissue Act 1986 (c.18)
Cornwall and Devon Roads Act 1770 (c.87)
Cornwall and Devon Roads Act 1777 (c.79)
Cornwall Duchy Act 1760 (c.11)
Cornwall Duchy Act 1793 (c.78)
Cornwall Duchy Act 1810 (c.6)
Cornwall Roads Act 1759 (c.42)
Cornwall Roads Act 1760 (c.27)
Cornwall Roads Act 1760 (c.32)
Cornwall Roads Act 1762 (c.46)
Cornwall Roads Act 1763 (c.52)
Cornwall Roads Act 1781 (c.78)
Cornwall Roads Act 1781 (c.90)
Cornwall Roads Act 1782 (c.104)
Cornwall Roads Act 1783 (c.27)
Cornwall Roads Act 1785 (c.108)
Cornwall Roads Act 1785 (c.114)
Cornwall Submarine Mines Act 1858 (c.109)
Coroners Act 1751 (c.29)
Coroners Act 1836 (c.89)
Coroners Act 1843 (c.12)
Coroners Act 1843 (c.83)
Coroners Act 1844 (c.92)
Coroners Act 1887 (c.71)
Coroners Act 1892 (c.56)
Coroners Act 1921 (c.30)
Coroners Act 1954 (c.31)
Coroners Act 1980 (c.38)
Coroners Act 1988 (c.13)
Coroners (Amendment) Act 1926 (c.59)
Coroners (Emergency Provisions) Act 1917 (c.19)
Coroners (Emergency Provisions Continuance) Act 1922 (c.2)
Coroners' Inquests, Bail Act 1859 (c.33)
Coroners' Inquests Expenses Act 1837 (c.68)
Coroners (Ireland) Act 1846 (c.37)
Coroners (Ireland) Act 1881 (c.35)
Coroners (Ireland) Act 1908 (c.37)
Coroners' Juries Act 1983 (c.31)
Corporate Bodies' Contracts Act 1960 (c.46)
Corporation of Dublin Act 1850 (c.55)
Corporations Act 1718 (c.6)
Correspondence with Enemies Act 1704 (c.13)
Correspondence with Enemies Act 1793 (c.27)
Correspondence with Foreign Parts Act 1801 (c.11)
Correspondence with James the Pretender (High Treason) Act 1701 (c.3)
Corrupt and Illegal Practices Prevention Act 1883 (c.51)
Corrupt and Illegal Practices Prevention Act 1895 (c.40)
Corrupt Practice (Municipal Elections) Act 1872 (c.60)
Corrupt Practices Act 1856 (c.84)
Corrupt Practices Act 1858 (c.87)
Corrupt Practices Act 1859 (c.48)
Corrupt Practices Act 1861 (c.122)
Corrupt Practices Act 1862 (c.109)
Corrupt Practices 1854 Act, Continuation Act 1860 (c.99)
Corrupt Practices at Elections Act 1735 (c.38)
Corrupt Practice Commission Expenses Act 1869 (c.21)
Corrupt Practices at Parliamentary Elections Act 1728 (c.24)
Corrupt Practices, Dublin City 1869 (c.65)
Corrupt Practices Prevention Act 1854 (c.102)
Corrupt Practices Prevention Act 1863 (c.29)
Corrupt Practices (Suspension of Election) Act 1882 (c.68)
Corrupt Practices (Suspension of Elections) Act 1881 (c.42)
Corrupt Practices (Suspension of Elections) Act 1883 (c.46)
Corrupt Practices (Suspension of Elections) Act 1884 (c.78)
Corruption of Blood Act 1814 (c.145)
Corsham to Bath Easton Bridge Road Act 1779 (c.112)
Cosford, Suffolk: Poor Relief Act 1779 (c.30)
Cosham to Chichester Road Act 1762 (c.84)
Cosham to Chichester Road Act 1783 (c.32)
Costs Act 1803 (c.46)
Costs in Criminal Cases Act 1952 (c.48)
Costs in Criminal Cases Act 1908 (c.15)
Costs in Criminal Cases Act 1973 (c.14)
Costs of Action of Trespass Act 1840 (c.24)
Costs of Leases Act 1958 (c.52)
Cottier Tenant (Ireland) Act 1856 (c.65)
Cottingham, Yorks: Inclosure Act 1791 (c.20)
Cotton Act 1954 (c.24)
Cotton Association (Emergency Action) Act 1915 (c.69)
Cotton (Centralised Buying) Act 1947 (c.26)
Cotton Cloth Factories Act 1889 (c.62)
Cotton Cloth Factories Act 1897 (c.58)
Cotton Industry Act 1923 (c.22)
Cotton Industry Act 1928 (c.11)
Cotton Industry Act 1933 (c.30)
Cotton Industry Act 1938 (c.15)
Cotton Industry Act 1939 (c.9)
Cotton Industry Act 1959 (c.48)
Cotton Industry (Reorganisation) Act 1939 (c.54)
Cotton Industry (Reorganisation) (Postponement) Act 1939 (c.116)

Cotton Manufacture (Scotland) Act 1803 (c.151)
Cotton Manufacturing Industry (Temporary Provisions) Act 1934 (c.30)
Cotton Spinning Industry Act 1936 (c.21)
Cotton Spinning (Re-equipment Subsidy) Act 1948 (c.31)
Cotton Statistics Act 1868 (c.33)
Cotton Trade (Ireland) Act 1813 (c.75)
Council of India Act 1876 (c.7)
Council of India Act 1907 (c.35)
Council of India Reduction Act 1889 (c.65)
Councils of Conciliation Act 1867 (c.105)
Counter Inflation Act 1973 (c.9)
Counter Inflation (Temporary Provisions) Act 1972 (c.74)
Counterfeit Currency (Convention) Act 1935 (c.25)
Counterfeit Dollars and Tokens Act 1804 (c.71)
Counterfeit Medal Act 1883 (c.45)
Counterfeiting Act 1702 (c.3)
Counterfeiting Bank of England Tokens Act 1811 (c.110)
Counterfeiting Bank of Ireland Silver Tokens, etc. Act 1805 (c.42)
Counterfeiting Coin Act 1741 (c.28)
Counterfeiting Coin Act 1797 (c.126)
Counterfeiting, etc., of Gold Coin Act 1772 (c.71)
Counterfeiting of Bank of Ireland Tokens Act 1813 (c.106)
Counterfeiting of Copper Coin Act 1771 (c.40)
Counterfeiting of Tokens, etc. Act 1808 (c.31)
Counterfeiting of Tokens, etc. Act 1812 (c.138)
Countervailing Duties Act 1802 (c.27)
Countervailing Duties Act 1804 (c.27)
Countervailing Duties (Ireland) Act 1807 (c.18)
Countervailing Duties on Spirit Mixtures, etc. Act 1836 (c.72)
Countervailing Duty Act 1803 (c.154)
Counties and Boroughs (Ireland) Act 1840 (c.109)
Counties (Detached Parts) Act 1839 (c.82)
Counties (Detached Parts) Act 1844 (c.61)
Counties of Cities Act 1798 (c.52)
Counties of Cities Act 1811 (c.100)
Counties of Drogheda and Meath Act 1845 (c.121)
Countryside Act 1968 (c.41)
Countryside (Scotland) Act 1967 (c.86)
Countryside (Scotland) Act 1981 (c.44)
County and Borough Councils (Qualification) Act 1914 (c.21)
County and Borough Police Act 1856 (c.69)
County and Borough Police Act 1859 (c.32)
County and Borough Police Act 1919 (c.84)
County and City of Dublin Grand Juries Act 1873 (c.65)
County Boundaries (Ireland) Act 1872 (c.48)
County Bridges Act 1841 (c.49)
County Bridges Loans Extension Act 1880 (c.5)
County Buildings Act 1837 (c.24)
County Buildings Act 1847 (c.28)
County Buildings (Loans) Act 1872 (c.7)
County Cessation (Ireland) Act 1848 (c.32)
County Cessation (Ireland) Act 1849 (c.36)
County Cessation (Ireland) Act 1850 (c.1)
County Cessation (Ireland) Act 1859 (c.23)
County Cessation (Ireland) Act 1861 (c.58)
County Common Juries Act 1910 (c.17)
County Contributions to Prisons, etc. Act 1861 (c.12)
County Coroners Act 1860 (c.116)
County Council Association Expenses (Amendment) Act 1937 (c.27)
County Council (Elections) Act 1891 (c.68)
County Councils Association Expenses Act 1890 (c.3)
County Councils Association Expenses (Amendment) Act 1947 (c.13)
County Councils Association (Scotland) Expenses Act 1894 (c.5)
County Councils (Bills in Parliament) Act 1903 (c.9)
County Councils (Elections) Amendment Act 1900 (c.13)
County Councils Mortgages Act 1909 (c.38)
County Court Amendment (Ireland) Act 1882 (c.29)
County Court Appeals (Ireland) Act 1889 (c.48)
County Court (Buildings) Act 1870 (c.15)
County Court (Costs and Salaries) Act 1882 (c.57)
County Court Districts (England) Act 1858 (c.74)
County Court Judges Act 1859 (c.57)
County Court Judges (Retirement Pensions and Deputies) Act 1919 (c.70)
County Court Jurisdiction in Lunacy (Ireland) Act 1880 (c.39)
County Court (Penalties for Contempt) Act 1983 (c.45)
County Courts Act 1849 (c.101)
County Courts Act 1850 (c.61)
County Courts Act 1852 (c.54)
County Courts Act 1854 (c.16)
County Courts Act 1856 (c.108)
County Courts Act 1857 (c.36)
County Courts Act 1866 (c.14)
County Courts Act 1867 (c.142)
County Courts Act 1875 (c.50)
County Courts Act 1888 (c.43)
County Courts Act 1903 (c.42)
County Courts Act 1919 (c.73)
County Courts Act 1924 (c.17)
County Courts Act 1934 (c.53)
County Courts Act 1955 (c.8)
County Courts Act 1959 (c.22)
County Courts Act 1984 (c.28)
County Courts Admiralty Jurisdiction Act 1868 (c.71)

County Courts Admiralty Jurisdiction Amendment Act 1869 (c.51)
County Courts (Amendment) Act 1934 (c.17)
County Courts (Equity Jurisdiction) Act 1865 (c.99)
County Courts (Expenses) Act 1887 (c.3)
County Courts (Investment) Act 1900 (c.47)
County Courts (Jurisdiction) Act 1963 (c.5)
County Courts Westminster and Southwark Act 1859 (c.8)
County Debentures Act 1873 (c.35)
County Dublin Baronies Act 1838 (c.115)
County Dublin Grand Jury Act 1844 (c.106)
County Dublin Surveyors Act 1897 (c.2)
County Elections Act 1788 (c.36)
County Elections Act 1789 (c.13)
County Elections Act 1789 (c.18)
County Elections (Ireland) Act 1862 (c.62)
County Elections (Scotland) Act 1853 (c.28)
County Electors Act 1888 (c.10)
County Fermanagh Baronies Act 1837 (c.82)
County General Assessment (Scotland) Act 1868 (c.82)
County Infirmaries (Ireland) Act 1805 (c.111)
County Infirmaries (Ireland) Act 1807 (c.50)
County Infirmaries (Ireland) Act 1814 (c.62)
County Institutions (Ireland) Act 1838 (c.116)
County Law Procedure Act 1848 (c.31)
County of Clare Treasurer Act 1838 (c.104)
County of Dublin Jurors and Voters' Revision Act 1884 (c.35)
County of Durham Coroners Act 1837 (c.64)
County of Hertford Act 1878 (c.50)
County of Hertford and Liberty of St. Albans Act 1874 (c.45)
County of Roscommon Act 1840 (c.76)
County of Sussex Act 1865 (c.37)
County Officers and Courts (Ireland) Act 1877 (c.56)
County Officers and Courts (Ireland) Amendment Act 1885 (c.71)
County Palatine of Chester Act 1787 (c.43)
County Police Act 1839 (c.93)
County Police Act 1840 (c.88)
County Police Act 1856 (c.2)
County Property Act 1858 (c.92)
County Property Act 1871 (c.14)
County Rate Act 1866 (c.78)
County Rates Act 1815 (c.51)
County Rates Act 1816 (c.49)
County Rates Act 1844 (c.33)
County Rates Act 1845 (c.111)
County Rates Act 1852 (c.81)
County Rates (England) Act 1858 (c.33)
County Rates Within Boroughs Act 1849 (c.65)
County Surveyors, etc. (Ireland) Act 1861 (c.63)
County Surveyors (Ireland) Act 1862 (c.106)
County Surveyors (Ireland) Act 1893 (c.49)
County Surveyors (Ireland) Act 1900 (c.18)
County Surveyors Superannuation (Ireland) - Northern Irish Act 1875 (c.56)
County, Town and Parish Councils (Qualification) (Scotland) Act 1914 (c.39)
County Treasurers (Ireland) Act 1837 (c.54)
County Treasurers (Ireland) Act 1838 (c.53)
County Treasurers (Ireland) Act 1867 (c.46)
County Voters Registration Act 1865 (c.36)
County Votes Registration (Scotland) Act 1861 (c.83)
County Works (Ireland) Act 1846 (c.2)
County Works (Ireland) Act 1846 (c.78)
Court Funds Act 1829 (c.13)
Court House (Ireland) Act 1813 (c.131)
Court Houses (Ireland) Act 1815 (c.89)
Court Houses (Ireland) Act 1840 (c.102)
Court Houses (Ireland) Act 1841 (c.31)
Court-martial on Admiral Keppel Act 1779 (c.6)
Court of Admiralty Act 1854 (c.78)
Court of Admiralty (Ireland) Act 1867 (c.114)
Court of Admiralty (Ireland) Amendment Act 1876 (c.28)
Court of Appeal in Chancery Act 1867 (c.64)
Court of Appeal in Chancery Act 1868 (c.11)
Court of Bankruptcy (Ireland) Officers and Clerks Act 1881 (c.23)
Court of Chancery Act 1738 (c.24)
Court of Chancery Act 1763 (c.32)
Court of Chancery Act 1765 (c.28)
Court of Chancery Act 1769 (c.19)
Court of Chancery Act 1774 (c.43)
Court of Chancery Act 1806 (c.129)
Court of Chancery Act 1840 (c.94)
Court of Chancery Act 1841 (c.5)
Court of Chancery Act 1841 (c.52)
Court of Chancery Act 1842 (c.103)
Court of Chancery Act 1845 (c.105)
Court of Chancery Act 1848 (c.10)
Court of Chancery Act 1851 (c.83)
Court of Chancery Act 1852 (c.87(a))
Court of Chancery Act 1854 (c.100)
Court of Chancery Act 1855 (c.134)
Court of Chancery Act 1860 (c.149)
Court of Chancery and Exchequer Funds (Ireland) Act 1868 (c.88)
Court of Chancery Act 1852 (c.80)
Court of Chancery (England) Act 1850 (c.35)
Court of Chancery (England) Act 1853 (c.98)
Court of Chancery Examiners Act 1853 (c.22)
Court of Chancery (Funds) Act 1872 (c.44)
Court of Chancery (Ireland) Act 1823 (c.61)
Court of Chancery (Ireland) Act 1836 (c.74)
Court of Chancery (Ireland) Reg. Act 1850 (c.89)
Court of Chancery of Lancaster Act 1850 (c.43)
Court of Chancery of Lancaster Act 1854 (c.82)
Court of Chancery of Lancaster Act 1952 (c.49)
Court of Chancery of Lancaster (Amendment) Act 1961 (c.38)
Court of Chancery (Officers) Act 1867 (c.87)
Court of Chancery Offices Act 1848 (c.94)

Court of Chancery Procedure Act 1852 (c.86)
Court of Common Pleas Act 1850 (c.75)
Court of Common Pleas Act 1862 (c.96)
Court of Exchequer Chamber (Ireland) Act 1857 (c.6)
Court of Exchequer, Equity Side Act 1836 (c.112)
Court of Exchequer (Ireland) Act 1816 (c.122)
Court of Exchequer (Ireland) Act 1855 (c.50)
Court of Exchequer (Scotland) Act 1806 (c.154)
Court of Exchequer (Scotland) Act 1836 (c.73)
Court of Justice Act Act 1866 (c.63)
Court of Justiciary (Scotland) Act 1864 (c.30)
Court of Justiciary (Scotland) Act 1868 (c.95)
Court of Pleas of Durham Act 1839 (c.16)
Court of Probate Act 1857 (c.77)
Court of Probate Act 1858 (c.95)
Court of Probate Act (Ireland) 1859 (c.31)
Court of Probate (Ireland) Act 1861 (c.111)
Court of Queen's Bench Act 1843 (c.20)
Court of Session Act 1723 (c.19)
Court of Session Act 1808 (c.151)
Court of Session Act 1810 (c.112)
Court of Session Act 1813 (c.64)
Court of Session Act 1821 (c.38)
Court of Session Act 1825 (c.120)
Court of Session Act 1830 (c.69)
Court of Session Act 1838 (c.86)
Court of Session Act 1839 (c.36)
Court of Session Act 1850 (c.36)
Court of Session Act 1857 (c.56)
Court of Session Act 1868 (c.100)
Court of Session Act 1988 (c.36)
Court of Session Adjournment Act 1762 (c.27)
Court of Session Consignations (Scotland) Act 1895 (c.19)
Court of Session (Extracts) Act 1916 (c.49)
Court of Session (No. 2) Act 1838 (c.118)
Court of Session (Records) Act 1815 (c.70)
Court of Session (Scotland) Act 1745 (c.7)
Courts Act 1672 (c.40)
Courts Act 1971 (c.23)
Courts and Legal Services Act 1990 (c.41)
Courts Baron of High Peak and Castleton Act 1759 (c.31)
Courts Baron, Sheffield Act 1756 (c.37)
Courts (Colonial) Jurisdiction Act 1874 (c.27)
Courts (Emergency Powers) Act 1914 (c.78)
Courts (Emergency Powers) Act 1917 (c.25)
Courts (Emergency Powers) Act 1919 (c.64)
Courts (Emergency Powers) Act 1939 (c.67)
Courts (Emergency Powers) Act 1940 (c.37)
Courts (Emergency Powers) Act 1943 (c.19)
Courts (Emergency Powers) (Amendment) Act 1916 (c.13)
Courts (Emergency Powers) Amendment Act 1942 (c.36)
Courts (Emergency Powers) (Ireland) Act 1914 (c.19)
Courts (Emergency Power) (No. 2) Act 1916 (c.18)
Courts (Emergency Powers) (Scotland) Act 1939 (c.113)
Courts (Emergency Powers) (Scotland) Act 1944 (c.6)
Courts in Prince of Wales Island and India Act 1855 (c.93)
Courts in Wales and Chester Act 1732 (c.14)
Courts-Martial (Appeals) Act 1951 (c.46)
Courts-Martial (Appeals) Act 1968 (c.20)
Courts-Martial, East Indies Act 1760 (c.14)
Courts-Martial in India Act 1844 (c.18)
Courts-Martial on Troops of East India Company Act 1810 (c.87)
Courts, Newfoundland Act 1791 (c.29)
Courts, Newfoundland Act 1792 (c.46)
Courts, Newfoundland Act 1793 (c.76)
Courts, Newfoundland Act 1795 (c.25)
Courts, Newfoundland Act 1796 (c.37)
Courts, Newfoundland Act 1799 (c.16)
Courts, Newfoundland, etc. Act 1794 (c.44)
Courts of Common Law, Sittings Act 1838 (c.32)
Courts of Exchequer Act 1799 (c.67)
Courts of Judicature, India Act 1839 (c.34)
Courts of Justice (Additional Site) Act 1871 (c.57)
Courts of Justice Building Act 1865 (c.48)
Courts of Justice Building Amendment Act 1880 (c.29)
Courts of Justice, Canada Act 1803 (c.138)
Courts of Justice Concentration (Site) Act 1865 (c.49)
Courts of Justice (Salaries and Funds) Act 1869 (c.91)
Courts of Law Fees Act 1867 (c.122)
Courts of Law Fees (Scotland) Act 1868 (c.55)
Courts of Law Fees (Scotland) Act 1895 (c.14)
Covent Garden Market Act 1961 (c.49)
Covent Garden Market (Financial Provisions) Act 1977 (c.2)
Coventry Act 1842 (c.110)
Coventry Canal Act 1768 (c.36)
Coventry Canal Act 1786 (c.20)
Coventry Canal Act 1786 (c.30)
Coventry Freemen, etc. Act 1781 (c.54)
Coventry Gaol Act 1768 (c.40)
Coventry Grammar School Act 1864 (c.41)
Coventry Improvement Act 1763 (c.41)
Coventry–Oxford Canal Act 1775 (c.9)
Coventry Roads Act 1796 (c.133)
Coventry: Streets Act 1790 (c.77)
Coventry to Oxford Canal Act 1769 (c.70)
Coventry to Oxford Canal Act 1794 (c.103)
Coventry to Ticknall Canal Act 1794 (c.93)
Cowgil Parish; Marriages Confirmation, Park Gate Chapel Act 1869 (c.30)
Cowley's Charity Act 1858 (c.81)
Cran Measures Act 1908 (c.17)
Cranbourne Street Act 1864 (c.111)
Cranford and Maidenhead Road Act 1726 (c.31)

Credit-Sale Agreements (Scotland) Act 1961 (c.56)
Credit Unions Act 1979 (c.34)
Cremation Act 1902 (c.8)
Cremation Act 1952 (c.31)
Crew of a Certain Foreign Vessel Act 1786 (c.8)
Crewkerne Roads Act 1765 (c.61)
Crewkerne Roads Act 1786 (c.123)
Crime and Outrage (Ireland) Act 1850 (c.106)
Crime and Outrage (Ireland) Act 1852 (c.66)
Crime and Outrage (Ireland) Act 1853 (c.72)
Crime and Outrage (Ireland) Act 1854 (c.92)
Crimes and Outrage (Ireland) Act 1855 (c.112)
Criminal and Dangerous Lunatics (Scotland) Amendment Act 1871 (c.55)
Criminal Appeal Act 1907 (c.23)
Criminal Appeal Act 1964 (c.43)
Criminal Appeal Act 1966 (c.31)
Criminal Appeal Act 1968 (c.19)
Criminal Appeal Act 1995 (c.35)
Criminal Appeal (Amendment) Act 1908 (c.46)
Criminal Appeal (Northern Ireland) Act 1930 (c.45)
Criminal Appeal (Northern Ireland) Act 1968 (c.21)
Criminal Appeal (Northern Ireland) Act 1980 (c.47)
Criminal Appeal (Scotland) Act 1926 (c.15)
Criminal Appeal (Scotland) Act 1927 (c.26)
Criminal Attempts Act 1981 (c.47)
Criminal Costs (Dublin) Act 1815 (c.91)
Criminal Court, Norfolk Island Act 1794 (c.45)
Criminal Court, Norfolk Island Act 1795 (c.18)
Criminal Damage Act 1971 (c.48)
Criminal Evidence Act 1898 (c.36)
Criminal Evidence Act 1965 (c.20)
Criminal Evidence Act 1979 (c.16)
Criminal Injuries Compensation Act 1995 (c.53)
Criminal Injuries (Ireland) Act 1919 (c.14)
Criminal Jurisdiction Act 1802 (c.85)
Criminal Jurisdiction Act 1975 (c.59)
Criminal Justice Act 1855 (c.126)
Criminal Justice Act 1856 (c.118)
Criminal Justice Act 1925 (c.86)
Criminal Justice Act 1948 (c.58)
Criminal Justice Act 1961 (c.39)
Criminal Justice Act 1965 (c.26)
Criminal Justice Act 1967 (c.80)
Criminal Justice Act 1972 (c.71)
Criminal Justice Act 1982 (c.48)
Criminal Justice Act 1987 (c.38)
Criminal Justice Act 1988 (c.33)
Criminal Justice Act 1991 (c.53)
Criminal Justice Act 1993 (c.36)
Criminal Justice Administration Act 1851 (c.55)
Criminal Justice Administration Act 1914 (c.58)
Criminal Justice Administration Act 1956 (c.34)
Criminal Justice Administration Act 1962 (c.15)
Criminal Justice Administration (Amendment) Act 1959 (c.41)
Criminal Justice Administration (Postponement) Act 1914 (c.9)
Criminal Justice (Amendment) Act 1925 (c.13)
Criminal Justice (Amendment) Act 1981 (c.27)
Criminal Justice and Public Order Act 1994 (c.33)
Criminal Justice (International Co-operation) Act 1990 (c.5)
Criminal Justice (Scotland) Act 1949 (c.94)
Criminal Justice (Scotland) Act 1963 (c.39)
Criminal Justice (Scotland) Act 1980 (c.62)
Criminal Justice (Scotland) Act 1987 (c.41)
Criminal Justice (Scotland) Act 1995 (c.20)
Criminal Law Act 1722 (c.22)
Criminal Law Act 1772 (c.31)
Criminal Law Act 1776 (c.43)
Criminal Law Act 1778 (c.62)
Criminal Law Act 1779 (c.54)
Criminal Law Act 1781 (cc.68, 69)
Criminal Law Act 1782 (c.40)
Criminal Law Act 1782 (c.58)
Criminal Law Act 1826 (c.64)
Criminal Law Act 1967 (c.58)
Criminal Law Act 1977 (c.45)
Criminal Law Amendment Act 1867 (c.35)
Criminal Law Amendment Act 1871 (c.32)
Criminal Law Amendment Act 1880 (c.45)
Criminal Law Amendment Act 1885 (c.69)
Criminal Law Amendment Act 1912 (c.20)
Criminal Law Amendment Act 1922 (c.56)
Criminal Law Amendment Act 1928 (c.42)
Criminal Law Amendment Act 1951 (c.36)
Criminal Law and Procedure (Ireland) Act 1887 (c.20)
Criminal Law (Consolidation) (Scotland) Act 1995 (c.39)
Criminal Law (Ireland) Act 1828 (c.54)
Criminal Law (Scotland) Act 1829 (c.38)
Criminal Law (Scotland) Act 1830 (c.37)
Criminal Lunatic Asylums Act 1860 (c.75)
Criminal Lunatics Act 1800 (c.94)
Criminal Lunatics Act 1838 (c.14)
Criminal Lunatics Act 1867 (c.12)
Criminal Lunatics Act 1869 (c.78)
Criminal Lunatics Act 1884 (c.64)
Criminal Lunatics (Ireland) Act 1838 (c.27)
Criminal Lunatics (Scotland) Act 1935 (c.32)
Criminal Procedure Act 1694 (c.43)
Criminal Procedure Act 1701 (c.6)
Criminal Procedure Act 1848 (c.46)
Criminal Procedure Act 1851 (c.100)
Criminal Procedure Act 1853 (c.30)
Criminal Procedure Act 1865 (c.18)
Criminal Procedure and Investigations Act 1996 (c.25)
Criminal Procedure (Attendance of Witnesses) Act 1965 (c.69)

Criminal Procedure (Consequential Provisions) (Scotland) Act 1995 (c.40)
Criminal Procedure (Insanity) Act 1964 (c.84)
Criminal Procedure (Insanity and Unfitness to Plead) Act 1991 (c.25)
Criminal Procedure (Right of Reply) Act 1964 (c.34)
Criminal Procedure (Scotland) Act 1887 (c.35)
Criminal Procedure (Scotland) Act 1921 (c.50)
Criminal Procedure (Scotland) Act 1938 (c.48)
Criminal Procedure (Scotland) Act 1965 (c.39)
Criminal Procedure (Scotland) Act 1975 (c.21)
Criminal Procedure (Scotland) Act 1995 (c.46)
Criminal Prosecutions Fees (Ireland) Act 1809 (c.101)
Criminal Statutes Repeal Act 1861 (c.95)
Crinan Canal Act 1793 (c.104)
Crinan Canal Act 1805 (c.85)
Cripplegate: Church Building Act 1732 (c.21)
Crofter Forestry (Scotland) Act 1991 (c.18)
Crofters Commission (Delegation of Powers) Act 1888 (c.63)
Crofters Common Grazings Regulation Act 1891 (c.41)
Crofters Common Grazings Regulation Act 1908 (c.50)
Crofters Holdings (Scotland) Act 1886 (c.29)
Crofters Holdings (Scotland) Act 1887 (c.24)
Crofters (Scotland) Act 1955 (c.21)
Crofters (Scotland) Act 1961 (c.58)
Crofters (Scotland) Act 1993 (c.44)
Crofting Reform (Scotland) Act 1976 (c.21)
Cromarty Harbour Act 1785 (c.39)
Cromford Bridge to Langley Mill Road Act 1786 (c.124)
Cromford Canal Act 1789 (c.74)
Crossbows Act 1987 (c.32)
Crossed Cheques Act 1876 (c.81)
Crossford Bridge and Altrincham Road Act 1796 (c.143)
Crown Agents Act 1979 (c.43)
Crown Agents Act 1995 (c.24)
Crown Agents (Amendment) Act 1986 (c.43)
Crown Appointments, Colonies Act 1846 (c.91)
Crown Cases Act 1848 (c.78)
Crown Debt from Late Right Hon. R. Rigby Act 1794 (c.66)
Crown Debt of Abraham Goldsmid, etc. Act 1812 (c.75)
Crown Debtors Act 1785 (c.35)
Crown Debts Act 1541 (c.39)
Crown Debts Act 1801 (c.90)
Crown Debts Act 1824 (c.111)
Crown Debts and Judgments Act 1860 (c.115)
Crown Estate Act 1956 (c.73)
Crown Estate Act 1961 (c.55)
Crown Land, Revenues Act 1854 (c.68)
Crown Lands Act 1702 (c.1)
Crown Lands Act 1775 (c.33)
Crown Lands Act 1784 (c.57)
Crown Lands Act 1800 (c.78)
Crown Lands Act 1806 (c.151)
Crown Lands Act 1810 (c.65)
Crown Lands Act 1814 (c.70)
Crown Lands Act 1841 (c.1)
Crown Lands Act 1845 (c.99)
Crown Lands Act 1848 (c.102)
Crown Lands Act 1851 (c.42)
Crown Lands Act 1852 (c.62)
Crown Lands Act 1853 (c.56)
Crown Lands Act 1855 (c.16)
Crown Lands Act 1866 (c.62)
Crown Lands Act 1873 (c.36)
Crown Lands Act 1885 (c.79)
Crown Lands Act 1894 (c.43)
Crown Lands Act 1906 (c.28)
Crown Lands Act 1913 (c.8)
Crown Lands Act 1927 (c.23)
Crown Lands Act 1936 (c.47)
Crown Lands Act 1943 (c.7)
Crown Lands at Byfleet, Weybridge, etc., Surrey Act 1804 (c.25)
Crown Lands at Catterick and Tunstall, Yorkshire Act 1790 (c.51)
Crown Lands at Egham, Exchange King and David Jebb Act 1807 (c.77)
Crown Lands at Enfield, Middlesex Act 1776 (c.17)
Crown Lands at North Scotland Yard, Middlesex Act 1785 (c.98)
Crown Lands at Richmond, Surrey Act 1772 (c.35)
Crown Lands at Richmond, Surrey Act 1772 (c.59)
Crown Lands at Shilston Bay, Devon Act 1805 (c.116)
Crown Lands (Copyholds) Act 1851 (c.46)
Crown Lands, Escheats Act 1807 (c.24)
Crown Lands (Forfeited Estates) Act 1715 (c.50)
Crown Lands—Forfeited Estates Act 1717 (c.8)
Crown Lands—Forfeited Estates Act 1718 (c.22)
Crown Lands—Forfeited Estates Act 1719 (c.24)
Crown Lands—Forfeited Estates Act 1720 (c.22)
Crown Lands—Forfeited Estates Act 1726 (c.28)
Crown Lands—Forfeited Estates Act 1727 (c.21)
Crown Lands—Forfeited Estates Act 1728 (c.33)
Crown Lands—Forfeited Estates Act 1744 (c.37)
Crown Lands—Forfeited Estates Act 1746 (c.41)

Crown Lands—Forfeited Estates Act 1748 (c.52)
Crown Lands—Forfeited Estates Act 1751 (c.41)
Crown Lands, Forfeited Estates Act 1757 (c.16)
Crown Lands, Forfeited Estates Act 1762 (c.17)
Crown Lands—Forfeited Estates Act 1774 (c.22)
Crown Lands—Forfeited Estates Act 1794 (c.101)
Crown Lands—Forfeited Estates Act 1795 (c.69)
Crown Lands (Forfeited Estates): Greenwich Hospital Act 1737 (c.30)
Crown Lands, Forfeited Estates in Ireland Act 1793 (c.46)
Crown Lands, Forfeited Estates (Ireland) Act 1702 (c.18(a))
Crown Lands, Forfeited Estates (Ireland) Act 1702 (c.25)
Crown Lands, Forfeited Estates (Ireland) Act 1706 (c.25)
Crown Lands, Forfeited Estates (Ireland) Act 1778 (c.61)
Crown Lands Grant to Jame's Archbald Stuart Act 1772 (c.44)
Crown Lands—Greenwich Hospital Act 1778 (c.29)
Crown Lands in Fenchurch Street London Act 1772 (c.19)
Crown Lands in Holborn, London Act 1772 (c.43)
Crown Lands in Meath to Vest in Gerald Fitzgerald Act 1771 (c.56)
Crown Lands in Northamptonshire, Grant to Earl of Exeter Act 1796 (c.63)
Crown Lands in Northamptonshire, Grant to Earl of Upper Ossory Act 1795 (c.40)
Crown Lands in Northamptonshire, Grant to Earl of Westmorland Act 1796 (c.62)
Crown Lands in Privy Garden, Westminster Act 1792 (c.24)
Crown Lands (Ireland) Act 1822 (c.63)
Crown Lands - New Forest Act 1800 (c.86)
Crown Land Revenues, etc. Act 1786 (c.87)
Crown Lands, Savoy Act 1771 (c.4)
Crown Lands (Scotland) Act 1833 (c.69)
Crown Lands: Taxation Act 1801 (c.47)
Crown Lessees (Protection of Sub-Tenants) Act 1952 (c.40)
Crown Office Act 1860 (c.54)
Crown Office Act 1877 (c.41)
Crown Office Act 1890 (c.2)
Crown Pensioners Disqualification Act 1715 (c.56)
Crown Pre-Emption of Lead Ore Act 1815 (c.134)
Crown Private Estate Act 1800 (c.88)
Crown Private Estates Act 1862 (c.37)
Crown Private Estates Act 1873 (c.61)
Crown Proceedings Act 1947 (c.44)
Crown Proceedings (Armed Forces) Act 1987 (c.25)
Crown Land Revenues Act 1794 (c.75)
Crown Revenues (Colonies) Act 1852 (c.39)
Crown Suits Act 1769 (c.16)
Crown Suits Act 1855 (c.90)
Crown Suits Act 1861 (c.62)
Crown Suits, etc. Act 1865 (c.104)
Crown Suits (Isle of Man) Act 1862 (c.14)
Crown Suits (Scotland) Act 1857 (c.44)
Croydon Parish Church Act 1760 (c.38)
Cruelty to Animals Act 1849 (c.92)
Cruelty to Animals Act 1854 (c.60)
Cruelty to Animals Act 1876 (c.77)
Cruelty to Animals (Ireland) Act 1837 (c.66)
Cruelty to Animals (Scotland) Act 1850 (c.92)
Cruelty to Animals (Scotland) Act 1895 (c.13)
Cultivation, etc. of Trees Act 1766 (c.36)
Cultivation of Madder Act 1765 (c.18)
Cumberland and Westmorland Roads Act 1762 (c.81)
Cumberland and Westmorland Roads Act 1783 (c.108)
Cumberland Roads Act 1749 (c.40)
Cumberland Roads Act 1753 (c.37)
Cumberland Roads Act 1753 (c.49)
Cumberland Roads Act 1767 (c.83)
Cumberland Roads Act 1778 (c.108)
Cumberland Roads Act 1779 (c.97)
Cumberland Roads Act 1789 (c.97)
Cumberland Roads Act 1794 (c.143)
Cunard Agreement (Money) Act 1904 (c.22)
Cunard (Insurance) Agreement Act 1931 (c.2)
Curates, etc. Act 1796 (c.83)
Curragh of Kildare Act 1868 (c.60)
Curragh of Kildare Act 1870 (c.74)
Currency Act 1982 (c.3)
Currency Act 1983 (c.9)
Currency and Bank Notes Act 1914 (c.14)
Currency and Bank Notes Act 1928 (c.13)
Currency and Bank Notes Act 1939 (c.7)
Currency and Bank Notes Act 1954 (c.12)
Currency and Bank Notes (Amendment) Act 1914 (c.72)
Currency (Defence) Act 1939 (c.64)
Curriers, etc. Act 1738 (c.25)
Cursitor Baron of the Exchequer Act 1856 (c.86)
Custody of Children Act 1891 (c.3)
Custody of Children (Scotland) Act 1939 (c.4)
Custody of Infants Act 1839 (c.54)
Custody of Infants Act 1873 (c.12)
Custody of Insane Persons Act 1816 (c.117)
Custody of Napoleon Buonaparte Act 1816 (c.22)
Customs Act 1719 (c.12)
Customs Act 1722 (c.21)
Customs Act 1772 (c.50)
Customs Act 1772 (c.60)
Customs Act 1724 (c.7)
Customs Act 1736 (c.30)
Customs Act 1753 (c.12)

Customs Act 1763 (c.9)
Customs Act 1763 (c.22)
Customs Act 1766 (c.20)
Customs Act 1766 (c.28)
Customs Act 1766 (c.41)
Customs Act 1766 (c.45)
Customs Act 1766 (c.50)
Customs Act 1767 (c.58)
Customs Act 1768 (c.23)
Customs Act 1770 (c.17)
Customs Act 1770 (c.30)
Customs Act 1770 (c.43)
Customs Act 1775 (c.34)
Customs Act 1775 (c.35)
Customs Act 1775 (c.37)
Customs Act 1776 (c.12)
Customs Act 1776 (c.27)
Customs Act 1776 (c.41)
Customs Act 1776 (c.42)
Customs Act 1776 (c.43)
Customs Act 1776 (c.48)
Customs Act 1778 (c.4)
Customs Act 1778 (cc.24, 25)
Customs Act 1778 (c.27)
Customs Act 1778 (c.40)
Customs Act 1778 (c.58)
Customs Act 1779 (c.29)
Customs Act 1779 (c.41)
Customs Act 1779 (c.62)
Customs Act 1780 (c.7)
Customs Act 1780 (c.16)
Customs Act 1780 (c.25)
Customs Act 1780 (c.30)
Customs Act 1780 (c.32)
Customs Act 1782 (c.20)
Customs Act 1782 (c.21)
Customs Act 1782 (c.28)
Customs Act 1782 (c.49)
Customs Act 1782 (c.61)
Customs Act 1783 (c.11)
Customs Act 1783 (c.56)
Customs Act 1783 (c.74)
Customs Act 1784 (c.9)
Customs Act 1784 (c.16)
Customs Act 1784 (c.49)
Customs Act 1785 (c.25)
Customs Act 1785 (c.69)
Customs Act 1786 (c.42)
Customs Act 1786 (c.104)
Customs Act 1788 (c.27)
Customs Act 1788 (c.33)
Customs Act 1789 (c.59)
Customs Act 1789 (c.60)
Customs Act 1789 (c.64)
Customs Act 1790 (c.4)
Customs Act 1791 (c.15)
Customs Act 1791 (c.26)
Customs Act 1792 (c.32)
Customs Act 1792 (c.43)
Customs Act 1792 (c.54)
Customs Act 1793 (c.48)
Customs Act 1793 (c.70)
Customs Act 1793 (c.81)
Customs Act 1794 (c.51)
Customs Act 1794 (c.70)
Customs Act 1795 (c.20)
Customs Act 1796 (c.15)
Customs Act 1796 (cc.78, 79)
Customs Act 1796 (c.110)
Customs Act 1797 (c.110)
Customs Act 1798 (c.86)
Customs Act 1799 (c.61)
Customs Act 1800 (c.51)
Customs Act 1800 (c.59)
Customs Act 1800 (c.60)
Customs Act 1801 (c.87)
Customs Act 1801 (c.89)
Customs Act 1801 (c.94)
Customs Act 1802 (c.95)
Customs Act 1803 (c.68)
Customs Act 1803 (c.70)
Customs Act 1803 (c.128)
Customs Act 1803 (c.131)
Customs Act 1804 (c.53)
Customs Act 1805 (c.18)
Customs Act 1805 (c.29)
Customs Act 1805 (cc.44, 45)
Customs Act 1805 (c.88)
Customs Act 1805 (c.103)
Customs Act 1806 (c.150)
Customs Act 1807 (c.51)
Customs Act 1807 (c.61)
Customs Act 1808 (c.9)
Customs Act 1808 (c.26)
Customs Act 1808 (c.28)
Customs Act 1808 (cc.56, 57)
Customs Act 1808 (c.67)
Customs Act 1809 (c.46)
Customs Act 1809 (c.65)
Customs Act 1809 (c.98)
Customs Act 1810 (c.77)
Customs Act 1811 (c.52)
Customs Act 1811 (c.55)
Customs Act 1811 (c.71)
Customs Act 1811 (c.96)
Customs Act 1812 (c.2)
Customs Act 1812 (c.60)
Customs Act 1812 (c.89)
Customs Act 1812 (c.117)
Customs Act 1812 (c.141)
Customs Act 1813 (cc.26, 27)
Customs Act 1813 (c.29)
Customs Act 1813 (c.33)
Customs Act 1813 (c.47)
Customs Act 1813 (c.104)
Customs Act 1813 (c.105)
Customs Act 1814 (c.14)
Customs Act 1814 (c.50)
Customs Act 1814 (cc.64–66)
Customs Act 1814 (c.69)
Customs Act 1814 (c.77)
Customs Act 1814 (c.103)
Customs Act 1814 (c.122)
Customs Act 1815 (cc.22, 23)
Customs Act 1815 (c.24)
Customs Act 1815 (cc.32, 33)

Customs Act 1815 (c.36)
Customs Act 1815 (c.52)
Customs Act 1815 (c.95)
Customs Act 1815 (c.135)
Customs Act 1815 (c.163)
Customs Act 1815 (c.174)
Customs Act 1815 (c.181)
Customs Act 1816 (c.77)
Customs Act 1816 (c.93)
Customs Act 1835 (c.66)
Customs Act 1836 (c.60)
Customs Act 1838 (c.113)
Customs Act 1840 (c.19)
Customs Act 1840 (c.95)
Customs Act 1842 (c.47)
Customs Act 1843 (c.84)
Customs Act 1844 (c.16)
Customs Act 1844 (c.43)
Customs Act 1844 (c.73)
Customs Act 1845 (c.12)
Customs Act 1845 (c.84)
Customs Act 1845 (c.86)
Customs Act 1845 (c.92)
Customs Act 1846 (c.24)
Customs Act 1846 (c.58)
Customs Act 1846 (c.94)
Customs Act 1846 (c.102)
Customs Act 1847 (c.24)
Customs Act 1849 (c.90)
Customs Act 1850 (c.95)
Customs Act 1851 (c.62)
Customs Act 1853 (c.54)
Customs Act 1853 (c.106)
Customs Act 1854 (cc.28, 29)
Customs Act 1854 (c.122)
Customs Act 1855 (c.21)
Customs Act 1856 (c.75)
Customs Act 1857 (c.15)
Customs Act 1857 (c.62)
Customs Act 1858 (c.12)
Customs Act 1858 (c.16)
Customs Act 1859 (c.37)
Customs Act 1860 (c.22)
Customs Act 1860 (c.36)
Customs Act 1867 (c.82)
Customs Amendment Act 1842 (c.56)
Customs Amendment Act 1886 (c.41)
Customs and Excise Act 1711 (c.19)
Customs and Excise Act 1782 (c.66)
Customs and Excise Act 1787 (c.13)
Customs and Excise Act 1804 (c.67)
Customs and Excise Act 1806 (c.38)
Customs and Excise Act 1809 (c.116)
Customs and Excise Act 1814 (cc.120, 121)
Customs and Excise Act 1815 (c.118)
Customs and Excise Act 1816 (c.85)
Customs and Excise Act 1857 (c.61)
Customs and Excise Act 1952 (c.44)
Customs and Excise Duties (General Reliefs) Act 1979 (c.3)
Customs and Excise (Ireland) Act 1804 (c.103)
Customs and Excise (Ireland) Act 1805 (c.108)
Customs and Excise (Ireland) Act 1806 (c.58)
Customs and Excise (Ireland) Act 1807 (c.48)
Customs and Excise (Ireland) Act 1808 (c.62)
Customs and Excise (Ireland) Act 1816 (c.20)
Customs and Excise Management Act 1979 (c.2)
Customs and Excise Warehousing Act 1869 (c.103)
Customs and Income Tax Act 1871 (c.21)
Customs and Inland Revenue Act 1861 (c.20)
Customs and Inland Revenue Act 1863 (c.22)
Customs and Inland Revenue Act 1867 (c.23)
Customs and Inland Revenue Act 1870 (c.32)
Customs and Inland Revenue Act 1872 (c.20)
Customs and Inland Revenue Act 1873 (c.18)
Customs and Inland Revenue Act 1874 (c.16)
Customs and Inland Revenue Act 1875 (c.23)
Customs and Inland Revenue Act 1876 (c.16)
Customs and Inland Revenue Act 1878 (c.15)
Customs and Inland Revenue Act 1879 (c.21)
Customs and Inland Revenue Act 1880 (c.14)
Customs and Inland Revenue Act 1881 (c.12)
Customs and Inland Revenue Act 1882 (c.41)
Customs and Inland Revenue Act 1883 (c.10)
Customs and Inland Revenue Act 1884 (c.25)
Customs and Inland Revenue Act 1885 (c.51)
Customs and Inland Revenue Act 1886 (c.18)
Customs and Inland Revenue Act 1887 (c.15)
Customs and Inland Revenue Act 1888 (c.8)
Customs and Inland Revenue Act 1889 (c.7)
Customs and Inland Revenue Act 1890 (c.8)
Customs and Inland Revenue Act 1891 (c.25)
Customs and Inland Revenue Act 1892 (c.16)
Customs and Inland Revenue Act 1893 (c.7)
Customs and Inland Revenue Amendment Act 1877 (c.10)
Customs and Inland Revenue Buildings (Ireland) - Northern Irish Act 1882 (c.17)
Customs Buildings Act 1879 (c.36)
Customs Consolidation Act 1853 (c.107)
Customs Consolidation Act 1860 (c.110)
Customs Consolidation Act 1876 (c.36)
Customs Consolidation Act, 1876, Amendment 1887 (c.7)
Customs Consolidation Act, 1876, Amendment 1890 (c.56)
Customs Duties Act 1811 (cc.67, 68)
Customs Duties (Dumping and Subsidies) Act 1957 (c.18)
Customs Duties (Dumping and Subsidies) Act 1969 (c.16)
Customs Duties (Dumping and Subsidies) Amendment Act 1968 (c.33)
Customs Duties, etc. Act 1763 (c.15)
Customs, etc. Act 1721 (c.18)
Customs, etc. Act 1727 (c.17)
Customs, etc. Act 1728 (c.18)
Customs, etc. Act 1736 (c.27)
Customs, etc. Act 1765 (cc.29–32)
Customs, etc. Act 1765 (c.45)
Customs, etc. Act 1766 (cc.46, 47)
Customs, etc. Act 1766 (c.52)
Customs, etc. Act 1769 (c.35)

Customs, etc. Act 1769 (c.41)
Customs, etc. Act 1784 (c.7)
Customs, etc. Act 1798 (c.76)
Customs, etc. Act 1813 (c.36)
Customs, etc. Act 1814 (c.171)
Customs, etc. Act 1815 (cc.82, 83)
Customs, etc. Act 1816 (c.29)
Customs, etc. (Ireland) Act 1812 (c.76)
Customs, etc., Revenues Act 1725 (c.28)
Customs, etc., Revenues Act 1765 (c.43)
Customs, Excise and Taxes Act 1804 (c.26)
Customs (Exportation Prohibition) Act 1914 (c.64)
Customs (Exportation Restriction) Act 1914 (c.2)
Customs (Exportation Restriction) Act 1915 (c.52)
Customs (Import Deposits) Act 1968 (c.74)
Customs (Import Deposits) Act 1969 (c.64)
Customs, Inland Revenue, and Savings Banks Act 1877 (c.13)
Customs (Ireland) Act 1806 (c.87)
Customs (Ireland) Act 1807 (c.12)
Customs (Ireland) Act 1808 (c.80)
Customs (Isle of Man) Act 1870 (c.12)
Customs (Isle of Man) Tariff Act 1874 (c.46)
Customs (Manchester Bonding) Act 1850 (c.84)
Customs (Officers) Act 1881 (c.30)
Customs Refined Sugar Duties, Isle of Man Act 1870 (c.43)
Customs Rotulorum (Ireland) Act 1831 (c.17)
Customs Seizures Act 1790 (c.43)
Customs Sugar Duties (Isle of Man) Act 1873 (c.29)
Customs Tariff Act 1855 (c.97)
Customs Tariff Act 1876 (c.35)
Customs (War Powers) Act 1915 (c.31)
Customs (War Powers) Act 1916 (c.102)
Customs (War Powers) (No. 2) Act 1915 (c.71)
Customs (Wine Duty) Act 1888 (c.14)
Cutlery Trade Act 1819 (c.7)
Cycle Tracks Act 1984 (c.38)
Cyprus Act 1960 (c.52)
Czecho-Slovakia (Financial Assistance) Act 1939 (c.6)
Czecho-Slovakia (Financial Claims and Refugees) Act 1940 (c.4)
Czecho-Slovakia (Restrictions on Banking Accounts etc.) Act 1939 (c.11)

Dalkeith Beer Duties Act 1759 (c.53)
Dalkeith Beer Duties Act 1782 (c.18)
Damages Act 1996 (c.48)
Damages (Scotland) Act 1976 (c.13)
Damages (Scotland) Act 1993 (c.5)
Damaging of Hides Act 1801 (c.53)
Dangerous Dogs Act 1989 (c.30)
Dangerous Dogs Act 1991 (c.65)
Dangerous Drugs Act 1925 (c.74)
Dangerous Drugs Act 1931 (c.14)
Dangerous Drugs Act 1951 (c.48)
Dangerous Drugs Act 1964 (c.36)
Dangerous Drugs Act 1965 (c.15)
Dangerous Drugs Act 1967 (c.82)
Dangerous Drugs (Amendment) Act 1950 (c.7)
Dangerous Drugs and Poisons (Amendment) Act 1923 (c.5)
Dangerous Litter Act 1971 (c.35)
Dangerous Performances Act 1897 (c.52)
Dangerous Vessels Act 1985 (c.22)
Dangerous Wild Animals Act 1976 (c.38)
Danube Works Loan Act 1868 (c.126)
Darby Court, Westminster Act 1845 (c.104)
Dartford and Strood Road Act 1760 (c.40)
Dartford Roads Act 1766 (c.98)
Dartford Roads Act 1788 (c.84)
Dartford–Thurrock Crossing Act 1988 (c.20)
Data Protection Act 1984 (c.35)
Day Industrial Schools (Scotland) Act 1893 (c.12)
Deal Act 1711 (c.43)
Deal Chapel of Ease Act 1711 (c.43)
Deal: Improvement Act 1791 (c.64)
Deal: Improvement Act 1796 (c.45)
Dealers in Excisable Articles Act 1805 (c.52)
Dean and Chapter Act 1868 (c.19)
Dean and New Forests Act 1808 (c.72)
Dean Forest (Encroachments) Act 1838 (cc.39–41)
Dean Forest Act 1861 (c.40)
Dean Forest (Mines) Act 1838 (c.43)
Dean Forest (Mines) Act 1871 (c.85)
Dean Forest (Mines) Act 1871 (c.85)
Dean Forest Roads Act 1796 (c.131)
Deanery of Manchester Act 1906 (c.19)
Deans and Canons Resignation Act 1872 (c.8)
Dean's Yard, Westminster Act 1755 (c.54)
Death Duties (Killed in War) Act 1914 (c.76)
Debenture Stock Act 1871 (c.27)
Debt of City of Edinburgh, etc. Act 1838 (c.55)
Debtors Act 1869 (c.62)
Debtors Act 1878 (c.54)
Debtors and Creditors Act 1860 (c.147)
Debtors and Imprisonment Act 1758 (c.28)
Debtors Imprisonment Act 1758 (c.28)
Debtors (Ireland) Act 1840 (c.105)
Debtors (Ireland) Act 1872 (c.57)
Debtors, Middlesex Act 1785 (c.45)
Debtors' Prison, Devonshire Act 1753 (c.57)
Debtors Relief Act 1793 (c.5)
Debtors Relief Act 1801 (c.64)
Debtors Relief Act 1812 (c.34)
Debtors (Scotland) Act 1838 (c.114)
Debtors (Scotland) Act 1880 (c.34)
Debtors (Scotland) Act 1987 (c.18)
Debts Clearing Offices Act 1948 (c.2)
Debts Clearing Offices and Import Restrictions Act 1934 (c.31)
Debts Due to Swiss Government Act 1798 (c.45)
Debts Due to the Army Act 1702 (c.24)

Debts Due to the Army Act 1711 (c.38)
Debts Due to the Army Act 1714 (c.24)
Debts Due to the Army Act 1715 (c.35)
Debts Due to the Army Act 1716 (c.17)
Debts Due to the Army Act 1720 (c.30)
Debts Due to the Army, etc. Act 1701 (c.1)
Debts Due to the Army, etc. Act 1717 (c.9)
Debts Due to the Army, etc. Act 1718 (c.14)
Debts Due to the Army, etc. Act 1719 (c.17)
Debts Due to the United Provinces, etc. Act 1797 (c.28)
Debts of East India Company Act 1812 (c.121)
Debts of Traders Act 1807 (c.74)
Debts Recovery Act 1839 (c.60)
Debts Recovery Act 1848 (c.87)
Debts Recovery (Scotland) Act 1867 (c.96)
Debts Securities (Scotland) Act 1856 (c.91)
Deceased Brother's Widow's Marriage Act 1921 (c.24)
Deceased Wife's Sister's Marriage Act 1907 (c.47)
Decimal Currency Act 1967 (c.47)
Decimal Currency Act 1969 (c.19)
Declaration by Quakers, etc. Act 1837 (c.5)
Declaration of Title Act 1862 (c.67)
Declarations by Quakers, etc. on Acceptance of Offices Act 1838 (c.15)
Declarations Before Taking Office Act 1866 (c.22)
Deeds of Arrangement Act 1887 (c.57)
Deeds of Arrangement Act 1914 (c.47)
Deeds of Arrangement Amendment Act 1890 (c.24)
Deep Sea Mining (Temporary Provisions) Act 1981 (c.53)
Deeping Fen Drainage Act 1737 (c.39)
Deeping Fens Act 1774 (c.23)
Deer Act 1963 (c.36)
Deer Act 1980 (c.49)
Deer Act 1987 (c.28)
Deer Act 1991 (c.54)
Deer (Amendment) (Scotland) Act 1967 (c.37)
Deer (Amendment) (Scotland) Act 1982 (c.19)
Deer (Amendment) (Scotland) Act 1996 (c.44)
Deer (Scotland) Act 1959 (c.40)
Deer (Scotland) Act 1996 (c.58)
Deer Stealers Act 1718 (c.15)
Deer Stealing (England) Act 1802 (c.107)
Deer Stealing (England) Act 1811 (c.120)
Defacing the Coin Act 1853 (c.102)
Defamation Act 1952 (c.66)
Defamation Act 1996 (c.31)
Defective Premises Act 1972 (c.35)
Defence Act 1842 (c.94)
Defence Act 1854 (c.67)
Defence Act 1859 (c.12)
Defence Act 1860 (c.112)
Defence Act 1865 (c.65)
Defence Act Amendment Act 1864 (c.89)
Defence Acts Amendment Act 1873 (c.72)
Defence (Barracks) Act 1935 (c.26)
Defence Contracts Act 1958 (c.38)
Defence Loans Act 1937 (c.13)
Defence Loans Act 1939 (c.8)
Defence of the Realm Act 1797 (c.27)
Defence of the Realm Act 1803 (c.55)
Defence of the Realm Act 1803 (c.120)
Defence of the Realm Act 1803 (c.125)
Defence of the Realm Act 1804 (c.95)
Defence of the Realm Act 1806 (c.90)
Defence of the Realm Act 1808 (c.107)
Defence of the Realm Act 1914 (c.29)
Defence of the Realm (Acquisition of Land) Act 1916 (c.63)
Defence of the Realm (Acquisition of Land) Act 1920 (c.79)
Defence of the Realm (Amendment) Act 1915 (c.34)
Defence of the Realm (Amendment) (No. 2) Act 1915 (c.37)
Defence of the Realm (Amendment) (No. 3) Act 1915 (c.42)
Defence of the Realm (Beans, Peas and Pulse Orders) Act 1918 (c.12)
Defence of the Realm Consolidation Act 1914 (c.8)
Defence of the Realm (Employment Exchanges) Act 1918 (c.58)
Defence of the Realm (England) Act 1803 (c.82)
Defence of the Realm (England) Act 1803 (c.123)
Defence of the Realm, etc. Act 1803 (c.96)
Defence of the Realm, etc. Act 1804 (c.56)
Defence of the Realm, etc. Act 1804 (c.66)
Defence of the Realm, etc. Act 1804 (c.74)
Defence of the Realm (Food Profits) Act 1918 (c.9)
Defence of the Realm (Ireland) Act 1803 (c.85)
Defence of the Realm (Ireland) Act 1806 (c.63)
Defence of the Realm, London Act 1803 (c.101)
Defence of the Realm, London Act 1804 (c.96)
Defence of the Realm, London Act 1806 (c.144)
Defence of the Realm (No. 2) Act 1914 (c.63)
Defence of the Realm (Scotland) Act 1803 (c.83)
Defence of the Realm (Scotland) Act 1803 (c.124)
Defence (Transfer of Functions) Act 1964 (c.15)
Defranchisement of Sudbury Act 1844 (c.53)
Delamere Forest Act 1856 (c.13)
Delay Act 1387 (c.10)
Delay of Cause After Issue Joined Act 1740 (c.17)
Demise of Parts of Rolls Estate Act 1836 (c.49)

Demise of the Crown Act 1727 (c.5)
Demise of the Crown Act 1830 (c.43)
Demise of the Crown Act 1837 (c.31)
Demise of the Crown Act 1901 (c.5)
Denbigh and Carnarvon Roads Act 1757 (c.69)
Denbigh and Flint Roads Act 1769 (c.45)
Denbigh and Flint Roads Act 1790 (c.110)
Denbigh, Flint and Carnarvon Roads Act 1758 (c.55)
Denbigh, Flint and Carnarvon Roads Act 1779 (c.109)
Denbigh, Flint and Carnarvon Roads Act 1780 (c.97)
Denbigh, Flint, Salop. and Chester Roads Act 1767 (c.104)
Denbigh Roads Act 1756 (c.68)
Denbigh Roads Act 1762 (c.77)
Denbigh Roads Act 1763 (c.43)
Denbigh Roads Act 1777 (c.111)
Denbigh Roads Act 1788 (c.112)
Denbigh to Rutland Road Act 1781 (c.80)
Dentists Act 1878 (c.33)
Dentists Act 1921 (c.21)
Dentists Act 1923 (c.36)
Dentists Act 1956 (c.29)
Dentists Act 1957 (c.28)
Dentists Act 1983 (c.38)
Dentists Act 1984 (c.24)
Dentists (Amendment) Act 1973 (c.31)
Denver, etc., Drainage, Norfolk Act 1771 (c.72)
Denver, etc. (Norfolk and Cambridge) Drainage Act 1748 (c.16)
Deodands Act 1846 (c.62)
Department of Science and Art Act 1875 (c.68)
Department of Scientific and Industrial Research Act 1956 (c.58)
Department of Technical Co-operation Act 1961 (c.30)
Dependency of Ireland on Great Britain Act 1719 (c.5)
Deposit of Poisonous Waste Act 1972 (c.21)
Depredations on the Thames Act 1800 (c.87)
Depredations on the Thames Act 1807 (c.37)
Depredations on the Thames Act 1814 (c.187)
Deputy Lieutenants Act 1918 (c.19)
Deputy Speaker Act 1855 (c.84)
Derby and Cheshire Roads Act 1792 (c.128)
Derby and Chester Roads Act 1782 (c.107)
Derby and Leicester Roads Act 1794 (c.120)
Derby and Nottinghamshire Roads Act 1757 (c.60)
Derby and Nottinghamshire Roads Act 1764 (c.67)
Derby and Nottinghamshire Roads Act 1780 (c.74)
Derby and Nottinghamshire Roads Act 1790 (c.113)
Derby and Sheffield Roads Act 1756 (c.82)
Derby and Stafford Roads Act 1766 (c.79)
Derby and Stafford Roads Act 1787 (c.87)
Derby and Uttoxeter Road Act 1763 (c.57)
Derby and Yorkshire Roads Act 1764 (c.65)
Derby and Yorkshire Roads Act 1776 (c.73)
Derby and Yorkshire Roads Act 1779 (c.99)
Derby Bridge Act 1788 (c.77)
Derby Canal Act 1793 (c.102)
Derby Gaol Act 1756 (c.48)
Derby: Improvement Act 1792 (c.78)
Derby, Leicester and Warwick Roads Act 1759 (c.47)
Derby, Leicester and Warwick Roads Act 1781 (c.92)
Derby Roads Act 1737 (c.33)
Derby Roads Act 1743 (c.20)
Derby Roads Act 1759 (c.33)
Derby Roads Act 1764 (c.82)
Derby Roads Act 1766 (c.69)
Derby Roads Act 1766 (c.80)
Derby Roads Act 1766 (c.87)
Derby Roads Act 1777 (c.92)
Derby Roads Act 1777 (c.101)
Derby Roads Act 1785 (c.121)
Derby Roads Act 1786 (c.151)
Derby Roads Act 1788 (c.89)
Derby Roads Act 1793 (c.152)
Derby Roads Act 1795 (c.154)
Derby to Newcastle-under-Lyme Road Act 1758 (c.60)
Derbyshire Roads Act 1724 (c.13)
Derbyshire Roads Act 1738 (c.12)
Derbyshire Roads Act 1758 (c.43)
Derbyshire Roads Act 1759 (c.39)
Derbyshire Roads Act 1769 (c.81)
Derbyshire Roads Act 1779 (c.87)
Derbyshire Roads Act 1781 (c.81)
Derbyshire Roads Act 1781 (c.83)
Deregulation and Contracting Out Act 1994 (c.40)
Derelict Land Act 1982 (c.42)
Derelict Vessels (Report) Act 1896 (c.12)
Deritend and Bordesley, Warwick: Improvement Act 1791 (c.17)
Deritend Bridge, Birmingham: Rebuilding Act 1788 (c.70)
Derwent (Yorks.) Navigation Act 1702 (c.14)
Desertion of Seamen Act 1797 (c.73)
Design Copyright Act 1968 (c.68)
Designing and Printing of Linens, etc. Act 1787 (c.38)
Designing and Printing of Linens, etc. Act 1789 (c.19)
Destruction of Coal Works Act 1739 (c.21)
Destruction of Deer (England) Act 1718 (c.28)
Destruction of Prisons by Rioters Act 1780 (c.1)
Destruction of Property (S.) Act 1789 (c.46)
Destruction of Stocking Frames, etc. Act 1812 (c.16)
Destruction of Stocking Frames, etc. Act 1813 (c.42)
Destruction of Turnpikes, etc. Act 1727 (c.19)

Destruction of Turnpikes, etc. Act 1731 (c.33)
Destruction of Turnpikes, etc. Act 1734 (c.20)
Destructive Imported Animals Act 1932 (c.12)
Destructive Insects Act 1877 (c.68)
Destructive Insects and Pests Act 1907 (c.4)
Destructive Insects and Pests Act 1927 (c.32)
Detached Parts of Counties (England) Act 1858 (c.68)
Detached Portions of Counties (Ireland) Act 1871 (c.106)
Determination of Needs Act 1941 (c.11)
Development and Road Improvement Funds Act 1909 (c.47)
Development and Road Improvement Funds Act 1910 (c.7)
Development Board for Rural Wales Act 1991 (c.1)
Development Land Tax Act 1976 (c.24)
Development (Loan Guarantees and Grants) Act 1929 (c.7)
Development of Inventions Act 1948 (c.60)
Development of Inventions Act 1954 (c.20)
Development of Inventions Act 1958 (c.3)
Development of Inventions Act 1965 (c.21)
Development of Inventions Act 1967 (c.32)
Development of Rural Wales Act 1976 (c.75)
Development of Tourism Act 1969 (c.51)
Devizes Road Act 1784 (c.65)
Devizes Roads Act 1797 (c.154)
Devizes: Streets Act 1780 (c.36)
Devon Bridges Act 1757 (c.47)
Devon: Canal Act 1796 (c.46)
Devon, Dorset and Somerset Roads Act 1792 (c.144)
Devon Gaol Act 1787 (c.59)
Devon (Poor Relief) Act 1772 (c.18)
Devon Roads Act 1755 (c.49)
Devon Roads Act 1757 (c.51)
Devon Roads Act 1758 (c.52)
Devon Roads Act 1758 (c.68)
Devon Roads Act 1760 (c.34)
Devon Roads Act 1762 (c.50)
Devon Roads Act 1762 (c.64)
Devon Roads Act 1763 (c.38)
Devon Roads Act 1765 (cc.69, 70)
Devon Roads Act 1767 (c.62)
Devon Roads Act 1772 (c.86)
Devon Roads Act 1772 (c.93)
Devon Roads Act 1780 (c.79)
Devon Roads Act 1781 (c.84)
Devon Roads Act 1783 (c.26)
Devon Roads Act 1784 (c.63)
Devon Roads Act 1784 (c.67)
Devon Roads Act 1787 (c.74)
Devon Roads Act 1791 (c.117)
Devon, Shire Hall Act 1772 (c.16)
Devonshire: Poor Relief Act 1769 (c.82)
Dewsbury to Elland Road Act 1758 (c.54)
Dewsbury to Elland Road Act 1779 (c.88)
Diet of Soldiers on a March Act 1813 (c.83)
Differential Duties on Foreign Ships Act 1852 (c.47)
Dindings Agreement (Approval) Act 1934 (c.55)
Diocesan Boundaries Act 1871 (c.14)
Diocesan Boundaries Act 1872 (c.14)
Diocese of Norwich Act 1848 (c.61)
Diplomatic and Consular Premises Act 1987 (c.46)
Diplomatic and Other Privileges Act 1971 (c.64)
Diplomatic Immunities (Commonwealth Countries and Republic of Ireland) Act 1951 (c.18)
Diplomatic Immunities (Conferences with Commonwealth Countries and Republic of Ireland) Act 1961 (c.11)
Diplomatic Immunities Restriction Act 1955 (c.22)
Diplomatic Privileges Act 1708 (c.12)
Diplomatic Privileges Act 1964 (c.81)
Diplomatic Privileges (Extension) Act 1941 (c.7)
Diplomatic Privileges (Extension) Act 1944 (c.44)
Diplomatic Privileges (Extension) Act 1946 (c.66)
Diplomatic Privileges (Extension) Act 1950 (c.7)
Diplomatic Relations with See of Rome Act 1848 (c.108)
Diplomatic Salaries, etc. Act 1869 (c.43)
Directors' Liability Act 1890 (c.64)
Disability Discrimination Act 1995 (c.50)
Disability (Grants) Act 1993 (c.14)
Disability Living Allowance and Disability Working Allowance Act 1991 (c.21)
Disabled Men (Facilities for Employment) (Master and Servant) Act 1919 (c.22)
Disabled Persons Act 1981 (c.43)
Disabled Persons Act 1986 (c.33)
Disabled Persons (Employment) Act 1944 (c.10)
Disabled Persons (Employment) Act 1958 (c.33)
Disabled Persons (Northern Ireland) Act 1989 (c.10)
Disarming the Highlands, etc. Act 1745 (c.39)
Disarming the Highlands, etc. Act 1753 (c.29)
Discharge of a Crown Debt Act 1788 (c.32)
Discharge of Certain Imprisoned Debtors Act 1808 (c.123)
Discharge to Lady A. Jekyll's Executors Act 1772 (c.53)
Discharged Prisoners Act 1774 (c.20)
Discharged Prisoners' Aid Act 1862 (c.44)
Discharged Soldiers, etc. Act 1748 (c.44)
Discontinuance of Duties Act 1757 (c.7)
Discontinuance of Duties Act 1757 (c.14)
Discontinuance of Duties Act 1758 (c.12)
Discontinuance of Duties Act 1770 (c.8)
Discontinuance of Portsdown Fair, Southampton Act 1862 (c.34)
Discount on Newspapers Act 1809 (c.50)
Discovery of Longitude at Sea Act 1713 (c.14)
Discovery of Longitude at Sea Act 1762 (c.14)

Discovery of Longitude at Sea Act 1762 (c.18)
Discovery of Longitude at Sea Act 1765 (c.11)
Discovery of Longitude at Sea Act 1765 (c.20)
Discovery of Longitude at Sea Act 1770 (c.34)
Discovery of Longitude at Sea Act 1774 (c.66)
Discovery of Longitude at Sea Act 1790 (c.14)
Discovery of Longitude at Sea Act 1815 (c.75)
Discovery of Longitude at Sea, etc. Act 1803 (c.118)
Discovery of Longitude at Sea, etc. Act 1806 (c.77)
Discovery of Longitude at Seas Act 1753 (c.25)
Discovery of North-West Passage Act 1744 (c.17)
Discovery of Northern Passage Act 1776 (c.6)
Disease Among Cattle Act 1772 (c.51)
Diseased Sheep, etc. Act 1798 (c.65)
Diseases of Animals Act 1894 (c.57)
Diseases of Animals Act 1896 (c.15)
Diseases of Animals Act 1903 (c.43)
Diseases of Animals Act 1909 (c.26)
Diseases of Animals Act 1910 (c.20)
Diseases of Animals Act 1922 (c.8)
Diseases of Animals Act 1923 (c.3)
Diseases of Animals Act 1925 (c.63)
Diseases of Animals Act 1927 (c.13)
Diseases of Animals Act 1935 (c.31)
Diseases of Animals Act 1950 (c.36)
Diseases of Animals Act 1975 (c.40)
Diseases of Animals (Ireland) Act 1914 (c.40)
Diseases of Fish Act 1937 (c.33)
Diseases of Fish Act 1983 (c.30)
Diseases Prevention Act 1855 (c.116)
Diseases Prevention (Metropolis) Act 1883 (c.35)
Disfranchisement of Freemen, Great Yarmouth Act 1848 (c.24)
Disfranchisement of St. Alban's Act 1852 (c.9)
Disorderly Houses Act 1751 (c.36)
Dispensary Committees (Ireland) Act 1896 (c.10)
Dispensary Houses (Ireland) Act 1879 (c.25)
Disposal of Ulysses Fitzmaurice's Intestate Estate Act 1774 (c.40)
Disposal of Uncollected Goods Act 1952 (c.43)
Disposition of Copyhold Estates by Will Act 1815 (c.192)
Disputes Between Masters and Workmen Act 1800 (c.90)
Dissolved Boards of Management and Guardians Act 1870 (c.2)
Distemper Amongst Cattle Act 1745 (c.5)
Distemper Amongst Cattle Act 1746 (c.4)
Distemper Amongst Cattle Act 1749 (c.23)
Distemper Amongst Cattle Act 1750 (c.31)
Distemper Amongst Cattle Act 1754 (c.14)
Distemper Amongst Cattle Act 1755 (c.18)
Distemper Amongst Cattle Act 1757 (c.20)
Distemper Amongst Cattle Act 1770 (c.4)
Distemper Amongst Cattle Act 1770 (c.45)
Distillation Act 1757 (c.10)
Distillation Act 1757 (c.15)
Distillation Act 1759 (c.9)
Distillation, etc. Act 1702 (c.14)
Distillation, etc. Act 1774 (c.73)
Distillation, etc. of Spirits (Ireland) Act 1813 (c.52)
Distillation from Corn, etc. Act 1812 (c.118)
Distillation from Corn Prohibition, etc. Act 1812 (c.7)
Distillation from Wheat, etc. Act 1799 (c.7)
Distillation from Wheat, etc. Act 1800 (c.21)
Distillation from Wheat, etc., Prohibition Act 1795 (c.20)
Distillation from Wheat (Ireland) Act 1801 (c.15)
Distillation (Ireland) Act 1812 (c.47)
Distillation of Spirits Act 1803 (c.11)
Distillation of Spirits Act 1805 (c.100)
Distillation of Spirits Act 1808 (c.118)
Distillation of Spirits Act 1809 (c.7)
Distillation of Spirits Act 1809 (c.24)
Distillation of Spirits Act 1810 (c.5)
Distillation of Spirits Act 1812 (c.3)
Distillation of Spirits from Sugar Act 1847 (c.6)
Distillation of Spirits from Sugar, etc. Act 1848 (c.100)
Distillation of Spirits (Ireland) Act 1813 (c.145)
Distillation of Spirits (Ireland) Act 1813 (c.148)
Distillation of Spirits (Ireland) Act 1814 (c.150)
Distillation of Spirits (Ireland) Act 1815 (c.151)
Distillation of Spirits (Ireland) Act 1816 (c.112)
Distillation of Spirits (Scotland) Act 1808 (c.10)
Distillation of Spirits (Scotland) Act 1810 (c.79)
Distillation of Spirits (Scotland) Act 1813 (c.9)
Distilleries, etc. Act 1793 (c.61)
Distillers Act 1746 (c.39)
Distillers Act 1779 (c.50)
Distillers of Spirits Act 1811 (c.42)
Distress (Costs) Act 1817 (c.93)
Distress for Rates Act 1849 (c.14)
Distress for Rent Act 1737 (c.19)
Distress for Rent Act 1960 (c.12)
Distressed Unions Advances (Ireland) Act 1850 (c.14)
Distressed Unions (Ireland) Act 1852 (c.68)
Distresses Under Justices' Warrants Act 1754 (c.20)

Distribution of Certain Monies Act 1803 (c.39)
Distribution of Industry Act 1944 (c.36)
Distribution of Industry (Industrial Finance) Act 1958 (c.41)
District Auditors Act 1879 (c.6)
District Church Tithes Act 1865 (c.42)
District Councillors and Guardians (Term of Office) Act 1900 (c.16)
District Councils (Water Supply Facilities) Act 1897 (c.44)
District Courts and Prisons Act 1842 (c.53)
District Courts and Prisons Act 1844 (c.50)
District Courts (Scotland) Act 1975 (c.20)
Distribution of Germany Enemy Property Act 1949 (c.85)
Distribution of Industry Act 1950 (c.8)
Disused Burial Grounds Act 1884 (c.72)
Disused Burial Grounds (Amendment) Act 1981 (c.18)
Disused Public Buildings (Ireland) Act 1808 (c.113)
Divided Parishes and Poor Law Amendment Act 1876 (c.61)
Divided Parishes and Poor Law Amendment Act 1882 (c.58)
Dividends Act 1978 (c.54)
Dividends and Stock Act 1869 (c.104)
Dividends and Stock Act 1870 (c.47)
Division of Deanery of St. Burian Act 1850 (c.76)
Divorce Amendment Act 1868 (c.77)
Divorce (Insanity and Desertion) Act 1958 (c.54)
Divorce Jurisdiction, Court Fees and Legal Aid (Scotland) Act 1983 (c.12)
Divorce Reform Act 1969 (c.55)
Divorce (Scotland) Act 1938 (c.50)
Divorce (Scotland) Act 1964 (c.91)
Divorce (Scotland) Act 1976 (c.39)
Dock Work Regulation Act 1976 (c.79)
Dock Workers (Pensions) Act 1960 (c.39)
Dock Workers (Regulation of Employment) Act 1946 (c.22)
Docking and Nicking of Horses Act 1949 (c.70)
Docks and Harbours Act 1966 (c.28)
Docks and Ordnance Service Act 1804 (c.79)
Docks, etc., at Chatham, etc. Act 1806 (c.130)
Dockyard Act 1865 (c.25)
Dockyard Ports Regulation Act 1865 (c.125)
Dockyard Services Act 1986 (c.52)
Dockyards, etc., Protection Act 1772 (c.24)
Dockyards Protection Act Amendment Act 1863 (c.30)
Doctrine of the Trinity Act 1813 (c.160)
Documentary Evidence Act 1868 (c.37)
Documentary Evidence Act 1882 (c.9)
Documentary Evidence Act 1895 (c.9)
Dog Licences Act 1959 (c.55)
Dog Licences Act 1867 (c.5)
Dog Racecourse Betting (Temporary Provisions) Act 1947 (c.20)
Dog Stealing Act 1770 (c.18)
Dog Stealing Act 1845 (c.47)
Dogs Act 1865 (c.60)
Dogs Act 1871 (c.56)
Dogs Act 1906 (c.32)
Dogs (Amendment) Act 1928 (c.21)
Dogs Amendment Act 1938 (c.21)
Dogs (Fouling of Land) Act 1996 (c.20)
Dogs (Ireland) Act 1862 (c.59)
Dogs (Ireland) Act 1867 (c.116)
Dogs (Protection of Livestock) Act 1953 (c.28)
Dogs Regulation (Ireland) Act 1865 (c.50)
Dogs Regulation (Ireland) Act 1919 (c.81)
Dogs (Scotland) Act 1863 (c.100)
Domestic and Appellate Proceedings (Restriction of Publicity) Act 1968 (c.63)
Domestic Proceedings and Magistrates' Courts Act 1978 (c.22)
Domestic Violence and Matrimonial Proceedings Act 1976 (c.50)
Domicile Act 1861 (c.121)
Domicile and Matrimonial Proceedings Act 1973 (c.45)
Dominica Act 1938 (c.10)
Dominica Loan Act 1860 (c.57)
Dominica Loan Act 1867 (c.91)
Doncaster and Tadcaster Road Act 1740 (c.28)
Doncaster Road and Bridges Act 1795 (c.158)
Doncaster Roads Act 1785 (c.104)
Doncaster: Small Debts, Lighting, etc. Act 1763 (c.40)
Doncaster to Bawtry Road Act 1776 (c.71)
Doncaster to Chester Road Act 1789 (c.98)
Donnington to Southall Canal Act 1788 (c.73)
Dorchester Bridge and Causeway Act 1745 (c.24)
Dorchester: Streets Act 1776 (c.27)
Dorset and Devon Roads Act 1757 (c.43)
Dorset and Devon Roads Act 1765 (c.75)
Dorset and Somerset Roads Act 1765 (c.102)
Dorset and Somerset Roads Act 1767 (c.82)
Dorset and Wilts: Canal Act 1796 (c.47)
Dorset, Devon and Somerset Roads Act 1777 (c.89)
Dorset, etc., Roads Act 1762 (c.61)
Dorset Roads Act 1758 (c.50)
Dorset Roads Act 1760 (c.24)
Dorset Roads Act 1766 (c.68)
Dorset Roads Act 1766 (c.92)
Dorset Roads Act 1769 (c.47)
Dorset Roads Act 1777 (c.103)
Dorset Roads Act 1782 (c.101)
Dorset Roads Act 1788 (c.91)
Dorset Roads Act 1790 (c.95)
Dover and Rye Harbours Act 1764 (c.72)
Dover, Deal and Sandwich Road Act 1797 (c.156)
Dover Harbour Act 1703 (c.7)
Dover Harbour Act 1717 (c.13)
Dover Harbour Act 1722 (c.30)

Dover Harbour Act 1737 (c.7)
Dover Harbour Act 1757 (c.8)
Dover Harbour Act 1786 (c.11)
Dover Harbour Act 1794 (c.112)
Dover Streets Act 1778 (c.76)
Doveridge Roads, Derby Act 1769 (c.59)
Downpatrick Election Committee Act 1815 (c.98)
Drafts on Bankers Act 1856 (c.25)
Drafts on Bankers Act 1858 (c.79)
Drainage and Improvement of Land (Ireland) Act 1866 (c.40)
Drainage and Improvement of Land (Ireland) Act 1892 (c.65)
Drainage and Improvement of Land, Supplemental (Ireland) Act 1865 (c.13)
Drainage and Improvement of Land, Supplemental (Ireland) Act 1865 (c.50)
Drainage and Improvement of Land, Supplemental (Ireland) Act 1867 (c.43)
Drainage and Improvement of Lands Amendment (Ireland) Act 1865 (c.52)
Drainage and Improvement of Lands Amendment (Ireland) Act 1869 (c.72)
Drainage and Improvement of Lands Amendment (Ireland) Act 1872 (c.31)
Drainage and Improvement of Lands Amendment (Ireland) Act 1874 (c.32)
Drainage and Improvement of Lands (Ireland) Act 1853 (c.130)
Drainage and Improvement of Lands (Ireland) Act 1855 (c.110)
Drainage and Improvement of Lands (Ireland) Act 1863 (c.88)
Drainage and Improvement of Lands (Ireland) Act 1864 (c.72)
Drainage and Improvement of Lands (Ireland) Act 1878 (c.59)
Drainage and Improvement of Lands (Ireland) Act 1880 (c.27)
Drainage and Improvement of Lands Supplemental Act 1866 (c.61)
Drainage and Improvement of Lands, Supplemental (Ireland) Act 1864 (c.107)
Drainage and Improvement of Lands, Supplemental (Ireland) Act 1867 (c.139)
Drainage: Cambridge, Isle of Ely Act 1772 (c.26)
Drainage, etc. (Ireland) Act 1847 (c.106)
Drainage (Ireland) Act 1842 (c.89)
Drainage (Ireland) Act 1846 (c.4)
Drainage (Ireland) Act 1847 (c.79)
Drainage (Ireland) Act 1856 (c.62)
Drainage: Isle of Ely Act 1772 (c.27)
Drainage Haddenham Level Act 1726 (c.18)
Drainage Maintenance Act 1866 (c.49)
Drainage of Bogs, etc. (Ireland) Act 1809 (c.102)
Drainage of Lands Act 1849 (c.100)
Drainage Rates Act 1958 (c.37)
Drainage Rates Act 1962 (c.39)
Drainage Rates Act 1963 (c.10)
Drainage Rates (Disabled Persons) Act 1986 (c.17)
Dramatic and Musical Performers' Protection Act 1925 (c.46)
Dramatic and Musical Performers' Protection Act 1958 (c.44)
Dramatic and Musical Performers' Protection Act 1972 (c.32)
Drawback Act 1795 (c.98)
Drawback Act 1795 (c.110)
Drawback Act 1796 (c.106)
Drawback Act 1806 (c.114)
Drawback Act 1807 (c.49)
Drawback, etc. on Glass Act 1812 (c.77)
Drawback of Duties Act 1795 (c.39)
Drawback of Duty on Coals Act 1811 (c.83)
Drawback on Chocolate Act 1812 (c.11)
Drawback on Coals Act 1813 (c.18)
Drawback on Linens Act 1805 (c.98)
Drawback on Paper Act 1814 (c.153)
Drawback on Wines Act 1813 (c.44)
Drawbacks Act 1802 (c.17)
Drawbacks Act 1802 (c.60)
Drawbacks Act 1803 (c.5)
Drawbacks Act 1803 (c.10)
Drawbacks Act 1807 (c.20)
Drawbacks Act 1807 (c.62)
Drawbacks Act 1808 (c.43)
Drawbacks and Bounties Act 1795 (c.18)
Drawbacks and Bounties Act 1802 (c.11)
Drawbacks and Bounties Act 1805 (c.93)
Drawbacks, etc. Act 1798 (c.61)
Drawbacks, etc. (Ireland) Act 1805 (c.23)
Drawbacks, etc., on Sugar Act 1811 (c.12)
Drawbacks, etc. on Tobacco, etc. Act 1815 (c.129)
Drawbacks (Ireland) Act 1806 (c.14)
Drawbacks (Ireland) Act 1807 (c.19)
Drawbacks on Paper Act 1814 (c.106)
Drawbacks on Spirits Act 1811 (c.121)
Drawbacks upon Sugar Act 1806 (c.10)
Drayton and Edgehill Road Act 1753 (c.78)
Drill Grounds Act 1886 (c.5)
Driving of Cattle, Metropolis Act 1774 (c.87)
Driving of Cattle, Metropolis Act 1781 (c.67)
Droitwich Roads Act 1768 (c.39)
Drought Act 1976 (c.44)
Drouly Fund Act 1838 (c.89)
Drugging of Animals Act 1876 (c.13)
Drugs (Prevention of Misuse) Act 1964 (c.64)
Drug Trafficking Act 1994 (c.37)
Drug Trafficking Offences Act 1986 (c.32)
Drury Lane Theatre Act 1776 (c.13)
Dublin Amended Carriage Act 1854 (c.45)
Dublin Amended Carriage Act 1855 (c.65)
Dublin and Other Roads Turnpikes Abolition Act 1855 (c.69)
Dublin Baronies Act 1842 (c.96)
Dublin Carriage Act 1853 (c.112)
Dublin, Collection of Rates Act 1849 (c.91)
Dublin Collector-General of Rates Act 1870 (c.11)
Dublin Corporation Act 1849 (c.85)
Dublin Corporation Act 1850 (c.81)
Dublin Foundling Hospital 1814 (c.128)

Dublin, Four Courts Act 1858 (c.84)
Dublin General Post Office Act 1808 (c.48)
Dublin General Post Office Act 1809 (c.70)
Dublin Grand Jury Act 1845 (c.81)
Dublin Harbour Act 1815 (c.191)
Dublin Harbour Act 1816 (c.62)
Dublin Hospitals Act 1856 (c.110)
Dublin, Hotels and Restaurants Act 1910 (c.33)
Dublin Improvement Act 1849 (c.97)
Dublin Improvement Act 1861 (c.26)
Dublin Justices Act 1840 (c.103)
Dublin Justices Act 1875 (c.20)
Dublin National Gallery Act 1865 (c.71)
Dublin Parliamentary Revising Act 1853 (c.58)
Dublin Paying, etc., Inquiry Act 1806 (c.68)
Dublin, Phoenix Park Act 1860 (c.42)
Dublin Police Act 1836 (c.29)
Dublin Police Act 1837 (c.25)
Dublin Police Act 1839 (c.78)
Dublin Police Act 1842 (c.24)
Dublin Police Act 1848 (c.113)
Dublin Police Act 1859 (c.52)
Dublin Police District Act 1838 (c.63)
Dublin Police Magistrates Act 1808 (c.140)
Dublin, Public Offices Site Act 1903 (c.16)
Dublin, Purchase of Land Act 1841 (c.16)
Dublin Reconstruction Act 1916 (c.66)
Dublin Record Office Act 1814 (c.63)
Dublin Revising Barristers Act 1857 (c.68)
Dublin Revising Barristers Act 1861 (c.56)
Dublin, Sale of Game Act 1865 (c.2)
Dublin, Sale of Property Act 1842 (c.62)
Dublin Science and Art Museum Act 1884 (c.6)
Dublin, Site of Record Office Act 1814 (c.113)
Dublin Tramways Act 1876 (c.65)
Dublin Voters Disfranchisement Act 1870 (c.54)
Duchess of Kent's Annuity Act 1838 (c.8)
Duchies of Lancaster and Cornwall (Accounts) Act 1838 (c.101)
Duchy of Cornwall Act 1700 (c.13)
Duchy of Cornwall Act 1707 (c.52)
Duchy of Cornwall Act 1713 (c.25)
Duchy of Cornwall Act 1715 (c.37)
Duchy of Cornwall Act 1750 (c.50)
Duchy of Cornwall Act 1759 (c.10)
Duchy of Cornwall Act 1768 (c.26)
Duchy of Cornwall Act 1776 (c.10)
Duchy of Cornwall Act 1812 (c.123)
Duchy of Cornwall Act 1844 (c.65)
Duchy of Cornwall Act 1860 (c.53)
Duchy of Cornwall Lands Act 1862 (c.49)
Duchy of Cornwall Leases, etc. Act 1842 (c.2)
Duchy of Cornwall (Limitation of Actions, etc.) Act 1860 (c.53)
Duchy of Cornwall Management Act 1863 (c.49)
Duchy of Cornwall Management Act 1868 (c.35)
Duchy of Cornwall Management Act 1893 (c.20)
Duchy of Cornwall Management Act 1982 (c.47)
Duchy of Cornwall (No. 2) Act 1844 (c.105)
Duchy of Cornwall Office Act 1854 (c.93)
Duchy of Lancaster Lands Act 1855 (c.58)
Duchy of Lancaster Act 1779 (c.45)
Duchy of Lancaster Act 1787 (c.34)
Duchy of Lancaster Act 1796 (c.97)
Duchy of Lancaster Act 1808 (c.73)
Duchy of Lancaster Act 1812 (c.161)
Duchy of Lancaster Act 1920 (c.51)
Duchy of Lancaster Act 1988 (c.10)
Duchy of Lancaster (Application of Capital Moneys) Act 1921 (c.45)
Duchy of Lancaster (Precinct of Savoy) Act 1772 (c.42)
Dudley Canal Act 1776 (c.66)
Dudley Canal Act 1785 (c.87)
Dudley Canal Act 1796 (c.13)
Dudley: Improvement Act 1791 (c.79)
Duke of Connaught, Annuity Act 1878 (c.46)
Duke of Connaught's Leave Act 1887 (c.10)
Duke of Grafton's Annuity Act 1806 (c.79)
Duke of Marlborough; Pension Act 1706 (c.7)
Duke of Marlborough's Annuity Act 1839 (c.94)
Duke of Richmond's Annuity Act 1800 (c.43)
Duke of Wellington, Purchase of Estate for Act 1815 (c.186)
Duke of York's School (Chapel) Act 1910 (c.16)
Dulwich College Act 1857 (c.84)
Dunbar Beer Duties Act 1718 (c.16)
Dumbarton Road and Bridges Act 1786 (c.21)
Dumfries and Roxburgh Roads Act 1764 (c.85)
Dumfries Beer Duties Act 1716 (c.6)
Dumfries Beer Duties Act 1736 (c.7)
Dumfries Beer Duties Act 1762 (c.55)
Dumfries Beer Duties Act 1787 (c.57)
Dumfries Roads Act 1777 (c.107)
Dumfries Roads Act 1785 (c.120)
Dumfries Roads Act 1788 (c.114)
Dumfries Roads Act 1789 (c.87)
Dumping at Sea Act 1974 (c.20)
Dunbar Beer Duties Act 1736 (c.4)
Dunbar Beer Duties Act 1764 (c.46)
Dunbar Harbour Loan Act 1857 (c.63)
Dunbar Water Supply Act 1768 (c.57)
Dunchurch to Southam Road Act 1794 (c.128)
Dunchurch to Stone Bridge Road Act 1770 (c.90)
Dundee Beer Duties Act 1730 (c.11)
Dundee Beer Duties Act 1746 (c.17)
Dundee Beer Duties Act 1776 (c.16)
Dunstable Highways Act 1710 (c.34)
Dunstable Highways Act 1713 (c.29)
Dunstable Roads Act 1722 (c.11)
Dunstable to Hockliffe Road Act 1792 (c.159)
Durham and Northumberland Roads Act 1792 (c.113)

Durham and Tyne Bridge Road Act 1753 (c.48)
Durham Chancery Act 1869 (c.84)
Durham (County Palatine) Act 1836 (c.19)
Durham County Palatine Act 1858 (c.45)
Durham Roads Act 1747 (c.5)
Durham Roads Act 1749 (c.27)
Durham Roads Act 1750 (c.30)
Durham Roads Act 1754 (c.29)
Durham Roads Act 1756 (c.70)
Durham Roads Act 1759 (c.56)
Durham Roads Act 1773 (c.99)
Durham Roads Act 1777 (c.110)
Durham Roads Act 1789 (c.81)
Durham Roads Act 1792 (c.127)
Durham Roads Act 1793 (c.148)
Durham Roads Act 1793 (c.161)
Durham Roads Act 1795 (c.139)
Durham: Streets Act 1790 (c.67)
Durham to Tyne Bridge Road Act 1746 (c.12)
Duties and Drawbacks Act 1799 (c.12)
Duties and Drawbacks (Ireland) Act 1806 (c.12)
Duties and Drawbacks (Ireland) Act 1806 (c.62)
Duties, Bounties, etc. (Ireland) Act 1806 (c.120)
Duties Continuance Act 1801 (c.17)
Duties Continuance Act 1802 (c.31)
Duties Continuance Act 1803 (c.24)
Duties, Drawbacks, etc. (Ireland) Act 1809 (c.74)
Duties, etc. Act 1743 (c.31)
Duties, etc., India Act 1814 (c.105)
Duties, etc. (Ireland) Act 1803 (c.92)
Duties, etc., on Coffee, etc. Act 1802 (c.83)
Duties, etc., on Foreign Liquors, etc. Act 1812 (c.159)
Duties, etc., on Glass, etc. Act 1815 (c.113)
Duties, etc., on Glass (Ireland) Act 1814 (c.87)
Duties, etc., on Malt, etc. (Ireland) Act 1807 (c.40)
Duties, etc., on Soap Act 1816 (c.44)
Duties, etc., on Sugar, etc. Act 1803 (c.42)
Duties, etc., on Tobacco (Ireland) Act 1813 (c.73)
Duties in American Colonies Act 1765 (c.12)
Duties in American Colonies Act 1766 (c.11)
Duties (Logwood, etc.) Act 1766 (c.47)
Duties of Customs Act 1845 (c.90)
Duties of Customs and Tonnage Act 1802 (c.43)
Duties of Prisage and Butlerage (Ireland) Act (c.94)
Duties on Auctioneers, etc. Act 1803 (c.130)
Duties on Auctions (Ireland) Act 1808 (c.63)
Duties on Beer, etc. Act 1802 (c.38)
Duties on Beetroot Sugar Act 1837 (c.57)
Duties on Bricks Act 1839 (c.24)
Duties on Bricks and Tiles Act 1784 (c.24)
Duties on Bricks and Tiles Act 1785 (c.66)
Duties on Bricks and Tiles Act 1794 (c.15)
Duties on Buckwheat, etc. Act 1847 (c.3)
Duties on Calicoes, etc. Act 1807 (c.47)
Duties on Candles Act 1784 (c.36)
Duties on Candles Act 1792 (c.7)
Duties on Cape Wines Act 1813 (c.84)
Duties on Carriages, etc. (Ireland) Act 1813 (c.59)
Duties on Certain Goods Act 1806 (c.42)
Duties on Certain Licences Act 1784 (c.41)
Duties on Certain Licences Act 1808 (c.143)
Duties on Certain Woods, etc. Act 1811 (c.43)
Duties on Cider, etc. Act 1766 (c.14)
Duties on Cinnamon, etc. Act 1798 (c.68)
Duties on Cinnamon, etc. Act 1802 (c.24)
Duties on Cinnamon, etc. Act 1808 (c.18)
Duties on Clocks and Watches Act 1797 (c.108)
Duties on Coach Makers' Licences, etc. 1785 (c.49)
Duties on Coals, etc. Act 1785 (c.54)
Duties on Coals, etc. Act 1812 (c.9)
Duties on Copper and Lead Act 1848 (c.127)
Duties on Corn Act 1842 (c.14)
Duties on Corn, etc. Act 1847 (c.64)
Duties on Distillation Act 1800 (c.73)
Duties on Distilleries Act 1797 (c.11)
Duties on Distilleries Act 1797 (c.31)
Duties on Distilleries Act 1799 (c.31)
Duties on Distilleries (Scotland) Act 1799 (c.78)
Duties on Distilleries (Scotland), etc. Act 1796 (c.17)
Duties on Dogs Act 1796 (c.124)
Duties on East India Goods Act 1707 (c.37)
Duties on Epsom Salts Act 1815 (c.162)
Duties on Foreign Cambrics, etc. Act 1741 (c.29)
Duties on Foreign Hops Act 1800 (c.82)
Duties on Foreign Packets Act 1816 (c.9)
Duties on Game Certificates Act 1803 (c.23)
Duties on Glass Act 1795 (c.114)
Duties on Glass Act 1805 (c.122)
Duties on Glass Act 1811 (c.69)
Duties on Glass Act 1812 (c.54)
Duties on Glass Act 1813 (c.109)
Duties on Glass Act 1839 (c.25)
Duties on Glass Act 1840 (c.22)
Duties on Glass, etc. Act 1800 (c.45)
Duties on Glass, etc. (Ireland) Act 1814 (c.7)
Duties on Glass (Great Britain) Act 1814 (c.97)
Duties on Glass (Great Britain) Act 1816 (c.1)
Duties on Hair Powder, etc. Act 1800 (c.32)
Duties on Hats, etc., Repeal (Ireland) Act 1811 (c.60)
Duties on Hides, etc. Act 1815 (c.105)
Duties on Hides, etc. (Ireland) Act 1813 (c.60)
Duties on Hops Act 1800 (c.4)
Duties on Horse Dealers' Licences Act 1795 (c.17)
Duties on Horses Act 1784 (c.31)
Duties on Horses Act 1795 (cc.15, 16)
Duties on Horses Act 1797 (c.106)

Duties on Horses and Carriage Act 1789 (c.49)
Duties on Horses, etc. Act 1802 (c.100)
Duties on Horses Let for Hire Act 1853 (c.88)
Duties on Houses, etc. Act 1779 (c.59)
Duties on Houses, etc. Act 1786 (c.79)
Duties on Importation, etc. Act 1791 (c.42)
Duties on Income Act 1799 (c.13)
Duties on Income Act 1799 (c.22)
Duties on Income Act 1799 (c.42)
Duties on Income Act 1799 (c.72)
Duties on Income Act 1800 (c.49)
Duties on Income Act 1800 (c.96)
Duties on Kid Skins Act 1800 (c.63)
Duties on Killing Game Act 1814 (c.141)
Duties on Leather Act 1815 (c.102)
Duties on Linens Act 1784 (c.40)
Duties on Linens Act 1785 (c.72)
Duties on Madder Act 1816 (c.69)
Duties on Mahogany, etc. Act 1812 (c.36)
Duties on Malt Act 1803 (c.16)
Duties on Malt Act 1805 (c.1)
Duties on Malt Act 1806 (c.2)
Duties on Malt Act 1807 (c.3)
Duties on Malt, etc. Act 1780 (c.35)
Duties on Malt, etc. Act 1795 (c.1)
Duties on Malt, etc. Act 1796 (c.1)
Duties on Malt, etc. Act 1797 (c.4)
Duties on Malt, etc. Act 1801 (c.1)
Duties on Malt, etc. Act 1802 (c.3)
Duties on Malt, etc. Act 1805 (c.22)
Duties on Malt, etc. Act 1808 (c.2)
Duties on Malt, etc. Act 1809 (c.1)
Duties on Malt, etc. Act 1810 (c.1)
Duties on Malt, etc. Act 1811 (c.2)
Duties on Malt, etc. Act 1812 (c.1)
Duties on Malt, etc. Act 1812 (c.15)
Duties on Malt, etc. Act 1813 (c.2)
Duties on Malt, etc. Act 1814 (c.3)
Duties on Malt, etc. Act 1816 (c.3)
Duties on Malt, etc. Act 1816 (c.43)
Duties on Malt (Ireland) Act 1815 (c.99)
Duties on Norway Timber Act 1811 (c.93)
Duties on Offices and Pensions Act 1836 (c.97)
Duties on Paper Act 1805 (c.106)
Duties on Paper Act 1839 (c.23)
Duties on Paper (Ireland) Act 1815 (c.112)
Duties on Paper (Ireland) Act 1816 (c.78)
Duties on Pensions, etc. Act 1798 (c.3)
Duties on Pensions, etc. Act 1799 (c.3)
Duties on Pensions, etc. Act 1801 (c.2)
Duties on Pensions, etc. Act 1802 (c.4)
Duties on Pensions, etc. Act 1803 (c.17)
Duties on Pensions, etc. Act 1805 (c.2)
Duties on Pensions, etc. Act 1806 (c.3)
Duties on Pensions, etc. Act 1807 (c.4)
Duties on Plate Act 1797 (c.24)
Duties on Post Horses, etc. Act 1785 (c.51)
Duties on Property, etc. Act 1816 (c.65)
Duties on Property, etc. (Great Britain) Act 1815 (c.53)
Duties on Rape Seed, etc. Act 1816 (c.75)
Duties on Rape Seed, etc. Act 1816 (c.79)
Duties on Rum, etc. Act 1802 (c.20)
Duties on Rum, etc. Act 1841 (c.8)
Duties on Salt Act 1703 (c.16)
Duties on Salt Act 1795 (c.19)
Duties on Salt Act 1798 (c.43)
Duties on Salt, etc. Act 1706 (c.29)
Duties on Scotch Distilleries Act 1795 (c.59)
Duties on Servants Act 1780 (c.31)
Duties on Servants Act 1785 (c.43)
Duties on Servants Act 1785 (c.70)
Duties on Servants Act 1791 (c.3)
Duties on Servants Act 1797 (c.107)
Duties on Servants Act 1798 (c.80)
Duties on Servants, etc. Act 1797 (c.41)
Duties on Servants, etc. Act 1802 (c.37)
Duties on Shops Act 1785 (c.30)
Duties on Shops Act 1786 (c.9)
Duties on Shops Act 1789 (c.9)
Duties on Smalts, etc. Act 1783 (c.75)
Duties on Soap Act 1839 (c.63)
Duties on Soap Act 1840 (c.49)
Duties on Soap, etc. Act 1776 (c.52)
Duties on Spanish Red Wine Act 1805 (c.67)
Duties on Spirit Licences Act 1787 (c.30)
Duties on Spirit Mixtures, etc. Act 1842 (c.25)
Duties on Spirits Act 1784 (c.46)
Duties on Spirits Act 1795 (c.89)
Duties on Spirits Act 1799 (c.8)
Duties on Spirits Act 1808 (c.115)
Duties on Spirits Act 1808 (c.119)
Duties on Spirits Act 1811 (c.59)
Duties on Spirits Act 1843 (c.49)
Duties on Spirits Act 1845 (c.65)
Duties on Spirits Act 1848 (c.60)
Duties on Spirits and Coffee Act 1808 (cc.121, 122)
Duties on Spirits, etc. Act 1794 (cc.3, 4)
Duties on Spirits, etc. Act 1842 (c.15)
Duties on Spirits, etc. Act 1853 (c.37)
Duties on Spirits, etc. (Scotland) Act 1815 (c.155)
Duties on Spirits, etc. (Scotland) Act 1816 (c.106)
Duties on Spirits (Great Britain) Act 1813 (c.147)
Duties on Spirits (Ireland) Act 1806 (c.56)
Duties on Spirits (Ireland) Act 1806 (c.88)
Duties on Spirits (Ireland) Act 1807 (c.17)
Duties on Spirits (Ireland) Act 1808 (c.81)
Duties on Spirits (Ireland) Act 1809 (c.73)
Duties on Spirits (Ireland) Act 1810 (c.15)
Duties on Spirits (Ireland) Act 1812 (c.46)
Duties on Spirits (Ireland) Act 1812 (c.48)
Duties on Spirits (Ireland) Act 1814 (c.88)
Duties on Spirits (Ireland) Act 1815 (c.111)
Duties on Spirits (Ireland) Act 1816 (c.111)
Duties on Spirits (Scotland) Act 1814 (c.172)
Duties on Spirituous Liquors (Ireland) Act 1805 (c.104)
Duties on Starch Act 1779 (c.40)
Duties on Starch Act 1786 (c.51)
Duties on Starch and Soap Act 1784 (c.48)

Duties on Stills, etc. (Scotland) Act 1806 (c.102)
Duties on Stone Bottles Act 1812 (c.139)
Duties on Sugar Act 1813 (c.62)
Duties on Sugar Act 1845 (c.13)
Duties on Sugar Act 1865 (c.95)
Duties on Sugar Act 1867 (c.10)
Duties on Sugar, etc. Act 1799 (c.63)
Duties on Sugar, etc. Act 1800 (c.48)
Duties on Sugar, etc. Act 1802 (c.47)
Duties on Sweets, etc. (Ireland) Act 1815 (c.110)
Duties on Tea, etc. (American Plantations) Act 1766 (c.46)
Duties on Tobacco Act 1785 (c.81)
Duties on Tobacco Act 1811 (c.56)
Duties on Tobacco and Snuff Act 1789 (c.68)
Duties on Waggons, etc. Act 1783 (c.66)
Duties on Wagons, etc. Act 1792 (c.4)
Duties on Wash Made From Sugar Act 1800 (c.61)
Duties on Wheat, etc. Act 1843 (c.29)
Duties on Windows, etc. Act 1802 (c.34)
Duties on Wines, etc. Act 1783 (c.76)
Duties on Wines, etc. Act 1796 (c.123)
Duties on Worts or Wash Act 1808 (c.152)
Duties on Worts, Spirits, etc. Act 1791 (c.1)
Duties on Worts, Wash, etc. Act 1794 (c.2)
Duties upon Candles Act 1784 (c.11)
Duties upon East India Goods Act 1814 (c.10)
Duties upon Malt, etc. Act 1798 (c.2)
Duties upon Malt, etc. Act 1799 (c.2)
Duties upon Silks Act 1808 (c.117)
Duty of Spirits, Newfoundland Act 1812 (c.106)
Duty on Almanacks Act 1781 (c.56)
Duty on Coffee, etc., Warehoused Act 1807 (c.52)
Duty on Copper Act 1811 (c.31)
Duty on Corks Act 1816 (c.34)
Duty on Cotton Stuffs, etc. Act 1774 (c.72)
Duty on Foreign Spirits Act 1815 (c.164)
Duty on Hair Powder Act 1795 (c.49)
Duty on Hats Act 1796 (c.125)
Duty on Hats, etc., Repeal (Great Britain) Act 1811 (c.70)
Duty on Hawkers, etc. Act 1789 (c.26)
Duty on Hops Act 1805 (c.94)
Duty on Horses Act 1797 (c.134)
Duty on Horses Act 1801 (c.9)
Duty on Houses Act 1806 (c.36)
Duty on Lead (Great Britain) Act 1816 (c.18)
Duty on Linen Act 1811 (c.44)
Duty on Malt Act 1812 (c.9)
Duty on Malt (Ireland) Act 1804 (c.28)
Duty on Malt (Ireland) Act 1813 (c.74)
Duty on Malt (Ireland) Act 1816 (c.59)
Duty on Oil, etc. Act 1816 (c.118)
Duty on Paper Act 1816 (c.103)
Duty on Paper Hangings, etc. (Ireland) Act 1815 (c.106)
Duty on Pensions, etc. Act 1800 (c.8)
Duty on Pensions, etc. Act 1800 (c.31)
Duty on Racehorses Act 1856 (c.82)
Duty on Racehorses Act 1857 (c.16)
Duty on Rice Act 1812 (c.10)
Duty on Salt Act 1812 (c.107)
Duty on Salt Act 1813 (c.21)
Duty on Servants Act 1778 (c.30)
Duty on Silk Handkerchiefs Act 1815 (c.93)
Duty on Spanish Red Wines Act 1805 (c.107)
Duty on Spirits Act 1788 (c.4)
Duty on Spirits (Ireland) Act 1813 (c.94)
Duty on Spirits (Ireland) Act 1815 (c.139)
Duty on Stage Carriages Act 1839 (c.66)
Duty on Sugar Act 1809 (c.61)
Duty on Sugar, etc. Act 1810 (c.61)
Duty on Taxed Carts Act 1798 (c.93)
Duty on Tiles Act 1815 (c.176)
Duty on Tobacco Act 1794 (c.55)
Duty on Tobacco and Snuff Act 1790 (c.40)
Duty on Woollen Goods Act 1805 (c.82)
Duty on Worts, etc. Act 1801 (c.5)
Dwelling-houses for the Working Classes (Scotland) Act 1855 (c.88)
Dyeing Trade Act 1726 (c.24)
Dyeing Trade (Frauds) Act 1783 (c.15)
Dyers Act 1776 (c.33)
Dyestuffs (Import Regulations) Act 1920 (c.77)
Dyestuffs (Import Regulations) Act 1934 (c.6)
Dygart Beer Duties Act 1753 (c.44)

Ealing Church Act 1738 (c.7)
Ealing Roads Act 1767 (c.75)
Earl of Clanriccard's Estates Act 1708 (c.29)
Earldom of Mar Act 1885 (c.48)
East Africa Loans Act 1926 (c.62)
East Africa Loans (Amendment) Act 1931 (c.21)
East African Protectorates (Loans) Act 1914 (c.38)
East and West Flegg: Poor Relief Act 1775 (c.13)
East Greenwich Church: Burial Act 1751 (c.11)
East Grinstead Church Act 1790 (c.79)
East India Act 1797 (c.142)
East India Annuity Funds Act 1874 (c.12)
East India Company Act 1707 (c.71)
East India Company Act 1711 (c.35)
East India Company Act 1730 (c.14)
East India Company Act 1767 (c.49)
East India Company Act 1767 (c.57)
East India Company Act 1768 (c.11)
East India Company Act 1769 (c.24)
East India Company Act 1770 (c.47)
East India Company Act 1772 (c.7)
East India Company Act 1772 (c.9)
East India Company Act 1772 (c.63)
East India Company Act 1772 (c.64)
East India Company Act 1775 (c.44)
East India Company Act 1776 (c.8)
East India Company Act 1776 (c.51)
East India Company Act 1779 (c.61)

East India Company Act 1780 (c.56)
East India Company Act 1780 (c.58)
East India Company Act 1780 (c.70)
East India Company Act 1781 (c.65)
East India Company Act 1782 (c.51)
East India Company Act 1783 (c.2)
East India Company Act 1783 (c.3)
East India Company Act 1783 (c.36)
East India Company Act 1783 (c.83)
East India Company Act 1784 (c.25)
East India Company Act 1784 (c.34)
East India Company Act 1786 (c.16)
East India Company Act 1786 (c.57)
East India Company Act 1788 (c.8)
East India Company Act 1788 (c.29)
East India Company Act 1793 (c.52)
East India Company Act 1796 (c.120)
East India Company Act 1797 (c.31)
East India Company Act 1797 (c.74)
East India Company Act 1799 (c.89)
East India Company Act 1803 (c.48)
East India Company Act 1803 (c.63)
East India Company Act 1803 (c.137)
East India Company Act 1806 (c.85)
East India Company Act 1807 (c.41)
East India Company Act 1810 (c.86)
East India Company Act 1811 (c.75)
East India Company Act 1812 (c.10)
East India Company Act 1812 (c.135)
East India Company Act 1813 (c.155)
East India Company Act 1815 (c.64)
East India Company Bonds Act 1811 (c.64)
East India Company (Money) Act 1794 (c.41)
East India Company Stock Act 1786 (c.62)
East India Company Stock Act 1789 (c.65)
East India Company (Stock) Act 1791 (c.11)
East India Company (Stock) Act 1793 (c.47)
East India Company, Warehouses Act 1787 (c.48)
East India Company's Officers Superannuation Act 1897 (c.10)
East India Contracts Act 1870 (c.59)
East India Irrigation and Canal Act 1869 (c.7)
East India Unclaimed Stock Act 1885 (c.25)
East India Loan Act 1859 (c.11)
East India Loan Act 1860 (c.130)
East India Loan Act 1861 (c.25)
East India Loan Act 1861 (c.118)
East India Loan Act 1869 (c.106)
East India Loan Act 1873 (c.32)
East India Loan Act 1874 (c.3)
East India Loan Act 1877 (c.51)
East India Loan Act 1879 (c.60)
East India Loan Act 1885 (c.28)
East India Loan Act 1893 (c.70)
East India Loan Act 1898 (c.13)
East India Loan (East Indian Railway Debentures) Act 1880 (c.10)
East India Loan (Great Indian Peninsular Railway Debentures) Act 1901 (c.25)
East India Loan (No. 2) Act 1859 (c.39)
East India Loans Act 1858 (c.3)
East India Loans Act 1908 (c.54)
East India Loans Act 1923 (c.31)
East India Loans Act 1937 (c.14)
East India Loans (Railway and Irrigation) Act 1922 (c.9)
East India Loans (Railways) Act 1905 (c.19)
East India Loans (Railways and Irrigation) Act 1910 (c.5)
East India Merchants: Land for Warehouses etc. Act 1796 (c.127)
East India Merchants: Purchase of Land in City, etc. Act 1796 (c.119)
East India Prize Goods Act 1804 (c.72)
East India Stock Act 1860 (c.102)
East India Stock Dividend Redemption Act 1873 (c.17)
East India Trade Act 1774 (c.34)
East India Trade Act 1813 (c.34)
East India Trade Act 1813 (c.35)
East India Trade Act 1840 (c.56)
East India Trade, etc. Act 1814 (c.134)
East India Unclaimed Stock Act 1885 (c.25)
East Indian Loan (Annuities) Act 1879 (c.61)
East Indian Railway (Redemption of Annuities) Act 1879 (c.43)
East Indian Railway (Redemption of Annuities) Act 1881 (c.53)
East Indies Act 1791 (c.40)
East Kent: Drainage Act 1776 (c.62)
East Stonehouse Chapel Act 1787 (c.17)
East Tarbet Harbour Act 1707 (c.79(b))
Easter Act 1928 (c.35)
Eccles, Appointments Suspension Act 1836 (c.67)
Ecclesiastical Appointments Suspension Act 1838 (c.108)
Ecclesiastical Assessments (Scotland) Act 1900 (c.20)
Ecclesiastical Buildings and Glebes (Scotland) Act 1868 (c.96)
Ecclesiastical Commissioners Act 1836 (c.77)
Ecclesiastical Commissioners Act 1840 (c.113)
Ecclesiastical Commissioners Act 1840, Amendment 1885 (c.55)
Ecclesiastical Commissioners Act 1841 (c.39)
Ecclesiastical Commissioners Act 1847 (c.108)
Ecclesiastical Commissioners Act 1850 (c.94)
Ecclesiastical Commissioners Act 1860 (c.124)
Ecclesiastical Commissioners Act 1866 (c.111)
Ecclesiastical Commissioners Act 1868 (c.114)
Ecclesiastical Commissioners Act 1873 (c.64)
Ecclesiastical Commissioners Act 1875 (c.71)
Ecclesiastical Commissioners Act 1885 (c.31)

Ecclesiastical Commissioners (Exchange of Patronage) Act 1853 (c.50)
Ecclesiastical Commissioners (Superannuation) Act 1865 (c.68)
Ecclesiastical Commissioners (Takenhill Rectory) Act 1885 (c.31)
Ecclesiastical Courts Act 1813 (c.127)
Ecclesiastical Courts Act 1840 (c.93)
Ecclesiastical Courts Act 1844 (c.68)
Ecclesiastical Courts Act 1854 (c.47)
Ecclesiastical Courts Act 1855 (c.41)
Ecclesiastical Courts and Registries (Ireland) Act 1864 (c.54)
Ecclesiastical Courts Jurisdiction Act 1860 (c.32)
Ecclesiastical Dilapidations Act 1871 (c.43)
Ecclesiastical Dilapidations Act 1872 (c.96)
Ecclesiastical Districts in Forest of Dean Act 1842 (c.65)
Ecclesiastical Fees Act 1867 (c.135)
Ecclesiastical Fees Act 1875 (c.76)
Ecclesiastical Houses of Residence Act 1842 (c.26)
Ecclesiastical Jurisdiction Act 1842 (c.58)
Ecclesiastical Jurisdiction Act 1843 (c.60)
Ecclesiastical Jurisdiction Act 1847 (c.98)
Ecclesiastical Jurisdiction Act 1848 (c.67)
Ecclesiastical Jurisdiction Act 1849 (c.39)
Ecclesiastical Jurisdiction Act 1850 (c.47)
Ecclesiastical Jurisdiction Act 1851 (c.29)
Ecclesiastical Jurisdiction Act 1852 (c.17)
Ecclesiastical Jurisdiction Act 1853 (c.108)
Ecclesiastical Jurisdiction Act 1854 (c.65)
Ecclesiastical Jurisdiction Act 1855 (c.75)
Ecclesiastical Jurisdiction Act 1857 (c.10)
Ecclesiastical Jurisdiction Act 1858 (c.50)
Ecclesiastical Jurisdiction Act 1859 (c.45)
Ecclesiastical Leases Act 1800 (c.41)
Ecclesiastical Leases Act 1836 (c.20)
Ecclesiastical Leases Act 1842 (c.27)
Ecclesiastical Leases Act 1861 (c.104)
Ecclesiastical Leases Act 1862 (c.52)
Ecclesiastical Leases Act 1865 (c.57)
Ecclesiastical Leases Act 1765 (c.17)
Ecclesiastical Leases (Amendment) Act 1836 (c.64)
Ecclesiastical Leases (Isle of Man) Act 1866 (c.81)
Ecclesiastical Leasing Act 1842 (c.108)
Ecclesiastical Leasing Act 1858 (c.57)
Ecclesiastical Patronage (Ireland) Act 1845 (c.51)
Ecclesiastical Patronage (Ireland) Act 1848 (c.78)
Ecclesiastical Patronage (Ireland) Act 1848 (c.67)
Ecclesiastical Preferments (England) Act 1839 (c.55)
Ecclesiastical Proctors (Ireland) Act 1814 (c.68)
Ecclesiastical Property (Ireland) Act 1855 (c.28)
Ecclesiastical Property Valuation (Ireland) Act 1851 (c.74)
Ecclesiastical Services (Omission of Account on War) Act 1917 (c.5)
Ecclesiastical Suits Act 1787 (c.44)
Ecclesiastical Tithe Rentcharges (Rates) Act 1922 (c.58)
Ecclesiastical Titles Act 1851 (c.60)
Ecclesiastical Titles Act 1871 (c.53)
Ecclesiastical Unions, etc. (Ireland) Act 1848 (c.41)
Economy (Miscellaneous Provisions) Act 1926 (c.9)
Eddystone Lighthouse Act 1705 (c.7)
Eddystone Lighthouse Act 1709 (c.17)
Eden River, Cumberland (Temporary Tolls for Improvement) Act 1721 (c.14)
Edinburgh and Glasgow Roads Act 1757 (c.55)
Edinburgh and Leith Road Act 1750 (c.35)
Edinburgh and Linlithgow Roads Act 1764 (c.86)
Edinburgh Beer Duties Act 1716 (c.5)
Edinburgh Beer Duties Act 1722 (c.14)
Edinburgh Beer Duties Act 1727 (c.22)
Edinburgh Beer Duties Act 1751 (c.9)
Edinburgh Bridewell Act 1791 (c.57)
Edinburgh Bridges and Highways Act 1713 (c.30)
Edinburgh Buildings Act 1753 (c.36)
Edinburgh College of Surgeons Act 1787 (c.65)
Edinburgh Debt Act 1844 (c.20)
Edinburgh, etc., Roads Act 1795 (c.150)
Edinburgh General Register House Act 1896 (c.24)
Edinburgh: Improvement Act 1772 (c.15)
Edinburgh: Improvement Act 1786 (c.113)
Edinburgh: Improvement Act 1787 (c.51)
Edinburgh: Improvements Act 1766 (c.27)
Edinburgh, Linlithgow and Lanark Roads, etc. Act 1792 (c.120)
Edinburgh Roads Act 1755 (c.39)
Edinburgh Roads Act 1783 (c.18)
Edinburgh Roads Act 1789 (c.105)
Edinburgh (Slaughter of Animals) Act 1782 (c.52)
Edinburgh: Streets Act 1771 (c.36)
Edinburgh: Streets Act 1785 (c.28)
Edinburgh University Property Arrangement Act 1861 (c.90)
Edinburgh University (Transfer of Patronage) Act 1897 (c.13)
Edinburgh Water Act 1756 (c.74)
Edington, Somerset Drainage, etc. Act 1790 (c.58)
Education Act 1901 (c.11)
Education Act 1901 (Renewal) 1902 (c.19)
Education Act 1902 (c.42)
Education Act 1918 (c.39)
Education Act 1921 (c.51)
Education Act 1936 (c.41)
Education Act 1944 (c.31)
Education Act 1946 (c.50)
Education Act 1959 (c.60)

Education Act 1962 (c.12)
Education Act 1964 (c.82)
Education Act 1967 (c.3)
Education Act 1968 (c.17)
Education Act 1973 (c.16)
Education Act 1975 (c.2)
Education Act 1976 (c.81)
Education Act 1979 (c.49)
Education Act 1980 (c.20)
Education Act 1981 (c.60)
Education Act 1986 (c.40)
Education Act 1993 (c.35)
Education Act 1994 (c.30)
Education Act 1996 (c.56)
Education (Administrative Provisions) Act 1907 (c.43)
Education (Administrative Provisions) Act 1909 (c.29)
Education (Administrative Provisions) Act 1911 (c.32)
Education (Amendment) Act 1986 (c.1)
Education (Amendment) (Scotland) Act 1984 (c.6)
Education and Local Taxation Account (Scotland) Act 1892 (c.51)
Education (Choice of Employment) Act 1910 (c.37)
Education Code (1890) (c.22)
Education (Compliance with Conditions of Grants) Act 1919 (c.41)
Education (Deaf Children) Act 1937 (c.25)
Education Department Act 1856 (c.116)
Education (Emergency) Act 1939 (c.111)
Education (Emergency) (Scotland) Act 1939 (c.112)
Education Endowments (Scotland) Act 1931 (c.5)
Education (Exemptions) (Scotland) Act 1947 (c.36)
Education (Fees and Awards) Act 1983 (c.40)
Education (Grants and Awards) Act 1984 (c.11)
Education (Handicapped Children) Act 1970 (c.52)
Education (Institution Children) Act 1923 (c.38)
Education (Ireland) Act 1806 (c.122)
Education (Local Authorities) Act 1931 (c.6)
Education (Local Authority Default) Act 1904 (c.18)
Education (London) Act 1903 (c.24)
Education (Mentally Handicapped Children) (Scotland) Act 1974 (c.27)
Education (Milk) Act 1971 (c.74)
Education (Miscellaneous Provisions) Act 1948 (c.40)
Education (Miscellaneous Provisions) Act 1953 (c.33)
Education (Necessity of Schools) Act 1933 (c.29)
Education (Northern Ireland) Act 1978 (c.13)
Education (No. 2) Act 1968 (c.37)
Education (No. 2) Act 1986 (c.61)
Education of Blind and Deaf Children (Scotland) Act 1890 (c.43)
Education of Defective Children (Scotland) Act 1906 (c.10)
Education of Pauper Children Act 1855 (c.34)
Education (Provision of Meals) Act 1906 (c.57)
Education (Provision of Meals) Act 1914 (c.20)
Education (Provision of Meals) (Ireland) Act 1914 (c.35)
Education (Provision of Meals) (Ireland) Act 1916 (c.10)
Education (Provision of Meals) (Ireland) Act 1917 (c.53)
Education (Provision of the Working Balances) Act 1903 (c.10)
Education Reform Act 1988 (c.40)
Education (School-Leaving Dates) Act 1976 (c.5)
Education (School Milk) Act 1970 (c.14)
Education (Schools) Act 1992 (c.38)
Education (Scotland) Act 1872 (c.62)
Education (Scotland) Act 1878 (c.78)
Education (Scotland) Act 1883 (c.56)
Education (Scotland) Act 1897 (c.62)
Education (Scotland) Act 1901 (c.9)
Education (Scotland) Act 1908 (c.63)
Education (Scotland) Act 1913 (c.12)
Education (Scotland) Act 1918 (c.48)
Education (Scotland) Act 1925 (c.89)
Education (Scotland) Act 1928 (c.28)
Education (Scotland) Act 1930 (c.36)
Education (Scotland) Act 1936 (c.42)
Education (Scotland) Act 1942 (c.5)
Education (Scotland) Act 1944 (c.37)
Education (Scotland) Act 1945 (c.37)
Education (Scotland) Act 1946 (c.72)
Education (Scotland) Act 1949 (c.19)
Education (Scotland) Act 1956 (c.75)
Education (Scotland) Act 1962 (c.47)
Education (Scotland) Act 1963 (c.21)
Education (Scotland) Act 1965 (c.7)
Education (Scotland) Act 1969 (c.49)
Education (Scotland) Act 1971 (c.42)
Education (Scotland) Act 1973 (c.59)
Education (Scotland) Act 1976 (c.20)
Education (Scotland) Act 1980 (c.44)
Education (Scotland) Act 1981 (c.58)
Education (Scotland) Act 1996 (c.43)
Education (Scotland) (Glasgow Electoral Division) Act 1913 (c.13)
Education (Scotland) (Provision of Meals) Act 1914 (c.68)
Education (Scotland) (Superannuation) Act 1919 (c.17)
Education (Scotland) (Superannuation) Act 1922 (c.48)
Education (Scotland) (Superannuation) Act 1924 (c.13)
Education (Scotland) (Superannuation) Act 1925 (c.55)
Education (Scotland) (War Service Superannuation) Act 1914 (c.67)

Education (Scotland) (War Service Superannuation) Act 1939 (c.96)
Education (Small Population Grants) Act 1915 (c.95)
Education (Student Loans) Act 1990 (c.6)
Education (Student Loans) Act 1996 (c.9)
Education (Work Experience) Act 1973 (c.23)
Educational Endowments (Ireland) Act 1885 (c.78)
Educational Endowments (Scotland) Act 1882 (c.59)
Educational Endowments (Scotland) Act 1928 (c.30)
Educational Endowments (Scotland) Act 1935 (c.5)
Edw. Whitaker, Public Accountant Act 1702 (c.16)
Effects of Residents in France Act 1794 (c.79)
Egham and Bagshot Roads Act 1727 (c.6)
Egham and Bagshot Road Act 1738 (c.16)
Egham and Bagshot Road Act 1763 (c.47)
Egyptian Loan Act 1885 (c.11)
Egyptians Act 1783 (c.51)
Eire (Confirmation of Agreements) Act 1938 (c.25)
Eisteddfod Act 1959 (c.32)
Ejectment and Distress (Ireland) Act 1846 (c.111)
Elders Widows' Fund (India) Act 1878 (c.47)
Elected Authorities (Northern Ireland) Act 1989 (c.3)
Election Commissioners Act 1852 (c.57)
Election Commissioners Act 1949 (c.90)
Election Commissioners Expenses Act 1871 (c.61)
Election (Hours of Poll) Act 1884 (c.34)
Election in the Recess Act 1863 (c.20)
Election (Ireland) Act 1862 (c.92)
Election of Members During Recess Act 1858 (c.110)
Election of Members for Cheshire Act 1846 (c.44)
Election of Representative Peers (Ireland) Act 1882 (c.26)
Election Petitions Act 1794 (c.83)
Election Petitions Act 1839 (c.38)
Election Petitions Act 1848 (c.98)
Election Petitions Act 1865 (c.8)
Election Recognizances Act 1848 (c.18)
Elections and Jurors Act 1945 (c.21)
Elections and Registration Act 1915 (c.76)
Elections (Fraudulent Conveyance) Act 1711 (c.31)
Elections (Hours of Poll) Act 1885 (c.10)
Elections in Recess Act 1863 (c.20)
Elections (Northern Ireland) Act 1985 (c.2)
Elections (Scotland) (Corrupt and Illegal Practices) Act 1890 (c.55)
Elections (Welsh Forms) Act 1964 (c.31)
Electoral Disabilities (Military Service) Removal Act 1900 (c.8)
Electoral Disabilities (Naval and Military Service) Removal Act 1914 (c.25)
Electoral Disabilities Removal Act 1891 (c.11)
Electoral Registers Act 1949 (c.86)
Electoral Registers Act 1953 (c.8)
Electric Lighting Act 1882 (c.56)
Electric Lighting Act 1888 (c.12)
Electric Lighting Act 1909 (c.34)
Electric Lighting (Clauses) Act 1899 (c.19)
Electric Lighting (Scotland) Act 1890 (c.13)
Electric Lighting (Scotland) Act 1902 (c.35)
Electricity Act 1947 (c.54)
Electricity Act 1957 (c.48)
Electricity Act 1972 (c.17)
Electricity Act 1989 (c.29)
Electricity (Amendment) Act 1961 (c.8)
Electricity and Gas Act 1963 (c.59)
Electricity (Borrowing Powers) Act 1959 (c.20)
Electricity (Borrowing Powers) (Scotland) Act 1962 (c.7)
Electricity (Financial Provisions) Act 1982 (c.56)
Electricity (Financial Provisions) (Scotland) Act 1976 (c.61)
Electricity (Financial Provisions) (Scotland) Act 1982 (c.56)
Electricity (Financial Provisions) (Scotland) Act 1988 (c.37)
Electricity Reorganisation (Scotland) Act 1954 (c.60)
Electricity (Scotland) Act 1969 (c.1)
Electricity (Scotland) Act 1979 (c.11)
Electricity (Supply) Act 1919 (c.100)
Electricity (Supply) Act 1922 (c.46)
Electricity (Supply) Act 1926 (c.51)
Electricity (Supply) Act 1928 (c.4)
Electricity (Supply) Act 1933 (c.46)
Electricity Supply Act 1935 (c.3)
Electricity Supply (Meters) Act 1936 (c.20)
Electricity Supply (Meters) Act 1952 (c.32)
Elementary Education Act 1870 (c.75)
Elementary Education Act 1873 (c.86)
Elementary Education Act 1876 (c.79)
Elementary Education Act 1880 (c.23)
Elementary Education Act 1891 (c.56)
Elementary Education Act 1897 (c.16)
Elementary Education Act 1900 (c.53)
Elementary Education Act Amendment Act 1872 (c.27)
Elementary Education Amendment Act 1903 (c.13)
Elementary Education (Blind and Deaf Children) Act 1893 (c.42)
Elementary Education (Defective and Epileptic Children) Act 1899 (c.32)
Elementary Education (Defective and Epileptic Children) Act 1914 (c.45)
Elementary Education (Election) Act 1871 (c.94)
Elementary Education (Elections) Act 1872 (c.59)
Elementary Education (Fee Grant) Act 1916 (c.35)

Elementary Education (Industrial Schools) Act 1879 (c.48)
Elementary Education (Orders) Act 1874 (c.90)
Elementary Education (School Attendance) Act 1893 (c.51)
Elementary Education (School Attendance) Act (1893) Amendment 1899 (c.13)
Elementary Education (Wenlock) Act 1874 (c.39)
Elementary School Teachers (Superannuation) Act 1898 (c.57)
Elementary School Teachers (Superannuation) Act 1912 (c.12)
Elementary School Teachers Superannuation (Isle of Man) Act 1900 (c.38)
Elementary School Teachers Superannuation (Jersey) Act 1900 (c.40)
Elementary School Teachers (War Service Superannuation) Act 1914 (c.66)
Elgin Beer Duties Act 1721 (c.7)
Elizabeth Taylor's Patent Act 1776 (c.18)
Elland and Leeds Road Act 1753 (c.61)
Elland to Leeds Road Act 1777 (c.87)
Elland to Leeds Road Act 1795 (c.159)
Elland to Leeds Road Act 1740 (c.25)
Ellesmere and Chester Canal Act 1793 (c.91)
Ellesmere and Chester Canal Act 1796 (c.71)
Ellesmere and Chester Canal Act 1796 (c.96)
Ellesmere, Salop: Poor Relief Act 1791 (c.78)
Elloe, Lincoln: Small Debts Act 1775 (c.64)
Elver Fishing Act 1876 (c.34)
Ely Roads Act 1740 (c.14)
Embezzlement Act 1799 Act (c.85)
Embezzlement Act 1814 (c.60)
Embezzlement by Bankers, etc. Act 1812 (c.63)
Embezzlement by Collectors Act 1810 (c.59)
Embezzlement (Ireland) Act 1811 (c.38)
Embezzlement of Naval, etc., Stores Act 1812 (c.12)
Embezzlement of Public Stores Act 1800 (c.89)
Embezzlement of Public Stores Act (c.126)
Embezzlement of Public Stores Act 1815 (c.127)
Emergency Laws (Miscellaneous Provisions) Act 1947 (c.10)
Emergency Laws (Miscellaneous Provisions) Act 1953 (c.47)
Emergency Laws (Re-enactments and Repeals) Act 1964 (c.60)
Emergency Laws (Repeal) Act 1959 (c.19)
Emergency Laws (Transitional Provisions) Act 1946 (c.26)
Emergency Powers Act 1920 (c.55)
Emergency Powers Act 1964 (c.38)
Emergency Powers (Defence) Act 1939 (c.20)
Emergency Powers (Defence) Act 1939 (c.62)
Emergency Powers (Defence) Act 1944 (c.31)
Emergency Powers (Defence) (No. 2) Act 1939 (c.45)
Emergency Powers (Isle of Man—Defence) Act 1943 (c.36)
Emigration from Scotland Act 1851 (c.91)
Empire Settlement Act 1922 (c.13)
Empire Settlement Act 1937 (c.18)
Empire Settlement Act 1952 (c.26)
Employers and Workmen Act 1875 (c.90)
Employers' Liability Act 1880 (c.42)
Employers' Liability Act 1888 (c.58)
Employers' Liability (Compulsory Insurance) Act 1969 (c.57)
Employers' Liability (Defective Equipment) Act 1969 (c.37)
Employers' Liability Insurance Companies Act 1907 (c.46)
Employment Act 1980 (c.42)
Employment Act 1982 (c.46)
Employment Act 1988 (c.19)
Employment Act 1989 (c.38)
Employment Act 1990 (c.38)
Employment Agencies Act 1973 (c.35)
Employment and Training Act 1948 (c.46)
Employment and Training Act 1973 (c.50)
Employment and Training Act 1981 (c.57)
Employment (Continental Shelf) Act 1978 (c.46)
Employment Medical Advisory Service Act 1972 (c.28)
Employment of Children Act 1903 (c.45)
Employment of Children Act 1973 (c.24)
Employment of Poor Act 1847 (c.87)
Employment of Poor, etc. (I.) Act 1847 (c.80)
Employment of Women Act 1907 (c.10)
Employment of Women and Young Persons Act 1936 (c.24)
Employment of Women, Young Persons and Children Act 1920 (c.65)
Employment Protection Act 1975 (c.71)
Employment Protection (Consolidation) Act 1978 (c.44)
Employment Rights Act 1996 (c.18)
Employment Subsidies Act 1978 (c.6)
Encouragement of Manufacturers Act 1723 (c.11)
Encouragement of Seamen, etc. Act 1803 (c.160)
Endangered Species (Import and Export) Act 1976 (c.72)
Endowed Institutions (Scotland) Act 1869 (c.39)
Endowed Institutions (Scotland) Act 1878 (c.48)
Endowed School Acts Continuance 1879 (c.66)
Endowed Schools Act 1813 (c.107)
Endowed Schools Act 1860 (c.11)
Endowed Schools Act 1869 (c.56)
Endowed Schools Act 1868 (c.32)
Endowed Schools Act 1869 (c.56)
Endowed Schools Act 1873 (c.87)
Endowed Schools Act 1874 (c.87)
Endowed Schools Inquiries (Ireland) Act 1855 (c.59)

Endowed Schools (Ireland) Act 1813 (c.107)
Endowed Schools (Masters) Act 1908 (c.39)
Endowed Schools (Time of Address) Act 1873 (c.7)
Endowed Schools (Vested Interests) Act Continued 1875 (c.29)
Enduring Power of Attorney Act 1985 (c.29)
Enemy Property Act 1953 (c.52)
Energy Act 1976 (c.76)
Energy Act 1983 (c.25)
Energy Conservation Act 1981 (c.17)
Energy Conservation Act 1996 (c.38)
Enfranchisement of Copyholds Act 1841 (c.35)
English Industrial Estates Corporation Act 1981 (c.13)
Engraving Copyright Act 1734 (c.13)
Engraving Copyright Act 1766 (c.38)
Enlargement of Time for First Meetings Act 1757 (c.34)
Enlargement of Time for First Meetings Act 1759 (c.14)
Enlargement of Times for Executing Acts Act 1757 (c.37)
Enlargement of Times for Executing Acts Act 1765 (c.15)
Enlistment Act 1794 (c.43)
Enlistment of Foreigners Act 1804 (c.75)
Enlistment of Foreigners Act 1806 (c.23)
Enlistment of Foreigners Act 1815 (c.85)
Enlistment of Foreigners Act 1837 (c.29)
Enlistment of Foreigners Act 1855 (c.2)
Enlistment of Persons Transferred from the Indian Forces Act 1861 (c.74)
Enlistment in Foreign Service Act 1713 (c.10)
Entail Act 1838 (c.70)
Entail Amendment Act 1848 (c.36)
Entail Amendment Act 1853 (c.94)
Entail Amendment (Scotland) Act 1868 (c.84)
Entail Amendment (Scotland) Act 1875 (c.61)
Entail Amendment (Scotland) Act 1878 (c.28)
Entail Cottages Act 1860 (c.95)
Entail Improvement Act 1770 (c.51)
Entail Powers Act 1836 (c.42)
Entail (Scotland) Act 1882 (c.53)
Entail (Scotland) Act 1914 (c.43)
Entail Sites Act 1840 (c.48)
Entailed Estates Act 1800 (c.56)
Entailed Lands, etc. (Scotland) Act 1841 (c.24)
Enterprise and New Towns (Scotland) Act 1990 (c.35)
Entertainments Duty Act 1958 (c.9)
Entertainments (Increased Penalties) Act 1990 (c.20)
Environment Act 1995 (c.25)
Environment and Safety Information Act 1988 (c.30)
Environmental Protection Act 1990 (c.43)
Epidemic and Other Diseases Prevention Act 1883 (c.59)
Episcopal and Capitular Estates Act 1851 (c.104)
Episcopal and Capitular Estates Act 1854 (c.116)
Episcopal and Capitular Estates Act 1857 (c.74)
Episcopal and Capitular Estates Act 1859 (c.46)
Episcopal Church (Scotland) Act 1864 (c.94)
Episcopal Church (Scotland) Act 1964 (c.12)
Episcopal, etc., Estates Management Act 1856 (c.74)
Episcopal Jurisdiction (England) Act 1839 (c.9)
Episcopal Meeting Houses (Scotland) Act 1745 (c.38)
Epping and Ongar Road Act 1742 (c.19)
Epping and Ongar Road Act 1769 (c.63)
Epping Forest Act 1871 (c.93)
Epping Forest Act 1873 (c.5)
Epping Forest Act 1875 (c.6)
Epping Forest Act 1876 (c.3)
Epping Forest Act Amendment 1872 (c.95)
Equal Pay Act 1970 (c.41)
Equity Procedure Act 1731 (c.25)
Equivalent Act 1714 (c.27)
Equivalent Act 1716 (c.14)
Equivalent Company Act 1850 (c.63)
Equivalent Money Act 1707 (c.51)
Equivalent Money Act 1713 (c.12)
Erasures in Deeds (Scotland) Act 1836 (c.33)
Erection of Cottages Act 1775 (c.32)
Erection of Lighthouses Act 1786 (c.101)
Erection of Lighthouses Act 1788 (c.25)
Erection of Lighthouses Act 1789 (c.52)
Erewash Canal Act 1777 (c.69)
Erewash Canal Act 1790 (c.56)
Erskine Bridge Tolls Act 1968 (c.4)
Escape of Debtors from Prison Act 1702 (c.6)
Escheat (Procedure) Act 1887 (c.53)
Escrick Church, Yorks Act 1781 (c.76)
Essential Buildings and Plant (Repair of War Damage) Act 1939 (c.74)
Essential Commodities Reserves Act 1938 (c.51)
Essex and Hertfordshire Roads Act 1743 (c.9)
Essex and Hertfordshire Roads Act 1769 (c.51)
Essex and Hertfordshire Roads Act 1791 (c.99)
Essex Roads Act 1702 (c.10)
Essex Roads Act 1723 (c.9)
Essex Roads Act 1725 (c.23)
Essex Roads Act 1746 (c.7)
Essex Roads Act 1763 (c.58)
Essex Roads Act 1787 (c.69)
Essex Roads Act 1793 (c.145)
Essex Roads Act 1793 (c.149)
Essex Shire House Act 1789 (c.8)
Essex, Suffolk and Hertford Roads Act 1765 (c.60)
Established Church Act 1713 (c.7)
Estate Agents Act 1979 (c.38)
Estate of Benjamin Hopkins Act 1795 (c.103)

Estate of Hugh Naish Act 1737 (c.38)
Estates Held for the Barrack Service Act 1805 (c.69)
Estates of Duke of Wellington Act 1839 (c.4)
Estates of Grenada and St. Vincent Traders Act 1806 (c.157)
Estates of Grenada and St. Vincent Traders Act 1806 (c.158)
Estates of Intestates, etc. Act 1852 (c.3)
Estates of Lunatics Act 1803 (c.75)
Estates Vest in Heirs, etc., of Mortgages Act 1838 (c.69)
Estreats Act 1716 (c.15)
European Assembly Elections Act 1978 (c.10)
European Assembly Elections Act 1981 (c.8)
European Assembly (Pay and Pensions) Act 1979 (c.50)
European Coal and Steel Community Act 1955 (c.4)
European Communities Act 1972 (c.68)
European Communities (Amendment) Act 1986 (c.58)
European Communities (Amendment) Act 1993 (c.32)
European Communities (Finance) Act 1985 (c.64)
European Communities (Finance) Act 1988 (c.46)
European Communities (Finance) Act 1995 (c.1)
European Communities (Greek Accession) Act 1979 (c.57)
European Communities (Spanish and Portuguese Accession) Act 1985 (c.75)
European Economic Area Act 1993 (c.51)
European Forces (India) Act 1860 (c.100)
European Free Trade Association Act 1960 (c.19)
European Monetary Agreement Act 1959 (c.11)
European Parliamentary Elections Act 1993 (c.41)
European Payments Union (Financial Provisions) Act 1950 (c.8)
European Troops in India Act 1859 (c.27)
European Union (Accessions) Act 1994 (c.38)
Everton, etc. (Nottinghamshire): Drainage, etc. Act 1796 (c.99)
Evesham Roads Act 1727 (c.11)
Evesham Roads Act 1778 (c.93)
Evesham Roads Act 1789 (c.103)
Evicted Tenants (Ireland) Act 1907 (c.56)
Evicted Tenants (Ireland) Act 1908 (c.22)
Eviction (Ireland) Act 1848 (c.47)
Evidence Act 1791 (c.35)
Evidence Act 1840 (c.26)
Evidence Act 1843 (c.85)
Evidence Act 1845 (c.113)
Evidence Act 1851 (c.99)
Evidence Act 1870 (c.49)
Evidence Act 1877 (c.14)
Evidence Act 1938 (c.28)
Evidence (Amendment) Act 1853 (c.83)
Evidence (Amendment) Act 1915 (c.94)
Evidence and Powers of Attorney Act 1940 (c.28)
Evidence and Powers of Attorney Act 1943 (c.18)
Evidence by Commission Act 1843 (c.82)
Evidence by Commission Act 1859 (c.20)
Evidence by Commission Act 1885 (c.74)
Evidence (Colonial Statutes) Act 1907 (c.16)
Evidence (Foreign, Dominion and Colonial Documents) Act 1933 (c.4)
Evidence Further Amendment Act 1869 (c.68)
Evidence Further Amendment Act 1874 (c.64)
Evidence Ireland Act 1815 (c.157)
Evidence (Proceedings in Other Jurisdictions) Act 1975 (c.34)
Evidence (Scotland) Act 1840 (c.59)
Evidence (Scotland) Act 1852 (c.27)
Evidence (Scotland) Act 1853 (c.20)
Evidence (Scotland) Act 1866 (c.112)
Examination of Drugs Act 1723 (c.20)
Excessive Loading of Vehicles, London and Westminster Act 1719 (c.6)
Exchange Control Act 1947 (c.14)
Exchange, Crown and Eton College Act 1842 (c.78)
Exchange Equalisation Account Act 1933 (c.18)
Exchange Equalisation Account Act 1937 (c.41)
Exchange Equalisation Account Act 1979 (c.30)
Exchange of American Prisoners Act 1782 (c.10)
Exchange of Crown Advowsons Act 1848 (c.57)
Exchange of Crown Lands in Perthshire Act 1766 (c.33)
Exchange of Ecclesiastical Patronage Act 1859 (c.9)
Exchequer Act 1728 (c.6)
Exchequer and Audit Departments Act 1866 (c.39)
Exchequer and Audit Departments Act 1921 (c.52)
Exchequer and Audit Departments Act 1950 (c.3)
Exchequer and Audit Departments Act 1957 (c.45)
Exchequer and Audit Departments (Temporary Provisions) Act 1939 (c.101)
Exchequer and Treasury Bills Act 1885 (c.44)
Exchequer Bills Act 1700 (c.1)
Exchequer Bills Act 1786 (c.97)
Exchequer Bills Act 1787 (c.23)
Exchequer Bills Act 1793 (c.29)
Exchequer Bills Act 1796 (cc.29, 30)
Exchequer Bills Act 1798 (c.91)
Exchequer Bills Act 1799 (c.6)

Exchequer Bills Act 1800 (c.33)
Exchequer Bills Act 1800 (c.109)
Exchequer Bills Act 1802 (c.41)
Exchequer Bills Act 1803 (c.60)
Exchequer Bills Act 1803 (c.148)
Exchequer Bills Act 1804 (c.73)
Exchequer Bills Act 1805 (c.27)
Exchequer Bills Act 1806 (c.93)
Exchequer Bills Act 1807 (c.28)
Exchequer Bills Act 1808 (c.7)
Exchequer Bills Act 1808 (cc.53, 54)
Exchequer Bills Act 1808 (c.97)
Exchequer Bills Act 1808 (c.114)
Exchequer Bills Act 1809 (cc.2, 3)
Exchequer Bills Act 1809 (c.52)
Exchequer Bills Act 1809 (c.93)
Exchequer Bills Act 1809 (c.114)
Exchequer Bills Act 1810 (cc.2, 3)
Exchequer Bills Act 1810 (cc.69, 70)
Exchequer Bills Act 1810 (cc.113, 114)
Exchequer Bills Act 1811 (cc.3, 4)
Exchequer Bills Act 1811 (c.15)
Exchequer Bills Act 1811 (cc.53, 54)
Exchequer Bills Act 1811 (c.85)
Exchequer Bills Act 1811 (c.112)
Exchequer Bills Act 1812 (cc.4, 5)
Exchequer Bills Act 1812 (c.16)
Exchequer Bills Act 1812 (c.86)
Exchequer Bills Act 1812 (c.114)
Exchequer Bills Act 1812 (c.164)
Exchequer Bills Act 1813 (c.18)
Exchequer Bills Act 1813 (cc.26, 27)
Exchequer Bills Act 1813 (c.39)
Exchequer Bills Act 1813 (c.42)
Exchequer Bills Act 1813 (cc.118, 119)
Exchequer Bills Act 1813 (c.161)
Exchequer Bills Act 1814 (cc.4, 5)
Exchequer Bills Act 1814 (c.53)
Exchequer Bills Act 1814 (cc.79, 80)
Exchequer Bills Act 1814 (c.188)
Exchequer Bills Act 1815 (cc.148, 149)
Exchequer Bills Act 1816 (c.4)
Exchequer Bills Act 1816 (c.28)
Exchequer Bills Act 1816 (c.54)
Exchequer Bills Act 1836 (c.2)
Exchequer Bills Act 1836 (c.113)
Exchequer Bills Act 1837 (c.16)
Exchequer Bills Act 1837 (c.38)
Exchequer Bills Act 1838 (c.12)
Exchequer Bills Act 1838 (c.26)
Exchequer Bills Act 1838 (c.93)
Exchequer Bills Act 1839 (c.8)
Exchequer Bills Act 1839 (c.90)
Exchequer Bills Act 1840 (c.12)
Exchequer Bills Act 1840 (c.106)
Exchequer Bills Act 1841 (c.19)
Exchequer Bills Act 1842 (c.21)
Exchequer Bills Act 1842 (c.66)
Exchequer Bills Act 1842 (c.86)
Exchequer Bills Act 1842 (c.115)
Exchequer Bills Act 1843 (c.17)
Exchequer Bills Act 1844 (c.14)
Exchequer Bills Act 1845 (c.23)
Exchequer Bills Act 1845 (c.129)
Exchequer Bills Act 1846 (c.15)
Exchequer Bills Act 1847 (c.19)
Exchequer Bills Act 1848 (c.16)
Exchequer Bills Act 1849 (c.20)
Exchequer Bills Act 1850 (c.10)
Exchequer Bills Act 1850 (c.22)
Exchequer Bills Act 1851 (c.9)
Exchequer Bills Act 1852 (c.10)
Exchequer Bills Act 1853 (c.25)
Exchequer Bills Act 1854 (c.3)
Exchequer Bills Act 1854 (c.12)
Exchequer Bills Act 1855 (c.8)
Exchequer Bills Act 1856 (c.19)
Exchequer Bills Act 1857 (c.17)
Exchequer Bills Act 1858 (c.13)
Exchequer Bills Act 1859 (c.22)
Exchequer Bills Act 1860 (c.20)
Exchequer Bills Act 1861 (c.5)
Exchequer Bills Act 1862 (c.3)
Exchequer Bills and Bonds Act 1855 (c.130)
Exchequer Bills and Bonds Act 1856 (c.44)
Exchequer Bills and Bonds Act 1866 (c.25)
Exchequer Bills and Bonds Act 1877 (c.5)
Exchequer Bills and Bonds Act 1878 (c.2)
Exchequer Bills and Bonds Act 1879 (c.62)
Exchequer Bills and Bonds Act 1880 (c.16)
Exchequer Bills and Bonds (Session 2) Act 1880 (c.21)
Exchequer Bills (Great Britain) Act 1815 (c.196)
Exchequer Bonds Act 1858 (c.14)
Exchequer Bonds Act 1862 (c.13)
Exchequer Bonds Act 1863 (c.16)
Exchequer Bonds Act 1864 (c.74)
Exchequer Bonds Act 1865 (c.29)
Exchequer Bonds Act 1867 (c.31)
Exchequer Bonds Act 1868 (c.27)
Exchequer Bonds Act 1869 (c.22)
Exchequer Bonds Act 1870 (c.41)
Exchequer Bonds Act 1871 (c.52)
Exchequer Bonds Act 1873 (c.54)
Exchequer Bonds Act 1876 (c.1)
Exchequer Bonds Act 1878 (c.7)
Exchequer Bonds and Bills Act 1854 (c.23)
Exchequer Bonds and Bills Act 1860 (c.132)
Exchequer Bonds and Bills (No. 2) Act 1878 (c.64)
Exchequer Bonds (No. 1) Act 1879 (c.3)
Exchequer Bonds (No. 2) Act 1878 (c.22)
Exchequer Court (Ireland) Act 1843 (c.55)
Exchequer Court (Ireland) Act 1843 (c.78)
Exchequer Court (Scotland) Act 1707 (c.53)
Exchequer Court (Scotland) Act 1779 (c.38)
Exchequer Court (Scotland) Act 1837 (c.65)
Exchequer Court (Scotland) Act 1856 (c.56)
Exchequer Equitable Jurisdiction (Ireland) Act 1850 (c.51)
Exchequer, etc., Courts (Scotland) Act 1790 (c.17)
Exchequer Extra Receipts Act 1868 (c.9)
Exchequer (Ireland) Act 1814 (c.83)
Excisable Goods on the Thames Act 1803 (c.115)

Excisable Liquors (Scotland) Act 1804 (c.55)
Excise Act 1719 (c.21)
Excise Act 1758 (c.29)
Excise Act 1772 (c.46)
Excise Act 1781 (c.55)
Excise Act 1781 (c.64)
Excise Act 1783 (c.70)
Excise Act 1785 (c.22)
Excise Act 1785 (c.47)
Excise Act 1785 (c.74)
Excise Act 1786 (c.59)
Excise Act 1786 (c.64)
Excise Act 1786 (cc.73, 74)
Excise Act 1786 (c.77)
Excise Act 1788 (c.37)
Excise Act 1788 (c.46)
Excise Act 1789 (c.63)
Excise Act 1790 (c.37)
Excise Act 1793 (c.59)
Excise Act 1795 (cc.10–13)
Excise Act 1795 (c.13)
Excise Act 1795 (c.97)
Excise Act 1795 (c.116)
Excise Act 1796 (c.14)
Excise Act 1798 (c.42)
Excise Act 1798 (c.54)
Excise Act 1800 (c.23)
Excise Act 1801 (c.91)
Excise Act 1802 (c.93)
Excise Act 1802 (c.96)
Excise Act 1803 (c.69)
Excise Act 1803 (c.81)
Excise Act 1803 (c.129)
Excise Act 1804 (c.49)
Excise Act 1805 (c.30)
Excise Act 1806 (c.39)
Excise Act 1806 (c.75)
Excise Act 1806 (c.112)
Excise Act 1806 (cc.138, 139)
Excise Act 1807 (c.27)
Excise Act 1807 (c.37)
Excise Act 1809 (c.63)
Excise Act 1809 (c.77)
Excise Act 1809 (c.80)
Excise Act 1809 (c.81)
Excise Act 1811 (c.32)
Excise Act 1812 (c.58)
Excise Act 1812 (c.61)
Excise Act 1812 (c.94)
Excise Act 1812 (c.128)
Excise Act 1813 (cc.56, 57)
Excise Act 1813 (c.88)
Excise Act 1813 (c.103)
Excise Act 1814 (c.73)
Excise Act 1814 (c.148)
Excise Act 1814 (c.183)
Excise Act 1815 (c.27)
Excise Act 1815 (c.30)
Excise Act 1815 (c.35)
Excise Act 1815 (c.62)
Excise Act 1815 (c.63)
Excise Act 1816 (c.17)
Excise Act 1816 (c.104)
Excise Act 1816 (c.108)
Excise Act 1836 (c.52)
Excise Act 1840 (c.17)
Excise Act 1848 (c.118)
Excise Act 1854 (c.27)
Excise Act 1855 (c.94)
Excise Act 1858 (c.15)
Excise Act 1860 (c.113)
Excise and Customs Act 1815 (c.66)
Excise and Stamps Act 1808 (c.41)
Excise and Stamps (Ireland) Act 1807 (c.14)
Excise and Taxes (Ireland) Act 1805 (c.19)
Excise Duties Act 1780 (c.17)
Excise Duties Act 1789 (c.45)
Excise Duties Act 1794 (c.33)
Excise Duties Act 1855 (c.22)
Excise Duties Act 1856 (c.34)
Excise Duties Act 1862 (c.84)
Excise Duties and Drawbacks Act 1807 (c.63)
Excise Duties and Licences (Ireland) Act 1815 (c.19)
Excise Duties and Taxes (Ireland) Act 1807 (c.18)
Excise Duties (Surcharges or Rebates) Act 1979 (c.8)
Excise Duty on Malt Act 1863 (c.3)
Excise Duty on Malt Act 1865 (c.66)
Excise, etc. Act 1811 (c.95)
Excise, etc. (Great Britain) Act 1807 (c.30)
Excise, etc. Act 1816 (c.30)
Excise (Great Britain) Act 1809 (c.117)
Excise (Ireland) Act 1807 (c.35)
Excise (Ireland) Act 1808 (c.82)
Excise (Ireland) Act 1809 (c.33)
Excise Incorporation (Scotland) Act 1835 (c.72)
Excise Laws, Glass Act 1792 (c.40)
Excise Management Act 1841 (c.20)
Excise Officers Act 1810 (c.44)
Excise Officers Allowance Act 1812 (c.81)
Excise on Spirits Act 1860 (c.129)
Excise (Scotland) Act 1793 (c.69)
Exclusive Trading (Ireland) Act 1846 (c.76)
Execution Act 1844 (c.96)
Execution (Ireland) Act 1848 (c.28)
Execution of Diligence (Scotland) Act 1926 (c.16)
Execution of Sentences (Scotland) Act 1730 (c.32)
Execution of Trusts (Emergency Provisions) Act 1939 (c.114)
Execution of Trusts (War Facilities) Act 1914 (c.13)
Execution of Trusts (War Facilities) Amendment Act 1915 (c.70)
Executions for Murder Act 1836 (c.30)
Executors (Scotland) Act 1900 (c.55)
Exemption from Coal Duty Act 1787 (c.21)
Exemption from Duties Act 1809 (c.44)
Exemption from Impressment Act 1739 (c.17)
Exemption from Toll Act 1812 (c.145)
Exemption of Bankers from Penalties Act 1813 (c.139)

Exercise Act 1723 (c.10)
Exercise Act 1727 (c.16)
Exercise of Trade by Soldiers Act 1784 (c.6)
Exercise of Trade by Soldiers, etc. Act 1802 (c.69)
Exercise of Trades by Soldiers, etc. Act 1816 (c.67)
Exercises of Trades Act 1712 (c.14)
Exercising Ground, Chatham Act 1808 (c.101)
Exeter: Lighting, etc. Act 1760 (c.28)
Exeter (Poor Relief) Act 1757 (c.53)
Exeter: Poor Relief Act 1774 (c.61)
Exeter: Poor Relief Act 1785 (c.21)
Exeter: Poor Relief Act 1788 (c.76)
Exeter Roads Act 1753 (c.74)
Exeter Roads Act 1756 (c.55)
Exeter Roads Act 1769 (c.93)
Exeter Roads Act 1770 (c.73)
Exeter Roads, etc. Act 1773 (c.109)
Exeter: Small Debts Act 1772 (c.27)
Exhibition Medals Act 1863 (c.119)
Exmoor Forest Act 1815 (c.138)
Ex-Officio Justice of the Peace (Scotland) Act 1898 (c.20)
Expenditure, etc., of Office of Works, etc. Act 1812 (c.41)
Expenditure in the West Indies Act 1800 (c.22)
Expenses of Fortifications for Protecting Royal Arsenals (No. 1) Act 1867 (c.24)
Expenses of Fortifications for Protecting Royal Arsenals (No. 2) Act 1867 (c.145)
Expenses of H.M. Forces, India Act 1791 (c.10)
Expenses of Prince Regent Act 1812 (c.7)
Expiring Laws Act 1922 (c.50)
Expiring Laws Act 1925 (c.76)
Expiring Laws Act 1931 (c.2)
Expiring Laws Act 1969 (c.61)
Expiring Laws Continuance Act 1841 (c.7)
Expiring Laws Continuance Act 1863 (c.95)
Expiring Laws Continuance Act 1864 (c.84)
Expiring Laws Continuance Act 1865 (c.119)
Expiring Laws Continuance Act 1866 (c.102)
Expiring Laws Continuance Act 1867 (c.143)
Expiring Laws Continuance Act 1868 (c.111)
Expiring Laws Continuance Act 1869 (c.85)
Expiring Laws Continuance Act 1870 (c.103)
Expiring Laws Continuance Act 1871 (c.95)
Expiring Laws Continuance Act 1872 (c.88)
Expiring Laws Continuance Act 1873 (c.75)
Expiring Laws Continuance Act 1874 (c.76)
Expiring Laws Continuance Act 1875 (c.72)
Expiring Laws Continuance Act 1876 (c.69)
Expiring Laws Continuance Act 1877 (c.67)
Expiring Laws Continuance Act 1878 (c.70)
Expiring Laws Continuance Act 1879 (c.67)
Expiring Laws Continuance Act 1880 (c.48)
Expiring Laws Continuance Act 1881 (c.70)
Expiring Laws Continuance Act 1882 (c.64)
Expiring Laws Continuance Act 1883 (c.40)
Expiring Laws Continuance Act 1884 (c.53)
Expiring Laws Continuance Act 1885 (c.59)
Expiring Laws Continuance Act 1886 (c.5)
Expiring Laws Continuance Act 1887 (c.63)
Expiring Laws Continuance Act 1888 (c.38)
Expiring Laws Continuance Act 1889 (c.67)
Expiring Laws Continuance Act 1890 (c.49)
Expiring Laws Continuance Act 1891 (c.60)
Expiring Laws Continuance Act 1892 (c.60)
Expiring Laws Continuance Act 1893 (c.59)
Expiring Laws Continuance Act 1894 (c.48)
Expiring Laws Continuance Act 1895 (c.1)
Expiring Laws Continuance Act 1896 (c.39)
Expiring Laws Continuance Act 1897 (c.54)
Expiring Laws Continuance Act 1898 (c.47)
Expiring Laws Continuance Act 1899 (c.34)
Expiring Laws Continuance Act 1900 (c.37)
Expiring Laws Continuance Act 1901 (c.33)
Expiring Laws Continuance Act 1902 (c.32)
Expiring Laws Continuance Act 1903 (c.40)
Expiring Laws Continuance Act 1904 (c.29)
Expiring Laws Continuance Act 1905 (c.21)
Expiring Laws Continuance Act 1906 (c.51)
Expiring Laws Continuance Act 1907 (c.34)
Expiring Laws Continuance Act 1908 (c.18)
Expiring Laws Continuance Act 1909 (c.46)
Expiring Laws Continuance Act 1910 (c.36)
Expiring Laws Continuance Act 1911 (c.22)
Expiring Laws Continuance Act 1912 (c.18)
Expiring Laws Continuance Act 1913 (c.15)
Expiring Laws Continuance Act 1914 (c.23)
Expiring Laws Continuance Act 1915 (c.63)
Expiring Laws Continuance Act 1916 (c.29)
Expiring Laws Continuance Act 1917 (c.38)
Expiring Laws Continuance Act 1918 (c.21)
Expiring Laws Continuance Act 1919 (c.39)
Expiring Laws Continuance Act 1920 (c.73)
Expiring Laws Continuance Act 1921 (c.53)
Expiring Laws Continuance Act 1923 (c.37)
Expiring Laws Continuance Act 1924 (c.1)
Expiring Laws Continuance Act 1926 (c.49)
Expiring Laws Continuance Act 1927 (c.34)
Expiring Laws Continuance Act 1928 (c.3)
Expiring Laws Continuance Act 1929 (c.12)
Expiring Laws Continuance Act 1931 (c.4)
Expiring Laws Continuance Act 1932 (c.2)
Expiring Laws Continuance Act 1933 (c.48)
Expiring Laws Continuance Act 1934 (c.57)
Expiring Laws Continuance Act 1935 (c.4)
Expiring Laws Continuance Act 1936 (c.4)
Expiring Laws Continuance Act 1937 (c.1)
Expiring Laws Continuance Act 1938 (c.1)
Expiring Laws Continuance Act 1939 (c.1)
Expiring Laws Continuance Act 1941 (c.3)
Expiring Laws Continuance Act 1942 (c.1)
Expiring Laws Continuance Act 1943 (c.1)
Expiring Laws Continuance Act 1944 (c.2)
Expiring Laws Continuance Act 1945 (c.9)
Expiring Laws Continuance Act 1947 (c.1)
Expiring Laws Continuance Act 1948 (c.3)
Expiring Laws Continuance Act 1949 (c.71)
Expiring Laws Continuance Act 1950 (c.1)
Expiring Laws Continuance Act 1951 (c.3)
Expiring Laws Continuance Act 1952 (c.5)

Expiring Laws Continuance Act 1953 (c.9)
Expiring Laws Continuance Act 1954 (c.69)
Expiring Laws Continuance Act 1955 (c.22)
Expiring Laws Continuance Act 1957 (c.2)
Expiring Laws Continuance Act 1958 (c.4)
Expiring Laws Continuance Act 1959 (c.4)
Expiring Laws Continuance Act 1960 (c.4)
Expiring Laws Continuance Act 1961 (c.4)
Expiring Laws Continuance Act 1962 (c.3)
Expiring Laws Continuance Act 1963 (c.58)
Expiring Laws Continuance Act 1964 (c.94)
Expiring Laws Continuance Act 1965 (c.77)
Expiring Laws Continuance Act 1966 (c.40)
Expiring Laws Continuance Act 1967 (c.89)
Expiring Laws Continuance Act 1968 (c.76)
Expiring Laws Continuance Act 1970 (c.58)
Explosive Substances Act 1883 (c.3)
Explosives Act 1875 (c.17)
Explosives Act 1923 (c.17)
Explosives (Age of Purchase) Act 1976 (c.26)
Export and Investment Guarantees Act 1991 (c.67)
Export Duty Act 1804 (c.57)
Export Guarantees Act 1937 (c.61)
Export Guarantees Act 1939 (c.5)
Export Guarantees Act 1944 (c.9)
Export Guarantees Act 1948 (c.54)
Export Guarantees Act 1949 (c.14)
Export Guarantees Act 1952 (c.21)
Export Guarantees Act 1957 (c.23)
Export Guarantees Act 1959 (c.63)
Export Guarantees Act 1967 (c.11)
Export Guarantees Act 1968 (c.26)
Export Guarantees Act 1975 (c.38)
Export Guarantees Amendment Act 1975 (c.19)
Export Guarantees and Overseas Investment Act 1978 (c.18)
Export Guarantees and Payments Act 1970 (c.14)
Export Guarantees and Payments Act 1970 (c.15)
Export of Salted Beef, etc. (Ireland) Act 1807 (c.10)
Exportation Act 1705 (c.19)
Exportation Act 1707 (c.44)
Exportation Act 1709 (c.2)
Exportation Act 1709 (c.7)
Exportation Act 1730 (c.29)
Exportation Act 1740 (c.3)
Exportation Act 1753 (c.11)
Exportation Act 1753 (c.15)
Exportation Act 1756 (cc.15, 16)
Exportation Act 1757 (c.1)
Exportation Act 1757 (c.9)
Exportation Act 1757 (c.37)
Exportation Act 1758 (c.8)
Exportation Act 1759 (c.15)
Exportation Act 1759 (c.28)
Exportation Act 1768 (c.24)
Exportation Act 1769 (c.1)
Exportation Act 1770 (c.1)
Exportation Act 1770 (c.10)
Exportation Act 1770 (c.31)
Exportation Act 1770 (c.38)
Exportation Act 1771 (c.37)
Exportation Act 1771 (c.39)
Exportation Act 1772 (cc.1, 2)
Exportation Act 1774 (c.5)
Exportation Act 1774 (c.10)
Exportation Act 1774 (c.11)
Exportation Act 1774 (c.26)
Exportation Act 1774 (c.71)
Exportation Act 1775 (c.5)
Exportation Act 1776 (c.28)
Exportation Act 1776 (c.37)
Exportation Act 1778 (c.16)
Exportation Act 1780 (c.37)
Exportation Act 1780 (c.46)
Exportation Act 1783 (c.14)
Exportation Act 1783 (c.81)
Exportation Act 1785 (c.5)
Exportation Act 1785 (c.62)
Exportation Act 1785 (c.67)
Exportation Act 1786 (c.2)
Exportation Act 1786 (c.76)
Exportation Act 1786 (c.89)
Exportation Act 1788 (c.16)
Exportation Act 1788 (c.38)
Exportation Act 1788 (c.45)
Exportation Act 1792 (c.2)
Exportation Act 1792 (c.9)
Exportation Act 1793 (c.3)
Exportation Act 1794 (c.34)
Exportation Act 1795 (c.5)
Exportation Act 1796 (c.53)
Exportation Act 1797 (c.10)
Exportation Act 1797 (c.29)
Exportation Act 1797 (c.125)
Exportation Act 1798 (c.67)
Exportation Act 1799 (c.26)
Exportation Act 1799 (c.96)
Exportation Act 1800 (c.1)
Exportation Act 1800 (c.2)
Exportation Act 1800 (c.91)
Exportation Act 1801 (c.21)
Exportation Act 1803 (c.49)
Exportation Act 1803 (c.105)
Exportation Act 1804 (c.22)
Exportation Act 1804 (c.70)
Exportation Act 1804 (c.101)
Exportation Act 1806 (c.11)
Exportation Act 1806 (c.17)
Exportation Act 1806 (c.115)
Exportation Act 1806 (c.116)
Exportation Act 1807 (c.9)
Exportation Act 1807 (c.30)
Exportation Act 1807 (c.49)
Exportation Act 1808 (c.29)
Exportation Act 1808 (cc.33–35)
Exportation Act 1808 (c.44)
Exportation Act 1808 (c.69)
Exportation Act 1809 (c.23)
Exportation Act 1809 (cc.30, 31)
Exportation Act 1810 (c.26)
Exportation Act 1810 (c.34)

Exportation Act 1810 (c.60)
Exportation Act 1810 (c.63)
Exportation Act 1810 (c.64)
Exportation Act 1811 (c.50)
Exportation Act 1811 (c.57)
Exportation Act 1812 (c.25)
Exportation Act 1812 (c.45)
Exportation Act 1812 (c.140)
Exportation Act 1813 (c.7)
Exportation Act 1813 (c.30)
Exportation Act 1813 (cc.31, 32)
Exportation Act 1813 (c.38)
Exportation Act 1813 (c.40)
Exportation Act 1813 (c.45)
Exportation Act 1813 (c.98)
Exportation Act 1813 (c.125)
Exportation Act 1814 (c.57)
Exportation Act 1814 (c.100)
Exportation Act 1814 (c.127)
Exportation Act 1814 (c.142)
Exportation Act 1814 (c.185)
Exportation Act 1815 (c.180)
Exportation Act 1815 (c.183)
Exportation Act 1816 (c.76)
Exportation Act 1816 (c.92)
Exportation Act 1816 (c.109)
Exportation Act 1816 (c.127)
Exportation and Importation Act 1768 (cc.1–3)
Exportation and Importation Act 1795 (c.3)
Exportation and Importation Act 1795 (c.4)
Exportation and Importation Act 1796 (c.7)
Exportation and Importation Act 1797 (c.83)
Exportation and Importation Act 1803 (c.12)
Exportation and Importation Act 1804 (c.65)
Exportation and Importation Act 1805 (c.33)
Exportation and Importation Act 1808 (c.27)
Exportation and Importation Act 1811 (c.14)
Exportation and Importation Act 1811 (c.86)
Exportation and Importation Act 1813 (c.67)
Exportation and Importation Act 1815 (c.31)
Exportation and Importation Act 1815 (c.37)
Exportation and Importation (Great Britain) Act 1810 (cc.18, 19)
Exportation and Importation (Ireland) Act 1810 (cc.16, 17)
Exportation, etc. Act 1716 (c.21)
Exportation, etc. Act 1749 (c.14)
Exportation, etc. Act 1758 (c.2)
Exportation, etc. Act 1769 (c.28)
Exportation etc. Act 1771 (c.1)
Exportation, etc. Act 1778 (c.55)
Exportation, etc. Act 1784 (c.50)
Exportation, etc. Act 1801 (c.36)
Exportation, etc. Act 1808 (c.22)
Exportation (Ireland) Act 1807 (c.58)
Exportation (Ireland) Act 1809 (c.76)
Exportation of Arms Act 1900 (c.44)
Exportation of Army Clothing Act 1775 (c.45)
Exportation of Gunpowder Act 1803 (c.52)
Exportation of Horses Act 1914 (c.15)
Exportation of Horses Act 1937 (c.42)
Exportations, etc. Act 1704 (c.7)
Exportations, etc. Act 1780 (c.59)
Exportations, etc. Act 1802 (cc.12, 13)
Exports Act 1786 (c.40)
Exports Act 1787 (c.31)
Extension of Polling Hours Act 1913 (c.6)
Extradition Act 1843 (cc.75, 76)
Extradition Act 1845 (c.120)
Extradition Act 1862 (c.70)
Extradition Act 1866 (c.121)
Extradition Act 1870 (c.52)
Extradition Act 1873 (c.60)
Extradition Act 1895 (c.33)
Extradition Act 1906 (c.15)
Extradition Act 1931 (c.39)
Extradition Act 1932 (c.39)
Extradition Act 1989 (c.33)
Extraordinary Tithe Act 1897 (c.23)
Extraordinary Tithe Redemption Act 1886 (c.54)
Extra-Parochial Places Act 1857 (c.19)
Eyemouth Harbour Act 1797 (c.49)
Eynsham Bridge Act 1767 (c.68)

Fabrics (Misdescription) Act 1913 (c.17)
Factories Act 1802 (c.73)
Factories Act 1937 (c.67)
Factories Act 1844 (c.15)
Factories Act 1847 (c.29)
Factories Act 1850 (c.54)
Factories Act 1853 (c.104)
Factories Act 1856 (c.38)
Factories Act 1948 (c.55)
Factories Act 1959 (c.67)
Factories Act 1961 (c.34)
Factors Act 1842 (c.39)
Factors Act 1889 (c.45)
Factors Acts Amendment 1877 (c.39)
Factors (Scotland) Act 1890 (c.40)
Factory Act 1874 (c.44)
Factory Acts Extension Act 1864 (c.48)
Factory Acts Extension Act 1867 (c.103)
Factory and Workshop Act 1870 (c.62)
Factory and Workshop Act 1871 (c.104)
Factory and Workshop Act 1878 (c.16)
Factory and Workshop Act 1883 (c.53)
Factory and Workshop Act 1891 (c.75)
Factory and Workshop Act 1895 (c.37)
Factory and Workshop Act 1901 (c.22)
Factory and Workshop Act 1907 (c.39)
Factory and Workshop Amendment (Scotland) Act 1888 (c.22)
Factory and Workshop (Cotton Cloth Factories) Act 1911 (c.21)
Factory and Workshop (Cotton Cloth Factories) Act 1929 (c.15)
Failure of Corn Crop Act 1783 (c.53)
Fair Employment (Northern Ireland) Act 1976 (c.25)
Fair Employment (Northern Ireland) Act 1989 (c.32)
Fair Trading Act 1973 (c.41)
Fairs Act 1868 (c.51)

Fairs Act 1871 (c.12)
Fairs Act 1873 (c.37)
Fairs and Market Act 1850 (c.23)
Fairs (Ireland) Act 1868 (c.12)
Falmouth Gaol Act 1865 (c.103)
False Alarms of Fire Act 1895 (c.28)
False Oaths (Scotland) Act 1933 (c.20)
False Personation Act 1874 (c.36)
False Weights and Scales Act 1770 (c.44)
Falsification of Accounts Act 1875 (c.24)
Families of Militiamen Act 1793 (c.8)
Families of Militiamen Act 1795 (c.81)
Families of Militiamen, etc. Act 1794 (c.47)
Families of Militiamen, etc. Act 1796 (c.114)
Family Allowances Act 1944 (c.41)
Family Allowances Act 1965 (c.53)
Family Allowances and National Insurance Act 1952 (c.29)
Family Allowances and National Insurance Act 1956 (c.50)
Family Allowances and National Insurance Act 1959 (c.18)
Family Allowances and National Insurance Act 1961 (c.6)
Family Allowances and National Insurance Act 1963 (c.10)
Family Allowances and National Insurance Act 1967 (c.90)
Family Allowances and National Insurance Act 1968 (c.40)
Family Income Supplements Act 1970 (c.55)
Family Law Act 1986 (c.55)
Family Law Act 1996 (c.27)
Family Law Reform Act 1969 (c.46)
Family Law Reform Act 1987 (c.42)
Family Law (Scotland) Act 1985 (c.37)
Family of Rt. Hon. S. Perceval Act 1812 (c.67)
Family Provision Act 1966 (c.35)
Farm and Garden Chemicals Act 1967 (c.50)
Farm Land and Rural Development Act 1988 (c.16)
Farnborough and Seven Oaks Road Act 1796 (c.128)
Farnborough to Seven Oaks Road Act 1773 (c.92)
Farnhurst, Chichester and Delkey Road Act 1797 (c.148)
Farriers (Registration) Act 1975 (c.35)
Farriers (Registration) (Amendment) Act 1977 (c.31)
Farringdon to Burford Road 1771 (c.84)
Fatal Accidents Act 1846 (c.93)
Fatal Accidents Act 1864 (c.95)
Fatal Accidents Act 1959 (c.65)
Fatal Accidents Act 1976 (c.30)
Fatal Accidents and Sudden Deaths Inquiry (Scotland) Act 1906 (c.35)
Fatal Accidents and Sudden Deaths Inquiry (Scotland) Act 1976 (c.14)
Fatal Accidents (Damages) Act 1908 (c.7)
Fatal Accidents Inquiry (Scotland) Act 1895 (c.36)
Faversham (Improvement) Act 1789 (c.69)
Faversham, Portsmouth, Plymouth Fortifications Act 1786 (c.94)
Federal Council of Australasia Act 1885 (c.60)
Federation of Malaya Independence Act 1957 (c.60)
Fee-Farm Rents (Ireland) Act 1851 (c.20)
Fees, etc., in Public Offices (Ireland) Act 1807 (c.41)
Fees etc., in Public Offices, etc. (Ireland) Act 1811 (c.81)
Fees for Pardons Act 1818 (c.29)
Fees in Public Offices, etc. Act 1809 (c.51)
Fees in Public Offices, etc. (Ireland) Act 1810 (c.81)
Fees in Public Offices, etc. (Ireland) Act 1812 (c.92)
Fees (Increase) Act 1923 (c.4)
Fees of Coroners (Ireland) Act 1810 (c.30)
Fees, Officers of the Exchequer Act 1786 (c.99)
Fees, Port of London, etc. Act 1806 (c.82)
Felony Act 1819 (c.27)
Felony Act 1841 (c.22)
Felony and Piracy Act 1772 (c.20)
Fencibles Act 1793 (c.36)
Fen Drainage Act 1749 (c.18)
Fen Drainage Act 1758 (c.13)
Fen Drainage Act 1774 (c.16)
Fen Drainage Act 1775 (c.65)
Fen Drainage Act 1776 (c.64)
Ferries (Acquisition by Local Authorities) Act 1919 (c.75)
Ferrybridge and Boroughbridge Road Act 1753 (c.77)
Fertilisers and Feeding Stuffs Act 1893 (c.56)
Fertilisers and Feeding Stuffs Act 1906 (c.27)
Fertilisers and Feeding Stuffs Act 1926 (c.45)
Festival of Britain (Additional Loans) Act 1951 (c.47)
Festival of Britain (Sunday Opening) Act 1951 (c.14)
Festival of Britain (Supplementary Provisions) Act (c.102)
Festival Pleasure Gardens 1952 (c.13)
Feudal Casualties (Scotland) Act 1914 (c.48)
Fever (Ireland) Act 1846 (c.6)
Fever (Ireland) Act 1847 (c.22)
Fever (Ireland) Act 1848 (c.131)
Field Monuments Act 1972 (c.43)
Fife (Country) Roads Act 1797 (c.180)
Fife Roads Act 1772 (c.83)
Fife Roads Act 1790 (c.93)
Fife Roads and Bridges Act 1774 (c.31)
Fifield, St. John's and Newbridge Road Act 1763 (c.29)
Fiji Independence Act 1970 (c.50)
Fiji Marriage Act 1878 (c.61)
Film Levy Finance Act 1981 (c.16)
Films Act 1960 (c.57)
Films Act 1964 (c.52)
Films Act 1966 (c.48)
Films Act 1970 (c.26)

Films Act 1979 (c.9)
Films Act 1980 (c.41)
Films Act 1985 (c.21)
Finance Act 1894 (c.30)
Finance Act 1895 (c.16)
Finance Act 1896 (c.28)
Finance Act 1897 (c.24)
Finance Act 1898 (c.10)
Finance Act 1899 (c.9)
Finance Act 1900 (c.7)
Finance Act 1901 (c.7)
Finance Act 1902 (c.7)
Finance Act 1903 (c.8)
Finance Act 1904 (c.7)
Finance Act 1905 (c.4)
Finance Act 1906 (c.8)
Finance Act 1907 (c.13)
Finance Act 1908 (c.16)
Finance (1909–10) Act 1910 (c.8)
Finance Act 1910 (c.35)
Finance Act 1911 (c.48)
Finance Act 1912 (c.8)
Finance Act 1913 (c.30)
Finance Act 1914 (c.10)
Finance Act 1915 (c.62)
Finance Act 1916 (c.24)
Finance Act 1917 (c.31)
Finance Act 1918 (c.15)
Finance Act 1919 (c.32)
Finance Act 1920 (c.18)
Finance Act 1921 (c.32)
Finance Act 1922 (c.17)
Finance Act 1923 (c.14)
Finance Act 1924 (c.21)
Finance Act 1925 (c.36)
Finance Act 1926 (c.22)
Finance Act 1927 (c.10)
Finance Act 1928 (c.17)
Finance Act 1929 (c.21)
Finance Act 1930 (c.28)
Finance Act 1931 (c.25)
Finance Act 1931 (c.28)
Finance Act 1932 (c.25)
Finance Act 1933 (c.19)
Finance Act 1934 (c.32)
Finance Act 1935 (c.24)
Finance Act 1936 (c.34)
Finance Act 1937 (c.54)
Finance Act 1938 (c.46)
Finance Act 1939 (c.41)
Finance Act 1940 (c.29)
Finance Act 1941 (c.30)
Finance Act 1942 (c.21)
Finance Act 1943 (c.28)
Finance Act 1944 (c.23)
Finance Act 1945 (c.24)
Finance Act 1946 (c.64)
Finance Act 1947 (c.35)
Finance Act 1948 (c.49)
Finance Act 1949 (c.47)
Finance Act 1950 (c.15)
Finance Act 1951 (c.43)
Finance Act 1952 (c.33)
Finance Act 1953 (c.34)
Finance Act 1954 (c.44)
Finance Act 1955 (c.15)
Finance Act 1956 (c.54)
Finance Act 1957 (c.49)
Finance Act 1958 (c.56)
Finance Act 1959 (c.58)
Finance Act 1960 (c.44)
Finance Act 1961 (c.36)
Finance Act 1962 (c.44)
Finance Act 1963 (c.25)
Finance Act 1964 (c.49)
Finance Act 1965 (c.25)
Finance Act 1966 (c.18)
Finance Act 1967 (c.54)
Finance Act 1968 (c.44)
Finance Act 1969 (c.32)
Finance Act 1970 (c.24)
Finance Act 1971 (c.68)
Finance Act 1972 (c.41)
Finance Act 1973 (c.51)
Finance Act 1974 (c.30)
Finance Act 1975 (c.7)
Finance Act 1976 (c.40)
Finance Act 1977 (c.36)
Finance Act 1978 (c.42)
Finance Act 1979 (c.25)
Finance Act 1980 (c.48)
Finance Act 1981 (c.35)
Finance Act 1982 (c.39)
Finance Act 1983 (c.28)
Finance Act 1984 (c.43)
Finance Act 1985 (c.54)
Finance Act 1986 (c.41)
Finance Act 1987 (c.16)
Finance Act 1988 (c.39)
Finance Act 1989 (c.26)
Finance Act 1990 (c.29)
Finance Act 1991 (c.31)
Finance Act 1992 (c.20)
Finance Act 1993 (c.34)
Finance Act 1994 (c.9)
Finance Act 1995 (c.4)
Finance Act 1996 (c.8)
Finance (Exchequer Bonds) Amendment Act 1916 (c.36)
Finance (Income Tax Reliefs) Act 1977 (c.53)
Finance (New Duties) Act 1916 (c.11)
Finance (No. 2) Act 1915 (c.89)
Finance (No. 2) Act 1931 (c.49)
Finance (No. 2) Act 1939 (c.109)
Finance (No. 2) Act 1940 (c.48)
Finance (No. 2) Act 1945 (c.13)
Finance (No. 2) Act 1947 (c.9)
Finance (No. 2) Act 1955 (c.17)
Finance (No. 2) Act 1964 (c.92)
Finance (No. 2) Act 1975 (c.45)
Finance (No. 2) Act 1979 (c.47)
Finance (No. 2) Act 1983 (c.49)
Finance (No. 2) Act 1987 (c.51)
Finance (No. 2) Act 1992 (c.48)
Finance (Session 2) Act 1914 (c.7)
Financial Emergency Enactments (Cont.) Act 1931 (c.13)

Financial Powers (U.S.A. Securities) Act 1941 (c.36)
Financial Services Act 1986 (c.60)
Findhorn Harbour Act 1778 (c.70)
Finding of the Longitude at Sea Act 1776 (c.48)
Finding of the Longitude at Sea Act 1780 (c.52)
Finding of the Longitude at Sea Act 1780 (c.61)
Fine Arts Copyright Act 1862 (c.68)
Fine or Imprisonment (Scotland and Ireland) Act 1899 (c.11)
Fines Act 1833 (c.99)
Fines Act (Ireland) 1851 (c.90)
Fines Act (Ireland) 1851, Amendment Act 1874 (c.72)
Fines Act (Ireland) 1874 (c.72)
Fines and Penalties (Ireland) Act 1839 (c.92)
Fines and Recoveries Act 1833 (c.74)
Fines and Recoveries Act 1842 (c.32)
Fines and Recoveries Act 1848 (c.70)
Fines and Recoveries (Ireland) Act 1834 (c.82)
Fines by Justices Act 1801 (c.85)
Fines, etc. (Ireland) Act 1838 (c.99)
Fines, etc. (Ireland) Act 1843 (c.56)
Fines (Ireland) Act 1851 (c.90)
Fines on Stills Act 1810 (c.100)
Finsbury Square Act 1791 (c.90)
Finsbury Square (Paving, Watching, etc.) Act 1795 (c.45)
Fire Brigade Pensions Act 1925 (c.47)
Fire Brigade Pensions Act 1929 (c.35)
Fire Brigades Act 1938 (c.72)
Fire Insurance Duty Act 1782 (c.48)
Fire Precautions Act 1971 (c.40)
Fire Precautions (Loans) Act 1973 (c.11)
Fire Prevention (Metropolis) Act 1774 (c.78)
Fire Safety and Safety of Places of Sport Act 1987 (c.27)
Fire Service College Board (Abolition) Act 1982 (c.13)
Fire Services Act 1947 (c.41)
Fire Services Act 1951 (c.27)
Fire Services Act 1959 (c.44)
Fire Services (Emergency Provisions) Act 1941 (c.22)
Firearms Act 1813 (c.115)
Firearms Act 1815 (c.59)
Firearms Act 1934 (c.16)
Firearms Act 1937 (c.12)
Firearms Act 1965 (c.44)
Firearms Act 1968 (c.27)
Firearms Act 1982 (c.31)
Firearms (Amendment) Act 1936 (c.39)
Firearms (Amendment) Act 1988 (c.45)
Firearms (Amendment) Act 1992 (c.31)
Firearms (Amendment) Act 1994 (c.31)
Firearms and Imitation Firearms (Criminal Use) Act 1933 (c.50)
Fires Prevention Act 1785 (c.77)
Fires Prevention Act 1838 (c.75)
Fireworks Act 1951 (c.58)
Fireworks Act 1964 (c.23)
First Meetings of Certain Commissioners Act 1786 (c.95)
First Meetings of Commissioners Act 1808 (c.133)
First Meetings of Commissioners, etc. Act 1776 (c.36)
First Meetings of Commissioners, etc. Act 1779 (c.55)
First Meetings of Commissioners, etc. Act 1782 (c.74)
First Offenders Act 1958 (c.31)
First Offenders (Scotland) Act 1960 (c.23)
First Public Health Supplemental Act 1852 (c.41)
Fish Act 1705 (c.8)
Fish Act 1714 (c.18)
Fish Act 1756 (c.39)
Fish Act 1759 (c.27)
Fish Act 1796 (c.118)
Fish Act 1801 (c.3)
Fish Act 1801 (c.99)
Fish Carriage Act 1762 (c.15)
Fish Market, Westminster Act 1748 (c.49)
Fish, Newfoundland, etc. Act 1801 (c.77)
Fish Teinds (Scotland) Act 1864 (c.33)
Fisheries Act 1780 (c.60)
Fisheries Act 1785 (c.65)
Fisheries Act 1786 (c.41)
Fisheries Act 1786 (c.81)
Fisheries Act 1787 (c.10)
Fisheries Act 1891 (c.37)
Fisheries Act 1955 (c.7)
Fisheries Act 1981 (c.29)
Fisheries Close Season (Ireland) Act 1895 (c.29)
Fisheries, Continuance of Laws Act 1801 (c.97)
Fisheries, Convention with France Act 1839 (c.96)
Fisheries, Convention with France Act 1840 (c.69)
Fisheries, Convention with France Act 1842 (c.63)
Fisheries (Dynamite) Act 1877 (c.65)
Fisheries in Greenland Seas, etc. Act 1799 (c.101)
Fisheries (Ireland) Act 1807 (c.22)
Fisheries (Ireland) Act 1842 (c.106)
Fisheries (Ireland) Act 1844 (c.108)
Fisheries (Ireland) Act 1845 (c.108)
Fisheries (Ireland) Act 1846 (c.3)
Fisheries (Ireland) Act 1846 (c.114)
Fisheries (Ireland) Act 1848 (c.92)
Fisheries (Ireland) Act 1850 (c.88)
Fisheries (Ireland) Act 1869 (c.92)
Fisheries (Ireland) Act 1901 (c.38)
Fisheries (Ireland) Act 1909 (c.25)
Fisheries (Norfolk and Suffolk) Act 1896 (c.18)
Fisheries (Oyster, Crab and Lobster) Act 1877 (c.42)

Fisheries (Oyster, Crab and Lobster) Act (1877) Amendment 1884 (c.26)
Fisheries (Scotland) Act 1726 (c.30)
Fisheries (Scotland) Act 1756 (c.23)
Fisheries (Severn and Verniew) Act 1778 (c.33)
Fishery Act 1791 (c.22)
Fishery Act 1794 (c.22)
Fishery Board (Scotland) Act 1882 (c.78)
Fishery Boards (Scotland) Extension of Powers Act 1894 (c.14)
Fishery Convention with France Act 1855 (c.101)
Fishery Harbours Act 1915 (c.48)
Fishery Harbours (Continuance of Powers) Act 1917 (c.39)
Fishery (Ireland) Act 1888 (c.30)
Fishery Limits Act 1964 (c.72)
Fishery Limits Act 1976 (c.86)
Fishery Treaty with United States Act 1855 (c.3)
Fishguard Roads Act 1791 (c.106)
Fishhouse Bridge Lancashire Act 1750 (c.36)
Fishing Vessel Grants Act 1967 (c.35)
Fishing Vessels (Safety Provisions) Act 1970 (c.27)
Flax and Cotton Manufactures Act 1789 (c.54)
Flax and Hemp Seed (Ireland) Act 1810 (c.82)
Flax Companies (Financial Assistance) Act 1918 (c.24)
Flax, etc., Manufacture Act 1783 (c.77)
Flax, etc. Manufacture (Great Britain) Act 1815 (c.178)
Flax Seed (Ireland) Act 1809 (c.29)
Fleet Ditch Act 1732 (c.22)
Flint and Carnarvon Roads Act 1779 (c.107)
Flint Canal Act 1788 (c.72)
Flint Roads Act 1769 (c.45)
Flint Roads Act 1771 (c.69)
Flint Roads Act 1788 (c.101)
Flintshire Roads Act 1763 (c.44)
Flood Prevention (Scotland) Act 1961 (c.41)
Folkestone: Improvement Act 1796 (c.49)
Folkestone Parish Church Act 1766 (c.63)
Food Act 1984 (c.30)
Food and Drugs Act 1938 (c.56)
Food and Drugs Act 1955 (c.16)
Food and Drugs (Amendment) Act 1954 (c.67)
Food and Drugs (Amendment) Act 1981 (c.26)
Food and Drugs (Amendment) Act 1982 (c.26)
Food and Drugs (Control of Food Premises) Act 1976 (c.37)
Food and Drugs (Milk) Act 1970 (c.3)
Food and Drugs (Milk and Dairies) Act 1944 (c.29)
Food and Drugs (Milk and Dairies and Artificial Cream) Act 1950 (c.35)
Food and Drugs (Scotland) Act 1956 (c.30)
Food and Environment Protection Act 1985 (c.48)
Food Safety Act 1990 (c.16)
Foods and Drugs (Adulteration) Act 1928 (c.31)
Foodstuffs (Prevention of Exploitation) Act 1931 (c.51)
Football (Offences) Act 1991 (c.19)
Football Spectators Act 1989 (c.37)
Forces Act 1922 (c.11)
Forces of East India Company Act 1799 (c.109)
Forces of East India Company Act 1805 (c.36)
Forces of East India Company Act 1812 (c.122)
Forcible Entry Act 1381 (c.7)
Forcible Entry Act 1429 (c.9)
Forcible Entry Act 1588 (c.1588)
Forcible Entry Act 1623 (c.15)
Forcible Entry (Ireland) Act 1786 (c.24)
Forehoe, Norfolk (Borrowing Powers of Guardians) Act 1783 (c.29)
Forehoe, Norfolk (Guardians' Borrowing Powers) Act 1789 (c.4)
Forehoe, Norfolk: Poor Relief Act 1776 (c.9)
Foreign and Protestants Naturalization Act 1708 (c.5)
Foreign Compensation Act 1950 (c.12)
Foreign Compensation Act 1962 (c.4)
Foreign Compensation Act 1969 (c.20)
Foreign Compensation (Amendment) Act 1993 (c.16)
Foreign Corporations Act 1991 (c.44)
Foreign Deserters Act 1852 (c.26)
Foreign Enlistment Act 1735 (c.30)
Foreign Enlistment Act 1756 (c.17)
Foreign Enlistment Act 1870 (c.90)
Foreign Judgments (Reciprocal Enforcement) Act 1933 (c.13)
Foreign Jurisdiction Act 1844 (c.94)
Foreign Jurisdiction Act 1875 (c.85)
Foreign Jurisdiction Act 1878 (c.67)
Foreign Jurisdiction Act 1890 (c.37)
Foreign Jurisdiction Act 1913 (c.16)
Foreign Jurisdiction Act Amendment Act 1865 (c.16)
Foreign Jurisdiction Act Amendment Act 1866 (c.87)
Foreign Jurisdiction Act Foreign Law Ascertainment Act 1861 (c.11)
Foreign Law Ascertainment Act 1861 (c.11)
Foreign Limitation Periods Act 1984 (c.16)
Foreign Marriage Act 1891 (c.74)
Foreign Marriage Act 1892 (c.23)
Foreign Marriage Act 1947 (c.33)
Foreign Marriage (Amendment) Act 1988 (c.44)
Foreign Prison-Made Goods Act 1897 (c.63)
Foreign Protestants Naturalization Act 1714 (c.29)
Foreign Service Act 1943 (c.35)
Foreign Service Act 1960 (c.11)

Foreign Ships Act 1797 (c.63)
Foreign Ships, etc. Act 1805 (c.32)
Foreign Tribunals Evidence Act 1856 (c.113)
Forest of Dean Act 1836 (c.3)
Forest of Dean Act 1844 (c.13)
Forest of Dean (Poor Relief) Act 1842 (c.48)
Forestalling, Regrating, etc. Act 1844 (c.24)
Forestry Act 1919 (c.58)
Forestry Act 1921 (c.61)
Forestry Act 1927 (c.6)
Forestry Act 1944 (c.35)
Forestry Act 1947 (c.21)
Forestry Act 1951 (c.61)
Forestry Act 1967 (c.10)
Forestry Act 1979 (c.21)
Forestry Act 1981 (c.39)
Forestry Act 1986 (c.30)
Forestry Act 1991 (c.43)
Forestry (Sale of Land) (Scotland) Act 1963 (c.23)
Forestry (Transfer of Woods) Act 1923 (c.21)
Forfar Roads Act 1789 (c.20)
Forfar Roads Act 1794 (c.100)
Forfeited and Unclaimed Prize Money Act 1811 (c.104)
Forfeited Estates Act 1703 (c.61)
Forfeited Estates—Derwentwater Estate Act 1731 (c.23)
Forfeited Estates, etc. Act 1718 (c.23)
Forfeited Estates—Greenwich Hospital Act 1734 (c.29)
Forfeited Estates (Ireland) Act 1705 (c.11)
Forfeited Estates (Ireland) Act 1703 (c.19)
Forfeited Estates (Ireland) etc. Act 1703 (c.21)
Forfeited Estates (Scotland) Act 1774 (c.65)
Forfeited Estates, Scotland Act 1786 (c.27)
Forfeited Estates (Time for Claims) Act 1716 (c.20)
Forfeiture Act 1870 (c.23)
Forfeiture Act 1982 (c.34)
Forfeiture upon Attainder of Treason Act 1799 (c.93)
Forged Exchequer Bills Act 1842 (c.11)
Forged Exchequer Bills Act 1843 (c.1)
Forged Transfers Act 1891 (c.43)
Forged Transfers Act 1892 (c.36)
Forgeries and Frauds in Bank Transfers Act 1793 (c.30)
Forgery Act 1733 (c.22)
Forgery Act 1778 (c.18)
Forgery Act 1797 (c.122)
Forgery Act 1830 (c.66)
Forgery Act 1837 (c.84)
Forgery Act 1861 (c.98)
Forgery Act 1870 (c.58)
Forgery Act 1913 (c.27)
Forgery and Counterfeiting Act 1981 (c.45)
Forgery of Bank of Ireland Notes, etc. Act 1809 (c.13)
Forgery of Banknotes Act 1801 (c.39)
Forgery of Foreign Bills Act 1803 (c.139)
Form of Deeds Act (Scotland) 1856 (c.89)
Former Enemy Aliens (Disabilities Removal) Act 1925 (c.43)
Forms of Pleading Act 1838 (c.100)
Forms of Pleading in High Court Act 1855 (c.26)
Forsyth's Indemnity Act 1866 (c.20)
Fort Marlborough in India Act 1802 (c.29)
Fort of Senegal Act 1763 (c.20)
Fort William in Bengal Act 1786 (c.25)
Fort William Pulp and Paper Mills Act 1963 (c.15)
Forth and Clyde and Monkland Canal Act 1790 (c.73)
Forth and Clyde Canal (Extinguishment of Rights of Navigation) Act 1962 (c.16)
Forth and Clyde Navigation Act 1768 (c.63)
Forth and Clyde, Navigation Act 1771 (c.62)
Forth and Clyde, Navigation Act 1773 (c.104)
Forth and Clyde: Navigation Act 1784 (c.59)
Forth and Clyde: Navigation Act 1787 (c.20)
Forth and Clyde: Navigation Act 1787 (c.55)
Fortifications Act 1708 (c.26)
Fortifications Act 1709 (c.23)
Fortifications Act 1757 (cc.38, 39)
Fortifications (Expenses) Act 1869 (c.76)
Fortifications for Royal Arsenals, etc. Act 1863 (c.80)
Fortifications for Royal Arsenals, etc. Act 1864 (c.109)
Fortifications - Portsmouth Act 1722 (c.32)
Fortifications - Portsmouth and Dover Act 1806 (c.105)
Fortifications, Portsmouth and Dover Act 1809 (c.39)
Fortifications, Royal Arsenals, etc. Act 1865 (c.61)
Fosdyke Bridge Act 1984 (c.17)
Foss, York: Navigation Act 1793 (c.99)
Foster Children Act 1980 (c.6)
Foster Children (Scotland) Act 1984 (c.56)
Foston Bridge and Witham Common Road Act 1725 (c.16)
Founding Hospital Act 1739 (c.29)
Foundling Hospital, Dublin Act 1801 (c.50)
Four and a Half Per Cent, Duties Repeal Act 1838 (c.92)
Four Courts Library Act 1894 (c.4)
Four Courts Marshalsea Discontinuance Act 1874 (c.21)
Four Courts Marshalsea (Ireland) Act 1842 (c.95)
Foyle College Act 1874 (c.79)
Frame Work Knitters Act 1766 (c.29)
Frampton Mansel Marriage Act 1868 (c.23)
Franchise Prisons Abolition Act 1858 (c.22)
Frauds by Boatmen and Others, etc. Act 1809 (c.122)
Frauds by Boatmen, etc. Act 1813 (c.87)
Frauds by Boatmen in Cinque Ports, etc. Act 1808 (c.130)
Frauds by Journeymen Shoemakers Act 1722 (c.27)
Frauds by Workmen Act 1748 (c.27)

Frauds by Workmen Act 1777 (c.56)
Frauds, etc., in Woollen Manufacturers Act 1774 (c.25)
Frauds in Excise Revenue Act 1791 (c.21)
Frauds in Excise Revenue Act 1792 (c.8)
Frauds in Manufacture of Clocks, etc. Act 1754 (c.7)
Frauds in Manufacture of Sweets Act 1815 (c.177)
Frauds in the Public Revenues, etc. Act 1738 (c.72)
Frauds of Workmen Act 1739 (c.8)
Frauds on Exportation Act 1810 (c.53)
Fraudulent Bankrupts (Scotland) Act 1827 (c.20)
Fraudulent Mediums Act 1951 (c.33)
Free Fishers of Whitstable Act 1793 (c.42)
Free Ports Act 1796 (c.55)
Free Ports Act 1797 (c.77)
Free Ports Act 1800 (c.23)
Free Ports, Jamaica Act 1774 (c.41)
Free Ports, West Indies, etc. Act 1766 (c.49)
Freeman (Admission) Act 1763 (c.15)
Freshwater and Salmon Fisheries (Scotland) Act 1976 (c.22)
Freshwater Fish (Scotland) Act 1902 (c.29)
Freshwater Fisheries Act 1878 (c.39)
Freshwater Fisheries Act 1884 (c.11)
Freshwater Fisheries Act 1886 (c.2)
Friendly and Industrial and Provident Societies Act 1968 (c.55)
Friendly Societies Act 1793 (c.54)
Friendly Societies Act 1795 (c.111)
Friendly Societies Act 1803 (c.111)
Friendly Societies Act 1809 (c.125)
Friendly Societies Act 1840 (c.73)
Friendly Societies Act 1846 (c.27)
Friendly Societies Act 1850 (c.115)
Friendly Societies Act 1852 (c.65)
Friendly Societies Act 1854 (c.101)
Friendly Societies Act 1855 (c.63)
Friendly Societies Act 1858 (c.101)
Friendly Societies Act 1860 (c.13)
Friendly Societies Act 1860 (c.58)
Friendly Societies Act 1875 (c.60)
Friendly Societies Act 1879 (c.9)
Friendly Societies Act 1887 (c.56)
Friendly Societies Act 1888 (c.66)
Friendly Societies Act 1889 (c.22)
Friendly Societies Act 1893 (c.30)
Friendly Societies Act 1895 (c.26)
Friendly Societies Act 1896 (c.25)
Friendly Societies Act 1908 (c.32)
Friendly Societies Act 1916 (c.54)
Friendly Societies Act 1924 (c.11)
Friendly Societies Act 1955 (c.19)
Friendly Societies Act 1971 (c.66)
Friendly Societies Act 1974 (c.46)
Friendly Societies Act 1981 (c.50)
Friendly Societies Act 1984 (c.62)
Friendly Societies Act 1992 (c.40)
Friendly Societies Amendment Act 1876 (c.32)
Friendly Society Amendment Act 1885 (c.27)
Friendly Societies Discharge Act 1854 (c.56)
Friendly Societies (Ireland) Act 1809 (c.58)
Friendly Societies (Quinquennial Returns) Act 1882 (c.35)
Frivolous Arrests Act 1725 (c.29)
Frivolous Arrests Act 1811 (c.124)
Frivolous Suits Act 1772 (c.51)
Frivolous Suits Act 1841 (c.28)
Frogmore House Act 1841 (c.2)
Frome Roads Act 1757 (c.39)
Frome Roads Act 1772 (c.94)
Frome Roads Act 1797 (c.175)
Fuel and Electricity (Control) Act 1973 (c.67)
Fugitive Offenders Act 1881 (c.69)
Fugitive Offenders Act 1967 (c.68)
Fugitive Offenders (Protected States) Act 1915 (c.39)
Fulbourne Church Act 1775 (c.49)
Fulham and Putney Bridge Act 1725 (c.36)
Fulham Bridge Act 1727 (c.18)
Fulham Roads Act 1730 (c.34)
Fulham Roads Act 1749 (c.16)
Fund for Fire Victims in Edinburgh Act 1727 (c.22)
Furnished Houses (Rent Control) Act 1946 (c.34)
Furnished Lettings (Rent Allowances) Act 1973 (c.6)
Further and Higher Education Act 1992 (c.13)
Further and Higher Education (Scotland) Act 1992 (c.37)
Further Education Act 1985 (c.47)

Gainsborough Bridge Act 1787 (c.15)
Gainsborough Church Act 1735 (c.22)
Gainsborough Church Act 1740 (c.15)
Gainsborough: Improvement Act 1769 (c.21)
Gainsborough: Inclosure Act 1796 (c.101)
Gainsborough Inclosure, etc. Act 1795 (c.82)
Galashiels Act 1867 (c.85)
Galashiels and Selkirk Act 1872 (c.47)
Galway Harbour Act 1859 (c.28)
Galway Harbour Act 1867 (c.56)
Gambia Independence Act 1964 (c.93)
Game Act 1706 (c.16)
Game Act 1710 (c.27)
Game Act 1716 (c.11)
Game Act 1721 (c.19)
Game Act 1755 (c.12)
Game Act 1762 (c.19)
Game Act 1766 (c.21)
Game Act 1770 (c.19)
Game Act 1773 (c.80)
Game Act 1796 (c.39)
Game Act 1796 (c.54)
Game Act 1831 (c.32)
Game Act 1970 (c.13)
Game Birds (Ireland) Act 1874 (c.11)
Game Certificates Act 1784 (c.43)
Game Certificates Act 1785 (c.50)
Game Certificates (Ireland) Act 1842 (c.81)

Game (England) Act 1772 (c.55)
Game Laws (Amendment) Act 1960 (c.36)
Game Laws Amendment (Scotland) Act 1877 (c.28)
Game Laws (England); Local Taxes, etc. (Scotland) Act 1836 (c.65)
Game Licences Act 1860 (c.90)
Game (Scotland) Act 1750 (c.34)
Game (Scotland) Act 1772 (c.54)
Game Trespass (Ireland) Act 1864 (c.67)
Gamekeepers Act 1808 (c.93)
Gaming Act 1710 (c.19)
Gaming Act 1738 (c.28)
Gaming Act 1739 (c.19)
Gaming Act 1744 (c.34)
Gaming Act 1802 (c.119)
Gaming Act 1845 (c.109)
Gaming Act 1892 (c.9)
Gaming Act 1922 (c.19)
Gaming Act 1968 (c.65)
Gaming Act (Northern Ireland) 1845 (c.109)
Gaming (Amendment) Act 1973 (c.12)
Gaming (Amendment) Act 1982 (c.22)
Gaming (Amendment) Act 1980 (c.8)
Gaming (Amendment) Act 1986 (c.11)
Gaming (Amendment) Act 1987 (c.11)
Gaming (Amendment) Act 1990 (c.26)
Gaming (Bingo) Act 1985 (c.35)
Gaming Houses Act 1854 (c.38)
Gaming Machines (Scotland) Act 1917 (c.23)
Gaming Transactions Act 1844 (c.7)
Gaol Fees Abolition Act 1815 (c.50)
Gaol Fees Abolition Act 1845 (c.114)
Gaols Act 1772 (c.58)
Gaols Act 1784 (c.54)
Gaols Act 1789 (c.67)
Gaols Act 1791 (c.46)
Garrotters Act 1863 (c.44)
Gas Act 1948 (c.67)
Gas Act 1960 (c.27)
Gas Act 1965 (c.36)
Gas Act 1972 (c.60)
Gas Act 1980 (c.37)
Gas Act 1986 (c.44)
Gas Act 1995 (c.45)
Gas and Electricity Act 1968 (c.39)
Gas and Electricity (Borrowing Powers) Act 1954 (c.52)
Gas and Steam Vehicles (Excise Duties) Act 1939 (c.6)
Gas and Water Works Facilities Act 1870 (c.70)
Gas and Water Works Facilities Act, 1870, Amendment 1873 (c.89)
Gas (Borrowing Powers) Act 1965 (c.60)
Gas (Exempt Supplies) Act 1993 (c.1)
Gas Levy Act 1981 (c.3)
Gas (Standard of Calorific Power) Act 1916 (c.25)
Gas Undertakings Act 1929 (c.24)
Gas Undertakings Act 1931 (c.40)
Gas Undertakings Act 1934 (c.28)
Gasworks Clauses Act 1847 (c.15)
Gasworks Clauses Act 1871 (c.41)
General Board of Health Act 1856 (c.85)
General Board of Health Act 1857 (c.38)
General Board of Health Continuance Act 1855 (c.115)
General de Lancey (Crown Claims) Act 1807 (c.69)
General de Lancey (Estates and Crown Claims) Act 1811 (c.102)
General Dealers (Ireland) Act 1903 (c.44)
General Pardon Act (c.19)
General Pardon Act 1707 (c.22)
General Pardon Act 1720 (c.29)
General Pardon Act 1746 (c.52)
General Pier and Harbour Act 1861 (c.45)
General Pier and Harbour Act, 1861, Amendment Act 1862 (c.19)
General Police and Improvement (Scotland) Act 1862 (c.101)
General Police and Improvement (Scotland) Act, 1862, Amendment Act 1877 (c.22)
General Police and Improvement (Scotland) Act, 1862, Amendment Act 1889 (c.51)
General Police and Improvement (Scotland) Act 1865 (c.7)
General Police and Improvement (Scotland) Act 1882 (c.6)
General Police and Improvement (Scotland) Amendment Act 1878 (c.30)
General Police and Improvement (Scotland) Supplemental Act 1863
General Police and Improvement (Scotland) Supplemental Act 1865 (c.7)
General Police and Improvement (Scotland) Supplemental Act 1866 (c.93)
General Police and Improvement (Scotland) Supplemental Act 1867 (c.79)
General Prisons (Ireland) Act 1877 (c.49)
General Rate Act 1967 (c.9)
General Rate Act 1970 (c.19)
General Rate Act 1975 (c.5)
General Rate (Public Utilities) Act 1977 (c.11)
General Register House, Edinburgh Act 1847 (c.20)
General Register Office Act 1852 (c.25)
Geneva Convention Act 1911 (c.20)
Geneva Convention Act 1937 (c.15)
Geneva Conventions Act 1957 (c.52)
Geneva Conventions (Amendment) Act 1995 (c.27)
Genocide Act 1969 (c.12)
Geological Survey Act 1845 (c.63)
German Conventions Act 1955 (c.2)
German Reparation (Recovery) Act 1921 (c.5)
Ghana (Consequential Provisions) Act 1960 (c.41)
Ghana Independence Act 1957 (c.6)
Gibraltar Lighthouse, etc. Act 1838 (c.66)
Gifts for Churches Act 1803 (c.108)
Gifts for Churches Act 1811 (c.115)
Glamorgan, Llansamlett–Llangevelach Bridge, River Tawey Act 1778 (c.68)

Glamorgan Roads Act 1764 (c.88)
Glamorgan Roads Act 1771 (c.77)
Glamorgan Roads Act 1779 (c.110)
Glamorgan Roads Act 1785 (c.122)
Glamorgan Roads Act 1793 (c.133)
Glamorganshire Canal Act 1796 (c.69)
Glamorganshire Election Act 1815 (c.72)
Glasgow and Dumbarton Roads Act 1772 (c.106)
Glasgow and Renfrew Road Act 1797 (c.161)
Glasgow and Renfrew Roads Act 1794 (c.140)
Glasgow and Shotts Road Act 1753 (c.81)
Glasgow Beer Duties Act 1715 (c.44)
Glasgow Beer Duties Act 1725 (c.27)
Glasgow Beer Duties Act 1735 (c.31)
Glasgow Beer Duties Act 1755 (c.29)
Glasgow Boundaries Act 1871 (c.68)
Glasgow (Improvement) Act 1768 (c.16)
Glasgow: Improvement Act 1793 (c.124)
Glasgow Parliamentary Divisions Act 1896 (c.17)
Glasgow Roads Act 1753 (c.90)
Glasgow Roads Act 1754 (c.27)
Glasgow Roads Act 1766 (c.82)
Glasgow Roads Act 1774 (c.102)
Glasgow Roads Act 1774 (c.105)
Glasgow Roads Act 1788 (c.92)
Glasgow Roads Act 1792 (c.152)
Glasgow Roads Act 1792 (c.154)
Glasgow Roads Act 1793 (c.160)
Glasgow Roads Act 1793 (c.174)
Glasgow Roads Act 1795 (c.155)
Glass Duties Act 1787 (c.28)
Glass Duties Act 1794 (c.27)
Glass Duties Act 1835 (c.77)
Glass Duties Act 1838 (c.44)
Glass Duties Repeal Act 1845 (c.6)
Glass, etc., Duties Act 1813 (c.70)
Glebe Exchange Act 1815 (c.147)
Glebe Exchange Act 1816 (c.52)
Glebe Houses (Ireland) Act 1803 (c.158)
Glebe (Ireland) Act 1851 (c.73)
Glebe Lands Act 1888 (c.20)
Glebe Lands Leasing Powers (Ireland) Act 1857 (c.47)
Glebe Lands, Representative Church Body, Ireland, Act 1875 (c.42)
Glebe Lands (Scotland) Act 1866 (c.71)
Glebe Loan Act 1870 (c.112)
Glebe Loan Act 1871 (c.100)
Glebe Loan (Ireland) Acts Amendment 1880 (c.2)
Glebe Loan (Ireland) Acts Amendment 1883 (c.8)
Glebe Loan (Ireland) Acts Amendment 1886 (c.6)
Glebe Loan (Ireland) Amendment Act 1875 (c.30)
Glebe Loan (Ireland) Amendment Act 1878 (c.6)
Glebe Loan (Ireland) Amendments Act 1871 (c.100)
Gloucester and Berkeley Canal Act 1793 (c.97)
Gloucester and Berkeley Canal Act 1797 (c.54)
Gloucester and Crickley Hull Road Act 1760 (c.30)
Gloucester and Hereford Roads Act 1746 (c.31)
Gloucester and Hereford Roads Act 1759 (c.34)
Gloucester and Hereford Roads Act 1769 (c.50)
Gloucester and Oxford Road Act 1750 (c.28)
Gloucester and Oxford Roads Act 1768 (c.41)
Gloucester and Oxford Roads Act 1787 (c.77)
Gloucester and Warwick Roads Act 1755 (c.47)
Gloucester and Wiltshire Roads Act 1756 (c.56)
Gloucester and Wiltshire Roads Act 1757 (c.61)
Gloucester and Wiltshire Roads Act 1762 (c.74)
Gloucester and Wiltshire Roads Act 1779 (c.118)
Gloucester and Wiltshire Roads Act 1792 (c.153)
Gloucester and Worcester Roads Act 1764 (c.79)
Gloucester and Worcester Roads Act 1794 (c.135)
Gloucester Gaol Act 1781 (c.74)
Gloucester Gaol Act 1785 (c.10)
Gloucester (Poor Relief, etc.) Act 1764 (c.60)
Gloucester Roads Act 1742 (c.21)
Gloucester Roads Act 1742 (c.22)
Gloucester Roads Act 1745 (c.18)
Gloucester Roads Act 1746 (c.23)
Gloucester Roads Act 1751 (c.13)
Gloucester Roads Act 1756 (c.58)
Gloucester Roads Act 1770 (c.74)
Gloucester Roads Act 1778 (c.102)
Gloucester Roads Act 1779 (c.93)
Gloucester Roads Act 1779 (c.115)
Gloucester Roads Act 1780 (c.70)
Gloucester Roads Act 1780 (c.84)
Gloucester Roads Act 1780 (c.93)
Gloucester Roads Act 1783 (c.104)
Gloucester Roads Act 1787 (c.68)
Gloucester Roads Act 1787 (c.78)
Gloucester Roads Act 1792 (c.146)
Gloucester Roads Act 1795 (c.140)
Gloucester Streets Act 1749 (c.15)
Gloucester to Stroud Road Act 1778 (c.98)
Gloucester Water Supply Act 1740 (c.11)
Gloucestershire Highways Act 1722 (c.31)
Gloucestershire Roads Act 1725 (c.24)
Gloucestershire Roads Act 1741 (c.15)
Gloucestershire Roads Act 1756 (c.51)
Gloucestershire Roads Act 1757 (c.54)
Gloucestershire Roads Act 1757 (c.64)

Gloucestershire Roads Act 1757 (c.65)
Gloucestershire Roads Act 1757 (c.70)
Gloucestershire Roads Act 1769 (c.58)
Gloucestershire Roads Act 1774 (c.111)
Gloucestershire Roads Act 1783 (c.106)
Gloucestershire: Small Debts Act 1792 (c.77)
Glove Duties Act 1785 (c.55)
Godmanchester to Cambridge Road Act 1793 (c.156)
Godstone to Highgate Road Act 1766 (c.58)
Gold and Silver (Export Control, etc.) Act 1920 (c.70)
Gold and Silver Thread Act 1702 (c.11)
Gold and Silver Thread Act 1741 (c.20)
Gold and Silver Thread Act 1788 (c.7)
Gold and Silver Wares Act 1844 (c.22)
Gold and Silver Wares Act 1854 (c.96)
Gold Currency Act 1812 (c.5)
Gold Currency Act 1814 (c.52)
Gold Currency and Bank Notes Act 1811 (c.127)
Gold Currency, etc. Act 1812 (c.50)
Gold Plate (Standard) Act 1798 (c.69)
Gold Standard Act 1925 (c.29)
Gold Standard (Amendment) Act 1931 (c.46)
Golden Square (Rates) Act 1750 (c.27)
Goodman's Fields Act 1778 (c.50)
Goods and Services (Price Control) Act 1941 (c.31)
Goods in Neutral Ships Act 1802 (c.80)
Goods Vehicles (Licensing of Operators) Act 1995 (c.23)
Gordon Memorial College at Khartoum Act 1899 (c.16)
Gosport: Improvement Act 1763 (c.56)
Goswell St., Middlesex Act 1780 (c.48)
Government and Other Stocks (Emergency Provisions) Act 1939 (c.100)
Government Annuities Act 1838 (c.49)
Government Annuities Act 1853 (c.45)
Government Annuities Act 1873 (c.44)
Government Annuities Act 1882 (c.51)
Government Annuities Act 1929 (c.29)
Government Annuities (Investments) Act 1864 (c.46)
Government Contractors Act 1815 (c.195)
Government of Burma Act 1935 (c.3)
Government of Burma (Temporary Provisions) Act 1944 (c.30)
Government of India Act 1800 (c.79)
Government of India Act 1833 (c.85)
Government of India Act 1853 (c.95)
Government of India Act 1854 (c.77)
Government of India Act 1858 (c.106)
Government of India Act 1859 (c.41)
Government of India Act 1865 (c.17)
Government of India Act 1869 (c.97)
Government of India Act 1870 (c.3)
Government of India Act 1912 (c.6)
Government of India Act 1915 (c.61)
Government of India Act 1919 (c.101)
Government of India Act 1935 (c.2)
Government of India Act 1935 (c.42)
Government of India (Aden) Act 1929 (c.2)
Government of India Amendment Act 1911 (c.25)
Government of India Amendment Act 1916 (c.37)
Government of India Amendment Act 1933 (c.23)
Government of India (Amendment) Act 1939 (c.66)
Government of India (Civil Services) Act 1925 (c.83)
Government of India (Indian Navy) Act 1927 (c.8)
Government of India (Leave of Absence) Act 1924 (c.28)
Government of India (Reprinting) Act 1935 (c.1)
Government of India (Statutory Commission) Act 1927 (c.24)
Government of Ireland Act 1914 (c.90)
Government of Ireland Act 1920 (c.67)
Government of New South Wales and Van Diemen's Land Act 1866 (c.74)
Government of New Zealand Act 1846 (c.103)
Government of Newfoundland Act 1847 (c.44)
Government of Northern Ireland (Loan Guarantee) Act 1922 (c.24)
Government of Soudan Loan Act 1919 (c.43)
Government of the Soudan Loan Act 1913 (c.10)
Government of the Soudan Loan Act 1914 (c.9)
Government of the Soudan Loan (Amendment) Act 1922 (c.15)
Government of New Zealand Act 1848 (c.5)
Government Offices Security Act 1810 (c.85)
Government Offices Security Act 1836 (c.28)
Government Offices Security Act 1838 (c.61)
Government Offices (Security) Act 1875 (c.64)
Government Trading Act 1990 (c.30)
Government Trading Funds Act 1973 (c.63)
Government War Obligations Act 1914 (c.11)
Government War Obligations Act 1915 (c.96)
Government War Obligations Act 1916 (c.70)
Government War Obligations Act 1918 (c.28)
Government War Obligations Act 1919 (c.44)
Governors, etc., of West Indies Islands Act 1794 (c.35)
Governors' Pension Act 1956 (c.64)
Governors' Pensions Act 1957 (c.62)
Grain Between Great Britain and Ireland Act 1806 (c.97)
Grammar Schools Act 1840 (c.77)
Grand Canal Branches (Ireland) Act 1844 (c.98)
Grand Canal (Ireland) Act 1813 (c.143)
Grand Junction Canal Act 1793 (c.80)
Grand Junction Canal Act 1794 (c.24)
Grand Junction Canal (No. 1) Act 1795 (c.8)
Grand Junction Canal (No. 2) Act 1795 (c.43)

Grand Junction Canal (No. 3) Act 1795 (c.85)
Grand Junction Canal (No. 4) Act 1795 (c.25)
Grand Juries Act 1856 (c.54)
Grand Juries (Ireland) Act 1843 (c.32)
Grand Juries (Suspension) Act 1917 (c.4)
Grand Jury Cess. Act 1846 (c.60)
Grand Jury Cess. Dublin Act 1838 (c.51)
Grand Jury Cess. (Dublin) Act 1851 (c.65)
Grand Jury Cess. (Ireland) Act 1848 (c.26)
Grand Jury Cess. (Ireland) Act 1849 (c.32)
Grand Jury Cess. (Ireland) Act 1850 (c.82)
Grand Jury Cess. (Ireland) Act 1853 (c.13)
Grand Jury Cess. (Ireland) Act 1857 (c.7)
Grand Jury (Ireland) Act 1816 (c.87)
Grand Jury (Ireland) Act 1836 Amendment 1908 (c.29)
Grand Jury (Ireland) Act 1836 (c.116)
Grand Jury (Ireland) Act 1837 (c.2)
Grand Jury (Ireland) Act 1838 (c.37)
Grand Jury (Ireland) Act 1853 (c.136)
Grand Jury (Ireland) Act 1856 (c.63)
Grand Jury (Ireland) Act 1857 (c.15)
Grand Jury (Ireland) Act 1872 (c.42)
Grand Jury (Ireland) Act 1873 (c.34)
Grand Jury (Ireland) Act 1895 (c.8)
Grand Jury Presentments (Ireland) Act 1842 (c.77)
Grand Jury Presentments (Ireland) Act 1843 (c.71)
Grant of Administration (Bonds) Act 1919 (c.26)
Grant of Feu Duties to John Francis Erskine Act 1815 (c.188)
Grant of Frogmore, etc. Act 1807 (c.45)
Grant of Manor of Corsham to Paul Methuen Act 1770 (c.13)
Grant of Military, etc. Commissions Act 1857 (c.4)
Grant to Duke of Marlborough Act 1704 (c.4)
Grant to J. Palmer, Esq. (Post Office Services) Act 1813 (c.157)
Grant to the House of Orange Act 1803 (c.149)
Grantham Canal Act 1793 (c.94)
Grantham Canal Act 1797 (c.30)
Grantham Town Hall Act 1787 (c.61)
Grants for Glebe Houses (I.) Act 1807 (c.23)
Grants of Life Annuities Act 1776 (c.26)
Grants of Officers Act 1812 (c.40)
Grants of Offices in Reversion, etc. Act 1808 (c.50)
Grants of Pensions Act 1811 (c.21)
Grants to George Keith Act 1760 (c.15)
Graves End: Streets Act 1772 (c.15)
Grease Butter from Ireland Act 1763 (c.20)
Great and Little Botton: Improvement Act 1792 (c.71)
Great Farringdon to Burford Road Act 1792 (c.150)
Great Grimsby (Lincoln) Harbour Act 1796 (c.98)
Great Marlow to Stokenchurch Road Act 1791 (c.135)
Great Seal Act 1851 (c.82)
Great Seal Act 1880 (c.10)
Great Seal Act 1884 (c.30)
Great Seal (Offices) Act 1874 (c.81)
Great Sessions in Wales Act 1768 (c.14)
Great Torrington Roads Act 1765 (c.58)
Great Torrington Roads Act 1786 (c.128)
Great Tower Hill: Improvement, etc. Act 1797 (c.87)
Great Yarmouth Haven Act 1749 (c.6)
Great Yarmouth: Improvement Act 1772 (c.14)
Great Yarmouth: Improvement Act 1785 (c.36)
Great Yarmouth Pier Act (c.10)
Greek Loan Act 1864 (c.40)
Greek Loan Act 1898 (c.4)
Greek Loan Guarantee Act 1836 (c.94)
Greek Marriages Act 1884 (c.20)
Greenland and Whale Fishery Act 1771 (c.38)
Greenland, etc., Fishery Act 1782 (c.19)
Greenland Fishery Act 1723 (c.16)
Greenland Fishery Act 1731 (c.78)
Greenland Fishery Act 1804 (c.23)
Greenland Trade Act 1702 (c.10)
Greenland Whale Fisheries Act 1802 (c.22)
Greenland Whale Fisheries Act 1815 (c.39)
Greenland Whale Fisheries, etc. Act (c.20)
Greenland Whale Fishery Act 1803 (c.32)
Greenland Whale Fishery Act 1805 (c.9)
Greenland Whale Fishery Act 1806 (c.9)
Greenland Whale Fishery Act 1810 (c.11)
Greenock Beer Duties Act 1750 (c.38)
Greenock: Improvement Act 1789 (c.43)
Greenock: Water Supply, etc. Act 1772 (c.28)
Greenwich Hospital Act 1728 (c.7)
Greenwich Hospital Act 1744 (c.31)
Greenwich Hospital Act 1751 (c.42)
Greenwich Hospital Act 1776 (c.24)
Greenwich Hospital Act 1806 (c.100)
Greenwich Hospital Act 1807 (c.52)
Greenwich Hospital Act 1814 (c.110)
Greenwich Hospital Act 1815 (c.56)
Greenwich Hospital Act 1829 (c.25)
Greenwich Hospital Act 1850 (c.24)
Greenwich Hospital Act 1865 (c.89)
Greenwich Hospital Act 1869 (c.44)
Greenwich Hospital Act 1870 (c.100)
Greenwich Hospital Act 1872 (c.67)
Greenwich Hospital Act 1883 (c.32)
Greenwich Hospital Act 1885 (c.42)
Greenwich Hospital Act 1898 (c.24)
Greenwich Hospital Act 1921 (c.41)
Greenwich Hospital Act 1942 (c.35)
Greenwich Hospital Act 1947 (c.5)
Greenwich Hospital Act 1967 (c.74)
Greenwich Hospital Act 1990 (c.13)
Greenwich Hospital (Disused Burial Ground) Act 1925 (c.58)
Greenwich Hospital, etc. Act 1711 (c.27)
Greenwich Hospital (Provision for Widows) Act 1863 (c.67)

Greenwich Markets Act 1849 (c.28)
Greenwich Out-Pensioners Act 1763 (c.16)
Grenada and St. Vincent Traders Act (c.11)
Grenada and St. Vincent Traders Act 1800 (c.27)
Grenada and St. Vincent Traders Act 1803 (c.40)
Grenada and St. Vincent Traders Act 1803 (c.104)
Grenada and St. Vincent Traders Act 1808 (c.135)
Gresham College, etc. Act 1768 (c.32)
Grey Seals Protection Act 1914 (c.3)
Grey Seals Protection Act 1931 (c.23)
Grosvenor Square: Paving, etc. Act 1774 (c.52)
Ground Game Act 1880 (c.47)
Ground Game (Amendment) Act 1906 (c.21)
Groundhurst Roads Act 1768 (c.35)
Growth of Coffee Act 1731 (c.24)
Growth of Coffee Act 1745 (c.23)
Growth of Coffee, etc. Act 1750 (c.35)
Growth of Hemp and Flax Act 1781 (c.58)
Growth of Raw Silk Act 1749 (c.20)
Guarantee by Companies Act 1867 (c.108)
Guard Dogs Act 1975 (c.50)
Guardians (Ireland) Act 1849 (c.4)
Guardianship Act 1973 (c.29)
Guardianship and Maintenance of Infants Act 1951 (c.56)
Guardianship of Infants Act 1886 (c.27)
Guardianship of Infants Act 1925 (c.45)
Guardianship of Minors Act 1971 (c.3)
Guardianship (Refugee Children) Act 1944 (c.8)
Guildford and Arundel Road Act 1757 (c.60)
Guildford and Farnham Road Act 1757 (c.78)
Guildford Hospital Act 1861 (c.32)
Guildford Streets Act 1758 (c.58)
Guildford to Farnham Road Act 1780 (c.96)
Gun Barrel Proof Act 1978 (c.9)
Gun Licence Act 1870 (c.57)
Gunpowder Act 1772 (c.61)
Gunpowder Act Amendment Act 1862 (c.98)
Gunpowder and Fireworks Act 1860 (c.139)
Gunpowder and Fireworks Act 1861 (c.130)
Gunpowder in Mersey Act 1851 (c.67)
Gunpowder Mill, Tonbridge Act 1772 (c.13)
Guyana Independence Act 1966 (c.14)
Guyana Republic Act 1970 (c.18)

Habeas Corpus Act 1679 (c.2)
Habeas Corpus Act 1803 (c.140)
Habeas Corpus Act 1804 (c.102)
Habeas Corpus Act 1816 (c.100)
Habeas Corpus Act 1862 (c.20)
Habeas Corpus (Ireland) Act 1868 (c.7)
Habeas Corpus Suspension Act 1707 (c.67)
Habeas Corpus Suspension Act 1715 (c.30)
Habeas Corpus Suspension Act 1722 (c.1)
Habeas Corpus Suspension Act 1743 (c.6)
Habeas Corpus Suspension Act 1745 (c.1)
Habeas Corpus Suspension Act 1745 (c.17)
Habeas Corpus Suspension Act 1746 (c.1)
Habeas Corpus Suspension Act 1776 (c.9)
Habeas Corpus Suspension Act 1778 (c.1)
Habeas Corpus Suspension Act 1779 (c.1)
Habeas Corpus Suspension Act 1780 (c.2)
Habeas Corpus Suspension Act 1782 (c.1)
Habeas Corpus Suspension Act 1794 (c.54)
Habeas Corpus Suspension Act 1795 (c.3)
Habeas Corpus Suspension Act 1797 (c.36)
Habeas Corpus Suspension Act 1799 (c.15)
Habeas Corpus Suspension Act 1799 (c.44)
Habeas Corpus Suspension Act 1800 (c.20)
Habeas Corpus Suspension Act 1800 (c.32)
Habeas Corpus Suspension Act 1801 (c.26)
Habeas Corpus Suspension, etc. Act 1714 (c.8)
Habeas Corpus Suspension (Ireland) Act 1803 (c.8)
Habeas Corpus Suspension (Ireland) Act 1801 (c.15)
Habeas Corpus Suspension (Ireland) Act 1803 (c.116)
Habeas Corpus Suspension (Ireland) Act 1805 (c.4)
Habeas Corpus Suspension (Ireland) Act 1848 (c.35)
Habeas Corpus Suspension (Ireland) Act 1849 (c.2)
Habeas Corpus Suspension (Ireland) Act 1866 (c.1)
Habeas Corpus Suspension (Ireland) Act 1866 (c.119)
Habeas Corpus Suspension (Ireland) Act 1867 (c.1)
Habeas Corpus Suspension (Ireland) Act 1867 (c.25)
Habitual Criminals Act 1869 (c.99)
Habitual Drunkards Act 1879 (c.19)
Hackney Carriages Act 1815 (c.159)
Hackney Carriages, Metropolis Act 1838 (c.79)
Hackney Chairs Act 1712 (c.15)
Hackney Chairs, etc. Act 1759 (c.25)
Hackney Coach Fares Act 1808 (c.87)
Hackney Coaches Act 1771 (c.24)
Hackney Coaches Act 1772 (c.49)
Hackney Coaches Act 1784 (c.27)
Hackney Coaches Act 1786 (c.72)
Hackney Coaches Act 1792 (c.47)
Hackney Coaches Act 1804 (c.88)
Hackney Coaches Act 1814 (c.147)
Hackney Coaches, etc. Act 1715 (c.57)
Hackney Coaches, etc., London Act 1800 (c.47)
Hackney Coaches, Metropolis Act 1802 (c.78)
Hackney Coachmen Act 1771 (c.28)
Hackney (Poor Relief etc.) Act 1764 (c.43)
Haddington County Roads Act 1749 (c.17)
Haddington Roads Act 1769 (c.74)
Haddington Roads Act 1793 (c.163)
Hagley and Birmingham Road Act 1753 (c.47)

Haileybury College Act 1838 (c.22)
Haileybury College Act 1855 (c.52)
Hainault Forest Act 1851 (c.43)
Hainault Forest (Allotment of Commons) Act 1858 (c.37)
Hair Powder Certificates, etc. Act 1795 (c.112)
Hairdressers' and Barbers' Shops (Sunday Closing) Act 1930 (c.35)
Hairdressers (Registration) Act 1964 (c.89)
Half-Pay and Pensions Act 1807 (c.25)
Half Pay of Officers, etc. 1815 (c.131)
Halifax and Sheffield Road Act 1797 (c.160)
Halifax Church Act 1795 Act (c.71)
Halifax to Manchester Canal Act 1794 (c.78)
Halifax to Sheffield Road Act 1777 (c.106)
Halifax to Sheffield Road Act 1793 (c.142)
Halifax: Water Supply Act 1762 (c.40)
Halifax: (Water Supply, etc.) Act 1768 (c.44)
Hallamshire Cutlers Act 1791 (c.58)
Halliwell and Finsbury Drainage Act 1778 (c.66)
Hallmarking Act 1973 (c.43)
Hall-marking of Foreign Plate Act 1904 (c.6)
Hall-marking of Foreign Plate Act 1939 (c.36)
Hamilton Bridge Act 1770 (c.93)
Hampshire and Berkshire Roads Act 1766 (c.86)
Hampshire and Dorset Roads Act 1762 (c.57)
Hampshire and Dorset Roads Act 1780 (c.92)
Hampshire and Wiltshire Fisheries Act 1797 (c.95)
Hampshire and Wiltshire Roads Act 1774 (c.104)
Hampshire, Kent, Sussex—Fortifications Act 1762 (c.37)
Hampshire, Kent, Sussex—Fortifications Act 1763 (c.35)
Hampshire Roads Act 1741 (c.14)
Hampshire Roads Act 1757 (c.73)
Hampshire Roads Act 1757 (c.74)
Hampshire Roads Act 1765 (c.95)
Hampstead Roads Act 1753 (c.80)
Hampstead: Streets Act 1775 (c.58)
Hampton Court Bridge Act 1749 (c.37)
Hampton to Staines Road Act 1773 (c.105)
Hampton to Staines Road Act 1793 (c.135)
Hanbury Church Act 1793 (c.45)
Hanley Chapel, Stafford Act 1787 (c.62)
Hans Town, Chelsea: Improvement Act 1790 (c.76)
Happing and Tunstead, Norfolk: Poor Relief Act 1785 (c.27)
Harbour Loans Act 1866 (c.30)
Harbour of Colombo Loan Act 1874 (c.24)
Harbour of Galle Loan Act 1869 (c.105)
Harbour of Howth Act 1805 (c.113)
Harbour of Leith Act 1800 (c.57)
Harbour of Leith Act 1805 (c.114)
Harbour Transfer Act 1865 (c.100)
Harbours Act 1745 (c.22)
Harbours Act 1814 (c.159)
Harbours Act 1964 (c.40)
Harbours (Amendment) Act 1970 (c.53)
Harbours and Passing Tolls etc. Act 1861 (c.47)
Harbours Development (Scotland) Act 1972 (c.64)
Harbours, Docks and Piers Clauses Act 1847 (c.27)
Harbours, Docks and Piers (Temporary Increase of Charges) Act 1922 (c.23)
Harbours (Ireland) Act 1805 (c.64)
Harbours (Loans) Act 1972 (c.16)
Harbours, Piers and Ferries (Scotland) Act 1937 (c.28)
Harbours, Piers and Ferries (Scotland) Act 1953 (c.11)
Harbours, Piers and Ferries (Scotland) Act 1972 (c.29)
Harbours (Scotland) Act 1982 (c.17)
Harbours Transfer Act 1862 (c.69)
Hardington and Old Stratford Road Act 1768 (c.52)
Hares Act 1848 (c.29)
Hares Preservation Act 1892 (c.8)
Hares Preservation (Ireland) Act 1879 (c.23)
Hares (Scotland) Act 1848 (c.30)
Harrogate to Ripon Road Act 1794 (c.121)
Hartlepool Pilotage Order Confirmation Act 1864 (c.58)
Hartley's Patent (Fire Prevention) Act 1776 (c.6)
Hartsmere, etc., Suffolk: Poor Relief Act 1779 (c.13)
Harvey's Charity, Folkestone Act 1858 (c.29)
Harwich, etc., Election Act 1842 (c.31)
Harwich Harbour Act 1863 (c.71)
Harwich Harbour Act 1864 (c.102)
Harwich Harbour Act 1865 (c.120)
Hastings: Improvement Act 1789 (c.27)
Hat Duties Act 1803 (c.22)
Hat Duties, etc. Act 1784 (c.51)
Hat Manufacture Act 1731 (c.22)
Hat Manufacture Act 1784 (c.21)
Hatfield Chase Act 1783 (c.13)
Hatfield Chase: Drainage Act 1787 (c.53)
Hawford–Droitwich Canal Act 1768 (c.37)
Hawkers Act 1717 (c.6)
Hawkers Act 1785 (c.78)
Hawkers Act 1810 (c.41)
Hawkers Act 1812 (c.108)
Hawkers Act 1888 (c.33)
Hawkers and Pedlars Act 1795 (c.91)
Hawkers (Scotland) Act 1815 (c.71)
Hay and Straw Act 1796 (c.88)
Hay and Straw Act 1856 (c.114)
Hay Bridge Over Wye Act 1756 (c.73)
Haydon, Chapel, Northumberland Act 1795 (c.47)
Heage to Duffield Road Act 1793 (c.177)
Health and Medicines Act 1988 (c.49)
Health and Safety at Work etc. Act 1974 (c.37)
Health and Social Security Act 1984 (c.48)
Health and Social Services and Social Security Adjudications Act 1983 (c.41)

Health Authorities Act 1995 (c.17)
Health of Prisoners Act 1774 (c.59)
Health Resorts and Watering Places Act 1921 (c.27)
Health Resorts and Watering Places Act 1936 (c.48)
Health Resorts, etc. (Ireland) Act 1909 (c.32)
Health Service Commissioners Act 1993 (c.46)
Health Service Commissioners (Amendment) Act 1996 (c.5)
Health Service Joint Consultative Committees (Access to Information) Act 1986 (c.24)
Health Services Act 1976 (c.83)
Health Services Act 1980 (c.53)
Health Services and Public Health Act 1968 (c.46)
Health Visiting and Social Work (Training) Act 1962 (c.33)
Hearing Aid Council Act 1968 (c.50)
Hearing Aid Council (Amendment) Act 1989 (c.12)
Hearing Aid Council (Extension) Act 1975 (c.39)
Heather Burning (Scotland) Act 1926 (c.30)
Heating Appliances (Fireguards) Act 1952 (c.42)
Heavy Commercial Vehicles (Controls and Regulations) Act 1973 (c.44)
Hedon Haven Act 1774 (c.106)
Heir Apparent's Establishment Act 1795 (c.125)
Hemingbrough to Market Weighton Road Act 1793 (c.159)
Hemlingford Riots Act 1793 (c.39)
Hemp and Flax Act 1770 (c.40)
Hemp and Flax Act 1786 (c.43)
Henley Grammar School Act 1778 (c.41)
Henley Improvement Act 1795 (c.79)
Henley to Oxford Road Act 1781 (c.97)
Henley-upon-Thames Bridge Act 1780 (c.33)
Hereditary Revenues Act 1856 (c.43)
Hereford and Bedford Roads Act 1769 (c.64)
Hereford and Gloucester Roads Act 1764 (c.62)
Hereford and Gloucester Roads Act 1789 (c.104)
Hereford and Salop Roads Act 1758 (c.66)
Hereford and Worcester Roads Act 1782 (c.100)
Hereford Cathedral Act 1792 (c.87)
Hereford (City) Roads Act 1730 (c.18)
Hereford, Radnor and Salop Roads Act 1778 (c.111)
Hereford Roads Act 1748 (c.15)
Hereford Roads Act 1748 (c.18)
Hereford Roads Act 1748 (c.26)
Hereford Roads Act 1751 (c.56)
Hereford Roads Act 1756 (c.65)
Hereford Roads Act 1770 (c.91)
Hereford Roads Act 1773 (c.95)
Hereford Roads Act 1773 (c.96)
Hereford Roads Act 1767 (c.67)
Hereford Roads Act 1769 (c.90)
Hereford Roads Act 1781 (c.105)
Hereford Roads Act 1782 (c.108)
Hereford Roads Act 1782 (c.112)
Hereford Roads Act 1784 (c.69)
Hereford Roads Act 1789 (c.108)
Hereford Roads Act 1791 (c.114)
Hereford Roads Act 1791 (c.130)
Hereford Roads Act 1794 (c.119)
Hereford Roads, etc. Act 1759 (c.58)
Hereford Streets Act 1774 (c.38)
Herefordshire and Gloucestershire Canal Act 1791 (c.89)
Herefordshire Roads Act 1740 (c.13)
Herefordshire Roads Act 1741 (c.17)
Heritable Jurisdictions (Scotland) Act 1746 (c.43)
Heritable Securities (Scotland) Act 1845 (c.31)
Heritable Securities (Scotland) Act 1847 (c.50)
Heritable Securities (Scotland) Act 1854 (c.62)
Heritable Securities (Scotland) Act 1860 (c.80)
Heritable Securities (Scotland) Act 1894 (c.44)
Herring Fisheries (Scotland) Act 1858 (c.69)
Herring Fisheries (Scotland) Act 1860 (c.92)
Herring Fisheries (Scotland) Act 1865 (c.22)
Herring Fisheries (Scotland) Act 1867 (c.52)
Herring Fishery Act 1749 (c.24)
Herring Fishery Act 1753 (c.9)
Herring Fishery Act 1755 (c.14)
Herring Fishery Act 1757 (c.30)
Herring Fishery Act 1765 (c.22)
Herring Fishery Act 1772 (c.58)
Herring Fishery Act 1851 (c.26)
Herring Fishery Barrels Act 1874 (c.25)
Herring Fishery (Scotland) Act 1808 (c.110)
Herring Fishery (Scotland) Act 1815 (c.94)
Herring Fishery (Scotland) Act 1889 (c.23)
Herring Fishery (Scotland) Act Amendment 1890 (c.10)
Herring Fishing (Branding) Act 1913 (c.9)
Herring Industry Act 1935 (c.9)
Herring Industry Act 1938 (c.42)
Herring Industry Act 1944 (c.32)
Hertford and Bedford Roads Act 1757 (c.43)
Hertford and Bedford Roads Act 1769 (c.87)
Hertford and Bedford Roads Act 1790 (c.115)
Hertford and Broadwater Road Act 1757 (c.45)
Hertford and Bucks. Roads Act 1762 (c.63)
Hertford and Cambridge Roads Act 1769 (c.86)
Hertford and Middlesex Roads Act 1791 (c.108)
Hertford and Ware Roads Act 1732 (c.15)
Hertford and Ware Roads Act 1753 (c.56)
Hertford Church Act 1765 (c.94)
Hertford College Act 1874 (c.55)

Hertford Highways Act 1721 (c.9)
Hertford: Improvement Act 1788 (c.75)
Hertford Prison Act 1775 (c.25)
Hertford Roads Act 1762 (c.48)
Hertford Roads Act 1771 (c.57)
Hertford Roads Act 1778 (c.90)
Hertford Roads Act 1778 (c.94)
Hertford Roads Act 1782 (c.91)
Hertford Roads Act 1783 (c.25)
Hertford Shire-House Act 1768 (c.58)
Hertfordshire and Gloucestershire Canal Act 1793 (c.119)
Hertfordshire and Huntingdonshire Highways Act 1713 (c.33)
Hertfordshire and Huntingdonshire Roads Act 1765 (c.77)
Hertfordshire and Huntingdonshire Roads Act 1790 (c.89)
Hertfordshire and Middlesex Roads Act 1770 (c.107)
Hertfordshire Highways Act 1706 (c.14)
Hertfordshire Highways Act 1710 (c.14)
Hertfordshire Highways Act 1719 (c.20)
Hertfordshire Roads Act 1724 (c.11)
Hertfordshire Roads Act 1725 (c.10)
Hertfordshire Roads Act 1726 (c.32)
Hertfordshire Roads Act 1731 (c.10)
Hertfordshire Roads Act 1732 (c.24)
Hertfordshire Roads Act 1742 (c.16)
Hertfordshire Roads Act 1763 (c.26)
Hexham Bridge Act 1778 (c.44)
Hexham: Inclosure Act 1792 (c.110)
Hexham to Alston Road Act 1778 (c.116)
Hides and Skins Act 1769 (c.39)
High Constables Act 1869 (c.47)
High Court and County Court (Judges) Act 1950 (c.4)
High Court of Admiralty Act 1859 (c.6)
High Court of Admiralty (E.) Act 1840 (c.66)
High Court of Justiciary (Scotland) Act 1892 (c.21)
High Highlands Act 1823 (c.79)
High Peak Mining Customs and Mineral Courts. Act 1851 (c.94)
Highgate and Chipping Barnet Road Act 1720 (c.18)
Highgate and Chipping Barnet Road Act 1763 (c.37)
Highgate and Hampstead Highways Act 1721 (c.5)
Highgate and Hampstead Roads Act 1734 (c.28)
Highgate and Hampstead Roads Act 1756 (c.88)
Highgate and Hampstead Roads Act 1776 (c.76)
Highgate and Hampstead Roads Act 1780 (c.78)
Highgate: Streets Act 1775 (c.43)
Highland Road and Bridges (Scotland) Act (c.43)
Highland Roads and Bridges Act 1851 (c.66)
Highland Roads and Bridges Act 1862 (c.105)
Highland Schools Act 1838 (c.87)
Highland Schools Act 1873 (c.53)
Highland Services Act 1715 (c.54)
Highlands and Islands Air Services (Scotland) Act 1980 (c.19)
Highlands and Islands Development (Scotland) Act 1965 (c.46)
Highlands and Islands Development (Scotland) Act 1968 (c.51)
Highlands and Islands (Medical Service) Additional Grant Act 1929 (c.13)
Highlands and Islands (Medical Service) Grant Act 1913 (c.26)
Highlands and Islands Shipping Services Act 1960 (c.31)
Highland Roads and Bridges Act 1862 (c.105)
Highland Services Act 1715 (c.54)
Highway Accounts Returns Act 1879 (c.39)
Highway Act 1794 (c.64)
Highway Act 1835 (c.50)
Highway Act 1841 (c.51)
Highway Act 1845 (c.71)
Highway Act 1863 (c.61)
Highway Act 1864 (c.101)
Highway Act Amendment 1885 (c.13)
Highway (Railway Crossing) Act 1839 (c.45)
Highway Rate Assessment and Expenditure Act 1882 (c.27)
Highway Rates Act 1836 (c.63)
Highway Rates Act 1839 (c.81)
Highway Rates Act 1840 (c.98)
Highway Rates Act 1843 (c.59)
Highway Rates Act 1845 (c.59)
Highway Rates Act 1846 (c.49)
Highway Rates Act 1847 (c.93)
Highway Rates Act 1848 (c.66)
Highway Rates Act 1849 (c.54)
Highway Rates Act 1850 (c.58)
Highway Rates Act 1851 (c.30)
Highway Rates Act 1852 (c.19)
Highway Rates Act 1853 (c.66)
Highway Rates Act 1854 (c.52)
Highway Rates Act 1860 (c.67)
Highway (Scotland) Act 1718 (c.30)
Highway (Scotland) Act 1771 (c.53)
Highway (Scotland) Act 1803 (c.80)
Highways Act 1707 (c.56)
Highways Act 1710 (c.23)
Highways Act 1714 (c.11)
Highways Act 1715 (c.52)
Highways Act 1718 (c.12)
Highways Act 1733 (c.9)
Highways Act 1742 (c.29)
Highways Act 1749 (c.28)
Highways Act 1750 (c.43)
Highways Act 1753 (c.28)
Highways Act 1765 (c.38)
Highways Act 1766 (c.42)
Highways Act 1766 (c.43)
Highways Act 1768 (c.5)
Highways Act 1773 (c.78)
Highways Act 1794 (c.74)

Highways Act 1839 (c.40)
Highways Act 1854 (c.69)
Highways Act 1862 (c.61)
Highways Act 1959 (c.25)
Highways Act 1971 (c.41)
Highways Act 1980 (c.66)
Highways (Amendment) Act 1965 (c.30)
Highways (Amendment) Act 1986 (c.13)
Highways and Bridges Act 1891 (c.63)
Highways and Locomotives (Amendment) Act 1878 (c.77)
Highways and Turnpike Roads Act 1753 (c.30)
Highways and Turnpike Roads Act 1755 (c.17)
Highways and Turnpike Roads Act 1757 (cc.27, 28)
Highways (England) Act 1814 (c.109)
Highways, etc. (England) Act 1815 (c.68)
Highways, etc. (Scotland) Act 1845 (c.41)
Highways (Ireland) Act 1805 (c.43)
Highways (Ireland) Act 1805 (c.96)
Highways (Ireland) Act 1806 (c.134)
Highways (Ireland) Act 1809 (c.84)
Highways (Ireland) Act 1810 (c.29)
Highways (Ireland) Act 1811 (c.40)
Highways (Ireland) Act 1811 (c.92)
Highways (Ireland) Act 1813 (c.76)
Highways (Ireland) Act 1813 (c.146)
Highways (Ireland) Act 1814 (c.135)
Highways (Isle of Wight) Act 1881 (c.72)
Highways (Miscellaneous Provisions) Act 1961 (c.63)
Highways, Old Stratford to Dunchurch Act 1757 (c.77)
Highways (Provision of Cattle Grids) Act 1950 (c.24)
Highways Returns Act 1849 (c.35)
Highways, South Wales Act 1851 (c.16)
Highways, South Wales Act 1854 (c.7)
Highworth, Wiltshire (Workhouse and Additional Overseer) Act 1789 (c.29)
Hijacking Act 1971 (c.70)
Hill Farming Act 1946 (c.73)
Hill Farming Act 1954 (c.23)
Hill Farming Act 1956 (c.72)
Hill Farming Act 1985 (c.32)
Hill to Lyde Way Road Act 1782 (c.109)
Hinckley and Coventry Road Act 1756 (c.66)
Hinckley and Coventry Road Act 1762 (c.69)
Hinckley to Melbourne Common Road Act 1774 (c.110)
Hire-Purchase Act 1938 (c.53)
Hire-Purchase Act 1954 (c.51)
Hire-Purchase Act 1964 (c.53)
Hire-Purchase Act 1965 (c.66)
Hire-Purchase (Scotland) Act 1965 (c.67)
Historic Buildings and Ancient Monuments Act 1953 (c.49)
Hockliffe to Stony Stratford Road Act 1786 (c.143)
Holborn: Improvement Act 1766 (c.100)
Holborn: Poor Relief Act 1770 (c.79)
Holborn: Poor Relief Act 1770 (c.80)
Holderness: Drainage Act 1774 (c.107)
Holderness to Beverley Road Act 1782 (c.90)
Holdings of County Courts Act 1732 (c.23)
Holidays Extension Act 1875 (c.13)
Holidays With Pay Act 1938 (c.70)
Holloway Prison Act 1852 (c.70)
Holy Island: Inclosure Act 1791 (c.92)
Holy Trinity Church, Bristol Act 1785 (c.95)
Holyhead Banks (Ireland) Act 1850 (c.111)
Holyhead Harbour Act 1810 (c.93)
Holyhead Harbour Act 1816 (c.84)
Holyhead Harbour Act 1847 (c.76)
Holyhead Harbour Railway Act 1859 (c.60)
Holyhead Harbours Act 1854 (c.44)
Holyhead Old Harbour Road Act 1874 (c.30)
Holyhead Road Act 1861 (c.28)
Holyhead Roads Act 1775 (c.69)
Holyhead Roads Act 1815 (c.152)
Holyhead Roads Act 1840 (c.104)
Home Counties (Music and Dancing) Licensing Act 1926 (c.31)
Home Energy Conservation Act 1995 (c.10)
Home Guard Act 1951 (c.8)
Home Purchase Assistance and Housing Corporation Guarantee Act 1978 (c.27)
Home Safety Act 1961 (c.20)
Homes Insulation Act 1978 (c.48)
Homicide Act 1957 (c.11)
Honiton: Improvement Act 1790 (c.25)
Honorary Freedom of Boroughs Act 1885 (c.29)
Honourable Lady Hylton-Foster's Annuity Act 1965 (c.70)
Hong Kong Act 1985 (c.15)
Hong Kong Economic and Trade Office Act 1996 (c.63)
Hong Kong (Overseas Public Servants) Act 1996 (c.2)
Hong Kong (War Wives and Widows) Act 1996 (c.41)
Hop (Prevention of Frauds) Act 1866 (c.37)
Hop Trade Act 1800 (c.81)
Hop Trade Act 1814 (c.123)
Hops Act 1774 (c.68)
Hops Act 1808 (c.134)
Hops Marketing Act 1982 (c.5)
Horse Breeding Act 1918 (c.13)
Horse Breeding Act 1958 (c.43)
Horse Duty Act 1811 (c.76)
Horse Patrol, Metropolis Act 1836 (c.50)
Horse Racing Act 1840 (c.5)
Horserace Betting Levy Act 1969 (c.14)
Horserace Betting Levy Act 1981 (c.30)
Horserace Totalisator and Betting Levy Boards Act 1972 (c.69)
Horses (Protective Headgear for Young Riders) Act 1990 (c.25)
Horsham Roads Act 1792 (c.115)
Horsleytown Parish Act 1732 (c.11)
Horticultural Produce Act 1986 (c.20)
Horticultural Products (Emergency Customs Duties) Act 1931 (c.3)

Horticultural Produce (Sales on Commission) Act 1926 (c.39)
Horticulture Act 1960 (c.22)
Horticulture (Special Payments) Act 1974 (c.5)
Hosiery Act 1845 (c.77)
Hosiery Manufacture (Wages) Act 1874 (c.48)
Hospital Complaints Procedure Act 1985 (c.42)
Hospital Endowments (Scotland) Act 1953 (c.41)
Hospital Endowments (Scotland) Act 1971 (c.8)
Hospitals and Infirmaries (Ireland) Act 1806 (c.95)
Hospitals (Ireland) Act 1807 (c.44)
Hospitals (Ireland) Act 1809 (c.36)
Hospitals (Ireland) Act 1814 (c.112)
Hotel Proprietors Act 1956 (c.62)
Hours of Employment (Conventions) Act 1936 (c.22)
House and Window Duties Act 1766 (c.38)
House Duties Act (c.105)
House Duty Act 1778 (c.26)
House Duty (Ireland) Act 1814 (c.132)
House Letting and Rating (Scotland) Act 1911 (c.53)
House Letting and Rating (Scotland) Act 1920 (c.8)
House Occupiers Disqualification Removal Act 1878 (c.3)
House Occupiers Disqualification Removal (Scotland) Act 1878 (c.5)
House Occupiers in Counties Disqualification Removal (Scotland) Act 1880 (c.6)
House of Commons Act 1800 (c.92)
House of Commons Act 1855 (c.10)
House of Commons Act 1859 (c.5)
House of Commons (Administration) Act 1978 (c.36)
House of Commons (Clergy Disqualification) Act 1801 (c.63)
House of Commons (Commissions in H.M.'s Forces) Act 1914 (c.3)
House of Commons Cost Taxation Act 1847 (c.69)
House of Commons Costs Taxation Act 1879 (c.17)
House of Commons Disqualification Act 1741 (c.22)
House of Commons (Disqualification) Act 1782 (c.45)
House of Commons Disqualification Act 1957 (c.20)
House of Commons Disqualification Act 1975 (c.24)
House of Commons Disqualification (Declaration of Law) Act 1931 (c.13)
House of Commons Disqualification (Declaration of Law) Act 1935 (c.38)
House of Commons Disqualification (Temporary Provisions) Act 1941 (c.8)
House of Commons Disqualifications (Temporary Provisions) Act 1943 (c.10)
House of Commons Disqualification (Temporary Provisions) Act 1944 (c.11)
House of Commons (Disqualifications) Act 1801 (c.52)
House of Commons (Disqualifications) Act 1813 (c.16)
House of Commons (Electors) Act 1786 (c.100)
House of Commons (Indemnification of Certain Members) Act 1949 (c.46)
House of Commons Members' Fund Act 1939 (c.49)
House of Commons Members' Fund Act 1948 (c.36)
House of Commons Members' Fund Act 1957 (c.24)
House of Commons Members' Fund Act 1960 (c.50)
House of Commons Members' Fund Act 1962 (c.53)
House of Commons Members' Fund and Parliamentary Pensions Act 1981 (c.7)
House of Commons Officers Act 1834 (c.70)
House of Commons (Offices) Act 1812 (c.11)
House of Commons Offices Act 1846 (c.77)
House of Commons Offices Act 1849 (c.72)
House of Commons Offices Act 1856 (c.1)
House of Commons Qualification Act 1838 (c.48)
House of Commons (Redistribution of Seats) Act 1944 (c.41)
House of Commons (Redistribution of Seats) Act 1947 (c.10)
House of Commons (Redistribution of Seats) Act 1949 (c.66)
House of Commons (Redistribution of Seats) Act 1958 (c.26)
House of Commons (Redistribution of Seats) Act 1979 (c.15)
House of Commons (Service in His Majesty's Forces) Act 1939 (c.85)
House of Commons (Speaker) Act 1832 (c.105)
House of Correction Act (1852) (c.70)
House of Lords Costs Taxation Act 1849 (c.78)
House of Lords Oath Act 1843 (c.6)
House Purchase and Housing Act 1959 (c.33)
House Purchase Assistance and Housing Corporation Guarantee Act 1978 (c.27)
House Tax Act 1803 (c.161)
House Tax Act 1808 (c.55)
House Tax Act 1851 (c.36)
House Tax Act 1871 (c.103)
House to House Collections Act 1939 (c.44)
Houses of Correction Act 1782 (c.64)
Houses of Correction Act 1784 (c.55)
Houses of Industry, etc. (I.) Act 1841 (c.41)
Houses of Parliament Act 1806 (c.89)
Houses of Parliament Act 1810 (c.119)

Houses of Parliament Act 1837 (c.7)
Houses of Parliament Act 1867 (c.40)
Housing Act 1914 (c.31)
Housing Act 1921 (c.19)
Housing Act 1925 (c.14)
Housing Act 1930 (c.39)
Housing Act 1935 (c.40)
Housing Act 1936 (c.51)
Housing Act 1949 (c.60)
Housing Act 1952 (c.53)
Housing Act 1957 (c.56)
Housing Act 1961 (c.65)
Housing Act 1964 (c.56)
Housing Act 1969 (c.33)
Housing Act 1971 (c.76)
Housing Act 1974 (c.44)
Housing Act 1980 (c.51)
Housing Act 1985 (c.68)
Housing Act 1988 (c.50)
Housing Act 1996 (c.52)
Housing (Agricultural Population) (Scotland) Act 1938 (c.38)
Housing (Agricultural Population) (Scotland) Act 1943 (c.22)
Housing (Amendment) Act 1973 (c.5)
Housing (Amendment) (Scotland) Act 1965 (c.40)
Housing (Amendment) (Scotland) Act 1970 (c.5)
Housing (Amendment) (Scotland) Act 1976 (c.11)
Housing (Amendment) (Scotland) Act 1981 (c.72)
Housing and Building Control Act 1984 (c.29)
Housing and Planning Act 1986 (c.63)
Housing and Town and Development (Scotland) Act 1957 (c.38)
Housing Associations Act 1985 (c.69)
Housing (Consequential Provisions) Act 1985 (c.71)
Housing Defects Act 1984 (c.50)
Housing (Emergency Powers) Act 1939 (c.73)
Housing, etc. Act 1923 (c.24)
Housing Finance Act 1972 (c.47)
Housing Finance (Special Provisions) Act 1975 (c.67)
Housing (Financial and Miscellaneous Provisions) Act 1946 (c.48)
Housing (Financial Provisions) Act 1924 (c.35)
Housing (Financial Provisions) Act 1933 (c.15)
Housing (Financial Provisions) Act 1938 (c.16)
Housing (Financial Provisions) Act 1958 (c.42)
Housing (Financial Provisions) (Scotland) Act 1933 (c.16)
Housing (Financial Provisions) (Scotland) Act 1946 (c.54)
Housing (Financial Provisions) (Scotland) Act 1967 (c.20)
Housing (Financial Provisions) (Scotland) Act 1968 (c.31)
Housing (Financial Provisions) (Scotland) Act 1972 (c.46)
Housing (Financial Provisions) (Scotland) Act 1978 (c.14)
Housing Grants, Construction and Regeneration Act 1996 (c.53)
Housing (Homeless Persons) Act 1977 (c.48)
Housing (Ireland) Act 1919 (c.45)
Housing (No. 2) Act 1914 (c.52)
Housing (No. 2) (Amendment) Act 1914 (c.71)
Housing of the Working Classes Act 1885 (c.72)
Housing of the Working Classes Act 1890 (c.70)
Housing of the Working Classes Act, 1890, Amendment (Scotland) 1892 (c.22)
Housing of the Working Classes Act, 1890, Amendment (Scotland) 1896 (c.31)
Housing of the Working Classes Act 1894 (c.55)
Housing of the Working Classes Act 1900 (c.59)
Housing of the Working Classes Act 1903 (c.39)
Housing of the Working Classes Act 1908 (c.61)
Housing of the Working Classes (Ireland) Act 1893 (c.33)
Housing of the Working Classes (Ireland) Act 1896 (c.11)
Housing of the Working Classes (Ireland) Act 1908 (c.61)
Housing Rents and Subsidies Act 1975 (c.6)
Housing Rents and Subsidies (Scotland) Act 1975 (c.28)
Housing Repairs and Rents Act 1954 (c.53)
Housing (Repairs and Rents) (Scotland) Act 1954 (c.50)
Housing (Revision of Contributions) Act 1929 (c.6)
Housing (Rosyth Dockyard) Act 1915 (c.49)
Housing (Rural Authorities) Act 1931 (c.39)
Housing (Rural Workers) Act 1926 (c.56)
Housing (Rural Workers) Act 1942 (c.32)
Housing (Rural Workers) Amendment Act 1931 (c.22)
Housing (Rural Workers) Amendment Act 1938 (c.35)
Housing (Scotland) Act 1920 (c.71)
Housing (Scotland) Act 1921 (c.33)
Housing (Scotland) Act 1925 (c.15)
Housing (Scotland) Act 1930 (c.40)
Housing (Scotland) Act 1935 (c.41)
Housing (Scotland) Act 1944 (c.39)
Housing (Scotland) Act 1949 (c.61)
Housing (Scotland) Act 1950 (c.34)
Housing (Scotland) Act 1952 (c.63)
Housing (Scotland) Act 1962 (c.28)
Housing (Scotland) Act 1966 (c.49)
Housing (Scotland) Act 1969 (c.34)

Housing (Scotland) Act 1974 (c.45)
Housing (Scotland) Act 1986 (c.65)
Housing (Scotland) Act 1987 (c.26)
Housing (Scotland) Act 1988 (c.43)
Housing (Slum Clearance Compensation) Act 1965 (c.81)
Housing Subsidies Act 1956 (c.33)
Housing Subsidies Act 1967 (c.29)
Housing (Temporary Accommodation) Act 1944 (c.36)
Housing (Temporary Accommodation) Act 1945 (c.39)
Housing (Temporary Accommodation) Act 1947 (c.6)
Housing (Temporary Provisions) Act 1944 (c.33)
Housing, Town Planning etc. Act 1919 (c.35)
Housing, Town Planning, etc. Act 1909 (c.44)
Housing, Town Planning, etc. (Scotland) Act 1919 (c.60)
Housing (Underground Rooms) Act 1959 (c.34)
Hovercraft Act 1968 (c.59)
Howth Harbour Act 1810 (c.72)
Howth Harbour Act 1863 (c.72)
Hubberston and Pill, Pembroke: Docks and Piers Act 1790 (c.55)
Huddersfield Burial Ground Act 1852 (c.41)
Huddersfield Burial Ground Act 1855 (c.89)
Huddersfield Roads Act 1788 (c.103)
Huddersfield to Ashton-under-Lyne Canal Act 1794 (c.53)
Hudson's Bay Company Act 1868 (c.105)
Hue and Cry Act 1734 (c.16)
Hue and Cry Act 1748 (c.24)
Hull: Drainage Act 1792 (c.109)
Hull: Improvement Act 1795 (c.46)
Hull, Poor Relief Act 1741 (c.10)
Hulmes Chapel and Chelpord Road Act 1797 (c.157)
Human Fertilisation and Embryology Act 1990 (c.37)
Human Fertilisation and Embryology (Disclosure of Information) Act 1992 (c.54)
Human Organ Transplants Act 1989 (c.31)
Human Tissue Act 1961 (c.54)
Humber Bridge (Debts) Act 1996 (c.1)
Hundred Foot River and Ouse: Bedford Level Act 1756 (c.22)
Hungerford to Leckford Road Act 1793 (c.168)
Huntingdon Clergy Charity Act 1775 (c.24)
Huntingdon: Drainage Act 1772 (c.39)
Huntingdon: Improvement Act 1785 (c.9)
Huntingdon Roads Act 1755 (c.26)
Huntingdon Roads Act 1765 (c.51)
Huntingdonshire and Cambridgeshire Roads Act 1744 (c.23)
Huntingdonshire and Northamptonshire Roads Act 1750 (c.59)
Huntingdonshire and Northamptonshire Roads Act 1771 (c.80)
Huntingdonshire Roads Act 1727 (c.4)
Huntingdonshire Roads Act 1757 (c.51)
Huntingdonshire Roads Act 1774 (c.118)
Huntingdonshire Roads Act 1779 (c.86)
Huntingdonshire Roads Act 1790 (c.103)
Hyde Park Act 1842 (c.19)
Hyde Park (Underground Parking) Act 1961 (c.26)
Hydrocarbon Oil (Customs and Excise) Act 1971 (c.12)
Hydrocarbon Oil Duties Act 1979 (c.5)
Hydrocarbon Oil Duties (Temporary Increase) Act 1956 (c.2)
Hydro-Electric Development (Scotland) Act 1943 (c.32)
Hydro-Electric Undertaking (Valuation for Rating) (Scotland) Act 1944 (c.34)
Hydro-Electricity Development (Scotland) Act 1952 (c.22)
Hydrogen Cyanide (Fumigation) Act 1937 (c.45)
Hypnotism Act 1952 (c.46)
Hypothec Abolition (Scotland) Act 1880 (c.12)
Hypothec Amendment (Scotland) Act 1867 (c.42)

Idiots Act 1886 (c.25)
Ilfracombe Harbour Act 1730 (c.19)
Illegal Trawling (Scotland) Act 1934 (c.18)
Illegitimate Children (Scotland) Act 1930 (c.33)
Illicit Distillation (Ireland) Act 1813 (c.32)
Illicit Distillation (Ireland) Act 1831 (c.55)
Illicit Distillation (Ireland) Act 1857 (c.40)
Immature Spirits (Restriction) Act 1915 (c.46)
Immigration Act 1971 (c.77)
Immigration Act 1988 (c.14)
Immigration Appeals Act 1969 (c.21)
Immigration (Carriers' Liability) Act 1987 (c.24)
Immoral Traffic (Scotland) Act 1902 (c.11)
Imperial Defence Act 1888 (c.32)
Imperial Institute (Management) Act 1916 (c.8)
Imperial Telegraphs Act 1929 (c.7)
Imperial Telegraphs Act 1938 (c.57)
Imperial War Graves Endowment Fund Act 1926 (c.14)
Imperial War Museum Act 1920 (c.16)
Imperial War Museum Act 1955 (c.14)
Import and Export Control Act 1990 (c.45)
Import and Export Duties Act 1802 (c.117)
Import Duties Act 1931 (c.8)
Import Duties Act 1958 (c.6)
Import Duties (Emergency Provisions) Act 1939 (c.97)
Import Duty Act 1804 (c.85)
Import, Export and Customs Powers (Defence) Act 1939 (c.69)
Import of Live Fish (England and Wales) Act 1980 (c.27)
Import of Live Fish (Scotland) Act 1978 (c.35)

Importation Act 1702 (c.8)
Importation Act 1702 (cc. 21, 22)
Importation Act 1703 (c.15)
Importation Act 1704 (c.9)
Importation Act 1706 (c.19)
Importation Act 1707 (c.60)
Importation Act 1711 (c.36)
Importation Act 1712 (c.9)
Importation Act 1714 (c.15)
Importation Act 1715 (c.40)
Importation Act 1719 (c.14)
Importation Act 1721 (c.12)
Importation Act 1726 (c.5)
Importation Act 1726 (c.25)
Importation Act 1728 (c.9)
Importation Act 1730 (c.12)
Importation Act 1730 (c.15)
Importation Act 1731 (c.9)
Importation Act 1732 (c.7)
Importation Act 1738 (c.36)
Importation Act 1740 (c.36)
Importation Act 1743 (c.36)
Importation Act 1753 (c.8)
Importation Act 1755 (c.21)
Importation Act 1757 (c.3)
Importation Act 1763 (c.6)
Importation Act 1763 (c.28)
Importation Act 1765 (c.1)
Importation Act 1765 (c.3)
Importation Act 1765 (c.10)
Importation Act 1765 (c.48)
Importation Act 1766 (cc.11, 12)
Importation Act 1766 (c.13)
Importation Act 1766 (c.19)
Importation Act 1766 (c.22)
Importation Act 1766 (c.30)
Importation Act 1766 (c.43)
Importation Act 1768 (c.9)
Importation Act 1769 (c.4)
Importation Act 1769 (c.9)
Importation Act 1770 (c.2)
Importation Act 1771 (c.8)
Importation Act 1771 (c.41)
Importation Act 1771 (cc.49, 50)
Importation Act 1772 (c.7)
Importation Act 1772 (cc.32, 33)
Importation Act 1772 (c.67)
Importation Act 1774 (c.9)
Importation Act 1774 (c.74)
Importation Act 1775 (c.1)
Importation Act 1775 (c.7)
Importation Act 1776 (c.8)
Importation Act 1776 (c.35)
Importation Act 1776 (c.41)
Importation Act 1778 (c.56)
Importation Act 1779 (c.28)
Importation Act 1780 (c.6)
Importation Act 1781 (c.62)
Importation Act 1782 (c.7)
Importation Act 1782 (c.30)
Importation Act 1782 (c.38)
Importation Act 1782 (c.72)
Importation Act 1782 (c.78)
Importation Act 1783 (c.1)
Importation Act 1783 (cc.9, 10)
Importation Act 1783 (c.14)
Importation Act 1788 (c.39)
Importation Act 1789 (c.16)
Importation Act 1790 (c.28)
Importation Act 1790 (c.41)
Importation Act 1791 (c.37)
Importation Act 1791 (c.38)
Importation Act 1792 (c.49)
Importation Act 1793 (c.63)
Importation Act 1794 (c.50)
Importation Act 1795 (c.4)
Importation Act 1795 (c.15)
Importation Act 1795 (c.100)
Importation Act 1795 (c.115)
Importation Act 1795 (c.117)
Importation Act 1796 (c.8)
Importation Act 1796 (c.81)
Importation Act 1796 (c.113)
Importation Act 1797 (c.3)
Importation Act 1797 (c.25)
Importation Act 1797 (c.72)
Importation Act 1797 (c.84)
Importation Act 1799 (c.27)
Importation Act 1799 (c.75)
Importation Act 1799 (c.87)
Importation Act 1799 (c.95)
Importation Act 1799 (c.98)
Importation Act 1799 (c.111)
Importation Act 1799 (c.112)
Importation Act 1800 (c.11)
Importation Act 1800 (c.18)
Importation Act 1800 (c.25)
Importation Act 1800 (c.83)
Importation Act 1800 (c.107)
Importation Act 1801 (c.7)
Importation Act 1801 (c.16)
Importation Act 1801 (c.37)
Importation Act 1801 (c.41)
Importation Act 1801 (c.93)
Importation Act 1802 (c.44)
Importation Act 1804 (cc.29, 30)
Importation Act 1806 (c.74)
Importation Act 1806 (c.103)
Importation Act 1806 (c.113)
Importation Act 1806 (c.117)
Importation Act 1806 (c.121)
Importation Act 1807 (c.24)
Importation Act 1807 (cc.25, 26)
Importation Act 1807 (c.27)
Importation Act 1807 (c.67)
Importation Act 1808 (c.11)
Importation Act 1808 (c.19)
Importation Act 1808 (cc.23, 24)
Importation Act 1808 (c.125)
Importation Act 1809 (c.9)
Importation Act 1809 (c.16)
Importation Act 1809 (cc.25, 26)
Importation Act 1809 (c.60)
Importation Act 1809 (c.105)
Importation Act 1810 (c.55)
Importation Act 1810 (c.80)

Importation Act 1811 (c.48)
Importation Act 1811 (c.58)
Importation Act 1811 (c.62)
Importation Act 1812 (c.18)
Importation Act 1812 (c.33)
Importation Act 1812 (c.119)
Importation Act 1813 (c.34)
Importation Act 1813 (c.37)
Importation Act 1813 (c.41)
Importation Act 1814 (c.51)
Importation Act 1814 (c.124)
Importation Act 1814 (c.125)
Importation Act 1815 (c.26)
Importation Act 1815 (c.34)
Importation Act 1815 (c.86)
Importation Act 1816 (c.2)
Importation Act 1816 (cc.25, 26)
Importation Act 1816 (c.36)
Importation Act 1816 (c.37)
Importation Act 1840 (c.32)
Importation Act 1844 (c.100)
Importation Act 1847 (c.2)
Importation Act 1847 (c.86)
Importation and Exportation Act 1766 (cc.1–5)
Importation and Exportation Act 1772 (cc. 1–5)
Importation and Exportation Act 1772 (cc.69, 70)
Importation and Exportation Act 1772 (cc.72, 73)
Importation and Exportation Act 1787 (c.27)
Importation and Exportation Act 1789 (c.58)
Importation and Exportation Act 1790 (c.1)
Importation and Exportation Act 1790 (c.29)
Importation and Exportation Act 1790 (c.42)
Importation and Exportation Act 1791 (c.4)
Importation and Exportation Act 1791 (c.30)
Importation and Exportation Act 1791 (c.47)
Importation and Exportation Act 1792 (c.37)
Importation and Exportation Act 1793 (c.50)
Importation and Exportation Act 1793 (c.65)
Importation and Exportation Act 1797 (c.39)
Importation and Exportation Act 1799 (c.88)
Importation and Exportation Act 1800 (c.58)
Importation and Exportation Act 1804 (c.109)
Importation and Exportation Act 1805 (c.57)
Importation and Exportation Act 1805 (c.86)
Importation and Exportation Act 1807 (c.34)
Importation and Exportation Act 1810 (cc.12, 13)
Importation and Exportation Act 1810 (c.21)
Importation and Exportation Act 1812 (c.8)
Importation and Exportation Act 1812 (c.69)
Importation and Exportation Act 1812 (c.79)
Importation and Exportation Act 1813 (c.55)
Importation and Exportation Act 1814 (c.81)
Importation and Exportation Act 1814 (c.129)
Importation and Exportation Act 1815 (c.117)
Importation and Exportation (Ireland) Act 1807 (c.1)
Importation and Exportation (Ireland) Act 1807 (c.16)
Importation and Exportation (Ireland) Act 1810 (c.97)
Importation, etc. Act 1750 (c.32)
Importation, etc. Act 1766 (c.28)
Importation, etc. Act 1766 (c.36)
Importation, etc. Act 1780 (c.45)
Importation, etc. Act 1801 (c.68)
Importation, etc. Act 1804 (c.35)
Importation, etc. Act 1804 (c.89)
Importation, etc. Act 1806 (c.53)
Importation, etc. Act 1809 (c.18)
Importation, etc. Act 1809 (c.22)
Importation, etc. Act 1812 (c.2)
Importation, etc. Act 1812 (c.20)
Importation, etc. Act 1814 (cc.8, 9)
Importation, etc. Act 1814 (c.111)
Importation, Exportation, etc. Act 1805 (c.26)
Importation in Neutral Vessel, etc. Act 1803 (c.153)
Importation into Isle of Man Act 1813 (c.110)
Importation into Quebec Act 1763 (c.19)
Importation into Quebec Act 1766 (c.42)
Importation into Scotland Act 1740 (c.7)
Importation (Ireland) Act 1807 (c.31)
Importation of Animals Act 1922 (c.5)
Importation of Arms, etc. (Ireland) Act 1841 (c.25)
Importation of Milk Act 1983 (c.37)
Importation of Pedigree Animals Act 1925 (c.30)
Importation of Plumage (Prohibition) Act 1921 (c.16)
Importation of Prize Goods Act 1711 (c.30)
Importation of Silk Act 1779 (c.9)
Imprisonment for Debt (Scotland) Act 1835 (c.70)
Imprisonment for Debts Abroad Act 1801 (c.106)
Imprisonment of Certain Traitors Act 1702 (c.23)
Imprisonment of Certain Traitors Act 1714 (c.7)
Imprisonment of Certain Traitors Act 1727 (c.4)
Imprisonment of Debtors, etc. Act 1786 (c.38)
Imprisonment (Temporary Provisions) Act 1980 (c.57)
Imprisonment with Hard Labour Act 1813 (c.162)
Improvement at Westminster Act 1814 (c.154)
Improvement of Commons Act 1801 (c.20)
Improvement of Land Act 1864 (c.114)
Improvement of Land Act 1899 (c.46)
Improvement of Land Act (1899) Amendment Act 1925 (c.48)
Improvement of Land (Scotland) Act 1893 (c.34)
Improvement of Lands (Ecclesiastical Benefices) Act 1854 (c.67)
Improvement of Live Stock (Licensing of Bulls) Act 1931 (c.43)
Improvements, Metropolis Act 1844 (c.1)

Incapacitated Bishops Act 1843 (c.62)
Incest Act 1567 (c.14)
Incest and Related Offences (Scotland) Act 1986 (c.36)
Incitement to Disaffection Act 1934 (c.56)
Incitement to Mutiny Act 1797 (c.70)
Incitement to Mutiny Act 1814 (c.158)
Inciting to Mutiny, etc. Act 1815 (c.171)
Inclosure Act 1773 (c.81)
Inclosure Act 1801 (c.109)
Inclosure Act 1836 (c.115)
Inclosure Act 1840 (c.31)
Inclosure Act 1845 (c.118)
Inclosure Act 1846 (c.70)
Inclosure Act 1852 (c.79)
Inclosure Act 1854 (c.97)
Inclosure Act 1857 (c.31)
Inclosure Act 1866 (c.94)
Inclosure Act 1867 (c.20)
Inclosure Act 1867 (c.71)
Inclosure, etc., Expenses Act 1868 (c.89)
Inclosures Act 1846 (c.16)
Inclosures Act 1846 (c.117)
Inclosures Act 1847 (c.25)
Income and Corporation Taxes Act 1970 (c.10)
Income and Corporation Taxes Act 1988 (c.1)
Income and Corporation Taxes (No. 2) Act 1970 (c.54)
Income Tax Act 1803 (c.122)
Income Tax Act 1804 (c.37)
Income Tax Act 1804 (c.83)
Income Tax Act 1805 (c.15)
Income Tax Act 1805 (c.49)
Income Tax Act 1805 (c.110)
Income Tax Act 1806 (c.65)
Income Tax Act 1842 (c.35)
Income Tax Act 1844 (c.38)
Income Tax Act 1845 (c.4)
Income Tax Act 1846 (c.81)
Income Tax Act 1871 (c.5)
Income Tax Act 1873 (c.8)
Income Tax Act 1918 (c.40)
Income Tax Act 1944 (c.32)
Income Tax Act 1952 (c.10)
Income Tax Assessment Act 1870 (c.4)
Income Tax (Employments) Act 1943 (c.45)
Income Tax, etc. Act 1810 (c.106)
Income Tax (Foreign Dividends) Act 1842 (c.80)
Income Tax Management Act 1964 (c.37)
Income Tax (Offices and Employment) Act 1944 (c.12)
Income Tax Procedure (Emergency Provisions) Act 1939 (c.99)
Income Tax (Public Offices) Act 1872 (c.82)
Income Tax (Repayment of Post-War Credits) Act 1959 (c.28)
Income Tax Repeal, etc. Act 1802 (c.42)
Increase of Rent and Mortgage Interest (Restrictions) Act 1919 (c.7)
Increase of Rent and Mortgage Interest (Restrictions) Act 1920 (c.17)
Increase of Rent and Mortgage Interest (Restrictions) Act 1935 (c.13)
Increase of Rent and Mortgage Interest (Restrictions) Act 1938 (c.26)
Increase of Rent and Mortgage Interest Restrictions Act 1923 (c.7)
Increase of Rent and Mortgage Interest (War Restrictions) Act 1915 (c.97)
Increase of Rent, etc. (Amendment) Act 1918 (c.7)
Increase of Rent, etc. (Amendment) Act 1919 (c.90)
Increased Assessments Act 1861 (c.27)
Incumbents Act 1868 (c.117)
Incumbents and Benefices Loans Extension Act 1881 (c.25)
Incumbents of Benefices Loans Act 1887 (c.8)
Incumbents of Benefices Loans Extension Act 1886 (c.34)
Incumbents of Benefices Loans Extension Act 1896 (c.13)
Incumbents Resignation Act 1871 (c.44)
Incumbents Resignation Act, 1871, Amendment 1887 (c.23)
Indecent Advertisements (Amendment) Act 1970 (c.47)
Indecent Advertisements Act 1889 (c.18)
Indecent Displays (Control) Act 1981 (c.42)
Indecency with Children Act 1960 (c.33)
Indemnity Act 1715 (c.39)
Indemnity Act 1727 (c.23)
Indemnity Act 1728 (c.31)
Indemnity Act 1730 (c.6)
Indemnity Act 1732 (c.4)
Indemnity Act 1733 (c.10)
Indemnity Act 1734 (c.4)
Indemnity Act 1734 (c.17)
Indemnity Act 1735 (c.6)
Indemnity Act 1736 (c.13)
Indemnity Act 1737 (c.31)
Indemnity Act 1738 (c.6)
Indemnity Act 1739 (c.6)
Indemnity Act 1740 (c.18)
Indemnity Act 1742 (c.30)
Indemnity Act 1754 (c.13)
Indemnity Act 1755 (c.3)
Indemnity Act 1755 (c.24)
Indemnity Act 1757 (c.9)
Indemnity Act 1763 (c.31)
Indemnity Act 1765 (c.4)
Indemnity Act 1766 (c.7)
Indemnity Act 1766 (c.31)
Indemnity Act 1766 (c.51)
Indemnity Act 1768 (c.6)
Indemnity Act 1769 (c.12)
Indemnity Act 1770 (c.42)
Indemnity Act 1771 (c.18)
Indemnity Act 1772 (c.12)
Indemnity Act 1772 (c.31)
Indemnity Act 1772 (c.76)
Indemnity Act 1774 (c.47)
Indemnity Act 1775 (c.17)

Indemnity Act 1776 (c.37)
Indemnity Act 1776 (c.50)
Indemnity Act 1778 (c.39)
Indemnity Act 1779 (c.47)
Indemnity Act 1780 (c.47)
Indemnity Act 1782 (c.55)
Indemnity Act 1783 (c.30)
Indemnity Act 1784 (c.58)
Indemnity Act 1785 (c.82)
Indemnity Act 1786 (c.98)
Indemnity Act 1787 (c.40)
Indemnity Act 1788 (c.22)
Indemnity Act 1789 (c.40)
Indemnity Act 1790 (c.12)
Indemnity Act 1791 (c.8)
Indemnity Act 1791 (c.27)
Indemnity Act 1793 (c.12)
Indemnity Act 1794 (c.12)
Indemnity Act 1795 (c.50)
Indemnity Act 1796 (c.11)
Indemnity Act 1796 (c.57)
Indemnity Act 1797 (c.14)
Indemnity Act 1797 (c.93)
Indemnity Act 1799 (c.17)
Indemnity Act 1800 (c.19)
Indemnity Act 1800 (c.31)
Indemnity Act 1801 (c.66)
Indemnity Act 1802 (c.6)
Indemnity Act 1802 (c.23)
Indemnity Act 1803 (c.7)
Indemnity Act 1805 (c.6)
Indemnity Act 1806 (c.7)
Indemnity Act 1807 (c.5)
Indemnity Act 1807 (c.3)
Indemnity Act 1807 (c.35)
Indemnity Act 1808 (c.40)
Indemnity Act 1809 (c.15)
Indemnity Act 1810 (c.4)
Indemnity Act 1811 (cc.17, 18)
Indemnity Act 1811 (c.98)
Indemnity Act 1812 (c.26)
Indemnity Act 1813 (c.5)
Indemnity Act 1815 (c.17)
Indemnity Act 1816 (c.33)
Indemnity Act 1836 (c.7)
Indemnity Act 1837 (c.12)
Indemnity Act 1838 (c.16)
Indemnity Act 1840 (c.16)
Indemnity Act 1841 (c.11)
Indemnity Act 1842 (c.10)
Indemnity Act 1843 (c.9)
Indemnity Act 1844 (c.10)
Indemnity Act 1845 (c.24)
Indemnity Act 1846 (c.13)
Indemnity Act 1847 (c.18)
Indemnity Act 1866 (c.116)
Indemnity Act 1867 (c.88)
Indemnity as to Certain Books Act 1809 (c.69)
Indemnity, etc. Act 1735 (c.26)
Indemnity for Certain Acts Act 1801 (c.46)
Indemnity for Certain Orders of Council Act 1805 (c.97)
Indemnity (Ireland) Act 1801 (c.49)
Indemnity (Ireland) Act 1802 (c.53)
Indemnity (Ireland) Act 1803 (c.77)
Indemnity, Masters in Chancery Act 1724 (c.2)
Indemnity (O. in C., West Indies Importation) Act 1812 (c.12)
Indemnity of Innkeepers Act 1774 (c.60)
Indemnity, Suppression of Riots Act 1780 (c.63)
Indemnity to Certain Governors Act 1836 (c.48)
Indemnity to Certain Governors, etc. Act 1795 (c.57)
Indemnity to Certain Persons Act 1838 (c.112)
Indemnity to Certain Printers Act 1801 (c.80)
Indemnity to Governor of Surinam Act 1800 (c.108)
Indemnity to Governors of West Indies Act 1796 (c.32)
Indemnity to Governors of West Indies Act 1797 (c.64)
Indemnity to Governors of West Indies Act 1798 (c.72)
Indemnity to Governors of West Indies Act 1799 (c.57)
Indemnity to Printers Act 1800 (c.95)
Indemnity to Proprietors, etc., of Newspapers Act 1792 (c.61)
Indemnity, West Indies Act 1800 (c.76)
Independent Broadcasting Authority Act 1973 (c.19)
Independent Broadcasting Authority Act 1974 (c.16)
Independent Broadcasting Authority Act 1978 (c.43)
Independent Broadcasting Authority Act 1979 (c.35)
Independent Broadcasting Authority (No. 2) Act 1974 (c.42)
India and Burma (Emergency Provisions) Act 1940 (c.33)
India and Burma (Existing Laws) Act 1937 (c.9)
India and Burma (Miscellaneous Amendments) Act 1940 (c.5)
India and Burma (Postponement of Elections) Act 1941 (c.44)
India and Burma (Temporary and Miscellaneous Provisions) Act 1942 (c.39)
India (Attachment of States) Act 1944 (c.14)
India (Central Government and Legislature) Act 1946 (c.39)
India (Consequential Provisions) Act 1949 (c.92)
India (Estate Duty) Act 1945 (c.7)
India (Federal Court Judges) Act 1942 (c.7)
India Government, etc. Act 1807 (c.68)
India Home (Appointments) Act 1875 (c.73)
India (Home Charges Arrears) Act 1882 (c.79)
India (Inam Lands) Act 1869 (c.29)
India Independence Act 1947 (c.30)

India Military Funds Act 1866 (c.18)
India (Miscellaneous Provisions) Act 1944 (c.38)
India Office Auditor Act 1881 (c.63)
India Officers' Salaries Act 1837 (c.47)
India Pay (Temporary Abatements) Act 1933 (c.7)
India (Proclamations of Emergency) Act 1946 (c.23)
India Stock Certificate Act 1863 (c.73)
India Stock Dividends Act 1871 (c.29)
India Stock (Powers of Attorney) Act 1880 (c.11)
India Stock Transfer Act 1862 (c.7)
Indian Advance Act 1879 (c.45)
Indian and Colonial Divorce Jurisdiction Act 1926 (c.40)
Indian and Colonial Divorce Jurisdiction Act 1939 (c.35)
Indian Army Pension Deficiency Act 1885 (c.67)
Indian Bishops Act 1842 (c.119)
Indian Bishops Act 1871 (c.62)
Indian Church Act 1927 (c.40)
Indian Civil Service (Temporary Provisions) Act 1915 (c.87)
Indian Councils Act 1869 (c.98)
Indian Councils Act 1871 (c.34)
Indian Councils Act 1874 (c.91)
Indian Councils Act 1892 (c.14)
Indian Councils Act 1904 (c.26)
Indian Councils Act 1909 (c.4)
Indian Divorce Act 1945 (c.5)
Indian Divorces (Validity) Act 1921 (c.18)
Indian Franchise Act 1945 (c.2)
Indian Guaranteed Railways Act 1879 (c.41)
Indian High Courts Act 1911 (c.18)
Indian High Courts Act 1922 (c.20)
Indian Independence Act 1947 (c.30)
Indian Loan Act 1881 (c.54)
Indian Marine Service Act 1884 (c.38)
Indian Pay (Temporary Abatements) Act 1931 (c.7)
Indian Pay (Temporary Abatements) Act 1934 (c.8)
Indian Presidency Towns Act 1815 (c.84)
Indian Prize Money Act 1866 (c.47)
Indian Prize Money Act 1868 (c.38)
Indian Railway Companies Act 1868 (c.26)
Indian Railway Companies Act 1873 (c.43)
Indian Railways Act 1894 (c.12)
Indian Railways Act Amendment 1906 (c.9)
Indian Salaries and Allowances Act 1880 (c.3)
Indian Securities Act 1860 (c.5)
Indictable Offences Act 1848 (c.42)
Indictable Offences Act Amendment 1868 (c.107)
Indictments Act 1915 (c.90)
Indus Basin Development Fund Act 1960 (c.1)
Industrial and Providence Societies Act 1952 (c.17)
Industrial and Providence Societies Act 1961 (c.28)
Industrial and Provident Societies Act 1867 (c.117)
Industrial and Provident Societies Act 1871 (c.80)
Industrial and Provident Societies Act 1876 (c.45)
Industrial and Provident Societies Act 1893 (c.39)
Industrial and Provident Societies Act 1894 (c.8)
Industrial and Provident Societies Act 1965 (c.12)
Industrial and Provident Societies Act 1967 (c.48)
Industrial and Provident Societies Act 1975 (c.41)
Industrial and Provident Societies Act 1978 (c.34)
Industrial and Provident Societies (Amendment) Act 1895 (c.30)
Industrial and Provident Societies (Amendment) Act 1913 (c.31)
Industrial and Provident Societies (Amendment) Act 1928 (c.4)
Industrial and Providence Societies (Amendment) Act 1954 (c.43)
Industrial Assurance Act 1923 (c.8)
Industrial Assurance and Friendly Societies Act 1929 (c.28)
Industrial Assurance and Friendly Societies Act 1948 (c.39)
Industrial Assurance and Friendly Societies Act 1948 (Amendment) Act 1958 (c.27)
Industrial Assurance and Friendly Societies (Emergency Protection from Forfeiture) Act 1940 (c.10)
Industrial Assurance (Juvenile Societies) Act 1926 (c.35)
Industrial Common Ownership Act 1976 (c.78)
Industrial Courts Act 1919 (c.69)
Industrial Development Act 1966 (c.34)
Industrial Development Act 1982 (c.52)
Industrial Development Act 1985 (c.25)
Industrial Development (Ships) Act 1970 (c.2)
Industrial Diseases (Notification) Act 1981 (c.25)
Industrial Expansion Act 1968 (c.32)
Industrial Injuries and Diseases (Northern Ireland Old Cases) Act 1975 (c.17)
Industrial Injuries and Diseases (Old Cases) Act 1967 (c.34)
Industrial Injuries and Diseases (Old Cases) Act 1975 (c.16)
Industrial Organisations and Development Act 1947 (c.40)
Industrial Relations Act 1971 (c.72)
Industrial Reorganisation Corporation Act 1966 (c.50)
Industrial Schools Act 1866 (c.118)

Industrial Schools Act Amendment 1880 (c.15)
Industrial Schools Acts Amendment 1894 (c.33)
Industrial Schools (Ireland) Act 1868 (c.25)
Industrial Schools (Ireland) Act 1885 (c.19)
Industrial Training Act 1954 (c.16)
Industrial Training Act 1964 (c.16)
Industrial Training Act 1982 (c.10)
Industrial Training Act 1986 (c.15)
Industrial Tribunals Act 1996 (c.17)
Industry Act 1971 (c.17)
Industry Act 1972 (c.63)
Industry Act 1975 (c.68)
Industry Act 1979 (c.32)
Industry Act 1980 (c.33)
Industry Act 1981 (c.6)
Industry Act 1982 (c.18)
Industry (Amendment) Act 1976 (c.73)
Inebriates Act 1888 (c.19)
Inebriates Act 1898 (c.60)
Inebriates Act 1899 (c.35)
Inebriates Amendment (Scotland) Act 1900 (c.28)
Infant Felons Act 1840 (c.90)
Infant Life (Preservation) Act 1929 (c.34)
Infant Life Protection Act 1872 (c.38)
Infant Life Protection Act 1897 (c.57)
Infant Suitors in Equity Entitled to Stock Act 1812 (c.32)
Infant Trustees and Mortgages Act 1763 (c.16)
Infanticide Act 1922 (c.18)
Infanticide Act 1938 (c.36)
Infants Property Act 1830 (c.65)
Infants Relief Act 1874 (c.62)
Infants' Settlements Act 1855 (c.43)
Infectious Diseases (Notification) Act 1889 (c.72)
Infectious Diseases (Notification) Extension Act 1899 (c.8)
Infectious Diseases (Prevention) Act 1890 (c.34)
Infeftment Act 1845 (c.35)
Inferior Courts Act 1779 (c.70)
Inferior Courts Act 1844 (c.19)
Inferior Courts Judgments Extension Act 1882 (c.31)
Informal Attestation of Certain Deeds Act 1814 (c.168)
Information in Nature of Quo Warranto Act 1792 (c.58)
Inhabited House Duties Act 1791 (c.2)
Inhabited House, etc., Duties Act 1797 (c.40)
Inheritance (Family Provision) Act 1938 (c.45)
Inheritance (Provision for Family and Dependants) Act 1975 (c.63)
Inheritance Tax (Formerly Capital Transfer Tax) Act 1984 (c.51)
Injured Animals Act 1894 (c.22)
Injured Animals Act 1907 (c.5)
Injuries in War (Compensation) Act 1914 (c.30)
Injuries in War Compensation Act 1914 (Session 2) (c.18)
Injuries in War (Compensation) Act 1915 (c.24)
Inland Excise and Taxes (Ireland) Act 1812 (c.97)
Inland Fisheries (Ireland) Act 1838 (c.76)
Inland Navigation (Ireland) Act 1813 (c.144)
Inland Navigation (Ireland) Act 1815 (c.182)
Inland Revenue Act 1866 (c.64)
Inland Revenue Act 1868 (c.124)
Inland Revenue Act 1880 (c.20)
Inland Revenue Buildings Act 1881 (c.10)
Inland Revenue Regulation Act 1890 (c.21)
Inland Revenue Repeal Act 1870 (c.99)
Inner Urban Areas Act 1978 (c.50)
Innkeepers Act 1878 (c.38)
Inquiries by Board of Trade Act 1872 (c.18)
Inquiry into Certain Frauds and Abuses Act 1802 (c.16)
Inquiry into Fees, Public Offices Act 1785 (c.19)
Inquiry into Fees, Public Offices Act 1786 (c.66)
Inquiry into Fees, Public Offices Act 1787 (c.35)
Inquiry into Military Departments Act 1805 (c.47)
Inquiry into Military Departments Act 1807 (c.33)
Inquiry into Military Departments Act 1808 (c.61)
Inquiry into Military Departments Act 1809 (c.111)
Inquiry into Military Expenditure, etc. Act 1811 (c.19)
Inquiry into Naval Departments Act 1805 (c.46)
Inquiry into Public Expenditure Act 1805 (c.70)
Inquiry into Public Offices (Ireland) Act 1804 (c.106)
Inquiry into Public Offices (Ireland) Act (c.65)
Inquiry into Public Offices (Ireland) Act 1813 (c.130)
Inrolment of Grants of Annuities Act (c.141)
Insane Prisoners Act 1840 (c.54)
Inshore Fishing Industry Act 1945 (c.11)
Inshore Fishing (Scotland) Act 1984 (c.26)
Inshore Fishing (Scotland) Act 1994 (c.27)
Insolvency Act 1976 (c.60)
Insolvency Act 1985 (c.65)
Insolvency Act 1986 (c.45)
Insolvency Act 1994 (c.7)
Insolvency (No. 2) Act 1994 (c.12)
Insolvency Services (Accounting and Investment) Act 1970 (c.8)
Insolvent Act 1812 (c.163)
Insolvent Debtors Act 1839 (c.39)
Insolvent Debtors Act 1842 (c.116)
Insolvent Debtor's Discharge Act 1794 (c.69)
Insolvent Debtor's Discharge Act 1795 (c.88)
Insolvent Debtors, East Indies Act 1836 (c.47)

Insolvent Debtors (England) Act 1813 (c.23)
Insolvent Debtors (England) Act 1813 (c.102)
Insolvent Debtors (England) Act 1816 (c.102)
Insolvent Debtors (England) Act 1836 (c.44)
Insolvent Debtors, etc., Relief Act 1774 (c.77)
Insolvent Debtors, India Act 1840 (c.80)
Insolvent Debtors, India Act 1846 (c.14)
Insolvent Debtors (Ireland) Act 1810 (c.47)
Insolvent Debtors (Ireland) Act 1813 (c.138)
Insolvent Debtors (Ireland) Act 1814 (c.114)
Insolvent Debtors (Ireland) Act 1816 (c.126)
Insolvent Debtors (Ireland) Act 1836 (c.23)
Insolvent Debtors (Ireland) Act 1840 (c.14)
Insolvent Debtors (Ireland) Act 1840 (c.107)
Insolvent Debtors (Ireland) Act 1841 (c.47)
Insolvent Debtors Relief Act 1702 (c.19)
Insolvent Debtors Relief Act 1703 (c.10)
Insolvent Debtors' Relief Act 1711 (c.29)
Insolvent Debtors' Relief Act 1724 (c.21)
Insolvent Debtors' Relief Act 1728 (c.20)
Insolvent Debtors' Relief Act 1730 (c.27)
Insolvent Debtors' Relief Act 1737 (c.9)
Insolvent Debtors' Relief Act 1755 (c.13)
Insolvent Debtors' Relief Act 1765 (c.41)
Insolvent Debtors' Relief Act 1769 (c.26)
Insolvent Debtors Relief Act 1776 (c.38)
Insolvent Debtors Relief Act 1781 (c.63)
Insolvent Debtors Relief Act 1801 (c.70)
Insolvent Debtors Relief Act 1804 (c.108)
Insolvent Debtors Relief Act 1805 (c.3)
Insolvent Debtors Relief Act 1806 (c.108)
Insolvent Debtors Relief Act 1809 (c.54)
Insolvent Debtors Relief Act 1809 (c.115)
Insolvent Debtors Relief Act 1812 (c.13)
Insolvent Debtors Relief Act 1812 (c.165)
Insolvent Debtors Relief (England) Act 1811 (c.125)
Insolvent Debtors Relief (England) Act 1812 (c.6)
Insolvent Debtors Relief (England) Act 1813 (c.28)
Insolvent Debtors' Relief, etc. Act 1719 (c.22)
Insolvent Debtors Relief, etc. Act 1778 (c.52)
Insolvent Debtors Relief (Ireland) Act 1811 (c.123)
Insurance Brokers (Registration) Act 1977 (c.46)
Insurance Companies Act 1958 (c.72)
Insurance Companies Act 1974 (c.49)
Insurance Companies Act 1980 (c.25)
Insurance Companies Act 1981 (c.31)
Insurance Companies Act 1982 (c.50)
Insurance Companies Amendment Act 1973 (c.58)
Insurance Companies Reserves Act 1995 (c.29)
Insurance Contracts (War Settlement) Act 1952 (c.56)
Insurance (Fees) Act 1985 (c.46)
Insurances on Ships, etc. Act 1785 (c.44)
Insurrection and Disturbances (Ireland) Act 1807 (c.13)
Intelligence Services Act 1994 (c.13)
Interception of Communications Act 1985 (c.56)
Interchange of Grain Between Great Britain and Ireland Act 1807 (c.7)
Intercourse Between Jamaica and St. Domingo Act 1812 (c.3)
Intercourse with St. Helena Act 1816 (c.23)
Interest on Damages (Scotland) Act 1958 (c.61)
Interest on Damages (Scotland) Act 1971 (c.31)
Intermediate Education (Ireland) Act 1878 (c.66)
Intermediate Education (Ireland) Act 1882 (c.69)
Intermediate Education (Ireland) Act 1900 (c.43)
Intermediate Education (Ireland) Act 1913 (c.29)
Intermediate Education (Ireland) Act 1914 (c.41)
Interments (Felo de se) Act 1882 (c.19)
International Bank and Monetary Fund Act 1959 (c.17)
International Carriage of Perishable Foodstuffs Act 1976 (c.58)
International Cocoa Agreement Act 1973 (c.46)
International Copyright Act 1838 (c.59)
International Copyright Act 1844 (c.12)
International Copyright Act 1875 (c.12)
International Copyright Act 1886 (c.33)
International Development Association Act 1960 (c.35)
International Development Association Act 1964 (c.13)
International Finance Corporation Act 1955 (c.5)
International Finance, Trade and Aid Act 1977 (c.6)
International Headquarters and Defence Organisations Act 1964 (c.5)
International Monetary Arrangements Act 1983 (c.51)
International Monetary Fund Act 1962 (c.20)
International Monetary Fund Act 1968 (c.58)
International Monetary Fund Act 1970 (c.49)
International Monetary Fund Act 1979 (c.29)
International Organisations Act 1968 (c.48)
International Organisations Act 1981 (c.9)
International Organisations (Immunities and Privileges) Act 1950 (c.14)
International Parliamentary Organisations (Registration) Act 1989 (c.19)
International Road Haulage Permits Act 1975 (c.46)
International Sugar Organisation Act 1973 (c.68)
International Transport Conventions Act 1983 (c.14)
Internationally Protected Persons Act 1978 (c.17)
Interpleader (Ireland) Act 1846 (c.64)

Interpretation Act 1889 (c.63)
Interpretation Act 1978 (c.30)
Interpretation of Terms Act 1837 (c.39)
Intestate Husband's Estate (Scotland) Act 1911 (c.10)
Intestate Husband's Estate (Scotland) Act 1919 (c.9)
Intestate Husband's Estate (Scotland) Act 1959 (c.21)
Intestate Moveable Succession (Scotland) Act 1919 (c.61)
Intestates Act 1873 (c.52)
Intestates Act 1875 (c.27)
Intestates' Estates Act 1884 (c.71)
Intestates' Estates Act 1890 (c.29)
Intestates' Estates Act 1952 (c.64)
Intestates' Widows and Children (Scotland) Act 1875 (c.41)
Institute of Management (Customs) Act 1951 (c.51)
Intoxicating Liquor (Sales to Persons Under Eighteen) Act 1923 (c.28)
Intoxicating Liquor (Temporary Restriction) Act 1914 (c.77)
Intoxicating Liquors (Ireland) Act 1906 (c.39)
Intoxicating Liquors (Licences Suspension) Act 1871 (c.88)
Intoxicating Liquors (Sale to Children) Act 1886 (c.56)
Intoxicating Liquors (Sale to Children) Act 1901 (c.27)
Intoxicating Substances (Supply) Act 1985 (c.26)
Inventories (Scotland) Act 1816 (c.107)
Inverness and Elgin County Boundaries Act 1870 (c.16)
Inverness Beer Duties Act 1718 (c.17)
Inverness Beer Duties Act 1737 (c.16)
Inverness Gaol Act 1788 (c.69)
Inverness Roads Act 1793 (c.118)
Investment and Building Grants Act 1971 (c.51)
Investment of Certain Money Act 1808 (c.21)
Investments of Trust Funds Act 1867 (c.132)
Ionian Islands Commissioners Act 1868 (c.128)
Ipswich and Stowmarket Navigation Act 1790 (c.57)
Ipswich and Stowmarket Navigation Act 1793 (c.20)
Ipswich and Yaxley Roads Act 1793 (c.128)
Ipswich: Improvement Act 1793 (c.92)
Ipswich: Improvement, etc. Act 1797 (c.44)
Iran (Temporary Powers) Act 1980 (c.28)
Ireland Act 1949 (c.41)
Ireland (Confirmation of Agreement) Act 1925 (c.77)
Ireland Development Grant Act 1903 (c.23)
Irish and Scotch Paupers Removal Act 1837 (c.10)
Irish Appeals Act 1780 (c.28)
Irish Appeals Act 1783 (c.28)
Irish Bankrupt and Insolvent Act 1857 (c.60)
Irish Charges Act 1801 (c.32)
Irish Church Act 1869 (c.42)
Irish Church Act Amendment Act 1881 (c.71)
Irish Church Act (1869) Amendment Act 1872 (c.90)
Irish Church Amendment Act 1872 (c.13)
Irish Constabulary Act 1874 (c.80)
Irish Education Act 1892 (c.42)
Irish Education Act 1893 (c.41)
Irish Free State (Agreement) Act 1922 (c.4)
Irish Free State (Confirmation of Agreement) Act 1924 (c.41)
Irish Free State (Confirmation of Agreement) Act 1929 (c.4)
Irish Free State (Consequential Provisions) Act 1922 (c.2)
Irish Free State Constitution Act 1922 (c.1)
Irish Free State Land Purchase (Loan Guarantee) Act 1924 (c.3)
Irish Free State (Special Duties) Act 1931 (c.30)
Irish Handloom Weavers Act 1909 (c.21)
Irish Land Act 1903 (c.37)
Irish Land Act 1904 (c.34)
Irish Land Act 1907 (c.38)
Irish Land Act 1909 (c.42)
Irish Land (Provisions for Sailors and Soldiers) Act 1919 (c.82)
Irish Lighthouses Act 1811 (c.66)
Irish Loans Act 1880 (c.44)
Irish Mariners, etc. Act 1802 (c.61)
Irish Militia Act 1805 (c.38)
Irish Militia Act 1806 (c.124)
Irish Militia Act 1807 (c.6)
Irish Police Constables (Naval and Military Service) Act 1914 (c.84)
Irish Police (Naval and Military Service) Act 1915 (c.32)
Irish Presbyterian Church Act 1871 (c.24)
Irish Railways (Confirmation of Agreement) Act 1919 (c.78)
Irish Reformatory Schools Act 1868 (c.59)
Irish Reproductive Loan Fund Act 1883 (c.33)
Irish Reproductive Loan Fund Amendment Act 1882 (c.16)
Irish Sailors and Soldiers Land Trust Act 1952 (c.58)
Irish Sailors and Soldiers Land Trust Act 1967 (c.67)
Irish Sailors and Soldiers Land Trust Act 1987 (c.48)
Irish Tobacco Act 1907 (c.3)
Irish Universities Act 1908 (c.38)
Iron and Steel Act 1949 (c.72)
Iron and Steel Act 1953 (c.15)
Iron and Steel Act 1967 (c.17)
Iron and Steel Act 1969 (c.45)
Iron and Steel Act 1972 (c.12)
Iron and Steel Act 1975 (c.64)
Iron and Steel Act 1981 (c.46)
Iron and Steel Act 1982 (c.25)
Iron and Steel (Amendment) Act 1976 (c.41)
Iron and Steel (Amendment) Act 1978 (c.41)

Iron and Steel (Borrowing Powers) Act 1981 (c.2)
Iron and Steel (Financial Provisions) Act 1960 (c.26)
Irvine Beer Duties Act 1735 (c.27)
Island of Rockall Act 1972 (c.2)
Isle of Axholme: Inclosure, etc. Act 1795 (c.107)
Isle of Ely and Norfolk Roads Act 1767 (c.100)
Isle of Ely: Drainage Act 1757 (c.19)
Isle of Ely: Drainage Act 1772 (c.20)
Isle of Ely: Drainage Act 1791 (c.81)
Isle of Ely: Drainage Act 1792 (c.108)
Isle of Ely: Drainage Act 1795 (c.48)
Isle of Ely: Drainage Act 1797 (c.96)
Isle of Ely, etc.: Drainage Act 1772 (c.19)
Isle of Ely, etc.: Drainage Act 1772 (c.60)
Isle of Ely, etc.: Drainage Act 1775 (c.66)
Isle of Ely: Small Debts Act 1778 (c.36)
Isle of Ely to Ramsey Road Act 1794 (c.127)
Isle of Man Act 1780 (c.42)
Isle of Man 1865 (c.28)
Isle of Man Act 1958 (c.11)
Isle of Man Act 1979 (c.58)
Isle of Man (Church Building and New Parishes) Act 1897 (c.33)
Isle of Man (Customs) Act 1810 (c.42)
Isle of Man (Customs) Act 1887 (c.5)
Isle of Man (Customs) Act 1888 (c.7)
Isle of Man (Customs) Act 1892 (c.28)
Isle of Man (Customs) Act 1895 (c.38)
Isle of Man (Customs) Act 1898 (c.27)
Isle of Man (Customs) Act 1899 (c.39)
Isle of Man (Customs) Act 1900 (c.31)
Isle of Man (Customs) Act 1901 (c.32)
Isle of Man (Customs) Act 1902 (c.23)
Isle of Man (Customs) Act 1903 (c.35)
Isle of Man (Customs) Act 1904 (c.25)
Isle of Man (Customs) Act 1905 (c.16)
Isle of Man (Customs) Act 1906 (c.18)
Isle of Man (Customs) Act 1907 (c.26)
Isle of Man (Customs) Act 1908 (c.9)
Isle of Man (Customs) Act 1909 (c.45)
Isle of Man (Customs) Act 1910 (c.18)
Isle of Man (Customs) Act 1911 (c.14)
Isle of Man (Customs) Act 1912 (c.9)
Isle of Man (Customs) Act 1913 (c.18)
Isle of Man (Customs) Act 1914 (c.19)
Isle of Man (Customs) Act 1915 (c.67)
Isle of Man (Customs) Act 1916 (c.27)
Isle of Man (Customs) Act 1917 (c.35)
Isle of Man (Customs) Act 1918 (c.41)
Isle of Man (Customs) Act 1919 (c.74)
Isle of Man (Customs) Act 1921 (c.40)
Isle of Man (Customs) Act 1922 (c.36)
Isle of Man (Customs) Act 1923 (c.26)
Isle of Man (Customs) Act 1924 (c.24)
Isle of Man (Customs) Act 1925 (c.56)
Isle of Man (Customs) Act 1926 (c.27)
Isle of Man (Customs) Act 1927 (c.20)
Isle of Man (Customs) Act 1928 (c.38)
Isle of Man (Customs) Act 1929 (c.1)
Isle of Man (Customs) Act 1930 (c.42)
Isle of Man (Customs) Act 1931 (c.16)
Isle of Man (Customs) Act 1931 (c.34)
Isle of Man (Customs) Act 1931 (c.41)
Isle of Man (Customs) Act 1933 (c.40)
Isle of Man (Customs) Act 1934 (c.46)
Isle of Man (Customs) Act 1935 (c.34)
Isle of Man (Customs) Act 1936 (c.45)
Isle of Man (Customs) Act 1937 (c.64)
Isle of Man (Customs) Act 1938 (c.68)
Isle of Man (Customs) Act 1939 (c.49)
Isle of Man (Customs) Act 1939 (c.53)
Isle of Man (Customs) Act 1941 (c.32)
Isle of Man (Customs) Act 1942 (c.25)
Isle of Man (Customs) Act 1943 (c.37)
Isle of Man (Customs) Act 1944 (c.27)
Isle of Man (Customs) Act 1945 (c.14)
Isle of Man (Customs) Act 1946 (c.69)
Isle of Man (Customs) Act 1947 (c.50)
Isle of Man (Customs) Act 1948 (c.61)
Isle of Man (Customs) Act 1949 (c.58)
Isle of Man (Customs) Act 1950 (c.19)
Isle of Man (Customs) Act 1952 (c.51)
Isle of Man (Customs) Act 1953 (c.44)
Isle of Man (Customs) Act 1954 (c.54)
Isle of Man (Customs) Act 1955 (c.17)
Isle of Man Customs Duties Act 1867 (c.86)
Isle of Man (Detention) Act 1941 (c.16)
Isle of Man Harbours Act 1771 (c.52)
Isle of Man Harbours Act 1814 (c.143)
Isle of Man Harbours Act 1840 (c.63)
Isle of Man Harbours Act 1872 (c.23)
Isle of Man Harbours Act 1874 (c.8)
Isle of Man Harbours Act 1883 (c.9)
Isle of Man Harbours Act 1884 (c.7)
Isle of Man Harbours Act 1911 (c.33)
Isle of Man (Harbours) Act 1947
Isle of Man Harbours Amendment Act 1864 (c.62)
Isle of Man Loans Act 1880 (c.8)
Isle of Man Loans Act 1931 (c.38)
Isle of Man (Officers) Act 1876 (c.43)
Isle of Man (Officers) Act 1882 (c.46)
Isle of Man Purchase Act 1765 (c.26)
Isle of Man Smuggling Act 1810 (c.62)
Isle of Man Trade Act 1798 (c.63)
Isle of Man Trade Act 1801 (c.54)
Isle of Man Trade Act 1802 (c.98)
Isle of Man Trade Act 1845 (c.94)
Isle of Man (War Legislation) Act 1914 (c.62)
Isle of Man (War Legislation) Act 1939 (c.86)
Isle of Wight, Carriage Rates Act 1783 (c.19)
Isle of Wight Guardians Act 1776 (c.53)
Isle of Wight: Poor Relief Act 1771 (c.43)
Islington: Poor Relief, etc. Act 1776 (c.5)
Islington: Poor Relief, etc. Act 1795 (c.147)
Isolation Hospitals Act 1893 (c.68)
Isolation Hospitals Act 1901 (c.8)
Issue and Payment of Exchequer Bills Act 1808 (c.1)
Issue, etc., of Gold and Silver Tokens Act 1813 (c.19)
Issue, etc., of Gold and Silver Tokens Act 1813 (c.114)

Issue of Bank Notes (Scotland) Act 1797 (c.2)
Issue of Bank Notes (Scotland) Act 1799 (c.10)
Issue of Bank Notes (Scotland) Act 1799 (c.25)
Issue of Bank Notes (Scotland) Act 1799 (c.48)

Jamaica Act 1866 (c.12)
Jamaica and St. Domingo Act 1812 (c.35)
Jamaica Independence Act 1962 (c.40)
Jamaica Loan Act 1854 (c.54)
Jamaica Loan Act 1862 (c.55)
Jamaica Loans Act 1869 (c.69)
James Watt's Fire Engines Patent Act 1775 (c.61)
Japanese Treaty of Peace Act 1951 (c.6)
Jedburgh Beer Duties Act 1720 (c.25)
Jeremy's Ferry Bridge, River Lee Act 1778 (c.10)
Jersey and Guernsey (Financial Provisions) Act 1947 (c.2)
Jews Act 1860 (c.63)
Jews Relief Act 1858 (c.49)
Joanna Stephens' Reward (Cure for Stone) Act 1738 (c.23)
Job Release Act 1977 (c.8)
Jobseekers Act 1995 (c.18)
John F. Kennedy Memorial Act 1964 (c.85)
John Whitehill, Esq Act 1782 (c.69)
John Whitehill, Esq Act 1783 (c.19)
John Wilkinson's Estate Act 1794 (c.67)
John Yeldham's Estate Act 1797 (c.47)
Joint Stock Banking Companies Act 1839 (c.68)
Joint Stock Banking Companies Act 1842 (c.85)
Joint Stock Banking Companies Act 1857 (c.49)
Joint Stock Banks Act 1838 (c.96)
Joint Stock Banks Act 1844 (c.113)
Joint Stock Banks Act 1856 (c.100)
Joint Stock Banks Act 1858 (c.91)
Joint Stock Banks (Scotland) Act 1856 (c.3)
Joint Stock Banks (Scotland) and (Ireland) Act 1846 (c.75)
Joint Stock Companies Act 1840 (c.111)
Joint Stock Companies Act 1844 (cc.110, 111)
Joint Stock Companies Act 1847 (c.78)
Joint Stock Companies Act 1848 (c.45)
Joint Stock Companies Act 1849 (c.108)
Joint Stock Companies Act 1856 (c.47)
Joint Stock Companies Act 1857 (c.14)
Joint Stock Companies Act 1857 (c.80)
Joint Stock Companies Act 1858 (c.60)
Joint Stock Companies Arrangements Act 1870 (c.104)
Joint Stock Companies (Ireland) Act 1845 (c.98)
Joint Stock Companies Winding-up Amendment Act 1857 (c.78)
Journeymen Tailors Act 1720 (c.13)
Journeymen Tailors, London Act 1768 (c.17)
Judges Jurisdiction Act 1870 (c.6)
Judges' Lodgings Act 1839 (c.69)
Judges' Lodgings (Ireland) Act 1801 (c.88)
Judges' Pensions Act 1799 (c.110)
Judges' Pensions Act 1813 (c.153)
Judges' Pensions (India and Burma) Act 1948 (c.4)
Judges' Pensions (Ireland) Act 1814 (c.95)
Judges' Pensions (Scotland) Act 1808 (c.145)
Judges' Remuneration Act 1954 (c.27)
Judges' Remuneration Act 1965 (c.61)
Judges' Salaries Act 1765 (c.47)
Judges' Salaries Act 1872 (c.51)
Judgment Mortgage (Ireland) Act 1850 (c.29)
Judgment Mortgage (Ireland) Act 1858 (c.105)
Judgment of Death Act 1823 (c.48)
Judgments Act 1838 (c.110)
Judgments Act 1839 (c.11)
Judgments Act 1840 (c.82)
Judgments Act 1855 (c.15)
Judgments Act 1864 (c.112)
Judgments Extension Act 1868 (c.54)
Judgments (Ireland) Act 1844 (c.90)
Judgments (Ireland) Act 1849 (c.95)
Judgments Registry Act 1871 (c.72)
Judgments Registry (Ireland) Act 1850 (c.74)
Judgments Registry (Ireland) Act 1871 (c.72)
Judgments, Wales and Counties Palatine Act 1721 (c.25)
Judicature (Northern Ireland) Act 1978 (c.23)
Judicature (Rule Committee) Act 1909 (c.11)
Judicial Committee Act 1833 (c.41)
Judicial Committee Act 1843 (c.38)
Judicial Committee Act 1844 (c.69)
Judicial Committee Act 1845 (c.30)
Judicial Committee Act 1871 (c.91)
Judicial Committee Act 1881 (c.3)
Judicial Committee Act 1915 (c.92)
Judicial Committee Amendment Act 1895 (c.44)
Judicial Factors Act 1849 (c.51)
Judicial Factors (Scotland) Act 1880 (c.4)
Judicial Factors (Scotland) Act 1889 (c.39)
Judicial Offices (Salaries and Pensions) Act 1957 (c.46)
Judicial Officers (Salaries, etc.) Act 1952 (c.12)
Judicial Pensions Act 1959 (c.9)
Judicial Pensions Act 1981 (c.20)
Judicial Pensions and Retirement Act 1993 (c.8)
Judicial Proceedings (Regulation of Reports) Act 1926 (c.61)
Judicial Ratifications (Scotland) Act 1836 (c.43)
Judicial Statistics (Scotland) Act 1869 (c.33)
Judicial Trustees Act 1896 (c.35)
Juries Act 1730 (c.7)
Juries Act 1730 (c.25)

Juries Act 1756 (c.19)
Juries Act 1825 (c.50)
Juries Act 1862 (c.107)
Juries Act 1870 (c.77)
Juries Act 1871 (c.2)
Juries Act 1871 (c.65)
Juries Act 1918 (c.23)
Juries Act 1922 (c.11)
Juries Act 1949 (c.27)
Juries Act 1954 (c.41)
Juries Act 1974 (c.23)
Juries Detention Act 1897 (c.18)
Juries (Disqualification) Act 1984 (c.34)
Juries (Emergency Provisions) Act 1920 (c.78)
Juries (Emergency Provisions) (Renewal) Act 1921 (c.36)
Juries, etc. Act 1750 (c.18)
Juries (Ireland) Act 1839 (c.48)
Juries (Ireland) Act 1845 (c.67)
Juries (Ireland) Act 1868 (c.75)
Juries (Ireland) Act 1871 (c.65)
Juries (Ireland) Act 1872 (c.25)
Juries (Ireland) Act 1873 (c.27)
Juries (Ireland) Act 1874 (c.28)
Juries (Ireland) Act 1875 (c.37)
Juries (Lighthouse Keepers' Exemption) Act 1869 (c.36)
Juries Procedure (Ireland) Act 1876 (c.78)
Juries (Scotland) Act 1826 (c.8)
Jurisdiction in Homicides Act 1862 (c.65)
Jurisdiction in Rating Act 1877 (c.11)
Jurisdiction in Siam Act 1857 (c.75)
Jurors Act 1587 (c.54)
Jurors Affirmation (Scotland) Act 1868 (c.39)
Jurors (Enrolment of Women) (Scotland) Act 1920 (c.53)
Jurors (Ireland) Amendment Act 1894 (c.49)
Jurors Prize Money Act 1868 (c.38)
Jurors Qualification (Ireland) Act 1876 (c.21)
Jurors (Scotland) Act 1745 (c.9)
Jurors (Scotland) Act 1825 (c.22)
Jury Trials Amendment (Scotland) Act 1910 (c.31)
Jury Trials (Scotland) Act 1815 (c.42)
Jury Trials (Scotland) Act 1819 (c.35)
Jury Trials (Scotland) Act 1837 (c.14)
Jury Trials (Scotland) Act 1854 (c.59)
Jury Trials (Scotland) Act 1859 (c.7)
Justice of Assize Act 1809 (c.91)
Justice of Assizes Act 1850 (c.25)
Justice of the Peace Act 1906 (c.16)
Justice of the Peace, Metropolis Act 1811 (c.119)
Justice of the Peace, the Metropolis Act 1792 (c.53)
Justices Act 1753 (c.27)
Justices' Clerks Act 1877 (c.43)
Justices' Clerks' Fees Act 1753 (c.14)
Justices' Clerks' Fees (Middlesex) Act 1754 (c.16)
Justices Commitment Act 1741 (c.24)
Justices Commitment Act 1743 (c.5)
Justices (Ireland) Act 1842 (c.46)
Justices (Ireland) Act 1843 (c.8)
Justices Jurisdiction Act 1742 (c.18)
Justices Jurisdiction Act 1852 (c.38)
Justices of Assize Act 1738 (c.27)
Justices of Assize Act 1839 (c.22)
Justices of the Peace Act 1361 (c.1)
Justices of the Peace Act 1661 (c.38)
Justices of the Peace Act 1788 (c.49)
Justices of the Peace Act 1867 (c.115)
Justices of the Peace Act 1906 (c.16)
Justices of the Peace Act 1949 (c.101)
Justices of the Peace Act 1965 (c.28)
Justices of the Peace Act 1968 (c.69)
Justices of the Peace Act 1979 (c.55)
Justices of the Peace in Metropolis Act 1837 (c.37)
Justices of the Peace, Nottingham Act 1803 (c.45)
Justices of the Peace Small Debt (Scotland) Act 1825 (c.48)
Justices of the Peace Small Debt (Scotland) Act 1849 (c.34)
Justices Oaths Act 1766 (c.9)
Justices Proceedings Confirmation (Sussex) Act 1864 (c.100)
Justices Protection Act 1803 (c.141)
Justices Protection Act 1848 (c.44)
Justices Protection (Ireland) Act 1849 (c.16)
Justices Qualification Act 1731 (c.18)
Justices Qualification Act 1744 (c.20)
Justices' Qualification Act 1760 (c.13)
Justices Qualification Act 1871 (c.18)
Justices Qualification Act 1875 (c.54)
Justices Quorum Act 1766 (c.21)
Justices (Scotland) Act 1856 (c.48)
Justices (Supplement List) Act 1941 (c.27)
Justiciary and Circuit Courts (Scotland) Act 1783 (c.45)
Justiciary Court (Scotland) Act 1868 (c.95)
Justiciary Courts (Scotland) Act 1814 (c.67)
Justiciary (Scotland) Act 1848 (c.79)
Juvenile Convict Prison (Ireland) Act 1856 (c.24)
Juvenile Courts (Metropolis) Act 1920 (c.68)
Juvenile Offenders Act 1847 (c.82)
Juvenile Offenders (Ireland) Act 1848 (c.59)

Keeper of Holyrood Park, etc. Act 1843 (c.64)
Keeping, etc., of Gunpowder Act 1748 (c.38)
Keeping, etc., of Gunpowder Act 1771 (c.35)
Keeping of Gunpowder Act 1718 (c.26)
Keeping of Gunpowder Act 1724 (c.23)
Keeping of Gunpowder Act 1741 (c.32)
Keighley to Bradford Road Act 1795 (c.135)
Keighley to Halifax Road Act 1795 (c.151)
Keighley to Kirby Kendal Road Act 1778 (c.113)
Kelso Beer Duties Act 1758 (c.56)
Kelso Beer Duties Act 1780 (c.11)
Kennet and Avon: Canal Act 1796 (c.44)
Kennington Common Act 1852 (c.29)

Kensington, Chelsea and Fulham: Improvements Act 1767 (c.101)
Kensington, Chelsea and Fulham Roads (Toll Continuation) Act 1740 (c.16)
Kensington, Chelsea and Fulham Roads (Tolls) Act 1725 (c.37)
Kensington: Improvement Act 1795 (c.74)
Kensington: Poor Relief Act 1777 (c.64)
Kensington Road Act 1795 (c.142)
Kensington Station and North and South London Junction Railway Act 1872 (c.80)
Kent and Surrey Roads Act 1765 (c.68)
Kent and Surrey Roads Act 1770 (c.62)
Kent and Surrey Roads Act 1781 (c.100)
Kent and Surrey Roads Act 1787 (c.70)
Kent and Surrey Roads Act 1792 (c.151)
Kent and Sussex Roads Act 1740 (c.12)
Kent and Sussex Roads Act 1762 (c.67)
Kent and Sussex Roads Act 1766 (c.56)
Kent and Sussex Roads Act 1767 (c.84)
Kent and Sussex Roads Act 1767 (c.86)
Kent and Sussex Roads Act 1770 (c.108)
Kent and Sussex Roads Act 1772 (c.92)
Kent and Sussex Roads Act 1787 (c.80)
Kent and Sussex Roads Act 1788 (c.85)
Kent and Sussex Roads Act 1789 (c.85)
Kent, Devon Fortifications Act 1794 (c.76)
Kent Fortifications Act 1797 (c.66)
Kent Roads Act 1724 (c.5)
Kent Roads Act 1724 (c.15)
Kent Roads Act 1730 (c.15)
Kent Roads Act 1735 (c.7)
Kent Roads Act 1737 (c.37)
Kent Roads Act 1743 (c.4)
Kent Roads Act 1748 (c.4)
Kent Roads Act 1748 (c.8)
Kent Roads Act 1751 (c.8)
Kent Roads Act 1753 (c.68)
Kent Roads Act 1754 (c.26)
Kent Roads Act 1759 (c.40)
Kent Roads Act 1762 (c.65)
Kent Roads Act 1762 (c.76)
Kent Roads Act 1764 (c.78)
Kent Roads Act 1765 (c.63)
Kent Roads Act 1765 (c.71)
Kent Roads Act 1766 (c.91)
Kent Roads Act 1766 (c.93)
Kent Roads Act 1767 (c.91)
Kent Roads Act 1767 (c.103)
Kent Roads Act 1769 (c.43)
Kent Roads Act 1769 (c.49)
Kent Roads Act 1769 (c.76)
Kent Roads Act 1769 (c.78)
Kent Roads Act 1769 (c.92)
Kent Roads Act 1773 (c.98)
Kent Roads Act 1773 (c.114)
Kent Roads Act 1776 (c.69)
Kent Roads Act 1782 (c.98)
Kent Roads Act 1782 (c.102)
Kent Roads Act 1785 (c.103)
Kent Roads Act 1785 (c.112)
Kent Roads Act 1786 (c.132)
Kent Roads Act 1786 (c.134)
Kent Roads Act 1786 (c.145)
Kent Roads Act 1788 (c.93)
Kent Roads Act 1789 (c.84)
Kent Roads Act 1789 (c.100)
Kent Roads Act 1790 (c.90)
Kent Roads Act 1791 (c.94)
Kent Roads Act 1792 (c.117)
Kent Roads Act 1793 (c.162)
Kent Roads Act 1793 (c.183)
Kent Roads Act 1795 (c.165)
Kent: Small Debts Act 1783 (c.8)
Kent: Small Debts Act 1786 (c.18)
Kent: Small Debts Act 1786 (c.22)
Kent: Small Debts Act 1786 (c.118)
Kent, Sussex Fortifications Act 1780 (c.10)
Kentish Town: Footpath Act 1771 (c.59)
Kenya Divorces (Validity) Act 1922 (c.10)
Kenya Independence Act 1963 (c.54)
Kenya Republic Act 1965 (c.5)
Kettering and Newport Pagnell Road Act 1754 (c.31)
Kettering to Newport Pagnell Roads Act 1773 (c.92)
Kettering to Newport Pagnell Road Act 1781 (c.103)
Kew Bridge (Building and Tolls) Act 1782 (c.42)
Kidderminster Church Act 1785 (c.94)
Kidderminster Roads Act 1777 (c.75)
Kidderminster: Small Debts Act 1772 (c.66)
Kilburn Road Act 1779 (c.120)
Kilmainham Hospital Act 1815 (c. 136)
Kilmainham Hospital Pensions Act 1807 (c.5)
Kilmainham Hospital (Pensions Commutation) Act 1813 (c.154)
Kimbolton Road Act 1755 (c.33)
Kincardine (County) Roads Act 1796 (c.132)
Kinghorn Beer Duties Act 1748 (c.13)
Kinghorn Beer Duties Act 1774 (c.28)
King's Bench Prison Act 1754 (c.17)
King's Bench Prison: Poor Relief Act 1783 (c.23)
King's Lynn: Pilotage Act 1772 (c.30)
King's Lynn: Small Debts Act 1770 (c.20)
Kingsholm District Act 1871 (c.54)
Kingston to Sheetbridge Road Act 1792 (c.119)
Kingston-upon-Hull: Improvement Act 1755 (c.27)
Kingston-upon-Hull: Improvement Act 1762 (c.70)
Kingston-upon-Hull: Improvement Act 1764 (c.74)
Kingston-upon-Hull: Improvement Act 1783 (c.55)
Kingston-upon-Hull Port Act 1774 (c.56)
Kingston-upon-Hull Roads Act 1744 (c.4)
Kingston-upon-Hull Roads Act 1767 (c.70)
Kingston-upon-Hull Roads Act 1788 (c.95)
Kingston-upon-Hull: Small Debts Act 1762 (c.38)
Kingston-upon-Thames: Streets Act 1772 (c.61)

Kingston-upon-Thames to Street Bride Road Act 1768 (c.56)
Kingstown and Dublin Harbours Act 1838 (c.36)
Kingstown Harbour Act 1836 (c.117)
Kingstown Harbour Act 1865 (c.67)
Kingstown Township Act 1898 (c.52)
Kinross and Alloa Road Act 1797 (c.171)
Kirby Kendal and Kirkby Ireleth Road Act 1763 (c.33)
Kirby Kendal to Kirkby Ireleth Road Act 1783 (c.23)
Kirby, Westmorland: Small Debts Act 1764 (c.41)
Kiribati Act 1979 (c.27)
Kirkby Lonsdale and Milnthorpe Road Act 1797 (c.165)
Kirkcaldy Beer Duties Act 1741 (c.8)
Kirkcaldy Beer Duties Act 1757 (c.69)
Kirkcaldy Beer Duties Act 1791 (c.82)
Kirkcudbright Roads Act 1780 (c.24)
Kirkcudbright Roads Act (c.153)
Knackers Act 1786 (c.71)
Knackers Act 1844 (c.87)
Knaresborough and Greenhammerton Road Act 1771 (c.65)
Knaresborough Inclosure Act 1789 (c.76)
Knaresborough: Water Supply Act 1764 (c.93)

L.C.C. (Money) Act 1890 (c.41)
L.C.C. (Money) Act 1891 (c.62)
Labour Bureaux (London) Act 1902 (c.13)
Labour Exchange Act 1909 (c.7)
Labourers' Cottages and Allotments (Ireland) Act 1882 (c.60)
Labourers (Ireland) Act 1883 (c.60)
Labourers (Ireland) Act 1885 (c.77)
Labourers (Ireland) Act 1886 (c.59)
Labourers (Ireland) Act 1891 (c.71)
Labourers (Ireland) Act 1892 (c.7)
Labourers (Ireland) Act 1896 (c.53)
Labourers (Ireland) Act 1906 (c.37)
Labourers (Ireland) Act 1911 (c.19)
Labourers (Ireland) Act 1914 (c.32)
Labourers (Ireland) Act 1918 (c.20)
Labourers (Ireland) Act 1919 (c.55)
Labouring Classes Lodging Houses and Dwellings (Ireland) Act 1866 (c.44)
Lairy Embankment (Plymouth) Act 1802 (c.32)
Lambeth Water Works Act 1785 (c.89)
Lanark and Hamilton Roads Act 1792 (c.122)
Lanark and Renfrew Roads Act 1789 (c.92)
Lanark Prisons Act 1868 (c.50)
Lanark Roads Act 1772 (c.82)
Lanark Roads Act 1792 (c.124)
Lancashire Roads Act 1730 (c.31)
Lancashire Roads Act 1774 (c.99)
Lancashire Roads Act 1784 (c.68)
Lancaster and Westmorland Roads Act 1782 (c.88)
Lancaster Bridge Act 1782 (c.57)
Lancaster Canal Act 1793 (c.107)
Lancaster County Clerk Act 1871 (c.73)
Lancaster: Drainage Act 1779 (c.33)
Lancaster Marsh: Drainage Act 1795 (c.11)
Lancaster Palatine Courts Act 1794 (c.58)
Lancaster Roads Act 1771 (c.91)
Lancaster Roads Act 1785 (c.106)
Lancaster Roads Act 1789 (c.107)
Lancaster Roads Act 1789 (c.110)
Lancaster Roads Act 1792 (c.139)
Lancaster Roads Act 1793 (c.181)
Lancaster Roads Act 1795 (c.144)
Land at Snaith Yorks. Act 1773 (c.85)
Land Charges Act 1900 (c.26)
Land Charges Act 1925 (c.22)
Land Charges Act 1972 (c.61)
Land Charges Registration and Searches Act 1888 (c.51)
Land Clauses Consolidation Act 1845 (c.18)
Land Clauses Consolidation Acts Amendment Act 1860 (c.106)
Land Clauses (Umpire) Act 1883 (c.15)
Land Commisssion Act 1967 (c.1)
Land Commission (Dissolution) Act 1971 (c.18)
Land Commissioners (Ireland) Salaries Act 1892 (c.45)
Land Compensation Act 1961 (c.33)
Land Compensation Act 1967 (c.1)
Land Compensation Act 1973 (c.26)
Land Compensation (Scotland) Act 1963 (c.51)
Land Compensation (Scotland) Act 1973 (c.56)
Land Drainage Act 1845 (c.56)
Land Drainage Act 1914 (c.4)
Land Drainage Act 1918 (c.17)
Land Drainage Act 1926 (c.24)
Land Drainage Act 1929 (c.8)
Land Drainage Act 1930 (c.44)
Land Drainage Act 1961 (c.48)
Land Drainage Act 1976 (c.70)
Land Drainage Act 1991 (c.59)
Land Drainage Act 1994 (c.25)
Land Drainage (Amendment) Act 1976 (c.17)
Land Drainage (Rating) Act 1743 (c.37)
Land Drainage (Scotland) Act 1930 (c.20)
Land Drainage (Scotland) Act 1935 (c.19)
Land Drainage (Scotland) Act 1941 (c.13)
Land Drainage (Scotland) Act 1958 (c.24)
Land Drainage Supplemental (No. 2) Act 1866 (c.80)
Land Drained at Great Carlton, Lincolnshire Act 1792 (c.91)
Land for Ordnance Services Act 1803 (cc. 65, 66)
Land for Prisons (Ireland) Act 1847 (c.26)
Land Law (Ireland) Act 1881 (c.49)
Land Law (Ireland) Act 1887 (c.33)
Land Law (Ireland) Act 1888 (c.13)
Land Law (Ireland) Act, 1888, Amendment 1889 (c.59)

Land Law (Ireland) Act 1896 (c.47)
Land Law (Ireland) Act 1881 (c.49)
Land Law (Ireland) Act 1887 (c.33)
Land Powers (Defence) Act 1958 (c.30)
Land Registers (Scotland) Act 1868 (c.64)
Land Registers (Scotland) Act 1995 (c.14)
Land Registration Act 1925 (c.21)
Land Registration Act 1936 (c.26)
Land Registration Act 1966 (c.39)
Land Registration Act 1986 (c.26)
Land Registration Act 1988 (c.3)
Land Registration and Land Charges Act 1971 (c.54)
Land Registration (Scotland) Act 1979 (c.33)
Land Registry Act 1862 (c.53)
Land Registry Act 1886 (c.1)
Land Registry (Middlesex Deeds) Act 1891 (c.64)
Land Registry (New Buildings) Act 1900 (c.19)
Land Revenue of the Crown Act 1815 (c.55)
Land Revenues of the Crown Act 1790 (c.50)
Land Settlement Amendment Act 1921 (c.43)
Land Settlement (Facilities) Act 1919 (c.59)
Land Settlement (Facilities) Amendment Act 1925 (c.85)
Land Settlement (Scotland) Act 1919 (c.97)
Land Settlement (Scotland) Act 1934 (c.35)
Land Tax Act 1702 (c.1)
Land Tax Act 1704 (c.1)
Land Tax Act 1705 (c.1)
Land Tax Act 1707 (c.35)
Land Tax Act 1708 (c.1)
Land Tax Act 1710 (c.1)
Land Tax Act 1711 (c.1)
Land Tax Act 1712 (c.1)
Land Tax Act 1713 (c.1)
Land Tax Act 1714 (c.1)
Land Tax Act 1715 (c.31)
Land Tax Act 1717 (c.1)
Land Tax Act 1718 (c.1)
Land Tax Act 1719 (c.1)
Land Tax Act 1720 (c.4)
Land Tax Act 1721 (c.1)
Land Tax Act 1723 (c.1)
Land Tax Act 1724 (c.1)
Land Tax Act 1725 (c.1)
Land Tax Act 1726 (c.1)
Land Tax Act 1727 (c.5)
Land Tax Act 1728 (c.4)
Land Tax Act 1729 (c.1)
Land Tax Act 1730 (c.4)
Land Tax Act 1732 (c.10)
Land Tax Act 1733 (c.7)
Land Tax Act 1734 (c.23)
Land Tax Act 1735 (c.3)
Land Tax Act 1736 (c.3)
Land Tax Act 1737 (c.14)
Land Tax Act 1746 (c.2)
Land Tax Act 1757 (c.4)
Land Tax Act 1757 (c.7)
Land Tax Act 1771 (c.5)
Land Tax Act 1772 (c.3)
Land Tax Act 1772 (c.8)
Land Tax Act 1774 (c.1)
Land Tax Act 1774 (c.17)
Land Tax Act 1775 (c.3)
Land Tax Act 1775 (c.26)
Land Tax Act 1776 (c.1)
Land Tax Act 1776 (c.4)
Land Tax Act 1776 (c.14)
Land Tax Act 1778 (c.2)
Land Tax Act 1778 (c.23)
Land Tax Act 1780 (c.2)
Land Tax Act 1780 (c.3)
Land Tax Act 1780 (c.23)
Land Tax Act 1782 (c.2)
Land Tax Act 1782 (c.9)
Land Tax Act 1783 (c.3)
Land Tax Act 1783 (c.4)
Land Tax Act 1783 (c.10)
Land Tax Act 1785 (c.4)
Land Tax Act 1785 (c.20)
Land Tax Act 1786 (c.3)
Land Tax Act 1786 (c.54)
Land Tax Act 1786 (c.103)
Land Tax Act 1786 (c.105)
Land Tax Act 1786 (c.121)
Land Tax Act 1787 (c.5)
Land Tax Act 1787 (c.47)
Land Tax Act 1788 (c.2)
Land Tax Act 1789 (c.6)
Land Tax Act 1790 (c.2)
Land Tax Act 1790 (c.13)
Land Tax Act 1791 (c.6)
Land Tax Act 1791 (c.14)
Land Tax Act 1792 (c.5)
Land Tax Act 1792 (c.23)
Land Tax Act 1793 (c.7)
Land Tax Act 1794 (c.8)
Land Tax Act 1795 (c.2)
Land Tax Act 1795 (c.17)
Land Tax Act 1796 (c.2)
Land Tax Act 1796 (c.89)
Land Tax Act 1797 (c.5)
Land Tax Act 1797 (c.26)
Land Tax Act 1797 (c.35)
Land Tax Act 1797 (c.128)
Land Tax Act 1800 (c.68)
Land Tax Act 1805 (c.48)
Land Tax Act 1808 (c.102)
Land Tax Act 1809 (c.55)
Land Tax Act 1809 (c.67)
Land Tax Act 1813 (c.142)
Land Tax Act 1814 (c.190)
Land Tax Act 1842 (c.37)
Land Tax, Assessed Tax, and Income Tax Act 1843 (c.24)
Land Tax Certificates Forgery Act 1812 (c.143)
Land Tax Commissioners Act 1798 (c.48)
Land Tax Commissioners Act 1844 (c.79)
Land Tax Commissioners Act 1867 (c.51)
Land Tax Commissioners Act 1906 (c.52)
Land Tax Commissioners Act 1927 (c.16)
Land Tax Commissioners Act 1937 (c.18)

Land Tax Commissioners (Appointment) Act 1836 (c.80)
Land Tax Commissioners (Appointment) Act 1838 (c.57)
Land Tax Commissioners (Appointment) Act 1866 (c.59)
Land Tax Commissioners (Appointment) Act 1869 (c.64)
Land Tax Commissioners (Appointment) Act 1874 (c.18)
Land Tax Commissioners (Names) Act 1879 (c.52)
Land Tax Commissioners (Names) Act 1881 (c.16)
Land Tax Commissioners Names Act 1886 (c.47)
Land Tax Commissioners Names Act 1893 (c.27)
Land Tax Commissioners Names Act 1899 (c.25)
Land, Tax, etc. Act 1806 (c.107)
Land, Tax, etc. Act 1815 (c.150)
Land Tax, Forfeited Estates, etc. Act 1702 (c.6)
Land Tax Perpetuation Act 1798 (c.60)
Land Tax Redemption Act 1799 (c.10)
Land Tax Redemption Act 1799 (c.21)
Land Tax Redemption Act 1799 (c.40)
Land Tax Redemption Act 1799 (c.43)
Land Tax Redemption Act 1799 (c.108)
Land Tax Redemption Act 1800 (c.28)
Land Tax Redemption Act 1800 (c.30)
Land Tax Redemption Act 1801 (c.72)
Land Tax Redemption Act 1802 (c.116)
Land Tax Redemption Act 1803 (c.51)
Land Tax Redemption Act 1805 (c.77)
Land Tax Redemption Act 1806 (c.133)
Land Tax Redemption Act 1810 (c.58)
Land Tax Redemption Act 1812 (c.80)
Land Tax Redemption Act 1813 (c.123)
Land Tax Redemption Act 1814 (c.173)
Land Tax Redemption Act 1837 (c.17)
Land Tax Redemption Act 1838 (c.58)
Land Tax Redemption, etc. Act 1798 (c.6)
Land Tenure Reform (Scotland) Act 1974 (c.38)
Land Transfer Act 1875 (c.87)
Land Transfer Act 1897 (c.65)
Landed Estates Court (Ireland) Act 1858 (c.72)
Landed Estates Court (Ireland) Act 1866 (c.99)
Landed Property Improvement (Ireland) Act 1847 (c.32)
Landing of Merchandise Act 1796 (c.82)
Landlord and Tenant Act 1709 (c.18(i))
Landlord and Tenant Act 1730 (c.28)
Landlord and Tenant Act 1871 (c.92)
Landlord and Tenant Act 1927 (c.36)
Landlord and Tenant Act 1954 (c.56)
Landlord and Tenant Act 1959 (c.64)
Landlord and Tenant Act 1962 (c.50)
Landlord and Tenant Act 1985 (c.70)
Landlord and Tenant Act 1987 (c.31)
Landlord and Tenant Act 1988 (c.26)
Landlord and Tenant (Covenants) Act 1995 (c.30)
Landlord and Tenant (Ireland) Act 1870 (c.46)
Landlord and Tenant (Ireland) Act 1871 (c.92)
Landlord and Tenant (Ireland) Act 1872 (c.32)
Landlord and Tenant Law Amendment Act Ireland 1860 (c.154)
Landlord and Tenant (Licensed Premises) Act 1990 (c.39)
Landlord and Tenant (Rent Control) Act 1949 (c.40)
Landlord and Tenant (Requisitioned Land) Act 1942 (c.13)
Landlord and Tenant (Requisitioned Land) Act 1944 (c.5)
Landlord and Tenant (Temporary Provisions) Act 1958 (c.68)
Landlord and Tenant (War Damage) Act 1939 (c.72)
Landlord and Tenant (War Damage) (Amendment) Act 1941 (c.41)
Lands at Sheerness and Chatham Act 1816 (c.74)
Lands Clauses Consolidation Act 1845 (c.18)
Lands Clauses Consolidation Act 1869 (c.18)
Lands Clauses Consolidation (Scotland) Act 1845 (c.19)
Lands Clauses (Taxation of Costs) Act 1895 (c.11)
Lands for Ordnance Services, Woolwich Act 1802 (c.89)
Lands for Ordnance Services, Woolwich Act 1803 (c.35)
Lands for the Defence of the Realm Act 1809 (c.112)
Lands of Earl of Pembroke Act 1783 (c.61)
Lands Tribunal Act 1949 (c.42)
Lands Valuation Amendment (Scotland) Act 1982 (c.57)
Lands Valuation (Scotland) Act 1854 (c.91)
Lands Valuation (Scotland) Act 1857 (c.58)
Lands Valuation (Scotland) Amendment Act 1895 (c.41)
Lands Valuation (Scotland) Amendment Act 1902 (c.25)
Lane End Chapel, Stoke upon Trent 1792 (c.88)
Langbaurgh Coroners Act 1873 (c.81)
Lapworth to Kingswood Canal Act 1795 (c.72)
Larceny Act 1808 (c.129)
Larceny Act 1868 (c.116)
Larceny Act 1896 (c.52)
Larceny Act 1901 (c.10)
Larceny Act 1916 (c.50)
Larceny (Advertisements) Act 1870 (c.65)
Late Earl of Seaforth Act 1734 (c.22)
Late Night Refreshment Houses Act 1969 (c.53)

Latent Damage Act 1986 (c.37)
Launceston: Poor Relief Act 1784 (c.17)
Launceston Roads Act 1781 (c.86)
Law Agents and Notaries Public (Scotland) Act 1891 (c.30)
Law Agents Apprenticeship (War Service) (Scotland) Act 1914 (c.20)
Law Agents Apprenticeship (War Service) (Scotland) Act 1919 (c.24)
Law Agents (Scotland) Act 1873 (c.63)
Law Agents (Scotland) Act Amendment 1896 (c.49)
Law and Procedure (Emergency Provisions) (Ireland) Act 1916 (c.46)
Law Commissions Act 1965 (c.22)
Law Costs (Ireland) Act 1823 (c.89)
Law of Commons Amendment Act 1893 (c.57)
Law of Distress Amendment Act 1888 (c.21)
Law of Distress Amendment Act 1895 (c.24)
Law of Distress Amendment Act 1908 (c.53)
Law of Distress and Small Debts (Ireland) Act 1888 (c.47)
Law of Distress and Small Debts (Ireland) Act 1893 (c.36)
Law of Libel Amendment Act 1888 (c.64)
Law of Property Act 1922 (c.16)
Law of Property Act 1925 (c.20)
Law of Property Act 1969 (c.59)
Law of Property Act (Postponement) Act 1924 (c.4)
Law of Property Amendment Act 1859 (c.35)
Law of Property Amendment Act 1860 (c.38)
Law of Property (Amendment) Act 1924 (c.5)
Law of Property (Amendment) Act 1926 (c.11)
Law of Property (Amendment) Act 1926 (c.14)
Law of Property (Amendment) Act 1929 (c.9)
Law of Property (Entailed Interests) Act 1931 (c.27)
Law of Property (Joint Tenants) Act 1964 (c.63)
Law of Property (Miscellaneous Provisions) Act 1989 (c.34)
Law of Property (Miscellaneous Provisions) Act 1994 (c.36)
Law Officers Act 1944 (c.25)
Law Officers' Fees Act 1872 (c.70)
Law Reform (Contributory Negligence) Act 1945 (c.28)
Law Reform (Damages and Solatium) (Scotland) Act 1962 (c.42)
Law Reform (Diligence) (Scotland) Act 1973 (c.22)
Law Reform (Enforcement of Contracts) Act 1954 (c.34)
Law Reform (Frustrated Contracts) Act 1943 (c.40)
Law Reform (Husband and Wife) Act 1962 (c.48)
Law Reform (Husband and Wife) (Scotland) Act 1984 (c.15)
Law Reform (Jurisdiction in Delict) (Scotland) Act 1971 (c.55)
Law Reform (Limitation of Actions etc.) Act 1954 (c.36)
Law Reform (Married Women and Tortfeasors) Act 1935 (c.30)
Law Reform (Miscellaneous Provisions) Act 1934 (c.41)
Law Reform (Miscellaneous Provisions) Act 1949 (c.100)
Law Reform (Miscellaneous Provisions) Act 1970 (c.33)
Law Reform (Miscellaneous Provisions) Act 1971 (c.43)
Law Reform (Miscellaneous Provisions) (Scotland) Act 1940 (c.42)
Law Reform (Miscellaneous Provisions) (Scotland) Act 1966 (c.19)
Law Reform (Miscellaneous Provisions) (Scotland) Act 1968 (c.70)
Law Reform (Miscellaneous Provisions) (Scotland) Act 1980 (c.55)
Law Reform (Miscellaneous Provisions) (Scotland) Act 1985 (c.73)
Law Reform (Miscellaneous Provisions) (Scotland) Act 1990 (c.40)
Law Reform (Parent and Child) (Scotland) Act 1986 (c.9)
Law Reform (Personal Injuries) Act 1948 (c.41)
Law Reform (Personal Injuries) Amendment Act 1948 (c.7)
Law Reform (Personal Injuries) Amendment Act 1953 (c.7)
Law Reform (Succession) Act 1995 (c.41)
Law Reform (Year and a Day Rule) Act 1996 (c.19)
Laws Continuation, etc. Act 1739 (c.18)
Laws in Wales Act 1542 (c.39)
Laying of Documents before Parliament (Interpretation) Act 1948 (c.59)
Lazarets Act 1772 (c.57)
Lead Paint (Protection Against Poisoning) Act 1926 (c.37)
Lease of Exeter Castle Act 1710 (c.24)
Leasehold Property Act and Long Leases (Scotland) Act Extension Act 1953 (c.12)
Leasehold Property (Repairs) Act 1938 (c.34)
Leasehold Property (Temporary Provisions) Act 1951 (c.38)
Leasehold Reform Act 1967 (c.88)
Leasehold Reform Act 1979 (c.44)
Leasehold Reform, Housing and Urban Development Act 1993 (c.28)
Leases and Sales of Settled Estates Amendment Act 1874 (c.33)
Leases for Schools (Ireland) Act 1881 (c.65)
Leases (Ireland) Act 1846 (c.112)
Leases of Episcopal Lands (Ireland) Act 1813 (c.92)
Leasing-making, etc. (Scotland) Act 1837 (c.5)
Leasing-making (Scotland) Act 1825 (c.47)

Leasing Powers Amendment Act for Religious Purposes in Ireland Act 1875 (c.11)
Leasing Powers for Religious Worship in Ireland Act 1855 (c.39)
Leatherhead and Guildford Road Act 1757 (c.77)
Lecturers and Parish Clerks Act 1844 (c.59)
Lectures Copyright Act 1835 (c.65)
Ledbury Highways Act 1720 (c.23)
Ledbury Roads Act 1793 (c.132)
Leddon and Clavering, Norfolk: Poor Relief Act 1764 (c.90)
Leeds and Blackburn Roads Act 1781 (c.102)
Leeds and Halifax Roads Act 1740 (c.32)
Leeds and Halifax Roads Act 1751 (c.55)
Leeds and Halifax Roads Act 1783 (c.94)
Leeds and Harrogate Road Act 1796 (c.138)
Leeds and Liverpool Canal Act 1770 (c.114)
Leeds and Liverpool Canal Act 1783 (c.47)
Leeds and Wakefield Road Act 1770 (c.61)
Leeds Bridge Act 1759 (c.54)
Leeds Church Act 1792 (c.89)
Leeds Coal Supply Act 1779 (c.11)
Leeds Coal Supply Act 1793 (c.86)
Leeds Corporation (Consolidation) Act 1905 (c.1)
Leeds: Lighting, etc. Act 1755 (c.41)
Leeds to Liverpool Canal Act 1790 (c.65)
Leeds to Liverpool Canal Act 1794 (c.94)
Leeds to Otley Road Act 1781 (c.98)
Leeds to Sheffield Road Act 1760 (c.33)
Leeds to Wakefield Road Act 1792 (c.131)
Leeds University Act 1904 (c.12)
Leeds: Water Supply Act 1790 (c.68)
Leeward Islands Act 1871 (c.107)
Leeward Islands Act 1956 (c.23)
Legacy Duty Act 1796 (c.52)
Legacy Duty Act 1797 Act (c.135)
Legacy Duty Act 1799 (c.73)
Legacy Duty Act 1805 (c.28)
Legal Advice and Assistance Act 1972 (c.50)
Legal Aid Act 1960 (c.28)
Legal Aid Act 1964 (c.30)
Legal Aid Act 1974 (c.4)
Legal Aid Act 1979 (c.26)
Legal Aid Act 1982 (c.44)
Legal Aid Act 1988 (c.34)
Legal Aid and Advice Act 1949 (c.51)
Legal Aid and Solicitors (Scotland) Act 1949 (c.63)
Legal Aid (Scotland) Act 1967 (c.43)
Legal Aid (Scotland) Act 1986 (c.47)
Legal Practitioners Act 1875 (c.79)
Legal Practitioners Act 1876 (c.66)
Legal Practitioners (Ireland) Act 1876 (c.44)
Legal Proceedings Against Enemies Act 1915 (c.36)
Legal Rate of Interest Act 1774 (c.79)
Legislative Council for Canada Act 1854 (c.118)
Legislative Council of Canada Act 1859 (c.10)
Legislative Council, New Zealand Act 1868 (c.57)
Legitimacy Act 1926 (c.60)
Legitimacy Act 1959 (c.73)
Legitimacy Act 1976 (c.31)
Legitimacy Declaration Act 1858 (c.93)
Legitimacy Declaration Act (Ireland) 1868 (c.20)
Legitimation (Re-registration of Births) Act 1957 (c.39)
Legitimation (Scotland) Act 1968 (c.22)
Leicester and Derby Roads Act 1759 (c.46)
Leicester and Notts. Roads Act 1762 (c.82)
Leicester and Stafford Roads Act 1753 (c.85)
Leicester and Stafford Roads Act 1779 (c.85)
Leicester and Warwick Roads Act 1754 (c.42)
Leicester and Warwick Roads Act 1781 (c.85)
Leicester Navigation Act 1791 (c.65)
Leicester Navigation Act 1797 (c.51)
Leicester Road Act 1725 (c.5)
Leicester Roads Act 1745 (c.10)
Leicester Roads Act 1753 (c.46)
Leicester Roads Act 1757 (c.44)
Leicester Roads Act 1759 (c.41)
Leicester Roads Act 1764 (c.84)
Leicester Roads Act 1769 (c.91)
Leicester Roads Act 1776 (c.81)
Leicester Roads Act 1777 (c.108)
Leicester Roads Act 1779 (c.90)
Leicester Roads Act 1781 (c.89)
Leicester Roads Act 1783 (c.107)
Leicester Roads Act 1785 (c.113)
Leicester Roads Act 1788 (c.100)
Leicester Roads Act 1790 (c.92)
Leicester to Peterborough Road Act 1754 (c.30)
Leicester, Warwick and Coventry Roads Act 1762 (c.80)
Leicestershire and Northamptonshire Union Canal Act 1793 (c.98)
Leicestershire Roads Act 1757 (c.49)
Leicestershire Roads Act 1762 (c.54)
Leicestershire Roads Act 1771 (c.88)
Leigh and Deerhurst Canal Act 1792 (c.83)
Leith and Bruntisland Ferries, etc. Act 1792 (c.93)
Leith Harbour Act 1754 (c.8)
Leith Harbour Act 1788 (c.58)
Leith Harbour and Docks Act 1847 (c.114)
Leith Harbour and Docks Act 1860 (c.48)
Leominster Canal Act 1791 (c.69)
Leominster Canal Act 1796 (c.70)
Leominster Roads Act 1728 (c.13)
Leominster Roads Act 1777 (c.85)
Leominster Roads Act 1797 (c.176)
Lesotho Independence Act 1966 (c.24)
Letter Stealing (Scotland) Act 1836 (c.21)
Letters of Marque Act 1801 (c.76)
Letters Patent for Inventions Act 1835 (c.83)
Levant Trade Act 1753 (c.18)
Level Crossings Act 1983 (c.16)

Lewes and Brighton Road Act 1770 (c.64)
Lewes and Eastbourne Road Act 1758 (c.67)
Lewes: Improvement Act 1791 (c.86)
Lewes to Brighton Road Act 1791 (c.115)
Lewis (Estates and Crown Claims) Act 1806 (c.131)
Lewisham Church Act 1774 (c.93)
Liabilities (War-Time Adjustment) Act 1941 (c.24)
Liabilities (War-Time Adjustment) Act 1944 (c.40)
Liabilities (War-Time Adjustment) (Scotland) Act 1944 (c.29)
Liability for War Damage (Miscellaneous Provisions) Act 1939 (c.102)
Liardet's Cement Patent Act 1776 (c.29)
Libel Act 1792 (c.60)
Libel Act 1843 (c.96)
Libel Act 1845 (c.75)
Libel (Ireland) Act 1868 (c.69)
Liberties Act 1836 (c.87)
Liberties Act 1850 (c.105)
Liberty of Ely Act 1837 (c.53)
Liberty of Religious Worship Act 1855 (c.86)
Libraries Offences Act 1898 (c.53)
Licences for Retailing Beer, etc. Act 1784 (c.30)
Licence to J. Porter etc. to Import Silk Act 1740 (c.4)
Licensed Premises (Exclusion of Certain Persons) Act 1980 (c.32)
Licensed Premises in New Towns 1952 (c.65)
Licensing (Abolition of State Management) Act 1971 (c.65)
Licensing Act 1842 (c.44)
Licensing Act 1872 (c.94)
Licensing Act 1874 (c.49)
Licensing Act 1902 (c.28)
Licensing Act 1904 (c.23)
Licensing Act 1906 (c.42)
Licensing Act 1921 (c.42)
Licensing Act 1949 (c.59)
Licensing Act 1953 (c.46)
Licensing Act 1961 (c.61)
Licensing Act 1964 (c.26)
Licensing Act 1988 (c.17)
Licensing (Airports) Act 1956 (c.37)
Licensing (Alcohol Education and Research) Act 1981 (c.28)
Licensing (Amendment) Act 1967 (c.51)
Licensing (Amendment) Act 1976 (c.18)
Licensing (Amendment) Act 1977 (c.26)
Licensing (Amendment) Act 1980 (c.40)
Licensing (Amendment) Act 1981 (c.40)
Licensing (Amendment) Act 1985 (c.40)
Licensing (Amendment) Act 1989 (c.20)
Licensing Amendment (Scotland) Act 1897 (c.50)
Licensing (Amendment) (Scotland) Act 1992 (c.18)
Licensing (Amendment) (Scotland) Act 1993 (c.20)
Licensing (Amendment) (Scotland) Act 1996 (c.36)
Licensing (Certificates in Suspense) (Scotland) Act 1967 (c.14)
Licensing (Consolidation) Act 1910 (c.24)
Licensing (Evidence) Act 1884 (c.29)
Licensing (Ireland) Act 1836 (c.38)
Licensing (Ireland) Act 1855 (c.62)
Licensing (Ireland) Act 1860 (c.35)
Licensing (Ireland) Act 1874 (c.69)
Licensing (Ireland) Act 1902 (c.18)
Licensing (Ireland) Act 1905 (c.3)
Licensing (Low Alcohol Drinks) Act 1990 (c.21)
Licensing (Occasional Permissions) Act 1983 (c.24)
Licensing of Alehouses Act 1792 (c.59)
Licensing (Permitted Hours) Act 1934 (c.26)
Licensing Planning (Temporary Provisions) Act 1944 (c.15)
Licensing Planning (Temporary Provisions) Act 1946 (c.53)
Licensing (Restaurant Meals) Act 1987 (c.2)
Licensing (Retail Sales) Act 1988 (c.25)
Licensing (Scotland) Act 1903 (c.25)
Licensing (Scotland) Act 1959 (c.51)
Licensing (Scotland) Act 1962 (c.51)
Licensing (Scotland) Act 1969 (c.13)
Licensing (Scotland) Act 1976 (c.66)
Licensing (Seamen's Canteens) Act 1954 (c.11)
Licensing (Sunday Hours) Act 1995 (c.33)
Lichfield Roads Act 1728 (c.5)
Lieutenancy Clerks Allowances Act 1887 (c.36)
Life Annuities Act 1808 (c.142)
Life Annuities Act 1809 (c.104)
Life Assurance Act 1774 (c.48)
Life Assurance Companies Act 1870 (c.61)
Life Assurance Companies Act 1871 (c.58)
Life Assurance Companies Act 1872 (c.41)
Life Insurance Companies (Payment into Court) Act 1896 (c.8)
Life Insurance (Ireland) Act 1866 (c.42)
Life Peerages Act 1958 (c.21)
Light Locomotives (Ireland) Act 1903 (c.2)
Light Railways Act 1896 (c.48)
Light Railways Act 1912 (c.19)
Light Railways Commissioners (Salaries) Act 1901 (c.36)
Light Railways (Ireland) Act 1889 (c.66)
Light Railways (Ireland) Act 1893 (c.50)
Light Silver Coin Act 1774 (c.42)
Lighthouses Act 1836 (c.79)
Lighthouses (Ireland) Act 1810 (c.95)
Lighting, etc., of Cities (Ireland) Act 1807 (c.42)
Lighting of Towns (Ireland) Act 1857 (c.12)
Lights on Vehicles Act 1907 (c.45)
Limehouse, Stepney Parish Act 1730 (c.17)
Limehouse, Stepney: Streets Act 1782 (c.87)
Limerick Harbour Act 1867 (c.53)
Limitation Act 1939 (c.21)

Limitation Act 1963 (c.47)
Limitation Act 1975 (c.54)
Limitation Act 1980 (c.58)
Limitation Amendment Act 1980 (c.24)
Limitation (Enemies and War Prisoners) Act 1945 (c.16)
Limitation of Action Act 1843 (c.54)
Limitation of Time (Ireland) (Canal Companies) Act 1815 (c.90)
Limitations of Actions and Costs Act 1842 (c.97)
Limited Liability Act 1855 (c.133)
Limited Owners Reservoirs and Water Supply Further Facilities Act 1877 (c.31)
Limited Owners Residence Act 1870 (c.56)
Limited Owners Residences Act (1870) Amendment Act 1871 (c.84)
Limited Partnerships Act 1907 (c.24)
Limited Penalties Act 1864 (c.110)
Lincoln and Northampton Roads Act 1757 (c.68)
Lincoln and Northamptonshire Roads Act 1765 (c.106)
Lincoln and Nottinghamshire Roads Act 1758 (c.57)
Lincoln and Nottinghamshire Roads Act 1766 (c.83)
Lincoln and Nottinghamshire Roads Act 1767 (c.78)
Lincoln and Nottinghamshire Roads Act 1767 (c.79)
Lincoln and Nottinghamshire Roads Act 1780 (c.73)
Lincoln and Nottinghamshire Roads Act 1782 (c.94)
Lincoln and Nottinghamshire Roads Act 1787 (c.71)
Lincoln and Peterborough Roads Act 1756 (c.85)
Lincoln and Rutland Roads Act 1762 (c.73)
Lincoln and Rutland Roads Act 1786 (c.159)
Lincoln (City) Roads Act 1738 (c.10)
Lincoln (City) Roads Act 1797 (c.168)
Lincoln: Drainage Act 1777 (c.70)
Lincoln: Drainage Act 1785 (c.14)
Lincoln: Drainage Act 1787 (c.66)
Lincoln: Drainage Act 1789 (c.32)
Lincoln: Drainage Act 1789 (c.70)
Lincoln: Drainage Act 1793 (c.116)
Lincoln: Drainage Act 1797 (c.67)
Lincoln: Drainage, etc. Act 1794 (c.102)
Lincoln: Improvement Act 1791 (c.80)
Lincoln: Poor Relief Act 1796 (c.102)
Lincoln Roads Act 1738 (c.8)
Lincoln Roads Act 1756 (c.84)
Lincoln Roads Act 1758 (c.44)
Lincoln Roads Act 1764 (c.53)
Lincoln Roads Act 1764 (c.80)
Lincoln Roads Act 1765 (c.73)
Lincoln Roads Act 1765 (c.88)
Lincoln Roads Act 1765 (c.96)
Lincoln Roads Act 1777 (c.109)
Lincoln Roads Act 1778 (c.104)
Lincoln Roads Act 1780 (c.75)
Lincoln Roads Act 1783 (c.34)
Lincoln Roads Act 1785 (c.123)
Lincoln Roads Act 1786 (c.137)
Lincoln Roads Act 1786 (c.138)
Lincoln Roads Act 1786 (c.141)
Lincoln Roads Act 1786 (c.146)
Lincoln Roads Act 1793 (c.150)
Lincoln: Small Debts Act 1778 (c.43)
Lincoln's Inn Fields Rate Act 1734 (c.26)
Lincolnshire Coroners Act 1899 (c.48)
Lincolnshire: Small Debts Act 1777 (c.62)
Lincolnshire: Small Debts Act 1778 (c.34)
Lincolnshire: Small Debts Act 1779 (c.43)
Linen and Hemp Manufacturers Act 1750 (c.31)
Linen and Hempen Manufacturers (Scotland) Act 1726 (c.26)
Linen, etc., Manufacturers (Ireland) Act 1850 (c.48)
Linen, etc., Manufacturers (Ireland) Act 1852 (c.13)
Linen, etc., Manufacturers (Ireland) Act 1853 (c.103)
Linen, etc., Manufacturers (Ireland) Act 1854 (c.46)
Linen, etc., Manufacturers (Ireland) Act 1859 (c.25)
Linen Manufacture (Ireland) Act 1802 (c.75)
Linen Manufacture (Ireland) Act 1804 (c.42)
Linen Manufacture (Ireland) Act 1804 (c.69)
Linen Manufacture, (Scotland) Act (c.23)
Linen Manufacture (Scotland) Act 1753 (c.20)
Linen Manufacturers, etc. (Ireland) Act 1838 (c.52)
Linen Manufacturers (Ireland) Act 1844 (c.47)
Linen (Trade Marks) Act 1743 (c.30)
Linen (Trade Marks) Act 1744 (c.24)
Linens, etc. Act 1794 (c.23)
Linlithgow and Stirling Roads Act 1790 (c.108)
Linlithgow Beer Duties Act 1732 (c.18)
Linlithgow Roads Act 1771 (c.79)
Linlithgow Roads Act 1781 (c.79)
Linlithgow Roads Act 1790 (c.105)
Linlithgow Roads and Bridges Act 1779 (c.12)
Liqueur Act 1848 (c.121)
Liquidation Act 1868 (c.68)
Lis. Pendens Act 1867 (c.47)
Liston, Essex Roads Act 1790 (c.84)
Litchfield Roads Act 1743 (c.24)
Literary and Scientific Institution Act 1854 (c.112)
Literary Copyright Act 1842 (c.45)
Litigants in Person (Costs and Expenses) Act 1975 (c.47)
Litter Act 1958 (c.34)
Litter Act 1983 (c.35)
Little Bowden to Rockingham Road Act 1793 (c.143)

Little Cumbrae Lighthouse Act 1756 (c.20)
Littlehampton Harbour Act 1732 (c.12)
Littlehampton Harbour Act 1793 (c.100)
Liverpool, Admiralty District Registrar Act 1970 (c.45)
Liverpool and Prescot Road Act 1725 (c.21)
Liverpool and Preston Road Act 1771 (c.93)
Liverpool Church Act 1792 (c.76)
Liverpool Churches Act 1767 (c.80)
Liverpool Court of Passage Act 1896 (c.21)
Liverpool Courts of Passage Act 1893 (c.37)
Liverpool Dock Act 1737 (c.32)
Liverpool Docks Act 1709 (c.8)
Liverpool Harbour Act 1762 (c.86)
Liverpool Harbour Act 1785 (c.15)
Liverpool, Improvement Act 1749 (c.24)
Liverpool: Improvement Act 1762 (c.68)
Liverpool: Improvement Act 1786 (c.12)
Liverpool: Improvement Act 1788 (c.13)
Liverpool Note Issue Act 1793 (c.31)
Liverpool Rectory Act 1786 (c.15)
Liverpool Theatre Act 1771 (c.16)
Liverpool to Preston Road Act 1786 (c.126)
Livestock Industry Act 1937 (c.50)
Livestock Rearing Act 1951 (c.18)
Llandilo Rhynws Bridge Act 1784 (c.66)
Llandovery Bridge Act 1773 (c.111)
Llanfyllin Market House Act 1789 (c.24)
Llangollen International Musical Eisteddfod Act 1967 (c.49)
Llanyblodwell to Newtown Canal Act 1794 (c.39)
Lloyd's Signal Stations Act 1888 (c.29)
Loan Act 1901 (c.12)
Loan Act 1902 (c.4)
Loan from Bank of England Act 1815 (c.16)
Loan Societies Act 1840 (c.110)
Loan Societies Act 1841 (c.55)
Loan Societies Act 1842 (c.5)
Loan Societies Act 1843 (c.41)
Loan Societies Act 1844 (c.54)
Loan Societies Act 1845 (c.60)
Loan Societies Act 1846 (c.52)
Loan Societies Act 1848 (c.64)
Loan Societies Act 1849 (c.37)
Loan Societies Act 1850 (c.45)
Loan Societies Act 1851 (c.31)
Loan Societies Act 1852 (c.15)
Loan Societies Act 1853 (c.109)
Loan Societies Act 1857 (c.41)
Loan Societies Act 1858 (c.19)
Loan Societies Act 1863 (c.56)
Loan Societies (Ireland) Act 1836 (c.55)
Loan Societies (Ireland) Act 1838 (c.78)
Loan Societies (Ireland) Act 1843 Amendment Act 1872 (c.17)
Loan to Emperor of Germany Act 1795 (c.93)
Loan to Emperor of Germany Act 1797 (c.59)
Loan to South Australia Act 1841 (c.13)
Loans for Erection of Workhouses Act 1802 (c.74)
Loans for Erection of Workhouses Act 1803 (c.110)
Loans for Parsonages, etc. (Ireland) Act 1803 (c.106)
Loans for Public Works (Ireland) Act 1846 (c.85)
Loans for Public Works (Ireland) Act 1846 (c.108)
Loans for Public Works (Ireland) Act 1851 (c.51)
Loans for Relief of Certain Merchants Act 1799 (c.5)
Loans for Schools, etc. (Ireland) Act 1884 (c.22)
Loans (Incumbents of Benefices) Amendment Act 1918 (c.42)
Loans of Exchequer Bills Act 1771 (c.25)
Loans of Exchequer Bills Act 1792 (cc.15, 16)
Loans of Exchequer Bills Act 1798 (cc.82–84)
Loans of Exchequer Bills Act 1799 (cc.68–71)
Loans or Exchequer Bills Act 1793 (cc.17, 18)
Loans or Exchequer Bills Act 1774 (c.69)
Loans or Exchequer Bills Act 1775 (c.38)
Loans or Exchequer Bills Act 1776 (c.35)
Loans or Exchequer Bills Act 1776 (c.38)
Loans or Exchequer Bills Act 1776 (c.45)
Loans or Exchequer Bills Act 1776 (c.51)
Loans or Exchequer Bills Act 1778 (c.38)
Loans or Exchequer Bills Act 1778 (c.57)
Loans or Exchequer Bills Act 1778 (c.64)
Loans or Exchequer Bills Act 1779 (cc.63, 64)
Loans or Exchequer Bills Act 1779 (c.73)
Loans or Exchequer Bills Act 1780 (cc.41, 42)
Loans or Exchequer Bills Act 1780 (c.43)
Loans or Exchequer Bills Act 1780 (c.53)
Loans or Exchequer Bills Act 1780 (c.57)
Loans or Exchequer Bills Act 1781 (c.59)
Loans or Exchequer Bills Act 1782 (c.36)
Loans or Exchequer Bills Act 1782 (c.76)
Loans or Exchequer Bills Act 1783 (c.12)
Loans or Exchequer Bills Act 1783 (c.72)
Loans or Exchequer Bills Act 1783 (c.84)
Loans or Exchequer Bills Act 1784 (c.33)
Loans or Exchequer Bills Act 1784 (c.52)
Loans or Exchequer Bills Act 1785 (cc.11, 12)
Loans or Exchequer Bills Act 1785 (c.33)
Loans or Exchequer Bills Act 1786 (cc.32, 33)
Loans or Exchequer Bills Act 1787 (c.24)
Loans or Exchequer Bills Act 1788 (cc.18,19)
Loans or Exchequer Bills Act 1789 (cc.34, 35)
Loans or Exchequer Bills Act 1790 (cc.15, 16)
Loans or Exchequer Bills Act 1790 (c.24)
Loans or Exchequer Bills Act 1791 (cc.48–50)
Loans or Exchequer Bills Act 1794 (cc.28, 29)
Loans or Exchequer Bills Act 1794 (c.62)
Loans or Exchequer Bills Act 1795 (cc.21, 22)
Loans or Exchequer Bills Act 1795 (c.37)
Loans or Exchequer Bills Act 1796 (c.31)
Loans or Exchequer Bills Act 1797 (c.8)
Loans or Exchequer Bills Act 1797 (c.20)
Loans or Exchequer Bills Act 1797 (c.114)
Loans or Exchequer Bills Act 1799 (c.4)
Loans or Exchequer Bills Act 1799 (c.18)
Loans or Exchequer Bills Act 1799 (c.33)

Loans or Exchequer Bills Act 1799 (c.41)
Loans or Exchequer Bills Act 1800 (cc.102–104)
Loans or Exchequer Bills Act 1801 (c.9)
Loans or Exchequer Bills Act 1801 (cc.81–83)
Loans or Exchequer Bills Act 1802 (c.5)
Loans or Exchequer Bills Act 1802 (c.17)
Loans or Exchequer Bills Act 1802 (c.21)
Loans or Exchequer Bills Act 1802 (cc.110, 111)
Loans or Exchequer Bills Act 1803 (c.15)
Loans or Exchequer Bills Act 1803 (c.36)
Loans or Exchequer Bills Act 1803 (c.93)
Loans or Exchequer Bills Act 1803 (cc.146, 147)
Loans or Exchequer Bills Act 1804 (c.31)
Loans or Exchequer Bills Act 1804 (cc.45, 46)
Loans or Exchequer Bills Act 1804 (c.81)
Loans or Exchequer Bills Act 1805 (c.7)
Loans or Exchequer Bills Act 1806 (c.6)
Loans or Exchequer Bills Act 1806 (cc.25, 26)
Loans or Exchequer Bills Act 1806 (c.41)
Loans or Exchequer Bills Act 1807 (c.2)
Loans or Exchequer Bills Act 1807 (cc.6, 7)
Loans or Exchequer Bills Act 1807 (c.73)
Loans or Exchequer Bills Act 1812 (c.137)
Loans or Exchequer Bills, etc. Act 1805 (cc.118–120)
Loans to A. Houston and Co., etc. Act 1800 (c.101)
Loans to Grenada and St. Vincent Traders Act 1796 (c.27)
Loans to Grenada and St. Vincent Traders Act 1799 (c.13)
Lobsters (Scotland) Act 1735 (c.33)
Local Acts, Preliminary Inquiries Act 1846 (c.106)
Local Acts, Preliminary Inquiries Act 1848 (c.129)
Local and Personal (Durham University) Act 1861 (c.82)
Local and Personal (Inverness Bridge (Treasury Grant)) Act 1855 (c.113)
Local and Personal (River Suck Drainage) Act 1890 (c.12)
Local Authorities (Admission of the Press to Meetings) Act 1908 (c.43)
Local Authorities (Disqualification Relief) Act 1914 (c.10)
Local Authorities (Emergency Provisions) Act 1923 (c.6)
Local Authorities (Emergency Provisions) Act 1924 (c.29)
Local Authorities (Emergency Provisions) Act 1926 (c.10)
Local Authorities (Emergency Provisions) Act 1928 (c.9)
Local Authorities (Expenditure on Special Purposes) (Scotland) Act 1961 (c.32)
Local Authorities (Expenditure Powers) Act 1983 (c.52)
Local Authorities (Expenses) Act 1887 (c.72)
Local Authorities (Expenses) Act 1956 (c.36)
Local Authorities (Financial Provisions) Act 1921 (c.67)
Local Authorities (Goods and Services) Act 1970 (c.39)
Local Authorities (Historic Buildings) Act 1962 (c.36)
Local Authorities (Ireland) (etc.) Act 1911 (c.35)
Local Authorities (Land) Act 1963 (c.29)
Local Authorities Loans Act 1945 (c.18)
Local Authorities Loans (Scotland) Act 1891 (c.34)
Local Authorities Loans (Scotland) Act, 1891, Amendment 1893 (c.8)
Local Authorities Loans (Scotland) Act 1924 (c.36)
Local Authorities' Mutual Investment Trust Act 1968 (c.25)
Local Authorities (Publicity) Act 1931 (c.17)
Local Authorities (Qualification of Members) Act 1971 (c.7)
Local Authorities (Restoration of Works Powers) Act 1977 (c.47)
Local Authorities (Treasury Powers) Act 1906 (c.33)
Local Authority Social Services Act 1970 (c.42)
Local Bankruptcy (Ireland) Act 1888 (c.44)
Local Commissioners Relief Act 1838 (c.65)
Local Education Authorities (Medical Treatment) Act 1909 (c.13)
Local Elections and Register of Electors (Temporary Provisions) Act 1939 (c.115)
Local Elections and Register of Electors (Temporary Provisions) Act 1940 (c.3)
Local Elections and Register of Electors (Temporary Provisions) Act 1941 (c.3)
Local Elections and Register of Electors (Temporary Provisions) Act 1941 (c.49)
Local Elections and Register of Electors (Temporary Provisions) Act 1942 (c.38)
Local Elections and Register of Electors (Temporary Provisions) Act 1943 (c.2)
Local Elections and Register of Electors (Temporary Provisions) Act 1944 (c.3)
Local Elections (Expenses) Act 1919 (c.13)
Local Elections (Service Abroad) Act 1945 (c.1)
Local Employment Act 1960 (c.18)
Local Employment Act 1963 (c.19)
Local Employment Act 1970 (c.7)
Local Employment Act 1972 (c.5)
Local (Forfeited Estates: Scotland) Act 1789 (c.28)
Local Government Act 1858 (c.98)
Local Government Act 1888 (c.41)
Local Government Act 1894 (c.73)
Local Government Act 1897 (c.1)
Local Government Act 1929 (c.17)
Local Government Act 1933 (c.51)
Local Government Act 1948 (c.26)
Local Government Act 1958 (c.55)

Local Government Act 1966 (c.42)
Local Government Act 1972 (c.70)
Local Government Act 1974 (c.7)
Local Government Act 1978 (c.39)
Local Government Act 1985 (c.51)
Local Government Act 1986 (c.10)
Local Government Act 1987 (c.44)
Local Government Act 1988 (c.9)
Local Government Act 1992 (c.19)
Local Government (Access to Information) Act 1985 (c.43)
Local Government (Adjustments) Act 1913 (c.19)
Local Government (Adjustments) (Scotland) Act 1914 (c.74)
Local Government (Allotments and Land Cultivation) (Ireland) Act 1917 (c.30)
Local Government (Amendment) Act 1863 (c.17)
Local Government (Amendment) Act 1993 (c.27)
Local Government and Housing Act 1989 (c.42)
Local Government and Miscellaneous Financial Provisions (Scotland) Act 1958 (c.64)
Local Government and Other Officers' Superannuation Act 1922 (c.59)
Local Government and Other Officers Superannuation (Temporary Provisions) Act 1933 (c.43)
Local Government and Planning (Amendment) Act 1981 (c.41)
Local Government and Planning (Scotland) Act 1982 (c.43)
Local Government Board Act 1871 (c.70)
Local Government Board (Ireland) Act 1872 (c.69)
Local Government Board (Ireland) Amendment Act 1881 (c.28)
Local Government Boundaries Act 1871 (c.70)
Local Government (Boundaries) Act 1887 (c.61)
Local Government (Boundary Commission) Act 1944 (c.38)
Local Government Boundary Commission (Dissolution) Act 1949 (c.83)
Local Government (Clerks) Act 1931 (c.45)
Local Government (County Boroughs and Adjustments) Act 1926 (c.38)
Local Government (Determination of Differences) Act 1896 (c.9)
Local Government (Development and Finance) (Scotland) Act 1964 (c.67)
Local Government (Elections) Act 1896 (c.1)
Local Government Elections Act 1956 (c.43)
Local Government (Elections) (No. 2) Act 1896 (c.4)
Local Government (Emergency Provisions) Act 1916 (c.12)
Local Government Emergency Provisions (No. 2) Act 1916 (c.55)
Local Government etc. (Scotland) Act 1994 (c.39)
Local Government Finance Act 1982 (c.32)
Local Government Finance Act 1987 (c.6)
Local Government Finance Act 1988 (c.41)
Local Government Finance Act 1992 (c.14)
Local Government Finance and Valuation Act 1991 (c.51)
Local Government Finance (Publicity for Auditors' Reports) Act 1991 (c.15)
Local Government (Financial Provisions) Act 1937 (c.22)
Local Government (Financial Provisions) Act 1941 (c.33)
Local Government (Financial Provisions) Act 1946 (c.24)
Local Government (Financial Provisions) Act 1963 (c.46)
Local Government (Financial Provisions) (Scotland) Act 1937 (c.29)
Local Government (Financial Provisions) (Scotland) Act 1941 (c.45)
Local Government (Financial Provisions) (Scotland) Act 1946 (c.25)
Local Government (Financial Provisions) (Scotland) Act 1954 (c.13)
Local Government (Financial Provisions) (Scotland) Act 1963 (c.12)
Local Government (Financial Provisions etc.) (Scotland) Act 1962 (c.9)
Local Government (Footpath and Open Spaces) (Scotland) Act 1970 (c.28)
Local Government (General Exchequer Contributions) Act 1933 (c.8)
Local Government Grants (Social Need) Act 1969 (c.2)
Local Government (Hours of Poll) Act 1938 (c.59)
Local Government (Interim Provisions) Act 1984 (c.53)
Local Government (Ireland) Act 1871 (c.109)
Local Government (Ireland) Act 1898 (c.37)
Local Government (Ireland) Act (1898) Amendment 1906 (c.31)
Local Government (Ireland) Act 1900 (c.63)
Local Government (Ireland) Act 1901 (c.28)
Local Government (Ireland) Act 1902 (c.38)
Local Government (Ireland) Act 1919 (c.19)
Local Government (Ireland) (No. 2) Act 1900 (c.41)
Local Government (Joint Committees) Act 1897 (c.40)
Local Government (Members' Travelling Expenses) Act 1937 (c.36)
Local Government (Miscellaneous Provisions) Act 1953 (c.26)
Local Government (Miscellaneous Provisions) Act 1976 (c.57)
Local Government (Miscellaneous Provisions) Act 1982 (c.30)
Local Government (Miscellaneous Provisions) (Scotland) Act 1981 (c.23)
Local Government Act 1898 (c.37)
Local Government (Omnibus Shelters and Queue Barriers) (Scotland) Act 1958 (c.50)

Local Government (Overseas Assistance) Act 1993 (c.25)
Local Government (Pecuniary Interests) Act 1964 (c.77)
Local Government (Pecuniary Interests) (Scotland) Act 1966 (c.7)
Local Government, Planning and Land Act 1980 (c.65)
Local Government (Records) Act 1962 (c.56)
Local Government (Scotland) Act 1889 (c.50)
Local Government (Scotland) Act 1894 (c.58)
Local Government (Scotland) Act, 1894, Amendment 1895 (c.1)
Local Government (Scotland) Act 1908 (c.62)
Local Government (Scotland) Act 1929 (c.25)
Local Government (Scotland) Act 1939 (c.28)
Local Government (Scotland) Act 1947 (c.43)
Local Government (Scotland) Act 1951 (c.15)
Local Government (Scotland) Act 1965 (c.41)
Local Government (Scotland) Act 1966 (c.51)
Local Government (Scotland) Act 1973 (c.65)
Local Government (Scotland) Act 1975 (c.30)
Local Government (Scotland) Act 1978 (c.4)
Local Government (Scotland) Act 1947 (Amendment) Act 1965 (c.41)
Local Government Staffs (War Service) Act 1939 (c.94)
Local Government (Stock Transfer) Act 1895 (c.32)
Local Government (Street Works) (Scotland) (Amendment) Act 1956 (c.40)
Local Government Superannuation Act 1937 (c.68)
Local Government Superannuation Act 1939 (c.18)
Local Government Superannuation Act 1953 (c.25)
Local Government Superannuation (Scotland) Act 1937 (c.69)
Local Government Supplemental Act 1859 (c.31)
Local Government Supplemental Act 1860 (c.44)
Local Government Supplemental Act 1861 (c.39)
Local Government Supplemental Act 1862 (c.25)
Local Government Supplemental Act 1863 (c.32)
Local Government Supplemental Act 1864 (c.26)
Local Government Supplemental Act 1865 (c.24)
Local Government Supplemental Act 1866 (c.24)
Local Government Supplemental Act 1867 (c.21)
Local Government Supplemental (No. 2) Act 1859 (c.11)
Local Government Supplemental (No. 2) Act 1860 (c.118)
Local Government Supplemental (No. 2) Act 1861 (c.128)
Local Government Supplemental (No. 2) Act 1863 (c.64)
Local Government Supplemental (No. 2) Act 1864 (c.83)
Local Government Supplemental (No. 2) Act 1865 (c.25)
Local Government Supplemental (No. 2) Act 1866 (c.79)
Local Government Supplemental (No. 3) Act 1865 (c.41)
Local Government Supplemental (No. 3) Act 1866 (c.106)
Local Government Supplemental (No. 3) Act 1867 (c.49)
Local Government Supplemental (No. 4) Act 1865 (c.110)
Local Government Supplemental (No. 4) Act 1866 (c.107)
Local Government Supplemental (No. 5) Act 1865 (c.108)
Local Government Supplemental (No. 5) Act 1867 (c.83)
Local Government Supplemental (No. 6) Act 1867 (c.123)
Local Government (Termination of Reviews) Act 1967 (c.18)
Local Government (Transfer of Powers) Act 1903 (c.15)
Local Government (Wales) Act 1994 (c.19)
Local Land Charges Act 1975 (c.76)
Local Light Dues Reduction Act 1876 (c.27)
Local Loans Act 1875 (c.83)
Local Loans Sinking Funds Act 1885 (c.30)
Local Militia Ballot Suspension Act 1816 (c.38)
Local Militia (England) Act 1808 (c.111)
Local Militia (England) Act 1809 (c.40)
Local Militia (England) Act 1812 (c.38)
Local Militia (England) Act 1813 (c.28)
Local Militia (Exemption) Act 1812 (c.116)
Local Militia (Great Britain) Act 1809 (c.82)
Local Militia (Great Britain) Act 1813 (c.19)
Local Militia (Great Britain) Act 1815 (c.76)
Local Militia (Ireland) Act 1813 (c.48)
Local Militia Pay (Great Britain) Act 1814 (c.176)
Local Militia Pay (Great Britain) Act 1815 (c.166)
Local Militia Pay (Great Britain) Act 1816 (c.45)
Local Militia (Scotland) Act 1808 (c.150)
Local Militia (Scotland) Act 1809 (c.48)
Local Militia (Scotland) Act 1812 (c.68)
Local Officers Superannuation (Ireland) Act 1869 (c.79)
Local (Redstone Bridge, Severn) Act 1773 (c.113)
Local Registration of Title (Ireland) Act 1891 (c.66)
Local Registration of Title (Ireland) Act 1909 (c.36)
Local Registration of Title (Ireland) Amendment Act 1908 (c.58)

Local (Rutland Roads) Act 1773 (c.108)
Local Stamp Act 1869 (c.49)
Local Tax Act 1731 (c.5)
Local Taxation Account (Scotland) Act 1898 (c.56)
Local Taxation (Customs and Excise) Act 1890 (c.60)
Local Taxation (Ireland) Estate Duty Act 1896 (c.41)
Local Taxation Returns Act 1860 (c.51)
Local Taxation Returns Act 1877 (c.66)
Local Taxation Returns (Scotland) Act 1881 (c.6)
Local (Westminster Streets) Act 1765 (c.13)
Locomotive Act 1861 (c.70)
Locomotive Threshing Engines Act 1894 (c.37)
Locomotives Act 1865 (c.83)
Locomotives Act 1898 (c.29)
Locomotives Amendment (Scotland) Act 1878 (c.58)
Locomotives on Highways Act 1896 (c.36)
Lodgers' Goods Protection Act 1871 (c.79)
Lodgers' Goods Protection Societies Act 1871 (c.80)
Lodging Houses Act 1851 (c.34)
Lodgings of Justices of Assize Act 1799 (c.46)
Loes and Wilford, Suffolk: Poor Relief Act 1791 (c.72)
Lombs's Silk Engines Act 1731 (c.8)
London Act 1532 (c.16)
London and Hertford Hospitals Act 1795 (c.104)
London and Holyhead Road Act 1836 (c.35)
London Assurance Act 1796 (c.27)
London Barbers and Surgeons Act 1744 (c.15)
London Bridge Act 1756 (c.40)
London Bridge Act 1757 (c.20)
London Bridge Act 1762 (c.30)
London Bridge Act 1771 (c.26)
London Bridge Act 1842 (c.64)
London Bridge Approaches Act 1848 (c.124)
London Bridge Approaches Act 1850 (c.103)
London Bridge Approaches Fund Act 1847 (c.115)
London Brokers Relief Act 1870 (c.60)
London Brokers Relief Act 1884 (c.3)
London Cab Act 1896 (c.27)
London Cab Act 1968 (c.7)
London Cab Act 1973 (c.20)
London Cab and Stage Carriage Act 1907 (c.55)
London, City Road Act 1760 (c.26)
London, City Road Act 1783 (c.102)
London Coal and Wine Duties Cont. Act 1863 (c.46)
London Coal and Wine Duties Cont. Act 1868 (c.17)
London Coal Duties Abolition Act 1889 (c.17)
London: Coal Trade Act 1786 (c.14)
London Council (Money) Act 1889 (c.61)
London County Council Electors Qualification Act 1900 (c.29)
London County Council (General Powers) Act 1947 (c.45)
London County Council (Improvements) Act 1962 (c.49)
London Diocese Act 1863 (c.36)
London Docks (Warehousing of Goods) Act (c.100)
London Electric Lighting Areas Act 1904 (c.13)
London Electric Lighting Areas Act 1904 (c.13)
London (Equalization of Rates) Act 1894 (c.53)
London Flour Company Act 1800 (c.97)
London Government Act 1899 (c.14)
London Government Act 1939 (c.40)
London Government Act 1950 (c.22)
London Government Act 1963 (c.33)
London Government Act 1967 (c.5)
London Hackney Carriage Act 1831 (c.22)
London Hackney Carriage Act 1853 (c.33)
London Hackney Carriage (No. 2) Act 1853 (c.127)
London Hackney Carriages Act 1843 (c.86)
London Hackney Carriages Act 1850 (c.7)
London Hospitals Act 1782 (c.77)
London Institution (Transfer) Act 1912 (c.13)
London Militia Act 1795 (c.27)
London Militia Act 1796 (c.91)
London Museum Site Act 1868 (c.8)
London Naval Treaty Act 1930 (c.48)
London Naval Treaty Act 1937 (c.65)
London Park and Works Act 1887 (c.34)
London Passenger Transport Act 1933 (c.14)
London Paving and Lighting Act 1766 (c.26)
London Regional Transport Act 1984 (c.32)
London Regional Transport Act 1996 (c.21)
London Regional Transport (Amendment) Act 1985 (c.10)
London Roads Act 1839 (c.80)
London Street Lighting Act 1743 (c.29)
London Streets Act 1762 (c.21)
London: Streets Act 1771 (c.54)
London: Streets Act 1772 (c.17)
London Streets Act 1772 (c.69)
London: Streets Act 1775 (c.54)
London: Streets Act 1776 (c.22)
London: Streets Act 1776 (c.23)
London: Streets Act 1778 (c.71)
London: Streets Act 1778 (c.73)
London: Streets Act 1782 (c.84)
London (Streets and Sewers) Act 1793 (c.75)
London Streets, City Act 1759 (c.30)
London: Thames Embankment Act 1771 (c.34)
London Traffic Act 1924 (c.34)
London Widening of Passages etc. Act 1766 (c.27)
Londonderry School Act 1808 (c.77)
Long Leases (Scotland) Act 1954 (c.49)
Long Leases (Temporary Provisions) (Scotland) Act 1951 (c.28)

Longitude and Latitude Act 1740 (c.39)
Longitude at Sea Act 1796 (c.107)
Lord Alcester's Grant Act 1883 (c.16)
Lord Blessington's Will Act 1772 (c.17)
Lord Chancellor of Ireland Act 1802 (c.105)
Lord Chancellor (Tenure of Office and Discharge of Ecclesiastical Functions) Act 1974 (c.25)
Lord Chancellor's Augmentation Act 1863 (c.120)
Lord Chancellor's Pension Act 1832 (c.111)
Lord Clerk Register (Scotland) Act 1861 (c.81)
Lord Clerk Register (Scotland) Act 1879 (c.44)
Lord Dundonald's Patent (Tar, Pitch, etc.) Act 1785 (c.42)
Lord High Commission (Church of Scotland) Act 1959 (c.8)
Lord High Commissioner (Church of Scotland) Act 1948 (c.30)
Lord High Commissioner (Church of Scotland) Act 1974 (c.19)
Lord Napier Act 1869 (c.3)
Lord Napier's Salary Act 1869 (c.3)
Lord Nelson, Purchase of Estate for Act 1815 (c.96)
Lord Powerscourt's Mansion Act 1807 (c.78)
Lord Wolseley's Grant Act 1883 (c.17)
Lords Justices Act 1837 (c.72)
Losses During Rebellion in Ireland Act 1805 (c.79)
Losses from Cession of East Florida Act 1786 (c.75)
Losses from Cession of East Florida Act 1788 (c.31)
Lost Property (Scotland) Act 1965 (c.27)
Lotteries Act 1710 (c.6)
Lotteries Act 1721 (c.2)
Lotteries Act 1787 (c.41)
Lotteries Act 1790 (c.30)
Lotteries Act 1802 (c.54)
Lotteries Act 1803 (c.91)
Lotteries Act 1804 (c.93)
Lotteries Act 1805 (c.74)
Lotteries Act 1806 (c.148)
Lotteries Act 1807 (c.9)
Lotteries Act 1808 (c.139)
Lotteries Act 1809 (c.94)
Lotteries Act 1810 (c.94)
Lotteries Act 1811 (c.113)
Lotteries Act 1812 (c.19)
Lotteries Act 1812 (c.125)
Lotteries Act 1813 (c.93)
Lotteries Act 1814 (c.74)
Lotteries Act 1815 (c.73)
Lotteries Act 1816 (c.61)
Lotteries Act 1836 (c.66)
Lotteries Act 1845 (c.74)
Lotteries Act 1975 (c.58)
Lotteries (Amendment) Act 1984 (c.9)
Lotteries and Amusements Act 1976 (c.32)
Lotteries and Gaming Act 1962 (c.55)
Lotteries (Ireland) Act 1780 (c.14)
Lottery Act 1771 (c.47)
Lottery Act 1785 (c.59)
Lottery Act 1786 (c.65)
Lottery Act 1787 (c.1)
Lottery Act 1788 (c.21)
Lottery Act 1789 (c.33)
Lottery Act 1791 (c.53)
Lottery Act 1792 (c.28)
Lottery Act 1793 (c.62)
Lottery Act 1794 (c.40)
Lottery Act 1795 (c.36)
Lottery Act 1796 (c.104)
Lottery Act 1797 (c.113)
Lottery Act 1798 (c.75)
Lottery Act 1799 (c.91)
Lottery Act 1800 (c.52)
Lottery Act 1801 (c.6)
Lottery Act 1801 (c.27)
Lottery Office Keepers Act 1779 (c.21)
Lottery Office Keepers Act 1782 (c.47)
Lottery Regulations Act 1802 (c.104)
Lough Corrib Act 1850 (c.112)
Lough Corrib Navigation Act 1874 (c.71)
Loughborough: Navigation Act 1766 (c.94)
Loughborough Navigation Act 1776 (c.65)
Louth, Lincoln, Roads Act 1770 (c.109)
Louth Roads Act 1780 (c.94)
Lower Canada Government Act 1838 (c.9)
Lower Canada Government Act 1839 (c.53)
Lower Ouse: Navigation Act 1791 (c.76)
Ludlow and Monk's Bridge Road Act 1750 (c.29)
Ludlow Roads Act 1756 (c.59)
Ludlow Roads Act 1779 (c.114)
Ludlow, Salop: Improvement Act 1793 (c.25)
Lunacy Act 1771 (c.20)
Lunacy Act 1842 (c.84)
Lunacy Act 1855 (c.13)
Lunacy Act 1890 (c.5)
Lunacy Act 1891 (c.65)
Lunacy Act 1908 (c.47)
Lunacy Act 1911 (c.40)
Lunacy Act 1922 (c.60)
Lunacy Act Amendment Act 1865 (c.80)
Lunacy Acts Amendment 1885 (c.52)
Lunacy Acts Amendment 1889 (c.41)
Lunacy Acts Amendments Act 1826 (c.111)
Lunacy Acts Amendments Act 1862 (c.111)
Lunacy Board (Scotland) Act 1864 (c.59)
Lunacy Board (Scotland) Salaries and Clerks Act 1900 (c.54)
Lunacy Districts (Scotland) Act 1887 (c.39)
Lunacy (Ireland) Act 1867 (c.118)
Lunacy (Ireland) Act 1901 (c.17)
Lunacy Regulation Act 1853 (c.70)
Lunacy Regulation Act 1855 (c.105)
Lunacy Regulation Act 1862 (c.86)
Lunacy Regulation Act 1871 (c.22)
Lunacy Regulation Amendment Act 1882 (c.82)
Lunacy Regulation (Ireland) Act 1871 (c.22)
Lunacy (Scotland) Act 1857 (c.71)

Lunacy (Scotland) Act 1862 (c.54)
Lunacy (Scotland) Act 1866 (c.51)
Lunacy (Vacating of Seats) Act 1886 (c.16)
Lunatic Asylums Act 1842 (c.87)
Lunatic Asylums Act 1853 (c.97)
Lunatic Asylums Act 1856 (c.87)
Lunatic Asylums, etc. Act 1846 (c.84)
Lunatic Asylums (Ireland) Act 1846 (c.79)
Lunatic Asylums (Ireland) Act 1846 (c.115)
Lunatic Asylums (Ireland) Act 1849 (c.56)
Lunatic Asylums (Ireland) Act 1851 (c.45)
Lunatic Asylums (Ireland) Act 1875 (c.67)
Lunatic Asylums (Ireland) Accounts Audit Act 1868 (c.97)
Lunatic Asylums Loans (Ireland) Act 1878 (c.24)
Lunatic Asylums Repayment of Advances (Ireland) Act 1855 (c.109)
Lunatic Asylums, Superannuations (Ireland) Act 1856 (c.99)
Lunatic Paupers or Criminals Act 1808 (c.96)
Lunatic Paupers, etc. (England) Act 1811 (c.79)
Lunatics Act 1730 (c.10)
Lunatics Act 1838 (c.73)
Lunatics Act 1845 (c.100)
Lunatics Act 1845 (c.126)
Lunatics Removal (India) Act 1851 (c.81)
Lunatics (Scotland) Act 1858 (c.89)
Lunatics (Scotland) Act 1867 (c.55)
Luton and St. Albans Road Act 1726 (c.17)
Luton and St. Albans Road Act 1742 (c.23)
Lying-in Hospitals Act 1773 (c.82)
Lyme Regis Roads Act 1770 (c.59)
Lymington Roads Act 1765 (c.59)
Lymington Roads Act 1786 (c.156)
Lyon King of Arms Act 1867 (c.17)

Macclesfield and Buxton Road Act 1958 (c.41)
Macclesfield to Buxton Road Act 1780 (c.91)
Macclesfield Grammar School Act 1774 (c.51)
Madder Act 1957 (c.12)
Madhouses Act 1774 (c.49)
Madhouses Act 1779 (c.15)
Madhouses Act 1786 (c.91)
Magdalen Hospital, London Act 1769 (c.31)
Magistrates' Courts Act 1952 (c.55)
Magistrates' Courts Act 1957 (c.29)
Magistrates' Courts Act 1980 (c.43)
Magistrates' Courts (Appeals from Binding Over Orders) Act 1956 (c.44)
Maidenhead and Reading, etc. Roads Act 1727 (c.3)
Maidenhead Bridge Act 1772 (c.41)
Maidenhead, Reading etc. Roads Act 1763 (c.46)
Maidenhead Road Act 1743 (c.19)
Maidenhead Roads Act 1779 (c.84)
Maidstone Gaol, Kent (Expenses) Act 1735 (c.12)
Maidstone, Kent: Improvement Act 1791 (c.62)
Maidstone: Poor Relief Act 1780 (c.22)
Maidstone to Ashford Road Act 1973 (c.173)
Maidstone to Cranbrook Road Act 1759 (c.57)
Maidstone to Cranbrook Road Act 1768 (c.43)
Mail to Spain Act 1793 (c.60)
Mail Ships Act 1902 (c.36)
Maintenance Agreements Act 1957 (c.35)
Maintenance Enforcement Act 1991 (c.17)
Maintenance of Church of England Act 1706 (c.8)
Maintenance of Live Stock Act 1915 (c.65)
Maintenance Orders Act 1950 (c.37)
Maintenance Orders Act 1958 (c.39)
Maintenance Orders Act 1968 (c.36)
Maintenance Orders (Facilities for Enforcement) Act 1920 (c.33)
Maintenance Orders (Reciprocal Enforcement) Act 1972 (c.18)
Maintenance Orders (Reciprocal Enforcement) Act 1992 (c.56)
Making of Bread Act 1957 (c.29)
Making of Indigo Act 1755 (c.25)
Making of indigo, etc. 1770 (c.37)
Making of Sail Cloth Act 1741 (c.35)
Malawi Independence 1964 (c.46)
Malaysia Act 1963 (c.35)
Malaysian Act 1963 (c.60)
Malicious Communications Act 1988 (c.27)
Malicious Damage Act 1812 (c.130)
Malicious Damage Act 1861 (c.97)
Malicious Damage Act 1964 (c.76)
Malicious Damage (Scotland) Act 1816 (c.125)
Malicious Injury Act 1769 (c.29)
Mall Approach (Improvement) Act 1914 (c.28)
Malmesbury Roads Act 1778 (c.114)
Malt Duties, etc. Act 1714 (c.2)
Malt Duties, etc. Act 1725 (c.4)
Malt Duties, etc. Act 1759 (c.7)
Malt Duties Act 1762 (c.13)
Malt Duties Act 1762 (c.2)
Malt Duties Act 1766 (c.6)
Malt Duties Act 1768 (c.4)
Malt Duties Act 1769 (c.2)
Malt Duties Act 1770 (c.5)
Malt Duties Act 1772 (c.6)
Malt Duties Act 1772 (c.6)
Malt Duties Act 1837 (c.49)
Malt Duties Act 1971 (c.2)
Malt Duties Act 1774 (c.2)
Malt Duties Act 1775 (c.2)
Malt Duties Act 1776 (c.1)
Malt Duties Act 1776 (c.2)
Malt Duties Act 1778 (c.3)
Malt Duties Act 1779 (c.3)
Malt Duties Act 1780 (c.3)
Malt Duties Act 1780 (c.4)
Malt Duties Act 1782 (c.3)

Malt Duties Act 1782 (c.4)
Malt Duties Act 1783 (c.64)
Malt Duties Act 1783 (c.1)
Malt Duties Act 1785 (c.2)
Malt Duties Act 1786 (c.6)
Malt Duties Act 1788 (c.1)
Malt Duties Act 1789 (c.10)
Malt Duties Act 1790 (c.3)
Malt Duties Act 1791 (c.2)
Malt Duties Act 1791 (c.7)
Malt Duties Act 1791 (c.6)
Malt Duties Act 1791 (c.18)
Malt Duties Act 1793 (c.11)
Malt Duties Act 1794 (c.7)
Malt, etc. Duties Act 1765 (c.2)
Malta Constitution Act 1932 (c.43)
Malta Independence Act 1964 (c.86)
Malta (Letters Patent) Act 1936 (c.29)
Malta (Reconstruction) Act 1947 (c.9)
Malta Republic Act 1975 (c.31)
Malton and Pickering Road Act 1765 (c.108)
Manchester and Oldham Canal Act 1792 (c.84)
Manchester-Oldham Canal Act 1974 (c.26)
Manchester and Salford: Improvement Act 1792 (c.69)
Manchester and Stockport Canal Act 1793 (c.21)
Manchester, Bolton and Bury Canal Act 1791 (c.68)
Manchester Canal Act 1794 (c.37)
Manchester Church Act 1753 (c.45)
Manchester Church Act 1769 (c.60)
Manchester, Church Building 1708 (c.28)
Manchester General Improvement Act 1851 (c.119)
Manchester Improvement Act 1765 (c.81)
Manchester: Poor Relief Act 1790 (c.81)
Manchester Roads Act 1731 (c.10)
Manchester Roads Act 1749 (c.5)
Manchester Roads Act 1771 (c.82)
Manchester Roads Act 1772 (c.88)
Manchester, School Mills Act 1758 (c.61)
Manchester Square: Improvement Act 1789 (c.5)
Manchester: Streets Act 1776 (c.63)
Manchester Theatre Act 1775 (c.47)
Manchester to Buxton Road Act 1793 (c.171)
Manchester to Chester Roads Act 1793 (c.139)
Manchester to Wilmslow Road Act 1793 (c.170)
Mandated and Trust Territories Act 1947 (c.8)
Manning of the Navy, etc. Act 1793 (c.66)
Manning of the Navy Act 1795 (c.5)
Manning of the Navy Act 1795 (c.9)
Manning of the Navy Act 1795 (c.19)
Manning of the Navy Act 1795 (c.29)
Manoeuvres Act 1958 (c.7)
Mansfield and Chesterfield Road Act 1958 (c.37)
Mansfield to Chesterfield Road Act 1780 (c.72)
Manufacture of Cambrics 1763 (c.37)
Manufacture of Hats Act 1776 (c.55)
Manufacture of Leather Act 1784 (c.19)
Manufacture of Ounce Thread Act 1788 (c.17)
Manufacture of Sail Cloth Act 1730 (c.27)
Manufacture of Sail Cloth Act 1735 (c.37)
Manufacture of Serges, etc. Act 1719 (c.13)
Manufacture of Serges, etc. Act 1723 (c.18)
Maplin Development Act 1973 (c.64)
Maplin Development Authority (Dissolution) Act 1976 (c.51)
Mar Peerage Restoration Act 1824 (c.59)
March, Cambridge, Isle of Ely: Drainage Act 1957 (c.36)
Margate Pier Act 1724 (c.3)
Margate Theatre Act 1786 (c.29)
Marine and Aviation Insurance (War Risks) Act 1952 (c.57)
Marine Duty Act 1791 (c.17)
Marine, etc. Broadcasting Offences Act 1967 (c.41)
Marine Insurance Act 1745 (c.37)
Marine Insurance Act 1788 (c.56)
Marine Insurance Act 1906 (c.41)
Marine Insurance (Gambling Policies) Act 1909 (c.12)
Marine Mutiny Act 1755 (c.11)
Marine Mutiny Act 1757 (c.11)
Marine Mutiny Act 1757 (c.6)
Marine Mutiny Act 1757 (c.9)
Marine Mutiny Act 1759 (c.8)
Marine Mutiny Act 1760 (c.8)
Marine Mutiny Act 1761 (c.12)
Marine Mutiny Act 1762 (c.3)
Marine Mutiny Act 1763 (c.8)
Marine Mutiny Act 1765 (c.6)
Marine Mutiny Act 1766 (c.10)
Marine Mutiny Act 1766 (c.13)
Marine Mutiny Act 1768 (c.12)
Marine Mutiny Act 1769 (c.7)
Marine Mutiny Act 1770 (c.7)
Marine Mutiny Act 1771 (c.7)
Marine Mutiny Act 1772 (c.5)
Marine Mutiny Act 1772 (c.11)
Marine Mutiny Act 1774 (c.4)
Marine Mutiny Act 1775 (c.4)
Marine Mutiny Act 1776 (c.7)
Marine Mutiny Act 1776 (c.4)
Marine Mutiny Act 1778 (c.5)
Marine Mutiny Act 1779 (c.8)
Marine Mutiny Act 1780 (c.13)
Marine Mutiny Act 1780 (c.9)
Marine Mutiny Act 1782 (c.5)
Marine Mutiny Act 1782 (c.7)
Marine Mutiny Act 1783 (c.17)
Marine Mutiny Act 1785 (c.3)
Marine Mutiny Act 1786 (c.7)
Marine Mutiny Act 1788 (c.3)
Marine Mutiny Act 1789 (c.3)
Marine Mutiny Act 1790 (c.7)
Marine Mutiny Act 1791 (c.9)
Marine Mutiny Act 1793 (c.6)

Marine Mutiny Act 1794 (c.6)
Marine Mutiny Act 1795 (c.7)
Marine Mutiny Act 1840 (c.8)
Marine Society Act 1772 (c.67)
Marine Works (Ireland) Act 1902 (c.24)
Marines Act 1792 (c.67)
Maritime Conventions Act 1911 (c.57)
Market Harborough and Brampton Road Act 1751 (c.57)
Market Harborough and Brampton Road Act 1754 (c.28)
Market Harborough and Brampton Road Act 1759 (c.38)
Market Harborough to Coventry Road Act 1755 (c.40)
Market Harborough to Coventry Road Act 1779 (c.82)
Market Harborough to Loughborough Road Act 1793 (c.176)
Market Weighton Act 1772 (c.37)
Markets and Fairs Clauses Act 1847 (c.14)
Markets and Fairs (Weighing of Cattle) Act 1887 (c.27)
Markets and Fairs (Weighing of Cattle) Act 1891 (c.70)
Markets and Fairs (Weighing of Cattle) Act 1926 (c.21)
Marriage Act 1939 (c.33)
Marriage Act 1949 (c.76)
Marriage Act 1983 (c.32)
Marriage Act 1949 (Amendment) 1954 (c.47)
Marriage Act 1994 (c.34)
Marriage Acts Amendment Act 1958 (c.29)
Marriage Ceremony (Prescribed Words) Act 1996 (c.34)
Marriage Confirmation Act 1830 (c.18)
Marriage (Enabling) Act 1960 (c.29)
Marriage (Extension of Hours) Act 1934 (c.13)
Marriage Law (Ireland) Amendment Act 1873 (c.16)
Marriage (Members of His Majesty's Forces) Act 1941 (c.47)
Marriage (Naval, Military and Air Force Chapels) Act 1932 (c.31)
Marriage Notice (Scotland) Act 1878 (c.43)
Marriage of British Subjects (Facilities) Act 1915 (c.40)
Marriage of British Subjects (Facilities) Amendment 1916 (c.21)
Marriage of Lunatics Act 1941 (c.30)
Marriage (Prohibited Degrees of Relationship) Act 1931 (c.31)
Marriage (Prohibited Degrees of Relationship) Act 1986 (c.16)
Marriage (Registrar General's Licence Act 1970 (c.34)
Marriage (Registration of Buildings) Act 1990 (c.33)
Marriage (Scotland) Act 1834 (c.28)
Marriage (Scotland) Act 1916 (c.7)
Marriage (Scotland) Act 1939 (c.34)
Marriage (Scotland) Act 1942 (c.20)
Marriage (Scotland) Act 1956 (c.70)
Marriage (Scotland) Act 1977 (c.15)
Marriage (Scotland) Emergency Provisions Act 1940 (c.30)
Marriage (Secretaries of Synagogues) Act 1959 (c.13)
Marriage (Wales) Act 1986 (c.7)
Marriage (Wales and Monmouthshire) Act 1962 (c.32)
Marriage with Foreigners Act 1906 (c.40)
Marriages (Confirmation) Act 1804 (c.77)
Marriages (Confirmation) Act 1808 (c.127)
Marriages (Confirmation) Act 1825 (c.92)
Marriages in Japan (Validity) Act 1912 (c.15)
Marriages (Ireland) Act 1844 (c.81)
Marriages (Ireland) Act 1846 (c.72)
Marriages (Ireland) Act 1918 (c.2)
Marriages Legalisation Act 1901 (c.23)
Marriages Legalisation Act 1903 (c.26)
Marriages (Validity) Act 1939 (c.35)
Marriages Validity (Provisional Orders) Act 1924 (c.20)
Married Women (Maintenance) Act 1920 (c.63)
Married Women (Restraint Upon Anticipation) Act 1949 (c.78)
Married Women's Policies of Assurance Act 1880 (c.26)
Married Women's Policies of Assurance (Scotland) (Amendment) Act 1980 (c.56)
Married Women's Property Act 1882 (c.75)
Married Women's Property Act 1907 (c.18)
Married Women's Property Act 1908 (c.27)
Married Women's Property Act 1964 (c.19)
Married Women's Property (Scotland) Act 1881 (c.21)
Married Women's Property (Scotland) Act 1920 (c.64)
Married Women's Reversionary Interests Act 1857 (c.57)
Marshall Aid Commemoration Act 1953 (c.39)
Marshall Scholarships Act 1959 (c.3)
Marylebone Act 1783 (c.110)
Marylebone: Improvement Act 1768 (c.46)
Marylebone Road Act 1720 (c.26)
Marylebone Road Act 1734 (c.8)
Maryport Harbour Act 1748 (c.6)
Maryport Harbour Act 1756 (c.57)
Maryport Harbour Act 1791 (c.23)
Master and Servant Act 1889 (c.24)
Matches and Mechanical Lighters Duties Act 1979 (c.6)
Maternity and Child Welfare Act 1918 (c.29)
Maternity Services (Scotland) Act 1937 (c.30)
Matrimonial and Family Proceedings Act 1984 (c.42)
Matrimonial Causes Act 1907 (c.12)
Matrimonial Causes Act 1923 (c.19)
Matrimonial Causes Act 1937 (c.57)
Matrimonial Causes Act 1950 (c.25)
Matrimonial Causes Act 1963 (c.45)
Matrimonial Causes Act 1965 (c.72)

Matrimonial Causes Act 1967 (c.56)
Matrimonial Causes Act 1973 (c.18)
Matrimonial Causes and Marriage Law (Ireland) Amendment Act 1871 (c.49)
Matrimonial Causes (Dominions Troops) Act 1919 (c.28)
Matrimonial Causes (Property and Maintenance) Act 1958 (c.35)
Matrimonial Causes (War Marriages) Act (c.43)
Matrimonial Homes Act 1967 (c.75)
Matrimonial Homes Act 1983 (c.19)
Matrimonial Homes and Property Act 1981 (c.24)
Matrimonial Homes (Family Protection) (Scotland) 1981 (c.59)
Matrimonial Proceedings and Property Act 1970 (c.45)
Matrimonial Proceedings (Children) Act 1958 (c.40)
Matrimonial Proceedings (Magistrates' Courts) Act 1960 (c.48)
Matrimonial Proceedings (Polygamous Marriages) Act 1972 (c.38)
Matrimonial Proceedings (Transfers) Act 1988 (c.18)
Mauritius Independence Act 1968 (c.8)
Mauritius Loan (Guarantee) Act 1931 (c.26)
Mauritius Republic Act 1992 (c.45)
Measurement of Coal Wagons, etc. Act 1775 (c.27)
Medical Act 1858 (c.90)
Medical Act 1860 (c.66)
Medical Act 1876 (c.41)
Medical Act 1886 (c.48)
Medical Act 1950 (c.29)
Medical Act 1956 (c.76)
Medical Act 1969 (c.40)
Medical Act 1978 (c.12)
Medical Act 1983 (c.54)
Medical Act (1886) Amendment 1904 (c.14)
Medical Act 1956 (Amendment) Act 1958 (c.58)
Medical Act (Royal College of Surgeons of England) 1875 (c.43)
Medical Act (University of London) 1873 (c.55)
Medical and Dentists Acts Amendment Act 1927 (c.39)
Medical Practitioners and Pharmacists Act 1947 (c.11)
Medical (Professional Performance) Act 1995 (c.51)
Medical Qualifications (Amendment) Act 1991 (c.38)
Medicinal Products: Prescription by Nurses, etc. Act 1992 (c.28)
Medicine Duties Act 1785 (c.79)
Medicines Act 1968 (c.67)
Medicines Act 1971 (c.69)
Mediterranean Passes Act 1730 (c.18)
Medway Fisheries Act 1757 (c.21)
Medway: Navigation Act 1792 (c.105)
Medway Oyster Fishery Act 1728 (c.19)
Melton Mowbray to Grantham Road Act 1780 (c.95)
Members of Local Authorities Relief Act 1900 (c.46)
Memorials of Grants of Annuities Act 1822 (c.92)
Mental Deficiency Act 1913 (c.28)
Mental Deficiency Act 1927 (c.33)
Mental Deficiency Act 1938 (c.43)
Mental Deficiency (Amendment) Act 1925 (c.53)
Mental Deficiency and Lunacy (Amendment) Act 1919 (c.85)
Mental Deficiency (Scotland) Act 1940 (c.8)
Mental Health Act 1959 (c.72)
Mental Health Act 1983 (c.20)
Mental Health (Amendment) Act 1975 (c.29)
Mental Health (Amendment) Act 1982 (c.51)
Mental Health (Amendment) Act 1994 (c.6)
Mental Health (Amendment) (Scotland) Act 1983 (c.39)
Mental Health (Detention) (Scotland) Act 1991 (c.47)
Mental Health (Patients in the Community) Act 1995 (c.52)
Mental Health (Scotland) Act 1960 (c.61)
Mental Health (Scotland) Act 1984 (c.36)
Mental Treatment Act 1930 (c.23)
Mercantile Law Amendment Act 1856 (c.97)
Mercantile Law Amendment (Scotland) Act 1856 (c.60)
Mercers Company, London Act 1751 (c.7)
Mercers Company, London Act 1764 (c.50)
Mercers, London Act 1747 (c.32)
Merchandise Marks Act 1911 (c.31)
Merchandise Marks Act 1926 (c.53)
Merchandise Marks Act 1953 (c.48)
Merchandise Marks (Ireland) Act 1909 (c.24)
Merchant Seamen Act 1728 (c.36)
Merchant Seamen Act 1746 (c.38)
Merchant Seamen Act 1762 (c.31)
Merchant Seamen (Payment of Wages and Rating) Act 1880 (c.16)
Merchant Shipping Act 1786 (c.86)
Merchant Shipping Act 1791 (c.39)
Merchant Shipping Act 1794 (c.68)
Merchant Shipping Act 1872 (c.73)
Merchant Shipping Act 1894 (c.60)
Merchant Shipping Act 1906 (c.48)
Merchant Shipping Act 1907 (c.52)
Merchant Shipping Act 1911 (c.42)
Merchant Shipping Act 1921 (c.28)
Merchant Shipping Act 1937 (c.23)
Merchant Shipping Act 1948 (c.44)
Merchant Shipping Act 1950 (c.9)
Merchant Shipping Act 1952 (c.14)
Merchant Shipping Act 1954 (c.18)
Merchant Shipping Act 1964 (c.47)
Merchant Shipping Act 1965 (c.47)
Merchant Shipping Act 1967 (c.26)
Merchant Shipping Act 1970 (c.36)
Merchant Shipping Act 1974 (c.43)

Merchant Shipping Act 1979 (c.39)
Merchant Shipping Act 1981 (c.11)
Merchant Shipping Act 1983 (c.13)
Merchant Shipping Act 1984 (c.5)
Merchant Shipping Act 1988 (c.12)
Merchant Shipping Act 1995 (c.21)
Merchant Shipping Acts (Amendment) 1923 (c.40)
Merchant Shipping (Amendment) Act 1920 (c.2)
Merchant Shipping (Carriage of Munitions to Spain) Act 1936 (c.1)
Merchant Shipping (Certificates) Act 1914 (c.42)
Merchant Shipping (Convention) Act 1914 (c.50)
Merchant Shipping (Equivalent Provisions) Act 1925 (c.37)
Merchant Shipping (International Labour Convention) Act 1925 (c.42)
Merchant Shipping (Liability of Shipowners and Others) Act 1900 (c.32)
Merchant Shipping (Liability of Shipowners and Others) Act 1958 (c.62)
Merchant Shipping (Line-throwing Appliances) Act 1928 (c.40)
Merchant Shipping (Liner Conferences) Act 1982 (c.37)
Merchant Shipping (Load Lines) Act 1967 (c.27)
Merchant Shipping (Mercantile Marine Fund) Act 1898 (c.44)
Merchant Shipping (Minicoy Lighthouse) 1960 (c.42)
Merchant Shipping (Oil Pollution) Act 1971 (c.59)
Merchant Shipping (Registration, etc.) Act 1993 (c.22)
Merchant Shipping (Safety and Load Line Conventions) Act 1932 (c.9)
Merchant Shipping (Safety Convention) Act 1949 (c.43)
Merchant Shipping (Safety Convention) Act 1977 (c.24)
Merchant Shipping (Salvage and Pollution) Act 1994 (c.28)
Merchant Shipping (Scottish Fishing Boats) Act 1920 (c.39)
Merchant Shipping (Seamen's Allotment) Act 1911 (c.8)
Merchant Shipping (Salvage) Act 1916 (c.41)
Merchant Shipping (Salvage) Act 1940 (c.43)
Merchant Shipping (Spanish Frontiers Observation) Act 1937 (c.19)
Merchant Shipping (Stevedores and Trimmers) Act 1911 (c.41)
Merchant Shipping (Superannuation Contributions) Act 1937 (c.4)
Merchant Shipping (Wireless Telegraphy) Act 1919 (c.38)
Merioneth Roads Act 1777 (c.96)
Merioneth Roads Act 1969 (c.56)
Mersey Canal Act 1775 (c.20)
Methylated Spirits (Sale by Retail) (Scotland) Act 1937 (c.48)
Metropolis Gas Act 1860 (c.125)
Metropolis Gas Act 1861 (c.79)
Metropolis Water Act 1899 (c.41)
Metropolis Water Act 1902 (c.41)
Metropolitan Ambulances Act 1909 (c.17)
Metropolitan Board of Works (Money) Act 1884 (c.50)
Metropolitan Board of Works (Money) Act 1886 (c.44)
Metropolitan Buildings Act 1772 (c.73)
Metropolitan Improvements (Funds) Act 1904 (c.2)
Metropolitan Magistrates' Courts Act 1959 (c.45)
Metropolitan Police Act 1829 (c.44)
Metropolitan Police Act 1838 (c.47)
Metropolitan Police Act 1839 (c.47)
Metropolitan Police Act 1856 (c.2)
Metropolitan Police Act 1860 (c.135)
Metropolitan Police Act 1884 (c.17)
Metropolitan Police Act 1886 (c.22)
Metropolitan Police Act 1912 (c.4)
Metropolitan Police Act 1918 (c.61)
Metropolitan Police Act 1933 (c.33)
Metropolitan Police Act 1958 (c.48)
Metropolitan Police (Borrowing Powers) Act 1935 (c.16)
Metropolitan Police (Borrowing Powers) Act 1952 (c.19)
Metropolitan Police (Commission) Act 1906 (c.6)
Metropolitan Police (Courts) Act 1839 (c.71)
Metropolitan Police (Courts) Act 1897 (c.26)
Metropolitan Police (Employment in Scotland) Act (c.44)
Metropolitan Police (Receiver) Act 1867 (c.39)
Metropolitan Police (Staff Superannuation and Police Fund) Act 1931 (c.12)
Metropolitan Streets Act 1903 (c.17)
Mevagissey Pier, Cornwall Act 1775 (c.62)
Michaelmas Term Act 1750 (c.48)
Middlesex and Essex Roads Act 1785 (c.124)
Middlesex and Hertford Highways Act 1711 (c.3)
Middlesex and Hertford Roads Act 1730) (c.10)
Middlesex and Hertford Roads Act 1743 (c.14)
Middlesex and Hertford Roads Act 1770 (c.71)
Middlesex and Hertford Roads Act 1772 (c.84)
Middlesex and Hertfordshire Roads Act 1748 (c.14)
Middlesex and Surrey Roads Act 1791 (c.134)
Middlesex Deeds Act 1940 (c.34)
Middlesex Gaol Act 1786 (c.55)
Middlesex Highways Act 1711 (c.4)
Middlesex Highways Act 1723 (c.6)

Middlesex Registry Act 1708 (c.20)
Middlesex (Registry of Deeds) Act 1751 (c.4)
Middlesex Road Act 1767 (c.88)
Middlesex Roads Act 1733 (c.26)
Middlesex Roads Act 1741 (c.9)
Middlesex Roads Act 1767 (c.102)
Middlesex Roads Act 1778 (c.84)
Middlesex Roads Act 1789 (c.96)
Middlesex Roads Act 1794 (c.131)
Middlesex Roads Act 1937 (c.6)
Middlesex Sessions Act 1792 (c.48)
Middlesex Sessions House Act 1778 (c.67)
Midwives Act 1902 (c.17)
Midwives Act 1918 (c.43)
Midwives Act 1926 (c.32)
Midwives Act 1936 (c.40)
Midwives Act 1951 (c.53)
Midwives (Amendment) Act 1950 (c.13)
Midwives (Ireland) Act 1918 (c.59)
Midwives (Scotland) Act 1915 (c.91)
Midwives (Scotland) Act 1927 (c.17)
Midwives (Scotland) Act 1951 (c.54)
Milbank New Church Act 1728 (c.15)
Mile End Night Watch Act 1777 (c.66)
Milford Fortifications Act 1758 (c.26)
Milford Haven Conservancy Act 1958 (c.23)
Milford to Portsmouth Road Act 1764 (c.63)
Milford to Portsmouth Road Act 1787 (c.95)
Milk (Special Designations) Act (c.34)
Military Aircraft (Loans) Act 1966 (c.15)
Military and Air Forces (Prolongation of Service) Act 1939 (c.90)
Military Lands Act 1900 (c.56)
Military Lands Act 1903 (c.47)
Military Manoeuvres Act 1911 (c.44)
Military Service Act 1916 (c.104)
Military Service Act 1918 (c.66)
Military Service (No. 2) Act 1918 (c.5)
Military Service (Review of Exceptions) Act 1917 (c.12)
Military Service (Session 2) 1916 (c.15)
Military Training Act 1939 (c.25)
Military Tramways Act 1887 (c.65)
Military Works Act 1901 (c.40)
Military Works Act 1903 (c.29)
Militia Act 1700 (c.8)
Militia Act 1701 (c.17)
Militia Act 1702 (c.15(d))
Militia Act 1703 (c.14(e))
Militia Act 1704 (c.15(l))
Militia Act 1705 (c.10)
Militia Act 1706 (c.28)
Militia Act 1707 (c.63)
Militia Act 1708 (c.23)
Militia Act 1709 (c.22)
Militia Act 1710 (c.31)
Militia Act 1712 (c.8)
Militia Act 1766 (c.15)
Militia Act 1786 (c.107)
Militia Act 1714 (c.14)
Militia Act 1733 (c.23)
Militia Act 1745 (c.2)
Militia Act 1757 (c.25)
Militia Act 1757 (c.26)
Militia Act 1758 (c.20)
Militia Act 1759 (c.2)
Militia Act 1759 (c.2)
Militia Act 1762 (c.20)
Militia Act 1763 (c.17)
Militia Act 1765 (c.36)
Militia Act 1769 (c.40)
Militia Act 1771 (c.32)
Militia Act 1776 (c.3)
Militia Act 1778 (c.14)
Militia Act 1779 (c.76)
Militia Act 1780 (c.8)
Militia Act 1780 (c.44)
Militia Act 1780 (c.7)
Militia Act 1780 (c.18)
Militia Act 1782 (c.6)
Militia Act 1782 (c.62)
Militia Act 1794 (c.81)
Militia Act 1802 (c.90)
Militia Act 1882 (c.49)
Militia and Yeomanry Act 1901 (c.14)
Militia and Yeomanry Act 1902 (c.39)
Militia (City of London) Act 1820 (c.100)
Militia, Derbyshire Act 1795 (c.16)
Militia, etc. Act 1711 (c.33)
Militia, etc. Act 1713 (c.9(c))
Militia, etc. Act 1778 (c.59)
Militia, etc. Act 1779 (c.72)
Militia Pay Act 1757 (c.30)
Militia Pay Act 1758 (c.21)
Militia Pay Act 1759 (c.24)
Militia Pay Act 1760 (c.22)
Militia Pay Act 1762 (c.35)
Militia Pay Act 1762 (c.10)
Militia Pay Act 1763 (c.30)
Militia Pay Act 1765 (c.34)
Militia Pay Act 1768 (c.20)
Militia Pay Act 1770 (c.9)
Militia Pay Act 1772 (c.13)
Militia Pay Act 1772 (c.23)
Militia Pay Act 1774 (c.18)
Militia Pay Act 1775 (c.8)
Militia Pay Act 1776 (c.19)
Militia Pay Act 1776 (c.10)
Militia Pay Act 1779 (c.19)
Militia Pay Act 1780 (c.13)
Militia Pay Act 1780 (c.21)
Militia Pay Act 1782 (c.24)
Militia Pay Act 1783 (c.35)
Militia Pay Act 1785 (c.8)
Militia Pay Act 1786 (c.69)
Militia Pay Act 1788 (c.11)
Militia Pay Act 1789 (c.15)
Militia Pay Act 1790 (c.9)
Militia Pay Act 1791 (c.16)
Militia Pay Act 1791 (c.26)
Militia Pay Act 1793 (c.19)
Militia Pay Act 1794 (c.16)
Militia Pay Act 1794 (c.30)
Militia Pay, etc. Act 1766 (c.30)
Militia Pay, etc. Act 1766 (c.17)
Militia Pay, etc. Act 1783 (c.13)

Militia (Scotland) Act 1802 (c.91)
Militia (Storehouse) Act 1882 (c.12)
Militia, Sussex Act 1793 (c.79)
Milk Act 1934 (c.51)
Milk (Amendment) 1937 (c.66)
Milk and Dairies Act 1914 (c.49)
Milk and Dairies Act Postponement Act 1915 (c.59)
Milk and Dairies (Amendment) 1922 (c.54)
Milk and Dairies (Consolidation) Act 1915 (c.66)
Milk and Dairies (Scotland) Act 1914 (c.46)
Milk (Cessation of Production) Act 1985 (c.4)
Milk (Extension and Amendment) 1938 (c.61)
Milk (Extension of Temporary Provisions) Act 1936 (c.9)
Milk Industry Act 1939 (c.46)
Milk (Special Designations) Act 1949 (c.34)
Mine Adventurers of England Act (c.26(d))
Minehead Harbour Act 1700 (c.9)
Minehead Harbour Act 1711 (c.32)
Minehead Harbour Act 1770 (c.26)
Minehead Harbour Act 1937 (c.8)
Minehead Roads Act 1786 (c.136)
Mineral Exploration and Investment Grants Act 1972 (c.9)
Mineral Workings Act 1951 (c.60)
Mineral Workings Act 1971 (c.71)
Mineral Workings Act 1985 (c.12)
Mineral Workings (Offshore Installations) Act 1971 (c.61)
Miners Welfare Act 1952 (c.23)
Mines Accidents (Rescue and Aid) Act 1910 (c.15)
Mines and Quarries Act 1954 (c.70)
Mines and Quarries Act 1969 (c.10)
Mines and Quarries (Tips) Act 1969 (c.10)
Mines Management Act 1971 (c.20)
Mines (Prohibition of Child Labour Underground) Act 1900 (c.21)
Mines (Working Facilities) Act 1934 (c.27)
Mines (Working Facilities and Support) Act 1923 (c.20)
Mines (Working Facilities and Support) Act 1966 (c.4)
Mines (Working Facilities and Support) Act 1974 (c.36)
Mining Industry Act 1920 (c.50)
Mining Industry Act 1926 (c.28)
Mining Industry (Amendment) Act 1939 (c.45)
Mining Industry (Welfare Fund) Act 1925 (c.80)
Mining Industry (Welfare Fund) Act 1931 (c.23)
Mining Industry (Welfare Fund) Act 1934 (c.9)
Mining Industry (Welfare Fund) Act 1939 (c.9)
Mining Industry (Welfare Fund) Act 1943 (c.3)
Minister of Agriculture and Fisheries Act 1919 (c.91)
Minister of Food (Continuance) Act 1920 (c.47)
Minister of Health Act 1919 (c.21)
Minister of Pensions 1916 (c.65)
Minister of the Crown Act 1964 (c.98)
Minister of Transport Act 1919 (c.50)
Ministerial and Other Pensions and Salaries Act 1991 (c.5)
Ministerial and other Salaries Act 1971 (c.3)
Ministerial and other Salaries Act 1975 (c.27)
Ministerial Salaries Act 1946 (c.55)
Ministerial Salaries Act 1957 (c.47)
Ministerial Salaries and Members' Pensions Act 1965 (c.11)
Ministerial Salaries Consolidation 1965 (c.58)
Ministeries of Munitions and Shipping (Cessation) Act 1921 (c.8)
Ministers of the Crown Act 1951 (c.9)
Ministers of the Crown Act 1964 (c.98)
Ministers of the Crown Act 1974 (c.21)
Ministers of the Crown Act 1975 (c.26)
Ministers of the Crown (Parliamentary Secretaries) Act 1960 (c.6)
Ministers of the Crown (Parliamentary Under-Secretaries) Act 1951 (c.9)
Ministers of the Crown (Transfer of Functions) Act 1964 (c.31)
Ministers Widows Fund (Scotland) Act 1779 (c.20)
Ministry of Civil Aviation Act 1945 (c.21)
Ministry of Defence Police Act 1987 (c.4)
Ministry of Food (Financial Powers) Act 1949 (c.15)
Ministry of Fuel and Power Act 1945 (c.19)
Ministry of Materials Act 1951 (c.42)
Ministry of Munitions Act 1915 (c.51)
Ministry of Munitions Act 1918 (c.60)
Ministry of National Insurance Act 1944 (c.46)
Ministry of National Service Act 1917 (c.6)
Ministry of Religion (Removal of Disqualifications) Act 1925 (c.54)
Ministry of Social Security Act 1966 (c.20)
Ministry of Supply Act 1939 (c.38)
Ministry of the Crown Act 1937 (c.38)
Ministry of the Crown and House of Commons Disqualification Act 1942 (c.11)
Ministry of the Crown (Emergency Appointments) Act 1939 (c.77)
Ministry of the Crown (Transfer of Functions) Act 1946 (c.31)
Ministry of the Crown (Treasury Secretaries) Act 1947 (c.5)
Ministry of Town and Country Planning Act 1943 (c.5)
Ministry of Transport Act 1919 (c.50)
Ministry of Works Act 1942 (c.23)
Minority of Heir to the Crown Act 1765 (c.27)
Minority of Successor to Crown Act 1750 (c.24)
Minors' Contracts Act 1987 (c.13)
Mint Prosecutions Expenses Act 1776 (c.46)
Miscellaneous Financial Provisions Act 1946 (c.40)
Miscellaneous Financial Provisions Act 1950 (c.21)

Miscellaneous Financial Provisions Act 1955 (c.6)
Miscellaneous Financial Provisions Act 1968 (c.75)
Miscellaneous Financial Provisions Act 1983 (c.29)
Mischief by Fire 1724 (c.28)
Mischiefs by Fire 1708 (c.17)
Mischiefs from Fire 1707 (c.58)
Misrepresentation Act 1967 (c.7)
Misuse of Drugs Act 1971 (c.38)
Mitford and Launditch, Norfolk: Poor Relief Act 1775 (c.59)
Mobile Homes Act 1975 (c.49)
Mobile Homes Act 1983 (c.34)
Mock Auctions Act 1961 (c.47)
Money Payments (Justices Procedure) Act 1935 (c.46)
Moneylenders Act 1900 (c.51)
Moneylenders Act 1911 (c.38)
Moneylenders Act 1927 (c.21)
Moneylenders (Crown Agents) Act 1975 (c.81)
Monkland, Glasgow: Navigation, etc. Act 1770 (c.105)
Monmouth and Gloucester Roads Act 1757 (c.44)
Monmouth Roads Act 1755 (c.31)
Monmouth Roads Act 1770 (c.106)
Monmouth Roads Act 1777 (c.96)
Monmouth Roads Act 1793 (c.169)
Monmouthshire Canal: Navigation Act 1792 (c.102)
Monopolies and Mergers Act 1965 (c.50)
Monopolies and Restrictive Practices Commission (Inquiry and Control) Act 1948 (c.66)
Monopolies and Restrictive Practices Commission Act 1953 (c.51)
Montgomery: Poor Relief Act 1792 (c.96)
Montgomery, Salop and Denbigh Roads Act 1788 (c.96)
Montrose Beer Duties Act 1719 (c.7)
Montrose Beer Duties Act 1732 (c.5)
Montrose Beer Duties Act 1769 (c.57)
Montrose Bridge Act 1792 (c.38)
Morden College Kent Act 1771 (c.10)
Morpeth and Elsdon Road Act 1751 (c.33)
Morpeth to Elsdon Road Act 1778 (c.107)
Morrison's Haven and Fort, East Lothian (repair) 1708 (c.27)
Mortmain and Charitable Uses Act 1888 (c.42)
Mortgage Act 1733 (c.20)
Mortuaries (Bangor, etc.) Abolition Act 1713 (c.6)
Mortuaries (Chester) Act 1755 (c.6)
Moss Troopers Act 1700 (c.6)
Moss Troopers Act 1712 (c.10)
Motor Car Act 1903 (c.36)
Motor Car (International Circulation) Act 1909 (c.37)
Motor-Cycle Crash-Helmets (Religious Exemption) Act 1976 (c.62)
Motor-Cycle Crash-Helmets (Restriction of Liability) Act 1985 (c.28)
Motor-Cycle Noise Act 1987 (c.34)
Motor Spirit (Regulations) Act 1948 (c.34)
Motor Vehicles (International Circulation) Act 1952 (c.39)
Motor Vehicles (Passenger Insurance) Act 1971 (c.36)
Motor Vehicles (Safety Equipment for Children) Act 1991 (c.14)
Motor Vehicles (Wearing of Rear Seat Belts by Children) Act 1988 (c.23)
Mr Speaker Clifton Brown's Retirement Act 1951 (c.2)
Mr Speaker King's Retirement Act 1970 (c.13)
Mr Speaker Morrison's Retirement Act 1959 (c.1)
Mr Speaker's Retirement Act 1904 (c.5)
Mr Speaker's Retirement Act 1921 (c.10)
Mr Speaker's Retirement Act 1928 (c.16)
Much Wenlock Roads Act 1756 (c.60)
Much Wenlock Roads Act 1778 (c.89)
Multilateral Investment Guarantee Agency Act 1988 (c.8)
Municipal Corporations Act 1882 (c.50)
Municipal Corporations Act 1883 (c.18)
Municipal Corporations Amendment 1906 (c.12)
Municipal Corporations Amendment 1910 (c.19)
Municipal Corporations (Audit) Act 1933 (c.28)
Municipal Corporations (Ireland) Act 1840 (c.108)
Municipal Corporations (Mandamus) Act 1772 (c.21)
Municipal Elections Act 1924 (c.4)
Municipal Elections (Corrupt and Illegal Practices) Act 1884 (c.70)
Municipal Elections (Corrupt and Illegal Practices) Act 1911 (c.7)
Municipal Offices Act 1710 (c.25)
Municipal Rate (Edinburgh) Act 1868 (c.42)
Municipal Savings Banks (War Loan Investment) Act 1916 (c.47)
Munitions (Liability for Explosion) Act 1916 (c.61)
Munitions of War Act 1915 (c.54)
Munitions of War Act 1917 (c.45)
Munitions of War Amendment 1916 (c.99)
Murder (Abolition of Death Penalty) Act 1965 (c.71)
Murder Act 1728 (c.21)
Murder Act 1751 (c.37)
Murders Abroad Act 1817 (c.53)
Murderers of Captain Porteous Act 1735 (c.35)
Museums and Galleries Admission Charges Act 1972 (c.73)
Museums and Gymnasiums Act 1891 (c.22)
Museum of London Act 1965 (c.17)
Museum of London Act 1986 (c.8)

Museums and Galleries Act 1992 (c.44)
Musical Copyright Act 1906 (c.36)
Musical (Summary Proceedings) Copyright Act 1902 (c.15)
Mutford and Lothingland, Suffolk (Poor Relief) Act 1764 (c.89)
Mutiny Act 1701 (c.2)
Mutiny Act 1702 (c.20)
Mutiny Act 1703 (c.17)
Mutiny Act 1704 (c.5)
Mutiny Act 1705 (c.22)
Mutiny Act 1706 (c.18)
Mutiny Act 1707 (c.74)
Mutiny Act 1708 (c.4)
Mutiny Act 1709 (c.6)
Mutiny Act 1710 (c.9)
Mutiny Act 1711 (c.13)
Mutiny Act 1712 (c.13)
Mutiny Act 1713 (c.4)
Mutiny Act 1714 (c.3)
Mutiny Act 1714 (c.9)
Mutiny Act 1715 (c.34)
Mutiny Act 1716 (c.2)
Mutiny Act 1717 (c.4)
Mutiny Act 1718 (c.5)
Mutiny Act 1719 (c.3)
Mutiny Act 1720 (c.6)
Mutiny Act 1721 (c.3)
Mutiny Act 1722 (c.4)
Mutiny Act 1723 (c.3)
Mutiny Act 1724 (c.6)
Mutiny Act 1725 (c.3)
Mutiny Act 1726 (c.2)
Mutiny Act 1727 (c.2)
Mutiny Act 1728 (c.2)
Mutiny Act 1729 (c.2)
Mutiny Act 1730 (c.2)
Mutiny Act 1731 (c.2)
Mutiny Act 1732 (c.3)
Mutiny Act 1733 (c.2)
Mutiny Act 1734 (c.2)
Mutiny Act 1735 (c.2)
Mutiny Act 1736 (c.2)
Mutiny Act 1737 (c.2)
Mutiny Act 1738 (c.2)
Mutiny Act 1739 (c.10)
Mutiny Act 1740 (c.9)
Mutiny Act 1741 (c.4)
Mutiny Act 1742 (c.14)
Mutiny Act 1743 (c.16)
Mutiny Act 1744 (c.7)
Mutiny Act 1745 (c.11)
Mutiny Act 1746 (c.11)
Mutiny Act 1747 (c.6)
Mutiny Act 1747 (c.13)
Mutiny Act 1748 (c.5)
Mutiny Act 1749 (c.4)
Mutiny Act 1750 (c.6)
Mutiny Act 1751 (c.2)
Mutiny Act 1753 (c.5)
Mutiny Act 1754 (c.5)
Mutiny Act 1755 (c.4)
Mutiny Act 1756 (c.3)
Mutiny Act 1757 (c.6)
Mutiny Act 1757 (c.5)
Mutiny Act 1758 (c.5)
Mutiny Act 1759 (c.6)
Mutiny Act 1760 (c.6)
Mutiny Act 1761 (c.11)
Mutiny Act 1762 (c.7)
Mutiny Act 1763 (c.3)
Mutiny Act 1765 (c.7)
Mutiny Act 1766 (c.8)
Mutiny Act 1766 (c.10)
Mutiny Act 1768 (c.7)
Mutiny Act 1769 (c.7)
Mutiny Act 1770 (c.3)
Mutiny Act 1770 (c.15)
Mutiny Act 1771 (c.6)
Mutiny Act 1772 (c.4)
Mutiny Act 1772 (c.10)
Mutiny Act 1774 (c.3)
Mutiny Act 1775 (c.6)
Mutiny Act 1776 (c.2)
Mutiny Act 1776 (c.3)
Mutiny Act 1778 (c.4)
Mutiny Act 1779 (c.16)
Mutiny Act 1780 (c.12)
Mutiny Act 1782 (c.4)
Mutiny Act 1783 (c.17)
Mutiny Act 1783 (c.24)
Mutiny Act 1783 (c.52)
Mutiny Act 1783 (c.11)
Mutiny Act 1785 (c.6)
Mutiny Act 1786 (c.10)
Mutiny Act 1788 (c.12)
Mutiny Act 1789 (c.2)
Mutiny Act 1790 (c.6)
Mutiny Act 1791 (c.13)
Mutiny Act 1791 (c.19)
Mutiny Act 1793 (c.9)
Mutiny Act 1794 (c.13)
Mutiny Act 1795 (c.6)
Mutiny, America Act 1765 (c.33)
Mutiny, America Act 1768 (c.19)
Mutiny, East Indies Act 1754 (c.9)
Mutiny in America Act 1766 (c.18)
Mutiny in America Act 1767 (c.55)
Mutiny in America Act 1769 (c.18)
Mutiny in America Act 1771 (c.11)
Mutiny in America Act 1772 (c.12)
Mutiny in America Act 1773 (c.24)
Mutiny in America Act 1774 (c.6)
Mutiny in America Act 1775 (c.15)
Mutiny in America Act 1776 (c.11)

Namibia Act 1991 (c.4)
Nantwich Canal Act 1777 (c.67)
Nantwich Canal Act 1778 (c.21)
Nantwich to Chester Road Act 1789 (c.91)
Nar: Navigation Act 1750 (c.19)
National Assistance Act 1948 (c.29)
National Assistance Act 1948 (Amendment) Act 1962 (c.24)
National Assistance Act 1959 (c.52)

National Assistance (Amendment) Act 1951 (c.57)
National Assistance (Amendment) Act 1959 (c.30)
National Audit Act 1983 (c.44)
National Coal Board (Additional Powers) Act 1966 (c.47)
National Coal Board (Finance) Act 1976 (c.1)
National Debt Act 1714 (c.2)
National Debt Act 1714 (c.12)
National Debt Act 1714 (c.19)
National Debt Act 1714 (c.21)
National Debt Act 1716 (c.7)
National Debt Act 1716 (c.9)
National Debt Act 1717 (c.10)
National Debt Act 1718 (c.3)
National Debt Act 1718 (c.9)
National Debt Act 1718 (c.19)
National Debt Act 1719 (c.4)
National Debt Act 1719 (c.10)
National Debt Act 1720 (c.5)
National Debt Act 1721 (c.1)
National Debt Act 1721 (c.20)
National Debt Act 1721 (c.22)
National Debt Act 1722 (cc.5, 6)
National Debt Act 1722 (c.12)
National Debt Act 1723 (c.5)
National Debt Act 1724 (c.17)
National Debt Act 1726 (c.3)
National Debt Act 1726 (c.21)
National Debt Act 1730 (c.16)
National Debt Act 1730 (c.5)
National Debt Act 1730 (c.9)
National Debt Act 1731 (c.17)
National Debt Act 1732 (c.28)
National Debt Act 1735 (c.34)
National Debt Act 1736 (c.17)
National Debt Act 1737 (c.27)
National Debt Act 1741 (c.19)
National Debt Act 1742 (cc.12, 13)
National Debt Act 1743 (c.18)
National Debt Act 1744 (c.9)
National Debt Act 1745 (c.12)
National Debt Act 1746 (c.3)
National Debt Act 1746 (c.10)
National Debt Act 1747 (c.2)
National Debt Act 1748 (c.23)
National Debt Act 1749 (c.1)
National Debt Act 1749 (c.16)
National Debt Act 1750 (c.2)
National Debt Act 1750 (c.11)
National Debt Act 1751 (c.25)
National Debt Act 1751 (c.27)
National Debt Act 1753 (c.1)
National Debt Act 1753 (c.23)
National Debt Act 1755 (c.15)
National Debt Act 1756 (c.7)
National Debt Act 1757 (c.19)
National Debt Act 1758 (c.22)
National Debt Act 1759 (c.12)
National Debt Act 1760 (c.7)
National Debt Act 1761 (cc.9, 10)
National Debt Act 1762 (c.9)
National Debt Act 1762 (c.12)
National Debt Act 1763 (c.18)
National Debt Act 1763 (c.25)
National Debt Act 1765 (c.16)
National Debt Act 1765 (c.23)
National Debt Act 1765 (c.42)
National Debt Act 1766 (c.21)
National Debt Act 1766 (c.39)
National Debt Act 1766 (cc.24–26)
National Debt Act 1768 (c.29)
National Debt Act 1768 (c.31)
National Debt Act 1770 (c.36)
National Debt Act 1770 (c.46)
National Debt Act 1772 (c.63)
National Debt Act 1774 (c.76)
National Debt Act 1775 (c.41)
National Debt Act 1776 (c.46)
National Debt Act 1778 (c.22)
National Debt Act 1779 (c.18)
National Debt Act 1782 (c.8)
National Debt Act 1782 (c.34)
National Debt Act 1783 (c.35)
National Debt Act 1784 (c.10)
National Debt Act 1784 (c.37)
National Debt Act 1784 (c.39)
National Debt Act 1785 (c.32)
National Debt Act 1785 (c.71)
National Debt Act 1786 (c.34)
National Debt Act 1789 (c.37)
National Debt Act 1793 (c.28)
National Debt Act 1793 (c.32)
National Debt Act 1794 (c.1)
National Debt Act 1794 (c.21)
National Debt Act 1795 (c.14)
National Debt Act 1795 (c.23)
National Debt Act 1795 (c.32)
National Debt Act 1958 (c.6)
National Debt Act 1972 (c.65)
National Debt (Conversion of Stock) Act 1884 (c.23)
National Debt (No. 2) Act 1749 (c.22)
National Debt Reduction Act 1724 (c.9)
National Debt Reduction Act 1786 (c.31)
National Economy Act 1931 (c.48)
National Film Finance Corporation Act 1981 (c.15)
National Fire Service Regulations (Indemnity) Act 1944 (c.35)
National Galleries of Scotland Act 1906 (c.50)
National Galleries of Scotland Act 1959 (c.61)
National Gallery and St. James's Park Act 1911 (c.23)
National Gallery and Tate Gallery Act 1954 (c.65)
National Gallery Enlargement Act 1866 (c.83)
National Gallery Enlargement Act 1867 (c.41)
National Gallery (Overseas Loans) Act 1935 (c.18)
National Gallery (Purchase of Adjacent Land) Act 1901 (c.16)
National Health (Hospital Boards) Act 1964 (c.32)
National Health Insurance Act 1918 (c.62)

National Health Insurance Act 1919 (c.36)
National Health Insurance Act 1920 (c.10)
National Health Insurance Act 1921 (c.25)
National Health Insurance Act 1922 (c.38)
National Health Insurance Act 1924 (c.38)
National Health Insurance Act 1928 (c.14)
National Health Insurance Act 1936 (c.32)
National Health Insurance (Amendment) Act 1937 (c.24)
National Health Insurance (Amendment) Act 1938 (c.14)
National Health Insurance and Contributory Pensions Act 1932 (c.52)
National Health Insurance and Contributory Pensions Act 1935 (c.44)
National Health Insurance and Contributory Pensions (Emergency Provisions) Act 1939 (c.84)
National Health Insurance, Contributory Pensions and Workmen's Compensation Act 1941 (c.39)
National Health Insurance (Cost of Medical Benefit) Act 1924 (c.10)
National Health Insurance (Juvenile Contributors and Young Persons) Act 1937 (c.3)
National Health Insurance (Prolongation of Insurance) Act 1921 (c.66)
National Health Insurance (Prolongation of Insurance) Act 1931 (c.5)
National Health Insurance (Prolongation of Insurance) Act 1932 (c.6)
National Health Service Act 1946 (c.81)
National Health Service Act 1951 (c.31)
National Health Service Act 1952 (c.25)
National Health Service Act 1961 (c.19)
National Health Service Act 1966 (c.8)
National Health Service Act 1977 (c.49)
National Health Service (Amendment) Act 1949 (c.93)
National Health Service (Amendment) Act 1957 (c.44)
National Health Service (Amendment) Act 1986 (c.66)
National Health Service (Amendment) Act 1995 (c.31)
National Health Service and Community Care Act 1990 (c.19)
National Health Service Contributions Act 1957 (c.34)
National Health Service Contributions Act 1961 (c.13)
National Health Service Contributions Act 1965 (c.54)
National Health Service Contributions Act 1970 (c.16)
National Health Service (Family Planning) Act 1967 (c.39)
National Health Service (Family Planning) Amendment Act 1972 (c.72)
National Health Service (Hospital Boards) Act 1964 (c.32)
National Health Service (Invalid Direction) Act 1980 (c.15)
National Health Service Reorganisation Act 1973 (c.32)
National Health Service (Residual Liabilities) Act 1996 (c.15)
National Health Service (Scotland) Act 1947 (c.27)
National Health Service (Scotland) Act 1972 (c.58)
National Health Service (Scotland) Act 1978 (c.29)
National Health Service (Vocational Training) Act 1976 (c.59)
National Heritage Act 1980 (c.17)
National Heritage Act 1983 (c.47)
National Heritage (Scotland) Act 1985 (c.16)
National Insurance Act 1911 (c.55)
National Insurance Act 1913 (c.37)
National Insurance Act 1946 (c.67)
National Insurance Act 1947 (c.37)
National Insurance Act 1949 (c.56)
National Insurance Act 1951 (c.34)
National Insurance Act 1953 (c.29)
National Insurance Act 1955 (c.29)
National Insurance Act 1956 (c.47)
National Insurance Act 1957 (c.26)
National Insurance Act 1959 (c.47)
National Insurance Act 1960 (c.5)
National Insurance Act 1963 (c.7)
National Insurance Act 1965 (c.51)
National Insurance Act 1966 (c.6)
National Insurance Act 1967 (c.73)
National Insurance Act 1969 (c.4)
National Insurance Act 1969 (c.44)
National Insurance Act 1971 (c.50)
National Insurance Act 1972 (c.57)
National Insurance Act 1974 (c.14)
National Insurance &c Act 1964 (c.96)
National Insurance and Supplementary Benefit Act 1973 (c.42)
National Insurance (Amendment) Act 1972 (c.36)
National Insurance, etc. Act 1969 (c.4)
National Insurance (Industrial) Act 1953 (c.43)
National Insurance (Industrial Injuries) Act 1946 (c.62)
National Insurance (Industrial Injuries) Act 1948 (c.42)
National Insurance (Industrial Injuries) Act 1965 (c.52)
National Insurance (Industrial Injuries) (Amendment) Act 1967 (c.25)
National Insurance Land Purchase (Winding-up) Act 1935 (c.21)
National Insurance (Miscellaneous Provisions) Act 1928 (c.24)
National Insurance (Miscellaneous Provisions) Act 1932 (c.11)
National Insurance (Miscellaneous Provisions) Act 1945 (c.12)
National Insurance (Navy and Army) Act (c.81)
National Insurance (Navy and Army) (Session 2) Act 1914 (c.15)

National Insurance (No. 2) Act 1957 (c.1)
National Insurance (Old Persons' and Widows' Pensions and Attendance Allowance) Act 1970 (c.51)
National Insurance (Pt. I Amendment) Act 1915 (c.29)
National Insurance (Pt. I Amendment) Act 1917 (c.15)
National Insurance (Pt. II Amendment) Act 1914 (c.57)
National Insurance (Pt. II Amendment) Act 1914 (c.27)
National Insurance (Pt. II) (Munition Workers) Act 1916 (c.20)
National Insurance Regulations (Validation) Act 1972 (c.4)
National Insurance Surcharge Act 1976 (c.85)
National Insurance Surcharge Act 1982 (c.55)
National Insurance (Temporary Employment in Agriculture) Act 1916 (c.53)
National Insurance (Unemployment) Act 1918 (c.63)
National Insurance (Unemployment) Act 1919 (c.77)
National Library of Scotland Act 1925 (c.73)
National Loans Act 1939 (c.117)
National Loans Act 1940 (c.3)
National Loans Act 1941 (c.18)
National Loans Act 1942 (c.14)
National Loans Act 1943 (c.13)
National Loans Act 1944 (c.19)
National Loans Act 1945 (c.23)
National Loans Act 1968 (c.13)
National Loans (No. 2) Act 1940 (c.23)
National Lottery etc. Act 1993 (c.39)
National Maritime Museum Act 1934 (c.43)
National Maritime Museum Act 1989 (c.8)
National Mod (Scotland) Act 1969 (c.41)
National Museum of Antiquities of Scotland Act 1954 (c.14)
National Parks and Access to the Countryside Act 1949 (c.97)
National Portrait Gallery Act 1889 (c.25)
National Registration Act 1915 (c.60)
National Registration Act 1939 (c.91)
National Registration (Amendment) Act 1918 (c.60)
National Savings Bank Act 1971 (c.29)
National Service Act 1941 (c.15)
National Service Act 1942 (c.3)
National Service Act 1947 (c.31)
National Service Act 1948 (c.64)
National Service Act 1950 (c.30)
National Service Act 1955 (c.11)
National Service (Amendment) Act 1948 (c.6)
National Service (Armed Forces) Act 1939 (c.81)
National Service (Armed Forces) Act 1940 (c.22)
National Service (Channel Islands) Act 1940 (c.24)
National Service (Foreign Countries) Act 1942 (c.30)
National Service (No. 2) Act 1941 (c.4)
National Service (Release of Conscientious Objectors) Act 1946 (c.38)
National Theatre Act 1949 (c.16)
National Theatre Act 1969 (c.11)
National Theatre Act 1974 (c.55)
National Theatre and Museum of London Act 1973 (c.2)
Nationalised Industries Loans Act 1958 (c.19)
Natural Heritage (Scotland) Act 1991 (c.28)
Natural-born Children of Aliens Act 1776 (c.52)
Naturalisation Act 1711 (c.9)
Naturalisation Act 1714 (c.4)
Naturalisation Act 1739 (c.7)
Naturalisation Act 1762 (c.25)
Naturalisation Act 1763 (c.4)
Naturalisation Act 1772 (c.25)
Naturalisation Act 1774 (c.84)
Naturalisation of Jews Act 1753 (c.26)
Naturalisation of Jews Act 1754 (c.1)
Nature Conservancy Council Act 1973 (c.54)
Naval Agency and Distribution Act 1864 (c.24)
Naval and Marine Forces (Temporary Release from Service) Act 1941 (c.4)
Naval and Marine Pay and Pensions Act 1865 (c.73)
Naval and Marine Reserves Pay Act 1957 (c.32)
Naval and Military War Pensions, etc. Act 1915 (c.83)
Naval and Military War Pensions, etc. (Admin. Expenses) Act 1917 (c.14)
Naval and Military War Pension, etc. (Committees) Act 1917 (c.54)
Naval and Military War Pensions, etc. (Expenses) Act 1916 (c.4)
Naval and Military War Pensions, etc. (Transfer of Powers) Act 1917 (c.37)
Naval Billeting, etc. Act 1914 (c. 70)
Naval Courts-Martial Act 1779 (c.17)
Naval Discipline Act 1909 (c.41)
Naval Discipline Act 1915 (c.30)
Naval Discipline Act 1917 (c.34)
Naval Discipline Act 1922 (c.37)
Naval Discipline Act 1957 (c.53)
Naval Discipline (Amendment) Act 1938 (c.64)
Naval Discipline (Amendment) Act 1941 (c.29)
Naval Discipline (Delegation of Powers) Act 1916 (c.17)
Naval Discipline (Delegation of Powers) Act 1917 (c.11)
Naval Discipline (Dominion Naval Forces) Act 1911 (c.47)
Naval Discipline (No. 2) Act 1915 (c.73)
Naval Enlistment Act 1884 (c.46)
Naval Establishments in British Possessions Act 1909 (c.18)

Naval Forces Act 1903 (c.6)
Naval Forces (Enforcement of Maintenance Liabilities) Act 1947 (c.24)
Naval Forces (Extension of Services) Act 1944 (c.13)
Naval Forces (Service on Shore) Act 1916 (c.101)
Naval Knights of Windsor (Dissolution) Act 1892 (c.34)
Naval Lands (Volunteers) Act 1908 (c.25)
Naval Marriages Act 1908 (c.26)
Naval Marriages Act 1915 (c.35)
Naval Medical Compassionate Fund Act 1915 (c.28)
Naval, Military and Air Force Service Act 1919 (c.15)
Naval Pensions Act 1884 (c.44)
Naval Prize Act 1739 (c.4)
Naval Prize Act 1743 (c.34)
Naval Prize Act 1746 (c.24)
Naval Prize Act 1758 (c.25)
Naval Prize Act 1772 (c.25)
Naval Prize Act 1864 (c.25)
Naval Prize Act 1918 (c.30)
Naval Prize Act 1928 (c.36)
Naval Prize etc. Act 1756 (c.34)
Naval Prize Money Act 1820 (c.85)
Naval Prize (Procedure) Act 1916 (c.2)
Naval Reserve Act 1900 (c.52)
Naval Reserve (Mobilisation) Act 1900 (c.17)
Naval Reserve (Officers) Act 1926 (c.41)
Naval Stores Act 1745 (c.36)
Naval Volunteers Act 1853 (c.73)
Naval Works Act 1901 (c.39)
Naval Works Act 1903 (c.22)
Naval Works Act 1904 (c.20)
Navigation Act 1703 (c.6)
Navigation Act 1755 (c.16)
Navigation Act 1756 (c.11)
Navigation Act 1776 (c.20)
Navigation Act 1776 (c.34)
Navigation Act 1778 (c.6)
Navigation Act 1779 (c.14)
Navigation Act 1780 (c.19)
Navigation Act 1782 (c.16)
Navigation, Norfolk Act 1754 (c.12)
Navru Island Agreement Act 1920 (c.27)
Navy Act 1705 (c.6)
Navy Act 1727 (c.14)
Navy Act 1740 (c.38)
Navy Act 1744 (c.35)
Navy Act 1747 (c.11)
Navy Act 1748 (c.33)
Navy Act 1756 (c.27)
Navy Act 1756 (c.10)
Navy Act 1762 (c.16)
Navy Act 1769 (c.30)
Navy Act 1779 (c.67)
Navy Act 1779 (c.75)
Navy Act 1780 (c.23)
Navy Act 1780 (c.15)
Navy Act 1786 (c.63)
Navy Act 1791 (c.33)
Navy Act 1791 (c.34)
Navy and Marines Act 1795 (c.28)
Navy and Marines (Wills) Act 1914 (c.17)
Navy and Marines (Wills) Act 1930 (c.38)
Navy and Marines (Wills) Act 1939 (c.87)
Navy and Marines (Wills) Act 1953 (c.24)
Navy and Victualling Bills Act 1794 (c.56)
Navy, Army and Air Force Reserves Act 1954 (c.10)
Navy, Army and Air Force Reserves Act 1959 (c.10)
Navy, Army and Air Force Reserves Act 1964 (c.11)
Navy, etc. Act 1714 (c.25)
Navy, etc. Act 1780 (c.11)
Navy (Pledging of Certificates, etc.) Act 1914 (c.89)
Neath Canal Act 1791 (c.85)
Negotiations of Certain Bonds Act 1782 (c.11)
Negotiations of Notes and Bills 1775 (c.51)
Negotiations of Notes and Bills Act 1802 (c.1)
Nether Knutsford Church Act 1740 (c.5)
New Forest Act 1949 (c.69)
New Forest Act 1964 (c.83)
New Forest Act 1970 (c.21)
Newfoundland (Consequential Provisions) Act 1949 (c.5)
New Hebrides Act 1980 (c.16)
New Malton, Yorks. (Searching, Sealing, etc. of Butter) Act 1743 (c.8)
New Method of Tanning Act 1794 (c.63)
New Ministries Act 1917 (c.44)
New Ministries and Secretaries Act 1916 (c.68)
New Office of Excise Act 1770 (c.32)
New Palace Yard, Westminster 1706 (c.15)
New Parishes Act 1843 (c.37)
New Parishes Act 1844 (c.94)
New Parishes Act 1856 (c.104)
New Parishes Acts and Church Building Acts Amendment Act 1869 (c.94)
New Parishes Acts and Church Building Acts Amendment Act 1884 (c.65)
New Roads and Street Works Act 1991 (c.22)
New Sarum: Poor Relief Act 1770 (c.81)
New Shoreham Harbour Act 1759 (c.35)
New Shoreham Harbour Act 1789 (c.21)
New Streets Act 1951 (c.40)
New Streets Act 1951 (Amendment) Act 1957 (c.33)
New Towns Act 1946 (c.68)
New Towns Act 1952 (c.27)
New Towns Act 1953 (c.38)
New Towns Act 1955 (c.4)
New Towns Act 1958 (c.12)
New Towns Act 1959 (c.62)
New Towns Act 1965 (c.59)
New Towns Act 1966 (c.44)
New Towns Act 1969 (c.5)
New Towns Act 1971 (c.81)
New Towns Act 1975 (c.42)
New Towns Act 1977 (c.23)

New Towns Act 1980 (c.36)
New Towns Act 1981 (c.64)
New Towns Act 1982 (c.7)
New Towns (No. 2) Act 1964 (c.68)
New Towns (Amendment) Act 1976 (c.68)
New Towns (Amendment) Act 1994 (c.5)
New Towns and Urban Development Corporations Act 1985 (c.5)
New Towns (Scotland) Act 1968 (c.16)
New Towns (Scotland) Act 1977 (c.16)
New Valuation Lists (Postponement) Act 1952 (c.4)
New Woodstock, Kiddington, etc. Roads Act 1757 (c.48)
New Zealand Constitution (Amendment) 1947 (c.4)
Newbury and Marlborough Roads Act 1744 (c.12)
Newbury to Bath Canal Act 1794 (c.90)
Newbury to Marlborough Road Act 1725 (c.8)
Newcastle and Gateshead Bridge Act 1788 (c.78)
Newcastle and Sunderland: Coals Act 1790 (c.78)
Newcastle: Improvement Act 1763 (c.55)
Newcastle (Sale of Coal by Measured Keel) Act 1791 (c.36)
Newcastle: Streets Act 1786 (c.39)
Newcastle to Buckton Burn Road Act 1794 (c.130)
Newcastle to Carlisle Road Act 1786 (c.160)
Newfoundland Act 1933 (c.2)
Newfoundland (Consequential Provisions) Act 1950 (c.5)
Newfoundland Fisheries Act 1775 (c.31)
Newfoundland Fisheries Act 1786 (c.26)
Newfoundland Fisheries Act 1788 (c.35)
Newgate Gaol Delivery Act 1785 (c.18)
Newgate Gaol and Session House Act 1778 (c.48)
Newhaven Bridge Act 1783 (c.21)
Newhaven Harbour Act 1730 (c.17)
Newmarket and Cambridge Road Act 1763 (c.32)
Newmarket to Cambridge Road Act 1775 (c.68)
Newspaper Duty Act 1772 (c.65)
Newspaper Libel and Registration Act 1881 (c.60)
Newspapers, Printers and Reading Rooms Repeal Act 1869 (c.24)
Newport, Isle of Wight: Improvement Act 1786 (c.119)
Niall Macpherson Indemnity 1954 (c.29)
Nigeria Independence Act 1960 (c.55)
Nigeria (Remission of Payments) Act 1937 (c.63)
Nigeria Republic Act 1963 (c.57)
Night Poaching Act 1828 (c.69)
Night Watch Westminster Act (c.15)
Nisi Prius, Middlesex Act 1725 (c.31)
Nith Fisheries Act 1792 (c.94)
Noise Act 1996 (c.37)
Noise Abatement Act 1960 (c.68)
Noise and Statutory Nuisance Act 1993 (c.40)
Nonconformist Relief Act 1779 (c.44)
Non-Domestic Rating Act 1992 (c.46)
Non-Domestic Rating Act 1993 (c.17)
Non-Domestic Rating Act 1994 (c.3)
Non-Domestic Rating (Information) Act 1996 (c.13)
Non-Ferrous Metal Industry Act 1917 (c.67)
Norfolk and Suffolk Broads Act 1988 (c.4)
Norfolk: Drainage Act 1783 (c,9)
Norfolk Highways Act 1708 (c.8)
Norfolk: Improvement Act 1725 (c.15)
Norfolk Roads Act 1765 (c.83)
Norfolk Roads Act 1765 (c.101)
Norfolk Roads Act 1767 (c.76)
Norfolk Roads Act 1770 (c.54)
Norfolk Roads Act 1770 (c.85)
Norfolk Roads Act 1770 (c.86)
Norfolk Roads Act 1786 (c.127)
Norfolk Roads Act 1790 (c.87)
Norfolk Roads Act 1790 (c.104)
Norfolk Roads Act 1791 (c.100)
Norfolk Roads Act 1791 (c.112)
Norfolk Roads Act 1791 (c.113)
Norfolk Roads Act 1792 (c.148)
Norfolk Roads Act 1792 (c.158)
Norfolk Roads Act 1794 (c.114)
North American Fisheries Act 1819 (c.38)
North Atlantic Shipping Act 1934 (c.10)
North Kyme Drainage Act 1788 (c.14)
North River, Norfolk: Navigation Act 1772 (c.37)
North Shields to Newcastle Road Act 1774 (c.115)
North Shields: Water Supply Act 1786 (c.110)
Northampton and Lincoln Roads Act 1756 (c.76)
Northampton and Lincoln Roads Act 1776 (c.72)
Northampton and Oxford Roads Act 1778 (c.87)
Northampton and Warwick Roads Act 1724 (c.25)
Northampton Highways Act (c.9)
Northampton: Improvement Act 1778 (c.79)
Northampton Roads Act 1748 (c.17)
Northampton Roads Act 1749 (c.8)
Northampton Roads Act 1753 (c.88)
Northampton Roads Act 1754 (c.23)
Northampton Roads Act 1778 (c.112)
Northampton Roads Act 1781 (c.94)
Northampton Roads Act 1783 (c.28)
Northampton Roads Act 1794 (c.126)
Northern Ireland Act 1929 (c.14)
Northern Ireland Act 1947 (c.37)
Northern Ireland Act 1955 (c.8)
Northern Ireland Act 1962 (c.30)
Northern Ireland Act 1972 (c.10)
Northern Ireland Act 1974 (c.28)
Northern Ireland Act 1982 (c.38)
Northern Ireland Assembly Act 1973 (c.17)

Northern Ireland Assembly Disqualifications Act 1975 (c.25)
Northern Ireland (Border Poll) Act 1972 (c.77)
Northern Ireland Compensation (for Compulsory Purchase) Act 1957 (c.14)
Northern Ireland Constitution Act 1973 (c.36)
Northern Ireland Constitution (Amendment) Act 1973 (c.69)
Northern Ireland (Emergency Provisions) Act 1973 (c.53)
Northern Ireland (Emergency Provisions) Act 1978 (c.5)
Northern Ireland (Emergency Provisions) Act 1987 (c.30)
Northern Ireland (Emergency Provisions) Act 1991 (c.24)
Northern Ireland (Emergency Provisions) Act 1996 (c.22)
Northern Ireland (Emergency Provisions) Amendment Act 1975 (c.62)
Northern Ireland (Emergency Provisions) (Amendment) Act 1977 (c.34)
Northern Ireland (Entry to Negotiations, etc) Act 1996 (c.11)
Northern Ireland (Financial Provisions) Act 1972 (c.76)
Northern Ireland (Foyle Fisheries) Act 1952 (c.11)
Northern Ireland Land Act 1925 (c.34)
Northern Ireland Land Act 1929 (c.14)
Northern Ireland Land Purchase (Winding Up) Act 1935 (c.21)
Northern Ireland (Loans) Act 1975 (c.83)
Northern Ireland (Loans) Act 1985 (c.76)
Northern Ireland (Miscellaneous Provisions) Act 1928 (c.24)
Northern Ireland (Miscellaneous Provisions) Act 1932 (c.11)
Northern Ireland (Miscellaneous Provisions) Act 1945 (c.12)
Northern Ireland (Remission of Sentences) Act 1995 (c.47)
Northern Ireland (Temporary Provisions) Act 1972 (c.22)
Northern Ireland (Young Persons) Act 1974 (c.33)
Northern Roads, London Act 1735 (c.39)
Northumberland Fishery Act 1789 (c.25)
Northumberland and Durham Roads Act 1792 (c.145)
Northumberland Roads Act 1746 (c.9)
Northumberland Roads Act 1748 (c.7)
Northumberland Roads Act 1748 (c.9)
Northumberland Roads Act 1751 (c.18)
Northumberland Roads Act 1751 (c.46)
Northumberland Roads Act 1751 (c.48)
Northumberland Roads Act 1757 (c.52)
Northumberland Roads Act 1776 (c.68)
Northumberland Roads Act 1776 (c.83)
Northumberland Roads Act 1778 (c.83)
Northumberland Roads Act 1778 (c.115)
Northumberland Roads Act 1779 (c.95)
Norton Folley, Middlesex, Lighting etc. Act 1758 (c.49)
Norwich Assizes Act 1746 (c.21)
Norwich and Swaffham Road Act 1770 (c.67)
Norwich and Thetford Road Act 1725 (c.22)
Norwich and Thetford Road Act 1746 (c.16)
Norwich and Watton Road Act 1770 (c.77)
Norwich Mayors, Sheriffs, etc. 1922 (c.9)
Norwich Roads Act 1790 (c.86)
Norwich to Bixley Roads Act 1790 (c.85)
Norwich to New Buckingham Road Act 1772 (c.95)
Norwich to Scole Bridge Road Act 1969 (c.66)
Norwich to Scole Bridge Road Act 1772 (c.76)
Norwich to Thetford Road Act 1792 (c.111)
Norwich to Swaffham Road Act 1792 (c.112)
Norwich to Yarmouth Road Act 1969 (c.68)
Norwich Water Act 1790 (c.21)
Norwich Workhouse Act 1711 (c.15)
Notice of Accidents Act 1906 (c.53)
Notification of Births Act 1907 (c.40)
Notification of Births (Extension) Act 1915 (c.64)
Nottingham Roads Act 1770 (c.92)
Nottingham Roads Act 1774 (c.101)
Nottingham Roads Act 1785 (c.107)
Nottingham and Derby Road Act 1758 (c.38)
Nottingham and Derby Roads Act 1764 (c.83)
Nottingham and Derby Roads Act 1765 (c.90)
Nottingham and Derby Roads Act 1783 (c.24)
Nottingham and Derby Roads Act 1788 (c.87)
Nottingham and Derby Roads Act 1788 (c.99)
Nottingham and Leicester Highways Act 1721 (c.13)
Nottingham and Leicester Roads Act 1737 (c.3)
Nottingham and Leicester Roads Act 1754 (c.22)
Nottingham and Lincoln Roads Act 1765 (c.85)
Nottingham Canal Act 1792 (c.100)
Nottingham, Leicester, Rutland and Northampton Roads Act 1780 (c.81)
Nottingham: Lighting etc. Act 1762 (c.47)
Nottingham Roads Act 1765 (c.54)
Nottingham Roads Act 1791 (c.131)
Nottingham Roads Act 1791 (c.132)
Nottingham, Shire Hall Act 1769 (c.62)
Nottingham to Mansfield Road Act 1787 (c.76)
Nuclear Industry (Finance) Act 1977 (c.7)
Nuclear Industry (Finance) Act 1981 (c.71)
Nuclear Installations Act 1959 (c.46)
Nuclear Installations Act 1965 (c.57)
Nuclear Installations Act 1969 (c.18)
Nuclear Installations (Amendment) Act 1965 (c.6)
Nuclear Materials (Offences) Act 1983 (c.18)
Nuclear Safeguards and Electricity (Finance) Act 1978 (c.25)
Nuisances Removal (Scotland) Act 1856 (c.103)
Nullity of Marriage Act 1971 (c.44)
Nurseries and Child Minders Regulation Act 1948 (c.53)

Nursery Education and Grant-Maintained Schools Act 1996 (c.50)
Nurses Act 1943 (c.17)
Nurses Act 1945 (c.6)
Nurses Act 1949 (c.73)
Nurses Act 1957 (c.15)
Nurses Act 1964 (c.44)
Nurses Act 1969 (c.47)
Nurses Registration Act 1919 (c.94)
Nurses Registration (Ireland) Act 1919 (c.96)
Nurses Registration (Scotland) Act 1919 (c.95)
Nurses (Scotland) Act 1943 (c.33)
Nurses (Scotland) Act 1949 (c.95)
Nurses (Scotland) Act (c.55)
Nurses Agencies Act 1957 (c.16)
Nurses (Amendment) Act 1961 (c.14)
Nurses, Midwives and Health Visitors Act 1979 (c.36)
Nurses, Midwives and Health Visitors Act 1992 (c.16)
Nurses (Scotland) Act 1951 (c.55)
Nursing Homes Act 1963 (c.13)
Nursing Homes Act 1975 (c.37)
Nursing Homes Registration Act 1927 (c.38)
Nursing Homes Registration (Scotland) Act 1938 (c.73)

OECD Support Fund Act 1975 (c.80)
Oakham Canal Act 1793 (c.103)
Oakhampton Roads Act 1782 (c.92)
Oaths, etc. Act 1714 (c.3)
Oaths Act 1775 (c.39)
Oaths Act 1838 (c.105)
Oaths Act 1888 (c.46)
Oaths Act 1909 (c.39)
Oaths Act 1961 (c.21)
Oaths Act 1978 (c.19)
Oaths and Evidence (Overseas Authorities) (Land) Act 1963 (c.27)
Oaths at Parliamentary Elections Act 1794 (c.84)
Oaths of Justices of the Peace Act 1745 (c.13)
Obscene Publications Act 1857 (c.83)
Obscene Publications Act 1959 (c.66)
Obscene Publications Act 1964 (c.74)
Observance of Lord's Day by Bakers Act 1794 (c.61)
Obtaining Money by False Pretences, etc. Act 1757 (c.24)
Occasional Licences and Young Persons 1956 (c.42)
Occupiers' Liability Act 1957 (c.31)
Occupiers' Liability Act 1984 (c.3)
Occupier's Liability (Scotland) Act 1960 (c.30)
Odiham to Farnham Roads Act 1789 (c.89)
Offences Against Customs and Excise Laws Act 1935 (c.35)
Offences Against Customs or Excise Act 1745 (c.34)
Offences Against Excise Laws Act 1758 (c.17)
Offences Against Excise Laws Act 1791 (c.10)
Offences Against the Person Act 1861 (c.100)
Offences Against Persons and Property Act 1936 (c.32)
Offences at Sea Act 1806 (c.54)
Offenders (Conveyance) Act 1753 (c.3)
Offensive Weapons Act 1996 (c.26)
Offices Act 1960 (c.47)
Office and Oath Act 1867 (c.75)
Offices of Court of Chancery Act 1792 (c.42)
Offices, Shops and Railway Premises Act 1963 (c.41)
Officers of Inland Revenue Act (1849) (c.58)
Officer of Late Wine Licences Office Act 1791 (c.28)
Officers of the Royal Naval Reserve Act 1863 (c.69)
Official Secrets Act 1911 (c.28)
Official Secrets Act 1920 (c.75)
Official Secrets Act 1939 (c.121)
Official Secrets Act 1989 (c.6)
Official Solicitor Act 1919 (c.30)
Offshore Petroleum Development (Scotland) Act 1975 (c.8)
Offshore Safety Act 1992 (c.15)
Offshore Safety (Protection against Victimisation) Act 1992 (c.24)
Oil and Gas (Enterprise) Act 1982 (c.23)
Oil and Pipelines Act 1985 (c.62)
Oil in Navigable Waters Act 1922 (c.39)
Oil Burners (Standards) Act 1960 (c.53)
Oil in Navigable Waters Act 1963 (c.28)
Oil in Navigable Waters Act 1955 (c.25)
Oil in Navigable Waters Act 1971 (c.21)
Oil in Tobacco Act 1900 (c.35)
Oil Taxation Act 1975 (c.22)
Oil Taxation Act 1983 (c.56)
Okehampton Roads Act 1759 (c.36)
Old Age and Widows Pensions Act 1940 (c.13)
Old Age Pensions Act 1908 (c.40)
Old Age Pensions Act 1911 (c.16)
Old Age Pensions Act 1919 (c.102)
Old Age Pensions Act 1924 (c.33)
Old Age Pensions Act 1936 (c.31)
Old Age and Widows' Pensions Act 1940 (c.13)
Old Brentford Bridge Act 1757 (c.63)
Old Brentford Bridge Act 1757 (c.46)
Old Palace Yard Act 1966 (c.32)
Old Shoreham, Bridge, Sussex Act 1780 (c.35)
Old Stratford to Dunchurch Road Act 1757 (c.57)
Old Stratford to Dunchurch Road Act 1775 (c.73)
Old Street Road Act 1753 (c.87)
Old Street Road Act 1756 (c.44)
Old Street Road Act 1772 (c.99)

Old Street Road Act 1789 (c.82)
Old Swineford: Small Debts Act 1776 (c.19)
Oldham to Alton Road Act 1793 (c.182)
Olympic Symbol etc. (Protection) Act 1995 (c.32)
Opencast Coal Act 1958 (c.69)
Open Spaces Act 1887 (c.32)
Open Spaces Act 1906 (c.25)
Open Space Act 1986 (c.38)
Opticians Act 1958 (c.32)
Opticians Act 1989 (c.44)
Orders, etc. of the Master of the Rolls Act 1730 (c.30)
Ordination of Aliens Act 1783 (c.35)
Ordnance Board Transfer Act 1855 (c.117)
Ordnance Factories and Military Services Act 1984 (c.59)
Ordnance Property Act 1821 (c.69)
Orkney and Shetland Small Piers and Harbours Act 1896 (c.32)
Orphans, London Act 1947 (c.29)
Osborne Estate Act 1902 (c.37)
Osborne Estate Act 1914 (c.36)
Osteopaths Act 1993 (c.21)
Oswestry: Poor Relief Act 1791 (c.24)
Ottawa Agreements Act 1932 (c.53)
Ouse: Navigation Act 1790 (c.52)
Ouse: Navigation Act 1790 (c.83)
Outdoor Relief (Friendly Societies) Act 1904 (c.32)
Outer Space Act 1986 (c.38)
Output of Beer (Restriction) Act 1916 (c.26)
Output of Beer (Restriction) Amendment Act 1916 (c.57)
Ouze Navigation Act 1731 (c.15)
Overseas Aid Act 1966 (c.21)
Overseas Aid Act 1968 (c.57)
Overseas Development and Co-operation Act 1980 (c.63)
Overseas Development and Service Act 1965 (c.38)
Overseas Investment and Export Guarantees Act 1972 (c.40)
Overseas Pensions Act 1973 (c.21)
Overseas Resources Act 1969 (c.36)
Overseas Resources Development Act 1947 (c.15)
Overseas Resources Development Act 1949 (c.65)
Overseas Resources Development Act 1951 (c.20)
Overseas Resources Development Act 1954 (c.71)
Overseas Resources Development Act 1956 (c.71)
Overseas Resources Development Act 1958 (c.15)
Overseas Resources Development Act 1959 (c.23)
Overseas Resources Development Act 1969 (c.36)
Overseas Service Act 1958 (c.14)
Overseas Service Act 1961 (c.10)
Overseas Superannuation Act 1991 (c.16)
Overseas Trade Act 1929 (c.12)
Overseas Trade Act 1930 (c.31)
Overseas Trade Act 1934 (c.12)
Overseas Trade (Credits and Insurance) Act 1920 (c.29)
Overseas Trade (Credits and Insurance) Amendment Act 1921 (c.26)
Overseas Trade Department (Secretary) Act 1918 (c.3)
Overseas Trade Guarantees Act 1939 (c.47)
Oxford and Berkshire Roads Act 1778 (c.81)
Oxford and Buckinghamshire Roads Act 1755 (c.42)
Oxford and Buckinghamshire Roads Act 1781 (c.77)
Oxford and Fifield Road Act 1767 (c.66)
Oxford and Gloucester Roads Act 1743 (c.10)
Oxford and Gloucester Roads Act 1730 (c.23)
Oxford and Gloucester Roads Act 1753 (c.70)
Oxford and Gloucester Roads Act 1765 (c.80)
Oxford and Gloucester Roads Act 1791 (c.111)
Oxford and Leicester Roads Act 1765 (c.105)
Oxford and Northampton Roads Act 1791 (c.128)
Oxford, Gloucester and Nottingham Roads Act 1770 (c.101)
Oxford: Improvement Act 1771 (c.19)
Oxford: Improvements Act 1780 (c.47)
Oxford: Poor Relief Act 1771 (c.14)
Oxford Roads Act 1750 (c.21)
Oxford Roads Act 1768 (c.34)
Oxford Roads Act 1771 (c.73)
Oxford Roads Act 1777 (c.88)
Oxford Roads Act 1778 (c.91)
Oxford Roads Act 1781 (c.87)
Oxford Roads Act 1789 (c.90)
Oxfordshire Roads Act 1739 (c.15)
Oxfordshire Roads Act 1730 (c.21)
Oxfordshire Roads Act 1757 (c.48)
Oxfordshire Roads Act 1762 (c.41)
Oyster and Mussel Fisheries Orders Confirmation Act 1869 (No. 2) (c.31)
Oyster Fisheries Act 1791 (c.51)

Pacific Cable Act 1901 (c.31)
Pacific Cable Act 1911 (c.36)
Pacific Cable Act 1924 (c.19)
Pacific Cable Act 1927 (c.9)
Pacific Cable Amendment Act 1902 (c.26)
Pacific Islands Protection Act 1875 (c.51)
Pacific Islands Regulations (Validation) Act 1916 (c.9)
Packing, etc. of Butter Act 1798 (c.73)
Paddington Churchyard Act 1753 (c.43)
Paddington (Improvement) Act 1763 (c.50)
Paddington Parish Church Act 1788 (c.74)

Paddington Parish Church Act 1793 (c.43)
Paisley Beer Duties Act 1753 (c.96)
Pakistan Act 1973 (c.48)
Pakistan Act 1974 (c.34)
Pakistan Act 1990 (c.14)
Pakistan (Consequential Provisions) Act 1956 (c.31)
Palestine Act 1948 (c.27)
Palestine Loan Act 1934 (c.33)
Pangbourn Bridge Act 1792 (c.97)
Paper Bills of Credit Act 1763 (c.34)
Paper Bills of Credit, American Colonies Act 1951 (c.53)
Paper Currency in America Act 1772 (c.57)
Paper Duties Act 1780 (c.24)
Paper Duties Act 1784 (c.18)
Paper Duties Act 1786 (c.78)
Paper Duties Act 1794 (c.20)
Papists Act 1715 (c.55)
Papists Act 1716 (c.18)
Papists Act 1722 (c.24)
Papists Act 1723 (c.4)
Papists Act 1732 (c.5)
Papists Act 1734 (c.25)
Papists Act 1737 (c.11)
Papists Act 1738 (c.14)
Papists Act 1740 (c.21)
Papists Act 1745 (c.16)
Papists Act 1753 (c.24)
Papists Act 1755 (c.10)
Papists Act 1757 (c.21)
Papists Act 1759 (c.13)
Papists Act 1762 (c.26)
Papists Act 1763 (c.38)
Papists Act 1766 (c.34)
Papists Act 1772 (c.10)
Papists Act 1774 (c.37)
Papists Act 1776 (c.45)
Papists Act 1778 (c.46)
Papists Act 1778 (c.60)
Papists Act 1780 (c.51)
Papists Act 1782 (c.23)
Papists Act 1783 (c.22)
Papists Act 1783 (c.16)
Papists Act 1787 (c.42)
Papists Act 1788 (c.47)
Papists Act 1789 (c.36)
Papists Act 1790 (c.19)
Papua New Guinea, Western Samoa and Nauru (Miscellaneous Provisions) Act 1980 (c.2)
Parish Apprentices Act 1778 (c.47)
Parish Apprentices Act 1792 (c.57)
Parish Church of St. Marylebone Act 1770 (c.112)
Parish Councils Act 1957 (c.42)
Parish Councils and Burial Authorities (Miscellaneous Provisions) Act 1970 (c.29)
Parish of The Trinity, Coventry Act 1779 (c.57)
Parish Officers Act 1793 (c.55)
Parish: Spittlefields, Stepney Act 1727 (c.10)
Park Lane Improvement Act 1958 (c.63)
Parking Act 1989 (c.16)
Parks Regulation Act 1872 (c.15)
Parks Regulation (Amendment) Act 1926 (c.36)
Parks Regulation (Amendment) Act 1974 (c.29)
Parliament Act 1710 (c.5)
Parliament Act 1712 (cc.5,6)
Parliament Act 1712 (c.16)
Parliament Act 1775 (c.36)
Parliament Act 1780 (c.1)
Parliament Act 1780 (c.50)
Parliament Act 1780 (c.43)
Parliament Act 1782 (c.29)
Parliament Act 1782 (c.41)
Parliament Act 1911 (c.13)
Parliament Act 1949 (c.103)
Parliament of Canada Act 1875 (c.38)
Parliament and Local Elections Act 1916 (c.44)
Parliament and Local Elections Act 1917 (c.13)
Parliament and Local Elections Act 1918 (c.22)
Parliament and Local Elections (No.2) Act 1917 (c.50)
Parliament and Registration Act 1916 (c.100)
Parliament (Elections and Meeting) Act 1943 (c.48)
Parliament (Qualification of Women) Act 1918 (c.47)
Parliamentary and Health Service Commissioners Act 1987 (c.39)
Parliamentary and Other Pensions Act 1972 (c.48)
Parliamentary and Other Pensions Act 1987 (c.45)
Parliamentary and Other Pensions and Salaries Act 1976 (c.48)
Parliamentary Commissioner Act 1967 (c.13)
Parliamentary Commissioner Act 1994 (c.14)
Parliamentary Commissioner (Consular Complaints) Act 1981 (c.11)
Parliamentary Constituencies Act 1986 (c.56)
Parliamentary Corporate Bodies Act 1992 (c.27)
Parliamentary Documents Deposit Act 1837 (c.83)
Parliamentary Elections Act 1734 (c.30)
Parliamentary Elections Act 1742 (c.11)
Parliamentary Elections Act 1744 (c.18)
Parliamentary Elections Act 1745 (c.28)
Parliamentary Elections Act 1757 (c.14)
Parliamentary Elections Act 1763 (c.24)
Parliamentary Elections Act 1770 (c.16)
Parliamentary Elections Act 1770 (c.41)
Parliamentary Elections Act 1771 (c.42)
Parliamentary Elections Act 1774 (c.15)
Parliamentary Elections Act 1774 (c.58)
Parliamentary Elections Act 1774 (c.81)
Parliamentary Elections Act 1780 (c.17)

Parliamentary Elections Act 1785 (c.84)
Parliamentary Elections Act 1790 (c.35)
Parliamentary Elections Act 1793 (c.64)
Parliamentary Elections Act 1795 (c.65)
Parliamentary Elections Act 1868 (c.125)
Parliamentary Elections, Cricklade Act 1782 (c.31)
Parliamentary Elections (Fraudulent Conveyances) Act 1739 (c.20)
Parliamentary Elections, New Shoreham Act 1771 (c.55)
Parliamentary Elections, Norwich 1730 (c.8)
Parliamentary Elections (Returning Officers) Act (1875) Amendment Act 1886 (c.57)
Parliamentary Elections Corrupt Practices Act 1879 (c.75)
Parliamentary Elections (Scotland) Act (c.16)
Parliamentary Elections (Soldiers) Act 1919 (c.10)
Parliamentary Electors (War-time Registration) Act 1944 (c.24)
Parliamentary Papers Act 1840 (c.9)
Parliamentary Pensions Act 1978 (c.56)
Parliamentary Pensions etc. Act 1984 (c.52)
Parliamentary Privilege Act 1770 (c.50)
Parliamentary Privilege Act 1937 (c.24)
Parliamentary Witnesses Act 1858 (c.78)
Parliamentary Witnesses Oaths Act 1871 (c.83)
Parochial Libraries Act 1708 (c.14)
Parochial Registers Act 1812 (c.146)
Parsonages Act 1838 (c.23)
Parsonages Act 1911 (c.29)
Participation Agreements Act 1978 (c.1)
Partition Act 1868 (c.40)
Partnership Act 1890 (c.39)
Parton, Cumberland, Harbour Act 1724 (c.16)
Parton Harbour, Cumberland Act 1731 (c.13)
Partridges Act 1799 (c.34)
Party Processions (Ireland) Act 1832 (c.118)
Party Processions (Ireland) Act 1844 (c.63)
Party Wall etc. Act 1996 (c.40)
Passage from Charing Cross Act 1757 (c.36)
Passenger Ships Act 1845 (c.14)
Passenger Vehicles (Experimental Areas) Act 1977 (c.21)
Patent Law Amendment Act 1852 (c.83)
Patents Act 1901 (c.18)
Patents Act 1902 (c.34)
Patents Act 1949 (c.87)
Patents Act 1957 (c.13)
Patents Act 1977 (c.37)
Patents and Designs Act 1907 (c.29)
Patents and Designs Act 1908 (c.4)
Patents and Designs Act 1914 (c.18)
Patents and Designs Act 1919 (c.80)
Patents and Designs Act 1927 (c.3)
Patents and Designs Act 1932 (c.32)
Patents and Designs Act 1942 (c.6)
Patents and Designs Act 1946 (c.44)
Patents and Designs Act 1949 (c.62)
Patents and Designs (Amendment) Act 1907 (c.28)
Patents and Designs (Limits of Time) Act 1939 (c.32)
Patents and Designs (Partial Suspension) Act 1915 (c.85)
Patents and Designs (Renewals, Extensions and Fees) Act 1961 (c.25)
Patents, Designs and Marks Act 1986 (c.39)
Patents, Designs and Trade Marks Act 1883 (c.57)
Patents, Designs and Trade Marks (Temporary Rules) Act 1914 (c.27)
Patents, Designs and Trade Marks (Temporary Rules) Amendment 1914 (c.73)
Patents, Designs, Copyright and Trade Marks (Emergency) Act 1939 (c.107)
Patents etc. (International Conventions) Act 1938 (c.29)
Patriotic Fund Act 1866 (c.120)
Patriotic Fund Reorganisation Act 1903 (c.20)
Pauper Children (Ireland) Act 1902 (c.16)
Paving, etc. of London Act 1768 (c.21)
Pawnbrokers Act 1784 (c.42)
Pawnbrokers Act 1785 (c.48)
Pawnbrokers Act 1787 (c.37)
Pawnbrokers Act 1788 (c.50)
Pawnbrokers Act 1789 (c.57)
Pawnbrokers Act 1791 (c.52)
Pawnbrokers Act 1793 (c.53)
Pawnbrokers Act 1872 (c.93)
Pawnbrokers Act 1922 (c.5)
Pawnbrokers Act 1960 (c.24)
Paymaster General Act 1782 (c.81)
Paymaster General Act 1783 (c.50)
Paymaster General Act 1835 (c.35)
Paymaster General Act 1848 (c.55)
Paymaster General, Balance, etc. Act 1780 (c.48)
Payment of Certain Regiments Act 1705 (c.12)
Payment of Charges of Constables Act 1778 (c.19)
Payment of Creditors (Scotland) Act 1780 (c.41)
Payment of Creditors (Scotland) Act 1783 (c.18)
Payment of Creditors (Scotland) Act 1789 (c.5)
Payment of Creditors (Scotland) Act 1793 (c.74)
Payment of Creditors (Scotland) Act 1804 (c.24)
Payment of Creditors (Scotland) Act 1813 (c.65)
Payment of Lace Makers' Wages Act 1779 (c.49)
Payment of Wages Act 1960 (c.37)
Pedlars Act 1871 (c.96)
Peebles Road Act 1753 (c.93)
Peebles Road Act 1771 (c.85)
Peebles Road Act 1775 (c.71)
Peebles Roads Act 1792 (c.123)
Peerage Act 1963 (c.48)

Pembroke Gaol Act 1779 (c.46)
Pembroke Road Act 1771 (c.96)
Pembroke Roads Act 1788 (c.102)
Pembroke Roads Act 1790 (c.91)
Pembroke Roads Act 1791 (c.102)
Pembroke Roads Act 1791 (c.109)
Pembroke Roads Act 1791 (c.126)
Penal Servitude Act 1891 (c.69)
Penal Servitude Act 1926 (c.58)
Penalties for Drunkenness Act 1962 (c.52)
Penicillin Act 1947 (c.29)
Penicillin (Merchant Ships) 1951 (c.13)
Penitentiary for Convicts Act 1794 (c.84)
Penny Post Act 1794 (c.17)
Pension Duties Act 1720 (c.27)
Pension Duties Act 1725 (c.2)
Pension Duties Act 1757 (c.22)
Pension Duties Act 1758 (c.33)
Pension Schemes Act 1993 (c.48)
Pension Schemes (Northern Ireland) Act 1993 (c.49)
Pensioners and Family Income Supplement Payments Act 1972 (c.75)
Pensioners' Payments Act 1974 (c.54)
Pensioners Payments Act 1977 (c.51)
Pensioners Payments Act 1978 (c.58)
Pensioners' Payments and National Insurance Act 1973 (c.61)
Pensioners' Payments and National Insurance Contributions Act 1972 (c.80)
Pensioners' Payments and Social Security Act 1979 (c.48)
Pensions Act 1839 (c.51)
Pensions Act 1995 (c.26)
Pensions and Determination of Needs Act 1943 (c.27)
Pensions and Yeomanry Pay Act 1884 (c.55)
Pensions Appeal Tribunals Act 1943 (c.39)
Pensions Appeal Tribunals Act 1949 (c.12)
Pensions Commutation Act 1871 (c.36)
Pensions Commutation Act 1882 (c.44)
Pensions Commutation Act 1984 (c.7)
Pensions (Governors of Dominions, etc.) Act 1911 (c.24)
Pensions (Governors of Dominions, etc.) Act 1929 (c.16)
Pensions (Governors of Dominions, etc.) Act 1936 (c.25)
Pensions (Governors of Dominions, etc.) Act 1947 (c.12)
Pensions (Governors of Dominions, etc.) Amendment 1913 (c.26)
Pensions (Increase) Act 1920 (c.36)
Pensions (Increase) Act 1924 (c.32)
Pensions (Increase) Act 1944 (c.21)
Pensions (Increase) Act 1946 (c.7)
Pensions (Increase) Act 1952 (c.45)
Pensions (Increase) Act 1954 (c.25)
Pensions (Increase) Act 1956 (c.39)
Pensions (Increase) Act 1962 (c.2)
Pensions (Increase) Act 1965 (c.78)
Pensions (Increase) Act 1969 (c.7)
Pensions (Increase) Act 1971 (c.56)
Pensions (Increase) Act 1974 (c.9)
Pensions (India, Pakistan and Burma) Act 1955 (c.22)
Pensions (Mercantile Marine) Act 1942 (c.26)
Pensions (Miscellaneous Provisions) Act 1990 (c.7)
Pensions (Navy, Army, Air Force and Mercantile Marine) Act 1939 (c.83)
Pensions to Seamen, etc. Act 1814 (c.1)
Performers' Protection Act 1963 (c.53)
Performers' Protection Act 1972 (c.32)
Performing Animals (Regulation) Act 1925 (c.38)
Perjury Act 1727 (c.25)
Perjury Act 1911 (c.6)
Perpetuation and Amendment of Acts 1904 (c.16)
Perpetuation, etc. of Acts 1708 (c.25)
Perpetuation of Acts, etc. Act 1719 (c.19)
Perpetuation of Testimony Act 1842 (c.69)
Perpetuation of Various Laws Act 1732 (c.37)
Perpetuities and Accumulations Act 1964 (c.55)
Persons Going Armed or Disguised Act 1758 (c.18)
Persons Going Armed and Disguised Act 1754 (c.15)
Personal Injuries (Emergency Provisions) Act 1939 (c.82)
Persuading Soldiers to Desert, etc. Act 1715 (c.47)
Perth: Highways and Bridge Act 1785 (c.13)
Perth Roads Act 1753 (c.91)
Perth Roads Act 1765 (c.89)
Perth Roads Act 1789 (c.17)
Perth Roads Act 1793 (c.158)
Pesticides (Fees and Enforcement) Act 1989 (c.27)
Pests Act 1954 (c.68)
Pet Animals Act 1951 (c.35)
Pet Animals Act 1951 (Amendment) Act 1983 (c.26)
Peterborough: Streets Act 1790 (c.66)
Petersham: Streets Act 1772 (c.42)
Petersfield Highways Act 1710 (c.33(f))
Petersfield to Portsmouth Road Act 1725 (c.19)
Petroleum Act 1879 (c.47)
Petroleum Act 1926 (c.25)
Petroleum Act 1975 (c.74)
Petroleum Act 1987 (c.12)
Petroleum (Amendment) 1928 (c.21)
Petroleum and Submarine Pipelines Act 1975 (c.74)
Petroleum (Consolidation) Act 1928 (c.32)
Petroleum (Production) Act 1918 (c.52)
Petroleum (Production) Act 1934 (c.36)
Petroleum Revenue Tax Act 1980 (c.1)
Petroleum Royalties (Relief) Act 1983 (c.59)
Petroleum Royalties (Relief) and Continental Shelf Act 1989 (c.1)
Petroleum Royalties (Relief) Act 1983 (c.59)
Petroleum (Transfer of Licences) Act 1936 (c.27)

Petty Sessions Act 1849 (c.18)
Petty Sessions Clerks and Fines (Ireland) Act 1878 (c.69)
Petty Sessions (Ireland) Act 1851 (c.93)
Petty Sessions Clerk (Ireland) (Amendment) Act 1901 (c.22)
Pharmacy Act 1929 (c.31)
Pharmacy Act 1953 (c.19)
Pharmacy Act 1954 (c.61)
Pharmacy and Medicines Act 1941 (c.42)
Pharmacy and Poisons Act 1933 (c.25)
Pharmacy and Poisons (Amendment) Act 1964 (c.35)
Physical Training and Recreation Act 1937 (c.46)
Physical Training and Recreation Act 1958 (c.36)
Piccadilly Act 1844 (c.88)
Piccadilly; Watering Act 1775 (c.57)
Pig Industry Levy Act 1983 (c.4)
Pilchard Fisheries Act 1791 (c.45)
Pilchard Fishery Act 1785 (c.58)
Pilchard Fishery Act 1786 (c.45)
Pilchard Fishery, Cornwall Act 1776 (c.36)
Pillory Abolition Act 1816 (c.138)
Pilotage Act 1716 (c.13)
Pilotage Act 1731 (c.20)
Pilotage Act 1913 (c.31)
Pilotage Act 1983 (c.21)
Pilotage Act 1987 (c.21)
Pilotage Authorities (Limitation of Liability) Act 1936 (c.36)
Pipelines Act 1962 (c.58)
Piracy Act 1717 (c.11)
Piracy Act 1721 (c.24)
Piracy Act 1744 (c.30)
Piracy Act 1837 (c.88)
Pistols Act 1903 (c.18)
Pittenweem Beer Duties Act 1719 (c.9)
Places of Religious Worship Act 1812 (c.155)
Places of Worship (Enfranchisement) Act 1920 (c.56)
Places of Worship Registration Act 1855 (c.81)
Planning and Compensation Act 1991 (c.34)
Planning (Consequential Provisions) Act 1990 (c.11)
Planning (Hazardous Substances) Act 1990 (c.10)
Planning Inquiries (Attendance of Public) Act 1982 (c.21)
Planning (Listed Buildings and Conservation Areas) Act 1990 (c.9)
Plant Health Act 1967 (c.8)
Plant Varieties Act 1983 (c.17)
Plant Varieties and Seeds Act 1964 (c.14)
Plantation Trade etc., Act 1741 (c.31)
Plate Act 1696 (c.8)
Plate Assay Act 1700 (c.3)
Plate Assay (Sheffield) Act 1784 (c.20)
Plate Assay (Sheffield and Birmingham) Act 1772 (c.52)
Plate Duties Act 1784 (c.53)
Plate (Duties, Drawbacks) Act 1785 (c.64)
Plate Duty Act 1719 (c.11)
Plate (Duty on Dealer's Licence) Act 1757 (c.32)
Plate (Duty on Dealer's Licence) Act 1757 (c.24)
Plate Glass Manufacture Act 1772 (c.38)
Plate (Offences) Act 1738 (c.26)
Plate (Offences) Act 1772 (c.59)
Plate (Scotland) Act 1836 (c.69)
Plays and Wine Licences 1736 (c.28)
Pleading Act 1711 (c.28)
Pleading in Misdemeanour Act 1819 (c.4)
Pluralities Act 1838 (c.106)
Pluralities Act 1850 (c.98)
Pluralities Act 1887 (c.68)
Pluralities of Living Act 1801 (c.102)
Plymouth and Portsmouth Fortifications Act 1758 (c.30)
Plymouth Dock Act 1766 (c.102)
Plymouth Dock to Torpoint: Ferry Act 1790 (c.61)
Plymouth: Fortifications Act 1774 (c.50)
Plymouth Fortifications Act 1781 (c.61)
Plymouth Fortifications Act 1782 (c.12)
Plymouth Improvement Act 1770 (c.14)
Plymouth Improvement Act 1772 (c.8)
Plymouth: Poor Relief Act 1758 (c.59)
Plymouth: Poor Relief Act 1786 (c.19)
Plymouth: Poor Relief etc, Act 1781 (c.72)
Plymouth, Sheerness, Gravesend, Tilbury-Fortifications Act 1780 (c.38)
Plymouth: Streets Act 1774 (c.8)
Plymouth Water Supply Act 1793 (c.85)
Plymouth Workhouse 1707 (c.46(d))
Pneumoconiosis and Byssinosis Benefit Act 1951 (c.4)
Pneumoconiosis etc. (Workers' Compensation) Act 1979 (c.41)
Poaching Prevention Act 1862 (c.114)
Poisons Act 1972 (c.66)
Poisons and Pharmacy Act 1908 (c.55)
Polehampton Estates Act 1885 (c.40)
Police Act 1909 (c.40)
Police Act 1919 (c.46)
Police Act 1964 (c.48)
Police Act 1969 (c.63)
Police Act 1972 (c.39)
Police Act 1976 (c.46)
Police Act 1996 (c.16)
Police and Criminal Evidence Act 1984 (c.60)
Police and Firemen (War Service) Act 1939 (c.103)
Police and Firemen (War Service) Act 1944 (c.22)
Police and Magistrates' Courts Act 1994 (c.29)
Police (Appeals) Act 1927 (c.19)
Police (Appeals) Act 1943 (c.8)
Police Army Act 1946 (c.46)
Police Constables (Naval and Military Service) Act 1914 (c.80)
Police Constables (Naval and Military Service) Act 1917 (c.36)

Police (Emergency Provisions) Act 1915 (c.41)
Police Factories, etc. (Miscellaneous Provisions) Act 1916 (c.31)
Police Federation Act 1959 (c.38)
Police Federations Act 1962 (c.25)
Police Federation Act 1961 (c.51)
Police, Fire and Probation Officers' Remuneration Act 1956 (c.1)
Police (His Majesty's Inspectors of Constabulary) Act 1945 (c.11)
Police (Liverpool Inquiry) Act 1909 (c.35)
Police Magistrates (Superannuation) Act 1915 (c.74)
Police Magistrates Superannuation Amendment Act 1929 (c.37)
Police Negotiating Board Act 1980 (c.10)
Police Officers (Central Service) Act 1989 (c.11)
Police (Overseas Service) Act 1945 (c.17)
Police (Pensions) Act 1918 (c.51)
Police (Pensions) Act 1921 (c.31)
Police Pensions Act 1926 (c.34)
Police Pensions Act 1948 (c.24)
Police Pensions Act 1961 (c.35)
Police Pensions Act 1976 (c.35)
Police (Property) Act 1897 (c.30)
Police Revenue and Consolidated Fund Charges Act 1854 (c.94)
Police (Scotland) Act 1857 (c.72)
Police (Scotland) Act 1856 (c.26)
Police (Scotland) Act 1890 (c.67)
Police (Scotland) Act 1946 (c.71)
Police (Scotland) Act 1966 (c.52)
Police (Scotland) Act 1967 (c.77)
Police (Scotland) Act (1890) Amendment Act 1910 (c.10)
Police (Scotland) (Limit of Age) Act 1914 (c.69)
Police Reservists Act 1902 (c.10)
Police Reservists (Allowances) Act 1900 (c.9)
Police Reservists (Allowances) Act 1914 (c.34)
Police (Superannuation) Act 1906 (c.7)
Police (Superannuation) Act 1908 (c.5)
Police (Weekly Rest Day) Act 1910 (c.13)
Police (Weekly Rest Day) (Scotland) Act 1914 (c.8)
Policing of Airports Act 1974 (c.41)
Policyholders Protection Act 1975 (c.75)
Polish Resettlement Act 1947 (c.19)
Polling Arrangements (Parliamentary Boroughs) Act 1908 (c.14)
Polling Districts (County Councils) Act 1908 (c.13)
Polling Districts and Registration of Voters (Ireland) Act 1908 (c.35)
Ponies Act 1969 (c.28)
Pool Betting Act 1954 (c.33)
Pool Competitions Act 1971 (c.57)
Pool Harbour Act 1756 (c.10)
Poole Roads Act 1756 (c.52)
Poole Roads Act 1757 (c.52)
Poole Roads Act 1757 (c.66)
Poole Roads Act 1777 (c.104)
Poole to Blandford Road Act 1777 (c.86)
Poor Act 1762 (c.22)
Poor Act 1766 (c.39)
Poor Act 1776 (c.40)
Poor Act 1793 (c.35)
Poor Act 1912 (c.18)
Poor Apprentices Act 1780 (c.36)
Poor Law Act 1927 (c.14)
Poor Law Act 1930 (c.17)
Poor Law Act 1934 (c.59)
Poor Law Amendment Act 1844 (c.101)
Poor Law (Amendment) Act 1938 (c.23)
Poor Law Authorities (Transfer of Property) Act 1904 (c.20)
Poor Law (Dissolution of School Districts and Adjustments) Act 1903 (c.19)
Poor Law Emergency Provisions (Scotland) Act 1921 (c.64)
Poor Law Emergency Provisions (Scotland) Act 1927 (c.3)
Poor Law Emergency Provisions Continuance (Scotland) Act 1924 (c.9)
Poor Law Emergency Provisions Continuance (Scotland) Act 1925 (c.35)
Poor Law, Hull Act 1709 (c.24)
Poor Law Officers' Superannuation Act 1896 (c.50)
Poor Law (Scotland) Act 1934 (c.52)
Poor Persons 1495 (c.12)
Poor Prisoners' Defence Act 1903 (c.38)
Poor Prisoners' Defence Act 1930 (c.32)
Poor Prisoners Relief Act 1737 (c.20)
Poor Prisoners (Scotland) Act 1825 (c.62)
Poor Rate Act 1743 (c.3)
Poor Rate Exemption Act 1833 (c.30)
Poor Relief Act 1722 (c.7)
Poor Relief Act 1743 (c.38)
Poor Relief Act 1769 (c.37)
Poor Relief (Deserted Wives and Children) Act 1718 (c.8)
Poor Relief: Gloucester Act 1726 (c.19)
Poor Relief (Ireland) Act 1838 (c.56)
Poor Relief (Ireland) Act 1849 (c.104)
Poor Relief (Ireland) Act 1900 (c.45)
Poor Relief (Ireland) Act 1914 (c.14)
Poor Removal Act 1900 (c.23)
Poor, Staffordshire Act 1791 (c.20)
Population (Statistics) Act 1938 (c.13)
Population (Statistics) Act 1960 (c.32)
Porcelain Patent Act 1775 (c.52)
Port Glasgow Harbour Act 1772 (c.16)
Port of Liverpool Act 1766 (c.61)
Port of London (Financial Assistance) Act 1980 (c.31)
Portman Square: Improvement Act 1782 (c.85)
Ports Act 1991 (c.52)
Ports (Finance) Act 1985 (c.30)
Ports (Financial Assistance) Act 1981 (c.21)
Ports (Reduction of Debt) Act 1983 (c.22)

Portsea Chapel Act 1787 (c.64)
Portsea Common Chapel Act 1753 (c.58)
Portsea: Improvement Act 1792 (c.103)
Portsmouth, Chatham Fortifications Act 1782 (c.80)
Portsmouth, Chatham Fortifications Act 1783 (c.71)
Portsmouth, Faversham Fortifications Act 1783 (c.87)
Portsmouth Improvement Act 1768 (c.62)
Portsmouth, Plymouth Fortifications Act 1784 (c.29)
Portsmouth: Streets Act 1776 (c.59)
Portsmouth Water Supply (Farlington) Act 1740 (c.43)
Possession of Mortgaged Land (Emergency Provisions) Act 1939 (c.108)
Postage Act 1730 (c.33)
Postage Act 1763 (c.24)
Postage Act 1765 (c.25)
Postage Act 1782 (c.70)
Postage Act 1783 (c.69)
Postage Act 1784 (c.8)
Postage Act 1787 (c.9)
Postage Act 1794 (c.18)
Postage Act 1796 (c.18)
Postage Act 1805 (c.11)
Postage Act 1805 (c.21)
Post Fines Act 1758 (c.14)
Post Horse Duties Act 1787 (c.26)
Post Horse Duties Act 1790 (c.23)
Post Horse Duties Act 1793 (c.71)
Post Horse Duties Act 1796 (c.84)
Post Office Act 1748 (c.25)
Post Office Act 1904 (c.14)
Post Office Act 1908 (c.48)
Post Office Act 1913 (c.11)
Post Office Act 1918 (c.10)
Post Office Act 1953 (c.36)
Post Office Act 1961 (c.15)
Post Office Act 1969 (c.48)
Post Office Act 1977 (c.44)
Post Office (Amendment) Act 1935 (c.15)
Post Office and Telegraph Act 1915 (c.82)
Post Office and Telegraph Act 1920 (c.40)
Post Office and Telegraph Act 1940 (c.25)
Post Office and Telegraph (Money) Act 1928 (c.37)
Post Office and Telegraph (Money) Act 1931 (c.20)
Post Office and Telegraph (Money) Act 1935 (c.14)
Post Office and Telegraph (Money) Act 1937 (c.51)
Post Office and Telegraph (Money) Act 1939 (c.42)
Post Office and Telegraph (Money) Act 1942 (c.24)
Post Office and Telegraph (Money) Act 1946 (c.51)
Post Office and Telegraph (Money) Act 1947 (c.16)
Post Office and Telegraph (Money) Act 1950 (c.2)
Post Office and Telegraph (Money) Act 1952 (c.34)
Post Office and Telegraph (Money) Act 1953 (c.4)
Post Office and Telegraph (Money) Act 1955 (c.14)
Post Office and Telegraph (Money) Act 1957 (c.5)
Post Office and Telegraph (Money) Act 1950 (c.2)
Post Office (Banking Services) Act 1976 (c.10)
Post Office (Borrowing Powers) Act 1967 (c.15)
Post Office (Borrowing Powers) Act 1972 (c.79)
Post Office (Data Processing Service) Act 1967 (c.62)
Post Office (Literature for the Blind) Act 1906 (c.22)
Post Office (Money Orders) Act 1903 (c.12)
Post Office (Money Orders) Act 1906 (c.4)
Post Office Offences and Isle of Man Postage Act 1767 (c.50)
Post Office (Parcels) Act 1922 (c.49)
Post Office (Pneumatic Tubes Acquisition) Act 1922 (c.43)
Post Office (Protection) Act 1884 (c.76)
Post Office (Revenues) Act 1710 (c.11(p))
Post Office Savings Bank Act 1908 (c.8)
Post Office Savings Bank Act 1954 (c.62)
Post Office Savings Bank Act 1965 (c.12)
Post Office Savings Bank (Public Trustee) Act 1908 (c.52)
Post Office (Subway) Act 1966 (c.25)
Post Office Works Act 1959 (c.43)
Post Roads in Scotland Act 1951 (c.28)
Post Works Loans Act 1957 (c.4)
Postponement of Enactments (Miscellaneous Provisions) Act 1939 (c.2)
Postponement of Payments Act 1914 (c.11)
Postponement of Polling Day Act 1945 (c.40)
Pot and Pearl Ashes Act 1750 (c.51)
Poultry Act 1911 (c.11)
Powers of Attorney Act 1971 (c.27)
Powers of Criminal Courts Act 1973 (c.62)
Prescription Act 1832 (c.71)
Prescription and Limitation (Scotland) Act 1973 (c.52)
Prescription and Limitation (Scotland) Act 1984 (c.45)
Prescription (Scotland) Act 1987 (c.36)
Presentation of Benefices Act 1713 (c.13)
Preservation of Fish and Conies Act 1965 (c.14)
Preservation of House Doves, etc. Act 1762 (c.29)
Preservation of Roads Act 1740 (c.42)
Preservation of Timber Act 1772 (c.33)
Preservation of Timber Trees Act 1715 (c.48)
Preservation of Timber Trees Act 1766 (c.48)
Preservation of Timber Trees (Scotland) Act 1719 (c.16)

Preservation of Trees, America Act 1710 (c.22)
Preservation of Woods, America Act 1728 (c.35)
President of the Board of Trade 1932 (c.21)
Presteigne Road Act 1756 (c.94)
Preston Bridge Act 1757 (c.55)
Prestonpans Beer Duties Act 1753 (c.79)
Prestonpans Beer Duties Act 1757 (c.52)
Presumption of Death (Scotland) Act 1977 (c.27)
Presumption of Life Limitation (Scotland) Act 1891 (c.29)
Prevention and Treatment of Blindness (Scotland) Act 1938 (c.32)
Prevention of Corruption Act 1906 (c.34)
Prevention of Corruption Act 1916 (c.64)
Prevention of Crimes Act 1871 (c.112)
Prevention of Crime Act 1908 (c.59)
Prevention of Crime Act 1953 (c.14)
Prevention of Cruelty to Children Act 1904 (c.15)
Prevention of Damage by Pests Act 1949 (c.55)
Prevention of Damage by Rabbits 1939 (c.43)
Prevention of Eviction Act 1924 (c.18)
Prevention of Fraud (Investments) Act 1939 (c.16)
Prevention of Fraud (Investments) Act 1958 (c.45)
Prevention of Offences Act 1851 (c.19)
Prevention of Oil Pollution Act 1971 (c.60)
Prevention of Oil Pollution Act 1986 (c.6)
Prevention of Terrorism (Additional Powers) Act 1996 (c.7)
Prevention of Terrorism (Temporary Provisions) Act 1974 (c.55)
Prevention of Terrorism (Temporary Provisions) Act 1976 (c.8)
Prevention of Terrorism (Temporary Provisions Act 1984 (c.8)
Prevention of Terrorism (Temporary Provisions) Act 1989 (c.4)
Prevention of Violence (Temporary Provisions) Act 1939 (c.50)
Previous Conviction Act 1836 (c.111)
Price Commission Act 1977 (c.33)
Price Commission (Amendment) Act 1979 (c.1)
Price Control and Other Orders (Indemnity) Act 1951 (c.59)
Price Control (Regulation of Disposal of Stocks) Act 1943 (c.47)
Price of Coal (Limitation) Act 1915 (c.75)
Prices Act 1974 (c.24)
Prices Act 1975 (c.32)
Prices and Incomes Act 1966 (c.33)
Prices and Incomes Act 1967 (c.53)
Prices and Incomes Act 1968 (c.42)
Prices of Goods Act 1939 (c.118)
Princess Elizabeth's and Duke of Edinburgh's Annuities Act 1947 (c.14)
Printer's Imprint Act 1961 (c.31)
Prison Act 1952 (c.52)
Prison Officers (Pensions) Act (c.9)
Prison Security Act 1992 (c.25)
Prisoners and Criminal Proceedings (Scotland) Act 1993 (c.9)
Prisoners' Earnings Act 1996 (c.33)
Prisoners of War (Escape) Act 1812 (c.156)
Prisoners (Return to Custody) Act 1995 (c.16)
Prisoners (Temporary Discharge for Ill-Health) Act 1913 (c.4)
Prisons (Ireland) Act 1819 (c.100)
Prisons (Ireland) Act 1907 (c.19)
Prisons (Scotland) Act 1839 (c.42)
Prisons (Scotland) Act 1844 (c.34)
Prisons (Scotland) Act 1904 (c.35)
Prisons (Scotland) Act 1909 (c.27)
Prisons (Scotland) Act 1926 (c.57)
Prisons (Scotland) Act 1952 (c.61)
Prisons (Scotland) Act 1989 (c.45)
Private International Law (Miscellaneous Provisions) Act 1995 (c.42)
Private Legislation Procedure (Scotland) Act 1933 (c.37)
Private Legislation Procedure (Scotland) Act 1936 (c.52)
Private Place of Entertainment (Licensing) Act 1967 (c.19)
Private Street Works Act 1961 (c.24)
Prize Act 1939 (c.65)
Prize Act 1948 (c.9)
Prize Causes Act 1797 (c.38)
Prize Courts Act 1915 (c.57)
Prize Courts (Procedure) Act 1914 (c.13)
Prize Goods Act 1803 (c.134)
Prize Salvage Act 1943 (c.7)
Prize Salvage Act 1944 (c.7)
Probate and Legacy Duties Act 1808 (c.149)
Probate and Legacy Duties (Ireland) Act 1814 (c.92)
Probate Duty Act 1801 (c.86)
Probate Duty Act 1859 (c.36)
Probate Duty Act 1860 (c.15)
Probate Duty Act 1861 (c.92)
Probate Duty (Ireland) Act 1816 (c.56)
Probates and Letters of Administration Act (Ireland) 1857 (c.79)
Probation of Offenders Act 1907 (c.17)
Probation of Offenders (Scotland) Act 1931 (c.30)
Probation Officers (Superannuation) Act 1947 (c.38)
Probation Service Act 1993 (c.47)
Proceedings Against Estates Act 1970 (c.17)
Proceeds of Crime Act 1995 (c.11)
Proceeds of Crime (Scotland) Act 1995 (c.43)
Professional Cavalry Act 1796 (c.23)
Professions Supplementary to Medicine Act 1960 (c.66)
Profiteering Act 1919 (c.66)
Profiteering Amendment Act 1920 (c.13)
Profiteering (Cont.) Act 1919 (c.87)

Profits Tax Act 1949 (c.64)
Prohibition of Female Circumcision Act 1985 (c.38)
Prolongation of Parliament Act 1940 (c.53)
Prolongation of Parliament Act 1941 (c.48)
Prolongation of Parliament Act 1942 (c.37)
Prolongation of Parliament Act 1943 (c.46)
Prolongation of Parliament Act 1944 (c.45)
Promissory Oaths Act 1868 (c.72)
Promissory Oaths Act 1871 (c.48)
Property Misdescriptions Act 1991 (c.29)
Property Services Agency and Crown Suppliers Act 1990 (c.12)
Prosecution of Offences Act 1879 (c.22)
Prosecution of Offences Act 1884 (c.58)
Prosecution of Offences Act 1908 (c.3)
Prosecution of Offences Act 1979 (c.31)
Prosecution of Offences Act 1985 (c.23)
Protection Against Cruel Tethering Act 1988 (c.31)
Protection from Eviction Act 1964 (c.97)
Protection from Eviction Act 1977 (c.43)
Protection of Aircraft Act 1973 (c.47)
Protection of Animals Act 1911 (c.27)
Protection of Animals Act 1934 (c.21)
Protection of Animals Act (1911) Amendment 1921 (c.14)
Protection of Animals (Amendment) 1927 (c.27)
Protection of Animals (Amendment) Act 1954 (c.40)
Protection of Animals (Amendment) Act 1988 (c.29)
Protection of Animals (Anaesthetics) Act 1954 (c.46)
Protection of Animals (Anaesthetics) Act 1964 (c.39)
Protection of Animals (Cruelty to Dogs) Act 1933 (c.17)
Protection of Animals (Cruelty to Dogs) (Scotland) Act 1934 (c.25)
Protection of Animals (Penalties) Act 1987 (c.35)
Protection of Animals (Scotland) Act 1912 (c.14)
Protection of Animals (Scotland) Act, 1912, Amendment Act 1921 (c.22)
Protection of Animals (Scotland) Act 1993 (c.15)
Protection of Birds Act 1925 (c.31)
Protection of Birds Act 1933 (c.52)
Protection of Birds Act 1954 (c.30)
Protection of Birds Act 1967 (c.46)
Protection of Birds Act 1954 (Amendment) Act 1964 (c.59)
Protection of Birds (Amendment) Act 1976 (c.42)
Protection of Children Act 1978 (c.37)
Protection of Children (Tobacco) Act 1986 (c.34)
Protection of Depositors Act 1963 (c.16)
Protection of Lapwings Act 1928 (c.2)
Protection of Military Remains Act 1986 (c.35)
Protection of Trading Interests Act 1980 (c.11)
Protection of Wrecks Act 1973 (c.33)
Provident Nominations and Small Intestacies Act 1883 (c.47)
Provisional Collection of Taxes 1913 (c.3)
Provisional Collection of Taxes Act 1968 (c.2)
Provisional Order Confirmation (Turnpikes) Act 1854 (c.51)
Provisional Order Confirmation (Turnpikes) Act 1855 (c.102)
Provisional Order Confirmation (Turnpikes) Act 1857 (c.9)
Provisional Order Confirmation (Turnpikes) Act 1858 (c.80)
Provisional Order Confirmation (Turnpikes) Act 1859 (c.33)
Provisional Order Confirmation (Turnpikes) Act 1860 (c.70)
Provisional Orders Confirmation (Turnpikes) Act 1862 (c.69)
Provisional Order Confirmation (Turnpikes) Act 1863 (c.98)
Provisional Order Confirmation (Turnpikes) Act 1864 (c.79)
Provisional Order (Marriages) Act 1904 (c.23)
Public Accounts Act 1804 (c.58)
Public Accounts and Charges Act 1891 (c.24)
Public and Other Schools (War Conditions) Act 1941 (c.20)
Public Authorities (Allowances) Act 1961 (c.43)
Public Authorities and Bodies (Loans) Act 1916 (c.69)
Public Bodies (Admission to Meetings) Act 1960 (c.67)
Public Bodies Corrupt Practices Act 1889 (c.69)
Public Buildings Expenses Act 1903 (c.41)
Public Buildings Expenses Act 1913 (c.14)
Public Entertainment Act 1875 (c.21)
Public Expenditure and Receipts Act 1968 (c.14)
Public Health Act 1875 (c.55)
Public Health Act 1904 (c.16)
Public Health Act 1908 (c.6)
Public Health Act 1925 (c.71)
Public Health Act 1936 (c.49)
Public Health Act (London) Act 1936 (c.50)
Public Health Act 1961 (c.64)
Public Health Acts Amendment Act 1890 (c.59)
Public Health Acts Amendment Act 1907 (c.53)
Public Health (Borrowing Powers) (Ireland) Act (c.35)
Public Health (Cleansing of Shellfish) Act 1932 (c.28)
Public Health (Coal Mine Refuse) Act 1939 (c.58)
Public Health (Coal Mine Refuse) (Scotland) Act 1939 (c.23)

Public Health (Confirmation of Byelaws) Act 1884 (c.12)
Public Health (Control of Disease) Act 1984 (c.22)
Public Health (Drainage of Trade Premises) Act 1937 (c.40)
Public Health (Interments) Act 1879 (c.31)
Public Health (Ireland) Act 1878 (c.52)
Public Health (Ireland) Act 1896 (c.54)
Public Health (Ireland) Act 1900 (c.10)
Public Health (Ireland) Act 1911 (c.12)
Public Health (Laboratory Service) Act 1960 (c.49)
Public Health (Laboratory Service) Act 1979 (c.23)
Public Health (London) Act 1936 (c.50)
Public Health (Medical Treatment, etc.) (Ireland) Act 1919 (c.16)
Public Health (Notification of Births) Act 1965 (c.42)
Public Health (Officers) Act 1921 (c.23)
Public Health Officers (Deputies) Act 1957 (c.19)
Public Health (Prevention and Treatment of Disease) Act 1913 (c.23)
Public Health (Prevention, etc. of Disease) (Ireland) Act 1917 (c.40)
Public Health (Recurring Nuisances) Act 1969 (c.25)
Public Health (Regulations as to Food) Act 1907 (c.32)
Public Health (Scotland) Act 1897 (c.38)
Public Health (Scotland) Amendment Act 1907 (c.30)
Public Health (Scotland) Act (1897) Amendment 1911 (c.30)
Public Health (Scotland) Amendment 1925 (c.75)
Public Health (Scotland) Act 1945 (c.15)
Public Health (Smoke Abatement) Act 1926 (c.43)
Public Health (Tuberculosis) Act 1921 (c.12)
Public Health (Water and Sewerage) (Scotland) Act 1935 (c.36)
Public Lavatories (Turnstiles) Act 1963 (c.32)
Public Lending Right Act 1979 (c.10)
Public Libraries Act 1884 (c.37)
Public Libraries Act 1901 (c.19)
Public Libraries Act 1919 (c.93)
Public Libraries (etc.) Act (Ireland) Act 1911 (c.9)
Public Libraries Act (Ireland) 1855 (c.40)
Public Libraries and Museums Act 1964 (c.75)
Public Libraries Consolidation (Scotland) Act 1887 (c.42)
Public Libraries (Ireland) Amendment Act 1877 (c.15)
Public Libraries (Ireland) Act 1894 (c.38)
Public Libraries (Ireland) Act 1902 (c.20)
Public Libraries (Ireland) Act 1920 (c.25)
Public Libraries (Scotland) Act 1894 (c.20)
Public Libraries (Scotland) Act 1899 (c.5)
Public Libraries (Scotland) Act 1920 (c.45)
Public Libraries (Scotland) Act 1955 (c.27)
Public Meeting Act 1908 (c.66)
Public Notaries (Articled Clerks) Act 1919 (c.25)
Public Notaries (Ireland) Act 1821 (c.36)
Public Notaries (War Service of Articled Clerks) Act 1946 (c.79)
Public Officers Protection (Ireland) Act 1803 (c.143)
Public Offices Fees Act 1879 (c.58)
Public Offices (Site) Act 1947 (c.45)
Public Order Act 1936 (c.6)
Public Order Act 1963 (c.52)
Public Order Act 1986 (c.64)
Public Order (Amendment) Act 1996 (c.59)
Public Parks (Scotland) Act 1878 (c.8)
Public Passenger Vehicles Act 1981 (c.14)
Public Records Act 1958 (c.51)
Public Records Act 1967 (c.44)
Public Records (Scotland) Act 1937 (c.43)
Public Registers and Records (Scotland) Act 1948 (c.57)
Public Registers and Records (Scotland) Act 1949 (c.11)
Public Roads (Ireland) Act 1911 (c.45)
Public Schools Act 1868 (c.118)
Public Schools (Eton College Property) Act 1873 (c.62)
Public Service Vehicles (Arrest of Offenders) Act 1975 (c.53)
Public Service Vehicles (Travel Concessions) Act 1955 (c.26)
Public Stores Act 1875 (c.25)
Public Trustee Act 1906 (c.55)
Public Trustee and Administration of Funds Act 1986 (c.57)
Public Trustee (Fees) Act 1957 (c.12)
Public Trustee (General Deposit Fund) Act 1939 (c.51)
Public Utilities Street Works Act 1950 (c.39)
Public Utility Companies (Capital Issues) Act 1920 (c.9)
Public Utility Transfers and Water Charges Act 1988 (c.15)
Public Works Facilities Act 1930 (c.50)
Public Works (Festival of Britain) Act 1949 (c.26)
Public Works Loans Act 1900 (c.36)
Public Works Loans Act 1901 (c.35)
Public Works Loans Act 1902 (c.22)
Public Works Loans Act 1903 (c.28)
Public Works Loans Act 1904 (c.22)
Public Works Loans Act 1904 (c.36)
Public Works Loans Act 1906 (c.29)
Public Works Loans Act 1907 (c.36)
Public Works Loans Act 1908 (c.23)
Public Works Loans Act 1909 (c.6)
Public Works Loans Act 1910 (c.21)
Public Works Loans Act 1911 (c.17)
Public Works Loans Act 1912 (c.11)
Public Works Loans Act 1913 (c.22)
Public Works Loans Act 1914 (c.33)

Public Works Loans Act 1915 (c.68)
Public Works Loans Act 1916 (c.28)
Public Works Loans Act 1917 (c.32)
Public Works Loans Act 1918 (c.27)
Public Works Loans Act 1919 (c.52)
Public Works Loans Act 1920 (c.61)
Public Works Loans Act 1921 (c.54)
Public Works Loans Act 1922 (c.33)
Public Works Loans Act 1923 (c.29)
Public Works Loans Act 1924 (c.26)
Public Works Loans Act 1925 (c.62)
Public Works Loans Act 1926 (c.2)
Public Works Loans Act 1927 (c.1)
Public Works Loans Act 1928 (c.5)
Public Works Loans Act 1930 (c.49)
Public Works Loans Act 1931 (c.47)
Public Works Loans Act 1932 (c.42)
Public Works Loans Act 1934 (c.48)
Public Works Loans Act 1935 (c.5)
Public Works Loans Act 1937 (c.11)
Public Works Loans Act 1939 (c.2)
Public Works Loans Act 1941 (c.14)
Public Works Loans Act 1944 (c.16)
Public Works Loans Act 1946 (c.41)
Public Works Loans Act 1947 (c.13)
Public Works Loans Act 1948 (c.48)
Public Works Loans Act 1949 (c.82)
Public Works Loans Act 1950 (c.5)
Public Works Loans Act 1951 (c.5)
Public Works Loans Act 1952 (c.3)
Public Works Loans Act 1953 (c.6)
Public Works Loans Act 1955 (c.11)
Public Works Loans Act 1956 (c.65)
Public Works Loans Act 1964 (c.9)
Public Works Loans Act 1965 (c.63)
Public Works Loans Act 1966 (c.16)
Public Works Loans Act 1967 (c.61)
Public Works Loans (No. 2) Act 1927 (c.28)
Public Works Loans (No. 2) Act 1937 (c.7)
Punishment of Incest Act 1908 (c.45)
Purchase of Land (Ireland) Act 1885 (c.73)
Purchase of Land (Ireland) Act 1891 (c.48)
Purchase of Land (Ireland) Act 1901 (c.3)
Purchase of Land (Ireland) (No. 2) Act 1901 (c.30)
Purchase Tax Act 1963 (c.9)

Quail Protection Act 1937 (c.5)
Quakers and Moravians Act 1833 (c.49)
Quakers and Moravians Act 1838 (c.77)
Qualification of Women (County and Borough Councils) Act 1907 (c.33)
Qualification of Women (County and Town Councils) Act 1907 (c.48)
Quarantine Act 1797 (c.33)
Quarantine Act 1800 (c.80)
Quarantine Act 1805 (c.10)
Quarantine Act 1810 (c.20)
Quarantine Act 1811 (c.46)
Quarantine Act 1825 (c.78)
Quarantine Act (Great Britain) Act 1806 (c.98)
Quarantine, etc., Act 1800 (c.30)
Quarries Act 1894 (c.42)
Quarry (Fencing) Act 1887 (c.19)
Quarter Sessions Act 1814 (c.84)
Quarter Sessions Act 1837 (c.4)
Quarter Sessions Act 1842 (c.38)
Quarter Sessions Act 1849 (c.45)
Quarter Sessions Act 1894 (c.6)
Quarter Sessions (Ireland) Act 1845 (c.80)
Quarter Sessions Jurors (Ireland) Act 1897 (c.20)
Quarter Sessions (London) Act 1896 (c.55)
Quartering of Soldiers Act 1795 (c.64)
Quartering of Soldiers Act 1796 (c.36)
Quartering of Soldiers Act 1797 (c.32)
Quartering of Soldiers Act 1797 (c.41)
Quartering of Soldiers Act 1799 (c.36)
Quartering of Soldiers Act 1800 (c.39)
Quartering of Soldiers Act 1801 (c.35)
Quartering of Soldiers Act 1802 (c.108)
Quartering of Soldiers Act 1803 (c.41)
Quartering of Soldiers Act 1804 (c.38)
Quartering of Soldiers Act 1805 (c.37)
Quartering of Soldiers Act 1806 (c.126)
Quartering of Soldiers Act 1807 (c.54)
Quartering of Soldiers Act 1808 (c.39)
Quartering of Soldiers Act 1809 (c.37)
Quartering of Soldiers Act 1810 (c.28)
Quartering of Soldiers Act 1810 (c.96)
Quartering of Soldiers Act 1811 (c.28)
Quartering of Soldiers Act 1812 (c.43)
Quartering of Soldiers Act 1813 (c.43)
Quartering of Soldiers Act 1814 (c.55)
Quartering of Soldiers Act 1815 (c.154)
Quartering of Soldiers Act 1816 (c.32)
Quartering of Soldiers Act 1817 (c.78)
Quartering of Soldiers Act 1818 (c.22)
Quartering of Soldiers Act 1819 (c.26)
Quartering of Soldiers Act 1820 (c.38)
Quartering of Soldiers Act 1821 (c.25)
Quartering of Soldiers Act 1822 (c.20)
Quartering of Soldiers Act 1823 (c.20)
Quartering of Soldiers Act 1824 (c.31)
Quartering of Soldiers Act 1825 (c.20)
Quartering of Soldiers Act 1826 (c.14)
Quartering of Soldiers Act 1826 (c.24)
Quartering of Soldiers Act 1828 (c.8)
Quartering of Soldiers Act 1828 (c.9)
Quays, etc. Between Tower and London Bridge Act 1832 (c.66)
Quebec Act 1774 (c.88)
Quebec Act 1852 (c.53)
Quebec Civil Government Charges Act 1831 (c.23)
Queen Anne's Bounty Act 1714 (c.10)
Queen Anne's Bounty Act 1803 (c.107)
Queen Anne's Bounty Act 1805 (c.84)
Queen Anne's Bounty Act 1838 (c.20)
Queen Anne's Bounty Act 1840 (c.20)
Queen Anne's Bounty (Superannuation) Act 1870 (c.89)
Queen's Bench (Ireland) Procedure Act 1872 (c.28)

Queen Caroline's Servants' Pension Act 1822 (c.98)
Queen's Colleges (Ireland) Act 1845 (c.66)
Queen's Prison Act 1842 (c.22)
Queen's Prison Act 1848 (c.7)
Queen's Prison Act 1860 (c.60)
Queen's Prison Discontinuance Act 1862 (c.104)
Queen's Remembrance Act 1859 (c.21)
Queensferry, Firth of Forth: Finance Act 1814 (c.138)

Rabies Act 1974 (c.17)
Race Relations Act 1965 (c.73)
Race Relations Act 1968 (c.71)
Race Relations Act 1976 (c.74)
Race Relations (Remedies) Act 1994 (c.10)
Racecourse Betting Act 1928 (c.41)
Racecourse Licensing Act 1879 (c.18)
Radioactive Material (Road Transport) Act 1991 (c.27)
Radioactive Substances Act 1948 (c.37)
Radioactive Substances Act 1960 (c.34)
Radioactive Substances Act 1993 (c.12)
Radiological Protection Act 1970 (c.46)
Rag Flock Act 1911 (c.52)
Rag Flock Act (1911) Amendment Act 1928 (c.39)
Rag Flock and Other Filling Materials Act 1951 (c.63)
Railways Act 1848 (c.3)
Railways Act 1974 (c.48)
Railway and Canal Commission (Abolition) Act 1949 (c.11)
Railway and Canal Commission (Consents) Act 1922 (c.47)
Railway and Canal Traffic Act 1854 (c.31)
Railway and Canal Traffic Act 1888 (c.25)
Railway and Canal Traffic Act 1892 (c.44)
Railway and Canal Traffic Act 1894 (c.54)
Railway and Canal Traffic Act 1913 (c.29)
Railway and Canal Traffic (Provisional Orders) Amendment Act 1891 (c.12)
Railway Assessors (Scotland) Superannuation Act 1897 (c.12)
Railway Clauses Act 1863 (c.92)
Railway Companies Act 1867 (c.127)
Railway Companies Act 1868 (c.79)
Railway Companies Act 1875 (c.31)
Railway Companies (Accounts and Returns) Act 1911 (c.34)
Railway Companies Arbitration Act 1859 (c.59)
Railway Companies (Ireland) Act 1867 (c.138)
Railway Companies (Ireland) Temporary Advances Act 1866 (c.95)
Railway Companies (Ireland) Temporary Advances Act 1868 (c.94)
Railway Companies Meetings Act 1869 (c.6)
Railway Companies Mortgage Trans. (Scotland) Act 1861 (c.50)
Railway Companies' Powers Act 1864 (c.120)
Railway Companies (Scotland) Act 1867 (c.126)
Railway Companies Securities Act 1866 (c.108)
Railway Employment (Prevention of Accidents) Act 1900 (c.27)
Railway Fires Act 1904 (c.11)
Railway Freight Rebates Act 1936 (c.2)
Railway Freight Rebates Act 1943 (c.23)
Railway Heritage Act 1996 (c.42)
Railway Passenger Duty Act 1917 (c.3)
Railway Regulation Act 1851 (c.64)
Railway Regulation Act 1893 (c.29)
Railway Regulation Act (Returns of Signal Arrangements, Working &c.) Act 1873 (c.76)
Railway Returns (Continuous Brakes) Act 1878 (c.20)
Railways Act 1921 (c.55)
Railways Act 1993 (c.43)
Railways (Agreement) Act 1935 (c.6)
Railways Agreement (Powers) Act 1941 (c.5)
Railways and Canals Act 1860 (c.41)
Railways (Authorisation of Works) Act 1923 (c.30)
Railways Clauses Act 1863 (c.92)
Railways Clauses Consolidation Act 1845 (c.20)
Railways Clauses Consolidation (Scotland) Act 1845 (c.33)
Railways Commission Act 1846 (c.105)
Railway Companies Dissolution 1846 (c.28)
Railways Construction Amendment (Ireland) Act 1880 (c.31)
Railways Construction Facilities Act 1864 (c.121)
Railways (Conveyance of Mails) Act 1838 (c.98)
Railways (Electrical Power) Act 1903 (c.30)
Railways Employment (Prevention of Accidents) Act 1900 (c.27)
Railways (Extension of Time) Act 1868 (c.18)
Railway Fires Act 1905 (c.11)
Railway Fires Act (1905) Amendment Act 1923 (c.27)
Railways (Ireland) Act 1856 (c.72)
Railways (Ireland) Act 1858 (c.34)
Railways (Ireland) Act 1864 (c.71)
Railways (Ireland) Act 1867 (c.104)
Railways (Ireland) Act 1890 (c.52)
Railways (Ireland) Act 1896 (c.34)
Railway Passenger Duty Act 1842 (c.79)
Railway Passenger Duty Act 1847 (c.42)
Railways (Powers and Construction) Acts, 1864, Amendment Act 1870 (c.19)
Railways (Private Sidings) Act 1904 (c.19)
Railway Regulation Act 1840 (c.97)
Railway Regulation Act 1842 (c.55)
Railway Regulation Act 1844 (c.85)
Railway Regulation (Gauge) Act 1846 (c.57)
Railway Rolling Stock Protection Act 1872 (c.50)

Railway (Sales and Leases) Act 1845 (c.96)
Railways Act 1921 (c.55)
Railways Act (Ireland) 1851 (c.70)
Railways Act (Ireland) 1860 (c.97)
Railways (Private Sidings) Act 1904 (c.19)
Railways (Settlement of Claims) Act 1921 (c.59)
Railways Traverse Act 1868 (c.70)
Railways (Valuation for Rating) Act 1930 (c.24)
Railways (Valuation for Rating) Act 1946 (c.61)
Ramsey (Huntingdonshire): Drainage, etc. Act 1796 (c.72)
Ramsgate Harbour Act 1797 (c.86)
Ramsgate: Improvement Act 1796 (c.43)
Ranges Act 1891 (c.54)
Rate in Aid of Distressed Unions Act 1849 (c.24)
Rate Rebate Act 1973 (c.28)
Rate of Interest Act 1821 (c.51)
Rate of Interest Act 1822 (c.47)
Rate Support Grants Act 1986 (c.54)
Rate Support Grants Act 1987 (c.5)
Rate Support Grants Act 1988 (c.51)
Rateable Property (Ireland) Act 1846 (c.110)
Rates Act 1984 (c.33)
Rates of Carriage of Goods Act 1827 (c.39)
Rates (Proceedings for Recovery) Act 1914 (c.85)
Rating Act 1874 (c.54)
Rating Act 1966 (c.9)
Rating Act 1971 (c.39)
Rating and Valuation Act 1925 (c.90)
Rating and Valuation Act 1928 (c.8)
Rating and Valuation Act 1932 (c.18)
Rating and Valuation Act 1937 (c.60)
Rating and Valuation Act 1957 (c.17)
Rating and Valuation Act 1959 (c.36)
Rating and Valuation Act 1961 (c.45)
Rating and Valuation (Air-Raid Works) Act 1938 (c.65)
Rating and Valuation (Air-Raid Works) (Scotland) Act 1938 (c.66)
Rating and Valuation (Amendment) (Scotland) Act 1984 (c.31)
Rating and Valuation (Apportionment) Act 1928 (c.44)
Rating and Valuation (Miscellaneous Provisions) Act 1955 (c.9)
Rating and Valuation (No. 2) Act 1932 (c.33)
Rating and Valuation (Postponement of Valuations) Act 1938 (c.19)
Rating and Valuation (Postponement of Valuations) Act 1940 (c.12)
Rating and Valuation (Scotland) Act 1952 (c.47)
Rating (Caravan Sites) Act 1976 (c.15)
Rating (Charity Shops) Act 1976 (c.45)
Rating (Disabled Persons) Act 1978 (c.40)
Rating Exemption (Scotland) Act 1874 (c.20)
Rating (Interim Relief) Act 1964 (c.18)
Rating of Small Tenements Act 1850 (c.99)
Rating of Small Tenements Act 1851 (c.39)
Rating (Revaluation Rebates) (Scotland) Act 1985 (c.33)
Rating (Scotland) Act 1926 (c.47)
Rating (Scotland) Amendment Act 1928 (c.6)
Rating (War Damage Insurance) Act 1941 (c.25)
Rating (War Damages) (Scotland) Act 1941 (c.25)
Ratings (Caravans and Boats) Act 1996 (c.12)
Rats and Mice (Destruction) Act 1919 (c.72)
Reading Charities Act 1861 (c.23)
Ready Money Football Betting Act 1920 (c.52)
Real Estate Charges Act 1854 (c.113)
Real Estate Charges Act 1867 (c.69)
Real Etate Charges Act 1877 (c.34)
Real Property Act 1845 (c.106)
Real Property Limitation Act 1833 (c.27)
Real Property Limitation Act 1837 (c.28)
Real Property Limitation Act 1874 (c.57)
Real Rights Act 1693 (c.22)
Rebuilding of London Bridge Act 1823 (c.50)
Recall of Army and Air Force Pensions Act 1948 (c.8)
Recaptured British-built Ships Act 1809 (c.41)
Receipt and Remittance of Taxes, etc. Act 1831 (c.18)
Receipt Stamps Act 1828 (c.27)
Receiver General of Stamps Act 1806 (c.76)
Receivers of Crown Rents Act 1816 (c.16)
Receivers of Stolen Goods, etc., Act 1822 (c.24)
Recess Elections Act 1784 (c.26)
Recess Elections Act 1975 (c.66)
Reclamation of Lands, etc. Act 1842 (c.105)
Reclamation of Lands, etc. (Ireland) Act 1831 (c.57)
Recognition of Divorces and Legal Separations Act 1971 (c.53)
Recognition of Trusts Act 1987 (c.14)
Recognizances (Ireland) Act 1809 (c.83)
Recognizances (Ireland) Act 1817 (c.56)
Record of Title (Ireland) Act 1865 (c.88)
Recorded Delivery Service Act 1962 (c.27)
Recorders' Courts of Quarter Sessions Act 1837 (c.19)
Recorders, Magistrates and Clerks of the Peace Act 1888 (c.23)
Recorders, Stipendiary Magistrates and Clerks of the Peace Act 1906 (c.46)
Recoveries in Copyhold, etc. Courts Act 1807 (c.8)
Recovery of Advowsons in Ireland Act 1844 (c.27)
Recovery of Alimony (Ireland) Act 1867 (c.11)
Recovery of Possession by Landlords Act 1820 (c.87)
Recovery of Small Tithes Act 1826 (c.15)
Recovery of Tenements, etc. (Ireland) Act 1816 (c.88)

Recovery of Tenements, etc. (Ireland) Act 1818 (c.39)
Recovery of Tenements (Ireland) Act 1820 (c.41)
Recovery of Tithes (Ireland) Act 1832 (c.41)
Recovery of Wages (Ireland) Act 1814 (c.116)
Recovery of Wages (Ireland) Act 1849 (c.15)
Recreation Grounds Act 1859 (c.27)
Recreational Charities Act 1958 (c.17)
Rectifying of Spirits (Ireland) Act 1807 (c.19)
Rectory of Ewelme Act 1871 (c.23)
Rectory of Ledbury Act 1855 (c.92)
Red Sea and India Telegraph Company Act 1861 (c.4)
Red Sea and India Telegraph Company Act 1862 (c.39)
Redemption of Rent (Ireland) Act 1891 (c.57)
Redemption of Standard Securities (Scotland) Act 1971 (c.45)
Redistribution of Seats Act 1885 (c.23)
Redistribution of Seats (Ireland) Act 1918 (c.65)
Redstone Bridge, Severn Act 1795 (c.108)
Reduction of Annuity Tax Act 1867 (c.107)
Reduction of Duty on Rum Act 1863 (c.102)
Reduction of National Debt 1809 (c.64)
Reduction of National Debt Act 1822 (c.9)
Reduction of National Debt Act 1858 (c.38)
Reduction of National Debt Act 1860 (c.71)
Reductions Ex Capite Lecti Abolished Act 1871 (c.81)
Redundancy Fund Act 1981 (c.5)
Redundancy Payments Act 1965 (c.62)
Redundancy Rebates Act 1969 (c.8)
Redundancy Rebates Act 1977 (c.22)
Redundant Churches and Other Religious Buildings Act 1969 (c.22)
Re-election of Ministers Act 1915 (c.50)
Re-election of Ministers Act 1916 (c.22)
Re-election of Ministers Act 1919 (c.2)
Re-election of Ministers Act (1919) Amendment 1926 (c.19)
Re-election of Ministers (No.2) Act 1916 (c.56)
Referendum Act 1975 (c.33)
Refined Sugar Bounties Act 1824 (c.35)
Reformatory and Industrial Schools Act 1891 (c.23)
Reformatory and Industrial Schools Acts Amendment Act 1872 (c.21)
Reformatory and Industrial Schools (Channel Islands Children) Act 1895 (c.17)
Reformatory and Industrial Schools (Manx Children) Act 1884 (c.40)
Reformatory, etc. Schools Act 1856 (c.109)
Reformatory Institutions (Ireland) Act 1881 (c.29)
Reformatory Schools Act 1856 (c.28)
Reformatory Schools Act 1866 (c.117)
Reformatory Schools Act 1893 (c.15)
Reformatory Schools Act 1893 (c.48)
Reformatory Schools Act 1899 (c.12)
Reformatory Schools (England) Act 1854 (c.74)
Reformatory Schools (England) Act 1857 (c.55)
Reformatory Schools (Ireland) Act 1858 (c.103)
Refreshment Houses Act 1860 (c.27)
Refreshment Houses Act 1964 (c.88)
Refreshment Houses Act 1967 (c.38)
Refreshment Houses (Ireland) Act 1860 (c.107)
Refuse Disposal (Amenity) Act 1978 (c.3)
Regency Act 1830 (c.2)
Regency Act 1840 (c.52)
Regency Act 1910 (c.26)
Regency Act 1937 (c.16)
Regency Act 1943 (c.42)
Regency Act 1953 (c.1)
Regency Act Amendment Act 1838 (c.24)
Regent's Park, Regent Street Act 1851 (c.95)
Regent's Park, Regent Street, etc. Act 1817 (c.24)
Regent's Park, Regent Street, etc. Act 1824 (c.100)
Regent's Park, Regent Street, etc. Act 1831 (c.29)
Regent's Park, Regent Street, etc. Act 1832 (c.56)
Regent's Quadrant Colonnade Act 1848 (c.50)
Regent Street, etc. Act 1825 (c.38)
Regent Street Act 1828 (c.64)
Regent Street Act 1829 (c.61)
Regent Street, Caslton Place Act 1826 (c.77)
Regent Street, etc. Act 1828 (c.70)
Regiment of Cornwall and Devon Miners Act 1798 (c.74)
Regimental Accounts Act 1808 (c.128)
Regimental Benefit Societies Act 1849 (c.71)
Regimental Charitable Funds Act 1935 (c.11)
Regimental Debts Act 1863 (c.57)
Regimental Debts Act 1893 (c.5)
Regimental Debts (Deposit of Wills) (Scotland) Act 1919 (c.89)
Regimental Exchange Act 1875 (c.16)
Regional Commissioners Act 1939 (c.76)
Regional Development Grants (Termination) Act 1988 (c.11)
Register of Sasines Act 1828 (c.19)
Register of Sasines (Scotland) Act 1987 (c.23)
Registered Designs Act 1949 (c.88)
Registered Establishments (Scotland) Act 1987 (c.40)
Registered Homes Act 1984 (c.23)
Registered Homes (Amendment) Act 1991 (c.20)
Registering of British Vessels Act 1845 (c.89)
Registering of Vessels Act 1823 (c.41)
Registers of Sasines (Scotland) Act 1848 (c.74)
Registrar General (Scotland) Act 1920 (c.69)
Registration Acceleration Act 1894 (c.32)

Registration Act 1885 (c.15)
Registration Act 1908 (c.21)
Registration Amendment (Ireland) Act 1868 (c.112)
Registration Amendment (Scotland) Act 1885 (c.)
Registration Appeals (Ireland) Act 1885 (c.66)
Registration (Ireland) Act 1898 (c.2)
Registration of Aliens Act 1836 (c.11)
Registration of Assurances (Ireland) Act 1850 (c.72)
Registration of Births and Deaths (Ireland) Act 1863 (c.11)
Registration of Births, Deaths and Marriages (Army) Act 1879 (c.8)
Registration of Births, Deaths and Marriages (Scotland) Act 1854 (c.80)
Registration of Births, Deaths and Marriages (Scotland) Act 1855 (c.29)
Registration of Births, Deaths and Marriages (Scotland) Act 1860 (c.85)
Registration of Births, Deaths and Marriages (Scotland) Act 1965 (c.49)
Registration of Births, Deaths and Marriages (Scotland) Amendment Act 1910 (c.32)
Registration of Births, Deaths and Marriages (Scotland) (Amendment) Act 1934 (c.19)
Registration of Births, Deaths and Marriages (Special Provisions) Act 1957 (c.58)
Registration of Births, etc. Act 1836 (c.1)
Registration of Burials Act 1864 (c.97)
Registration of Business Names Act 1916 (c.58)
Registration of Certain Writs (Scotland) Act 1891 (c.9)
Registration of Clubs (Ireland) Act 1904 (c.9)
Registration of County Electors (Extension of Time) Act 1889 (c.19)
Registration of County Voters (Ireland) Act 1864 (c.22)
Registration of Deeds (Ireland) Act 1864 (c.76)
Registration of Electors 1891 (c.18)
Registration of Leases (Scotland) Act 1857 (c.26)
Registration of Leases (Scotland) Amendment Act 1877 (c.36)
Registration of Marriages (Ireland) Act 1863 (c.90)
Registration of Still-Births (Scotland) Act 1938 (c.55)
Registration of Voters (Ireland) Act 1973 (c.30)
Registration Service Act 1953 (c.37)
Registry Courts (Ireland) Amendment Act 1879 (c.71)
Registry, etc. of Colonial Slaves Act 1819 (c.120)
Registry of Admiralty Court Act 1813 (c.151)
Registry of Boats, etc. Act 1795 (c.58)
Registry of Deeds Act 1822 (c.116)
Registry of Deeds Act 1832 (c.87)
Registry of Deeds Act 1875 (c.5)
Registry of Deeds, etc. (Ireland) Act 1828 (c.57)
Registry of Deeds Office (Ireland) Holidays Act 1883 (c.20)
Registry of Ships Act 1796 (c.112)
Registry of Ships Built in India Act 1815 (c.116)
Registry of Wool Act 1821 (c.81)
Regrating and Ingrossing of Oaken Bark Act 1807 (c.53)
Regular and Elders' Widows' Funds Act 1897 (c.11)
Regulation of Factories Act 1834 (c.1)
Regulation of Railways Act 1868 (c.119)
Regulation of Railways Act 1871 (c.78)
Regulation of Railways Act 1873 (c.48)
Regulation of Railways Acts, 1873 and 1874, Continuance Act 1879 (c.56)
Regulation of Railways Act 1889 (c.57)
Regulation of the Forces Act 1871 (c.86)
Regulation of the Forces Act 1881 (c.57)
Rehabilitation of Offenders Act 1974 (c.53)
Reinstatement in Civil Employment Act 1944 (c.15)
Reinstatement in Civil Employment Act 1950 (c.10)
Reinsurance (Acts of Terrorism) Act 1993 (c.18)
Released Persons (Poor Law Relief) Act 1907 (c.14)
Relief as to Transferable Stocks, etc. Act 1812 (c.158)
Relief of Bankers Act 1824 (c.73)
Relief of Certain Bishops Act 1843 (c.57)
Relief of Certain Curates (England) Act 1803 (c.2)
Relief of Certain Incumbents Act 1824 (c.89)
Relief of Debtors Act 1799 (c.50)
Relief of Debtors in Prison Act 1812 (c.160)
Relief of Discharged Soldiers and Sailors Act 1803 (c.61)
Relief of Distress Act 1849 (c.63)
Relief of Distress (Ireland) Act 1880 (c.4)
Relief of Distress (Ireland) Amendment Act 1880 (c.14)
Relief of Distressed Unions (Ireland) Act 1883 (c.24)
Relief of Families of Militiamen Act 1803 (c.47)
Relief of Families of Militiamen (Scotland) Act 1809 (c.90)
Relief of Families of Militiamen (Ireland) Act 1811 (c.78)
Relief of Families of Militiamen Act 1812 (c.28)
Relief of Insolvent Debtors Act 1797 (c.112)
Relief of Prisoners Act 1797 (c.85)
Relief of Prisoners for Debt Act 1809 (c.6)
Relief of the Poor Act 1795 (c.23)
Relief of the Poor Act 1810 (c.50)
Relief of the Poor Act 1812 (c.73)
Relief of Revenue Prisoners Act 1795 (c.96)

Relief of Rutson & Company Act 1820 (c.30)
Relief of Sailors Abroad Act 1818 (c.38)
Relief of Shipwrecked Mariners, etc. Act 1814 (c.126)
Relief of Stress (Ireland) Act 1849 (c.5)
Relief of Traders for Grenada, etc. Act (c.127)
Relief to Chelsea, etc. Pensioners Act 1825 (c. 27)
Relief to Holders of Certain Securities Act 1818 (c.93)
Religious Congregations, etc. (Scotland) Act 1850 (c.13)
Religious Disabilities Act 1846 (c.59)
Remedies Against the Hundred (England) Act 1827 (c.31)
Remission of Penalties Act 1859 (c.32)
Remission of Penalties Act 1875 (c.80)
Remission of Rates (London) Act 1940 (c.32)
Removal of Goods Act 1812 (c.142)
Removal of Goods for Exportation, etc. Act 1808 (c.126)
Removal of Indictments into King's Bench Act 1835 (c.33)
Removal of Offensive Matter Act 1906 (c.45)
Removal of Prisoners in Custody Act 1854 (c.115)
Removal of Slaves Act 1820 (c.50)
Removal of Wool Act 1814 (c.78)
Removal of Wrecks Act 1877 (c.16)
Removal of Wrecks Act, 1877, Amendment Act 1889 (c.5)
Removal Terms Act 1886 (c.50)
Removal Terms (Burghs) (Scotland) Act 1881 (c.39)
Removal Terms (Scotland) Act, 1886, Amendment Act 1890 (c.36)
Remuneration, Charges and Grants Act 1975 (c.57)
Remuneration of Teachers Act 1963 (c.20)
Remuneration of Teachers Act 1965 (c.3)
Remuneration of Teachers (Scotland) Act 1967 (c.36)
Renewable Leasehold Conversion Act 1849 (c.105)
Renewable Leasehold Conversion (Ireland) Act 1868 (c.62)
Renewal of Leases (Ireland) Act 1838 (c.62)
Rent Act 1957 (c.25)
Rent Act 1965 (c.75)
Rent Act 1968 (c.23)
Rent Act 1974 (c.51)
Rent Act 1977 (c.42)
Rent (Agricultural) Amendment Act 1977 (c.17)
Rent (Agriculture) Act 1976 (c.80)
Rent (Amendment) Act 1985 (c.24)
Rent and Mortgage Interest Restrictions Act 1923 (c.32)
Rent and Mortgage Interest Restriction Act 1939 (c.71)
Rent and Mortgage Interest Restrictions (Amendment) Act 1933 (c.32)
Rent and Mortgage Interest (Restrictions Continuance) Act 1925 (c.32)
Rent (Control of Increases) Act 1969 (c.62)
Rent of Furnished Houses Control (Scotland) Act 1943 (c.44)
Rent Rebate Act 1973 (c.28)
Rent Restrictions (Notices of Increase) Act 1923 (c.13)
Rent (Scotland) Act 1971 (c.28)
Rent (Scotland) Act 1984 (c.58)
Rentcharges Act 1977 (c.30)
Rents of the Rolls Estate, etc. Act 1820 (c.107)
Reorganisation of Offices (Scotland) Act 1928 (c.34)
Reorganisation of Offices (Scotland) Act 1939 (c.20)
Repair of Blenheim Palace Act 1840 (c.43)
Repair of Roads and Bridges (Ireland) Act 1825 (c.101)
Repair of War Damage Act 1941 (c.34)
Repatriation of Prisoners Act 1984 (c.47)
Repayment of Advances (Ireland) Act 1852 (c.16)
Repayment of Certain Loans Act 1802 (c.39)
Repayment of Duty in Certain Cases Act 1810 (c.39)
Repeal of Acts Concerning Importation Act 1822 (cc.41, 42)
Repeal of 39 Eliz. c.17 Act 1812 (c.31)
Repeal of 41 Geo. 3 (Great Britain) 1801 (c.4)
Repeal of Certain Duties Act 1800 (c.69)
Repeal of Certain Duties Act 1824 (c.22)
Repeal, etc. of Certain Duties Act 1802 (c.103)
Repeal of a Certain Tax Act 1801 (c.100)
Repeal of Obsolete Statutes Act 1856 (c.64)
Repeal of Part of 15 Geo.3.c.31 Act 1850 (c.80)
Repeal of Salt Duties Act 1824 (c.65)
Repeal of Sir J. Barnard's Act 1860 (c.28)
Repeal of Nore Tolls Act 1859 (c.29)
Representation of the People Act 1832 (c.45)
Representation of the People Act 1832 (c.88)
Representation of the People Act 1867 (c.102)
Representation of the People Act 1884 (c.3)
Representation of the People Act 1918 (c.64)
Representation of the People Act 1920 (c.15)
Representation of the People Act 1921 (c.34)
Representation of the People Act 1922 (c.12)
Representation of the People Act 1945 (c.5)
Representation of the People Act 1948 (c.65)
Representation of the People Act 1949 (c.68)
Representation of the People Act 1968 (c.15)
Representation of the People Act 1969 (c.15)
Representation of the People Act 1974 (c.10)
Representation of the People Act 1977 (c.9)
Representation of the People Act 1978 (c.32)
Representation of the People Act 1979 (c.40)
Representation of the People Act 1980 (c.3)
Representation of the People Act 1981 (c.34)
Representation of the People Act 1983 (c.2)
Representation of the People Act 1985 (c.50)
Representation of the People Act 1989 (c.28)

Representation of the People Act 1990 (c.32)
Representation of the People Act 1991 (c.11)
Representation of the People Act 1993 (c.29)
Representation of the People (Amendment) Act 1918 (c.50)
Representation of the People Amendment Act 1957 (c.43)
Representation of the People Amendment Act 1958 (c.9)
Representation of the People (Armed Forces) Act 1976 (c.29)
Representation of the People (Equal Franchise) Act 1928 (c.12)
Representation of the People (Ireland) Act 1850 (c.69)
Representation of the People (Ireland) Act 1861 (c.60)
Representation of the People (Ireland) Act 1868 (c.49)
Representation of the People (No. 2) Act 1920 (c.35)
Representation of the People (No. 2) Act 1922 (c.41)
Representation of the People (No. 2) Act 1974 (c.13)
Representation of the People (Reading University) Act 1928 (c.25)
Representation of the People (Returning Officers' Expenses) Act 1919 (c.8)
Representation of the People (Scotland) Act 1832 (c.65)
Representation of the People (Scotland) Act 1868 (c.48)
Representative Peers (Ireland) Act 1857 (c.33)
Representative Peers (Scotland) Act 1847 (c.52)
Representative Peers (Scotland) Act 1851 (c.87)
Representative Peers (Scotland) Act 1852 (c.35)
Reprisals Against Foreign Ships, etc. Act 1808 (c.132)
Reproductive Loan Fund Act 1874 (c.86)
Republic of Gambia Act 1970 (c.37)
Republic of South Africa (Temporary Provisions) Act 1961 (c.23)
Requirements of Writing (Scotland) Act 1995 (c.7)
Requisitioned Houses Act 1960 (c.20)
Requisitioned Houses and Housing (Amendment) Act 1955 (c.24)
Requisitioned Land and War Works Act 1945 (c.43)
Requisitioned Land and War Works Act 1947 (c.17)
Requisitioned Land and War Works Act 1948 (c.17)
Resale Prices Act 1964 (c.58)
Resale Prices Act 1976 (c.53)
Rescue Act 1821 (c.88)
Reserve and Auxiliary Forces Act 1939 (c.24)
Reserve and Auxiliary Forces (Protection of Civil Interests) Act 1951 (c.65)
Reserve and Auxiliary Forces (Training) Act 1951 (c.23)
Reserve Force Act 1859 (c.42)
Reserve Force Act 1867 (c.110)
Reserve Forces Act 1870 (c.67)
Reserve Forces Act 1882 (c.48)
Reserve Forces Act 1890 (c.42)
Reserve Forces Act 1899 (c.40)
Reserve Forces Act 1900 (c.62)
Reserve Forces Act 1906 (c.11)
Reserve Forces Act 1937 (c.17)
Reserve Forces Act 1966 (c.30)
Reserve Forces Act 1980 (c.9)
Reserve Forces Act 1982 (c.14)
Reserve Forces Act 1996 (c.14)
Reserve Forces and Militia Act 1898 (c.9)
Reserve Forces (Safeguard of Employment) Act 1985 (c.17)
Reservoirs Act 1975 (c.23)
Reservoirs (Safety Provisions) Act 1930 (c.51)
Residence in France During the War Act 1798 (c.79)
Residence of Incumbents Act 1869 (c.109)
Residence on Benefices, etc. (England) Act 1814 (c.175)
Residence on Benefices, etc. (England) Act 1816 (c.6)
Residence on Benefices, etc. (England) Act 1816 (c.123)
Residence on Benefices, etc. (England) Act 1817 (c.99)
Resident Magistrates and Police Commissioners Salaries Act 1874 (c.23)
Resident Magistrates (Belfast) Act 1911 (c.58)
Resident Magistrates (Ireland) Act 1920 (c.38)
Resident Magistrates (Ireland) Act 1853 (c.60)
Residential Homes Act 1980 (c.7)
Resignation Bonds Act 1827 (c.25)
Responsibility of Shipowners Act 1813 (c.159)
Restoration of Order in Ireland Act 1920 (c.31)
Restoration of Order In Ireland (Indemnity) Act 1923 (c.12)
Restoration of Pre-War Practices Act 1919 (c.42)
Restoration of Pre-War Trade Practices Act 1942 (c.9)
Restoration of Pre-War Trade Practices Act 1950 (c.9)
Restriction of Advertisement (War Risks Insurance) Act 1939 (c.120)
Restriction of Offensive Weapons Act 1959 (c.37)
Restriction of Ribbon Development (Temporary Development) Act 1943 (c.34)
Restrictions of Ribbon Development Act 1935 (c.47)
Restriction on Cash Payments Act 1797 (c.1)

Restriction on Cash Payments Act 1797 (c.45)
Restriction on Cash Payments Act 1797 (c.91)
Restriction on Cash Payments Act 1802 (c.40)
Restriction on Cash Payments Act 1802 (c.45)
Restriction on Cash Payments Act 1803 (c.1)
Restriction on Cash Payments Act 1803 (c.18)
Restriction on Cash Payments Act 1803 (c.44)
Restriction on Cash Payments Act 1814 (c.99)
Restriction on Cash Payments Act 1814 (c.130)
Restriction on Cash Payments Act 1815 (c.28)
Restriction on Cash Payments Act 1815 (c.41)
Restriction on Cash Payments Act 1816 (c.40)
Restriction on Cash Payments Act 1816 (c.48)
Restriction on Cash Payments Act 1818 (c.37)
Restriction on Cash Payments Act 1818 (c.60)
Restriction on Cash Payments (Ireland) Act 1804 (c.21)
Restrictive Practices Court Act 1976 (c.33)
Restrictive Trade Practices Act 1956 (c.68)
Restrictive Trade Practices Act 1968 (c.66)
Restrictive Trade Practices Act 1976 (c.34)
Restrictive Trade Practices Act 1977 (c.19)
Restrictive Trade Practices (Stock Exchange) Act 1984 (c.2)
Resumption of Cash Payments Act 1819 (c.49)
Resumption of Cash Payments Act 1819 (c.99)
Retail Brewers Act 1828 (c.68)
Retail Meat Dealers' Shops (Sunday Closing) Act 1936 (c.30)
Retailing of Spirits (Scotland) Act 1818 (c.13)
Retail of Sweets, etc. Act 1834 (c.77)
Retired Officers (Civil Employment) Act 1919 (c.40)
Retirement of Officers on Half Pay Act 1811 (c.103)
Retirement of Officers on Half Pay Act 1812 (c.151)
Retirement of Teachers (Scotland) Act 1976 (c.65)
Return of Persons Committed, etc. Act 1815 (c.49)
Returning Officers Act 1854 (c.57)
Returning Officers (Scotland) Act 1886 (c.58)
Returning Officers (Scotland) Act 1891 (c.49)
Returning Officers (Scotland) Act 1977 (c.14)
Returns to Secretary of State Act 1858 (c.67)
Revenue Act 1845 (c.76)
Revenue Act 1862 (c.22)
Revenue Act 1863 (c.33)
Revenue Act 1865 (c.30)
Revenue Act 1866 (c.36)
Revenue Act 1867 (c.114)
Revenue Act 1867 (c.90)
Revenue Act 1868 (c.28)
Revenue Act 1869 (c.14)
Revenue Act 1883 (c.55)
Revenue Act 1884 (c.62)
Revenue Act 1889 (c.42)
Revenue Act 1898 (c.46)
Revenue Act 1903 (c.46)
Revenue Act 1906 (c.20)
Revenue Act 1909 (c.43)
Revenue Act 1911 (c.2)
Revenue Act 1968 (c.11)
Revenue Buildings, Liverpool Act 1832 (c.14)
Revenue Departments Accounts Act 1861 (c.93)
Revenue, Friendly Societies and National Debt Act 1882 (c.72)
Revenue (Ireland) Act 1806 (c.106)
Revenue (Ireland) Act 1821 (c.90)
Revenue Inquiry Act 1824 (c.7)
Revenue (No. 1) Act 1861 (c.21)
Revenue (No. 1) Act 1864 (c.18)
Revenue (No. 2) Act 1861 (c.91)
Revenue (No. 2) Act 1864 (c.56)
Revenue (No. 2) Act 1865 (c.96)
Revenue of Scotland Act 1718 (c.20)
Revenue Officers' Disabilities Act 1868 (c.73)
Revenue Officers' Disabilities Removal Act 1874 (c.22)
Revenue Offices (Scotland) Holidays Act 1880 (c.17)
Revenue Solicitors Act 1828 (c.25)
Revenue (Transfer of Charges) Act 1856 (c.59)
Revenues of Archbishopric of Armagh Act 1864 (c.81)
Reverend J. G. MacManaway's Indemnity Act 1951 (c.29)
Reverter of Sites Act 1987 (c.15)
Review of Justices' Decisions Act 1872 (c.26)
Revising Barristers Act 1866 (c.54)
Revising Barristers Act 1873 (c.70)
Revising Barristers Act 1874 (c.53)
Revising Barristers Act 1885 (c.57)
Revising Barristers Act 1886 (c.42)
Revising Barristers (Ireland) Act 1886 (c.43)
Revision of the Army and Air Force Acts (Transitional Provisions) Act 1955 (c.20)
Revival of Expired Laws, etc. Jamaica Act 1839 (c.26)
Rhodesia and Nyasaland Federation Act 1953 (c.30)
Rhodesia and Nyasaland Act 1963 (c.34)
Richmond Lunatic Asylum Act 1815 (c.107)
Richmond Lunatic Asylum Act 1830 (c.22)
Richmond Lunatic Asylum Act 1831 (c.13)
Richmond Penitentiary, etc. Act 1836 (c.51)
Richmond to Lancaster Road Act 1795 (c.157)

Riding Establishments Act 1939 (c.56)
Riding Establishments Act 1964 (c.70)
Riding Establishments Act 1970 (c.32)
Rifle Volunteer Grounds Act 1860 (c.140)
Rifle Volunteer Grounds Act 1862 (c.41)
Right of Light Act 1959 (c.56)
Rights of Entry (Gas and Electricity Boards) Act 1954 (c.21)
Rights of Way Act 1932 (c.45)
Rights of Way Act 1990 (c.24)
Rights of Way Near Aldershot Camp Act 1856 (c.66)
Riot Act 1714 (c.5)
Riot (Damages) Act 1886 (c.38)
Riotous Assemblies (Scotland) Act 1822 (c.33)
River Boards Act 1948 (c.32)
River Itchin: Navigation Act 1795 (c.86)
River Ivel: Navigation Act 1795 (c.105)
River Liffey, Dublin Act 1833 (c.26)
River Ness Act 1855 (c.113)
River Navigation Improvement (Ireland) Act 1914 (c.55)
River Ouze: Navigation Act 1795 (c.77)
River Poddle Act 1840 (c.58)
River Thames and Isis: Navigation Act 1795 (c.106)
Rivers Pollution Prevention Act 1876 (c.75)
Rivers Pollution Prevention Act 1893 (c.31)
Rivers Pollution Prevention (Border Councils) Act 1898 (c.34)
Rivers (Prevention of Pollution) Act 1951 (c.64)
Rivers (Prevention of Pollution) Act 1961 (c.50)
Rivers (Prevention of Pollution) (Scotland) Act 1951 (c.66)
Rivers (Prevention of Pollution) (Scotland) Act 1965 (c.13)
Road and Rail Traffic Act 1933 (c.53)
Road Haulage Wages Act 1938 (c.44)
Road Safety Act 1967 (c.30)
Road Traffic Act 1930 (c.43)
Road Traffic Act 1934 (c.50)
Road Traffic Act 1937 (c.44)
Road Traffic Act 1956 (c.67)
Road Traffic Act 1959 (c.16)
Road Traffic Act 1960 (c.16)
Road Traffic Act 1962 (c.59)
Road Traffic Act 1964 (c.45)
Road Traffic Act 1967 (c.21)
Road Traffic Act 1972 (c.20)
Road Traffic Act 1974 (c.50)
Road Traffic Act 1988 (c.52)
Road Traffic Act 1991 (c.40)
Road Traffic (Amendment) Act 1931 (c.32)
Road Traffic (Amendment) Act 1960 (c.51)
Road Traffic (Amendment) Act 1967 (c.70)
Road Traffic and Roads Improvement Act 1960 (c.63)
Road Traffic (Consequential Provisions) Act 1988 (c.54)
Road Traffic (Disqualification) Act 1970 (c.23)
Road Traffic (Driving Instruction by Disabled Persons) Act 1993 (c.31)
Road Traffic (Driver Licensing and Information Systems) Act 1989 (c.22)
Road Traffic (Drivers' Ages and Hours of Work) Act 1976 (c.3)
Road Traffic (Driving Instruction) Act 1967 (c.79)
Road Traffic (Driving Instruction) Act 1984 (c.13)
Road Traffic (Driving Licences) Act 1936 (c.23)
Road Traffic (Driving Licences) Act 1946 (c.8)
Road Traffic (Driving Licences) Act 1983 (c.43)
Road Traffic (Driving of Motor Cycles) Act 1960 (c.69)
Road Traffic (Foreign Vehicles) Act 1972 (c.27)
Road Traffic (New Drivers) Act 1995 (c.13)
Road Traffic Offenders Act 1988 (c.53)
Road Traffic (Production of Documents) Act 1985 (c.34)
Road Traffic Regulation Act 1967 (c.76)
Road Traffic Regulation Act 1984 (c.27)
Road Traffic Regulation (Parking) Act 1986 (c.27)
Road Traffic Regulation (Special Events) Act 1994 (c.11)
Road Traffic (Temporary Restrictions) Act 1991 (c.26)
Road Transport Lighting Act 1927 (c.37)
Road Transport Lighting Act 1953 (c.21)
Road Transport Lighting Act 1957 (c.51)
Road Transport Lighting Act 1967 (c.55)
Road Transport Lighting (No. 2) Act (c.22)
Road Transport Lighting (Amendment) Act 1958 (c.22)
Roads Act 1920 (c.72)
Roads Amendment Act 1880 (c.7)
Roads and Bridges (Scotland) Act 1848 (c.40)
Roads and Bridges (Scotland) Act 1878 (c.51)
Roads and Bridges (Scotland) Amendment Act 1892 (c.12)
Roads and Bridges (Scotland) Act 1878 Amendment Act 1888 (c.9)
Roads and Streets in Police Burghs (Scotland) Act 1891 (c.32)
Roads and Streets in Police Burghs (Scotland) Act 1925 (c.82)
Roads between London and Holyhead Act 1819 (c.48)
Roads, etc. (Ireland) Act 1827 (c.23)
Roads, etc. (Ireland) Act 1829 (c.40)
Roads, etc. (Scotland) Act 1833 (c.33)
Roads (Ireland) Act 1835 (c.31)
Roads Improvement Act 1925 (c.68)
Roads in Lanarkshire, etc. Act 1823 (c.10)
Roads (London to Chirk) Act 1820 (c.70)
Roads (Scotland) Act 1970 (c.20)
Roads (Scotland) Act 1984 (c.54)

Roasted Malt for Colouring Beer Act 1842 (c.30)
Robbery from the Person Act 1837 (c.87)
Rochdale Canal Company Act 1798 (c.49)
Rochdale Road Act 1795 (c.160)
Rochdale and Bury Road Act 1797 (c.145)
Rochdale and Bury and Sudden Roads Act 1797 (c.146)
Rochdale to Bury Road Act 1794 (c.124)
Rochdale Vicarage Act 1866 (c.86)
Rochdale Vicarage Appointment Act 1865 (c.117)
Rock Salt Act 1811 (c.82)
Roe Deer (Close Seasons) Act 1977 (c.4)
Rogue Money Act (Scotland) 1839 (c.65)
Roll of Valuation (1748) (c.29)
Rolls Estate Act 1837 (c.46)
Rolls-Royce (Purchase) Act 1971 (c.9)
Roman Catholic Act 1844 (c.102)
Roman Catholic Charities Act 1831 (c.115)
Roman Catholic Charities Act 1856 (c.76)
Roman Catholic Charities Act 1857 (c.76)
Roman Catholic Charities Act 1858 (c.51)
Roman Catholic Charities Act 1859 (c.50)
Roman Catholic Charities Act 1860 (c.134)
Roman Catholic Relief Act 1791 (c.32)
Roman Catholic Relief Act 1803 (c.30)
Roman Catholic Relief Act 1813 (c.128)
Roman Catholic Relief Act 1829 (c.7)
Roman Catholic Relief Act 1926 (c.55)
Roosevelt Memorial Act 1946 (c.83)
Ropeworks Act 1846 (c.40)
Rothwell Gaol Act 1845 (c.72)
Royal and Parliamentary Titles Act 1927 (c.4)
Royal Arsenals, etc. Act 1862 (c.78)
Royal Assent Act 1967 (c.23)
Royal Burghs (Scotland) Act 1822 (c.91)
Royal Burghs (Scotland) Act 1833 (c.76)
Royal Burghs, etc. (Scotland) Act 1834 (c.87)
Royal Canal Act 1818 (c.35)
Royal Canal Company Act 1813 (c.101)
Royal Exchange Assurance Act 1796 (c.26)
Royal Household, etc., Act 1812 (c.8)
Royal Irish Constabulary Act 1873 (c.74)
Royal Irish Constabulary (Widows' Pensions) Act 1954 (c.17)
Royal (Late Indian) Ordinance Corps Act 1874 (c.61)
Royal Marines Act 1820 (c.91)
Royal Marines Act 1847 (c.63)
Royal Marines Act 1857 (c.1)
Royal Marines Act 1914 (c.16)
Royal Marines Act 1916 (c.23)
Royal Marines Act 1939 (c.88)
Royal Marines Act 1946 (c.4)
Royal Marines Act 1948 (c.25)
Royal Military Asylum, Chelsea Act 1854 (c.61)
Royal Military Asylum Chelsea (Transfer) Act 1884 (c.32)
Royal Military Canal Act 1837 (c.20)
Royal Military Canal Act 1867 (c.140)
Royal Military Canal Act 1872 (c.66)
Royal Naval Asylum Act 181 (c.105)
Royal Naval Asylum, etc. Act 1825 (c.26)
Royal Naval Reserve Act 1902 (c.5)
Royal Naval Reserve Act 1927 (c.18)
Royal Naval Reserve (Volunteer) Act 1859 (c.40)
Royal Naval Reserve Volunteer Act 1896 (c.33)
Royal Naval Volunteer Reserve Act 1917 (c.22)
Royal Naval Volunteer Reserve Act 1942 (c.18)
Royal Niger Company Act 1899 (c.43)
Royal Patriotic Fund Corporation Act 1949 (c.10)
Royal Pavilion, Brighton, etc. Act 1849 (c.102)
Royal Scottish Museum (Extension) Act 1912 (c.16)
Royal Signature by Commission Act 1830 (c.23)
Royal Tithes Act 1876 (c.10)
Royal Titles Act 1901 (c.15)
Royal Titles Act 1952 (c.9)
Royal University of Ireland Act 1881 (c.52)
Rules Publication Act 1893 (c.66)
Rural Water Supplies Act 1934 (c.7)
Rural Water Supplies and Sewerage Act 1944 (c.26)
Rural Water Supplies and Sewerage Act 1951 (c.45)
Rural Water Supplies and Sewerage Act 1955 (c.13)
Rural Water Supplies and Sewerage Act 1961 (c.29)
Rural Water Supplies and Sewerage Act 1965 (c.80)
Rural Water Supplies and Sewerage Act 1971 (c.49)
Rural Water Supplies and Sewerage (No. 2) Act 1955 (c.15)
Rural Water Supplies and Sewerage (Scotland) Act 1969 (c.6)
Russian Dutch Loan Act 1815 (c.115)
Russian Dutch Loan Act 1832 (c.81)
Russian Dutch Loan Act 1891 (c.26)
Russian Goods (Import Prohibition) Act 1933 (c.10)
Russian Government Securities Act 1854 (c.123)
Ruthin Charities Act 1863 (c.59)
Rye Harbour Act 1797 (c.130)

Sacramental Test Act 1828 (c.17)
Sacramental Test (Ireland) Act 1832 (c.7)
Sailcloth Manufacture, etc. Act 1805 (c.68)
Safety at Sea Act 1986 (c.23)
Safety of Sports Grounds Act 1975 (c.52)
Safeguarding of Industries Act 1921 (c.47)
Safeguarding of Industries (Customs Duties) Act 1925 (c.79)
Sailors and Soldiers (Gifts for Land Settlement) Act 1916 (c.60)

Salaries of Bishops, etc. in West Indies Act 1826 (c.4)
Salaries of Chief Baron, etc. Act 1809 (c.127)
Salaries of County Officers (Ireland) Act 1823 (c.43)
Salaries of County Officers (Ireland) Act 1824 (c.93)
Salaries of Judges (Scotland) Act 1806 (c.49)
Salaries of Scotch Judges Act 1800 (c.55)
Salary of Lord Lieutenant Act 1811 (c.89)
Salary of Sir J. Lawrence Act 1864 (c.2)
Salcey Forest Act 1825 (c.132)
Sale and Supply of Goods Act 1994 (c.35)
Sale of Advowsons Act 1856 (c.50)
Sale of Beer Act 1795 (c.113)
Sale of Beer, etc. on Sunday Act 1848 (c.49)
Sale of Beer, etc. Act 1854 (c.79)
Sale of Bread, etc. Act 1800 (c.16)
Sale of Bread Act 1800 (c.71)
Sale of Bread Act 1800 (c.18)
Sale of Bread Act 1801 (c.12)
Sale of Butter Act 1796 (c.86)
Sale of Certain Lands in Worcester Act 1819 (c.137)
Sale of Certain Stock Act 1812 (c.148)
Sale, etc. of Certain Stocks Act 1829 (c.48)
Sale of Church Patronages Belonging to Municipal Corporations Act 1838 (c.31)
Sale of Crown Lands Act 1826 (c.51)
Sale of Crown Rents (Ireland) Act 1806 (c.123)
Sale of Crown Rents, etc. (Ireland) Act 1807 (c.16)
Sale of Exhausted Parish Lands Act 1876 (c.62)
Sale of Farming Stock Act 1816 (c.50)
Sale of Fish Act 1834 (c.20)
Sale of Food and Drugs Act 1875 (c.63)
Sale of Food and Drugs Act 1899 (c.51)
Sale of Food and Drugs Act 1927 (c.5)
Sale of Food and Drugs Amendment Act 1879 (c.30)
Sale of Food (Weights and Measures) Act 1926 c.63)
Sale of Gas Act 1859 (c.66)
Sale of Gas Act 1860 (c.146)
Sale of Gas (Scotland) Act 1864 (c.96)
Sale of Goods Act 1893 (c.71)
Sale of Goods Act 1979 (c.54)
Sale of Goods (Amendment) Act 1994 (c.32)
Sale of Goods (Amendment) Act 1995 (c.28)
Sale of Hares (Ireland) Act 1863 (c.19)
Sale of H. M.'s Bakehouse in Windsor Act 1862 (c.57)
Sale of Horseflesh, etc. Regulation Act 1889 (c.11)
Sale of Land by Auction Act 1867 (c.48)
Sale of Liquors by Retail (Ireland) Act 1807 (c.12)
Sale of Liquors on Sunday Act 1878 (c.72)
Sale of Mill Sites, etc. (Ireland) Act 1863 (c.42)
Sale of Muriate of Potash, etc. Act 1813 (c.97)
Sale of Offices Act 1809 (c.126)
Sale of Post Office Buildings Act 1831 (c.27)
Sale of Prize Ship Constantia Maria Act 1808 (c.147)
Sale of Spirits Act 1862 (c.38)
Sale of Spirits (England) Act 1820 (c.76)
Sale of Spirits, etc. (Ireland) Act 1839 (c.79)
Sale of Spirituous Liquors Act 1805 (c.50)
Sale of Spirituous Liquors, etc. Act 1813 (c.137)
Sale of Tea Act 1922 (c.29)
Sale of Venison (Scotland) Act 1968 (c.38)
Sale of Wine, etc. Act 1801 (c.48)
Sale of Workhouses Act 1821 (c.56)
Sales of Reversions Act 1867 (c.4)
Salmon Act 1696 (c.35)
Salmon Act 1986 (c.62)
Salmon Acts Amendment Act 1863 (c.10)
Salmon Acts Amendment Act 1870 (c.33)
Salmon and Fisheries Act 1965 (c.68)
Salmon and Freshwater Fisheries Act 1886 (c.39)
Salmon and Freshwater Fisheries Act 1892 (c.50)
Salmon and Freshwater Fisheries Act 1907 (c.15)
Salmon and Freshwater Fisheries Act 1921 (c.38)
Salmon and Freshwater Fisheries Act 1923 (c.16)
Salmon and Freshwater Fisheries Act 1923 (Amendment) Act 1964 (c.27)
Salmon and Freshwater Fisheries Act 1935 (c.43)
Salmon and Freshwater Fisheries Act 1972 (c.37)
Salmon and Freshwater Fisheries Act 1975 (c.51)
Salmon and Freshwater Fisheries (Amendment) Act 1929 (c.39)
Salmon and Freshwater Fisheries (Protection) (Scotland) Act 1951 (c.26)
Salmon Fisheries Act 1843 (c.33)
Salmon Fisheries Act 1848 (c.52)
Salmon Fisheries (England) Act 1818 (c.43)
Salmon Fisheries (Scotland) Act 1828 (c.39)
Salmon Fisheries (Scotland) Act 1844 (c.95)
Salmon Fisheries (Scotland) Act 1862 (c.97)
Salmon Fisheries (Scotland) Act 1863 (c.50)
Salmon Fisheries (Scotland) Act 1864 (c.118)
Salmon Fisheries (Scotland) Act 1868 (c.123)
Salmon Fishery Act 1861 (c.109)
Salmon Fishery Act 1865 (c.121)
Salmon Fishery Act 1873 (c.71)
Salmon Fishery Act 1876 (c.19)
Salmon Fishery Commissioners Act 1873 (c.13)
Salmon Fishery (Ireland) Act 1863 (c.114)
Salmon Fishery (Ireland) Act 1869 (c.9)
Salmon Fishery Law Amendment Act 1879 (c.26)

Salop Roads Act 1794 (c.123)
Salop Roads Act 1797 (c.172)
Salop and Hereford Roads Act 1794 (c.122)
Salt Duties Act 1798 (c.89)
Salt Duties Act 1799 (c.77)
Salt Duties Act 1805 (c.14)
Salt Duties Act 1813 (c.22)
Salt Duty Act 1813 (c.124)
Salt Duty Act 1815 (c.179)
Salt Duty Act 1816 (c.94)
Saltcoates Harbour 1797 (c.132)
Saltpetre Act 1800 (c.38)
Sand-Grouse Protection Act 1888 (c.55)
Sandhurst Act 1862 (c.33)
Sanitary Act 1866 (c.90)
Sanitary Act 1868 (c.115)
Sanitary Act 1870 (c.53)
Sanitary Act 1873 (c.78)
Sanitary Act, 1866, Amendment (Ireland) Act 1869 (c.108)
Sanitary Act (Dublin) Amendment Act 1870 (c.106)
Sanitary Inspectors (Change of Designation) Act 1956 (c.66)
Sanitary Law Amendment Act 1874 (c.89)
Sanitary Law (Dublin) Amendment Act 1875 (c.95)
Sanitary Loans Act 1869 (c.100)
Sardinia Loan Act 1855 (c.17)
Sardinian Loan Act 1856 (c.39)
Satisfied Terms Act 1845 (c.112)
Saving Banks Act 1824 (c.62)
Saving Bank Act 1828 (c.92)
Saving Bank Act 1833 (c.14)
Saving Bank Act 1835 (c.57)
Saving Bank Act 1844 (c.83)
Saving Banks Act 1852 (c.60)
Saving Banks Act 1880 (c.36)
Saving Banks Act 1887 (c.40)
Savings Banks Act 1891 (c.21)
Savings Bank Act 1893 (c.69)
Savings Bank Act 1904 (c.8)
Savings Banks Act 1920 (c.12)
Savings Banks Act 1929 (c.27)
Savings Banks Act 1949 (c.13)
Savings Banks and Friendly Societies Act 1854 (c.50)
Savings Banks (Barrister) Act 1876 (c.52)
Savings Bank (Charitable Societies) Act 1859 (c.53)
Savings Bank (England) Act 1817 (c.130)
Savings Bank (England) Act 1818 (c.48)
Savings Bank (England) Act 1820 (c.83)
Savings Bank Investment Act 1863 (c.25)
Savings Bank Investment Act 1866 (c.5)
Savings Bank Investment Act 1869 (c.59)
Savings Bank (Ireland) Act 1817 (c.105)
Savings Bank (Ireland) Act 1848 (c.133)
Savings Bank (Ireland) Act 1850 (c.110)
Savings Banks (Ireland) Act 1859 (c.17)
Savings Banks (Ireland) Cont. Act 1862 (c.75)
Savings Bank (Scotland) Act 1819 (c.62)
School Board Conference Act 1897 (c.32)
School Boards Act 1885 (c.38)
School Boards (Scotland) Act 1988 (c.47)
School Crossing Patrols Act 1953 (c.45)
School Districts Act 1850 (c.11)
School Grants Act 1855 (c.131)
School Inspections Act 1996 (c.57)
School of Physic (Ireland) Amendment Act 1867 (c.9)
School Sites Act 1841 (c.38)
School Sites Act 1844 (c.37)
School Sites Act 1849 (c.49)
School Sites Act 1851 (c.24)
School Sites Act 1852 (c.49)
School Sites (Ireland) Act 1810 (c.32)
School Teachers Pay and Conditions Act 1991 (c.49)
School Teachers (Superannuation) Act 1918 (c.55)
School Teachers (Superannuation) Act 1922 (c.42)
School Teachers (Superannuation) Act 1924 (c.12)
Schools for Science and Art Act 1891 (c.61)
Science and Technology Act 1965 (c.4)
Scientific Societies Act 1843 (c.36)
Scotch and Irish Paupers Act 1840 (c.27)
Scotch and Irish Paupers Removal Act 1844 (c.42)
Scotch Distilleries Act 1797 (c.102)
Scotch Distilleries Act 1798 (c.92)
Scotch Whisky Act 1988 (c.22)
Scotland Act 1978 (c.51)
Scottish Board of Health Act 1919 (c.20)
Scottish Development Agency Act 1975 (c.69)
Scottish Development Agency Act 1987 (c.56)
Scottish Episcopal and other Clergy Act 1840 (c.33)
Scottish Episcopalians Act 1711 (c.10)
Scottish Episcopalians Relief Act 1792 (c.63)
Scottish Fisheries Advisory Council Act 1941 (c.1)
Scottish Land Court Act 1938 (c.31)
Scottish Land Court Act 1993 (c.45)
Scottish Universities (Emergency Powers) Act 1915 (c.78)
Scrabster Harbour Act 1841 (c.1)
Scrap Metal Dealers Act 1964 (c.69)
Sculpture Copyright Act 1814 (c.56)
Sea and Coast Fisheries Fund (Ireland) Act 1884 (c.21)
Sea Birds Preservation Act 1869 (c.17)
Sea Fish (Conservation) Act 1967 (c.84)
Sea Fish (Conservation) Act 1992 (c.60)
Sea Fish Industry Act 1938 (c.30)
Sea Fish Industry Act 1951 (c.30)
Sea Fish Industry Act 1959 (c.7)
Sea Fish Industry Act 1962 (c.31)
Sea Fish Industry Act 1970 (c.11)
Sea Fish Industry Act 1973 (c.3)
Sea Fish Industry Act 1980 (c.35)

Sea Fisheries Act 1817 (c.69)
Sea Fisheries Act 1843 (c.79)
Sea Fisheries Act 1868 (c.45)
Sea Fisheries Act 1875 (c.15)
Sea Fisheries Act 1883 (c.22)
Sea Fisheries Act 1884 (c.27)
Sea Fisheries Act 1967 (c.83)
Sea Fisheries Act 1968 (c.77)
Sea Fisheries (Clam and Bait Beds) Act 1881 (c.11)
Sea Fisheries (Compensation) (Scotland) Act 1959 (c.27)
Sea Fisheries (Ireland) Act 1818 (c.94)
Sea Fisheries (Ireland) Act 1883 (c.26)
Sea Fisheries Regulation Act 1888 (c.54)
Sea Fisheries Regulation Act 1966 (c.38)
Sea Fisheries (Regulation) Expenses Act 1930 (c.41)
Sea Fisheries Regulation (Scotland) Act 1895 (c.42)
Sea Fisheries (Scotland) Act 1810 (c.108)
Sea Fisheries (Scotland) Application of Penalties Act 1907 (c.42)
Sea Fisheries (Scotland) Act 1810 (c.108)
Sea Fisheries (Scotland) Amendment Act 1885 (c.70)
Sea Fisheries (Shellfish) Act 1967 (c.83)
Sea Fisheries (Shellfish) Act 1973 (c.30)
Sea Fisheries (Shellfish) Regulation Act 1894 (c.26)
Sea Fisheries (Wildlife Conservation) Act 1992 (c.36)
Sea Fishing Boats (Scotland) Act 1886 (c.53)
Sea Fishing Industry Act 1933 (c.45)
Sea Insurances (Stamping of Policies) Amendment Act 1876 (c.6)
Seal Fisheries (North Pacific) Act 1895 (c.21)
Seal Fisheries (North Pacific) Act 1912 (c.10)
Seal Fishery Act 1875 (c.18)
Seal Fishery (Behring's Sea) Act 1891 (c.19)
Seal Fishery (North Pacific) Act 1893 (c.23)
Seal Office in Courts of Queen's Bench and Common Pleas Act 1845 (c.34)
Seamen Act 1836 (c.15)
Seamen's and Soldiers' False Characters Act 1906 (c.5)
Seamen's Clothing Act 1869 (c.57)
Seamen's Fund Winding-up Act 1851 (c.102)
Seamen's Hospital Society Act 1832 (c.9)
Seamen's Savings Bank Act 1856 (c.41)
Seats for Shop Assistants Act 1899 (c.21)
Second Session (Explanation) Act 1899 (c.3)
Secret Service Money (Repeal) Act 1886 (c.2)
Secretary at War Abolition Act 1863 (c.12)
Secretary for Scotland Act 1885 (c.61)
Secretary for Scotland Act 1887 (c.52)
Secretary for Scotland Act 1889 (c.16)
Secretary for State 1904 (c.27)
Secretaries of State Act 1926 (c.18)
Securities (Validation) Act 1940 (c.55)
Securities (Validation) Act 1942 (c.10)
Security of Public Officers Act 1812 (c.66)
Security of Rents, Durham Act 1830 (c.11)
Security Service Act 1989 (c.5)
Security Service Act 1996 (c.35)
Seditious Meetings Act 1795 (c.8)
Seditious Meetings Act 1817 (c.19)
Seditious Meetings Act 1846 (c.33)
Seditious Meetings, etc. Act 1819 (c.6)
Seditious Meetings Prevention Act 1801 (c.30)
Seed Potatoes and Seed Oats Supply (Ireland) Act 1908 (c.19)
Seed Potatoes Supply (Ireland) Act 1891 (c.1)
Seed Potatoes Supply (Ireland) Act 1891 (c.7)
Seed Potatoes Supply (Ireland) Act 1895 (c.2)
Seed Potatoes Supply (Ireland) Act 1906 (c.3)
Seed Supply and Potato Spraying (Ireland) Act 1898 (c.50)
Seed Supply (Ireland) Act 1880 (c.1)
Seeds Act 1920 (c.54)
Seeds Amendment Act 1925 (c.66)
Sees of St. Asaph and Bangor Act 1842 (c.112)
Seizure of Arms Act 1819 (c.2)
Seizure of Crops (Ireland) Act 1863 (c.62)
Selective Employment Payments Act 1966 (c.32)
Self-Governing Schools etc. (Scotland) Act 1989 (c.39)
Senior Member of Council, India Act 1860 (c.87)
Senior Public Elementary Schools (Liverpool) Act (c.60)
Sentence of Death (Expectant Mothers) Act 1931 (c.24)
Separatists' Affirmations Act 1833 (c.82)
Sequestration Act 1849 (c.67)
Sequestration Act 1871 (c.45)
Sergeants at Law Act 1825 (c.95)
Servants' Characters Act 1792 (c.56)
Servants' Wages (Ireland) Act 1807 (c.43)
Service of Heirs (Scotland) Act 1847 (c.47)
Service of Process (Justices) Act 1933 (c.42)
Service of Process out of the Jurisdiction (England and Ireland) Act 1832 (c.33)
Service of Process out of the Jurisdiction (England and Ireland) Act 1834 (c.82)
Session Court (Scotland) Act 1810 (c.31)
Session of the Peace, Dublin Act 1843 (c.81)
Sessions Houses, Westminster, etc. Act 1804 (c.61)
Sessions of the Peace, Westminster Act 1828 (c.9)
Settled Estates Act 1840 (c.55)
Settled Estates Act 1856 (c.120)
Settled Estates Act 1858 (c.77)
Settled Estates Act 1876 (c.30)
Settled Estates Act 1877 (c.18)
Settled Estates Act Amendment Act 1864 (c.45)

Settled Land Act 1882 (c.38)
Settled Land Act 1884 (c.18)
Settled Land Act 1889 (c.36)
Settled Land Act 1890 (c.69)
Settled Land Act 1925 (c.18)
Settled Land Acts (Amendment) Act 1887 (c.30)
Settled Land and Trustee Acts (Courts General Powers) Act 1943 (c.25)
Settled Land (Ireland) Act 1847 (c.46)
Settlement of Estate on Lord Nelson Act 1813 (c.134)
Settlement of the Poor (England) Act 1819 (c.50)
Settlements on Coast of Africa and Falkland Islands Act 1843 (c.13)
Severn Bridge Tolls Act 1965 (c.24)
Severn Bridge Act 1992 (c.3)
Sewage Utilisation Act 1865 (c.75)
Sewage Utilisation Act 1867 (c.113)
Sewerage (Scotland) Act 1968 (c.47)
Sewers Act 1833 (c.22)
Sewers Act 1841 (c.45)
Sewers Act 1849 (c.50)
Sex Discrimination Act 1975 (c.65)
Sex Discrimination Act 1986 (c.59)
Sex Disqualification (Removal) Act 1919 (c.71)
Sexual Offences Act 1956 (c.69)
Sexual Offences Act 1967 (c.60)
Sexual Offences Act 1985 (c.44)
Sexual Offences Act 1993 (c.30)
Sexual Offences (Amendment) Act 1976 (c.82)
Sexual Offences (Amendment) Act 1992 (c.34)
Sexual Offences (Conspiracy and Incitement) Act 1996 (c.29)
Sexual Offences (Scotland) Act 1976 (c.67)
Seychelles Act 1976 (c.19)
Shannon Act 1874 (c.60)
Shannon Act 1885 (c.41)
Shannon Navigation Act 1839 (c.61)
Shannon Navigation Act 1847 (c.74)
Sharing of Church Buildings Act 1969 (c.38)
Sheep and Cattle Disease Prevention Act 1850 (c.71)
Sheep, etc. Diseases Act 1851 (c.69)
Sheep, etc. Disorders Prevention Act 1852 (c.11)
Sheep Stealers (Ireland) Act 1849 (c.30)
Sheep Stocks Valuation (Scotland) Act 1937 (c.34)
Sheffield University Act 1914 (c.4)
Sheriff and Sheriff Clerk of Chancery (Scotland) Act 1854 (c.72)
Sheriff Court Houses Act 1860 (c.79)
Sheriff Court Houses (Scotland) Act 1866 (c.53)
Sheriff Court Houses (Scotland) Amendment Act 1884 (c.42)
Sheriff Courts and Legal Officers (Scotland) Act 1927 (c.35)
Sheriff Courts (Civil Jurisdiction and Procedure) (Scotland) Act 1963 (c.22)
Sheriff Courts Consignations (Scotland) Act 1893 (c.44)
Sheriff Courts (Scotland) Act 1825 (c.23)
Sheriff Courts (Scotland) Act 1838 (c.119)
Sheriff Courts (Scotland) Act 1853 (c.80)
Sheriff Courts (Scotland) Act 1870 (c.86)
Sheriff Courts (Scotland) Act 1876 (c.70)
Sheriff Courts (Scotland) Act 1877 (c.50)
Sheriff Courts (Scotland) Act 1907 (c.51)
Sheriff Courts (Scotland) Act 1913 (c.28)
Sheriff Courts (Scotland) Act 1939 (c.98)
Sheriff Courts (Scotland) Act 1971 (c.58)
Sheriff Courts (Scotland) Amendment 1914 (c.5)
Sheriff Courts (Scotland) Extracts Act 1892 (c.17)
Sheriff Deputies, etc. Act 1799 (c.66)
Sheriff of Lanarkshire Act 1887 (c.41)
Sheriff of Selkirkshire Act 1832 (c.101)
Sheriff of Westmoreland Act 1849 (c.42)
Sheriff of Westmoreland Act 1850 (c.30)
Sheriff Substitute (Scotland) Act 1875 (c.81)
Sheriffs Act 1817 (c.68)
Sheriffs Act 1887 (c.55)
Sheriffs Fees Act 1837 (c.55)
Sheriffs (Ireland) Act 1835 (c.55)
Sheriffs (Ireland) Act 1920 (c.26)
Sheriffs of Edinburgh and Lanark Act 1822 (c.49)
Sheriffs' Pension (Scotland) Act 1961 (c.42)
Sheriffs (Scotland) Act 1853 (c.92)
Sheriff's Substitute Act 1864 (c.106)
Sheriff's Tenure of Office (Scotland) Act 1898 (c.8)
Sheriffs, Wales Act 1845 (c.11)
Sherwood Forest Act 1818 (c.100)
Shipbuilding Act 1979 (c.59)
Shipbuilding Act 1982 (c.4)
Shipbuilding Act 1985 (c.14)
Shipbuilding Credit Act 1964 (c.7)
Shipbuilding Industry Act 1967 (c.40)
Shipbuilding Industry Act 1968 (c.6)
Shipbuilding Industry Act 1971 (c.46)
Shipbuilding (Redundancy Payments) Act 1978 (c.11)
Shipowners' Liability for Losses by Fire Act 1836 (c.61)
Shipowners' Negligence (Remedies) Act 1904 (c.10)
Shipping Act 1795 (c.80)
Shipping Act 1799 (c.32)
Shipping Act 1816 (c.114)
Shipping and Trading Interests (Protection) Act 1995 (c.22)
Shipping Casualties Investigations Act 1879 (c.72)
Shipping Dues Exemption Act 1867 (c.15)
Shipping Dues Exemption Act Amendment Act 1869 (c.52)
Shipping Duties Exemption Act 1870 (c.50)
Shipping, etc. Act 1845 (c.88)

Shipping Offences Act 1793 (c.67)
Shipping under Treaties of Commerce Act 1826 (c.5)
Ships and Aircraft (Transfer Restriction) Act 1939 (c.70)
Shoeburyness Artillery Rangers Act 1862 (c.36)
Shooting Hares (Scotland) Act 1808 (c.94)
Shop Clubs Act 1902 (c.21)
Shop Hours Act 1892 (c.62)
Shop Hours Act 1893 (c.67)
Shop Hours Act 1895 (c.5)
Shop Hours Act 1904 (c.31)
Shop Hours Regulation Act 1886 (c.55)
Shops Act 1911 (c.54)
Shops Act 1912 (c.3)
Shops Act 1913 (c.24)
Shops Act 1934 (c.42)
Shops Act 1936 (c.28)
Shops Act 1950 (c.28)
Shops (Airports) Act 1962 (c.35)
Shops (Early Closing) Act 1920 (c.58)
Shops (Early Closing) Act (1920) Amendment Act 1921 (c.60)
Shops (Early Closing Days) Act 1965 (c.35)
Shops (Hours of Closing) Act 1928 (c.33)
Shops (Sunday Trading Restrictions) Act 1936 (c.53)
Shorncliffe Military Canal, etc. Act 1807 (c.70)
Short Titles Act 1892 (c.10)
Short Titles Act 1896 (c.14)
Shrewsbury and Holyhead Road Act 1845 (c.73)
Shrewsbury Improvement Act 1756 (c.78)
Shrewsbury to Bangor Road Act 1835 (c.21)
Shrewsbury to Holyhead Act 1819 (c.30)
Shubenaccasie Canal, Nova Scotia Act 1830 (c.34)
Siam and Straits Settlement Jurisdiction Act 1870 (c.55)
Sierra Leone Act 1853 (c.86)
Sierra Leone Company Act 1807 (c.44)
Sierra Leone Independence Act 1961 (c.16)
Sierra Leone Offences Act 1861 (c.31)
Sierra Leone Republic Act 1972 (c.1)
Sikes' Hydrometer Act 1816 (c.140)
Silk, etc. Bounties Act 1821 (c.91)
Silk Duties Act 1828 (c.23)
Silk Manufacture Act 1811 (c.7)
Silk Manufacture, etc. Act 1821 (c.11)
Silk Manufacture (Ireland) Act 1810 (c.27)
Silk Manufactures Act 1809 (c.20)
Silk Manufactures Act 1824 (c.21)
Silk Manufactures Act 1824 (c.66)
Silk Weavers Act 1845 (c.128)
Silver Coin Act 1798 (c.59)
Silver Plate Act 1790 (c.31)
Simony Act 1588 (c.6)
Singapore Act 1966 (c.29)
Sinking Fund Act 1875 (c.45)
Sir H. Pottinger's Annuity Act 1845 (c.49)
Sir J. Soane's Museum Act 1862 (c.9)
Sir John Port's Charity, Repton Act 1867 (c.99)
Sir R. Hitcham's Charity Act 1863 (c.58)
Site for Docks, etc. Dublin Act 1819 (c.82)
Site for Record Office (Ireland) Act 1826 (c.13)
Sites for Schoolrooms Act 1836 (c.70)
Sites of Parish Churches (Ireland) Act 1813 (c.66)
Six Clerks in Chancery (Ireland) Act 1813 (c.129)
Slander of Women Act 1891 (c.51)
Slate Mines (Gunpowder) Act 1882 (c.3)
Slaughter of Animals Act 1914 (c.75)
Slaughter of Animals Act 1933 (c.39)
Slaughter of Animals Act 1958 (c.8)
Slaughter of Animals (Amendment) Act 1951 (c.49)
Slaughter of Animals (Amendment) Act 1954 (c.59)
Slaughter of Animals (Pigs) Act 1953 (c.27)
Slaughter of Animals (Scotland) Act 1928 (c.29)
Slaughter of Animals (Scotland) Act 1949 (c.52)
Slaughter of Animals (Scotland) Act 1980 (c.13)
Slaughter of Poultry Act 1967 (c.24)
Slaughterhouses Act 1954 (c.42)
Slaughterhouses Act 1958 (c.70)
Slaughterhouses Act 1974 (c.3)
Slaughterhouses etc. (Metropolis) Act 1874 (c.67)
Slave Trade Act 1795 (c.90)
Slave Trade Act 1797 (c.104)
Slave Trade Act 1797 (c.118)
Slave Trade Act 1798 (c.88)
Slave Trade Act 1799 (c.80)
Slave Trade Act 1806 (c.52)
Slave Trade Act 1806 (c.119)
Slave Trade Act 1811 (c.23)
Slave Trade Act 1813 (c.112)
Slave Trade Act 1814 (c.59)
Slave Trade Act 1818 (c.36)
Slave Trade Act 1818 (c.49)
Slave Trade Act 1818 (c.85)
Slave Trade Act 1818 (c.98)
Slave Trade Act 1819 (c.97)
Slave Trade Act 1824 (c.17)
Slave Trade Act 1824 (c.113)
Slave Trade Act 1828 (c.84)
Slave Trade Act 1833 (c.72)
Slave Trade Act 1835 (cc.60, 61)
Slave Trade Act 1836 (c.81)
Slave Trade Act 1837 (c.62)
Slave Trade Act 1843 (c.46)
Slave Trade Act 1843 (c.98)
Slave Trade Act 1844 (c.26)
Slave Trade Act 1848 (c.116)
Slave Trade Act 1849 (c.84)
Slave Trade Act 1873 (c.88)
Slave Trade Act 1876 (c.46)
Slave Trade, Brazil Act 1845 (c.122)

Slave Trade Convention with Brazil Act 1827 (c.74)
Slave Trade (East African Courts) Act 1873 (c.59)
Slave Trade (East African Courts) Act 1879 (c.38)
Slave Trade Jurisdiction (Zanzibar) Act 1869 (c.75)
Slave Trade (Muscat) Act 1848 (c.128)
Slave Trade Suppression Act 1838 (c.47)
Slave Trade Suppression Act 1838 (c.102)
Slave Trade Suppression Act 1839 (c.57)
Slave Trade Suppression Act 1839 (c.73)
Slave Trade Suppression Act 1840 (c.64)
Slave Trade Suppression Act 1842 (c.42)
Slave Trade Suppression Act 1842 (c.59)
Slave Trade Suppression Act 1842 (c.91)
Slave Trade Suppression Act 1842 (c.101)
Slave Trade Suppression Act 1842 (c.114)
Slave Trade Suppression, African Treaty Act 1855 (c.85)
Slave Trade Suppression, Netherlands Act 1819 (c.16)
Slave Trade Suppression, Portugal Act 1819 (c.17)
Slave Trade Suppression Treaties with Sohar and New Grenada Act 1853 (cc.16, 17)
Slave Trade Suppression Treaty with Spain Act 1836 (c.6)
Slave Trade Suppression Treaty with Venezuela Act 1840 (c.67)
Slave Trade Treaties Act 1838 (cc.39–41)
Slave Trade Treaties Act 1838 (cc.83, 84)
Slave Trade Treaties Act 1843 (cc.50–53)
Slave Trade Treaties with Bolivia, Texas, Uruguay Act 1843 (cc.14-16)
Slave Trade, Treaty with Sweden Act 1827 (c.54)
Slavery Abolition Act 1833 (c.73)
Sligo and Cashel Disfranchisement Act 1870 (c.38)
Slough Roads Act 1796 (c.140)
Slum Clearance (Compensation) Act 1956 (c.57)
Small Debt Amendment (Scotland) Act 1889 (c.26)
Small Debt (Scotland) Act 1837 (c.41)
Small Debt (Scotland) Act 1924 (c.16)
Small Debt (Scotland) Act 1932 (c.38)
Small Debts Act 1795 (c.123)
Small Debts Act 1845 (c.127)
Small Debts Recovery (Ireland) Act 1837 (c.43)
Small Debts (Scotland) Act 1800 (c.46)
Small Debts (Scotland) Act 1825 (c.24)
Small Debts (Scotland) Act 1829 (c.55)
Small Dwellings Acquisition Act 1899 (c.44)
Small Estates (Representation) Act 1961 (c.37)
Small Holdings Act 1892 (c.31)
Small Holdings Act 1910 (c.34)
Small Holdings and Allotments Act 1907 (c.54)
Small Holdings and Allotments Act 1908 (c.36)
Small Holdings and Allotments Act 1926 (c.52)
Small Holding Colonies Act 1916 (c.38)
Small Holding Colonies (Amendment) Act 1918 (c.26)
Small Landholders and Agricultural Holdings (Scotland) Act 1931 (c.44)
Small Landholders (Scotland) Act 1911 (c.49)
Small Livings Act 1806 (c.60)
Small Lotteries and Gaming Act 1956 (c.45)
Small Lotteries and Gaming Act 1959 (c.35)
Small Penalties Act 1865 (c.127)
Small Penalties (Ireland) Act 1873 (c.82)
Small Tenements Recovery Act 1838 (c.74)
Small Testate Estates (Scotland) Act 1876 (c.24)
Smithfield Market Act 1851 (c.61)
Smoke Abatement, London Act 1853 (c.128)
Smoke Abatement, London Act 1856 (c.107)
Smoke Detectors Act 1991 (c.37)
Smoke Nuisance (Scotland) Act 1857 (c.73)
Smoke Nuisance (Scotland) Act 1865 (c.102)
Smoke of Furnaces (Scotland) Act 1861 (c.17)
Smugglers' Families Act 1830 (c.10)
Smuggling Act 1795 (c.31)
Smuggling Act 1802 (c.82)
Smuggling Act 1803 (c.157)
Smuggling Act 1805 (c.121)
Smuggling Act 1807 (c.66)
Smuggling Act 1819 (c.121)
Smuggling Act 1822 (c.110)
Smuggling Act 1834 (c.13)
Smuggling Customs Regulations etc. Act 1809 (c.62)
Smuggling, etc. Act 1805 (c.99)
Smuggling, etc. Act 1808 (c.84)
Smuggling, etc. Act 1818 (c.76)
Smuggling, etc. Act 1820 (c.43)
Soap Duty Allowances Act 1835 (c.15)
Soap Duties Act 1839 (c.32)
Soap Duties Allowances Act 1842 (c.16)
Soap Duties Allowances Act 1844 (c.51)
Soap Duties Allowances Act 1847 (c.41)
Soap Duties Allowances Act 1849 (c.40)
Soap Duties Allowances Act 1851 (c.59)
Soap Duties Repeal Act 1853 (c.39)
Social Fund (Maternity and Funeral Expenses) Act 1987 (c.7)
Social Security Act 1971 (c.73)
Social Security Act 1973 (c.38)
Social Security Act 1975 (c.14)
Social Security Act 1979 (c.18)
Social Security Act 1980 (c.30)
Social Security Act 1981 (c.33)
Social Security Act 1985 (c.53)
Social Security Act 1986 (c.50)
Social Security Act 1988 (c.7)
Social Security Act 1989 (c.24)
Social Security Act 1990 (c.27)

Social Security Act 1993 (c.3)
Social Security Administration Act 1992 (c.5)
Social Security Administration (Northern Ireland) Act 1992 (c.8)
Social Security Amendment Act 1974 (c.58)
Social Security and Housing Benefits Act 1982 (c.24)
Social Security and Housing Benefits Act 1983 (c.36)
Social Security Benefits Act 1975 (c.11)
Social Security (Consequential Provisions) Act 1975 (c.18)
Social Security (Consequential Provisions) Act 1992 (c.6)
Social Security (Consequential Provisions) (Northern Ireland) Act 1992 (c.9)
Social Security (Contributions) Act 1981 (c.1)
Social Security (Contributions) Act 1982 (c.2)
Social Security (Contributions) Act 1991 (c.42)
Social Security (Contributions) Act 1994 (c.1)
Social Security Contributions and Benefits Act 1992 (c.4)
Social Security Contributions and Benefits (Northern Ireland) Act 1992 (c.7)
Social Security (Incapacity for Work) Act 1994 (c.18)
Social Security (Miscellaneous Provisions) Act 1977 (c.5)
Social Security (Mortgage Interest Payments) Act 1992 (c.33)
Social Security (Northern Ireland) Act 1975 (c.15)
Social Security (No. 2) Act 1980 (c.39)
Social Security (Overpayments) Act 1996 (c.51)
Social Security Pensions Act 1975 (c.60)
Social Services (Northern Ireland Agreement) Act 1949 (c.23)
Social Work (Scotland) Act 1968 (c.49)
Social Work (Scotland) Act 1972 (c.24)
Societies' Borrowing Powers Act 1898 (c.15)
Societies (Miscellaneous Provisions) Act 1940 (c.19)
Societies (Suspension of Meetings) Act 1917 (c.16)
Sodor and Man Act 1838 (c.30)
Solicitor (Ireland) Act 1822 (c.16)
Solicitors Act 1837 (c.56)
Solicitors Act 1843 (c.73)
Solicitors Act 1860 (c.127)
Solicitors Act 1877 (c.25)
Solicitors Act 1888 (c.65)
Solicitors Act 1894 (c.9)
Solicitors Act 1899 (c.4)
Solicitors Act 1906 (c.24)
Solicitors Act 1919 (c.56)
Solicitors Act 1922 (c.57)
Solicitors Act 1928 (c.22)
Solicitors Act 1932 (c.37)
Solicitors Act 1933 (c.24)
Solicitors Act 1934 (c.45)
Solicitors Act 1936 (c.35)
Solicitors Act 1941 (c.46)
Solicitors Act 1950 (c.6)
Solicitors Act 1957 (c.27)
Solicitors Act 1965 (c.31)
Solicitors Act 1974 (c.47)
Solicitors (Amendment) Act 1956 (c.41)
Solicitors (Amendment) Act 1959 (c.42)
Solicitors (Amendment) Act 1974 (c.26)
Solicitors (Articled Clerks) Act 1918 (c.16)
Solicitors (Articled Clerks) Act 1919 (c.27)
Solicitors (Clerks) Act 1839 (c.33)
Solicitors (Clerks) Act 1844 (c.86)
Solicitors (Disciplinary Committee) Act 1939 (c.110)
Solicitors (Emergency Provisions) Act 1940 (c.15)
Solicitors (Examination) Act 1917 (c.43)
Solicitors (Ireland) Act 1821 (c.48)
Solicitors (Ireland) Act 1849 (c.53)
Solicitors (Ireland) Act 1861 (c.68)
Solicitors (Ireland) Act 1898 (c.17)
Solicitors, Public Notaries, etc. Act 1949 (c.21)
Solicitors Remuneration Act 1881 (c.44)
Solicitors (Scotland) Act 1933 (c.21)
Solicitors (Scotland) Act 1958 (c.28)
Solicitors (Scotland) Act 1965 (c.29)
Solicitors (Scotland) Act 1976 (c.6)
Solicitors (Scotland) Act 1980 (c.46)
Solicitors (Scotland) Act 1988 (c.42)
Solitary Confinement Act 1837 (c.90)
Solomon Islands Act 1978 (c.15)
Solvent Abuse (Scotland) Act 1983 (c.33)
Somerset: Canal Act 1796 (c.48)
Somerset House Act 1853 (c.8)
Somerset House Act 1984 (c.21)
Somerset House (King's College Lease) Act 1873 (c.4)
Somersham Rectory Act 1882 (c.81)
Sound Broadcasting Act 1972 (c.31)
Sound Dues Redemption Act 1857 (c.12)
South Africa Act 1877 (c.47)
South Africa Act 1909 (c.9)
South Africa Act 1962 (c.23)
South Africa Act 1995 (c.3)
South African Loans and War Contribution Act 1903 (c.27)
South African Offences Act 1863 (c.35)
South American Loans Guarantee Act 1852 (c.4)
South Australia Act 1834 (c.95)
South Australia Act 1842 (c.61)
South Australia Government Act 1838 (c.60)
South Indian Railway Purchase Act 1890 (c.6)
South Sea Company Act 1807 (c.23)
South Sea Company Act 1815 (c.57)
South Sea Company Act 1820 (c.2)
South Sea Company's Privileges Act 1815 (c.141)
South Sea Trade Act 1821 (c.60)
South Wales Bridges Act 1881 (c.14)
South Wales Highways Act 1860 (c.68)

South Wales Highway Act Amendment Act 1878 (c.34)
South Wales Turnpike Roads Act 1847 (c.72)
South Wales Turnpike Roads Amendment Act 1882 (c.67)
South Wales Turnpike Trusts Amendment Act 1875 (c.35)
Southampton to New Sarum Canal Act 1795 (c.51)
Southampton, Portsmouth and Sheet Bridge Roads Act 1796 (c.135)
Southern Rhodesia Act 1965 (c.76)
Southern Rhodesia Act 1979 (c.52)
Southern Rhodesia (Constitution) Act 1961 (c.2)
Southern Whale Fisheries Act 1795 (c.92)
Southern Whale Fisheries Act 1797 (c.121)
Southern Whale Fisheries Act 1798 (c.57)
Southern Whale Fisheries Act 1808 (c.124)
Southern Whale Fishery Act 1802 (c.18)
Southern Whale Fishery Act 1802 (c.114)
Southern Whale Fishery Act 1803 (c.90)
Southern Whale Fishery Act 1805 (c.96)
Southern Whale Fishery Act 1811 (c.34)
Southern Whale Fishery Act 1812 (c.103)
Southern Whale Fishery Act 1813 (c.111)
Southern Whale Fishery Act 1815 (c.45)
Southern Whale Fishery Act 1819 (c.113)
Spalding Road Act 1795 (c.166)
Special Acts (Extension of Time) Act 1915 (c.72)
Special Areas (Amendment) Act 1937 (c.31)
Special Areas (Development and Improvement) Act 1935 (c.1)
Special Areas Reconstruction (Agreement) Act 1936 (c.19)
Special Commission Act 1888 (c.35)
Special Commission (Belfast Prison) Act 1918 (c.44)
Special Commission (Dardanelles and Mesopotamia) Act 1916 (c.34)
Special Constables Act 1831 (c.41)
Special Constables Act 1835 (c.43)
Special Constables Act 1838 (c.80)
Special Constables Act 1914 (c.61)
Special Constables Act 1923 (c.11)
Special Constables (Ireland) Act 1832 (c.108)
Special Constables (Ireland) Act 1845 (c.46)
Special Constables (Scotland) Act 1914 (c.53)
Special Constables (Scotland) Act 1915 (c.47)
Special Enactments (Extension of Time) Act 1940 (c.16)
Special Juries Act 1898 (c.6)
Special Roads Act 1949 (c.32)
Spencer Perceval's Pensions Act 1813 (c.122)
Spirit, etc. Licences (Ireland) Act 1806 (c.70)
Spirit Licences Act 1799 (c.86)
Spirit of Wine Act 1855 (c.38)
Spirit Trade Act 1814 (c.149)
Spirits Act 1805 (c.39)
Spirits Act 1832 (c.74)
Spirits Act 1860 (c.114)
Spirits Act 1880 (c.24)
Spirits (Ireland) Act 1809 (c.99)
Spirits (Ireland) Act 1815 (c.104)
Spirits (Ireland) Act 1844 (c.82)
Spirits (Ireland) Act 1845 (c.64)
Spirits (Ireland) Act 1849 (c.17)
Spirits (Ireland) Act 1854 (c.89)
Spirits (Ireland) Act 1855 (c.103)
Spirits (Scotland): Spirits (Ireland) Act 1832 (c.29)
Spirits (Strength Ascertainment) Act 1818 (c.28)
Spiritual Duties Act 1839 (c.30)
Spitalfields and Shoreditch New Street Act 1853 (c.52)
Spitalfields Improvements Act 1850 (c.109)
Sporting Events (Control of Alcohol etc.) Act 1985 (c.57)
Sporting Events (Control of Alcohol etc.) (Amendment) Act 1992 (c.57)
Sporting Lands Rating (Scotland) Act 1886 (c.15)
Spray Irrigation (Scotland) Act 1964 (c.90)
Spring Assizes Act 1879 (c.1)
Spring Guns Act 1827 (c.18)
Sri Lanka Republic Act 1972 (c.55)
St. Albans Bribery Commission Act 1851 (c.106)
St. Albans Roads Act 1794 (c.113)
St. Briavels Small Debts Court Act 1842 (c.83)
St. Bride's Church, City Act 1796 (c.35)
St. David's College Act 1824 (c.101)
St. Helena Act 1833 (c.85)
St. John's Church, Hackney Act 1795 (c.70)
St. John's, Newfoundland Act 1820 (c.51)
St. John's, Newfoundland, etc. Act 1811 (c.45)
St. Martin Outwich Church, City Act 1796 (c.103)
St. Mary Magdalen Hospital, Bath Act 1856 (c.45)
St. Mary Somerset's Church, London Act 1868 (c.127)
St. Marylebone: Improvement Act 1795 (c.73)
St. Marylebone Rectory, Purchase of Act 1817 (c.98)
St. Michael, Cornhill: Building Act 1716 (c.5)
St. Pancras: Improvements, etc. Act 1797 (c.80)
St. Paul, Covent Garden: Church Rebuilding Act 1796 (c.65)
St. Vincent and Grenada Constitution Act 1876 (c.47)
Stables at Windsor Castle Act 1839 (c.20)
Stafford Election Act 1833 (c.20)
Stafford Election Act 1836 (c.10)
Stafford Roads Act 1770 (c.113)
Staffordshire Potteries Stipendiary Justice Act 1839 (c.15)

Stage Carriages Act 1832 (c.120)
Stage Coach duties Act 1796 (c.16)
Stage Coaches, etc. Act 1806 (c.136)
Stage Coaches, etc. (Great Britain) Act 1810 (c.48)
Stage Coaches, etc. (Ireland) Act 1810 (c.32)
Stage Coaches (Scotland) Act 1820 (c.4)
Stamford to Greetham Road Act 1795 (c.152)
Stamp Act 1795 (c.30)
Stamp Act 1795 (c.55)
Stamp Act 1795 (c.63)
Stamp Act 1796 (c.19)
Stamp Act 1796 (c.80)
Stamp Act 1797 (c.60)
Stamp Act 1797 (c.90)
Stamp Act 1797 (c.111)
Stamp Act 1797 (c.136)
Stamp Act 1798 (c.56)
Stamp Act 1798 (c.85)
Stamp Act 1799 (c.39)
Stamp Act 1799 (c.92)
Stamp Act 1799 (c.107)
Stamp Act 1804 (c.98)
Stamp Act 1815 (c.184)
Stamp Act 1853 (c.59)
Stamp Act 1854 (c.83)
Stamp Act 1864 (c.90)
Stamp Act 1870 (c.97)
Stamp Act 1891 (c.39)
Stamp Duties Act 1828 (c.49)
Stamp Duties Act 1848 (c.9)
Stamp Duties Act 1850 (c.97)
Stamp Duties Act 1860 (c.111)
Stamp Duties, etc. (Ireland) Act 1812 (c.87)
Stamp Duties (Court of Chancery) (Ireland) Act 1823 (c.78)
Stamp Duties (Ireland) Act 1815 (c.100)
Stamp Duties (Ireland) Act 1826 (c.20)
Stamp Duties in Law Proceedings (Ireland) Act 1821 (c.112)
Stamp Duties (Ireland) Act 1842 (c.82)
Stamp Duties (Ireland) Act 1850 (c.114)
Stamp Duties Management Act 1870 (c.98)
Stamp Duties Management Act 1891 (c.38)
Stamp Duties on Cards and Dice Act 1828 (c.18)
Stamp Duties on Newspapers Act 1836 (c.76)
Stamp Duty Composition (Ireland) Act 1867 (c.89)
Stamp Duty on Certain Leases Act 1870 (c.44)
Stamp Duty (Temporary Provisions) Act 1992 (c.2)
Stamps Act 1800 (c.84)
Stamps Act 1801 (c.58)
Stamps Act 1802 (c.99)
Stamps Act 1803 (c.21)
Stamps Act 1803 (cc.126, 127)
Stamps Act 1810 (c.35)
Stamps Act 1813 (c.108)
Stamps Act 1814 (c.144)
Stamps Act 1815 (c.101)
Stamps Act 1821 (c.55)
Stamps Act 1822 (c.117)
Stamps Act 1824 (c.41)
Stamps Act 1825 (c.41)
Stamps Act 1826 (c.44)
Stamps Act 1832 (c.91)
Stamps Act 1833 (c.23)
Stamps Act 1834 (c.57)
Stamps Act 1838 (c.85)
Stamps Act 1840 (c.79)
Stamps Act 1841 (c.34)
Stamps Act 1843 (c.72)
Stamps Act 1844 (c.21)
Stamps Act 1845 (c.2)
Stamps Act 1849 (c.80)
Stamps Act 1851 (c.18)
Stamps Act 1852 (c.21)
Stamps Act 1856 (c.22)
Stamps Act 1856 (c.81)
Stamps Act 1858 (c.20)
Stamps Act 1858 (c.24)
Stamps Act 1871 (c.4)
Stamps and Excise Act 1836 (c.45)
Stamps and Taxes Act 1835 (c.20)
Stamps, etc. Act 1833 (c.97)
Stamps (Great Britain) Act 1814 (c.133)
Stamps (Ireland) Act 1804 (c.68)
Stamps (Ireland) Act 1805 (c.20)
Stamps (Ireland) Act 1805 (c.51)
Stamps (Ireland) Act 1806 (c.35)
Stamps (Ireland) Act 1806 (c.64)
Stamps (Ireland) Act 1807 (c.50)
Stamps (Ireland) Act 1810 (c.76)
Stamps (Ireland) Act 1812 (c.126)
Stamps (Ireland) Act 1814 (c.118)
Stamps (Ireland) Act 1815 (cc.78, 79)
Stamps (Ireland) Act 1815 (c.80)
Stamps (Ireland) Act 1815 (c.81)
Stamps on Fire Insurances Act 1828 (c.13)
Standards of Weights, Measures and Coinage Act 1866 (c.82)
Stanhope and Wolsingham Rectories Act 1858 (c.58)
Stannaries Act 1836 (c.106)
Stannaries Act 1839 (c.58)
Stannaries Act 1855 (c.32)
Stannaries Act 1869 (c.19)
Stannaries Act 1887 (c.43)
Stannaries Court (Abolition) Act 1896 (c.45)
Stannaries Court of Cornwall Act 1834 (c.42)
Starch and Soap Duties Allowances Act 1822 (c.25)
State Hospitals (Scotland) Act 1994 (c.16)
State Immunity Act 1978 (c.33)
State of Singapore Act 1958 (c.59)
Statement of Rates Act 1919 (c.31)
Statistics of Trade Act 1947 (c.39)
Status of Aliens Act 1914 (c.17)
Statute Duty Act 1804 (c.52)
Statute of Frauds Amendment Act 1828 (c.14)
Statute of Westminster Act 1932 (c.4)
Statute Law (Repeals) Act 1969 (c.52)

Statute Law (Repeals) Act 1971 (c.52)
Statute Law (Repeals) Act 1973 (c.39)
Statute Law (Repeals) Act 1974 (c.22)
Statute Law (Repeals) Act 1975 (c.10)
Statute Law (Repeals) Act 1976 (c.16)
Statute Law (Repeals) Act 1977 (c.18)
Statute Law (Repeals) Act 1978 (c.45)
Statute Law (Repeals) Act 1981 (c.19)
Statute Law (Repeals) Act 1986 (c.12)
Statute Law (Repeals) Act 1989 (c.43)
Statute Law (Repeals) Act 1993 (c.50)
Statute Law (Repeals) Act 1995 (c.44)
Statute Law Revision Act 1861 (c.101)
Statute Law Revision Act 1863 (c.125)
Statute Law Revision Act 1867 (c.59)
Statute Law Revision Act 1870 (c.69)
Statute Law Revision Act 1871 (c.116)
Statute Law Revision Act 1872 (c.63)
Statute Law Revision Act 1873 (c.91)
Statute Law Revision Act 1874 (c.35)
Statute Law Revision Act 1875 (c.66)
Statute Law Revision Act 1878 (c.79)
Statute Law Revision Act 1883 (c.39)
Statute Law Revision Act 1887 (c.59)
Statute Law Revision Act 1888 (c.3)
Statute Law Revision Act 1890 (c.33)
Statute Law Revision Act 1891 (c.67)
Statute Law Revision Act 1892 (c.19)
Statute Law Revision Act 1893 (c.14)
Statute Law Revision Act 1894 (c.56)
Statute Law Revision Act 1898 (c.22)
Statute Law Revision Act 1908 (c.49)
Statute Law Revision Act 1927 (c.42)
Statute Law Revision Act 1948 (c.62)
Statute Law Revision Act 1950 (c.6)
Statute Law Revision Act 1953 (c.5)
Statute Law Revision Act 1958 (c.46)
Statute Law Revision Act 1959 (c.68)
Statute Law Revision Act 1960 (c.56)
Statute Law Revision Act 1963 (c.30)
Statute Law Revision Act 1964 (c.79)
Statute Law Revision Act 1966 (c.5)
Statute Law Revision Act 1969 (c.52)
Statute Law Revision Act 1971 (c.52)
Statute Law Revision and Civil Procedure Act 1881 (c.59)
Statute Law Revision and Civil Procedure Act 1883 (c.49)
Statute Law Revision (Consequential Repeals) Act 1965 (c.55)
Statute Law Revision (Ireland) Act 1872 (c.98)
Statute Law Revision (Ireland) Act 1878 (c.57)
Statute Law Revision (Ireland) Act 1879 (c.24)
Statute Law Revision (Isle of Man) Act 1991 (c.61)
Statute Law Revision (Northern Ireland) Act 1973 (c.55)
Statute Law Revision (Northern Ireland) Act 1976 (c.12)
Statute Law Revision (Northern Ireland) Act 1980 (c.59)
Statute Law Revision (No. 2) Act 1872 (c.97)
Statute Law Revision (No. 2) Act 1874 (c.96)
Statute Law Revision (No. 2) Act 1888 (c.57)
Statute Law Revision (No. 2) Act 1890 (c.51)
Statute Law Revision (No. 2) Act 1893 (c.54)
Statute Law Revision (Scotland) Act 1906 (c.38)
Statute Law Revision (Scotland) Act 1964 (c.80)
Statute Law Revision (Substituted Enactments) Act 1876 (c.20)
Statute of Frauds 1677 (c.3)
Statute of Frauds Amendment Act 1828 (c.14)
Statute of Westminster 1931 (c.4)
Statutes (Definition of Time) Act 1880 (c.9)
Statutory Commissioners Act 1823 (c.35)
Statutory Companies (Redeemable Stock) Act 1915 (c.44)
Statutory Corporations (Financial Provisions) Act 1974 (c.8)
Statutory Corporations (Financial Provisions) Act 1975 (c.55)
Statutory Declarations Act 1835 (c.62)
Statutory Gas Companies (Electricity Supply Powers) Act 1925 (c.44)
Statutory Instruments Act 1946 (c.36)
Statutory Instruments (Production and Sale) Act 1996 (c.54)
Statutory Orders (Special Procedure) Act 1945 (c.18)
Statutory Orders (Special Procedure) Act 1965 (c.43)
Statutory Salaries Act 1937 (c.35)
Statutory Salaries (Restoration) Act 1934 (c.24)
Statutory Sick Pay Act 1991 (c.3)
Statutory Sick Pay Act 1994 (c.2)
Statutory Undertakings (Temporary Increase of Charges) Act 1918 (c.34)
Statutory Water Companies Act 1991 (c.58)
Stealing from Bleaching Grounds (Ireland) Act 1811 (c.39)
Stealing from Gardens Act 1826 (c.69)
Stealing in Shops, etc. Act 1820 (c.117)
Stealing of Linen, etc. Act 1811 (c.41)
Stealing of Records, etc. Act 1824 (c.30)
Stealing Property from Mines Act 1816 (c.73)
Steam Engines Furnaces Act 1821 (c.41)
Steam Navigation Act 1846 (c.100)
Steam Navigation Act 1848 (c.81)
Steam Navigation Act 1851 (c.79)
Steam Trawling (Ireland) Act 1889 (c.74)
Steam Whistles Act 1872 (c.61)
Steeping of Barley Act 1801 (c.31)
Stepney: Improvements, Poor Relief Act 1797 (c.79)
Still-Birth (Definition) Act 1992 (c.29)
Still Licences Act 1846 (c.90)
Stipendiary Curates Act 1813 (c.149)
Stipendiary Magistrate, Manchester Act 1813 (c.72)
Stipendiary Magistrate, Manchester and Salford Act 1854 (c.20)

Stipendiary Magistrate, Staffs Act 1846 (c.65)
Stipendiary Magistrates Act 1858 (c.73)
Stipendiary Magistrates Act 1863 (c.97)
Stipendiary Magistrates Act 1869 (c.34)
Stipendiary Magistrates Jurisdiction (Scotland) Act 1897 (c.48)
Stipendiary Magistrate for Manchester Act 1844 (c.30)
Stirling Roads Act 1794 (c.138)
Stirling, Dumbarton and Perth Roads Act 1794 (c.129)
Stockbridge Roads Act 1797 (c.149)
Stockbrokers (Ireland) Act 1868 (c.31)
Stockbrokers (Ireland) Act 1918 (c.46)
Stock Exchange (Completion of Bargains) Act 1976 (c.47)
Stock Transfer Act 1963 (c.18)
Stock Transfer Act 1982 (c.41)
Stocks, etc. of Lunatics Act 1821 (c.15)
Stoke Poges Hospital Act 1856 (c.111)
Stoke to Newcastle Canal Act 1795 (c.87)
Straits Settlements Act 1866 (c.115)
Straits Settlements and Johore Territorial Waters (Agreement) Act 1928 (c.23)
Straits Settlements (Ecclesiastic) Act 1869 (c.88)
Straits Settlements Offences Act 1874 (c.38)
Straits Settlements (Repeal) Act 1946 (c.37)
Stratified Ironstone Mines (Gunpowder) Act 1881 (c.26)
Stratford and Long Compton Hill Roads Act 1797 (c.152)
Street Betting Act 1906 (c.43)
Street Collections Regulations (Scotland) Act 1915 (c.88)
Street from Coventry Street to Long Acre Act 1841 (c.12)
Street Offences Act 1959 (c.57)
Street Playgrounds Act 1938 (c.37)
Submarine Telegraph Act 1885 (c.49)
Submarine Telegraph Act 1886 (c.3)
Subscriptions to Loan Act 1797 (c.82)
Subscriptions to Loan Act 1847 (c.36)
Substitution of Punishments for Death Act 1841 (c.56)
Succession Duty Act 1853 (c.51)
Succession (Scotland) Act 1964 (c.41)
Succession (Scotland) Act 1973 (c.25)
Succession to the Crown Act 1707 (c.41)
Sudan (Special Payments) Act 1955 (c.11)
Sudbury Bribery Commission Act 1843 (c.97)
Sudbury Disfranchisement Act 1842 (c.52)
Sudbury Disfranchisement Act 1843 (c.11)
Suez Canal (Shares) Act 1876 (c.67)
Suffragan Bishops Act 1898 (c.11)
Suffragans Nomination Act 1888 (c.56)
Sugar Act 1956 (c.48)
Sugar Bounties, etc. Act 1811 (c.13)
Sugar Convention Act 1903 (c.21)
Sugar Duties Act 1828 (c.36)
Sugar Duties Act 1829 (c.39)
Sugar Duties Act 1830 (c.50)
Sugar Duties Act 1831 (c.23)
Sugar Duties Act 1832 (c.22)
Sugar Duties Act 1832 (c.95)
Sugar Duties Act 1834 (c.5)
Sugar Duties Act 1836 (c.26)
Sugar Duties Act 1837 (c.27)
Sugar Duties Act 1838 (c.33)
Sugar Duties Act 1839 (c.21)
Sugar Duties Act 1840 (c.23)
Sugar Duties Act 1840 (c.57)
Sugar Duties Act 1841 (c.29)
Sugar Duties Act 1842 (c.34)
Sugar Duties Act 1843 (c.27)
Sugar Duties Act 1844 (c.28)
Sugar Duties Act 1845 (c.5)
Sugar Duties Act 1846 (c.29)
Sugar Duties Act 1846 (c.41)
Sugar Duties Act 1846 (c.63)
Sugar Duties Act 1848 (c.97)
Sugar Duties Act 1854 (c.30)
Sugar Duties (Ireland) Act 1820 (c.80)
Sugar Duties and Exchequer Bills Act 1835 (c.12)
Sugar, etc. Act 1820 (c.64)
Sugar in Brewing Act 1847 (c.5)
Sugar Industry Act 1942 (c.16)
Sugar Industry (Reorganisation) Act 1936 (c.18)
Suicide Act 1961 (c.60)
Suits Against Spiritual Persons Act 1814 (c.54)
Summary Convictions, etc. Act 1824 (c.18)
Summary Convictions (Ireland) Act 1834 (c.93)
Summary Convictions (Ireland) Act 1849 (c.70)
Summary Jurisdiction Act 1848 (c.43)
Summary Jurisdiction Act 1857 (c.43)
Summary Jurisdiction Act 1863 (c.77)
Summary Jurisdiction Act 1879 (c.49)
Summary Jurisdiction Act 1884 (c.43)
Summary Jurisdiction Act 1899 (c.22)
Summary Jurisdiction (Appeals) Act 1933 (c.38)
Summary Jurisdiction Cinque Ports, etc. Act 1864 (c.80)
Summary Jurisdiction (Ireland) Act 1850 (c.102)
Summary Jurisdiction (Ireland) Act 1851 (c.92)
Summary Jurisdiction (Ireland) Act 1862 (c.50)
Summary Jurisdiction (Ireland) Act 1908 (c.24)
Summary Jurisdiction (Ireland) Act 1918 (c.18)
Summary Jurisdiction (Ireland) Amendment Act 1871 (c.76)
Summary Jurisdiction (Married Women) Act 1895 (c.39)
Summary Jurisdiction over Children (Ireland) Act 1884 (c.19)
Summary Jurisdiction (Process) Act 1881 (c.24)

Summary Jurisdiction (Scotland) Act 1881 (c.33)
Summary Jurisdiction (Scotland) Act 1908 (c.65)
Summary Jurisdiction (Scotland) Act 1909 (c.28)
Summary Jurisdiction (Scotland) Act 1954 (c.48)
Summary Jurisdiction (Separation and Maintenance) Act 1925 (c.51)
Summary Proceedings Act 1822 (c.23)
Summary Procedure (Domestic Proceedings) Act 1937 (c.58)
Summary Procedure on Bills of Exchange Act 1855 (c.67)
Summary Procedure on Bills of Exchange (Ireland) Act 1861 (c.43)
Summary Procedure (Scotland) Act 1864 (c.53)
Summary Prosecutions Appeals (Scotland) Act 1875 (c.62)
Summer Time Act 1916 (c.14)
Summer Time Act 1922 (c.22)
Summer Time Act 1925 (c.64)
Summer Time Act 1947 (c.16)
Summer Time Act 1972 (c.6)
Summons and Process Servers' Fees (Ireland) Act 1919 (c.4)
Sunday and Ragged Schools (Exemption from Rating) Act 1869 (c.40)
Sunday Cinema Act 1972 (c.19)
Sunday Closing (Wales) Act 1881 (c.61)
Sunday Entertainments Act 1932 (c.51)
Sunday Observance Act 1833 (c.31)
Sunday Observation Prosecution Act 1871 (c.87)
Sunday Performances (Temporary Regulation) Act 1931 (c.52)
Sunday Theatre Act 1972 (c.26)
Sunday Trading Act 1994 (c.20)
Sunderland Pilotage Order Confirmation Act 1865 (c.59)
Superannuation Act 1834 (c.24)
Superannuation Act 1859 (c.26)
Superannuation Act 1860 (c.89)
Superannuation Act 1866 (c.68)
Superannuation Act 1872 (c.12)
Superannuation Act 1875 (c.4)
Superannuation Act 1876 (c.53)
Superannuation Act 1881 (c.43)
Superannuation Act 1884 (c.57)
Superannuation Act 1887 (c.67)
Superannuation Act 1892 (c.40)
Superannuation Act 1909 (c.10)
Superannuation Act 1914 (c.86)
Superannuation Act 1935 (c.23)
Superannuation Act 1946 (c.60)
Superannuation Act 1949 (c.44)
Superannuation Act 1950 (c.2)
Superannuatin Act 1957 (c.37)
Superannuation Act 1965 (c.74)
Superannuation Act 1972 (c.11)
Superannuation Allowances Act 1824 (c.104)
Superannuation Act Amendment Act 1834 (c.45)
Superannuation Acts Amendment Act 1873 (c.23)
Superannuation Amendment Act 1965 (c.10)
Superannuation and Other Trust Funds (Validation) Act 1927 (c.41)
Superannuation, etc. Act 1828 (c.79)
Superannuation (Diplomatic Service) Act 1929 (c.11)
Superannuation (Ecclesiastical Commissioners and Queen Anne's Bounty) Act 1914 (c.5)
Superannuation (Ecclesiastical Commissioners and Queen Anne's Bounty) Act 1933 (c.47)
Superannuation (Mercantile Marine Fund Officers) Act 1877 (c.44)
Superannuation (Metropolis) Act 1866 (c.31)
Superannuation (Miscellaneous Provisions) Act 1948 (c.33)
Superannuation (Miscellaneous Provisions) Act 1967 (c.28)
Superannuation Post Office and War Office Act 1876 (c.68)
Superannuation (President of Industrial Court) Act 1954 (c.37)
Superannuation (Prison Officers) Act 1919 (c.67)
Superannuation Schemes (War Service) Act 1940 (c.26)
Superannuation (Various Services) Act 1938 (c.13)
Superannuation (War Department) Act 1890 (c.18)
Superintending Magistrates, etc. (Ireland) Act 1814 (c.13)
Superintending Magistrates, etc. (Ireland) Act 1817 (c.22)
Superior Courts (Officers) Act 1837 (c.30)
Supplemental Customs Consolidation Act 1855 (c.96)
Supplemental War Loan Act 1900 (c.61)
Supplemental War Loan (No. 2) Act 1900 (c.1)
Supplementary Benefits Act 1976 (c.71)
Supplementary Benefit (Amendment) Act 1976 (c.56)
Supplementary Militia Act 1797 (c.18)
Supplementary Militia Act 1797 (c.19)
Supplementary Militia Act 1799 (c.14)
Supplies and Services (Defence Purposes) Act 1951 (c.25)
Supplies and Services (Extended Purpose) Act 1947 (c.55)
Supplies and Services (Translation Powers) Act 1945 (c.10)
Supply Act 1820 (c.10)
Supply Act 1821 (c.4)
Supply Act 1821 (c.7)
Supply Act 1823 (c.6)
Supply Act 1823 (c.21)
Supply Act 1824 (c.3)

Supply Act 1824 (c.42)
Supply Act 1825 (c.1)
Supply Act 1825 (c.14)
Supply Act 1826 (c.1)
Supply Act 1827 (c.16)
Supply Act 1827 (c.42)
Supply Act 1828 (c.1)
Supply Act 1828 (c.10)
Supply Act 1828 (c.19)
Supply Act 1828 (c.28)
Supply Act 1828 (c.30)
Supply Act 1829 (c.3)
Supply Act 1830 (c.1)
Supply Act 1830 (c.2)
Supply Act 1830 (c.4)
Supply Act 1830 (c.28)
Supply Act 1831 (cc.9–10)
Supply Act 1831 (c.28)
Supply Act 1832 (c.1)
Supply Act 1832 (c.6)
Supply Act 1832 (c.30)
Supply Act 1832 (c.55)
Supply Act 1833 (c.18)
Supply Act 1834 (c.2)
Supply Act 1834 (c.12)
Supply Act 1835 (c.3)
Supply Act 1835 (c.9)
Supply Act 1836 (c.1)
Supply Act 1836 (c.18)
Supply Act 1837 (c.6)
Supply Act 1837 (c.11)
Supply Act 1838 (c.11)
Supply Act 1838 (c.21)
Supply Act 1839 (c.2)
Supply Act 1839 (c.6)
Supply Act 1840 (c.4)
Supply Act 1840 (c.7)
Supply Act 1841 (c.4)
Supply Act 1842 (c.8)
Supply Act 1843 (c.5)
Supply Act 1843 (c.87)
Supply Act 1844 (c.6)
Supply Act 1845 (c.1)
Supply Act 1846 (c.7)
Supply Act 1846 (c.47)
Supply Act 1847 (c.8)
Supply Act 1848 (c.4)
Supply Act 1848 (c.33)
Supply Act 1849 (c.3)
Supply Act 1849 (c.44)
Supply Act 1850 (c.3)
Supply Act 1851 (c.3)
Supply Act 1852 (c.1)
Supply Act 1853 (c.12)
Supply Act 1853 (c.31)
Supply Act 1854 (c.2)
Supply Act 1854 (c.21)
Supply Act 1855 (cc.5, 6)
Supply Act 1855 (c.37)
Supply Act 1856 (c.4)
Supply Act 1856 (c.7)
Supply Act 1857 (c.4)
Supply Act 1858 (cc.5, 6)
Supply Act 1858 (c.17)
Supply Act 1859 (cc.6, 7)
Supply Act 1859 (c.2)
Supply Act 1860 (cc.2, 3)
Supply Act 1860 (c.12)
Supply Act 1860 (c.25)
Supply Act 1860 (c.103)
Supply Act 1861 (c.2)
Supply Act 1861 (c.6)
Supply Act 1861 (c.19)
Supply Act 1862 (cc.1, 2)
Supply Act 1862 (c.31)
Supply Act 1863 (c.6)
Supply Act 1863 (c.15)
Supply Act 1864 (cc.5, 6)
Supply Act 1864 (c.11)
Supply Act 1864 (c.73)
Supply Act 1865 (c.4)
Supply Act 1865 (c.10)
Supply Act 1866 (c.6)
Supply Act 1866 (c.13)
Supply Act 1867 (c.4)
Supply Act 1867 (c.7)
Supply Act 1867 (c.30)
Supply Act 1867 (c.1)
Supply Act 1868 (c.10)
Supply Act 1868 (c.13)
Supply Act 1868 (c.16)
Supply Act 1869 (c.1)
Supply Act 1869 (c.8)
Supply Act 1870 (c.5)
Supply Act 1870 (c.31)
Supply Act 1871 (cc.6, 7)
Supply Act 1871 (c.20)
Supply Act 1871 (c.51)
Supply Act 1872 (c.1)
Supply Act 1872 (c.11)
Supply Act 1872 (c.37)
Supply Act 1873 (c.26)
Supply Act 1873 (c.3)
Supply Act 1874 (cc.1, 2)
Supply Act 1874 (c.10)
Supply Act 1875 (cc.1, 2)
Supply Act 1875 (c.10)
Supply Act 1876 (c.2)
Supply Act 1876 (c.4)
Supply Act 1876 (c.15)
Supply Act 1877 (c.1)
Supply Act 1877 (c.6)
Supply Act 1877 (c.12)
Supply Act 1877 (c.24)
Supply Act 1878 (c.1)
Supply Act 1878 (c.9)
Supply Act 1878 (c.21)
Supply Act 1878 (c.45)
Supply, etc., Act 1742 (c.25)
Supply of Goods and Services Act 1982 (c.29)
Supply of Goods (Implied Terms) Act 1973 (c.13)
Supply of Seamen Act 1803 (c.64)
Supply of Water in Bulk Act 1934 (c.15)
Supply Powers Act 1975 (c.9)

Support of Captured Slaves Act 1815 (c.172)
Support of Commercial Credit (Ireland) Act 1820 (c.39)
Support of Commercial Credit (Ireland) Act 1822 (c.22)
Support of Commercial Credit (Ireland) Act 1822 (c.118)
Support of Commercial Credit (Ireland) Act 1823 (c.42)
Suppression of Insurrections (Ireland) Act 1822 (c.1)
Suppression of Insurrections (Ireland) Act 1822 (c.80)
Suppression of Insurrection, etc. (Ireland) Act 1810 (c.78)
Suppression of Rebellion Act 1801 (c.14)
Suppression of Rebellion Act 1801 (c.61)
Suppression of Rebellion Act 1801 (c.104)
Suppression of Rebellion, etc. Act 1803 (c.117)
Suppression of Rebellion, etc. (Ireland) Act 1803 (c.9)
Suppression of Rebellion, etc. (Ireland) Act 1803 (c.117)
Suppression of Terrorism Act 1978 (c.26)
Supreme Court Act 1981 (c.54)
Supreme Court Act (Northern Ireland) 1942 (c.2)
Supreme Court (England) Act 1850 (c.16)
Supreme Court (England) Act 1864 (c.15)
Supreme Court (Ireland) Act 1850 (c.18)
Supreme Court (Ireland) Act 1850 (c.19)
Supreme Court (Ireland) (Master of the Rolls) Act 1815 (c.114)
Supreme Court, Madras Act 1830 (c.75)
Supreme Court (Northern Ireland) Act 1942 (c.2)
Supreme Court of Judicature Act 1873 (c.66)
Supreme Court of Judicature Act 1875 (c.77)
Supreme Court of Judicature Act 1877 (c.9)
Supreme Court of Judicature Act 1881 (c.68)
Supreme Court of Judicature Act 1884 (c.61)
Supreme Court of Judicature Act 1890 (c.44)
Supreme Court of Judicature Act 1891 (c.53)
Supreme Court of Judicature Act 1899 (c.6)
Supreme Court of Judicature Act 1902 (c.31)
Supreme Court of Judicature Act 1910 (c.12)
Supreme Court of Judicature (Amendment) Act 1935 (c.2)
Supreme Court of Judicature (Amendment) Act 1938 (c.67)
Supreme Court of Judicature (Amendment) Act 1944 (c.9)
Supreme Court of Judicature (Amendment) Act 1948 (c.20)
Supreme Court of Judicature (Amendment) Act 1959 (c.39)
Supreme Court of Judicature (Circuit Officers) Act 1946 (c.78)
Supreme Court of Judicature (Commencement) Act 1874 (c.83)
Supreme Court of Judicature (Consolidation) Act 1925 (c.49)
Supreme Court of Judicature (Funds, etc.) Act 1883 (c.29)
Supreme Court of Judicature Act (Ireland) Act 1877 (c.57)
Supreme Court of Judicature (Ireland) Act 1882 (c.70)
Supreme Court of Judicature (Ireland) Act 1887 (c.6)
Supreme Court of Judicature (Ireland) Act 1897 (c.17)
Supreme Court of Judicature (Ireland) Act 1907 (c.44)
Supreme Court of Judicature (Ireland) Act 1877, Amendment Act 1878 (c.27)
Supreme Court of Judicature (Ireland) Amendment Act 1888 (c.27)
Supreme Court of Judicature (Ireland) (No. 2) Act 1897 (c.66)
Supreme Court of Judicature of Northern Ireland 1926 (c.44)
Supreme Court of Judicature (London Causes) Act 1891 (c.14)
Supreme Court of Judicature (Officers) Act 1878 (c.35)
Supreme Court of Judicature (Officers) Act 1879 (c.78)
Supreme Court of Judicature (Procedure) Act 1894 (c.16)
Supreme Court Officers (Pensions) Act 1954 (c.38)
Supreme Court Officers (Retirement, Pensions, etc.) Act 1921 (c.56)
Surrey Act 1856 (c.61)
Surrogacy Arrangements Act 1985 (c.49)
Survey Act 1870 (c.13)
Survey, Great Britain Act 1851 (c.22)
Survey (Great Britain) Continuance Act 1875 (c.32)
Suspension of Certain Appointments Act 1837 (c.71)
Suspensory Act 1914 (c.88)
Swansea Harbour Act 1796 (c.93)
Swaziland Independence Act 1968 (c.56)
Sydney Branch Mint Act 1863 (c.74)

Tancred's Charities 1871 (c.117)
Tanganyika Agricultural Corporation Act 1957 (c.54)
Tanganyika and British Honduras Loans Act 1932 (c.17)
Tanganyika Independence Act 1961 (c.1)
Tanganyika Republic Act 1962 (c.1)
Tanners, Curriers, Shoemakers, etc. Act 1808 (c.60)
Tanners' Indemnity, etc. Act 1799 (c.54)
Taking of Hostages Act 1982 (c.28)
Tanzania Act 1969 (c.29)
Tattooing of Minors Act 1969 (c.24)
Tavistock Canal Act 1796 (c.67)
Taxation Act 1797 (c.16)
Taxation Act 1798 (c.81)
Taxation Act 1801 (c.8)

Taxation Act 1801 (c.10)
Taxation Act 1801 (c.33)
Taxation Act 1801 (c.40)
Taxation Act 1801 (c.42)
Taxation Act 1801 (c.44)
Taxation Act 1801 (c.51)
Taxation Act 1801 (c.62)
Taxation Act 1801 (c.69)
Taxation Act 1801 (c.71)
Taxation Act 1801 (c.74)
Taxation Act 1801 (c.75)
Taxation Act 1805 (c.5)
Taxation Act 1806 (c.84)
Taxation of Chargeable Gains Act 1992 (c.12)
Taxation of Colonies Act 1778 (c.12)
Taxes Act 1797 (c.69)
Taxes Act 1803 (c.99)
Taxes Act 1805 (c.71)
Taxes Act 1810 (c.105)
Taxes Act 1821 (c.113)
Taxes Act 1856 (c.80)
Taxes Management Act 1880 (c.19)
Taxes Management Act 1970 (c.9)
Taxes on Carriages, etc., (Ireland) Act 1809 (c.75)
Taxes (Regulation of Remuneration) Act 1891 (c.13)
Taxes (Regulation of Remuneration) Amendment Act 1892 (c.25)
Taxes (Scotland) Act 1803 (c.150)
Taxes (Scotland) Act 1805 (c.95)
Taxes (Scotland) 1812 (c.95)
Taxes (Scotland) Act 1815 (c.161)
Taxing Masters (Ireland) Act 1848 (c.132)
Taxing Officer (Ireland) Act 1853 (c.55)
Tea Duties Act 1833 (c.101)
Tea Duties Act 1835 (c.32)
Tea Duties Act 1855 (c.9)
Teachers of Nursing Act 1967 (c.16)
Teachers of Schools (Ireland) Act 1844 (c.8)
Teachers' Pay and Conditions Act 1987 (c.1)
Teachers' (Superannuation) Act 1925 (c.59)
Teachers' (Superannuation) Act 1928 (c.10)
Teachers' (Superannuation) Act 1933 (c.22)
Teachers' (Superannuation) Act 1935 (c.35)
Teachers' (Superannuation) Act 1937 (c.47)
Teachers' (Superannuation) Act 1945 (c.14)
Teachers' Superannuation Act 1965 (c.83)
Teachers' Superannuation Act 1967 (c.12)
Teachers' Superannuation (Scotland) Act 1968 (c.12)
Teachers' Superannuation (War Service) Act 1939 (c.95)
Teaching Council (Scotland) Act 1965 (c.19)
Teaching Council (Scotland) Act 1970 (c.2)
Technical and Industrial Institutions Act 1892 (c.29)
Technical Instruction Act 1889 (c.76)
Technical Instruction Act 1891 (c.4)
Technical Instruction Amendment (Scotland) Act 1892 (c.63)
Technical Schools (Scotland) Act 1887 (c.64)
Teinds Act 1808 (c.138)
Teinds Act 1810 (c.84)
Teinds Act 1824 (c.72)
Telecommunications Act 1984 (c.12)
Telegraph Act 1869 (c.73)
Telegraph Act 1870 (c.88)
Telegraph Act 1873 (c.83)
Telegraph Act 1885 (c.58)
Telegraph Act 1954 (c.28)
Telegraph Act 1863 (c.112)
Telegraph Act 1868 (c.110)
Telegraph Act 1878 (c.76)
Telegraph Act 1892 (c.59)
Telegraph Act 1899 (c.38)
Telegraph Act 1943 (c.26)
Telegraph Act 1949 (c.80)
Telegraph Act 1951 (c.37)
Telegraph Act 1962 (c.14)
Telegraph Act Amendment Act 1866 (c.3)
Telegraph (Arbitration) Act 1909 (c.20)
Telegraph (Construction) Act 1908 (c.33)
Telegraph (Construction) Act 1911 (c.39)
Telegraph (Construction) Act 1916 (c.40)
Telegraph (Isle of Man) Act 1889 (c.34)
Telegraph (Money) Act 1871 (c.75)
Telegraph (Money) Act 1876 (c.5)
Telegraph (Money) Act 1896 (c.40)
Telegraph (Money) Act 1898 (c.33)
Telegraph (Money) Act 1904 (c.3)
Telegraph (Money) Act 1907 (c.6)
Telegraph (Money) Act 1913 (c.24)
Telegraph (Money) Act 1920 (c.37)
Telegraph (Money) Act 1921 (c.57)
Telegraph (Money) Act 1922 (c.45)
Telegraph (Money) Act 1924 (c.25)
Telegraph (Money) Act 1925 (c.65)
Telegraphs (Money) Act 1877 (c.30)
Telephone Act 1951 (c.52)
Telephone Transfer Act 1911 (c.26)
Telephone Transfer Amendment Act 1911 (c.56)
Television Act 1954 (c.55)
Television Act 1963 (c.50)
Television Act 1964 (c.21)
Temperance (Scotland) Act 1913 (c.33)
Temple Balsall Hospital Act 1861 (c.24)
Temple Bar, etc. Act 1795 (c.126)
Temporary Migration of Children (Guardianship) Act 1941 (c.23)
Temporary Removal of Convicts Act 1823 (c.82)
Tenancy of Shops (Scotland) Act 1949 (c.25)
Tenancy of Shops (Scotland) Act 1964 (c.50)
Tenants Compensation 1890 (c.57)
Tenants' Rights, etc. (Scotland) Act 1980 (c.52)
Tenants' Rights, etc. (Scotland) Amendment Act 1980 (c.61)
Tenants' Rights, etc. (Scotland) Amendment Act 1984 (c.18)
Tension's Charity Act 1860 (c.43)
Tenures Abolition Act 1660 (c.24)
Term and Quarter Days (Scotland) Act 1990 (c.22)

Termination of the Present War (Definition) Act 1918 (c.59)
Terms and Conditions of Employment Act 1959 (c.26)
Territorial and Reserve Forces Act 1907 (c.9)
Territorial Army and Militia Act 1921 (c.37)
Territorial Sea Act 1987 (c.49)
Territorial Waters Jurisdiction Act 1878 (c.73)
Test Abolition Act 1867 (c.62)
Textile Manufacturers (Ireland) Act 1840 (c.91)
Textile Manufacturers (Ireland) Act 1842 (c.68)
Textile Manufacturers (Ireland) Act 1867 (c.60)
Thames: Ballastage Act 1795 (c.84)
Thames and Isis, Navigation Act 1771 (c.45)
Thames and Severn Canal Act 1796 (c.34)
Thames Conservancy Act 1864 (c.113)
Thames Embankment Act 1852 (c.71)
Thames Embankment Act 1853 (c.87)
Thames Embankment Act 1862 (c.93)
Thames Embankment Act 1863 (c.75)
Thames Embankment Act 1873 (c.40)
Thames Embankment, etc. (Loans) Act 1864 (c.61)
Thames Embankment, etc. (Loans) Act 1868 (c.43)
Thames Navigation Act 1866 (c.89)
Thames Preservation Act 1885 (c.76)
Thatched House Court and Little St. James's Street, Westminster Act 1843 (c.19)
The Chest at Chatham Act 1803 (c.119)
Theatres Act 1843 (c.68)
Theatres Act 1968 (c.54)
Theatres Trust Act 1976 (c.27)
Theatres Trust (Scotland) Act 1978 (c.24)
Theatrical Employers Act 1928 (c.46)
Theatrical Employers Registration Act 1925 (c.50)
Theatrical Employers Registration (Amendment) Act 1928 (c.46)
Theft Act 1968 (c.60)
Theft Act 1978 (c.31)
Theft (Amendment) Act 1996 (c.62)
Theft of Turnips, etc. Act 1802 (c.67)
Therapeutic Substances Act 1925 (c.60)
Therapeutic Substances Act 1953 (c.32)
Therapeutic Substances Act 1956 (c.25)
Thermal Insulation (Industrial Buildings) Act 1957 (c.40)
Third Parties (Rights against Insurers) Act 1930 (c.25)
Thirlage Act 1799 (c.55)
Thirsk Roads Act 1794 (c.118)
Thomas Macklin's Paintings Act 1797 (c.133)
Thread Lace Manufacture (England) Act 1806 (c.81)
Threatening Letters Act 1825 (c.19)
Threatening Letters, etc. Act 1847 (c.66)
Threshing Machines Act 1878 (c.12)
Threshing Machines, Remedies for Damage Act 1832 (c.72)
Timber (Ireland) Act 1888 (c.37)
Timber Ships Act 1845 (c.45)
Timber Ships, America Act 1842 (c.17)
Timber Ships, British North America Act 1839 (c.44)
Timber Ships, British North America Act 1840 (c.36)
Time (Ireland) Act 1916 (c.45)
Time of Service in the Army Act 1847 (c.37)
Timeshare Act 1992 (c.35)
Tithe Act 1832 (c.100)
Tithe Act 1836 (c.71)
Tithe Act 1837 (c.69)
Tithe Act 1838 (c.64)
Tithe Act 1839 (c.62)
Tithe Act 1840 (c.15)
Tithe Act 1842 (c.54)
Tithe Act 1846 (c.73)
Tithe Act 1847 (c.104)
Tithe Act 1860 (c.93)
Tithe Act 1878 (c.42)
Tithe Act 1891 (c.8)
Tithe Act 1918 (c.54)
Tithe Act 1925 (c.87)
Tithe Act 1936 (c.43)
Tithe Act 1951 (c.62)
Tithe Annuities Apportionment Act 1921 (c.20)
Tithe Arrears Act 1839 (c.3)
Tithe Commutation Acts Amendment Act 1873 (c.42)
Tithe Composition Act 1837 (c.58)
Tithe Compositions (Ireland) Act 1836 (c.95)
Tithe Compositions (Ireland) Act 1841 (c.37)
Tithe Compositions (Ireland) Act 1841 (c.6)
Tithe (Ireland) Act 1840 (c.13)
Tithe Rentcharge (Ireland) Act 1838 (c.109)
Tithe Rentcharge (Ireland) Act 1848 (c.80)
Tithe Rentcharge (Ireland) Act 1900 (c.58)
Tithe Rentcharge (Rates) Act 1899 (c.17)
Tithe Rentcharge Redemption Act 1885 (c.32)
Tithes Act 1841 (c.36)
Tithes Prescription Act 1834 (c.83)
Tithes Rating Act 1851 (c.50)
Title Act 1846 (c.73)
Title Act 1925 (c.87)
Title Act 1936 (c.43)
Title Act 1951 (c.62)
Tin Duties Act 1838 (c.120)
Titles Deprivation Act 1917 (c.47)
Titles to Land Consolidation (Scotland) Act 1868 (c.101)
Titles to Land Consolidation (Scotland) Amendment Act 1869 (c.116)
Titles to Land (Scotland) Act 1858 (c.76)
Titles to Land (Scotland) Act 1860 (c.143)
Tobacco Act 1840 (c.18)
Tobacco Act 1842 (c.93)
Tobacco Cultivation Act 1831 (c.13)
Tobacco Growing (Scotland) Act 1908 (c.10)
Tobacco Products Duty Act 1979 (c.7)
Tokens Act 1812 (c.157)

Tokens Act 1813 (c.4)
Tokens Act 1817 (c.46)
Tokens Act 1817 (c.113)
Tokens Act 1825 (c.98)
Tokyo Convention Act 1967 (c.52)
Tolls for Certain Carriages Act 1813 (c.82)
Tolls (Ireland) Act 1817 (c.108)
Tonga Act 1970 (c.22)
Tonnage Duties Act 1822 (c.48)
Tonnage, etc. of Ships Act 1835 (c.56)
Tonnage Rates (Port of London) Act 1834 (c.32)
Tonnage of Steam Vessels Act 1819 (c.5)
Tortola Trade Act 1802 (c.102)
Tortola Trade, etc. Act 1803 (c.133)
Tortola Trade Act 1806 (c.72)
Torts (Interference with Goods) Act 1977 (c.32)
Tourism (Overseas Promotion) (Scotland) Act 1984 (c.4)
Tourism (Overseas Promotion) (Wales) Act 1992 (c.26)
Towcaser to Hardington Road Act 1795 (c.153)
Tower Burial Ground Act 1811 (c.116)
Tower Hamlets Militia Act 1797 (c.75)
Town and Country Amenities Act 1974 (c.32)
Town and Country Planning Act 1932 (c.48)
Town and Country Planning Act 1943 (c.5)
Town and Country Planning Act 1944 (c.47)
Town and Country Planning Act 1947 (c.51)
Town and Country Planning Act 1953 (c.16)
Town and Country Planning Act 1954 (c.72)
Town and Country Planning Act 1959 (c.53)
Town and Country Planning Act 1962 (c.38)
Town and Country Planning Act 1963 (c.17)
Town and Country Planning Act 1968 (c.72)
Town and Country Planning Act 1969 (c.30)
Town and Country Planning Act 1971 (c.78)
Town and Country Planning Act 1984 (c.10)
Town and Country Planning Act 1990 (c.8)
Town and Country Planning (Amendment) Act 1951 (c.19)
Town and Country Planning (Amendment) Act 1972 (c.42)
Town and Country Planning (Amendment) Act 1977 (c.29)
Town and Country Planning (Amendment) Act 1985 (c.52)
Town and Country Planning (Compensation) Act 1985 (c.19)
Town and Country Planning (Costs of Inquiries etc.) Act 1995 (c.49)
Town and Country Planning (Interim Development) Act 1943 (c.29)
Town and Country Planning (Interim Development) (Scotland) Act 1943 (c.43)
Town and Country Planning (Minerals) Act 1981 (c.36)
Town and Country Planning Regulations (London) (Indemnity) Act 1970 (c.57)
Town and Country Planning (Scotland) Act 1932 (c.49)
Town and Country Planning (Scotland) Act 1945 (c.33)
Town and Country Planning (Scotland) Act 1947 (c.53)
Town and Country Planning (Scotland) Act 1954 (c.73)
Town and Country Planning (Scotland) Act 1959 (c.70)
Town and Country Planning (Scotland) Act 1972 (c.52)
Town and Country Planning (Scotland) Act 1977 (c.10)
Town and Country (Scotland) Act 1969 (c.30)
Town Council and Local Bds. Act 1880 (c.17)
Town Councils (Scotland) Act 1900 (c.49)
Town Councils (Scotland) Act 1903 (c.34)
Town Councils (Scotland) Act 1923 (c.41)
Town Development Act 1952 (c.54)
Town Gardens Protection Act 1863 (c.13)
Town Planning Act 1925 (c.16)
Town Planning (Scotland) Act 1925 (c.17)
Town Police Clauses Act 1847 (c.89)
Town Police Clauses Act 1889 (c.14)
Town Tenants (Ireland) Act 1906 (c.54)
Towns Improvements Clauses Act 1847 (c.34)
Towns Improvement (Ireland) Act 1854 (c.103)
Towyn Trewan Common Act 1963 (c.4)
Trade Act 1807 (c.38)
Trade Act 1814 (c.72)
Trade Act 1822 (cc.44,45)
Trade, America, etc. Act 1817 (c.29)
Trade, American Colonies and West Indies Act 1823 (c.2)
Trade Between Bermuda and America Act 1817 (c.28)
Trade Between Great Britain and Ireland Act 1802 (c.14)
Trade Between Great Britain and Ireland Act 1803 (c.78)
Trade Between Europe and British America Act 1809 (c.47)
Trade Between Ireland and East Indies Act 1808 (c.30)
Trade Boards Act 1909 (c.22)
Trade Boards Act 1918 (c.32)
Trade Boards and Road Haulage Wages (Emergency Provisions) Act 1940 (c.7)
Trade Descriptions Act 1968 (c.29)
Trade Descriptions Act 1972 (c.34)
Trade Disputes Act 1906 (c.47)
Trade Disputes Act 1965 (c.48)
Trade Disputes and Trade Unions Act 1927 (c.22)
Trade Disputes and Trade Unions Act 1946 (c.52)
Trade During Hostilities Act 1803 (c.57)
Trade, East Indies and Mediterranean Act 1817 (c.36)
Trade, Europe and American Colonies Act 1811 (c.97)
Trade Facilities Act 1921 (c.65)

Trade Facilities Act 1924 (c.8)
Trade Facilities Act 1925 (c.13)
Trade Facilities Act 1926 (c.3)
Trade Facilities and Loans Guarantee Act 1922 (c.4)
Trade in Grain, etc. Act 1802 (c.35)
Trade in Spirits Act 1815 (c.132)
Trade in Spirits Act 1816 (c.105)
Trade in Spirits Act 1817 (c.72)
Trade in Spirits Act 1818 (c.26)
Trade in Spirits Act 1819 (c.75)
Trade in Spirits Act 1820 (c.77)
Trade Marks Act 1904 (c.15)
Trade Marks Act 1905 (c.15)
Trade Marks Act 1914 (c.16)
Trade Marks Act 1919 (c.79)
Trade Marks Act 1938 (c.22)
Trade Marks Act 1994 (c.26)
Trade Marks (Amendment) Act 1937 (c.49)
Trade Marks (Amendment) Act 1984 (c.19)
Trade Marks Registration Act 1875 (c.91)
Trade Marks Registration Amendment Act 1876 (c.33)
Trade Marks, Registration etc. Act 1877 (c.37)
Trade of British Possessions Act 1845 (c.93)
Trade of Canada Act 1812 (c.55)
Trade of Demerara, etc. Act 1816 (c.91)
Trade of Malta, etc. Act 1814 (c.182)
Trade of Malta, Act 1815 (c.29)
Trade of Nova Scotia, etc. Act 1809 (c.49)
Trade of West Indies Act 1812 (c.100)
Trade of West Indies Act 1814 (c.48)
Trade of West Indies, etc. Act 1814 (c.49)
Trade to the Levant Sea Act 1799 (c.99)
Trade Union Act 1871 (c.31)
Trade Union Act Amendment Act 1876 (c.22)
Trade Union Act 1913 (c.30)
Trade Union Act 1984 (c.49)
Trade Union (Amalgamation) Act 1917 (c.24)
Trade Union (Amalgamations, etc.) Act 1964 (c.24)
Trade Union and Labour Relations Act 1974 (c.52)
Trade Union and Labour Relations (Amendment) Act 1976 (c.7)
Trade Union and Labour Relations (Consolidation) Act 1992 (c.52)
Trade Union Commissions Act 1967 (c.8)
Trade Union Commissions Act Extension 1867 (c.74)
Trade Union (Provident Funds) Act 1893 (c.2)
Trade Union Funds Protection Act 1869 (c.61)
Trade Union Reform and Employment Rights Act 1993 (c.19)
Trade with America Act 1795 (c.26)
Trade with America Act 1796 (c.58)
Trade with America Act 1801 (c.95)
Trade with America Act 1808 (c.85)
Trade with British Possession Act 1831 (c.24)
Trade with French Colonies Act 1815 (c.146)
Trade with India Act 1797 (c.117)
Trade with New South Wales Act 1819 (c.122)
Trade with South America Act 1808 (c.109)
Trade with United States Act 1797 (c.37)
Trade with United States Act 1809 (c.59)
Trade with United States Act 1815 (c.193)
Trade of Tanners and Curriers Act 1816 (c.110)
Trading Partnerships Act 1841 (c.14)
Trading Representations (Disabled Persons) Act 1958 (c.49)
Trading Representations (Disabled Persons) Amendment Act 1972 (c.45)
Trading Schemes Act 1996 (c.32)
Trading Stamps Act 1964 (c.71)
Trading with the Enemy Act 1914 (c.87)
Trading with the Enemy Act 1939 (c.89)
Trading with the Enemy Amendment Act 1914 (c.12)
Trading with the Enemy Amendment Act 1915 (c.79)
Trading with the Enemy Amendment Act 1916 (c.105)
Trading with the Enemy (Amendment) Act 1918 (c.31)
Trading with the Enemy and Export of Prohibited Goods Act 1916 (c.52)
Trading with the Enemy (Copyright) Act 1916 (c.32)
Trading with the Enemy (Extension of Powers) Act 1915 (c.98)
Trafalgar Estates Act 1947 (c.34)
Trafalgar Square Act 1844 (c.60)
Traffic Calming Act 1992 (c.30)
Tralee Navigation and Harbour Act 1844 (c.99)
Tralee Navigation Loan Act 1841 (c.46)
Tramway Act (1865) (c.74)
Tramways Act 1870 (c.78)
Tramways and Public Companies Act 1884 (c.5)
Tramways and Public Companies (Ireland) Act 1883 (c.43)
Tramways and Public Companies (Ireland) Amendment Act 1884 (c.28)
Tramways (Ireland) Act 1860 (c.152)
Tramways (Ireland) Act 1895 (c.20)
Tramways (Ireland) Act 1900 (c.60)
Tramways (Ireland) Amendment Act 1861 (c.102)
Tramways (Ireland) Amendment Act 1871 (c.114)
Tramways (Ireland) Amendment Act 1881 (c.17)
Tramways (Ireland) Amendment Act 1891 (c.42)
Tramways (Scotland) Act 1861 (c.69)
Tramways (Temporary Increase of Charges) Act 1920 (c.14)
Transfer of Aids Act 1853 (c.6)
Transfer of Property Act 1844 (c.76)
Transfer of Railways (Ireland) Act 1891 (c.2)
Transfer of Uster Canal Act 1865 (c.109)

Transfer of Balance of Fees Act 1830 (c.1)
Transfer of Contracts, etc. Act 1816 (c.31)
Transfer of Public Funds Act 1821 (c.73)
Transfer of Scotch Excise Charity, etc. Act (c.82)
Transfer of Singapore to East India Company, etc., Act 1824 (c.108)
Transfer of Stock Act 1800 (c.36)
Transfer of Stock (Ireland) Act 1820 (c.5)
Transfer of Stock of Hertford College Act 1816 (c.95)
Transfer of Stocks Act 1817 (c.79)
Transfer of Stocks Act 1818 (c.80)
Transfer of Trust Estates Act 1830 (c.60)
Transfer of Trust Estates, etc. (Ireland) Act 1826 (c.43)
Transfer of Works (Ireland) Act 1856 (c.37)
Transfer to Admiralty of Postal Contracts Act 1837 (c.3)
Transferrence of Lands (Scotland) Act 1847 (cc.48, 49)
Transitional Payments Act (Determination of Need) Act 1932 (c.54)
Transitional Payments Prolongation (Unemployed Persons) Act 1932 (c.19)
Transmission of Moveable Property (Scotland) Act 1862 (c.85)
Transport Act 1947 (c.49)
Transport Act 1953 (c.13)
Transport Act 1962 (c.46)
Transport Act 1968 (c.73)
Transport Act 1978 (c.55)
Transport Act 1980 (c.34)
Transport Act 1981 (c.56)
Transport Act 1982 (c.49)
Transport Act 1983 (c.10)
Transport Act 1985 (c.67)
Transport Act 1962 (Amendment) Act 1981 (c.32)
Transport and Works Act 1992 (c.42)
Transport (Borrowing Papers) Act 1954 (c.10)
Transport (Borrowing Papers) Act 1959 (c.16)
Transport Charges, etc. (Miscellaneous Provisions) Act 1954 (c.64)
Transport (Disposal of Road Haulage Property) Act 1956 (c.56)
Transport (Finance) Act 1982 (c.6)
Transport Finances Act 1966 (c.17)
Transport (Financial Provisions) Act 1977 (c.20)
Transport (Grants) Act 1972 (c.15)
Transport Holding Company Act 1968 (c.10)
Transport Holding Company Act 1972 (c.14)
Transport (London) Act 1969 (c.35)
Transport (London) Amendment Act 1969 (c.60)
Transport Police (Jurisdiction) Act 1994 (c.8)
Transport (Railway Finances) Act 1957 (c.9)
Transport (Scotland) Act 1989 (c.23)
Transportation Act 1799 (c.51)
Transportation Act 1802 (c.15)
Transportation Act 1802 (c.28)
Transportation, etc. Act 1806 (c.28)
Transportation Act 1813 (c.39)
Transportation Act 1813 (c.30)
Transportation Act 1815 (c.156)
Transportation Act 1816 (c.27)
Transportation Act 1819 (c.101)
Transportation Act 1821 (c.6)
Transportation Act 1824 (c.84)
Transportation Act 1825 (c.69)
Transportation Act 1830 (c.39)
Transportation Act 1834 (c.67)
Transportation Act 1843 (c.7)
Transportation Act 1846 (c.26)
Transportation Act 1847 (c.67)
Transportation (Ireland) Act 1849 (c.27)
Transvaal Loan (Guarantee) Act 1907 (c.37)
Travel Concessions Act 1964 (c.95)
Travel Concessions (London) Act 1982 (c.12)
Trawling in Prohibited Areas Prevention Act 1909 (c.8)
Treachery Act 1940 (c.21)
Treason Act 1708 (c.21)
Treason Act 1746 (c.30)
Treason Act 1795 (c.7)
Treason Act 1800 (c.93)
Treason Act 1814 (c.146)
Treason Act 1817 (c.6)
Treason Act 1842 (c.51)
Treason Act 1945 (c.44)
Treason Felony Act 1848 (c.12)
Treason (Ireland) Act 1821 (c.24)
Treason (Ireland) Act 1854 (c.26)
Treason in Scotland Act 1714 (c.20)
Treason Outlawries (Scotland) Act 1748 (c.48)
Treasure Act 1996 (c.24)
Treasurer of the Navy Act 1807 (c.56)
Treasurer of the Navy Act 1808 (c.8)
Treasurer of the Navy, etc. Act 1817 (c.121)
Treasurer of the Navy Act 1821 (c.74)
Treasurer of the Navy Act 1830 (c.42)
Treasurers of Counties (Ireland) Act 1855 (c.74)
Treasury Bills Act 1806 (c.32)
Treasury Bills Act 1807 (c.10)
Treasury Bills Act 1877 (c.2)
Treasury Bills Act 1899 (c.2)
Treasury Bills (Ireland) Act 1803 (c.114)
Treasury Bills (Ireland) Act 1804 (c.97)
Treasury Bills (Ireland) Act 1807 (c.72)
Treasury Bills (Ireland) Act 1808 (c.112)
Treasury Bills (Ireland) Act 1809 (c.79)
Treasury Bills (Ireland) Act 1810 (c.98)
Treasury Bills (Ireland) Act 1811 (c.5)
Treasury Bills (Ireland) Act 1811 (c.88)
Treasury Bills (Ireland) Act 1812 (c.90)
Treasury Bills (Ireland) Act 1812 (c.113)
Treasury Bills (Ireland) Act 1813 (c.80)
Treasury Bills (Ireland) Act 1814 (c.75)
Treasury Bills (Ireland) Act 1815 (c.40)
Treasury Bills (Ireland) Act 1816 (cc.41, 42)
Treasury Bills (Ireland) Act 1816 (c.47)

Treasury Bills (Ireland) Act 1817 (c.81)
Treasury Bills (Ireland) Act 1818 (c.87)
Treasury Bills (Ireland) Act 1819 (c.132)
Treasury Bills (Ireland) Act 1820 (c.46)
Treasury Bills (Ireland) Act 1821 (c.80)
Treasury Chest Fund Act 1861 (c.127)
Treasury Chest Fund Act 1873 (c.56)
Treasury Chest Fund Act 1877 (c.45)
Treasury Chest Fund Act 1893 (c.18)
Treasury Instruments (Signature) Act 1849 (c.89)
Treasury of the Ordnance Act 1806 (c.45)
Treasury Solicitor Act 1876 (c.18)
Treasury (Temporary Borrowing) Act 1910 (c.1)
Treaties of Peace (Austria and Bulgaria) Act 1920 (c.6)
Treaties of Peace (Italy, Roumania, Bulgaria, Hungary and Finland) Act 1947 (c.23)
Treaties of Washington Act 1922 (c.21)
Treaty of Commerce, etc. with America Act 1805 (c.35)
Treaty of Commerce, etc. with America Act 1806 (c.16)
Treaty of Commerce, etc. with America Act 1807 (c.2)
Treaty of Commerce, etc. with America Act 1808 (c.6)
Treaty of Peace Act 1919 (c.33)
Treaty of Peace (Hungary) Act 1921 (c.11)
Treaty of Peace (Turkey) Act 1924 (c.7)
Treaty of Washington Act 1872 (c.45)
Treaty with Hayti Act 1842 (c.41)
Treaty with United States 1797 (c.97)
Treaty with United States Act 1819 (c.54)
Trees Act 1970 (c.43)
Trent and Markham Bridges Act 1837 (c.15)
Trespass (Scotland) Act 1865 (c.56)
Trial of Felonies in Certain Boroughs Act 1834 (c.27)
Trial of Lunatics Act 1883 (c.38)
Trial of Offences (Ireland) Act 1833 (c.79)
Trial of Peers (Scotland) Act 1825 (c.66)
Trials for Felony Act 1836 (c.114)
Trials of Murders, etc., in Honduras Act 1819 (c.44)
Tribunals and Inquiries Act 1958 (c.66)
Tribunals and Inquiries Act 1966 (c.43)
Tribunals and Inquiries Act 1971 (c.62)
Tribunals and Inquiries Act 1992 (c.53)
Tribunals of Inquiry (Evidence) Act 1921 (c.7)
Trinidad and Tobago Act 1887 (c.44)
Trinidad and Tobago Independence Act 1962 (c.54)
Trinidad and Tobago Republic Act 1976 (c.54)
Trinity College, Dublin Act 1855 (c.82)
Trout (Scotland) Act 1845 (c.26)
Trout (Scotland) Act 1860 (c.45)
Trout (Scotland) Act 1933 (c.35)
Truck Act 1831 (c.37)
Truck Act 1837 (c.37)
Truck Act 1896 (c.44)
Truck Act 1940 (c.38)
Truck Amendment Act 1887 (c.46)
Truck Commission Act 1870 (c.105)
Trunk Roads Act 1936 (c.5)
Trunk Roads Act 1946 (c.30)
Truro Bishopric and Chapter Acts Amendment Act 1887 (c.12)
Truro Chapter Act 1878 (c.44)
Trust Investment Act 1889 (c.32)
Trust Property, Escheat Act 1834 (c.23)
Trust (Scotland) Amendment Act 1884 (c.63)
Trustee Act 1850 (c.60)
Trustee Act 1852 (c.55)
Trustee Act 1888 (c.59)
Trustee Act 1893 (c.53)
Trustee Act 1925 (c.19)
Trustee Act 1893 Amendment Act 1894 (c.10)
Trustee Appointment Act 1850 (c.28)
Trustee Appointment Act 1869 (c.26)
Trustee Churches (Ireland) Act 1884 (c.10)
Trustee Investments Act 1961 (c.62)
Trustee Savings Banks Act 1863 (c.87)
Trustee Savings Banks Act 1887 (c.47)
Trustee Savings Banks Act 1918 (c.4)
Trustee Savings Banks Act 1946 (c.6)
Trustee Savings Banks Act 1954 (c.63)
Trustee Savings Banks Act 1957 (c.8)
Trustee Savings Banks Act 1969 (c.50)
Trustee Savings Banks Act 1976 (c.4)
Trustee Savings Banks Act 1978 (c.16)
Trustee Savings Banks Act 1981 (c.65)
Trustee Savings Banks Act 1985 (c.58)
Trustee Savings Banks (Pensions) Act 1954 (c.12)
Trustee Savings Banks (Special Investments) Act 1934 (c.37)
Trustee (War Damage Insurance) Act 1941 (c.28)
Trustees Appointment Act 1890 (c.19)
Trustees Relief Act 1847 (c.96)
Trustees Relief Act 1849 (c.74)
Trustees Relief (Ireland) Act 1848 (c.68)
Trustees Savings Banks Act 1968 (c.6)
Trusts of Land and Appointment of Trustees Act 1996 (c.47)
Trusts (Scotland) Act 1861 (c.84)
Trusts (Scotland) Act 1867 (c.97)
Trusts (Scotland) Act 1897 (c.8)
Trusts (Scotland) Act 1898 (c.42)
Trusts (Scotland) Act, 1867, Amendment Act 1887 (c.18)
Trusts (Scotland) Amendment Act 1891 (c.44)
Trustee (Scotland) Act 1910 (c.22)
Trusts (Scotland) Act 1921 (c.58)
Trusts (Scotland) Act 1961 (c.57)
Tuberculosis Prevention (Ireland) Act 1908 (c.56)
Tuberculosis Prevention (Ireland) Act 1913 (c.25)
Tumultuous Petitioning Act 1661 (c.5)
Tumultuous Risings (Ireland) Act 1831 (c.44)

Tunnel Between Devonport and Keyham Act 1854 (c.15)
Turbary (Ireland) Act 1891 (c.45)
Turkish Loan Act 1855 (c.99)
Turks and Caicos Islands Act 1873 (c.6)
Turnpike Acts Act 1843 (c.69)
Turnpike Acts Continuance 1800 (c.26)
Turnpike Acts Continuance Act 1831 (c.6)
Turnpike Acts Continuance Act 1834 (c.10)
Turnpike Acts Continuance Act 1835 (c.49)
Turnpike Acts Continuance Act 1836 (c.62)
Turnpike Acts Continuance Act 1837 (c.18)
Turnpike Acts Continuance Act 1838 (c.68)
Turnpike Acts Continuance Act 1839 (c.31)
Turnpike Acts Continuance Act 1840 (c.45)
Turnpike Acts Continuance Act 1841 (c.9)
Turnpike Acts Continuance Act 1842 (c.60)
Turnpike Acts Continuance Act 1845 (c.53)
Turnpike Acts Continuance Act 1848 (c.96)
Turnpike Acts Continuance Act 1849 (c.87)
Turnpike Acts Continuance Act 1857 (c.24)
Turnpike Acts Continuance Act 1858 (c.63)
Turnpike Acts Continuance Act 1866 (c.105)
Turnpike Acts Continuance (Ireland) Act 1851 (c.44)
Turnpike Acts, Great Britain Act 1844 (c.41)
Turnpike Acts, Great Britain Act 1846 (c.51)
Turnpike Acts, Great Britain Act 1847 (c.105)
Turnpike Acts, Great Britain Act 1852 (c.58)
Turnpike Acts, Great Britain Act 1855 (c.98)
Turnpike Acts, Great Britain Act 1856 (c.49)
Turnpike Acts (Ireland) Act 1838 (c.72)
Turnpike Acts (Ireland) Act 1842 (c.23)
Turnpike Acts (Ireland) Act 1843 (c.21)
Turnpike Acts (Ireland) Act 1844 (c.36)
Turnpike Acts (Ireland) Act 1845 (c.125)
Turnpike Acts (Ireland) Act 1848 (c.73)
Turnpike Acts (Ireland) Act 1849 (c.47)
Turnpike Acts (Ireland) Act 1852 (c.22)
Turnpike Acts (Ireland) Act 1853 (c.76)
Turnpike Acts (Ireland) Act 1854 (c.42)
Turnpike Acts (Ireland) Act 1855 (c.83)
Turnpike Acts, Ireland, Continuance Act 1836 (c.40)
Turnpike Acts, Ireland, Continuance Act 1840 (c.46)
Turnpike Acts, Ireland, Continuance Act 1850 (c.34)
Turnpike Acts, Ireland, Continuance Act 1856 (c.71)
Turnpike Debts Act 1852 (c.33)
Turnpike Roads Act 1815 (c.119)
Turnpike Roads Act 1817 (c.37)
Turnpike Roads Act 1822 (c.126)
Turnpike Roads Act 1823 (c.95)
Turnpike Roads Act 1824 (c.69)
Turnpike Roads Act 1827 (c.24)
Turnpike Roads Act 1828 (c.77)
Turnpike Roads (England) Act 1853 (c.135)
Turnpike Roads (England) Act 1854 (c.58)
Turnpike Roads in Yorkshire Act 1852 (c.45)
Turnpike Roads (Ireland) Act 1834 (c.91)
Turnpike Roads (Ireland) Act 1841 (c.6)
Turnpike Roads (Ireland) Act 1846 (c.89)
Turnpike Roads (Ireland) Act 1847 (c.35)
Turnpike Roads (Scotland) Act 1823 (c.49)
Turnpike Roads (Scotland) Act 1831 (c.43)
Turnpike Roads (Scotland) Act 1849 (c.31)
Turnpike Roads (Tolls on Lime) Act 1823 (c.16)
Turnpike Roads Trusts Act 1820 (c.95)
Turnpike Tolls Act 1835 (c.18)
Turnpike Tolls Act 1839 (c.46)
Turnpike Tolls Act 1840 (c.51)
Turnpike Tolls Act 1841 (c.33)
Turnpike Tolls (Allowance of Wagon Weights) Act 1834 (c.81)
Turnpike Trusts Act 1856 (c.12)
Turnpike Trusts Arrangements Act 1867 (c.66)
Turnpike Trusts Arrangements Act 1868 (c.66)
Turnpike Trusts Arrangements Act 1872 (c.72)
Turnpike Trusts: Making of Provisional Orders Act 1851 (c.38)
Turnpike Trusts Relief Act 1861 (c.46)
Turnpike Trusts Returns Act 1833 (c.80)
Turnpike Trusts, South Wales Act 1845 (c.61)
Turnpikes Abolition (Ireland) Act 1857 (c.16)
Turnpikes Act 1831 (c.25)
Turnpikes Act 1832 (c.124)
Turnpikes Act 1840 (c.39)
Turnpikes Acts Continuation Act 1849 (c.87)
Turnpikes (Provisional Orders Confirmation) Act 1865 (c.91)
Turnpikes (Provisional Orders Confirmation) Act 1866 (c.92)
Turnpikes (Provisional Orders Confirmation) Act 1870 (c.22)
Turnpikes, South Wales Act 1844 (c.91)
Tuvalu Act 1978 (c.20)
Tweed Fisheries Act 1797 (c.48)
Tyne Pilotage Order Confirmation Act 1865 (c.44)
Tyne Pilotage Order Confirmation Act 1867 (c.78)

Uganda Act 1964 (c.20)
Uganda Railway Act 1896 (c.38)
Uganda Railway Act 1900 (c.11)
Uganda Railway Act 1902 (c.40)
Ugandan Independence Act 1962 (c.57)
Ulster Defence Regiment Act 1969 (c.65)
Ulster Defence Regiment Act 1973 (c.34)
Ulster Society 1704 (c.19)
Ulverstone Canal Act 1793 (c.105)
Unclaimed Prize Money, etc. Act 1812 (c.132)
Under Secretaries of State Act 1929 (c.9)
Under Secretary of State Indemnity Act 1864 (c.21)
Underground Works (London) Act 1956 (c.59)

Unemployed Workers' Dependants (Temporary Provisions) Act 1921 (c.62)
Unemployed Workmen Act 1904 (c.18)
Unemployment Act 1934 (c.29)
Unemployment and Family Allowances (Northern Ireland Agreement) Act 1946 (c.3)
Unemployment Assistance (Emergency Powers) Act 1939 (c.93)
Unemployment Assistance (Temporary Provisions) Act 1935 (c.6)
Unemployment Assistance (Temporary Provisions) (Amendment) Act 1937 (c.10)
Unemployment Assistance (Temporary Provisions) (Extension) Act 1936 (c.7)
Unemployment Assistance (Temporary Provisions) (No. 2) Act 1935 (c.22)
Unemployment Insurance Act 1920 (c.30)
Unemployment Insurance Act 1921 (c.1)
Unemployment Insurance Act 1922 (c.7)
Unemployment Insurance Act 1923 (c.2)
Unemployment Insurance Act 1924 (c.1)
Unemployment Insurance Act 1925 (c.69)
Unemployment Insurance Act 1926 (c.12)
Unemployment Insurance Act 1927 (c.30)
Unemployment Insurance Act 1928 (c.1)
Unemployment Insurance Act 1929 (c.3)
Unemployment Insurance Act 1930 (c.16)
Unemployment Insurance Act 1931 (c.8)
Unemployment Insurance Act 1935 (c.8)
Unemployment Insurance Act 1938 (c.8)
Unemployment Insurance Act 1939 (c.29)
Unemployment Insurance Act 1940 (c.44)
Unemployment Insurance (Agriculture) Act 1936 (c.13)
Unemployment Insurance (Crediting of Contributions) Act 1935 (c.33)
Unemployment Insurance (Emergency Powers) Act 1939 (c.92)
Unemployment Insurance (Expiring Enactments) Act 1933 (c.26)
Unemployment Insurance (Eire Volunteers) Act 1946 (c.76)
Unemployment Insurance (Increase of Benefit) Act 1944 (c.42)
Unemployment Insurance (Northern Ireland Agreement) Act 1926 (c.4)
Unemployment Insurance (Northern Ireland Agreement) Act 1929 (c.18)
Unemployment Insurance (No. 2) Act 1921 (c.15)
Unemployment Insurance (No. 2) Act 1922 (c.30)
Unemployment Insurance (No. 2) Act 1924 (c.30)
Unemployment Insurance (No. 2) Act 1930 (c.19)
Unemployment Insurance (No. 2) Act 1931 (c.25)
Unemployment Insurance (No. 3) Act 1924 (c.6)
Unemployment Insurance (No. 3) Act 1930 (c.47)
Unemployment Insurance (No. 3) Act 1931 (c.36)
Unemployment Insurance (No. 4) Act 1931 (c.3)
Unemployment Insurance (Temporary Provisions Amendment) 1920 (c.82)
Unemployment Insurance (Transitional Provisions Amendment) Act 1929 (c.19)
Unemployment (Northern Ireland Agreement) Act 1936 (c.10)
Unemployment Relief Works 1920 (c.57)
Unfair Contract Terms Act 1977 (c.50)
Unfunded Debt Act 1761 (c.7)
Unfunded Debt Act 1765 (c.19)
Unfunded Debt Act 1766 (c.15)
Unfunded Debt Act 1766 (c.16)
Unfunded Debt Act 1768 (c.18)
Unfunded Debt Act 1769 (c.15)
Unfunded Debt Act 1770 (c.11)
Unfunded Debt Act 1772 (c.39)
Unfunded Debt Act 1772 (c.66)
Unfunded Debt Act 1801 (c.4)
Uniform Laws on International Sales Act 1967 (c.45)
Uniformity of Worship Act 1749 (c.28)
Uniforms Act 1894 (c.45)
Union and Parish Property Act 1837 (c.50)
Union Assessment Act 1880 (c.7)
Union Assessment Committee Act 1862 (c.103)
Union Assessment Committee Amendment Act 1864 (c.39)
Union Between England and Scotland Act 1702 (c.8)
Union Chargeability Act 1865 (c.79)
Union Loans Act 1869 (c.45)
Union of Benefices Act 1860 (c.142)
Union of Benefices Act 1898 (c.23)
Union of Benefices Act 1919 (c.98)
Union of Benefices Acts Amendment Act 1871 (c.90)
Union of Benefices, etc. Act 1855 (c.127)
Union of England and Scotland 1704 (c.6)
Union of England and Scotland 1705 (c.15)
Union of Parishes Act 1827 (c.43)
Union of Parishes, etc. (Ireland) Act 1832 (c.67)
Union of Turnpike Trusts Act 1849 (c.46)
Union Officers (Ireland) Act 1872 (c.89)
Union Officers (Ireland) Act 1885 (c.80)
Union Officers Superannuation (Ireland) Act 1865 (c.26)
Union Relief Aid Act 1862 (c.110)
Union Relief Aid Act 1863 (c.91)
Union Relief Aid Continuance Act 1863 (c.4)
Union Relief Aid Continuance Act 1864 (c.10)
Union with Ireland Act 1800 (c.67)
Union with Scotland Act 1706 (c.11)
Union with Scotland (Amendment) Act 1707 (c.40)
United Nations Act 1946 (c.45)
United Parishes (Scotland) Act 1868 (c.30)
United Parishes (Scotland) Act 1876 (c.11)

United States of America Veterans' Pensions (Administration) Act 1949 (c.45)
United States of America (Visiting Forces) Act 1942 (c.31)
Universities Act 1825 (c.97)
Universities and College (Emergency Powers) Act 1914 (c.22)
Universities and College (Emergency Provisions) Act 1939 (c.106)
Universities and College Estates Act 1858 (c.44)
Universities and College Estates Act 1898 (c.55)
Universities and College Estates Act 1925 (c.24)
Universities and College Estates Act 1964 (c.51)
Universities and College Estates Act Extension Act 1860 (c.59)
Universities and College Estates Amendment Act 1880 (c.46)
Universities and Colleges (Trust) Act 1943 (c.9)
Universities Election Act 1868 (c.65)
Universities Elections Amendment (Scotland) Act 1881 (c.40)
Universities of Oxford and Cambridge Act 1859 (c.19)
Universities of Oxford and Cambridge Act 1877 (c.48)
Universities of Oxford and Cambridge Act 1880 (c.11)
Universities of Oxford and Cambridge Act 1923 (c.33)
Universities (Scotland) Act 1853 (c.89)
Universities (Scotland) Act 1858 (c.83)
Universities (Scotland) Act 1859 (c.24)
Universities (Scotland) Act 1862 (c.28)
Universities (Scotland) Act 1889 (c.55)
Universities (Scotland) Act 1922 (c.31)
Universities (Scotland) Act 1932 (c.26)
Universities (Scotland) Act 1966 (c.13)
Universities Tests Act 1871 (c.26)
University Education (Ireland) Act 1879 (c.65)
University Elections Act 1861 (c.53)
University of Dublin Registration Act 1842 (c.74)
University of Dublin Tests 1873 (c.21)
University of Durham Act 1908 (c.20)
University of Durham Act 1935 (c.29)
University of Liverpool Act 1904 (c.11)
University of London Act 1898 (c.62)
University of London Act 1899 (c.24)
University of London Act 1926 (c.46)
University of London Medical Graduates Act 1854 (c.114)
University of Oxford Act 1869 (c.20)
University of St. Andrews Act 1746 (c.32)
University of St. Andrews Act 1953 (c.40)
University of Wales Act 1902 (c.14)
University of Wales (Medical Graduates) Act 1911 (c.43)
Universities (Wine Licences) Act 1743 (c.40)
Unlawful Combinations (Ireland) Act 1803 (c.86)
Unlawful Combinations (Ireland) Act 1814 (c.180)
Unlawful Combinations (Ireland) Act 1848 (c.89)
Unlawful Combinations of Workmen Act 1799 (c.81)
Unlawful Combinations of Workmen Act 1800 (c.106)
Unlawful Distillation, etc. (Ireland) Act 1814 (c.12)
Unlawful Drilling Act 1819 (c.1)
Unlawful Games Act 1728 (c.28)
Unlawful Oaths Act 1797 (c.123)
Unlawful Oaths Act 1810 (c.102)
Unlawful Oaths Act 1812 (c.104)
Unlawful Oaths Act 1823 (c.87)
Unlawful Oaths (Ireland) Act 1810 (c.102)
Unlawful Oaths (Ireland) Act 1844 (c.78)
Unlawful Oaths (Ireland) Act 1845 (c.55)
Unlawful Oaths (Ireland) Act 1851 (c.48)
Unlawful Oaths (Ireland) Act 1856 (c.78)
Unlawful Oaths (Ireland) Act 1862 (c.32)
Unlawful Pawning Act 1786 (c.92)
Unlawful Societies Act 1799 (c.79)
Unlawful Societies (Ireland) Act 1839 (c.74)
Unlawful Weights (Ireland) Act 1824 (c.110)
Unreasonable Withholding of Food Supplies Act 1914 (c.51)
Unsolicited Goods and Services Act 1971 (c.30)
Unsolicited Goods and Services (Amendment) Act 1975 (c.13)
Urban Development Corporations (Financial Limits) Act 1987 (c.57)
Use of Clarke's Hydrometer Act 1802 (c.97)
Use of Corn in Distillation of Spirits, etc. Act 1800 (c.3)
Use of Fine Flow Act 1801 (cc.1, 2)
Use of Fire on Steamboats Act 1828 (c.11)
Use of Highland Dress Act 1782 (c.63)
Use of Horsehides etc. Act 1800 (c.66)
Use of Plate Act 1769 (c.11)
Use of Rice in Distillation Act 1856 (c.51)
Use of Salt Duty Free, etc. Act 1800 (c.21)
Use of Sugar in Brewing Act 1800 (c.62)
Use of Sugar in Brewing Act 1812 (c.1)
Use of Sugar in Brewing Act 1812 (c.65)
Use of Wheat in Making Starch Act 1800 (c.25)
Usury Act 1713 (c.15)
Usury Act 1837 (c.80)
Usury Act 1839 (c.37)
Usury Act 1840 (c.83)
Usury Act 1841 (c.54)
Usury Act 1843 (c.45)
Usury Act 1845 (c.102)
Usury Act 1850 (c.56)
Usury Laws Repeal Act 1854 (c.90)
Uttoxeter to Stoke Road Act 1793 (c.131)
Uxbridge: Streets Act 1785 (c.16)

Vacant Ecclesiastical Dignities, etc. Act 1835 (c.30)
Vaccination Act 1840 (c.29)
Vaccination Act 1841 (c.32)
Vaccination Act 1853 (c.100)
Vaccination Act 1867 (c.84)
Vaccination Act 1871 (c.98)
Vaccination Act 1874 (c.75)
Vaccination Act 1898 (c.49)
Vaccination Act 1907 (c.31)
Vaccination Acts Amendment Act 1861 (c.59)
Vaccination Amendment (Ireland) Act 1868 (c.87)
Vaccination Amendment (Ireland) Act 1879 (c.70)
Vaccination (Ireland) Act 1858 (c.64)
Vaccination (Ireland) Act 1863 (c.52)
Vaccination (Scotland) Act 1863 (c.108)
Vaccination (Scotland) Act 1907 (c.49)
Vaccine Damage Payments Act 1979 (c.17)
Vagrance (Ireland) Amendment Act 1865 (c.33)
Vagrancy Act 1824 (c.83)
Vagrancy Act 1838 (c.38)
Vagrancy Act 1898 (c.39)
Vagrancy Act 1935 (c.20)
Vagrancy (England) Act 1822 (c.40)
Vagrancy (Ireland) Act 1847 (c.84)
Vagrant Act Amendment Act 1868 (c.52)
Vagrant Act Amendment Act 1873 (c.38)
Vagrants Act 1706 (c.32)
Vagrants Act 1713 (c.26)
Vagrants Act 1739 (c.24)
Vagrants Act 1821 (c.64)
Vagrants and Criminals Act 1787 (c.11)
Validation of Acts of Hate, Chief Justice of Bombay Act 1858 (c.32)
Validation of Elections Act 1955 (c.10)
Validation of Elections (No. 2) Act 1955 (c.12)
Validation of Elections (No. 3) Act 1955 (c.13)
Validation of Elections (Northern Ireland) Act 1956 (c.35)
Validation of War-time Leases Act 1944 (c.34)
Validity of Certain Contracts Act 1838 (c.10)
Validity of Certain Oaths Act 1812 (c.21)
Validity of Certain Orders in Council, etc. Act 1808 (c.37)
Validity of Certain Proceedings, etc. Act 1854 (c.37)
Validity of Proceedings in the House of Commons Act 1855 (c.33)
Valuation and Rating (Exempted Classes) (Scotland) Act 1976 (c.64)
Valuation and Rating (Scotland) Act 1956 (c.60)
Valuation (Ireland) Act 1834 (c.55)
Valuation (Ireland) Act 1852 (c.63)
Valuation (Ireland) Act 1853 (c.7)
Valuation (Ireland) Act 1854 (c.8)
Valuation (Ireland) Act 1864 (c.52)
Valuation (Ireland) Act 1901 (c.37)
Valuation (Ireland) Amendment Act 1874 (c.70)
Valuation (Metropolis) Act 1869 (c.67)
Valuation Metropolis Amendment Act 1884 (c.5)
Valuation Metropolis Amendment Act 1925 (c.40)
Valuation of Lands (Ireland) Act 1826 (c.62)
Valuation of Lands (Ireland) Act 1831 (c.51)
Valuation of Lands (Ireland) Act 1832 (c.73)
Valuation of Lands (Ireland) Act 1836 (c.84)
Valuation for Rating Act 1953 (c.42)
Valuation for Rating (Scotland) Act 1970 (c.4)
Valuation of Lands (Scotland) Acts Amendment Act 1894 (c.36)
Valuation of Lands (Scotland) Amendment Act 1867 (c.80)
Valuation of Lands (Scotland) Amendment Act 1879 (c.42)
Valuation of Lands (Scotland) Amendment Act 1887 (c.51)
Value Added Tax Act 1983 (c.55)
Value Added Tax Act 1994 (c.23)
Van Diemen's Land Act 1842 (c.3)
Van Diemen's Land Co. Act 1825 (c.39)
Van Diemen's Land Co. Act 1847 (c.57)
Vancouver's Island Act 1849 (c.48)
Variation of Trusts Act 1958 (c.53)
Vehicle and Driving Licences Act 1969 (c.27)
Vehicle Excise and Registration Act 1994 (c.22)
Vehicles (Excise) Act 1949 (c.89)
Vehicles (Excise) Act 1962 (c.13)
Vehicles (Excise) Act 1971 (c.10)
Vendor and Purchaser Act 1874 (c.78)
Venereal Disease Act 1917 (c.21)
Vessels Built at Malta, etc. Act 1820 (c.9)
Vessels Protection Act 1967 (c.85)
Vesting in Crown of Lands at Sandhurst Act 1812 (c.124)
Vestries Act 1818 (c.69)
Vestries Act 1819 (c.85)
Vestries Act 1831 (c.60)
Vestries Act 1850 (c.57)
Vestries Act 1853 (c.65)
Vesty Cess Abolition Act 1864 (c.17)
Veterinary Surgeons Act 1881 (c.62)
Veterinary Surgeons Act 1948 (c.52)
Veterinary Surgeons Act 1966 (c.36)
Veterinary Surgeons Act (1881) Amendment 1920 (c.20)
Veterinary Surgeons Amendment 1900 (c.24)
Veterinary Surgeons (Irish Free State Agreement) Act 1932 (c.10)
Vexatious Actions Act 1896 (c.51)
Vexatious Actions (Scotland) Act 1898 (c.35)
Vexatious Arrests Act 1747 (c.3)
Vexatious Arrests Act 1817 (c.101)
Vexatious Indictments Act 1859 (c.17)
Vice-Admiralty Courts Act 1816 (c.82)
Vice-Admiralty Courts Act 1832 (c.51)
Vice-Admiralty Courts Act 1863 (c.24)
Vice-Admiralty Courts Act Amendment Act 1867 (c.45)

Victoria Constitution Act 1855 (c.55)
Victoria Park Act 1842 (c.20)
Victoria Park Act 1872 (c.53)
Victoria University Act 1888 (c.45)
Victualling Establishment, Plymouth Act 1824 (c.49)
Video Recordings Act 1984 (c.39)
Video Recordings Act 1993 (c.24)
Vinegar Act 1844 (c.25)
Viscount Hardinge's Annuity Act 1846 (c.21)
Visiting Forces Act 1952 (c.67)
Visiting Forces (British Commonwealth) Act 1933 (c.6)
Voluntary Conveyances Act 1893 (c.21)
Voluntary Hospitals (Paying Patients) Act 1936 (c.17)
Voluntary Schools Act 1897 (c.5)
Volunteer Act 1863 (c.65)
Volunteer Act 1869 (c.81)
Volunteer Act 1895 (c.23)
Volunteer Act 1897 (c.47)
Volunteer Act 1900 (c.39)
Volunteer Act 1916 (c.62)
Volunteers Act 1780 (c.37)
Volunteers Act 1782 (c.79)
Volunteers Act 1861 (c.126)
Volunteers and Local Militia Act 1809 (c.113)
Volunteers and Yeomanry (Great Britain) Act 1803 (c.18)
Volunteer Corps Act 1794 (c.31)

Wadeshill and Royston Road Act 1796 (c.129)
Wages Act 1708 (c.16)
Wages Act 1986 (c.48)
Wages and Prize Money, etc. in the Navy Act 1809 (c.108)
Wages Arrestment Act 1845 (c.39)
Wages Arrestment Limitation (Amendment) (Scotland) Act 1960 (c.21)
Wages Arrestment Limitation (Scotland) Act 1870 (c.63)
Wages Attachment Abolition Act 1870 (c.30)
Wages Councils Act 1945 (c.17)
Wages Councils Act 1948 (c.7)
Wages Councils Act 1959 (c.69)
Wages Councils Act 1979 (c.12)
Wages Councils (Northern Ireland) Act 1945 (c.21)
Wages, etc. of Artificers, etc. Act 1813 (c.40)
Wages of Artificers, etc. Act 1820 (c.93)
Wages of Certain Deceased Seamen Act 1819 (c.59)
Wages of Merchant Seamen Act 1819 (c.58)
Wages (Temporary Regulations) Act 1918 (c.61)
Wages (Temporary Regulations) Extension Act 1919 (c.18)
Wakefield Church Act 1791 (c.74)
Wakefield, etc. Roads Act 1740 (c.19)
Wakefield and Halifax Roads Act 1793 (c.129)
Wakefield and Sheffield Road Act 1797 (c.159)
Wakefield (Improvement) Act 1771 (c.44)
Wakefield: Improvement Act 1796 (c.50)
Wakefield Roads Act 1778 (c.85)
Wakefield to Abberford Road Act 1789 (c.86)
Wakefield to Abberford Road Act 1793 (c.179)
Wakefield to Austerlands Road Act 1758 (c.48)
Wakefield to Sheffield Road Act 1778 (c.105)
Walcot, Somerset: Improvement Act 1793 (c.89)
Wales Act 1978 (c.52)
Wales and Berwick Act 1746 (c.42)
Wales, Chester, etc. (Courts) Act 1793 (c.68)
Wallingford: Improvement Act 1795 (c.75)
Walmer Vesting Act 1863 (c.54)
Walmore and Bearce Commons, Forest of Dean Act 1866 (c.70)
Walton - Shepperton Bridge (Building and Tolls) Act 1746 (c.22)
Walton - Shepperton Bridge (Rebuilding and Tolls) Act 1780 (c.32)
Wangford, Suffolk: Poor Relief Act 1764 (c.91)
Wapping, Stepney Act 1728 (c.30)
Wapping, Stepney: Poor Relief Act 1782 (c.35)
Wapping, Stepney: Poor Relief, etc. Act 1783 (c.32)
Wapping, Stepney: Improvement Act 1782 (c.86)
War Charges (Validity) Act 1925 (c.6)
War Charities Act 1916 (c.43)
War Charities Act 1940 (c.31)
War Charities Act (Scotland) 1919 (c.12)
War Crimes Act 1991 (c.13)
War Damage Act 1941 (c.12)
War Damage Act 1943 (c.21)
War Damage Act 1949 (c.36)
War Damage Act 1964 (c.25)
War Damage Act 1965 (c.18)
War Damage (Amendment) Act 1942 (c.28)
War Damages (Amendment) Act 1943 (c.12)
War Damage (Clearance Payments) Act 1960 (c.25)
War Damage (Extension of Risk Period) Act 1941 (c.37)
War Damage (Public Utility Undertakings, etc.) Act 1949 (c.36)
War Damage to Land (Scotland) Act 1939 (c.80)
War Damage to Land (Scotland) Act 1941 (c.40)
War Damage (Valuation Appeals) Act 1945 (c.8)
War Damaged Sites Act 1949 (c.84)
War Department Property Act 1938 (c.49)
War Department Stores Act 1867 (c.128)
War Department Tramway (Devon) Act 1865 (c.74)
War Emergency Laws (Continuance) Act 1920 (c.5)

War Loan Act 1900 (c.2)
War Loan Act 1914 (c.60)
War Loan Act 1915 (c.55)
War Loan Act 1916 (c.67)
War Loan Act 1917 (c.41)
War Loan Act 1918 (c.25)
War Loan Act 1919 (c.37)
War Loan (Redemption) Act 1910 (c.2)
War Loan (Supplemental Provisions) Act 1915 (c.93)
War Memorials (Local Authorities' Powers) Act 1923 (c.18)
War Office Act 1879 (c.17)
War Orphans Act 1942 (c.8)
War Pensions Act 1920 (c.23)
War Pensions Act 1921 (c.49)
War Pensions (Administrative Provisions) Act 1918 (c.57)
War Pensions (Administrative Provisions) Act 1919 (c.53)
War Risks Insurance Act 1939 (c.57)
War Risks (Insurance by Truskes) Act 1916 (c.6)
War Service Canteens (Disposal of Surplus) Act 1922 (c.53)
War Stores (Commission) Act 1904 (c.7)
Warden of Fleet Prison Act 1728 (c.32)
Warden of the Fleet Prison Act 1819 (c.64)
Wareham and Purbeck Roads Act 1786 (c.122)
Wareham: Improvement Act 1763 (c.54)
Warehoused British Spirits Act 1867 (c.27)
Warehoused Goods Act 1809 (c.106)
Warehoused Tobacco, etc. Act 1793 (c.57)
Warehousing of British Compounded Spirits Act 1865 (c.98)
Warehousing of British Spirits Act 1864 (c.12)
Warehousing of Foreign Goods, Manchester Act 1844 (c.31)
Warehousing of Goods Act 1799 (c.59)
Warehousing of Goods Act 1803 (c.132)
Warehousing of Goods Act 1823 (c.24)
Warehousing of Goods Act 1845 (c.91)
Warehousing of Spirits (Ireland) Act 1812 (c.30)
Warehousing of Wines, etc. Act 1795 (c.118)
Warminster Roads Act 1726 (c.16)
Warminster Roads Act 1742 (c.5)
Warminster Roads Act 1765 (c.62)
Warminster Roads Act 1792 (c.141)
Warrants of Attorney Act 1822 (c.39)
Warrants of Attorney Act 1843 (c.66)
Warrick Election Act 1834 (c.17)
Warrington and Wigan Road Act 1726 (c.10)
Warrington and Wigan Road Act 1770 (c.70)
Warrington to Wigan Road Act 1746 (c.8)
Warrington to Wigan Road Act 1793 (c.164)
Warwick and Birmingham Canal Act 1793 (c.38)
Warrington and Birmingham Canal Act 1796 (c.42)
Warwick and Gloucester Roads Act 1773 (c.97)
Warwick and Gloucester Roads Act 1791 (c.116)
Warwick and Napton Canal Act 1794 (c.38)
Warwick and Napton Canal Act 1796 (c.95)
Warwick and Northampton Road Act 1765 (c.107)
Warwick Assizes Act 1854 (c.35)
Warwick, etc. Roads Act 1739 (c.5)
Warwick to Northampton Road Act 1776 (c.80)
Warwick and Northampton Roads Act 1781 (c.106)
Warwick and Northamptonshire Roads Act 1759 (c.44)
Warwick and Oxford Roads Act 1755 (c.46)
Warwick and Oxford Roads Act 1780 (c.69)
Warwick and Worcester Roads Act 1754 (c.36)
Warwick and Worcester Roads Act 1767 (c.81)
Warwick and Worcester Roads Act 1780 (c.71)
Warwick and Worcester Roads Act 1781 (c.88)
Warwick Bridge Act 1788 (c.9)
Warwick Gaol Act 1777 (c.58)
Warwick, Stafford and Worcester Roads Act 1794 (c.117)
Warwick Roads Act 1723 (c.15)
Warwick Roads Act 1730 (c.9)
Warwick Roads Act 1738 (c.18)
Warwick Roads Act 1739 (c.22)
Warwick Roads Act 1742 (c.20)
Warwick Roads Act 1743 (c.12)
Warwick Roads Act 1744 (c.32)
Warwick Roads Act 1753 (c.73)
Warwick Roads Act 1760 (c.36)
Warwick Roads Act 1767 (c.77)
Warwick Roads Act 1770 (c.63)
Warwick Roads Act 1770 (c.69)
Warwick Roads Act 1770 (c.94)
Warwick Roads Act 1772 (c.91)
Warwick Roads Act 1780 (c.80)
Warwick Roads Act 1785 (c.115)
Warwick Roads Act 1788 (c.107)
Warwick Roads Act 1791 (c.98)
Warwick Roads Act 1792 (c.116)
Warwick Roads Act 1794 (c.115)
Warwick Roads Act 1794 (c.116)
Warwick Shire Hall Act 1757 (c.56)
Warwick, Stafford and Worcester Roads Act 1772 (c.110)
Warwick, Worcester and Stafford Roads Act 1787 (c.73)
Warwickshire and Northamptonshire Roads 1736 (c.11)
Warwickshire Roads Act 1744 (c.19)
Washington Treaty (Claims) Act 1875 (c.52)
Waste Lands, Australia Act 1846 (c.104)
Waste Lands, Van Diemen's Land Act 1845 (c.95)
Watch Rates in Boroughs Act 1840 (c.28)
Watching: City of London Act 1736 (c.22)

Watching: Holborn Act 1736 (c.25)
Watching, St. Margaret and St. John, Westminster 1735 (c.17)
Watching, St. Martin's in the Fields Act 1735 (c.8)
Watching, St. Paul (Covent Garden) 1735 (c.13)
Watching, Westminster 1735 (c.19)
Watchett (Somerset) Harbour Act 1707 (c.69)
Watchett (Somerset) Harbour Act 1720 (c.14)
Watchett Harbour Act 1770 (c.24)
Water Act 1945 (c.42)
Water Act 1948 (c.22)
Water Act 1958 (c.67)
Water Act 1973 (c.37)
Water Act 1981 (c.12)
Water Act 1983 (c.23)
Water Act 1989 (c.15)
Water Charges Act 1976 (c.9)
Water Charges Equalisation Act 1977 (c.41)
Water Companies (Regulation of Powers) Act 1887 (c.21)
Water Consolidation (Consequential Provisions) Act 1991 (c.60)
Water (Fluoridation) Act 1985 (c.63)
Water Industry Act 1991 (c.60)
Water Measure of Fruit 1702 (c.9)
Water Officers Compensation Act 1960 (c.15)
Water Rate Definition Act 1885 (c.34)
Water Resources Act 1963 (c.38)
Water Resources Act 1968 (c.35)
Water Resources Act 1971 (c.34)
Water Resources Act 1991 (c.57)
Water (Scotland) Act 1946 (c.42)
Water (Scotland) Act 1949 (c.31)
Water (Scotland) Act 1967 (c.78)
Water (Scotland) Act 1980 (c.45)
Water Supplies (Exceptional Shortage Orders) Act 1934 (c.20)
Water Supply, London Act 1747 (c.8)
Water Undertakings (Modification of Charges) Act 1921 (c.44)
Waterbeach Level (Cambridge, Isle of Ely): Drainage Act 1797 (c.88)
Waterbeach Level: Drainage Act 1790 (c.74)
Waterbeach Level, Northampton: Drainage Act 1740 (c.24)
Waterford Hospital Act 1839 (c.19)
Waterfront House of Industry Act 1838 (c.13)
Waterloo Subscription Fund Act 1819 (c.34)
Waterworks Clauses Act 1847 (c.17)
Waterworks Clauses Act 1863 (c.93)
Watford Churchyard and Workhouse Act 1772 (c.28)
Wear Coal Trade Act 1792 (c.29)
Wear Navigation Act 1758 (c.64)
Wear Navigation Act 1758 (c.65)
Wearmouth and Tyne Bridge Road Act 1796 (c.136)
Wedding Rings Act 1855 (c.60)
Wednesfield Chapel Act 1746 (c.27)
Weedon Barracks Act 1804 (c.78)
Weeds Act 1959 (c.54)
Weeds and Agricultural Seeds (Ireland) Act 1909 (c.31)
Weights and Measures Act 1795 (c.102)
Weights and Measures Act 1797 (c.143)
Weights and Measures Act 1815 (c.43)
Weights and Measures Act 1824 (c.74)
Weights and Measures Act 1825 (c.12)
Weights and Measures Act 1834 (c.49)
Weights and Measures Act 1855 (c.72)
Weights and Measures Act 1859 (c.56)
Weights and Measures Act 1862 (c.76)
Weights and Measures Act 1878 (c.49)
Weights and Measures Act 1889 (c.21)
Weights and Measures Act 1893 (c.19)
Weights and Measures Act 1904 (c.28)
Weights and Measures Act 1936 (c.38)
Weights and Measures Act 1963 (c.31)
Weights and Measures Act 1979 (c.45)
Weights and Measures Act 1985 (c.72)
Weights and Measures (Amendment) Act 1926 (c.8)
Weights and Measures, Dublin Act 1867 (c.94)
Weights and Measures etc. Act 1976 (c.77)
Weights and Measures (Ireland) Act 1860 (c.119)
Weights and Measures (Leather Measurement) Act 1919 (c.29)
Weights and Measures (Metric System) Act 1897 (c.46)
Weights and Measures (Northern Ireland) Act 1967 (c.6)
Weights and Measures (Purchase) Act 1892 (c.18)
Weights and Measures, Sale of Coal (Scotland) Act 1936 (c.54)
Weights in Sales of Bullion Act 1853 (c.29)
Weights for Coin in the Mint Act 1774 (c.92)
Weights for Coin in the Mint Act 1775 (c.30)
Welfare of Animals at Slaughter Act 1991 (c.30)
Welford and Leicester Road Act 1765 (c.78)
Welford Bridge to Milston Lane Road Act 1786 (c.148)
Wellingborough and Northampton Road Act 1797 (c.167)
Wellington Museum Act 1947 (c.46)
Wells Harbour Act 1769 (c.8)
Wells Roads Act 1753 (c.76)
Wells, Somerset: Improvement Act 1779 (c.31)
Welsh Cathedrals Act 1843 (c.77)
Welsh Church Act 1914 (c.91)
Welsh Church (Amendment) Act 1938 (c.39)
Welsh Church (Burial Grounds) Act 1945 (c.27)
Welsh Church (Temporalities) Act 1919 (c.65)
Welsh Courts Act 1942 (c.40)
Welsh Development Agency Act 1975 (c.70)
Welsh Development Agency Act 1988 (c.5)
Welsh Development Agency Act 1991 (c.69)

Welsh Intermediate Education Act 1889 (c.40)
Welsh Language Act 1967 (c.66)
Welsh Language Act 1993 (c.38)
Welsh National Opera Company 1971 (c.37)
Wendover and Buckingham Road Act 1766 (c.71)
Wern and Bron-y-Garth Road Act 1797 (c.151)
Wesleyan Methodists (Appointments During the War) Act 1917 (c.29)
West Africa Offences Act 1871 (c.8)
West Coast of Africa and Falkland Islands Act 1860 (c.121)
West Coast of Africa Possessions Act 1821 (c.28)
West Cowgate and Alemouth Road Act 1797 (c.163)
West Highland Railway Guarantee Act 1896 (c.58)
West India Island Relief Act 1845 (c.50)
West India Islands Relief Act 1840 (c.40)
West India Loans Act 1848 (c.38)
West India Loans Act 1855 (c.71)
West India Loans Act 1879 (c.16)
West India Relief Commissioners Act 1856 (c.35)
West Indian Bishops, etc. Act 1825 (c.88)
West Indian Court of Appeal Act 1919 (c.47)
West Indian Courts of Appeal Act 1850 (c.15)
West Indian Incumbered Estates Act 1854 (c.117)
West Indian Incumbered Estates Act 1858 (c.96)
West Indian Incumbered Estates Act 1862 (c.45)
West Indian Incumbered Estates Act 1864 (c.108)
West Indian Islands Relief Act 1844 (c.17)
West Indian Islands (Telegraph) Act 1924 (c.14)
West Indian Loans Act 1848 (c.130)
West Indian Mortgages Act 1772 (c.14)
West Indian Prisons Act 1838 (c.67)
West Indies Act 1806 (c.80)
West Indies Act 1962 (c.19)
West Indies Act 1967 (c.4)
West Indies (Encumbered Estates) Act 1872 (c.9)
West Indies (Encumbered Estates) Act 1886 (c.36)
West Indies Relief Act 1843 (c.63)
West Indies (Salaries) Act 1868 (c.120)
West Riding Inclosures Act 1712 (c.4)
West Riding: Small Debts Act 1780 (c.65)
West Riding: Small Debts Act 1793 (c.84)
Westbury, Wilts (Additional Oversees) Act 1786 (c.23)
Western Australia Constitution Act 1890 (c.26)
Western Australia Government Act 1835 (c.14)
Western Australia Government Act 1836 (c.68)
Western Australia Government Act 1838 (c.46)
Western Australia Government Act 1841 (c.43)
Western Australia Government Act 1842 (c.88)
Western Australia Government Act 1844 (c.57)
Western Australia Government Act 1846 (c.35)
Western Highlands and Islands (Transport Services) Act 1928 (c.6)
Western Highlands and Islands (Scotland) Works Act 1891 (c.58)
Westminster Act 1756 (c.25)
Westminster Act 1757 (c.17)
Westminster 1861 (c.78)
Westminster Abbey Act 1888 (c.11)
Westminster Bridge Act 1735 (c.29)
Westminster Bridge Act 1736 (c.16)
Westminster Bridge Act 1737 (c.25)
Westminster Bridge Act 1738 (c.33)
Westminster Bridge Act 1739 (c.16)
Westminster Bridge Act 1740 (c.40)
Westminster Bridge Act 1741 (c.26)
Westminster Bridge Act 1743 (c.32)
Westminster Bridge Act 1744 (c.29)
Westminster Bridge Act 1756 (c.38)
Westminster Bridge Act 1757 (c.34)
Westminster Bridge Act 1853 (c.46)
Westminster Bridge Act 1859 (c.58)
Westminster Bridge Act 1864 (c.88)
Westminster Corn and Grain Market Act 1757 (c.25)
Westminster Election Act 1813 (c.152)
Westminster Fish Market Act 1790 (c.54)
Westminster Fish Market Act 1802 (c.19)
Westminster: Improvement Act 1778 (c.72)
Westminster: Improvement Act 1787 (c.54)
Westminster: Improvements Act 1790 (c.53)
Westminster, Improvements Act 1821 (c.45)
Westminster, King's Street Act 1753 (c.101)
Westminster Market Act 1749 (c.14)
Westminster Offices Act 1855 (c.95)
Westminster Offices Act 1859 (c.19)
Westminster Offices Act 1861 (c.33)
Westminster Offices Act 1862 (c.74)
Westminster Offices Act 1864 (c.51)
Westminster Offices Act 1865 (c.31)
Westminster Offices Act 1865 (c.32)
Westminster Parliamentary Elections Act 1811 (c.126)
Westminster Parliamentary Elections Act 1819 (c.2)
Westminster Streets Act 1728 (c.11)
Westminster Streets Act 1763 (c.39)
Westminster Streets Act 1765 (c.50)
Westminster Streets Act 1777 (c.61)
Westminster: Streets Act 1782 (c.44)
Westminster: Streets Act 1783 (c.42)
Westminster: Streets Act 1783 (c.43)
Westminster: Streets Act 1783 (c.89)
Westminster: Streets Act 1783 (c.90)

Westminster: Streets Act 1786 (c.102)
Westminster: Watching Act 1774 (c.90)
Westminster: Watching Act 1786 (c.112)
Westminster (Water Supply) Act 1721 (c.26)
Westmoreland Canals Act 1792 (c.101)
Westmoreland Gaol, etc. Act 1776 (c.54)
Westmoreland Roads Act 1742 (c.3)
Westmoreland Roads Act 1760 (c.43)
Westmoreland Roads Act 1753 (c.67)
Westmoreland Roads Act 1758 (c.69)
Westmoreland Roads Act 1779 (c.106)
Westmoreland Roads Act 1779 (c.108)
Westmoreland Roads Act 1780 (c.88)
Westmoreland Roads Act 1782 (c.111)
Westmoreland and Yorkshire Roads Act 1784 (c.70)
Wetherby to Grassington Road Act 1758 (c.71)
Wetherby to Grassington Road Act 1774 (c.98)
Wetherby to Knaresborough Road Act 1783 (c.103)
Wexford Grand Jury Act 1867 (c.77)
Weyhill and Lyde Way Road Act 1762 (c.60)
Weymouth Harbour Act 1748 (c.22)
Weymouth: Improvement Act 1776 (c.57)
Weymouth: Water Supply Act 1797 (c.129)
Whale Fishery Act 1732 (c.33)
Whale Fishery Act 1748 (c.45)
Whale Fishery Act 1755 (c.20)
Whale Fishery Act 1763 (c.22)
Whale Fishery Act 1768 (c.27)
Whale Fishery, etc. Act 1776 (c.47)
Whale Fisheries Act 1789 (c.53)
Whale Fisheries (Scotland) Act 1907 (c.41)
Whale Fisheries (Scotland) Act Amendment 1922 (c.34)
Whales Fisheries (Ireland) Act 1908 (c.31)
Whaling Industry (Regulation) Act 1934 (c.49)
Wharves Between London Bridge and Temple Act 1821 (c.89)
Wheat Act 1932 (c.24)
Wheat (Amendment) Act 1939 (c.37)
Whichwood Disafforesting Act 1853 (c.36)
Whichwood Disafforesting Act 1856 (c.32)
Whipping Act 1820 (c.57)
Whipping Act 1862 (c.18)
Whipping of Female Offenders, Abolition Act 1817 (c.75)
Whitby Harbour Act 1734 (c.10)
Whitby Harbour Act 1749 (c.39)
Whitby Harbour Act 1766 (c.81)
Whitby Harbour Act 1780 (c.12)
Whitby Harbour Act 1796 (c.121)
Whitby: Improvement Act 1764 (c.73)
Whitby: Improvement Act 1789 (c.12)
Whitby Piers 1702 (c.13)
Whitby Piers Act 1708 (c.7)
Whitby Roads Act 1785 (c.111)
Whitchurch, Salop: Poor Relief Act 1792 (c.85)
White Cross and Beverley Roads Act 1760 (c.42)
White Fish and Herring Industries Act 1948 (c.51)
White Fish and Herring Industries Act 1953 (c.17)
White Fish and Herring Industries Act 1957 (c.22)
White Fish and Herring Industries Act 1961 (c.18)
White Herring Fisheries Act 1771 (c.31)
White Herring Fishery Act 1779 (c.26)
White Herring Fishery (Scotland) Act 1821 (c.79)
White Herring Fishery (Scotland) Act 1861 (c.72)
White Phosphorus Matches Prohibition Act 1908 (c.42)
Whitechapel Highways Act 1721 (c.30)
Whitechapel: Improvement Act 1778 (c.37)
Whitechapel: Improvement Act 1778 (c.80)
Whitechapel (Poor Relief) Act 1763 (c.53)
Whitechapel: Poor Relief Act 1766 (c.74)
Whitechapel Roads Act 1736 (c.36)
Whitechapel, Stepney: Improvement Act 1793 (c.82)
Whitechapel: Streets Act 1783 (c.91)
Whitechapel to Aldermaston Road Act 1770 (c.88)
Whitehaven Harbour Act 1708 (c.9)
Whitehaven Harbour Act 1710 (c.17)
Whitehaven Harbour Improvement Act 1739 (c.14)
Whitehaven Harbour Impovement Act 1760 (c.44)
Whitehaven Harbour Improvement Act 1762 (c.87)
Whitehaven: Improvement Act 1788 (c.61)
Whitgift, Yorks (Drainage) Act 1793 (c.108)
Whitney Bridge, Hereford Act 1797 (c.56)
Whitney Bridge, Wye Act 1780 (c.27)
Whittlesey Drainage Act 1797 (c.68)
Whittlewood Disafforesting Act 1853 (c.42)
Whittlewood Forest Act 1824 (c.99)
Wicklow Harbour Act 1897 (c.55)
Wide Streets and Coal Trade, Dublin Act 1809 (c.72)
Wide Streets, Dublin Act 1811 (c.10)
Widows', Orphans' and Old Age Contributory Pensions Act 1925 (c.70)
Widows', Orphans' and Old Age Contributory Pensions Act 1929 (c.10)
Widows', Orphans' and Old Age Contributory Pensions Act 1931 (c.19)
Widows', Orphans' and Old Age Contributory Pensions Act 1936 (c.33)
Widows', Orphans' and Old Age Contributory Pensions (Voluntary Contributors) Act 1937 (c.39)
Wigan to Preston Road Act 1726 (c.9)
Wigan to Preston Road Act 1779 (c.92)
Wigan to Preston Road Act 1795 (c.145)
Wigan: Water Supply Act 1764 (c.75)
Wiggenhall Drainage Act 1757 (c.32)
Wigtown Roads Act 1778 (c.7)

Wild Animals in Captivity Protection Act 1900 (c.33)
Wild Animals in Captivity Protection (Scotland) Act 1909 (c.33)
Wild Birds (Duck and Geese) Protection Act 1939 (c.19)
Wild Birds Protection Act 1880 (c.35)
Wild Birds Protection Act 1881 (c.51)
Wild Birds Protection Act 1894 (c.24)
Wild Birds (Protection) Act 1896 (c.56)
Wild Birds Protection Act 1902 (c.6)
Wild Birds Protection Act 1904 (c.4)
Wild Birds Protection Act 1908 (c.11)
Wild Birds Protection (St. Kilda) Act 1904 (c.10)
Wild Creatures and Forest Laws Act 1971 (c.47)
Wild Mammals (Protection) Act 1996 (c.3)
Wilden Ferry Bridge Act 1757 (c.59)
Wildlife and Countryside Act 1981 (c.69)
Wildlife and Countryside (Amendment) Act 1985 (c.31)
Wildlife and Countryside (Amendment) Act 1991 (c.39)
Wildlife and Countryside (Service of Notices) Act 1985 (c.59)
Will of Sir Joseph Jekyll Act 1746 (c.34)
Willian Preston Indemnity Act 1925 (c.7)
Wills Act 1703 (c.5)
Wills Act 1751 (c.6)
Wills Act 1837 (c.26)
Wills Act 1861 (c.114)
Wills Act 1963 (c.44)
Wills Act 1968 (c.28)
Wills Act Amendment Act 1852 (c.24)
Wills, etc. of Seamen, etc. Act 1815 (c.60)
Wills (Soldiers and Sailors) Act 1918 (c.58)
Wiltshire Highways 1706 (c.26)
Wiltshire Highways Act 1707 (c.76)
Wiltshire Highways Act 1713 (c.17)
Wiltshire Highways Act 1728 (c.12)
Wiltshire Roads Act 1724 (c.27)
Wiltshire Roads Act 1725 (c.7)
Wiltshire Roads Act 1725 (c.11)
Wiltshire Roads Act 1736 (c.6)
Wiltshire Roads Act 1740 (c.29)
Wiltshire Roads Act 1742 (c.10)
Wiltshire Roads Act 1743 (c.23)
Wiltshire Roads Act 1743 (c.27)
Wiltshire Roads Act 1744 (c.14)
Wiltshire Roads Act 1750 (c.9)
Wiltshire Roads Act 1751 (c.5)
Wiltshire Roads Act 1751 (c.12)
Wiltshire Roads Act 1753 (c.42)
Wiltshire Roads Act 1755 (c.44)
Wiltshire Roads Act 1756 (c.67)
Wiltshire Roads Act 1757 (c.41)
Wiltshire Roads Act 1757 (c.68)
Wiltshire Roads Act 1758 (c.63)
Wiltshire Roads Act 1760 (c.37)
Wiltshire Roads Act 1762 (c.49)
Wiltshire Roads Act 1762 (c.51)
Wiltshire Roads Act 1762 (c.59)
Wiltshire Roads Act 1762 (c.66)
Wiltshire Roads Act 1766 (c.57)
Wiltshire Roads Act 1768 (c.49)
Wiltshire Roads Act 1769 (c.48)
Wiltshire Roads Act 1769 (c.73)
Wiltshire Roads Act 1771 (c.81)
Wiltshire Roads Act 1772 (c.74)
Wiltshire Roads Act 1772 (c.85)
Wiltshire Roads Act 1773 (c.101)
Wiltshire Roads Act 1777 (c.72)
Wiltshire Roads Act 1777 (c.98)
Wiltshire Roads Act 1779 (c.111)
Wiltshire Roads Act 1780 (c.82)
Wiltshire Roads Act 1780 (c.98)
Wiltshire Roads Act 1783 (c.30)
Wiltshire Roads Act 1783 (c.111)
Wiltshire Roads Act 1788 (c.86)
Wiltshire Roads Act 1790 (c.96)
Wiltshire Roads Act 1790 (c.98)
Wiltshire Roads Act 1791 (c.121)
Wiltshire Roads Act 1792 (c.114)
Wiltshire Roads Act 1795 (c.136)
Wiltshire and Berkshire Roads Act 1757 (c.66)
Wiltshire, Dorset and Somerset Roads Act 1753 (c.60)
Wiltshire, Dorset and Somerset Roads Act 1756 (c.92)
Wiltshire, Dorset and Somerset Roads Act 1756 (c.54)
Wiltshire and Dorset Roads Act 1777 (c.83)
Wiltshire, Dorset and Somerset Roads Act 1779 (c.94)
Wiltshire and Gloucester Roads Act 1751 (c.59)
Wiltshire and Gloucester Roads 1778 (c.103)
Wiltshire and Hampshire Roads 1764 (c.47)
Wiltshire and Somerset Roads Act 1751 (c.17)
Wiltshire and Somerset Roads Act 1751 (c.52)
Wiltshire and Somerset Roads Act 1751 (c.24)
Wiltshire and Somerset Roads Act 1757 (c.46)
Wiltshire and Somerset Roads Act 1768 (c.49)
Wiltshire and Somerset Roads Act 1777 (c.93)
Wiltshire and Somerset Roads Act 1777 (c.99)
Wiltshire and Somerset Roads Act 1792 (c.137)
Wiltshire and Somerset Roads Act 1793 (c.155)
Wiltshire and Southampton Roads Act 1753 (c.66)
Wiltshire and Southampton Roads Act 1756 (c.45)
Wiltshire and Southampton Roads Act 1782 (c.110)
Wincanton Roads 1756 (c.49)
Winchester: Improvement Act 1771 (c.9)

Window Duties Act 1747 (c.10)
Window Duties Act 1753 (c.17)
Window Duties Act 1761 (c.8)
Window Duties (Scotland) Act 1817 (c.128)
Window Duty (Ireland) Act 1810 (c.75)
Windows Duties Act 1796 (c.117)
Windsor Bridge Act 1735 (c.15)
Windsor Castle Act 1848 (c.53)
Windsor Forest Act 1806 (c.143)
Windsor Forest Act 1813 (c.158)
Windsor Forest Act 1815 (c.122)
Windsor Forest Act 1816 (c.132)
Windsor Forest Boundary Commission Act 1807 (c.46)
Windsor Forest Road Act 1758 (c.46)
Windsor Lands Act 1702 (c.27)
Windward Islands Appeal Court Act 1889 (c.33)
Wine and Beerhouse Act 1869 (c.27)
Wine and Beerhouse Amendment Act 1870 (c.29)
Wine, etc. Duties Act 1825 (c.13)
Wine Licences Act 1758 (c.19)
Winfrith Heath Act 1957 (c.61)
Winter Assizes Act 1876 (c.57)
Winter Assizes Act 1877 (c.46)
Winterbourne Parish Act 1841 (c.42)
Wireless Telegraph (Blind Person' Facilities) Act 1926 (c.54)
Wireless Telegraphy Act 1904 (c.24)
Wireless Telegraphy Act 1906 (c.13)
Wireless Telegraphy Act 1949 (c.54)
Wireless Telegraphy Act 1955 (c.10)
Wireless Telegraphy Act 1967 (c.72)
Wireless Telegraphy (Explanation) Act 1925 (c.67)
Wireless Telegraphy (Validation of Charges) Act 1954 (c.2)
Wisbech Canal Act 1794 (c.92)
Wisbech Roads Act 1786 (c.133)
Witchcraft Act 1735 (c.5)
Witchcraft, etc. (Ireland) Act 1821 (c.18)
Witford, etc. Suffolk: Poor Relief Act 1765 (c.97)
Witham Drainage Act 1762 (c.32)
Witnesses Act 1806 (c.37)
Witnesses' Indemnity, Penryn Act 1828 (c.13)
Witnesses on Petitions Act 1801 (c.105)
Witnesses on Trial for Treason 1702 (c.9)
Witnesses (Public Inquiries) Protection Act 1892 (c.64)
Witney to Chanfield Road Act 1793 (c.137)
Wiveliscombe Roads Act 1786 (c.135)
Wolverhampton Church Act 1755 (c.34)
Wolverhampton: Improvements Act 1776 (c.25)
Wolverhampton Parish Act 1848 (c.95)
Wolverhampton Roads Act 1772 (c.101)
Wolverhampton Roads 1747 (c.25)
Wolverhampton Roads Act 1793 (c.147)
Wolverhampton Roads Act 1794 (c.133)
Wolverhampton Roads Act 1796 (c.146)
Women and Young Persons (Employment in Lead Processes) Act 1920 (c.62)
Woods and Forest Act 1803 (c.31)
Woods and Forests Act 1806 (c.142)
Woodstock, Oxford, Roads Act 1784 (c.61)
Wool Act 1738 (c.21)
Wool Act 1780 (c.55)
Wool Duties, etc. Act 1824 (c.47)
Woolcombers Act 1795 (c.124)
Woollen Cloths Act 1707 (c.43)
Woollen Cloths Act 1708 (c.13)
Woollen, etc. Manufacturers Act 1710 (c.32)
Woollen, etc. Manufacturers 1735 (c.4)
Woollen, etc. Manufactures Act 1720 (c.7)
Woollen, etc. Manufactures, Bedfordshire Act 1785 (c.40)
Woollen, etc. Manufactures, Norfolk Act 1791 (c.56)
Woollen Manufacturers Act 1702 (c.22)
Woollen Manufacture Act 1711 (c.26)
Woollen Manufacture Act 1714 (c.15)
Woollen Manufacture Act 1715 (c.41)
Woollen Manufactures Act 1725 (c.34)
Woollen Manufactures Act 1726 (c.23)
Woollen Manufactures Act 1731 (c.21)
Woollen Manufacture Act 1756 (c.33)
Woollen Manufactures Act 1757 (c.12)
Woollen Manufactures Act 1803 (c.136)
Woollen Manufacture Act 1804 (c.64)
Woollen Manufacture Act 1805 (c.83)
Woollen Manufacture Act 1806 (c.18)
Woollen Manufacture Act 1807 (c.43)
Woollen Manufacture Act 1808 (c.131)
Woollen Manufacture Act 1809 (c.109)
Woollen Manufacture Act 1810 (c.83)
Woollen Manufactures, Suffolk Act 1784 (c.3)
Woollen Trade Act 1833 (c.28)
Woolmer Forest Act 1812 (c.71)
Woolmer Forest Act 1855 (c.46)
Woolwich Church Act 1738 (c.9)
Woolwich Dockyard Act 1833 (c.65)
Woolwich Fortifications Act 1780 (c.46)
Worcester Roads Act 1725 (c.14)
Worcester Roads Act 1736 (c.5)
Worcester Roads act 1743 (c.13)
Worcester Roads Act 1753 (c.50)
Worcester Roads Act 1759 (c.50)
Worcester Roads Act 1767 (c.65)
Worcester Roads Act 1782 (c.95)
Worcester Roads Act 1783 (c.98)
Worcester Roads Act 1788 (c.88)
Worcester Roads Act 1789 (c.102)
Worcester Roads Act 1793 (c.175)
Worcester Roads Act 1795 (c.133)
Worcester and Birmingham Canal Act 1791 (c.59)
Worcester Bridge Act 1769 (c.84)
Worcester Bridge Act 1779 (c.42)
Worcester to Droitwich Road Act 1725 (c.20)
Worcester: Improvement Act 1770 (c.22)
Worcester: Poor Relief, Burial Ground and Hopmarket 1703 (c.8)
Worcester: Poor Relief, Burial Ground and Hopmarket Act 1730 (c.23)

Worcester: Poor Relief, Burial Ground and Hopmarket Act 1730 (c.25)
Worcester: Poor Relief, Burial Ground and Hopmarket Act 1792 (c.99)
Worcester and Salop Roads Act 1762 (c.78)
Worcester and Salop Roads Act 1763 (c.51)
Worcester, Salop and Stafford Roads Act 1790 (c.102)
Worcester: Streets Act 1780 (c.21)
Worcester and Warwick Roads Act 1767 (c.68)
Worcester and Warwick Roads Act 1771 (c.92)
Worcester and Warwick Roads Act 1773 (c.106)
Worcester and Warwick Roads Act 1773 (c.107)
Worcester and Warwick Roads Act 1788 (c.115)
Worcester and Warwick Roads Act 1789 (c.106)
Worcester and Warwick Roads Act 1792 (c.140)
Worcester and Warwick Roads Act 1794 (c.136)
Worcester, Warwick and Gloucester Roads Act 1757 (c.64)
Worcester: Water Supply, etc., Act 1771 (c.13)
Worcestershire Highways Act 1713 (c.27)
Worcestershire Roads Act 1748 (c.43)
Worcestershire Roads Act 1751 (c.60)
Worcestershire Roads Act 1755 (c.48)
Worcestershire Roads Act 17776 (c.78)
Worcestershire Roads Act 1779 (c.89)
Worcestershire, Staffordshire, Shropshire Roads Act 1781 (c.93)
Workhouses Act 1790 (c.49)
Workhouse Act 1816 (c.129)
Workhouses (Ireland) Act 1849 (c.86)
Workhouse Sites Act 1857 (c.13)
Workhouse, Westminster Act 1772 (c.34)
Working Classes Dwellings Act 1890 (c.16)
Working Men's Dwellings Act 1874 (c.59)
Working of Jews on Sunday Act 1871 (c.19)
Workmen's Compensation Act 1897 (c.37)
Workmen's Compensation Act 1900 (c.22)
Workmen's Compensation Act 1906 (c.58)
Workmen's Compensation Act 1909 (c.16)
Workmen's Compensation Act 1923 (c.42)
Workmen's Compensation Act 1925 (c.84)
Workmen's Compensation Act 1926 (c.42)
Workmen's Compensation Act 1931 (c.18)
Workmen's Compensation Act 1943 (c.6)
Workmen's Compensation (Amendment) Act 1938 (c.27)
Workmen's Compensation and Benefit (Amendment) Act 1965 (c.79)
Workmen's Compensation and Benefit (Byssinosis) Act 1940 (c.56)
Workmen's Compensation and Benefit (Supplementation) Act 1956 (c.51)
Workmen's Compensation (Coal Mines) Act 1934 (c.23)
Workmen's Compensation (Illegal Employment) Act 1918 (c.8)
Workmen's Compensation (Pneumoconiosis) Act 1945 (c.16)
Workmen's Compensation (Silicosis) Act 1918 (c.14)
Workmen's Compensation (Silicosis) Act 1924 (c.40)
Workmen's Compensation (Silicosis and Asbestosis) Act 1930 (c.29)
Workmen's Compensation (Supplementary Allowances) Act 1940 (c.47)
Workmen's Compensation (Supplementation) Act 1951 (c.22)
Workmen's Compensation (Temporary Increase) Act 1943 (c.49)
Workmen's Compensation (Transfer of Funds) Act 1927 (c.15)
Workmen's Compensation (War Addition) Act 1917 (c.42)
Workmen's Compensation (War Addition) Amendment Act 1919 (c.83)
Works and Public Buildings Act 1874 (c.84)
Works of Utility, etc. Indemnity Act 1858 (c.102)
Workshop Regulation Act 1867 (c.146)
Worksop and Attercliffe Road Act 1764 (c.52)
Worksop and Attercliffe Road Act 1786 (c.125)
Worsley Brook: Navigation Act 1736 (c.9)
Worstead Act 1776 (c.11)
Wreak and Eye: Navigation Act 1791 (c.77)
Wreck and Salvage Act 1846 (c.99)
Wrecking (Ireland) Act 1803 (c.79)
Wrexham to Barnhill Road Act 1782 (c.105)
Writ of Subpoena Act 1805 (c.92)
Writs Execution (Scotland) Act 1877 (c.40)
Writs of Assistance Act 1814 (c.46)
Writs of Error Act 1718 (c.13)
Writs of Error Act 1825 (c.96)
Writs of Execution Act 1833 (c.67)
Writs of Mandamus Act 1843 (c.67)
Writs Registration (Scotland) Act 1868 (c.34)

Yarmouth Coal Import Duties 1706 (c.10)
Yarmouth Coal Import Duties (Privileges of Freemen, etc.) 1782 (c.22)
Yarmouth Haven Act 1746 (c.40)
Yarmouth Haven and Pier Repairs 1702 (c.7)
Yarmouth Naval Hospital Act 1931 (c.15)
Yarmouth Naval Hospital Transfer Act 1957 (c.3)
Yarmouth: Small Debts Act 1757 (c.24)
Yarmouth to Gorleston Road Act 1775 (c.67)
Yarmouth to Gorleston Road Act 1795 (c.132)
Yaxley: Drainage Act 1772 (c.46)
Yeomanry Act 1804 (c.54)
Yeomanry Act 1817 (c.44)
Yeomanry Act 1826 (c.58)
Yeomanry (Accounts) Act 1804 (c.94)
Yeomanry Cavalry Act 1798 (c.51)

Yeomanry (Ireland) Act 1802 (c.68)
Yeomanry (Training) Act 1816 (c.39)
Yeomanry and Volunteers Act 1802 (c.66)
Yeomanry and Volunteers Act 1803 (c.121)
Yeomanry Corps, etc. (Ireland) Act 1814 (c.178)
Yeomanry Corps (Ireland) Act 1816 (c.72)
Yeomanry Corps (Ireland) Act 1818 (c.40)
Yeomanry Corps (Ireland) Act 1820 (c.48)
Yeomanry Corps (Ireland) Act 1823 (c.15)
Yeomanry Corps (Ireland) Act 1828 (c.30)
Yeomanry, etc. Act 1806 (c.125)
York and Boroughbridge Road Act 1749 (c.38)
York and Boroughbridge Road Act 1771 (c.66)
York and Boroughbridge Road Act 1797 (c.149)
York and Durham Roads Act 1753 (c.95)
York Buildings Company, Sale of Scottish Estates Act 1776 (c.24)
York Buildings: Rates Act 1756 (c.90)
York Butter Trade Supervision Act 1721 (c.27)
York House and Victoria Park Act 1841 (c.27)
York: Lighting and Watching Act 1763 (c.48)
York Roads Act 1765 (c.99)
York Roads Act 1792 (c.155)
Yorkshire Registries Act 1884 (c.54)
Yorkshire Registries Amendment Act 1884 (c.4)
Yorkshire Registries Amendment Act 1885 (c.26)
Yorkshire Roads Act 1740 (c.23)
Yorkshire Roads Act 1742 (c.7)
Yorkshire Roads Act 1743 (c.22)
Yorkshire Roads Act 1743 (c.25)
Yorkshire Roads Act 1744 (c.6)
Yorkshire Roads Act 1744 (c.16)
Yorkshire Roads Act 1748 (c.39)
Yorkshire Roads Act 1751 (c.47)
Yorkshire Roads Act 1751 (c.53)
Yorkshire Roads Act 1751 (c.58)
Yorkshire Roads Act 1755 (c.50)
Yorkshire Roads Act 1756 (c.71)
Yorkshire Roads Act 1756 (c.83)
Yorkshire Roads Act 1757 (c.54)
Yorkshire Roads Act 1758 (c.70)
Yorkshire Roads Act 1759 (c.55)
Yorkshire Roads Act 1760 (c.35)
Yorkshire Roads Act 1762 (c.71)
Yorkshire Roads Act 1764 (c.66)
Yorkshire Roads Act 1764 (c.69)
Yorkshire Roads Act 1765 (c.72)
Yorkshire Roads Act 1766 (c.59)
Yorkshire Roads Act 1766 (c.62)
Yorkshire Roads Act 1767 (c.71)
Yorkshire Roads Act 1768 (c.54)
Yorkshire Roads Act 1769 (c.54)
Yorkshire Roads Act 1769 (c.75)
Yorkshire Roads Act 1769 (c.79)
Yorkshire Roads Act 1771 (c.63)
Yorkshire Roads Act 1771 (c.68)
Yorkshire Roads Act 1771 (c.71)
Yorkshire Roads Act 1774 (c.117)
Yorkshire Roads Act 1777 (c.73)
Yorkshire Roads Act 1777 (c.77)
Yorkshire Roads Act 1777 (c.78)
Yorkshire Roads Act 1777 (c.80)
Yorkshire Roads Act 1777 (c.102)
Yorkshire Roads Act 1778 (c.96)
Yorkshire Roads Act 1780 (c.86)
Yorkshire Roads Act 1780 (c.89)
Yorkshire Roads Act 1781 (c.96)
Yorkshire Roads Act 1782 (c.97)
Yorkshire Roads Act 1783 (c.29)
Yorkshire Roads Act 1783 (c.95)
Yorkshire Roads Act 1786 (c.142)
Yorkshire Roads Act 1786 (c.144)
Yorkshire Roads Act 1787 (c.86)
Yorkshire Roads Act 1788 (c.106)
Yorkshire Roads Act 1788 (c.108)
Yorkshire Roads Act 1788 (c.110)
Yorkshire Roads Act 1789 (c.109)
Yorkshire Roads Act 1790 (c.99)
Yorkshire Roads Act 1792 (c.132)
Yorkshire Roads Act 1792 (c.133)
Yorkshire Roads Act 1792 (c.136)
Yorkshire Roads Act 1793 (c.157)
Yorkshire Roads Act 1794 (c.134)
Yorkshire and Chester Roads Act 1767 (c.94)
Yorkshire and Derby Roads Act 1757 (c.62)
Yorkshire and Derby Roads Act 1768 (c.47)
Yorkshire and Derby Roads Act 1771 (c.76)
Yorkshire and Derby Roads Act 1779 (c.96)
Yorkshire and Derby Roads Act 1795 (c.164)
Yorkshire, Derby and Chester Roads Act 1793 (c.140)
Yorkshire and Derbyshire Roads Act 1793 (c.184)
Yorkshire and Durham Roads Act 1746 (c.28)
Yorkshire and Durham Roads Act 1748 (c.32)
Yorkshire and Durham Roads Act 1755 (c.51)
Yorkshire and Durham Roads Act 1756 (c.80)
Yorkshire and Durham Roads Act 1760 (c.41)
Yorkshire and Durham Roads Act 1779 (c.80)
Yorkshire and Durham Roads Act 1782 (c.93)
Yorkshire and Durham Roads Act 1792 (c.118)
Yorkshire and Durham Roads Act 1792 (c.135)
Yorkshire and Lancaster Roads Act 1755 (c.59)
Yorkshire and Lancaster Roads Act 1755 (c.60)
Yorkshire and Lancaster Roads Act 1756 (c.91)
Yorkshire and Lancaster Roads Act 1759 (c.48)
Yorkshire and Lancaster Roads Act 1777 (c.90)
Yorkshire and Nottinghamshire Roads Act 1766 (c.67)
Yorkshire and Westmorland Roads Act 1753 (c.86)
Yorkshire and Westmorland Roads Act 1791 (c.122)

Yorkshire Coroners Act 1897 (c.39)
Yorkshire: Drainage Act 1789 (c.78)
Yorkshire (East Riding) Land Registry Act 1707 (c.62)
Yorkshire (North Riding) Land Registry Act 1734 (c.6)
Yorkshire: Small Debts Act 1776 (c.15)
Yorkshire (West Riding) Land Registry Act 1703 (c.4)
Yorkshire (West Riding) Land Registry 1706 (c.20)
Youghal Rectory Act 1827 (c.26)
Young Persons (Employment) Act 1938 (c.69)
Young Persons (Employment) Act 1964 (c.66)
Youthful Offenders Act 1855 (c.87)
Youthful Offenders Act 1901 (c.20)
Youthful Offenders, Great Britain Act 1854 (c.86)
Yule Vacance Act 1711 (c.22)
Yule Vacance Act 1714 (c.28)

Zambia Independence Act 1964 (c.65)
Zanzibar Act 1963 (c.55)
Zanzibar Indemnity Act 1894 (c.31)
Zimbabwe Act 1979 (c.60)
Zoo Licensing Act 1981 (c.37)

INDEX

This is the third part of the Current Law Statutes Index 1996 and is up to date to February 5, 1997. References, *e.g.* 6/33, are to the Statutes of 1996, Chapter 6, section 33.

ACQUISITION OF LAND,
by agreement,
for Channel Tunnel Rail Link, **61**/48
compulsory,
for Channel Tunnel Rail Link, **61**/4, 5, Sched. 4
for improvements to A2 and M2, **61**/45, Sched. 13
ADMIRALTY LAW,
arbitration proceedings, **23**/11
ADVERTISEMENTS,
trading standards, **32**/2
AIR PASSENGER DUTY,
pleasure flights, **8**/13
AIRCRAFT,
British-controlled, **39**/1
evidence: inquiries by consular officer, **39**/2
foreign aircraft UK bound, **39**/1
hovercraft: adaption, **8**/28
ALIBI DEFENCE,
procedural amendments, **25**/5(7–8), 74
Allied Irish Banks Act 1996 (c.vii)
ANIMALS AND BIRDS,
deer in Scotland, *see* SCOTS LAW
dogs fouling land,
byelaws, effect on, **20**/6
fixed penalty notices, **20**/4
land,
applicable, **20**/1
designation of, **20**/2
offence, **20**/3
wild mammals,
confiscation and destruction of vehicles and equipment, **3**/6
constable's powers, **3**/4
definition, **3**/3
lawful killing, **3**/2
offence against, **3**/1
penalties, **3**/5
suffering, intent to inflict, **3**/1
Appropriation Act 1996 (c.45)
ARBITRATION,
admiralty proceedings, **23**/11
agreements,
commencement of proceedings, **23**/12–14, *see also* commencement of proceedings
consumer, *see* consumer arbitration agreements
death of party, **23**/8
domestic, *see* domestic arbitration agreements
meaning of, **23**/6

ARBITRATION—*cont.*
agreements—*cont.*
separability of, **23**/7
stay of legal proceedings, **23**/9–12, *see also* stay of legal proceedings
writing, need for, **23**/5
applicable law, **23**/4
arbitral tribunal,
arbitrators,
appointment: failure of procedure, **23**/18
death of, **23**/26
fees and expenses, **23**/28, 56
filling vacancies, **23**/27
immunity of, **23**/29
immunity of appointors, **23**/74
judges as, **23**/93, Sched. 2
number of, **23**/15
procedure, **23**/16
removal of, **23**/24
resignation of, **23**/25
revocation of authority of, **23**/23
sole arbitrator, **23**/17
awards,
additional, **23**/57
appeals against,
on point of law, **23**/69
provisions as to, **23**/70
serious irregularity, **23**/68
substantive jurisdiction, **23**/67
choice of law, **23**/46
correction of, **23**/57
costs of, **23**/61, 62
date of, **23**/54
on different issues, **23**/47
effect of, **23**/58
enforcement of, **23**/66
extension of time for making, **23**/50
foreign, *see* foreign awards
form of, **23**/52
interest, **23**/49
notification of, **23**/54
place where made, **23**/53
provisional, **23**/39
remedies, **23**/48
settlement, **23**/51
withholding where non-payment of fees, **23**/56
chairman,
decision-making where no chairman, **23**/22
functions, **23**/20

Arbitration—*cont.*
arbitral tribunal—*cont.*
court's powers and,
attendance of witnesses, **23**/43
enforcement of awards, **23**/66
generally, **23**/44
point of law, determination of, **23**/45
jurisdiction,
determination of preliminary point, **23**/32
objection to, **23**/31
ruling on its own, **23**/30
notices, **23**/76, 80
objection to proceedings, **23**/73
party taking no part in proceedings, **23**/72
proceedings,
concurrent hearings, **23**/35
consolidation of, **23**/35
decisions as to, **23**/34
default of party, **23**/41
duty of parties, **23**/40
experts, advisers and assessors, **23**/37
general duty, **23**/33
legal representation, **23**/36
powers of tribunal, **23**/38
service of documents, **23**/77
time limits, **23**/78, 79
umpire, **23**/21, 22
arbitration,
general principles, **23**/1
mandatory provisions, **23**/3, Sched. 1
non-mandatory provisions, **23**/4
object of, 1
seat of, **23**/2, 3
statutory, *see* statutory arbitration
awards, *see* arbitral tribunal
choice of law, **23**/4, 46
commencement of arbitral proceedings,
Limitation Acts, application of, **23**/13
parties' agreement as to, **23**/14
time for beginning, **23**/12
common law, application of, **23**/81
consumer arbitration agreements, 23/89–91
costs of,
agreement,
as to liability, **23**/62
to pay in any event, **23**/60
arbitrator's fees and expenses,
liability of parties, **23**/28
recoverable, **23**/64
witholding award for non-payment, 23/56
award of, **23**/61, 62
meaning of, **23**/59
recoverable,
of arbitration, **23**/63
of arbitrator, **23**/64
limitation of, **23**/65
solicitor's costs, **23**/75
court's powers,
agreement to exclude in domestic agreements, **23**/87
in arbitral proceedings, *see* arbitral proceedings
jurisdiction, **23**/105
see also stay of legal proceedings

Arbitration—*cont.*
Crown application, **23**/106
death of party, **23**/8
domestic arbitration agreements,
exclusion of court's jurisdiction, **23**/87
modified provisions as to, **23**/85
power to repeal provisions as to, **23**/88
staying of legal proceedings, **23**/86
for Channel Tunnel Rail Link, **61**/43
foreign awards,
Geneva Convention awards, **23**/99
New York Convention awards, **23**/100–104
immunity of arbitral institutions, **23**/74
interest awards, **23**/49
interpleader issues, **23**/10
irregularities, **23**/68
judges as arbitrators, **23**/93, Sched. 2
parties' agreement, **23**/1, 4
remedies, **23**/48
separability, **23**/7
settlement of dispute, **23**/51
small claims, **23**/92
solicitor's costs, **23**/75
statutory, **23**/94–98
stay of legal proceedings,
Admiralty proceedings, **23**/11
application for, **23**/9
domestic agreements, **23**/86
interpleader reference, **23**/10
umpire, **23**/21
unfair terms, **23**/89–91
Arbitration Act 1996 (c.23)
Architects Registration Board,
code of practice, **53**/122
constitution and functions, **53**/118, Sched. 2
discipline, **53**/121
Education Fund, **53**/124
practising while unregistered: offence, **53**/123
Registrar of Architects, **53**/119
registration, **53**/120
staff, **53**/119
Armed Forces Act 1996 (c.46)
Armed Services,
community supervision orders, **46**/10, Sched. 3
complaints,
employment rights, **46**/26, 27
equal treatment, **46**/24, 25
racial discrimination, **46**/23
redress of procedures, **46**/20
sex discrimination,
Great Britain, **46**/21
Northern Ireland, **46**/22
courts martial, *see* trial and punishment of offences
Criminal Procedure and Evidence Act 1996: application of Act, **25**/78
discharge certificates, **46**/3
drug testing programmes, **46**/32
employment rights, **18**/192, **46**/26, 27
enlistment,
for local service, **46**/2
regulations, **46**/4

ARMED SERVICES—*cont.*
equal treatment, **46**/24, 25
fingerprints and samples, **46**/11
Firearms Act 1968: exemptions, **46**/28, 29
Greenwich Hospital, **46**/30
Hong Kong war wives and widows: British nationality, **41**/1, 2
Independent Assessor of Military Complaints Procedures in Northern Ireland, **22**/51, Sched. 4
industrial tribunals, **46**/21
local service, **46**/2
racial discrimination, **46**/23
reserve forces *see* RESERVE FORCES
Royal Naval College, Greenwich, **46**/31
Service Acts,
continuation of, **46**/1
offences under, *see* Trial and punishment of offenders
sex discrimination: Northern Ireland, **46**/22
and terrorism, *see* NORTHERN IRELAND, emergency provisions
trial and punishment of offences,
abrogation of corroboration rules, **46**/6
community supervision orders, **46**/10, Sched. 3
evidence from children, **46**/7
findings of unfitness to stand trial and insanity, **46**/8, Sched. 2
fingerprints and samples, **46**/11
postponement of sentences of courts-martial, **46**/9
procedure, **46**/5, Sched. 1
rehabilitation of offenders, **46**/13, 14, Sched. 4
review and appeal,
abolition of confirmation, **46**/15
appeals against sentence, **46**/17
deceased persons, appeals on behalf of, **46**/19
Registrar's powers, **46**/18
review of findings, **46**/16, Sched. 5
visiting forces, **46**/33
ARREST POWERS,
deer offences (Scots Law), **58**/28
immigration offences and, **49**/7
non-molestation orders and, **27**/46, Sched. 5
terrorism and, *see* NORTHERN IRELAND, emergency provisions
without warrant for carrying offensive weapons, **26**/1
witness summonses and, **25**/51
ASSAULT,
on constables, **16**/89
procedure and investigations, **25**/1(2)(d)
ASSURED TENANCIES, *see* LANDLORD AND TENANT, repossession
ASYLUM, *see* IMMIGRATION
Asylum and Immigration Act 1996 (c.49)
ATTEMPT,
to commit offences in relation to deer, **58**/24
AUDIT COMMISSION,
extension of functions, **10**/1, 2
AUDIT COMMISSION—*cont.*
financial years, **10**/3, 4
publication, **10**/5
remuneration of members, **10**/6
Audit (Miscellaneous Provisions) Act 1996 (c.10)
Australia and New Zealand Banking Group Act 1996 (c.ii)

BANKING LAW,
Allied Irish Banks p.l.c.: fusion of businesses, **vii**/1-17
ANZ Grindlays Bank p.l.c.,
continuation of legal identity, **ii**/4(2)
registration in Victoria, **ii**/3
removal from register in England, **ii**/4
ANZ Holding (UK) p.l.c.,
continuation of legal identity, **ii**/4(2)
registration in Victoria, **ii**/3
removal from register in England, **ii**/4
Australia and New Zealand Banking Group Limited (ANZ),
transfer of business to, **ii**/5–11
Belfast Charitable Society Act 1996 (c.vi)
BERNERAY CAUSEWAY,
confirmation of provisional order, **xii**
BLIND PERSONS, *see* HANDICAPPED PERSONS
BOATS,
rating, **12**/1
BODIES CORPORATE,
and deer offences, **58**/23
offences under Housing Act 1996, **52**/223
BRIDGES, *see* HIGHWAYS AND BRIDGES
BROADCASTING,
advertising, **55**/31
ancillary services, **55**/87
BBC,
BBC companies, services provided by, **55**/136, Sched. 8
enforcement of licences, **55**/35
reservation of digital capacity in local radio multiplex licences, **55**/49
transmission schemes,
agreements as to, **55**/133
power to make, **55**/131, Sched. 5
Secretary of State's powers as to, **55**/132
successor companies, **55**/134, Sched. 6
taxation provisions, **55**/136, Sched. 7
Broadcasting Complaints Commission,
dissolution of, **55**/128, Sched. 4
transfer of assets to Broadcasing Standards Commission, **55**/128
transitional provisions as to complaints, **55**/129
Broadcasting Standards Commission,
annual reports, **55**/125
codes,
broadcasting standards generally, **55**/108
interference with privacy, **55**/107
unjust or unfair treatment, **55**/107
complaints,
action taken on findings: reports, **55**/120

Broadcasting—*cont.*
Broadcasting Standards Commission—*cont.*
complaints—*cont.*
allowances for persons attending hearings, **55**/118
as to fairness, **55**/111
committee to consider, **55**/112
consideration of, **55**/115
form of, **55**/114
general functions, **55**/110
publication of findings, **55**/119
qualified privilege for matters published, **55**/121
recordings, duty to retain, **55**/117
as to standards,
conditions to be met, **55**/113
consideration of, **55**/116
taste decency etc., **55**/113
transitional provisions, **55**/129
establishment of, **55**/106, Sched. 3
funding of, **55**/127
monitoring of standards, **55**/109
publicising, **55**/124
reports to Secretary of State, **55**/126
representing Government interests on international bodies, **55**/123
research, power to commission, **55**/122
transfer of assets of existing boards, **55**/128
Broadcasting Standards Council,
dissolution of, **55**/128, Sched. 4
transfer of assets to Broadcasting Standards Commission, **55**/128
Channel 3,
licences subject to conditions, **55**/86
Channel 4,
extension of powers of, **55**/84
funding of,
application of excess revenues, **55**/83
multiplex revenue to be taken into account, **55**/82
complaints, *see* Broadcasting Standards Commission
copyright,
licensing, **55**/139
statutory amendments, **55**/138, Sched. 9
unauthorised decoders, **55**/140
unauthorised reception: apparatus, **55**/141
visual images in news reporting, **55**/137
deaf people,
digital programme code for, **55**/20–22
decency, **55**/113
digital additional services (radio),
licences,
application for, **55**/64
conditions of, **55**/65
duration of, **55**/65
enforcement of, **55**/66
meaning of, **55**/63
digital additional services (television),
licences,
application for, **55**/25

Broadcasting—*cont.*
digital additional services (television)—*cont.*
licences—*cont.*
conditions of, **55**/26
duration of, **55**/26
enforcement of, **55**/27
meaning of, **55**/24
digital broadcasting,
advertisements in qualifying services, **55**/31
equal opportunities, **55**/34
financial penalties, **55**/36
Gaelic programmes, **55**/32
by independent analogue broadcasters, **55**/28
qualifying teletext service, **55**/30
S4C service, **55**/29
television: review, **55**/33
digital programme services,
code relating to deaf and visually impaired, **55**/20-22
licences,
applications, **55**/18
conditions of, **55**/19
duration of, **55**/19
enforcement of, **55**/23
meaning of, **55**/1
digital radio broadcasting,
equal opportunities, **55**/68
licences, application for, **55**/60
review of, **55**/67
digital sound programme services,
licences,
conditions of, **55**/61
duration of, **55**/61
enforcement of, **55**/62
meaning of, **55**/60
digital terrestrial sound broadcasting,
independent national broadcaster, 55/41
licences,
general conditions, **55**/4, 43
grant of, **55**/42
local radio multiplex,
applications for, **55**/50
award of, **55**/51
conditions attached to, **55**/54
duration, **55**/58
enforcement of, **55**/59
failure to provide service, **55**/53
financial penalties on revocation, **55**/53
renewal of, **55**/58
reservation of capacity for BBC, **55**/49
two or more to one person, **55**/52
national radio multiplex,
additional payments, **55**/55
conditions attached, **55**/54
duration, **55**/58
enforcement of, **55**/59
renewal of, **55**/58
restrictions on holding, **55**/44

INDEX

BROADCASTING—*cont.*
digital terrestrial sound broadcasting—*cont.*
radio multiplex services,
assignment of frequencies, **55**/45
attribution of, to licence holder and others, **55**/57
award of, **55**/47
meaning of, **55**/40
national radio multiplex licences, **55**/46
reservation of capacity for independent national broadcasters, **55**/48
revenue, **55**/56
computation of, **55**/70, Sched. 1
simulcast radio service, **55**/41
digital terrestrial television broadcasting,
licences,
grant of, **55**/3
restrictions on holding, **55**/5
meaning of terms, **55**/1, 2
see also multiplex services
equal opportunities, **55**/34, 68
events of national interest,
categories of service, **55**/98
code of guidance, **55**/104
contracts for,
exclusive rights: void, **55**/99
specifying category of service, **55**/100
listed events, **55**/97
penalties in connection with, **55**/102
reports to Secretary of State, **55**/103
restriction on televising, **55**/101
Gaelic programmes,
digital broadcasting of, **55**/32
financing of sound programmes, **55**/95
independent analogue broadcasters,
meaning of, **55**/2
services provided by, **55**/28, *see also* digital broadcasting
independent national broadcasters, **55**/41
Independent Television Commission,
power to suspend licences for non-domestic satellite service, **55**/89
international bodies, **55**/123
licences (general),
disposal of receipts from, **55**/38
disqualification on grounds of political objects, **55**/143
enforcement of, to provide licensable programme services, **55**/90
false information, **55**/144–146
restrictions on holding, **55**/73, Sched. 2
local delivery service, **55**/91
multiplex services (radio), **55**/40, *see also* digital terrestrial sound broadcasting,
assignment of frequencies, **55**/6
multiplex services (television),
enforcement of, **55**/17
equal opportunities, **55**/34
financial penalties, **55**/36
licences,
applications for, **55**/7
award of, **55**/8
conditions attached, **55**/12
duration of, **55**/16

BROADCASTING—*cont.*
multiplex services (television)—*cont.*
licences—*cont.*
failure to begin to provide service, **55**/11
multiple licences subject to conditions, **55**/10
percentage of revenue as additional payment, **55**/13
renewal of, **55**/16
revocation: financial penalties, **55**/11
two or more to one person, **55**/9
meaning of, **55**/1
revenue,
attribution to licence holder and others, **55**/15
calculation of, **55**/14
computation of, **55**/37, Sched. 1
news, *see* copyright: Regional Channel 3 services
privacy,
code relating to interference with, **55**/107
qualifying service,
meaning of, **55**/2
regional Channel 3 services,
modification of networking arrangements, **55**/79
news,
appointment of news providers, **55**/75, 76
modification of Restrictive Trade Practices Act 1976, **55**/77
provision of news programmes, **55**/74
variation of licence following change of control, **55**/78
research, **55**/122
S4C,
digital service, duty of Welsh Authority as to, **55**/29
extension of powers of, **55**/84
funding of, **55**/80
multiplex revenue to be taken into account, **55**/82
public service fund, **55**/81
satellite services,
non-domestic,
enforcement of licences, **55**/88
power to suspend licences, **55**/89
suspension of licences, **55**/96
sexual conduct, code on, **55**/108
Sianel Pedwar Cymru, *see* S4C
simulcast radio service, **55**/41
sound broadcasting,
Gaelic programmes: financing, **55**/95
local,
renewal of licences, **55**/94
variation of licences following change of control, **55**/93
national: renewal of licences, **55**/92
suspension of licences to provide satellite service, **55**/96
sporting events, *see* events of national interest
taste, **55**/113
teletext service, **55**/30
television, *see* digital terrestrial television broadcasting

BROADCASTING—*cont.*
television services, restricted, **55**/85
transmission systems: standards, **55**/142
unjust or unfair treatment,
code for avoidance of, **55**/107
complaints as to, *see* Broadcasting Standards Commission
violence: code on, **55**/108
visually impaired people: digital programme code for, **55**/20-22
Broadcasting Act 1996 (c.55)
BURIAL GROUNDS,
on Channel Tunnel Rail Link, **61**/39, Sched. 11
BUSINESS PROPERTY RELIEF, **8**/184

CAPITAL GAINS TAX,
chargeable gains: reliefs,
overseas petroleum licences, **8**/181
retirement relief: age limits, **8**/176
oil licences: disposal, **8**/180
reinvestment relief: disposal of qualifying corporate bond, **8**/177
CARAVANS,
rating, **12**/1
CHANNEL TUNNEL RAIL LINK,
A2 and M2 improvement works, *see* HIGHWAYS
arbitration, **61**/43
burial grounds: removal of remains and monuments, **61**/39, Sched. 11
bye-laws, **61**/15
co-operation, duty as to, **61**/37
competition,
anti-competitive practices, **61**/25, 26
monopoly situations, **61**/24, 26
Rail Regulator's functions, **61**/22
restrictive trade practices, **61**/23, 26
controls, disapplication of, **61**/38, Sched. 10
deposited plans, correction of, **61**/53
development agreement, variation of, **61**/41
financial matters, **61**/55
expenditure for securing construction, **61**/31
financial assistance: undertakings, **61**/33
reserved capacity, **61**/32
heritage,
disapplication of controls, **61**/12, Sched. 7
rights of entry, **61**/13, Sched. 8
injurious affection: compensation, **61**/36
land,
compulsory acquisition of outside limits of deposited plans, **61**/5
shown on deposited plans, **61**/4, Sched. 4
private rights of way: extinguishment, **61**/7
statutory undertakers' rights: extinguishment, **61**/8
temporary possession and use, **61**/6, Sched. 5
landlord and tenant law, application of, **61**/40
noise,
control of construction sites: appeals, **61**/29
insulation, **61**/49
statutory nuisance: defence, **61**/30

CHANNEL TUNNEL RAIL LINK—*cont.*
nominated undertaker, **61**/34
operation, **61**/14
overhead lines, **61**/50, Sched. 14
planning,
conditions, **61**/9(5), Sched. 6
deemed permission, **61**/9(1), 9(6)–(9)
fees for planning applications, **61**/11
general, **61**/9
permitted development: time limits, **61**/10
protective provisions, **61**/52, Sched. 15
Rail Regulator, functions of,
duty to exercise, **61**/21
restriction of, in relation to competition, **61**/22
railway legislation, application of, **61**/20, Sched. 9
access agreements, **61**/17
closures, **61**/18
licensing, **61**/16
railway administration orders, **61**/19
service of documents, **61**/54
Transport and Works Act 1992, application of, **61**/42
trees,
disapplication of controls, **61**/28
power to deal with neighbouring, **61**/27
works,
construction and maintenance, **61**/1
highways, **61**/3, Sched. 3
scheduled works, **61**/1(1), Sched. 1
supplementary provisions, **61**/2, Sched. 2
transfer of functions relating to, **61**/35
Channel Tunnel Rail Link Act 1996 (c.61)
CHARITIES,
Belfast Charitable Society,
objects, powers, constitution and management of, **vi**/1–10
charitable donations: payroll deduction scheme, **8**/109
charitable property of disbanded units of Reserve Forces, **14**/120, Sched. 3
grants for repair of parsonages and charity property, **53**/95
and Housing Act 1996, **52**/58
public collections (London), **ix**/26
tax relief, **8**/146
CHEMICAL WEAPONS,
annual reports on, **6**/33
definition of, **6**/1
forfeiture, **6**/30
information, **6**/21–3, 32
inspections,
entry rights, **6**/25
offences, **6**/26
privileges and immunities, **6**/27
types of, **6**/24
legitimate military purposes, **6**/1(4)
offences, **6**/29–31
permitted purposes,
definition, **6**/1
licences, **6**/20
restrictions on use, **6**/19

CHEMICAL WEAPONS—*cont.*
premises for producing,
compensation payments, **6**/16
destruction or alteration, **6**/13, 17, 18
enforcement procedure, **6**/14
notices as to suspicious equipment or buildings, **6**/12–15
offences, **6**/17
use of, 11
search powers, **6**/29
suspicious objects,
compensation for destruction, **6**/8
destruction of, **6**/6, 10
entry powers, **6**/7
notices as to, **6**/4
offences, **6**/9
removal of, **6**/5
toxic chemicals,
definition, **6**/5, Sched.
restrictions on use, **6**/19
use of, **6**/2–3
Chemical Weapons Act 1996 (c.6)
CHEQUERS ESTATE ACT 1917, **47**/25(3)
CHEVENING ESTATE ACT 1959, **47**/25(3)
CHILD BENEFIT,
persons subject to immigration control, **49**/10
CHILDREN AND YOUNG PERSONS,
Criminal Procedure and Investigation Act 1996: application of Act, **25**/1(2)(c)
evidence from, **46**/7
family law,
emergency protection orders, **46**/52, Sched. 6
interests of, in marital breakdown, **27**/1
interim care orders, **27**/52, Sched. 6
non-molestation orders, **27**/43
separate representation in family proceedings, **27**/64
welfare of in orders preventing divorce, **27**/11
and scheduled offences, *see* NORTHERN IRELAND, emergency provisions
CHOICE OF LAW,
in arbitration proceedings, **23**/4, 46
CHURCH OF ENGLAND,
grants for repair of parsonages, **53**/95
City of Edinburgh Council Order Confirmation Act 1996 (c.x)
City of London (Approved Premises for Marriage) Act 1996 (c.iv)
City of Westminster Act 1996 (c.viii)
CIVIL SERVICE, *see* HONG KONG PUBLIC SERVANTS
CLEARANCE AREAS, *see* HOUSING GRANTS; relocation grants
COMMISSION FOR NEW TOWNS,
orders for dissolution, **53**/145
COMMITTAL PROCEEDINGS, *see* CRIMINAL PROCEDURE AND INVESTIGATIONS
COMMONEALTH DEVELOPMENT CORPORATION,
powers of, **28**/1
COMMONWEALTH,
Hong Kong war wives and widows: British nationality, **41**/1, 2
Commonwealth Development Corporation Act 1996 (c.28)
COMMUNITY CARE,
direct payments for services,
decision to make, **30**/1(1)(a)
Mental Health Act 1983 care, **30**/1(3)
Northern Ireland provisions, **30**/6
person providing service, **30**/1(4)
rate of, **30**/1(2)
recipient, **30**/1(1)(b)
regulations, **30**/1(7)–(8)
relationship with authority's other functions, **30**/2
repayment of, **30**/1(6)
residential accommodation, **30**/1(5)
Scottish provisions, **30**/4, 5
services, meaning of, **30**/1(9)
Community Care (Direct Payments) Act 1996 (c.30)
COMMUNITY SUPERVISION ORDERS, **46**/10, Sched. 3
COMPANY LAW,
close companies,
loans to participators, **8**/173
non-resident: attribution of gains to participators, **8**/174
controlled foreign companies:
accounting periods, **8**/178
directors' liability (London), **ix**/30
registration in France, **v**/3
removal from register in England, **v**/4
COMPETITION,
and Channel Tunnel Rail Link, **61**/22–26
COMPULSORY ACQUISITION OF LAND, *see* ACQUISITION OF LAND
COMPUTER RECORDS,
and school inspections, **57**/42
CONSERVATION,
control and management of deer, *see* SCOTS LAW, deer
Consolidated Fund Act 1996 (c.4)
CONSPIRACY,
to commit sexual acts outside UK, *see* SEXUAL OFFENCES
CONSTRUCTION CONTRACTS,
adjudication, **53**/108
construction operations: meaning, **53**/105
Crown application, **53**/117
general, **53**/104
payment, **53**/109,
conditional: prohibition, **53**/113
dates for, **53**/110
notice of intention to withhold, **53**/111
performance suspended for non-payment, **53**/112
reckoning periods of time, **53**/116
residential occupier, **53**/106
Scheme for Construction Contracts, **53**/114
service of notices, **53**/115
in writing, **53**/107
CONSTRUCTION INDUSTRY,
sub-contractors: registration cards, **8**/178
CONSUMER LAW,
trading standards extension of Fair Trading Act 1973, **32**/1, *see also* TRADING STANDARDS, 2

CONSUMER LAW—*cont.*
unfair terms in arbitration agreements, **23**/89, 90
CONTRACT LAW,
cases before Industrial Tribunals, **17**/8
construction contracts, *see* CONSTRUCTION CONTRACTS
CONVERSION,
abolition of doctrine, **47**/3, *see also* TRUSTS AND TRUSTEES
COPYRIGHT,
broadcasting, *see* BROADCASTING
CORONERS,
inquests into treasure, **24**/7-9
CORPORATE BONDS, **8**/177
CORPORATION TAX,
accounting periods, **8**/138, Sched. 24
charge and rate for 1996, **8**/77
chargeable gains,
premiums for leases, **8**/142
roll-over relief, **8**/141
transfer of company's assets to investment trust, **8**/140
Schedule C: abolition of charge, **8**/79, Sched. 7
surrenders of advance corporation tax, **8**/139, Sched. 25
Taxes Act 1988, **8**/137, Sched. 23
COURTS MARTIAL, *see* ARMED SERVICES, trial and punishment of offences
CRIMINAL LAW,
criminal libel, *see* DEFAMATION
defence of due diligence (London), **ix**/29 *see also* THEFT
investigations, *see* CRIMINAL PROCEDURE AND INVESTIGATIONS
offensive weapons, *see* OFFENSIVE WEAPONS
procedure, *see* CRIMINAL PROCEDURE AND INVESTIGATIONS
scheduled offences, *see* NORTHERN IRELAND, emergency provisions
serious crime: prevention and detection, **35**/1, 2
sexual acts outside UK, *see* SEXUAL OFFENCES
warrants issued to Security Service, 35/2
CRIMINAL PROCEDURE AND INVESTIGATIONS,
alibi defence,
procedural amendments, **25**/5(7)–(8), 74
armed forces: application of Act, **25**/78
assault, **25**/1(2)(d)
bill of indictment, **25**/1(2)(e)
children: cases involving, **25**/1(2)(c)
code of practice, **25**/23
committal,
proceedings, **25**/47, Sched. 1
restatement of provisions, **25**/44
defence statements,
for court and prosecutor, **25**/5
faults in, **25**/11
voluntary disclosure, **25**/6
secondary disclosure by prosecutor, **25**/7
CRIMINAL PROCEDURE AND INVESTIGATIONS —*cont.*
derogatory assertions,
orders: provisions for making, **25**/58
reporting,
offences, **25**/60, 61
restrictions, **25**/59
disclosure,
by accused,
compulsory disclosure, **25**/5
faults in, **25**/11
voluntary disclosure, **25**/6
application by accused for, **25**/8
application of Act, **25**/1
code of practice, 23
common law rules as to, **25**/21
confidentiality, **25**/17
contravention, **25**/18
defence statements,
for court and prosecutor, **25**/5
faults in, **25**/11
time limits, **25**/12
interpretation, **25**/2
of prosecution material,
copies, **25**/3(3)–(4)
document obtained under Code of Practice, **25**/4
duty of prosecutor, **25**/3(1)
inspection, **25**/3(5)
meaning of, **25**/3(2)
obtained by interception under warrant, **25**/3(7)
against public interest, **25**/3(6)
recording, **25**/3(3)-(4)
relevant period, **25**/3(8)
by prosecutor,
continuing duty, **25**/9
primary disclosure, **25**/3, 4
secondary disclosure, **25**/7
time limits, failure to observe, **25**/10
public interest provisions, **25**/3(6), 7(5), 8(5), 9(8), 14–16
rules of court, **25**/19
statutory rules as to, **25**/20
evidence,
blood or urine samples, **25**/63
fingerprints, checks against, **25**/64
television links, **25**/62
video recordings, **25**/62
written statements and depositions, **25**/68, Sched. 2
fraud,
serious or complex, **25**/1(2)(b), 72, Sched. 3
indictable offences,
committal for trial, **25**/1(2)(a)
serious or complex fraud, **25**/1(2)(b)
with summary trial, **25**/1(1)(c)
transfer to Crown Court, **25**/1(2)(b)–(c)
investigations,
code of practice, **25**/23
effect of, **25**/26
examples of disclosure provisions, 25/24
operation and revision of, **25**/25
disclosure, *see* DISCLOSURE

CRIMINAL PROCEDURE AND INVESTIGATIONS —*cont.*
investigations—*cont.*
meaning of, **25**/1(4), 22
not begun before appointed day, **25**/1(3)
justices, indemnity of, **25**/70
justices' clerks, indemnity of, **25**/70
Magistrates' Courts,
attachment of earnings order, **25**/53
either way offences: accused's intention as to plea, **25**/49
fines: enforcement of payment, **25**/50
non-appearance of accused: issue of warrant, **25**/48
powers, **25**/76
remand in custody, **25**/52
witnesses: summons and warrant for arrest, **25**/51
Northern Ireland provisions, **25**/79, Sched. 4
offences triable either way, **25**/1(1)(b)
orders and regulations, **25**/77
pre-trial hearings, **25**/39
preliminary stage of proceedings, **25**/71
preparatory hearings,
appeals from, **25**/35, 36
application of Act, **25**/28
arraignment, **25**/30
conduct of, **25**/31
Crown Court Rules, **25**/33
later stages of trial, **25**/34
orders before, **25**/32
power to order, **25**/29
reporting restrictions, **25**/37
offences in connection with, **25**/38
start of trial, **25**/30
prosecution material,
application for, **25**/8
disclosure,
continuing duty, **25**/9
faults in, **25**/11
primary, **25**/3, 4
secondary, **25**/7
time limits, **25**/12, 13
failure to observe, **25**/10
public interest, **25**/14–16
road traffic,
device for blood or urine samples, **25**/63
rulings,
application of Act, **25**/43
power to make, **25**/40
pre-trial hearings, **25**/39
reporting restrictions, **25**/41
offences in connection with, **25**/42
Scotland: criminal procedure amendments, **25**/73
summary offences, **25**/1(1)(A)
tainted acquittals,
application of Act, **25**/54
conditions for making order, **25**/55
supplementary provisions, **25**/57
time limits for proceedings, **25**/56
transfer of trial,
notices of, **25**/45
restatement of provisions, **25**/44
war crimes, **25**/46

CRIMINAL PROCEDURE AND INVESTIGATIONS —*cont.*
war crimes: abolition of transfer procedure, **25**/46
witness orders and summonses, **25**/51, 65, 66, 67
year and a day rule,
abolition, **19**/1
proceedings for fatal offence, **19**/2
Criminal Procedure and Investigations Act 1996 (c.25)
CROWN COURT,
Northern Ireland hearings, **22**/10
CROWN EMPLOYMENT,
employment rights,
applicability of 1996 Act, **18**/191
armed forces, **18**/192, 217
national security, **18**/193
parliamentary staff, **18**/194, 195
CROWN LAND,
compulsory purchase powers, **52**/221
CROWN RIGHTS,
party walls, **40**/19
in treasure, **24**/4, 10

DAMAGES,
assumed rate of return on investment of, **48**/1
consent orders for periodical payments, **48**/2
provisional damages and fatal accident claims, **48**/3
public sector settlements: guarantees, 48/6, Sched.
structured settlements,
enhanced protection for, **48**/4
meaning of, **48**/5
Damages Act 1996 (c.48)
DEER, *see* SCOTS LAW
Deer (Scotland) Act 1996 (c.58)
Deer (Scotland) (Amendment) Act 1996 (c.44)
DEFAMATION,
author,
defendant not author, **31**/1(1)
meaning of, **31**/1(2)–(4)
criminal libel, **31**/20(2)
editor,
defendant not editor, **31**/1(1)
meaning of, **31**/1(2)–(4)
evidence,
of convictions, **31**/12
of proceedings in Parliament, **31**/13
limitation of actions, **31**/5, 6
Northern Ireland provisions, **31/31**/6, 11
offer to make amends,
accepting, **31**/3
compensation provisions, **31**/3
defence preventing offer being made, **31**/2(5)
failure to accept, **31**/4
form of, **31**/2(2)–(4)
power to make, **31**/2(1)
proceedings, **31**/3(10)

DEFAMATION—*cont.*
offer to make amends—*cont.*
Scottish provisions, **31**/3(9)
withdrawal of, **31**/2(6)
privilege,
absolute, **31**/14
qualified, **31**/15, Sched. 1
publication,
reasonable care as to, **31**/1(5)
responsibility for, **31**/1
publisher,
defendant not publisher, **31**/1(1)
meaning of, **31**/1(2)–(4)
statements, ruling on meaning of, **31**/7
summary disposal of claim,
court's powers, **31**/8
Northern Ireland provisions, **31**/11
rules of court, **31**/10
summary relief, meaning of, **31**/9
Defamation Act 1996 (c.31)
DEFERRED ACTION NOTICES, *see* HOUSES IN MULTIPLE OCCUPATION
DIVORCE, *see* FAMILY LAW
Dogs (Fouling of Land) Act 1996 (c.20)
DOMESTIC VIOLENCE, *see* FAMILY LAW
DOMICILE,
overseas electors, **8**/200
DRUGS,
drug testing programmes (armed services), **46**/32

EARNINGS,
prisoners' earnings, *see* Wages
EDINBURGH,
General Reserve Fund: confirmation of provisional order, **x**
Merchant Company
borrowing powers, **xi**/Sched. para. 138
Darling Fund, **xi**/Sched. paras. 39–40
donations, **xi**/Sched. para. 139
fees payable, **xi**/Sched. paras. 15–18
Fraser Trust, **xi**/Sched. paras. 113–121
funds and property, **xi**/Sched. paras. 19–21
investment powers, **xi**/Sched. para. 137
joint committee, **xi**/Sched. paras. 128–135
master's court, **xi**/Sched. para. 30–38
meetings, **xi**/Sched. paras. 5–9
office bearers, **xi**/Sched. paras. 10–12
officials, **xi**/Sched. paras. 13–14
powers of, **xi**/Sched. para. 4
rule-making, **xi**/Sched. para. 29
Russell and Foster Endowment, **xi**/Sched. paras. 122–126
variation of trusts, **xi**/Sched. para. 127
widows' fund, **xi**/Sched. paras. 41–91
Edinburgh Assay Office Order Confirmation Act 1996 (c.i)
Edinburgh Merchant Company Order Confirmation Act 1996 (c.xi)
EDUCATION,
admissions, *see* school admissions
aided schools,
conduct and staffing of, *see* conduct and staffing
decision as to status of, **56**/48

EDUCATION—*cont.*
aided schools—*cont.*
disapplication of restriction on disposals, **56**/75
financial assistance for,
grants,
for preliminary expenditure, **56**/66
for premises and equipment, **56**/65
by LEAs, **56**/68, 70
loans for initial expenses, **56**/67
government of, *see* government of aided and special agreement schools
obligations of LEAs to provide new sites, **56**/61
as voluntary schools, **56**/32
ancillary functions, *see* governing bodies; LEAs: Secretary of State
assisted places, *see* independent schools
attendance, *see* school attendance
charges,
information as to, **56**/459
interpretation, **56**/462
maintained school: meaning, **56**/449
permitted, **56**/455
articles to be owned by pupil, **56**/454(2)
board and lodging, **56**/458
music teaching, **56**/451(3)
recovery of, **56**/461
regulation of, **56**/456
and remission policies, **56**/457
tuition outside school hours, **56**/451(4), 452
wasted examination fees, **56**/453
prohibited,
admission charges, **56**/450
examination fees, **56**/453
incidental charges, **56**/454
provision of education, **56**/451
voluntary contributions, **56**/460
Chief Education Officer, **56**/138, 532
City Colleges,
agreements for establishment, **56**/482
characteristics, **56**/482(2)
financial provisions, **56**/483
names of, **56**/482(3)
cleanliness of pupils, *see* local education authorities, ancillary functions
community schools,
staffing, **56**/140
compulsory education, *see* statutory system of education
conduct and staffing of schools,
articles of government,
making and altering: procedure, **56**/128
overriding and amendment of, **56**/129
requiremnt for, **56**/127
conduct,
general, **56**/130
non-urgent cases, **56**/131
separate departments treated as separate schools, **56**/132
control of premises,
outside school hours, **56**/149
voluntary schools, **56**/150
transfer of control agreements, **56**/151
use outside school hours, **56**/152

EDUCATION—*cont.*
conduct and staffing of schools—*cont.*
discipline,
breakdown: LEA's reserve powers, **56**/155
corporal punishment, **56**/548-550
exclusion,
appeals against, **56**/159, 160
duty to inform parents, **56**/157
head's powers, **56**/156
pending cleansing, **56**/524
and recoupment of grants, **56**/494
reinstatement of excluded pupil, **56**/158, Sched. 15
restriction on power, **56**/307
general, **56**/154
information by governors and head teacher, **56**/165
instruction outside school premises, **56**/153
new schools, **56**/166, Sched. 19
religious education teachers,
appointment, **56**/143, 144
reports, meetings and information,
annual parents' meetings, **56**/162, Sched. 18
grouped schools, **56**/164
special and boarding schools, **56**/163
governors' annual reports, **56**/161, Sched. 17
grouped schools, **56**/164
sessions, **56**/148
staffing,
aided schools with delegated budgets, **56**/137
advisory rights of chief education officer, **56**/138
amendment of articles relating to, **56**/141
maintained special schools, **56**/142
non-school activities in community schools, **56**/140
religious education teachers: dismissal, **56**/145
religious opinions of staff, **56**/146
schools with delegated budgets, **56**/136, Sched. 14
dismissal payments, **56**/139
schools without delegated budgets, **56**/133, Sched. 13
appointment of clerk, **56**/135
terms and holidays, **56**/147
construction,
changes to school not amounting to discontinuance, **56**/574
Education Acts, **56**/578
employment, **56**/576
meaning of expressions, **56**/573
minor authorities, **56**/577
parent: meaning of, **56**/576
controlled schools,
financial assistance for,
execution of works by LEA, **56**/74
payment by LEAs,
of expenses of enlarging, **56**/64
of expenses of establishing, **56**/63
as voluntary schools, **56**/32

EDUCATION—*cont.*
corporal punishment: no right to give, **56**/548–550
county schools,
change of status,
compensation payable by governing body to LEA, **56**/56
objections to, **56**/53
order by Secretary of State, **56**/54
proposal, **56**/52
on repayment of grant under special agreement, **56**/58
variations of order, **56**/55
where governing body fails to carry out financial obligations, **56**/57
decision as to status of, **56**/48
establishment, alteration or new site,
approval of school premises, **56**/39, Sched. 6
approval or rejection of, **56**/37
determination by LEA whether to implement, **56**/38
implementation of, **56**/40
objections to, **56**/36
proposals, **56**/35
government of, *see* government of county schools . . .
proposals for division of, **56**/50
curriculum,
basic, **56**/352
complaints, **56**/409
enforcement, **56**/409
external qualifications, courses leading to, **56**/400
senior pupils and further education students, **56**/401
general duties as to, **56**/351
information provision, **56**/408
maintained school: meaning, **56**/350
and nursery education, **56**/410
politics,
balanced treatment of issues, **56**/407
indoctrination, **56**/406
public examinations, obligations as to, **56**/402
religious education,
agreed syllabuses, **56**/375, Sched. 31, 382
required provision for,
aided and special agreement schools, **56**/378
appropriate agreed syllabus, **56**/382
changes in, **56**/383
controlled schools, **56**/377
county schools, **56**/376
duties as to, **56**/384
grant-maintained schools,
former aided or special, agreement schools, **56**/381
former controlled schools, **56**/380
former county schools, **56**/379
new schools, **56**/381
religious worship,
access to meetings and documents, **56**/397
collective, **56**/385

EDUCATION—*cont.*
curriculum—*cont.*
secular education,
Curriculum and Assessment Authority for Wales,
functions, **56**/361
membership, status and constitution, **56**/360, Sched. 30
governing body's functions, **56**/371, 373, 374
head teacher's functions, **56**/372, 373, 374
National Curriculum,
core subjects, **56**/354
development work and experiments, **56**/362
establishment of, **56**/356
exceptions, **56**/363
for individual pupils, **56**/365–367
general, **56**/353
implementation of, **56**/357
key stages, **56**/355
orders and regulations, **56**/368
pupils with statements of special needs, **56**/364
research in Wales, **56**/369
policy of LEAs, **56**/370
School Curriculum and Assessment Authority,
functions, **56**/359
membership, status and constitution, **56**/358, Sched. 29
sex education,
exemption from, **56**/405
manner of provision, **56**/403
statement of policy, **56**/404
day nurseries, **56**/515
disability statements, **56**/528
discipline, *see* conduct and staffing
discontinuance of schools,
proposals for, **56**/167
approval or rejection of, **56**/169
duty to implement, **56**/171
LEA's decision whether to implement, **56**/170
objections to, **56**/168
restrictions on LEA taking steps, **56**/172
voluntary school: by governing body, **56**/173
LEA conducting school, **56**/174
proposed further education corporation, **56**/175
documents and evidence,
birth certificates and registrar's returns, **56**/564
educational records, **56**/563
presumptions as to age, **56**/445, 565
signed documents, **56**/566
Education Associations, *see* SCHOOL INSPECTIONS
education supervision orders, **56**/447
educational institutions, *see* statutory system of education
educational trusts, **56**/553
religious, *see* religious education
employment law,
during financial delegation, **56**/178

EDUCATION—*cont.*
employment of children and young persons,
meaning of "child," **56**/558
prohibited or restricted, **56**/559
work experience, **56**/560
examinations,
fees for, **56**/453
obligations as to, **56**/402
exclusion of pupils, *see* conduct and staffing of schools, discipline
financing of LEA schools,
delegation,
apart from schemes, **56**/125
and new schools, **56**/126, Sched. 12
schemes of delegation, **56**/101
applicable schools, **56**/115
budget shares,
application of formula, **56**/106
calculation of LEA's aggregated budget, **56**/105
delegation,
conditions as to, **56**/109
effect of, **56**/116
initial implementation, **56**/110
optional, **56**/108
requirement, **56**/107
employment law, application of, **56**/178
extension of, to maintained special schools, **56**/120
information,
certification of statements by Audit Commission, **56**/123
financial statements, **56**/122, 124, Sched. 11
publication of schemes, **56**/121
LEA requirement as to, **56**/103
preparation and imposition of, **56**/104
revision of by LEA,
general, **56**/111
minor revisions, **56**/113
significant variations, **56**/112
revision of by Secretary of State, **56**/114
schools to be covered by, **56**/102
funding authorities,
Authorities,
Funding Agency for Schools, **56**/20, Sched. 2
Schools Funding Council for Wales, 56/21, Sched. 2
functions,
generally, **56**/22
supervision of, by Secretary of State, **56**/24
transferred to by Secretary of State, **56**/22(3), Sched. 3
value-for-money studies of grant-maintained schools, **56**/23
grants to, **56**/25
information, provision of, **56**/30
LEA's functions: resolution of disputes, **56**/28
meaning of, **56**/26
responsibility for providing sufficient school places, **56**/27

EDUCATION—*cont.*
further education,
definition, **56**/2
disability statements relating to, **56**/528
distribution of information about institutions, **56**/541
further education corporation,
proposal to establish, **56**/175
in grant-maintained schools, **56**/293
local education authority's functions, **56**/14
provision of, **56**/176
pupils of compulsory school age, **56**/400, 401
governing bodies,
ancillary functions,
day nurseries, **56**/535
medical arrangements, **56**/536
provision of services, **56**/533
school meals (grant-maintained schools), **56**/535
new schools,
temporary bodies, **56**/98–99, Sched. 9
provision of information by,
distribution of,
further education institutions, **56**/541
secondary education, **56**/540
grant-maintained schools, **56**/539
regulations as to, **56**/537
to Secretary of State, **56**/538
see also government of... schools
government of aided and special agreement schools,
governing body,
constitution, **56**/84
to reflect current circumstances of school, **56**/86
sponsor governors for aided secondary schools, **56**/85
government of county, voluntary and maintained special schools,
governing bodies,
adjustment in number of governors, **56**/83
appointment of parent governors, **56**/81
appointment of representative governors, **56**/80
categories of governor, **56**/78
circumstances of school: change in, **56**/87
constitution, **56**/79
grouping under single body,
alterating instrument, **56**/92
consents to, **56**/90, 91
consultation as to, **56**/91
governors, **56**/93
LEA's powers, **56**/89
review of, **56**/94
termination of, **56**/95
incorporation, **56**/88(1), Sched. 7
membership and proceedings, **56**/88 (2), Sched. 8
new schools,
grouping of, **56**/100
temporary bodies, **56**/96, 97

EDUCATION—*cont.*
government of county, voluntary and maintained special schools—*cont.*
governing bodies—*cont.*
reflecting circumstances, **56**/86
review of constitution, **56**/82
instruments of government,
contents of, **56**/76
procedure for making and altering, **56**/77
grant-maintained schools,
acquisition of status,
ballot,
duty of governors to consider, 56/185
eligible voters, **56**/190
of parents, **56**/189–93
publication of proposals, **56**/193, Sched. 20
second, if insufficient votes cast, **56**/191
void for irregularity, **56**/192
eligible schools, **56**/184
information as to parents, **56**/188
initiation of procedure,
by governors, **56**/186
by parents, **56**/187
interpretation, **56**/200
proposals for,
by alteration of county school, **56**/198, 199
approval of, **56**/194
exercising powers before status achieved, **56**/196, Sched. 21
expenses, **56**/197
incorporation of governing body, **56**/195
publication of, **56**/193, Sched. 20
appeal committees, **56**/308
benefits and services to pupils, **56**/295
discontinuance of,
proposals for,
approval, adoption or rejection of, **56**/269
by funding authority, **56**/268
by governing body, **56**/267
implementation of, **56**/270
transfer of functions, **56**/271
winding-up and disposal of property,
disposal of property, **56**/277, 278
grants to governing body in liquidation, **56**/276
order for, **56**/274
surplus money and investments, **56**/279
timetable for, **56**/275
withdrawal of grant where school unsuitable, **56**/272, 273
disposal,
by funding authority, **56**/300
by trustees, **56**/299
exclusion of pupils: restriction on power, **56**/307
funding of,
capital grants, **56**/246, 248
loans, **56**/255
maintenance grants, **56**/244, 248

EDUCATION—*cont.*
grant-maintained schools—*cont.*
funding of—*cont.*
recovery from local funds, **56**/256–258
requirements on governing body on receipt of grant, **56**/247
special purpose grants, **56**/245, 248
Wales,
capital grants, **56**/252, 254
maintenance grants, **56**/250, 254
requirements on governing body on receipt of grant, **56**/253
special purpose grants, **56**/251, 254
transitional arrangements, **56**/249
further education, **56**/293
government of,
articles of government, **56**/218, Sched. 23
subsequent, **56**/221
instrument of government, **56**/218, Sched. 22
initial, **56**/219
subsequent, **56**/220
interpretation, **56**/243
joint schemes, **56**/232
making and varying, **56**/233
notifications to governors, **56**/309
powers of governing body, **56**/231
governors,
additional, **56**/230
categories, **56**/222, Sched. 24
first, **56**/226
determination of initial, **56**/236
replacement of, **56**/227
replacement of initial, **56**/238
foundation, **56**/228
determination of initial, **56**/236
replacement of initial, **56**/238
head teacher, **56**/225
of new schools, **56**/241
parent, **56**/223
determination of initial, **56**/234, 235, 239, Sched. 8
replacement of initial, **56**/237
savings for defects, **56**/242
sponsor, **56**/229
initial, **56**/240
teacher, **56**/224
determination of initial, **56**/234, 235, 239, Sched. 8
replacement of initial, **56**/237
groups of,
acquisition of grant-maintained status, **56**/290
government of,
additional governors, **56**/287
core governors, **56**/285, 286, Sched. 25
head teacher governors, **56**/284
instrument and articles of government, **56**/281
parent governors, **56**/282
powers of governing body, **56**/288
teacher governors, **56**/283
maintenance grants, application of, **56**/289
nature of group, **56**/280

EDUCATION—*cont.*
grant-maintained schools—*cont.*
inspection of accounts, **56**/310
interpretation, **56**/311
meaning of, **56**/183
middle schools, **56**/292
modification of instruments,
land held for voluntary schools, **56**/303
variation of trust deeds, **56**/302
new, establishment of,
initial governors, **56**/241
interpretation, **56**/217
proposals,
approval, adoption or rejection of, **56**/214
exercise of powers before implementation, **56**/216
by funding authority, **56**/211, 213
implementation of, **56**/215
by promoters, **56**/212, 213, Sched. 20
nursery education in, **56**/292, 343
power to borrow, **56**/7
property,
change of purpose for which held, **56**/208
contracts,
control of, **56**/206
wrongful, **56**/207
land,
control of disposals, **56**/204
wrongful disposals, **56**/205
LEA's duty to convey interest, **56**/210
"pending" procedure, **56**/203
transfer of, **56**/201
proposals for change of character,
approval, adoption or rejection of, **56**/261
approval of school premises, **56**/262
approved before grant-maintained status, **56**/265
by funding authority, **56**/260
by governing body, **56**/259
implementation of, **56**/263
interpretation, **56**/266
transfer of functions, **56**/264
religious opinions of staff,
change in religious character of schools, **56**/306
former county schools, **56**/304
former voluntary schools, **56**/305
staff,
restriction on changes, **56**/209
transfer of, **56**/202
teacher training in, **56**/294
transfer and disposal of premises,
interpretation, **56**/301
to new site, **56**/297
under s.201, **56**/298
to trustees, **56**/296
value-for-money studies of, **56**/23
grants,
in aid of educational services or research, **56**/485, 489
to bodies for promotion of learning or research, **56**/486, 489
education in Wales, **56**/487, 489

EDUCATION—*cont.*
grants—*cont.*
education of travellers and displaced persons, **56**/488, 489
education support and training, **56**/484, 489
payment of school fees and expenses, **56**/491
recoupment of,
cross-border provisions, **56**/493
excluded pupils, **56**/494
provision for, **56**/492
special provision for ethnic minorities, **56**/490
guidance, **56**/571
inapplicabilty of 1996 Act, **56**/561, 562
independent schools,
assisted places scheme,
incidental expenses of pupils, **56**/481
participation agreements, **56**/479, Sched. 35
regulations, **56**/480
complaints about,
determination of,
by Independent Schools Tribunal, **56**/470
by Secretary of State, **56**/471
notice of, **56**/469
disqualification, **56**/470(2)(f)
effect of personal, **56**/472
enforcement of, **56**/473, 478
removal of, **56**/474
in Scotland, **56**/477
Independent Schools Tribunal, **56**/470, 476, Sched. 34
meaning of, **56**/463
providing special education, approval of, **56**/347
registration,
enforcement of: offences, **56**/466, 478
for England and Wales, **56**/464
information about, **56**/467
order for deletion from register, **56**/475
provisional and final, **56**/465
striking off for breach of employment regulations, **56**/468
inspections of schools, *see* SCHOOL INSPECTIONS
local education authorities,
allocation of responsibility for providing sufficient school places, **56**/27, Sched. 4
ancillary functions,
acquisition and holding of property,
by agreement, **56**/531
compulsory purchase of land, **56**/530
gifts for educational purposes, 56/529
allowances for governors, **56**/519
chief education officer's appointment, **56**/532
cleanliness of pupils,
arrangements for cleansing, **56**/523
compulsory cleansing, **56**/522
examination for, **56**/521
exclusion of pupil pending examination or cleansing, **56**/524
offence of neglecting, **56**/525

EDUCATION—*cont.*
local education authorities—*cont.*
allocation of responsibility for providing sufficient school places—*cont.*
disability statements relating to further education, **56**/528
educational conferences, **56**/527
educational research, **56**/526
medical arrangements, **56**/520
payment of fees at non-maintained schools, **56**/517
provision of,
board and lodging, **56**/514
clothing, **56**/510, 511
meals at maintained schools, **56**/512
meals at non-maintained schools, **56**/513
services, **56**/508
teaching services for day nurseries, **56**/515
transport, **56**/509
supply of goods and services, **56**/516
authorities and their areas, **56**/12
disapplication of restriction on disposals, **56**/75
establishment of schools,
nursery schools: powers, **56**/17
power to establish, maintain and assist primary and secondary schools, **56**/16
funding authorities' functions: resolution of disputes, **56**/28
general functions,
further education, **56**/15
general responsibility for education, **56**/13
primary and secondary schools, **56**/15
information, provision of, **56**/29
obligations to provide new sites,
for aided and special agreement schools, **56**/61, 62
for controlled schools (and buildings), **56**/60, 62
provision of education,
exceptional, in pupil referral units, **56**/19, Sched. 1
non-maintained schools, **56**/18
schools maintained by,
meaning of "maintain," **56**/34
see also under types of school
maintained nursery schools; meaning of, **56**/33(1)
maintained schools; meaning of, **56**/350
maintained special schools,
conduct and staffing of, *see* conduct and staffing
government of, *see* government...
meaning of, **56**/33(1)
medical examinations, **56**/506, 520, 536
middle schools,
grant-maintained, **56**/291
proposals for establishment of, **56**/49
music teaching, **56**/451(3)
national curriculum, *see* curriculum
non-maintained schools: special education provision, **56**/348
nursery education,
and admission to schools, **56**/436
day nurseries, **56**/515, 535
in grant-maintained schools, **56**/292, 343

EDUCATION—*cont.*
nursery education—*cont.*
grants for, **50**/8
arrangements for making, **49**/1
children with special educational needs, **50**/4
delegation powers, **50**/2
disclosure of information, **50**/6, Sched. 2
inspections, **50**/5, Sched. 1
requirements for, **50**/3
local education authority's powers, **56**/17
National Curriculum, non-applicability of, **56**/410
orders, regulations and directions, **56**/568–70
parental choice and parents' wishes, *see* school admissions: statutory system of education
politics, *see* curriculum
premises, *see* school premises
primary education,
conditions for being county school, **56**/31(1)
conditions for being voluntary school, **56**/31(2)
definition, **56**/2
local education authority and,
functions, **56**/14
powers to establish, maintain and assist, **56**/16
pupil,
definition, **56**/3
Pupil Referral Units, **56**/19, Sched. 1
religious education,
change in religious character of schools, **56**/306
collective,
broadly Christian, **56**/386
disapplication of requirement, **56**/387, 394
duty to secure participation in, **56**/388
religious educational trusts,
orders for new provision for use of endowments, **56**/554
contents of, **56**/556
procedure, **56**/555
statutory trusts, adoption of, **56**/557, Sched. 36
religious opinions of staff, **56**/146, 304, 305
school inspections, **57**/23, Sched. 4
staffing,
appointments, **56**/143, 144
dismissals, **56**/145
see also curriculum
religious worship,
exceptions and special arrangements, **56**/389
standing advisory councils,
constitution, **56**/390
duty to constitute, **56**/393
functions, **56**/391
Secretary of State's powers over, **56**/396

EDUCATION—*cont.*
religious worship—*cont.*
standing advisory councils—*cont.*
supplementary provisions, **56**/392
where Christian collective worship not to apply, **56**/394
review of determinations, **56**/395
Sunday school, no requirement to attend, **56**/398
whether in accordance with trust deed, **56**/399
rights,
employment rights of teachers in aided schools, **18**/134
school admissions,
appeal arrangements, **56**/423, Sched. 33
co-ordinated arrangements, **56**/430
consultations as to, **56**/412
direction powers, **56**/431, 432
grant-maintained schools,
appeal arrangements, **56**/429
arrangements and information about, **56**/425
minimum numbers, **56**/426
alteration of by funding authority, **56**/428
alteration of by Secretary of State, **56**/427
information as to, **56**/414
new schools, **56**/422
numbers,
for county and voluntary schools,
admission authority: meaning, **56**/415
fixing, **56**/416
standard,
for primary schools, **56**/418, 419
review of, **56**/421
for secondary schools, **56**/417
variation of, **56**/420, Sched. 32
for nursery education, **56**/436
nursery schools, **56**/424
parental preference, **56**/411
preserving character of aided or special agreement schools, **56**/413
rationalisation of school places, see, Secretary of State, ancillary powers
registration of pupils, **56**/434
responsibility for finding sufficient places, **56**/27
special schools, **56**/424
time for, **56**/433
withdrawal of pupils, **56**/435
school attendance,
duration of school day, **56**/551
education supervision orders, **56**/447
exemption for child attaining five during term, **56**/448
offences,
failure to comply with order, **56**/443
failure to secure regular attendance, **56**/444
institution of proceedings, **56**/446
presumptions of age, **56**/445, 565
parents' general duty as to, **56**/7

EDUCATION—*cont.*
school attendance—*cont.*
school attendance orders,
service of, **56**/437
with statement of special needs,
choice of school, **56**/441
revocation of order, **56**/442
without statement of special needs, **56**/438
amendment of, **56**/440
specification of schools, **56**/439
school day, **56**/551
school inspections, *see* SCHOOL INSPECTIONS
school premises,
approval of, **56**/544
boarding hostels, **56**/544
control of harmful materials, **56**/546
exemption from byelaws, **56**/545
nuisance or disturbance on, **56**/547
offensive weapons on, **26**/1, 3
prescribed standards, **56**/542
relaxation of, **56**/543
secondary schools,
conditions for being county school, **56**/31(1)
conditions for being voluntary school, **56**/31(2)
local education authority and,
functions, **56**/14
powers to establish, maintain and assist, **56**/16
secondary education: definition, **56**/2
Secretary of State's functions,
ancillary functions,
appointment of governors, **56**/498
committee membership, **56**/499
determination of disputes, **56**/495
general default power, **56**/497
local inquiries, **56**/507
medical examinations, **56**/506
preventing unreasonable exercise of functions, **56**/496
rationalisation of school places,
additional provision, **56**/501
adoption of proposals, **56**/504
public inquiry into proposals, **56**/503
publication of proposals, **56**/502
remedies for excessive provision, **56**/500
supplementary provisions, **56**/505
general duty, **56**/10
primary, secondary and further education, **56**/11
secular education, *see* curriculum
sex education, *see* curriculum
single-sex schools, **56**/552
special agreement schools,
disapplication of restriction on disposals, **56**/75
financial assistance for, **56**/67
assistance by LEAs, **56**/68
grants for preliminary expenditure, **56**/66
grants for premises and equipment, **56**/65

EDUCATION—*cont.*
special agreement schools—*cont.*
government of, *see* government obligations of LEAs to provide new sites, **56**/61
"special agreement", meaning of, **56**/32 (5), Sched. 5
as voluntary schools, **56**/32
special educational needs,
code of practice,
issue of, **56**/313
making and approval of, **56**/314
definitions, **56**/312
government of, **56**/344, Sched. 28
identification and assessment,
assessment, **56**/323, Sched. 26
children under two, **56**/331
notification to parent, **56**/332
at request of governing body, **56**/330
at request of parent, **56**/329
review of, **56**/328
general duty of LEA, **56**/321
help from Health Authority or local authority, **56**/322
statement of special educational needs,
access to schools for, **56**/327
appeal against contents, **56**/326
appeal against decision, **56**/325
duty to make, **56**/324, Sched. 27
and National Curriculum, **56**/364
independent school providing, approval of, **56**/347
at non-maintained schools, **56**/348
payment of fees by local authority, **56**/517, 518
provision of,
duties of governing body or LEA, **56**/317
goods and services, **56**/318
in mainstream schools, **56**/316
otherwise than in schools, **56**/319
outside England and Wales, **56**/320
review of arrangements, **56**/315
Special Educational Needs Tribunal,
constitution, **56**/333
President and members, **56**/334
procedure, **56**/336
remuneration and expenses, **56**/335
special schools,
approval of, **56**/342
categories of, **56**/337
grant-maintained, **56**/338
grouping of, **56**/346
maintained or grant-maintained schools, **56**/339
approval of premises, **56**/341
proposals, procedure for dealing with, **56**/340
maintained special schools becoming grant-maintained special schools, **56**/345
variation of trust deeds, **56**/349
staffing, *see* conduct and staffing of schools

EDUCATION—*cont.*
statutory system of education,
compulsory education,
compulsory school age, **56**/8
parents' duties, **56**/7
educational institutions,
middle schools, **56**/5
nursery schools, **56**/6
primary schools, **56**/5
schools: general, **56**/4
secondary schools, **56**/5
further education: definition, **56**/2
parents' wishes, education in accordance with, **56**/9
primary education: definition, **56**/2
pupil: definition, **56**/3
secondary education: definition, **56**/2
stages of education, **56**/1
student loans,
subsidy in respect of private sector loans, **9**/1, 2
teacher training, **56**/177, 294
trust deeds,
ex officio trustees, **56**/180
modification of, **56**/179
vocational training, **8**/129, 144
voluntary schools,
categories of, **56**/32
conduct and staffing of, *see* conduct and staffing
disapplication of restriction on disposals, **56**/75
financial assistance,
endowments, **56**/72
by LEAs,
default in maintaining: Secretary of State's powers, **56**/71
for promoters of new schools, **56**/69, 70
letting or hiring fees, **56**/73
funding of,
obligations of governing bodies, **56**/59
obligations of LEAs,
to provide new sites and buildings, **56**/60
to provide new sites for aided and special agreement schools, **56**/61
government of, *see* government ...
proposals for division of, **56**/51
proposals for establishment, alteration or new site,
approval of school premises, **56**/44
approval or rejection of, **56**/43
establishment of new school in substitution for old school, **56**/46
general, **56**/41
implementation of, **56**/45
objections to, **56**/42
order authorising transfer to new site, **56**/47
proposals for middle school, **56**/49
status of new school: controlled or aided, **56**/48

EDUCATION—*cont.*
Wales,
Curriculum and Assessment Authority, **56**/360, 361, Sched. 30
funding of grant-maintained schools, *see* funding authorities: grant-maintained schools, funding of
grants for education, **56**/487, 489
research into National Curriculum matters, **56**/369
work experience, **56**/560
Education Act 1996 (c.56)
EDUCATION FINANCING OF LEA SCHOOLS,
schemes of delegation,
delegation,
suspension of, **56**/117–19
Education (Student Loans) Act 1996 (c.9)
EMPLOYMENT,
children and young persons,
local authority's power to restrict, **56**/559
work experience, **56**/560
civilian police employees, **16**/15
Employment Appeal Tribunal, *see* INDUSTRIAL TRIBUNALS
living accommodation for employees, **8**/106
Parliamentary staff and Industrial Tribunals, **17**/39
persons subject to immigration control: restrictions on, **49**/8
Reserve Forces and,
employee agreements, **14**/38–42
employment safeguards, **14**/122
rights,
armed services, **18**/192, **46**/26, 217, 27
betting workers, **18**/233
continuous employment,
change of employer, **18**/218
employment abroad, **18**/215
industrial disputes, **18**/91(2), 143, 144, 216
intervals in employment, **18**/213
meaning of, **18**/210
periods of, **18**/211
redundancy payments and, **18**/214
and reinstatement or re-engagement, **18**/219
weeks counting in computation, **18**/212
contracting out, restrictions on, **18**/203
Crown employment,
applicability of 1996 Act, **18**/191
armed forces, **18**/192
national security, **18**/193
parliamentary staff, **18**/194, 195
death of employer or employee,
redundancy payments, **18**/174–176
rights and liabilities accruing, **18**/207
tribunal proceedings, 206
unfair dismissal and, **18**/133
detriment in employment,
employee representatives, **18**/47
enforcement, **18**/48, 49
health and safety cases, **18**/44
right not to suffer, **18**/44
Sunday working, **18**/45

EMPLOYMENT—*cont.*
rights—*cont.*
detriment in employment—*cont.*
trustees of pension schemes, **18**/46
domestic servants, **18**/161
employee representatives,
time off work, **18**/61-63
unfair dismissal, **18**/103
employee representatives,
and detriment in employment, **18**/47
employment outside Great Britain, **18**/196, 215
employment particulars,
accessibility to document of agreement, **18**/6
enforcement, **18**/11, 12
exclusion from rights to, **18**/5
orders, **18**/7, 10
pay statement, **18**/8, 9
statement of changes, **18**/4
statement of initial particulars, **18**/1–3
fixed-term contracts, **18**/197
guarantee payments,
calculation of, **18**/30
contractual remuneration, **18**/32
exemption orders, **18**/35
limits on, **18**/31
power to modify, **18**/33
references to industrial tribunals, **18**/34
right to, **18**/28, 29
industrial disputes, **18**/91(2), 143, 144, 216
industrial tribunals, references to,
detriment in employment, **18**/48
employment particulars, **18**/11, 12
full extent of remedy, **18**/205
guarantee payments, **18**/34
redundancy of employer, **18**/188
statement of reasons for dismissal, **18**/93
suspension, **18**/70
time off work, **18**/51
ante-natal care, **18**/57
employee representatives, **18**/63
pension scheme trustees, **18**/60
redundant employees, **18**/54
wages, **18**/23–26
unfair dismissal, *see* unfair dismissal
information, restrictions on disclosure, **18**/202
insolvency of employers,
appropriate date, **18**/185
debts applicable, **18**/184
industrial tribunal, complaints to, **18**/188
information, power to obtain, **18**/190
insolvency: meaning, **18**/183
limit on amount payable, **18**/186
relevant officer, role of, **18**/187
rights and remedies transferred to Secretary of State, **18**/189
law governing employment, **18**/204
mariners, **18**/199

EMPLOYMENT—*cont.*
rights—*cont.*
maternity rights,
leave,
commencement, **18**/72
contractual rights to, **18**/78
duration of, **18**/73
general right to, **18**/71
intention to return: duty to notify, **18**/76
notification of date, **18**/74
pregnancy, duty to notify, **18**/75
redundancy during, **18**/77, 81
unfair dismissal and, **18**/127
right to return to work,
contractual rights, **18**/85
dismissal after leave, **18**/84
exercise of rights, **18**/82
failure to permit: dismissal, **18**/96
general right, **18**/79
notification, duty of, **18**/80
notified day of return, **18**/83
redundancy before return, **18**/77, 81
suspension from work on maternity grounds, **18**/66–68
unfair dismissal, **18**/99
national security, **18**/193, 202
normal working hours, **18**/234
occupation pension fund trustees and detriment in employment, **18**/46
time off work, **18**/58–60
unfair dismissal, **18**/102
offshore employment, **18**/201
police officers, **18**/200
public duties, **18**/50
redundancy payments,
amount of, **18**/162
claims, **18**/164
death of employee, **18**/176
death of employer, **18**/174, 175
employment not under contract, **18**/171
equivalent payments, **18**/177
general exclusions from right **18**/155–161
general right to, **18**/135
payment by person other than employer, **18**/173
payments by Secretary of State, **18**/166–170
by reason of lay-off or short time, **18**/147, 148–152
by reason of redundancy, **18**/136–139
exclusions, **18**/140–144
references to industrial tribunals, **18**/163
termination of employment by statute, **18**/172
written particulars, **18**/165
shop workers, **18**/232
cash shortages, *see* wages
short-term employment, **18**/198
Sunday working,
contracts of employment, **18**/37, 38
opted-out workers, **18**/40–43
protected shop and betting workers, **18**/36

EMPLOYMENT—*cont.*
rights—*cont.*
suspension from work,
calculation of remuneration, **18**/69
complaints to industrial tribunals, **18**/70
on maternity grounds, **18**/66–68
on medical grounds, **18**/64, 65
teachers in aided schools, **18**/134
termination of employment,
death of employer or employee, **18**/133, 174–176
minimum period of notice, **18**/86–91
written statement of reasons, **18**/92, 93
time off work,
ante-natal care, **18**/55–57
Occupation pension scheme trustees, **18**/58–60
complaints to industrial tribunals, **18**/51
employee representatives, **18**/61–63
public duties, **18**/50
redundant employees, **18**/52–54
unfair dismissal,
death of employer or employee, **18**/133, 174–176
dismissal, **18**/95–97
exclusion of right, **18**/108–110
fairness, **18**/98–107
remedies for,
compensation, **18**/118–127
complaints to industrial tribunal, **18**/111
interim relief, **18**/128–132
orders and compensation, **18**/112
orders for reinstatement, **18**/113–117
wages,
cash shortages and stock deficiencies, **18**/17–22
deductions by employer, **18**/13, 14
enforcement, **18**/23–26
payments to employer, **18**/15, 16
week's pay,
calculation date, **18**/225, 226
calculation of, **18**/220
employments with no normal working hours, **18**/224
employments with normal working hours, **18**/221–223
maximum amount, **18**/227
new employment and special cases, 18/ 228, 229
Employment Rights Act 1996 (c.18)
ENERGY CONSERVATION,
energy efficiency schemes, **53**/142
residential accommodation: extended meaning of, **38**/1
Energy Conservation Act 1996 (c.38)
ENTAILED INTERESTS, **47**/25(4), *see also* TRUSTS AND TRUSTEES
ENTRY POWERS,
Channel Tunnel Rail Link, **61**/13, Sched. 8
deer offences (Scots Law), **58**/15
for noise at night, **37**/10
ENTRY POWERS—*cont.*
to search for offensive weapons, **26**/4
terrorism and, *see* NORTHERN IRELAND, emergency provisions
ENVIRONMENTAL LAW,
London, **ix**/24
EQUAL OPPORTUNITIES,
in broadcasting, **55**/34, 68
equal treatment in armed services, **46**/24, 25
EUROPEAN COMMISSION,
VAT Simplification Directive, **8**/25–29, *see also* VALUE ADDED TAX
EVIDENCE,
aircraft: inquiries by consular officer, **39**/2
blood or urine samples, **25**/63
from children, **46**/7
in defamation cases,
of convictions, **31**/12
proceedings in Parliament, **31**/13
fingerprints,
armed services, **46**/11
checks against, **25**/64
noise at night: measuring devices, **37**/7
television links, **25**/62
terrorist offences, *see* NORTHERN IRELAND, emergency provisions
video recordings, **25**/62
written statements and depositions, **25**/68, Sched. 2
see also CRIMINAL PROCEDURE AND INVESTIGATIONS
EXCISE DUTIES,
air passenger duty, **8**/13
alcoholic liquor duties, **8**/1–3
amusement machine licence duty, **8**/12
betting duties, **8**/10, 11
drawbacks and allowances: repeals, **8**/24
hydrocarbon oil duties, **8**/4–8, Sched. 1
tobacco products duty, **8**/9
vehicle excise duty, *see* VEHICLE EXCISE DUTY
EXCISE DUTY,
see also HYDROCARBON OIL DUTIES
EXPERT WITNESSES,
in arbitration proceedings, **23**/37

FAMILY HOME, *see* FAMILY LAW
FAMILY LAW,
children,
and applications for non-molestation orders, **27**/43
continuing relationship with parents, **27**/1(c)(ii)
distress to be avoided, **27**/1(c)(i)
interim care orders and emergency protection orders, **27**/52, Sched. 6
risk of violence to be avoided, 27/1(d)
separate representation in proceedings, **27**/64
welfare of, in orders preventing divorce, **27**/11

FAMILY LAW—*cont.*
divorce and separation,
commencement of marital proceedings, **27**/20
connected proceedings, **27**/25
divorce orders,
circumstances in which made, **27**/3
effect of, **27**/2(1)(a)
financial provision,
in magistrates' courts, **27**/18
orders as to, **27**/15, Sched. 2
pension rights, **27**/16
pension rights (Scotland), **27**/17
jurisdiction and proceedings, **27**/19
separate representation for children, **27**/64
stay of proceedings, **27**/19(5), Sched. 3
marital breakdown,
requirements for, **27**/5
statement of, **27**/6, 12
marriage support services,
funding for, **27**/22
marriage counselling, **27**/23
mediation, **27**/13
orders preventing divorce,
hardship, **27**/10
welfare of children, **27**/11
reflection and consideration,
arrangements for future, **27**/9, Sched. 1
information meetings, **27**/8
period for, **27**/7
resolution of disputes,
adjournment of proceedings, **27**/14
directions as to mediation, **27**/13
separation orders,
circumstances in which made, **27**/3
conversion to divorce order, **27**/4
effect of, **27**/2(1)(b)
intestacy, effect of, **27**/21
see also marriage
domestic violence, *see* family homes and domestic violence
family homes and domestic violence,
appeals, **27**/61
children,
as applicants for non-molestation orders, **27**/43
interim care orders and emergency protection orders, **27**/52, Sched. 6
interpretation, **27**/62, 63
jurisdiction, **27**/57, 59
magistrates' courts' jurisdiction, **27**/59
magistrates' courts' powers,
guardianship orders, **27**/51
hospital admission orders, **27**/51
to suspend execution of committal order, **27**/50
mortgages,
action by mortgagees,
joining connected persons, **27**/55
service of notices, **27**/56
dwellinghouses subject to, **27**/54

FAMILY LAW—*cont.*
family homes and domestic violence—*cont.*
non-molestation orders,
arrest for breach of, **27**/47, Sched. 5
children under sixteen, **27**/43
evidence of agreement to marry, **27**/44
ex parte orders, **27**/45
power to make, **27**/42
remand for medical examination and report, **27**/48
undertakings, **27**/46
variation and discharge of, **27**/49
occupation orders,
effect of, where charge on dwelling-house, **27**/34
neither cohabitant entitled to occupy, **27**/38
neither spouse entitled to occupy, **27**/37
one cohabitant with no right to occupy, **27**/36
one former spouse with no right to occupy, **27**/35
provisions (additional) that may be included, **27**/40
supplementary provisions, **27**/39
where applicable, **27**/33
proceedings,
contempt proceedings, **27**/58
Lord Chancellor's orders as to, **27**/57
separate representation for children, **27**/64
third parties acting on behalf of victims, **27**/60
right to occupy matrimonial home,
charge on dwelling-house, **27**/31
conditions as to, **27**/30
and Matrimonial Homes Act 1983, **27**/32, Sched. 4
transfer of tenancies, **27**/53, Sched. 7
legal aid for mediation in family matters,
civil legal aid, **27**/29
interpretation, **27**/26
payment for, **27**/28
provision and availability of, **27**/27
marriage,
to be supported, **27**/1(a)
irretrievable breakdown,
conditions for, **27**/5
general principles as to, **27**/1(c)
statement of, **27**/6, 12
see also DIVORCE AND SEPARATION
marriage support services,
funding for, **27**/22
marriage counselling, **27**/23
steps to save, **27**/1(b)
support services, **27**/22, 23
violence in, **27**/1(d)
matrimonial home, *see* family home and domestic violence
mortgages, *see* family home and domestic violence
non-molestation orders, *see* family home and domestic violence
separation orders, *see* divorce and separation

Family Law Act 1996 (c.27)
Finance Act 1996 (c.8)
FINGERPRINTS, *see* EVIDENCE
FIRE SAFETY (LONDON), **ix**/20–23
FIREARMS,
deer offences (Scots Law),
illegal possession, **44**/9
wilfully injuring deer, **58**/21(5)
exemption from Firearms Act 1968 (armed services), **46**/28, 29
FRANCE,
registration of company in, **v**/3
FRAUD, SERIOUS OR COMPLEX, **25**/1(2)(b), 72, Sched. 3
FRIENDLY SOCIETIES,
life or endowment business, **8**/171

GAELIC LANGUAGE PROGRAMMES, **55**/32, 95
GENEVA CONVENTION,
in arbitration proceedings, **23**/99
GREENWICH HOSPITAL, **46**/30

HALLMARKS,
Edinburgh Assay Office, confirmation of powers of, **c.i**
HANDICAPPED PERSONS,
blind (visually impaired) persons,
broadcasting: digital programme code, **55**/20–22
and dog-fouling, **20**/3(3)
tax relief, **8**/75
digital decoding for deaf, **55**/20–22
disabled facilities grant, *see* HOUSING GRANTS
HEALTH,
school medical examinations, **56**/506, 520, 536
HEALTH SERVICE COMMISSIONERS, *see* NATIONAL HEALTH SERVICE
Health Service Commissioners (Amendment) Act 1996 (c.5)
Henry Johnson, Sons & Co., Limited Act 1996 (c.v)
HERITAGE,
Channel Tunnel Rail Link: disapplication of controls, **61**/12, Sched. 7
HIGHWAYS,
A2 and M2 improvement works,
acquisition of land, **61**/45, Sched. 13
authorised works, **61**/44, Sched. 12
blight: compensation for pre-enactment acquisition, **61**/46
bus lanes (London), **ix**/3–9
Channel Tunnel Rail Link: works, **61**/3
closure of, **22**/27
interference with, **22**/26
HIGHWAYS AND BRIDGES,
Humber Bridge debts, **1**
HOME REPAIR ASSISTANCE, *see* HOUSING GRANTS
HOMELESSNESS,
accommodation available for occupation: meaning, **52**/176
applications for assistance,
generally, **52**/183
inquiries into, **52**/184

HOMELESSNESS—*cont.*
associated person: meaning, **52**/178
asylum seekers, **52**/186, *see also* IMMIGRATION
discharge of local authority's functions, **52**/205
accommodation provided, **52**/207
co-operation between housing authorities and bodies, **52**/213
methods available, **52**/206
out-of-area placements, **52**/208
private landlord arrangements, **52**/209
protection of homeless person's property, **52**/211, 212
suitability of accommodation, **52**/210
duties to homeless persons,
after minimum period of duty, **52**/194
intentionally homeless, **52**/190, 191
not in priority need and not intentionally homeless, **52**/192
with priority need and not intentionally homeless, **52**/193
suitable accommodation available, **52**/197
threatened homelessness, **52**/195
intentional, **52**/196
eligibility for assistance,
asylum-seekers, **52**/186
information by Secretary of State, **52**/187
persons from abroad, **52**/185
general provisions,
consequential amendments, **52**/216(3), Sched. 17
definitions, **52**/217
false statements, **52**/214
index of defined expressions, **52**/218
regulations and orders, **52**/215
transitional provisions, **52**/216
guidance by Secretary of State, **52**/182
housing authority's functions,
advisory services, **52**/179
assistance for voluntary organisations, **52**/180
interim duty to accommodate where priority need,
generally, **52**/188
those with priority need, **52**/189
meaning of, **52**/175
reasonableness of continuing to occupy, **52**/177
referral to another local housing authority,
duties to applicant, **52**/200
generally, **52**/198
local connection, **52**/199
review of decisions,
appeal on point of law, **52**/204
procedure on, **52**/203
right to request, **52**/202
terms and conditions of assistance, **52**/181
threatened: meaning, **52**/175
HONG KONG,
war wives and widows acquiring British citizenship,
conditions for, **41**/1

HONG KONG—*cont.*
war wives and widows acquiring British citizenship—*cont.*
consequential nationality provisions, **41**/2
Hong Kong Economic and Trade Office Act 1996 (c.63)
Hong Kong (Overseas Public Servants) Act 1996 (c.2)
HONG KONG PUBLIC SERVANTS,
definition, **2**/1
early retirement, **2**/3
income tax provisions, **2**/5(5)
other overseas public service payments, **2**/5(3)–(4)
payments to,
amount and method of, **2**/5
authority for, **2**/2
pension supplements, **2**/4
Special Administrative Region, **2**/2
HONG KONG SPECIAL ADMINISTRATIVE REGION,
offices in UK: privileges and immunities, **63**/1
HOUSE-BOATS,
definition of, **38**/1
home repair assistance for, **53**/78
HOUSES IN MULTIPLE OCCUPATION,
codes of practice, **52**/77
common lodging houses, **52**/80
deferred action notices,
appeals against, **53**/83
defined expressions, **53**/91
definitions, **53**/90
form of, **53**/89
guidance by Secretary of State, **53**/85
meaning of, **53**/81
review of, **53**/84
service of, **53**/82
duty to keep premises fit for number of occupants, **52**/73
fines, **52**/78
HMO grants,
approval of application, **53**/28
availability of, **53**/1(5)
certificates required, **53**/26
conditions as to occupation, **53**/50
interest of applicant in property, **53**/25
purposes for which grant may be given, **53**/27
repayment on disposal, **53**/47
limit on number of occupants: local land charge, **52**/74
means of escape from fire, **52**/75
minor amendments, **52**/79
registration schemes, **52**/65
control provisions, **52**/66
existing, **52**/70
information requirements, **52**/69
offences in connection with, **52**/68
special control provisions, **52**/67
works notices,
enforcement procedures, **52**/76
recovery of expenses of, **52**/72
restrictions, **52**/71
HOUSING,
Architects, *see* ARCHITECTS REGISTRATION BOARD
HOUSING—*cont.*
construction contracts, *see* CONSTRUCTION CONTRACTS
grants, *see* HOUSING GRANTS
houses in multiple occupation, *see* HOUSES IN MULTIPLE OCCUPATION
Housing for Wales, **52**/56(1)
persons subject to immigration control, **49**/9
register, *see* social sector
social sector,
allocation of housing accommodation,
adverse decision,
notification of, **52**/164
right to review, **52**/164
procedure on, **52**/165
allocation scheme,
allocation in accordance with, **52**/167
information about, **52**/168
co-operation on, **52**/170
consequential amendments, **52**/173, Sched. 16
false statements and witholding information, **52**/171
generally, **52**/159
guidance to authorities, **52**/169
housing register,
establishment and maintenance of, **52**/162
information about, **52**/166
operation of, **52**/163
persons from abroad, **52**/161(2)
qualifying persons, **52**/161
immigration control, **52**/161(2), 185(2)
index of defined expressions, **52**/174
non-applicability of provisions, **52**/160
regulations, **52**/172
Housing Corporation, *see* HOUSING CORPORATION
Industrial and Provident Societies, **52**/57
offences by bodies corporate, **52**/223
Registered Social Landlords, *see* REGISTERED SOCIAL LANDLORDS
see also Homelessness
HOUSING ACTION TRUSTS,
orders for dissolution, **53**/144
HOUSING BENEFIT,
administration of, **52**/121, Sched. 12
consequential amendments, **52**/123, Sched. 13
payment to third parties, **52**/120
rent officers' functions, **52**/122
HOUSING CORPORATION,
determinations by, **52**/54
general powers, **52**/30
housing management,
entry powers, **52**/37
penalty for obstructing, **52**/38
guidelines, **52**/36
information,
disclosure by Corporation, **52**/33
disclosure to Corporation, **52**/32
enforcement of notices, **52**/31

HOUSING CORPORATION—*cont.*
information—*cont.*
as to levels of performance, **52**/35
meaning of, **52**/56(2)
standards of performance, **52**/34
see also REGISTERED SOCIAL LANDLORDS
HOUSING GRANTS,
common parts grant,
applications for, **53**/15
approval of application, **53**/18
availability of, **53**/1(1)
certificates required, **53**/16
purpose for which grant can be made, **53**/17
repayment on disposal, **53**/46
tenant's application: apportionment, **53**/32
disabled facilities grant,
applications, **53**/19
approval of application, **53**/24
availability of, **53**/1(3)
certificates required, **53**/21–22
change of circumstances, **53**/41
disabled occupant, **53**/20
disabled person: meaning, **53**/100
purposes for which grant may be made, **53**/23
energy efficiency schemes, **53**/142
existing: exempt disposal, **53**/141
group repair schemes,
approval of schemes, **53**/63
conditions of participation,
cessation on payment of balance of cost, **53**/73
disposals, **53**/72
general, **53**/69
occupation, **53**/71
payment of balance of costs on disposal, **53**/70
defined expressions, **53**/75
directions as to modification of provisions, **53**/74
generally, **53**/60
participation in,
certificate of completion date, **53**/66
contribution by participants, **53**/67
persons eligible, **53**/64
restriction on works, **53**/65
scheme consent, **53**/65
qualifying buildings, **53**/61
scheme works, **53**/62
variation of, **53**/68
home repair assistance,
availability of, **53**/1(1), 76
defined expressions, **53**/80
entitlement to, **53**/77
for house-boats, **53**/78
for mobile homes, **53**/78
regulations as to, **53**/79
for houses in multiple occupation *see* HOUSES IN MULTIPLE OCCUPATION
regeneration, development and relocation,
financial assistance for,
forms of assistance, **53**/127
Secretary of State's powers, **53**/126
HOUSING GRANTS—*cont.*
regeneration, development and relocation—*cont.*
financial assistance for—*cont.*
terms on which given, **53**/128
Welsh Development Agency, **53**/130
relocation grants in clearance areas,
amount, **53**/134
applications and payments, **53**/132
conditions,
cessation of, on repayment, **53**/137
liability to repay as charge on dwelling, **53**/138
owner-occupation, **53**/136
repayment on disposal, **53**/135
contributions by Secretary of State, **53**/139
definitions, **53**/140
qualifying persons and dwellings, **53**/133
resolution to pay, **53**/131
for renewal of private sector housing,
age of property, **53**/4
applications for, **53**/2
availability of, **53**/1
charities, **53**/95
conditions,
availability for letting (renovation grants), **53**/**53**/49
cessation of, on repayment, **53**/55
compensation claims: repayment from, **53**/51
disposals,
exempt, **53**/54
relevant, meaning of, **53**/53
as local authority thinks fit, **53**/52
occupation (HMO grants), **53**/**53**/50
owner-occupation: renovation grants, **53**/48
repayment (general), **53**/44
repayment on disposal, **53**/45–47
conditions for, **53**/3
consent of Secretary of State, **53**/94
consequential amendments, **53**/103, Sched. 1
contributions by Secretary of State, **53**/92
recovery of, **53**/93
death of applicant, **53**/56
decision on application and notification, **53**/34
defective dwellings, **53**/6
defined expressions, **53**/59
definitions, **53**/58, **53**/101
excluded descriptions of works, **53**/5
existing grants: exempt disposals, **53**/141
family and connected persons: meaning, **53**/98
fitness for human habitation: meaning, **53**/97, *see also* unfit houses
interpretation, **53**/96–101
landlord's application: amount of grant, **53**/31
local authority's powers to carry out works, **53**/57
mandatory grants, **53**/24(1)

HOUSING GRANTS—*cont.*
for renewal of private sector housing—*cont.*
maximum amount of, **53**/33
means testing, **53**/30
owner: meaning, **53**/99
parsonages, **53**/95
payment of,
applicant ceasing to be entitled, **53**/40
change of circumstances affecting disabled occupant, **53**/41
conditions as to carrying out works, **53**/37
conditions as to contractors employed, **53**/38
to contractor, **53**/39
delayed payment of mandatory grant, **53**/36
general, **53**/35
recalculated, withheld or repaid, **53**/42
repayment where applicant not entitled, **53**/43
reasonable repair: meaning, **53**/96
restrictions on grant aid, **53**/29
transitional provisions, **53**/102
renovation grants,
applications (generally), **53**/7
approval of application, **53**/13
availability of, **53**/1(2)
conditions,
as to availability for letting, **53**/49
as to owner-occupation, **53**/48
landlord's application: amount of grant, **53**/31
means testing, **53**/30
owners' applications: certificates required, **53**/8
prior qualifying period, **53**/10-11
purposes for which grant can be given, **53**/12
repayment on disposal, **53**/45
tenants' applications: certificates required, **53**/9
restrictions on grant aid, **53**/29
unfit houses,
defined expressions, **53**/91
definitions, **53**/90
fitness for human habitation: meaning, **53**/97
power to charge for enforcement action, **53**/87–88
power to improve enforcement procedures, **53**/86
see also deferred action notices
Housing Grants, Construction and Regeneration Act 1996 (c.53)
Humber Bridge (Debts) Act 1996 (c.1)
HYDROCARBON OIL DUTIES,
marine voyages: relief, **8**/8
marked oil for road vehicles, **8**/7
rates and rebate, **8**/4
rebated kerosene misuse of, **8**/5
rebated oil, mixing of, **8**/6, Sched. 1

IMMIGRATION,
asylum claims,
extension of special appeals procedure, **49**/1

IMMIGRATION—*cont.*
asylum claims—*cont.*
removal to safe third countries, **49**/2
appeals against, **49**/3
social security benefits and, **49**/11, Sched. 1
control: housing allocation, **52**/161(2), 185(2)
immigration offences,
arrest powers, **49**/7
assisting claimants and persons seeking leave by deception, **49**/5
deception, **49**/4, 5
increased penalties, **49**/6
obtaining leave by deception, **49**/4
search warrants, **49**/7
persons subject to immigration control,
entitlements,
child benefit, **49**/10
housing accommodation and assistance, **49**/9
savings for social security regulations, **49**/11, Sched. 1
restrictions on employment, **49**/8
port and border controls: terrorism, **7**/3
IMPRISONMENT,
prisoners' wages, *see* WAGES
INCITEMENT,
to commit sexual acts outside UK, *see* SEXUAL OFFENCES
INCOME TAX,
blind person's allowance, **8**/75
charge and rates for 1996, **8**/72
insurance premiums, *see* INSURANCE
interest: limit on relief, **8**/76
loan relationships,
collective investment schemes, **8**/98, Sched. 10
computational provisions,
accounting methods, **8**/85–90, Sched. 9
debts and credits brought into account, **8**/84, Sched. 9
payments subject to deduction of tax, **8**/91
convertible securities, **8**/94–96
debt contract and option, **8**/101(2), Sched. 12
discounted securities, **8**/102, Sched. 13
financial instruments, **8**/101
imputed interest, **8**/100
interest on judgments, **8**/100
meaning of, **8**/81
Schedule E charge,
beneficial loans, **8**/107
charitable donations: payroll deduction scheme, **8**/109
living accommodation for employees, **8**/106
Members of Parliament: incidental benefits, **8**/108
PAYE settlement agreements, 110
lower rate: application to savings income, **8**/73, Sched. 6
personal allowances for 1996–97, **8**/74

INCOME TAX—*cont.*
reliefs,
agricultural property, **8**/185
annual payments in residuary cases, **8**/149
business property, **8**/184
charities, **8**/146
Class 4 contributions, **8**/147
interest: limits, **8**/76
non-resident EEA nationals: personal relief, **8**/145
personal injury cases: exemptions, **8**/150, Sched. 26
personal pensions: mis-sold, **8**/148
retirement: age limits, **8**/176
roll-over, **8**/141
self assessment, **8**/128, Sched. 17
vocational training, **8**/144
self assessment,
general management,
appeals, **8**/136, Sched. 22
claims and enquiries, **8**/133, Sched. 19
discretions, **8**/134, Sched. 20
medical insurance relief, **8**/129
no return delivered, **8**/125
notices, **8**/130
notional deductions and payments, **8**/122
overdue tax, **8**/131, 132, Sched. 18
partners' liability, **8**/123
PAYE regulations, **8**/126
records: retention, **8**/124
reliefs involving two or more years, **8**/128, Sched. 17
repayment postponed pending enquiries, **8**/127
returns, **8**/121
time limit for claims, **8**/135, Sched. 21
vocational training relief, **8**/129
INDICTABLE OFFENCES,
see CRIMINAL PROCEDURE AND INVESTIGATIONS
INDUSTRIAL AND PROVIDENT SOCIETIES,
and social housing, **52**/57
INDUSTRIAL TRIBUNALS,
complaints from armed services, personnel, **46**/21–27
conciliation, **17**/18, 19
Employment Appeal Tribunal,
continuance of, **17**/20(1)
costs and expenses, **17**/34
decisions and further appeals, **17**/35–37
jurisdiction, **17**/21
membership, **17**/22–25, 27, 28
procedure, **17**/29, 30
publicity, **17**/31, 32
situation, **17**/20(2)
status, **17**/20(3)
vexatious proceedings, **17**/33
employment rights complaints, *see* EMPLOYMENT, rights
establishment of, **17**/1
jurisdiction, **17**/2, 3
membership, **17**/4, 5
Parliamentary staff, **17**/39
INDUSTRIAL TRIBUNALS—*cont.*
procedure,
conduct of hearings, **17**/6
contract cases, **17**/8
costs and expenses, **17**/13
enforcement of orders, **17**/15
interest on sums payable, **17**/14
national security and, **17**/10
pre-hearing reviews, **17**/9
private sittings, **17**/10
publicity, **17**/11, 12
regulations, **17**/7
recoupment of social security benefits, **17**/16, 17
Industrial Tribunals Act 1996 (c.17)
INHERITANCE TAX,
agricultural property relief, **8**/185
business property relief, **8**/184
rate bands, **8**/183
INJURIOUS AFFECTION,
Channel Tunnel Rail Link, **61**/36
INNS OF COURT,
approval of premises for marriage, **iv**/4
party walls, **40**/18
INQUESTS,
into treasure, **24**/7–9
INSTITUTE OF CHILD HEALTH,
dissolution of, **iii**/4
INSTITUTE OF NEUROLOGY,
dissolution of, **iii**/4
INSURANCE,
annual payments: relief, **8**/143
medical: relief, **8**/129
qualifying life policies, **8**/162
INSURANCE COMPANIES,
annual payments: decuctions, **8**/168
capital redemption business, **8**/168, Sched. 33
equilisation reserves, **8**/166, Sched. 32
expenses relief: limits, **8**/164
industrial assurance business, **8**/167
life assurance business losses, **8**/163, Sched. 31
loan relationship, **8**/99, Sched. 11
pension business: provisional repayments, **8**/169, Sched. 11
returns: time for amending, **8**/170
INTEREST,
in arbitration proceedings, **23**/49
imputed, **8**/100
on judgments, **8**/100
setting rates, **8**/197
on sums awarded by Industrial Tribunals, **17**/14
INTERNATIONAL LAW,
acquisition of British citizenship, **41**/1
Convention on Prohibition, etc., of Chemical Weapons and on their Destruction, *see* CHEMICAL WEAPONS
foreign aircraft, UK bound, **39**/1
foreign arbitral awards, **23**/99–104
INTRODUCTORY TENANCIES, *see* LANDLORD AND TENANT

ISLES OF SCILLY,
Education Act 1996, application of, **56**/581
Police Act 1996, application of, **16**/35

JIM CLARK MEMORIAL RALLY,
confirmation of provisional order, **xii**
JUDGES,
as arbitrators, **23**/93, Sched. 2
JUSTICES,
indemnity of, **25**/70
JUSTICES' CLERKS,
indemnity of, **25**/70

LANDFILL TAX,
administration, **8**/47–50
bankruptcy, **8**/58(4)
basic provisions, **8**/39–42
bodies corporate, **8**/58(3)
Commissioners' decisions, **8**/54
credit, **8**/51–53
disposal,
as landfill, **8**/65
as waste, **8**/64
groups of companies, **8**/59
information, **8**/60, Sched. 5
operators, **8**/67
orders and regulations, **8**/71
partnerships, **8**/58(1)
qualifying material, **8**/63
review and appeal, **8**/55, 56
sites, **8**/66
taxable activities, **8**/69
taxable disposals, **8**/61, 62
transfer of business, **8**/58(5)–(6)
unincorporated bodies, **8**/58(2)
weight of material, **8**/68
LANDLORD AND TENANT,
assured agricultural occupancies, **52**/103
assured non-shorthold tenancies, **52**/96, Sched. 7
assured shorthold tenancies,
definition of, **52**/96, Sched. 7
false statement, **52**/102
grounds for possession: non-payment of rent, **52**/101
notices under S.21 Housing Act 1988, **52**/98
rent determination: application time limit, **52**/100
restriction on recovery of possession, **52**/99
statement of terms of, **52**/97
and Channel Tunnel Rail Link, **61**/40
compulsory acquisition of landlord's interest, **52**/88
conduct of tenants, see: introductory tenancies, injunctions against anti-social behaviour: repossession
introductory tenancies,
assignment, **52**/134
consultation on housing management, **52**/137
county court's jurisdiction, **52**/138
duration of, **52**/125

LANDLORD AND TENANT—*cont.*
introductory tenancies—*cont.*
dwelling-house: meaning, **52**/139
family members: meaning, **52**/140
general provisions, **52**/124
information about tenancies, **52**/136
injunctions against anti-social behaviour,
arrest powers,
arrest and remand, **52**/155, Sched. 15
for breach of injunction, **52**/153
ex-parte applications, **52**/154
remand for medical examination, **52**/156
supplementary provisions, **52**/157
power to grant, **52**/152
proceedings for possession,
effect of, **52**/130
generally, **52**/127
notice of, **52**/128
review of decision to seek possession, **52**/129
regulations and orders, **52**/142
repairs, **52**/135
succession on death of tenant, **52**/131–133
leasehold reform,
collective enfranchisement,
multiple freeholders, **52**/107, Sched. 10
compensation for landlords for ineffective claims, **52**/116, Sched. 11
costs determination, **52**/115
estate management schemes for enfranchisement, **52**/118
low rent test,
extension of rights, **52**/106, Sched. 9
nil rateable values, **52**/105
minor amendment, **52**/114
pre-trial review: leasehold valuation tribunals, **52**/119
priority of interests on grant of new lease, **52**/117
trusts,
satisfaction of residence condition,
collective enfranchisement, **52**/111
new leases, **52**/112
trustees' powers, **52**/113
valuation,
collective enfranchisement,
professional valuation not needed, **52**/108
valuation principles, **52**/109
new leases: valuation principles, **52**/110
leasehold valuation panel, **52**/86, 87, Sched. 5
legal advice on residential tenancies, **52**/94
Registered Social Landlords, *see* REGISTERED SOCIAL LANDLORDS
repossession,
assured tenancies,
annoyance to adjoining occupiers, **52**/148
domestic violence, **52**/149, 150
early commencement of proceedings, **52**/151
notice requirements, **52**/147

Landlord and Tenant—*cont.*
repossession—*cont.*
secure tenancies,
annoyance to neighbours, **52**/144
domestic violence, **52**/145
false statements, **52**/146
secure tenancies, *see* repossession
social sector,
definitions, **52**/56–63
tenants' rights,
county court's jurisdiction, **52**/95
forfeiture,
notice under S.146 Law of Property Act 1925, **52**/82
service charge, restriction on termination for failure to pay, **52**/81
managers: appointment by court, **52**/85
right of first refusal,
application in relation to contracts, **52**/89
new landlord to inform tenant of rights, **52**/93
tenant's rights,
right of first refusal,
notice to landlord, **52**/90
offences by landlord, **52**/91
procedure, **52**/92, Sched. 6
tenants' rights,
service charges,
failure to pay, **52**/81
reasonableness of, **52**/83
surveyor to advise, **52**/84, Sched. 4
transfer of jurisdiction to leasehold valuation panel, **52**/86, 87, Sched. 5
see also Homelessness: Housing: Registered Social Landlords
Law Reform,
leasehold reform, *see* Landlord and Tenant
year and a day rule,
abolition, **19**/1
proceedings for fatal offence, **19**/2
Law Reform (Year and a Day Rule) Act 1996 (c.19)
Legal Aid,
for mediation in family matters, **27**/26–29, *see also* Family Law
for terrorist offences, **20**/4
Licensing,
conditions attached for certain events (Scots Law), **36**/1
game licences, **58**/38
Licensing (Amendment) (Scotland) Act 1996 (c.36)
Lieutenancies,
and Reserve Forces, **14**/121, Sched. 6
Loan Relationships, *see* Income Tax
Local Authorities,
bye-laws for Channel Tunnel Rail Link, **61**/15
see also London
control of sex establishments (Westminster), **viii**/1–8
direct payments for Community Care services, *see* Community Care
Local Authorities—*cont.*
dog-fouling,
and byelaws, **20**/6
designating land, **20**/2
fixed penalty notices, **20**/4
school inspections, *see* School Inspections
London,
approved premises for marriage, **iv**/1–5
audible alarms, **ix**/25
bus lanes, **ix**/3–9
City of London Police, **16**/22, 95
civilian employees, **16**/15
Common Council of the City of London
committee under Housing Act 1959, **52**/224
directors' liability, **ix**/30
due diligence defence, **ix**/29
entertainment licensing and fire safety, **ix**/20–23
environmental protection, **ix**/24
fire safety, **ix**/20–23
obstruction of authorised officer, **ix**/28
occasional sales, **ix**/10–19
public charitable collections, **ix**/26
Regional Transport,
contractors, agreements with, **21**/1
general powers, extension of, **21**/1
land acquisitions, **21**/2
operating powers, extension of, **21**/2
transfer of functions, **21**/3
University College Medical School transfer of property etc. of other medical schools to, **iii**/1–11
Westminster sex establishments, *see* Sex Establishments
London Local Authorities Act 1996 (c.ix)
London Regional Transport Act 1996 (c.21)

Magistrates' Courts,
powers and jurisdiction in family law matters, *see* Family Law
procedure, *see* Criminal Procedure and Investigations
Mammals, *see* Animals and Birds
Marriage,
approval of premises for (City of London), **iv**/1–5
ceremony: alternatives for prescribed words, **34**/1
irretrievable breakdown, *see* Family Law
Marriage Ceremony (Prescribed Words) Act 1996 (c.34)
Maternity Rights,
see Employment, rights
Matrimonial Home, *see* Family Law
Means Testing,
for housing grants, **53**/30
Mental Health,
direct payments for community services, **30**/1(3)
Mental Welfare Commission for Scotland: investigative procedure, 5/4

MENTAL WELFARE COMMISSION FOR SCOTLAND:
investigative procedure, **5**/4
MOBILE HOMES,
home repair assistance for, **53**/78
MODE OF TRIAL,
court- or civil court-martial, **14**/106
terrorism offences, *see* Northern Ireland, emergency provisions
MORTGAGES,
family homes and domestic violence cases, **27**/54–56
MOTOR VEHICLES,
involved in deer offences (Scots Law), **58**/19, 20
rally driving, **xii**

NATIONAL HEALTH SERVICE,
complaints,
and clinical judgment, **5**/6
fund-holding practices, **5**/2
general health services, **5**/7
information, **5**/11
other remedies, availability of, **5**/5
procedure, **5**/2
requirements to be met, **5**/9
Health Service Commissioners,
advisers, **5**/11(4)
investigative powers, **5**
personnel matters, **5**/8
reports, **5**/10
maladministration, **5**/2
service providers,
complaints against, **5**/2
investigations by Commissioners, **5**/1–2, Sched. 1
transfer of residual liabilities, **15**/1–3
National Health Service (Residual Liabilities) Act 1996 (c.15)
NATIONAL INTEREST,
events of, *see* BROADCASTING, events of national interest
NATIONAL PARKS,
restriction on disposal of houses in, **52**/13
NATIONAL SECURITY,
and employment rights, **18**/193, 202
and Industrial Tribunal hearings, **17**/10
NATIONALITY,
British citizenship,
acquisition of, by Hong Kong war wives and widows, **41**/1
otherwise than by descent, **41**/2
Noise Act 1996 (c.37)
NOISE,
and Channel Tunnel Rail Link, **61**/29–30, 40
NOISE AT NIGHT,
entry powers and seizure of equipment, 37/10
protection from personal liability, **37**/12
summary procedure for dealing with,
adoption of provisions by local authorities, **37**/1
evidence, **37**/7
excessive noise after notice: offence, **37**/4

NOISE AT NIGHT—*cont.*
summary procedure for dealing with—*cont.*
fixed penalty notices, **37**/8, 9
investigation of complaints, **37**/2
measuring devices, **37**/6
permitted level, **37**/5
warning notices, **37**/3
Non-Domestic Rating (Information) Act 1996 (c.13)
NON-MOLESTATION ORDERS, *see* FAMILY LAW
NORTHERN IRELAND,
election of delegates to forum for referendums,
delegates' allowances, **11**/6
elections, **11**/1, Sched. 1
forum, **11**/3, Sched. 2
negotiations, **11**/2
nominating representative of a party, **11**/5
referendums, **11**/4
emergency provisions,
admissions, **22**/12
arrest, search and seizure power,
examination of documents, **22**/24, 28(2)
explosives inspectors, **22**/22
force, exercise of, **22**/28
munitions, **22**/20
radio transmitters, **22**/20
records of searches, **22**/21, 28
stop and question powers, **22**/25
vessels, vehicles and aircraft, **22**/28
arrest, search and seizure powers,
constables' powers, **22**/17, 18
entry, general powers, **22**/26
entry and search for arresting terrorists, **22**/17
bail, **22**/3
children and young persons,
offences committed during remission period, **22**/16
treatment of, **22**/14
codes of practice,
Her Majesty's forces and, **22**/54
police powers, **22**/52
provisions as to, **22**/54
compensation for damage, **22**/55
Crown Court hearings, **22**/10
detention orders, **22**/36, Sched. 3
documents, examination of, **22**/24, 28
evidence and onus of proof, **22**/12, 13
entry powers,
general, **22**/26
premises, meaning of, **22**/28
property rights, interference with, **22**/26, 55, 56
to search for persons unlawfully maintained, **22**/23
Explosives Act licences, **22**/22
Her Majesty's forces,
codes of practice and, **22**/54
Independent Assessor of Military Complaints, **22**/51, Sched. 4
see also arrest, search and seizure powers

NORTHERN IRELAND—*cont.*
emergency provisions—*cont.*
highways,
closure of, **22**/27
general powers as to interference with, **22**/26
hoods in public places, **22**/35
Independent Assessor of Military Complaints Procedure, **22**/51, Sched. 4
legal aid, **22**/4
mode of trial, **22**/11
police custody,
codes of practice, **22**/52
fingerprinting, **22**/48
legal advice, access to, **22**/47
meaning of, **22**/45
right to have someone informed, **22**/46
terrorism provisions and, **22**/45
see also remand in custody
police powers: code of practice, **22**/52
private security services,
certificates,
application for, **22**/38
failure to hold: offence, **22**/37
directors' liability, **22**/43
employees' records, **22**/41
issue, duration and revocation, **22**/39
notification provisions, **22**/44
payments in respect of: offence, **22**/42
payments to uncertified persons, **22**/42
personnel changes: duty to notify, **22**/40
property rights,
compensation for damage, **22**/55, 56
interference with, **22**/26
proscribed articles, **22**/12
proscribed organisations, *see* terrorist organisations
prosecutions, **22**/57
public order offences,
possession of items for terrorist purposes, **22**/32
regulations to preserve peace, **22**/49
and terrorist organisations,
directing, **22**/29
display of support in public, **22**/31
proscribed, **22**/30
training in making or use of firearms etc., **22**/34
unlawful collection of information, **22**/33
wearing hoods in public places, **22**/35
remand in custody,
escape from custody, **22**/9
maximum period, **22**/5
young persons, **22**/6
remission,
offence committed during, **22**/16
restricted, **22**/15
scheduled offences,
bail powers, **22**/1
court, **22**/10

NORTHERN IRELAND—*cont.*
emergency provisions—*cont.*
scheduled offences—*cont.*
evidential rules,
admissions by person charged, **22**/12
onus of proof regarding stolen articles, **22**/13
legal aid, **22**/4
meaning of, **22**/1, Sched. 1
mode of trial, **22**/11
preliminary inquiries into, **22**/2
remand, *see* remand in custody
treatment of offenders, **22**/14, 15
search powers, *see* arrest, search and seizure powers
seizure powers, *see* arrest, search and seizure powers
stop and question powers, **22**/25
terrorist organisations,
directing, **22**/29
proscribed,
list of, **22**/30
membership or support of, **22**/30
public support for, **22**/31
terrorist purposes,
information for, **22**/33
items intended for, **22**/32
training for, **22**/34
video recordings, **22**/53
Housing Act 1996: applicability, **52**/226
and housing grants, **53**/149
police: jurisdiction of Metropolitan Police, **16**/99
social security overpayments, recovery of, **51**/2
Northern Ireland (Emergency Provisions) Act 1996 (c.22)
Northern Ireland (Entry to Negotiations) Act 1996 (c.11)
NUISANCE,
audible alarms (London), **ix**/25
statutory: defence, **61**/30
see also NOISE; NOISE AT NIGHT

OBSTRUCTION OF AUTHORISED OFFICER (LONDON), **ix**/28
OCCASIONAL SALES (LONDON), **ix**/10–19
OCCUPATION ORDERS, *see* FAMILY LAW
OFFENSIVE WEAPONS,
arrest without warrant, **26**/1
entry and search powers, **26**/4
knives or articles with blade or point,
having, in public place, **26**/1(1), 3
having, on school premises, **26**/1(1), 4
sale of, **26**/6
offences,
carrying without lawful authority or reasonable excuse, **26**/1(1)
having article with blade or point in public place, 3, **26**/1(1)
having article with blade or point on school premises, **26**/1(1), 4
penalties, **26**/2, 3
school premises, **26**/1(1), 3
Scots Law, **26**/5

Offensive Weapons Act 1996 (c.26)
OIL AND GAS LAW,
oil licences,
overseas petroleum, **8**/181
scientific research expenditure, **8**/180
oil licences: disposal, **8**/180
overseas petroleum licences, **8**/181
see also HYDROCARBON OIL DUTIES
OVERSEAS PUBLIC SERVANTS, *see* HONG KONG PUBLIC SERVANTS

PARKING, *see* ROAD LAW
PARLIAMENT,
evidence of proceedings in, **31**/13
Members' incidental benefits, **8**/108
staff's employment rights,
under Employment Rights Act 1996, **18**/194, 195
and Industrial Tribunals, **17**/39
statutory instruments, **54**/1
PARSONAGES,
and housing grants, **53**/95
PARTITION, **47**/7
PARTNERSHIPS,
self assessment, **8**/123
Party Wall etc. Act 1996 (c.40)
PARTY WALLS,
construction and repair on line of junction,
adjacent excavation and construction, **40**/6
Crown application, **40**/19
dispute resolution, **40**/10
expenses, **40**/11–14
new building, **40**/1
offences, **40**/16
party structure notices, **40**/3
counter notices, **40**/4
disputes under, **40**/5
recovery of sums, **40**/17
repair of party wall: rights of owner, **40**/2
rights,
compensation, **40**/7
easements, **40**/9
entry rights, **40**/8
Temples, **40**/18
PENSION SCHEMES,
occuational schemes' trustees and employment rights, **18**/46, 58–60, 102
PENSIONS,
pension rights on divorce, **27**/16, 17
personal pension schemes,
mis-sold pensions: relief, **8**/148
return of contributions on death of member, **8**/172
provisional repayments, **8**/150, Sched. 26
PLANNING LAW,
blight: compensation, **61**/46
and Channel Tunnel Rail Link, **61**/9–11, Sched. 6
concrete batching facilities at St Pancras, **61**/51
POLICE,
areas, **16**/1, Sched. 1
alteration of, **16**/32–34
Chief Constables and, **16**/100
assaults on constables, **16**/89
Assistant Chief Constables, **16**/12
attestation and declaration, **16**/4, Sched. 4
cadets, **16**/28, 52
capital expenditure, **16**/47
causing disaffection, **16**/91
central services, **16**/57
Chief Constables,
affected by area alterations, **16**/100
appointment and removal, **16**/11
functions of, **16**/10
reports, **16**/22, 44
City of London Police,
Commissioner's reports, **16**/22
fund, **16**/95
codes of practice, **16**/39, **22**/52
collaboration agreements, **16**/23
common services, **16**/57
community policing, **16**/96
complaints,
Police Complaints Authority, **16**/66, Sched. 5
constables,
attestation and declaration, **16**/29, Sched. 4
jurisdiction, **16**/30
constabularies other than police authorities, **16**/78
criminal statistics, **16**/45
cross-border aid, **16**/98
custody, *see* NORTHERN IRELAND, emergency provisions
disaffection, **16**/91
disciplinary proceedings, **16**/84–88, Sched. 6
employment rights of police officers, **18**/200
equipment standards, **16**/53
financial provisions, **16**/92–95
forces outside London,
aid of one by another, **16**/24
attestation and declaration of members, **16**/4
cadets, **16**/28
collaboration agreements, **16**/23
constables, **16**/29, 30
cross-border aid, **16**/98
maintenance of, **16**/2
police authorities, **16**/3
ranks, **16**/13
rewards for diligence, **16**/31
service outside force, **16**/97
special services, **16**/25
goods and services, **16**/18
handling, **16**/67–83
impersonation of member of force, **16**/90
information, disclosure of, **16**/22(5)
Inspectors of Constabulary, **16**/54–56
international organisations, **16**/26
local inquiries, **16**/49
local policing, **16**/7, 8

POLICE—*cont.*
Metropolitan Police Force,
fund, **16**/95
jurisdiction, **16**/99
national security, **16**/48
Northern Ireland,
jurisdiction, **16**/99
Police Advisory Boards, **16**/63
Police Authorities,
advice to international organisations, **16**/26
annual reports, **16**/9
appointments to office, **16**/17
budget minimum, **16**/41
clerk, **16**/16
codes of practice, **16**/39
designation of duties, **16**/17
establishment of, **16**/3
functions of, **16**/6
goods and services, **16**/18
inspections, **16**/40
legislative provisions, application of, **16**/21
local policing, **16**/7, 8
membership, **16**/4, Scheds. 2, 3
assistant chief constables, **16**/12
chief constables, **16**/10, 11
other ranks, **16**/13
objectives, **16**/37
performance targets, **16**/38
police fund, **16**/14
precepts, **16**/19
questions on, at council meetings, **16**/20
reduction in size, **16**/5
Police Federations, **16**/59, 60
Police Fund, **16**/14
Police Grant, **16**/46
Police Negotiating Board, **16**/61, 62
precepts, **16**/19
relevant force, **16**/97
Secretary of State's functions, **16**/36–53
special constables,
appointment, **16**/27
jurisdiction, **16**/30
regulations for, **16**/51
trade union membership, **16**/64
Police Act 1996 (c.16)
POLICE POWERS,
cordons, **7**/4, Sched.
see also Northern Ireland, emergency provisions SEARCH AND SEIZURE; STOP AND SEARCH: TERRORISM
PORTS,
border controls: terrorism, **7**/3
Prevention of Terrorism (Additional Powers) Act 1996 (c.7)
PRISONERS,
earnings, *see* WAGES
Prisoners' Earnings Act 1996 (c.33)
PRIVACY,
broadcasting code on interference with, **55**/107
PRIVATE SECURITY SERVICES,
see NORTHERN IRELAND, emergency provisions
PRIVILEGE, *see* DEFAMATION
PROFIT SHARING SCHEMES,
appropriate allowance, **8**/118
appropriate percentage, **8**/117
employee share ownership trusts, **8**/119, 120
release date, **8**/116
see also SHARE OPTIONS
PUBLIC INTEREST,
non-disclosure of material, **25**/3(6), 7(5), 8(5), 9(8)
opportunity to be heard on, **25**/16
reviews, **25**/14, 15
PUBLIC ORDER,
terrorism offences, *see* Northern Ireland, emergency provisions
PUBLIC SECTOR SETTLEMENTS, *see* DAMAGES
PUBLIC WORKS COMMISSIONERS,
loans to Registered Social Landlords, **52**/23

RACIAL DISCRIMINATION,
in armed services, **46**/23
Railway Heritage Act 1996 (c.42)
RAILWAYS,
heritage,
bodies holding records, artefacts, etc., **42**/1
committees,
establishment of, **42**/2(1)
function of, **42**/3
guidance and information, **42**/6
membership of, **42**/2(2)
provisions as to, **42**/2(2)
schemes establishing, **42**/2
records and artefacts,
designation of, **42**/3
disposal of, **42**/5
notice of proposed disposal, **42**/4
see also CHANNEL TUNNEL RAIL LINK
RATING,
caravans and boats, **12**/1
non-domestic: information from rating officials, **13**/1
Rating (Caravans and Boats) Act 1996 (c.12)
REGISTERED SOCIAL LANDLORDS,
charges by, **52**/219, 220
complaints against, **52**/51 Sched. 2
definitions,
associate, **52**/61
charity, **52**/58
family, **52**/62
index of defined expressions, **52**/64
industrial and provident societies, **52**/57
minor, **52**/63
officer, **52**/59
subsidiary, **52**/60
determinations by Corporation or Secretary of State, **52**/53
disposal of land,
control by Corporation,
consent required, **52**/9
exempt disposals, **52**/15
lettings not requiring consent, **52**/10

REGISTERED SOCIAL LANDLORDS—*cont.*
disposal of land—*cont.*
control by Corporation—*cont.*
options, treatment of, **52**/14
relevant disposals, **52**/15
repayment of discount,
covenant for, **52**/11
priority of charge for, **52**/12
restrictions on, in National Parks etc., **52**/13
moratorium on, on insolvency, **52**/42, 43
power as to, **52**/8
disposal of proceeds,
application or appropriation of, **52**/25
disposal of, **52**/24
power to require information, **52**/26
grants,
under Housing Act 1988, ss.50 to 55, **52**/28
land subject to housing management agreement, **52**/19
local authority assistance, **52**/22
Public Works Commissioners' loans, **52**/23
purchase grant,
where right to acquire exercised, **52**/20
where right to acquire not exercised, **52**/21
social housing grants, **52**/18
recovery of, **52**/27
special residual subsidy, commutation of, **52**/29
insolvency of,
moratorium on disposals, **52**/42, 43
notices to Corporation,
initial, **52**/40
subsequent, **52**/41
proposals as to ownership and management of land, **52**/44
application to court to secure compliance, **52**/50
assistance by Corporation, **52**/49
effect of, **52**/45
manager to implement,
appointment, **52**/46
powers of manager, **52**/47
transfer of engagements, **52**/48
scheme of provisions, **52**/39
orders by Secretary of State, **52**/52
registration, **52**/3(1)
application for, **52**/3(2)
eligibility for, **52**/2
notice of, **52**/3(3)
register, **52**/1
removal from register, **52**/4
appeal against, **52**/6
criteria for, **52**/5
regulation of, **52**/7 Sched. 1
tenant's right to acquire building, **52**/16–17
see also HOUSING CORPORATION
RESERVE FORCES,
absence without leave, *see* offences
additional duties commitment, **14**/25, *see also* training obligations
appeals, *see* Reserve Forces Appeal Tribunal

RESERVE FORCES—*cont.*
billetting, **14**/123
call-out,
on authority of call-out order,
acceptance into service, **14**/59
alteration of authority, **14**/61
call-out notice, **14**/58
content of order, **14**/58
exemption from liability, **14**/62
exercise of Secretary of State's functions, **14**/63
release from service, **14**/60
exemptions, **14**/78, 80–82
financial assistance, **14**/83–87
for permanent service,
general liability, **14**/50
geographical extent of liability, **14**/51
powers to authorise,
national danger, **14**/52, 53
necessary or desirable, **14**/56, 57
warlike operations in preparation, **14**/54, 55
special agreements, **14**/28–34
special members (employee agreements), **14**/43–49
charitable property of disbanded units, **14**/120, Sched. 3
command, **14**/20
death attributable to service, **14**/8(2)
desertion, *see* offences
discharge,
appeal against, **14**/14(3), 15(2)
by commanding officer, **14**/15
entitlement to, **14**/16
postponement of, **14**/17
power to, **14**/14
rights of men on, **14**/18
employee agreements,
call-out, *see* call-out
discharge of special members, **14**/42
effect of, **14**/38, 39(7)–(8)
employer's consent, **14**/39(2)–(4)
liability under, **14**/40, 41
purpose of, **14**/38
termination of, **14**/39(9)
terms of, **14**/39(5)–(6)
who may enter into, **14**/39(1)
employment safeguards, 122
enlistment,
enlisting officer, **14**/9
foreign nationals, **14**/10
land and air forces, **14**/12
power to enlist, **14**/9, Sched. 1
re-engagement, **14**/11
transfers between reserve forces, **14**/13
ex-regular reserve forces,
compulsory service, **14**/13
meaning, **14**/2(2)
transfer between, **14**/13
full-time service commitment, **14**/24
Lieutenancies and, **14**/121, Sched. 6
maintenance and composition, **14**/2–3
meaning of, **14**/1

RESERVE FORCES—*cont.*
necessary or desirable to use armed forces, **14**/56, 57
offences,
in connection with appeals, **14**/94
desertion and absence without leave,
failure to attend, **14**/96, 97
false pretence of illegal absence, **14**/99
inducing a person to desert, **14**/101
punishment, **14**/98
record of illegal absence, **14**/102
treatment of deserters, **14**/100, Sched. 2
voting, absence for, **14**/125
evidence, **14**/108, Sched. 3
against good order and discipline, 95
proceedings, **14**/107
trial,
by civil court, **14**/104, 105, 109
court-martial or civil court, **14**/106
under service law, **14**/103
pay and pensions, **14**/7
permanent staff, **14**/6
postings, **14**/20
re-engagement, **14**/11
recall for service,
duration of service, **14**/69
exemptions, **14**/79–82
financial assistance, **14**/83–87
general liability, **14**/65
geographical extent of liability, **14**/67
power to authorise, **14**/68
recall orders, **14**/70–77
who may be recalled, **14**/66
see also call-out
regular servicemen: postponement of transfer to reserve or discharge, **14**/126, Sched. 7
regulations and organisation, **14**/4–6
Reserve Associations, **14**/111–119, Sched. 4
Reserve Forces Appeal Tribunals, **14**/88–94
Royal Fleet Reserve, **14**/21
Royal Marines, **14**/21, 123
tolls, exemption from, **14**/124
training obligations,
additional duties,
commitment, 25
exemption from, **14**/23
full-time service commitment, **14**/24
general requirement, **14**/22
parliamentray control of, **14**/26
voluntary activities, **14**/27
volunteer reserve forces: meaning, **14**/2(3)
voting, absence for, **14**/125
warlike operations, **14**/54, 55
see also recall for service
Reserve Forces Act 1996 (c.14)
RESTRICTIVE TRADE PRACTICES,
and Channel Tunnel Rail Link, **61**/22–26
REVENUE AND FINANCE,
appropriation of grants, **46**/2
Consolidated Fund: issues, **46**/1
see also TAXATION
RIGHTS OF WAY,
extinguishment for Channel Tunnel Rail Link, **61**/7

ROAD LAW,
terrorism: parking restrictions, **7**/5
ROAD TRAFFIC LAW,
device for blood and urine samples, **25**/63
Jim Clark Memorial Rally, **xii**
ROYAL FREE HOSPITAL SCHOOL OF MEDICINE,
dissolution of, **iii**/4
ROYAL NAVAL COLLEGE, GREENWICH, **46**/31

SCHOOL INSPECTIONS,
by,
local authority inspection service, **57**/24
members of the Inspectorate, **57**/12
registered inspectors,
duties as to, **57**/18, Sched. 2
timing of, **57**/15
Chief Inspector of Schools, *see* Her Majesty's Inspectorate
computer records, **57**/42
Education Associations,
conduct of school, **57**/36
discontinuance of school conducted by, **57**/38
functions of, **57**/35
non-applicability of s.10, **57**/10(4)
power to establish, **57**/31, Sched. 5
regulations, **57**/41
reports showing school no longer requires special measures, **57**/41
schools acquiring grant-maintained status, **57**/37
supervision of, **57**/32
transfer of responsibiity for running school to, **57**/33–34
winding-up, **57**/39
financial provisions, **57**/43, 44
Her Majesty's Inspectorate for England,
Chief Inspector,
appointment, **57**/1(1)
functions of, **57**/2
power to arrange inspections, **57**/3
terms and conditions of service, **57**/1(4)–(5), Sched. 1
Inspectors of Schools,
appointment, **57**/1(2)
terms and conditions of service, **57**/1(3), Sched. 1
Her Majesty's Inspectorate for Wales,
Chief Inspector,
appointment, **57**/4(1)
functions of, **57**/5
power to arrange inspections, **57**/6
terms and conditions of service, **57**/4(4)–(5), Sched. 1
Inspectors of Schools,
appointment, **57**/4(2)
terms and conditions of service, **57**/4(3)
Inspectors of Schools,
appointment and terms of service, *see* Her Majesty's Inspectorate
inspections by, **57**/10, Sched. 3
register of inspectors,
appeals in relation to, **57**/9, Sched. 2

SCHOOL INSPECTIONS—*cont.*
Inspectors of Schools—*cont.*
register of inspectors—*cont.*
imposition of conditions, **57**/8
registration procedure, **57**/7
removal from register, **57**/8
local authority inspection service, **57**/24
procedure for, **57**/12
religious education, **57**/23, Sched. 4
reports (all schools), **57**/13
reports (s.10 schools),
destination of, **57**/16
of inspections by members of the Inspectorate, **57**/14
special measures following, **57**/17–19
reports (s.11(3) schools),
destination of reports, **57**/20
special measures following, **57**/21 monitoring, **57**/22
schools to be inspected, **57**/10(3)
special measure by appropriate authority,
applicable schools, **57**/26
powers over schools requiring,
appointment of additional governors, **57**/27
grouping and degrouping, **57**/29
prohibition of ballot, **57**/31
suspension of right to delegated budget, **57**/28
s.10 schools, **57**/17–18
monitoring, **57**/19
s.11(3) schools, **57**/21
monitoring, **57**/22
see also Education Associations
School Inspections Act 1996 (c.57)
SCOTS LAW,
armed services,
complaints to Industrial Tribunals, **46**/21, *see also* ARMED SERVICES
criminal procedure: amendments, **25**/73
deer,
arrest powers, **58**/28
authorisations, *see* Deer Commission for Scotland
close season, **43**/14(3), **44**/8
compensation for damage, **58**/41
conservation, control and management,
close seasons, **58**/5
control agreements, **58**/7
control areas, **58**/6
control schemes, **58**/8, 9, Sched. 2
Crown application, **58**/44
emergency measures,
to prevent damage by deer, **58**/10
to protect natural heritage (woodland), **58**/11
entry powers, **58**/15
equipment for, **58**/12
limitation of criminal liability, **58**/14
offences, **58**/13
payment of expenses, **58**/12
service of notices, **58**/16
control agreements and schemes, **44**/6
damage to natural heritage, **44**/5

SCOTS LAW—*cont.*
deer—*cont.*
Deer Commission for Scotland,
advice to Secretary of State, **58**/2
annual reports, **58**/2
appointment of, **58**/1
authorisations,
effect of, **58**/38
grant of, **58**/37
return of number of deer killed, **58**/40
constitution, **58**/1(7), Sched. 1
continuance of, **58**/1(1)
control agreements and control schemes, **44**/6
functions of, **44**/1(1)(b), **58**/1
guidance to facilitate exercise of functions, **58**/3
panels, appointment of, **44**/2, **58**/4
powers,
authorisation of certain acts, **44**/10
emergency, to authorise killing, **44**/4
particular, **44**/3
prevention of damage to natural heritage, **44**/5
Red Deer Commission name change, **44**/1(1)(a)
deer killed under authority,
authorisation by Commission of certain acts, **44**/10, **58**/39
disposal of, **44**/6, **58**/39
emergency powers as to, **44**/4
disposal of,
deer liable to forfeiture, **58**/32
killed by authority, **58**/39
farmed deer, **44**/11, **58**/43
firearms offences,
orders as to, **58**/21
wilfully injuring deer, **58**/21(5)
game licences, **58**/38
information for owner of land, **58**/42
offences,
arrest powers, **58**/28
attempts, **58**/24
bodies corporate, **58**/29
charged on one offence, conviction on another, **58**/30
court's powers on conviction, **58**/31
disposal of deer liable to forfeiture, **58**/32
firearms and ammunition: orders, **58**/21
illegal possession, **58**/23
illegal possession of deer, **44**/9, **58**/23
involving vehicles, **58**/19, 20
by more than one person, **58**/22
penalties, **58**/Sched. 3
search and seizure powers, **58**/27
taking or killing at night, **58**/18
unlawful killing, taking and injuring, **58**/17
use of vehicle to drive deer, **58**/19
by venison dealers, **58**/36

SCOTS LAW—*cont.*
deer—*cont.*
offences—*cont.*
exemptions,
occupiers' rights when deer causing damage, **58**/26
preventing suffering, **58**/25
panels, **44**/2, **58**/4
Red Deer Commission,
constitution, **4**/1
name change, **44**/1(1)(a)
search and seizure powers, **58**/27
venison dealers,
licensing, **58**/33
offences, **58**/36
reciprocal arrangements, **58**/35
records, **58**/34
divorce and separation: pension rights on, **27**/17
education,
accreditation, **43**/3
assessment of secondary school pupils, **43**/32
children under school age: grants for,
amounts, **43**/23(2)
availability of, **43**/23(1)
delegation of functions as to, **43**/25
disclosure of information, **43**/26
requirements for, 24, **43**/23(2)
independent schools: disqualification, **56**/477
placing requests, **43**/33
quality assurance, **43**/4
regulations and orders, **43**/35
reserved places, **43**/33
school boards,
amendments to School Boards (Scotland) Act 1988, **43**/31, Sched. 4
co-opted members, **43**/28
conflict of interest, **43**/30
elections to, **43**/28
terms of office of members, **43**/29
Scottish Borders Council (Jim Clark Memorial Rally) Order Confirmation Act 1996 (c.xii)
Scottish Examination Board,
annual report, **43**/11
constitution, **43**/1(5), Sched. 1
dissolution of, **43**/19, Sched. 2
establishment of, **43**/1(1)
financial provisions,
accounting records, **43**/16
accounts, **43**/16
Scottish Qualifications Authority (SQA),
financial provisions,
audit, **43**/16(4)
duties, **43**/12
grants payable, **43**/13
guaranteed borrowing, **43**/15
loans, **43**/14
functions,
accreditation, **43**/3
advisory, **43**/5
considerations underlying exercise of, **43**/7

SCOTS LAW—*cont.*
education—*cont.*
Scottish Qualifications Authority (SQA)—*cont.*
functions—*cont.*
general, **43**/2
incidental, **43**/6
quality assurance, **43**/4
Secretary of State's directions as to, **43**/9
services to and collaboration with others, **43**/8
information to be provided by, **43**/10
membership of, **43**/1(2)–(4)
property transfers to, **43**/17, 19, Sched. 2
staff transfers to, **43**/18, 19, Sched. 2
transitional provisions, **43**/20, Sched. 3
Scottish Vocational Council dissolution of, **43**/19, Sched. 2
service of documents, **43**/22
Gaelic broadcasts, **55**/32, 95
jurisdiction of Metropolitan Police, **16**/99
licensing,
conditions attached for certain events, **36**/1
for existing licences, **36**/1
licensing divisions, **36**/2
offensive weapons, **26**/5, *see also* OFFENSIVE WEAPONS
see also BERNERAY CAUSEWAY; EDINBURGH; JIM CLARK MEMORIAL RALLY
SCOTTISH HEALTH SERVICE,
transfer of residual liabilities, **15**/1–3
SEARCH AND SEIZURE,
chemical weapons: premises, **6**/7, 29
equipment making noise at night, **37**/10
for offensive weapons, **26**/4
in relation to deer offences, **58**/27
terrorism and, *see* NORTHERN IRELAND, emergency provisions
non-residential premises, **7**/2
unaccompanied goods, **7**/3
wild mammals; offence, **3**/4
SEARCH WARRANTS,
immigration offences and, **49**/7
SECURITIES,
convertible: and loan relationships, **8**/94–96
discounted, **8**/102, Sched. 13
electronic transfer of: stamp duty, **8**/186
gilt-edged: and loan relationships, **8**/94–96
gilt stripping, **8**/202
quotation or listing, **8**/199, Sched. 38
SECURITY SERVICE,
functions of, **35**/1
warrants, **35**/2
Security Service Act 1996 (c.35)
SEIZURE POWERS, *see* SEARCH AND SEIZURE POWERS
SEPARATION, *see* FAMILY LAW
SETTLED LAND ACT SETTLEMENTS, SEE TRUSTS AND TRUSTEES
SEX DISCRIMINATION,
in armed services, **46**/21, 22
SEX EDUCATION, *see* EDUCATION, curriculum

INDEX

SEX ESTABLISHMENTS,
control of, in Westminster,
closure notices, **viii**/3
closure orders, **viii**/4
appeals against, **viii**/5
enforcement, **viii**/6
offences by bodies corporate, **viii**/7
service of notices, **viii**/8
SEXUAL CONDUCT,
broadcasting code on, **55**/108
SEXUAL OFFENCES,
sexual acts outside UK,
British citizenship: immateriality of, **29**/3(6)
conspiracy to commit,
conditions for, **29**/1
defences, **29**/3
offences under foreign law, 1(6), 3(1), **29**/1(3)
incitement to commit,
conditions for, **29**/2
defences, **29**/3
by messages, **29**/2(3)
listed offences, **29**/5, Sched.
offences under foreign law, 2(1)(c), 3, 3(1), **29**/1(3), **29**/2(1)(c)
defence's notice as to, **29**/3
what accused had in view, 3(3)(b), 29/2
relevant conduct, **29**/3(2)–(3)
Scottish provisions, **29**/6
Sexual Offences (Conspiracy and Incitement) Act 1996 (c.29)
SHARE OPTIONS,
approved schemes, **8**/114, Sched. 16
consideration for, **8**/111
release and replacement, **8**/112
savings-related schemes, **8**/113
see also PROFIT SHARING SCHEMES
SHIPPING LAW,
mariners' employment rights, **18**/199
roll-over relief: ships, **8**/179, Sched. 35
SIANEL PEDWAR CYMRU, *see* BROADCASTING, S4C
SMALL CLAIMS,
arbitration proceedings, **23**/92
SOCIAL SECURITY,
asylum seekers: benefits, **49**/11
child benefit,
persons subject to immigration control, **49**/10
housing benefit, *see* HOUSING BENEFIT
overpayments, recovery of, **51**/1, 2
recoupment of benefits in Industrial Tribunal hearings, **17**/16, 17
SOCIAL SERVICES,
direct payments for community care services, *see* COMMUNITY CARE
SPORTING EVENTS, *see* BROADCASTING, events of national interest, JIM CLARK MEMORIAL RALLY
STAMP DUTY,
clearance services: election, **8**/196
on electronic transfers of securities, **8**/186
STAMP DUTY—*cont.*
stamp duty reserve tax, **8**/186–190
STATUTORY INSTRUMENTS, **54**/1
Statutory Instruments (Production and Sale) Act 1996 (c.54)
STATUTORY UNDERTAKERS,
extinguishment of rights: Channel Tunnel Rail Link, **61**/8
STAY OF PROCEEDINGS,
in arbitration proceedings, **23**/9–11, 86
STOP AND QUESTION POWERS, **22**/25
see also NORTHERN IRELAND, emergency provisions
STOP AND SEARCH,
pedestrians: prevention of terrorism, **7**/1
wild mammals; offence, **3**/4
STRUCTURED SETTLEMENTS, *see* DAMAGES

TAXATION,
anti-avoidance provisions, **8**/31, Sched. 4
extra-statutory concessions, **8**/201, Sched. 39
fiscal warehousing, **8**/26, Sched. 3
gilt stripping, **8**/202
indirect, **8**/197
of investments,
accrued income scheme: transfers on death, **8**/158
cancellation of advantages, **8**/175
foreign income dividends, **8**/153, Sched. 27
FOTRA Securities, **8**/154, Sched. 9
in housing, **8**/160, Sched. 30
income from savings, **8**/73, Sched. 6
manufactured payments, repos etc., **8**/159
paying and collecting agents, **8**/156, Sched. 29
payment without deduction of tax, directions for, **8**/155
stock lending fees, **8**/157
transfer by electronic transfer: stamp duty, **8**/186
venture capital trusts: control of companies, **8**/161
loan relationships,
gilt-edged securities, **8**/94–96
insurance companies, **8**/99, Sched. 11
linked to value of asset, **8**/93
manufactured interest, **8**/97
taxation of profits and gains, **8**/80–83, Sched. 8
see also EXCISE DUTIES
TERRORISM,
consent to prosecutions, **7**/6
non-residential premises: search powers, **7**/2
parking prohibitions, **7**/5
pedestrians, **7**/1
police cordons, **7**/4, Sched.
port and border controls, **7**/3
scheduled offences, *see* Northern Ireland, emergency provisions
stop and search powers, **7**/1
unaccompanied goods: search powers, **7**/3

THEFT,
dishonestly obtaining a wrongful credit, **62**/2
obtaining a money transfer by deception, **62**/1
obtaining services by deception, **62**/4
Theft (Amendment) Act 1996 (c.62)
TOBACCO PRODUCTS DUTY, **8**/9
TORT,
damages, *see* DAMAGES
TRADE UNIONS,
police membership, **16**/64
TRADING SCHEMES, **32**/1
TRADING STANDARDS,
distribution of advertisements, **32**/2
extension of Fair Trading Act 1973, **32**/1
trading schemes, **32**/1
Trading Standards Act 1996 (c.32)
TRANSFER OF TRIAL, *see* CRIMINAL PROCEDURE AND INVESTIGATIONS
TRANSPORT,
London Regional, *see* LONDON *see also* RAILWAYS
TREASURE,
codes of practice, **24**/11
coroners' jurisdiction,
duty of finder to notify coroner, **24**/8
inquests,
notifications required, **24**/9
without jury, **24**/7(4)
when exercisable, **24**/7
Crown rights,
rewards, **24**/10
treasure vesting in Crown, 6, **24**/4(1)(b)
franchisees, 5, **24**/4(1)(a)
meaning of, **24**/1
power to alter, **24**/2
terms used, **24**/3
Northern Ireland application, **24**/13
ownership of
Crown, 6, **24**/4(1)(b)
franchisee, 5, **24**/4(1)(a)
reports of operation of Treasure Act 1996, **24**/12
rewards, **24**/10
wrecks, **24**/3(7)
Treasure Act 1996 (c.24)
TREES,
and Channel Tunnel Rail Link, **61**/27, 28
TRIBUNALS, *see* INDUSTRIAL TRIBUNALS
TRUSTS AND TRUSTEES,
education trust deeds, **56**/179, 180
religious education trusts, **56**/554–557, Sched. 36
trusts of land and appointment of trustees,
beneficiary, meaning of, **47**/22
Chequers Estate Act 1917, **47**/25(3)
Chevenings Estate Act 1959, **47**/25(3)
consents, **47**/10
consultation with beneficiaries, **47**/11
conversion: abolition of doctrine, **47**/3
Crown application, **47**/24
deaths, effect of, **47**/25(5)
entailed interests, **47**/25(4)

TRUSTS AND TRUSTEES—*cont.*
trusts of land and appointment of trustees—*cont.*
orders of court,
applications for, **47**/14
relevant matters in determining, **47**/15
partition, **47**/7
personal representatives, **47**/18
proceeds of sale, **47**/17
purchaser protection, **47**/16
right to occupy,
beneficiaries' right, **47**/12
exclusion and restriction of, **47**/13
Settled Land Act settlements,
as trusts of land, **47**/2, Sched. 1
trustees,
appointment,
at instance of beneficiaries, **47**/19, 21
of substitute for incapable trustee, **47**/20
retirement at instance of beneficiaries, **47**/19, 21
trustees of land,
applications for order of court, **47**/14, 15
delegation powers, **47**/9
exclusion and restriction of powers, **47**/8
general powers, **47**/6
partition by, **47**/7
trusts for sale,
implied trusts: amendments, **47**/5, Sched. 2
power to postpone sale, **47**/4
as trusts of land, **47**/4, 5
trusts of land,
beneficiaries' right to occupy, *see* right to occupy
consents, **47**/10
consultations with beneficiaries, **47**/11
meaning, **47**/1
protection of purchaser, **47**/16
settlements as, **47**/2, Sched. 1
trusts for sale as, **47**/4, 5
trusts of proceeds of sale, **47**/17
TRUSTS FOR SALE, *see* TRUSTS AND TRUSTEES
Trusts of Land and Appointment of Trustees Act 1996 (c.47)

UNIVERSITY COLLEGE, LONDON,
transfer of property etc. of other medical schools to, **iii**/1–11
University College London Act 1996 (c.iii)
UNJUST OR UNFAIR TREATMENT,
broadcasting code on, 107
URBAN DEVELOPMENT CORPORATIONS,
pre-dissolution transfers, **53**/143

VALUE ADDED TAX,
anti-avoidance provisions, **8**/31, Sched. 4
EC Second VAT Simplification, **8**/25–29
payment and enforcement, **8**/34–37
refunds, **8**/30
small gifts, **8**/33
supply: gold etc., **8**/32

INDEX

VEHICLE EXCISE DUTY,
electrically propelled vehicles, 15
general rate, **8**/14
licensing and registration regulations, **8**/23, Sched. 2
load-carrying vehicles, **8**/17
Northern Ireland provisions, **8**/21, 22
old vehicles, **8**/18, 19
special concessionary vehicles, **8**/16
steam powered vehicles, **8**/16
testing vehicles: exemptions, **8**/20, 21
VENTURE CAPITAL TRUSTS, **8**/161
VIOLENCE,
broadcasting code on, **55**/108
crimes involving: detection and warrants, **35**/1, 2
domestic, *see* FAMILY LAW
VOCATIONAL TRAINING, **8**/129, 144

WAGES,
employment rights,
cash shortages and stock, deficiencies, **18**/17–22
deductions by employer, **18**/13, Sched. 14
enforcement, **18**/23–26
payments to employer, **18**/15, Sched. 16
prisoners earnings: deductions and levies, **33**/1
application of, **33**/2

WAGES—*cont.*
prisoners earnings: deductions and levies—*cont.*
statement of account, **33**/3
WALES,
applicability of Education Act 1996, *see* EDUCATION
Housing for Wales, **52**/56(1)
marriage ceremony: alternatives for prescribed words, **34**/1
S4C (Sianel Pedwar Cymru), *see* BROADCASTING
school inspections, *see* SCHOOL INSPECTIONS
Welsh Development Agency, **53**/130
WAR CRIMES,
abolition of transfer procedure, **25**/46
WATER LAW,
house-boats,
home repair assistance for, **53**/78
houseboats,
definition, **38**/1
mariners' employment rights, **18**/199
rating of boats, **12**/1
Western Isles Council (Berneray Causeway) Order Confirmation Act 1996 (c.xiii)
Wild Mammals (Protection) Act 1996 (c.3)
WRECKS,
and treasure, **24**/3(7)

YEAR AND A DAY RULE,
abolition, **19**/1